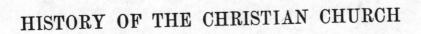

HISTORY OF THE CHRISTIAN CHURCH

HISTORY

OF THE

CHRISTIAN CHURCH

BY

PHILIP SCHAFF

Christianus sum. Christiani nihil a me alienum puto

VOLUME II

ANTE-NICENE CHRISTIANITY

A. D. 100–325.

WM. B. EERDMANS PUBLISHING COMPANY

GRAND RAPIDS   MICHIGAN

*Reproduced by special arrangement
with the original publisher*

Library of Congress Number 39-3700

ISBN 0-8028-8048-7

Reprinted, July 1987

PHOTOLITHOPRINTED BY EERDMANS PRINTING COMPANY
GRAND RAPIDS, MICHIGAN, UNITED STATES OF AMERICA

PREFACE TO THE THIRD EDITION REVISED

A few months after the appearance of the revised edition of this volume, Dr. Bryennios, the learned Metropolitan of Nicomedia, surprised the world by the publication of the now famous *Didache*, which he had discovered in the Jerusalem Monastery of the Most Holy Sepulchre at Constantinople. This led me, in justice to myself and to my readers, to write an independent supplement under the title: *The Oldest Church Manual, called the Teaching of the Twelve Apostles*, etc., which is now passing through the press.

At the same time I have taken advantage of a new issue of this *History*, without increasing the size and the price, to make in the plates all the necessary references to the *Didache* where it sheds new light on the post-apostolic age (especially on pages 140, 184, 185, 202, 226, 236, 239, 241, 247, 249, 379, 640).

I have also brought the literature up to date, and corrected a few printing errors, so that this issue may be called a revised edition. A learned and fastidious German critic and professional church historian has pronounced this work to be far in advance of any German work in the fullness of its digest of the discoveries and researches of the last thirty years. ("Theolog. Literatur-Zeitung," for March 22, 1884.) But the Bryennios discovery, and the extensive literature which it has called forth, remind me of the imperfect character of historical books in an age of such rapid progress as ours.

THE AUTHOR.

NEW YORK, April 22, 1885.

FIFTH EDITION

The fourth edition (1886) was a reprint of the third, with a few slight improvements. In this fifth edition I have made numerous additions to the literature, and adapted the text throughout to the present stage of research, which continues to be very active and fruitful in the Ante-Nicene period.

Several topics connected with the catechetical instruction, organization, and ritual (baptism and eucharist) of the early Church are more fully treated in my supplementary monograph, *The Teaching of the Twelve Apostles*, or *The Oldest Church Manual*, which first appeared in June, 1885, and in a third edition, revised and enlarged, January, 1889 (325 pages).

P. S.

NEW YORK, July, 1889.

PREFACE TO THE SECOND EDITION

THIS second volume contains the history of Christianity from the end of the Apostolic age to the beginning of the Nicene.

The first Edict of Toleration, A. D. 311, made an end of persecution; the second Edict of Toleration, 313 (there is no third), prepared the way for legal recognition and protection; the Nicene Council, 325, marks the solemn inauguration of the imperial state-church. Constantine, like Eusebius, the theologian, and Hosius the statesman, of his reign, belongs to both periods and must be considered in both, though more fully in the next.

We live in an age of discovery and research, similar to that which preceded the Reformation. The beginnings of history, the beginnings of civilization, the beginnings of Christianity are now absorbing the attention of scholars.

During the present generation early church history has been vastly enriched by new sources of information, and almost revolutionized by independent criticism. Among the recent literary discoveries and publications the following deserve special mention:

The SYRIAC IGNATIUS (by Cureton 1845 and 1849), which opened a new chapter in the Ignatian controversy so closely connected with the rise of Episcopacy and Catholicism; the PHILOSOPHUMENA of HIPPOLYTUS (by Miller 1851, and by Duncker and Schneidewin, 1859), which have shed a flood of light on the ancient heresies and systems of thought, as well as on the doctrinal and disciplinary commotions in the Roman church in the early part of the third century; the TENTH BOOK of THE PSEUDO-CLEMENTINE HOMILIES (by Dressel, 1853), which supplements our knowledge of a curious type of distorted Christianity in the post-apostolic age, and furnishes, by an undoubted quotation, a valuable contribution to the solution of the Johannean problem; the GREEK HERMAS from Mt. Athos (the Codex Lipsiensis, published by Anger and Tischendorf, 1856); a new and complete Greek MS. of the FIRST EPISTLE of the ROMAN CLEMENT with several important new chapters and the oldest written Christian prayer (about one-tenth of the whole), found in a Convent Library at Constantinople (by Bryennios, 1875); and in the same codex the SECOND (so called) EPISTLE of CLEMENT, or post-Clementine HOMILY rather, in its complete form (20 chs. instead of 12), giving us the first post-apostolic sermon, besides a new Greek text of the Epistle of BARNABAS; a SYRIAC Version of CLEMENT in the library of Jules Mohl, now at Cambridge (1876); fragments of TATIAN's DIATESSARON with EPHRÆM's COMMENTARY on it, in an Armenian version (Latin by Mösinger 1878); fragments of the apologies of MELITO (1858), and ARISTIDES (1878); the complete Greek text of the ACTS of THOMAS (by Max Bonnet, 1883); and the crowning discovery of all, the CODEX SINAITICUS, the only complete uncial MS. of the Greek Testament, together with the GREEK BARNABAS and the GREEK HERMAS (by Tischendorf, 1862), which, with the facsimile edition of the VATICAN CODEX (1868–1881, 6 vols.), marks an epoch in the science of textual criticism of the Greek Testament and of those two Apostolic Fathers, and establishes the fact of the ecclesiastical use of all our canonical books in the age of Eusebius.

In view of these discoveries we would not be surprised if the EXPOSITION of THE LORD's ORACLES by PAPIAS, which was still in existence at Nismes in 1215, the MEMORIALS of HEGESIPPUS, and the whole GREEK original of IRENÆUS, which were recorded by a librarian as extant in the sixteenth century, should turn up in some old convent.

In connection with these fresh sources there has been a corresponding activity on the part of scholars. The Germans have done and are doing an astonishing amount of *Quellenforschung* and *Quellenkritik* in numerous monographs and periodicals, and have given us the newest and best critical editions of the Apostolic Fathers and Apologists. The English with their strong common sense, judicial calmness, and conservative tact are fast wheeling into the line of progress, as is evident from the collective works on *Christian Antiquities*, and *Christian Biography*, and from Bp. Lightfoot's *Clementine Epistles*, which are soon to be followed by his edition of the *Ignatian Epistles*. To the brilliant French genius and learning of Mr. Renan we owe a graphic picture of the secular surroundings of early Christianity down to the time of Marcus Aurelius, with sharp glances into the literature and life of the church. His *Histoire des Origines du Christianisme*, now completed in seven volumes, after twenty years' labor, is well worthy to rank with Gibbon's immortal work. The Rise and Triumph of Christianity is a grander theme than the contemporary Decline and Fall of the Roman Empire, but no historian can do justice to it without faith in the divine character and mission of that peaceful Conqueror of immortal souls, whose kingdom shall have no end.

The importance of these literary discoveries and investigations should not blind us to the almost equally important monumental discoveries and researches of Cavalier de Rossi, Garrucci, and other Italian scholars who have illuminated the subterranean mysteries of the church of Rome and of early Christian art. Neander, Gieseler, and Baur, the greatest church historians of the nineteenth century, are as silent about the catacombs as Mosheim and Gibbon were in the eighteenth. But who could now write a history of the first three centuries without recording the lessons of those rude yet expressive pictures, sculptures and epitaphs from the homes of confessors and martyrs? Nor should we overlook the gain which has come to us from the study of monumental inscriptions, as for instance in rectifying the date of Polycarp's martyrdom who is now brought ten years nearer to the age of St. John.

Before long there will be great need of an historic architect who will construct a beautiful and comfortable building out of the vast material thus brought to light. The Germans are historic miners, the French and English are skilled manufacturers; the former understand and cultivate the science of history, the latter excel in the art of historiography. A master of both would be the ideal historian. But God has wisely distributed his gifts, and made individuals and nations depend upon and supplement each other.

The present volume is an entire reconstruction of the corresponding part of the first edition (vol. I. p. 144–528), which appeared twenty-five years ago. It is more than double in size. Some chapters (e. g. VI. VII. IX.) and several sections (e. g. 90–93, 103, 155–157, 168, 171, 184, 189, 190, 193, 198–204, etc.) are new, and the rest has been improved and enlarged, especially the last chapter on the literature of the church. My endeavor has been to bring the book up to the present advanced state of knowledge, to record every important work (German, French, English, and American) which has come under my notice, and to make the results of the best scholarship of the age available and useful to the rising generation.

In conclusion, I may be permitted to express my thanks for the kind reception which has been accorded to this revised edition of the work of my youth. It will stimulate me to new energy in carrying it forward as far as God may give time and strength. The third volume needs no reconstruction, and a new edition of the same with a few improvements will be issued without delay.

PHILIP SCHAFF.

UNION THEOLOGICAL SEMINARY,
October, 1883.

CONTENTS.

CHAPTER V.

Christian Worship.

CHAPTER VI.

Beginnings of Christian Art.

CHAPTER VII.

The Church in the Catacombs.

CHAPTER VIII.

The Christian Life in Contrast with Pagan Corruption.

CHAPTER IX.

ASCETIC TENDENCIES.

CHAPTER X.

MONTANISM.

CHAPTER XI.

THE HERESIES OF THE ANTE-NICENE AGE.

CHAPTER XII

The Development of Catholic Theology.

CHAPTER XIII

Ecclesiastical Literature of the Ante-Nicene Age, and Biographical Sketches of the Church Fathers.

SECOND PERIOD

ANTE-NICENE CHRISTIANITY

OR,

THE AGE OF PERSECUTION AND MARTYRDOM

FROM THE

DEATH OF JOHN THE APOSTLE TO CONSTANTINE THE GREAT

A. D. 100–325.

"THE BLOOD OF MARTYRS IS THE SEED OF THE CHURCH."

SECOND PERIOD

ANTE-NICENE CHRISTIANITY

OR,

THE AGE OF PERSECUTION AND MARTYRDOM.

FROM THE

DEATH OF JOHN THE APOSTLE TO CONSTANTINE THE GREAT

§ 1. *Literature on the Ante-Nicene Age.*

I. SOURCES.

1. The writings of the Apostolic Fathers, the Apologists, and all the ecclesiastical authors of the 2nd and 3rd, and to some extent of the 4th and 5th centuries; particularly CLEMENT OF ROME, IGNATIUS, POLYCARP, JUSTIN MARTYR, IRENÆUS, HIPPOLYTUS, TERTULLIAN, CYPRIAN, CLEMENT OF ALEXANDRIA, ORIGEN, EUSEBIUS, JEROME, EPIPHANIUS, and THEODORET.

2. The writings of the numerous heretics, mostly extant only in fragments.

3. The works of the pagan opponents of Christianity, as CELSUS, LUCIAN, PORPHYRY, JULIAN THE APOSTATE.

4. The occasional notices of Christianity, in the contemporary classical authors, TACITUS, SUETONIUS, the younger PLINY, DION CASSIUS.

II. COLLECTIONS OF SOURCES, (besides those included in the comprehensive Patristic Libraries):

GEBHARDT, HARNACK, and ZAHN: *Patrum Apostolicorum Opera.* Lips., 1876; second ed. 1878 sqq.

FR. XAV. FUNK (R. C.): *Opera Patrum Apost.* Tubing., 1878, 1881, 1887, 2 vols. The last edition includes the *Didache.*

I. C. TH. OTTO: *Corpus Apologetarum Christianorum sæculi secundi.* Jenæ, 1841 sqq., in 9 vols.; 2nd ed. 1847–1861; 3rd ed. 1876 sqq. ("*plurimum aucta et emendata*").

ROBERTS AND DONALDSON : *Ante-Nicene Christian Library.* Edinburgh
(T. & T. Clark), 1868–'72, 25 volumes. American edition, chronologically arranged and enlarged by Bishop A. C. COXE, D. D., with
a valuable *Bibliographical Synopsis* by E. C. RICHARDSON. New
York (Christian Literature Company), 1885–'87, 9 large vols.

The fragments of the earliest Christian writers, whose works are
lost, may be found collected in GRABE : *Spicilegium Patrum ut et
Haereticorum Saeculi I. II. et III.* (Oxon. 1700; new ed. Oxf. 1714,
3 vols.); in ROUTH : *Reliquiæ Sacræ, sive auctorum fere jam perdi-
torum secundi, tertiique saeculi fragmenta, quae supersunt* (Oxon. 1814
sqq. 4 vols.; 2nd ed. enlarged, 5 vols. Oxf. 1846–48); and in DOM.
I. B. PITRA (O. S. B., a French Cardinal since 1863) : *Spicilegium
Solesmense, complectens sanctorum patrum scriptorumque eccles. anec-
dota hactenus opera, selecta e Graecis, Orientialibus et Latinis codicibus*
(Paris, 1852–'60, 5 vols.). Comp. also BUNSEN : *Christianity and Mankind,* etc. Lond. 1854, vols. V., VI. and VII., which contain the
Analecta Ante-Nicaena (*reliquiæ literariæ, canonicæ, liturgicæ*).

The *hæreseological* writings of Epiphanius, Philastrius, Pseudo-
Tertullian, etc. are collected in FRANC. OEHLER : *Corpus hæreseolo-
gicum.* Berol. 1856–61, 3 vols. They belong more to the next period.

The *Jewish* and *Heathen* Testimonies are collected by N. LARDNER,
1764, new ed. by Kippis, Lond. 1838.

III. HISTORIES.

1. Ancient Historians.

HEGESIPPUS (a Jewish Christian of the middle of the second century) : 'Υπομνήματα τῶν ἐκκλησιαστικῶν πράξεων (quoted under the
title πέντε ὑπομνήματα and πέντε συγγράμματα). These ecclesiastical
Memorials are only preserved in fragments (on the martyrdom of
James of Jerusalem, the rise of heresies, etc.) in Eusebius *H. Eccl.,*
collected by Grabe (*Spicileg.* II. 203–214), Routh (*Reliqu. Sacræ,*
vol. I. 209–219), and Hilgenfeld ("Zeitschrift für wissenschaftliche
Theol." 1876, pp. 179 sqq.). See art. of Weizsäcker in Herzog, 2nd
ed., V. 695; and of Milligan in Smith & Wace, II. 875. The work
was still extant in the 16th century, and may be discovered yet; see
Hilgenfeld's "Zeitschrift" for 1880, p. 127. It is strongly *Jewish*-
Christian, yet not Ebionite, but Catholic.

* EUSEBIUS (bishop of Cæsarea in Palestine since 315, died 340, "the
father of Church History," "the Christian Herodotus," confidential
friend, adviser, and eulogist of Constantine the Great) : 'Εκκλησιαστικὴ
ἱστορία, from the incarnation to the defeat and death of Licinius 324.
Chief edd. by *Stephens,* Paris 1544 (*ed. princeps*) ; *Valesius* (with the
other Greek church historians), Par. 1659; *Reading,* Cambr. 1720;
Zimmermann, Francof. 1822; *Burton,* Oxon. 1838 and 1845 (2 vols.);
Schwegler, Tub. 1852; *Lämmer,* Scaphus. 1862 (important for the
text); *F. A. Heinichen,* Lips. 1827, second ed. improved 1868–'70,
3 vols. (the most complete and useful edition of all the *Scripta His-*

torica of Eus.); *G. Dindorf*, Lips., 1871. Several versions (German, French, and English); one by *Hanmer* (Cambridge; 1683, etc.); another by *C. F. Crusé* (an Am. Episc., London, 1842, Phil., 1860, included in Bagster's edition of the *Greek Eccles. Historians*, London, 1847, and in Bohn's *Eccles. Library*); the best with commentary by *A. C. McGiffert* (to be published by "The Christian Lit. Comp.," New York, 1890).

The other historical writings of Eusebius, including his *Chronicle*, his *Life of Constantine*, and his *Martyrs of Palestine*, are found in Heinichen's ed., and also in the ed. of his *Opera omnia*, by MIGNE, "Patrol. Græca," Par. 1857, 5 vols. Best ed. of his *Chronicle*, by ALFRED SCHÖNE, Berlin, 1866 and 1875, 2 vols.

Whatever may be said of the defects of Eusebius as an historical critic and writer, his learning and industry are unquestionable, and his Church History and Chronicle will always remain an invaluable collection of information not attainable in any other ancient author. The sarcastic contempt of Gibbon and charge of willful suppression of truth are not justified, except against his laudatory over-estimate of Constantine, whose splendid services to the church blinded his vision. For a just estimate of Eusebius see the exhaustive article of Bishop Lightfoot in Smith & Wace, II. 308–348.

2. Modern Historians.

WILLIAM CAVE (died 1713): *Primitive Christianity.* Lond. 4th ed. 1682, in 3 parts. The same: *Lives of the most eminent Fathers of the Church that flourished in the first four centuries*, 1677–'83, 2 vols.; revised by ed. *H. Carey*, Oxford, 1840, in 3 vols. Comp. also CAVE'S *Scriptorum ecclesiasticorum historia literaria, a Christo nato usque ad sæculum* XIV; best ed. Oxford, 1740–'43, 2 vols. fol.

* J. L. MOSHEIM: *Commentarii de rebus Christianis ante Constantinum M.* Helmst. 1753. The same in English by *Vidal*, 1813 sqq., 3 vols., and by *Murdock*, New Haven, 1852, 2 vols.

* EDWARD GIBBON: *The History of the Decline and Fall of the Roman Empire.* London, 1776–'88, 6 vols.; best edd. by *Milman*, with his own, Guizot's and Wenck's notes, and by *William Smith*, including the notes of Milman, etc. Reprinted, London, 1872, 8 vols., New York, Harpers, 1880, in 6 vols. In Chs. 15 and 16, and throughout his great work, Gibbon dwells on the outside, and on the defects rather than the virtues of ecclesiastical Christianity, without entering into the heart of spiritual Christianity which continued beating through all ages; but for fullness and general accuracy of information and artistic representation his work is still unsurpassed.

H. G. TZSCHIRNER: *Der Fall des Heidenthums.* Leipz. 1829.

EDW. BURTON: *Lectures upon the Ecclesiastical History of the first three Centuries.* Oxf. 1833, in 3 parts (in 1 vol. 1845). He made also collections of the ante-Nicene testimonies to the Divinity of Christ, and the Holy Spirit.

HENRY H. MILMAN: *The History of Christianity from the Birth of Christ*

to the Abolition of Paganism in the Roman Empire. Lond. 1840.
3 vols.; 2nd ed. 1866. Comp. also the first book of his *History of
Latin Christianity,* 2d ed. London and New York, 1860, in 8 vols.

JOHN KAYE (Bishop of Lincoln, d. 1853): *Ecclesiastical History of the
Second and Third Centuries, illustrated from the writings of Tertullian.*
Lond. 1845. Comp. also his books on *Justin Martyr, Clement of
Alex.,* and the *Council of Nicœa* (1853).

F. D. MAURICE : *Lectures on the Eccles. Hist. of the First and Second
Cent.* Cambr. 1854.

* A. RITSCHL: *Die Entstehung der alt-katholischen Kirche.* Bonn, 1850;
2nd ed. 1857. The second edition is partly reconstructed and more
positive.

* E. DE PRESSENSÉ (French Protestant): *Histoire de trois premiers siècles
de l'église chrétienne.* Par. 1858 sqq. The same in German trans. by *E.
Fabarius.* Leipz. 1862–'63, 4 vols. English transl. by *Annie Harwood-
Holmden,* under the title: *The Early Years of Christianity. A Comprehensive History of the First Three Centuries of the Christian Church,*
4 vols. Vol. I. The Apost. Age; vol. II. Martyrs and Apologists; vol.
III. Heresy and Christian Doctrine; vol. IV. Christian Life and Practice. London (Hodder & Stoughton), 1870 sqq., cheaper ed., 1879.
Revised edition of the original, Paris, 1887 sqq.

W. D. KILLEN (Presbyterian): *The Ancient Church traced for the first
three centuries.* Edinb. and New York, 1859. New ed. N. Y., 1883.

AMBROSE MANAHAN (R. Cath.): *Triumph of the Catholic Church in the
Early Ages.* New York, 1859.

ALVAN LAMSON (Unitarian): *The Church of the First Three Centuries,
with special reference to the doctrine of the Trinity; illustrating its
late origin and gradual formation.* Boston, 1860.

MILO MAHAN (Episcopalian): *A Church History of the First Three centuries.*
N. York, 1860. Second ed., 1878 (enlarged).

J. J. BLUNT: *History of the Christian Church during the first three centuries.* London, 1861.

JOS. SCHWANE (R. C.): *Dogmengeschichte der vornicänischen Zeit.*
Münster, 1862.

TH. W. MOSSMAN: *History of the Cath. Church of J. Christ from the
death of St. John to the middle of the second century.* Lond. 1873.

* ERNEST RENAN: *L' Histoire des origines du Christianisme.* Paris, 1863–
1882, 7 vols. The last two vols., *l' église Chrétienne,* 1879, and *Marc
Aurèle,* 1882, belong to this period. Learned, critical, and brilliant,
but thoroughly secular, and skeptical.

* GERHARD UHLHORN: *Der Kampf des Christenthums mit dem Heidenthum.* 3d improved ed. Stuttgart, 1879. English transl. by Profs.
Egbert C. Smyth and *C. J. H. Ropes: The Conflict of Christianity,* etc.
N. York, 1879. An admirable translation of a graphic and inspiring
account of the heroic conflict of Christianity with heathen Rome.

*THEOD. KEIM, (d. 1879): *Rom und das Christenthum.* Ed. from the author's MSS. by *H. Ziegler.* Berlin, 1881. (667 pages).

CHR. WORDSWORTH (Bishop of Lincoln): *A Church History to the Council of Nicæa, A. D.* 325. Lond. and N. York, 1881. Anglo-Catholic.

A. PLUMMER : *The Church of the Early Fathers,* London, 1887.

Of the general works on Church History, those of BARONIUS, TILLEMONT (R. C.), SCHRÖCKH, GIESELER, NEANDER, and BAUR (the third revised ed. of vol. 1st, Tüb. 1853, pp. 175–527 ; the same also transl. into English) should be noticed throughout on this period; but all these books are *partly* superseded by more recent discoveries and discussions of special points, which will be noticed in the respective sections.

§ 2. *General Character of Ante-Nicene Christianity.*

We now descend from the primitive apostolic church to the Graeco-Roman; from the scene of creation to the work of preservation; from the fountain of divine revelation to the stream of human development; from the inspirations of the apostles and prophets to the productions of enlightened but fallible teachers. The hand of God has drawn a bold line of demarcation between the century of miracles and the succeeding ages, to show, by the abrupt transition and the striking contrast, the difference between the work of God and the work of man, and to impress us the more deeply with the supernatural origin of Christianity and the incomparable value of the New Testament. There is no other transition in history so radical and sudden, and yet so silent and secret. The stream of divine life in its passage from the mountain of inspiration to the valley of tradition is for a short time lost to our view, and seems to run under ground. Hence the close of the first and the beginning of the second centuries, or the age of the Apostolic Fathers is often regarded as a period for critical conjecture and doctrinal and ecclesiastical controversy rather than for historical narration.

Still, notwithstanding the striking difference, the church of the second and third centuries is a legitimate continuation of that of the primitive age. While far inferior in originality, purity, energy, and freshness, it is distinguished for conscientious fidelity in preserving and propagating the sacred writings and traditions of the apostles, and for untiring zeal in imitating their holy lives amidst the greatest difficulties and dangers, when the religion of Christ was prohibited by law and the profession of it punished as a political crime.

The second period, from the death of the apostle John to the end of the persecutions, or to the accession of Constantine, the first Christian emperor, is the classic age of the *ecclesia pressa*, of heathen persecution, and of Christian martyrdom and heroism, of cheerful sacrifice of possessions and life itself for the inheritance of heaven. It furnishes a continuous commentary on the Saviour's words: "Behold, I send you forth as sheep in the midst of wolves;" "I came not to send peace on earth, but a sword."[1] No merely human religion could have stood such an ordeal of fire for three hundred years. The final victory of Christianity over Judaism and heathenism, and the mightiest empire of the ancient world, a victory gained without physical force, but by the moral power of patience and perseverance, of faith and love, is one of the sublimest spectacles in history, and one of the strongest evidences of the divinity and indestructible life of our religion.

But equally sublime and significant are the intellectual and spiritual victories of the church in this period over the science and art of heathenism, and over the assaults of Gnostic and Ebionitic heresy, with the copious vindication and development of the Christian truth, which the great mental conflict with those open and secret enemies called forth.

The church of this period appears poor in earthly possessions and honors, but rich in heavenly grace, in world-conquering faith, love, and hope; unpopular, even outlawed, hated, and persecuted, yet far more vigorous and expansive than the philosophies of Greece or the empire of Rome; composed chiefly of persons of the lower social ranks, yet attracting the

[1] Comp. Matt. 10: 17–39; 5: 10, 12; 13: 21; 16: 24; 20: 22 sq.; 1 Cor. 15: 31; 2 Cor. 4: 10; Rom. 8: 35; Phil. 3: 10 sq.; Col. 1: 24 sq.; 1 Pet. 2: 21.

noblest and deepest minds of the age, and bearing in her bosom the hope of the world; "as unknown, yet well-known, as dying, and behold it lives;" conquering by apparent defeat, and growing on the blood of her martyrs; great in deeds, greater in sufferings, greatest in death for the honor of Christ and the benefit of generations to come.[1]

The condition and manners of the Christians in this age are most beautifully described by the unknown author of the "Epistola ad Diognetum" in the early part of the second century.[2] "The Christians," he says, "are not distinguished from other men by country, by language, nor by civil institutions. For they neither dwell in cities by themselves, nor use a peculiar tongue, nor lead a singular mode of life. They dwell in the Grecian or barbarian cities, as the case may be; they follow the usage of the country in dress, food, and the other affairs of life. Yet they present a wonderful and confessedly paradoxical conduct. They dwell in their own native lands, but as strangers. They take part in all things, as citizens; and they suffer all things, as foreigners. Every foreign country is a fatherland to them, and every native land is a foreign. They marry, like all others; they have children; but they do not cast away their offspring. They have the table in common, but not wives. They are in the flesh, but do not live after the flesh. They

---

[1] Isaac Taylor, in his *Ancient Christianity*, which is expressly written against a superstitious over-valuation of the patristic age, nevertheless admits (vol. i. p. 37): "Our brethren of the early church challenge our respect, as well as affection; for theirs was the fervor of a steady faith in things unseen and eternal; theirs, often, a meek patience under the most grievous wrongs; theirs the courage to maintain a good profession before the frowning face of philosophy, of secular tyranny, and of splendid superstition; theirs was abstractedness from the world and a painful self-denial; theirs the most arduous and costly labors of love; theirs a munificence in charity, altogether without example; theirs was a reverent and scrupulous care of the sacred writings; and this one merit, if they had no other, is of a superlative degree, and should entitle them to the veneration and grateful regards of the modern church. How little do many readers of the Bible, nowadays, think of what it cost the Christians of the second and third centuries, merely to rescue and hide the sacred treasures from the rage of the heathen!"

[2] C. 5 and 6 (p. 69 sq. ed. Otto. Lips. 1852).

live upon the earth, but are citizens of heaven. They obey the existing laws, and excel the laws by their lives. They love all, and are persecuted by all. They are unknown, and yet they are condemned. They are killed and are made alive. They are poor and make many rich. They lack all things, and in all things abound. They are reproached, and glory in their reproaches. They are calumniated, and are justified. They are cursed, and they bless. They receive scorn, and they give honor. They do good, and are punished as evil-doers. When punished, they rejoice, as being made alive. By the Jews they are attacked as aliens, and by the Greeks persecuted; and the cause of the enmity their enemies cannot tell. In short, what the soul is in the body, the Christians are in the world. The soul is diffused through all the members of the body, and the Christians are spread through the cities of the world. The soul dwells in the body, but it is not of the body; so the Christians dwell in the world, but are not of the world. The soul, invisible, keeps watch in the visible body; so also the Christians are seen to live in the world, but their piety is invisible. The flesh hates and wars against the soul, suffering no wrong from it, but because it resists fleshly pleasures; and the world hates the Christians with no reason, but that they resist its pleasures. The soul loves the flesh and members, by which it is hated; so the Christians love their haters. The soul is inclosed in the body, but holds the body together; so the Christians are detained in the world as in a prison; but they contain the world. Immortal, the soul dwells in the mortal body; so the Christians dwell in the corruptible, but look for incorruption in heaven. The soul is the better for restriction in food and drink; and the Christians increase, though daily punished. This lot God has assigned to the Christians in the world; and it cannot be taken from them."

The community of Christians thus from the first felt itself, in distinction from Judaism and from heathenism, the salt of the earth, the light of the world, the city of God set on a hill, the immortal soul in a dying body; and this its impression respecting itself was no proud conceit, but truth and reality, acting in life and in death, and opening the way through hatred and persecution even to an outward victory over the world.

The ante-Nicene age has been ever since the Reformation a battle-field between Catholic and Evangelical historians and polemics, and is claimed by both for their respective creeds. But it is a sectarian abuse of history to identify the Christianity of this martyr period either with Catholicism, or with Protestantism. It is rather the common root out of which both have sprung, Catholicism (Greek and Roman) first, and Protestantism afterwards. It is the natural transition from the apostolic age to the Nicene age, yet leaving behind many important truths of the former (especially the Pauline doctrines) which were to be derived and explored in future ages. We can trace in it the elementary forms of the Catholic creed, organization and worship, and also the germs of nearly all the corruptions of Greek and Roman Christianity.

In its relation to the secular power, the ante-Nicene church is simply the continuation of the apostolic period, and has nothing in common either with the hierarchical, or with the Erastian systems. It was not opposed to the secular government in its proper sphere, but the secular heathenism of the government was opposed to Christianity. The church was altogether based upon the voluntary principle, as a self-supporting and self-governing body. In this respect it may be compared to the church in the United States, but with this essential difference that in America the secular government, instead of persecuting Christianity, recognizes and protects it by law, and secures to it full freedom of public worship and in all its activities at home and abroad.

The theology of the second and third centuries was mainly apologetic against the paganism of Greece and Rome, and polemic against the various forms of the Gnostic heresy. In this conflict it brings out, with great force and freshness, the principal arguments for the divine origin and character of the Christian religion and the outlines of the true doctrine of Christ and the holy trinity, as afterwards more fully developed in the Nicene and post-Nicene ages.

The organization of this period may be termed primitive episcopacy, as distinct from the apostolic order which preceded, and the metropolitan and patriarchal hierarchy which succeeded it. In worship it forms likewise the transition from apostolic simplicity to the liturgical and ceremonial splendor of full-grown Catholicism.

The first half of the second century is comparatively veiled in obscurity, although considerable light has been shed over it by recent discoveries and investigations. After the death of John only a few witnesses remain to testify of the wonders of the apostolic days, and their writings are few in number, short in compass and partly of doubtful origin: a volume of letters and historical fragments, accounts of martyrdom, the pleadings of two or three apologists; to which must be added the rude epitaphs, faded pictures, and broken sculptures of the subterranean church in the catacombs. The men of that generation were more skilled in acting out Christianity in life and death, than in its literary defence. After the intense commotion of the apostolic age there was a breathing spell, a season of unpretending but fruitful preparation for a new productive epoch. But the soil of heathenism had been broken up, and the new seed planted by the hands of the apostles gradually took root.

Then came the great literary conflict of the apologists and doctrinal polemics in the second half of the same century; and towards the middle of the third the theological schools of Alexandria, and northern Africa, laying the foundation the one for the theology of the Greek, the other for that of the Latin church. At the beginning of the fourth century the church east and west was already so well consolidated in doctrine and discipline that it easily survived the shock of the last and most terrible persecution, and could enter upon the fruits of its long-continued sufferings and take the reins of government in the old Roman empire.

CHAPTER I.

SPREAD OF CHRISTIANITY.

§ 3. *Literature.*

I. Sources.

No statistics or accurate statements, but only scattered hints in
Pliny (107): *Ep.* x. 96 sq. (the letter to Trajan). Ignatius (about 110):
Ad Magnes. c. 10. *Ep. ad Diogn.* (about 120) c. 6.
Justin Martyr (about 140): *Dial.* 117; *Apol.* I. 53.
Irenaeus (about 170): *Adv. Haer.* I. 10; III. 3, 4; v. 20, etc.
Tertullian (about 200): *Apol.* I. 21, 37, 41, 42; *Ad Nat.* I. 7; *Ad
Scap.* c. 2, 5; *Adv. Jud.* 7, 12, 13.
Origen (d. 254): *Contr. Cels.* I. 7, 27; II. 13, 46; III. 10, 30; *De
Princ.* 1. IV. c. 1, § 2; *Com. in Matth.* p. 857, ed. *Delarue.*
Eusebius (d. 340): *Hist. Eccl.* III. 1; v. 1; vii, 1; viii. 1, also books ix.
and x. Rufinus: *Hist. Eccles.* ix. 6.
Augustin (d. 430): *De Civitate Dei.* Eng. translation by *M. Dods*, Edin-
burgh, 1871; new ed. (in Schaff's "Nicene and Post-Nicene Library"),
N. York, 1887.

II. Works.

Mich. Le Quien (a learned Dominican, d. 1733): *Oriens Christianus.*
Par. 1740. 3 vols. fol. A complete ecclesiastical geography of the
East, divided into the four patriarchates of Constantinople, Alexan-
dria, Antioch, and Jerusalem.

Mosheim: *Historical Commentaries*, etc. (ed. Murdock) I. 259–290.

Gibbon: *The Decline and Fall of the Roman Empire.* Chap. xv.

A. Beugnot: *Histoire de la destruction du paganisme en Occident.* Paris
1835, 2 vols. Crowned by the *Académie des inscriptions et belles-
letters.*

Etienne Chastel: *Histoire de la destruction du paganisme dans l'
empire d' Orient.* Paris 1850. Prize essay of the *Académie.*

Neander: *History of the Christian Relig. and Church* (trans. of Torrey),
I. 68–79.

Wiltsch: *Handbuch der kirchl. Geographie u. Statistik.* Berlin 1846.
I. p. 32 sqq.

Chs. Merivale: *Conversion of the Roman Empire* (Boyle Lectures for
1864), republ. N. York 1865. Comp. also his *History of the Romans
under the Empire*, which goes from Julius Cæsar to Marcus Aurelius,
Lond. & N. York, 7 vols.

Edward A. Freeman: *The Historical Geography of Europe.* Lond. &
N. York 1881. 2 vols. (vol. I. chs. II. & III. pp. 18–71.)

Comp. Friedländer, *Sittengesch. Roms.* III. 517 sqq.; and Renan:
Marc-Aurèle. Paris 1882, ch. xxv. pp. 447–464 (*Statistique et extension géographique du Christianisme*).

V. Schultze: *Geschichte des Untergangs des griech-römischen. Heidenthums.* Jena, 1887.

13

§ 4. *Hindrances and Helps.*

For the first three centuries Christianity was placed in the most unfavorable circumstances, that it might display its moral power, and gain its victory over the world by spiritual weapons alone. Until the reign of Constantine it had not even a legal existence in the Roman empire, but was first ignored as a Jewish sect, then slandered, proscribed, and persecuted, as a treasonable innovation, and the adoption of it made punishable with confiscation and death. Besides, it offered not the slightest favor, as Mohammedanism afterwards did, to the corrupt inclinations of the heart, but against the current ideas of Jews and heathen it so presented its inexorable demand of repentance and conversion, renunciation of self and the world, that more, according to Tertullian, were kept out of the new sect by love of pleasure than by love of life. The Jewish origin of Christianity also, and the poverty and obscurity of a majority of its professors particularly offended the pride of the Greeks and Romans. Celsus, exaggerating this fact, and ignoring the many exceptions, scoffingly remarked, that "weavers, cobblers, and fullers, the most illiterate persons" preached the "irrational faith," and knew how to commend it especially "to women and children."

But in spite of these extraordinary difficulties Christianity made a progress which furnished striking evidence of its divine origin and adaptation to the deeper wants of man, and was employed as such by Irenæus, Justin, Tertullian, and other fathers of that day. Nay, the very hindrances became, in the hands of Providence, means of promotion. Persecution led to martyrdom, and martyrdom had not terrors alone, but also attractions, and stimulated the noblest and most unselfish form of ambition. Every genuine martyr was a living proof of the truth and holiness of the Christian religion. Tertullian could exclaim to the heathen : " All your ingenious cruelties can accomplish nothing ; they are only a lure to this sect. Our number increases the more you destroy us. The blood of the Christians is their seed." The moral earnestness of the Christians contrasted powerfully with the prevailing corruption of the age, and while it repelled the frivolous and voluptuous, it could not fail to impress most strongly the deepest and noblest minds. The predilection of the poor and oppressed for the gospel attested its comforting and redeeming power. But others also, though not many, from the higher and educated classes, were from the first attracted to the new religion; such men as Nicodemus, Joseph of Arimathæa, the apostle Paul, the proconsul Sergius Paulus, Dionysius of Athens, Erastus of Corinth, and some members of the imperial household. Among the sufferers in Domitian's persecution were his own near kinswoman Flavia Domitilla and her husband Flavius Clemens. In the oldest part of the Catacomb of Callistus, which is named after St. Lucina, members of the illustrious *gens Pomponia*, and perhaps also of the Flavian house, are interred. The senatorial and equestrian orders furnished several converts open or concealed. Pliny laments, that in Asia Minor men of every rank (*omnis ordinis*) go over to the Christians. Tertullian asserts that the tenth part of Carthage, and among them senators and ladies of the noblest descent and the nearest relatives of the proconsul of Africa professed Christianity. The numerous church fathers from the middle of the second century, a Justin Martyr, Irenæus, Hippolytus, Clement, Origen, Tertullian, Cyprian, excelled, or at least equalled in talent and culture, their most eminent heathen contemporaries.

Nor was this progress confined to any particular localities. It extended alike over all parts of the empire. "We are a people of yesterday," says Tertullian in his Apology, "and yet we have filled every place belonging to you—cities, islands, castles, towns, assemblies, your very camp, your tribes, companies, palace, senate, forum! We leave you your temples only. We can count your armies; our numbers in a single province will be greater." All these facts expose the injustice of the odious charge of Celsus, repeated by a modern sceptic, that the new sect was almost entirely composed of the dregs of the populace—of peasants and mechanics, of boys and women, of beggars and slaves.

§ 5. *Causes of the Success of Christianity.*

The chief positive cause of the rapid spread and ultimate triumph of Christianity is to be found in its own absolute intrinsic worth, as the universal religion of salvation, and in the perfect teaching and example of its divine-human Founder, who proves himself to every believing heart a Saviour from sin and a giver of eternal life. Christianity is adapted to all classes, conditions, and relations among men, to all nationalities and races, to all grades of culture, to every soul that longs for redemption from sin, and for holiness of life. Its value could be seen in the truth and self-evidencing power of its doctrines; in the purity and sublimity of its precepts; in its regenerating and sanctifying effects on heart and life; in the elevation of woman and of home life over which she presides; in the amelioration of the condition of the poor and suffering; in the faith, the brotherly love, the beneficence, and the triumphant death of its confessors.

To this internal moral and spiritual testimony were added the powerful outward proof of its divine origin in the prophecies and types of the Old Testament, so strikingly fulfilled in the New; and finally, the testimony of the miracles, which, according to the express statements of Quadratus, Justin Martyr, Irenæus, Tertullian, Origen, and others, continued in this period to accompany the preaching of missionaries from time to time, for the conversion of the heathen.

Particularly favorable outward circumstances were the extent, order, and unity of the Roman empire, and the prevalence of the Greek language and culture.

In addition to these positive causes, Christianity had a powerful negative advantage in the hopeless condition of the Jewish and heathen world. Since the fearful judgment of the destruction of Jerusalem, Judaism wandered restless and accursed, without national existence. Heathenism outwardly held sway, but was inwardly rotten and in process of inevitable decay. The popular religion and public morality were undermined by a sceptical and materialistic philosophy; Grecian science and art had lost their creative energy; the Roman empire rested only on the power of the sword and of temporal interests; the moral bonds of society were sundered; unbounded avarice and vice of every kind, even by the confession of a Seneca and a Tacitus, reigned in Rome and in the provinces, from the throne to the hovel. Virtuous emperors, like Antoninus Pius and Marcus Aurelius, were the exception, not the rule, and could not prevent the progress of moral decay. Nothing, that classic antiquity in its fairest days had produced, could heal the fatal wounds of the age, or even give transient relief. The only star of hope in the gathering night was the young, the fresh, the dauntless religion of Jesus, fearless of death, strong in faith, glowing with love, and destined to commend itself more and more to all reflecting minds as the only living religion of the present and the future. While the world was continually agitated by wars, and revolutions, and public calamities, while systems of philosophy, and dynasties were rising and passing away, the new religion, in spite of fearful opposition from without and danger from within, was silently and steadily progressing with the irresistible force of truth, and worked itself gradually into the very bone and blood of the race.

"Christ appeared," says the great Augustin, "to the men of the decrepit, decaying world, that while all around them was withering away, they might through Him receive new, youthful life."

NOTES.

GIBBON, in his famous fifteenth chapter, traces the rapid progress of Christianity in the Roman empire to five causes: the zeal of the early Christians, the belief in future rewards and punishment, the power of miracles, the austere (pure) morals of the Christian, and the compact church organization. But these causes are themselves the effects of a cause which Gibbon ignores, namely, the divine truth of Christianity, the perfection of Christ's teaching and Christ's example. See the strictures of Dr. John Henry Newman, *Grammar of Assent*, 445 sq., and Dr. George P. Fisher, *The Beginnings of Christianity*, p. 543 sqq. "The zeal" [of the early Christians], says Fisher, "was zeal for a person, and for a cause identified with Him; the belief in the future life sprang out of faith in Him who had died and risen again, and ascended to Heaven; the miraculous powers of the early disciples were consciously connected with the same source; the purification of morals, and the fraternal unity, which lay at the basis of ecclesiastical association among the early Christians, were likewise the fruit of their relation to Christ, and their common love to Him. The victory of Christianity in the Roman world was the victory of Christ, who was lifted up that He might draw all men unto Him."

Lecky (*Hist. of Europ. Morals*, I. 412) goes deeper than Gibbon, and accounts for the success of early Christianity by its intrinsic excellency and remarkable adaptation to the wants of the times in the old Roman empire. "In the midst of this movement," he says, "Christianity gained its ascendancy, and we can be at no loss to discover the cause of its triumph. No other religion, under such circumstances, had ever combined so many distinct elements of power and attraction. Unlike the Jewish religion, it was bound by no local ties, and was equally adapted for every nation and for every class. Unlike Stoicism, it appealed in the strongest manner to the affections, and offered all the charm of a sympathetic worship. Unlike the Egyptian religion, it united with its distinctive teaching a pure and noble system of ethics, and proved itself capable of realizing it in action. It proclaimed, amid a vast movement of social and national amalgamation, the universal brotherhood of mankind. Amid the softening influence of philosophy and civilization, it taught the supreme sanctity of love. To the slave, who had never before exercised so large an influence over Roman religious life, it was the religion of the suffering and the oppressed. To the philosopher it was at once the echo of the highest ethics of the later Stoics, and the expansion of the best teaching of the school of Plato. To a world thirsting for prodigy, it offered a history replete with wonders more strange than those of Apollonius; while the Jew and the Chaldean could scarcely rival its exorcists, and the legends of continual miracles circulated among its followers. To a world deeply conscious of political dissolution, and prying eagerly and anxiously into the future, it proclaimed with a thrilling power the immediate destruction of the globe— the glory of all its friends, and the damnation of all its foes. To a world that had grown very weary gazing on the cold passionless grandeur which Cato realized, and which Lucan sung, it presented an ideal of compassion and of love—an ideal destined for centuries to draw around it all that was greatest, as well as all that was noblest upon earth—a Teacher who could weep by the sepulchre of His friend, who was touched with the feeling of our infirmities. To a world, in fine, distracted by hostile creeds and colliding philosophies, it taught its doctrines, not as a human speculation, but as a Divine revelation, authenticated much less by reason than by faith. 'With the heart man believeth unto righteousness;' 'He that doeth the will of my Father will know the doctrine, whether it be of God;' 'Unless you believe you cannot understand;' 'A heart naturally Christian;' 'The heart makes the theologian,' are the phrases which best express the first action of Christianity upon the world. Like all great religions, it was more concerned with modes of feeling than with modes of thought. The chief cause of its success was the congruity of its teaching with the spiritual nature of mankind. It was because it was true of the moral sentiments of the age, because it represented faithfully the supreme type of excellence to which men were then tending, because it corresponded with their religious wants, aims, and emotions, because the whole spiritual being could then expand and expatiate under its influence, that it planted its roots so deeply in the hearts of men.''

MERIVALE (*Convers. of the Rom. Emp.*, Preface) traces the conversion of the Roman empire chiefly to four causes : 1) the external evidence of the apparent fulfilment of recorded prophecy and miracles to the truth of Christianity ; 2) the internal evidence of satisfying the acknowledged need of a redeemer and sanctifier; 3) the goodness and holiness manifested in the lives and deaths of the primitive believers; 4) the temporal success of Christianity under Constantine, which "turned the mass of mankind, as with a sweeping revolution, to the rising sun of revealed truth in Christ Jesus."

RENAN discusses the reasons for the victory of Christianity in the 31st chapter of his *Marc-Aurèle* (Paris 1882), pp. 561–588. He attributes it chiefly "to the new discipline of life," and "the moral reform," which the world required, which neither philosophy nor any of the established religions could give. The Jews indeed rose high above the corruptions of the times. " *Gloire éternelle et unique, qui doit faire oublier bien des folies et des violences ! Les Juifs sont les révolutionnaires du 1er et du 2e siècle de notre ère.*" They gave to the world Christianity. "*Les populations se précipitèrent, par une sorte du mouvement instinctif, dans une secte qui satisfaisait leur aspirations les plus intimes et ouvrait des éspérances infinies.*" Renan makes much account of the belief in immortality and the offer of complete pardon to every sinner, as allurements to Christianity ; and, like Gibbon, he ignores its real power as a religion of *salvation.* This accounts for its success not only in the old Roman empire, but in every country and nation where it has found a home.

§ 6. *Means of Propagation.*

It is a remarkable fact that after the days of the Apostles no names of great missionaries are mentioned till the opening of the middle ages, when the conversion of nations was effected or introduced by a few individuals as St. Patrick in Ireland, St. Columba in Scotland, St. Augustine in England, St. Boniface in Germany, St. Ansgar in Scandinavia, St. Cyril and Methodius among the Slavonic races. There were no missionary societies, no missionary institutions, no organized efforts in the ante-Nicene age; and yet in less than 300 years from the death of St. John the whole population of the Roman empire which then represented the civilized world was nominally christianized.

To understand this astonishing fact, we must remember that the foundation was laid strong and deep by the apostles themselves. The seed scattered by them from Jerusalem to Rome, and fertilized by their blood, sprung up as a bountiful harvest. The word of our Lord was again fulfilled on a larger scale: "One soweth, and another reapeth. I sent you to reap that whereon ye have not labored: others have labored, and ye are entered into their labor" (John 4 : 38).

Christianity once established was its own best missionary. It grew naturally from within. It attracted people by its very presence. It was a light shining in darkness and illuminating the darkness. And while there were no professional missionaries devoting their whole life to this specific work, every congregation was a missionary society, and every Christian believer a missionary, inflamed by the love of Christ to convert his fellow-men. The example had been set by Jerusalem and Antioch, and by those brethren who, after the martyrdom of Stephen, "were scattered abroad and went about preaching the Word."[1] Justin Martyr was converted by a venerable old man whom he met walking on the shore of the sea. "Every Christian laborer," says Tertullian, "both finds out God and manifests him, though Plato affirms that it is not easy to discover the Creator, and difficult when He is found to make him known to all." Celsus scoffingly remarks that fullers and workers in wool and leather, rustic and ignorant persons, were

---

[1] Acts 8 : 4 ; 11 : 19.

the most zealous propagators of Christianity, and brought it first to women and children. Women and slaves introduced it into the home-circle. It is the glory of the gospel that it is preached to the poor and by the poor to make them rich. Origen informs us that the city churches sent their missionaries to the villages. The seed grew up while men slept, and brought forth fruit, first the blade, then the ear, after that the full corn in the ear. Every Christian told his neighbor, the laborer to his fellow-laborer, the slave to his fellow-slave, the servant to his master and mistress, the story of his conversion, as a mariner tells the story of the rescue from shipwreck.

The gospel was propagated chiefly by living preaching and by personal intercourse; to a considerable extent also through the sacred Scriptures, which were early propagated and translated into various tongues, the Latin (North African and Italian), the Syriac (the Curetonian and the Peshito), and the Egyptian (in three dialects, the Memphitic, the Thebaic, and the Bashmuric). Communication among the different parts of the Roman empire from Damascus to Britain was comparatively easy and safe. The highways built for commerce and for the Roman legions, served also the messengers of peace and the silent conquests of the cross. Commerce itself at that time, as well as now, was a powerful agency in carrying the gospel and the seeds of Christian civilization to the remotest parts of the Roman empire.

The particular mode, as well as the precise time, of the introduction of Christianity into the several countries during this period is for the most part uncertain, and we know not much more than the fact itself. No doubt much more was done by the apostles and their immediate disciples, than the New Testament informs us of. But on the other hand the mediæval tradition assigns an apostolic origin to many national and local churches, which cannot have arisen before the second or third century. Even Joseph of Arimathæa, Nicodemus, Dionysius the Areopagite, Lazarus, Martha and Mary were turned by the legend into missionaries to foreign lands.

§ 7. *Extent of Christianity in the Roman Empire.*

Justin Martyr says, about the middle of the second century: "There is no people, Greek or barbarian, or of any other race, by whatsoever appellation or manners they may be distinguished, however ignorant of arts or agriculture, whether they dwell in tents or wander about in covered wagons — among whom prayers and thanksgivings are not offered in the name of the crucified Jesus to the Father and Creator of all things." Half a century later, Tertullian addresses the heathen defiantly: "We are but of yesterday, and yet we already fill your cities, islands, camps, your palace, senate and forum; we have left to you only your temples."[1] These, and similar passages of Irenæus and Arnobius, are evidently rhetorical exaggerations. Origen is more cautious and moderate in his statements. But it may be fairly asserted, that about the end of the third century the name of Christ was known, revered, and persecuted in every province and every city of the empire. Maximian, in one of his edicts, says that "almost all" had abandoned the worship of their ancestors for the new sect.

In the absence of statistics, the number of the Christians must be purely a matter of conjecture. In all probability it amounted at the close of the third and the beginning of the fourth century to nearly one-tenth or one-twelfth of the subjects of Rome, that is to about ten millions of souls.

But the fact, that the Christians were a closely united body, fresh, vigorous, hopeful, and daily increasing, while the heathen were for the most part a loose aggregation, daily diminishing, made the true prospective strength of the church much greater.

The propagation of Christianity among the barbarians in the provinces of Asia and the north-west of Europe beyond the

---

[1] "*Sola vobis relinquimus templa.*" *Apol.* c. 37. Long before Tertullian the heathen Pliny, in his famous letter to Trajan (*Epp.* x. 97) had spoken of "*desolata templa*" and "*sacra solemnia diu intermissa*," in consequence of the spread of the Christian superstition throughout the cities and villages of Asia Minor.

Roman empire, was at first, of course, too remote from the current of history to be of any great immediate importance. But it prepared the way for the civilization of those regions, and their subsequent position in the world.

NOTES.

Gibbon and Friedländer (III. 531) estimate the number of Christians at the accession of Constantine (306) probably too low at one-twentieth ; Matter and Robertson too high at one-fifth of his subjects. Some older writers, misled by the hyperbolical statements of the early Apologists, even represent the Christians as having at least equalled if not exceeded the number of the heathen worshippers in the empire. In this case common prudence would have dictated a policy of toleration long before Constantine. Mosheim, in his *Hist. Commentaries*, etc. (Murdock's translation I. p. 274 sqq.) discusses at length the number of Christians in the second century without arriving at definite conclusions. Chastel estimates the number at the time of Constantine at $\frac{1}{15}$ in the West, $\frac{1}{10}$ in the East, $\frac{1}{12}$ on an average (*Hist. de la destruct. du paganisme*, p. 36). According to Chrysostom, the Christian population of Antioch in his day (380) was about 100,000, or one-half of the whole.

§ 8. *Christianity in Asia.*

Asia was the cradle of Christianity, as it was of humanity and civilization. The apostles themselves had spread the new religion over Palestine, Syria, and Asia Minor. According to the younger Pliny, under Trajan, the temples of the gods in Asia Minor were almost forsaken, and animals of sacrifice found hardly any purchasers. In the second century Christianity penetrated to Edessa in Mesopotamia, and some distance into Persia, Media, Bactria, and Parthia; and in the third, into Armenia and Arabia. Paul himself had, indeed, spent three years in Arabia, but probably in contemplative retirement, preparing for his apostolic ministry. There is a legend, that the apostles Thomas and Bartholomew carried the gospel to India. But a more credible statement is, that the Christian teacher Pantænus of Alexandria journeyed to that country about 190, and that in the fourth century churches were found there.

The transfer of the seat of power from Rome to Constantinople, and the founding of the East Roman empire under Constantine I. gave to Asia Minor, and especially to Constantinople, a commanding importance in the history of the Church for several centuries. The seven Œcumenical Councils from 325 to 787 were all held in that city or its neighborhood, and the doctrinal controversies on the Trinity and the person of Christ were carried on chiefly in Asia Minor, Syria, and Egypt.

In the mysterious providence of God those lands of the Bible and the early church have been conquered by the prophet of Mecca, the Bible replaced by the Koran, and the Greek church reduced to a condition of bondage and stagnation; but the time is not far distant when the East will be regenerated by the undying spirit of Christianity. A peaceful crusade of devoted missionaries preaching the pure gospel and leading holy lives will reconquer the holy land and settle the Eastern question.

§ 9. *Christianity in Egypt.*

In Africa Christianity gained firm foothold first in Egypt, and there probably as early as the apostolic age. The land of the Pharaohs, of the pyramids and sphinxes, of temples and tombs, of hieroglyphics and mummies, of sacred bulls and crocodiles, of despotism and slavery, is closely interwoven with sacred history from the patriarchal times, and even imbedded in the Decalogue as " the house of bondage." It was the home of Joseph and his brethren, and the cradle of Israel. In Egypt the Jewish Scriptures were translated more than two hundred years before our era, and this Greek version used even by Christ and the apostles, spread Hebrew ideas throughout the Roman world, and is the mother of the peculiar idiom of the New Testament. Alexandria was full of Jews, the literary as well as commercial centre of the East, and the connecting link between the East and the West. There the largest libraries were collected; there the Jewish mind came into close contact with the Greek, and the religion of Moses with the philosophy of Plato and Aristotle. There Philo wrote, while Christ taught in Jerusalem and Galilee, and his works were destined to exert a great influence on Christian exegesis through the Alexandrian fathers.

Mark, the evangelist, according to ancient tradition, laid the foundation of the church of Alexandria. The Copts in old Cairo, the Babylon of Egypt, claim this to be the place from which Peter wrote his first epistle (5 : 13); but he must mean either the Babylon on the Euphrates, or the mystic Babylon of Rome. Eusebius names, as the first bishops of Alexandria, Annianos (A. D. 62–85), Abilios (to 98), and Kerdon (to 110). This see naturally grew up to metropolitan and patriarchal importance and dignity. As early as the second century a theological school flourished in Alexandria, in which Clement and Origen taught as pioneers in biblical learning and Christian philosophy. From Lower Egypt the gospel spread to Middle and Upper Egypt and the adjacent provinces, perhaps (in the fourth century) as far as Nubia, Ethiopia, and Abyssinia. At a council of Alexandria in the year 235, twenty bishops were present from the different parts of the land of the Nile.

During the fourth century Egypt gave to the church the Arian heresy, the Athanasian orthodoxy, and the monastic piety of St. Antony and St. Pachomius, which spread with irresistible force over Christendom.

The theological literature of Egypt was chiefly Greek. Most of the early manuscripts of the Greek Scriptures—including probably the invaluable Sinaitic and Vatican MSS.—were written in Alexandria. But already in the second century the Scriptures were translated into the vernacular language, in three different dialects. What remains of these versions is of considerable weight in ascertaining the earliest text of the Greek Testament.

The Christian Egyptians are the descendants of the Pharaonic Egyptians, but largely mixed with negro and Arab blood. Christianity never fully penetrated the nation, and was almost swept away by the Mohammedan conquest under the Caliph Omar (640), who burned the magnificent libraries of Alexandria under the plea that if the books agreed with the Koran, they were useless, if not, they were pernicious and fit for destruction. Since that time Egypt almost disappears from church history, and is still groaning, a house of bondage under new masters. The great mass of the people are Moslems, but the Copts—about half a million of five and a half millions—perpetuate the nominal Christianity of their ancestors, and form a mission field for the more active churches of the West.

§ 10. *Christianity in North Africa.*

BÖTTIGER: *Geschichte der Carthager.* Berlin, 1827.

MOVERS: *Die Phönizier.* 1840–56, 4 vols. (A standard work.)

TH. MOMMSEN: *Röm. Geschichte*, I. 489 sqq. (Book III. chs. 1–7, 5th ed.)

N. DAVIS: *Carthage and her Remains.* London & N. York, 1861.

R. BOSWORTH SMITH: *Carthage and the Carthaginians.* Lond. 2nd ed. 1879. By the same: *Rome and Carthage.* N. York, 1880.

OTTO MELTZER: *Geschichte der Karthager.* Berlin, vol. I. 1879.

　　These books treat of the secular history of the ancient Carthaginians, but help to understand the situation and antecedents.

JULIUS LLOYD; *The North African Church.* London, 1880. Comes down to the Moslem Conquest.

The inhabitants of the provinces of Northern Africa were of Semitic origin, with a language similar to the Hebrew, but became Latinized in customs, laws, and language under the Roman rule. The church in that region therefore belongs to Latin Christianity, and plays a leading part in its early history.

The Phœnicians, a remnant of the Canaanites, were the English of ancient history. They carried on the commerce of the world; while the Israelites prepared the religion, and the Greeks the civilization of the world. Three small nations, in small countries, accomplished a more important work than the colossal empires of Assyria, Babylon, and Persia, or even Rome. Occupying a narrow strip of territory on the Syrian coast, between Mount Lebanon and the sea, the Phœnicians sent their merchant vessels from Tyre and Sidon to all parts of the old world from India to the Baltic, rounded the Cape of Good Hope two thousand years before Vasco de Gama, and brought back sandal wood from Malabar, spices from Arabia, ostrich plumes from Nubia, silver from Spain, gold from the Niger, iron from Elba, tin from England, and amber from the Baltic.

They furnished Solomon with cedars from Lebanon, and helped him to build his palace and the temple. They founded on the northernmost coast of Africa, more than eight hundred years before Christ, the colony of Carthage.[1] From that favorable position they acquired the control over the northern coast of Africa from the pillars of Hercules to the Great Syrtes, over Southern Spain, the islands of Sardinia and Sicily, and the whole Mediterranean sea. Hence the inevitable rivalry between Rome and Carthage, divided only by three days' sail; hence the three Punic wars which, in spite of the brilliant military genius of Hannibal, ended in the utter destruction of the capital of North Africa (B. C. 146).[2] "*Delenda est Carthago,*" was the narrow and cruel policy of the elder Cato. But under Augustus, who carried out the wiser plan of Julius Cæsar, there arose a new Carthage on the ruins of the old, and became a rich and prosperous city, first heathen, then Christian, until it was captured by the barbarous Vandals (A. D. 439), and finally destroyed by a race cognate to its original founders, the Mohammedan Arabs (647). Since that time "a mournful and solitary silence" once more brooded over its ruins.[3]

Christianity reached proconsular Africa in the second, perhaps already at the close of the first century, we do not know when and how. There was constant intercourse with Italy. It spread very rapidly over the fertile fields and burning sands of Mauritania and Numidia. Cyprian could assemble in 258 a

---

[1] The Phœnician or Punic name is *Karthada*, the Greek *Karchedon* (Καρχηδών), the Latin *Carthago*. It means New City (Neapolis). The word *Kereth* or *Carth* enters also into the names of other cities of Phœnician origin, as *Cirta* in Numidia.

[2] See the masterly comparison of Rome and Carthage by Mommsen, Book III. ch. 1. (vol. I. 506), of the destruction of Carthage in Book IV. ch. 1. (vol. II. 22 sqq.)

[3] On the ruins of Carthage see the descriptions of N. Davis and B. Smith (*Rome and Carthage*, ch. xx. 263–291). The recent conquest of Tunis by France (1881) gives new interest to the past of that country, and opens a new chapter for its future. Smith describes Tunis as the most Oriental of Oriental towns, with a gorgeous mixture of races—Arabs, Turks, Moors, and Negroes—held together by the religion of Islam.

synod of eighty-seven bishops, and in 308 the schismatical Donatists held a council of two hundred and seventy bishops at Carthage. The dioceses, of course, were small in those days.

The oldest Latin translation of the Bible, miscalled "Itala" (the basis of Jerome's "Vulgata"), was made probably in Africa and for Africa, not in Rome and for Rome, where at that time the Greek language prevailed among Christians. Latin theology, too, was not born in Rome, but in Carthage. Tertullian is its father. Minutius Felix, Arnobius, and Cyprian bear witness to the activity and prosperity of African Christianity and theology in the third century. It reached its highest perfection during the first quarter of the fifth century in the sublime intellect and burning heart of St. Augustin, the greatest among the fathers, but soon after his death (430) it was buried first beneath the Vandal barbarism, and in the seventh century by the Mohammedan conquest. Yet his writings led Christian thought in the Latin church throughout the dark ages, stimulated the Reformers, and are a vital force to this day.

§ 11. *Christianity in Europe.*

"Westward the course of Empire takes its way."

This law of history is also the law of Christianity. From Jerusalem to Rome was the march of the apostolic church. Further and further West has been the progress of missions ever since.

The church of ROME was by far the most important one for all the West. According to Eusebius, it had in the middle of the third century one bishop, forty-six presbyters, seven deacons with as many sub-deacons, forty-two acolyths, fifty readers, exorcists, and door-keepers, and fifteen hundred widows and poor persons under its care. From this we might estimate the number of members at some fifty or sixty thousand, *i. e.* about one-twentieth of the population of the city, which cannot be accurately determined indeed, but must have exceeded one million during the reign of the Antonines.[1] The strength of Chris-

[1] Gibbon, in his thirty-first chapter, and Milman estimate the population of

tianity in Rome is also confirmed by the enormous extent of the catacombs where the Christians were buried.

From Rome the church spread to all the cities of ITALY. The first Roman provincial synod, of which we have information, numbered twelve bishops under the presidency of Telesphorus (142–154). In the middle of the third century (255) Cornelius of Rome held a council of sixty bishops.

The persecution of the year 177 shows the church already planted in the south of GAUL in the second century. Christianity came hither probably from the East; for the churches of Lyons and Vienne were intimately connected with those of Asia Minor, to which they sent a report of the persecution, and Irenæus, bishop of Lyons, was a disciple of Polycarp of Smyrna. Gregory of Tours states, that in the middle of the third century seven missionaries were sent from Rome to Gaul. One of these, Dionysius, founded the first church of Paris, died a martyr at Montmartre, and became the patron saint of France. Popular superstition afterwards confounded him with Dionysius the Areopagite, who was converted by Paul at Athens.

SPAIN probably became acquainted with Christianity likewise in the second century, though no clear traces of churches and bishops there meet us till the middle of the third. The council of Elvira in 306 numbered nineteen bishops. The apostle Paul once formed the plan of a missionary journey to Spain, and according to Clement of Rome he preached there, if we understand that country to be meant by "the limit of the West," to which he says that Paul carried the gospel.[1] But there is no trace of his labors in Spain on record. The legend, in defiance of all chronology, derives Christianity in that country from James

Rome at 1,200,000; Hoeck (on the basis of the Monumentum Ancyranum), Zumpt and Howson at two millions; Bunsen somewhat lower; while Dureau de la Malle tries to reduce it to half a million, on the ground that the walls of Servius Tullius occupied an area only one-fifth of that of Paris. But these walls no longer marked the limits of the city since its reconstruction after the conflagration under Nero, and the suburbs stretched to an unlimited extent into the country. Comp. vol. I. p. 359.

[1] Rom. 15: 24; Clem. R. *Ad Cor.* c. 5 (τὸ τέρμα τῆς δύσεως).

the Elder, who was executed in Jerusalem in 44, and is said to be buried at Campostella, the famous place of pilgrimage, where his bones were first discovered under Alphonso II., towards the close of the eighth century. [1]

When Irenæus speaks of the preaching of the gospel among the GERMANS and other barbarians, who, " without paper and ink, have salvation written in their hearts by the Holy Spirit," he can refer only to the parts of Germany belonging to the Roman empire (*Germania cisrhenana*).

According to Tertullian BRITAIN also was brought under the power of the cross towards the end of the second century. The Celtic church existed in England, Ireland, and Scotland, independently of Rome, long before the conversion of the Anglo-saxons by the Roman mission of Augustine; it continued for some time after that event and sent offshoots to Germany, France, and the Low Countries, but was ultimately at different dates incorporated with the Roman church. It took its origin probably from Gaul, and afterwards from Italy also. The legend traces it to St. Paul and other apostolic founders. The venerable Bede (†735) says, that the British king Lucius (about 167) applied to the Roman bishop Eleutherus for missionaries. At the council of Arles, in Gaul (Arelate), in 314, three British bishops, of Eboracum (York), Londinum (London), and Colonia Londinensium (*i. e.* either Lincoln or more probably Colchester), were present.

The conversion of the barbarians of Northern and Western Europe did not begin in earnest before the fifth and sixth centuries, and will claim our attention in the history of the Middle Ages.

---

[1] See J. B. Gams (R. C.): *Die Kirchengeschichte von Spanien*, Regensburg, 1862–1879, 5 vols. The first vol. (422 pages) is taken up with the legendary history of the first three centuries. 75 pages are given to the discussion of Paul's journey to Spain. Gams traces Christianity in that country to Paul and to seven disciples of the Apostles sent to Rome, namely, Torquatus, Ctesiphon, Secundus, Indaletius, Cäcilius, Hesychius, and Euphrasius (according to the Roman Martyrologium, edited by Baronius, 1586).

CHAPTER II.

PERSECUTION OF CHRISTIANITY AND CHRISTIAN MARTYRDOM.

"Semen est sanguis Christianorum."—Tertullian.

§ 12. *Literature.*

I. SOURCES:

EUSEBIUS : *H. E.*, particularly Lib. viii. and ix.

LACTANTIUS : *De Mortibus persecutorum.*

The Apologies of JUSTIN MARTYR, MINUCIUS FELIX, TERTULLIAN, and ORIGEN, and the Epistles of CYPRIAN.

THEOD. RUINART : *Acta primorum martyrum sincera et selecta.* Par. 1689; 2nd ed. Amstel. 1713 (covering the first four cent.).

Several biographies in the *Acta Sanctorum.* Antw. 1643 sqq.

Les Acts des martyrs depuis l'origine de l'église Chrétienne jusqu'à nos temps. Traduits et publiés par les R.R. P.P. bénédictins de la congreg. de France. Par. 1857 sqq.

The *Martyrol. Hieronymianum* (ed. Florentini, Luc. 1668, and in Migne's *Patrol. Lat. Opp. Hieron.* xi. 434 sqq.); the *Martyrol. Romanum* (ed. Baron. 1586), the *Menolog. Græc.* (ed. Urbini, 1727); DE ROSSI, ROLLER, and other works on the Roman Catacombs.

II. WORKS.

JOHN FOXE (or Fox, d. 1587): *Acts and Monuments of the Church* (commonly called *Book of Martyrs*), first pub. at Strasburg 1554, and Basle 1559; first complete ed. fol. London 1563 ; 9th ed. fol. 1684, 3 vols. fol. ; best ed. by G. Townsend, Lond. 1843, 8 vols. 8o. ; also many abridged editions. Foxe exhibits the entire history of Christian martyrdom, including the Protestant martyrs of the middle age and the sixteenth century, with polemical reference to the church of Rome as the successor of heathen Rome in the work of bloody persecution. "The Ten Roman persecutions " are related in the first volume.

KORTHOLDT : *De persecutionibus eccl. primævæ.* Kiel, 1629.

GIBBON : chap. xvi.

MÜNTER : *Die Christen im heidnischen Hause vor Constantin.* Copenh. 1828.

SCHUMANN VON MANSEGG (R. C.): *Die Verfolgungen der ersten christ-lichen Kirche.* Vienna, 1821.

W. Ad. Schmidt: *Geschichte der Denk u. Glaubensfreiheit im ersten Jahrhundert der Kaiserherrschaft und des Christenthums.* Berl. 1847.

Kritzler: *Die Heldenzeiten des Christenthums.* Vol. i. *Der Kampf mit dem Heidenthum.* Leipz. 1856.

Fr. W. Gass: *Das christl. Märtyrerthum in den ersten Jahrhunderten.* 1859–60 (in Niedner's "Zeitschrift für hist. Theol." for 1859, pp. 323–392, and 1860, pp. 315–381).

F. Overbeck: *Gesetze der röm. Kaiser gegen die Christen,* in his *Studien zur Gesch. der alten Kirche,* I. Chemn. 1875.

B. Aubé: *Histoire des persécutions de l'église jusqu' à la fin des Antonins.* 2nd ed. Paris 1875 (Crowned by the Académie française). By the same: *Histoire des persécutions de l'église, La polémique païenne à la fin du II. siècle,* 1878. *Les Chréstiens dans l'empire romain, de la fin des Antonins au milieu du IIIe siècle (180–249),* 1881. *L'église et l'état dans la seconde moitié du IIIe siècle,* 1886.

K. Wieseler: *Die Christenverfolgungen der Cäsaren, hist. und chronol. untersucht.* Gütersloh, 1878.

Gerh. Uhlhorn: *Der Kampf des Christenthums mit dem Heidenthum.* 3d ed. Stuttgart, 1879. Engl. transl. by Smyth & Ropes, 1879.

Theod. Keim: *Rom und das Christenthum.* Berlin, 1881.

E. Renan: *Marc-Aurèle.* Paris, 1882, pp. 53–69.

§ 13. *General Survey.*

The persecutions of Christianity during the first three centuries appear like a long tragedy: first, foreboding signs; then a succession of bloody assaults of heathenism upon the religion of the cross; amidst the dark scenes of fiendish hatred and cruelty the bright exhibitions of suffering virtue; now and then a short pause; at last a fearful and desperate struggle of the old pagan empire for life and death, ending in the abiding victory of the Christian religion. Thus this bloody baptism of the church resulted in the birth of a Christian world. It was a repetition and prolongation of the crucifixion, but followed by a resurrection.

Our Lord had predicted this conflict, and prepared His disciples for it. "Behold, I send you forth as sheep in the midst of wolves. They will deliver you up to councils, and in their synagogues they will scourge you; yea and before governors and kings shall ye be brought for My sake, for a testimony to them and to the Gentiles. And brother shall deliver up brother to death, and the father his child: and children shall rise up against parents, and cause them to be put to death. And ye shall be hated of all men for My name's sake: but he that endureth to the end, the same shall be saved." These, and similar words, as well as the recollection of the crucifixion and resurrection, fortified and cheered many a confessor and martyr in the dungeon and at the stake.

The persecutions proceeded first from the Jews, afterwards from the Gentiles, and continued, with interruptions, for nearly three hundred years. History reports no mightier, longer and deadlier conflict than this war of extermination waged by heathen Rome against defenseless Christianity. It was a most unequal struggle, a struggle of the sword and of the cross; carnal power all on one side, moral power all on the other. It was a struggle for life and death. One or the other of the combatants must succumb. A compromise was impossible. The future of the world's history depended on the downfall of heathenism and the triumph of Christianity. Behind the scene were the powers of the invisible world, God and the prince of darkness. Justin, Tertullian, and other confessors traced the persecutions to Satan and the demons, though they did not ignore the human and moral aspects; they viewed them also as a punishment for past sins, and a school of Christian virtue. Some denied that martyrdom was an evil, since it only brought Christians the sooner to God and the glory of heaven. As war brings out the heroic qualities of men, so did the persecutions develop the patience, the gentleness, the endurance of the Christians, and prove the world-conquering power of faith.

Number of Persecutions.

From the fifth century it has been customary to reckon ten great persecutions: under Nero, Domitian, Trajan, Marcus Aurelius, Septimius Severus, Maximinus, Decius, Valerian, Aurelian, and Diocletian.[1] This number was suggested by the

---

[1] So Augustin, *De Civit. Dei*, xviii. 52, but he mentions Antoninus for Marcus Aurelius. Lactantius counts six, Sulpitius Severus nine persecutions.

ten plagues of Egypt taken as types (which, however, befell the enemies of Israel, and present a contrast rather than a parallel), and by the ten horns of the Roman beast making war with the Lamb, taken for so many emperors.[1] But the number is too great for the general persecutions, and too small for the provincial and local. Only two imperial persecutions—those of Decius and Diocletian — extended over the empire; but Christianity was always an illegal religion from Trajan to Constantine, and subject to annoyance and violence everywhere.[2] Some persecuting emperors—Nero, Domitian, Galerius, were monstrous tyrants, but others — Trajan, Marcus Aurelius, Decius, Diocletian—were among the best and most energetic emperors, and were prompted not so much by hatred of Christianity as by zeal for the maintenance of the laws and the power of the government. On the other hand, some of the most worthless emperors—Commodus, Caracalla, and Heliogabalus—were rather favorable to the Christians from sheer caprice. All were equally ignorant of the true character of the new religion.

The Result.

The long and bloody war of heathen Rome against the church, which is built upon a rock, utterly failed. It began in Rome under Nero, it ended near Rome at the Milvian bridge, under Constantine. Aiming to exterminate, it purified. It called forth the virtues of Christian heroism, and resulted in the consolidation and triumph of the new religion. The

---

[1] Ex. chs. 5–10; Rev. 17: 12 sqq. Augustin felt the impropriety of referring to the Egyptian plagues, and calls this a mere conjecture of the human mind which "sometimes hits the truth and sometimes is deceived." He also rectifies the number by referring to the persecutions before Nero, mentioned in the N. T., and to the persecutions after Diocletian, as that of Julian, and the Arian emperors. "When I think of these and the like things," he says, "it does not seem to me that the number of persecutions with which the church is to be tried can be definitely stated."

[2] On the relation of Christianity to the laws of the Roman empire, see Aubé, *De la legalité du Christianisme dans l'empire Romain au Ier siècle.* Paris 1866.

philosophy of persecution is best expressed by the terse word of Tertullian, who lived in the midst of them, but did not see the end: "The blood of the Christians is the seed of the Church."

Religious Freedom.

The blood of persecution is also the seed of civil and religious liberty. All sects, schools, and parties, whether religious or political, when persecuted, complain of injustice and plead for toleration; but few practise it when in power. The reason of this inconsistency lies in the selfishness of human nature, and in mistaken zeal for what it believes to be true and right. Liberty is of very slow, but sure growth.

The ancient world of Greece and Rome generally was based upon the absolutism of the state, which mercilessly trampled under foot the individual rights of men. It is Christianity which taught and acknowledged them.

The Christian apologists first proclaimed, however imperfectly, the principle of freedom of religion, and the sacred rights of conscience. Tertullian, in prophetic anticipation as it were of the modern Protestant theory, boldly tells the heathen that everybody has a natural and inalienable right to worship God according to his conviction, that all compulsion in matters of conscience is contrary to the very nature of religion, and that no form of worship has any value whatever except as far as it is a free voluntary homage of the heart.[1]

Similar views in favor of religious liberty were expressed by

---

[1] See the remarkable passage *Ad Scapulam*, c. 2: "*Tamen humani juris et naturalis potestatis est unicuique quod putaverit colere, nec alii obest, aut prodest alterius religio. Sed nec religionis est cogere religionem, quœ sponte suscipi debeat non vi, cum et hostiae ab animo libenti expostulentur. Ita etsi nos compuleritis ad sacrificandum, nihil prœstabitis diis vestris. Ab invitis enim sacrificia non desiderabunt, nisi si contentiosi sunt; contentiosus autem deus non est.*" Comp. the similar passage in Tertullian, *Apolog.* c. 24, where after enumerating the various forms of idolatry which enjoyed free toleration in the empire he continues: "*Videte enim ne et hoc ad irreligiositatis elogium concurrat, adimere libertatem religionis et interdicere optionem divinitatis, ut non liceat mihi colere quem velim sed cogar colere quem nolim. Nemo se ab invito coli volet, ne homo quidem.*"

Justin Martyr,[1] and at the close of our period by Lactantius, who says: "Religion cannot be imposed by force; the matter must be carried on by words rather than by blows, that the will may be affected. Torture and piety are widely different; nor is it possible for truth to be united with violence, or justice with cruelty. Nothing is so much a matter of free will as religion." [2]

The Church, after its triumph over paganism, forgot this lesson, and for many centuries treated all Christian heretics, as well as Jews and Gentiles, just as the old Romans had treated the Christians, without distinction of creed or sect. Every state-church from the times of the Christian emperors of Constantinople to the times of the Russian Czars and the South American Republics, has more or less persecuted the dissenters, in direct violation of the principles and practice of Christ and the apostles, and in carnal misunderstanding of the spiritual nature of the kingdom of heaven.

§ 14. *Jewish Persecution.*

Sources.

I. Dio Cassius: *Hist. Rom.* LXVIII. 32; LXIX. 12–14; Justin M.: *Apol.* I. 31, 47; Eusebius: *H. Eccl.* IV. 2. and 6. Rabbinical traditions in Derenbourg: *Histoire de la Palestine depuis Cyrus jusqu' à Adrien* (Paris 1867), pp. 402–438.
II. Fr. Münter: *Der Jüdische Krieg unter Trajan u. Hadrian.* Altona and Leipz. 1821.
Deyling: *Aeliae Capitol. origines et historiæ.* Lips. 1743.
Ewald: *Gesch. des Volkes Israel,* VII. 373–432.
Milman: *History of the Jews,* Books 18 and 20.
Grätz: *Gesch. der Juden.* Vol. IV. (Leipz. 1866).
Schürer: *Neutestam. Zeitgeschichte* (1874), pp. 350–367.

The Jews had displayed their obstinate unbelief and bitter hatred of the gospel in the crucifixion of Christ, the stoning of Stephen, the execution of James the Elder, the repeated incarcerations of Peter and John, the wild rage against Paul, and the

---

[1] *Apol.* I. c. 2, 4, 12.   [2] *Instit. div.* V. 20.

murder of James the Just. No wonder that the fearful judgment of God at last visited this ingratitude upon them in the destruction of the holy city and the temple, from which the Christians found refuge in Pella.

But this tragical fate could break only the national power of the Jews, not their hatred of Christianity. They caused the death of Symeon, bishop of Jerusalem (107); they were particularly active in the burning of Polycarp of Smyrna; and they inflamed the violence of the Gentiles by calumniating the sect of the Nazarenes.

The Rebellion under Bar-Cochba. Jerusalem again Destroyed.

By severe oppression under Trajan and Hadrian, the prohibition of circumcision, and the desecration of Jerusalem by the idolatry of the pagans, the Jews were provoked to a new and powerful insurrection (A. D. 132–135). A pseudo-Messiah, Bar-Cochba (son of the stars, Num. 24: 17), afterwards called Bar-Cosiba (son of falsehood), put himself at the head of the rebels, and caused all the Christians who would not join him to be most cruelly murdered. But the false prophet was defeated by Hadrian's general in 135, more than half a million of Jews were slaughtered after a desperate resistance, immense numbers sold into slavery, 985 villages and 50 fortresses levelled to the ground, nearly all Palestine laid waste, Jerusalem again destroyed, and a Roman colony, Aelia Capitolina, erected on its ruins, with an image of Jupiter and a temple of Venus. The coins of Aelia Capitolina bear the images of Jupiter Capitolinus, Bacchus, Serapis, Astarte.

Thus the native soil of the venerable religion of the Old Testament was ploughed up, and idolatry planted on it. The Jews were forbidden to visit the holy spot of their former metropolis upon pain of death.[1] Only on the anniversary of the destruc-

---

[1] As reported by Justin M., a native of Palestine and a cotemporary of this destruction of Jerusalem. *Apol.* I. c. 47. Tertullian also says (*Adv. Jud.* c. 13), that "an interdict was issued forbidding any one of the Jews to linger in the confines of the district."

tion were they allowed to behold and bewail it from a distance. The prohibition was continued under Christian emperors to their disgrace. Julian the Apostate, from hatred of the Christians, allowed and encouraged them to rebuild the temple, but in vain. Jerome, who spent the rest of his life in monastic retirement at Bethlehem (d. 419), informs us in pathetic words that in his day old Jewish men and women, "*in corporibus et in habitu suo iram Domini demonstrantes*," had to buy from the Roman watch the privilege of weeping and lamenting over the ruins from mount Olivet in sight of the cross, "*ut qui quondam emerant sanguinem Christi, emant lacrymas suas, et ne fletus quidem eis gratuitus sit.*"[1] The same sad privilege the Jews now enjoy under Turkish rule, not only once a year, but every Friday beneath the very walls of the Temple, now replaced by the Mosque of Omar.[2]

The Talmud.

After this the Jews had no opportunity for any further independent persecution of the Christians. Yet they continued to circulate horrible calumnies on Jesus and his followers. Their learned schools at Tiberias and Babylon nourished this bitter hostility. The Talmud, *i. e.* Doctrine, of which the first part (the Mishna, *i. e.* Repetition) was composed towards the end of the second century, and the second part (the Gemara, *i. e.* Completion) in the fourth century, well represents the Judaism of its day, stiff, traditional, stagnant, and anti-Christian. Subsequently the Jerusalem Talmud was eclipsed by the Babylonian (430-521), which is four times larger, and a still more distinct expression of Rabbinism. The terrible imprecation on apostates

---

[1] *Ad Zephan.* 1 : 15 sqq. Schürer quotes the passage, p. 363.

[2] "The Wailing Place of the Jews" at the cyclopean foundation wall is just outside of the Mosque El Aska, and near "Robinson's Arch." There I saw on Good Friday, 1877, a large number of Jews, old and young, men and women, venerable rabbis with patriarchal beards, others dirty and repulsive, kissing the stone wall and watering it with their tears, while repeating from Hebrew Bibles and prayer-books the Lamentations of Jeremiah, Psalms 76th and 79th, and various litanies. Comp. Tobler, *Topographie von Jerusalem,* I. 629.

(*precatio hæreticorum*), designed to deter Jews from going over to the Christian faith, comes from the second century, and is stated by the Talmud to have been composed at Jafna, where the Sanhedrin at that time had its seat, by the younger Rabbi Gamaliel.

The Talmud is the slow growth of several centuries. It is a chaos of Jewish learning, wisdom, and folly, a continent of rubbish, with hidden pearls of true maxims and poetic parables. Delitzsch calls it "a vast debating club, in which there hum confusedly the myriad voices of at least five centuries, a unique code of laws, in comparison with which the law-books of all other nations are but lilliputian." It is the Old Testament misinterpreted and turned against the New, in fact, though not in form. It is a rabbinical Bible without inspiration, without the Messiah, without hope. It shares the tenacity of the Jewish race, and, like it, continues involuntarily to bear testimony to the truth of Christianity. A distinguished historian, on being asked what is the best argument for Christianity, promptly replied : the Jews.[1]

Unfortunately this people, still remarkable even in its tragical end, was in many ways cruelly oppressed and persecuted by the Christians after Constantine, and thereby only confirmed in its fanatical hatred of them. The hostile legislation began with the prohibition of the circumcision of Christian slaves, and the intermarriage between Jews and Christians, and proceeded already in the fifth century to the exclusion of the Jews from all civil and political rights in Christian states. Even our enlightened age has witnessed the humiliating spectacle of a cruel *Judenhetze* in Germany and still more in Russia (1881). But through all changes of fortune God has preserved this ancient

[1] On the literature of the Talmud see the articles in Herzog, and in McClintock & Strong, and especially Schürer, *Neutestamentl. Zeitgeschichte* (Leipz. 1874), pp. 45–49, to which I add Schürer's essay: *Die Predigt Jesu Christi in ihrem Verhältniss zum Alten Testament und zum Judenthum*, Darmstadt, 1882. The relation of the Talmud to the Sermon on the Mount and the few resemblances is discussed by Pick in McClintock & Strong, vol. ix. 571.

race as a living monument of his justice and his mercy; and
he will undoubtedly assign it an important part in the consummation of his kingdom at the second coming of Christ.

§ 15. *Causes of Roman Persecution.*

The policy of the Roman government, the fanaticism of the
superstitious people, and the self-interest of the pagan priests
conspired for the persecution of a religion which threatened to
demolish the tottering fabric of idolatry; and they left no ex-
pedients of legislation, of violence, of craft, and of wickedness
untried, to blot it from the earth.

To glance first at the relation of the Roman state to the Christian religion.

Roman Toleration.

The policy of imperial Rome was in a measure tolerant. It
was repressive, but not preventive. Freedom of thought was
not checked by a censorship, education was left untrammelled to
be arranged between the teacher and the learner. The armies
were quartered on the frontiers as a protection of the empire,
not employed at home as instruments of oppression, and the
people were diverted from public affairs and political discontent
by public amusements. The ancient religions of the conquered
races were tolerated as far as they did not interfere with the
interests of the state. The Jews enjoyed special protection since
the time of Julius Cæsar.

Now so long as Christianity was regarded by the Romaus as
a mere sect of Judaism, it shared the hatred and contempt, indeed, but also the legal protection bestowed on that ancient
national religion. Providence had so ordered it that Christianity
had already taken root in the leading cities of the empire before
its true character was understood. Paul had carried it, under
the protection of his Roman citizenship, to the ends of the empire, and the Roman proconsul at Corinth refused to interfere
with his activity on the ground that it was an internal question
of the Jews, which did not belong to his tribunal. The heathen

statesmen and authors, even down to the age of Trajan, including the historian Tacitus and the younger Pliny, considered the Christian religion as a vulgar superstition, hardly worthy of their notice.

But it was far too important a phenomenon, and made far too rapid progress to be long thus ignored or despised. So soon as it was understood as a *new* religion, and as, in fact, claiming universal validity and acceptance, it was set down as unlawful and treasonable, a *religio illicita;* and it was the constant reproach of the Christians: "You have no right to exist." [1]

Roman Intolerance.

We need not be surprised at this position. For with all its professed and actual tolerance the Roman state was thoroughly interwoven with heathen idolatry, and made religion a tool of its policy. Ancient history furnishes no example of a state without some religion and form of worship. Rome makes no exception to the general rule. "The Romano-Hellenic state-religion" (says Mommsen), "and the Stoic state-philosophy inseparably combined with it were not merely a convenient instrument for every government-oligarchy, democracy, or monarchy—but altogether indispensable, because it was just as impossible to construct the state wholly without religious elements as to discover any new state religion adapted to form a substitute for the old." [2]

The piety of Romulus and Numa was believed to have laid the foundation of the power of Rome. To the favor of the deities of the republic, the brilliant success of the Roman arms was attributed. The priests and Vestal virgins were supported out of the public treasury. The emperor was ex-officio the *pontifex maximus,* and even an object of divine worship. The gods were national; and the eagle of Jupiter Capitolinus moved as a good genius before the world-conquering legions. Cicero lays down as a principle of legislation, that no one should be allowed

---

[1] "*Non licet esse vos.*" Tertullian, *Apol.* 4.
[2] *The History of Rome,* translated by Dickson, vol. IV. P. II. p. 559.

to worship foreign gods, unless they were recognized by public statute.[1] Mæcenas counselled Augustus: "Honor the gods according to the custom of our ancestors, and compel[2] others to worship them. Hate and punish those who bring in strange gods."

It is true, indeed, that *individuals* in Greece and Rome enjoyed an almost unlimited liberty for expressing sceptical and even impious sentiments in conversation, in books and on the stage. We need only refer to the works of Aristophanes, Lucian, Lucretius, Plautus, Terence. But a sharp distinction was made then, as often since by Christian governments, between liberty of private thought and conscience, which is inalienable and beyond the reach of legislation, and between the liberty of public worship, although the latter is only the legitimate consequence of the former. Besides, wherever religion is a matter of state-legislation and compulsion, there is almost invariably a great deal of hypocrisy and infidelity among the educated classes, however often it may conform outwardly, from policy, interest or habit, to the forms and legal acquirements of the established creed.

The senate and emperor, by special edicts, usually allowed conquered nations the free practice of their worship even in Rome; not, however, from regard for the sacred rights of conscience, but merely from policy, and with the express prohibition of making proselytes from the state religion; hence severe laws were published from time to time against transition to Judaism.

Obstacles to the Toleration of Christianity.

To Christianity, appearing not as a national religion, but claiming to be the only true universal one, making its converts among every people and every sect, attracting Greeks and Romans in much larger numbers than Jews, refusing to compromise with any form of idolatry, and threatening in fact the very existence of the Roman state religion, even this limited

---

[1] "*Nisi publice adscitos.*"   [2] ἀνάγκαζε, according to Dion Cassius.

toleration could not be granted. The same all-absorbing political interest of Rome dictated here the opposite course, and Tertullian is hardly just in charging the Romans with inconsistency for tolerating the worship of all false gods, from whom they had nothing to fear, and yet prohibiting the worship of the only true God who is Lord over all.[1] Born under Augustus, and crucified under Tiberius at the sentence of the Roman magistrate, Christ stood as the founder of a spiritual universal empire at the head of the most important epoch of the Roman power, a rival not to be endured. The reign of Constantine subsequently showed that the free toleration of Christianity was the death-blow to the Roman state religion.

Then, too, the conscientious refusal of the Christians to pay divine honors to the emperor and his statue, and to take part in any idolatrous ceremonies at public festivities, their aversion to the imperial military service, their disregard for politics and depreciation of all civil and temporal affairs as compared with the spiritual and eternal interests of man, their close brotherly union and frequent meetings, drew upon them the suspicion of hostility to the Cæsars and the Roman people, and the unpardonable crime of conspiracy against the state.[2]

The common people also, with their polytheistic ideas, abhorred the believers in the one God as atheists and enemies of the gods. They readily gave credit to the slanderous rumors of all sorts of abominations, even incest and cannibalism, practised by the Christians at their religious assemblies and love-feasts, and regarded the frequent public calamities of that age as punishments justly inflicted by the angry gods for the disregard of their worship. In North Africa arose the proverb: "If God does not send rain, lay it to the Christians." At every inundation, or drought, or famine, or pestilence, the fanatical populace cried: "Away with the atheists! To the lions with the Christians!"

---

[1] *Apolog.* c. 24 at the close: *"Apud vos quodvis colere jus est praeter Deum verum, quasi non hic magis omnium sit Deus, cuius omnes sumus."*

[2] Hence the reproachful designation, *"Hostes Cæsarum et populi Romani."*

Finally, persecutions were sometimes started by priests, jugglers, artificers, merchants, and others, who derived their support from the idolatrous worship. These, like Demetrius at Ephesus, and the masters of the sorceress at Philippi, kindled the fanaticism and indignation of the mob against the new religion for its interference with their gains.[1]

§ 16. *Condition of the Church before the Reign of Trajan.*

The imperial persecutions before Trajan belong to the Apostolic age, and have been already described in the first volume. We allude to them here only for the sake of the connection. Christ was born under the first, and crucified under the second Roman emperor. Tiberius (A. D. 14–37) is reported to have been frightened by Pilate's account of the crucifixion and resurrection, and to have proposed to the senate, without success, the enrolment of Christ among the Roman deities; but this rests only on the questionable authority of Tertullian. The edict of Claudius (42–54) in the year 53, which banished the Jews from Rome, fell also upon the Christians, but as Jews with whom they were confounded. The fiendish persecution of Nero (54–68) was intended as a punishment, not for Christianity, but for alleged incendiarism (64). It showed, however, the popular temper, and was a declaration of war against the new religion. It became a common saying among Christians that Nero would reappear as Antichrist.

During the rapidly succeeding reigns of Galba, Otho, Vitellius, Vespasian, and Titus, the church, so far as we know, suffered no very serious persecution.

But Domitian (81–96), a suspicious and blasphemous tyrant, accustomed to call himself and to be called "Lord and God," treated the embracing of Christianity as a crime against the state, and condemned to death many Christians, even his own cousin, the consul Flavius Clemens, on the charge of atheism; or confiscated their property, and sent them, as in the case of

[1] Comp. Arts. 19 : 24; 16 : 16.

Domitilla, the wife of the Clemens just mentioned, into exile. His jealousy also led him to destroy the surviving descendants of David; and he brought from Palestine to Rome two kinsmen of Jesus, grandsons of Judas, the "brother of the Lord," but seeing their poverty and rustic simplicity, and hearing their explanation of the kingdom of Christ as not earthly, but heavenly, to be established by the Lord at the end of the world, when He should come to judge the quick and the dead, he let them go. Tradition (in Irenæus, Eusebius, Jerome) assigns to the reign of Domitian the banishment of John to Patmos (which, however, must be assigned to the reign of Nero), together with his miraculous preservation from death in Rome (attested by Tertullian), and the martyrdom of Andrew, Mark, Onesimus, and Dionysius the Areopagite. The Martyrium of Ignatius speaks of "many persecutions under Domitian."

His humane and justice-loving successor, Nerva (96–98), recalled the banished, and refused to treat the confession of Christianity as a political crime, though he did not recognise the new religion as a *religio licita*.

§ 17. *Trajan. A. D.* 98–117—*Christianity Forbidden—Martyrdom of Symeon of Jerusalem, and Ignatius of Antioch.*

I. Sources.

PLINIUS, jun.: *Epist.* x. 96 and 97 (al. 97 sq.). TERTULLIAN: *Apol.* c. 2; EUSEBIUS: *H. E.* III. 11, 32, 33, 36. *Chron. pasch.* p. 470 (ed. Bonn.). *Acta Martyrii Ignatii*, in RUINART, p. 8 sqq.; recent edd. by THEOD. ZAHN, in *Patrum Apost. Opera* (Lips. 1876), vol. II. pp. 301 sqq.; FUNK, *Opera Patr. Apost.*, vol. I. 254–265; II. 218–275; and LIGHTFOOT: *S. Ignatius* and *S. Polyc.*, II. 1, 473–570.

II. Works.

On Trajan's reign in general see TILLEMONT, *Histoire des Empereurs;* MERIVALE, *History of the Romans under the Empire.*
On Ignatius: THEOD. ZAHN: *Ignatius von Antiochien.* Gotha 1873 (631 pages). LIGHTFOOT: *S. Ignatius* and *S. Polyc.*, London 1885, 2 vols.
On the chronology: ADOLPH HARNACK: *Die Zeit des Ignatius.* Leipzig, 1878 (90 pages); comp. KEIM, *l. c.* 510–562; but especially LIGHTFOOT, *l. c.* II. 1, 390 sqq.
The Epistles of Ignatius will be discussed in chapter XIII. on ecclesiastical literature, §§ 164 and 165.

Trajan, one of the best and most praiseworthy emperors, honored as the "father of his country," but, like his friends, Tacitus and Pliny, wholly ignorant of the nature of Christianity, was the first to pronounce it in form a proscribed religion, as it had been all along in fact. He revived the rigid laws against all secret societies,[1] and the provincial officers applied them to the Christians, on account of their frequent meetings for worship. His decision regulated the governmental treatment of the Christians for more than a century. It is embodied in his correspondence with the younger Pliny, who was governor of Bithynia in Asia Minor from 109 to 111.

Pliny came in official contact with the Christians. He himself saw in that religion only a "depraved and immoderate superstition," and could hardly account for its popularity. He reported to the emperor that this superstition was constantly spreading, not only in the cities, but also in the villages of Asia Minor, and captivated people of every age, rank, and sex, so that the temples were almost forsaken, and the sacrificial victims found no sale. To stop this progress, he condemned many Christians to death, and sent others, who were Roman citizens, to the imperial tribunal. But he requested of the emperor further instructions, whether, in these efforts, he should have respect to age; whether he should treat the mere bearing of the Christian name as a crime, if there were no other offence.

To these inquiries Trajan replied: "You have adopted the right coûrse, my friend, with regard to the Christians; for no universal rule, to be applied to all cases, can be laid down in this matter. They should not be searched for; but when accused and convicted, they should be punished; yet if any one denies that he has been a Christian, and proves it by action, namely,

---

[1] Or prohibited clubs. This is the meaning of *hetœria* (ἑταιρεία or ἑταιρία), *collegium, sodalitas, sodalitium*, company, brotherhood, especially a private political club or union for party purposes. The Roman sodalities were festive clubs or lodges, and easily available for political and revolutionary ends. Trajan refused to sanction a company of firemen in Nicomedia (Pliny, *Ep.* X. 34, al. 43). Comp. Büttner, *Geschichte der politischen Hetärien in Athen* (1840). and Mommsen, *De collegiis et sodali-üs Romanorum* (Kiel, 1843).

by worshipping our gods, he is to be pardoned upon his repentance, even though suspicion may still cleave to him from his antecedents. But anonymous accusations must not be admitted in any criminal process; it sets a bad example, and is contrary to our age" (*i. e.* to the spirit of Trajan's government).

This decision was much milder than might have been expected from a heathen emperor of the old Roman stamp. Tertullian charges it with self-contradiction, as both cruel and lenient, forbidding the search for Christians and yet commanding their punishment, thus declaring them innocent and guilty at the same time. But the emperor evidently proceeded on political principles, and thought that a transient and contagious enthusiasm, as Christianity in his judgment was, could be suppressed sooner by leaving it unnoticed, than by openly assailing it. He wished to ignore it as much as possible. But every day it forced itself more and more upon public attention, as it spread with the irresistible power of truth.

This rescript might give occasion, according to the sentiment of governors, for extreme severity towards Christianity as a secret union and a *religio illicita.* Even the humane Pliny tells us that he applied the rack to tender women. Syria and Palestine suffered heavy persecutions in this reign.

Symeon, bishop of Jerusalem, and, like his predecessor James, a kinsman of Jesus, was accused by fanatical Jews, and crucified A. D. 107, at the age of a hundred and twenty years.

In the same year (or probably between 110 and 116) the distinguished bishop Ignatius of Antioch was condemned to death, transported to Rome, and thrown before wild beasts in the Colosseum. The story of his martyrdom has no doubt been much embellished, but it must have some foundation in fact, and is characteristic of the legendary martyrology of the ancient church.

Our knowledge of Ignatius is derived from his disputed epistles,[1] and a few short notices by Irenæus and Origen. While

[1] In three recensions, two in Greek, and one in Syriac. The seven shorter Greek Ep. are genuine. See below § 165.

his existence, his position in the early Church, and his martyrdom are admitted, everything else about him is called in question. How many epistles he wrote, and when he wrote them, how much truth there is in the account of his martyrdom, and when it took place, when it was written up, and by whom—all are undecided, and the subject of protracted controversy. He was, according to tradition, a pupil of the Apostle John, and by his piety so commended himself to the Christians in Antioch that he was chosen bishop, the second after Peter, Euodius being the first. But although he was a man of apostolic character, and governed the church with great care, he was personally not satisfied, until he should be counted worthy of sealing his testimony with his blood, and thereby attaining to the highest seat of honor. The coveted crown came to him at last, and his eager and morbid desire for martyrdom was gratified. The emperor Trajan, in 107, came to Antioch, and there threatened with persecution all who refused to sacrifice to the gods. Ignatius was tried for this offence, and proudly confessed himself a "Theophorus" ("bearer of God") because, as he said, he had Christ within his breast. Trajan condemned him to be thrown to the lions at Rome. The sentence was executed with all haste. Ignatius was immediately bound in chains, and taken over land and sea, accompanied by ten soldiers, whom he denominated his "leopards," from Antioch to Seleucia, to Smyrna, where he met Polycarp, and whence he wrote to the churches, particularly to that in Rome; to Troas, to Neapolis, through Macedonia to Epirus, and so over the Adriatic to Rome. He was received by the Christians there with every manifestation of respect, but would not allow them to avert or even to delay his martyrdom. It was on the 20th day of December, 107, that he was thrown into the amphitheater: immediately the wild beasts fell upon him, and soon naught remained of his body but a few bones, which were carefully conveyed to Antioch as an inestimable treasure. The faithful friends who had accompanied him from home dreamed that night that they saw him; some that he was standing by Christ, dropping with sweat as if he had just come from his great labor. Comforted by these dreams they returned with the relics to Antioch.

Note on the Date of the Martyrdom of Ignatius.

The date A. D. 107 has in its favor the common reading of the best of the martyrologies of Ignatius (*Colbertinum*) ἐννάτῳ ἔτει, *in the ninth year*, *i. e.* from Trajan's accession, A. D. 98. From this there is no good reason to depart in favor of another reading τέταρτον ἔτος, *the nineteenth year*, *i. e.* A. D. 116. Jerome makes the date A. D. 109. The fact that the names of the Roman consuls are correctly given in the *Martyrium Colbertinum*, is proof of the correctness of the date, which is accepted by such critics as Ussher, Tillemont, Möhler, Hefele, and Wieseler. The latter, in his work *Die Christenverfolgungen der Cäsaren*, 1878, pp. 125 sqq., finds confirmation of this date in Eusebius's statement that the martyrdom took place *before* Trajan came to Antioch, which was in his 10th year; in the short interval between the martyrdom of Ignatius and Symeon, son of Klopas (*Hist. Ecc.* III. 32); and finally, in the letter of Tiberian to Trajan, relating how many pressed forward to martyrdom—an effect, as Wieseler thinks, of the example of Ignatius. If 107 be accepted, then another supposition of Wieseler is probable. It is well known that in that year Trajan held an extraordinary triumph on account of his Dacian victories: may it not have been that the blood of Ignatius reddened the sand of the amphitheatre at that time?

But 107 A. D. is by no means universally accepted. Keim (*Rom und das Christenthum*, p. 540) finds the *Martyrium Colbertinum* wrong in stating that the death took place under the first consulate of Sura and the second of Senecio, because in 107 Sura was consul for the third and Senecio for the fourth time. He also objects that Trajan was not in Antioch in 107, but in 115, on his way to attack the Armenians and Parthians. But this latter objection falls to the ground if Ignatius was not tried by Trajan personally in Antioch. Harnack concludes that it is only barely possible that Ignatius was martyred under Trajan. Lightfoot assigns the martyrdom to between 110 and 118.

§ 18. *Hadrian.* *A. D.* 117–138.

See GREGOROVIUS: *Gesch. Hadrians und seiner Zeit* (1851); RENAN: *L'Église chrétienne* (1879), 1–44, and WAGENMANN in Herzog, vol. v. 501–506.

Hadrian, of Spanish descent, a relative of Trajan, and adopted by him on his death-bed, was a man of brilliant talents and careful education, a scholar, an artist, a legislator and administrator, and altogether one of the ablest among the Roman emperors, but of very doubtful morality, governed by changing moods, attracted in opposite directions, and at last lost in self-contradictions and utter disgust of life. His mausoleum (Moles Hadriani) still adorns, as the castle of Sant' Angelo, the bridge of the Tiber in Rome. He is represented both as a friend and foe of the church. He was devoted to the religion of the state, bitterly opposed to Judaism, indifferent to Christianity from ignorance of it. He insulted the Jews and the Christians alike by erecting temples of Jupiter and Venus over the site of the temple and the supposed spot of the crucifixion. He is said to have directed the Asiatic proconsul to check the popular fury against the Christians, and to punish only those who should be, by an orderly judicial process, convicted of transgression of the laws.[1] But no doubt he regarded, like Trajan, the mere profession of Christianity as itself such a transgression.

The Christian apologies, which took their rise under this emperor, indicate a very bitter public sentiment against the Christians, and a critical condition of the church. The least encouragement from Hadrian would have brought on a bloody persecution. Quadratus and Aristides addressed their pleas for their fellow-Christians to him, we do not know with what effect.

Later tradition assigns to his reign the martyrdom of St. Eustachius, St. Symphorosa and her seven sons, of the Roman bishops Alexander and Telesphorus, and others whose names are scarcely known, and whose chronology is more than doubtful.

§ 19. *Antoninus Pius. A. D.* 137–161. *The Martyrdom of Polycarp.*

COMTE DE CHAMPAGNY (R. C.): *Les Antonins.* (A. D. 69–180), Paris, 1863; 3d ed. 1874. 3 vols., 8vo. MERIVALE'S *History.*

MARTYRIUM POLYCARPI (the oldest, simplest, and least objectionable of the martyr-acts), in a letter of the church of Smyrna to the Christians in Pontus or Phrygia, preserved by EUSEBIUS, *H. Eccl.* IV. 15, and separately edited from various MSS. by Ussher (1647) and in nearly all the editions of the Apostolic Fathers, especially by O. v. Gebhardt, Harnack, and Zahn, II. 132–168, and Prolog. L–LVI. The recension of the text is by Zahn, and departs from the text of the Bollandists in 98 places. Best edition by LIGHT-

---

[1] The rescript of Hadrian to Minucius Fundanus (124 or 128), preserved by Eusebius in a Greek translation, (*H. E.*, IV. 8, 9), is almost an edict of toleration, and hence doubted by Baur, Keim, Aubé, but defended as genuine by Neander (I. 101, Engl. ed.), Wieseler, Funk, Renan (*l. c.* p. 32 sqq.). Renan represents Hadrian as a *rieur spirituel, un Lucian couronné prenant le monde comme un jeu frivole* (p. 6), and therefore more favorable to religious liberty than the serious Trajan and the pious Antoninus and Marcus Aurelius. But Friedländer (III. 492) accepts the report of Pausanias that Hadrian was zealously devoted to the worship of the gods. Keim regards him as a visionary and hostile to Christianity as well as to Judaism.

FOOT, *S. Ign.* and *S. Polycarp*, I. 417 sqq., and II. 1005–1047. Comp. the Greek *Vita Polycarpi*, in Funk, II. 315 sqq.

IGNATIUS : *Ad. Polycarpum.* Best ed., by Lightfoot, *l. c.*

IRENAEUS: *Adv. Hær.* III. 3. 4. His letter to Florinus in EUSEB. v. 20.

POLYCRATES of Ephesus (c. 190), in EUSEB. v. 24.

On the date of Polycarp's death :

WADDINGTON : *Mémoire sur la chronologie de la vie du rhéteur Aelius Aristide* (in "Mém. de l' Acad. des inscript. et belles letters," Tom. XXVI. Part II. 1867, pp. 232 sqq.), and in *Fastes des provinces Asiatiques*, 1872, 219 sqq.

WIESELER : *Das Martyrium Polykarp's und dessen Chronologie*, in his *Christenverfolgungen*, etc. (1878), 34–87.

KEIM : *Die Zwölf Märtyrer von Smyrna und der Tod des Bishops Polykarp*, in his *Aus dem Urchristenthum* (1878), 92–133.

E. EGLI : *Das Martyrium des Polyk.*, in Hilgenfeld's " Zeitschrift für wissensch. Theol." for 1882, pp. 227 sqq.

Antoninus Pius protected the Christians from the tumultuous violence which broke out against them on account of the frequent public calamities. But the edict ascribed to him, addressed to the deputies of the Asiatic cities, testifying to the innocence of the Christians, and holding them up to the heathen as models of fidelity and zeal in the worship of God, could hardly have come from an emperor, who bore the honorable title of Pius for his conscientious adherence to the religion of his fathers;[1] and in any case he could not have controlled the conduct of the provincial governors and the fury of the people against an illegal religion.

The persecution of the church at Smyrna and the martyrdom of its venerable bishop, which was formerly assigned to the year 167, under the reign of Marcus Aurelius, took place, according to more recent research, under Antoninus in 155, when Statius Quadratus was proconsul in Asia Minor.[2] Polycarp was a per-

[1] He always offered sacrifice himself as high-priest. Friedländer III. 492.

[2] So Waddington, who has made it almost certain that Quadratus was Roman consul A. D. 142, and proconsul in Asia from 154 to 155, and that Polycarp died Feb. 23, 155. He is followed by Renan (1873), Ewald (1873), Aubé (1875), Hilgenfeld (1874), Lightfoot (1875), Lipsius (1874), O. v. Gebhardt (1875), Zahn, Harnack (1876), Egli (1882), and again by Lightfoot (1885, *l. c.* I. 647 sqq). Wieseler and Keim learnedly defend the old date (166–167), which rests on the authority of Eusebius and Jerome, and was held by Masson and Clinton. But Lightfoot refutes their objections (I. 647, sqq.), and sustains Waddington.

sonal friend and pupil of the Apostle John, and chief presbyter of the church at Smyrna, where a plain stone monument
still marks his grave. He was the teacher of Irenæus of Lyons,
and thus the connecting link between the apostolic and post-
apostolic ages. As he died 155 at an age of eighty-six years or
more, he must have been born A. D. 69, a year before the destruction of Jerusalem, and may have enjoyed the friendship of
St. John for twenty years or more. This gives additional weight
to his testimony concerning apostolic traditions and writings.
We have from him a beautiful epistle which echoes the apostolic
teaching, and will be noticed in another chapter.

Polycarp steadfastly refused before the proconsul to deny his
King and Saviour, whom he had served six and eighty years,
and from whom he had experienced nothing but love and
mercy. He joyfully went up to the stake, and amidst the
flames praised God for having deemed him worthy " to.be numbered among his martyrs, to drink the cup of Christ's sufferings,
unto the eternal resurrection of the soul and the body in the
incorruption of the Holy Spirit." The slightly legendary account in the letter of the church of Smyrna states, that the
flames avoided the body of the saint, leaving it unharmed, like
gold tried in the fire; also the Christian bystanders insisted, that
they perceived a sweet odor, as of incense. Then the executioner thrust his sword into the body, and the stream of blood
at once extinguished the flame. The corpse was burned after
the Roman custom, but the bones were preserved by the church,
and held more precious than gold and diamonds. The death of
this last witness of the apostolic age checked the fury of the
populace, and the proconsul suspended the persecution.

§ 20. *Persecutions under Marcus Aurelius. A. D.* 161–180.

MARCUS AURELIUS ANTONINUS: (b. 121, d. 180): Τῶν εἰς ἑαυτὸν βιβλία
ιβ', or *Meditations*. It is a sórt of diary or common place book, in
which the emperor wrote down, towards the close of his life, partly
amid the turmoil of war " in the land of the Quadi " (on the
Danube in Hungary), for his self-improvement, his own moral reflections) together with striking maxims of wise and virtuous men.

Ed. princeps by *Xylander* Zurich 1558, and Basle 1568; best ed with a new Latin trans. and very full notes by *Gataker*, Lond. 1643, Cambr. 1652, and with additional notes from the French by Dacier, Lond. 1697 and 1704. New ed. of the Greek text by *J. M. Schultz*, 1802 (and 1821); another by *Adamantius Coraïs*, Par. 1816. English translation by *George Long*, Lond. 1863, republ. Boston, revised edition, London, 1880. There are translations into most European languages, one in Italian by the Cardinal Francis Barberini (nephew of Pope Urban VIII), who dedicated his translation to his own soul, "to make it redder than his purple at the sight of the virtues of this Gentile." Comp. also the letters of the famous rhetorician *M. Corn. Fronto*, the teacher of M. Aurelius, discovered and published by Angelo Mai, Milan 1815 and Rome 1823 (*Epistolarum ad Marcum Cæsarem Lib. V.*, etc.) They are, however, very unimportant, except so far as they show the life-long congenial friendship between the amiable teacher and his imperial pupil.

ARNOLD BODEK: *Marcus Aurelius Antoninus als Freund und Zeitgenosse des Rabbi Jehuda ha-Nasi.* Leipz. 1868. (Traces the connection of this emperor with the Jewish monotheism and ethics.)

E. RENAN: *Marc-Aurèle et la fin du monde antique.* Paris 1882. This is the seventh and the last vol. of his work of twenty years' labor on the "Histoire des Origines du Christianisme." It is as full of genius, learning and eloquence, and as empty of positive faith as the former volumes. He closes the period of the definite formation of Christianity in the middle of the second century, but proposes in a future work to trace it back to Isaiah (or the "Great Unknown") as its proper founder.

EUSEBIUS: *H. E.* V. 1–3. The Letter of the Churches of Lyons and Vienne to the Christians of Asia Minor. *Die Akten des Karpus, des Papylus und der Agathonike, untersucht von* AD. HARNACK. Leipz., 1888.

On the legend of the *Legio fulminatrix* see TERTULLIAN: *Apol.* 5; EUSEB.: *H. E.* V. 5.; and DION CASS.: *Hist.* LXXI. 8, 9.

Marcus Aurelius, the philosopher on the throne, was a well-educated, just, kind, and amiable emperor, and reached the old Roman ideal of self-reliant Stoic virtue, but for this very reason he had no sympathy with Christianity, and probably regarded it as an absurd and fanatical superstition. He had no room in his cosmopolitan philanthropy for the purest and most innocent of his subjects, many of whom served in his own army. He was flooded with apologies of Melito, Miltiades, Athenagoras in behalf of the persecuted Christians, but turned a deaf ear to them. Only once, in his Meditations, does he

allude to them, and then with scorn, tracing their noble enthusiasm for martyrdom to "sheer obstinacy" and love for
theatrical display.[1] His excuse is ignorance. He probably
never read a line of the New Testament, nor of the apologies
addressed to him.[2]

Belonging to the later Stoical school, which believed in an
immediate absorption after death into the Divine essence, he
considered the Christian doctrine of the immortality of the soul,
with its moral consequences, as vicious and dangerous to the
welfare of the state. A law was passed under his reign, punishing every one with exile who should endeavor to influence
people's mind by fear of the Divinity, and this law was, no
doubt, aimed at the Christians.[3] At all events his reign was a
stormy time for the church, although the persecutions cannot be
directly traced to him. The law of Trajan was sufficient to
justify the severest measures against the followers of the "forbidden" religion.

About the year 170 the apologist Melito wrote: "The race

---

[1] *Med.* xi. 3 : Μὴ κατὰ ψιλὴν παράταξιν, ὡς οἱ Χριστιανοὶ, ἀλλὰ λελογισμένως καὶ
σεμνῶς καὶ, ὥστε καὶ ἄλλον πεῖσαι, ἀτραγῴδως.

[2] Bodek (*l. c.* p. 82 sqq.) maintains, contrary to the common view, that Marcus
Aurelius was *personally* indifferent to heathenism and Christianity, that his acts
of respect for the worship of the gods, related by Capitolinus and others, were
simply *official* tributes, and that the persecutions of the Christians did probably
not originate with him. "*Er war eben so wenig ein Feind des Christenthums,
als er ein Feind des Heidenthums war : was wie religiöser Fanatismus aussah,
war in Wahrheit nur politischer Conservatismus*" (p. 87). On the other hand,
Bodek claims for him a friendly sympathy with Judaism in its monotheistic
and ethical features, and assumes that he had intimate relations with a
Jewish rabbi. But there is nothing in his twelve books "*De seipso et
ad seipsum,*" which is inconsistent with an enlightened heathen piety under the
unconscious influence of Christianity, yet hostile to it partly from ignorance
of its true nature, partly from a conscientious regard to his duty as the pontifex
maximus of the state religion. The same was the case with Trajan and Decius.
Renan (p. 262 sqq.) calls the Meditations of Marcus Aurelius "*le livre le plus
purement humain qu'il y ait. Il ne tranche aucune question controversée. En
théologie, Marc Aurèle flotte entre le déisme pur, le polythéisme enterprété dans
un sens physique, à la façon des stoïciens, et une sorte de panthéisme cosmique.*"

[3] "*Si quis aliquid fecerit, quo leves hominum animi superstitione numinis
terrerentur, Divus Marcus hujusmodi homines in insulam relegari rescripsit.*"
Dig. XLVIII. tit. 19. 1. 13, quoted by Lecky in *Hist. of Europ. Morals,* I. 448.

of the worshippers of God in Asia is now persecuted by new edicts as it never has been heretofore; shameless, greedy sycophants, finding occasion in the edicts, now plunder the innocent day and night." The empire was visited at that time by a number of conflagrations, a destructive flood of the Tiber, an earthquake, insurrections, and particularly a pestilence, which spread from Ethiopia to Gaul. This gave rise to bloody persecutions, in which government and people united against the enemies of the gods and the supposed authors of these misfortunes. Celsus expressed his joy that "the demon" [of the Christians] was "not only reviled, but banished from every land and sea," and saw in this judgment the fulfilment of the oracle: "the mills of the gods grind late." But at the same time these persecutions, and the simultaneous literary assaults on Christianity by Celsus and Lucian, show that the new religion was constantly gaining importance in the empire.

In 177, the churches of Lyons and Vienne, in the South of France, underwent a severe trial. Heathen slaves were forced by the rack to declare, that their Christian masters practised all the unnatural vices which rumor charged them with; and this was made to justify the exquisite tortures to which the Christians were subjected. But the sufferers, "strengthened by the fountain of living water from the heart of Christ," displayed extraordinary faith and steadfastness, and felt, that "nothing can be fearful, where the love of the Father is, nothing painful, where shines the glory of Christ."

The most distinguished victims of this Gallic persecution were the bishop Pothinus, who, at the age of ninety years, and just recovered from a sickness, was subjected to all sorts of abuse, and then thrown into a dismal dungeon, where he died in two days; the virgin Blandina, a slave, who showed almost superhuman strength and constancy under the most cruel tortures, and was at last thrown to a wild beast in a net; Ponticus, a boy of fifteen years, who could be deterred by no sort of cruelty from confessing his Saviour. The corpses of the martyrs, which covered the streets, were shamefully mutilated, then burned, and the ashes cast into the Rhone, lest any remnants of the enemies of the gods might desecrate the soil. At last the people grew weary of slaughter, and a considerable number of Christians survived. The martyrs of Lyons distinguished themselves by true humility, disclaiming in their prison that title of honor, as due only, they said, to the faithful and true witness, the First-born from the dead, the Prince of life (Rev.1: 5), and to those of his followers who had already sealed their fidelity to Christ with their blood.

About the same time a persecution of less extent appears to have visited Autun (Augustodunum) near Lyons. Symphorinus, a young man of good family, having refused to fall down before the image of Cybele, was condemned to be beheaded. On his way to the place of execution his own mother called to him: "My son, be firm and fear not that death, which so surely leads to life. Look to Him who reigns in heaven. To-day is thy earthly life not taken from thee, but transferred by a blessed exchange into the life of heaven."

The story of the "thundering legion"[1] rests on the fact of a remarkable deliverance of the Roman army in Hungary by a sudden shower, which quenched their burning thirst and fright-ened their barbarian enemies, A. D. 174. The heathens, how-ever, attributed this not to the prayers of the Christian soldiers, but to their own gods. The emperor himself prayed to Jupiter: "This hand, which has never yet shed human blood, I raise to thee." That this event did not alter his views respecting the Christians, is proved by the persecution in South Gaul, which broke out three years later.

Of isolated cases of martyrdom in this reign, we notice that of Justin Martyr, at Rome, in the year 166. His death is traced to the machinations of Crescens, a Cynic philosopher.

Marcus Aurelius was succeeded by his cruel and contemptible son, Commodus (180–192), who wallowed in the mire of every

---

[1] *Legio fulminatrix,* κεραυνοφόρος. The twelfth legion bore the name *Fulminata* as far back as the time of Trajan; and hence it cannot be derived from this event.

sensual debauchery, and displayed at the same time like Nero the most ridiculous vanity as dancer and singer, and in the character of buffoon; but he was accidentally made to favor the Christians by the influence of a concubine,[1] Marcia, and accordingly did not disturb them. Yet under his reign a Roman senator, Apollonius, was put to death for his faith.

§ 21. Condition of the Church from Septimius Severus to Philip the Arabian. A. D. 193–249.

CLEMENS ALEX.: *Strom.* II. 414. TERTULL.: *Ad Scapulam,* c. 4, 5; *Apol.* (A. D. 198), c. 7, 12, 30, 37, 49.

Respecting the Alexandrian martyrs comp. EUSEB.: VI. 1 and 5.

The Acts of the Carthaginian martyrs, which contain their *ipsissima verba* from their diaries in the prisons, but bear a somewhat Montanistic stamp, see in RUINART, p. 90 sqq.

LAMPRIDIUS: *Vita Alex. Severi,* c. 22, 29, 49.

On Philip the Arabian see EUSEB.: VI. 34, 36. HIERON.: *Chron.* ad ann. 246.

J. J. MÜLLER: *Staat und Kirche unter Alex. Severus.* Zürich 1874.

F. GÖRRES: *Kaiser Alex. Severus und das Christenthum.* Leipz., 1877.

JEAN RÉVILLE: *La religion à Rome sous les Sévères.* Paris, 1886 (vii and 302 pp); Germ. transl. by *Krüger,* 1888.

With Septimius Severus (193–211), who was of Punic descent and had a Syrian wife, a line of emperors (Caracalla, Heliogabalus, Alexander Severus) came to the throne, who were rather Oriental than Roman in their spirit, and were therefore far less concerned than the Antonines to maintain the old state religion. Yet towards the close of the second century there was no lack of local persecutions; and Clement of Alexandria wrote of those times: "Many martyrs are daily burned, confined, or beheaded, before our eyes."

In the beginning of the third century (202) Septimius Severus, turned perhaps by Montanistic excesses, enacted a rigid law against the further spread both of Christianity and of Judaism. This occasioned violent persecutions in Egypt and in North Africa, and produced some of the fairest flowers of martyrdom. In Alexandria, in consequence of this law, Leonides, father

---

[1] φιλόθεος παλλακή.

of the renowned Origen, was beheaded. Potamiæna, a virgin of rare beauty of body and spirit, was threatened by beastly passion with treatment worse than death, and, after cruel tortures, slowly burned with her mother in boiling pitch. One of the executioners, Basilides, smitten with sympathy, shielded them somewhat from abuse, and soon after their death embraced Christianity, and was beheaded. He declared that Potamiæna had appeared to him in the night, interceded with Christ for him, and set upon his head the martyr's crown.

In Carthage some catechumens, three young men and two young women, probably of the sect of the Montanists, showed remarkable steadfastness and fidelity in the dungeon and at the place of execution. Perpetua, a young woman of noble birth, resisting, not without a violent struggle, both the entreaties of her aged heathen father and the appeal of her helpless babe upon her breast, sacrificed the deep and tender feelings of a daughter and a mother to the Lord who died for her. Felicitas, a slave, when delivered of a child in the same dungeon, answered the jailor, who reminded her of the still keener pains of martyrdom: "Now I suffer, what I suffer; but then another will suffer for me, because I shall suffer for him." All remaining firm, they were cast to wild beasts at the next public festival, having first interchanged the parting kiss in hope of a speedy reunion in heaven.

The same state of things continued through the first years of Caracalla (211–217), though this gloomy misanthrope passed no laws against the Christians.

The abandoned youth, El-Gabal, or Heliogabalus (218–222), who polluted the throne by the blackest vices and follies, tolerated all the religions in the hope of at last merging them in his favorite Syrian worship of the sun with its abominable excesses. He himself was a priest of the god of the sun, and thence took his name.[1]

His far more worthy cousin and successor, Alexander Severus

---

[1] Unless we should prefer to derive it from אֵל and גְּבָל, "mountain of God."

(222–235), was addicted to a higher kind of religious eclecticism and syncretism, a pantheistic hero-worship. He placed the busts of Abraham and Christ in his domestic chapel with those of Orpheus, Apollonius of Tyana, and the better Roman emperors, and had the gospel rule, "As ye would that men should do to you, do ye even so to them," engraven on the walls of his palace and on public monuments.[1] His mother, Julia Mammaea, was a patroness of Origen.

His assassin, Maximinus the Thracian (235–238), first a herdsman, afterwards a soldier, resorted again to persecution out of mere opposition to his predecessor, and gave free course to the popular fury against the enemies of the gods, which was at that time excited anew by an earthquake. It is uncertain whether he ordered the entire clergy or only the bishops to be killed. He was a rude barbarian who plundered also heathen temples.

The legendary poesy of the tenth century assigns to his reign the fabulous martyrdom of St. Ursula, a British princess, and her company of eleven thousand (according to others, ten thousand) virgins, who, on their return from a pilgrimage to Rome, were murdered by heathens in the neighborhood of Cologne. This incredible number has probably arisen from the misinterpretation of an inscription, like "Ursula et Undecimilla" (which occurs in an old missal of the Sorbonne), or "Ursula et XI M. V.," *i. e. Martyres Virgines*, which, by substituting *milia* for *martyres*, was increased from eleven martyrs to eleven thousand virgins. Some historians place the fact, which seems to form the basis of this legend, in connexion with the retreat of the Huns after the battle of Chalons, 451. The abridgment of *Mil.*, which may mean soldiers (*milites*) as well as thousands (*milia*), was another fruitful source of mistakes in a credulous and superstitious age.

Gordianus (238–244) left the church undisturbed. Philip the Arabian (244–249) was even supposed by some to be a Chris-

---

[1] Yet he meant no more than toleration, as Lampridius says, 22 (21): *Judæis privilegia reservavit, Christianos esse passus est.*

tian, and was termed by Jerome " primus omnium ex Romanis imperatoribus Christianus." It is certain that Origen wrote letters to him and to his wife, Severa.

This season of repose, however, cooled the moral zeal and brotherly love of the Christians; and the mighty storm under the following reign served well to restore the purity of the church.

§ 22. *Persecutions under Decius, and Valerian. A. D.* 249–260. *Martyrdom of Cyprian.*

DIONYSIUS ALEX., in Euseb. VI. 40–42; VII. 10, 11.

CYPRIAN: *De Lapsis,* and particularly his *Epistles* of this period. On Cyprian's martyrdom see the *Proconsular Acts,* and PONTIUS: *Vita Cypriani.*

FRANZ GÖRRES: *Die Toleranzedicte des Kaisers Gallienus,* in the " Jahrbücher für protest. Theol.," 1877, pp. 606–630. By the same: *Die angebliche Christenverfolgung zur Zeit der Kaiser Numerianus und Carinus,* in Hilgenfeld's "Zeitschrift für wissenschaftl. Theologie." 1880 pp. 31–64.

Decius Trajan (249–251), an earnest and energetic emperor, in whom the old Roman spirit once more awoke, resolved to root out the church as an atheistic and seditious sect, and in the year 250 published an edict to all the governors of the provinces, enjoining return to the pagan state religion under the heaviest penalties. This was the signal for a persecution which, in extent, consistency, and cruelty, exceeded all before it. In truth it was properly the first which covered the whole empire, and accordingly produced a far greater number of martyrs than any former persecution. In the execution of the imperial decree confiscation, exile, torture, promises and threats of all kinds, were employed to move the Christians to apostasy. Multitudes of nominal Christians,[1] especially at the beginning, sacrificed to the gods (*sacrificati, thurificati*), or procured from the magistrate a false certificate that they had done so (*libellatici*), and were then excommunicated as apostates (*lapsi*); while hundreds

---

[1] " *Maximus fratrum numerus,*" says Cyprian.

rushed with impetuous zeal to the prisons and the tribunals, to obtain the confessor's or martyr's crown. The confessors of Rome wrote from prison to their brethren of Africa: "What more glorious and blessed lot can fall to man by the grace of God, than to confess God the Lord amidst tortures and in the face of death itself; to confess Christ the Son of God with lacerated body and with a spirit departing, yet free; and to become fellow-sufferers with Christ in the name of Christ? Though we have not yet shed our blood, we are ready to do so. Pray for us, then, dear Cyprian, that the Lord, the best captain, would daily strengthen each one of us more and more, and at last lead us to the field as faithful soldiers, armed with those divine weapons (Eph. 6 : 2) which can never be conquered."

The authorities were specially severe with the bishops and officers of the churches. Fabianus of Rome, Babylas of Antioch, and Alexander of Jerusalem, perished in this persecution. Others withdrew to places of concealment; some from cowardice; some from Christian prudence, in hope of allaying by their absence the fury of the pagans against their flocks, and of saving their own lives for the good of the church in better times.

Among the latter was Cyprian, bishop of Carthage, who incurred much censure by his course, but fully vindicated himself by his pastoral industry during his absence, and by his subsequent martyrdom. He says concerning the matter: "Our Lord commanded us in times of persecution to yield and to fly. He taught this, and he practised it himself. For since the martyr's crown comes by the grace of God, and cannot be gained before the appointed hour, he who retires for a time, and remains true to Christ, does not deny his faith, but only abides his time."

The poetical legend of the seven brothers at Ephesus, who fell asleep in a cave, whither they had fled, and awoke two hundred years afterwards, under Theodosius II. (447), astonished to see the once despised and hated cross now ruling over city and country, dates itself internally from the time of Decius, but is not mentioned before Gregory of Tours in the sixth century.

Under Gallus (251–253) the persecution received a fresh im
pulse through the incursions of the Goths, and the prevalence of
a pestilence, drought, and famine. Under this reign the Roman
bishops Cornelius and Lucius were banished, and then condemned to death.

Valerian (253–260) was at first mild towards the Christians ;
but in 257 he changed his course, and made an effort to check
the progress of their religion without bloodshed, by the banishment of ministers and prominent laymen, the confiscation of
their property, and the prohibition of religious assemblies.
These measures, however, proving fruitless, he brought the death
penalty again into play.

The most distinguished martyrs of this persecution under
Valerian are the bishops Sixtus II. of Rome, and Cyprian of
Carthage.

When Cyprian received his sentence of death, representing
him as an enemy of the Roman gods and laws, he calmly answered : " Deo gratias ! " Then, attended by a vast multitude
to the scaffold, he prayed once more, undressed himself, covered
his eyes, requested a presbyter to bind his hands, and to pay the
executioner, who tremblingly drew the sword, twenty-five pieces
of gold, and won the incorruptible crown (Sept. 14, 258). His
faithful friends caught the blood in handkerchiefs, and buried
the body of their sainted pastor with great solemnity.

Gibbon describes the martyrdom of Cyprian with circum-
stantial minuteness, and dwells with evident satisfaction on the
small decorum which attended his execution. But this is no
fair average specimen of the style in which Christians were executed throughout the empire. For Cyprian was a man of the
highest social standing and connection from his former eminence
as a rhetorician and statesman. His deacon, Pontius, relates
that " numbers of eminent and illustrious persons, men of mark
and family and secular distinction, often urged him, for the sake
of their old friendship with him, to retire." We shall return
to Cyprian again in the history of church government, where
he figures as a typical, ante-Nicene high-churchman, advocating

both the visible unity of the church and episcopal independence of Rome.

The much lauded martyrdom of the deacon St. Laurentius of Rome, who pointed the avaricious magistrates to the poor and sick of the congregation as the richest treasure of the church, and is said to have been slowly roasted to death (Aug. 10, 258), is scarcely reliable in its details, being first mentioned by Ambrose a century later, and then glorified by the poet Prudentius. A Basilica on the Via Tiburtina celebrates the memory of this saint, who occupies the same position among the martyrs of the church of Rome as Stephen among those of Jerusalem.

§ 23. *Temporary Repose.* A. D. 260–303.

Gallienus (260–268) gave peace to the church once more, and even acknowledged Christianity as a religio licita. And this calm continued forty years; for the edict of persecution, issued by the energetic and warlike Aurelian (270–275), was rendered void by his assassination; and the six emperors who rapidly followed, from 275 to 284, let the Christians alone.

The persecutions under Carus, Numerianus and Carinus from 284 to 285 are not historical, but legendary.[1]

During this long season of peace the church rose rapidly in numbers and outward prosperity. Large and even splendid houses of worship were erected in the chief cities, and provided with collections of sacred books and vessels of gold and silver for the administration of the sacraments. But in the same proportion discipline relaxed, quarrels, intrigues, and factions increased, and worldliness poured in like a flood.

Hence a new trial was a necessary and wholesome process of purification.[2]

---

[1] See Franz Görres, *l. c.*   [2] Eusebius. *H. E.* VIII. 1.

§ 24. *The Diocletian Persecution.* *A. D.* 303–311.

I. Sources.

Eusebius: *H. E.* Lib. VIII.–X; *De Martyr. Palæst.* (ed. Cureton, Lond. 1861); *Vita Const.* (ed. Heinichen, Lips. 1870).

Lactantius: *De Mortibus Persec.* c. 7 sqq. Of uncertain authorship.

Basilius M.: *Oratio in Gordium mart.; Oratio in Barlaham mart.*

II. Works.

Baronius: *Annal. ad ann.* 302–305.

Gibbon: Chrs. XIII., XIV. and XVI.

Jak. Burckhardt: *Die Zeit Constantins des Gr.* Basel, 1853, p. 325.

Th. Keim: *Der Uebertritt Constantins des Gr. zum Christenthum.* Zürich 1852. The same: *Die römischen Toleranzedicte für das Christenthum* (311–313), in the "Tüb. Theol. Jahrb." 1852. (His. *Rom und das Christenthum* only comes down to A. D. 192.)

Alb. Vogel: *Der Kaiser Diocletian.* Gotha 1857.

Bernhardt: *Diokletian in s. Verhältnisse zu den Christen.* Bonn, 1862.

Hunziker: *Regierung und Christenverfolgung des Kaisers Diocletianus und seiner Nachfolger.* Leipz. 1868.

Theod. Preuss: *Kaiser Diocletian und seine Zeit.* Leipz. 1869.

A. J. Mason: *The Persecution of Diocletian.* Cambridge, 1876. Pages 370. (Comp. a review by Ad. Harnack in the "Theol. Literaturzeitung" for 1877. No. 7. f. 169.)

Theod. Zahn: *Constantin der Grosse und die Kirche.* Hannover, 1876.

Brieger: *Constantin der Gr. als Religionspolitiker.* Gotha, 1880. Comp. the Lit. on Constantine, in vol. III., 10, 11.

The forty years' repose was followed by the last and most violent persecution, a struggle for life and death.

"The accession of the Emperor Diocletian is the era from which the Coptic Churches of Egypt and Abyssinia still date, under the name of the 'Era of Martyrs.' All former persecutions of the faith were forgotten in the horror with which men looked back upon the last and greatest: the tenth wave (as men delighted to count it) of that great storm obliterated all the traces that had been left by others. The fiendish cruelty of Nero, the jealous fears of Domitian, the unimpassioned dislike of Marcus, the sweeping purpose of Decius, the clever devices of Valerian, fell into obscurity when compared with the concentrated terrors of that final grapple, which resulted in the destruction of the old Roman Empire and the establishment of the Cross as the symbol of the world's hope." [1]

Diocletian (284–305) was one of the most judicious and able emperors who, in a trying period, preserved the sinking state from dissolution. He was the son of a slave or of obscure parentage, and worked himself up to supreme power. He converted the Roman republican empire into an Oriental despotism, and prepared the way for Constantine and Constantinople. He associated with himself three subordinate co-regents, Maximian (who committed suicide, 310), Galerius (d. 311), and Constantius Chlorus (d. 306, the father of Constantine the Great), and divided with them the government of the immense empire; thereby quadrupling the personality of the sovereign, and imparting vigor to provincial administration, but also sowing the seed of discord and civil war. [2] Gibbon calls him a second Augustus, the founder of a new empire, rather than the restorer of the old. He also compares him to Charles V., whom he somewhat resembled in his talents, temporary success and ultimate failure, and voluntary retirement from the cares of government.

In the first twenty years of his reign Diocletian respected the toleration edict of Gallienus. His own wife Prisca, his daughter Valeria, and most of his eunuchs and court officers, besides many of the most prominent public functionaries, were Christians, or at least favorable to the Christian religion. He

---

[1] So Arthur James Mason begins his book on the *Persecution of Diocletian.*

[2] Maximian (surnamed Herculius) ruled in Italy and Africa, Galerius (Armentarius) on the banks of the Danube, and afterwards in the East, Constantius (Chlorus) in Gaul, Spain, and Britain; while Diocletian reserved to himself Asia, Egypt, and Thrace, and resided in Nicomedia. Galerius married a daughter of Diocletian (the unfortunate Valeria), Constantius a (nominal) daughter of Maximian (Theodora), after repudiating their former wives. Constantine, the son of the divorced Helena, married Fausta, the daughter of Maximian as his second wife (father and son being married to two sisters). He was raised to the dignity of Cæsar, July 25, 306. See Gibbon, chs. XIII. and XIV.

himself was a superstitious heathen and an oriental despot. Like Aurelian and Domitian before him, he claimed divine honors, as the vicar of Jupiter Capitolinus. He was called, as the Lord and Master of the world, *Sacratissimus Dominus Noster ;* he guarded his Sacred Majesty with many circles of soldiers and eunuchs, and allowed no one to approach him except on bended knees, and with the forehead touching the ground, while he was seated on the throne in rich vestments from the far East. "Ostentation," says Gibbon, " was the first principle of the new system instituted by Diocletian." As a practical statesman, he must have seen that his work of the political restoration and consolidation of the empire would lack a firm and permanent basis without the restoration of the old religion of the state. Although he long postponed the religious question, he had to meet it at last. It could not be expected, in the nature of the case, that paganism should surrender to its dangerous rival without a last desperate effort to save itself.

But the chief instigator of the renewal of hostility, according to the account of Lactantius, was Diocletian's co-regent and son-in-law, Galerius, a cruel and fanatical heathen.[1] He prevailed at last on Diocletian in his old age to authorize the persecution which gave to his glorious reign a disgraceful end.

In 303 Diocletian issued in rapid succession three edicts, each more severe than its predecessor. Maximian issued the fourth, the worst of all, April 30, 304. Christian churches were to be destroyed ; all copies of the Bible were to be burned ; all Christians were to be deprived of public office and civil rights ; and at last all, without exception, were to sacrifice to the gods upon pain of death. Pretext for this severity was afforded by the occurrence of fire twice in the palace of Nicomedia in Bithynia, where Diocletian resided.[2] It was strengthened by

---

[1] Lactantius (*De Mort. Persec.* c. 9), calls him "a wild beast," in whom dwelt "a native barbarity and a savageness foreign to Roman blood." He died at last of a terrible disease, of which Lactantius gives a minute account (ch. 33).

[2] Lactantius charges the incendiarism on Galerius who, as a second Nero,

the tearing down of the first edict by an imprudent Christian (celebrated in the Greek church under the name of John), who vented in that way his abhorrence of such "godless and tyrannical rulers," and was gradually roasted to death with every species of cruelty. But the conjecture that the edicts were occasioned by a conspiracy of the Christians who, feeling their rising power, were for putting the government at once into Christian hands, by a stroke of state, is without any foundation in history. It is inconsistent with the political passivity of the church during the first three centuries, which furnish no example of rebellion and revolution. At best such a conspiracy could only have been the work of a few fanatics; and they, like the one who tore down the first edict, would have gloried in the deed and sought the crown of martyrdom.[1]

The persecution began on the twenty-third day of February, 303, the feast of the *Terminalia* (as if to make an end of the Christian sect), with the destruction of the magnificent church in Nicomedia, and soon spread over the whole Roman empire, except Gaul, Britain, and Spain, where the co-regent Constantius Chlorus, and especially his son, Constantine the Great (from 306), were disposed, as far as possible, to spare the Christians. But even here the churches were destroyed, and many martyrs of Spain (St. Vincentius, Eulalia, and others celebrated by Prudentius), and of Britain (St. Alban) are assigned by later tradition to this age.

endangered the residence for the purpose of punishing the innocent Christians. Constantine, who then resided at the Court, on a solemn occasion at a later period, attributes the fire to lightning (*Orat. ad Sanct.* c. 25), but the repetition of the occurrence strengthens the suspicion of Lactantius.

[1] Gibbon, ch. XVI., intimates the probability of a political plot. In speaking of the fire in the imperial palace of Nicomedia, he says: "The suspicion naturally fell on the Christians; and it was suggested, *with some degree of probability*, that those desperate fanatics, provoked by their present sufferings, and apprehensive of impending calamities, had entered into a conspiracy with their faithful brethren, the eunuchs of the palace, against the lives of two emperors, whom they detested as the irreconcilable enemies of the church of God." The conjecture of Gibbon was renewed by Burkhardt in his work on *Constantine*, pp. 332 ff., but without any evidence. Baur rejects it as artificial and very improbable. (*Kirchengesch.* I. 452, note). Mason (p. 97 sq.) refutes it.

The persecution raged longest and most fiercely in the East under the rule of Galerius and his barbarous nephew Maximin Daza, who was intrusted by Diocletian before his retirement with the dignity of Cæsar and the extreme command of Egypt and Syria.[1] He issued in autumn, 308, a fifth edict of persecution, which commanded that all males with their wives and servants, and even their children, should sacrifice and actually taste the accursed offerings, and that all provisions in the markets should be sprinkled with sacrificial wine. This monstrous law introduced a reign of terror for two years, and left the Christians no alternative but apostasy or starvation.[2] All the pains, which iron and steel, fire and sword, rack and cross, wild beasts and beastly men could inflict, were employed to gain the useless end.

Eusebius was a witness of this persecution in Cæsarea, Tyre, and Egypt, and saw, with his own eyes, as he tells us, the houses of prayer razed to the ground, the Holy Scriptures committed to the flames on the market places, the pastors hunted, tortured, and torn to pieces in the amphitheatre. Even the wild beasts, he says, not without rhetorical exaggeration, at last refused to attack the Christians, as if they had assumed the part of men in place of the heathen Romans; the bloody swords became dull and shattered; the executioners grew weary, and had to relieve each other; but the Christians sang hymns of praise and thanksgiving in honor of Almighty God, even to their latest breath. He describes the heroic sufferings and death of several martyrs, including his friend, " the holy and blessed Pamphilus," who after two years of imprisonment won

---

[1] See Lactant., *De Morte Persec.* ch. 18 and 19, 32, and Gibbon, ch. XIV. (vol. II. 16 in Smith's edition). The original name of Maximin was Daza. He must not be confounded with Maximian (who was older and died three years before him). He was a rude, ignorant and superstitious tyrant, equal to Galerius in cruelty, and surpassing him in incredible debauchery (See Lact. *l. c.* ch. 37 sqq.). He died of poison after being defeated by Licinius, in 313.

[2] See on this edict of Maximin, Euseb. *Mart. Pal.* IX. 2; the Acts of Martyrs in Boll., May 8, p. 291, and Oct. 19, p. 428; Mason, *l. c.* 284 sqq.

the crown of life (309), with eleven others—a typical company that seemed to him to be "a perfect representation of the church."

Eusebius himself was imprisoned, but released. The charge of having escaped martyrdom by offering sacrifice is without foundation.[1]

In this, as in former persecutions, the number of apostates who preferred the earthly life to the heavenly, was very great. To these was now added also the new class of the *traditores*, who delivered the holy Scriptures to the heathen authorities, to be burned. But as the persecution raged, the zeal and fidelity of the Christians increased, and martyrdom spread as by contagion. Even boys and girls showed amazing firmness. In many the heroism of faith degenerated to a fanatical courting of death; confessors were almost worshipped, while yet alive; and the hatred towards apostates distracted many congregations, and produced the Meletian and Donatist schisms.

The number of martyrs cannot be estimated with any degree of certainty. The seven episcopal and the ninety-two Palestinian martyrs of Eusebius are only a select list bearing a similar relation to the whole number of victims as the military lists of distinguished fallen officers to the large mass of common soldiers, and form therefore no fair basis for the calculation of Gibbon, who would reduce the whole number to less than two thousand. During the eight years[2] of this persecution the number of victims, without including the many confessors who were barbarously mutilated and condemned to a lingering death in the prisons and mines, must have been much larger. But there is no truth in the tradition (which figures in older church histories) that the tyrants erected trophies in Spain and elsewhere with such inscriptions as announce the suppression of the Christian sect.[3]

---

[1] Lightfoot vindicates him in his learned art. *Euseb.* in Smith and Wace, *Dict. of Christ. Biogr.* II. 311.

[2] Or ten years, if we include the local persecutions of Maximin and Licinius after the first edict of toleration (311–313).

[3] As "*Nomine Christianorum deleto; superstitione Christiana ubique deleta, et cultu Deorum propagato.*" See the inscriptions in full in Baronius *ad ann.* 304,

The martyrologies date from this period several legends, the germs of which, however, cannot now be clearly sifted from the additions of later poesy. The story of the destruction of the legio Thebaica is probably an exaggeration of the martyrdom of St. Mauritius, who was executed in Syria, as *tribunus militum*, with seventy soldiers, at the order of Maximin. The martyrdom of Barlaam, a plain, rustic Christian of remarkable constancy, and of Gordius, a centurion (who, however, was tortured and executed a few years later under Licinius, 314) has been eulogized by St. Basil. A maiden of thirteen years, St. Agnes, whose memory the Latin church has celebrated ever since the fourth century, was, according to tradition, brought in chains before the judgment-seat in Rome; was publicly exposed, and upon her steadfast confession put to the sword; but afterwards appeared to her grieving parents at her grave with a white lamb and a host of shining virgins from heaven, and said: "Mourn me no longer as dead, for ye see that I live. Rejoice with me, that I am forever united in heaven with the Saviour, whom on earth I loved with all my heart." Hence the lamb in the paintings of this saint; and hence the consecration of lambs in her church at Rome at her festival (Jan. 21), from whose wool the pallium of the archbishop is made. Agricola and Vitalis at Bologna, Gervasius and Protasius at Milan, whose bones were discovered in the time of Ambrose Janurius, bishop of Benevent, who became the patron saint of Naples, and astonishes the faithful by the annual miracle of the liquefaction of his blood, and the British St. Alban, who delivered himself to the authorities in the place of the priest he had concealed in his house, and converted his executioner, are said to have attained martyrdom under Diocletian.[1]

no. 8, 9; but they are inconsistent with the confession of the failure in the edict of toleration, and acknowledged to be worthless even by Gams (*K. Gesh. v. Spanien*, I. 387).

[1] For details see the Martyrologies, the "Lives of Saints," also Baronius *Annal.* This historian is so fully convinced of the "*insigne et perpetuum miraculum sanguinis S. Januarii*," that he thinks it unnecessary to produce any witness, since "*tota Italia, et totus Christianus orbis testis est locupletissimus!*" *Ad ann.* 305 no. 6.

§ 25. *The Edicts of Toleration.* A. D. 311–313.

See Lit. in § 24, especially KEIM, and MASON (*Persecution of Diocletian,* pp. 299 and 326 sqq.)

This persecution was the last desperate struggle of Roman heathenism for its life. It was the crisis of utter extinction or absolute supremacy for each of the two religions. At the close of the contest the old Roman state religion was exhausted. Diocletian retired into private life in 305, under the curse of the Christians; he found greater pleasure in planting cabbages at Salona in his native Dalmatia, than in governing a vast empire, but his peace was disturbed by the tragical misfortunes of his wife and daughter, and in 313, when all the achievements of his reign were destroyed, he destroyed himself.

Galerius, the real author of the persecution, brought to reflection by a terrible disease, put an end to the slaughter shortly before his death, by a remarkable edict of toleration, which he issued from Nicomedia in 311, in connexion with Constantine and Licinius. In that document he declared, that the purpose of reclaiming the Christians from their wilful innovation and the multitude of their sects to the laws and discipline of the Roman state, was not accomplished; and that he would now grant them permission to hold their religious assemblies, provided they disturbed not the order of the state. To this he added in conclusion the significant instruction that the Christians, "after this manifestation of grace, should pray *to their God* for the welfare of the emperors, of the state, and of themselves, that the state might prosper in every respect, and that they might live quietly in their homes." [1]

---

[1] M. de Broglie (*L'Église et l'Empire,* I. 182) well characterizes this manifesto: "*Singulier document, moitié insolent, moitié suppliant, qui commence par insulter les chrétiens et finit par leur demander de prier leur maître pour lui.*" Mason (*l. c.* p. 299): "The dying emperor shows no penitence, makes no confession, except his impotence. He wishes to dupe and outwit the angry Christ, by pretending to be not a persecutor but a reformer. With a curse, he dashes his edict of toleration in the church's face, and hopes superstitiously that it will win him indemnity."

This edict virtually closes the period of persecution in the Roman empire.

For a short time Maximin, whom Eusebius calls "the chief of tyrants," continued in every way to oppress and vex the church in the East, and the cruel pagan Maxentius (a son of Maximian and son-in-law of Galerius) did the same in Italy.

But the young Constantine, who hailed from the far West, had already, in 306, become emperor of Gaul, Spain, and Britain. He had been brought up at the court of Diocletian at Nicomedia (like Moses at the court of Pharaoh) and destined for his successor, but fled from the intrigues of Galerius to Britain, and was appointed by his father and proclaimed by the army as his successor. He crossed the Alps, and under the banner of the cross, he conquered Maxentius at the Milvian bridge near Rome, and the heathen tyrant perished with his army of veterans in the waters of the Tiber, Oct. 27, 312. A few months afterwards Constantine met at Milan with his co-regent and brother-in-law, Licinius, and issued a new edict of toleration (313), to which Maximin also, shortly before his suicide (313), was compelled to give his consent at Nicomedia.[1] The second edict went beyond the first of 311; it was a decisive step from hostile neutrality to friendly neutrality and protection, and prepared the way for the legal recognition of Christianity, as the religion of the empire. It ordered the full restoration of all confiscated church property to the *Corpus Christianorum*, at the expense of the imperial treasury, and directed the provincial magistrates to execute this order at once with all energy, so that peace may be fully established and the continuance of the Divine favor secured to the emperors and their subjects.

This was the first proclamation of the great principle that

---

[1] It is usually stated (also by Keim, *l. c.*, Gieseler, Baur, vol. I. 454 sqq.), that Constantine and Licinius issued two edicts of toleration, one in the year 312, and one from Milan in 313, since the last refers to a previous edict; but the reference seems to be to directions now lost for officials which accompanied the edict of Galerius (311), of which Constatine was a co-signatory. There is no edict of 312. See Zahn and especially Mason (p. 328 sq.), also Uhlhorn (*Conflict*, etc., p. 497, Engl. translation).

every man had a right to choose his religion according to the dictates of his own conscience and honest conviction, without compulsion and interference from the government.[1] Religion is worth nothing except as an act of freedom. A forced religion is no religion at all. Unfortunately, the successors of Constantine from the time of Theodosius the Great (383–395) enforced the Christian religion to the exclusion of every other; and not only so, but they enforced orthodoxy to the exclusion of every form of dissent, which was punished as a crime against the state.

Paganism made another spasmodic effort. Licinius fell out with Constantine and renewed the persecution for a short time in the East, but he was defeated in 323, and Constantine became sole ruler of the empire. He openly protected and favored the church, without forbidding idolatry, and upon the whole remained true to his policy of protective toleration till his death (337). This was enough for the success of the church, which had all the vitality and energy of a victorious power; while heathenism was fast decaying at its root.

With Constantine, therefore, the last of the heathen, the first of the Christian, emperors, a new period begins. The church ascends the throne of the Cæsars under the banner of the once despised, now honored and triumphant cross, and gives new vigor and lustre to the hoary empire of Rome. This sudden political and social revolution seems marvellous; and yet it was only the legitimate result of the intellectual and moral revolution which Christianity, since the second century, had silently and imperceptibly wrought in public opinion. The very violence of the Diocletian persecution betrayed the inner weakness of heathenism. The Christian minority with its ideas already controlled the deeper current of history. Constantine, as a

---

[1] "Ut daremus et Christianis et omnibus liberam potestatem sequendi religionem, quam quiscunque voluisset." See Euseb. H. E. X. 5; Lactant. De Mort. Pers. c. 48. Mason (p. 327) says of the Edict of Milan: "It is the very first announcement of that doctrine which is now regarded as the mark and principle of civilization, the foundation of solid liberty, the characteristic of modern politics. In vigorous and trenchant sentences it sets forth perfect freedom of conscience, the unfettered choice of religion."

sagacious statesman, saw the signs of the times and followed them. The motto of his policy is well symbolized in his military standard with the inscription : " *Hoc signo vinces.*"[1] What a contrast between Nero, the first imperial persecutor, riding in a chariot among Christian martyrs as burning torches in his gardens, and Constantine, seated in the Council of Nicæa among three hundred and eighteen bishops (some of whom—as the blinded Confessor Paphnutius, Paul of Neocæsarea, and the ascetics from Upper Egypt clothed in wild raiment—wore the insignia of torture on their maimed and crippled bodies), and giving the highest sanction of civil authority to the decree of the eternal deity of the once crucified Jesus of Nazareth! Such a revolution the world has never seen before or since, except the silent, spiritual, and moral reformation wrought by Christianity itself at its introduction in the first, and at its revival in the sixteenth century.

§ 26. *Christian Martyrdom.*

I. SOURCES.

IGNATIUS : *Epistolæ. Martyrium Polycarpi.* TERTULLIAN : *Ad Martyres.* ORIGENES : *Exhortatio ad martyrium* (προτρεπτικὸς λόγος εἰς μαρτύριον.) CYPRIAN : *Ep.* 11 *ad mart.* PRUDENTIUS : Περὶ στεφάνων *hymni* XIV. Comp. Lit. § 12.

II. WORKS.

SAGITTARIUS : *De mart. cruciatibus,* 1696.

H. DODWELL : *De paucitate martyrum, in his Dissertationes Cyprianicæ.* Lond. 1684.

RUINART (R. C.) : *Præfatio generalis in Acta Martyrum.*

F. W. GASS : *Das christl. Märtyrerthum in den ersten Jahrhunderten,* in *Niedner's* "Zeitschrift f. hist. Theol." 1859 and '60.

E. DE PRESSENSÉ : *The Martyrs and Apologists.* Translated from the French. London and N. Y. 1871. (Ch. II. p. 67 sqq.).

CHATEAUBRIAND : *Les martyrs ou le triomphe de la rel. chrêt.* 2 vols. Paris 1809 and often (best Engl. trsl. by *O. W. Wight,* N. York, 1859.) Has no critical or historical value, but merely poetical.

Comp. in part Mrs. JAMESON : *Sacred and Legendary Art.* Lond. 1848. 2 vols.

---

[1] For a fuller account of Constantine and his relation to the Church, see the next volume.

To these protracted and cruel persecutions the church opposed no revolutionary violence, no carnal resistance, but the moral heroism of suffering and dying for the truth. But this very heroism was her fairest ornament and stanchest weapon. In this very heroism she proved herself worthy of her divine founder, who submitted to the death of the cross for the salvation of the world, and even prayed that his murderers might be forgiven. The patriotic virtues of Greek and Roman antiquity reproduced themselves here in exalted form, in selfdenial for the sake of a heavenly country, and for a crown that fadeth not away. Even boys and girls became heroes, and rushed with a holy enthusiasm to death. In those hard times men had to make earnest of the words of the Lord: "Whosoever doth not bear his cross and come after me, cannot be my disciple." "He, that loveth father and mother more than me, is not worthy of me." But then also the promise daily proved itself true: "Blessed are they, who are persecuted for righteousness' sake; for theirs is the kingdom of heaven." "He, that loseth his life for my sake, shall find it." And it applied not only to the martyrs themselves, who exchanged the troubled life of earth for the blessedness of heaven, but also to the church as a whole, which came forth purer and stronger from every persecution, and thus attested her indestructible vitality.

These suffering virtues are among the sweetest and noblest fruits of the Christian religion. It is not so much the amount of suffering which challenges our admiration, although it was terrible enough, as the spirit with which the early Christians bore it. Men and women of all classes, noble senators and learned bishops, illiterate artisans and poor slaves, loving mothers and delicate virgins, hoary-headed pastors and innocent children approached their tortures in no temper of unfeeling indifference and obstinate defiance, but, like their divine Master, with calm self-possession, humble resignation, gentle meekness, cheerful faith, triumphant hope, and forgiving charity. Such spectacles must have often overcome even the inhuman murderer. "Go on," says Tertullian tauntingly to the heathen governors, "rack, torture, grind us to powder: our numbers increase in proportion as ye mow us down. The blood of Christians is their harvest seed. Your very obstinacy is a teacher. For who is not incited by the contemplation of it to inquire what there is in the core of the matter? And who, after having joined us, does not long to suffer?"[1]

Unquestionably there were also during this period, especially after considerable seasons of quiet, many superficial or hypocritical Christians, who, the moment the storm of persecution broke forth, flew like chaff from the wheat, and either offered incense to the gods (*thurificati*, *sacrificati*), or procured false witness of their return to paganism (*libellatici*, from *libellum*), or gave up the sacred books (*traditores*). Tertullian relates with righteous indignation that whole congregations, with the clergy at the head, would at times resort to dishonorable bribes in order to avert the persecution of heathen magistrates.[2] But these were certainly cases of rare exception. Generally speaking the three sorts of apostates (*lapsi*) were at once excommunicated, and in many churches, through excessive rigor, were even refused restoration.

Those who cheerfully confessed Christ before the heathen magistrate at the peril of life, but were not executed, were honored as *confessors*.[3] Those who suffered abuse of all kind and death itself, for their faith, were called *martyrs* or *blood-witnesses*.[4]

Among these confessors and martyrs were not wanting those in whom the pure, quiet flame of enthusiasm rose into the wild fire of fanaticism, and whose zeal was corrupted with impatient haste, heaven-tempting presumption, and pious ambition; to whom that word could be applied: "Though I give my body

---

[1] Comp. a similar passage in the anonymous *Ep. ad Diognetum*, c. 6 and 7 at the close, and in Justin M., *Dial. c. Tryph. Jud.* c. 110.

[2] *De fuga in persec.* c. 13: "*Massaliter totœ ecclesiae tributum sibi irrogaverunt.*"

[3] Ὁμολογῆται, confessores, Matt. 10: 32; 1 Tim. 6: 12.

Μάρτυρες, Acts 22: 20; Heb. 12: 1; 1 Pet. 5: 1; Rev. 17: 6.

to be burned, and have not love, it profiteth me nothing."
They delivered themselves up to the heathen officers, and in
every way sought the martyr's crown, that they might merit
heaven and be venerated on earth as saints. Thus Tertullian
tells of a company of Christians in Ephesus, who begged martyrdom from the heathen governor, but after a few had been
executed, the rest were sent away by him with the words:
"Miserable creatures, if you really wish to die, you have pre-
cipices and halters enough." Though this error was far less
discreditable than the opposite extreme of the cowardly fear of
man, yet it was contrary to the instruction and the example of
Christ and the apostles,[1] and to the spirit of true martyrdom,
which consists in the union of sincere humility and power, and
possesses divine strength in the very consciousness of human
weakness. And accordingly intelligent church teachers censured this stormy, morbid zeal. The church of Smyrna speaks
thus: "We do not commend those who expose themselves; for
the gospel teaches not so." Clement of Alexandria says:
"The Lord himself has commanded us to flee to another
city when we are persecuted; not as if the persecution were an
evil; not as if we feared death; but that we may not lead or
help any to evil doing." In Tertullian's view martyrdom per-
fects itself in divine patience; and with Cyprian it is a gift of
divine grace, which one cannot hastily grasp, but must patiently
wait for.

But after all due allowance for such adulteration and degeneracy, the martyrdom of the first three centuries still
remains one of the grandest phenomena of history, and an
evidence of the indestructible, divine nature of Christianity.

No other religion could have stood for so long a period the
combined opposition of Jewish bigotry, Greek philosophy, and
Roman policy and power; no other could have triumphed at
last over so many foes by purely moral and spiritual force,
without calling any carnal weapons to its aid. This compre-

---

[1] Comp. Matt. 10: 23; 24: 15–20; Phil. 1: 20–25; 2 Tim. 4: 6–8.

hensive and long-continued martyrdom is the peculiar crown and glory of the early church; it pervaded its entire literature and gave it a predominantly apologetic character; it entered deeply into its organization and discipline and the development of Christian doctrine; it affected the public worship and private devotions; it produced a legendary poetry; but it gave rise also, innocently, to a great deal of superstition, and undue exaltation of human merit; and it lies at the foundation of the Catholic worship of saints and relics.

Sceptical writers have endeavored to diminish its moral effect by pointing to the fiendish and hellish scenes of the papal crusades against the Albigenses and Waldenses, the Parisian massacre of the Huguenots, the Spanish Inquisition, and other persecutions of more recent date. Dodwell expressed the opinion, which has been recently confirmed by the high authority of the learned and impartial Niebuhr, that the Diocletian persecution was a mere shadow as compared with the persecution of the Protestants in the Netherlands by the Duke of Alva in the service of Spanish bigotry and despotism. Gibbon goes even further, and boldly asserts that "the number of Protestants who were executed by the Spaniards in a single province and a single reign, far exceeded that of the primitive martyrs in the space of three centuries and of the Roman empire." The victims of the Spanish Inquisition also are said to outnumber those of the Roman emperors.[1]

---

[1] The number of Dutch martyrs under the Duke of Alva amounted, according to Grotius, to over 100,000; according to P. Sarpi, the R. Cath. historian, to 50,000. Motley, in his *History of the Rise of the Dutch Republic*, vol. II. 504, says of the terrible reign of Alva: "The barbarities committed amid the sack and ruin of those blazing and starving cities are almost beyond belief; unborn infants were torn from the living bodies of their mothers; women and children were violated by the thousands; and whole populations burned and hacked to pieces by soldiers in every mode which cruelty, in its wanton ingenuity, could devise." Buckle and Friedländer (III. 586) assert that during the eighteen years of office of Torquemada, the Spanish Inquisition punished, according to the lowest estimate, 105,000 persons, among whom 8,800 were burnt. In Andalusia 2000 Jews were *executed*, and 17,000 *punished* in a single year.

Admitting these sad facts, they do not justify any sceptical conclusion. For Christianity is no more responsible for the crimes and cruelties perpetrated in its name by unworthy professors and under the sanction of an unholy alliance of politics and religion, than the Bible for all the nonsense men have put into it, or God for the abuse daily and hourly practised with his best gifts. But the number of martyrs must be judged by the total number of Christians who were a minority of the population. The want of particular statements by contemporary writers leaves it impossible to ascertain, even approximately, the number of martyrs. Dodwell and Gibbon have certainly underrated it, as far as Eusebius, the popular tradition since Constantine, and the legendary poesy of the middle age, have erred the other way. This is the result of recent discovery and investigation, and fully admitted by such writers as Renan. Origen, it is true, wrote in the middle of the third century, that the number of Christian martyrs was small and easy to be counted; God not permitting that all this class of men should be exterminated.[1] But this language must be understood as referring chiefly to the reigns of Caracalla, Heliogabalus, Alexander Severus and Philippus Arabs, who did not persecute the Christians. Soon afterwards the fearful persecution of Decius broke out, in which Origen himself was thrown into prison and cruelly treated. Concerning the preceding ages, his statement must be qualified by the equally valid testimonies of Turtullian, Clement of Alexandria (Origen's teacher), and the still older Irenæus, who says expressly, that the church, for her love to God, " sends in all places and at all times a multitude of martyrs to the Father."[2] Even the heathen Tacitus speaks of an " immense multitude " (*ingens multitudo*) of Christians, who were murdered in the city of Rome alone during the

---

[1] Ὀλίγοι κατὰ καιροὺς καὶ σφόδρα εὐαρίθμητοι τεθνήκασι. *Adv. Cels.* III. 8. The older testimony of Melito of Sardis, in the well-known fragment from his Apology, preserved by Eusebius IV. 26, refers merely to the small number of *imperial* persecutors before Marcus Aurelius.

[2] *Adv. Haer.* IV. c. 33, § 9 : *Ecclesia omni in loco ob eam, quam habet erga Deum dilectionem, multitudinem martyrum in omni tempore praemittit ad Patrem.*

Neronian persecution in 64. To this must be added the silent, yet most eloquent testimony of the Roman catacombs, which, according to the calculation of Marchi and Northcote, extended over nine hundred English miles, and are said to contain nearly seven millions of graves, a large proportion of these including the relics of martyrs, as the innumerable inscriptions and instruments of death testify. The sufferings, moreover, of the church during this period are of course not to be measured merely by the number of actual executions, but by the far more numerous insults, slanders, vexations, and tortures, which the cruelty of heartless heathens and barbarians could devise, or any sort of instrument could inflict on the human body, and which were in a thousand cases worse than death.

Finally, while the Christian religion has at all times suffered more or less persecution, bloody or unbloody, from the ungodly world, and always had its witnesses ready for any sacrifice; yet at no period since the first three centuries was the whole church denied the right of a peaceful legal existence, and the profession of Christianity itself universally declared and punished as a political crime. Before Constantine the Christians were a helpless and proscribed minority in an essentially heathen world, and under a heathen government. Then they died not simply for particular doctrines, but for the facts of Christianity. Then it was a conflict, not for a denomination or sect, but for Christianity itself. The importance of ancient martyrdom does not rest so much on the number of victims and the cruelty of their sufferings as on the great antithesis and the ultimate result in saving the Christian religion for all time to come. Hence the first three centuries are the classical period of heathen persecution and of Christian martyrdom. The martyrs and confessors of the ante-Nicene age suffered for the common cause of all Christian denominations and sects, and hence are justly held in reverence and gratitude by all.

NOTES.

Dr. Thomas Arnold, who had no leaning to superstitious and idolatrous saint-worship, in speaking of a visit to the church of San Stefano at Rome, remarks: "No doubt many of the particular stories thus painted will bear no critical examination; it is likely enough, too, that Gibbon has truly accused the general statements of exaggeration. But this is a thankless labor. Divide the sum total of the reported martyrs by twenty—by fifty, if you will; after all you have a number of persons of all ages and sexes suffering cruel torments and death for conscience' sake, and for Christ's; and by their sufferings manifestly with God's blessing ensuring the triumph of Christ's gospel. Neither do I think that we consider the excellence of this martyr spirit half enough. I do not think that pleasure is a sin; but though pleasure is not a sin, yet surely the contemplation of suffering for Christ's sake is a thing most needful for us in our days, from whom in our daily life suffering seems so far removed. And as God's grace enabled rich and delicate persons, women and even children, to endure all extremities of pain and reproach, in times past; so there is the same grace no less mighty now; and if we do not close ourselves against it, it might be in us no less glorious in a time of trial."

Lecky, a very able and impartial historian, justly censures the unfeeling chapter of Gibbon on persecution. "The complete absence," he says (*History of European Morals*, I. 494 sqq.), "of all sympathy with the heroic courage manifested by the martyrs, and the frigid, and in truth most unphilosophical severity with which the historian has weighed the words and actions of men engaged in the agonies of a deadly struggle, must repel every generous nature, while the persistence with which he estimates persecutions by the number of deaths rather than the amount of suffering, diverts the mind from the really distinctive atrocities of the Pagan persecutions. . . . . . It is true that in one Catholic country they introduced the atrocious custom of making the spectacle of men burnt alive for their religious opinions an element in the public festivities. It is true, too, that the immense majority of the acts of the martyrs are the transparent forgeries of lying monks; but it is also true that among the authentic records of Pagan persecutions there are histories which display, perhaps more vividly than any other, both the depth of cruelty to which human nature may sink, and the heroism of resistance it may attain. There was a time when it was the just boast of the Romans, that no refinement of cruelty, no prolongations of torture, were admitted in their stern but simple penal code. But all this was changed. Those hateful games, which made the spectacle of human suffering and death the delight of all classes, had spread their brutalising influence wherever the Roman name was known, had rendered millions absolutely indifferent to the sight of human suffering, had produced in many, in the very centre of an advanced civilisation, a relish and a passion for torture, a rapture and an exultation in watching the spasms of extreme agony, such as an African or an American savage alone can equal. The most horrible recorded instances of torture were usually inflicted, either by the populace, or in their presence, in the arena. We read of Christians bound in chains of red-hot iron, while the stench of their half-consumed flesh rose in a suffocating cloud to heaven; of others who were torn to the very bone by shells, or hooks of iron; of holy virgins given over to the lust of the gladiator or to the mercies of the pander; of two hundred and twenty-seven converts sent on one occasion to the mines, each with the sinews of one leg severed by a red-hot iron, and with an eye scooped from its socket; of fires so slow that the victims writhed for hours in their agonies; of bodies torn limb from limb, or sprinkled with burning lead; of mingled salt and vinegar poured over the flesh that was bleeding from the rack; of tortures prolonged and varied through entire days. For the love of their Divine Master, for the cause they believed to be true, men, and even weak girls, endured these things without flinching, when one word would have freed them from their sufferings. *No opinion we may form of the proceedings of priests in a later age should impair the reverence with which we bend before the martyr's tomb.*

§ 27. *Rise of the Worship of Martyrs and Relics.*

I. Sources.

In addition to the works quoted in §§ 12 and 26, comp. Euseb. *H. E.* IV. 15; *De Mart. Palaest.* c. 7. Clem. Alex.: *Strom.* IV. p. 596. Orig.: *Exhort. ad mart.* c. 30 and 50. *In Num. Kom.* X. 2. Tertull.: *De cor. mil.* c. 3; *De Resurr. carn.* c. 43. Cypr.: *De lapsis*, c. 17; *Epist.* 34 and 57. Const. Apost.: l. 8.

II. Works.

C. Sagittarius: *De natalitiis mart.* Jen. 1696.
Schwabe: *De insigni veneratione, quae obtinuit erga martyres in primit. eccl.* Altd. 1748.

In thankful remembrance of the fidelity of this " noble army of martyrs," in recognition of the unbroken communion of saints, and in prospect of the resurrection of the body, the church paid to the martyrs, and even to their mortal remains, a veneration, which was in itself well-deserved and altogether natural, but which early exceeded the scriptural limit, and afterwards degenerated into the worship of saints and relics. The heathen hero-worship silently continued in the church and was baptized with Christian names.

In the church of Smyrna, according to its letter of the year 155, we find this veneration still in its innocent, childlike form: " They [the Jews] know not, that we can neither ever forsake Christ, who has suffered for the salvation of the whole world of the redeemed, nor worship another. Him indeed we adore (προσκυνοῦμεν) as the Son of God; but the martyrs we love as they deserve (ἀγαπῶμεν ἀξίως), for their surpassing love to their King and Master, as we wish also to be their companions and fellow-disciples." [1] The day of the death of a martyr was called his heavenly birth-day,[2] and was celebrated annually at his grave (mostly in a cave or catacomb), by prayer, reading of a history of his suffering and victory, oblations, and celebration of the holy supper.

But the early church did not stop with this. Martyrdom was taken, after the end of the second century, not only as a higher grade of Christian virtue, but at the same time as a baptism of fire and blood,[3] an ample substitution for the baptism of water, as purifying from sin, and as securing an entrance into heaven. Origen even went so far as to ascribe to the sufferings of the martyrs an atoning virtue for others, an efficacy like that of the sufferings of Christ, on the authority of such passages as 2 Cor. 12: 15; Col. 1: 24; 2 Tim. 4: 6. According to Tertullian, the martyrs entered immediately into the blessedness of heaven, and were not required, like ordinary Christians, to pass through the intermediate state. Thus was applied the benediction on those who are persecuted for righteousness' sake, Matt. 5: 10–12. Hence, according to Origen and Cyprian, their prayers before the throne of God came to be thought peculiarly efficacious for the church militant on earth, and, according to an example related by Eusebius, their future intercessions were bespoken shortly *before* their death.

In the Roman Catacombs we find inscriptions where the departed are requested to pray for their living relatives and friends.

The veneration thus shown for the persons of the martyrs was transferred in smaller measure to their remains. The church of Smyrna counted the bones of Polycarp more precious than gold or diamonds.[4] The remains of Ignatius were held in

---

[1] *Martyrium Polycarpi*, cap. 17; comp. Eusebius, *H. E.* IV. 15.

[2] Ἡμέρα γενέθλιος, γενέθλια, natales, natalitia martyrum.

[3] *Lavacrum sanguinis*, βάπτισμα διὰ πυρός, comp. Matt. 20: 22; Luke 12: 50; Mark 10: 39.

[4] It is worthy of note, however, that some of the startling phenomena related in the *Martyrium Polycarpi* by the congregation of Smyrna are omitted in the narrative of Eusebius (IV. 15), and may be a later interpolation.

equal veneration by the Christians at Antioch. The friends of Cyprian gathered his blood in handkerchiefs, and built a chapel over his tomb.

A veneration frequently excessive was paid, not only to the deceased martyrs, but also the surviving confessors. It was made the special duty of the deacons to visit and minister to them in prison. The heathen Lucian in his satire, "De morte Peregrini," describes the unwearied care of the Christians for their imprisoned brethren; the heaps of presents brought to them; and the testimonies of sympathy even by messengers from great distances; but all, of course, in Lucian's view, out of mere good-natured enthusiasm. Tertullian the Montanist censures the excessive attention of the Catholics to their confessors. The *libelli pacis*, as they were called—intercessions of the confessors for the fallen—commonly procured restoration to the fellowship of the church. Their voice had peculiar weight in the choice of bishops, and their sanction not rarely overbalanced the authority of the clergy. Cyprian is nowhere more eloquent than in the praise of their heroism. His letters to the imprisoned confessors in Carthage are full of glorification, in a style somewhat offensive to our evangelical ideas. Yet after all, he protests against the abuse of their privileges, from which he had himself to suffer, and earnestly exhorts them to a holy walk; that the honor they have gained may not prove a snare to them, and through pride and carelessness be lost. He always represents the crown of the confessor and the martyr as a free gift of the grace of God, and sees the real essence of it rather in the inward disposition than in the outward act. Commodian conceived the whole idea of martyrdom in its true breadth, when he extended it to all those who, without shedding their blood, endured to the end in love, humility, and patience, and in all Christian virtue.

CHAPTER III.

LITERARY CONTEST OF CHRISTIANITY WITH JUDAISM AND HEATHENISM.

§ 28. *Literature.*

I. SOURCES.

TACITUS (Consul 97, d. about 117): *Annal.* xv. 44. Comp. his picture of the Jews, *Hist.* v. 1–5.

PLINIUS (d. about 114): *Ep.* x. 96, 97.

CELSUS (flourished about 150): ᾿Αληθὴς λόγος. Preserved in fragments in Origen's Refutation (8 books Κατὰ Κέλσου); reconstructed, translated and explained by THEODOR KEIM: *Celsus' Wahres Wort. Aelteste wissenschaftliche Streitschrift antiker Weltanschauung gegen das Christenthum,* Zürich 1873 (293 pages).

LUCIAN (d. about 180): Περὶ τῆς Περεγρίνου τελευτῆς, c. 11–16; and ᾿Αληθὴς ἱστορία, I. 22, 30; II. 4, 11.

PORPHYRIUS (about 300): Κατὰ Χριστιανῶν λόγοι. Only fragments preserved, and collected by HOLSTEIN, Rom. 1630. His most important works are lost. Those that remain are ed. by A. NAUCK, 1860.

II. WORKS.

NATH. LARDNER: *Collection of Ancient Jewish and Heathen Testimonies to the Truth of the Christian Religion* (Lond. 1727–'57) in the VI. and VII. vols. of his *Works,* ed. by Kippis, London, 1838. Very valuable.

MOSHEIM: Introduction to his Germ. translation of *Origen against Celsus.* Hamb. 1745.

BINDEMANN: *Celsus und seine Schriften gegen die Christen,* in Illgen's "Zeitschr. für hist. Theol." Leipz. 1842. N. 2, p. 58–146.

AD. PLANCK: *Lukian u. das Christenthum,* in the "Studien u. Kritiken," 1851. N. 4; translated in the "Bibliotheca Sacra," Andover, 1852.

F. CHR. BAUR: *Das Christenthum der 3 ersten Jahrh.* Tüb. secd. ed. 1860 (and 1863) pp. 370–430.

NEANDER: *General History of the Christian Religion and Church;* Engl. trans. by *Torrey,* vol. I., 157–178. (12th Boston ed.)

85

RICHARD VON DER ALM: *Die Urtheile heidnischer und jüdischer Schriftsteller der vier ersten Jahrh. über Jesus und die ersten Christen.* Leipz. 1865. (An infidel book.)

H. KELLNER (R. C.): *Hellenismus und Christenthum oder die geistige Reaction des antiken Heidenthums gegen das Christenthum.* Köln 1866 (454 pp.)

B. AUBÉ: *De l'Apologétique chrétienne au IIe siècle. St. Justin, philosophe et martyr,* 2nd ed. Paris 1875. By the same: *Histoire des Persecutions de l'église.* The second part, also under the title *La polémique païenne à la fin du IIe siècle.* Paris 1878.

E. RENAN: *Marc-Aurèle* (Paris 1882), pp. 345 (*Celse et Lucien*), 379 sqq. (*Nouvelles apologies*).

J. W. FARRAR: *Seekers after God.* London, 1869, new ed. 1877. (Essays on Seneca, Epictetus, and Marcus Aurelius, compared with Christianity.)

Comp. the Lit. quoted in § 12, especially UHLHORN and KEIM (1881), and the monographs on Justin M., Tertullian, Origen, and other Apologists, which are noticed in sections treating of these writers.

§ 29. *Literary Opposition to Christianity.*

Besides the external conflict, which we have considered in the second chapter, Christianity was called to pass through an equally important intellectual and literary struggle with the ancient world ; and from this also it came forth victorious, and conscious of being the perfect religion for man. We shall see in this chapter, that most of the objections of modern infidelity against Christianity were anticipated by its earliest literary opponents, and ably and successfully refuted by the ancient apologists for the wants of the church in that age. Both unbelief and faith, like human nature and divine grace, are essentially the same in all ages and among all nations, but vary in form, and hence every age, as it produces its own phase of opposition, must frame its own mode of defense.

The Christian religion found at first as little favor with the representatives of literature and art as with princes and statesmen. In the secular literature of the latter part of the first century and the beginning of the second, we find little more than ignorant, careless and hostile allusions to Christianity as a new form of superstition which then began to attract the attention of the Roman government. In this point of view also Christ's kingdom was not of the world, and was compelled to force its way through the greatest difficulties; yet it proved at last the mother of an intellectual and moral culture far in advance of the Græco-Roman, capable of endless progress, and full of the vigor of perpetual youth.

The pious barbarism of the Byzantine emperors Theodosius II. and Valentinian III. ordered the destruction of the works of Porphyrius and all other opponents of Christianity, to avert the wrath of God, but considerable fragments have been preserved in the refutations of the Christian Fathers, especially Origen, Eusebius, Cyril of Alexandria (against Julian), and scattered notices of Jerome and Augustin.

§ 30. *Jewish Opposition. Josephus and the Talmud.*

The hostility of the Jewish Scribes and Pharisees to the gospel is familiar from the New Testament. Josephus mentions Jesus once in his Archæology, but in terms so favorable as to agree ill with his Jewish position, and to subject the passage to the suspicion of interpolation or corruption.[1] His writings, however, contain much valuable testimony to the truth of the gospel history. His "Archæology" throughout is a sort of fifth Gospel in illustration of the social and political environments of the life of Christ.[2] His "History of the Jewish War," in particular, is undesignedly a striking commentary on the Saviour's predictions concerning the destruction of the city and temple of Jerusalem, the great distress and affliction of the Jewish people at that time, the famine, pestilence, and earthquake, the rise of false prophets and impostors, and the flight of his disciples at the approach of these calamities.[3]

The attacks of the later Jews upon Christianity are essentially mere repetitions of those recorded in the Gospels—denial

[1] Joseph. *Antiqu.* l. XVIII. c. 3, sect. 3. Comp. on this much disputed passage, vol. I., p. 92.

[2] It is the special merit of Keim to have thoroughly utilized Josephus for the biography of Jesus.

[3] These coincidences have been traced out in full by Lardner, *Works*, ed. Kippis, vol. VI. p. 406 ff.

of the Messiahship of Jesus, and horrible vituperation of his confessors. We learn their character best from the dialogue of Justin with the Jew Trypho. The fictitious disputation on Christ by Jason and Papiscus, first mentioned by Celsus, was lost since the seventh century.[1] It seems to have been a rather poor apology of Christianity against Jewish objections by a Jewish Christian, perhaps by Aristo of Pella.

The Talmud is the Bible of Judaism separated from, and hostile to, Christianity, but it barely notices it except indirectly. It completed the isolation of the Jews from all other people.

§ 31. *Pagan Opposition. Tacitus and Pliny.*

The Greek and Roman writers of the first century, and some of the second, as Seneca, the elder Pliny, and even the mild and noble Plutarch, either from ignorance or contempt, never allude to Christianity at all.

Tacitus and the younger Pliny, contemporaries and friends of the emperor Trajan, are the first to notice it; and they speak of it only incidentally and with stoical disdain and antipathy, as an " *exitiabilis superstitio,*" "*prava et immodica superstitio,*" " *inflexibilis obstinatio.*" These celebrated and in their way altogether estimable Roman authors thus, from manifest ignorance, saw in the Christians nothing but superstitious fanatics, and put them on a level with the hated Jews; Tacitus, in fact, reproaching them also with the " *odium generis humani.*" This will afford some idea of the immense obstacles which the new religion encountered in public opinion, especially in the cultivated circles of the Roman empire. The Christian apologies of the second century also show, that the most malicious and gratuitous slanders against the Christians were circulated among the common people, even charges of incest and cannibalism,[2] which may have arisen in part from a misappre-

---

[1] Ἰάσονος καὶ Παπίσκου ἀντιλογία περὶ Χριστοῦ. Origenes *Contra Cels.* IV. 51. Celsus says, that he read the book which defends the allegorical interpretation, with pity and hatred. Comp. Harnack, *Altchristl. Literatur*, vol. I. (1882), p. 115 sqq.

[2] Οἰδιπόδειοι μίξεις, *incesti concubitus;* and θυεστεῖα δεῖπνα, *Thyesteæ epulæ.*

hension of the intimate brotherly love of the Christians, and their nightly celebration of the holy supper and love-feasts.

Their indirect Testimony to Christianity.

On the other hand, however, the scanty and contemptuous allusions of Tacitus and Pliny to Christianity bear testimony to a number of facts in the Gospel History. Tacitus, in giving an account of the Neronian persecution, incidentally attests, that Christ was put to death as a malefactor by Pontius Pilate in the reign of Tiberius; that he was the founder of the Christian sect, that the latter took its rise in Judæa and spread in spite of the ignominious death of Christ and the hatred and contempt it encountered throughout the empire, so that a "vast multitude" (*multitudo ingens*) of them were most cruelly put to death in the city of Rome alone as early as the year 64. He also bears valuable testimony, in the fifth book of his History, together with Josephus, from whom he mainly, though not exclusively takes his account, to the fulfilment of Christ's prophecy concerning the destruction of Jerusalem and the overthrow of the Jewish theocracy.

As to Pliny's famous letter to Trajan, written about 107, it proves the rapid spread of Christianity in Asia Minor at that time among all ranks of society, the general moral purity and steadfastness of its professors amid cruel persecution, their mode and time of worship, their adoration of Christ as God, their observance of a "stated day," which is undoubtedly Sunday, and other facts of importance in the early history of the Church. Trajan's rescript in reply to Pliny's inquiry, furnishes evidence of the innocence of the Christians; he notices no charge against them except their disregard of the worship of the gods, and forbids them to be sought for. Marcus Aurelius testifies, in one brief and unfriendly allusion, to their eagerness for the crown of martyrdom.

§ 32. Direct Assaults. Celsus.

The direct assault upon Christianity, by works devoted to the purpose, began about the middle of the second century, and was very ably conducted by a Grecian philosopher, Celsus, other-wise unknown; according to Origen, an Epicurean with many Platonic ideas, and a friend of Lucian. He wrote during the persecuting reign of Marcus Aurelius.[1]

Celsus, with all his affected or real contempt for the new religion, considered it important enough to be opposed by an extended work entitled "A True Discourse," of which Origen, in his Refutation, has faithfully preserved considerable frag-ments.[2] These represent their author as an eclectic philosopher of varied culture, skilled in dialectics, and familiar with the Gospels, Epistles, and even the writings of the Old Testament. He speaks now in the frivolous style of an Epicurean, now in the earnest and dignified tone of a Platonist. At one time he advocates the popular heathen religion, as, for instance, its doc-trine of demons; at another time he rises above the polytheistic notions to a pantheistic or sceptical view. He employs all the aids which the culture of his age afforded, all the weapons of learning, common sense, wit, sarcasm, aud dramatic animation of style, to disprove Christianity; and he anticipates most of the arguments and sophisms of the deists and infidels of later times. Still his book is, on the whole, a very superficial, loose, and light-minded work, and gives striking proof of the ina-bility of the natural reason to understand the Christian truth. It has no savor of humility, no sense of the corruption of hu-man nature, and man's need of redemption; it is full of heathen passion and prejudice, utterly blind to any spiritual realities, and could therefore not in the slightest degree appreciate the glory of the Redeemer and of his work. It needs no refuta-tion, it refutes itself.

[1] Origen (I. 8) indefinitely assigns him to the reign of Hadrian and the Antonines; most historians (Mosheim, Gieseler, Baur, Friedländer) to A. D. 150 or later; others (Tillemont, Neander, Zeller) to about 160 or 170; Keim (*l. c.* p. 267) to A. D. 178. As the place of composition Keim (p. 274) sug-gests Rome, others Alexandria. He ably defends his identity with the friend of Lucian (p. 291), but makes him out a Platonist rather than an Epicurean (p. 203 sqq.).

[2] See the restoration of Celsus from these fragments by Dr. Keim, quoted above.

Celsus first introduces a Jew, who accuses the mother of Jesus of adultery with a soldier named Panthera;[1] adduces the denial of Peter, the treachery of Judas, and the death of Jesus as contradictions of his pretended divinity; and makes the resurrection an imposture. Then Celsus himself begins the attack, and begins it by combating the whole idea of the supernatural, which forms the common foundation of Judaism and Christianity. The controversy between Jews and Christians appears to him as foolish as the strife about the shadow of an ass. The Jews believed, as well as the Christians, in the prophecies of a Redeemer of the world, and thus differed from them only in that they still expected the Messiah's coming. But then, to what purpose should God come down to earth at all, or send another down? He knows beforehand what is going on among men. And such a descent involves a change, a transition from the good to the evil, from the lovely to the hateful, from the happy to the miserable; which is undesirable, and indeed impossible, for the divine nature. In another place he says, God troubles himself no more about men than about monkeys and flies. Celsus thus denies the whole idea of revelation, now in pantheistic style, now in the levity of Epicurean deism; and thereby at the same time abandons the ground of the popular heathen religion. In his view Christianity has no rational foundation at all, but is supported by the imaginary terrors of future punishment. Particularly offensive to him are the promises of the gospel to the poor and miserable, and the doctrines of forgiveness of sins and regeneration, and of the resurrection of the body. This last he scoffingly calls a hope of worms, but not of rational souls. The appeal to the omnipotence of God, he thinks, does not help the matter, be-

---

[1] Πάνθηρ, *panthera*, here, and in the Talmud, where Jesus is likewise called יֵשׁוּ בֶּן פַּנְדִּירָא, is used, like the Latin *lupa*, as a type of ravenous lust hence as a symbolical name for μοιχείρ. So Nitzsch and Baur. But Keim (p. 12) takes it as a designation of the wild rapacious (πᾶν θηρῶν) Roman soldier. The mother of Jesus was, according to the Jewish informant of Celsus, a poor seamstress, and engaged to a carpenter, who plunged her into disgrace and misery when he found out her infidelity.

cause God can do nothing improper and unnatural. He reproaches the Christians with ignorance, credulity, obstinacy, innovation, division, and sectarianism, which they inherited mostly from their fathers, the Jews. They are all uncultivated, mean, superstitious people, mechanics, slaves, women, and children. The great mass of them he regarded as unquestionably deceived. But where there are deceived, there must be also deceivers; and this leads us to the last result of this polemical sophistry. Celsus declared the first disciples of Jesus to be deceivers of the worst kind; a band of sorcerers, who fabricated and circulated the miraculous stories of the Gospels, particularly that of the resurrection of Jesus; but betrayed themselves by contradictions. The originator of the imposture, however, is Jesus himself, who learned that magical art in Egypt, and afterwards made a great noise with it in his native country.

But here, this philosophical and critical sophistry virtually acknowledges its bankruptcy. The hypothesis of deception is the very last one to offer in explanation of a phenomenon so important as Christianity was even in that day. The greater and more permanent the deception, the more mysterious and unaccountable it must appear to reason.

Chrysostom made the truthful remark, that Celsus bears witness to the antiquity of the apostolic writings. This heathen assailant, who lived almost within hailing distance of St. John, incidentally gives us an abridgement of the history of Christ as related by the Gospels, and this furnishes strong weapons against modern infidels, who would represent this history as a later invention. "I know everything," he says; "we have had it all from your own books, and need no other testimony; ye slay yourselves with your own sword." He refers to the Gospels of Matthew, Luke, and John, and makes upon the whole about eighty allusions to, or quotations from, the New Testament. He takes notice of Christ's birth from a virgin in a small village of Judæa, the adoration of the wise men from the East, the slaughter of the infants by order of Herod, the flight to Egypt, where he supposed Christ learned the charms of magicians, his residence in Nazareth, his baptism and the descent of the Holy Spirit in the shape of a dove and the voice from heaven, the election of disciples, his friendship with publicans and other low people, his supposed cures of the lame and the blind, and raising of the dead, the betrayal of Judas, the denial of Peter, the principal circumstances in the history of the passion and crucifixion, also the resurrection of Christ.[1]

It is true he perverts or abuses most of these facts; but according to his own showing they were then generally and had always been believed by the Christians. He alludes to some of the principal doctrines of the Christians, to their private assemblies for worship, to the office of presbyters. He omits the grosser charges of immorality, which he probably disowned as absurd and incredible.

In view of all these admissions we may here, with Lardner, apply Samson's riddle: " Out of the eater came forth meat, and out of the strong came forth sweetness."[2]

§ 33. Lucian.

Edd. of Lucian's works by *Hemsterhuis* and *Reiz* (1743 sqq.), *Jacobitz* (1836–39), *Dindorf* (1840 and 1858), *Bekker* (1853), *Franc. Fritzsche* (1860–'69). The pseudo-Lucianic dialogue *Philopatris* (φιλόπατρις, loving one's country, patriot) in which the Christians are ridiculed and condemned as enemies of the Roman empire, is of a much later date, probably from the reign of Julian the Apostate (363). See Gesner: *De œtate et auctore Philopatridis*, Jen. 1714.

[1] Keim (*Geschichte Jesu von Nazara*, I. 22) says of Celsus: " *Von der Jungfraugeburt bis zum Jammer des Todes bei Essig und Galle, bis zu den Wundern des Todes und der Auferstehung hat er unsere Evangelien verfolgt, und anderen Quellen, welche zum Theil heute noch fliessen, hat er den Glauben an die Hässlichkeit Jesu und an die Sündhaftigkeit seiner Jünger abgewonnen.*" Comp. *Keim's* monograph on *Celsus*, pp. 219–231. On the bearing of his testimony on the genuineness of the Gospel of John, see vol. I. p. 708.

[2] Judges xiv. 14. Comp. Lardner's *Works*, vol. VII. pp. 210–270. Dr. Doddridge and Dr. Leland made good use of Celsus against the Deists of the last century. He may with still greater effect be turned against the more radical theories of Strauss and Renan. For Keim's estimate, see his *Celsus*, 253–261.

JACOB: *Charakteristik Lucians.* Hamburg 1822.
G. BERNAYS: *Lucian und die Cyniker.* Berlin. 1879.
Comp. KEIM: *Celsus,* 143–151; ED. ZELLER: *Alexander und Peregrinus,*
in the " Deutsche Rundschau," for Jan. 1877; HENRY COTTERILL:
Peregrinus Proteus (Edinb. 1879); AD. HARNACK in Herzog (ed.
II.), VIII. 772–779; and the Lit. quoted in ? 28.

In the same period the rhetorician Lucian (born at Samosata
in Syria about 120, died in Egypt or Greece before 200),
the Voltaire of Grecian literature, attacked the Christian religion with the same light weapons of wit and ridicule, with
which, in his numerous elegantly written works, he assailed the
old popular faith and worship, the mystic fanaticism imported
from the East, the vulgar life of the Stoics and Cynics of that
day, and most of the existing manners and customs of the distracted period of the empire.   An Epicurean, worldling, and
infidel, as he was, could see in Christianity only one of the many
vagaries and follies of mankind; in the miracles, only jugglery;
in the belief of immortality, an empty dream; and in the contempt of death and the brotherly love of the Christians, to
which he was constrained to testify, a silly enthusiasm.

Thus he represents the matter in an historical romance on the
life and death of Peregrinus Proteus, a contemporary Cynic
philosopher, whom he makes the basis of a satire upon Christianity, and especially upon Cynicism.   Peregrinus is here presented as a perfectly contemptible man, who, after the meanest
and grossest crimes, adultery, sodomy, and parricide, joins the
credulous Christians in Palestine, cunningly imposes on them,
soon rises to the highest repute among them, and, becoming one
of the confessors in prison, is loaded with presents by them, in
fact almost worshipped as a god, but is afterwards excommunicated for eating some forbidden food (probably meat of the
idolatrous sacrifices); then casts himself into the arms of the
Cynics, travels about everywhere, in the filthiest style of that
sect; and at last about the year 165, in frantic thirst for fame,
plunges into the flames of a funeral pile before the assembled
populace of the town of Olympia, for the triumph of philosophy.

This fiction of the self-burning was no doubt meant for a parody on the Christian martyrdom, perhaps with special reference to Polycarp, who a few years before had suffered death by fire at Smyrna (155).[1]

Lucian treated the Christians rather with a compassionate smile, than with hatred. He nowhere urges persecution. He never calls Christ an impostor, as Celsus does, but a "crucified sophist;" a term which he uses as often in a good sense as in the bad. But then, in the end, both the Christian and the heathen religions amount, in his view, to imposture; only, in his Epicurean indifferentism, he considers it not worth the trouble to trace such phenomena to their ultimate ground, and attempt a philosophical explanation.[2]

The merely negative position of this clever mocker of all religions injured heathenism more than Christianity, but could not be long maintained against either; the religious element is far too deeply seated in the essence of human nature. Epicureanism and scepticism made way, in their turns, for Platonism, and for faith or superstition. Heathenism made a vigorous effort to regenerate itself, in order to hold its ground against the steady advance of Christianity. But the old religion itself could not help feeling more and more the silent influence of the new.

§ 34. Neo-Platonism.

I. SOURCES.

PLOTINUS: *Opera Omnia*, ed. Oxf. 1835, 3 vols.; ed. Kirchhoff, Lips. 1856; ed. Didot, Par. 1856; H. F. Müller, Berlin 1878–80.

PORPHYRIUS: Κατὰ Χριστιανῶν λόγοι (fragments collected in Holstein: *Dissert. de vita et scriptis Porphyr.* Rom. 1630). His biographies of Pythagoras, Plotinus, and other works were ed. by A. Nauck, 1860.

---

[1] Harnack, *l. c.* denies a reference to Polycarp.

[2] Berneys (*l. c.* p. 43) characterizes Lucian very unfavorably: "*ein anscheinend nicht sehr glücklisher Advocat, ist er ohne ernste Studien ins Literatenthum übergegangen; unwissend und leichtfertig trägt er lediglich eine nihilistische Oede in Bezug auf alle religiösen und metaphysischen Fragen zur Schau und reisst alles als verkehrt und lächerlish herunter.*" Berneys thinks that the Peregrinus Proteus is not directed against the Christians, but against the Cynic philosophers, and more particularly against the then still living Theagenes.

HIEROCLES: Λόγοι φιλαλήθεις πρὸς Χριστιανούς (fragments in Euseb.: *Contra Hierocl. lib.*, and probably also in Macarius Magnes: ''Αποκριτικὸς ἢ Μονογενής, Par. 1876).

PHILOSTRATUS: *De Vita Apollonii Tyanensis libri octo* (Greek and Latin), Venet. 1501; ed. Westerman, Par. 1840; ed. Kayser, Zürich, 1853, 1870. Also in German, French and English translations.

II. WORKS.

VOGT: *Neuplatonismus u. Christenthum.* Berl. 1836.

RITTER: *Gesch. der Philos.* vol. 4th, 1834 (in English by Morrison, Oxf. 1838).

NEANDER: *Ueber das neunte Buch in der zweiten Enneade des Plotinus.* 1843. (vid. Neander's *Wissenschaftl. Abhandlungen*, published by Jacobi, Berl. 1851, p. 22 sqq.)

ULLMANN: *Einflus des Christenthums auf Porphyrius*, in "Stud. u. Krit." 1832.

KIRCHNER: *Die Philosophie des Plotin.* Halle, 1854.

F. CHR. BAUR: *Apollonius von Tyana u. Christus.* Tüb. 1832, republ. by Ed. Zeller, in *Drei Abhandlungen zur Gesch. der alten Philosophie u. ihres Verh. zum Christenthum.* Leipzig, 1876, pp. 1–227.

JOHN H. NEWMAN: *Apollonius Tyanæus.* Lond. 1849 (Encycl. Metropol. Vol. X., pp. 619–644).

A..CHASSANG: *Ap. de T., sa vie, ses voyages, ses prodiges*, etc. Paris, 1862. Translation from the Greek, with explanatory notes.

H. KELLNER: *Porphyrius und sein Verhältniss zum Christenthum*, in the Tübingen "Theol. Quartalschrift," 1865. No. I.

ALBERT RÉVILLE: *Apollonius of Tyana, the Pagan Christ of the third century*, translated from the French. Lond. 1866.

K. MÖNKEBERG: *Apollonius v. Tyana.* Hamb. 1877.

FR. UEBERWEG: *History of Philosophy* (Eng. transl. N. York, 1871), vol. I. 232–259.

ED. ZELLER: *Philosophie der Griechen*, III. 419 sqq.

More earnest and dignified, but for this very reason more lasting and dangerous, was the opposition which proceeded directly and indirectly from Neo-Platonism. This system presents the last phase, the evening red, so to speak, of the Grecian philosophy; a fruitless effort of dying heathenism to revive itself against the irresistible progress of Christianity in its freshness and vigor. It was a pantheistic eclecticism and a philosophico-religious syncretism, which sought to reconcile Platonic and Aristotelian philosophy with Oriental religion and theosophy, polytheism with monotheism, superstition with culture, and to hold, as with convulsive grasp, the old popular religion in a refined and idealized form. Some scattered Christian ideas also were unconsciously let in; Christianity already filled the atmosphere of the age too much, to be wholly shut out. As might be expected, this compound of philosophy and religion was an extravagant, fantastic, heterogeneous affair, like its contemporary, Gnosticism, which differed from it by formally recognising Christianity in its syncretism. Most of the Neo-Platonists, Jamblichus in particular, were as much hierophants and theurgists as philosophers, devoted themselves to divination and magic, and boasted of divine inspirations and visions. Their literature is not an original, healthy natural product, but an abnormal after-growth.

In a time of inward distraction and dissolution the human mind hunts up old and obsolete systems and notions, or resorts to magical and theurgic arts. Superstition follows on the heels of unbelief, and atheism often stands closely connected with the fear of ghosts and the worship of demons. The enlightened emperor Augustus was troubled, if he put on his left shoe first in the morning, instead of the right; and the accomplished elder Pliny wore amulets as protection from thunder and lightning. In their day the long-forgotten Pythagoreanism was conjured from the grave and idealized. Sorcerers like Simon Magus, Elymas, Alexander of Abonoteichos, and Apollonius of Tyana (d. A. D. 96), found great favor even with the higher classes, who laughed at the fables of the gods. Men turned wishfully to the past, epecially to the mysterious East, the land of primitive wisdom and religion. The Syrian cultus was sought out; and all sorts of religions, all tne sense and all the nonsense of antiquity found a rendezvous in Rome. Even a succession of Roman emperors, from Septimius Severus, at the close of the second century, to Alexander Severus, embraced this religious syncretism, which, instead of supporting the old Roman state religion, helped to undermine it.[1]

[1] The oldest apostle of this strange medley of Hellenic, Persian, Chaldean,

After the beginning of the third century this tendency found philosophical expression and took a reformatory turn in Neo-Platonism. The magic power, which was thought able to reanimate all these various elements and reduce them to harmony, and to put deep meaning into the old mythology, was the philosophy of the divine Plato; which in truth possessed essentially a mystical character, and was used also by learned Jews, like Philo, and by Christians, like Origen, in their idealizing efforts and their arbitrary allegorical expositions of offensive passages of the Bible. In this view we may find among heathen writers a sort of forerunner of the Neo-Platonists in the pious and noble-minded Platonist, Plutarch of Bœotia (d. 120), who likewise saw a deeper sense in the myths of the popular polytheistic faith, and in general, in his comparative biographies and his admirable moral treatises, looks at the fairest and noblest side of the Græco-Roman antiquity, but often wanders off into the trackless regions of fancy.

The proper founder of Neo-Platonism was Ammonius Saccas, of Alexandria, who was born of Christian parents, but apostatized, and died in the year 243. His more distinguished pupil, Plotinus, also an Egyptian (204–269), developed the Neo-Platonic ideas in systematic form, and gave them firm foothold and wide currency, particularly in Rome, where he taught philosophy. The system was propagated by his pupil Porphyry of Tyre (d. 304), who likewise taught in Rome, by Jamblichus

and Egyptian mysteries in Rome was Nigidius Figulus, who belonged to the strictest section of the aristocracy, and filled the prætorship in 696 A. U. (58 B. C.) He foretold the father of the subsequent emperor Augustus on the very day of his birth his future greatness. The system was consecrated by the name of Pythagoras, the primeval sage of Italian birth, the miracle-worker and necromancer. The new and old wisdom made a profound impression on men of the highest rank and greatest learning, who took part in the citation of spirits, as in the nineteenth century spirit-rapping and table-moving exercised for a while a similar charm. "These last attempts to save the Roman theology, like the similar efforts of Cato in the field of politics, produce at once a comical and a melancholy impression. We may smile at the creed and its propagators, but still it is a grave matter when all men begin to addict themselves to absurdity." Th. Mommsen, *History of Rome*, vol. IV. p. 563 (Dickson's translation. Lond. 1867.)

of Chalcis in Cœlo-Syria (d. 333), and by Proclus of Constantinople (d. 485). It supplanted the popular religion among the educated classes of later heathendom, and held its ground until the end of the fifth century, when it perished of its own internal falsehood and contradictions.

From its love for the ideal, the supernatural, and the mystical, this system, like the original Platonism, might become for many philosophical minds a bridge to faith; and so it was even to St. Augustin, whom it delivered from the bondage of scepticism, and filled with a burning thirst for truth and wisdom. But it could also work against Christianity. Neo-Platonism was, in fact, a direct attempt of the more intelligent and earnest heathenism to rally all its nobler energies, especially the forces of Hellenic philosophy and Oriental mysticism, and to found a universal religion, a pagan counterpart to the Christian. Plotinus, in his opposition to Gnosticism, assailed also, though not expressly, the Christian element it contained. On their syncretistic principles the Neo-Platonists could indeed reverence Christ as a great sage and a hero of virtue, but not as the Son of God. They ranked the wise men of heathendom with him. The emperor Alexander Severus (d. 235) gave Orpheus and Apollonius of Tyana a place in his lararium by the side of the bust of Jesus.

The rhetorician Philostratus, the elder, about the year 220, at the request of Julia Domna, the wife of Septimius Severus, and a zealous patron of the reform of paganism, idealized the life of the pagan magician and soothsayer Apollonius, of the Pythagorean school, and made him out an ascetic saint, a divinely inspired philosopher, a religious reformer and worker of miracles, with the purpose, as is generally assumed, though without direct evidence, of holding him up as a rival of Christ with equal claims to the worship of men.[1]

[1] Philostratus himself gives no intimation of such design on his part, and simply states that he was requested by the empress Julia Domna (A. D. 217), to draw up a biography of Apollonius from certain memoranda of Damis, one of his friends and followers. The name of Christ is never mentioned by him;

The points of resemblance are chiefly these: Jesus was the Son of God, Apollonius the son of Jupiter; the birth of Christ was celebrated by the appearance of angels, that of Apollonius by a flash of lightning; Christ raised the daughter of Jairus, Apollonius a young Roman maiden, from the dead; Christ cast out demons, Apollonius did the same; Christ rose from the dead, Apollonius appeared after his death. Apollonius is made to combine also several characteristics of the apostles, as the miraculous gift of tongues, for he understood all the languages of the world. Like St. Paul, he received his earlier education at Tarsus, labored at Antioch, Ephesus, and other cities, and was persecuted by Nero. Like the early Christians, he was falsely accused of sacrificing children with certain mysterious ceremonies.[1]

With the same secret polemical aim Porphyry and Jamblichus embellished the life of Pythagoras, and set him forth as the highest model of wisdom, even a divine being incarnate, a Christ of heathenism.

These various attempts to Christianize paganism were of course as abortive as so many attempts to galvanize a corpse. They made no impression upon their age, much less upon ages following. They were indirect arguments in favor of Christianity: they proved the internal decay of the false, and the irresistible progress of the true religion, which began to mould the spirit of the age and to affect public opinion outside of the church. By inventing false characters in imitation of Christ

nor does he allude to the Gospels, except in one instance, where he uses the same phrase as the dæmon in St. Luke (viii. 28): "I beseech thee, torment me not (μή με βασανίσῃς.). *Vita Apoll.* IV. 25. Bishop Samuel Parker, in a work on the Divine Authority of the Christian Religion (1681), Lardner, Neander (*K. G.* I. 298), and J. S. Watson (in a review of Réville's *Apoll. of T.*, in the "Contemporary Review" for 1867, p. 199 ff.), deny the commonly received opinion, first maintained by Bishop Daniel Hust, and defended by Baur, Newman, and Réville, that Philostratus intended to draw a parallel between his hero and Christ. The resemblance is studied and fictitious, and it is certain that at a later date Hierocles vainly endeavored to lower the dignity of Christ by raising this Pythagorean adventurer as portrayed by Philostratus, to a level with the eternal Son of God.

[1] Comp. the account of the resemblance by Baur, *l. c.* pp. 138 sqq.

they indirectly conceded to the historical Christ his claim to the admiration and praise of mankind.

§ 35. *Porphyry and Hierocles.*

See the Lit. in § 34.

One of the leading Neo-Platonists made a direct attack upon Christianity, and was, in the eyes of the church fathers, its bitterest and most dangerous enemy. Towards the end of the third century Porphyry wrote an extended work against the Christians, in fifteen books, which called forth numerous refutations from the most eminent church teachers of the time, particularly from Methodius of Tyre, Eusebius of Cæsarea, and Apollinaris of Laodicea. In 448 all the copies were burned by order of the emperors Theodosius II. and Valentinian III., and we know the work now only from fragments in the fathers.

Porphyry attacked especially the sacred books of the Christians, with more knowledge than Celsus. He endeavored, with keen criticism, to point out the contradictions between the Old Testament and the New, and among the apostles themselves; and thus to refute the divinity of their writings. He represented the prophecies of Daniel as *vaticinia post eventum*, and censured the allegorical interpretation of Origen, by which transcendental mysteries were foisted into the writings of Moses, contrary to their clear sense. He took advantage, above all, of the collision between Paul and Peter at Antioch (Gal. 2: 11), to reproach the former with a contentious spirit, the latter with error, and to infer from the whole, that the doctrine of such apostles must rest on lies and frauds. Even Jesus himself he charged with equivocation and inconsistency, on account of his conduct in John 7: 8 compared with verse 14.

Still Porphyry would not wholly reject Christianity. Like many rationalists of more recent times, he distinguished the original pure doctrine of Jesus from the second-handed, adulterated doctrine of the apostles. In another work[1] on the

---

[1] Περὶ τῆς ἐκ λογίων φιλοσοφίας. Fabricius, Mosheim, Neander, and others, treat the work as genuine, but Lardner denies it to Porphyry.

"Philosophy of Oracles," often quoted by Eusebius, and also by Augustin,[1] he says, we must not calumniate Christ, who was most eminent for piety, but only pity those who worship him as God. "That pious soul, exalted to heaven, is become, by a sort of fate, an occasion of delusion to those souls from whom fortune withholds the gifts of the gods and the knowledge of the immortal Zeus." Still more remarkable in this view is a letter to his wife Marcella, which A. Mai published at Milan in 1816, in the unfounded opinion that Marcella was a Christian. In the course of this letter Porphyry remarks, that what is born of the flesh is flesh; that by faith, love, and hope we raise ourselves to the Deity; that evil is the fault of man; that God is holy; that the most acceptable sacrifice to him is a pure heart; that the wise man is at once a temple of God and a priest in that temple. For these and other such evidently Christian ideas and phrases he no doubt had a sense of his own, which materially differed from their proper scriptural meaning. But such things show how Christianity in that day exerted, even upon its opponents, a power, to which heathenism was forced to yield an unwilling assent.

The last literary antagonist of Christianity in our period is Hierocles, who, while governor of Bythynia, and afterwards of Alexandria under Diocletian, persecuted that religion also with the sword, and exposed Christian maidens to a worse fate than death. His "Truth-loving Words to the Christians" has been destroyed, like Porphyry's work, by the mistaken zeal of Christian emperors, and is known to us only through the answer of Eusebius of Cæsarea.[2] He appears to have merely repeated the objections of Celsus and Porphyry, and to have drawn a

---

[1] *De Civit. Dei*, l. XIX. c. 22, 23; comp. also Eusebius, *Demonstr. Evang.* III. 6.

[2] To this may be added the extracts from an unnamed heathen philosopher (probably Hierocles or Porphyrius) in the apologetic work of Macarius Magnes (about 400), which was discovered at Athens in 1867, and published by Blondel, Paris 1876. See L. Duchesne, *De Marcario Magnete et scriptis ejus*, Par. 1877, and Zöckler in Herzog, ed. II. vol. IX. 160.

comparison between Christ and Apollonius of Tyana, which resulted in favor of the latter. The Christians, says he, consider Jesus a God, on account of some insignificant miracles falsely colored up by his apostles; but the heathens far more justly declare the greater wonder-worker Apollonius, as well as an Aristeas and a Pythagoras, simply a favorite of the gods and a benefactor of men.

§ 36. *Summary of the Objections to Christianity.*

In general the leading arguments of the Judaism and heathenism of this period against the new religion are the following:

1. Against Christ: his illegitimate birth; his association with poor, unlettered fishermen, and rude publicans: his form of a servant, and his ignominious death. But the opposition to him gradually ceased. While Celsus called him a downright impostor, the Syncretists and Neo-Platonists were disposed to regard him as at least a distinguished sage.

2. Against Christianity: its novelty; its barbarian origin; its want of a national basis; the alleged absurdity of some of its facts and doctrines, particularly of regeneration and the resurrection; contradictions between the Old and New Testaments, among the Gospels, and between Paul and Peter; the demand for a blind, irrational faith.

3. Against the Christians: atheism, or hatred of the gods; the worship of a crucified malefactor; poverty, and want of culture and standing; desire of innovation; division and sectarianism; want of patriotism; gloomy seriousness; credulity; superstition, and fanaticism. Sometimes they were charged even with unnatural crimes, like those related in the pagan mythology of Oedipus and his mother Jocaste (*concubitus Oedipodei*), and of Thyestes and Atreus (*epulæ Thyesteæ*). Perhaps some Gnostic sects ran into scandalous excesses; but as against the Christians in general this charge was so clearly unfounded, that it is not noticed even by Celsus and

Lucian. The senseless accusation, that they worshipped an ass's head, may have arisen, as Tertullian already intimates,[1] from a story of Tacitus, respecting some Jews, who were once directed by a wild ass to fresh water, and thus relieved from the torture of thirst; and it is worth mentioning, only to show how passionate and blind was the opposition with which Christianity in this period of persecution had to contend.

§ 37. *The Apologetic Literature of Christianity.*

Comp. Lit. in § 1 and 12.

I. The sources are all the writings of the Apologists of the second and third centuries; particularly JUSTIN M.: *Apologia I.* and *II.;* TERTULL.: *Apologeticus;* MINUCIUS FELIX: *Octavius;* ORIGEN: *Contra Celsum* (κατὰ Κέλσου) libr. VIII. ARISTIDIS, *Philosophi Atheniensis, Sermones duo,* Venetiis 1878. (From an Armenian translation). Complete editions of the Apologists: *Apologg. Christ. Opp.* ed. Prud. Maranus, Par. 1742; *Corpus Apologetarum Christianorum sœculi secundi,* ed. Th. Otto, Jenae, 1847 sqq. ed. III. 1876 sqq. A new ed. by O. v. Gebhardt and E. Schwartz, begun 1888.

II. FABRICIUS: *Delectus argumentorum et Syllabus scriptorum, qui veritatem rel. Christ. asseruerunt.* Hamb. 1725.

TZSCHIRNER: *Geschichte der Apologetik.* Lpz. 1805 (unfinished).

G. H. VAN SANDEN: *Gesch. der Apol.* translated from Dutch into German by Quack and Binder. Stuttg. 1846. 2 vols.

SEMISCH: *Justin der Märt.* Bresl. 1840. II. 56–225.

W. B. COLTON: *The Evidences of Christianity as exhibited in the writings of its Apologists down to Augustine* (Hulsean Prize Essay, 1852), republ. in Boston, 1854.

KARL WERNER (R. C.): *Geschichte der apologetischen und polemischen Literatur der christl. Theologie.* Schaffhausen, 1861–'65. 5 vols. (vol. I. belongs here).

JAMES DONALDSON: *A Critical History of Christian Literature and Doctrine from the Death of the Apostles to the Nicene Council.* London, 1864–66. 3 vols.

ADOLF HARNACK: *Die Ueberlieferung der Griechischen Apologeten des zweiten Jahrhunderts in der alten Kirche und im Mittelalter.* Band I. Heft 1 and 2. Leipz. 1882.

These assaults of argument and calumny called forth in the second century the Christian apologetic literature, the vindica-

---

[1] *Apol.* c. 16: "*Somniastis caput asininum esse deum nostrum. Hanc Cornelius Tacitus suspicionem ejusmodi dei inseruit,*" etc.

tion of Christianity by the pen, against the Jewish zealot, the Grecian philosopher, and the Roman statesman. The Christians were indeed from the first "ready always to give an answer to every man that asked them a reason of the hope that was in them." But when heathenism took the field against them not only with fire and sword, but with argument and slander besides, they had to add to their simple practical testimony a theoretical self-defence. The Christian apology against non-Christian opponents, and the controversial efforts against Christian errorists, are the two oldest branches of theological science.

The apologetic literature began to appear under the reign of Hadrian, and continued to grow till the end of our period. Most of the church teachers took part in this labor of their day. The first apologies, by Quadratus, bishop of Athens, Aristides, philosopher of Athens, and Aristo of Pella, which were addressed to the emperor Hadrian, and the later works of Melito of Sardis, Claudius Apollinaris of Hierapolis, and Miltiades, who lived under Marcus Aurelius, were either entirely lost, or preserved only in scattered notices of Eusebius. But some interesting fragments of Melito and Aristides have been recently discovered.[1] More valuable are the apologetical works of the Greek philosopher and martyr, Justin (d. 166), which we possess in full. After him come, in the Greek church, Tatian, Athenagoras, Theophilus of Antioch, and Hermias in the last half of the second century, and Origen, the ablest of all, in the first half of the third.

The most important Latin apologists are Tertullian (d. about 220), Minucius Felix (d. between 220 and 230; according to some, between 161 and 200), the later Arnobius and Lactantius, all of North Africa.

Here at once appears the characteristic difference between the

---

[1] See on the works of these Apologists, lost and partly recovered, Harnack, l. c. pp. 100 sqq.; 240 sqq.; and Renan, L'egl. chrét. p. 40 sqq. We shall refer to them in the chapter on Christian literature.

Greek and the Latin minds. The Greek apologies are more learned and philosophical, the Latin more practical and juridical in their matter and style. The former labor to prove the truth of Christianity and its adaptedness to the intellectual wants of man; the latter plead for its legal right to exist, and exhibit mainly its moral excellency and salutary effect upon society. The Latin also are in general more rigidly opposed to heathenism, while the Greek recognize in the Grecian philosophy a certain affinity to the Christian religion.

The apologies were addressed in some cases to the emperors (Hadrian, Antoninus Pius, Marcus Aurelius) or the provincial governors; in others, to the intelligent public. Their first object was to soften the temper of the authorities and people towards Christianity and its professors by refuting the false charges against them. It may be doubtful whether they ever reached the hands of the emperors; at all events the persecution continued.[1] Conversion commonly proceeds from the heart and will, not from the understanding and from knowledge. No doubt, however, these writings contributed to dissipate prejudice among honest and susceptible heathens, to spread more favorable views of the new religion, and to infuse a spirit of humanity into the spirit of the age, the systems of moral philosophy and the legislation of the Antonines.

Yet the chief service of this literature was to strengthen believers and to advance theological knowledge. It brought the church to a deeper and clearer sense of the peculiar nature of the Christian religion, and prepared her thenceforth to vindicate it before the tribunal of reason and philosophy; whilst Judaism and heathenism proved themselves powerless in the combat, and were driven to the weapons of falsehood and vituperation. The sophisms and mockeries of a Celsus and a Lucian have none but a historical interest; the Apologies of Justin and the Apologeticus of Tertullian, rich with indestructible truth and

---

[1] Orosius, however, relates in his *Hist.* vii. 14, that Justin M., by his Apology, made the emperor Antoninus Pius "*benignum erga Christianos.*"

glowing piety, are read with pleasure and edification to this day. The apologists do not confine themselves to the defensive, but carry the war aggressively into the territory of Judaism and heathenism. They complete their work by positively demonstrating that Christianity is the divine religion, and the only true religion for all mankind.

§ 38. *The Argument against Judaism.*

In regard to the controversy with Judaism, we have two principal sources : the Dialogue of Justin Martyr with the Jew Trypho,[1] based, it appears, on real interviews of Justin with Trypho; and Tertullian's work against the Jews.[2] Another work from the first half of the second century by Aristo of Pella, entitled " A Disputation of Jason and Papiscus concerning Christ," is lost.[3] It was known to Celsus who speaks contemptuously of it on account of its allegorical interpretation. Origen deems it useful for ordinary readers, though not calculated to make much impression on scholars. It was intended to show the fulfillment of the old prophecies in Christ, and ends with the conviction of the Jew Papiscus and his baptism by Jason. The author was a Jewish Christian of Pella, the city of refuge for the Christians of Jerusalem before the destruction.

I. The DEFENSIVE apology answered the Jewish objections thus :

(1) Against the charge, that Christianity is an apostasy from the Jewish religion, it was held, that the Mosaic law, as far as it relates to outward rites and ceremonies was only a temporary institution for the Jewish nation foreshadowing the substance of Christianity, while its moral precepts as contained in the Decalogue were kept in their deepest spiritual sense only by

---

[1] Διάλογος πρὸς Τρίφωνα 'Ιουδαῖον.

[2] *Adversus Judæos.* Also Cyprian's *Testimonia adv. Judæos.*

[3] 'Ιάσωνος καὶ Παπίσκου ἀντιλογία περὶ Χριστοῦ. Comp. the discussion of Harnack, *l. c.* pp. 115-130. He assigns the book to A. D. 135 or soon after. It disappeared in the seventh century.

Christians; that the Old Testament itself points to its own dissolution and the establishment of a new covenant;[1] that Abraham was justified before he was circumcised, and women, who could not be circumcised, were yet saved.

(2) Against the asertion, that the servant-form of Jesus of Nazareth, and his death by the cross, contradicted the Old Testament idea of the Messiah, it was urged, that the appearance of the Messiah is to be regarded as twofold, first, in the form of a servant, afterwards in glory; and that the brazen serpent in the wilderness, and the prophecies of David in Psalm 22, of Isaiah in ch. 53, and Zech. 13, themselves point to the sufferings of Christ as his way to glory.

(3) To the objection, that the divinity of Jesus contradicts the unity of God and is blasphemy, it was replied, that the Christians believe likewise in only one God; that the Old Testament itself makes a distinction in the divine nature; that the plural expression: " Let us make man,"[2] the appearance of the three men at Mamre,[3] of whom one was confessedly God,[4] yet distinct from the Creator,[5] indicate this; and that all theophanies (which in Justin's view are as many christophanies), and the Messianic Psalms,[6] which ascribe divine dignity to the Messiah, show the same.

II. The AGGRESSIVE apology or polemic theology urges as evidence against Judaism :

(1) First and mainly that the prophecies and types of the Old Testament are fulfilled in Jesus Christ and his church. Justin finds all the outlines of the gospel history predicted in the Old Testament: the Davidic descent of Jesus, for example, in Isa. 11: 1; the birth from a virgin in 7: 14; the birth at Bethlehem in Micah 5: 1; the flight into Egypt in Hosea 11: 1 (rather than Ps. 22: 10 ?); the appearance of the Baptist

---

[1] Is. 51: 4 sqq.; 55: 3 sqq.; Jer. 31: 31 sqq.
[2] Gen. 1: 26; comp. 3: 22.   [3] Gen. 18: 1 sqq.
                [4] 21: 12.   [5] 19: 24.
         [6] Ps. 110: 1 sqq.; 45: 7 sqq.; 72: 2–19, and others.

in Is. 40: 1–17; Mal. 4: 5; the heavenly voice at the baptism
of Jesus in Ps. 2: 7; the temptation in the wilderness under
the type of Jacob's wrestling in Gen. 32: 24 sqq.; the miracles
of our Lord in Is. 35: 5; his sufferings and the several circumstances of his crucifixion in Is. 53 and Ps. 22. In this
effort, however, Justin wanders also, according to the taste of
his uncritical age, into arbitrary fancies and allegorical conceits;
as when he makes the two goats, of which one carried away the
sins into the wilderness, and the other was sacrificed, types of
the first and second advents of Christ; and sees in the twelve
bells on the robe of the high priest a type of the twelve
apostles, whose sound goes forth into all the world.[1]

(2) The destruction of Jerusalem, in which Judaism, according to the express prediction of Jesus, was condemned by God
himself, and Christianity was gloriously vindicated. Here the
Jewish priest and historian Josephus, who wrote from personal
observation a graphic description of this tragedy, had to furnish
a powerful historical argument against his own religion and for
the truth of Christianity. Tertullian sums up the prophetic
predictions of the calamities which have befallen the Jews for
rejecting Christ, " the sense of the Scriptures harmonizing with
the events." [2]

§ 39. *The Defense against Heathenism.*

I. The various OBJECTIONS and ACCUSATIONS of the heathens,
which we have collected in § 36, were founded for the most
part on ignorance or hatred, and in many cases contradicted
themselves.

(1) The attack upon the miraculous in the evangelical history
the apologists could meet by pointing to the similar element in
the heathen mythology; of course proposing this merely in the
way of *argumentum ad hominem*, to deprive the opposition of
the right to object. For the credibility of the miraculous
accounts in the Gospels, particularly that of the resurrection of

[1] Ps. 19: 4; comp. Rom. 10: 18.   [2] *Adv. Jud. c.* 13.

Jesus, Origen appealed to the integrity and piety of the nar-
rators, to the publicity of the death of Jesus, and to the effects
of that event.

(2) The novelty and late appearance of Christianity were
justified by the need of historical preparation in which the
human race should be divinely trained for Christ; but more
frequently it was urged also, that Christianity existed in the
counsel of God from eternity, and had its unconscious votaries,
especially among the pious Jews, long before the advent of
Christ. By claiming the Mosaic records, the apologists had
greatly the advantage as regards antiquity over any form of
paganism, and could carry their religion, in its preparatory state,
even beyond the flood and up to the very gates of paradise.
Justin and Tatian make great account of the fact that Moses is
much older than the Greek philosophers, poets, and legislators.
Athenagoras turns the tables, and shows that the very names
of the heathen gods are modern, and their statues creations of
yesterday.   Clement of Alexandria calls the Greek philosophers
thieves and robbers, because they stole certain portions of truth
from the Hebrew prophets and adulterated them. Tertullian, Minucius Felix and others raise the same charge of plagiarism.

(3) The doctrine of the resurrection of the body, so peculiarly
offensive to the heathen and Gnostic understanding, was supported, as to its possibility, by reference to the omnipotence of
God, and to the creation of the world and of man; and its
propriety and reasonableness were argued from the divine
image in man, from the high destiny of the body to be the
temple of the Holy Spirit, and from its intimate connection
with the soul, as well as from the righteousness and goodness
of God.   The argument from analogy was also very generally
used, but often without proper discrimination.   Thus, Theophilus
alludes to the decline and return of the seasons, the alternations
of day and night, the renewal of the waning and waxing moon,
the growth of seeds and fruits.   Tertullian expresses his surprise that anybody should deny the possibility and probability

of the resurrection in view of the mystery of our birth and the daily occurrences of surrounding nature. "All things," he says, "are preserved by dissolution, renewed by perishing; and shall man . . . . . the lord of all this universe of creatures, which die and rise again, himself die only to perish forever?" [1]

(4) The charge of immoral conduct and secret vice the apologists might repel with just indignation, since the New Testament contains the purest and noblest morality, and the general conduct of the Christians compared most favorably with that of the heathens. "Shame! shame!" they justly cried; "to roll upon the innocent what you are openly guilty of, and what belongs to you and your gods!" Origen says in the preface to the first book against Celsus: "When false witness was brought against our blessed Saviour, the spotless Jesus, he held his peace, and when he was accused, returned no answer, being fully persuaded that the tenor of his life and conduct among the Jews was the best apology that could possibly be made in his behalf. . . . . . And even now he preserves the same silence, and makes no other answer than the unblemished lives of his sincere followers; they are his most cheerful and successful advocates, and have so loud a voice that they drown the clamors of the most zealous and bigoted adversaries."

II. To their defence the Christians, with the rising consciousness of victory, added direct ARGUMENTS AGAINST HEATHENISM, which were practically sustained by its dissolution in the following period.

(1) The popular religion of the heathens, particularly the doctrine of the gods, is unworthy, contradictory, absurd, immoral, and pernicious. The apologists and most of the early church teachers looked upon the heathen gods not as mere imaginations or personified powers of nature or deifications of

---

[1] *Apolog.* c. 43. Comp. his special tract *De Resurrectione Carnis*, c. 12, where he defends the doctrine more fully against the Gnostics and their radical misconception of the nature and import of the body.

distinguished men, but as demons or fallen angels. They took this view from the Septuagint version of Ps. 96 : 5,[1] and from the immorality of those deities, which was charged to demons (even sexual intercourse with fair daughters of men, according to Gen. 6 : 2).

" What sad fates," says Minucius Felix, " what lies, ridiculous things, and weaknesses we read of the pretended gods! Even their form, how pitiable it is! Vulcan limps; Mercury has wings to his feet; Pan is hoofed; Saturn in fetters; and Janus has two faces, as if he walked backwards. . . . . . . Sometimes Hercules is a hostler, Apollo a cow-herd, and Neptune, Laomedon's mason, cheated of his wages. There we have the thunder of Jove and the arms of Aeneas forged on the same anvil (as if the heavens and the thunder and lightning did not exist before Jove was born in Crete); the adultery of Mars and Venus; the lewdness of Jupiter with Ganymede, all of which were invented for the gods to authorize men in their wickedness." " Which of the poets," asks Tertullian, " does not calumniate your gods? One sets Apollo to keep sheep; another hires out Neptune to build a wall; Pindar declares Æsculapius was deservedly scathed for his avarice in exercising the art of medicine to a bad purpose; whilst the writers of tragedy and comedy alike, take for their subjects the crimes or the miseries of the deities. Nor are the philosophers behindhand in this respect. Out of pure contempt, they would swear by an oak, a goat, a dog. Diogenes turned Hercules into ridicule; and the Roman Cynic Varro introduces three hundred Joves without heads." From the stage abuser the sarcastic African father selects, partly from his own former observation, those of Diana being flogged, the reading of Jupiter's will after his decease, and the three half-starved Herculesses! Justin brings up the infanticide of Saturn, the parricide, the anger, and the adultery of Jupiter, the drunkenness of Bacchus, the voluptuousness of Venus, and he appeals to the judgment of the better heathens,

---

[1] Πάντες οἱ θεοὶ τῶν ἐθνῶν δαιμόνια.   Comp. 1 Cor. 10 : 20.

who were ashamed of these scandalous histories of the gods; to Plato, for example, who for this reason banishes Homer from his ideal State. Those myths, which had some resemblance to the Old Testament prophecies or the gospel history, Justin regards as caricatures of the truth, framed by demons by abuse of Scripture. The story of Bacchus, for instance, rests in his fanciful view, on Gen. 49: 11 sq.; the myth of the birth of Perseus from a virgin, on Is. 7: 14; that of the wandering of Hercules, on Ps. 19: 6; the fiction of the miracles of Esculapius on Is. 35: 1 sqq.

Origen asks Celsus, why it is that he can discover profound mysteries in those strange and senseless accidents, which have befallen his gods and goddesses, showing them to be polluted with crimes and doing many shameful things; whilst Moses, who says nothing derogatory to the character of God, angel, or man, is treated as an impostor. He challenges any one to compare Moses and his laws with the best Greek writers; and yet Moses was as far inferior to Christ, as he was superior to the greatest of heathen sages and legislators.

(2) The Greek philosophy, which rises above the popular belief, is not suited to the masses, cannot meet the religious wants, and confutes itself by its manifold contradictions. Socrates, the wisest of all the philosophers, himself acknowledged that he knew nothing. On divine and human things Justin finds the philosophers at variance among themselves; with Thales water is the ultimate principle of all things; with Anaximander, air; with Heraclitus, fire; with Pythagoras, number. Even Plato not seldom contradicts himself; now supposing three fundamental causes (God, matter, and ideas), now four (adding the world-soul); now he considers matter as unbegotten, now as begotten; at one time he ascribes substantiality to ideas, at another makes them mere forms of thought, etc. Who, then, he concludes, would intrust to the philosophers the salvation of his soul?

(3) But, on the other hand, the Greek apologists recognized also elements of truth in the Hellenic literature, especially in

the Platonic and Stoic philosophy, and saw in them, as in the law and the prophecies of Judaism, a preparation of the way for Christianity. Justin attributes all the good in heathenism to the divine Logos, who, even before his incarnation, scattered the seeds of truth (hence the name " Logos spermaticos "), and incited susceptible spirits to a holy walk. Thus there were Christians before Christianity ; and among these he expressly reckons Socrates and Heraclitus.[1] Besides, he supposed that Pythagoras, Plato, and other educated Greeks, in their journeys to the East, became acquainted with the Old Testament writings, and drew from them the doctrine of the unity of God, and other like truths, though they in various ways misunderstood them, and adulterated them with pagan errors. This view of a certain affinity between the Grecian philosophy and Christianity, as an argument in favor of the new religion, was afterwards further developed by the Alexandrian fathers, Clement and Origen.[2]

The Latin fathers speak less favorably of the Greek philosophy ; yet even Augustin acknowledges that the Platonists approach so nearly to Christian truth that with a change of some expressions and sentences they would be true Christians (in theory).[3]

§ 40. *The Positive Apology.*

The Christian apology completed itself in the positive demonstration of the divinity of the new religion ; which was at the same time the best refutation of both the old ones. As

---

[1] Also the Stoics and some of the poets as far as their moral teaching went, comp. Just. *Apol.* II. c. 8, and 13.

[2] See the introduction of E. Spiess to his *Logos spermatikos,* Leipz. 1871.

[3] *De Vera Religione* IV. 7 : " *Proxime Platonici a veritate Christiana absunt vel veri Christiani sunt paucis mutatis verbis atque sententiis.*" *Retract.* I. 13 : " *Res ipsa quae nunc religio Christiana nuncupatur, erat apud antiquos, nec defuit ab initio generis humani, quousque Christus veniret in carnem, unde vera religio, quae jam erat, coepit appellari Christiana.*" Comp. Lactantius, *De Falsa Religione,* I. 5 ; *De Vita Beata,* VII. 7 ; Minucius Fel., *Octav.* 20.

early as this period the strongest historical and philosophical arguments for Christianity were brought forward, or at least indicated, though in connection with many untenable adjuncts.

1. The great argument, not only with Jews, but with heathens also, was the PROPHECIES ; since the knowledge of future events can come only from God. The first appeal of the apologists was, of course, to the prophetic writings of the Old Testament, in which they found, by a very liberal interpretation, every event of the gospel history and every lineament of our Saviour's character and work. In addition to the Scriptures, even such fathers as Clement of Alexandria, and, with more caution, Origen, Eusebius, St. Jerome, and St. Augustin, employed also, without hesitation, apocryphal prophecies, especially the Sibylline oracles, a medley of ancient heathen, Jewish, and in part Christian fictions, about a golden age, the coming of Christ, the fortunes of Rome, and the end of the world.[1] And indeed, this was not all error and pious fraud. Through all heathenism there runs, in truth, a dim, unconscious presentiment and longing hope of Christianity. Think of the fourth Eclogue of Virgil, with its predictions of the "virgo" and "nova progenies" from heaven, and the "puer," with whom, after the blotting out of sin and the killing of the serpent, a golden age of peace was to begin. For this reason Virgil was the favorite poet of the Latin church during the middle ages, and figures prominently in Dante's Divina Comedia as his guide through the dreary regions of the Inferno and Purgatorio to the very gates of Paradise. Another pseudo-prophetic book used

---

[1] Comp. DR. FRIEDLIEB: Die Sibyllinischen Weissagungen vollständig gesammelt, mit kritischem Commentare und metrischer Uebersetzung. Leipz. 1852. Another edition with a Latin version by C. ALEXANDRE, Paris 1841, second ed. 1869, 2 tom. We have at present twelve books of χρησμοί σιβυλλιακοί in Greek hexameters, and some fragments. They have been critically discussed by Blondel (1649), Bleek (1819), Volkmann (1853), Ewald (1858), Lüben (1875), Reuss, and Schürer (see lit. in his N. T. Zeitgesch. p. 513). The Sibyl figures in the Dies Irae alongside with King David (teste David cum Sibylla), as prophesying the day of judgment.

by the fathers (Tertullian, Origen, and apparently Jerome) is
"The Testaments of the Twelve Patriarchs," written by a
Jewish Christian between A. D. 100 and 120. It puts into the
mouth of the twelve sons of Jacob farewell addresses and predictions of the coming of Christ, his death and resurrection,
of baptism and the Lord's Supper, the rejection of the gospel
by the Jews, and the preaching of Paul, the great apostle of the
Gentiles, the destruction of Jerusalem and the end of the
world.[1]

2. The TYPES. These, too, were found not only in the Old
Testament, but in the whole range of nature. Justin saw
everywhere, in the tree of life in Eden, in Jacob's ladder, in
the rods of Moses and Aaron, nay, in every sailing ship, in the
wave-cutting oar, in the plough, in the human countenance,
in the human form with outstretched arms, in banners and
trophies—the sacred form of the cross, and thus a prefiguration
of the mystery of redemption through the crucifixion of the
Lord.[2]

3. The MIRACLES of Jesus and the apostles, with those which
continued to be wrought in the name of Jesus, according to the
express testimony of the fathers, by their contemporaries. But
as the heathens also appealed to miraculous deeds and appearances in favor of their religion, Justin, Arnobius, and particularly Origen, fixed certain criteria, such as the moral purity
of the worker, and his intention to glorify God and benefit
man, for distinguishing the true miracles from Satanic juggleries.
"There might have been some ground," says Origen, "for the
comparison which Celsus makes between Jesus and certain

---

[1] Best edition by ROBERT SINKER from the Cambridge MS., Cambridge,
1869, and an Appendix, 1879; an English translation by Sinker, in the "Ante-
Nicene Library," vol. XXII. (Edinb. 1871). Discussions by Nitzsch (1810),
Ritschl (1850 and 1857), Vorstmann (1857), Kayser (1851), Lücke (1852),
Dillmann (in Herzog, first ed. XII. 315), Lightfoot (1875), and Warfield (in
"Presbyt. Review," N. York, January, 1880, on the apologetical value of the
work for its allusions to various books of the N. T.).

[2] *Apol.* I. c. 55; *Dial. c. Tryph.* c. 91.

wandering magicians, if there had appeared in the latter the slightest tendency to beget in persons a true fear of God, and so to regulate their actions in prospect of the day of judgment. But they attempt nothing of the sort. Yea, they themselves are guilty of the most grievous crimes; whereas the Saviour would have his hearers to be convinced by the native beauty of religion and the holy lives of its teachers, rather than by even the miracles they wrought."

The subject of *post*-apostolic miracles is surrounded by much greater difficulties in the absence of inspired testimony, and in most cases even of ordinary immediate witnesses. There is an antecedent probability that the power of working miracles was not suddenly and abruptly, but gradually withdrawn, as the necessity of such outward and extraordinary attestation of the divine origin of Christianity diminished and gave way to the natural operation of truth and moral suasion. Hence St. Augustin, in the fourth century, says: "Since the establishment of the church God does not wish to perpetuate miracles even to our day, lest the mind should put its trust in visible signs, or grow cold at the sight of common marvels." * But it is impossible to fix the precise termination, either at the death of the apostles, or their immediate disciples, or the conversion of the Roman empire, or the extinction of the Arian heresy, or any subsequent era, and to sift carefully in each particular case the truth from legendary fiction.

It is remarkable that the genuine writings of the ante-Nicene church are more free from miraculous and superstitious elements than the annals of the Nicene age and the middle

---

* On the other hand, however, St. Augustin lent the authority of his name to some of the most incredible miracles of his age, wrought by the bones of St. Stephen, and even of Gervasius and Protasius. Comp. the treatise of Fr. Nitzsch (jun.) on Augustin's Doctrine of Miracles, Berlin 1865; and on the general subject J. H. Newman's *Two Essays on Biblical and Ecclesiastical Miracles*, third ed. London 1873; and J. B. Mozley's Bampton Lectures *On Miracles*. Oxford and Lond. (1865), fifth ed. 1880, Lect. VIII. which treats of false miracles.

ages. The history of monasticism teems with miracles even greater than those of the New Testament. Most of the statements of the apologists are couched in general terms, and refer to extraordinary cures from demoniacal possession (which probably includes, in the language of that age, cases of madness, deep melancholy, and epilepsy) and other diseases, by the invocation of the name of Jesus.[1] Justin Martyr speaks of such cures as a frequent occurrence in Rome and all over the world, and Origen appeals to his own personal observation, but speaks in another place of the growing scarcity of miracles, so as to suggest the gradual cessation theory as held by Dr. Neander, Bishop Kaye, and others. Tertullian attributes many if not most of the conversions of his day to supernatural dreams and visions, as does also Origen, although with more caution. But in such psychological phenomena it is exceedingly difficult to draw the line of demarcation between natural and supernatural causes, and between providential interpositions and miracles proper. The strongest passage on this subject is found in Irenæus, who, in contending against the heretics, mentions, besides prophecies and miraculous cures of demoniacs, even the raising of the dead among contemporary events taking place in the Catholic church;[2] but he specifies no particular case or name; and it should be remembered also, that his youth still bordered almost on the Johannean age.

4. The MORAL effect of Christianity upon the heart and life of its professors. The Christian religion has not only taught the purest and sublimest code of morals ever known among men, but actually exhibited it in the life, sufferings, and death of its founder and true followers. All the apologists, from the author of the Epistle to Diognetus down to Origen, Cyprian, and Augustin, bring out in strong colors the infinite superiority

---

[1] They are analogous to the "faith-cures," real or pretended, of our own age.

[2] *Adv. Haer.* II. 31, § 2, and II. 32, § 4: Ἤδη δὲ καὶ νεκροὶ ἠγέρθησαν καὶ παρέμεινον σὺν ἡμῖν ἱκανοῖς ἔτεσι. These two passages can hardly be explained, with Heumann and Neander, as referring merely to cases of *apparent* death.

of Christian ethics over the heathen, and their testimony is fully corroborated by the practical fruits of the church, as we shall have occasion more fully to show in another chapter. "They think us senseless," says Justin, "because we worship this Christ, who was crucified under Pontius Pilate, as God next to the Father. But they would not say so, if they knew the mystery of the cross. By its fruits they may know it. We, who once lived in debauchery, now study chastity; we, who dealt in sorceries, have consecrated ourselves to the good, the increate God; we, who loved money and possessions above all things else, now devote our property freely to the general good, and give to every needy one; we, who fought and killed each other, now pray for our enemies; those who persecute us in hatred, we kindly try to appease, in the hope that they may share the same blessings which we enjoy."[1]

5. The rapid SPREAD of Christianity by purely moral means, and in spite of the greatest external obstacles, yea, the bitter persecution of Jews and Gentiles. The anonymous apologetic Epistle to Diognetus which belongs to the literature of the Apostolic Fathers, already thus urges this point: "Do you not see the Christians exposed to wild beasts, that they may be persuaded to deny the Lord, and yet not overcome? Do you not see that the more of them are punished, the greater becomes the number of the rest? This does not seem to be the work of man: this is the power of God; these are the evidences of his manifestation."[2] Justin Martyr and Tertullian frequently go on in a similar strain. Origen makes good use of this argument against Celsus, and thinks that so great a success as Christianity met among Greeks and barbarians, learned and unlearned persons in so short a time, without any force or other worldly means, and in view of the united opposition of emperors, senate, governors, generals, priests, and people, can only be rationally accounted for on the ground of an ex-

---

[1] *Apol.* I. c. 13 and 14.　　　　　[2] *Ad Diogn.* c. 7.

traordinary providence of God and the divine nature of Christ.

6. The REASONABLENESS of Christianity, and its agreement with all the true and the beautiful in the Greek philosophy and poesy. All who had lived rationally before Christ were really, though unconsciously, already Christians. Thus all that is Christian is rational, and all that is truly rational is Christian. Yet, on the other hand, of course, Christianity is supra-rational (not irrational).

7. The ADAPTATION of Christianity to the deepest needs of human nature, which it alone can meet. Here belongs Tertullian's appeal to the "*testimonia animae naturaliter Christianae;*" his profound thought, that the human soul is, in its inmost essence and instinct, predestined for Christianity, and can find rest and peace in that alone. "The soul," says he, "though confined in the prison of the body, though perverted by bad training, though weakened by lusts and passions, though given to the service of false gods, still no sooner awakes from its intoxication and its dreams, and recovers its health, than it calls upon God by the one name due to him: 'Great God! good God!'—and then looks, not to the capitol, but to heaven; for it knows the abode of the living God, from whom it proceeds." [1]

This deep longing of the human soul for the living God in Christ, Augustin, in whom Tertullian's spirit returned purified and enriched, afterwards expressed in the grand sentence: "Thou, O God, hast made us for thee, and our heart is restless, till it rests in thee." [2]

---

[1] Tert. *Apolog.* c. 17. Comp. the beautiful passage in *De Testim. Animœ*, c. 2: "*Si enim anima aut divina aut a Deo data est, sine dubio datorem suum novit, et si novit, utique et timet . . . . O testimonium veritatis, quœ apud ipsa dœmonia testem efficit Christianorum.*"

[2] Aug. *Confess.* I. 1: "*Fecisti nos ad Te, et inquietum est cor nostrum, donec re quiescat in Te.*"

CHAPTER IV.

ORGANIZATION AND DISCIPLINE OF THE CHURCH.

I. The chief sources for this chapter are the Epistles of IGNATIUS, the works of IRENÆUS, TERTULLIAN, and especially CYPRIAN, and the so-called CONSTITUTIONES APOSTOLICÆ,

II. See the Literature in vol. I. § 58 (p. 481 sqq.), particularly the works of ROTHE, RITSCHL, LIGHTFOOT, and HATCH.

§ 41. *Progress in Consolidation.*

IN the external organization of the church, several important changes appear in the period before us. The distinction of clergy and laity, and the sacerdotal view of the ministry becomes prominent and fixed; subordinate church offices are multiplied; the episcopate arises; the beginnings of the Roman primacy appear; and the exclusive unity of the Catholic church develops itself in opposition to heretics and schismatics. The apostolical organization of the first century now gives place to the old Catholic episcopal system; and this, in its turn, passes into the metropolitan, and after the fourth century into the patriarchal. Here the Greek church stopped, and is governed to this day by a hierarchical oligarchy of patriarchs equal in rank and jurisdiction; while the Latin church went a step further, and produced in the middle ages the papal monarchy. The germs of this papacy likewise betray themselves even in our present period, particularly in Cyprian, together with a protest against it. Cyprian himself is as much a witness for consolidated primacy, as for independent episcopacy, and hence often used and abused alike by Romanists and Anglicans for sectarian purposes.

The characteristics, however, of the pre-Constantinian hierarchy, in distinction from the post-Constantinian, both Greek and Roman, are, first, its grand simplicity, and secondly, its spirituality, or freedom from all connection with political power and worldly splendor. Whatever influence the church acquired and exercised, she owed nothing to the secular government, which continued indifferent or positively hostile till the protective toleration edict of Constantine (313). Tertullian thought it impossible for an emperor to be a Christian, or a Christian to be an emperor; and even after Constantine, the Donatists persisted in this view, and cast up to the Catholics the memory of the former age: "What have Christians to do with kings? or what have bishops to do in the palace?"[1] The ante-Nicene fathers expected the ultimate triumph of Christianity over the world from a supernatural interposition at the second Advent. Origen seems to have been the only one in that age of violent persecution who expected that Christianity, by continual growth, would gain the dominion over the world.[2]

The consolidation of the church and its compact organization implied a restriction of individual liberty, in the interest of order, and a temptation to the abuse of authority. But it was demanded by the diminution of spiritual gifts, which were poured out in such extraordinary abundance in the apostolic age. It made the church a powerful republic within the Roman empire, and contributed much to its ultimate success. "In union is strength," especially in times of danger and persecution such as the church had to pass through in the ante-Nicene age. While we must deny a divine right and perpetual obligation to any peculiar form of government as far as it departs from the simple principles of the New Testament, we may concede a historical necessity and great relative importance to the ante-Nicene and subsequent organizations of the church. Even the papacy was by no means an unmixed evil, but a training school for the barbarian nations during the middle ages.

---

[1] "*Quid Christianis cum regibus? aut quid episcopis cum palatio?*"

[2] *Contra Cels.* VIII. 68.   Comp. the remarks of Neander, I. 129 (Boston ed.).

Those who condemn, in principle, all hierarchy, sacerdotalism, and ceremonialism, should remember that God himself appointed the priesthood and ceremonies in the Mosaic dispensation, and that Christ submitted to the requirements of the law in the days of his humiliation.

§ 42. *Clergy and Laity.*

The idea and institution of a special priesthood, distinct from the body of the people, with the accompanying notion of sacrifice and altar, passed imperceptibly from Jewish and heathen reminiscences and analogies into the Christian church. The majority of Jewish converts adhered tenaciously to the Mosaic institutions and rites, and a considerable part never fully attained to the height of spiritual freedom proclaimed by Paul, or soon fell away from it. He opposed legalistic and ceremonial tendencies in Galatia and Corinth; and although sacerdotalism does not appear among the errors of his Judaizing opponents, the Levitical priesthood, with its three ranks of high-priest, priest, and Levite, naturally furnished an analogy for the threefold ministry of bishop, priest, and deacon, and came to be regarded as typical of it. Still less could the Gentile Christians, as a body, at once emancipate themselves from their traditional notions of priesthood, altar, and sacrifice, on which their former religion was based. Whether we regard the change as an apostasy from a higher position attained, or as a reaction of old ideas never fully abandoned, the change is undeniable, and can be traced to the second century. The church could not long occupy the ideal height of the apostolic age, and as the pentecostal illumination passed away with the death of the apostles, the old reminiscences began to reassert themselves.[1]

[1] Renan, looking at the gradual development of the hierarchy out of the primitive democracy, from his secular point of view, calls it "the most profound transformation" in history, and a triple abdication: first the club (the congregation) committing its power to the bureau or the committee (the college of presbyters), then the bureau to its president (the bishop) who could say:

In the apostolic church preaching and teaching were not confined to a particular class, but every convert could proclaim the
gospel to unbelievers, and every Christian who had the gift
could pray and teach and exhort in the congregation.[1] The
New Testament knows no spiritual aristocracy or nobility, but
calls all believers "saints," though many fell far short of their
vocation. Nor does it recognize a special priesthood in distinction from the people, as mediating between God and the laity.
It knows only one high-priest, Jesus Christ, and clearly teaches
the universal priesthood, as well as universal kingship, of believers.[2] It does this in a far deeper and larger sense than the
Old;[3] in a sense, too, which even to this day is not yet fully
realized. The entire body of Christians are called "clergy"
($\varkappa\lambda\tilde{\eta}\rho o\iota$), a peculiar people, the heritage of God.[4]

On the other hand it is equally clear that there was in the
apostolic church a ministerial office, instituted by Christ, for the
very purpose of raising the mass of believers from infancy and
pupilage to independent and immediate intercourse with God,

"*Je suis le club,*" and finally the presidents to the pope as the universal and
infallible bishop; the last process being completed in the Vatican Council of
1870. See his *L'Église chrétienne*, p. 88, and his *English Conferences* (Hibbert
Lectures, 1880), p. 90.

[1] Comp. Acts 8: 4; 9: 27; 13: 15; 18: 26, 28; Rom. 12: 6; 1 Cor. 12:
10, 28; 14: 1–6, 31. Even in the Jewish Synagogue the liberty of teaching
was enjoyed, and the elder could ask any member of repute, even a stranger,
to deliver a discourse on the Scripture lesson (Luke 4: 17; Acts 17: 2).

[2] 1 Pet. 2: 5, 9; 5: 3; Rev. 1: 6; 5: 10; 20: 6. See Neander, Lightfoot,
Stanley, etc., and vol. I. 486 sqq. I add a passage from Hatch's Bampton
Lectures on *The Organization of the Early Christian Churches* (1881), p. 139:
"In earlier times there was a grander faith. For the kingdom of God was a
kingdom of priests. Not only the 'four and twenty elders' before the throne,
but the innumerable souls of the sanctified upon whom 'the second death had
no power,' were 'kings and priests unto God.' Only in that high sense was
priesthood predicable of Christian men. For the shadow had passed: the
reality had come: the one High Priest of Christianity was Christ."

[3] Exod. 19: 6.

[4] 1 Pet. 5: 3. Here Peter warns his fellow-presbyters not to lord it
($\kappa\upsilon\rho\iota\epsilon\acute{\upsilon}\epsilon\iota\nu$) over the $\kappa\lambda\tilde{\eta}\rho o\iota$ or the $\kappa\lambda\eta\rho o\nu o\mu\acute{\iota}\alpha$, *i. e.*, the lot or inheritance of the
Lord, the charge allotted to them. Comp. Deut. 4: 20; 9: 29 (LXX).

to that prophetic, priestly, and kingly position, which in principle and destination belongs to them all.[1] This work is the gradual process of church history itself, and will not be fully accomplished till the kingdom of glory shall come. But these ministers are nowhere represented as priests in any other sense than Christians generally are priests with the privilege of a direct access to the throne of grace in the name of their one and eternal high-priest in heaven. Even in the Pastoral Epistles which present the most advanced stage of ecclesiastical organization in the apostolic period, while the teaching, ruling, and pastoral functions of the presbyter-bishops are fully discussed, nothing is said about a sacerdotal function. The Apocalypse, which was written still later, emphatically teaches the universal priesthood and kingship of believers. The apostles themselves never claim or exercise a special priesthood. The sacrifice which all Christians are exhorted to offer is the sacrifice of their person and property to the Lord, and the spiritual sacrifice of thanksgiving and praise.[2] In one passage a Christian "altar" is spoken of, in distinction from the Jewish altar of literal and daily sacrifices, but this altar is the cross on which Christ offered himself once and forever for the sins of the world.[3]

After the gradual abatement of the extraordinary spiritual elevation of the apostolic age, which anticipated in its way the ideal condition of the church, the distinction of a regular class of teachers from the laity became more fixed and prominent. This appears first in Ignatius, who, in his high episcopalian spirit, considers the clergy the necessary medium of access for the people to God. "Whoever is within the sanctuary (or altar), is pure; but he who is outside of the sanctuary is not pure; that

[1] Comp. Eph. 4: 11–13.
[2] Rom. 12: 1; Phil. 2: 17; 1 Pet. 2: 5; Heb. 13: 16.
[3] Heb. 13: 10. So θυσιαστήριον is understood by Thomas Aquinas, Bengel, Bleek, Lünemann, Riehm, etc. Others explain it of the Lord's table, Lightfoot (p. 263) of the congregation assembled for common worship.

is, he who does anything without bishop and presbytery and deacon, is not pure in conscience."[1] Yet he nowhere represents the ministry as a sacerdotal office. The *Didache* calls "the prophets" *high-priests*, but probably in a spiritual sense.[2] Clement of Rome, in writing to the congregation at Corinth, draws a significant and fruitful parallel between the Christian presiding office and the Levitical priesthood, and uses the expression "layman" (λαϊκος ἄνθρωπος) as antithetic to high-priest, priests, and Levites.[3] This parallel contains the germ of the whole system of sacerdotalism. But it is at best only an argument by *analogy*. Tertullian was the first who expressly and directly asserts sacerdotal claims on behalf of the Christian ministry, and calls it "*sacerdotium*," although he also strongly affirms the universal priesthood of all believers. Cyprian (d. 258) goes still further, and applies all the privileges, duties, and responsibilities of the Aaronic priesthood to the officers of the Christian church, and constantly calls them *sacerdotes* and *sacerdotium*. He may therefore be called the proper father of the sacerdotal conception of the Christian ministry as a mediating agency between God and the people. During the third century it became customary to apply the term "priest" directly and

---

[1] *Ad Trall.* c. 7: ὁ ἐντὸς θυσιαστηρίου ὢν καθαρός ἐστιν ὁ δὲ ἐκτὸς θυσιαστηρίου ὢν οὐ καθαρός ἐστιν· τουτέστιν, ὁ χωρὶς ἐπισκόπου καὶ πρεσβυτερίου καὶ διακόνου πράσσων τι, οὗτος οὐ καθαρός ἐστιν τῇ συνειδήσει. Funk's ed. I. 208. Some MSS. omit the second clause, perhaps from homœoteleuton. Von Gebhardt and Harnack also omit it in the Greek text, but retain it in the Latin (*qui extra altare est, non mundus est*). The τουτέστιν evidently requires the clause.

[2] Cf. ch. 13. See note in Schaff's edition, p. 206.

[3] *Ad Cor.* 40: "Unto the high-priest his proper services have been intrusted, and to the priests their proper office is appointed, and upon the levites their proper ministrations are laid. The layman is bound by the layman's ordinances (ὁ λαϊκὸς ἄνθρωπος τοῖς λαϊκοῖς προστάγμασιν δέδεται)." The passage occurs in the text of Bryennios as well as in the older editions, and there is no good reason to suspect it of being an interpolation in the hierarchical interest, as Neander and Milman have done. Bishop Lightfoot, in his *St. Clement of Rome*, p. 128 sq., puts a mild construction upon it, and says that the analogy does not extend to the *three* orders, because Clement only knows two (bishops and deacons), and that the high priesthood of Christ is wholly different in kind from the Mosaic high priesthood, and exempt from those very limitations on which Clement dwells in that chapter.

exclusively to the Christian ministers, especially the bishops.[1] In the same manner the whole ministry, and it alone, was called "clergy," with a double reference to its presidency and its peculiar relation to God.[2] It was distinguished by this name from the Christian people or "laity."[3] Thus the term "clergy," which first signified the lot by which office was assigned (Acts 1 : 17, 25), then the office itself, then the persons holding that office, was transferred from the Christians generally to the ministers exclusively.

Solemn "ordination" or consecration by the laying on of hands was the form of admission into the "ordo ecclesiasticus" or "sacerdotalis." In this order itself there were again three degrees, "ordines majores," as they were called : the diaconate, the presbyterate, and the episcopate—held to be of divine institution. Under these were the "ordines minores," of later date, from sub-deacon to ostiary, which formed the stepping-stone between the clergy proper and the people.[4]

---

[1] *Sacerdos*, also *summus sacerdos* (Tertullian, *De Bapt.* 7), and once *pontifex maximus* (*De Pudic.* 1, with ironical reference, it seems, to the Roman bishop); *ordo sacerdotalis* (*De Exhort. Cast.* 7); ἱερεύς and sometimes ἀρχιερεύς (*Apost. Const.* II. 34, 35, 36, 57; III. 9; vi. 15, 18, etc.). Hippolytus calls his office an ἀρχιερατεία and διδασκαλία (*Ref. Haer.* I. prooem.). Cyprian generally applies the term *sacerdos* to the bishop, and calls his colleagues *consacerdotales*

[2] Κλῆρος, *clerus*, τάξις, *ordo, ordo sacerdotalis* (Tertull., *De Exhort. Cast.* 7), *ordo ecclesiasticus* or *ecclesiae* (*De Monog.* 11; *De Idolol.* 7); κληρικοί, *clerici*. The first instance perhaps of the use of *clerus* in the sense of clergy is in Tertullian, *De Monog.* c. 12 : "*Unde enim episcopi et clerus?*" and : "*Extollimur et inflamur adversus clerum.*" Jerome (*Ad Nepotian.*) explains this exclusive application of *clerus* to ministers, "*vel quia de sorte sunt Domini, vel quia ipse Dominus sors, id est, pars clericorum est.*" The distinction between the *regular* clergy, who were also monks, and the *secular* clergy or parish priests, is of much later date (seventh or eighth century).

[3] Λαός, λαϊκοί, *plebs.* In Tertullian, Cyprian, and in the Apostolic Constitutions the term "layman" occurs very often. Cyprian speaks (250) of a "conference held with bishops, presbyters, deacons, confessors, and also with laymen who stood firm" (in persecution), *Ep.* 30, *ad Rom.*

[4] Occasionally, however. we find a somewhat wider terminology. Tertullian mentions, *De Monog.* c. 12, the *ordo viduarum* among the *ordines ecclesiastici*, and even the much later Jerome (see *In Jesaiam.* 1. v. c. 19, 18), enumerates *quinque ecclesiae ordines, episcopos. presbyteros, diaconos, fideles, catechumenos.*

Thus we find, so early as the third century, the foundations of a complete hierarchy; though a hierarchy of only moral power, and holding no sort of outward control over the conscience. The body of the laity consisted of two classes: the faithful, or the baptized and communicating members, and the catechumens, who were preparing for baptism. Those church members who lived together in one place,[1] formed a church in the narrower sense.[2]

With the exaltation of the clergy appeared the tendency to separate them from secular business, and even from social relations—from marriage, for example—and to represent them, even outwardly, as a caste independent of the people, and devoted exclusively to the service of the sanctuary. They drew their support from the church treasury, which was supplied by voluntary contributions and weekly collections on the Lord's Day. After the third century they were forbidden to engage in any secular business, or even to accept any trusteeship. Celibacy was not yet in this period enforced, but left optional. Tertullian, Gregory of Nyssa, and other distinguished church teachers, lived in wedlock, though theoretically preferring the unmarried state. Of an official clerical costume no certain trace appears before the fourth century; and if it came earlier into use, as may have been the case, after the example of the Jewish church, it must have been confined, during the times of persecution, to the actual exercises of worship.

With the growth of this distinction of clergy and laity, however, the idea of the universal priesthood continued from time to time to assert itself: in Irenæus,[3] for example, and in an eccentric form in the Montanists, who even allowed women to teach publicly in the church. So Tertullian, with whom *clerus* and *laici* were at one time familiar expressions, inquires, as the champion of the Montanistic reaction against the Catholic hierarchy: "Are not we laymen priests also?"[4]   It is written,

---

[1] Πάροικοι, παρεπίδημοι, Eph. 2: 19; 1 Pet. 2: 11.   [2] or parish, παροικία.
[3] *Adv. Haer.* iv. 8, § 3.   [4] *Nonne et laici sacerdotes sumus?*

he continues : " He hath made us kings and priests (Rev. 1 : 6). It is the authority of the church alone which has made a distinction between clergy and laity. Where there is no college of ministers, you administer the sacrament, you baptize, you are a priest for yourself alone. And where there are three of you, there is a church, though you be only laymen. For each one lives by his own faith, and there is no respect of persons with God." [1] All, therefore, which the clergy considered peculiar to them, he claimed for the laity as the common sacerdotal privilege of all Christians.

Even in the Catholic church an acknowledgment of the general priesthood showed itself in the custom of requiring the baptized to say the Lord's Prayer before the assembled congregation. With reference to this, Jerome says : " *Sacerdotium laici, id est, baptisma.*" The congregation also, at least in the West, retained for a long time the right of approval and rejection in the choice of its ministers, even of the bishop. Clement of Rome expressly requires the assent of the whole congregation for a valid election ; [2] and Cyprian terms this an apostolic and almost universal regulation.[3] According to his testimony it obtained also in Rome, and was observed in the case of his contemporary, Cornelius.[4] Sometimes in the filling of a vacant bishopric the " suffragium" of the people preceded the "judicium" of the clergy of the diocese. Cyprian, and afterwards Athanasius, Ambrose, Augustin, and other eminent prelates, were in a manner pressed into the bishopric in this democratic way. Cyprian, with all his high-church proclivities, declares it his principle to do nothing as bishop without the advice of the presbyters and deacons, and the consent of the people.[5] A pe-

---

[1] *De Exhort. Cast.* c. 7. Comp. also *De Monog.* 7, 12 ; *De Bapt.* 17 ; *De Orat.* 18.

[2] *Ad Cor.* 44 : Συνευδοκάσης τῆς ἐκκλησίας πάσης, *consentiente universa ecclesia.*

[3] *Ep.* lx. 3–4 (ed. Goldhorn).

[4] *Ep.* lv. 7 : " *Factus est Cornelius episcopus de Dei et Christi ejus judicio, de clericorum pœne omnium testimonio, de plebis quæ tum adfuit suffragio, et de sacerdotum antiquorum et bonorum virorum collegio.*"

[5] *Sine consensu plebis.*

culiar influence, which even the clergy could not withstand, attached to the "confessors," and it was sometimes abused by them, as in their advocacy of the lapsed, who denied Christ in the Decian persecution.

Finally, we notice cases where the function of teaching was actually exercised by laymen. The bishops of Jerusalem and Cæsarea allowed the learned Origen to expound the Bible to their congregations before his ordination, and appealed to the example of several bishops in the East.[1] Even in the Apostolical Constitutions there occurs, under the name of the Apostle Paul, the direction: " Though a man be a layman, if experienced in the delivery of instruction, and reverent in habit, he may teach; for the Scripture says: ' They shall be all taught of God.' "[2] The fourth general council at Carthage (398) prohibited laymen from teaching in the presence of clergymen and without their consent; implying at the same time, that with such permission the thing might be done.[3]

It is worthy of notice that a number of the most eminent church teachers of this period, Hermas, Justin Martyr, Athenagoras, Clement of Alexandria, Origen, Tertullian, Arnobius,

[1] Euseb., *H. E.* VI. 19: "There [in Cæsarea] he [Origen] was also requested by the bishops to expound the sacred Scriptures publicly in the church, although he had not yet obtained the priesthood by the imposition of hands." It is true this was made the ground of a charge against him by Demetrius, bishop of Alexandria; but the charge was that Origen had preached "in the presence of bishops," not that he had preached as a layman. And the bishops of Jerusalem and Cæsarea adduced several examples of holy bishops inviting capable laymen to preach to the people. Prudentius and Aedesius, while laymen, founded the church in Abyssinia, Socrates, *Hist. Eccl.* I. 19.

[2] *Const. Apost.* VIII. 31. Ambrosiaster, or Hilary the Deacon, in his Com. *Ad Eph.* 4: 11, 12, says that in early times "*omnes docebant et omnes baptizabant.*"

[3] Can. 98: " *Laicus præsentibus clericis, nisi ipsis jubentibus, docere non audeat.*" The 99th canon forbids women, no matter how "learned or holy," to "presume to teach men in a meeting." Pope Leo I. (*Ep.* 92 and 93) forbids lay preaching in the interest of ecclesiastical order. Charlemagne enacted a law that "a layman ought not to recite a lesson in church, nor to say the Hallelujah, but only the Psalm or responses without the Hallelujah."

and Lactantius, were either laymen, or at most only presbyters. Hermas, who wrote one of the most popular and authoritative books in the early church, was probably a layman; perhaps also the author of the homily which goes under the name of the Second Epistle of Clement of Rome, and has recently been discovered in full both in the original Greek and in a Syriac translation; for he seems to distinguish himself and his hearers from the presbyters.[1]

§ 43. *New Church Officers.*

The expansion of the church, the development of her cultus, and the tendency towards hierarchical pomp, led to the multiplication of offices below the diaconate, which formed the *ordines minores*. About the middle of the third century the following new officers are mentioned:

1. SUB-DEACONS, or under-helpers;[2] assistants and deputies of the deacons; the only one of these subordinate offices for which a formal ordination was required. Opinions differ as to its value.

2. READERS,[3] who read the Scriptures in the assembly and had charge of the church books.

3. ACOLYTHS,[4] attendants of the bishops in their official duties and processions.

4. EXORCISTS,[5] who, by prayer and the laying on of hands, cast out the evil spirit from the possessed,[6] and from catechumens,

---

[1] The Greek text (of which only a fragment was known before) was found and published by Bryennios, 1875, the Syriac version by Bensley, 1876. See Harnack's ed. in the *Patres Apost.* vol. I., and Lightfoot, *S. Clement of Rome, Appendix* (1877). Harnack, Hilgenfeld, and Hatch (*l. c.* 114; note) suppose that the homily was delivered by a layman, but Lightfoot (p. 304) explains the language above alluded to as a common rhetorical figure by which the speaker places himself on a level with his audience.

[2] Ὑποδιάκονοι, *subdiaconi*, perhaps the same as the ὑπηρέται of the New Testament and the earlier fathers.

[3] Ἀναγνῶσται, *lectores*, mentioned by Tertullian.

[4] Ἀκόλυθοι, *acolythi*. [5] Ἐξορκισταί, *exorcistae*. [6] Δαιμονιζόμενοι, ἐνεργούμενοι.

and frequently assisted in baptism. This power had been formerly considered a free gift of the Holy Spirit.

5. PRECENTORS,[1] for the musical parts of the liturgy, psalms,
benedictions, responses, etc.

6. JANITORS or sextons,[2] who took care of the religious meet-
ing-rooms, and at a later period also of the church-yards.

7. Besides these there were in the larger churches CATE-
CHISTS, and, where the church language in the worship was not
understood, INTERPRETERS ; but the interpreting was commonly
done by presbyters, deacons, or readers.

The bishop Cornelius of Rome (d. 252), in a letter on the
Novatian schism,[3] gives the number of officers in his church as
follows : Forty-six presbyters, probably corresponding to the
number of the meeting-houses of the Christians in the city ;
seven deacons, after the model of the church at Jerusalem (Acts
vi) ; seven sub-deacons ; forty-two acolyths, and fifty-two exorcists, readers, and janitors.

As to the *ordines majores*, the deacons during this period rose
in importance. In addition to their original duties of caring
for the poor and sick, they baptized, distributed the sacramental
cup, said the church prayers, not seldom preached, and were
confidential advisers, sometimes even delegates and vicars of the
bishops. This last is true especially of the "archdeacon," who
does not appear, however, till the fourth century. The presbyters, on the contrary, though above the deacons, were now over-
topped by the new office of bishop, in which the entire government of the church became centred.

§ 44. *Origin of the Episcopate.*

Besides the works already cited, compare the special works and essays
on the *Ignatian* controversy, published since 1837, by ROTHE (close
of his *Anfänge*, etc.), HEFELE (R. C.), BAUR, HILGENFELD,
BUNSEN, PETERMANN, CURETON, LIPSIUS, UHLHORN, ZAHN,
LIGHTFOOT (I. 376 sqq). Also R. D. HITCHCOCK on the *Origin*

---

[1] Ψάλται, *psalmistae cantores.*   [2] Θυρωροί, πυλωροί, *ostiarii janitores.*
[3] In Euseb. vi. 43.

of Episcopacy, N. Y. 1867 (in the "Am. Presbyt. & Theol. Review" for Jan. 1867, pp. 133–169); LIGHTFOOT on the *Christian Ministry* (1873); HATCH on the *Organization of the Early Christian Church* (1881); RENAN, *L' Eglise chrétienne* (1879), ch. VI. *Progrès de l'épiscopat;* and GORE, *The Ministry of the Church* (1889).

The most important and also the most difficult phenomenon of our period in the department of church organization is the rise and development of the episcopate as distinct from the presbyterate. This institution comes to view in the second century as the supreme spiritual office, and is retained to this day by all Roman and Greek Christendom, and by a large part of the Evangelical church, especially the Anglican communion. A form of government so ancient and so widely adopted, can be satisfactorily accounted for only on the supposition of a religious need, namely, the need of a tangible outward representation and centralization, to illustrate and embody to the people their relation to Christ and to God, and the visible unity of the church. It is therefore inseparable from the catholic principle of authority and mediation; while the protestant principle of freedom and direct intercourse of the believer with Christ, consistently carried out, infringes the strict episcopal constitution, and tends to ministerial equality. Episcopacy in the full sense of the term requires for its base the idea of a real priesthood and real sacrifice, and an essential distinction between clergy and laity. Divested of these associations, it resolves itself into a mere superintendency.[1]

During the lifetime of the apostles, those eye- and ear-witnesses of the divine-human life of Jesus, and the inspired organs of the Holy Spirit, there was no room for proper bishops; and those who were so called, must have held only a

---

[1] Such is the Swedish and Danish Lutheran, the American Methodist, and the Moravian episcopate, which recognizes the validity of non-episcopal orders. The Anglican church harbors a high-church and a low-church theory of episcopacy, the one derived from the mediæval hierarchy, the other from the Reformation, but repudiates the primacy as an antichristian usurpation, although it must be confessed to be almost as old as episcopacy, its roots going back to Clement of Rome, or at all events to the age of Irenæus.

subordinate place. The church, too, in the first century was as yet a strictly supernatural organization, a stranger in this world, standing with one foot in eternity, and longing for the second coming of her heavenly bridegroom. But in the episcopal constitution the church provided an extremely simple but compact and freely expansible organization, planted foot firmly upon earth, became an institution for the education of her infant people, and, as chiliastic hopes receded, fell into the path of quiet historical development; yet unquestionably she thus incurred also the danger of a secularization which reached its height just when the hierarchy became complete in the Roman church, and which finally necessitated a reformation on the basis of apostolical Christianity. That this secularization began with the growing power of the bishops even before Constantine and the Byzantine court orthodoxy, we perceive, for instance, in the lax penitential discipline, the avarice, and the corruption with which Hippolytus, in the ninth book of his *Philosophumena*, reproaches Zephyrinus and Callistus, the Roman bishops of his time (202–223); also in the example of the bishop Paul of Samosata, who was deposed in 269 on almost incredible charges, not only against his doctrine, but still more against his moral character.[1] Origen complains that there are, especially in the larger cities, overseers of the people of God, who seek to outdo the pomp of heathen potentates, would surround themselves, like the emperors, with a body-guard, and make themselves terrible and inaccessible to the poor.[2]

We consider, first, the ORIGIN of the episcopate. The unreliable character of our documents and traditions from the transition period between the close of the apostolic church and the beginning of the post-apostolic, leaves large room here for critical research and combination. First of all comes the question: Was the episcopate directly or indirectly of apostolic

---

[1] Comp. Euseb. vii. 27–30.

[2] See the passages quoted by Gieseler, vol. I. 282 sq. (Harpers' ed. of New York.)

(Johannean) origin?[1] Or did it arise after the death of the apostles, and develope itself from the presidency of the congregational presbytery?[2] In other words, was the episcopate a continuation and contraction of, and substitute for, the apostolate, or was it an expansion and elevation of the presbyterate?[3] The later view is more natural and better sustained by facts. Most of its advocates date the change from the time of Ignatius in the first quarter of the second century, while a few carry it further back to the close of the first, when St. John still lived in Ephesus.

I. For the APOSTOLIC origin of episcopacy the following points may be made:

(1) The position of James, who evidently stood at the head of the church at Jerusalem,[4] and is called bishop, at least in the pseudo-Clementine literature, and in fact supreme bishop of the whole church.[5] This instance, however, stands quite alone, and does not warrant an inference in regard to the entire church.

(2) The office of the assistants and delegates of the apostles, like Timothy, Titus, Silas, Epaphroditus, Luke, Mark, who had a sort of supervision of several churches and congregational officers, and in a measure represented the apostles in special missions. But, in any case, these were not limited, at least during the life of the apostles, each to a particular diocese; they were itinerant evangelists and legates of the apostles; only

[1] This is the Greek, the Roman Catholic, and the high Anglican theory. It is advocated by a very few Continental Protestants as Chevalier Bunsen, Rothe and Thiersch (an Irvingite), who trace episcopacy to John in Ephesus.

[2] So the Lutheran, Presbyterian, and some eminent Episcopal writers. We mention Mosheim, Neander, Lightfoot, Stanley, Hatch. Also Baur and Renan, who judge as mere critics.

[3] Bishop Lightfoot (l. c. p. 194) thus states the question with his own answer: "The episcopate was formed, not out of the apostolic order by localization, but out of the presbyterial by elevation; and the title, which originally was common to all, came at length to be appropriated to the chief among them."

[4] Acts 15: 13; 21: 18. Comp. vol. I. 264 sqq.

[5] Ἐπίσκοπος ἐπισκόπων.

the doubtful tradition of a later day assigns them distinct bishoprics. If bishops at all, they were missionary bishops.

(3) The angels of the seven churches of Asia,[1] who, if regarded as individuals, look very like the later bishops, and indicate a monarchical shaping of the church government in the days of John. But, apart from the various interpretations of the Apocalyptic ἄγγελοι, that office appears not co-ordinate with the apostolate of John, but subordinate to it, and was no more than a congregational superintendency.

(4) The testimony of Ignatius of Antioch, a disciple of John, in his seven (or three) epistles from the beginning of the second century (even according to the shorter Syriac version), presupposes the episcopate, in distinction from the presbyterate, as already existing, though as a new institution, yet in its growth.

(5) The statement of Clement of Alexandria,[2] that John instituted bishops after his return from Patmos; and the accounts of Irenæus,[3] Tertullian,[4] Eusebius,[5] and Jerome,[6] that the same apostle nominated and ordained Polycarp (with whom Irenæus was personally acquainted) bishop of Smyrna.

(6) The uncertain tradition in Eusebius, who derived it probably from Hegesippus, that the surviving apostles and disciples of the apostles, soon after the destruction of Jerusalem, elected Symeon, the son of Klopas and a cousin of Jesus, bishop of that city and successor of James. But this arrangement at best was merely local, and not general.[7]

(7) The tradition of the churches of Antioch and Rome,

---

[1] Rev. 1: 20. For the different views see vol. I. 497.

[2] *Quis dives salvus*, c. 42.   [3] *Adv. Haer.* III. 3.

[4] *De Praescr. Haer.* c. 32.   [5] *H. E.* III. 36.

[6] *Catal.* sub Polyc.

[7] *H. E.* III. 11. Comp. the fragment of Hegesippus, in IV. 22. Lightfoot (*Philippians*, p. 202) remarks against Rothe's inference: "The account of Hegesippus confines the object of this gathering to the appointment of a successor of St. James. If its deliberations had exerted that vast and permanent influence on the future of the church which Rothe's theory supposes, it is scarcely possible that this early historian should have been ignorant of the fact, or knowing it should have passed it over in silence."

which trace their line of bishops back to apostolic institution,
and kept the record of an unbroken succession.

(8) A passage in the second of the Pfaff Fragments of
Irenæus, which speaks of " second ordinances of the apostles "
(δεύτεραι τῶν ἀποστόλων διατάξεις). Rothe understands by
these the institution of the episcopate. But aside from the
doubtful genuineness of the Fragments, these words are at all
events of unsettled interpretation, and, according to the connection, relate not to the government of the church at all, but
to the celebration of the eucharist.

(9) Equally uncertain is the conclusion drawn from an
obscure passage in the Epistle of Clement of Rome to the
Corinthians, which admits of different interpretations.[1] The
apostles, it is said, foreseeing the future controversy about the
name of the episcopal office, appointed bishops and deacons,
and *afterwards* made the disposition,[2] that when *they* should

---

[1] *Ad Corinth.* c. 44: Οἱ ἀπόστολοι ἡμῶν ἔγνωσαν διὰ τοῦ κυρίου ἡμῶν
'Ιησοῦ Χριστοῦ ὅτι ἔρις ἔσται ἐπὶ τοῦ ὀνόματος τῆς ἐπισκοπῆς. Διὰ
ταύτην οὖν τὴν αἰτίαν πρόγνωσιν εἰληφότες τελείαν κατέστησαν τοὺς
προειρημένους καὶ μεταξὺ ἐπινομὴν [or ἐπιμονὴν] ἔδωκαν, ὅπως, ἐὰν
κοιμηθῶσιν, διαδέξωνται ἕτεροι δεδοκιμασμένοι ἄνδρες τὴν λειτουργίαν
αὐτῶν. "Our apostles knew through our Lord Jesus Christ that there would
be strife over the name of the bishop's office [*i. e.*, the office of the ministry
in general; comp. Acts 1 : 20; Sept. Num. 4 : 16 ; Ps. 109 : 8 ; 2 Chr. 23 : 18].
For this cause, therefore, having complete foreknowledge, they appointed the
aforesaid persons [*i. e.*, presbyter-bishops and deacons; comp. c. 42 and 57],
and afterwards they made the disposition [or provided a continuance, if we
read with Lightfoot ἐπιμονήν], that if these should fall asleep, other approved
men should succeed to their ministration."

[2] The reading is obscure and disputed. The Alexandrian MS. reads :
ἐπινομήν, the Constantinopolitan : ἐπιδομήν (both have ΕΠΙ-ΟΜΗΝ). The
former word is rare (from νέμω, or from νόμος), the latter is not found in the
dictionaries ; and hence various emendations have been proposed, as ἀπονομήν
(Junius), ἐπιδοχήν (Bryennios), ἐπιβολήν (von Gebhardt and Harnack),
ἐπιμονήν (Bunsen, Lightfoot), ἐπιτροπήν (Hilgenfeld), ἐπιλογήν, ἐπινομίαν,
ἐπιστολήν, ἐπιταγήν, ἔτι νόμον. Rothe (*Anfänge*, p. 374) ingeniously translates ἐπινομήν "testamentary disposition" (*testamentarische Verfügung* =
ἐπινομίς, an after-enactment, a codicil), and identifies it with the δεύτεραι
διατάξεις of the fragment of Irenæus. But this is rejected by the latest
editors as untenable. Lightfoot (with Bunsen) reads ἐπιμονήν, permanence
(**not** "life-tenure," as Bunsen rendered it). The drift of the passage, how-

fall asleep, other approved men should follow *them* in office. Rothe refers "they" and "them" to the apostles as the main subject. But these words naturally refer to the congregational officers just before mentioned, and in this case the "other approved men" are not successors of the apostles, but of the presbyter-bishops and deacons.[1] This view is sustained by the connection. The difficulty in the Corinthian congregation was a rebellion, not against a single bishop, but against a number of presbyter-bishops, and Clement reminds them that the apostles instituted this office not only for the first generation, but provided for a permanent succession, and that the officers were appointed for life, and could therefore not be deposed so long as they discharged their duties. Hence he goes on to say, immediately after the disputed passage in chapter 44 : "Wherefore we think that those cannot justly be thrown out of their ministry who were appointed either by them (the apostles), or afterwards by other eminent men, with the consent of the whole congregation; and who have with all lowliness and innocency ministered to the flock of Christ, in peace, and without self-interest, and were for a long time commended by all."

(10) Finally, the philosophical consideration, that the universal and uncontested spread of the episcopate in the second century cannot be satisfactorily explained without the presumption of at least the indirect sanction of the apostles. By the same argument the observance of Sunday and infant baptism are usually traced to apostolic origin. But it is not quite con-

---

ever, does not so much depend upon the meaning of this word as upon the question whether the apostles, or the congregational officers are the grammatical subjects of the following verb, κοιμηθῶσιν.

[1] See also Gebhardt and Harnack (*presbyteri et diaconi illi, quos apostoli ipsi constituerunt*), the Roman Catholic editor Funk (" κοιμηθῶσιν, sc. episcopi et diaconi de quorum successione Clemens agit"), and Bishop Lightfoot ("the first generation of presbyters appointed by the apostles themselves"). Comp. also on this whole passage Lightfoot, *Philippians*, p. 203, where he refutes Rothe's interpretation; Baur *Ursprung des Episcopats*, p. 53; Ewald, *Gesch. des Volkes Israel*, VII. 300; Ritschl, *Altkath. K.* 358 and 413, and Hilgenfeld, *Apost. Väter*, 70.

clusive, since most of the apostles died before the destruction of Jerusalem. It could only apply to John, who was the living centre of the church in Asia Minor to the close of the first century.[1]

II. The theory of the POST-APOSTOLIC origin of the episcopate as a *separate* office or order, and its rise out of the presidency of the original congregational presbyterate, by way of human, though natural and necessary, development, is supported by the following facts:

(1) The undeniable identity of presbyters and bishops in the New Testament,[2] conceded even by the best interpreters among the church fathers, by Jerome, Chrysostom, and Theodoret, and by the best scholars of recent times.

(2) Later, at the close of the first and even in the second century, the two terms are still used in like manner for the same office. The Roman bishop Clement, in his First Epistle to the Corinthians says, that the apostles, in the newly-founded churches, appointed the first fruits of the faith, *i. e.*, the first converts, "bishops and deacons."[3] He here omits the πρεσβύτεροι, as Paul does in Phil. 1: 1, for the simple reason that they are in his view identical with ἐπίσκοποι; while conversely, in c. 57, he enjoins subjection to presbyters, without mentioning bishops.[4]

---

[1] Hence Rothe traces the institution to John. And Bishop Lightfoot (*Philippians*, p. 204) is inclined to this view: "Asia Minor was the nurse, if not the mother of episcopacy in the Gentile churches. So important an institution, developed in a Christian community of which St. John was the living centre and guide, could hardly have grown up without his sanction: and early tradition very distinctly connects his name with the appointment of bishops in these parts." He repeats the same view more confidently in his *Ignat. and Polyc.*, I. 377.

[2] Acts 20: 17, 28; Phil. 1: 1; Tit. 1: 5; 1 Tim. 3: 1–7, 8–13; 1 Pet. 5: 1, 2. Comp. the author's *Hist. of the Apost. Ch.* §§ 132, 133, pp. 522–531 (N. York ed.); and vol. I. p. 492 sqq.

[3] C. 42. Comp. the Commentary of Lightfoot. "It is impossible that he should have omitted the presbyters, more especially as his one object is to defend their authority, which had been assailed. The words ἐπίσκοπος and πρεσβύτερος therefore are synonymes in Clement, as they are in the apostolic writers. In Ignatius and Polycarp they first appear as distinct titles."

[4] The ἡγούμενοι, c. 1, also, and the προηγούμενοι, c. 21, are not bishops, but congregational officers collectively, as in Heb. 13 : 7, 17, 24.

The *Didache* mentions bishops and deacons, but no presbyters.[1] Clement of Alexandria distinguishes, it is true, the deaconate, the presbyterate, and the episcopate; but he supposes only a two-fold official character, that of presbyters, and that of deacons—a view which found advocates so late as the middle ages, even in pope Urban II., A. D. 1091. Lastly, Irenæus, towards the close of the second century, though himself a bishop, makes only a relative difference between *episcopi* and *presbyteri;* speaks of successions of the one in the same sense as of the other; terms the office of the latter *episcopatus;* and calls the bishops of Rome "presbyters."[2] Sometimes, it is true, he appears to use the term "presbyters" in a more general sense, for the old men, the fathers.[3] But in any case his language shows that the distinction between the two offices was at that time still relative and indefinite.

(3) The express testimony of the learned Jerome, that the churches originally, before divisions arose through the instigation of Satan, were governed by the common council of the presbyters, and not till a later period was one of the presbyters placed at the head, to watch over the church and suppress schisms.[4] He traces the difference of the office simply to "ecclesiastical" custom as distinct from divine institution.[5]

(4) The custom of the church of Alexandria, where, from the evangelist Mark down to the middle of the third century, the twelve presbyters elected one of their number president, and called him bishop. This fact rests on the authority of Je-

[1] Ch. 15 : Χειροτονήσατε ἑαυτοῖς ἐπισκόπους καὶ διακόνους. See Schaff's monograph on the *Didache*, p. 211 sq.

[2] *Adv. Haer.* iii. 2, ? 2 ; 3, ? 2 ; iv. 26, ? 2, ? 4 and ? 5. Comp. also the letter of Irenæus to the Roman bishop Victor in Euseb., v. 24.

[3] Comp. 2 Jno. 1. and 3 Jno. 1.

[4] *Ad Titum* i. 7. Comp. *Epist.* 83 and 85.

[5] *Ad Tit.* i. 7 : "*Sicut ergo presbyteri sciunt, see ex ecclesiæ consuetudine ei, qui sibi præpositus fuerit, esse subjectos, ita episcopi noverint, se magis consuetudine quam dispositionis Dominicæ veritate presbyteris esse majores et in commune debere ecclesiam regere.*" The Roman deacon Hilary (Ambrosiaster) says, *ad* 1 *Tim.* 3: 10: "*Hic enim episcopus est, qui inter presbyteros primus est.*" Comp. also Chrysostom *Hom.* xi. *in Epist,* 1 *ad Tim.* 3: 8.

rome,[1] and is confirmed independently by the Annals of the Alexandrian patriarch, Eutychius, of the tenth century.[2] The latter states that Mark instituted in that city a patriarch (this is an anachronism) and twelve presbyters, who should fill the vacant patriarchate by electing and *ordaining* to that office one of their number and then electing a new presbyter, so as always to retain the number twelve. He relates, moreover, that down to the time of Demetrius, at the end of the second century, there was no bishop in Egypt besides the one at Alexandria; consequently there could have been no episcopal ordination except by going out of the province.

III. CONCLUSION. The only satisfactory conclusion from these various facts and traditions seems to be, that the episcopate proceeded, both in the descending and ascending scale, from the apostolate and the original presbyterate conjointly, as a contraction of the former and an expansion of the latter, without either express concert or general regulation of the apostles, neither of which, at least, can be historically proved. It arose, instinctively, as it were, in that obscure and critical transition period between the end of the first and the middle of the second century. It was not a sudden creation, much less the invention of a single mind. It grew, in part, out of the general demand for a continuation of, or substitute for, the

---

[1] *Epist. ad Evangelum* (*Opp.* iv. p. 802, ed. **Martinay**): *Alexandriœ a Marco evangelista usque ad Heraclam et Dionysium episcopos presbyteri semper unum ex se electum in excelsiori gradu collocatum episcopum nominabant, quomodo si exercitus imperatorem faciat, aut diaconi elegant de se, quem industrium noverint et archidiaconum vocent.*

[2] Ed. Oxon. 1658, p. 331: "*Constituit evangelista Marcus una cum Hakania patriarcha duodecim presbyteros, qui nempe cum patriarcha manerent, adeo ut eum vacaret patriachatus, unum e duodecim presbyteris eligerent, cnius capiti reliqui undecim manus imponentes ipsi benedicerent et patriarcham crearent, deinde virum aliquem insignem eligerent, quem secum presbyterum constituerent, loco ejus, qui factus est patriarcha, ut ita semper exstarent duodecim. Neque desiit Alexandriae institutum hoc de presbyteris, ut scilcet patriarchas crearent ex presbyteris duodecim, usque ad tempora Alexandri patriarchae Alexandriae. Is autem vetuit, ne deinceps patriarcham presbyteri crearent. Et decrervit, ut mortuo patriarcha convenient episcopi, qui patriarcham ordinarent.*"

apostolic church government, and this, so far as it was trans-
missible at all, very naturally passed first to the most eminent
disciples and fellow-laborers of the apostles, to Mark, Luke,
Timothy, Clement, Ignatius, Polycarp, Papias, which accounts
for the fact that tradition makes them all bishops in the prominent sense of the term. It was further occasioned by the need
of a unity in the presbyterial government of congregations,
which, in the nature of the case and according to the analogy
of the Jewish ἀρχισυνάγωγος,[1] required a head or president.
This president was called bishop, at first only by eminence, as
primus inter pares; afterwards in the exclusive sense. In the
smaller churches there was, perhaps, from the beginning, only
one presbyter, who of himself formed this centre, like the
chorepiscopi or country-bishops in the fourth century. The
dioceses of the bishops in Asia Minor and North Africa, owing
to their large number, in the second and third centuries, can
hardly have exceeded the extent of respectable pastoral charges.
James of Jerusalem, on the other hand, and his immediate
successors, whose positions in many respects were altogether
peculiar, seem to have been the only bishops in Palestine.
Somewhat similar was the state of things in Egypt, where,
down to Demetrius (A. D. 190–232), we find only the one bishop
of Alexandria.

We cannot therefore assume any strict uniformity. But the
whole church spirit of the age tended towards centralization;
it everywhere felt a demand for compact, solid unity; and this
inward bent, amidst the surrounding dangers of persecution and
heresy, carried the church irresistibly towards the episcopate.
In so critical and stormy a time, the principle, union is strength,
division is weakness, prevailed over all. In fact, the existence
of the church at that period may be said to have depended in a
great measure on the preservation and promotion of unity, and
that in an outward, tangible form, suited to the existing grade
of culture. Such a unity was offered in the bishop, who held a

[1] Mark 5: 35, 36, 38; Luke 8: 41–49; Acts 18: 8–17.

monarchical, or more properly a patriarchal relation to the congregation. In the bishop was found the visible representative of Christ, the great Head of the whole church. In the bishop, therefore, all sentiments of piety found a centre. In the bishop the whole religious posture of the people towards God and towards Christ had its outward support and guide. And in proportion as every church pressed towards a single centre, this central personage must acquire a peculiar importance and subordinate the other presbyters to itself; though, at the same time, as the language of Clement and Irenæus, the state of things in Egypt, and even in North Africa, and the testimony of Jerome and other fathers, clearly prove, the remembrance of the original equality could not be entirely blotted out, but continued to show itself in various ways.

Besides this there was also a powerful practical reason for elevating the powers of the bishop. Every Christian congregation was a charitable society, regarding the care of the widow and orphan, the poor and the stranger as a sacred trust; and hence the great importance of the bishop as the administrative officer by whom the charitable funds were received and the alms disbursed. In Greek communities the title bishop (ἐπίσκοπος, ἐπιμελιτής) was in wide use for financial officers. Their administrative functions brought them in close relation to the deacons, as their executive aids in the care of the poor and sick. The archdeacon became the right arm, the "eye" and "heart" of the bishop. In primitive times every case of poverty or suffering was separately brought to the notice of the bishop and personally relieved by a deacon. Afterwards institutions were founded for widows and orphans, poor and infirm, and generally placed under the superintendence of the bishop; but personal responsibility was diminished by this organized charity, and the deacons lost their original significance and became subordinate officers of public worship.[1]

---

[1] The philanthropic and financial aspect of episcopacy has been brought out very fully by Hatch, in his Bampton Lectures on *The Organization of the Early Christian Churches*, Lect. II.

Whatever may be thought, therefore, of the origin and the divine right of the episcopate, no impartial historian can deny its adaptation to the wants of the church at the time, and its historical necessity.

But, then, this primitive catholic episcopal system must by no means be confounded with the later hierarchy. The dioceses, excepting those of Jerusalem, Ephesus, Alexandria, Antioch, and Rome, must have long remained very small, if we look at the number of professing Christians. In the Apocalypse seven such centres of unity are mentioned within a comparatively small compass in Asia Minor, and at a time when the number of Christians was insignificant. In the year 258, Cyprian assembled a council of eighty-seven bishops of North Africa. The functions of the bishops were not yet strictly separated from those of the presbyters, and it was only by degrees that ordination, and, in the Western church, confirmation also, came to be intrusted exclusively to the bishops.

§ 45. *Development of the Episcopate. Ignatius.*

It is matter of fact that the episcopal form of government was universally established in the Eastern and Western church as early as the middle of the second century. Even the heretical sects, at least the Ebionites, as we must infer from the commendation of the episcopacy in the pseudo-Clementine literature, were organized on this plan, as well as the later schismatic parties of Novatians, Donatists, etc. But it is equally undeniable, that the episcopate reached its complete form only step by step. In the period before us we must note three stages in this development connected with the name of Ignatius in Syria (d. 107 or 115), Irenæus in Gaul (d. 202), and Cyprian in North Africa (d. 258).

The episcopate first appears, as distinct from the presbyterate, but as a congregational office only (in distinction from the diocesan idea), and as yet a young institution, greatly needing commendation, in the famous seven (or three) Epistles of Ignatius of Antioch, a disciple of the apostles, and the second bishop of that see (Evodius being the first, and Hero the third). He is also the first who uses the term " *catholic church*," as if episcopacy and catholicity sprung up simultaneously. The whole story of Ignatius is more legendary than real, and his writings are subject to grave suspicion of fraudulent interpolation. We have three different versions of the Ignatian Epistles, but only one of them can be genuine; either the smaller Greek version, or the lately discovered Syriac.[1] In the latter, which contains only three epistles, most of the passages on the episcopate are wanting, indeed; yet the leading features of the institution appear even here, and we can recognise *ex ungue leonem.*[2] In any case they reflect the public sentiment before the middle of the second century.

The substance of these epistles (with the exception of that to the Romans, in which, singularly enough, not a word is said about bishops[3]), consists of earnest exhortations to obey the

---

[1] The question of the genuineness will be discussed in § 165 (p. 660). Cureton (1845) Bunsen, Lipsius, and others accept the Syriac version as the original form of the Ignatian epistles, and regard even the short Greek text as corrupt, but yet as dating from the middle of the second century. Rothe, Hefele, Schaff (first ed.), Düsterdieck, Uhlhorn, Zahn, Harnack, defend the genuineness of the shorter Greek recension. The larger Greek recension is universally given up as spurious. The origin of the hierarchical system is obscured by pious frauds. See below, §§ 164 and 165.

[2] In the Syriac Ep. to *Polycarp*, the word *bishop* occurs four times; in the Syriac Ep. to the *Ephesians*, God is blessed for having given them such a bishop as Onesimus. In the shorter Greek Ep. to *Polycarp* episcopacy is mentioned in the salutation, and in three of the eight chapters (ch. 5 twice, ch. 6 twice, ch. 8 once). In the 21 chapters of the Greek Ep. to the *Ephesians*, the word *bishop* occurs thirteen times, *presbyter* three times, and *deacon* once (in the first six chapters, and ch. 21). In the Greek *Trallians*, the bishop appears nine times; in the *Magnesians*, eleven times; in the *Philadelphians*, eight times; in the *Smyrnœans*, nine times. Thus in the three Syriac Epistles the bishop is mentioned but six times; in the seven shorter Greek Epistles about fifty times; but one of the strongest passages is found in the Syriac Epistle to *Polycarp* (ch. 5. and 6.).

[3] Except that Ignatius speaks of himself as " the bishop of Syria," who " has found favor with God, being sent from the East to the West" (ch. 2). The verb ἐπισκοπέω is also used, but of Christ (ch. 9).

bishop and maintain the unity of the church against the Judaistic and docetic heresies.   With the near prospect and the most
ardent desire for martyrdom, the author has no more fervent
wish than the perfect inward and outward unity of the faithful; and to this the episcopate seems to him indispensable.   In
his view Christ is the invisible supreme head, the one great
universal bishop of all the churches scattered over the earth.
The human bishop is the centre of unity for the single congregation, and stands in it as the vicar of Christ and even of God.[1]
The people, therefore, should unconditionally obey him, and do
nothing without his will.   Blessed are they who are one with
the bishop, as the church is with Christ, and Christ with the
Father, so that all harmonizes in unity.   Apostasy from the
bishop is apostasy from Christ, who acts in and through the
bishops as his organs.

We shall give passages from the shorter Greek text (as edited
by Zahn):

"If any one is able to continue in purity (ἐν ἁγνείᾳ, i. e., in the
state of celibacy), to the honor of the flesh of our Lord, let him
continue so without boasting; if he boasts, he is lost (ἀπώλετο);
if he become known more than the bishop,[2] he is corrupt
(ἔφθαρται).   It is becoming, therefore, to men and women who
marry, that they marry by the counsel of the bishop, that the
marriage may be in the Lord, and not in lust.   Let every thing
be done for the honor of God.   Look to the bishop, that God
also [may look] upon you.   I will be in harmony with those
who are subject to the bishop, and the presbyters, and the
deacons; with them may I have a portion near God!"   This
passage is one of the strongest, and occurs in the Syriac Epistle
to Polycarp as well as in the shorter Greek recension.[3]   It
characteristically connects episcopacy with celibacy: the as-

[1] Ἐπίσκοπος εἰς τόπον θεοῦ προκαθήμενος, each bishop being thus a sort of pope.

[2] Zahn reads, *Ad Polyc.* cap. 5: ἐὰν γνωσθῇ πλέον τοῦ ἐπισκόπου, *i. e.* if he be
better known or more esteemed than the bishop.   The other reading is, πλήν,
beyond, or apart from.

[3] *Ad Polyc.* cap. 5 and 6.   The Greek text varies but little from the Syriac.

cetic system of Catholicism starts in celibacy, as the hierarchical organization of Catholicism takes its rise in episcopacy. " It becomes you to be in harmony with the mind (or sentence, γνώμη) of the bishop, as also ye do. For your most estimable presbytery, worthy of God, is fitted to the bishop as the strings are to the harp."¹ " It is evident that we should look upon the bishop as we do upon the Lord himself."² " I exhort you that ye study to do all things with a divine concord: the bishop presiding in the place of God (εἰς τόπον θεοῦ), and presbyters in the place of the college of the apostles, (εἰς τόπον συνεδρίου τῶν ἀποστόλων), and the deacons, most dear to me, being intrusted with the ministry (διακονίαν) of Jesus Christ, who was with the Father before all ages, and in the end appeared to us."³ " Be subject to the bishop, and to one another, as Christ [was subject] to the Father according to the flesh, and the apostles to Christ and to the Father and to the Spirit, in order that the union be carnal (σαρκική), as well as spiritual."⁴ " It is necessary, as is your habit, to do nothing without the bishop, and that ye should be subject also to the presbytery (τῷ πρεσβυτερίῳ), as to the apostles of Jesus Christ."⁵ " As many as are of God and of Jesus Christ, are also with their bishop."⁶ " Let all of you follow the bishop, as Jesus Christ [follows] the Father; and the presbytery as ye would the apostles; and reverence the deacons as the ordinance of God. Without the bishop let no one do anything connected with the church. Let that eucharist be accounted valid which is [offered] under the bishop or by one he has appointed. Wherever the bishop is found, there let the people be; as wherever Christ is, there is the *catholic* church.

---

¹ *Ad Ephes.* c. 4: Ὅυτως συνήρμοσται τῷ ἐπισκόπῳ, ὡς χορδαὶ κιθάρᾳ.

² *Ad Ephes.* c. 6: Τὸν οὖν ἐπίσκοπον δῆλον ὅτι ὡς αὐτὸν τὸν κύριον δεῖ προσβλέπειν.

³ *Ad Magnes.* c. 6.

⁴ *Ibid.* c. 13. The desire for "carnal" unity is significant.

⁵ *Ad Trallian.* c. 2: Ἀναγκαῖον ἐστὶν, ὥσπερ ποιεῖτε, ἄνευ τοῦ ἐπισκόπου μηδὲν πράσσειν ὑμᾶς, κ. τ. λ.

⁶ *Ad Philad.* c. 3.

Without the bishop it is not lawful either to baptize or to celebrate a love-feast."[1]

This is the first time that the term "catholic" is applied to the church, and that episcopacy is made a condition of catholicity.

"He that honors the bishop, shall be honored by God; he that does anything without the knowledge of the bishop serves the devil."[2]

This is making salvation pretty much depend upon obedience to the bishop; just as Leo I., three centuries later, in the controversy with Hilary of Arles, made salvation depend upon obedience to the pope by declaring every rebel against the pope to be a servant of the devil! Such daring superabundance of episcopalianism clearly betrays some special design and raises the suspicion of forgery or large interpolations. But it may also be explained as a special pleading for a novelty which to the mind of the writer was essential to the very existence of the church.

The peculiarity in this Ignatian view is that the bishop appears in it as the head and centre of a *single congregation*, and not as equally the representative of the whole church; also, that (as in the pseudo-Clementine Homilies) he is the *vicar of Christ*, and not, as in the later view, merely the successor of the apostles,—the presbyters and deacons around him being represented as those successors; and finally, that there are no distinctions of order among the bishops, no trace of a primacy; all are fully *coördinate* vicars of Christ, who provides for himself in them, as it were, a sensible, perceptible omnipresence in the church. The Ignatian episcopacy, in short, is congregational, not diocesan; a new and growing institution, not a settled policy of apostolic origin.

---

[1] *Ad. Smyrn.* c. 8: "Ὅπου ἂν φανῇ ὁ ἐπίσκοπος, ἐκεῖ τὸ πλῆθος ἔστω, ὥσπερ ὅπου ἂν ᾖ Χριστὸς Ἰησοῦς, ἐκεῖ ἡ καθολικὴ ἐκκλησία.

[2] *Ad Smyrn.* c. 9: Ὁ τιμῶν ἐπίσχοπον ὑπὸ θεοῦ τετίμηται· ὁ λάθρα ἐπισκόπου τι πράσσων τῷ διαβόλῳ λατρεύει.

§ 46. *Episcopacy at the time of Irenæus and Tertullian.*

In all these points the idea of the episcopate in Irenæus, the great opponent of Gnosticism (about 180), is either lower or higher. This father represents the institution as a diocesan office, and as the continuation of the apostolate, as the vehicle of the catholic tradition, and the support of doctrinal unity in opposition to heretical vagaries. He exalts the bishops of the original apostolic churches, above all the church of Rome, and speaks with great emphasis of an unbroken episcopal succession as a test of apostolic teaching and a bulwark against heresy.[1]

At the same time the wavering terminology of Irenæus in the interchangeable use of the words "bishop" and "presbyter" reminds us of Clement of Rome, and shows that the distinction of the two orders was not yet fully fixed.[2]

---

[1] Comp. *Adv. Hær.* III. 3, § 1, 2; 4, 1; IV. 33, § 8. I remember what great stress the late Dr. Pusey, when I saw him at Oxford in 1844, laid on the testimony of Irenæus for the doctrine of an unbroken episcopal succession, as the indispensable mark of a genuine Catholic church ; while he ignored the simultaneous growth of the primacy, which a year afterwards carried his friend, J. H. Newman, over to the church of Rome. The New Testament is the only safe guide and ultimate standard in all matters of faith and discipline. The teaching of Irenæus on episcopacy is well set forth by Lightfoot (*l. c.* p. 237): "Irenæus followed Ignatius after an interval of about two generations. With the altered circumstances of the Church, the aspect of the episcopal office has also undergone a change. The religious atmosphere is now charged with heretical speculations of all kinds. Amidst the competition of rival teachers, all eagerly bidding for support, the perplexed believer asks for some decisive test by which he may try the claims of disputants. To this question Irenæus supplies an answer. 'If you wish,' he argues, ' to ascertain the doctrine of the Apostles, apply to the Church of the Apostles.' In the succession of bishops tracing their descent from the primitive age and appointed by the Apostles themselves, you have a guarantee for the transmission of the pure faith, which no isolated, upstart, self-constituted teacher can furnish. There is the Church of Rome for instance, whose episcopal pedigree is perfect in all its links, and whose earliest bishops, Linus and Clement, associated with the Apostles themselves : there is the Church of Smyrna again, whose bishop Polycarp, the disciple of St. John, died only the other day. Thus the episcopate is regarded now not so much as the *centre of ecclesiastical unity*, but rather as the *depositary of apostolic tradition*."

[2] Comp. *Adv. Haer.* III. 2, § 2; IV. 26; V. 20; and his letter to Victor of Rome in Eusebius, *H. E.* V. 24.

The same view of the episcopal succession as the preserver of apostolic tradition and guardian of orthodox doctrine, we find also, though less frequently, in the earlier writings of Tertullian, with this difference that he uniformly and clearly distinguishes bishops and presbyters, and thus proves a more advanced state of the episcopal polity at his time (about 200).[1] But afterwards, in the chiliastic and democratic cause of Montanism, he broke with the episcopal hierarchy, and presented against it the antithesis that the church does not consist of bishops, and that the laity are also priests.[2]

§ 47. *Cyprianic Episcopacy.*

The old catholic episcopalianism reached its maturity in the middle of the third century in the teaching and example of Cyprian, bishop and martyr of the church in North Africa. He represents the claims of episcopacy in close connection with the idea of a special priesthood and sacrifice.[3] He is the typical high-churchman of the ante-Nicene age. He vigorously put into practice what he honestly believed. He had a good opportunity to assert his authority in the controversy about the lapsed during the Decian persecution, in the schism of Felicissimus, and in the controversy on heretical baptism.

Cyprian considers the bishops as the bearers of the Holy Spirit, who passed from Christ to the apostles, from them by ordination to the bishops, propagates himself in an unbroken line of succession, and gives efficacy to all religious exercises. Hence they are also the pillars of the unity of the church; nay, in a certain sense they are the church itself. "The bishop,"

---

[1] *De Praescr. Hær.* c. 32, 36.

[2] *Non ecclesia numerus episcoporum.* *De Pudic.* c. 21. Comp. § 42, p. 128.

[3] "As Cyprian crowned the edifice of episcopal power, so also was he the first to put forward without relief or disguise the sacerdotal assumptions; and so uncompromising was the tone in which he asserted them, that nothing was left to his successors but to enforce his principles and reiterate his language." Lightfoot *l. c.* p. 257. "If with Ignatius the bishop is the centre of Christian unity, if with Irenæus he is the depository of apostolic tradition, with Cyprian he is the *absolute vicegerent of Christ* in things spiritual." *Ibid.* p. 238.

says he, " is in the church, and the church in the bishop, and if any one is not with the bishop he is not in the church." [1] And this is the same with him as to say, he is no Christian. Cyprian is thoroughly imbued with the idea of the solidary unity of the episcopate,—the many bishops exercising only one office *in solidum*, each within his diocese, and each at the same time representing in himself the whole office.[2]

But with all this, the bishop still appears in Cyprian in the closest connexion with the presbyters. He undertook no important matter without their advice. The fourth general council, at Carthage, A.D. 398, even declared the sentence of a bishop, without the concurrence of the lower clergy, void, and decreed that in the ordination of a presbyter, all the presbyters, with the bishop, should lay their hands on the candidate.[3]

The ordination of a bishop was performed by the neighboring bishops, requiring at least three in number. In Egypt, however, so long as there was but one bishop there, presbyters must have performed the consecration, which Eutychius [4] and Hilary the Deacon [5] expressly assert was the case.

§ 48. *The Pseudo-Clementine Episcopacy.*

Besides this orthodox or catholic formation of the episcopate, the kindred monarchical hierarchy of the Ebionitic sect deserves attention, as it meets us in the pseudo-Clementine Homilies. Chronologically this falls in the middle of the second century, between Ignatius and Irenæus, and forms a sort

---

[1] *Epist.* lxvi. 3. Comp. *Ep.* lv. 20 : *Christianus non est, qui in Christi ecclesia non est.*

[2] *De Unit. Eccl.* c. 5 : *Episcopatus unus est, cujus a singulis in solidum pars tenetur.* Comp. *Ep.* lv. 20 : *Quum sit a Christo una ecclesia per totum mundum in multa membra divisa, item episcopatus unus episcoporum multorum concordi numerositate diffusus.*

[3] Can. 3 : *Presbyter quum ordinatur, episcopo eum benedicente et manum super caput ejus tenente, etiam omnes presbyteri, qui praesentes sunt, manus suas juxta manum episcopi super caput illius teneant.*

[4] *Eutychii Patriarchæ Alexandr. Annal. interpr. Pocockio* (Oxon. 1658, I. p. 331). See the passage quoted, p. 141.

[5] Or Ambrosiaster, *Ad Eph.* iv. 11.

of transition from the former to the latter; though it cannot exactly be said to have influenced the Catholic church. It is rather a heretical counterpart of the orthodox episcopate. The organization which consolidated the Catholic church answered the same purpose for a sect. The author of the pseudo-Clementina, like Ignatius, represents the bishop as the vicar of Christ,[1] and at the same time, according to the view of Irenæus, as the vicar and successor of the apostles;[2] but outstrips both in his high hierarchical expressions, such as κάθεδρα θρόνος τοῦ ἐπισκόπου, and in his idea of the primacy, or of a universal church monarchy, which he finds, however, not as Irenæus suggests and Cyprian more distinctly states, in Peter and the Roman see, but, agreeably to his Judaistic turn, in James of Jerusalem, the "bishop of bishops."[3]

The Manichæans had likewise a hierarchical organization (as the Mormons in modern times).

Montanism, on the other hand, was a democratic reaction against the episcopal hierarchy in favor of the general priesthood, and the liberty of teaching and prophesying, but it was excommunicated and died out, till it reappeared under a different form in Quakerism.

§ 49. *Beginnings of the Metropolitan and Patriarchal Systems.*

Though the bishops were equal in their dignity and powers as successors of the apostles, they gradually fell into different ranks, according to the ecclesiastical and political importance of their several districts.

1. On the lowest level stood the bishops of the country churches, the *chorepiscopi* who, though not mentioned before the beginning of the fourth century, probably originated at an earlier period.[4] They stood between the presbyters and the city

---

[1] *Hom.* iii. 60, 62, 66, 70.   *Ep. Clem. ad Jac.* 17.   Comp. *Recogn.* iii. 66.

[2] *Hom.* xi. 36; *Recogn.* iii. 66; vi. 15.

[3] Ἐπίσκοπος ἐπισκόπων, *Hom.* xi. 35; *Recogn.* iv. 35.

[4] The country bishops (χωρεπίσκοποι) appear first in the councils of Ancyra and Neo-Cæsarea, 314, and again in the Council of Nicæa. They continued to

bishops, and met the wants of episcopal supervision in the villages of large dioceses in Asia Minor and Syria, also in Gaul.

2. Among the city bishops the *metropolitans* rose above the rest, that is, the bishops of the capital cities of the provinces.[1] They presided in the provincial synods, and, as *primi inter pares*, ordained the bishops of the province. The metropolitan system appears, from the Council of Nicæa in 325, to have been already in operation at the time of Constantine and Eusebius, and was afterwards more fully carried out in the East. In North Africa the oldest bishop, hence called *senex*, stood as primas, at the head of his province; but the bishop of Carthage enjoyed the highest consideration, and could summon general councils.

3. Still older and more important is the distinction of *apostolic mother-churches*,[2] such as those at Jerusalem, Antioch, Alexandria, Ephesus, Corinth, and Rome. In the time of Irenæus and Tertullian they were held in the highest regard, as the chief bearers of the pure church tradition. Among these Antioch, Alexandria, and Rome were most prominent, because they were the capitals respectively of the three divisions (*eparchiæ*) of the Roman empire, and centres of trade and intercourse, combining with their apostolic origin the greatest political weight. To the bishop of Antioch fell all Syria as his metropolitan district; to the bishop of Alexandria, all Egypt; to the bishop of Rome, central and lower Italy, without definite boundaries.

4. Here we have the germs of the *eparchal* or *patriarchal* system, to which the Greek church to this day adheres. The name *patriarch* was at first, particularly in the East, an honorary title for all bishops, and was not till the fourth century exclusively

exist in the East till the 9th century, when they were superseded by the exarchs (ἔξαρχοι). In the West, the *chorepiscopi* performed regular episcopal functions, without proper subordination to the diocesans, and hence excited jealousy and hostility till the office was abolished under Charlemagne, and continued only as a title of various cathedral dignitaries. See Haddan in Smith & Cheetham, *Dict. Chr. Ant.* I. 354, and the authorities quoted there.

1 Μητροπόλεις. Hence μητροπολῖται.

2 *Sedes apostolicæ, matrices ecclesiæ.*

appropriated to the bishops of the three ecclesiastical and political capitals of the Roman empire, Antioch, Alexandria and Rome, and also to the bishop of Jerusalem *honoris causa,* and the bishop of Constantinople or New Rome. So in the West the term *papa* afterwards appropriated by the Roman bishop, as *summus pontifex, vicarius Christi,* was current for a long time in a more general application.

§ 50. *Germs of the Papacy.*

Comp. the Lit. in vol. I. ₹ 25 (p. 245).

BLONDEL: *Traité historique de la primauté en l'église.* Genéve, 1641.

SALMASIUS: *De Primatu Papœ.* Lugd. Bat. 1645.

IS. BARROW: *The Pope's Supremacy.* Lond. 1680 (new ed. Oxf. 1836. N. York, 1845).

ROTHENSEE (R. C.): *Der Primat Des Papstes in allen christlichen Jahrhunderten,* 3 vols. Mainz, 1836–38 (I. 1–98).

KENRICK (R. C., archbishop of Baltimore, d. 1853): *The Primacy of the Apostolic See vindicated.* N. York, 4th ed. 1855.

R. I. WILBERFORCE (formerly archdeacon in the Anglican church; died in the Roman church, 1857): *An Inquiry into the Principles of Church Authority; or Reasons for Recalling my subscriptions to the Royal Supremacy.* Lond. 1854 (ch. vi.–x.).

J. E. RIDDLE: *The History of the Papacy to the Period of the Reformation.* Lond. 1856. 2 vols. (Chapter 1, p. 2–113; chiefly taken from Schröckh and Planck).

THOMAS GREENWOOD: *Cathedra Petri. A Political History of the great Latin Patriarchate.* Lond. 1856–1872. 6 vols. Vol. I. ch. I.–VI. (A work of independent and reliable learning.)

JOH. FRIEDRICH (Old Cath.): *Zur ältesten Geschichte des Primates in der Kirche.* Bonn, 1879.

E. RENAN: *Conferences d'Angleterre. Rome et le christianisme.* Paris 1880. The Hibbert Lectures delivered in Lond. 1880. English translation by *Charles Beard,* London (Williams & Norgate) 1880, another by *Erskine Clement* (Boston, 1880). Consists mostly of extracts from his books on the Origin of Christianity, skillfully put together.

H. FORMBY (R. C.): *Ancient Rome and its connection with the Christian Religion.* London 1880.

JOS. LANGEN (Old Cath.): *Geschichte der römischen Kirche bis zum Pontificate Leo's I.* Bonn, 1881.

R. F. LITTLEDALE (Anglo-Cath.): *The Petrine Claims. A Critical Inquiry.* London 1889. Controversial.

Among the great bishops of Antioch, Alexandria, and Rome, the Roman bishop combined all the conditions for a primacy, which, from a purely honorary distinction, gradually became the basis of a supremacy of jurisdiction. The same propension to monarchical unity, which created out of the episcopate a centre, first for each congregation, then for each diocese, pressed on towards a visible centre for the whole church. Primacy and episcopacy grew together. In the present period we already find the faint beginnings of the papacy, in both its good and its evil features; and with them, too, the first examples of earnest protest against the abuse of its power. In the Nicene age the bishop of Jerusalem was made an honorary patriarch in view of the antiquity of that church, though his diocese was limited; and from the middle of the fourth century the new patriarch of Constantinople or New Rome, arose to the primacy among the eastern patriarchs, and became a formidable rival of the bishop of old Rome.

The Roman church claims not only human but divine right for the papacy, and traces its institution directly to Christ, when he assigned to Peter an eminent position in the work of founding his church, against which even the gates of hades shall never prevail. This claim implies several assumptions, viz. (1) that Peter by our Lord's appointment had not simply a primacy of personal excellency, or of honor and dignity (which must be conceded to him), but also a supremacy of jurisdiction over the other apostles (which is contradicted by the fact that Peter himself never claimed it, and that Paul maintained a position of perfect independence, and even openly rebuked him at Antioch, Gal. 2: 11); (2) that the privileges of this primacy and supremacy are not personal only (as the peculiar gifts of Paul or John undoubtedly were), but official, hereditary and transferable; (3) that they were actually transferred by Peter, not upon the bishop of Jerusalem, or Antioch (where Peter certainly was), but upon the bishop of Rome; (4) that Peter was not only at Rome (which is very probable after 63, though not as certain as Paul's presence and martyrdom in Rome), but acted there as bishop till his martyrdom, and appointed a successor (of which there is not the slightest historical evidence); and (5) that the bishops of Rome, as successors of Peter, have always enjoyed and exercised an universal jurisdiction over the Christian church (which is not the case as a matter of fact, and still less as a matter of conceded right).

Leaving a full discussion of most of these points to polemical theology, we are here concerned with the papacy as a growth of history, and have to examine the causes which have gradually raised it to its towering eminence among the governing institutions of the world.

The historical influences which favored the ascendency of the Roman see were:

(1) The high antiquity of the Roman church, which had been honored even by Paul with the most important doctrinal epistle of the New Testament. It was properly the only apostolic mother-church in the West, and was thus looked upon from the first by the churches of Italy, Gaul, and Spain, with peculiar reverence.

(2) The labors, martyrdom, and burial at Rome of Peter and Paul, the two leading apostles. The whole Roman congregation passed through the fearful ordeal of martyrdom during the Neronian persecution, but must soon afterwards have been reorganized, with a halo of glory arising from the graves of the victims.

(3) The political pre-eminence of that metropolis of the world, which was destined to rule the European races with the sceptre of the cross, as she had formerly ruled them with the sword.

(4) The executive wisdom and the catholic orthodox instinct of the Roman church, which made themselves felt in this period in the three controversies on the time of Easter, the penitential discipline, and the validity of heretical baptism.

To these may be added, as secondary causes, her firmness under persecutions, and her benevolent care for suffering brethren, even in distant places, as celebrated by Dionysius of Corinth (180), and by Eusebius.

From the time of St. Paul's Epistle (58), when he bestowed high praise on the earlier Roman converts, to the episcopate of Victor at the close of the second century, and the unfavorable account by Hippolytus of Pope Zephyrinus and Pope Callistus, we have no express and direct information about the internal state of the Roman church. But incidentally it is more frequently mentioned than any other. Owing to its metropolitan position, it naturally grew in importance and influence with the spread of the Christian religion in the empire. Rome was the battle-field of orthodoxy and heresy, and a resort of all sects and parties. It attracted from every direction what was true and false in philosophy and religion. Ignatius rejoiced in the prospect of suffering for Christ in the centre of the world; Polycarp repaired hither to settle with Anicetus the paschal controversy; Justin Martyr presented there his defense of Christianity to the emperors, and laid down for it his life; Irenæus, Tertullian, and Cyprian conceded to that church a position of singular pre-eminence. Rome was equally sought as a commanding position by heretics and theosophic jugglers, as Simon Magus, Valentine, Marcion, Cerdo, and a host of others. No wonder, then, that the bishops of Rome at an early date were looked upon as metropolitan pastors, and spoke and acted accordingly with an air of authority which reached far beyond their immediate diocese.

Clement of Rome.

The first example of the exercise of a sort of papal authority is found towards the close of the first century in the letter of the Roman bishop Clement (d. 102) to the bereaved and distracted church of Corinth. This epistle, full of beautiful exhortations to harmony, love, and humility, was sent, as the very address shows,[1] not in the bishop's own name, which is not

---

[1] Ἡ ἐκκλησία τοῦ θεοῦ, ἡ παροικοῦσα Ῥώμην τῇ ἐκκλησίᾳ τοῦ θεοῦ, τῇ παροικούσῃ Κόρινθον. "The church of God which sojourns at Rome to the church of God which sojourns at Corinth." Πάροικος is a temporary, κάτοικος a permanent, resident. The Christians appear here as strangers and pilgrims in this world, who have their home in heaven; comp. 1 Pet. 1: 17; 2: 11; Heb. 11: 13.

mentioned at all, but in that of the Roman congregation, which speaks always in the first person plural. It was a service of love, proffered by one church to another in time of need. Similar letters of instruction, warning and comfort were written to other congregations by Ignatius, Polycarp, Dionysius of Corinth, Irenæus. Nevertheless it can hardly be denied that the document reveals the sense of a certain superiority over all ordinary congregations. The Roman church here, without being asked (as far as appears), gives advice, with superior administrative wisdom, to an important church in the East, dispatches messengers to her, and exhorts her to order and unity in a tone of calm dignity and authority, as the organ of God and the Holy Spirit.[1] This is all the more surprising if St. John, as is probable, was then still living in Ephesus, which was nearer to Corinth than Rome. The hierarchical spirit arose from the domineering spirit of the Roman church, rather than the Roman bishop or the presbyters who were simply the organs of the people.[2] But a century later the bishop of Rome was substituted for the church of Rome, when Victor in his *own* name excommunicated the churches of Asia Minor for a trifling difference of ritual. From this hierarchical assumption there was only one step towards the papal absolutism of a Leo and Hildebrand, and this found its ultimate doctrinal climax in the Vatican dogma of papal infallibility.

Ignatius.

Ignatius, in his Epistle to the Romans (even in the Syriac recension), applies to that congregation a number of high-sounding titles, and describes her as "presiding in the place of the

[1] This is very evident towards the close from the newly discovered portions, chs. 59, 62 and 63 (edition of Bryennios, Const. 1875). These chapters shed new light on the origin of the papal domination. Comp. the judicious remarks of Lightfoot in his *Appendix to S. Clement of Rome* (Lond. 1877), p. 252 sqq.

[2] It is quite evident from the Epistle itself that at that time the Roman congregation was still governed by a college of presbyters (*collegialisch, nicht monarchisch*, as Langen, *l. c.* p. 81, expresses it).

region of the Romans," and as "taking the lead in charity."[1] This
is meant as a commendation of her practical benevolence for which
she was famous. Dionysius of Corinth in his letter to Soter of
Rome, testifies to it as saying : " This practice has prevailed with
you from the very beginning, to do good to all the brethren in
every way, and to send contributions to many churches in every
city."[2] The Roman church was no doubt more wealthy than
any other, and the liberal use of her means must have greatly
increased her influence. Beyond this, Ignatius cannot be quoted
as a witness for papal claims. He says not a word of the
primacy, nor does he even mention Clement or any other
bishop of Rome. The church alone is addressed throughout.
He still had a lively sense of the difference between a bishop
and an apostle. " I do not *command* you," he writes to the
Romans, " as if I were Peter or Paul; they were apostles."

Irenæus.

Irenæus calls Rome the greatest, the oldest(?) church, acknowledged by all, founded by the two most illustrious apostles, Peter
and Paul, the church, with which, on account of her more important precedence, all Christendom must agree, or (according to
another interpretation) to which (as the metropolis of the world)
all other churches must resort.[3] The " more important pre-

---

[1] Προκαθημένη τῆς ἀγάπης, *præsidens in caritate.* Inscription. Zahn in his
ed., p. 75, says: " *In caritatis operibus semper primum locum sibi vindicavit ecclesia
Romana.*" Some Roman Catholic writers (as Möhler, *Patrol.* I. 144) explain
the phrase very artificially and hierarchically: "head of the love-union of
Christendom (*Vorsteherin des Liebesbundes).*" *Agape* never means church, but
either love, or love-feast. See Langen, *l. c.* p. 94.

[2] Euseb., *Hist. Eccl.* IV. 23, 10 : ἐξ ἀρχῆς ὑμῖν ἔθος ἐστὶ τοῦτο, πάντας μὲν
ἀδελφοὺς ποικίλως εὐεργετεῖν, ἐκκλησίαις τε πολλαῖς ταῖς ματὰ πᾶσαν πόλιν ἐφόδια
πέμπειν.

[3] The famous passage, *Adv. Haer.* iii. § 2, is only extant in Latin, and of
disputed interpretation : " *Ad hanc enim ecclesiam propter potentiorem* (according
to Massuet's conjecture : *potiorem*) *principalitatem necesse est omnem convenire
ecclesiam, hoc est, eos qui sunt undique fideles, in qua semper ab his, qui sunt
undique, conservata est ab apostolis traditio.*" In the original Greek it probably
read : Πρός ταύτην γὰρ τὴν ἐκκλησίαν διὰ τὴν ἱκανωτέραν πρωτεῖαν συμβαίνειν (or,
in the local sense, συνέρχεσθαι) δεῖ (according to others : ἀνάγκη, natural necessity) πᾶσαν τὴν ἐκκλησίαν, etc. The stress lies on *principalitas*, which stands

cedence" places her above the other apostolic churches, to which likewise a precedence is allowed.

This is surely to be understood, however, as a precedence only of honor, not of jurisdiction. For when Pope Victor, about the year 190, in hierarchical arrogance and intolerance, broke fellow- ship with the churches of Asia Minor, for no other reason but because they adhered to their tradition concerning the celebration of Easter, the same Irenæus, though agreeing with him on the disputed point itself, rebuked him very emphatically as a trou- bler of the peace of the church, and declared himself against a forced uniformity in such unessential matters. Nor did the Asiatic churches allow themselves to be intimidated by the dicta- tion of Victor. They answered the Roman tradition with that of their own *sedes apostolicae.* The difference continued until the council at Nicæa at last settled the controversy in favor of the Roman practice, but even long afterwards the old British churches differed from the Roman practice in the Easter observance to the time of Gregory I.

Hippolytus.

The celebrated Hippolytus, in the beginning of the third century, was a decided antagonist of the Roman bishops, Zephy- rinus and Callistus, both for doctrinal and disciplinary reasons. Nevertheless we learn from his work called *Philosophumena,* that at that time the Roman bishop already claimed an absolute

probably for πρωτεία (so Thiersch and Gieseler). Comp. Iren. IV. 38, 3, where πρωτεύει is rendered *principalitatem habet.* Stieren and Ziegler (*Irenæus,* 1871, p. 152), however, translate *propter potentiorem principalitatem*: οιά τὴν ἱκανωτέραν ἀρχαιότητα, "on account of the higher *antiquity.*" Comp. on the whole passage an essay by Thiersch in the "Studien und Kritiken" 1842, 512 sqq.; Gieseler I. 1. p. 214 (§ 51); Schneemann: *Sancti Irenœi de ecclesiœ Romanœ principatu testimonium commentatum et defensum,* Freiburg i. B. 1870, and Langen, *l. c.* p. 170 sqq. Langen (who is an Old Catholic of the Döllinger school) explains: "*Die potior principalitas bezeichnet den Vorrang, welchen die Kirche der Hauptstadt als solche vor allen übrigen Kirchen besass . . . . die Haupstadt war das Centrum des damaligen Weltverkehrs, und in Folge dessen der Sammelplatz von Christen aller Art.*" He defends the *local* sense of *convenire* by parallel passages from Herveus of Bordeaux and Hugo Eterianus (p. 172 sq.). But the moral sense (*to agree*) seems more natural.

power within his own jurisdiction; and that Callistus, to the great grief of part of the presbytery, laid down the principle, that a bishop can never be deposed or compelled to resign by the presbytery, even though he have committed a mortal sin.

Tertullian.

Tertullian points the heretics to the apostolic mother churches, as the chief repositories of pure doctrine; and among these gives especial prominence to that of Rome, where Peter was crucified, Paul beheaded, and John immersed unhurt in boiling oil (?) and then banished to the island. Yet the same father became afterwards an opponent of Rome. He attacked its loose penitential discipline, and called the Roman bishop (probably Zephyrinus), in irony and mockery, "*pontifex maximus*" and "*episcopus episcoporum.*"

Cyprian.

Cyprian is clearest, both in his advocacy of the fundamental idea of the papacy, and in his protest against the mode of its application in a given case. Starting from the superiority of Peter, upon whom the Lord built his church, and to whom he intrusted the feeding of his sheep, in order to represent thereby the unity in the college of the apostles, Cyprian transferred the same superiority to the Bishop of Rome, as the successor of Peter, and accordingly called the Roman church the chair of Peter, and the fountain of priestly unity,[1] the root, also, and mother of the catholic church.[2] But on the other side, he asserts with equal energy the equality and relative independence of the bishops, as successors of the apostles, who had all an equally direct appointment from Christ. In his correspondence he uniformly addresses the Roman bishop as "brother" and "colleague," conscious of his own equal dignity and authority. And

---

[1] *Petri cathedram atque ecclesiam principalem, unde unitas sacerdotalis exorta est. Epist.* lv. c. 19 (ed. Bal.) *Ad Cornelium episc. Rom.* In Goldhorn's ed., *Ep.* lix. 19.

[2] *Ecclesiae catholicae radicem et matricem.* Ep. xl. 2 ed. Bal. (xlviii. ed. Goldh.). Other passages in Cyrian favorable to the Roman see are either interpolations or corruptions in the interest of the papacy.

in the controversy about heretical baptism, he opposes Pope Stephen with almost Protestant independence, accusing him of error and abuse of his power, and calling a tradition without truth an old error.   Of this protest he never retracted a word.

Firmilian.

Still more sharp and unsparing was the Cappadocian bishop, Firmilian, a disciple of Origen, on the bishop of Rome, while likewise implying a certain acknowledgment of his primacy. Firmilian charges him with folly, and with acting unworthily of his position; because, as the successor of Peter, he ought rather to further the unity of the church than to destroy it, and ought to abide on the rock foundation instead of laying a new one by recognising heretical baptism.   Perhaps the bitterness of Firmilian was due partly to his friendship and veneration for Origen, who had been condemned by a council at Rome.

Nevertheless, on this question of baptism, also, as on those of Easter, and of penance, the Roman church came out victorious in the end.

Comparative Insignificance of the first Popes.

From these testimonies it is clear, that the growing influence of the Roman see was rooted in public opinion and in the need of unity in the ancient church.   It is not to be explained at all by the talents and the ambition of the incumbents.   On the contrary, the personality of the thirty popes of the first three centuries falls quite remarkably into the background; though they are all canonized saints, and, according to a later but extremely doubtful tradition, were also, with two exceptions, martyrs.[1]   Among them, and it may be said down to Leo the Great, about the middle of the fifth century, there was hardly one, perhaps Clement, who

---

[1] Irenæus recognizes among the Roman bishops from Clement to Eleutherus (177), all of whom he mentions by name, only *one* martyr, to wit, Telesphorus, of whom he says: Ὃς καὶ ἐνδόξως ἐμαρτύρησε, *Adv. Haer.* III., c. 3, § 3.   So Eusebius, *H. E.* V. 6.   From this we may judge of the value of the Roman Catholic tradition on this point.   It is so remote from the time in question as to be utterly unworthy of credit.

could compare, as a church leader, with an Ignatius, a Cyprian, and an Ambrose; or, as a theologian, with an Irenæus, a Tertullian, an Athanasius, and an Augustin.[1] Jerome, among his hundred and thirty-six church celebrities, of the first four centuries, brings in only four Roman bishops, Clement, Victor, Cornelius, and Damasus, and even these wrote only a few epistles. Hippolytus, in his *Philosophumena*, written about 225, even presents two contemporaneous popes, St. Zephyrinus (202–218) and Callistus (St. Calixtus I., 218–223), from his own observation, though not without partisan feeling, in a most unfavorable light; charging the first with ignorance and avarice,[2] the second with scandalous conduct (he is said to have been once a swindler and a fugitive slave rescued from suicide), and both of them with the Patripassian heresy. Such charges could not have been mere fabrications with so honorable an author as Hippolytus, even though he was a schismatic rival bishop to Callistus; they must have had at least some basis of fact.

§ 51. *Chronology of the Popes.*

I. SOURCES.

The principal sources for the obscure chronology of the early bishops of Rome are the catalogues of popes. These are divided into two classes, the oriental or Greek, and the occidental or Latin. To the first belong the lists of Hegesippus and Irenæus, from the second century, that of Eusebius (in his *Chronicle*, and his *Church History*), and his successors from the fourth century and later. This class is followed by Lipsius and Harnack. The second class embraces the catalogues of Augustin (*Ep.* 55, al. 165), Optatus of Mileve (*De schism. Donat.* II. 3), the "Catalogus Liberianus" (coming down to Liberius, 354), the "Catalogus Felicianus" (to 530), the

---

[1] Cardinal Newman says (*Apologia*, p. 407): "The see of Rome possessed no great mind in the whole period of persecution. Afterwards for a long time it had not a single doctor to show. The great luminary of the western world is St. Augustin; he, no infallible teacher, has formed the intellect of Europe." Dean Stanley remarks (*Christian Institutions*, p. 241): "There have been occupants of the sees of Constantinople, Alexandria, and Canterbury, who have produced more effect on the mind of Christendom by their utterances than any of the popes."

[2] He calls him in the ninth book of the *Philosophumena* an ἀνήρ ἰδιώτης καὶ αἰσχροκέρδης.

"Catalogus Cononianus," based perhaps on the "Catalogus Leoninus" (to 440), the "Liber Pontificalis" (formerly supposed to be based on the preceding catalogues, but according to the Abbé Duchesne and Waitz, older than the "Liber Felicianus"). The "Liber Pontif." itself exists in different MSS., and has undergone many changes. It is variously dated from the fifth or seventh century.

To these may be added the "Martyrologia" and "Calendaria" of the Roman Church, especially the "Martyrologium Hieronymianum," and the "Martyrologium Romanum parvum" (both of the seventh or eighth century).

The inscriptions on the papal tombs discovered in Rome since 1850, contain names and titles, but no dates.

On the "Catalogus Liberianus," see especially the critical essay of Mommsen " *Ueber den Chronographen des Jahres* 354," in the "Transactions of the Royal Saxon Society of Sciences," Philos. histor. Section, vol. I. (1850), p. 631 sqq. The text of the Catalogue is given, p. 634–'37, and by Lipsius, *Chronologie der röm. Bischöfe*, Append. p. 265–268. The oldest MSS. of the "Liber Pontificalis" date from the seventh and eighth centuries, and present a text of A. D. 641, but with many variations. "*Mit wahrer Sicherheit*," says Waitz, "*gelangen wir in der Geschichte des Papsthums nicht über das 7te Jahrhundert hinauf.*"

II. Works.

Phil. Jaffé: *Regesta Pontificum Romanorum ab condita ecclesia ad ann.* 1198. Berolini 1851, *ed. secunda correcta et aucta auspiciis* Gul. Wattenbach. Lips. 1881 sqq. Continued by Potthast from 1198–1304, and supplemented by Harttung (Bd.I. A. D. 748–1198, Gotha 1880).

R. A. Lipsius: *Chronologie der röm. Bischöfe bis zur Mitte des 4ten Jahrh.* Kiel, 1869. Comp. Hort's review of this book in the "Academy" for Sept. 15, 1871. Lipsius: *Neue Studien zur Papstchronologie,* in the "Jahrbücher für Protest. Theol." Leipz. 1880 (pp. 78–126 and 233–307). Lipsius denies that Peter ever was at Rome.

Abbé L. Duchesne: *Étude sur le Liber Pontificalis.* Paris, 1887. *La date et les recensions du Liber Pontificalis.* 1879. *Le Liber Pontificalis. Texte, introduction et commentaire.* Paris, 1884 and 1889, 2 vols. 4° (with fac similes).

Adolf Harnack: *Die Zeit des Ignatius und die Chronologie der antiochenischen Bischöfe bis Tyrannus.* Leipz. 1878 (p. 73).

G. Waitz: *Ueber die verschiedenen Texte des Liber Pontificalis,* in the " Archiv der Gesellschaft für ältere deutsche Geschichtskunde," IV; and his review of Duchesne, and Lipsius, in H. v. Sybel's " Histor. Zeitschrift" for 1880, p. 135 sqq.

The oldest links in the chain of Roman bishops are veiled in impenetrable darkness. Tertullian and most of the Latins (and the pseudo-Clementina), make Clement (Phil. 4: 3), the first successor of Peter;[1] but Irenæus, Eusebius, and other Greeks, also Jerome and the Roman Catalogue, give him the third place, and put Linus (2 Tim. 4: 21), and Anacletus (or Anincletus), between him and Peter.[2] In some lists Cletus is substituted for Anacletus, in others the two are distinguished. Perhaps Linus and Anacletus acted during the life time of Paul and Peter as assistants, or presided only over one part of the church, while Clement may have had charge of another branch; for at that early day, the government of the congregation composed of Jewish and Gentile Christian elements was not so centralized as it afterwards became. Furthermore, the earliest fathers, with a true sense of the distinction between the apostolic and episcopal offices, do not reckon Peter among the bishops of Rome at all; and the Roman Catalogue in placing Peter in the line of bishops, is strangely regardless of Paul, whose independent labors in Rome are attested not only by tradition, but by the clear witness of his own epistles and the book of Acts.

Lipsius, after a laborious critical comparison of the different catalogues of popes, arrives at the conclusion that Linus, Anacletus, and Clement were Roman presbyters (or presbyter-bishops in the N. T. sense of the term), at the close of the first century, Evaristus and Alexander presbyters at the beginning of the second, Xystus I. (Latinized: Sixtus), presbyter for ten years

---

[1] Or at least the first appointed by Peter. Tertullian *De Praescr. Hær.* c. 32 "*Romanorum Clementem a Petro ordinatum.*" The *Apost. Const.* VII. 6 make Linus (comp. 2 Tim. 4: 21) the first bishop, appointed by Paul, Clement the next, appointed by Peter. According to Epiphanius (*Hær.* XXVII. 6) Clement was ordained by Peter, but did not enter upon his office till after the death of Linus and Anacletus.

[2] The catalogue of Irenæus (*Adv. Hær.* III. 3, 3) down to his own time (A. D. 177) is this: The *apostles* Peter and Paul, Linos, Anacletos, Clement, Evaristus, Alexander, Xystos, Telesphoros, who died gloriously as a martyr, Hyginos, Pios, Aniketos, Soter, Eleutheros, who then held "the inheritance of the episcopate in the twelfth place from the apostles." Irenæus adds: "In this order and by this succession, the ecclesiastical tradition from the apostles and the preaching of the truth have come down to us."

till about 128, Telesphorus for eleven years, till about 139, and his next successors diocesan bishops.[1]

It must in justice be admitted, however, that the list of Roman bishops has by far the preëminence in age, completeness, integrity of succession, consistency of doctrine and policy, above every similar catalogue, not excepting those of Jerusalem, Antioch, Alexandria, and Constantinople; and this must carry great weight with those who ground their views chiefly on external testimonies, without being able to rise to the free Protestant conception of Christianity and its history of development on earth.

§ 51. List of the Roman Bishops and Roman Emperors during the First Three Centuries.

From the lists of Eusebius (till Silvester), Jaffé (Regesta), Potthast (Bibliotheca Hist. Medii Aevi), Lipsius and others compared. See a continuation of the list in my History of Mediæval Christianity, p. 205 sqq.

A. D.	POPES.	EMPERORS.	B. C.
		Augustus,	27
		Tiberius,	A.D. 14–37
		Caligula,	37–41
		Claudius.	41–54
? 42– 67	Petrus-Apostolus.[2]	Nero,	54–68
(63–64)			
? 67– 79	Linus-Presbyter.	Galba, ⎫	68
		Otho, ⎬	
		Vitellius, ⎭	68–69
		Vespasian,	70–79
? 79– 91	Cletus or Anacletus.	Titus,	79–81
		Domitian,	81–96
? 91–100	Clemens I.	Nerva,	96–98
		Trajan,	98–117
?100–109	Evaristus.		
?109–119	Alexander I.	Hadrian,	117–138
?119–128	Xystus or Sixtus I.		
?128–139	Telesphorus (Martyr).	Antoninus Pius,	138–161

[1] Langen (l. c. p. 100 sqq.) carries the line of Roman presbyter-bishops down to Alexander, and dates the monarchical constitution of the Roman church (i. e. the diocesan episcopacy) from the age of Trajan or Hadrian. Irenæus (in Euseb. V. 27) calls the Roman bishops down to Anicetus (154) πρεσβύτεροι.

[2] The best historians agree that Peter cannot have been in Rome before A. D. 63, and that the Roman tradition of a twenty-five years' episcopate is a fable.

A. D.	POPES.	EMPERORS.	B. C.
? 139–142	Hyginus.		
? 142–154	Pius I.		
? 154–168	Anicetus.	Marcus Aurelius,	161–180
? 168–176	Soter.		
? 177–190	Eleutherus.	Commodus,	180–190
? 190–202	Victor I.	Pertinax,	190–191
		Didius Julianus,	191–192
		Niger,	192–193
		Septimius Severus,	193–211
202–218	Zephyrinus.	Caracalla, ⎫	211–217
		Geta (d. 212), ⎭	
		M. Opilius Macrinus,	217–218
218–223	Callistus, or Calixtus I.	Heliogabalus,	218–222
	(Hippolytus, Antipope).		
? 223–230	Urbanus I.	Alexander Severus,	222–235
? 230–235	Pontianus (resigned in exile).		
235–236	Anterus.	Maximin I: (the Thracian),	235–237
236–250	Fabianus, Martyr.	The two Gordians, ⎫	
		Maximus Pupienus, ⎬	237–238
		Balbinus, ⎭	
		Gordian the Younger,	238–244
		Philip,	244–249
250–251	The See vacant till March 251.	Decius,	249–251
? 251–252	Cornelius (in exile).	Gallus.	251–252
? 251	(Novatianus, Antipope).		
252–253	Lucius I.	Volusian,	252–253
? 253–257	Stephanus I.	Æmilian,	253–268
		Valerian,	256–259
		Gallienus.	259–268
? 257–258	Xystus (Sixtus) II.		
Till July 21, 259.	The See vacant.		
259–269	Dionysius.	Claudius II.	268–270
269–274	Felix I.	Aurelian,	270–275
275–283	Eutychianus.	Tacitus,	275–276
		Probus,	276–282
283–296	Gajus (Caius).	Carus,	282–284
		Carinus, ⎫	284–286
		Numerian, ⎭	
		Diocletian (d. 313),	284–305
		Maximian, joint Emp. ⎫	286–305
		with Diocletian, ⎭	
296–304	Marcellinus.	Constantius (d. 306), ⎫	
304–307	The See vacant.	Galerius (d. 311), ⎬	304 or 307
		Licinius (d. 323), ⎭	
		Maximin II. (Daza),	308–309
		Constantine the Great, ⎫	
		Galerius (d. 311), ⎪	
308–309	Marcellus,	Licinius (d. 323), ⎪	309–323
309–310	Eusebius, d. Sept. 26 (?) 309.	Maximin (d. 313), ⎬	
		Maxentius (d. 312), ⎪	
		reigning jointly. ⎭	
309–310	The See vacant.		
311–314	Miltiades (Melchiades)		
314–335	Silvester I.	Constantine the Great, sole ruler.	323–337

The whole number of popes, from the Apostle Peter to Leo XIII. (1878) is two hundred and sixty-three. This would allow about seven years on an average to each papal reign. The traditional twenty-five years of Peter were considered the maximum which none of his successors was permitted to reach, except Pius IX., the first infallible pope, who reigned twenty-seven years (1846–1878). The average term of office of the archbishops of Canterbury is fourteen years.

§ 53. *The Catholic Unity.*

J. A. Möhler (R. C.): *Die Einheit der Kirche oder das Princip des Katholicismus.* Tübingen 1825. Full of Catholic enthusiasm for the unity of the church.

R. Rothe: *Die Anfänge der christl. Kirche.* Wittenb. 1837 (pp. 553–711). A Protestant counterpart of Möhler's book.

Huther: *Cyprian's Lehre von der Einheit der Kirche.* Hamb. 1839.

J. W. Nevin: *Cyprian;* four articles in the "Mercersburg Review," 1852. Comp. Varien's strictures on these articles in the same "Review" for 1853, p. 555 sqq.

Joh. Peters (Ultramontane): *Die Lehre des heil. Cyprian von der Einheit der Kirche gegenüber den beiden Schismen in Carthago und Rom.* Luxemb. 1870.

Jos. H. Reinkens (Old Cath. Bishop): *Die Lehre des heil. Cyprian von der Einheit der Kirche.* Würzburg, 1873.

Comp. also Hartel's ed. of Cyprian's *Opera* (3 Parts, Vienna, 1868–'71), and the monographs on Cyprian by Rettberg (1831), Peters (1877), Fechtrup (1878), and O. Ritschl (1883).

On the basis of Paul's idea of the unity, holiness, and universality of the church, as the mystical body of Christ; hand in hand with the episcopal system of government; in the form of fact rather than of dogma; and in perpetual conflict with heathen persecution from without, and heretical and schismatic tendencies within—arose the idea and the institution of "*the Holy Catholic Church,*" as the Apostles' Creed has it;[1] or, in

---

[1] The Church of England retained the term "catholic" in the Creed, and the ante-papal and anti-papal use of this term (= general, universal); while Luther in his Catechism, and the Moravian church (in her liturgy) substituted the word "Christian," and surrendered the use of "catholic" to the *Roman* Catholics. "Roman" is a sectarian term (in opposition to Greek Catholic and Evangelical Catholic).

the fuller language of the Nicene-Constantinopolitan, " the *One Holy Catholic Apostolic Church.*" In both the œcumenical symbols, as even in the more indefinite creeds of the second and third centuries, on which those symbols are based, the church appears as an article of faith,[1] presupposing and necessarily following faith in the Father, the Son, and the Holy Spirit; and as a holy fellowship,[2] within which the various benefits of grace, from the forgiveness of sins to the life everlasting, are enjoyed.

Nor is any distinction made here between a visible and an invisible church. All catholic antiquity thought of none but the actual, historical church, and without hesitation applied to this, while yet in the eyes of the world a small persecuted sect, those four predicates of unity, holiness, universality, and apostolicity, to which were afterwards added exclusiveness, infallibility and indestructibility. There sometimes occur, indeed, particularly in the Novatian schism, hints of the incongruity between the empirical reality and the ideal conception of the church; and this incongruity became still more palpable, in regard to the predicate of holiness, after the abatement of the spiritual elevation of the apostolic age, the cessation of persecution, and the decay of discipline. But the unworthiness of individual members and the external servant-form of the church were not allowed to mislead as to the general objective character, which belonged to her in virtue of her union with her glorious heavenly Head.

The fathers of our period all saw in the church, though with different degrees of clearness, a divine, supernatural order of things, in a certain sense the continuation of the life of Christ on earth, the temple of the Holy Spirit, the sole repository of the powers of divine life, the possessor and interpreter of the Holy Scriptures, the mother of all the faithful. She is holy

---

[1] *Credo ecclesiam;* yet not *in* (εἰς) *ecclesiam,* as in the case of the Divine persons.

[2] *Communio sanctorum.* This clause, however, is not found in the original Creed of the Roman church before the fifth century.

because she is separated from the service of the profane world, is animated by the Holy Spirit, forms her members to holiness, and exercises strict discipline. She is catholic, that is (according to the precise sense of ὅλος, which denotes not so much numerical totality as wholeness), complete, and alone true, in distinction from all parties and sects. Catholicity, strictly taken, includes the three marks of universality, unity, and exclusiveness, and is an essential property of the church as the body and organ of Christ, who is, in fact, the only Redeemer for all men. Equally inseparable from her is the predicate of apostolicity, that is, the historical continuity or unbroken succession, which reaches back through the bishops to the apostles, from the apostles to Christ, and from Christ to God. In the view of the fathers, every theoretical departure from this empirical, tangible, catholic church is heresy, that is, arbitrary, subjective, ever changing human opinion; every practical departure, all disobedience to her rulers is schism, or dismemberment of the body of Christ; either is rebellion against divine authority, and a heinous, if not the most heinous, sin. No heresy can reach the conception of the church, or rightly claim any one of her predicates; it forms at best a sect or party, and consequently falls within the province and the fate of human and perishing things, while the church is divine and indestructible.

This is without doubt the view of the ante-Nicene fathers, even of the speculative and spiritualistic Alexandrians. The most important personages in the development of the doctrine concerning the church are, again, Ignatius, Irenæus, and Cyprian. Their whole doctrine of the episcopate is intimately connected with their doctrine of the catholic unity, and determined by it. For the episcopate is of value in their eyes only as the indispensable means of maintaining and promoting this unity: while they are compelled to regard the bishops of heretics and schismatics as rebels and antichrists.

1. In the Epistles of IGNATIUS the unity of the church, in the form and through the medium of the episcopate, is the fundamental thought and the leading topic of exhortation. The

author calls himself a man prepared for union.[1] He also is the first to use the term "catholic" in the ecclesiastical sense, when he says:[2] "Where Christ Jesus is, there is the catholic church;" that is, the closely united and full totality of his people. Only in her, according to his view, can we eat the bread of God; he, who follows a schismatic, inherits not the kingdom of God.[3]

We meet similar views, although not so clearly and strongly stated, in the Roman Clement's First Epistle to the Corinthians, in the letter of the church of Smyrna on the martyrdom of Polycarp, and in the Shepherd of Hermas.

2 IRENÆUS speaks much more at large respecting the church. He calls her the haven of rescue, the way of salvation, the entrance to life, the paradise in this world, of whose trees, to wit, the holy Scriptures, we may eat, excepting the tree of knowledge of good and evil, which he takes as a type of heresy. The church is inseparable from the Holy Spirit; it is his home, and indeed his only dwelling-place on earth. "Where the church is," says he, putting the church first, in the genuine catholic spirit, "there is the Spirit of God, and where the Spirit of God is there is all grace."[4] Only on the bosom of the church, continues he, can we be nursed to life. To her must we flee, to be made partakers of the Holy Spirit; separation from her is separation from the fellowship of the Holy Spirit. Heretics, in his view, are enemies of the truth and sons of Satan, and will be swallowed up by hell, like the company of Korah, Dathan, and Abiram. Characteristic in this respect is the well-known legend, which he relates, about the meeting of the apostle John with the Gnostic Cerinthus, and of Polycarp with Marcion, the "first-born of Satan."

3. TERTULLIAN is the first to make that comparison of the church with Noah's ark, which has since become classical in

---

[1] ἄνθρωπον εἰς ἕνωσιν κατηρτισμένον.   [2] Ad Smyrn. c. 8.
[3] Ad Ephes. c. 5.   Ad Trall. c. 7.   Ad Philad. c. 3, etc.
[4] Adv. Hœr. iii. 24. "Ubi ecclesia ibi et Spiritus Dei, et ubi Spiritus Dei, illic ecclesia et omnis gratia." Protestantism would say, conversely, putting the Spirit first: "Ubi Spiritus Dei, ibi ecclesia et omnis gratia."

Roman catholic theology; and he likewise attributes heresies to the devil, without any qualification. But as to schism, he was himself guilty of it since he joined the Montanists and bitterly opposed the Catholics in questions of discipline. He has therefore no place in the Roman Catholic list of the *patres*, but simply of the *scriptores ecclesiæ*.

4. Even CLEMENT of Alexandria, and ORIGEN, with all their spiritualistic and idealizing turn of mind, are no exception here. The latter, in the words : "Out of the church no man can be saved,"[1] brings out the principle of the catholic exclusiveness as unequivocally as Cyprian. Yet we find in him, together with very severe judgments of heretics, mild and tolerant expressions also; and he even supposes, on the ground of Rom. 2 : 6 sqq., that in the future life honest Jews and heathens will attain a suitable reward, a low grade of blessedness, though not the "life everlasting" in the proper sense. In a later age he was himself condemned as a heretic.

Of other Greek divines of the third century, Methodius in particular, an opponent of Origen, takes high views of the church, and in his *Symposion* poetically describes it as "the garden of God in the beauty of eternal spring, shining in the richest splendor of immortalizing fruits and flowers;" as the virginal, unspotted, ever young and beautiful royal bride of the divine Logos.

5. Finally, CYPRIAN, in his Epistles, and most of all in his classical tract : *De Unitate Ecclesiæ*, written in the year 251, amidst the distractions of the Novatian schism, and not without an intermixture of hierarchical pride and party spirit, has most distinctly and most forcibly developed the old catholic doctrine of the church, her unity, universality, and exclusiveness. He is the typical champion of visible, tangible church unity, and would have made a better pope than any pope before Leo I.; yet after all he was anti-papal and anti-Roman when he differed from the pope. Augustin felt this inconsistency, and thought

---

[1] *Hom. 3 in Josuam,* c. 5. "*Extra hanc domum, id est extra ecclesiam, nemo salvatur.*"

that he had wiped it out by the blood of his martyrdom. But he never gave any sign of repentance. His views are briefly as follows:

The Catholic church was founded from the first by Christ on St. Peter alone, that, with all the equality of power among the apostles, unity might still be kept prominent as essential to her being. She has ever since remained one, in unbroken episcopal succession; as there is only one sun, though his rays are everywhere diffused. Try once to separate the ray from the sun; the unity of the light allows no division. Break the branch from the tree; it can produce no fruit. Cut off the brook from the fountain; it dries up. Out of this empirical orthodox church, episcopally organized and centralized in Rome, Cyprian can imagine no Christianity at all;[1] not only among the Gnostics and other radical heretics, but even among the Novatians, who varied from the Catholics in no essential point of doctrine, and only elected an opposition bishop in the interest of their rigorous penitential discipline. Whoever separates himself from the catholic church is a foreigner, a profane person, an enemy, condemns himself, and must be shunned. No one can have God for his father, who has not the church for his mother.[2] As well might one out of the ark of Noah have escaped the flood, as one out of the church be saved;[3] because she alone is the bearer of the Holy Spirit and of all grace.

In the controversy on heretical baptism, Cyprian carried out the principle of exclusiveness even more consistently than the Roman church. For he entirely rejected such baptism, while Stephen held it valid, and thus had to concede, in strict consistency, the possibility of regeneration, and hence of salvation, outside the Catholic church. Here is a point where even the Roman system, generally so consistent, has a loophole of liberality, and practically gives up her theoretical principle of

[1] "Christianus non est, qui in Christi ecclesia non est."

[2] "Habere non potest Deum patrem, qui ecclesiam non habet matrem."

[3] "Extra ecclesiam nulla salus." Yet he nowhere says "extra ecclesiam Romanam nulla salus."

exclusiveness. But in carrying out this principle, even in persistent opposition to the pope, in whom he saw the successor of Peter and the visible centre of unity, Cyprian plainly denied the supremacy of Roman jurisdiction and the existence of an infallible tribunal for the settlement of doctrinal controversies, and protested against identifying the church in general with the church of Rome. And if he had the right of such protest in favor of strict exclusiveness, should not the Greek church, and above all the Evangelical, much rather have the right of protest against the Roman exclusiveness, and in favor of a more free and comprehensive conception of the church?

We may freely acknowledge the profound and beautiful truth at the bottom of this old catholic doctrine of the church, and the historical importance of it for that period of persecution, as well as for the great missionary work among the barbarians of the middle ages; but we cannot ignore the fact that the doctrine rested in part on a fallacy, which, in course of time, after the union of the church with the state, or, in other words, with the world, became more and more glaring, and provoked an internal protest of ever-growing force. It blindly identified the spiritual unity of the church with unity of organization, insisted on outward uniformity at the expense of free development, and confounded the faulty empirical church, or a temporary phase of the development of Christianity, with the ideal and eternal kingdom of Christ, which will not be perfect in its manifestation until the glorious second coming of its Head. The Scriptural principle: "Out of *Christ* there is no salvation," was contracted and restricted to the Cyprianic principle: "Out of the (visible) *church* there is no salvation;" and from this there was only one step to the fundamental error of Romanism: "Out of the *Roman* Church there is no salvation."

No effort after outward unity could prevent the distinction of an Oriental and Occidental church from showing itself at this early period, in language, customs, and theology;—a distinction which afterwards led to a schism to this day unhealed.

It may well be questioned whether our Lord intended an

outward visible unity of the church in the present order of things. He promised that there should be "one flock, one shepherd," but not "one fold."[1] There may be one flock, and yet many folds or church organizations. In the sacerdotal prayer, our Lord says not one word about church, bishops or popes, but dwells upon that spiritual unity which reflects the harmony between the eternal Father and the eternal Son. "The true communion of Christian men—'the communion of saints' upon which all churches are built—is not the common performance of external acts, but a communion of soul with soul and of the soul with Christ. It is a consequence of the nature which God has given us that an external organization should help our communion with one another: it is a consequence both of our twofold nature, and of Christ's appointment that external acts should help our communion with Him. But subtler, deeper, diviner than anything of which external things can be either the symbol or the bond is that inner reality and essence of union—that interpenetrating community of thought and character—which St. Paul speaks of as the 'unity of the Spirit,' and which in the sublimest of sublime books, in the most sacred words, is likened to the oneness of the Son with the Father and of the Father with the Son."[2]

§ 54. *Councils.*

Best Collections of Acts of Councils by HARDUIN (1715, 12 vols.), and MANSI (1759, 31 vols.).

C. J. HEFELE (R. C. Bishop of Rottenburg, and member of the Vatican Council of 1870): *Conciliengeschichte,* Freiburg 1855; second ed. 1873 sqq., 7 vols. down to the Council of Florence, A. D. 1447 (See vol. I., pp. 83–242). English translation by *W. R. Clark* and *H. R. Oxenham* (Edinb. 1871, 2d vol. 1876, 3d vol. 1883).

E. B. PUSEY (d. 1882): *The Councils of the Church, from the Council of Jerusalem, A. D. 51, to the Council of Constantinople, A. D. 381;*

---

[1] John 10: 16. It was a characteristic, we may say, an ominous mistake of the Latin Vulgate to render ποίμνη by *ovile* (confounding it with αὐλή). The Authorized Version has copied the mischievous blunder ("one fold"), but the Revision of 1881 has corrected it.

[2] Hatch, *l. c.* p. 187 sq.

chiefly as to their constitution, but also as to their object and history.
Lond. 1857.

A. W. DALE: *The Synod of Elvira* [A. D. 306] *and Christian Life in the
Fourth Century.* Lond. 1882.

Comp. the article *Council* in SMITH and CHEETHAM and Lect. VII. in
HATCH, Bampton Lect. on the *Organization of the Early Christian
Church.* Lond. 1881, pp. 165 sqq.

Councils or Synods were an important means of maintaining
and promoting ecclesiastical unity, and deciding questions of
faith and discipline.[1] They had a precedent and sanction in
the apostolic Conference of Jerusalem for the settlement of the
circumcision controversy.[2] They were suggested moreover by the
deliberative political assemblies of the provinces of the Roman
empire, which met every year in the chief towns.[3] But we have
no distinct trace of Councils before the middle of the second
century (between 50 and 170), when they first appear, in the
disputes concerning Montanism and Easter.

There are several kinds of Synods according to their size,
DIOCESAN, PROVINCIAL (or METROPOLITAN), NATIONAL, PATRI-
ARCHAL, and OECUMENICAL (or UNIVERSAL).[4] Our period
knows only the first three. Diocesan synods consist of the

---

[1] *Concilium,* first used in the ecclesiastical sense by Tertullian, *De Iejun.* c. 13,
De Pudic. c. 10; σύνοδος, assembly, meeting for deliberation (Herodotus,
Thucydides, Plato, Demosthenes, etc.), first used of Christian assemblies in the
pseudo-Apostolical *Constit.* V. 20, and the *Canons,* c. 36 or 38. It may designate a diocesan, or provincial, or general Christian convention for either elec-
tive, or judicial, or legislative, or doctrinal purposes.

[2] A. D. 50. Acts 15 and Gal. 2. Comp. also the Lord's promise to be present where even the smallest number are assembled in *his* name, Matt. 18: 19,
20. See vol. I. ₰ 64, p. 503 sqq.

[3] On the provincial councils of the Roman empire see Marquardt, *Römische
Staatsverwaltung,* I. 365–377, and Hatch, *l. c.* p. 164 sqq. The deliberations
were preceded by a sacrifice, and the president was called highpriest.

[4] That is, within the limits of the old Roman empire, as the *orbis terrarum.*
There never was an *absolutely* universal council. Even the seven Œcumenical
Councils from 325 to 787 were confined to the empire, and poorly attended by
Western bishops. The Roman Councils held after that time (down to the
Vatican Council in 1870) *claim* to be oecumenical, but exclude the Greek and
all evangelical churches.

bishop and his presbyters and deacons with the people assisting, and were probably held from the beginning, but are not mentioned before the third century. Provincial synods appear first in Greece, where the spirit of association had continued strong since the days of the Achæan league, and then in Asia Minor, North Africa, Gaul, and Spain. They were held, so far as the stormy times of persecution allowed, once or twice a year, in the metropolis, under the presidency of the metropolitan, who thus gradually acquired a supervision over the other bishops of the province. Special emergencies called out extraordinary sessions, and they, it seems, preceded the regular meetings. They were found to be useful, and hence became institutions.

The synodical meetings were public, and the people of the community around sometimes made their influence felt. In the time of Cyprian. presbyters, confessors, and laymen took an active part, a custom which seems to have the sanction of apostolic practice.[1] At the Synod which met about 256, in the controversy on heretical baptism, there were present eighty-seven bishops, very many priests and deacons, and " *maxima pars plebis;*"[2] and in the synods concerning the restoration of the *Lapsi*, Cyprian convened besides the bishops, his clergy, the " *confessores,*" and " *laicos stantes* " (*i. e.* in good standing).[3] Nor was this practice confined to North Africa. We meet it in Syria, at the synods convened on account of Paul of Samosata (264–269), and in Spain at the council of Elvira. Origen, who was merely a presbyter, was the leading spirit of two Arabian synods, and convinced their bishop Beryllus of his Christological

---

[1] Comp. Acts 15: 6, 7, 12, 13, 23, where the "brethren" are mentioned expressly, besides the apostles and elders, as members of the council, even at the final decision and in the pastoral letter. On the difference of reading, see vol. I. 505.

[2] Cyprian, *Opera*, p. 329, ed. Baluz. In the acts of this council, however (pp. 330–338), only the bishops appear as voters, from which some writers infer that the laity, and even the presbyters, had no *votum decisivum*. But in several old councils the presbyters and deacons subscribed their names after those of the bishops; see Harduin, *Coll. Conc.* I. 250 and 266; Hefele I. 19.

[3] *Epp.* xi., xiii., lxvi., lxxi.

error. Even the Roman clergy, in their letter to Cyprian,[1] speak of a common synodical consultation of the bishops with the priests, deacons, confessors, and laymen in good standing.

But with the advance of the hierarchical spirit, this republican feature gradually vanished. After the council of Nicæa (325) bishops alone had seat and voice, and the priests appear hereafter merely as secretaries, or advisers, or representatives of their bishops. The bishops, moreover, did not act as representatives of their churches, nor in the name of the body of the believers, as formerly, but in their own right as successors of the apostles. They did not as yet, however, in this period, claim infallibility for their decisions, unless we choose to find a slight approach to such a claim in the formula: " *Placuit nobis, Sancto Spiritu suggerente,*" as used, for example, by the council of Carthage, in 252.[2] At all events, their decrees at that time had only moral power, and could lay no claim to universal validity. Even Cyprian emphatically asserts absolute independence for each bishop in his own diocese. " To each shepherd," he says, " a portion of the Lord's flock has been assigned, and his account must be rendered to his Master."

The more important acts, such as electing bishops, excommunication, decision of controversies, were communicated to other provinces by *epistolæ synodicæ.* In the intercourse and the translation of individual members of churches, letters of recommendation[3] from the bishop were commonly employed or required as terms of admission. Expulsion from one church was virtually an expulsion from all associated churches.

The effect of the synodical system tended to consolidation. The Christian churches from independent communities held together by a spiritual fellowship of faith, became a powerful

---

[1] *Ep.* xxxi.

[2] Cyprian, *Ep.* liv., on the ground of the ἔδοξε τῷ ἁγίῳ πνεύματι καὶ ἡμῖν, *visum est Spiritui Sancto et nobis,* Acts 15: 28. So also, the council of Arles, A. D. 314: *Placuit ergo, presente Spiritu Sancto et angelis ejus* (Harduin, *Coll. Concil.* I. 262).

[3] *Epistolae formatae,* γράμματα τετυπωμένα.

confederation, a compact moral commonwealth within the political organization of the Roman empire.

As the episcopate culminated in the primacy, so the synodical system rose into the œcumenical councils, which represented the whole church of the Roman empire. But these could not be held till persecution ceased, and the emperor became the patron of Christianity. The first was the celebrated council of Nicæa, in the year 325. The state gave legal validity to the decrees of councils, and enforced them if necessary by all its means of coërcion. But the Roman government protected only the *Catholic* or *orthodox* church, except during the progress of the Arian and other controversies, before the final result was reached by the decision of an œcumenical Synod convened by the emperor.[1]

§ 55. *The Councils of Elvira, Arles, and Ancyra.*

Among the ante-Nicene Synods some were occasioned by the Montanist controversy in Asia Minor, some by the Paschal controversies, some by the affairs of Origen, some by the Novatian schism and the treatment of the *Lapsi* in Carthage and Rome, some by the controversies on heretical baptism (255, 256), three were held against Paul of Samosata in Antioch (264–269).

In the beginning of the fourth century three Synods, held at Elvira, Arles, and Ancyra, deserve special mention, as they approach the character of general councils and prepared the way for the first œcumenical council. They decided no doctrinal question, but passed important canons on church polity and

---

[1] This policy was inaugurated by Constantine I. A. D. 326 (*Cod. Theod.* 16, 5, 1). He confined the privileges and immunities which, in 313, he had granted to Christians in his later enactments to " *Catholicæ legis observatoribus.*" He ratified the Nicene creed and exiled Arius (325), although he afterwards wavered and was baptized by a semi-Arian bishop (337). His immediate successors wavered likewise. But as a rule the Byzantine emperors recognized the decisions of councils in dogma and discipline, and discouraged and ultimately prohibited the formation of dissenting sects. The state can, of course, not prevent dissent as an individual opinion; it can only prohibit and punish the open profession. Full religious liberty requires separation of church and state.

Christian morals. They were convened for the purpose of restoring order and discipline after the ravages of the Diocletian persecution. They deal chiefly with the large class of the Lapsed, and reflect the transition state from the ante-Nicene to the Nicene age. They are alike pervaded by the spirit of clericalism and a moderate asceticism.

1. The Synod of ELVIRA (Illiberis, or Eliberis, probably on the site of the modern Granada) was held in 306,[1] and attended by nineteen bishops, and twenty-six presbyters, mostly from the Southern districts of Spain. Deacons and laymen were also present. The Diocletian persecution ceased in Spain after the abdication of Diocletian and Maximian Herculeus in 305; while it continued to rage for several years longer in the East under Galerius and Maximin. The Synod passed eighty-one Latin canons against various forms of heathen immorality then still abounding, and in favor of church discipline and austere morals. The Lapsed were forbidden the holy communion even in *articulo mortis* (can. 1). This is more severe than the action of the Nicene Synod. The thirty-sixth canon prohibits the admission of sacred pictures on the walls of the church buildings,[2] and has often been quoted by Protestants as an argument against image worship as idolatrous; while Roman Catholic writers explain it either as a prohibition of representations of the deity only, or as a prudential measure against heathen desecration of holy things.[3] Otherwise the Synod is thoroughly catholic in spirit and tone. Another characteristic feature is the severity against the Jews

[1] Hefele, Gams, and Dale decide in favor of this date against the superscription which puts it down to the period of the Council of Nicæa (324). The chief reason is that Hosius, bishop of Cordova, could not be present in 324 when he was in the Orient, nor at any time after 307, when he joined the company of Constantine as one of his private councillors.

[2] "*Placuit picturas in ecclesia esse non debere, ne quod colitur et adoratur in parietibus depingatur.*" "There shall be no pictures in the church, lest what is worshipped [saints] and adored [God and Christ] should be depicted on the walls."

[3] The last is the interpretation of the canon by De Rossi, in *Roma sotteranea*, Tom. I., p. 97, and Hefele, I. 170. But Dale (p. 292 sqq.) thinks that it was aimed against the idolatry of Christians.

who were numerous in Spain. Christians are forbidden to marry Jews.[1]

The leading genius of the Elvira Synod and the second in the list was Hosius, bishop of Corduba (Cordova), who also attended the Council of Nicæa as the chief representative of the West. He was a native of Cordova, the birth-place of Lucan and Seneca, and more than sixty years in the episcopate. Athanasius calls him a man holy in fact as well as in name, and speaks of his wisdom in guiding synods. As a far-seeing statesman, he seems to have conceived the idea of reconciling the empire with the church and influenced the mind of Constantine in that direction. He is one of the most prominent links between the age of persecution and the age of imperial Christianity. He was a strong defender of the Nicene faith, but in his extreme old age he wavered and signed an Arian formula. Soon afterwards he died, a hundred years old (358).

2. The first Council of ARLES in the South of France[2] was held A. D. 314, in consequence of an appeal of the Donatists to Constantine the Great, against the decision of a Roman Council of 313, consisting of three Gallican and fifteen Italian bishops under the lead of Pope Melchiades. This is the first instance of an appeal of a Christian party to the secular power, and it turned out unfavorably to the Donatists who afterwards became enemies of the government. The Council of Arles was the first called by Constantine and the forerunner of the Council of

---

[1] The best accounts of the Synod of Elvira are given by Ferdinand de Mendoza, *De confirmando Concilio Illiberitano ad Clementem VIII.*, 1593 (reprinted in Mansi II. 57–397); Fr. Ant. Gonzalez, *Collect. Can. Ecclesiæ Hispaniæ*, Madrid, 1808, new ed. with Spanish version, 1849 (reprinted in Bruns, *Bibl. Eccl.* Tom. I. Pars II. 1 sqq.); Hefele, *Conciliengesch.* I. 148–192 (second ed., 1873; or 122 sqq., first ed.); Gams, *Kirchengesch. von Spanien* (1864), vol. II. 1–136; and Dale in his monograph on the *Synod of Elvira*, London, 1882.

[2] *Concilium Arelatense*, from *Arelate* or *Arelatum Sextanorum*, one of the chief Roman cities in South-Eastern Gaul, where Constantine at one time resided, and afterwards the West Gothic King Eurich. It was perhaps the seat of the first bishopric of Gaul, or second only to that of Lyons and Vienne. Several councils were held in that city, the second in 353 during the Arian controversy.

Nicæa. Augustin calls it even universal, but it was only Western at best. It consisted of thirty-three bishops[1] from Gaul, Sicily, Italy (exclusive of the Pope Sylvester, who, however, was represented by two presbyters and two deacons), North Africa, and Britain (three, from York, London, and probably from Cærleon on Usk), besides thirteen presbyters and twenty-three deacons. It excommunicated Donatus and passed twenty-two canons concerning Easter (which should be held on one and the same day), against the non-residence of clergy, against participation in races and gladiatorial fights (to be punished by excommunication), against the rebaptism of heretics, and on other matters of discipline. Clergymen who could be proven to have delivered sacred books or utensils in persecution (the *traditores*) should be deposed, but their official acts were to be held valid. The assistance of at least three bishops was required at ordination.[2]

3. The Council of ANCYRA, the capital of Galatia in Asia Minor, was held soon after the death of the persecutor Maximin (313), probably in the year 314, and represented Asia Minor and Syria. It numbered from twelve to eighteen bishops (the lists vary), several of whom eleven years afterwards attended the Council of Nicæa. Marcellus of Ancyra who acquired celebrity in the Arian controversies, presided, according to others Vitalis of Antioch. Its object was to heal the wounds of the Diocletian persecution, and it passed twenty-five canons relating chiefly to the treatment of those who had betrayed their faith or delivered the sacred books in those years of terror. Priests who had offered sacrifice to the gods, but afterwards repented, were prohibited from preaching and all sacerdotal functions, but allowed to retain their clerical dignity. Those who had sacrificed before baptism may be admitted to orders.

[1] Not 633, as McClintock & Strong's "Cyclop." has it sub Arles.

[2] See Eus. *H. E.* x. 5; Mansi, II. 463–468; München, *Das erste Concil von Arles* (in the "Bonner Zeitschrift für Philos. und kath. Theol.," No. 9, 26, 27), and Hefele I. 201–219 (2nd ed.).

Adultery is to be punished by seven years' penance, murder by life-long penance.[1]

A similar Council was held soon afterwards at Neo-Cæsarea in Cappadocia (between 314–325), mostly by the same bishops who attended that of Ancyra, and passed fifteen disciplinary canons.[2]

§ 56. Collections of Ecclesiastical Law. The Apostolical Constitutions and Canons.

SOURCES.

I. Διαταγαὶ τῶν ἁγίων 'Αποστόλων διὰ Κλήμεντος, etc., CONSTITUTIONES APOSTOLICÆ, first edited by *Fr. Turrianus*, Ven. 1563, then in *Cotelier's* ed. of the *Patres Apostolici* (I. 199 sqq.), in *Mansi* (*Collect. Concil.* I.), and *Harduin* (*Coll. Conc.* I.); newly edited by *Ueltzen*, Rost. 1853, and *P. A. de Lagarde*, Lips. and Lond. 1854 and 1862. Ueltzen gives the textus receptus improved. Lagarde aims at the oldest text, which he edited in Syriac (*Didascalia Apostolorum Syriace*, 1854), and in Greek (*Constit. Apostolorum Grœce*, 1862). *Hilgenfeld: Nov. Test. extra Canonem rec.*, Lips. (1866), ed. II. (1884), Fasc. IV. 110–121. He gives the Ap. Church Order under the title *Duœ Viœ vel Judicium Petri*.

THOS. PELL PLATT: *The Æthiopic Didascalia; or the Æthiopic Version of the Apostolical Constitutions, received in the Church of Abyssinia*, with an Engl Transl., Lond. 1834.

HENRY TATTAM: *The Apostolical Constitutions, or Canons of the Apostles in Coptic. With an Engl. translation.* Lond. 1848 (214 pages).

II. Κανόνες ἐκκλησιαστικοὶ τῶν ἁγ. 'Αποστόλων, CANONES, qui dicuntur *Apostolorum*, in most collections of church law, and in *Cotel.* (I. 437 sqq.), *Mansi*, and *Harduin* (tom. I.), and in the editions of the Ap. Constitutions at the close. Separate edd. by PAUL DE LAGARDE in Greek and Syriac: *Reliquiœ juris ecclesiastici antiquissimœ Syriace*, Lips. 1856; and *Reliquiœ juris ecclesiastici Grœce*, 1856 (both to be had at Trübner's, Strassburg). An Ethiopic translation of the Canons, ed. by WINAND FELL, Leipz. 1871.

W. G. BEVERIDGE (Bishop of St. Asaph, d. 1708): Συνόδικον, s. *Pandectœ Canonum S. G. Apostolorum et Conciliorum, ab Ecclesia Gr. recept.* Oxon. 1672–82, 2 vols. fol.

JOHN FULTON: *Index Canonum. In Greek and English. With a Complete Digest of the entire code of canon law in the undivided Primitive Church.* N. York 1872; revised ed. with Preface by P. Schaff, 1883.

---

[1] Hefele, vol. I. 222 sqq., gives the canons in Greek and German with explanation. He calls it a *Synodus plenaria*, i. e., a general council for the churches of Asia Minor and Syria. See also Mansi II. 514 sqq. Two Arian Synods were held at Ancyra in 358 and 375. [2] See Hefele I. 242–251.

CRITICAL DISCUSSIONS.

KRABBE: *Ueber den Ursprung u. den Inhalt der apost. Constitutionen des Clemens Romanus.* Hamb. 1829.

S. v. DREY (R. C.): *Neue Untersuchungen über die Constitut. u. Kanones der Ap.* Tüb. 1832.

J. W. BICKELL (d. 1848): *Gesch. des Kirchenrechts.* Giess. 1843 (I. 1, pp. 52–255). The second part appeared, Frankf., 1849.

CHASE: *Constitutions of the Holy Apostles, including the Canons; Whiston's version revised from the Greek; with a prize essay* (of Krabbe) *upon their origin and contents.* New York, 1848.

BUNSEN: *Hippolytus u. seine Zeit.*, Leipz. 1852 (I. pp. 418–525, and II. pp. 1–126); and in the 2d Engl. ed. *Hippolytus and his Age, or Christianity and Mankind,* Lond. 1854 (vols. V–VII).

HEFELE (R. C.): *Conciliengeschichte* I. p. 792 sqq. (second ed. 1873).

THE DIDACHE LITERATURE (fully noticed in Schaff's monograph).

PHILOTH. BRYENNIOS: Διδαχὴ τῶν δώδεκα ἀποστόλων. Constantinople, 1833.

AD. HARNACK: *Die Lehre der Zwölf Apostel.* Leipz., 1884. *Die Apostellehre und die jüdischen beiden Wege,* 1886.

PH. SCHAFF: *The Teaching of the Twelve Apostles, or the Oldest Church Manual.* N. York, 1885. 3d ed. revised and enlarged, 1889.

Several church manuals or directories of public worship, and discipline have come down to us from the first centuries in different languages. They claim directly or indirectly apostolic origin and authority, but are post-apostolic and justly excluded from the canon. They give us important information on the ecclesiastical laws, morals, and customs of the ante-Nicene age.

1. THE TEACHING OF THE TWELVE APOSTLES is the oldest and simplest church manual, of Jewish Christian (Palestinian or Syrian) origin, from the end of the first century, known to the Greek fathers, but only recently discovered and published by Bryennios (1883). It contains in 16 chapters (1) a summary of moral instruction based on the Decalogue and the royal commandment of love to God and man, in the parabolic form of two ways, the way of life and the way of death; (2) directions on the celebration of baptism and the eucharist with the agape; (3) directions on discipline and the offices of apostles (*i. e.* travelling evangelists), prophets, teachers, bishops (*i. e.* presbysters), and deacons; (4) an exhortation to watchfulness in view of the coming of the Lord and the resurrection of the saints. A very

remarkable book. Its substance survived in the seventh book
of the Apostolical Constitutions.

2. THE ECCLESIASTICAL CANONS OF THE HOLY APOSTLES
or APOSTOLICAL CHURCH ORDER, of Egyptian origin, probably
of the third century. An expansion of the former in the shape
of a fictitious dialogue of the apostles, first published in Greek
by Bickell (1843), and then also in Coptic and Syriac. It contains ordinances of the apostles on morals, worship, and discipline.

3. THE APOSTOLICAL CONSTITUTIONS, the most complete and
important Church Manual. It is, in form, a literary fiction,
professing to be a bequest of all the apostles, handed down
through the Roman bishop Clement, or dictated to him. It
begins with the words: " The apostles and elders, to all who
among the nations have believed in the Lord Jesus Christ.
Grace be with you, and peace." It contains, in eight books, a
collection of moral exhortations, church laws and usages, and
liturgical formularies, which had gradually arisen in the various
churches from the close of the first century, the time of the
Roman Clement, downward, particularly in Jerusalem, Antioch,
Alexandria, and Rome, partly on the authority of apostolic
practice. These were at first orally transmitted ; then committed
to writing in different versions, like the creeds; and finally
brought, by some unknown hand, into their present form. The
first six books, which have a strongly Jewish-Christian tone, were
composed, with the exception of some later interpolations, at the
end of the third century, in Syria. The seventh book is an expansion of the *Didache* of the Twelve Apostles. The eighth
book contains a liturgy, and, in an appendix, the apostolical
canons. The collection of the three parts into one whole
may be the work of the compiler of the eighth book. It
is no doubt of Eastern authorship, for the church of Rome
nowhere occupies a position of priority or supremacy.[1] The

---

[1] Harnack (*l. c.* 266–268) identifies Pseudo-Clement with Pseudo-Ignatius,
and assigns him to the middle of the fourth century.

design was, to set forth the ecclesiastical life for laity and clergy, and to establish the episcopal theocracy. These constitutions were more used and consulted in the East than any work of the fathers, and were taken as the rule in matters of discipline, like the Holy Scriptures in matters of doctrine. Still the collection, as such, did not rise to formal legal authority, and the second Trullan council of 692 (known as *quinisextum*), rejected it for its heretical interpolations, while the same council acknowledged the Apostolical Canons.[1]

The "APOSTOLICAL CANONS" consist of brief church rules or prescriptions, in some copies eighty-five in number, in others fifty, and pretend to be of apostolic origin, being drawn up by Clement of Rome from the directions of the apostles, who in several places speak in the first person. They are incorporated in the "Constitutions" as an appendix to the eighth book, but are found also by themselves, in Greek, Syriac, Æthiopic, and Arabic manuscripts. Their contents are borrowed partly from the Scriptures, especially the Pastoral Epistles, partly from tradition, and partly from the decrees of early councils at Antioch, Neo-Cæsarea, Nicæa, Laodicea, &c. (but probably not Chalcedon, 451). They are, therefore, evidently of gradual growth, and were collected either after the middle of the fourth century,[2] or not till the latter part of the fifth,[3] by some

---

[1] Turrianus, Bovius, and the eccentric Whiston regarded these pseudo-apostolic Constitutions as a genuine work of the apostles, containing Christ's teaching during the forty days between the Resurrection and Ascension. But Baronius, Bellarmin, and Petavius attached little weight to them, and the Protestant scholars, Daillé and Blondel, attacked and overthrew their genuineness and authority. The work is a gradual growth, with many repetitions, interpolations, and contradictions, and anachronisms. James, who was beheaded (A. D. 44), is made to sit in council with Paul (VI. 14), but elsewhere is represented as dead (V. 7). The apostles condemn post-apostolic heresies and heretics (VI. 8), and appoint days of commemoration of their death (VIII. 33). Episcopacy is extravagantly extolled. P. de Lagarde says: (*Rel juris eccles. ant.*, Preface, p. IV.): "*Communis vivorum doctorum fere omnium nunc invaluit opinio eas [constitutiones] sæculo tertio clam succrevisse et quum sex aliquando libris absolutæ fuissent, septimo et octavo unctas esse postea.*"

[2] As Bickell supposes. Beveridge put the collection in the third century.

[3] According to Daillé, Dr. von Drey, and Mejer.

unknown hand, probably also in Syria. They are designed to furnish a complete system of discipline for the clergy. Of the laity they say scarcely a word. The eighty-fifth and last canon settles the canon of the Scripture, but reckons among the New Testament books two epistles of Clement and the genuine books of the pseudo-Apostolic Constitutions.

The Greek church, at the Trullan council of 692, adopted the whole collection of eighty-five canons as authentic and binding, and John of Damascus placed it even on a parallel with the epistles of the apostle Paul, thus showing that he had no sense of the infinite superiority of the inspired writings. The Latin church rejected it at first, but subsequently decided for the smaller collection of fifty canons, which Dionysus Exiguus about the year 500 translated from a Greek manuscript.

§ 57. *Church Discipline.*

I. Several Tracts of TERTULLIAN (especially *De Pœnitentia*). The *Philosophumena* of HIPPOLYTUS (l. IX.). The *Epistles* of CYPRIAN, and his work *De Lapsis*. The *Epistolæ Canonicæ* of DIONYSIUS of Alex., GREGORY THAUMATURGUS (about 260), and PETER of Alex. (about 306), collected in ROUTH's *Reliquiæ Sacræ*, tom. III., 2nd ed. The CONSTIT. APOST. II. 16, 21–24. The CANONS of the councils of *Elvira*, *Arelate*, *Ancyra*, *Neo-Cœsarea*, and *Nicœa*, between 306 and 325 (in the Collections of Councils, and in ROUTH's *Reliq. Sacr.* tom. IV.).

II. MORINUS: *De Disciplina in administratione sacram pœnitentiæ*, Par. 1651 (Venet. 1702).

MARSHALL: *Penitential Discipline of the Primitive Church.* Lond. 1714 (new ed. 1844).

FR. FRANK: *Die Bussdisciplin der Kirche bis zum 7 Jahrh.* Mainz. 1868.

On the discipline of the Montanists, see BONWETSCH: *Die Geschichte des Montanismus* (1881), pp. 108–118.

The ancient church was distinguished for strict discipline. Previous to Constantine the Great, this discipline rested on purely moral sanctions, and had nothing to do with civil constraints and punishments. A person might be expelled from one congregation without the least social injury. But the more powerful the church became, the more serious were the consequences of her censures, and when she was united with the state, ecclesiastical offenses were punished as offenses against the state, in extreme cases even with death. The church always abhorred blood ("*ecclesia non sitit sanguinem*"), but she handed the offender over to the civil government to be dealt with according to law. The worst offenders for many centuries were heretics or teachers of false doctrine.

The object of discipline was, on the one hand, the dignity and purity of the church, on the other, the spiritual welfare of the offender; punishment being designed to be also correction. The extreme penalty was excommunication, or exclusion from all the rights and privileges of the faithful. This was inflicted for heresy and schism, and all gross crimes, such as theft, murder, adultery, blasphemy, and the denial of Christ in persecution. After Tertullian, these and like offences, incompatible with the regenerate state, were classed as mortal sins,[1] in distinction from venial sins or sins of weakness.[2]

Persons thus excluded passed into the class of penitents,[3] and could attend only the catechumen worship. Before they could be re-admitted to the fellowship of the church, they were required to pass through a process like that of the catechumens, only still more severe, and to prove the sincerity of their penitence by the absence from all pleasures, from ornament in dress, and from nuptial intercourse, by confession, frequent prayer, fasting, almsgiving, and other good works. Under pain of a troubled conscience and of separation from the only saving church, they readily submitted to the severest penances. The church teachers did not neglect, indeed, to inculcate the penitent spirit and the contrition of the heart as the main thing. Yet many of them laid too great stress on certain outward exercises.

---

[1] *Peccata mortalia*, or, *ad mortem;* after a rather arbitrary interpretation of 1 John 5: 16. Tertullian gives seven mortal sins: *Homicidium idololatria, fraus, negatio blasphemia, utique et moechia et fornicatio et si qua alia violatio templi Dei. De pudic.* c. 19. These he declares *irremissibilia, horum ultra exorator non erit Christus;* that is, if they be committed *after* baptism; for baptism washes away all former guilt. Hence he counselled delay of baptism.

[2] *Peccata venialia*.   [3] *Pœnitentes*.

Tertullian conceived the entire church penance as a "satisfaction" paid to God. This view could easily obscure to a dangerous degree the all-sufficient merit of Christ, and lead to that self-righteousness against which the Reformation raised so loud a voice.

The time and the particular form of the penances, in the second century, was left as yet to the discretion of the several ministers and churches. Not till the end of the third century was a rigorous and fixed system of penitential discipline established, and then this could hardly maintain itself a century. Though originating in deep moral earnestness, and designed only for good, it was not fitted to promote the genuine spirit of repentance. Too much formality and legal constraint always deadens the spirit, instead of supporting and regulating it. This disciplinary formalism first appears, as already familiar, in the council of Ancyra, about the year 314.[1]

Classes of Penitents.

The penitents were distributed into four classes:—

(1) The WEEPERS,[2] who prostrated themselves at the church doors in mourning garments and implored restoration from the clergy and the people.

(2) The HEARERS,[3] who, like the catechumens called by the same name, were allowed to hear the Scripture lessons and the sermon.

(3) The KNEELERS,[4] who attended the public prayers, but only in the kneeling posture.

(4) The STANDERS,[5] who could take part in the whole worship standing, but were still excluded from the communion.

---

[1] Can. 4 sqq. See Hefele, *Conciliengesch* (second ed.) I. 225 sqq. Comp. also the fifth canon of Neocæsarea, and Hefele, p. 246.

[2] Προσκλαίοντες, *flentes;* also called χειμάζοντες, *hiemantes*.

[3] Ἀκροώμενοι, *audientes*, or *auditores*. The fourteenth canon of Nicæa (Hefele I. 418) directs that "Catechumens who had fallen, should for three years be only hearers, but afterwards pray with the Catechumens."

[4] Γονυκλίνοντες, *genuflectentes:* also ὑποπίπτοντες, *substrati*. The term γόνυ κλίνων as designating a class of penitents occurs only in the 5th canon of the Council of Neocæsarea, held after 314 and before 325.

[5] Συνιστάμενοι, *consistentes*.

Those classes answer to the four stages of penance.[1] The course of penance was usually three or four years long, but, like the catechetical preparation, could be shortened according to circumstances, or extended to the day of death. In the East there were special penitential presbyters,[2] intrusted with the oversight of the penitential discipline.

Restoration.

After the fulfilment of this probation came the act of reconciliation.[3] The penitent made a public confession of sin, received absolution by the laying on of hands of the minister, and precatory or optative benediction,[4] was again greeted by the congregation with the brotherly kiss, and admitted to the celebration of the communion. For the ministry alone was he for ever disqualified. Cyprian and Firmilian, however, guard against the view, that the priestly absolution of hypocritical penitents is unconditional and infallible, and can forestall the judgment of God.[5]

Two Parties.

In reference to the propriety of any restoration in certain cases, there was an important difference of sentiment, which gave rise to several schisms. All agreed that the church punishment

---

[1] Πρόσκλανσις, fle⟨us; ἀκρόασις, auditus; ὑπόπτωσις, prostratio, humiliatio; σύστασις, consistentia. The last three classes are supposed to correspond to three classes of catechumens, but without good reason. There was only one class of catechumens, or at most two classes. See below, § 72.

[2] Πρεσβύτεροι ἐπὶ τῆς μετανοίας, presbyteri poenitentiarii.

[3] Reconciliatio.

[4] The declarative, and especially the direct indicative or judicial form of absolution seems to be of later origin.

[5] Cypr. Epist. LV., c. 15: "Neque enim prejudicamus Domino judicaturo, quominus si pœnitentiam plenam et justam peccatoris invenerit tunc ra⟨um faciat, quod a nobis fuerit hic statutum. Si vero nos aliquis pœnitentiæ simulatione deluserit, Deus, cui non deridetur, et qui cor hominis intuetur, de his, quæ nos minus perspeximus, judicet et servorum suorum sententiam Dominus emendet." Comp. the similar passages in Epist. LXXV. 4, and De Lapsis, c. 17. But if the church can err in imparting absolution to the unworthy, as Cyprian concedes, she can err also in withholding absolution and in passing sentence of excommunication.

could not forestall the judgment of God at the last day, but was merely temporal, and looked to the repentance and conversion of the subject. But it was a question whether the church should restore even the grossest offender on his confession of sorrow, or should, under certain circumstances, leave him to the judgment of God. The strict, puritanic party, to which the Montanists, the Novatians, and the Donatists belonged, and, for a time, the whole African and Spanish Church, took ground against the restoration of those who had forfeited the grace of baptism by a mortal sin, especially by denial of Christ; since, otherwise, the church would lose her characteristic holiness, and encourage loose morality. The moderate party, which prevailed in the East, in Egypt, and especially in Rome, and was so far the catholic party, held the principle that the church should refuse absolution and communion, at least on the death-bed, to no penitent sinner. Paul himself restored the Corinthian offender.[1]

The point here in question was of great practical moment in the times of persecution, when hundreds and thousands renounced their faith through weakness, but as soon as the danger was passed, pleaded for readmission into the church, and were very often supported in their plea by the potent intercessions of the martyrs and confessors, and their *libelli pacis*. The principle was: necessity knows no law. A mitigation of the penitential discipline seemed in such cases justified by every consideration of charity and policy. So great was the number of the lapsed in the Decian persecution, that even Cyprian found himself compelled to relinquish his former rigoristic views, all the more because he held that out of the visible church there was no salvation.

The strict party were zealous for the holiness of God; the moderate, for his grace. The former would not go beyond the revealed forgiveness of sins by baptism, and were content with urging the lapsed to repentance, without offering them hope of

---

[1] 1 Cor. 5: 1 sqq. Comp. 2 Cor. 2: 5 sqq.

absolution in this life. The latter refused to limit the mercy of God and expose the sinner to despair. The former were carried away with an ideal of the church which cannot be realized till the second coming of Christ; and while impelled to a fanatical separatism, they proved, in their own sects, the impossibity of an absolutely pure communion on earth. The others not rarely ran to the opposite extreme of a dangerous looseness, were quite too lenient, even towards mortal sins, and sapped the earnestness of the Christian morality.

It is remarkable that the lax penitential discipline had its chief support from the end of the second century, in the Roman church. Tertullian assails that church for this with bitter mockery. Hippolytus, soon after him, does the same; for, though no Montanist, he was zealous for strict discipline. According to his statement (in the ninth book of his *Philosophumena*), evidently made from fact, the pope Callistus, whom a later age stamped a saint because it knew little of him, admitted *bigami* and *trigami* to ordination, maintained that a bishop could not be deposed, even though he had committed a mortal sin, and appealed for his view to Rom. 14 : 4, to the parable of the tares and the wheat, Matt. 13 : 30, and, above all, to the ark of Noah, which was a symbol of the church, and which contained both clean and unclean animals, even dogs and wolves. In short, he considered no sin too great to be loosed by the power of the keys in the church. And this continued to be the view of his successors.

But here we perceive, also, how the looser practice in regard to penance was connected with the interest of the hierarchy. It favored the power of the priesthood, which claimed for itself the right of absolution ; it was at the same time matter of worldly policy ; it promoted the external spread of the church, though at the expense of the moral integrity of her membership, and facilitated both her subsequent union with the state and her hopeless confusion with the world. No wonder the church of Rome, in this point, as in others, triumphed at last over all opposition.

§ 58. *Church Schisms.*

I. On the Schism of HIPPOLYTUS: The *Philosophumena* of HIPPOL.
   lib. IX. (ed. Miller, Oxf. 1851, better by Duncker and Schneidewin,
   Gött. 1859), and the monographs on Hippolytus, by Bunsen, Döllinger, Wordsworth, Jacobi, and others (which will be noticed in.
   chapter XIII. § 183).

II. On the Schism of Felicissimus: CYPRIAN: *Epist.* 38–40, 42, 55.

III. On the Novatian Schism: HIPPOL.: *Philosoph.* 1. IX. CYPR.:
   Epist. 41–52; and the Epistles of CORNELIUS of Rome, and DIONYS.
   of Alex., in Euseb. *H. E.*, VI. 43–45; VII. 8. Comp. Lit. in § 200.

IV. On the Meletian Schism: Documents in Latin translation in MAFFEI:
   Osservationi Letterarie, Verona, 1738, tom. III. p. 11 sqq., and the
   Greek fragments from the *Liber de pœnitentia* of Peter of Alexandria
   in ROUTH: *Reliquiæ Sacr.* vol. II. pp. 21–51. EPIPHAN.: *Hær.* 68
   (favorable to Meletius); ATHANAS.: *Apol. contra Arianos,* § 59; and
   after him, SOCR., SOZOM., and THEOD. (very unfavorable to
   Meletius).

Out of this controversy on the restoration of the lapsed, proceeded four schisms during the third century; two in Rome, one
in North Africa, and one in Egypt. Montanism, too, was in
a measure connected with the question of penitential discipline,
but extended also to several other points of Christian life, and
will be discussed in a separate chapter.

I. The Roman schism of HIPPOLYTUS. This has recently
been brought to the light by the discovery of his *Philosophumena* (1851). Hippolytus was a worthy disciple of Irenæus,
and the most learned and zealous divine in Rome, during the
pontificates of Zephyrinus (202–217), and Callistus (217–222).
He died a martyr in 235 or 236. He was an advocate of strict
views on discipline in opposition to the latitudinarian practice which we have described in the previous section. He
gives a most unfavorable account of the antecedents of Callistus,
and charges him and his predecessor with the patripassian heresy.
The difference, therefore, was doctrinal as well as disciplinarian.
It seems to have led to mutual excommunication and a temporary schism, which lasted till A. D. 235. Hippolytus ranks
himself with the successors of the apostles, and seems to have
been bishop of Portus, the port of Rome (according to later

Latin tradition), or bishop of Rome (according to Greek writers). If bishop of Rome, he was the first schismatic pope, and forerunner of Novatianus, who was ordained anti pope in 251.[1] But the Roman Church must have forgotten or forgiven his schism, for she numbers him among her saints and martyrs, and celebrates his memory on the twenty-second of August. Prudentius, the Spanish poet, represents him as a Roman presbyter, who first took part in the Novatian schism, then returned to the Catholic church, and was torn to pieces by wild horses at Ostia on account of his faith. The remembrance of the schism was lost in the glory of his supposed or real martyrdom. According to the chronological catalogue of Popes from A. D. 354, a "presbyter" Hippolytus, together with the Roman bishop Pontianus, the successor of Callistus, was banished from Rome in the reign of Alexander Severus (235), to the mines of Sardinia.[2]

II. The schism of FELICISSIMUS, at Carthage, about the year 250, originated in the personal dissatisfaction of five presbyters with the hasty and irregular election of Cyprian to the bishopric, by the voice of the congregation, very soon after his baptism, A. D. 248. At the head of this opposition party stood the presbyter Novatus, an unprincipled ecclesiastical demagogue, of restless, insubordinate spirit and notorious character,[3] and the deacon Felicissimus, whom Novatus ordained, without the permission or knowledge of Cyprian, therefore illegally, whether with his own hands or through those of foreign bishops. The controversy cannot, however, from this circumstance, be construed, as it is by Neander and others, into a presbyterial reaction against episcopal autocracy. For the opponents themselves afterwards chose a bishop in the person of Fortunatus.

[1] See the particulars in § 183, and in Döllinger's *Hippol.* and *Call.*, Engl. transl. by A. Plummer (1876), p. 92 sqq.

[2] See Mommsen, *Ueber den Chronographen vom Jahr* 354 (1850), Lipsius, *Chronologie der röm. Bischöfe*, p. 40 sqq.; Döllinger, *l. c.* p. 332 sqq.; Jacobi in Herzog[2] VI. 142 sqq.

[3] Cyprian charges him with terrible cruelties, such as robbing widows and orphans, gross abuse of his father, and of his wife even during her pregnancy; and says, that he was about to be arraigned for this and similar misconduct when the Decian persecution broke out. *Ep.* 49.

The Novatians and the Meletians likewise had the episcopal form of organization, though doubtless with many irregularities in the ordination.

After the outbreak of the Decian persecution this personal rivalry received fresh nourishment and new importance from the question of discipline. Cyprian originally held Tertullian's principles, and utterly opposed the restoration of the lapsed, till further examination changed his views. Yet, so great was the multitude of the fallen, that he allowed an exception *in periculo mortis.* His opponents still saw even in this position an unchristian severity, least of all becoming him, who, as they misrepresented him, fled from his post for fear of death. They gained the powerful voice of the confessors, who in the face of their own martyrdom freely gave their peace-bills to the lapsed. A regular trade was carried on in these indulgences. An arrogant confessor, Lucian, wrote to Cyprian in the name of the rest, that he granted restoration to all apostates, and begged him to make this known to the other bishops. We can easily understand how this lenity from those who stood in the fire, might take more with the people than the strictness of the bishop, who had secured himself. The church of Novatus and Felicissimus was a resort of all the careless *lapsi.* Felicissimus set himself also against a visitation of churches and a collection for the poor, which Cyprian ordered during his exile.

When the bishop returned, after Easter, 251, he held a council at Carthage, which, though it condemned the party of Felicissimus, took a middle course on the point in dispute. It sought to preserve the integrity of discipline, yet at the same time to secure the fallen against despair. It therefore decided for the restoration of those who proved themselves truly penitent, but against restoring the careless, who asked the communion merely from fear of death. Cyprian afterwards, when the persecution was renewed, under Gallus, abolished even this limitation. He was thus, of course, not entirely consistent, but gradually accommodated his principles to circumstances and to the practice of the Roman church.[1] His antagonists elected their bishop, indeed, but were shortly compelled to yield to the united force of the African and Roman churches, especially as they had no moral earnestness at the bottom of their cause.

His conflict with this schismatical movement strengthened Cyprian's episcopal authority, and led him in his doctrine of the unity of the church to the principle of absolute exclusiveness.

III. The NOVATIAN schism in Rome was prepared by the controversy already alluded to between Hippolytus and Callistus. It broke out soon after the African schism, and, like it, in consequence of an election of bishop. But in this case the opposition advocated the strict discipline against the lenient practice of the dominant church. The Novatianists[2] considered themselves the only pure communion,[3] and unchurched all churches which defiled themselves by re-admitting the lapsed, or any other gross offenders. They went much farther than Cyprian, even as far as the later Donatists. They admitted the possibility of mercy for a mortal sinner, but denied the power and the right of the church to decide upon it, and to prevent, by absolution, the judgment of God upon such offenders. They also, like Cyprian, rejected heretical baptism, and baptized all who came over to them from other communions not just so rigid as themselves.

At the head of this party stood the Roman presbyter Novatian,[4] an earnest, learned, but gloomy man, who had come to faith through severe demoniacal disease and inward struggles. He fell out with Cornelius, who, after the Decian persecution in 251, was nominated bishop of Rome, and at once, to the grief of many, showed great indulgence towards the lapsed. Among his adherents the above-named Novatus of Carthage was particularly busy, either from a mere spirit of opposition to existing authority, or from having changed his former lax principles on his removal to Rome. Novatian, against his will, was chosen

---

[1] In *Ep.* 52, *Ad Antonianum,* he tried to justify himself in regard to this change in his views.　　[2] *Novatiani, Novatianenses.*　　[3] Καθαροί.

[4] Eusebius and the Greeks call him Ναυάτος, and confound him with Novatus of Carthage. Dionysius of Alex., however, calls him Ναυατιανός.

bishop by the opposition. Cornelius excommunicated him. Both parties courted the recognition of the churches abroad. Fabian, bishop of Antioch, sympathized with the rigorists. Dionysius of Alexandria, on the contrary, accused them of blaspheming the most gracious Lord Jesus Christ, by calling him unmerciful. And especially Cyprian, from his zeal for ecclesiastical unity and his aversion to Novatus, took sides with Cornelius, whom he regarded the legitimate bishop of Rome.

In spite of this strong opposition the Novatian sect, by virtue of its moral earnestness, propagated itself in various provinces of the West and the East down to the sixth century. In Phrygia it combined with the remnants of the Montanists. The council of Nicæa recognized its ordination, and endeavored, without success, to reconcile it with the Catholic church. Constantine, at first dealt mildly with the Novatians, but afterwards prohibited them to worship in public and ordered their books to be burnt.

IV. The MELETIAN schism in Egypt arose in the Diocletian persecution, about 305, and lasted more than a century, but, owing to the contradictory character of our accounts, it is not so well understood. It was occasioned by Meletius, bishop of Lycopolis in Thebais, who, according to one statement, from zeal for strict discipline, according to another, from sheer arrogance, rebelled against his metropolitan, Peter of Alexandria (martyred in 311), and during his absence encroached upon his diocese with ordinations, excommunications, and the like. Peter warned his people against him, and, on returning from his flight, deposed him as a disturber of the peace of the church. But the controversy continued, and spread over all Egypt. The council of Nicæa endeavored, by recognizing the ordination of the twenty-nine Meletian bishops, and by other compromise measures, to heal the division; but to no purpose. The Meletians afterwards made common cause with the Arians.

The DONATIST schism, which was more formidable than any of those mentioned, likewise grew out of the Diocletian persecution, but belongs more to the next period.

CHAPTER V.

CHRISTIAN WORSHIP.

I. The richest sources here are the works of JUSTIN M., TERTULLIAN, CYPRIAN, EUSEBIUS, and the so-called CONSTITUTIONES APOSTOLICÆ; also CLEMENT OF ROME (*Ad Cor.* 59–61), and the Homily falsely ascribed to him (fully publ. 1875).

II. See the books quoted in vol. I. 455, and the relevant sections in the archæological works of BINGHAM (*Antiquities of the Christian Church*, Lond. 1708–22. 10 vols.; new ed. Lond. 1852, in 2 vols.), AUGUSTI (whose larger work fills 12 vols., Leipz. 1817–31, and his *Handbuch der Christl. Archæol.* 3 vols. Leipz. 1836), BINTERIM (R. C.), SIEGEL, SMITH & CHEETHAM (*Dict. of Chr. Ant.*, Lond. 1875, 2 vols.), and GARRUCCI (*Storia della arte crist.*, 1872–80, 6 vols.)

§ 59. *Places of Common Worship.*

R. HOSPINIANUS: *De Templis*, etc. Tig. 1603. And in his *Opera*, Genev. 1681.

FABRICIUS: *De Templis vett. Christ.* Helmst. 1704.

MURATORI (R. C.): *De primis Christianorum Ecclesiis.* Arezzo, 1770.

HÜBSCH: *Altchristliche Kirchen.* Karlsruh, 1860.

JOS. MULLOOLY: *St. Clement and his Basilica in Rome.* Rome, 2nd ed. 1873.

DE VOGÜÉ: *Architecture civile et relig. du 1e au VIIe siècle. Paris,* 1877, 2 *vols.*

The numerous works on church architecture (by Fergusson, Brown, Bunsen, Kugler, Kinkel, Kreuser, Schnaase, Lübke, Voillet-le-Duc, De Vogüé, etc.) usually begin with the basilicas of the Constantinian age, which are described in vol. III. 541 sqq.

THE Christian worship, as might be expected from the humble condition of the church in this period of persecution, was very simple, strongly contrasting with the pomp of the Greek and Roman communion; yet by no means puritanic. We perceive here, as well as in organization and doctrine, the gradual and sure approach of the Nicene age, especially in the ritualistic solemnity of the baptismal service, and the mystical character of the eucharistic sacrifice.

Let us glance first at the places of public worship. Until about the close of the second century the Christians held their worship mostly in private houses, or in desert places, at the graves of martyrs, and in the crypts of the catacombs. This arose from their poverty, their oppressed and outlawed condition, their love of silence and solitude, and their aversion to all heathen art. The apologists frequently assert, that their brethren had neither temples nor altars (in the pagan sense of these words), and that their worship was spiritual and independent of place and ritual. Heathens, like Celsus, cast this up to them as a reproach; but Origen admirably replied: The humanity of Christ is the highest temple and the most beautiful image of God, and true Christians are living statues of the Holy Spirit, with which no Jupiter of Phidias can compare. Justin Martyr said to the Roman prefect: The Christians assemble wherever it is convenient, because their God is not, like the gods of the heathen, inclosed in space, but is invisibly present everywhere. Clement of Alexandria refutes the superstition, that religion is bound to any building.

In private houses the room best suited for worship and for the love-feast was the oblong dining-hall, the *triclinium*, which was never wanting in a convenient Greek or Roman dwelling, and which often had a semicircular niche, like the choir[1] in the later churches. An elevated seat[2] was used for reading the Scriptures and preaching, and a simple table[3] for the holy communion. Similar arrangements were made also in the catacombs, which sometimes have the form of a subterranean church.

The first traces of special houses of worship[4] occur in Tertul-

---

[1] *Chorus*, βῆμα. The two are sometimes identified, sometimes distinguished, the bema being the sanctuary proper for the celebration of the holy mysteries, the choir the remaining part of the chancel for the clergy; while the nave was for the laity.

[2] Ἄμβων, *suggestus, pulpitum.*

[3] Τράπεζα, *mensa sacra;* also *ara, altare.*

[4] Ἐκκλησία, ἐκκλησιαστήριον, κυριακά, οἶκος θεοῦ, *ecclesia, dominica, domus Dei, templum.* The names for a church building in the Teutonic and Slavonic lan-

lian, who speaks of going to church,[1] and in his contemporary, Clement of Alexandria, who mentions the double meaning of the word ἐκκλησία.[2] About the year 230, Alexander Severus granted the Christians the right to a place in Rome against the protest of the tavern-keepers, because the worship of God in any form was better than tavern-keeping. After the middle of the third century the building of churches began in great earnest, as the Christians enjoyed over forty years of repose (260–303), and multiplied so fast that, according to Eusebius, more spacious places of devotion became everywhere necessary. The Diocletian persecution began (in 303,) with the destruction of the magnificent church at Nicomedia, which, according to Lactantius, even towered above the neighboring imperial palace.[3] Rome is supposed to have had, as early as the beginning of the fourth century, more than forty churches. But of the form and arrangement of them we have no account. With Constantine the Great begins the era of church architecture, and its first style is the Basilica. The emperor himself set the example, and built magnificent churches in Jerusalem, Bethlehem, and Constantinople, which, however, have undergone many changes. His contemporary, the historian Eusebius, gives us the first account of a church edifice which Paulinus built in Tyre between A.D. 313 and 322.[4] It included a large portico (πρόπυλον); a quadrangular atrium (αἴθριον), surrounded by

guages (*Kirche, Church, Kerk, Kyrka, Tserkoff,* etc.) are derived from the Greek κυριακή. κυριακόν (belonging to the Lord, the Lord's house), through the medium of the Gothic; the names in the Romanic languages (*Chiesa, Igreja, Église,* etc.) from the Latin *ecclesia,* although this is also from the Greek, and means originally *assembly* (either a local congregation, or the whole body of Christians). Churches erected specially in honor of martyrs were called *martyria, memoriæ, tropæa, tituli.*

[1] *In ecclesiam, in domum Dei venire,*

[2] Τόπος and ἄθροισμα τῶν ἐκλεκτῶν.

[3] *De Mort. Persec.* c. 12. The Chronicle of Edessa (in Assem. *Bibl. Orient.* XI. 397) mentions the destruction of Christian temples A. D. 292.

[4] *Hist. Eccl.* X. 4. Eusebius also describes, in rhetorical exaggeration and looseness, the churches built by Constantine in Jerusalem, Antioch, and Constantinople (*Vita Const.* l. III. 50; IV. 58, 59). See De Vogüé, *Églises de la terre-sainte,* Hübsch, *l. c.,* and Smith & Cheetham, I. 368 sqq.

ranges of columns; a fountain in the centre of the atrium for the customary washing of hands and feet before entering the church; interior porticoes; the nave or central space (βασίλειος οἶκος) with galleries above the aisles, and covered by a roof of cedar of Lebanon; and the most holy altar (ἅγιον ἁγίων θυσιαστήριον). Eusebius mentions also the thrones (θρόνοι) for the bishops and presbyters, and benches or seats. The church was surrounded by halls and inclosed by a wall, which can still be traced. Fragments of five granite columns of this building are among the ruins of Tyre.

The description of a church in the Apostolic Constitutions,[1] implies that the clergy occupy the space at the east end of the church (in the choir), and the people the nave, but mentions no barrier between them. Such a barrier, however, existed as early as the fourth century, when the laity were forbidden to enter the enclosure of the altar.

§ 60. The Lord's Day.

See Lit. in vol. I. 476.

The celebration of the Lord's Day in memory of the resurrection of Christ dates undoubtedly from the apostolic age.[2] Nothing short of apostolic precedent can account for the universal religious observance in the churches of the second century. There is no dissenting voice. This custom is confirmed by the

---

[1] II. 57, ed. Ueltzen, p. 66 sqq.

[2] The original designations of the Christian Sabbath or weekly rest-day are: ἡ μία or μία σαββάτων, the first day of the week (Matt. 28: 1; Mark 16: 2; Luke 24: 1; John 21: 1; Acts 20: 7; 1 Cor. 16: 2), and ἡ ἡμέρα κυριακή, the Lord's Day, which first occurs in Rev. 1: 10, then in Ignatius and the fathers. The Latins render it Dominicus or Dominica dies. Barnabas calls it the eighth day, in contrast to the Jewish sabbath. After Constantine the Jewish term Sabbath and the heathen term Sunday (ἡμέρα τοῦ ἡλίου, dies Solis) were used also. In the edict of Gratian, A. D. 386, two are combined: "Solis die, quem Dominicum ritè dixere majores." On the Continent of Europe Sunday has ruled out Sabbath completely; while in England, Scotland, and the United States Sabbath is used as often as the other or oftener in religious literature. The difference is characteristic of the difference in the Continental and the Anglo-American observance of the Lord's Day.

testimonies of the earliest post-apostolic writers, as Barnabas,[1] Ignatius,[2] and Justin Martyr.[3] It is also confirmed by the younger Pliny.[4] The *Didache* calls the first day "the Lord's Day of the Lord."[5]

Considering that the church was struggling into existence, and that a large number of Christians were slaves of heathen masters, we cannot expect an unbroken regularity of worship and a universal cessation of labor on Sunday until the civil government in the time of Constantine came to the help of the church and legalized (and in part even enforced) the observance of the Lord's Day. This may be the reason why the religious observance of it was not expressly enjoined by Christ and the apostles; as for similar reasons there is no prohibition of polygamy and slavery by the letter of the New Testament, although its spirit condemns these abuses, and led to their abolition. We may go further and say that coërcive Sunday laws are against the genius and spirit of the Christian religion which appeals to the free will of man, and uses only moral means for its ends. A Christian government may and ought to *protect* the Christian Sabbath against open desecration, but its *positive* observance by attending public worship, must be left to the conscientious conviction of individuals. Religion cannot be forced by law. It looses its value when it ceases to be voluntary.

The fathers did not regard the Christian Sunday as a continuation of, but as a substitute for, the Jewish Sabbath, and based it not so much on the fourth commandment, and the primitive rest of God in creation, to which the commandment expressly refers, as upon the resurrection of Christ and the apostolic tradition. There was a disposition to disparage the Jewish law in

---

[1] *Ep.*, c. 15: "We celebrate the eighth day with joy, on which Jesus rose from the dead, and, after having appeared [to his disciples], ascended to heaven." It does not follow from this that Barnabas put the ascension of Christ likewise on a Sunday.

[2] *Ep. ad Magnes.* c. 8, 9.   [3] *Apol.* I. 67.

[4] "*Stato die*,' in his letter to Trajan, *Ep.* X. 97. This "stated day," on which the Christians in Bithynia assembled before day-light to sing hymns to Christ as a God, and to bind themselves by a *sacramentum*, must be the Lord's Day.

[5] Ch. 14: Κυριακὴ κυρίον, pleonastic The adjective in Rev. 1: 10.

the zeal to prove the independent originality of Christian institutions. The same polemic interest against Judaism ruled in the paschal controversies, and made Christian Easter a moveable feast. Nevertheless, Sunday was always regarded in the ancient church as a divine institution, at least in the secondary sense, as distinct from divine ordinances in the primary sense, which were directly and positively commanded by Christ, as baptism and the Lord's Supper. Regular public worship absolutely requires a stated day of worship.

Ignatius was the first who contrasted Sunday with the Jewish Sabbath as something done away with.[1] So did the author of the so-called Epistle of Barnabas.[2] Justin Martyr, in controversy with a Jew, says that the pious before Moses pleased God without circumcision and the Sabbath,[3] and that Christianity requires not one particular Sabbath, but a perpetual Sabbath.[4] He assigns as a reason for the selection of the first day for the purposes of Christian worship, because on that day God dispelled the darkness and the chaos, and because Jesus rose from the dead and appeared to his assembled disciples, but makes no allusion to the fourth commandment.[5] He uses the term " to sabbathize" (σαββατίζειν), only of the Jews, except in the passage just quoted, where he spiritualizes the Jewish law. Dionysius of Corinth mentions Sunday incidentally in a letter to the church of Rome, A.D., 170: " To-day we kept the Lord's

---

[1] *Ep. ad Magnes.* c. 8, 9 in the shorter Greek recension (wanting in the Syriac edition).

[2] Cap. 15. This Epistle is altogether too fierce in its polemics against Judaism to be the production of the apostolic Barnabas.

[3] *Dial c. Tryph. Jud.* 19, 27 (Tom. I. P. II. p. 68, 90, in the third ed. of Otto).

[4] *Dial.* 12 (II. p. 46): σαββατίζειν ὑμᾶς (so Otto reads, but ἡμᾶς would be better) ὁ καινὸς νόμος διὰ παντὸς (belongs to σαββατίζειν) ἐθέλει. Comp. Tertullian, *Contra Jud.* c. 4: " *Unde nos intelligimis magis, sabbatizare nos ab omni opere servili semper debere, et non tantum septimo quoque die, sed per omne tempus.*"

[5] *Apol.* I. 67 (I. p. 161): Τὴν δὲ τοῦ ἡλίου ἡμέραν κοινῇ πάντες τὴν συνέλευσιν ποιούμεθα, ἐπειδὴ πρώτη ἐστὶν ἡμέρα, ἐν ᾗ ὁ θεὸς τὸ σκότος καὶ τὴν ὕλην τρέψας, κόσμον ἐποίησε, καὶ Ἰησοῦς Χριστὸς ὁ ἡμέτερος σωτὴρ τῇ αὐτῇ ἡμέρᾳ ἐκ νεκρῶν ἀνέστη. κ. τ. λ.

Day holy, in which we read your letter."[1] Melito of Sardis wrote a treatise on the Lord's Day, which is lost.[2] Irenæus of Lyons, about 170, bears testimony to the celebration of the Lord's Day,[3] but likewise regards the Jewish Sabbath merely as a symbolical and typical ordinance, and says that "Abraham without circumcision and without observance of Sabbaths believed in God," which proves "the symbolical and temporary character of those ordinances, and their inability to make perfect."[4] Tertullian, at the close of the second and beginning of the third century, views the Lord's Day as figurative of rest from sin and typical of man's final rest, and says: "We have nothing to do with Sabbaths, new moons or the Jewish festivals, much less with those of the heathen. We have our own solemnities, the Lord's Day, for instance, and Pentecost. As the heathen confine themselves to their festivals and do not observe ours, let us confine ourselves to ours, and not meddle with those belonging to them." He thought it wrong to fast on the Lord's Day, or to pray kneeling during its continuance. "Sunday we give to joy." But he also considered it Christian duty to abstain from secular care and labor, lest we give place to the devil.[5] This is the first express evidence of cessation from labor on Sunday among Christians. The habit of standing in prayer on Sunday, which Tertullian regarded as essential to the festive character of the day, and which was sanctioned by an œcumenical council, was afterwards abandoned by the western church.

---

[1] Eusebius, *H. E.* IV. 23.

[2] Περὶ κυριακῆς λόγος. Euseb. IV. 26.

[3] In one of his fragments περὶ τοῦ πάσχα, and by his part in the Quartadecimanian controversy, which turned on the *yearly* celebration of the Christian Passover, but implied universal agreement as to the *weekly* celebration of the Resurrection. Comp. Hessey, *Bampton Lectures on Sunday.* London, 1860, p. 373.

[4] *Adv. Hær.* IV. 16.

[5] *De Orat.* c. 23: "*Nos vero sicut accepimus, solo die Dominicæ Resurrectionis non ab isto tantum* [the bowing of the knee], *sed omni anxietatis habitu et officio cavere debemus, differentes etiam negotia, ne quem diabolo locum demus.*" Other passages of Tertullian, Cyprian, Clement of Alex., and Origen see in Hessey, *l. c.,* pp. 375 ff.

The Alexandrian fathers have essentially the same view, with some fancies of their own concerning the allegorical meaning of the Jewish Sabbath.

We see then that the ante-Nicene church clearly distinguished the Christian Sunday from the Jewish Sabbath, and put it on independent Christian ground. She did not fully appreciate the perpetual obligation of the fourth commandment in its substance as a weekly day of rest, rooted in the physical and moral necessities of man. This is independent of those ceremonial enactments which were intended only for the Jews and abolished by the gospel. But, on the other hand, the church took no secular liberties with the day. On the question of theatrical and other amusements she was decidedly puritanic and ascetic, and denounced them as being inconsistent on *any* day with the profession of a soldier of the cross. She regarded Sunday as a sacred day, as the Day of the Lord, as the weekly commemoration of his resurrection and the pentecostal effusion of the Spirit, and therefore as a day of holy joy and thanksgiving to be celebrated even before the rising sun by prayer, praise, and communion with the risen Lord and Saviour.

Sunday legislation began with Constantine, and belongs to the next period.

The observance of the Sabbath among the Jewish Christians gradually ceased. Yet the Eastern church to this day marks the seventh day of the week (excepting only the Easter Sabbath) by omitting fasting, and by standing in prayer; while the Latin church, in direct opposition to Judaism, made Saturday a fast day. The controversy on this point began as early as the end of the second century.

WEDNESDAY,[1] and especially FRIDAY,[2] were devoted to the weekly commemoration of the sufferings and death of the Lord, and observed as days of penance, or watch-days,[3] and half-fasting (which lasted till three o'clock in the afternoon).[4]

---

[1] *Feria quarta.*

[2] *Feria sexta, ἡ παρασκευή.*

[3] *Dies stationum* of the *milites Christi.*

[4] *Semijejunia.*

§ 61. *The Christian Passover.* (*Easter*).

R. HOSPINIANUS: *Festa Christ., h. e. de origine, progressu, ceremoniis et ritibus festorum dierum Christ.* Tig. 1593, and often.

A. G. PILLWITZ: *Gesch. der heil. Zeiten in der abendländ. Kirche.* Dresden, 1842.

M. A. NICKEL (R. C.): *Die heil. Zeiten u. Feste nach ihrrer Gesch. u. Feier in der kath. Kirche.* Mainz, 1825–1838. 6 vols.

F. PIPER: *Gesch. des Osterfestes.* Berl. 1845.

LISCO: *Das christl. Kirchenjahr.* Berlin, 1840, 4th ed. 1850.

STRAUSS (court-chaplain of the King of Prussia, d. 1863): *Das evangel. Kirchenjahr.* Berlin, 1850.

BOBERTAG: *Das evangel. Kirchenjahr.* Breslau 1857.

H. ALT: *Der Christliche Cultus,* IInd Part: *Das Kirchenjahr,* 2nd ed. Berlin 1860.

L. HENSLEY: Art. *Easter* in Smith and Cheetham (1875), I. 586–595.

F. X. KRAUS (R. C.): Art. *Feste* in "*R. Encykl. der Christl. Alterthümer,*" vol. I. (1881), pp. 486–502, and the lit. quoted there. The article is written by several authors, the section on Easter and Pentecost by Dr. Funk of Tübingen.

The yearly festivals of this period were Easter, Pentecost, and Epiphany. They form the rudiments of the church year, and keep within the limits of the facts of the New Testament.

Strictly speaking the ante-Nicene church had two annual festive seasons, the *Passover* in commemoration of the suffering of Christ, and the *Pentecoste* in commemoration of the resurrection and exaltation of Christ, beginning with Easter and ending with Pentecost proper. But Passover and Easter were connected in a continuous celebration, combining the deepest sadness with the highest joy, and hence the term *pascha* (in Greek and Latin) is often used in a wider sense for the Easter season, as is the case with the French *pâque* or *pâques*, and the Italian *pasqua*. The Jewish passover also lasted a whole week, and after it began their Pentecost or feast of weeks. The death of Christ became fruitful in the resurrection, and has no redemptive power without it. The commemoration of the death of Christ was called the *pascha staurosimon* or the *Passover* proper.[1] The commemoration of the resurrection was called

---

[1] Pascha, πάσχα, is not from the verb πάσχειν, to suffer (though often con·

the *pascha anastasimon*, and afterwards *Easter*.[1] The former corresponds to the gloomy Friday, the other to the cheerful Sunday, the sacred days of the week in commemoration of those great events.

The Christian Passover naturally grew out of the Jewish Passover, as the Lord's Day grew out of the Sabbath; the paschal lamb being regarded as a prophetic type of Christ, the Lamb of God slain for our sins (1 Cor. 5: 7, 8), and the deliverance from the bondage of Egypt as a type of the redemption from sin. It is certainly the oldest and most important annual festival of the church, and can be traced back to the first century, or at all events to the middle of the second, when it was universally observed, though with a difference as to the day, and the extent of the fast connected with it. It is based on the view that Christ crucified and risen is the centre of faith. The Jewish Christians would very naturally from the beginning continue to celebrate the legal passover, but in the light of its fulfillment by the sacrifice of Christ, and would dwell chiefly

founded with it and with the Latin *passio* by the Fathers, who were ignorant of Hebrew), but from the Hebrew פֶּסַח, and the Chaldee פַּסְחָא, (comp. the verb פֶּסַח, to pass over, to spare). See Ex. chs. 12 and 13; Lev. 23: 4-9; Num. ch. 9. It has three meanings in the Sept. and the N. T. 1) the paschal festival, called "the feast of unleavened bread," and lasting from the fourteenth to the twentieth of Nisan, in commemoration of the sparing of the first-born and the deliverance of Israel from Egypt; 2) the paschal lamb which was slain between the two evenings (3-5 P. M.) on the 14th of Nisan; 3) the paschal supper on the evening of the same day, which marked the beginning of the 15th of Nisan, or the first day of the festival. In the first sense it corresponds to the Christian Easter-festival, as the type corresponds to the substance. Nevertheless the translation *Easter* for *Passover* in the English version, Acts 12: 4, is a strange anachronism (corrected in the Revision).

[1] Easter is the resurrection festival which follows the Passover proper, but is included in the same festive week. The English *Easter* (Anglo-Saxon *eáster, eástran*, German *Ostern*) is connected with *East* and sunrise, and is akin to ἠώς, *oriens, aurora* (comp. Jac. Grimm's *Deutsche Mythol.* 1835, p. 181 and 349, and Skeat's *Etym. Dict. E. Lang.* sub *Easter*). The comparison of sunrise and the natural spring with the new moral creation in the resurrection of Christ, and the transfer of the celebration of *Ostara*, the old German divinity of the rising, health-bringing light, to the Christian Easter festival, was easy and natural, because all nature is a symbol of spirit, and the heathen myths are dim presentiments and carnal anticipations of Christian truths.

on the aspect of the crucifixion. The Gentile Christians, for whom the Jewish passover had no meaning except through reflection from the cross, would chiefly celebrate the Lord's resurrection as they did on every Sunday of the week. Easter formed at first the beginning of the Christian year, as the month of Nisan, which contained the vernal equinox (corresponding to our March or April), began the sacred year of the Jews. Between the celebration of the death and the resurrection of Christ lay "the great Sabbath,"[1] on which also the Greek church fasted by way of exception; and "the Easter vigils,"[2] which were kept, with special devotion, by the whole congregation till the break of day, and kept the more scrupulously, as it was generally believed that the Lord's glorious return would occur on this night. The feast of the resurrection, which completed the whole work of redemption, became gradually the most prominent part of the Christian Passover, and identical with Easter. But the crucifixion continued to be celebrated on what is called "Good Friday."[3]

The paschal feast was preceded by a season of penitence and fasting, which culminated in "the holy week."[4] This fasting varied in length, in different countries, from one day or forty hours to six weeks;[5] but after the fifth century, through the

---

[1] Τὸ μέγα σάββατον, τὸ ἅγιον σάββατον, Sabbatum magnum.

[2] Παννυχίδες, vigiliæ paschæ, Easter Eve. Good Friday and Easter Eve were a continuous fast, which was prolonged till midnight or cock-crow. See Tertull. Ad uxor. II. 4; Euseb. H. E. VI. 34; Apost. Const. V. 18; VII. 23.

[3] Various names: πάσχα σταυρώσιμον (as distinct from π. ἀναστάσιμον), ἡμέρα σταυροῦ, παρασκευὴ μεγάλη or ἁγία, parasceue, feria sexta major, Good Friday, Charfreitag (from χάρις or from carus, dear). But the celebration seems not to have been universal; for Augustin says in his letter Ad Januar., that he did not consider this day holy. See Siegel, Handbuch der christl. kirchl. Alterthümer, I. 374 sqq.

[4] From Palm Sunday to Easter Eve. Ἑβδομὰς μεγάλη, or τοῦ πάσχα, hebdomas magna, hebdomas nigra (in opposition to dominica in albis), hebdomas crucis, Charwoche.

[5] Irenæus, in his letter to Victor of Rome (Euseb. V. 24): "Not only is the dispute respecting the day, but also respecting the manner of fasting. For some think that they ought to fast only one day, some two, some more days; some compute their day as consisting of forty hours night and day; and

influence of Rome, it was universally fixed at forty days,[1] with reference to the forty days' fasting of Christ in the wilderness and the Old Testament types of that event (the fasting of Moses and Elijah).[2]

§ 62. *The Paschal Controversies.*

I. The sources for the paschal controversies:

Fragments from MELITO, APOLLINARIUS, POLYCRATES, CLEMENT of Alexandria, IRENÆUS, and HIPPOLYTUS, preserved in EUSEB. *H. E.* IV. 3, 26; V. 23–25; VI. 13; the CHRONICON PASCH. I. 12 sqq., a passage in the *Philosophumena* of HIPPOLYTUS, Lib. VIII. cap. 18 (p. 435, ed. Duncker & Schneidewin, 1859), a fragment from EUSEBIUS in Angelo Mai's *Nova P. P. Bibl.* T. IV. 209–216, and the *Hæresies* of EPIPHANIUS, *Hær.* LXX. 1–3; LXX. 9.

II. Recent works, occasioned mostly by the Johannean controversy:

WEITZEL: *Die Christl. Passafeier der drei ersten Jahrh.* Pforzheim, 1848 (and in the "Studien und Kritiken," 1848, No. 4, against Baur).

BAUR: *Das Christenthum der 3 ersten Jahrh.* (1853). Tüb. 3rd ed. 1863, pp. 156–169. And several controversial essays against Steitz.

HILGENFELD: *Der Paschastreit und das Evang. Johannis* (in "Theol. Jahrbücher" for 1849); *Noch ein Wort über den Passahstreit* (ibid. 1858); and *Der Paschastreit der alten Kirche nach seiner Bedeutung für die Kirchengesch. und für die Evangelienforschung urkundlich dargestellt.* Halle 1860 (410 pages).

STEITZ: Several essays on the subject, mostly against Baur, in the "Studien u. Kritiken," 1856, 1857, and 1859; in the "Theol. Jahrbücher," 1857, and art. *Passah* in "Herzog's Encycl." vol. XII. (1859), p. 149 sqq., revised in the new ed., by Wagenmann, XI. 270 sqq.

WILLIAM MILLIGAN: *The Easter Controversies of the second century in their relation to the Gospel of St. John,* in the "Contemporary Review" for Sept. 1867 (p. 101–118).

EMIL SCHÜRER: *De Controversiis paschalibus sec. post Chr. sæc. exortis.* Lips. 1869. By the same: *Die Paschastreitigkeiten des 2ten Jahrh.,*

this diversity existing among those that observe it, is not a matter that has just sprung up in our times, but long ago among those before us, who perhaps not having ruled with sufficient strictness, established the practice that arose from their simplicity and ignorance."

[1] *Quadragesima.*

[2] Matt. 4: 2; comp. Ex. 34: 28; 1 Kings 19: 8.

in Kahnis' "Zeitschrift für hist. Theol." 1870, pp. 182–284. Very full and able.

C. JOS. VON HEFELE (R. C.): *Conciliengeschichte*, I. 86–101 (second ed. Freib. 1873; with some important changes).

ABBÉ DUCHESNE: *La question de la Pâque*, in "Revue des questions historiques," July 1880.

RENAN: *L'église chrêt.* 445–451; and *M. Aurèle*, 194–206 (*la question de la Pâque*).

Respecting the time of the Christian Passover and of the fast connected with it, there was a difference of observance which created violent controversies in the ancient church, and almost as violent controversies in the modern schools of theology in connection with the questions of the primacy of Rome, and the genuineness of John's Gospel.[1]

The paschal controversies of the ante-Nicene age are a very complicated chapter in ancient church-history, and are not yet sufficiently cleared up. They were purely ritualistic and disciplinary, and involved no dogma; and yet they threatened to split the churches; both parties laying too much stress on external uniformity. Indirectly, however, they involved the question of the independence of Christianity on Judaism.[2]

Let us first consider the difference of observance or the subject of controversy.

The Christians of Asia Minor, following the Jewish chronology, and appealing to the authority of the apostles John and Philip, celebrated the Christian Passover uniformly on the fourteenth of Nisan (which might fall on any of the seven days of the week) by a solemn fast; they fixed the close of the fast accordingly, and seem to have partaken on the evening of this day, as the close of the fast, not indeed of the Jewish paschal lamb, as has sometimes been supposed,[3] but of the commu-

---

[1] See note at the end of the section.

[2] So Renan regards the controversy, *Marc-Aurèle*, p. 194, as a conflict between two kinds of Christianity, "*le christianisme qui s'envisageait comme une suite du judaisme*," and "*le christianisme qui s'envisageait comme la destruction du judaisme.*"

[3] By Mosheim (*De rebus christ. ante Const. M. Com.*, p. 435 sqq.) and Neander (in the first edition of his Church Hist., I. 518, but not in the second I. 512,

nion and love-feast, as the Christian passover and the festival of the redemption completed by the death of Christ.[1] The communion on the evening of the 14th (or, according to the Jewish mode of reckoning, the day from sunset to sunset, on the beginning of the 15th) of Nisan was in memory of the last paschal supper of Christ. This observance did not exclude the idea that Christ died as the true paschal Lamb. For we find among the fathers both this idea and the other that Christ ate the regular Jewish passover with his disciples, which took place on the 14th.[2] From the day of observance the Asiatic Christians were afterwards called *Quartadecimanians.*[3] Hippolytus of Rome speaks of them contemptuously as a sect of contentious and ignorant persons, who maintain that "the pascha should be observed on the fourteenth day of the first month according to the law, no matter on what day of the week it might fall."[4] Nevertheless the Quartadecimanian observance was probably the oldest and in accordance with the Synoptic tradition of the last Passover of our Lord, which it commemorated.[5]

Germ. ed., I. 298 in Torrey's translation). There is no trace of such a Jewish custom on the part of the Quartadecimani. This is admitted by Hefele (I. 87), who formerly held to three parties in this controversy; but there were only two.

[1] The celebration of the eucharist is not expressly mentioned by Eusebius, but may be inferred. He says (*H. E.* V. 23): "The churches of all Asia, guided by older tradition (ὡς ἐκ παραδόσεως ἀρχαιοτέρας, older than that of Rome), thought that they were bound to keep the *fourteenth day* of the moon, on (or at the time of) the feast of the Saviour's Passover (ἐπὶ τῆς τοῦ σωτηρίον πάσχα ἑορτῆς), that day on which the Jews were commanded to kill the paschal lamb; it being incumbent on them by all means to regulate the close of the fast by that day on whatever day of the week it might happen to fall."

[2] Justin M. *Dial.* c. 111; Iren. *Adv. Hær.* II. 22, 3; Tert. *De Bapt.* 19; Origen, *In Matth.;* Epiph. *Hær.* XLII. St. Paul first declared Christ to be our passover (1 Cor. 5: 7), and yet his companion Luke, with whom his own account of the institution of the Lord's Supper agrees, represents Christ's passover meal as taking place on the 14th.

[3] The ιδ′=14, *quarta decima.* See Ex. 12: 6; Lev. 23: 5, where this day is prescribed for the celebration of the Passover. Hence Τεσσαρεσκαιδεκατῖται, *Quartodecimani,* more correctly *Quartadecimani.* This sectarian name occurs in the canons of the councils of Laodicea, 364, Constantinople, 381, etc.

[4] *Philosoph.* or *Refutat. of all Hæres.* VIII. 18.

[5] So also Renan regards it, *L'égl. chrét.,* p. 445 sq., but he brings it, like

The Roman church, on the contrary, likewise appealing to early custom, celebrated the death of Jesus always on a Friday, the day of the week on which it actually occurred, and his resurrection always on a Sunday after the March full moon, and extended the paschal fast to the latter day; considering it improper to terminate the fast at an earlier date, and to celebrate the communion before the festival of the resurrection. Nearly all the other churches agreed with the Roman in this observance, and laid the main stress on the resurrection-festival on Sunday. This Roman practice created an entire holy week of solemn fasting and commemoration of the Lord's passion, while the Asiatic practice ended the fast on the 14th of Nisan, which may fall sometimes several days before Sunday.

Hence a spectacle shocking to the catholic sense of ritualistic propriety and uniformity was frequently presented to the world, that one part of Christendom was fasting and mourning over the death of our Saviour, while the other part rejoiced in the glory of the resurrection. We cannot be surprised that controversy arose, and earnest efforts were made to harmonize the opposing sections of Christendom in the public celebration of the fundamental facts of the Christian salvation and of the most sacred season of the church-year.

The gist of the paschal controversy was, whether the Jewish paschal-day (be it a Friday or not), or the Christian Sunday, should control the idea and time of the entire festival. The Johannean practice of Asia represented here the spirit of adhesion to historical precedent, and had the advantage of an immovable Easter, without being Judaizing in anything but the observance of a fixed day of the month. The Roman custom represented the principle of freedom and discretionary change, and the independence of the Christian festival system. Dogmatically stated, the difference would be, that in the former case the chief stress was laid on the Lord's death; in the latter, on his resurrection. But the leading interest of the question for

Baur, in conflict with the chronology of the fourth Gospel. He traces the Roman custom from the pontificate of Xystus and Telesphorus, A. D. 120.

the early Church was not the astronomical, nor the dogmatical, but the ritualistic. The main object was to secure uniformity of observance, and to assert the originality of the Christian festive cycle, and its independence of Judaism; for both reasons the Roman usage at last triumphed even in the East. Hence Easter became a movable festival whose date varies from the end of March to the latter part of April.

The history of the controversy divides itself into three acts.

1. The difference came into discussion first on a visit of Polycarp, bishop of Smyrna, to Anicetus, bishop of Rome, between A.D. 150 and 155.[1] It was not settled; yet the two bishops parted in peace, after the latter had charged his venerable guest to celebrate the holy communion in his church. We have a brief, but interesting account of this dispute by Irenæus, a pupil of Polycarp, which is as follows:[2]

"When the blessed Polycarp sojourned at Rome in the days of Anicetus, and they had some little difference of opinion likewise with regard to other points,[3] they forthwith came to a peaceable understanding on this head [the observance of Easter], having no love for mutual disputes. For neither could Anicetus persuade Polycarp *not to observe*,[4] inasmuch as he [Pol.] had always *observed* with John, the disciple of our Lord, and the other apostles, with whom he had associated; nor did Polycarp persuade Anicetus to *observe* ($\tau\eta\rho\epsilon\tilde{\iota}\nu$), who said that he was bound to maintain the custom of the presbyters (= bishops) before him. These things being so, they communed together; and in the church Anicetus yielded to Polycarp, out of respect no doubt, the celebration of the eucharist ($\tau\dot{\eta}\nu\ \epsilon\dot{\upsilon}\chi\alpha\rho\iota\sigma\tau\acute{\iota}\alpha\nu$), and they separated from each other in peace, all the church being at peace, both those that observed and those that did not observe [the fourteenth of Nisan], maintaining peace."

This letter proves that the Christians of the days of Polycarp

---

[1] Renan (*l. c.*, p. 447) conjectures that Irenæus and Florinus accompanied Polycarp on that journey to Rome. Neander and others give a wrong date, 162. Polycarp died in 155, see § 19, p. 51. The pontificate of Anicetus began in 154 or before.

[2] In a fragment of a letter to the Roman bishop Victor, preserved by Eusebius, *H. E.* V. c. 24 (ed. Heinichen, I. 253).

[3] $\kappa\alpha\grave{\iota}\ \pi\epsilon\rho\grave{\iota}\ \ddot{\alpha}\lambda\lambda\omega\nu\ \tau\iota\nu\tilde{\omega}\nu\ \mu\iota\kappa\rho\grave{\alpha}\ \sigma\chi\acute{o}\nu\tau\epsilon\varsigma$ (or $\ddot{\epsilon}\chi o\nu\tau\epsilon\varsigma$) $\pi\rho\grave{o}\varsigma\ \dot{\alpha}\lambda\lambda\acute{\eta}\lambda o\upsilon\varsigma$.

[4] $\mu\grave{\eta}\ \tau\eta\rho\epsilon\tilde{\iota}\nu$, *i. e.* the fourteenth of Nisan, as appears from the connection and from ch. 23. The $\tau\eta\rho\epsilon\tilde{\iota}\nu$ consisted mainly in fasting, and probably also the celebration of the eucharist in the evening. It was a technical term for legal observances, comp. John 9: 16.

knew how to keep the unity of the Spirit without uniformity of rites and ceremonies. "The very difference in our fasting," says Irenæus in the same letter, "establishes the unanimity in our faith."

2. A few years afterwards, about A. D. 170, the controversy broke out in Laodicea, but was confined to Asia, where a difference had arisen either among the Quartadecimanians themselves, or rather among these and the adherents of the Western observance. The accounts on this interimistic sectional dispute are incomplete and obscure. Eusebius merely mentions that at that time Melito of Sardis wrote two works on the Passover.[1] But these are lost, as also that of Clement of Alexandria on the same topic.[2] Our chief source of information is Claudius Apolinarius (Apollinaris),[3] bishop of Hierapolis, in Phrygia, in two fragments of his writings upon the subject, which have been preserved in the *Chronicon Paschale*.[4] These are as follows:

"There are some now who, from ignorance, love to raise strife about these things, being guilty in this of a pardonable offence; for ignorance does not so much deserve blame as need instruction. And they say that *on the fourteenth* [of Nisan] *the Lord ate the paschal lamb* (τὸ πρόβατον ἔφαγε) with his disciples, but that He himself suffered on the great day of unleavened bread[5] [*i. e.* the fifteenth of Nisan]; and they interpret Matthew as favoring their view from which it appears that their view does not agree with the law,[6] and that the Gospels seem, according to them, to be at variance."[7]

[1] *H. E.* IV. 26.

[2] With the exception of a few fragments in the *Chronicon Paschale*.

[3] Eusebius spells his name ᾽Απολινάριος (IV. 21 and 26, 27, see Heinichen's ed.), and so do Photius, and the Chron. Paschale in most MSS. But the Latins spell his name *Apollinaris*. He lived under Marcus Aurelius (161–180), was apologist and opponent of Montanism which flourished especially in Phrygia, and must not be confounded with one of the two Apollinarius or Apollinaris, father and son, of Laodicea in *Syria*, who flourished in the fourth century.

[4] Ed. Dindorf I. 13; in Routh's *Reliquiæ Sacræ* I. p. 160. Quoted and discussed by Milligan, *l. c.* p. 109 sq.

[5] If this is the genuine Quartadecimanian view, it proves conclusively that it agreed with the Synoptic chronology as to the day of Christ's death, and that Weitzel and Steitz are wrong on this point.

[6] Since according to the view of Apolinarius, Christ as the true fulfillment of the law, must have died on the 14th, the day of the legal passover.

[7] This seems to be the meaning of στασιάζειν δοκεῖ, κατ᾽ αὐτοὺς, τὰ εὐαγγέλια,

" *Tʜᴇ fourteenth is the true Passover of the Lord,* the great sacrifice, the Son of God [1] in the place of the lamb . . . . who was lifted up upon the horns of the unicorn . . . . and who was buried on the day of the Passover, the stone having been placed upon his tomb."

Here Apolinarius evidently protests against the Quartadecimanian practice, yet simply as one arising from ignorance, and not as a blameworthy heresy.   He opposes it as a chronological and exegetical mistake, and seems to hold that the fourteenth, and not the fifteenth, is the great day of the death of Christ as the true Lamb of God, on the false assumption that this truth depends upon the chronological coincidence of the crucifixion and the Jewish passover.   But the question arises : Did he protest from the Western and Roman standpoint which had many advocates in the East,[2] or as a Quartadecimanian ?[3]   In the latter case we would be obliged to distinguish two parties of Quartadecimanians, the orthodox or catholic Quartadecimanians, who simply observed the 14th Nisan by fasting and the evening communion, and a smaller faction of heretical and schismatic Quartadecimanians, who adopted the Jewish practice of eating a paschal lamb on that day in commemoration of the Saviour's last passover.   But there is no evidence for this distinction in the above or other passages.   Such a grossly Judaizing party would have been treated with more severity by a catholic bishop. Even the Jews could no more eat of the paschal lamb after the destruction of the temple in which it had to be slain.   There is no trace of such a party in Irenæus, Hippolytus [4] and Eusebius who speak only of one class of Quartadecimanians.[5]

inter se pugnare, etc.   On the assumption namely that John fixes the death of Christ on the fourteenth of Nisan, which, however, is a point in dispute.   The opponents who started from the chronology of the Synoptists, could retort this objection.

[1] The same argument is urged in the fragments of Hippolytus in the Chronicon Paschale.   But that Jesus was the true Paschal Lamb is a doctrine in which all the churches were agreed.

[2] So Baur (p. 163 sq.) and the Tübingen School rightly maintain.

[3] As Weitzel, Steitz, and Lechler assume in opposition to Baur.

[4] In the passage of the *Philosoph.* above quoted, and in the fragments of the Paschal Chronicle.

[5] Epiphanius, it is true, distinguishes different opinions among the Quarta-

Hence we conclude that Apolinarius protests against the whole Quartadecimanian practice, although very mildly and charitably. The Laodicean controversy was a stage in the same controversy which was previously discussed by Polycarp and Anicetus in Christian charity, and was soon agitated again by Polycrates and Victor with hierarchical and intolerant violence.

3. Much more important and vehement was the third stage of the controversy between 190 and 194, which extended over the whole church, and occasioned many synods and synodical letters.[1] The Roman bishop Victor, a very different man from his predecessor Anicetus, required the Asiatics, in an imperious tone, to abandon their Quartadecimanian practice. Against this Polycrates, bishop of Ephesus, solemnly protested in the name of a synod held by him, and appealed to an imposing array of authorities for their primitive custom. Eusebius has preserved his letter, which is quite characteristic.

"We," wrote the Ephesian bishop to the Roman pope and his church, "We observe the genuine day; neither adding thereto nor taking therefrom. For in Asia great lights[2] have fallen asleep, which shall rise again in the day of the Lord's appearing, in which he will come with glory from heaven, and will raise up all the saints: Philip, one of the twelve apostles, who sleeps in Hierapolis, and his two aged virgin daughters; his other daughter, also, who having lived under the influence of the Holy Spirit, now likewise rests in Ephesus; moreover, John, who rested upon the bosom of our Lord,[3] who was also a priest, and bore the sacerdotal plate,[4] both a martyr and teacher; he is buried in Ephesus. Also Polycarp of Smyrna, both bishop and martyr, and Thrascas, both bishop and martyr of Eumenia, who sleeps in Smyrna. Why should I mention Sagaris, bishop and martyr, who sleeps in Laodicea; moreover, the blessed Papirius, and Melito, the eunuch

decimanians (*Hær.* L. cap. 1-3 *Contra Quartadecimanas*), but he makes no mention of the practice of eating a Paschal lamb, or of any difference in this chronology of the death of Christ.

[1] Eusebius, *H. E.*, V. 23-25.

[2] Μεγάλα στοιχεῖα in the sense of stars used *Ep. ad Diog.* 7; Justin *Dial.* c. 23 (τὰ οὐράνια στοιχεῖα).

[3] ὁ ἐπὶ τὸ στῆθος τοῦ κυρίου ἀναπεσών. Comp. John 13: 25; 21: 20. This designation, as Renan admits (*Marc-Aurèle*, p. 196, note 2), implies that Polycrates acknowledged the Gospel of John as genuine.

[4] τὸ πέταλον. On this singular expression, which is probably figurative for priestly holiness, see vol. 1. p. 431, note 1.

[celibate], who lived altogether under the influence of the Holy Spirit, who now rests in Sardis, awaiting the episcopate from heaven, in which he shall rise from the dead. All these *observed the fourteenth day of the passover according to the gospel*, deviating in no respect, but following the rule of faith.

"Moreover, I, Polycrates, who am the least of you, according to the tradition of my relatives, some of whom I have followed. For seven of my relatives were bishops, and I am the eighth; and my relatives always observed the day when the people of the Jews threw away the leaven. I, therefore, brethren, am now sixty-five years in the Lord, who having conferred with the brethren throughout the world, and having studied the whole of the Sacred Scriptures, am not at all alarmed at those things with which I am threatened, to intimidate me. For they who are greater than I have said, 'we ought to obey God rather than men.' . . . . I could also mention the bishops that were present, whom you requested me to summon, and whom I did call; whose names would present a great number, but who seeing my slender body consented to my epistle, well knowing that I did not wear my gray hairs for nought, but that I did at all times regulate my life in the Lord Jesus."[1]

Victor turned a deaf ear to this remonstrance, branded the Asiatics as heretics, and threatened to excommunicate them.[2]

But many of the Eastern bishops, and even Irenæus, in the name of the Gallic Christians, though he agreed with Victor on the disputed point, earnestly reproved him for such arrogance, and reminded him of the more Christian and brotherly conduct of his predecessors Anicetus, Pius, Hyginus, Telesphorus, and Xystus, who sent the eucharist to their dissenting brethren. He dwelt especially on the fraternal conduct of Anicetus to Polycarp. Irenæus proved himself on this occasion, as Eusebius remarks, a true peacemaker, and his vigorous protest seems to have prevented the schism.

We have from the same Irenæus another utterance on this controversy,[3] saying: "The apostles have ordered that we should 'judge no one in meat or in drink, or in respect to a feast-day or a new moon or a sabbath day' (Col. 2: 16). Whence then these wars? Whence these schisms? We keep the feasts, but in the leaven of malice by tearing the church of

[1] Euseb. V. 24 (ed. Heinichen, I. p. 250 sqq).

[2] He is probably the author of the pseudo-Cyprianic homily against dice-players (*De Aleatoribus*), which assumes the tone of a papal encyclical.

[3] In the third Fragment discovered by Pfaff, probably from his book against Blastus. See *Opera*. ad. Stieren, I. 887.

God and observing what is outward, in order to reject what is better, faith and charity. That such feasts and fasts are displeasing to the Lord, we have heard from the Prophets." A truly evangelical sentiment from one who echoes the teaching of St. John and his last words: "Children, love one another."

4. In the course of the third century the Roman practice gained ground everywhere in the East, and, to anticipate the result, was established by the council of Nicæa in 325 as the law of the whole church. This council considered it unbecoming in Christians to follow the usage of the unbelieving, hostile Jews, and ordained that Easter should always be celebrated on the first Sunday after the first full moon succeeding the vernal equinox (March 21), and always after the Jewish passover.[1] If the full moon occurs on a Sunday, Easter-day is the Sunday after. By this arrangement Easter may take place as early as March 22, or as late as April 25.

Henceforth the Quartadecimanians were universally regarded as heretics, and were punished as such. The Synod of Antioch, 341, excommunicated them. The Montanists and Novatians were also charged with the Quartadecimanian observance. The last traces of it disappeared in the sixth century.

But the desired uniformity in the observance of Easter was still hindered by differences in reckoning the Easter Sunday according to the course of the moon and the vernal equinox, which the Alexandrians fixed on the 21st of March, and the Romans on the 18th; so that in the year 387, for example, the Romans kept Easter on the 21st of March, and the Alexandrians not till the 25th of April. In the West also the computation changed

---

[1] In the Synodical letter which the fathers of Nicæa addressed to the churches of Egypt, Libya, and Pentapolis (Socrates, *H. E.* I. c. 9), it is said: " We have also gratifying intelligence to communicate to you relating to the unity of judgment on the subject of the most holy feast of Easter; . . . . that all the brethren in the East who have heretofore kept this festival at the same time as the Jews, will henceforth conform to the Romans and to us, and to all who from the earliest time have observed our period of celebrating Easter." Eusebius reports (*Vita Const.* III. 19) that especially the province of Asia acknowledged the decree. He thinks that only God and the emperor Constantine could remove this evil of two conflicting celebrations of Easter.

and caused a renewal of the Easter controversy in the sixth and seventh centuries. The old British, Irish and Scotch Christians, and the Irish missionaries on the Continent adhered to the older cycle of eighty-four years in opposition to the later Dionysian or Roman cycle of ninety-five years, and hence were styled "Quartadecimanians" by their Anglo-Saxon and Roman opponents, though unjustly; for they celebrated Easter always on a *Sunday* between the 14th and the 20th of the month (the Romans between the 15th and 21st). The Roman practice triumphed. But Rome again changed the calendar under Gregory XIII. (A. D. 1583). Hence even to this day the Oriental churches who hold to the Julian and reject the Gregorian calendar, differ from the Occidental Christians in the time of the observance of Easter.

All these useless ritualistic disputes might have been avoided if, with some modification of the old Asiatic practice as to the close of the fast, Easter, like Christmas, had been made an immovable feast at least as regards the week, if not the day, of its observance.

NOTE.

The bearing of this controversy on the Johannean origin of the fourth Gospel has been greatly overrated by the negative critics of the Tübingen School. Dr. Baur, Schwegler, Hilgenfeld, Straus (*Leben Jesu*, new ed. 1864, p. 76 sq.), Schenkel, Scholten, Samuel Davidson, Renan (*Marc-Aurèle*, p. 196), use it as a fatal objection to the Johannean authorship. Their argument is this: "The Asiatic practice rested on the belief that Jesus ate the Jewish Passover with his disciples on the evening of the 14th of Nisan, and died on the 15th; this belief is incompatible with the fourth Gospel, which puts the death of Jesus, as the true Paschal Lamb, on the 14th of Nisan, just before the regular Jewish Passover; therefore the fourth Gospel cannot have existed when the Easter controversy first broke out about A. D. 160; or, at all events, it cannot be the work of John to whom the Asiatic Christians so confidently appealed for their paschal observance."

But leaving out of view the early testimonies for the authenticity of John, which reach back to the first quarter of the second century, the minor premise is wrong, and hence the conclusion falls. A closer examination of the relevant passages of John leads to the result that he agrees with the Synoptic account, which puts the last Supper on the 14th, and

the crucifixion on the 15th of Nisan. (Comp. on this chronological difficulty vol. I. 133 sqq.; and the authorities quoted there, especially John
Lightfoot, Wieseler, Robinson, Lange, Kirchner, and McClellan.)

Weitzel, Steitz, and Wagenmann deny the inference of the Tübingen
School by disputing the major premise, and argue that the Asiatic observance (in agreement with the Tübingen school and their own interpretation of John's chronology) implies that Christ died as the true paschal
lamb on the 14th, and not on the 15th of Nisan. To this view we object:
1) It conflicts with the extract from Apolinarius in the Chronicon
Paschale as given p. 214. 2) There is no contradiction between the idea
that Christ died as the true paschal lamb, and the Synoptic chronology;
for the former was taught by Paul (1 Cor. 5: 7), who was quoted for the
Roman practice, and both were held by the fathers; the coincidence in
the time being subordinate to the fact. 3) A contradiction in the primitive tradition of Christ's death is extremely improbable, and it is much
easier to conform the Johannean chronology to the Synoptic than *vice
versa.*

It seems to me that the Asiatic observance of the 14th of Nisan was in
commemoration of the last passover of the Lord, and this of necessity
implied also a commemoration of his death, like every celebration of the
Lord's Supper. In any case, however, these ancient paschal controversies did not hinge on the chronological question or the true date of
Christ's death at all, but on the week-day and the manner of its *annual
observance.* The question was whether the paschal communion should
be celebrated on the 14th of Nisan, or on the Sunday of the resurrection
festival, without regard to the Jewish chronology.

§ 63. *Pentecost.*

Easter was followed by the festival of PENTECOST.[1] It
rested on the Jewish feast of harvest. It was universally observed, as early as the second century, in commemoration of the
appearances and heavenly exaltation of the risen Lord, and had
throughout a joyous character. It lasted through fifty days—
Quinquagesima—which were celebrated as a continuous Sunday,
by daily communion, the standing posture in prayer, and the
absence of all fasting. Tertullian says that all the festivals of
the heathen put together will not make up the one Pentecost of

---

[1] Πεντεκοστή (ἡμέρα), *Quinquagesima*, is the fiftieth day after the Passover
Sabbath, see vol. I. 225 sqq. It is used by the fathers in a wider sense for the
whole period of fifty days, from Easter to Whitsunday, and in a narrower sense
for the single festival of Whitsunday.

the Christians.[1] During that period the Acts of the Apostles were read in the public service (and are read to this day in the Greek church).

Subsequently the celebration was limited to the fortieth day as the feast of the Ascension, and the fiftieth day, or Pentecost proper (Whitsunday) as the feast of the outpouring of the Holy Spirit and the birthday of the Christian Church. In this restricted sense Pentecost closed the cycle of our Lord's festivals (the *semestre Domini*), among which it held the third place (after Easter and Christmas).[2] It was also a favorite time for baptism, especially the vigil of the festival.

§ 64. *The Epiphany.*

The feast of the EPIPHANY is of later origin.[3] It spread from the East towards the West, but here, even in the fourth century, it was resisted by such parties as the Donatists, and condemned as an oriental innovation. It was, in general, the feast of the appearance of Christ in the flesh, and particularly of the manifestation of his Messiahship by his baptism in the Jordan, the festival at once of his birth and his baptism. It was usually kept on the 6th of January. When the East adopted from the West the Christmas festival, Epiphany was restricted to the celebration of the baptism of Christ, and made one of the three great reasons for the administration of baptism.

In the West it was afterwards made a collective festival of several events in the life of Jesus, as the adoration of the Magi, the first miracle of Cana, and sometimes the feeding of the five

---

[1] *De Idol.* c. 12; comp. *De Bapt.* c. 19; *Const. Apost.* V. 20.

[2] In this sense *Pentecoste* is first used by the Council of Elvira (Granada) A. D. 306, can. 43. The week following was afterwards called *Hebdomadas Spiritus Sancti.*

[3] ἡ ἐπιφάνεια, τὰ ἐπιφάνια, ἡ θεοφάνεια, ἡμέρα τῶν φώτων: *Epiphania, Theophania, Dies Luminum, Festum Trium Regum,* etc. The feast is first mentioned by Clement of Alex. as the annual commemoration of the baptism of Christ by the Gnostic sect of the Basilidians (*Strom.* I. 21). Neander supposes that they derived it from the Jewish Christians in Palestine. Chrysostom often alludes to it.

[4] Augustin, *Serm.* 202, § 2.

thousand. It became more particularly the " feast of the three kings," that is, the wise men from the East, and was placed in special connexion with the mission to the heathen. The legend of the three kings (Caspar, Melchior, Baltazar) grew up gradually from the recorded gifts, gold, frankincense, and myrrh, which the Magi offered to the new-born King of the Jews.[1]

Of the CHRISTMAS festival there is no clear trace before the fourth century; partly because the feast of the Epiphany in a measure held the place of it; partly because the birth of Christ, the date of which, at any rate, was uncertain, was less prominent in the Christian mind than his death and resurrection. It was of Western (Roman) origin, and found its way to the East after the middle of the fourth century; for Chrysostom, in a Homily, which was probably preached Dec. 25, 386, speaks of the celebration of the separate day of the Nativity as having been recently introduced in Antioch.

§ 65. *The Order of Public Worship.*

The earliest description of the Christian worship is given us by a heathen, the younger Pliny, A. D. 109, in his well-known letter to Trajan, which embodies the result of his judicial investigations in Bithynia.[2] According to this, the Christians assembled on an appointed day (Sunday) at sunrise, sang responsively a song to Christ as to God,[3] and then pledged themselves by an oath (*sacramentum*) not to do any evil work, to commit no theft, robbery, nor adultery, not to break their word, nor sacrifice property intrusted to them. Afterwards (at evening) they assembled again, to eat ordinary and innocent food (the agape).

This account of a Roman official then bears witness to the

---

[1] Matt. 2 : 11. The first indistinct trace, perhaps, is in Tertullian, *Adv. Jud.* c. 9: *Nam et Magos reges fere habuit Oriens.*" The apocryphal Gospels of the infancy give us no fiction on that point.

[2] Comp. § 17, p. 46, and G. Boissier, *De l'authenticité de la lettre de Pline au sujet des Chrétiens,* in the " Revue Archéol.," 1876, p. 114–125.

[3] " *Quod essent soliti stato die ante lucem convenire, carmenque Christo, quasi Deo, dicere secum invicem.*"

primitive observance of Sunday, the separation of the love-feast from the morning worship (with the communion), and the worship of Christ as God in song.

Justin Martyr, at the close of his larger Apology,[1] describes the public worship more particularly, as it was conducted about the year 140. After giving a full account of baptism and the holy Supper, to which we shall refer again, he continues :

" On Sunday[2] a meeting of all, who live in the cities and villages, is held, and a section from the Memoirs of the Apostles (the Gospels) and the writings of the Prophets (the Old Testament) is read, as long as the time permits.[3] When the reader has finished, the president,[4] in a discourse, gives an exhortation[5] to the imitation of these noble things. After this we all rise in common prayer.[6] At the close of the prayer, as we have before described,[7] bread and wine with water are brought. The president offers prayer and thanks for them, according to the power given him,[8] and the congregation responds the Amen. Then the consecrated elements are distributed to each one, and partaken, and are carried by the deacons to the houses of the absent. The wealthy and the willing then give contributions according to their free will, and this collection is deposited with the president, who therewith supplies orphans and widows, poor

---

[1] *Apol.* I. c. 65–67 (*Opera*, ed. Otto III. Tom. I. P. I. 177–188). The passage quoted is from ch. 67.

[2] τῇ τοῦ Ἡλίου λεγομένῃ ἡμέρᾳ.

[3] Μέχρις ἐγχωρεῖ.

[4] Ὁ προεστώς, the presiding presbyter or bishop.

[5] Τὴν νουθεσίαν καὶ παράκλησιν.

[6] Εὐχὰς πέμπομεν, *preces emittimus.*

[7] Chap. 65.

[8] Ὅση δύναμις αὐτῷ, that is probably *pro viribus, quantum potest;* or like Tertullian's " *de pectore*" and "*ex proprio ingenio.*" Others translate wrongly : *totis viribus,* with all his might, or with a clear, loud voice. Comp. Otto, *l. c.* 187. The passages, however, in no case contain any *opposition* to forms of prayer which were certainly in use already at that time, and familiar without book to every worshipper; above all the Lord's Prayer. The whole liturgical literature of the fourth and fifth centuries presupposes a much older liturgical tradition. The prayers in the eighth book of the Apost. Constitutions are probably among the oldest portions of the work.

and needy, prisoners and strangers, and takes care of all who are in want. We assemble in common on Sunday, because this is the first day, on which God created the world and the light, and because Jesus Christ our Saviour on the same day rose from the dead and appeared to his disciples."

Here, reading of the Scriptures, preaching (and that as an episcopal function), prayer, and communion, plainly appear as the regular parts of the Sunday worship ; all descending, no doubt, from the apostolic age. Song is not expressly mentioned here, but elsewhere.[1] The communion is not yet clearly separated from the other parts of worship. But this was done towards the end of the second century.

The same parts of worship are mentioned in different places by Tertullian.[2]

The eighth book of the Apostolical Constitutions contains already an elaborate service with sundry liturgical prayers.[3]

§ 66.　Parts of Worship.

1. The READING OF SCRIPTURE LESSONS from the Old Testament with practical application and exhortation passed from the Jewish synagogue to the Christian church. The lessons from the New Testament came prominently into use as the Gospels and Epistles took the place of the oral instruction of the apostolic age. The reading of the Gospels is expressly mentioned by Justin Martyr, and the Apostolical Constitutions add the Epistles and the Acts.[4] During the Pentecostal season the Acts of the Apostles furnished the lessons. But there was no uniform system of selection before the Nicene age. Besides the canonical Scripture, post-apostolic writings, as the Epistle of Clement of Rome, the Epistle of Barnabas, and the Pastor of Hermas, were read in some congregations, and are found in

---

[1] Cap. 13.　Justin himself wrote a book entitled ψάλτης.

[2] See the passages quoted by Otto. *l. c.* 184 sq.

[3] B. VIII. 3 sqq.　Also VII. 33 sqq.　See translation in the "Ante-Nicene Library," vol. XVII., P. II. 191 sqq. and 212 sqq.

[4] BK. VII. 5.

important MSS. of the New Testament.[1] The Acts of Martyrs were also read on the anniversary of their martyrdom.

2. The SERMON [2] was a familiar exposition of Scripture and exhortation to repentance and a holy life, and gradually assumed in the Greek church an artistic, rhetorical character. Preaching was at first free to every member who had the gift of public speaking, but was gradually confined as an exclusive privilege of the clergy, and especially the bishop. Origen was called upon to preach before his ordination, but this was even then rather an exception. The oldest known homily, now recovered in full (1875), is from an unknown Greek or Roman author of the middle of the second century, probably before A. D. 140 (formerly ascribed to Clement of Rome). He addresses the hearers as " brothers" and " sisters," and read from manuscript.[3] The homily has no literary value, and betrays confusion and intellectual poverty, but is inspired by moral earnestness and triumphant faith. It closes with this doxology: "To the only God invisible, the Father of truth, who sent forth unto us the Saviour and Prince of immortality, through whom also He made manifest unto us the truth and the heavenly life, to Him be the glory forever and ever. Amen."[4]

3. PRAYER. This essential part of all worship passed like-

[1] The Ep. of Clemens in the Codex Alexandrinus (A); Barnabas and Hermas in the Cod. Sinaiticus.

[2] ‘Ομιλία, λόγος, sermo, tractatus.

[3] § 19, ἀναγινώσκω ὑμῖν. But the homily may have first been delivered extempore, and taken down by short-hand writers (ταχυγράφοι, notarii). See Lightfoot, p. 306.

[4] Ed. by Bryennios (1875), and in the Patr. Apost. ed. by de Gebhardt and Harnack, I. 111–143. A good translation by Lightfoot, S. Clement of Rome, Appendix, 380–390. Lightfoot says: " If the first Epistle of Clement is the earliest foreshadowing of a Christian liturgy, the so called Second Epistle is the first example of a Christian homily." He thinks that the author was a bishop; Harnack, that he was a layman, as he seems to distinguish himself from the presbyters. Lightfoot assigns him to Corinth, and explains in this way the fact that the homily was bound up with the letter of Clement to the Corinthians; while Harnack ably maintains the Roman origin from the time and circle of Hermas. Bryennios ascribes it to Clement of Rome (which is quite impossible), Hilgenfeld to Clement of Alexandria (which is equally impossible).

wise from the Jewish into the Christian service. The oldest prayers of post-apostolic times are the eucharistic thanksgivings in the *Didache*, and the intercession at the close of Clement's Epistle to the Corinthians, which seems to have been used in the Roman church.[1] It is long and carefully composed, and largely interwoven with passages from the Old Testament. It begins with an elaborate invocation of God in antithetical sentences, contains intercession for the afflicted, the needy, the wanderers, and prisoners, petitions for the conversion of the heathen, a confession of sin and prayer for pardon (but without a formula of absolution), and closes with a prayer for unity and a doxology. Very touching is the prayer for rulers then so hostile to the Christians, that God may grant them health, peace, concord and stability. The document has a striking resemblance to portions of the ancient liturgies which begin to appear in the fourth century, but bear the names of Clement, James and Mark, and probably include some primitive elements.[2]

The last book of the Apostolical Constitutions contains the pseudo- or post-Clementine liturgy, with special prayers for believers, catechumens, the possessed, the penitent, and even for the dead, and a complete eucharistic service.[3]

The usual posture in prayer was standing with outstretched arms in Oriental fashion.

4. SONG. The Church inherited the psalter from the synagogue, and has used it in all ages as an inexhaustible treasury of devotion. The psalter is truly catholic in its spirit and aim; it springs from the deep fountains of the human heart in its secret communion with God, and gives classic expression to the

---

[1] *Ad Cor.* ch. 59–61, discovered and first published by Bryennios, 1875. We give Clement's prayer below, p. 228 sq. The prayers of the *Didache* (chs. 9 and 10), brought to light by Bryennios, 1883, are still older, and breathe the spirit of primitive simplicity. See ¿ 68.

[2] See vol. III. 517 sqq., and add to the literature there quoted, PROBST (R. C.), *Die Liturgie der 3 ersten Jahrh.*, Tüb., 1870; C. A. HAMMOND, *Ancient Liturgies* (with introduction, notes, and liturgical glossary), Oxford and Lond., 1878.

[3] *Ap. Const.*, Bk. VIII., also in the liturgical collections of Daniel, Neale, Hammond, etc.

religious experience of all men in every age and tongue. This is the best proof of its inspiration. Nothing like it can be found in all the poetry of heathendom. The psalter was first enriched by the inspired hymns which saluted the birth of the Saviour of the world, the *Magnificat* of Mary, the *Benedictus* of Zacharias, the *Gloria in Excelsis* of the heavenly host, and the *Nunc Dimittis* of the aged Simeon. These hymns passed at once into the service of the Church, to resound through all successive centuries, as things of beauty which are "a joy forever." Traces of primitive Christian poems can be found throughout the Epistles and the Apocalypse. The angelic anthem (Luke 2: 14) was expanded into the *Gloria in Excelsis*, first in the Greek church, in the third, if not the second, century, and afterwards in the Latin, and was used as the morning hymn.[1] It is one of the classical forms of devotion, like the Latin *Te Deum* of later date. The evening hymn of the Greek church is less familiar and of inferior merit.

The following is a free translation :

"Hail! cheerful Light, of His pure glory poured,
   Who is th' Immortal Father, Heavenly, Blest,
Holiest of Holies—Jesus Christ our Lord!
   Now are we come to the Sun's hour of rest,
   The lights of Evening round us shine,
We sing the Father, Son, and Holy Ghost Divine!
   Worthiest art Thou at all times, to be sung
     With undefiled tongue,
Son of our God, Giver of Life alone!
Therefore, in all the world, Thy glories, Lord, we own."[2]

---

[1] *Const. Apost.* lib. VII. 47. Also in Daniel's *Thesaurus Hymnol.*, tom. III., p. 4, where it is called ὕμνος ἑωθινός (as in Cod. Alex.), and commences: Δόξα ἐν ὑψίστοις Θεῷ. Comp. Tom. II. 268 sqq. It is also called *hymnus angelicus*, while the *Ter Sanctus* (from Isa. 6: 3) came afterwards to be distinguished as *hymnus seraphicus*. Daniel ascribes the former to the third century, Routh to the second. It is found with slight variations at the end of the Alexandrian Codex of the Bible (in the British Museum), and in the Zurich Psalter reprinted by Tischendorf in his *Monumenta Sacra*. The Latin form is usually traced to Hilary of Poictiers in the fourth century.

[2] Daniel, *l. c.* vol. III. p. 5. Comp. in part *Const. Ap.* VIII. 37. The ὕμνος ἑσπερινός or ὕμνος τοῦ λυχνικοῦ, commences:

Φῶς ἱλαρὸν ἁγίας δόξης,
'Αθανάτου πατρὸς οὐρανίου.

An author towards the close of the second century[1] could appeal against the Artemonites, to a multitude of hymns in proof of the faith of the church in the divinity of Christ: " How many psalms and odes of the Christians are there not, which have been written from the beginning by believers, and which, in their theology, praise Christ as the Logos of God?" Tradition says, that the antiphonies, or responsive songs, were introduced by Ignatius of Antioch. The Gnostics, Valentine and Bardesanes, also composed religious songs; and the church surely learned the practice not from them, but from the Old Testament psalms.

The oldest Christian poem preserved to us which can be traced to an individual author is from the pen of the profound Christian philosopher, Clement of Alexandria, who taught theology in that city before A. D. 202. It is a sublime but somewhat turgid song of praise to the Logos, as the divine educator and leader of the human race, and though not intended and adapted for public worship, is remarkable for its spirit and antiquity.[2]

NOTES.

I. The Prayer of the Roman Church from the newly recovered portion of the Epistle of Clement to the Corinthians, ch. 59–61 (in Bishop Lightfoot's translation, *St. Clement of Rome*, Append. pp. 376–378) :

"Grant unto us, Lord, that we may set our hope on Thy Name which is the primal source of all creation, and open the eyes of our hearts, that we may know Thee, who alone *abidest Highest in the highest, Holy in the holy;* who *layest low the insolence of the proud:* who *scatterest the imaginings of nations;* who *settest the lowly on high,* and *bringest the lofty low;* who *makest rich and makest poor;* who *killest and makest alive;* who alone art the Benefactor of spirits and the God of all flesh; who *lookest into the abysses,* who scannest the works of

---

[1] In Euseb. *H. E.* V. 28.

[2] In the *Pædag.* III. 12 (p. 311 ed. Pott.); also in Daniel's *Thesaurus hymnologicus* III. p. 3 and 4. Daniel calls it "*vetustissimus hymnus ecclesiæ,*" but the *Gloria in Excelsis* may dispute this claim. The poem has been often translated into German, by Münter (in Rambach's *Anthologie christl. Gesänge,* I. p. 35); Dorner (*Christologie,* I. 293); Fortlage (*Gesänge christl. Vorzeit,* 1844, p. 38); and in rhyme by Hagenbach (*Die K. G. der 3 ersten Jahrh.* p. 222 sq.). An English translation may be found in Mrs. Charles: *The Voice of Christian Life in Song,* N. York, 1858, p. 44 sq., and a closer one in the " Ante-Nicene Christian Library," vol. V. p. 343 sq.

man; the Succor of them that are in peril, *the Saviour of them that are in despair;* the Creator and Overseer of every spirit; who multipliest the nations upon earth, and hast chosen out from all men those that love Thee through Jesus Christ, Thy beloved Son, through whom Thou didst instruct us, didst sanctify us, didst honor us. We beseech Thee, Lord and Master, to be our help and succor. Save those among us who are in tribulation; have mercy on the lowly; lift up the fallen; show Thyself unto the needy; heal the ungodly; convert the wanderers of Thy people; feed the hungry; release our prisoners; raise up the weak; comfort the faint-hearted. Let all the Gentiles know that *Thou art God alone,* and Jesus Christ is Thy Son, and *we are Thy people and the sheep of Thy pasture.*

"Thou through Thine operations didst make manifest the everlasting fabric of the world. Thou, Lord, didst create the earth. Thou that art faithful throughout all generations, righteous in Thy judgments, marvellous in strength and excellence. Thou that art wise in creating and prudent in establishing that which Thou hast made, that art good in the things which are seen and faithful with them that trust on Thee, pitiful and compassionate, forgive us our iniquities and our unrighteousnesses and our transgressions and shortcomings. Lay not to our account every sin of Thy servants and Thine handmaids, but cleanse us with the cleansing of Thy truth, and guide our steps to walk in holiness and righteousness and singleness of heart, and to do such things as are good and well-pleasing in Thy sight and in the sight of our rulers. Yea, Lord, make Thy face to shine upon us in peace for our good, that we may be sheltered by Thy mighty hand and delivered from every sin by Thine uplifted arm. And deliver us from them that hate us wrongfully. Give concord and peace to us and to all that dwell on the earth, as thou gavest to our fathers, when they called on Thee in faith and truth with holiness, that we may be saved, while we render obedience to Thine almighty and most excellent Name, and to our rulers and governors upon the earth.

"Thou, Lord and Master, hast given them the power of sovereignty through Thine excellent and unspeakable might, that we knowing the glory and honor which Thou hast given them may submit ourselves unto them, in nothing resisting Thy will. Grant unto them therefore, O Lord, health, peace, concord, stability, that they may administer the government which Thou hast given them without failure. For Thou, O heavenly Master, King of the ages, givest to the sons of men glory and honor and power over all things that are upon earth. Do Thou, Lord, direct their counsel according to that which is good and well pleasing in Thy sight, that, administering in peace and gentleness with godliness the power which Thou hast given them, they may obtain Thy favor. O Thou, who alone art able to do these things and things far more exceeding good than these for us, we praise Thee through the High-priest and Guardian of our souls, Jesus Christ, through whom be the glory and the majesty unto Thee both now and for all generations and for ever and ever. Amen."

II. A literal translation of the poem of Clement of Alexandria in praise of Christ. Ὕμνος τοῦ Σωτῆρος Χριστοῦ. (Στομίον πώλων ἀδάων).

" Bridle of untamed colts,
Wing of unwandering birds,
Sure Helm of babes,
Shepherd of royal lambs!
Assemble Thy simple children,
To praise holily,
To hymn guilelessly
With innocent mouths
Christ, the guide of children.

O King of saints,
All-subduing Word
Of the most high Father,
Prince of wisdom,
Support of sorrows,
That rejoicest in the ages,
Jesus, Saviour
Of the human race,
Shepherd, Husbandman,
Helm, Bridle,
Heavenly Wing,
Of the all holy flock,
Fisher of men
Who are saved,
Catching the chaste fishes
With sweet life
From the hateful wave
Of a sea of vices.

Guide [us], Shepherd
Of rational sheep;
Guide harmless children,
O holy King.

O footsteps of Christ,
O heavenly way,
Perennial Word,
Endless age,
Eternal Light,
Fount of mercy,
Performer of virtue.
Noble [is the] life of those
Who praise God,
O Christ Jesus,
Heavenly milk
Of the sweet breasts
Of the graces of the Bride,
Pressed out of Thy wisdom.

Babes, nourished
With tender mouths,
Filled with the dewy spirit
Of the spiritual breast,
Let us sing together
Simple praises
True hymns
To Christ [the] King,
Holy reward
For the doctrine of life.
Let us sing together,
Sing in simplicity
To the mighty Child.
O choir of peace,
The Christ begotten,
O chaste people
Let us praise together
The God of peace."

This poem was for sixteen centuries merely a hymnological curiosity, until an American Congregational minister, Dr. HENRY MARTYN DEXTER, by a happy reproduction, in 1846, secured it a place in modern hymn-books. While preparing a sermon (as he informs me) on "some prominent characteristics of the early Christians" (text, Deut. 32: 7, " Remember the days of old "), he first wrote down an exact translation of the Greek hymn of Clement, and then reproduced and modernized it for the use of his congregation in connection with the sermon. It is well known that many Psalms of Israel have inspired some of the noblest

Christian hymns. The 46th Psalm gave the key-note of Luther's triumphant war-hymn of the Reformation: *" Ein' feste Burg."* John Mason Neale dug from the dust of ages many a Greek and Latin hymn, to the edification of English churches, notably some portions of Bernard of Cluny's *De Contemptu Mundi,* which runs through nearly three thousand dactylic hexameters, and furnished the material for "Brief life is here our portion," "For thee, O dear, dear Country," and "Jerusalem the golden." We add Dexter's hymn as a fair specimen of a useful transfusion and rejuvenation of an old poem.

1. Shepherd of tender youth,
   Guiding in love and truth
      Through devious ways;
   Christ, our triumphant King,
   We come Thy name to sing;
   Hither our children bring
      To shout Thy praise!

2. Thou art our Holy Lord,
   The all-subduing Word,
      Healer of strife!
   Thou didst Thyself abase,
   That from sin's deep disgrace
   Thou mightest save our race,
      And give us life.

3. Thou art the great High Priest;
   Thou hast prepared the feast
      Of heavenly love;
   While in our mortal pain

None calls on Thee in vain;
Help Thou dost not disdain—
   Help from above.

4. Ever be Thou our Guide,
   Our Shepherd and our Pride,
      Our Staff and Song!
   Jesus, Thou Christ of God,
   By Thy perennial Word
   Lead us where Thou hast trod,
      Make our faith strong.

5. So now, and till we die,
   Sound we Thy praises high,
      And joyful sing:
   Infants, and the glad throng
   Who to Thy Church belong,
   Unite to swell the song
      To Christ our King!

§ 67. *Division of Divine Service. The Disciplina Arcani.*

RICHARD ROTHE: *De Disciplinæ Arcani, quæ dicitur, in Ecclesia Christ. Origine.* Heidelb. 1841; and his art. on the subject in the first ed. of Herzog (vol. I. 469–477).

C. A. GERH. VON ZEZSCHWITZ: *System der christl. kirchlichen Katechetik.* Leipz. 1863, vol. I. p. 154–227. See also his art. in the second ed. of Herzog, I. 637–645 (abridged in Schaff's "Rel. Enc.").

G. NATH. BONWETSCH (of Dorpat): *Wesen, Entstehung und Fortgang der Arkandisciplin,* in Kahnis' "Zeitschrift für hist. Theol." 1873, pp. 203 sqq.

J. P. LUNDY: *Monumental Christianity.* N. York, 1876, p. 62–86.

Comp. also A. W. HADDAN in Smith & Cheetham, I. 564–566; WAN-
DINGER, in Wetzer & Welte, new ed. vol. I. (1882), 1234–1238. Older
dissertations on the subject by SCHELSTRATE (1678), MEIER (1679),
TENZELL (1863), SCHOLLINER (1756), LIENHARDT (1829), TOKLOT
(1836), FROMMANN (1833), SIEGEL (1836, I. 506 sqq.).

The public service was divided from the middle of the second
century down to the close of the fifth, into the worship of the
catechumens,[1] and the worship of the faithful.[2] The former
consisted of scripture reading, preaching, prayer, and song, and
was open to the unbaptized and persons under penance. The
latter consisted of the holy communion, with its liturgical appendages; none but the proper members of the church could attend
it; and before it began, all catechumens and unbelievers left the
assembly at the order of the deacon,[3] and the doors were closed
or guarded.

The earliest witness for this strict separation is Tertullian,
who reproaches the heretics with allowing the baptized and the
unbaptized to attend the same prayers, and casting the holy even
before the heathens.[4] He demands, that believers, catechumens,
and heathens should occupy separate places in public worship.
The Alexandrian divines furnished a theoretical ground for this

---

[1] Λειτουργία τῶν κατηχουμένων, *Missa Catechumenorum.* The name *missa*
(from which our *mass* is derived) occurs first in Augustin and in the acts of
the council of Carthage, A.D. 398. It arose from the formula of dismission at
the close of each part of the service, and is equivalent to *missio, dismissio.*
Augustin (*Serm.* 49, c. 8): "Take notice, after the sermon the dismissal (*missa*)
of the catechumens takes place; the faithful will remain." Afterwards *missa*
came to designate exclusively the communion service. In the Greek church
λειτουργία or λιτουργία, *service,* is the precise equivalent for *missa.*

[2] Λειτουργία τῶν πιστῶν, *Missa Fidelium.*

[3] Μή τις τῶν κατηχουμένων, μή τις τῶν ἀκροωμένων, μή τις τῶν ἀπίστων, μή τις
ἑτεροδόξων, "Let none of the catechumens, let none of the hearers, let none of
the unbelievers, let none of the heterodox, stay here." *Const. Apost.* viii. 12.
Comp. Chrysostom, *Hom. in Matt.* xxiii.

[4] *De Prœscr. Hœr.* c. 41: "*Quis catechumenus, quis fidelis, incertum est*" (that
is, among the heretics); "*pariter adeunt, pariter orant, etiam ethnici, si superve-
nerint; sanctum canibus et porcis margaritas, licet non veras*" (since they have no
proper sacraments), "*jactabunt.*" But this does not apply to all heretics, least
of all to the Manichæans, who carried the notion of mystery in the sacraments
much further than the Catholics.

practice by their doctrine of a secret tradition for the esoteric. Besides the communion, the sacrament of baptism, with its accompanying confession, was likewise treated as a mystery for the initiated,[1] and withdrawn from the view of Jews and heathens.

We have here the beginnings of the Christian mystery-worship, or what has been called since 1679 "the Secret Discipline," (*Disciplina Arcani*), which is presented in its full development in the liturgies of the fourth century, but disappeared from the Latin church after the sixth century, with the dissolution of heathenism and the universal introduction of infant baptism.

The Secret Discipline had reference chiefly to the celebration of the sacraments of baptism and the eucharist, but included also the baptismal symbol, the Lord's Prayer, and the doctrine of the Trinity. Clement of Alexandria, Origen, Cyril of Jerusalem, and other fathers make a distinction between lower or elementary (exoteric) and higher or deeper (esoteric) doctrines, and state that the latter are withheld from the uninitiated out of reverence and to avoid giving offence to the weak and the heathen. This mysterious reticence, however, does not justify the inference that the Secret Discipline included transubstantiation, purgatory, and other Roman dogmas which are not expressly taught in the writings of the fathers. The argument from silence is set aside by positive proof to the contrary.[2] Modern Roman archæologists have pressed the whole symbolism of the Catacombs into the service of the Secret Discipline, but without due regard to the age of those symbolical representations.

The origin of the Secret Discipline has been traced by some to

---

[1] Μύηται, *initiati* = πιστοί, *fideles.*

[2] The learned Jesuit Emanuel von Schelstrate first used this argument in *Antiquitas illustrata* (Antv. 1678), and *De Disciplina Arcani* (Rom. 1685); but he was refuted by the Lutheran W. Ernst Tentzel, in his *Dissert. de Disc. Arcani*, Lips. 1683 and 1692. Tentzel, Casaubon, Bingham, Rothe, and Zetzschwitz are wrong, however, in confining the *Disc. Arc.* to the ritual and excluding the dogma. See especially Cyril of Jerus. *Katech.* XVI. 26; XVIII. 32, 33.

the apostolic age, on the ground of the distinction made between "milk for babes" and "strong meat" for those "of full age," and between speaking to "carnal" and to "spiritual" hearers.[1] But this distinction has no reference to public worship, and Justin Martyr, in his first Apology, addressed to a heathen emperor, describes the celebration of baptism and the eucharist without the least reserve. Others derive the institution from the sacerdotal and hierarchical spirit which appeared in the latter part of the second century, and which no doubt favored and strengthened it;[2] still others, from the Greek and Roman mystery worship, which would best explain many expressions and formulas, together with all sorts of unscriptural pedantries connected with these mysteries.[3] Yet the first motive must be sought rather in an opposition to heathenism; to wit, in the feeling of the necessity of guarding the sacred transactions of Christianity, the embodiment of its deepest truths, against profanation in the midst of a hostile world, according to Matt. 7: 6; especially when after Hadrian, perhaps even from the time of Nero, those transactions came to be so shamefully misunderstood and slandered. To this must be added a proper regard for modesty and decency in the administration of adult baptism by immersion. Finally—and this is the chief cause—the institution of the order of catechumens led to a distinction of half-Christians and full-Christians, exoteric and esoteric, and this distinction gradually became

---

[1] Heb. 5: 12–14; 1 Cor. 3: 1, 2. So some fathers who carry the *Disc. Arc.* back to the Lord's command, Matt. 7 : 6, and in recent times Credner (1844), and Wandinger (in the new ed. of Wetzer and Welte, I. 1237). St. Paul, 1 Cor. 14: 23–25, implies the presence of strangers in the public services, but not necessarily during the communion.

[2] So Bonwetsch, *l. c.*, versus Rothe and Zetzchwitz.

[3] The correspondence is very apparent in the ecclesiastical use of such terms as μυστήριον, σύμβολον, μύησις, μυσταγωγεῖν, κάθαρσις, τελείωσις, φωτισμός (of baptism), etc. On the Greek, and especially the Eleusinian cultus of mysteries, comp. Lobeck, *Aglaophanus*, Königsberg, 1829; several articles of Preller in Pauly's *Realencyklop. der Alterthumswissenschaft* III. 83 sqq., V. 311 sqq., Zetzschwitz, *l. c.* 156 sqq., and Lübker's *Reallex. des class. Alterthums*, 5th ed. by Erler (1877), p. 762. Lobeck has refuted the older view of Warburton and Creuzer, that a secret wisdom, and especially the traditions of a primitive revelation, were propagated in the Greek mysteries.

established in the liturgy. The secret discipline was therefore a temporary, educational and liturgical expedient of the ante-Nicene age. The catechumenate and the division of the acts of worship grew together and declined together. With the disappearance of *adult* catechumens, or with the general use of infant baptism and the union of church and state, disappeared also the secret discipline in the sixth century: " *cessante causa cessat effectus.*"

The Eastern church, however, has retained in her liturgies to this day the ancient form for the dismission of catechumens, the special prayers for them, the designation of the sacraments as "mysteries," and the partial celebration of the mass behind the veil; though she also has for centuries had no catechumens in the old sense of the word, that is, adult heathen or Jewish disciples preparing for baptism, except in rare cases of exception, or on missionary ground.

§ 68. *Celebration of the Eucharist.*

The celebration of the Eucharist or holy communion with appropriate prayers of the faithful was the culmination of Christian worship.[1] Justin Martyr gives us the following description, which still bespeaks the primitive simplicity:[2] "After the prayers [of the catechumen worship] we greet one another with the brotherly kiss. Then bread and a cup with water and wine are handed to the president (bishop) of the brethren. He receives them, and offers praise, glory, and thanks to the Father of all, through the name of the Son and the Holy Spirit, for these his gifts. When he has ended the prayers and thanksgiving, the whole congregation responds: 'Amen.' For 'Amen' in the Hebrew tongue means: 'Be it so.' Upon this the deacons, as we call them, give to each of those present some of the blessed bread,[3] and of the wine mingled with water, and carry it to the absent in their dwellings. This food is called with us

---

[1] Names: εὐχαριστία, κοινωνία, *eucharistia, communio, communicatio*, etc.
[2] *Apol.* I. c. 65, 66.
[3] Εὐχαριστηθέντος ἄρτου.

the *eucharist*, of which none can partake, but the believing and baptized, who live according to the commands of Christ. For we use these not as common bread and common drink; but like as Jesus Christ our Redeemer was made flesh through the word of God, and took upon him flesh and blood for our redemption; so we are taught, that the nourishment blessed by the word of prayer, by which our flesh and blood are nourished by trans-formation (assimilation), is the flesh and blood of the incarnate Jesus."

Then he relates the institution from the Gospels, and men-tions the customary collections for the poor.

We are not warranted in carrying back to this period the full liturgical service, which we find prevailing with striking unifor-mity in essentials, though with many variations in minor points, in all quarters of the church in the Nicene age. A certain sim-plicity and freedom characterized the period before us. Even the so-called Clementine liturgy, in the eighth book of the pseudo-Apostolical Constitutions, was probably not composed and written out in this form before the fourth century. There is no trace of *written* liturgies during the Diocletian persecution. But the germs date from the second century. The oldest eucharistic prayers have recently come to light in the *Didache*, which contains three thanksgivings for the cup, the broken bread, and for all mercies. (chs. 9 and 10.)

From scattered statements of the ante-Nicene fathers we may gather the following view of the eucharistic service as it may have stood in the middle of the third century, if not earlier.

The communion was a regular and the most solemn part of the Sunday worship; or it was the worship of God in the stricter sense, in which none but full members of the church could engage. In many places and by many Christians it was celebrated even daily, after apostolic precedent, and according to the very common mystical interpretation of the fourth petition of the Lord's prayer.[1] The service began, after the dismission of

---

[1] Cyprian speaks of daily sacrifices. *Ep.* 54: "*Sacerdotes qui sacrificia Dei quotidie celebramus.*" So Ambrose, *Ep.* 14 *ad Marcell.*, and the oldest liturgical

the catechumens, with the kiss of peace, given by the men to men, and by the women to women, in token of mutual recognitión as members of one redeemed family in the midst of a heartless and loveless world. It was based upon apostolic precedent, and is characteristic of the childlike simplicity, and love and joy of the early Christians.[1] The service proper consisted of two principal acts: the *oblation*,[2] or presenting of the offerings of the congregation by the deacons for the ordinance itself, and for the benefit of the clergy and the poor; and the *communion*, or partaking of the consecrated elements. In the oblation the congregation at the same time presented itself as a living thank-offering; as in the communion it appropriated anew in faith the sacrifice of Christ, and united itself anew with its Head. Both acts were accompanied and consecrated by prayer and songs of praise.

In the prayers we must distinguish, first, the general *thanksgiving* (the eucharist in the strictest sense of the word) for all the natural and spiritual gifts of God, commonly ending with the seraphic hymn, Isa. 6: 3; secondly, the prayer of *consecration*, or the invocation of the Holy Spirit[3] upon the people and

works. But that the observance was various, is certified by Augustin, among others. *Ep.* 118 *ad Januar.* c. 2: "*Alii quotidie communicant corpori et sanguini Dominico; alii certis diebus accipiunt; alibi nullus dies intermittitur quo non offeratur; alibi sabbato tantum et dominico; alibi tantum dominico.*" St. Basil says (*Ep.* 289): "We commune four times in the week, on the Lord's Day, the fourth day, the preparation day [Friday], and the Sabbath." Chrysostom complains of the small number of communicants at the daily sacrifice.

[1] Rom. 16: 16; 1 Cor. 16: 20; 2 Cor. 13: 12; 1 Thess. 5: 26; 1 Pet. 5: 14. The Kiss of Peace continued in the Latin church till the end of the thirteenth century, and was then transferred to the close of the service or exchanged for a mere form of words: *Pax tibi et ecclesiæ.* In the Russian church the clergy kiss each other during the recital of the Nicene Creed to show the nominal union of orthodoxy and charity (so often divided). In the Coptic church the primitive custom is still in force, and in some small Protestant sects it has been revived.

[2] Προσφορά.

[3] Ἐπίκλησις τοῦ Πν. Ἁγ. Irenæus derives this *invocatio Spiritus S.*, as well as the oblation and the thanksgiving, from apostolic instruction. See the 2nd fragment, in Stieren, I. 854. It appears in all the Greek liturgies. In the *Liturgia Jacobi* it reads thus: Καὶ ἐξαπόστειλον ἐφ᾽ ἡμᾶς καὶ ἐπὶ τὰ προσκείμενε

the elements, usually accompanied by the recital of the words of institution and the Lord's Prayer; and finally, the general *intercessions* for all classes, especially for the believers, on the ground of the sacrifice of Christ on the cross for the salvation of the world. The length and order of the prayers, however, were not uniform; nor the position of the Lord's Prayer, which sometimes took the place of the prayer of consecration, being reserved for the prominent part of the service. Pope Gregory I. says that it "was the custom of the Apostles to consecrate the oblation only by the Lord's Prayer." The congregation responded from time to time, according to the ancient Jewish and the apostolic usage, with an audible "Amen," or "Kyrie eleison." The "Sursum corda," also, as an incitement to devotion, with the response, "Habemus ad Dominum," appears at least as early as Cyprian's time, who expressly alludes to it, and in all the ancient liturgies. The prayers were spoken, not read from a book. But extemporaneous prayer naturally assumes a fixed form by constant repetition.

The elements were common or leavened bread[1] (except among the Ebionites, who, like the later Roman church from the seventh century, used unleavened bread), and wine mingled with water. This mixing was a general custom in antiquity, but came now to have various mystical meanings attached to it. The elements were placed in the hands (not in the mouth) of each communicant by the clergy who were present, or, according to Justin, by the deacons alone, amid singing of psalms by the congregation (Psalm 34), with the words: "The body of Christ;" "The blood of Christ, the cup of life;" to each of

δῶρα ταῦτα τὸ Πνεῦμά σου τὸ πανάγιον, τὸ κύριον καὶ ζωοποιὸν ... ἵνα ... ἁγιάσῃ καὶ ποιήσῃ τὸν μὲν ἄρτον τοῦτον σῶμα ἅγιον τοῦ Χριστοῦ σου, καὶ τὸ ποτήριον τοῦτο αἷμα τίμιον τοῦ Χρ. σου, ἵνα γένηται πᾶσι τοῖς ἐξ αὐτῶν μεταλαμβάνουσιν εἰς ἄφεσιν ἁμαρτιῶν καὶ εἰς ζωὴν αἰώνιον, εἰς ἁγιασμὸν ψυχῶν καὶ σωμάτων, εἰς καρποφορίαν ἔργων ἀγαθῶν.

[1] Κοινὸς ἄρτος, says Justin, while in view of its sacred import he calls it also uncommon bread and drink. The use of leavened or unleavened bread became afterwards, as is well known, a point of controversy between the Roman and Greek churches.

which the recipient responded "Amen."[1] The whole congregation thus received the elements, standing in the act.[2] Thanksgiving and benediction concluded the celebration.

After the public service the deacons carried the consecrated elements to the sick and to the confessors in prison. Many took portions of the bread home with them, to use in the family at morning prayer. This domestic communion was practised particularly in North Africa, and furnishes the first example of a *communio sub una specie*. In the same country, in Cyprian's time, we find the custom of infant communion (administered with wine alone), which was justified from John 6 : 53, and has continued in the Greek (and Russian) church to this day, though irreconcilable with the apostle's requisition of a preparatory examination (1 Cor. 11 : 28).

At first the communion was joined with a LOVE FEAST, and was then celebrated in the evening, in memory of the last supper of Jesus with his disciples. But so early as the beginning of the second century these two exercises were separated, and the communion was placed in the morning, the love feast in the evening, except on certain days of special observance.[3]

[1] This simplest form of distribution, "Σῶμα Χριστοῦ," and "Αἷμα Χρ., ποτήριον ζωῆς," occurs in the Clementine liturgy of the Apostolic Constitutions, VIII. 13, and seems to be the oldest. The *Didache* gives no form of distribution.

[2] The standing posture of the congregation during the principal prayers, and in the communion itself, seems to have been at first universal. For this was, indeed, the custom always on the day of the resurrection in distinction from Friday ("*stantes oramus, quod est signum resurrectionis*," says Augustin) ; besides, the communion was, in the highest sense, a ceremony of festivity and joy ; and finally, Justin expressly observes: "Then we all stand up to prayer." After the twelfth century, kneeling in receiving the elements became general, and passed from the Catholic church into the Lutheran and Anglican, while most of the Reformed churches returned to the original custom of standing. Sitting in the communion was first introduced after the Reformation by the Presbyterian church of Scotland, and is very common in the United States, the deacons or elders handing the bread and cup to the communicants in their pews. A curious circumstance is the *sitting* posture of the *Pope* in the communion, which Dean Stanley regards as a relic of the reclining or recumbent posture of the primitive disciples. See his *Christ. Instit.* p. 250 sqq.

[3] On Maundy-Thursday, according to Augustin's testimony, the communion continued to be celebrated in the evening, "*tanquam ad insigniorem*

Tertullian gives a detailed description of the Agape in refutation of the shameless calumnies of the heathens.[1] But the growth of the churches and the rise of manifold abuses led to the gradual disuse, and in the fourth century even to the formal prohibition of the Agape, which belonged in fact only to the childhood and first love of the church. It was a family feast, where rich and poor, master and slave met on the same footing, partaking of a simple meal, hearing reports from distant congregations, contributing to the necessities of suffering brethren, and encouraging each other in their daily duties and trials. Augustin describes his mother Monica as going to these feasts with a basket full of provisions and distributing them.

The communion service has undergone many changes in the course of time, but still substantially survives with all its primitive vitality and solemnity in all churches of Christendom,—a perpetual memorial of Christ's atoning sacrifice and saving love to the human race. Baptism and the Lord's Supper are institutions which proclaim from day to day the historic Christ, and can never be superseded by contrivances of human ingenuity and wisdom.

commemorationem." So on high feasts, as Christmas night, Epiphany, and Easter Eve, and in fasting seasons. See Ambrose, *Serm.* viii. *in Ps.* 118.

[1] *Apol.* c. 39: "About the modest supper-room of the Christians alone a great ado is made. Our feast explains itself by its name. The Greeks call it love. Whatever it costs, our outlay in the name of piety is gain, since with the good things of the feast we benefit the needy, not as it is with you, do parasites aspire to the glory of satisfying their licentious propensities, selling themselves for a belly-feast to all disgraceful treatment—but as it is with God himself, a peculiar respect is shown to the lowly. If the object of our feast be good, in the light of that consider its further regulations. As it is an act of religious service, it permits no vileness or immodesty. The participants, before reclining, taste first of prayer to God. As much is eaten as satisfies the cravings of hunger; as much is drunk as befits the chaste. They say it is enough, as those who remember that even during the night they have to worship God; they talk as those who know that the Lord is one of their auditors. After the washing of hands and the bringing in of lights, each is asked to stand forth and sing, as he can, a hymn to God, either one from the holy Scriptures or one of his own composing—a proof of the measure of our drinking. As the feast commenced with prayer, so with prayer it closed. We go from it, not like troops of mischief-doers, nor bands of roamers, nor to break out into licentious acts, but to have as much care of our modesty and chastity as if we had been at a school of virtue rather than a banquet." (Translation from the "Ante-Nicene Library").

§ 69. *The Doctrine of the Eucharist.*

Literature. See the works quoted, vol. I. 472, by WATERLAND (Episc. d. 1740), DÖLLINGER (R. Cath., 1826; since 1870 Old Cath.), EBRARD (Calvinistic, 1845), NEVIN (Calvinistic, 1846), KAHNIS (Luth. 1851, but changed his view in his *Dogmatik*), E. B. PUSEY (high Anglic., 1855), RÜCKERT (Rationalistic, 1856), VOGAN (high Anglic., 1871), HARRISON (Evang. Angl., 1871), STANLEY (Broad Church Episc., 1881), GUDE (Lutheran, 1887).

On the Eucharistic doctrine of Ignatius, Justin, Irenæus, and Tertullian, there are also special treatises by THIERSCH (1841), SEMISCH (1842), ENGELHARDT (1842), BAUR (1839 and 1857), STEITZ (1864), and others.

HÖFLING: *Die Lehre der ältesten Kirche vom Opfer im Leben und Cultus der Christen.* Erlangen, 1851.

Dean STANLEY: *The Eucharistic Sacrifice.* In "Christian Institutions" (N. Y. 1881) p. 73 sqq.

The doctrine concerning the sacrament of the Lord's Supper, not coming into special discussion, remained indefinite and obscure. The ancient church made more account of the worthy participation of the ordinance than of the logical apprehension of it. She looked upon it as the holiest mystery of the Christian worship, and accordingly celebrated it with the deepest devotion, without inquiring into the mode of Christ's presence, nor into the relation of the sensible signs to his flesh and blood. It is unhistorical to carry any of the later theories back into this age; although it has been done frequently in the apologetic and polemic discussion of this subject.

I. THE EUCHARIST AS A SACRAMENT.

The *Didache* of the Apostles contains eucharistic prayers, but no theory of the eucharist. Ignatius speaks of this sacrament in two passages, only by way of allusion, but in very strong, mystical terms, calling it the flesh of our crucified and risen Lord Jesus Christ, and the consecrated bread a medicine of immortality and an antidote of spiritual death.[1] This view,

---

[1] *Ad Smyrn.* c. 7; against the Docetists, who deny τὴν εὐχαριστίαν σάρκα εἶναι τοῦ σωτῆρος ἡμῶν Ἰ. Χρ., κ. τ. λ.; and *Ad Ephes.* c. 20: Ὅς (sc. ἄρτος) ἐστιν φάρμακον ἀθανασίας, ἀντίδοτος τοῦ μὴ ἀποθανεῖν, ἀλλὰ ζῆν ἐν Ἰησοῦ Χριστῷ διὰ παντός. Both passages are wanting in the Syriac version. But the first is

closely connected with his high-churchly tendency in general, no doubt involves belief in the real presence, and ascribes to the holy Supper an effect on spirit and body at once, with reference to the future resurrection, but is still somewhat obscure, and rather an expression of elevated feeling, than a logical definition.

The same may be said of Justin Martyr, when he compares the descent of Christ into the consecrated elements to his incarnation for our redemption.[1]

Irenæus says repeatedly, in combating the Gnostic Docetism,[2] that bread and wine in the sacrament become, by the presence of the Word of God, and by the power of the Holy Spirit, the body and blood of Christ, and that the receiving of them strengthens soul and body (the germ of the resurrection body) unto eternal life. Yet this would hardly warrant our ascribing either transubstantiation or consubstantiation to Irenæus. For in another place he calls the bread and wine, after consecration, "antitypes," implying the continued distinction of their substance from the body and blood of Christ.[3] This expression in itself, indeed, might be understood as merely contrasting here the Supper, as the substance, with the Old Testament passover, its type; as Peter calls baptism the antitype of the saving

cited by Theodoret, *Dial.* III. p. 231, and must therefore have been known even in the Syrian church in his time.

[1] *Apol.* I. 66 (I. 182, third ed. of Otto). Here also occurs already the term μεταβολή, which some Roman controversialists use at once as an argument for transubstantiation. Justin says: Ἐξ ἧς (*i. e.* τροφῆς) αἷμα καὶ σάρκες κατὰ μεταβολὴν τρέφονται ἡμῶν, *ex quo alimento sanguis et carnes nostræ per mutationem aluntur.* But according to the context, this denotes by no means a transmutation of the elements, but either the assimilation of them to the body of the receiver, or the operation of them upon the body, with reference to the future resurrection. Comp. John 6: 54 sqq., and like passages in Ignatius and Irenæus.

[2] *Adv. hær.* IV. 18, and *passim.*

[3] In the second of the Fragments discovered by Pfaff (*Opp.* Iren. ed. Stieren, vol. I. p. 855), which Maffei and other Roman divines have unwarrantably declared spurious. It is there said that the Christians, after the offering of the eucharistic sacrifice, call upon the Holy Ghost, ὅπως ἀποφήνῃ τὴν θυσίαν ταύτην καὶ τὸν ἄρτον σῶμα τοῦ Χριστοῦ, καὶ τὸ ποτήριον τὸ αἷμα τοῦ Χρ., ἵνα οἱ μεταλαβόντες τούτων τῶν ἀντιτύπων, τῆς ἀφέσεως τῶν ἁμαρτιῶν καὶ τῆς ζωῆς αἰωνίου τύχωσιν.

water of the flood.[1] But the connection, and the *usus loquendi*
of the earlier Greek fathers, require us to take the term antitype
in the sense of type, or, more precisely, as the antithesis of
archetype. The bread and wine represent and exhibit the body
and blood of Christ as the archetype, and correspond to them,
as a copy to the original. In exactly the same sense it is said
in Heb. 9 : 24—comp. 8 : 5—that the earthly sanctuary is the
antitype, that is the copy, of the heavenly archetype. Other
Greek fathers also, down to the fifth century, and especially the
author of the Apostolical Constitutions, call the consecrated
elements "antitypes" (sometimes, like Theodoretus, "types")
of the body and blood of Christ.[2]

A different view, approaching nearer the Calvinistic or Reformed, we meet with among the African fathers. Tertullian
makes the words of institution : *Hoc est corpus meum*, equivalent to : *figura corporis mei*, to prove, in opposition to Marcion's
docetism, the reality of the body of Jesus—a mere phantom
being capable of no emblematic representation.[3] This involves,
at all events, an essential distinction between the consecrated
elements and the body and blood of Christ in the Supper. Yet
Tertullian must not be understood as teaching a *merely* symbolical presence of Christ ; for in other places he speaks, according to his general realistic turn, in almost materialistic language
of an eating of the body of Christ, and extends the participation even to the body of the receiver.[4] Cyprian likewise ap-

---

[1] 1 Pet. 3 : 20, 21.

[2] Const. Apost. l. V. c. 14 : Τὰ ἀντίτυπα μυστήρια τοῦ τιμίου σώματος αὐτοῦ
καὶ αἵματος. So VI. 30, and in a eucharistic prayer, VII. 25. Other passages
of the Greek fathers see in Stieren, l. c. p. 884 sq. Comp. also Bleek's learned
remarks in his large *Com. on Heb.* 8 : 5, and 9 : 24.

[3] *Adv. Marc.* IV. 40 ; and likewise III. 19. This interpretation is plainly
very near that of Œcolampadius, who puts the figure in the predicate, and who
attached no small weight to Tertullian's authority. But the Zwinglian view,
which puts the figure in the ἐστι, instead of the predicate, appears also in Tertullian, *Adv. Marc.* I. 14, in the words : "*Panem qui ipsum corpus suum rep-
ræsentat.*" The two interpretations are only grammatical modifications of the
same symbolical theory.

[4] *De Resur. Carnis*, c. 8. "*Caro corpore et sanguine Christi vescitur, ut et anima
de Deo saginetur.*" *De Pudic.* c. 9, he refers the fatted calf, in the parable of

pears to favor a symbolical interpretation of the words of institution, yet not so clearly.   The idea of the real presence would
have much better suited his sacerdotal conception of the ministry.
In the customary mixing of the wine with water he sees a type
of the union of Christ with his church,[1] and, on the authority
of John 6 : 53, holds the communion of the Supper indispensable to salvation.   The idea of a sacrifice comes out very boldly
in Cyprian.

The Alexandrians are here, as usual, decidedly spiritualistic.
Clement twice expressly calls the wine a symbol or an allegory
of the blood of Christ, and says, that the communicant receives
not the physical, but the spiritual blood, the life, of Christ; as,
indeed, the blood is the life of the body.   Origen distinguishes
still more definitely the earthly elements from the heavenly
bread of life, and makes it the whole design of the supper to
feed the soul with the divine word.[2]   Applying his unsound
allegorical method here, he makes the bread represent the Old
Testament, the wine the New, and the breaking of the bread
the multiplication of the divine word !   But these were rather
private views for the initiated, and can hardly be taken as presenting the doctrine of the Alexandrian church.

We have, therefore, among the ante-Nicene fathers, three dif-

---

the prodigal son, to the Lord's Supper, and says : " *Opimitate Dominici corporis
vescitur, eucharistia scilicet.*" *De Orat.* c. 6 : " *Quod et corpus Christi in pane cense-
tur,*" which should probably be translated : is to be understood by the bread
(not contained in the bread).

[1] For this reason he considers the mixing essential.   *Epist.* 63 (ed. Bal.) c.
13 : "*Si vinum tantum quis offerat, sanguis Christi incipit esse sine nobis ; si vero
aqua sit sola, plebs incipit esse sine Christo.   Quando autem utrumque miscetur et
adunatione confusa sibi invicem copulatur, tunc sacramentum spirituale et cœleste
perficitur.*"

[2] *Comment. ser. in Matt.* c. 85 (III. 898): "*Panis iste, quem Deus Verbum
[Logos] corpus suum esse fatetur, verbum est nutritorium animarum, verbum de
Deo Verbo procedens, et panis de pani cœlesti. . . . . Non enim panem illum visi-
bilem, quem tenebat in manibus, corpus suum dicebat Deus Verbum, sed verbum, in
cuius mysterio fuerat panis ille frangendus.*"   Then the same of the wine.
Origen evidently goes no higher than the Zwinglian theory, while Clement
approaches the Calvinistic view of a spiritual real fruition of Christ's life in
the eucharist.

ferent views, an Oriental, a North-African, and an Alexandrian. The first view, that of Ignatius and Irenæus, agrees most nearly with the mystical character of the celebration of the eucharist, and with the catholicizing features of the age.

2. THE EUCHARIST AS A SACRIFICE.

This point is very important in relation to the doctrine, and still more important in relation to the cultus and life, of the ancient church. The Lord's Supper was universally regarded not only as a sacrament, but also as a sacrifice,[1] the true and eternal sacrifice of the new covenant, superseding all the provisional and typical sacrifices of the old; taking the place particularly of the passover, or the feast of the typical redemption from Egypt. This eucharistic sacrifice, however, the ante-Nicene fathers conceived not as an unbloody repetition of the atoning sacrifice of Christ on the cross, but simply as a commemoration and renewed appropriation of that atonement, and, above all, a thank-offering of the whole church for all the favors of God in creation and redemption. Hence the current name itself—*eucharist;* which denoted in the first place the prayer of thanksgiving, but afterwards the whole rite.[2]

The consecrated elements were regarded in a twofold light, as representing at once the natural and the spiritual gifts of God, which culminated in the self-sacrifice of Christ on the cross. Hence the eucharistic prayer, like that connected with the typical passover, related at the same time to creation and redemption, which were the more closely joined in the mind of the church for their dualistic separation by the Gnostics. The earthly gifts of bread and wine were taken as types and pledges of the heavenly gifts of the same God, who has both created and redeemed the world.

Upon this followed the idea of the self-sacrifice of the worshipper himself, the sacrifice of renewed self-consecration to

---

[1] Προσφορά, θυσία, *oblatio, sacrificium.*

[2] So among the Jews the cup of wine at the paschal supper was called "the cup of blessing," ποτήριον εὐλογίας = εὐχαριστίας, comp. 1 Cor. 10: 16.

Christ in return for his sacrifice on the cross, and also the sacrifice of charity to the poor. Down to the twelfth and thirteenth centuries the eucharistic elements were presented as a thank-offering by the members of the congregation themselves, and the remnants went to the clergy and the poor. In these gifts the people yielded themselves as a priestly race and a living thank-offering to God, to whom they owed all the blessings alike of providence and of grace. In later times the priest alone offered the sacrifice. But even the Roman Missal retains a recollection of the ancient custom in the plural form, " We offer," and in the sentence: " All you, both brethren and sisters, pray that my sacrifice and your sacrifice, which is equally yours as well as mine, may be meat for the Lord."

This subjective offering of the whole congregation on the ground of the objective atoning sacrifice of Christ is the real centre of the ancient Christian worship, and particularly of the communion. It thus differed both from the later Catholic mass, which has changed the thank-offering into a sin-offering, the congregational offering into a priest offering; and from the common Protestant cultus, which, in opposition to the Roman mass, has almost entirely banished the idea of sacrifice from the celebration of the Lord's Supper, except in the customary offerings for the poor.

The writers of the second century keep strictly within the limits of the notion of a congregational *thank*-offering. Thus Justin says expressly, prayers and thanksgivings alone are the true and acceptable sacrifices, which the Christians offer. Irenæus has been brought as a witness for the Roman doctrine, only on the ground of a false reading.[1] The African fathers, in the third century, who elsewhere incline to the symbolical interpretation of the words of institution, are the first to approach on

---

[1] *Adv. Hær.* IV. c. 18, § 4: " *Verbum* [the Logos] *quod offertur Deo;*" instead of which should be read, according to other manuscripts: " *Verbum per quod offertur,*"—which suits the connexion much better. Comp. IV. 17, § 6: "*Per Jes. Christum offert ecclesia.*"   Stieren reads " *Verbum quod,*" but refers it not to Christ, but to the word of the prayer. The passage is, at all events, too obscure and too isolated to build a dogma upon.

this point the later Roman Catholic idea of a sin-offering; especially Cyprian, the steadfast advocate of priesthood and of episcopal authority.[1] The ideas of priesthood, sacrifice, and altar, are intimately connected, and a Judaizing or paganizing conception of one must extend to all.

§ 70. *The Celebration of Baptism.*

The Lit. see in vol. I. § 54, p. 465 sq., especially WALL and HÖFLING. On the archæology of baptism see BINGHAM'S *Antiquities,* AUGUSTI'S *Denkwürdigkeiten,* the first vol. of BINTERIM, and the art. *Baptism* in SMITH and CHEETHAM, I. 155–172. Also SCHAFF, on the *Didache* (1885), p. 29–56. For pictorial illustrations see the monumental works of Cav. DE ROSSI, GARRUCCI, ROLLER, on the catacombs, and SCHAFF, *l. c.*

The "Teaching of the Twelve Apostles" (ch. 7,) enjoins baptism, after chatechetical instruction, in these words: "Baptize into the name of the Father, and of the Son, and of the Holy Ghost in living (running) water. But if thou hast not living water, baptize into other water; and if thou canst not in cold, then in warm. But if thou hast neither, pour (ἔχχεον) water upon the head thrice, into the name of the Father, Son, and Holy Ghost."

Justin Martyr gives the following account of baptism:[2] "Those who are convinced of the truth of our doctrine, and have promised to live according to it, are exhorted to prayer, fasting and repentance for past sins; we praying and fasting with them. Then they are led by us to a place where is water, and in this way they are regenerated, as we also have been regenerated; that is, they receive the water-bath in the name of God, the Father and Ruler of all, and of our Redeemer Jesus Christ, and of the Holy Ghost. For Christ says: Except ye be born again, ye cannot enter into the kingdom of heaven. (John 3 : 5.) Thus, from children of necessity and ignorance, we become

---

[1] *Epist.* 63 *ad Cœcil.* c. 14: "*Si Jesus Christus, Dominus et Deus noster, ipse est summus sacerdos Dei Patris et sacrificium Patri seipsum primus obtulit et hoc fieri in sui commemorationem præcepit: utique ille sacerdos vice Christi vere fungitur, qui id, quod Christus fecit, imitatur et sacrificium verum et plenum tunc offert.*"

[2] *Apol.* I., c. 61 (I. 164 ed. Otto).

children of choice and of wisdom, and partakers of the forgiveness of former sins. . . . . The baptismal bath is called
also illumination (φωτισμός), because those who receive it are
enlightened in the understanding."

This account may be completed by the following particulars
from Tertullian and later writers.

Before the act the candidate was required in a solemn vow to
renounce the service of the devil, that is, all evil,[1] give himself
to Christ, and confess the sum of the apostolic faith in God the
Father, the Son, and Holy Spirit.[2] The Apostles' Creed, therefore, is properly the baptismal symbol, as it grew, in fact, out of
the baptismal formula.

This act of turning from sin and turning to God, or of repentance and faith, on the part of the candidate, was followed by
an appropriate prayer of the minister, and then by the baptism
itself into the triune name, with three successive immersions in
which the deacons and deaconesses assisted. The immersion
consisted in thrice dipping the head of the candidate who stood
nude in the water.[3] Single immersion seems to have been

---

[1] *Abrenunciatio diaboli.* **Tertullian**: " *Renunciare diabolo et pompæ et angelis
jus.*" Const. Apost.: 'Αποτάσσομαι τῷ Σατανᾷ καὶ τοῖς ἔργοις αὐτοῦ καὶ ταῖς
πομπαῖς αὐτοῦ, καὶ ταῖς λατρείαις αὐτοῦ, καὶ πᾶσι τοῖς ὑπ' αὐτόν. This renunciation of the devil was made, at least in the fourth century, as we learn from
Cyril of Jerusalem, in the vestibule of the baptistery, with the face towards
the west, and the hand raised in the repelling posture, as if Satan were present
(ὡς παρόντι ἀποτάσσεσθε Σατανᾷ), and was sometimes accompanied with exsuf-
flations, or other signs of expulsion of the evil spirit.

[2] 'Ομολόγησις, *professio.* The creed was either said by the catechumen after
the priest, or confessed in answer to questions, and with the face turned east-
wards towards the light.

[3] See the authorities quoted in Smith and Cheetham, I. 161, and more fully in
Augusti. *l. c.* " *Ter mergitamur,*" says Tertullian. Immersion was very natural
in Southern climates. The baptisteries of the Nicene age, of which many re-
main in Asia, Africa, and Southern Europe, were built for immersion, and all
Oriental churches still adhere to this mode. Garrucci (*Storia della Arte
Cristiana,* I. 27) says: " *Antichissimo e solenne fu il rito d' immergere la persona
nell' acqua, e tre volte anche il capo, al pronunziare del ministro i tre nomi.*"
Schultze (*Die Katakomben,* p. 136): " *Die Taufdarstellungen vorkonstantinischer
Zeit, deren Zahl sich auf drei beläuft, zeigen sämmtlich erwachsene Täuflinge, in
zwei Fällen Knaben von etwa zwölf Jahren, im dritten Falle einen Jüngling. Der
Act wird durch Untertauchen vollzogen.*" Dean Stanley delights in pictorial

introduced by Eunomius about 360, but was condemned on pain
of degradation, yet it reappeared afterwards in Spain, and Pope
Gregory I. declared both forms valid, the trine immersion as
setting forth the Trinity, the single immersion the Unity of the
Godhead.[1] The Eastern church, however, still adheres strictly
to the trine immersion.[2] Baptism by *pouring* water from a
shell or vessel or from the hand on the head of the candidate
very early occurs also and was probably considered equivalent to immersion.[3] The *Didache* allows pouring in cases of
scarcity of water. But afterwards this mode was applied only
to infirm or sick persons; hence called *clinical* baptism.[4] The
validity of this baptism was even doubted by many in the third

exaggeration of the baptismal immersion in patristic times as contrasted with
modern sprinkling. "Baptism," he says, "was not only a bath, but a plunge—
an entire submersion in the deep water, a leap as into the rolling sea or the
rushing river, where for the moment the waves close over the bather's head,
and he emerges again as from a momentary grave; or it was a shock of a
shower-bath—the rush of water passed over the whole person from capacious
vessels, so as to wrap the recipient as within the veil of a splashing cataract.
This was the part of the ceremony on which the Apostles laid so much stress.
It was to them like a burial of the old former self and the rising up again of
the new self." *Christian Institutions,* (1881), p. 9. See Schaff, *l. c.* p. 41 sqq.

[1] *Ep.* I. 41 in reply to Leander, bishop of Hispala. Thomas Aquinas
(*Summa Theol.,* Tom. IV., f. 615, ed. Migne) quotes this letter with approval,
but gives the preference to *trina immersio,* as expressing "*triduum sepulturæ
Christi et etiam Trinitas personarum.*"

[2] The Russian Orthodox Catechism defines baptism as "a sacrament, in
which a man who believes, having his body *thrice plunged in water* in the name
of God the Father, the Son, and the Holy Ghost, dies to the carnal life of sin,
and is born again of the Holy Ghost to a life spiritual and holy." In the case
of infants the act is usually completed by pouring water over the head, the
rest of the body being immersed. So I was informed by a Greek priest.

[3] Pouring or affusion is the present practice of the Roman Catholic church.
It is first found on pictures in the Roman catacombs, one of which De
Rossi assigns to the second century (in the cemetry of Calixtus). "It is remarkable that in almost all the earliest representations of baptism that have
been preserved to us, this [the pouring of water from vessels over the body]
is the special act represented." Marriott in Smith and Cheetham, I. 168.
But the art of painting can only represent a part of the act, not the whole
process; and in all the Catacomb pictures the candidate stands with the feet in
water, and is undressed as for immersion, total or partial.

[4] "*Baptismus clinicorum*" (κλινικοί, from κλίνη, bed). *Clinicus* or *grabbatarius*
designated one who was *baptized* on the sick bed.

century ; and Cyprian wrote in its defence, taking the ground that the mode of application of water was a matter of minor importance, provided that faith was present in the recipient and ministrant.[1] According to ecclesiastical law clinical baptism at least incapacitated for the clerical office.[2] Yet the Roman bishop Fabian ordained Novatian a presbyter, though he had been baptized on a sick-bed by aspersion.[3]

---

[1] *Ep.* 69 (al. 75), *ad Magnum.* He answered the question as best he could in the absence of any ecclesiastical decision at that time. This Epistle, next to Tertullian's opposition to infant baptism, is the oldest document in the *controversial* baptismal literature. Cyprian quotes (ch. 12) several passages from the O. T. where "sprinkling" is spoken of as an act of cleansing (Ez. 36: 25, 26; Num. 8: 5–7; 19: 8–13), and then concludes: "Whence it appears that sprinkling also of water prevails equally with the salutary washing (*adspersionem quoque aquae instar salutaris lavacri obtinere*); and that when this is done in the church where the faith both of the receiver and the giver is sound (*ubi sit et accipientis et dantis fides integra*), all things hold and may be consummated and perfected by the majesty of the Lord and by the truth of faith." But in the same Ep., Cyprian denies the validity of heretical and schismatic baptism in any form. See below, § 74.

[2] The twelfth canon of the Council of Neo-Cæsarea (after 314) ordains: "Whosoever has received clinical baptism cannot be promoted to the priesthood, because his [profession of] faith was not from free choice, but from necessity (ἐξ ἀνάγκης, fear of death), unless he excel afterwards in zeal and faith, or there is a deficiency of [able] men." This canon passed into the *Corpus jur. can.* c. 1 Dist. 57. See Hefele, *Conciliengesch*, I. 249 (2nd ed.).

[3] Pouring and sprinkling were still exceptional in the ninth century according to Walafrid Strabo (*De Rel. Eccl.*, c. 26), but they made gradual progress with the spread of infant baptism, as the most convenient mode, especially in Northern climates, and came into common use in the West at the end of the thirteenth century. Thomas Aquinas (d. 1274) says, that although it may be safer to baptize by immersion, yet pouring and sprinkling are also allowable (*Summa Theol.* P. III. Qu. LXVI. *De Bapt.* art. 7 : in Migne's ed. Tom. IV. fol. 614): "*Si totum corpus aquâ non possit perfundi propter aquæ paucitatem, vel propter aliquam aliam causam, opportet caput perfundere, in quo manifestatur principium animalis vitæ.*" In Ireland aspersion seems to have been practiced very early along with immersion. "Trine immersion, *with the alternative of aspersion,* is ordered in the earliest extant Irish Baptismal Office, in the composition of which, however, Roman influence is strongly marked." F. E. Warren, *The Liturgy and Ritual of the Celtic Church*, Oxford (Clarendon Press), 1881, p. 65. Prof. Norman Fox and other Baptist writers, think that "neither infant baptism nor the use of pouring and sprinkling for baptism would ever have been thought of but for the superstitious idea that baptism was necessary to salvation." But this idea prevailed among the fathers and

Thanksgiving, benediction, and the brotherly kiss concluded the sacred ceremony.

Besides these essential elements of the baptismal rite, we find, so early as the third century, several other subordinate usages, which have indeed a beautiful symbolical meaning, but, like all redundancies, could easily obscure the original simplicity of this sacrament, as it appears in Justin Martyr's description. Among these appendages are the signing of the cross on the forehead and breast of the subject, as a soldier of Christ under the banner of the cross; giving him milk and honey (also salt) in token of sonship with God, and citizenship in the heavenly Canaan; also the unction of the head, the lighted taper, and the white robe.

Exorcism, or the expulsion of the devil, which is not to be confounded with the essential formula of renunciation, was probably practised at first only in special cases, as of demoniacal possession. But after the council of Carthage, A. D. 256, we find it a regular part of the ceremony of baptism, preceding the baptism proper, and in some cases, it would seem, several times repeated during the course of catechetical instruction. To understand fully this custom, we should remember that the early church derived the whole system of heathen idolatry, which it justly abhorred as one of the greatest crimes,[1] from the agency

in the Greek church fully as much as in the Roman, while it is rejected in most Protestant churches where sprinkling is practiced.

Luther sought to restore immersion, but without effect. Calvin took a similar view of the subject as Thomas Aquinas, but he went farther and declared the mode of application to be a matter of indifference, *Inst.* IV. ch. 15, § 19: "Whether the person who is baptized be wholly immersed (*mergatur totus*), and whether thrice or once, or whether water be only poured (*infusa*) or sprinkled upon him (*aspergatur*), is of no importance (*minimum refert*): but this should be left free to the churches according to the difference of countries. Yet the very word *baptize* signifies to immerse (*mergere*); and it is certain that immersion was the practice of the ancient church." Most Protestants agree with Calvin, except the Baptists, who revived the ancient practice, but only in part (*single* instead of *trine* immersion), and without the patristic ideas of baptismal regeneration, infant baptism, and the necessity of baptism for salvation. They regard baptism as a mere symbol which exhibits the fact that regeneration and conversion have already taken place.

[1] Tertullian calls it "*principale crimen generis humani*" (*De idol.* c. 1), and Cyprian, "*summum delictum*" (*Ep.* x.).

of Satan.   The heathen deities, although they had been eminent
men during their lives, were, as to their animating principle,
identified with demons—either fallen angels or their progeny.
These demons, as we may infer from many passages of Justin,
Minutius Felix, Tertullian, and others, were believed to traverse
the air, to wander over the earth, to deceive and torment
the race, to take possession of men, to encourage sacrifices, to
lurk in statues, to speak through the oracles, to direct the flights
of birds, to work the illusions of enchantment and necromancy,
to delude the senses by false miracles, to incite persecution
against Christianity, and, in fact, to sustain the whole fabric of
heathenism with all its errors and vices.   But even these evil
spirits were subject to the powerful name of Jesus.   Tertullian
openly challenges the pagan adversaries to bring demoniacs
before the tribunals, and affirms that the spirits which possessed
them, would bear witness to the truth of Christianity.

The institution of *sponsors*,[1] first mentioned by Tertullian, arose
no doubt from infant baptism, and was designed to secure Christian
training, without thereby excusing Christian parents from their
duty.

Baptism might be administered at any time, but was commonly
connected with Easter and Pentecost, and in the East with
Epiphany also, to give it the greater solemnity.   The favorite
hour was midnight lit up by torches.   The men were baptized
first, the women afterwards   During the week following, the
neophytes wore white garments as symbols of their purity.

Separate chapels for baptism, or BAPTISTERIES, occur first in
the fourth century, and many of them still remain in Southern
Europe.   Baptism might be performed in any place, where, as
Justin says, " water was."   Yet Cyprian, in the middle of the
third century, and the pseudo-Apostolical Constitutions, require
the element to be previously consecrated, that it may become the
vehicle of the purifying energy of the Spirit.   This corresponded
to the consecration of the bread and wine in the Lord's Supper, and involved no transformation of the substance.

---

[1] 'Ανάδοχοι, *sponsores, fideijussores.*

§ 71. *The Doctrine of Baptism.*

This ordinance was regarded in the ancient church as the sacrament of the new birth or regeneration, and as the solemn rite of initiation into the Christian Church, admitting to all her benefits and committing to all her obligations. It was supposed to be preceded, in the case of adults, by instruction on the part of the church, and by repentance and faith (*i. e.* conversion) on the part of the candidate, and to complete and seal the spiritual process of regeneration, the old man being buried, and the new man arising from the watery grave. Its effect consists in the forgiveness of sins and the communication of the Holy Spirit. Justin calls baptism "the water-bath for the forgiveness of sins and regeneration," and "the bath of conversion and the knowledge of God." It is often called also illumination, spiritual circumcision, anointing, sealing, gift of grace, symbol of redemption, death of sins, &c.[1] Tertullian describes its effect thus: "When the soul comes to faith, and becomes transformed through regeneration by water and power from above, it discovers, after the veil of the old corruption is taken away, its whole light. It is received into the fellowship of the Holy Spirit; and the soul, which unites itself to the Holy Spirit, is followed by the body." He already leans towards the notion of a magical operation of the baptismal water. Yet the subjective condition of repentance and faith was universally required. Baptism was not only an act of God, but at the same time the most solemn surrender of man to God, a vow for life and death, to live henceforth only to Christ and his people. The keeping of this vow was the condition of continuance in the church; the breaking of it must be followed either by repentance or excommunication.

From John 3: 5 and Mark 16: 16, Tertullian and other

---

[1] The patristic terms for baptism expressive of doctrine are ἀναγέννησις, παλιγγενεσία (and λουτρὸν παλιγγενεσίας, Tit. 3: 5), θεογένεσις, *regeneratio, secunda* or *spiritualis nativitas, renascentia;* also φωτισμός, φώτισμα, *illuminatio,* σφραγίς, *signaculum, seal,* μύησις, μυσταγωγία, *initiation into the mysteries* (the sacraments). The sign was almost identified with the thing itself.

fathers argued the necessity of baptism to salvation. Clement of Alexandria supposed, with the Roman Hermas and others, that even the saints of the Old Testament were baptized in Hades by Christ or the apostles. But exception was made in favor of the bloody baptism of martyrdom as compensating the want of baptism with water; and this would lead to the evangelical principle, that not the omission, but only the contempt of the sacrament, is damning.[1]

The effect of baptism, however, was thought to extend only to sins committed before receiving it. Hence the frequent postponement of the sacrament,[2] which Tertullian very earnestly recommends, though he censures it when accompanied with moral levity and presumption.[3] Many, like Constantine the Great, put it off to the bed of sickness and of death. They preferred the risk of dying unbaptized to that of forfeiting forever the baptismal grace. Death-bed baptisms were then what death-bed repentances are now.

But then the question arose, how the forgiveness of sins committed after baptism could be obtained? This is the starting point of the Roman doctrine of the sacrament of *penance.* Tertullian[4] and Cyprian[5] were the first to suggest that satisfaction must be made for such sins by self-imposed penitential exercises and good works, such as prayers and almsgiving. Tertullian held seven gross sins, which he denoted mortal sins, to be unpardonable after baptism, and to be left to the uncovenanted mercies of God; but the Catholic church took a milder view, and even received back the adulterers and apostates on their public repentance.

---

[1] "*Non defectus* (or *privatio*), *sed contemtus sacramenti damnat.*" This leaves the door open for the salvation of Quakers, unbaptized children, and elect heathen who die with a desire for salvation.

[2] *Procrastinatio baptismi.*

[3] So the author of the *Apost. Constit.*, VI. 15, disapproves those who say: ὅτι ὅταν τελευτῶ, βαπτίζομαι, ἵνα μὴ ἁμαρτήσω καὶ ῥυπανῶ τὸ βάπτισμα.

[4] *De Pœnitentia.*

[5] *De Opere et Eleemosynis.*

NOTES.

In reviewing the patristic doctrine of baptism which was sanctioned by the Greek and Roman, and, with some important modifications, also by the Lutheran and Anglican churches, we should remember that during the first three centuries, and even in the age of Constantine, *adult* baptism was the rule, and that the actual *conversion* of the candidate was required as a condition before administering the sacrament (as is still the case on missionary ground). Hence the preceding catechetical instruction, the renunciation of the devil, and the profession of faith. But when the same high view is applied without qualification to *infant* baptism, we are confronted at once with the difficulty that infants cannot comply with this condition. They may be *regenerated* (this being an act of God), but they cannot be *converted, i. e.* they cannot repent and believe, nor do they need repentance, having not yet committed any actual transgression. Infant baptism is an act of consecration, and looks to subsequent instruction and personal conversion, as a condition to full membership of the church. Hence confirmation came in as a supplement to infant baptism.

The strict Roman Catholic dogma, first clearly enunciated by St. Augustin (though with reluctant heart and in the mildest form), assigns all *unbaptized* infants to hell on the ground of Adam's sin and the absolute necessity of baptism for salvation. A *dogma horribile*, but *falsum*. Christ, who is the truth, blessed *unbaptized* infants, and declared: "To such belongs the kingdom of heaven." The Augsburg Confession (Art. IX.) still teaches against the Anabaptists: "*quod baptismus sit necessarius ad salutem*," but the leading Lutheran divines reduce the absolute necessity of baptism to a relative or ordinary necessity; and the Reformed churches, under the influence of Calvin's teaching, went further by making salvation depend upon divine election, not upon the sacrament, and now generally hold to the salvation of all infants dying in infancy. The Second Scotch Confession (A. D. 1580) was the first to declare its abhorrence of "the cruel [popish] judgment against infants departing without the sacrament," and the doctrine of "the absolute necessity of baptism."

§ 72. *Catechetical Instruction and Confirmation.*

LITERATURE.

I. CYRIL (Κυρίλλος) of Jerusalem (315–386): Eighteen *Catechetical Lectures*, addressed to Catechumens (Κατηχήσεις φωτιζουένων), and Five *Mystagogical Lectures*, addressed to the newly baptized. Best ed. by Touttée, Par. 1720, reprinted in Migne's *Patrol. Gr.* vol. 33.

AUGUSTIN (d. 430): *De Catechizandis Rudibus.*

II. BINGHAM: *Antiquities*, X. 2.

ZEZSCHWITZ (Luth.): *System der christl. kirchl. Katechetik.* Leipzig, vol. I. 1863; vol. II. in 2 Parts, 1869 and 1872.

JOH. MAYER (R. C.): *Geschichte des Katechumenats, and der Katechese in den ersten sechs Jahrh.* Kempten, 1866.

A. WEISS (R. C.): *Die altkirchliche Pädagogik dargestellt in Katechumenat und Katechese der ersten sechs Jahrh.* Freiburg, 1869.

Fr. X. Funk (R. C): *Die Katechumenats-classen des christl. Alterthums,*
in the Tübing. "Theol. Quartalschrift," Tüb. 1883, p. 41–77.

1. The Catechumenate or preparation for baptism was a
very important institution of the early church. It dates substantially from apostolic times. Theophilus was "instructed" in
the main facts of the gospel history; and Apollos was "instructed"
in the way of the Lord.[1] As the church was set in the midst of
a heathen world, and addressed herself in her missionary preaching in the first instance to the adult generation, she saw the
necessity of preparing the susceptible for baptism by special
instruction under teachers called "catechists," who were generally
presbyters and deacons.[2] The catechumenate preceded baptism
(of adults); whereas, at a later period, after the general introduction of infant baptism, it followed. It was, on the one hand,
a bulwark of the church against unworthy members; on the
other, a bridge from the world to the church, a Christian
novitiate, to lead beginners forward to maturity. The catechumens or hearers[3] were regarded not as unbelievers, but as half-
Christians, and were accordingly allowed to attend all the
exercises of worship, except the celebration of the sacraments.
They embraced people of all ranks, ages, and grades of culture,
even philosophers, statesmen, and rhetoricians,—Justin, Athenagoras, Clement of Alexandria, Tertullian, Cyprian, Arnobius,
Lactantius, who all embraced Christianity in their adult years.

The *Didache* contains in the first six chapters, a high-toned
moral catechism preparatory to baptism, based chiefly on the
Sermon on the Mount.

There was but one or at most two classes of Catechumens.
The usual division into three (or four) classes rests on confusion
with the classes of Penitents.[4]

[1] Luke 1: 4 (κατηχήθης); Acts 18: 25 (κατηχημένος); comp. Rom. 2: 18;
1 Cor. 14: 19; Gal. 6: 6; Heb. 5: 12. The verb κατηχέω means 1) to resound; 2) to teach by word of mouth; 3) in Christian writers, to instruct in
the elements of religion.

[2] Κατηχηταί, *doctores audientium.* The term designates a function, not a special office or class.

[3] Κατηχούμενοι, ἀκροαταί, *auditores, audientes.*

[4] Ἀκροώμενοι, or *audientes;* γονυκλίνοντες, or *genuflectentes;* and φωτιζόμενοι,
or *competentes.* So Ducange, Augusti, Neander, Höfling, Hefele (in the first
ed. of his *Conciliengesch.,* but modified in the second, vol. I. 246, 248), Zezsch-

The catechetical school of Alexandria was particularly renowned for its highly learned character.

The duration of this catechetical instruction was fixed sometimes at two years [1] sometimes at three,[2] but might be shortened according to circumstances. Persons of decent moral character and general intelligence were admitted to baptism without delay. The Councils allow immediate admission in cases of sickness.

2. CONFIRMATION [3] was originally closely connected with baptism, as its positive complement, and was performed by the imposition of hands, and the anointing of several parts of the body with fragrant balsam-oil, the chrism, as it was called. These acts were the medium of the communication of the Holy Spirit, and of consecration to the spiritual priesthood. Later, however, it came to be separated from baptism, especially in the case of infants, and to be regarded as a sacrament by itself. Cyprian is the first to distinguish the baptism with water and the baptism with the Spirit as two sacraments; yet this term, sacrament, was used as yet very indefinitely, and applied to all sacred doctrines and rites.

The Western church, after the third century, restricted the power of confirmation to bishops, on the authority of Acts 8 : 17 ; they alone, as the successors of the apostles, being able to impart the Holy Ghost. The Greek church extended this function to priests and deacons. The Anglican church retains the Latin practice. Confirmation or some form of solemn reception into full communion on personal profession of faith, after proper instruction, was regarded as a necessary supplement to infant baptism, and afterwards as a special sacrament.

witz, Herzog, and many others. Bona and Bingham add even a fourth class (ἐξωθούμενοι). But this artificial classification (as Dr. Funk has shown, *l. c.*) arose from a misunderstanding of the fifth canon of Neocæsarea (between 314 and 325), which mentions one γόνυ κλίνων, but as representing a class of penitents, not of catechumens. Suicer, Mayer, and Weiss assume but two classes, *audientes* and *competentes*. Funk maintains that the candidates for baptism (φωτιζόμενοι, *competentes* or *electi baptizandi*) were already numbered among the faithful (*fideles*), and that there was only one class of catechumens.

[1] Conc. of Elvira, *can.* 42.　　　　　[2] *Const. Apost.* VIII. 32.
[3] Σφραγίς, χρίσμα, *confirmatio, obsignatio, signaculum.*

§ 73. *Infant Baptism.*

On INFANT BAPTISM comp. JUST. M.: *Dial. c. Tryph.* Jud. c. 43. IREN.: *Adv. Hær.* II. 22, ¿ 4, compared with III. 17, ¿ 1, and other passages. TERTUL.: *De Baptismo*, c. 18. CYPR.: *Epist.* LIX. *ad Fidum.* CLEM. ALEX.: *Pædag.* III. 247. ORIG.: *Comm. in Rom.* V. *Opp.* IV. 565, and *Homil. XIV. in Luc.*

See Lit. in vol. I. 463 sq., especially WALL. Comp. also W. R. POWERS: *Irenæus and Infant Baptism*, in the "Am. Presb. and Theol. Rev." N. Y. 1867, pp. 239–267.

While the church was still a missionary institution in the midst of a heathen world, infant baptism was overshadowed by the baptism of adult proselytes; as, in the following periods, upon the union of church and state, the order was reversed. At that time, too, there could, of course, be no such thing, even on the part of Christian parents, as a *compulsory* baptism, which dates from Justinian's reign, and which inevitably leads to the profanation of the sacrament. Constantine sat among the fathers at the great Council of Nicæa, and gave legal effect to its decrees, and yet put off his baptism to his deathbed. The cases of Gregory of Nazianzum, St. Chrysostom, and St. Augustin, who had mothers of exemplary piety, and yet were not baptized before early manhood, show sufficiently that considerable freedom prevailed in this respect even in the Nicene and post-Nicene ages. Gregory of Nazianzum gives the advice to put off the baptism of children, where there is no danger of death, to their third year.[1]

At the same time it seems an almost certain fact, though by many disputed, that, with the baptism of converts, the *optional* baptism of the children of Christian parents in established congregations, comes down from the apostolic age.[2] Pious parents would naturally feel a desire to consecrate their offspring from the very beginning to the service of the Redeemer, and find a precedent in the ordinance of circumcision. This desire would

[1] *Orat.* XL.
[2] Comp. I. 469 sq. The fact is not capable of positive proof, but rests on strong probabilities. The Baptists deny it. So does Neander, but he approves the practice of infant baptism as springing from the *spirit* of Christianity.

be strengthened in cases of sickness by the prevailing notion of the necessity of baptism for salvation. Among the fathers, Tertullian himself not excepted—for he combats only its expediency—there is not a single voice against the lawfulness and the apostolic origin of infant baptism. No time can be fixed at which it was first introduced. Tertullian suggests, that it was usually based on the invitation of Christ: "Suffer the little children to come unto me, and forbid them not." The usage of sponsors, to which Tertullian himself bears witness, although he disapproves of it, and still more, the almost equally ancient abuse of infant communion, imply the existence of infant baptism. Heretics also practised it, and were not censured for it.

The apostolic fathers make, indeed, no mention of it. But their silence proves nothing; for they hardly touch upon baptism at all, except Hermas, and he declares it necessary to salvation, even for the patriarchs in Hades (therefore, as we may well infer, for children also). Justin Martyr expressly teaches the capacity of *all* men for spiritual circumcision by baptism; and his "all" can with the less propriety be limited, since he is here speaking to a Jew.[1] He also says that many old men and women of sixty and seventy years of age have been from childhood disciples of Christ.[2] Polycarp was eighty-six years a Christian, and must have been baptized in early youth. According to Irenæus, his pupil and a faithful bearer of Johannean tradition, Christ passed through all the stages of life, to sanctify them all, and came to redeem, through himself, "all who through him are *born again* unto God, *sucklings, children*, boys, youths, and adults."[3] This profound view seems to involve an

---

[1] *Dial. c. Tr.* c. 43.

[2] *Apol.* I. c. 15 (Otto I. 48): Οἱ ἐκ παίδων ἐμαθητεύθησαν τῷ Χριστῷ.

[3] *Adv. Hær.* II. 22, § 4: "*Omnes venit per semetipsum salvare; omnes, inquam, qui per eum renascuntur in Deum, infantes et parvulos et pueros et juvenes et seniores. Ideo per omnem venit aetatem, et infantibus infans factus, sanctificans infantes; in parvulis parvulus, sanctificans hanc ipsam habentes aetatem; simul et exemplum illis pietatis effectus et justitiæ et subjectionis, in juvenibus juvenis,*" etc. Neander, in discussing this passage remarks, that "from this idea, founded on what is inmost in Christianity, becoming prominent in the feelings of Christians, resulted the practice of infant baptism" (I. 312, Boston ed.)

acknowledgment not only of the idea of infant baptism. but also of the practice of it; for in the mind of Irenæus and the ancient church baptism and regeneration were intimately connected and almost identified.[1] In an infant, in fact, any regeneration but through baptism cannot be easily conceived. A moral and spiritual regeneration, as distinct from sacramental, would imply conversion, and this is a conscious act of the will, an exercise of repentance and faith, of which the infant is not capable.

In the churches of Egypt infant baptism must have been practised from the first. For, aside from some not very clear expressions of Clement of Alexandria, Origen distinctly derives it from the tradition of the apostles; and through his journeys in the East and West he was well acquainted with the practice of the church in his time.[2]

---

[1] Irenæus speaks of "the washing of regeneration," and of the "baptism of regeneration unto God," τὸ βάπτισμα τῆς εἰς θεὸν ἀναγεννήσεως (*Adv. Haer.* I. c. 21, § 1); he identifies the apostolic commission to baptize with the *potestas regenerationis in Deum* (III. 17, § 1); he says that Christ descending into Hades, regenerated the ancient patriarchs (III. c. 22, § 4; "*in sinum suum recipiens pristinos patres regeneravit eos in vitam Dei*"), by which he probably meant baptism (according to the fancy of Hermas, Clement of Alex., and others). Compare an examination of the various passages of Irenæus in the article by Powers, who comes to the conclusion (*l. c.* p. 267) that "Irenæus everywhere implies baptism in the regeneration he so often names."

[2] *In Ep. ad Rom.* (*Opera*, vol. IV. col. 1047 ed. Migne; or IV. 565 ed. Delarue): "*Pro hoc et Ecclesia ab apostolis traditionem suscepit, etiam parvulis baptismum dare.*" *In Levit. Hom. VIII.* (II. 496 in Migne), he says that "*secundum Ecclesiæ observantiam*" baptism was given also to children (*etiam parvulis*). Comp. his *Com. in Matt. XV.* (III. 1268 sqq.) where he seems to infer this custom from the example of Christ blessing little children. That Origen himself was baptized in childhood (185 or soon after), is nowhere expressly stated in his works (as far as I know), but may be inferred as probable from his descent of, and early religious instruction, by Christian parents (reported by Euseb *H. E.* VI. 19: τῷ Ὠριγένει τὰ τῆς κατὰ Χριστὸν διδασκαλίας ἐκ προγόνων ἐσώζετο), in connection with the Egyptian custom. Comp. Redepenning, *Origenes*, I. 49. It would certainly be more difficult to prove that he was *not* baptized in infancy. He could easily make room for infant baptism in his theological system, which involved the Platonic idea of a prehistoric fall of the individual soul. But the Cyprianic and Augustinian theology connected it with the historic fall of Adam, and the consequent hereditary depravity and guilt.

The only opponent of infant baptism among the fathers is the eccentric and schismatic Tertullian, of North Africa. He condemns the hastening of the innocent age to the forgiveness of sins, and intrusting it with divine gifts, while we would not commit to it earthly property.[1] Whoever considers the solemnity of baptism, will shrink more from the receiving, than from the postponement of it. But the very manner of Tertullian's opposition proves as much in favor of infant baptism as against it. He meets it not as an innovation, but as a prevalent custom; and he meets it not with exegetical nor historical arguments, but only with considerations of religious prudence. His opposition to it is founded on his view of the regenerating effect of baptism, and of the impossibility of having mortal sins forgiven in the church after baptism; this ordinance cannot be repeated, and washes out only the guilt contracted before its reception. On the same ground he advises healthy adults, especially the unmarried, to postpone this sacrament until they shall be no longer in danger of forfeiting forever the grace of baptism by committing adultery, murder, apostasy, or any other of the seven crimes which he calls mortal sins. On the same principle his advice applies only to healthy children, not to sickly ones, if we consider that he held baptism to be the indispensable condition of forgiveness of sins, and taught the doctrine of hereditary sin. With him this position resulted from moral earnestness, and a lively sense of the great solemnity of the baptismal vow. But many put off baptism to their death-bed, in moral levity and presumption, that they might sin as long as they could.

Tertullian's opposition, moreover, had no influence, at least no theoretical influence, even in North Africa. His disciple Cyprian differed from him wholly. In his day it was no question, whether the children of Christian parents might and

---

[1] " *Quid festinat innocens aetas ad remissionem peccatorum ?* " The "*innocens*" here is to be taken only in a relative sense; for Tertullian in other places teaches a *vitium originis*, or hereditary sin and guilt, although not as distinctly and clearly as Augustin.

should be baptized—on this all were agreed,—but whether they might be baptized so early as the second or third day after birth, or, according to the precedent of the Jewish circumcision, on the eighth day. Cyprian, and a council of sixty-six bishops held at Carthage in 253 under his lead, decided for the earlier time, yet without condemning the delay.[1] It was in a measure the same view of the almost magical effect of the baptismal water, and of its absolute necessity to salvation, which led Cyprian to hasten, and Tertullian to postpone the holy ordinance; one looking more at the beneficent effect of the sacrament in regard to past sins, the other at the danger of sins to come.

§ 74. *Heretical Baptism.*

On HERETICAL BAPTISM comp. EUSEBIUS: *H. E.* VII. 3–5. CYPRIAN: *Epist.* LXX.–LXXVI. The Acts of the Councils of Carthage, A. D. 255 and 256, and the anonymous tract, *De Rebaptismate*, among CYPRIAN'S works, and in ROUTH'S *Reliquiæ Sacræ*, vol. v. 283–328.
HEFELE: *Conciliengeschichte*, I. 117–132 (second ed.).
G. E. STEITZ: *Ketzertaufe*, in Herzog, rev. ed., VII. 652–661.

Heretical baptism was, in the third century, the subject of a violent controversy, important also for its bearing on the question of the authority of the Roman see.

Cyprian, whose Epistles afford the clearest information on this subject, followed Tertullian[2] in rejecting baptism by heretics as an inoperative mock-baptism, and demanded that all heretics coming over to the Catholic church be baptized (he would not say *re*-baptized). His position here was due to his high-church exclusiveness and his horror of schism. As the one Catholic church is the sole repository of all grace, there can be no forgiveness of sins, no regeneration or communication of the Spirit, no salvation, and therefore no valid sacraments, out of her bosom. So far he had logical consistency on his side. But,

---

[1] A later council of Carthage of the year 418 went further and decreed: "*Item placuit, ut quicunque parvulos recentes ab uteris matrum baptizandos negat . . . anathema sit.*"

[2] *De Bapt.* c. 15. Comp. also Clement of Alex., *Strom.* I. 375.

on the other hand, he departed from the objective view of the church, as the Donatists afterwards did, in making the efficacy of the sacrament depend on the subjective holiness of the priest. " How can one consecrate water," he asks, " who is himself unholy, and has not the Holy Spirit?" He was followed by the North African church, which, in several councils at Carthage in the years 255-6, rejected heretical baptism; and by the church of Asia Minor, which had already acted on this view, and now, in the person of the Cappadocian bishop Firmilian, a disciple and admirer of the great Origen, vigorously defended it against Rome, using language which is entirely inconsistent with the claims of the papacy.[1]

The Roman bishop Stephen (253-257) appeared for the opposite doctrine, on the ground of the ancient practice of his church.[2] He offered no argument, but spoke with the consciousness of authority, and followed a catholic instinct. He laid chief stress on the objective nature of the sacrament, the virtue of which depended neither on the officiating priest, nor on the receiver, but solely on the institution of Christ. Hence he considered heretical baptism valid, provided only it was administered with intention to baptize and in the right form, to wit, in the name of the Trinity, or even of Christ alone; so that heretics coming into the church needed only confirmation, or the ratification of baptism by the Holy Ghost. " Heresy," says he, " produces children and exposes them; and the church takes up the exposed children, and nourishes them as her own, though she herself has not brought them forth."

The doctrine of Cyprian was the more consistent from the

[1] See p. 162. Some Roman divines (Molkenkuhr and Tizzani, as quoted by Hefele, p. 121) thought that such an irreverent Epistle as that of Firmilian (the 75th among Cyprian's Epp.) cannot be historical, and that the whole story of the controversy between Pope Stephen and St. Cyprian must be a fabrication! Dogma versus facts.

[2] According to Hippolytus (*Philosoph.*), the rebaptism of heretics was unknown before Callistus, A.D. 218-223. Cyprian does not deny the antiquity of the Roman custom, but pleads that truth is better than custom ("*quasi consuetudo major sit veritate*"). Hefele, I. p. 121. The Epistles of Stephen are lost, and we must learn his position from his opponents.

hierarchical point of view; that of Stephen, from the sacramental. The former was more logical, the latter more practical
and charitable. The one preserved the principle of the exclusiveness of the church; the other, that of the objective force of
the sacrament, even to the borders of the *opus operatum* theory.
Both were under the direction of the same churchly spirit, and
the same hatred of heretics; but the Roman doctrine is after all
a happy inconsistency of liberality, an inroad upon the principle
of absolute exclusiveness, an involuntary concession, that baptism, and with it the remission of sin and regeneration, therefore
salvation, are possible outside of Roman Catholicism.[1]

The controversy itself was conducted with great warmth.
Stephen, though advocating the liberal view, showed the genuine papal arrogance and intolerance. He would not even admit
to his presence the deputies of Cyprian, who brought him the
decree of the African synod, and he called this bishop, who
in every respect excelled Stephen, and whom the Roman church
now venerates as one of her greatest saints, a false Christ and
false apostle.[2] He broke off all intercourse with the African
church, as he had already with the Asiatic. But Cyprian and
Firmilian, nothing daunted, vindicated with great boldness, the
latter also with bitter vehemence, their different view, and continued in it to their death. The Alexandrian bishop Dionysius
endeavored to reconcile the two parties, but with little success.
The Valerian persecution, which soon ensued, and the martyrdom of Stephen (257) and of Cyprian (258), suppressed this
internal discord.

In the course of the fourth century, however, the Roman
theory gradually gained on the other, received the sanction

---

[1] Unless it be maintained that the baptismal grace, if received outside of the
Catholic communion, is of no use, but rather increases the guilt (like the
knowledge of the heathen), and becomes available only by the subjective conversion and regular confirmation of the heretic. This was the view of Augustin; see Steitz, *l. c.*, p. 655 sq.

[2] "*Pseudochristum, pseudoapostolum, et dolosum operarium.*" Firmil. *Ad Cyp.*
towards the end (*Ep.* 75). Hefele (I. 120) calls this unchristian intolerance
of Stephen very mildly "*eine grosse Unfreundlichkeit.*"

of the œcumenical Council of Nicæa in 325, was adopted in North Africa during the Donatistic controversies, by a Synod of Carthage, 348, defended by the powerful dialectics of St. Augustin against the Donatists, and was afterwards confirmed by the Council of Trent with an anathema on the opposite view.

NOTE.

The Council of Trent declares (*Sessio Sept.*, March 3, 1547, canon 4): "If any one says that the baptism, which is even given by heretics in the name of the Father, and of the Son, and of the Holy Ghost, with the intention of doing what the church doth, is not true baptism: let him be anathema." The Greek church likewise forbids the repetition of baptism which has been performed in the name of the Holy Trinity, but requires trine immersion. See the *Orthodox Conf.* Quaest. CII. (in Schaff's *Creeds* II. 376), and the *Russian Catch.* (II. 493), which says: "Baptism is spiritual birth: a man is born but once, therefore he is also baptized but once." But the same Catechism declares "trine immersion" to be "most essential in the administration of baptism" (II. 491).

The Roman church, following the teaching of St. Augustin, bases upon the validity of heretical and schismatical baptism even a certain legal claim on all baptized persons, as virtually belonging to her communion, and a right to the forcible conversion of heretics under favorable circumstances.[1] But as there may be some doubt about the orthodox form and intention of heretical baptism in the mind of the convert (*e. g.* if he be a Unitarian), the same church allows a *conditional* rebaptism with the formula: "*If* thou art *not yet* baptized, I baptize thee," etc.

Evangelical creeds put their recognition of Roman Catholic or any other Christian baptism not so much on the theory of the objective virtue of the sacrament, as on a more comprehensive and liberal conception of the church. Where Christ is, there is the church, and there are true ordinances. The Baptists alone, among Protestants, deny the validity of any other baptism but by immersion (in this respect resembling the Greek church), but are very far on that account from denying the Christian status of other denominations, since baptism with them is only a *sign* (not a *means*) of regeneration or conversion, which *precedes* the rite and is independent of it.

---

[1] Augustin thus misinterpreted the "*Coge intrare*," Luke 14: 22, 23, as justifying persecution (*Ep. ad Bonifac.*, c. 6). If the holy bishop of Hippo had foreseen the fearful consequences of his exegesis, he would have shrunk from it in horror.

CHAPTER VI.

CHRISTIAN ART.

§ 75. *Literature.*

Comp. the Lit. on the Catacombs, ch. VII.

FR. MÜNTER: *Sinnbilder u. Kunstvorstellungen der alten Christen.* Altona, 1825.

GRÜNEISEN: *Ueber die Ursachen des Kunsthasses in den drei ersten Jahrhunderten.* Stuttg. 1831.

HELMSDÖRFER: *Christl. Kunstsymbolik u. Ikonographie.* Frkf. 1839.

F. PIPER: *Mythologie u. Symbolik der christl. Kunst.* 2 vols. Weimar, 1847–51. *Ueber den christl. Bilderkreis.* Berl. 1852 (p. 3–10). By the same: *Einleitung in die monumentale Theologie.* Gotha, 1867.

J. B. DE ROSSI (R. C.): *De Christianis monumentis ἰχθύν exhibentibus,* in the third volume of PITRA's "Spicilegium Solesmense." Paris, 1855. Also his great work on the Roman Catacombs (*Roma Sotteranea,* 1864–1867), and his Archæol. "Bulletin" (*Bulletino di Archeologia cristiana,* since 1863).

A. WELBY PUGIN (architect and Prof. of Eccles. Antiquities at Oscott, a convert to the R. C. Ch., d. 1852): *Glossary of Ecclesiastical Ornament and Costume.* Lond. 1844, 4°, third ed. 1868, revised and enlarged by B. Smith, with 70 plates. See the art. "Cross."

P. RAFFAELLE GARRUCCI (Jesuit): *Storia della Arte Cristiana nei primi otto secoli della chiesa.* Prato, 1872–'80, 6 vols. fol., with 500 magnificent plates and illustrations. A most important work, but intensely Romish. By the same: *Il crocifisso graffito in casa dei Cesari.* Rom. 1857.

FR. BECKER: *Die Darstellung Jesu Christi unter dem Bilde des Fisches auf den Monumenten der Kirche der Katakomben, erläutert.* Breslau, 1866. The same: *Das Spott-Crucifix der römischen Kaiserpaläste aus dem Anfang des dritten Jahrh.* Breslau, 1866 (44 pp.). The same: *Die Wand-und Deckengemälde der röm. Katakomben.* Gera, 1876.

Abbé JOS. AL. MARTIGNY: *Diction. des Antiquités Chrétiennes.* Paris, 1865, second ed., 1877. (With valuable illustrations).

F. X. KRAUS (R. C.): *Die christl. Kunst in ihren frühesten Anfängen.* Leipzig, 1873 (219 pages and 53 woodcuts). Also several articles in his "Real-Encyklop. der. christl. Alterthümer," Freiburg i. B. 1880 sqq. (The cuts mostly from Martigny).

H. ACHELIS : *Das Symbol d. Fisches u. d. Fischdenkmäler*, Marb., 1888.
C. W. BENNETT : *Christian Archæology*, N. York, 1888.

§ 76. *Origin of Christian Art.*

CHRISTIANITY owed its origin neither to art nor to science, and is altogether independent of both. But it penetrates and pervades them with its heaven-like nature, and inspires them with a higher and nobler aim. Art reaches its real perfection in worship, as an embodiment of devotion in beautiful forms, which afford a pure pleasure, and at the same time excite and promote devotional feeling. Poetry and music, the most free and spiritual arts, which present their ideals in word and tone, and lead immediately from the outward form to the spiritual substance, were an essential element of worship in Judaism, and passed thence, in the singing of psalms, into the Christian church.

Not so with the plastic arts of sculpture and painting, which employ grosser material—stone, wood, color—as the medium of representation, and, with a lower grade of culture, tend almost invariably to abuse when brought in contact with worship. Hence the strict prohibition of these arts by the Monotheistic religions. The Mohammedans follow in this respect the Jews; their mosques are as bare of images of living beings as the synagogues, and they abhor the image worship of Greek and Roman Christians as a species of idolatry.

The ante-Nicene church, inheriting the Mosaic decalogue, and engaged in deadly conflict with heathen idolatry, was at first averse to those arts. Moreover her humble condition, her contempt for all hypocritical show and earthly vanity, her enthusiasm for martyrdom, and her absorbing expectation of the speedy destruction of the world and establishment of the millennial kingdom, made her indifferent to the ornamental part of life. The rigorous Montanists, in this respect the forerunners of the Puritans, were most hostile to art. But even the highly cultivated Clement of Alexandria put the spiritual worship of God in sharp contrast to the pictorial representation of the divine. "The habit of daily view," he says, "lowers the dignity of the divine, which cannot be honored, but is only degraded, by sensible material."

Yet this aversion to art seems not to have extended to mere symbols such as we find even in the Old Testament, as the brazen serpent and the cherubim in the temple. At all events, after the middle or close of the second century we find the rude beginnings of Christian art in the form of significant symbols in the private and social life of the Christians, and afterwards in public worship. This is evident from Tertullian and other writers of the third century, and is abundantly confirmed by the Catacombs, although the age of their earliest pictorial remains is a matter of uncertainty and dispute.

The origin of these symbols must be found in the instinctive desire of the Christians to have visible tokens of religious truth, which might remind them continually of their Redeemer and their holy calling, and which would at the same time furnish them the best substitute for the signs of heathen idolatry. For every day they were surrounded by mythological figures, not only in temples and public places, but in private houses, on the walls, floors, goblets, seal-rings, and grave-stones. Innocent and natural as this effort was, it could easily lead, in the less intelligent multitude, to confusion of the sign with the thing signified, and to many a superstition. Yet this result was the less apparent in the first three centuries, because in that period artistic works were mostly confined to the province of symbol and allegory.

From the private recesses of Christian homes and catacombs artistic representations of holy things passed into public churches in the fourth century, but under protest which continued for a long time and gave rise to the violent image controversies which were not settled until the second Council of Nicæa (787), in favor of a limited image worship. The Spanish Council of Elvira (Granada) in 306 first raised such a protest, and prohibited (in the thirty-sixth canon) "pictures in the church (*picturas in ecclesia*), lest the objects of veneration and worship should be depicted on the walls." This sounds almost iconoclastic and puritanic; but in view of the numerous ancient pictures and sculptures in the catacombs, the prohibition must be probably understood as a temporary measure of expediency in that transition period.[1]

§ 77. *The Cross and the Crucifix.*

"*Religion des Kreuzes, nur du verknüpfest in Einem Kranze*
Der Demuth und Kraft doppelte Palme zugleich."—(SCHILLER).*

Comp. the works quoted in § 75, and the lists in Zöckler and Fulda.

JUSTUS LIPSIUS (R. C., d. 1606, as Prof. at Louvain): *De Cruce libri tres, ad sacram profanamque historiam utiles.* Antw., 1595, and later editions.

JAC. GRETSER (Jesuit): *De Cruce Christi rebusque ad eam pertinentibus.* Ingolst., 1598–1605, 3 vols. 4to; 3rd ed. revised, 1608; also in his *Opera*, Ratisb., 1734, Tom. I.–III.

WM. HASLAM: *The Cross and the Serpent: being a brief History of the Triumph of the Cross.* Oxford, 1849.

W. R. ALGER: *History of the Cross.* Boston, 1858.

GABR. DE MORTILLET: *Le Signe de la Croix avant le Christianisme.* Paris, 1866.

A. CH. A. ZESTERMANN: *Die bildliche Darstellung des Kreuzes und der Kreuzigung historisch entwickelt.* Leipzig, 1867 and 1868.

J. STOCKBAUER (R. C.): *Kunstgeschichte des Kreuzes.* Schaffhausen, 1870.

O. ZŒCKLER (Prof. in Greifswald): *Das Kreuz Christi. Religionshistorische und kirchlich-archæologische Untersuchungen.* Gütersloh, 1875 (484 pages, with a large list of works, pp. xiii.–xxiv.). English translation by M. G. Evans, Lond., 1878.

ERNST V. BUNSEN: *Das Symbol des Kreuzes bei allen Nationen und die Entstehung des Kreuzsymbols der christlichen Kirche.* Berlin, 1876. (Full of hypotheses.)

HERMANN FULDA: *Das Kreuz und die Kreuzigung. Eine antiquarische Untersuchung.* Breslau, 1878. Polemical against the received views since Lipsius. See a full list of literature in Fulda, pp. 299–328.

E. DOBBERT: *Zur Entstehungsgeschichte des Kreuzes*, Leipzig, 1880.

The oldest and dearest, but also the most abused, of the primitive Christian symbols is the CROSS, the sign of redemption, sometimes alone, sometimes with the Alpha and Omega, sometimes with the anchor of hope or the palm of peace. Upon this arose, as early as the second century, the custom of making the

---

[1] See above, p. 180.   * "*Der deutschen Muse schönstes Distichon.*"

sign of the cross[1] on rising, bathing, going out, eating, in short, on engaging in any affairs of every-day life; a custom probably attended in many cases, even in that age, with superstitious confidence in the magical virtue of this sign; hence Tertullian found it necessary to defend the Christians against the heathen charge of worshipping the cross (*staurolatria*).[2]

Cyprian and the Apostolical Constitutions mention the sign of the cross as a part of the baptismal rite, and Lactantius speaks of it as effective against the demons in the baptismal exorcism. Prudentius recommends it as a preservative against temptations and bad dreams. We find as frequently, particularly upon ornaments and tombs, the monogram of the name of Christ, X P, usually combined in the cruciform character, either alone, or with the Greek letters Alpha and Omega, "the first and the last;" in later cases with the addition: "In the sign."[3] Soon after Constantine's victory over Maxentius by the aid of the Labarum (312), crosses were seen on helmets, bucklers, standards, crowns, sceptres, coins and seals, in various forms.[4]

---

[1] *Signaculum* or *signum crucis.*

[2] *Apol.* c. 16; *Ad Nat.* I. 12.   Julian the Apostate raised the same charge against the Christians of his day.

[3] "*In signo*," i. e. "*In hoc signo vinces*," the motto of Constantine.

[4] Archæologists distinguish seven or more forms of the cross:

(a) *crux decussata* (St. Andrew's cross), ✗

(b) *crux commissa* (the Egyptian cross), T

(c) *crux immissa* or *ordinaria* (the upright Latin cross), ┤├

(d) The inverted Latin cross of St. Peter, who considered himself unworthy to suffer in the upright position like his Lord, ⊥

(e) The Greek cross, consisting of four equally long arms, ✛

(f) The double cross, ≠

(g) The triple cross (used by the Pope), ☰

The chief forms of the monogram are:

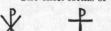

The story of the miraculous invention and raising of the true cross of Christ by Helena, the mother of Constantine, belongs to the Nicene age. The connection of the cross with the *a* and *ω* arose from the Apocalyptic designation of Christ (Rev. 1: 8; 21: 6; 22: 13), which is thus explained by Prudentius (*Cathem. hymn.* IX. 10–12):

The cross was despised by the heathen Romans on account of the crucifixion, the disgraceful punishment of slaves and the worst criminals; but the Apologists reminded them of the unconscious recognition of the salutary sign in the form of their standards and triumphal symbols, and of the analogies in nature, as the form of man with the outstretched arm, the flying bird, and the sailing ship.[1] Nor was the symbolical use of the cross confined to the Christian church, but is found among the ancient Egyptians, the Buddhists in India, and the Mexicans before the conquest, and other heathen nations, both as a symbol of blessing and a symbol of curse.[2]

The cross and the Lord's Prayer may be called the greatest martyrs in Christendom. Yet both the superstitious abuse and the puritanic protest bear a like testimony to the significance of the great fact of which it reminds us.

The CRUCIFIX, that is the sculptured or carved representation of our Saviour attached to the cross, is of much later date, and cannot be clearly traced beyond the middle of the sixth cen-

"Alpha et Omega cognominatus; ipse fons et clausula,
Omnia quæ sunt, fuerunt, quæque post futura sunt."

[1] Minut. Felix, *Octav.* c. 29: "*Tropæa vestra victricia non tantum simplicis crucis faciem, verum etiam adfixi hominis imitantur. Signum sane crucis naturaliter visimus in navi, cum velis tumentibus vehitur, cum expansis palmulis labitur; et cum erigitur jugum, crucis signum est; et cum homo porrectis manibus Deum pura mente veneratur. Ita signo crucis aut ratio naturalis innititur, aut vestra religio formatur.*" Comp. a very similar passage in Tertul., *Apol.* c. 16; and *Ad Nat.* I. 12; also Justin M., *Apol.* I. 55.

[2] When the temple of Serapis was destroyed (A. D. 390), signs of the cross were found beneath the hieroglyphics, and heathen and Christians referred it to their religion. Socrates, *H. E.* V. 17; Sozomenus, VII. 15; Theodoret, V. 22. On the Buddhist cross see Medhurst, *China*, p. 217. At the discovery of Mexico the Spaniards found the sign of the cross as an object of worship in the idol temples at Anahuac. Prescott, *Conquest of Mexico*, III. 338–340. See on the heathen use of the Cross, Haslam, Mortillet, Zöckler (*l. c.*, 7 sqq.), and Brinton, *Myths of the New World;* also an article on "*The pre-Christian Cross,*" in the "Edinburgh Review," Jan. 1870. Zöckler says (p. 95): "*Aller Fluch und Segen, alles Todeselend und alle Lebensherrlichkeit, die durch die vorchristliche Menschheit ausgebreitet gewesen, erscheinen in dem Kreuze auf Golgatha concentrirt zum wundervollsten Gebilde der religiös sittlichen Entwicklung unseres Geschlechtes.*"

tury. It is not mentioned by any writer of the Nicene and Chalcedonian age. One of the oldest known crucifixes, if not the very oldest, is found in a richly illuminated Syrian copy of the Gospels in Florence from the year 586.[1] Gregory of Tours (d. 595) describes a crucifix in the church of St. Genesius, in Narbonne, which presented the crucified One almost entirely naked.[2] But this gave offence, and was veiled, by order of the bishop, with a curtain, and only at times exposed to the people. The Venerable Bede relates that a crucifix, bearing on one side the Crucified, on the other the serpent lifted up by Moses, was brought from Rome to the British cloister of Weremouth in 686.[3]

NOTE.

The first symbol of the crucifixion was the cross alone; then followed the cross and the lamb—either the lamb with the cross on the head or shoulder, or the lamb fastened on the cross; then the figure of Christ in connection with the cross—either Christ holding it in his right hand (on the sarcophagus of Probus, d. 395), or Christ with the cross in the background (in the church of St. Pudentiana, built 398); at last Christ nailed to the cross.

An attempt has been made to trace the crucifixes back to the third or second century, in consequence of the discovery, in 1857, of a mock-crucifix on the wall in the ruins of the imperial palaces on the western declivity of the Palatine hill in Rome, which is preserved in the Museo Kircheriano. It shows the figure of a crucified man with the head of an ass or a horse, and a human figure kneeling before it, with the inscription: "Alexamenos worships his God."[4] This figure was no doubt scratched on the wall by some heathen enemy to ridicule a Christian slave or page of the imperial household, or possibly even the emperor Alexander Severus (222–235), who, by his religious syncretism, exposed himself to sarcastic criticism. The date of the caricature is uncertain ; but we know that in the second century the Christians, like the Jews

[1] See Becker, *l. c.*, p. 38, Westwood's *Palæographia Sacra*, and Smith and Cheetham, I. 515.

[2] " *Pictura, quae Dominum nostrum quasi praecinctum linteo indicat crucifixum.*" *De Gloria Martyrum*, lib. I. c. 28.

[3] *Opera,* ed. Giles, iv. p. 376. A crucifix is found in an Irish MS. written about 800. See Westwood, as quoted in Smith and Cheetham, I. 516.

[4] Ἀλεξάμενος σέβετ [αι] θεόν. The monument was first published by the Jesuit Garrucci, and is fully discussed by Becker in the essay quoted. A woodcut is also given in Smith and Cheetham, I. 516.

before them, were charged with the worship of an ass, and that at that time there were already Christians in the imperial palace.[1] After the third century this silly charge disappears. Roman archæologists (P. Garrucci, P. Mozzoni, and Martigny) infer from this mock-crucifix that crucifixes were in use among Christians already at the close of the second century, since the original precedes the caricature. But this conjecture is not supported by any evidence. The heathen Cæcilius in Minucius Felix (ch. 10) expressly testifies the absence of Christian *simulacra*. As the oldest pictures of Christ, so far as we know, originated not among the orthodox Christians, but among the heretical and half heathenish Gnostics, so also the oldest known representation of the *crucifix* was a mock-picture from the hand of a heathen—an excellent illlustration of the word of Paul that the preaching of Christ crucified is foolishness to the Greeks.

§ 78. *Other Christian Symbols.*

The following symbols, borrowed from the Scriptures, were frequently represented in the catacombs, and relate to the virtues and duties of the Christian life : The dove, with or without the olive branch, the type of simplicity and innocence;[2] the ship, representing sometimes the church, as safely sailing through the flood of corruption, with reference to Noah's ark, sometimes the individual soul on its voyage to the heavenly home under the conduct of the storm-controlling Saviour; the palm-branch, which the seer of the Apocalypse puts into the hands of the elect, as the sign of victory;[3] the anchor, the figure of hope;[4] the lyre, denoting festal joy and sweet harmony;[5] the cock, an admonition to watchfulness, with reference to Peter's fall;[6] the hart which pants for the fresh water-brooks;[7] and the vine which, with its branches and clusters, illustrates the union of

[1] Comp. on the supposed ὀνολατρεία of the Christians, Tertullian, *Apol.* c. 16 ("*Nam et somniastis caput asininum esse Deum nostrum,*" etc.) ; *Ad nationes* I. 11, 14; Minut. Felix, *Octav.* 9. Tertullian traces this absurdity to Cornelius Tacitus, who charges it upon the Jews (*Hist.* V. 4).

[2] Comp. Matt. 3: 16; 10: 16; Gen. 8: 11; Cant. 6: 9.

[3] Rev. 7: 9. The palm had a similar significance with the heathen. Horace writes (*Od.* I. 1): "*Palmaque nobilis Terrarum dominos evehit ad deos.*"

[4] Heb. 6: 19. Likewise among the heathen.

[5] Comp. Eph. 5: 19.

[6] Matt. 26: 34, and parallel passages.

[7] Ps. 42: 1.

the Christians with Christ according to the parable, and the richness and joyfulness of Christian life.[1]

The phenix, a symbol of rejuvenation and of the resurrection, is derived from the well-known heathen myth.[2]

§ 79. *Historical and Allegorical Pictures.*

From these emblems there was but one step to iconographic representations. The Bible furnished rich material for historical, typical, and allegorical pictures, which are found in the catacombs and ancient monuments. Many of them date from the third or even the second century.

The favorite pictures from the Old Testament are Adam and Eve, the rivers of Paradise, the ark of Noah, the sacrifice of Isaac, the passage through the Red Sea, the giving of the law, Moses smiting the rock, the deliverance of Jonah, Jonah naked under the gourd, the translation of Elijah, Daniel in the lions' den, the three children in the fiery furnace. Then we have scenes from the Gospels, and from apostolic and post-apostolic history, such as the adoration of the Magi, their meeting with Herod, the baptism of Jesus in the Jordan, the healing of the paralytic, the changing of water into wine, the miraculous feeding of five thousand, the ten virgins, the resurrection of Lazarus, the entry into Jerusalem, the Holy Supper, the portraits of St. Peter and St. Paul.[3]

[1] John 15: 1–6. The parables of the Good Shepherd, and of the Vine and the Branches, both recorded only by St. John, seem to have been the most prominent in the mind of the primitive Christians, as they are in the catacombs. "What they valued" (says Stanley, *Christ. Inst.*, p. 288), "what they felt, was a new moral influence, a new life stealing through their veins, a new health imparted to their frames, a new courage breathing in their faces, like wine to a weary laborer, like sap in the hundred branches of a spreading tree, like juice in the thousand clusters of a spreading vine." But more important than this was the idea of vital union of the believers with Christ and among each other, symbolized by the vine and its branches.

[2] The fabulous phenix is nowhere mentioned in the Bible, and is first used by Clement of Rome, *Ad Cor.* c. 25, and by Tertullian, *De Resurr.* c. 13. Comp. Pliny, *Hist. Nat.* XIII. 4.

[3] For details the reader is referred to the great illustrated works of Perret, De Rossi, Garrucci, Parker, Roller, Northcote and Brownlow, etc.

The passion and crucifixion were never represented in the early monuments, except by the symbol of the cross.

Occasionally we find also mythological representations, as Psyche with wings, and playing with birds and flowers (an emblem of immortality), Hercules, Theseus, and especially Orpheus, who with his magic song quieted the storm and tamed the wild beasts.

Perhaps Gnosticism had a stimulating effect in art, as it had in theology. At all events the sects of the Carpocratians, the Basilideans, and the Manichaeans cherished art. Nationality also had something to do with this branch of life. The Italians are by nature an artistic people, and shaped their Christianity accordingly. Therefore Rome is preëminently the home of Christian art.

The earliest pictures in the catacombs are artistically the best, and show the influence of classic models in the beauty and grace of form. From the fourth century there is a rapid decline to rudeness and stiffness, and a transition to the Byzantine type.

Some writers [1] have represented this primitive Christian art merely as pagan art in its decay, and even the Good Shepherd as a copy of Apollo or Hermes. But while the form is often an imitation, the spirit is altogether different, and the myths are understood as unconscious prophecies and types of Christian verities, as in the Sibylline books. The relation of Christian art to mythological art somewhat resembles the relation of biblical Greek to classical Greek. Christianity could not at once invent a new art any more than a new language, but it emancipated the old from the service of idolatry and immorality, filled it with a deeper meaning, and consecrated it to a higher aim.

The blending of classical reminiscences and Christian ideas is best embodied in the beautiful symbolic pictures of the Good Shepherd and of Orpheus. [2]

The former was the most favorite figure, not only in the Catacombs, but on articles of daily use, as rings, cups, and

[1] Raoul-Rochette (*Mémoires sur les antiquités chrétiennes;* and *Tableau des Catacombes*), and Renan (*Marc-Aurèle*, p. 542 sqq.).

[2] See the illustrations at the end of the volume.

lamps. Nearly one hundred and fifty such pictures have come down to us. The Shepherd, an appropriate symbol of Christ, is usually represented as a handsome, beardless, gentle youth, in light costume, with a girdle and sandals, with the flute and pastoral staff, carrying a lamb on his shoulder, standing between two or more sheep that look confidently up to him. Sometimes he feeds a large flock on green pastures. If this was the popular conception of Christ, it stood in contrast with the contemporaneous theological idea of the homely appearance of the Saviour, and anticipated the post-Constantinian conception.

The picture of Orpheus is twice found in the cemetery of Domitilla, and once in that of Callistus. One on the ceiling in Domitilla, apparently from the second century, is especially rich : it represents the mysterious singer, seated in the centre on a piece of rock, playing on the lyre his enchanting melodies to wild and tame animals—the lion, the wolf, the serpent, the horse, the ram—at his feet—and the birds in the trees ;[1] around the central figure are several biblical scenes, Moses smiting the rock, David aiming the sling at Goliath (?), Daniel among the lions, the raising of Lazarus. The heathen Orpheus, the reputed author of monotheistic hymns (the Orphica), the centre of so many mysteries, the fabulous charmer of all creation, appears here either as a symbol and type of Christ himself,[2] or rather, like the heathen Sibyl, as an antitype and unconscious prophet of Christ, announcing and foreshadowing Him as the conqueror of all the forces of nature, as the harmonizer of all discords, and as ruler over life and death.

§ 80. *Allegorical Representations of Christ.*

Pictures of Christ came into use slowly and gradually, as the conceptions concerning his personal appearance changed. The

---

[1] Comp. Horace, *De Arte Poët.*, 391 sqq.

Silvestres homines sacer interpresque deorum
Cœdibus et victu fœdo deterruit Orpheus,
Dictus ob hoc lenire tigres rabidosque leones.

[2] This is the explanation of nearly all archæologists since Bosio, except Schultze (*Die Katak.*, p. 105).

Evangelists very wisely keep profound silence on the subject, and no ideal which human genius may devise, can do justice to Him who was God manifest in the flesh.

In the ante-Nicene age the strange notion prevailed that our Saviour, in the state of his humiliation, was homely, according to a literal interpretation of the Messianic prophecy : " He hath no form nor comeliness." [1] This was the opinion of Justin Martyr,[2] Tertullian,[3] and even of the spiritualistic Alexandrian divines Clement,[4] and Origen.[5] A true and healthy feeling leads rather to the opposite view; for Jesus certainly had not the physiognomy of a sinner, and the heavenly purity and harmony of his soul must in some way have shone through the veil of his flesh, as it certainly did on the Mount of Transfiguration. Physical deformity is incompatible with the Old Testament idea of the priesthood, how much more with the idea of the Messiah.

Those fathers, however, had the state of humiliation alone in their eye. The exalted Redeemer they themselves viewed as clothed with unfading beauty and glory, which was to pass from Him, the Head, to his church also, in her perfect millennial state.[6] We have here, therefore, not an essential opposition

---

[1] Isa. 53 : 2, 3; 52 : 14; comp. Ps. 22.

[2] *Dial. c. Tryphone Judœo* c. 14 (εἰς τὴν π ρ ώ τ η ν παρουσίαν τοῦ Χριστοῦ, ἐν ᾗ καὶ ἄτιμος καὶ ἀειδὴς καὶ θνητὸς φανήσεσθαι κεκηρυγμένος ἐστίν); c. 49 (παθητὸς καὶ ἄτιμος καὶ ἀειδής); 85, 88, 100, 110, 121.

[3] *Adv. Jud.* c. 14 : " *ne aspectu quidem honestus,*" and then he quotes Isa. 53 : 2 sqq.; 8 : 14; Ps. 22. *De carne Christi,* c. 9 : "*nec humanœ honestatis corpus fuit, nedum cœlestis claritatis.*"

[4] *Paedag.* III. 1, p. 252; *Strom.* lib. II. c. 5, p. 440; III. c. 17, p. 559; VI. c. 17, p. 818 (ed. Potter).

[5] *Contr. Cels.* VI. c. 75, where Origen quotes from Celsus that Christ's person did not differ from others in grandeur or beauty or strength, but was, as the Christians report, "little, ill-favored and ignoble" (τὸ σῶμα μικρὸν καὶ δυσειδὲς καὶ ἀγενὲς ἦν). He admits the "ill-favored," but denies the "ignoble," and doubts the "little," of which there is no certain evidence. He then quotes the language of Isaiah 53, but adds the description of Ps. 45 : 3, 4 (Sept.), which represents the Messiah as a king arrayed in beauty. Celsus used this false tradition of the supposed uncomeliness of Jesus as an argument against his divinity, and an objection to the Christian religion.

[6] Comp. Tertullian, *Adv. Jud.* c. 14 (*Opera,* ed. Oehler II. 740), where he

made between holiness and beauty, but only a temporary separation.   Nor did the ante-Nicene fathers mean to deny that
Christ, even in the days of his humiliation, had a spiritual
beauty which captivated susceptible souls.   Thus Clement of
Alexandria distinguishes between two kinds of beauty, the outward beauty of the flesh, which soon fades away, and the
beauty of the soul, which consists in moral excellence and is
permanent.   "That the Lord Himself," he says, "was uncomely
in aspect, the Spirit testifies by Isaiah: 'And we saw Him, and
he had no form nor comeliness; but his form was mean, inferior
to men.'   Yet who was more admirable than the Lord?   But
it was not the beauty of the flesh visible to the eye, but the
true beauty of both soul and body, which He exhibited, which
in the former is beneficence; in the latter—that is, the flesh—
immortality." [1]   Chrysostom went further: he understood
Isaiah's description to refer merely to the scenes of the passion,
and took his idea of the personal appearance of Jesus from the
forty-fifth Psalm, where he is represented as "fairer than the
children of men."   Jerome and Augustin had the same view,
but there was at that time no authentic picture of Christ, and
the imagination was left to its own imperfect attempts to set
forth that human face divine which reflected the beauty of sinless holiness.

The first representations of Christ were purely *allegorical*.
He appears now as a shepherd, who lays down his life for the

quotes Dan. 7: 13 sq., and Ps. 45: 3, 4, for the heavenly beauty and
glory of the exalted Saviour, and says: "*Primo sordibus indutus est, id est
carnis passibilis et mortalis indignitate. . . . . . dehinc spoliatus pristina sorde,
exornatus podere et mitra et cidari munda, id est secundi adventus; quoniam
gloriam et honorem adeptus demonstratur.*" Justin Martyr makes the same distinction between the humility of the first and the glory of the second appearance.   *Dial. c. Tryph. Jud.* c. 14 and c. 49, etc.   So does Origen in the passage
just quoted.

[1] *Paedag.* lib. III. c. 1, which treats of true beauty.   Compare also the last
chapter in the second book, which is directed against the extravagant fondness
of females for dress and jewels, and contrasts with these meretricious ornaments the true beauty of the soul, which "blossoms out in the flesh, exhibiting
the amiable comeliness of self-control, whenever the character, like a beam of
light, gleams in the form."

sheep,[1] or carries the lost sheep on his shoulders;[2] now as a
lamb, who bears the sin of the world;[3] more rarely as a ram,
with reference to the substituted victim in the history of Abraham and Isaac;[4] frequently as a fisher.[5] Clement of Alexandria, in his hymn, calls Christ the "Fisher of men that are
saved, who with his sweet life catches the pure fish out of the
hostile flood in the sea of iniquity."

The most favorite symbol seems to have been that of the fish.
It was the double symbol of the Redeemer and the redeemed.
The corresponding Greek ICHTHYS is a pregnant anagram, containing the initials of the words: "Jesus Christ, Son of God,
Saviour."[6] In some pictures the mysterious fish is swimming
in the water with a plate of bread and a cup of wine on
his back, with evident allusion to the Lord's Supper. At the
same time the fish represented the soul caught in the net of
the great Fisher of men and his servants, with reference to
Matt. 4: 19; comp. 13: 47. Tertullian connects the symbol
with the water of baptism, saying:[7] "We little fishes
(*pisciculi*) are born by our Fish (*secundum* 'ΙΧΘΥΝ *nostrum*), Jesus Christ, in water, and can thrive only by continuing in the water;" that is if we are faithful to our bap-

---

[1] John 10: 11. Comp. above, p. 276.

[2] Luke 15: 3–7; comp. Isa. 40: 11; Ez. 34: 11–15; Ps. 23.

[3] John 1: 29; 1 Pet. 1: 19; Rev. 5: 12.   [4] Gen. 22: 13.

[5] Christ calls the apostles "fishers of men," Matt. 4: 19.

[6] 'ΙΧΘΥΣ = 'Ι-ησοῦς Χ-ριστὸς Θ-εοῦ Υ-ἱὸς Σ-ωτήρ. Comp. Augustin, *De Civit.
Dei* xviii. 23 (*Jesus Christus Dei Filius Salvator*). The acrostic in the
Sibylline Books (lib. viii. vs. 217 sqq.) adds to this word σταυρός, the cross.
Schultze (*Katak.*, p. 129), not satisfied with this explanation, goes back to Matt.
7: 10, where fish (ἰχθύς) and serpent (ὄφις) are contrasted, and suggested a
contrast between Christ and the devil (comp. Apoc. 12: 14, 15; 2 Cor. 11: 3).
Rather artificial. Merz derives the symbol from ὄψον (hence ὀψάριον in John
21: 9) in the sense of "fish, flesh." In Palestine fish was, next to bread, the
principal food, and a savory accompaniment of bread. It figures prominently
in the miraculous feeding of the multitude (John 6: 9, 11), and in the meal
of the risen Saviour on the shores of the Lake of Tiberias (John 21: 9,
ὀψάριον καὶ ἄρτον). By an allegorical stretch, the fish might thus become to
the mind of the early church a symbol of Christ's body, as the heavenly food
which he gave for the salvation of men (John 6: 51).

[7] *De Baptismo,* c. 1.

tismal covenant, and preserve the grace there received. The pious fancy made the fish a symbol of the whole mystery of the Christian salvation. The anagrammatic or hieroglyphic use of the Greek ICHTHYS and the Latin PISCIS-CHRISTUS belonged to the *Disciplina Arcani*, and was a testimony of the ancient church to the faith in Christ's person as the Son of God, and his work as the Saviour of the world. The origin of this symbol must be traced beyond the middle of the second century, perhaps to Alexandria, where there was a strong love for mystic symbolism, both among the orthodox and the Gnostic heretics.[1] It is familiarly mentioned by Clement of Alexandria, Origen, and Tertullian, and is found on ancient remains in the Roman catacombs, marked on the grave-stones, rings, lamps, vases, and wall-pictures.[2]

The Ichthys-symbol went out of use before the middle of the fourth century, after which it is only found occasionally as a reminiscence of olden times.

Previous to the time of Constantine, we find no trace of an image of Christ, properly speaking, except among the Gnostic Carpocratians,[3] and in the case of the heathen emperor Alexander Severus, who adorned his domestic chapel, as a sort of syncretistic Pantheon, with representatives of all religions.[4] The above-mentioned idea of the uncomely personal appearance

---

[1] So Pitra, *De Pisce symbolico*, in "Spicil. Solesm.," III. 524. Comp. Marriott, *The Testimony of the Catacombs*, p. 120 sqq.

[2] The oldest Ichthys-monument known so far was discovered in 1865 in the Cœmeterium Domitillæ, a hitherto inaccessible part of the Roman catacombs, and is traced by Cavalier De Rossi to the first century, by Becker to the first half of the second. It is in a wall picture, representing three persons with three loaves of bread and a fish. In other pictures we find fish, bread, and wine, with evident allusion to the miraculous feeding (Matt. 15: 17), and the meals of the risen Saviour with his disciples (Luke, ch. 24; John, ch. 21). Paulinus calls Christ "*panis ipse verus et aquæ vivæ piscis.*" See the interesting illustrations in Garrucci, Martigny, Kraus, and other archæological works.

[3] Irenæus, *Adv. Haer.* I. 25. The Carpocratians asserted that even Pilate ordered a portrait of Christ to be made. Comp. Hippolytus, *Philos.*, VII. c. 32; Epiphanius, *Adv. Hær.* XXVI. 6; Augustin, *De Hær.* c. 7.

[4] Apollonius, Orpheus, Abraham, and Christ. See Lampridius, *Vita Alex. Sev.* c. 29.

of Jesus, the entire silence of the Gospels about it, and the Old Testament prohibition of images, restrained the church from making either pictures or statues of Christ, until in the Nicene age a great change took place, though not without energetic and long-continued opposition. Eusebius gives us, from his own observation, the oldest report of a statue of Christ, which was said to have been erected by the woman with the issue of blood, together with her own statue, in memory of her cure, before her dwelling at Cæsarea Philippi (Paneas).[1] But the same historian, in a letter to the empress Constantia (the sister of Constantine and widow of Licinius), strongly protested against images of Christ, who had laid aside his earthly servant form, and whose heavenly glory transcends the conception and artistic skill of man.[2]

§ 81. *Pictures of the Virgin Mary.*

DE ROSSI: *Imagines selectœ Deiparœ Virginis* (Rome, 1863); MARRIOTT: *Catacombs* (Lond. 1870, pp. 1–63); MARTIGNY: *Dict.* sub "Vierge;" KRAUS: *Die christl. Kunst* (Leipz. 1873, p. 105); NORTHCOTE and BROWNLOW: *Roma Sotter.* (2nd ed. Lond. 1879, Pt. II. p. 133 sqq.); WITHROW: *Catacombs* (N. Y. 1874, p. 305 sqq.); SCHULTZE: *Die Marienbilder der altchristl. Kunst,* and *Die Katacomben* (Leipz. 1882, p. 150 sqq.); VON LEHNER: *Die Marienverehrung in den 3 ersten Jahrh.* (Stuttgart, 1881, p. 282 sqq.).

It was formerly supposed that no picture of the Virgin existed before the Council of Ephesus (431), which condemned Nestorius and sanctioned the *theotokos,* thereby giving solemn sanction and a strong impetus to the cultus of Mary. But several pictures are now traced, with a high degree of probability, to the third, if not the second century. From the first

---

[1] *H. E.* VII. 18. Comp. Matt. 9: 20. Probably that alleged statue of Christ was a monument of Hadrian, or some other emperor to whom the Phœnicians did obeisance, in the form of a kneeling woman. Similar representations are seen on coins, particularly from the age of Hadrian. Julian the Apostate destroyed the two statues, and substituted his own, which was riven by lightning (Sozom. V. 21).

[2] A fragment of this letter is preserved in the acts of the iconoclastic Council of 754, and in the sixth act of the Second Council of Nicæa, 787. See Euseb. *Opp.* ed. Migne, II. col. 1545, and Harduin, *Conc.* IV. 406.

five centuries nearly fifty representations of Mary have so far been brought to the notice of scholars, most of them in connection with the infant Saviour.

The oldest is a fragmentary wall-picture in the cemetery of Priscilla: it presents Mary wearing a tunic and cloak, in sitting posture, and holding at her breast the child, who turns his face round to the beholder. Near her stands a young and beardless man (probably Joseph) clothed in the *pallium*, holding a book-roll in one hand, pointing to the star above with the other, and looking upon the mother and child with the expression of joy; between and above the figures is the star of Bethlehem; the whole represents the happiness of a family without the supernatural adornments of dogmatic reflection.[1] In the same cemetery of Priscilla there are other frescos, representing (according to De Rossi and Garrucci) the annunciation by the angel, the adoration of the Magi, and the finding of the Lord in the temple. The adoration of the Magi (two or four, afterwards three) is a favorite part of the pictures of the holy family. In the oldest picture of that kind in the cemetery

---

[1] See the picture in De Rossi, Plate IV., Northcote and Brownlow, Plate xx (II. 140), and in Schultze, *Katak.*, p. 151. De Rossi (" Bulletino," 1865, 23, as quoted by N. and B.) declares it either coëval with the first Christian art, or little removed from it, either of the age of the Flavii or of Trajan and Hadrian, or at the very latest, of the first Antonines. "On 'the roof of this tomb there was figured in fine stucco the Good Shepherd between two sheep, and some other subject, now nearly defaced." De Rossi supports his view of the high antiquity of this Madonna by the superior, almost classical style of art, and by the fact that the catacomb of Priscilla, the mother of Pudens, is one of the oldest. But J. H. Parker, an experienced antiquary, assigns this picture to A. D. 523. The young man is, according to De Rossi, Isaiah or some other prophet; but Marriott and Schultze refer him to Joseph, which is more probable, although the later tradition of the Greek church derived from the Apocryphal Gospels and strengthened by the idea of the perpetual virginity, represents him as an old man with several children from a previous marriage (the brethren of Jesus, changed into cousins by Jerome and the Latin church). Northcote and Brownlow (II. 141) remark: "St. Joseph certainly appears in some of the sarcophagi; and in the most ancient of them as a young and beardless man, generally clad in a tunic. In the mosaics of St. Mary Major's, which are of the fifth century, and in which he appears four or five times, he is shown of mature age, if not old; and from that time forward this became the more common mode of representing him."

of SS. Peter and Marcellinus, Mary sits on a chair, holding the babe in her lap, and receiving the homage of two Magi, one on each side, presenting their gifts on a plate.[1] In later pictures the manger, the ox and the ass, and the miraculous star are added to the scene.

The frequent pictures of a lady in praying attitude, with uplifted or outstretched arms (*Orans* or *Orante*), especially when found in company with the Good Shepherd, are explained by Roman Catholic archæologists to mean the church or the blessed Virgin, or both combined, praying for sinners.[2] But figures of praying men as well as women are abundant in the catacombs, and often represent the person buried in the adjacent tomb, whose names are sometimes given. No *Ora pro nobis*, no *Ave Maria*, no *Theotokos* or *Deipara* appears there. The pictures of the *Orans* are like those of other women, and show no traces of Mariolatry. Nearly all the representations in the catacombs keep within the limits of the gospel history. But after the fourth century, and in the degeneracy of art, Mary was pictured in elaborate mosaics, and on gilded glasses, as the crowned queen of heaven, seated on a throne, in bejewelled purple robes, and with a nimbus of glory, worshipped by angels and saints.

The noblest pictures of Mary, in ancient and modern times, endeavor to set forth that peculiar union of virgin purity and motherly tenderness which distinguish "the Wedded Maid

---

[1] See Plate xx. in N. and B. ii. 140. Schultze (p. 153) traces this picture to the beginning of the third century.

[2] According to the usual Roman Catholic interpretation of the apocalyptic vision of the woman clothed with the sun, and bringing forth a man-child (12: 1, 5). Cardinal Newman reasons inconclusively in a letter to Dr. Pusey on his *Eirenicon* (p. 62): "I do not deny that, under the image of the woman, the church is signified; but . . . . the holy apostle would not have spoken of the church under this particular image unless there had existed a blessed Virgin Mary, who was exalted on high, and the object of veneration of all the faithful." When accompanied by the Good Shepherd the *Orans* is supposed by Northcote and Brownlow (II. 137) to represent Mary as the new Eve, as the Shepherd is the new Adam. It must be admitted that the parallel between Mary and Eve is as old as Irenæus, and contains the fruitful germ of Mariolatry, but in those pictures no such contrast is presented.

and Virgin Mother" from ordinary women, and exert such a powerful charm upon the imagination and feelings of Christendom.   No excesses of Mariolatry, sinful as they are, should blind us to the restraining and elevating effect of contemplating, with devout reverence,

"The ideal of all womanhood,
So mild, so merciful, so strong, so good,
So patient, peaceful, loyal, loving, pure."

CHAPTER VII.

THE CHURCH IN THE CATACOMBS.

§ 82. *Literature.*

Comp. the works quoted in ch. VI., especially GARRUCCI (6 vols.), and the Table of Illustrations at the end of this volume.

I. Older works. By BOSIO (*Roma Sotterranea*, Rom. 1632; abridged edition by P. GIOVANNI SEVERANI da S. Severino, Rom. 1710, very rare); BOLDETTI (1720); BOTTARI (1737); D'AGINCOURT (1825); RÖSTELL (1830); MARCHI (1844); MAITLAND (*The Church in the Catacombs*, Lond. 1847); LOUIS PERRET (*Catacombes de Rome*, etc. Paris, 1853 sqq. 5 vols., with 325 splendid plates, but with a text that is of little value, and superseded).

II. More recent works.

*GIOVANNI BATTISTA DE ROSSI (the chief authority on the Catacombs): *La Roma Sotterranea Cristiana descritta et illustrata*, publ. by order of Pope Pio Nono, Roma (cromolitografia Pontificia), Tom. I. 1864, Tom. II. 1867, Tom. III. 1877, in 3 vols. fol. with two additional vols. of plates and inscriptions. A fourth volume is expected. Comp. his articles in the bimonthly "Bulletino di archeologia Cristiana," Rom. 1863 sqq., and several smaller essays. Roller calls De Rossi " *le fouilleur le mieux qualifié, fervent catholique, mais critique sérieux.*"

*J. SPENCER NORTHCOTE (Canon of Birmingham) and W. R. BROWNLOW (Canon of Plymouth): *Roma Sotterranea*. London (Longmans, Green & Co., 1869; second edition, "rewritten and greatly enlarged," 1879, 2 vols. The first vol. contains the History, the second, Christian Art. This work gives the substance of the investigations of Commendatore De Rossi by his consent, together with a large number of chromo-lithographic plates and wood-engravings, with special reference to the cemetery of San Callisto. The vol. on Inscriptions is separate, see below.

F. X. KRAUS (R. C.), *Roma Sotterranea. Die Röm. Katakomben.* Freiburg. i. B. (1873), second ed. 1879. Based upon De Rossi and the first ed. of Northcote & Brownlow.

D. DE RICHEMONT: *Les catacombes de Rome.* Paris, 1870.

WHARTON B. MARRIOTT, B. S. F. S. A. (Ch. of England): *The Testi-*

mony of the Catacombs and of other Monuments of Christian Art from the second to the eighteenth century, concerning questions of Doctrine now disputed in the Church. London, 1870 (223 pages with illustrations). Discusses the monuments referring to the cultus of the Virgin Mary, the supremacy of the Pope, and the state after death.

F. Becker: *Roms altchristliche Cömeterien.* Leipzig, 1874.

W. H. Withrow (Methodist): *The Catacombs of Rome and their Testimony relative to Primitive Christianity.* New York (Nelson & Phillips), 1874. Polemical against Romanism. The author says (Pref., p. 6): "The testimony of the catacombs exhibits, more strikingly than any other evidence, the immense contrast between primitive Christianity and modern Romanism."

John P. Lundy (Episc.): *Monumental Christianity: or the Art and Symbolism of the Primitive Church as Witnesses and Teachers of the one Catholic Faith and Practice.* New York, 1876. New ed. enlarged, 1882, 453 pages, richly illustrated.

*John Henry Parker (Episc.): *The Archæology of Rome.* Oxford and London, 1877. Parts IX. and X.: Tombs in and near Rome, and Sculpture; Part XII.: The Catacombs. A standard work, with the best illustrations.

* Théophile Roller (Protest.): *Les Catacombes de Rome. Histoire de l'art et des croyances religieuses pendant les premiers siècles du Christianisme.* Paris, 1879–1881, 2 vols. fol. 720 pages text and 100 excellent plates en héliogravure, and many illustrations and inscriptions. The author resided several years at Naples and Rome as Reformed pastor.

M. Armellini (R. C.): *Le Catacombe Romane descritte.* Roma, 1880 (A popular extract from De Rossi, 437 pages). By the same the more important work: *Il Cimiterio di S. Agnese sulla via Nomentana.* Rom. 1880.

Dean Stanley: *The Roman Catacombs,* in his "Christian Institutions." Lond. and N. York, 1881 (pp. 272–295).

* Victor Schultze (Lutheran): *Archæologische Studien über altchristliche Monumente. Mit 26 Holzschnitten.* Wien, 1880; *Die Katakomben. Die altchristlichen Grabstätten. Ihre Geschichte und ihre Monumente* (with 52 illustrations). Leipzig, 1882 (342 pages); *Die Katakomben von San Gennaro dei Poveri in Neapel.* Jena, 1877. Also the pamphlet: *Der theolog. Ertrag der Katakombenforschung.* Leipz. 1882 (30 pages). The last pamphlet is against Harnack's review, who charged Schultze with overrating the gain of the catacomb-investigations (see the "Theol. Literaturzeitung," 1882.)

Bishop W. J. Kip: *The Catacombs of Rome as illustrating the Church of the First Three Centuries.* N. York, 1853, 6th ed., 1887 (212 pages).

K. Rönneke: *Rom's christliche Katakomben.* Leipzig, 1886.

Comp. also Edmund Venables in Smith and Cheetham, 1. 294–317;

HEINRICH MERZ in Herzog, VII. 559–568; THEOD. MOMMSEN on the *Roman Catac.* in "The Contemp. Review." vol. XVII. 160–175 (April to July, 1871); the relevant articles in the Archæol. Dicts. of MARTIGNY and KRAUS, and the *Archæology* of BENNETT (1888).

III. Christian Inscriptions in the catacombs and other old monuments.

*Commendatore J. B. DE ROSSI: *Inscriptiones Christianæ Urbis Romæ septimo seculo antiquiores.* Romæ, 1861 (XXIII. and 619 pages). Another vol. is expected. The chief work in this department. Many inscriptions also in his *Roma Sott.* and "Bulletino."

EDWARD LE BLANT: *Inscriptions chrétiennes de la Gaule anterieures au VIIIme siècle.* Paris, 1856 and 1865, 2 vols. By the same: *Manuel d'Épigraphie chrétienne.* Paris, 1869.

JOHN McCAUL: *Christian Epitaphs of the First Six Centuries.* Toronto, 1869. Greek and Latin, especially from Rome.

F. BECKER: *Die Inschriften der römischen Cömeterien.* Leipzig, 1878.

*J. SPENCER NORTHCOTE (R. C. Canon of Birmingham): *Epitaphs of the Catacombs or Christian Inscriptions in Rome during the First Four Centuries.* Lond., 1878 (196 pages).

G. T. STOKES on *Greek and Latin Christian Inscriptions;* two articles in the "Contemporary Review" for 1880 and 1881.

V. SCHULTZE discusses the Inscriptions in the fifth section of his work *Die Katakomben* (1882), pp. 235–274, and gives the literature.

The *Corpus Inscriptionum Græcarum* by BÖCKH, and KIRCHHOFF, and the *Corpus Inscriptionum Lat*, edited for the Berlin Academy by TH. MOMMSEN and others, 1863 sqq. (not yet completed), contain also Christian Inscriptions. Prof. E. HÜBNER has added those of Spain (1871) and Britain (1873). G. PETRIE has collected the Christian Inscriptions in the Irish language, ed. by STOKES. Dublin, 1870 sqq. Comp. the art. "Inscriptions," in Smith and Cheetham, I. 841.

§ 83. *Origin and History of the Catacombs.*

THE Catacombs of Rome and other cities open a new chapter of Church history, which has recently been dug up from the bowels of the earth. Their discovery was a revelation to the world as instructive and important as the discovery of the long lost cities of Pompeii and Herculaneum, and of Nineveh and Babylon. Eusebius says nothing about them; the ancient Fathers scarcely allude to them, except Jerome and Prudentius, and even they give us no idea of their extent and importance. Hence the historians till quite recently have passed them by in silence.[1] But since the great discoveries of Commendatore De Rossi and other archæologists they can no longer be ignored. They confirm, illustrate, and supplement our previous knowledge derived from the more important literary remains.

The name of the Catacombs is of uncertain origin, but is equivalent to subterranean cemeteries or resting-places for the dead.[2] First used of the Christian cemeteries in the neighborhood of Rome, it was afterwards applied to those of Naples, Malta, Sicily, Alexandria, Paris, and other cities.

It was formerly supposed that the Roman Catacombs were originally sand-pits (*arenariæ*) or stone-quarries (*lapidicinæ*), excavated by the heathen for building material, and occasionally used as receptacles for the vilest corpses of slaves and criminals.[3] But this view is now abandoned on account of the difference of construction and of the soil. A few of the catacombs, however, about five out of thirty, are more or less closely connected with abandoned sand-pits.[4]

[1] Mosheim and Gibbon in the last century, and even Neander, Gieseler, and Baur, in our age, ignore the very existence of the catacombs, except that Gieseler quotes the well-known passage of Jerome. But Dean Milman, in his *History of Christianity*, Hase, Kurtz, Kraus, and others, in their manuals, take brief notice of them.

[2] κατακύμβιον, *catacumba*, also (in some MSS.) *catatumba*. Various derivations: 1) From κατά (*down from*, *downwards*, as in καταβαίνω, κατάκειμαι, καταπέμπω), and τύμβος (compare the late Latin *tumba*, the French *tombe*, *tombeau*, and the English *tomb*, *grave*), *i. e.* a tomb down in the earth, as distinct from tombs on the surface. This corresponds best to the thing itself. 2) From κατά and κοιμάω (*to sleep*), which would make it equivalent to κοιμητήριον, *dormitorium*, *sleeping place*. 3) From κατά and κύμβη (*the hollow of a vessel*) or κύμβος (*cup*), κυμβίον (*a small cup*, Lat. *cymbium*), which would simply give us the idea of a hollow place. So Venables in Smith and Cheetham. Very unlikely. 4) A hybrid term from κατά and the Latin *decumbo*, *to lie down*, *to recline*. So Marchi, and Northcote and Brownlow (I. 263). The word first occurs in a Christian calendar of the third or fourth century (*in Catacumbas*), and in a letter of Gregory I. to the Empress Constantia, towards the end of the sixth century (*Epp.* III. 30), with a special local application to San Sebastian. The earlier writers use the terms κοιμητήρια, *cœmeteria* (whence our *cemetery*), also *cryptæ*, *crypts*.

[3] So Aringhi, Baronius, Severano, Bottari, Boldetti, and all writers prior to Marchi, and his pupils, the two brothers De Rossi, who turned the current of opinion. See Northcote and Br. I. 377 sqq.

[4] The sand-pits and stone-quarries were made wide enough for a horse and

The catacombs, therefore, with a few exceptions, are of Christian origin, and were excavated for the express purpose of Christian burial. Their enormous extent, and the mixture of heathen with Christian symbols and inscriptions, might suggest that they were used by heathen also; but this is excluded by the fact of the mutual aversion of Christians and idolaters to associate in life and in death. The mythological features are few, and adapted to Christian ideas.[1]

Another erroneous opinion, once generally entertained, regarded the catacombs as places of refuge from heathen persecution. But the immense labor required could not have escaped the attention of the police. They were, on the contrary, the result of toleration. The Roman government, although (like all despotic governments) jealous of secret societies, was quite liberal towards the burial clubs, mostly of the poorer classes, or associations for securing, by regular contributions, decent interment with religious ceremonies.[2] Only the worst criminals,

cart, and are cut in the *tufa litoide* and *pozzolana pura*, which furnish the best building material in Rome ; while the catacombs have generally very narrow passages, run in straight lines, often cross each other at sharp angles, and are excavated in the *tufa granulare*, which is too soft for building-stone, and too much mixed with earth to be used for cement, but easily worked, and adapted for the construction of galleries and chambers. See Northcote and Br. I. 376–390. The exceptions are also stated by these authors. J. H. Parker has discovered *loculi* for Christian burial in the recesses of a deserted sand-pit.

[1] See the remarks of Northcote and Br. I. 276 against J. H. Parker, who asserts the mixed use of the catacombs for heathens and Christians.

[2] This view is supported by Professor Mommsen, the Roman historian, who says (in "Contemporary Review," vol. xxvii. p. 168): "Associations of poor people who clubbed together for the burial of their members were not only tolerated but supported by the imperial government, which otherwise was very strict against associations. From this point of view, therefore, there was no legal impediment to the acquisition of these properties. Christian associations have from the very beginning paid great attention to their burials; it was considered the duty of the wealthier members to provide for the burial of the poor, and St. Ambrose still allowed churches to sell their communion plate, in order to enlarge the cemeteries of the faithful. The catacombs show what could be achieved by such means at Rome. Even if their fabulous dimensions are reduced to their right measure, they form an immense work, without beauty and ornament, despising in architecture and inscription not only pomp

traitors, suicides, and those struck down by lightning (touched by the gods) were left unburied.　The pious care of the dead is an instinct of human nature, and is found among all nations. Death is a mighty leveler of distinctions and preacher of toleration and charity ; even despots bow before it, and are reminded of their own vanity ; even hard hearts are moved by it to pity and to tears.　" *De mortuis nihil nisi bonum.*"

The Christians enjoyed probably from the beginning the privilege of common cemeteries, like the Jews, even without an express enactment.　Galienus restored them after their temporary confiscation during the persecution of Valerian (260).[1]

Being mostly of Jewish and Oriental descent, the Roman Christians naturally followed the Oriental custom of cutting their tombs in rocks, and constructing galleries.　Hence the close resemblance of the Jewish and Christian cemeteries in Rome.[2]　The ancient Greeks and Romans under the empire were in the habit of burning the corpses (*crematio*) for sanitary

and empty phraseology, but even nicety and correctness, avoiding the splendor and grandeur as well as the tinsel and vanity of the life of the great town that was hurrying and throbbing above, the true commentary of the words of Christ—'My kingdom is not of this world.' "

[1] Euseb. *H. E.* VII. 13: 1, τὰ τῶν καλουμένων κοιμητηρίων ἀπολαμβάνειν ἐπιτρέπων χωρία.

[2] Roller says (in Lichtenberger's *Encycl. des Sc. Rel.* II. 685).　"*Les juifs ensevelissaient dans le roc.　A Rome ils ont creusé de grandes catacombes presque identiques à celles des chrétiens.　Ceux-ci ont été leurs imitateurs.　Les Etrusques se servaient aussi de grottes; mais ils ne les reliaient point par des galeries illimitées.*"　Dean Stanley (*l. c.* p. 274) : "The Catacombs are the standing monuments of the Oriental and Jewish character, even of Western Christianity.　The fact that they are the counterparts of the rock-hewn tombs of Palestine, and yet more closely of the Jewish cemeteries in the neighborhood of Rome, corresponds to the fact that the early Roman Church was not a Latin but an Eastern community, speaking Greek and following the usages of Syria.　And again, the ease with which the Roman Christians had recourse to these cemeteries is an indication of the impartiality of the Roman law, which extended (as De Rossi has well pointed out) to this despised sect the same protection in regard to burial, even during the times of persecution, that was accorded to the highest in the land.　They thus bear witness to the unconscious fostering care of the Imperial Government over the infant church. They are thus monuments, not so much of the persecution as of the toleration which the Christians received at the hands of the Roman Empire."

reasons, but burial in the earth (*humatio*), outside of the city near the public roads, or on hills, or in natural grottos, was the older custom; the rich had their own sepulchres (*sepulcra*). In their catacombs the Christians could assemble for worship and take refuge in times of persecution. Very rarely they were pursued in these silent retreats. Once only it is reported that the Christians were shut up by the heathen in a cemetery and smothered to death.

Most of the catacombs were constructed during the first three centuries, a few may be traced almost to the apostolic age.[1] After Constantine, when the temporal condition of the Christians improved, and they could bury their dead without any disturbance in the open air, the cemeteries were located above ground, especially above the catacombs, and around the basilicas, or on other land purchased or donated for the purpose. Some catacombs owe their origin to individuals or private families, who granted the use of their own grounds for the burial of their brethren; others belonged to churches. The Christians wrote on the graves appropriate epitaphs and consoling thoughts, and painted on the walls their favorite symbols. At funerals they turned these dark and cheerless abodes into chapels; under the dim light of the terra-cotta lamps they committed dust to dust, ashes to ashes, and amidst the shadows of death they inhaled the breath of the resurrection and life everlasting. But it is an error to suppose that the catacombs served as the usual places of worship in times of persecution; for such a purpose they were entirely unfitted; even the largest could accommodate, at most, only twenty or thirty persons within convenient distance.[2]

[1] De Rossi (as quoted by Northcote and Brownlow, I. 112): "Precisely in those cemeteries to which history or tradition assigns apostolic origin, I see, in the light of the most searching archæological criticism, the cradle both of Christian subterranean sepulchres, of Christian art, and of Christian inscriptions; there I find memorials of persons who appear to belong to the times of the Flavii and of Trajan; and finally I discover precise dates of those times."

[2] Schultze (*Die Katak.*, p. 73 and 83) maintains in opposition to Marchi, that the catacombs were nothing but burial places, and used only for the burial service, and that the little chapels (*ecclesiolæ*) were either private sepulchral chambers or post-Constantinian structures.

The devotional use of the catacombs began in the Nicene age, and greatly stimulated the worship of martyrs and saints. When they ceased to be used for burial they became resorts of pious pilgrims. Little chapels were built for the celebration of the memory of the martyrs. St. Jerome relates,[1] how, while a school-boy, about A. D. 350, he used to go with his companions every Sunday to the graves of the apostles and martyrs in the crypts at Rome, "where in subterranean depths the visitor passes to and fro between the bodies of the entombed on both walls, and where all is so dark, that the prophecy here finds its fulfillment: The living go down into Hades.[2] Here and there a ray from above, not falling in through a window, but only pressing in through a crevice, softens the gloom; as you go onward, it fades away, and in the darkness of night which surrounds you, that verse of Virgil comes to your mind:

"Horror ubique animos, simul ipsa silentia terrent."[3]

The poet Prudentius also, in the beginning of the fifth century, several times speaks of these burial places, and the devotions held within them.[4]

Pope Damasus (366–384) showed his zeal in repairing and decorating the catacombs, and erecting new stair-cases for the convenience of pilgrims. His successors kept up the interest, but by repeated repairs introduced great confusion into the chronology of the works of art.

The barbarian invasions of Alaric (410), Genseric (455), Ricimer (472), Vitiges (537), Totila (546), and the Lombards (754), turned Rome into a heap of ruins and destroyed many valuable treasures of classical and Christian antiquity. But the pious barbarism of relic hunters did much greater damage.

---

[1] *Com. in Ez.* ch. 40.
[2] He refers to such passages as Ps. 55: 15; Num. 16: 33.
[3] *Aen.* II. 755:
"Horror on every side, and terrible even the silence."
Or in German:
"*Grauen rings um mich her, und schreckvoll selber die Stille.*"
[4] *Peristeph.* XI. 153 sqq.

The tombs of real and imaginary saints were rifled, and cart-loads of dead men's bones were translated to the Pantheon and churches and chapels for more convenient worship. In this way the catacombs gradually lost all interest, and passed into decay and complete oblivion for more than six centuries.

In the sixteenth century the catacombs were rediscovered, and opened an interesting field for antiquarian research. The first discovery was made May 31, 1578, by some laborers in a vineyard on the Via Salaria, who were digging *pozzolana*, and came on an old subterranean cemetery, ornamented with Christian paintings, Greek and Latin inscriptions and sculptured sarcophagi. "In that day," says De Rossi, "was born the name and the knowledge of Roma Sotterranea." One of the first and principal explorers was Antonio Bosio, "the Columbus of this subterranean world." His researches were published after his death (Roma, 1632). Filippo Neri, Carlo Borromeo, and other restorers of Romanism spent, like St. Jerome of old, whole nights in prayer amid these ruins of the age of martyrs. But Protestant divines discredited these discoveries as inventions of Romish divines seeking in heathen sand-pits for Christian saints who never lived, and Christian martyrs who never died.[1]

In the present century the discovery and investigation of the catacombs has taken a new start, and is now an important department of Christian archæology. The dogmatic and sectarian treatment has given way to a scientific method with the sole aim to ascertain the truth. The acknowledged pioneer in this subterranean region of ancient church history is the Cavalier John Baptist de Rossi, a devout, yet liberal Roman Catholic. His monumental Italian work (*Roma Sotterranea*, 1864–1877) has been made accessible in judicious condensations to French, German, and English readers by Allard (1871),

---

[1] *E. g.* Bishop Burnet (who visited the catacombs in 1685): *Letters from Italy and Switzerland* in 1685 and 1686. He believed that the catacombs were the common burial places of the ancient heathen. G. S. Cyprian (1699), J. Basnage (1699), and Peter Zorn (1703), wrote on the subject in polemical interest against Rome.

Kraus (1873 and 1879), Northcote & Brownlow (1869 and 1879). Other writers, Protestant as well as Roman Catholic, are constantly adding to our stores of information. Great progress has been made in the chronology and the interpretation of the pictures in the catacombs.

And yet the work is only begun. More than one half of ancient Christian cemeteries are waiting for future exploration. De Rossi treats chiefly of one group of Roman catacombs, that of Callistus. The catacombs in Naples, Syracuse, Girgenti, Melos, Alexandria, Cyrene, are very imperfectly known ; still others in the ancient apostolic churches may yet be discovered, and furnish results as important for church history as the discoveries of Ilium, Mycenæ, and Olympia for that of classical Greece.

§ 84. *Description of the Catacombs.*

The Roman catacombs are long and narrow passages or galleries and cross-galleries excavated in the bowels of the earth in the hills outside and around the city, for the burial of the dead. They are dark and gloomy, with only an occasional ray of light from above. The galleries have two or more stories, all filled with tombs, and form an intricate net-work or subterranean labyrinth. Small compartments (*loculi*) were cut out like shelves in the perpendicular walls for the reception of the dead, and rectangular chambers (*cubicula*) for families, or distinguished martyrs. They were closed with a slab of marble or tile. The more wealthy were laid in sarcophagi. The ceiling is flat, sometimes slightly arched. Space was economized so as to leave room usually only for a single person ; the average width of the passages being $2\frac{1}{2}$ to 3 feet. This economy may be traced to the poverty of the early Christians, and also to their strong sense of community in life and in death. The little oratories with altars and episcopal chairs cut in the tufa are probably of later construction, and could accommodate only a few persons at a time. They were suited for funeral services and private devotion, but not for public worship.

The galleries were originally small, but gradually extended to enormous length. Their combined extent is counted by hundreds of miles, and the number of graves by millions.[1]

The oldest and best known of the Roman cemeteries is that of St. SEBASTIAN, originally called *Ad Catacumbas*, on the Appian road, a little over two miles south of the city walls. It was once, it is said, the temporary resting-place of the bodies of St. Peter and St. Paul, before their removal to the basilicas named after them; also of forty-six bishops of Rome, and of a large number of martyrs.

The immense cemetery of Pope CALLISTUS (218–223) on the Via Appia consisted originally of several small and independent burial grounds (called Lucinæ, Zephyrini, Callisti, Hippoliti). It has been thoroughly investigated by De Rossi. The most ancient part is called after Lucina, and measures 100 Roman feet in breadth by 180 feet in length. The whole group bears the name of Callistus, probably because his predecessor, Zephyrinus "set him over the cemetery" (of the church of Rome).[2] He was then a deacon. He stands high in the estimation of the Roman church, but the account given of him by Hippolytus is quite unfavorable. He was certainly a remarkable man, who rose from slavery to the highest dignity of the church.

[1] I hesitate to state the figures. Roman archæologists, as Marchi, J. B. de Rossi and his brother Michael de R. (a practical mathematician), Martigny and others estimate the length of the Roman catacombs variously at from 350 to 900 miles, or as "more than the whole length of Italy" (Northcote and Brownlow, I. 2). Allowance is made for from four to seven millions of graves! It seems incredible that there should have been so many Christians in Rome in four centuries, even if we include the numerous strangers. All such estimates are purely conjectural. See Smith and Cheetham, I. 301. Smyth (*l. c.*. p. 15) quotes Rawlinson as saying that 7,000,000 of graves in 400 years' time gives an average population of from 500,000 to 700,000. Total population of Rome, 1,500,000 to 2,000,000 at the beginning of the empire.

[2] This is so stated by Hippolytus, *Philosoph.* IX. 11. Zephyrinus was buried there contrary to the custom of burying the popes in St. Peter's crypt in the Vatican. Callistus was hurled from a window in Trastevere, and hastily removed to the nearest cemetery on the Via Aurelia. The whole report of Hippolytus about Callistus is discredited by Northcote and Brownlow (I. 497 sqq.), but without good reason.

The cemetery of DOMITILLA (named in the fourth century St. Petronillæ, Nerei et Achillei) is on the Via Ardeatina, and its origin is traced back to Flavia Domitilla, grand-daughter or great-grand-daughter of Vespasian. She was banished by Domitian (about A. D. 95) to the island of Pontia "for professing Christ."[1] Her chamberlains (eunuchi cubicularii), Nerus and Achilleus, according to an uncertain tradition, were baptized by St. Peter, suffered martyrdom, and were buried in a farm belonging to their mistress. In another part of this cemetery De Rossi discovered the broken columns of a subterranean chapel and a small chamber with a fresco on the wall, which represents an elderly matron named "Veneranda," and a young lady, called in the inscription "PETRONILLA martyr," and pointing to the Holy Scriptures in a chest by her side, as the proofs of her faith. The former apparently introduces the latter into Paradise.[2] The name naturally suggests the legendary daughter of St. Peter.[3] But Roman divines, reluctant to admit that the first pope had any children (though his marriage is beyond a doubt from the record of the Gospels), understand Petronilla to be a spiritual daughter, as Mark was a spiritual son, of the apostle (1 Pet. 5 : 13), and make her the daughter of some Roman Petronius or Petro connected with the family of Domitilla.

Other ancient catacombs are those of Prætextatus, Priscilla (St. Silvestri and St. Marcelli), Basilla (S. Hermetis, Basillæ, Proti, et Hyacinthi), Maximus, St. Hippolytus, St. Laurentius, St. Peter and Marcellinus, St. Agnes, and the Ostrianum (Ad Nymphas Petri, or Fons Petri, where Peter is said to have baptized from a natural well). De Rossi gives a list of forty-two

---

[1] Eusebius, H. E. III. 18. De Rossi distinguishes two Christian Domitillas, and defends this view against Mommsen. See "Bulletino," 1875, pp. 69–77, and Mommsen, Corp. Inscript. Lat., Tom. VI. p. 172, as quoted by Northcote and Br. I. 86. See also Mommsen in "The Contemp. Review," XVII. 169 sq.; Lightfoot. Philippians, p. 22, and S. Clement of R., 257.

[2] See the picture in Northcote and Br. I. 182, and on the whole subject of Petronilla, pp. 122, 176–186.

[3] Acta Sanct. Maii, III. 11.

greater or lesser cemeteries, including isolated tombs of martyrs, in and near Rome, which date from the first four centuries, and are mentioned in ancient records.[1]

The FURNITURE of the catacombs is instructive and interesting, but most of it has been removed to churches and museums, and must be studied outside. Articles of ornament, rings, seals, bracelets, neck-laces, mirrors, tooth-picks, ear-picks, buckles, brooches, rare coins, innumerable lamps of clay (terra-cotta), or of bronze, even of silver and amber, all sorts of tools, and in the case of children a variety of playthings were inclosed with the dead. Many of these articles are carved with the monogram of Christ, or other Christian symbols. (The lamps in Jewish cemeteries bear generally a picture of the golden candlestick).

A great number of flasks and cups also, with or without ornamentation, are found, mostly outside of the graves, and fastened to the grave-lids. These were formerly supposed to have been receptacles for tears, or, from the red, dried sediment in them, for the blood of martyrs. But later archæologists consider them drinking vessels used in the agapæ and oblations. A superstitious habit prevailed in the fourth century, although condemned by a council of Carthage (397), to give to the dead the eucharistic wine, or to put a cup with the consecrated wine in the grave.[2]

The instruments of torture which the fertile imagination of

[1] See also the list in N. and Br. I. pp. xx–xxi, and in Smith and Cheetham, I. 315.

[2] The curious controversy about these blood-stained phials is not yet closed. Chemical experiments have led to no decided results. The Congregation of Rites and Relics decided, in 1668, that the *phiolæ cruentæ* or *ampullæ sanguinolentæ* were blood-vessels of martyrs, and Pius IX. confirmed the decision in 1863. It was opposed by distinguished Roman scholars (Mabillon, Tillemont, Muratori, the Jesuit Père de Buck (*De phialis rubricatis*, Brussels, 1855), but defended again, though cautiously and to a very limited extent by De Rossi (III. 602), Northcote and Brownlow (II. 330–343), and by F. X. Kraus (*Die Blutampullen der röm. Katakomben*, 1868, and *Ueber den gegenw. Stand der Frage nach dem Inhalt und der Bedeutung der röm. Blutampullen*, 1872). Comp. also Schultze: *Die sogen. Blutgläser der Röm. Kat.* (1880), and *Die Katakomben* (1882, pp. 226–232). Roller thinks that the phials contained probably perfumery, or perhaps eucharistic wine.

credulous people had discovered, and which were made to prove that almost every Christian buried in the catacombs was a martyr, are simply implements of handicraft. The instinct of nature prompts the bereaved to deposit in the graves of their kindred and friends those things which were constantly used by them. The idea prevailed also to a large extent that the future life was a continuation of the occupations and amusements of the present, but free from sin and imperfection.

On opening the graves the skeleton appears frequently even now very well preserved, sometimes in dazzling whiteness, as covered with a glistening glory; but falls into dust at the touch.

§ 85. *Pictures and Sculptures.*

The most important remains of the catacombs are the pictures, sculptures, and epitaphs.

I. Pictures. These have already been described in the preceding chapter. They are painted *al fresco* on the wall and ceiling, and represent Christian symbols, scenes of Bible history, and allegorical conceptions of the Saviour. A few are in pure classic style, and betray an early origin when Greek art still flourished in Rome; but most of them belong to the period of decay. Prominence is given to pictures of the Good Shepherd, and those biblical stories which exhibit the conquest of faith and the hope of the resurrection. The mixed character of some of the Christian frescos may be explained partly from the employment of heathen artists by Christian patrons, partly from old reminiscences. The Etrurians and Greeks were in the habit of painting their tombs, and Christian Greeks early saw the value of pictorial language as a means of instruction. In technical skill the Christian art is inferior to the heathen, but its subjects are higher, and its meaning is deeper.

II. The works of sculpture are mostly found on sarcophagi. Many of them are collected in the Lateran Museum. Few of them date from the ante-Nicene age.[1] They represent in relief

---

[1] Renan dates the oldest sculptures from the end of the third century : " *Les*

the same subjects as the wall-pictures, as far as they could be worked in stone or marble, especially the resurrection of Lazarus, Daniel among the lions, Moses smiting the rock, the sacrifice of Isaac.

Among the oldest Christian sarcophagi are those of St. Helena, the mother of Constantine (d. 328), and of Constantia, his daughter (d. 354), both of red porphyry, and preserved in the Vatican Museum. The sculpture on the former probably represents the triumphal entry of Constantine into Rome after his victory over Maxentius; the sculpture on the latter, the cultivation of the vine, probably with a symbolical meaning.[1]

The richest and finest of all the Christian sarcophagi is that of Junius Bassus, Prefect of Rome, A. D. 359, and five times Consul, in the crypt of St. Peter's in the Vatican.[2] It was found in the Vatican cemetery (1595). It is made of Parian marble in Corinthian style. The subjects represented in the upper part are the sacrifice of Abraham, the capture of St. Peter, Christ seated between Peter and Paul, the capture of Christ, and Pilate washing his hands; in the lower part are the temptation of Adam and Eve, suffering Job, Christ's entrance into Jerusalem, Daniel among the lions, and the capture of St. Paul.

§ 86. *Epitaphs.*

"Rudely written, but each letter
Full of hope, and yet of heart-break,
Full of all the tender pathos of the Here
    and the Hereafter."

To perpetuate, by means of sepulchral inscriptions, the

*sarcophages sculptés, représentant des scènes sacrées, apparaissent vers la fin du III*e *siècle. Comme les peintures chrétiennes, ils ne s'écartent guère, sauf pour le sujet, des habitudes de l'art païen du même temps."* (*Marc Auréle*, p. 546). Comp. also Schultze, *Die Katak.* 165–186, and especially the IXth part of John Henry Parker's great work, which treats on the *Tombs in and near Rome*, 1877.

[1] See photographs of both in Parker, Part IX, Nos. 209 and 210, and pp. 41 and 42.

[2] See a photograph in Parker, *l. c.*, Plate XIII; also in Lundy, *Monum. Christianity*, p. 112.

memory of relatives and friends, and to record the sentiments of love and esteem, of grief and hope, in the face of death and eternity, is a custom common to all civilized ages and nations. These epitaphs are limited by space, and often provoke rather than satisfy curiosity, but contain nevertheless in poetry or prose a vast amount of biographical and historical information. Many a grave-yard is a broken record of the church to which it belongs.

The Catacombs abound in such monumental inscriptions, Greek and Latin, or strangely mixed (Latin words in Greek characters), often rudely written, badly spelt, mutilated, and almost illegible, with and without symbolical figures. The classical languages were then in a process of decay, like classical eloquence and art, and the great majority of Christians were poor and illiterate people. One name only is given in the earlier epitaphs, sometimes the age, and the day of burial, but not the date of birth.

More than fifteen thousand epitaphs have been collected, classified, and explained by De Rossi from the first six centuries in Rome alone, and their number is constantly increasing. Benedict XIV. founded, in 1750, a Christian Museum, and devoted a hall in the Vatican to the collection of ancient sarcophagi. Gregory XVI. and Pius IX. patronized it. In this Lapidarian Gallery the costly pagan and the simple Christian inscriptions and sarcophagi confront each other on opposite walls, and present a striking contrast. Another important collection is in the Kircherian Museum, in the Roman College, another in the Christian Museum of the University of Berlin.[1] The entire field of ancient epigraphy, heathen and Christian in Italy and other countries, has been made accessible by the industry and learning of Gruter, Muratori, Marchi, De Rossi, Le

---

[1] Under the care of Professor Piper (a pupil of Neander), who even before De Rossi introduced a scientific knowledge of the sepulchral monuments and inscriptions. Comp. his "*Monumental Theology*," and his essay "*Ueber den kirchenhistorischen Gewinn aus Inschriften*, in the "Jahrbücher f. D. Theologie," 1875.

Blant, Boeckh, Kirchhoff, Orelli, Mommsen, Henzen, Hübner, Waddington, McCaul.

The most difficult part of this branch of archæology is the chronology (the oldest inscriptions being mostly undated).[1] Their chief interest for the church historian is their religion, as far as it may be inferred from a few words.

The key-note of the Christian epitaphs, as compared with the heathen, is struck by Paul in his words of comfort to the Thessalonians, that they should not sorrow like the heathen who have no hope, but remember that, as Jesus rose from the dead, so God will raise them also that are fallen asleep in Jesus.

Hence, while the heathen epitaphs rarely express a belief in immortality, but often describe death as an eternal sleep, the grave as a final home, and are pervaded by a tone of sadness, the Christian epitaphs are hopeful and cheerful. The farewell on earth is followed by a welcome from heaven. Death is but a short sleep; the soul is with Christ and lives in God, the body waits for a joyful resurrection: this is the sum and substance of the theology of Christian epitaphs. The symbol of Christ (*Ichthys*) is often placed at the beginning or end to show the ground of this hope. Again and again we find the brief, but significant words: " in peace; "[2] " he " or " she sleeps in peace; "[3] " live in God," or " in Christ; " " live forever."[4] " He rests well." " God quicken thy spirit." " Weep not, my child; death is not eternal." " Alexander is not dead, but lives above the stars, and his body rests in this tomb."[5] " Here

---

[1] De Rossi traces some up to the first century, but Renan (*Marc-Aurèle*, p. 536) maintains: "*Les inscriptions chrétiennes des catacombes ne remontent qu' au commencement du IIIe siècle.*"

[2] *In pace;* ἐν εἰρήνῃ. Frequent also in the Jewish cemeteries (*shalom*).

[3] *Dormit in pace; requiescit in pace; in pace Domini;* κοιμᾶται ἐν εἰρήνῃ. The pagan formula "*depositus*" also occurs, but with an altered meaning: a precious treasure intrusted to faithful keeping for a short time.

[4] *Vivas,* or *vive in Deo; vivas in æternum; vivas inter sanctos.* Contrast with these the pagan acclamations: *Sit tibi terra levis; Ossa tua bene quiescant; Ave; Vale.*

[5] This inscription in the cemetery of Callistus dates from the time of persecution, probably in the third century, and alludes to it in these words: "For while

Gordian, the courier from Gaul, strangled for the faith, with his whole family, rests in peace. The maid servant, Theophila, erected this." [1]

At the same time stereotyped heathen epitaphs continued to be used (but of course not in a polytheistic sense), as " sacred to the funeral gods," or " to the departed spirits." [2] The laudatory epithets of heathen epitaphs are rare,[3] but simple terms of natural affection very frequent, as " My sweetest child;" "Innocent little lamb;" "My dearest husband;" "My dearest wife;" "My innocent dove;" "My well-deserving father," or "mother." [4] A. and B. " lived together " (for 15, 20, 30, 50, or even 60 years) "without any complaint or quarrel, without taking or giving offence." [5] Such commemoration of conjugal happiness and commendations of female virtues, as modesty, chastity, prudence, diligence, frequently occur also on pagan monuments, and prove that there were many exceptions to the corruption of Roman society, as painted by Juvenal and the satirists.

Some epitaphs contain a request to the dead in heaven to pray for the living on earth.[6] At a later period we find requests

on his knees, and about to sacrifice to the true God, he was led away to execution. O sad times! in which among sacred rites and prayers, even in caverns, we are not safe. What can be more wretched than such a life? and what than such a death? when they cannot be buried by their friends and relations—still at the end they shine like stars in heaven (*tandem in cœlo corruscant*)." See Maitland, *The Church in the Cat.*, second ed. p. 40.

[1] This inscription is in Latin words, but in Greek uncial letters. See Perret, II. 152, and Aringhi, p. 387.

[2] *D. M.* or *D. M. S.* = *Dis Manibus sacrum* (others explain: *Deo Magno* or *Maximo*); *memoriæ æternæ*, etc. See Schultze, p. 250 sq. Sometimes the monogram of Christ is inserted before S, and then the meaning may be *Deo Magno Christo Sacrum*, or *Christo Salvatori.* So Northcote, p. 99, who refers to Tit. 2: 13.

[3] More frequent in those after the middle of the fourth century, as *incomparabilis, miræ sapientiæ* or *innocentiæ, rarissimi exempli, eximiæ bonitatis.*

[4] *Dulcis, dulcissimus,* or *dulcissima, carus.* or *cara. carissimus, optimus, incomparabilis, famulus Dei, puella Deo placita,* ἀγαϑός. ἅγιος, ϑεοσεβής, σεμνός, etc.

[5] *Sine ulla querela, sine ulla contumelia, sine læsione animi, sine ulla offensa, sine jurgio, sine lite molesta,* etc.

[6] "*Pete,* or *roga, ora, pro nobis, pro parentibus, pro conjuge, pro filiis, pro sorore.*" These petitions are comparatively rare among the thousands of undated in-

for intercession in behalf of the departed when once, chiefly through the influence of Pope Gregory I., purgatory became an article of general belief in the Western church.[1] But the overwhelming testimony of the oldest Christian epitaphs is that the pious dead are already in the enjoyment of peace, and this accords with the Saviour's promise to the penitent thief, and with St. Paul's desire to depart and be with Christ, which is far better.[2] Take but this example: "Prima, thou livest in the glory of God, and in the peace of our Lord Jesus Christ."[3]

NOTES.

I. SELECTION OF ROMAN EPITAPHS.

The following selection of brief epitaphs in the Roman catacombs is taken from De Rossi, and Northcote, who give *fac-similes* of the original Latin and Greek. Comp. also the photographic plates in Roller, vol. I. Nos. X, XXXI, XXXII, and XXXIII; and vol. II. Nos. LXI, LXII, LXV, and LXVI.

1. To dear Cyriacus, sweetest son. Mayest thou live in the Holy Spirit.

2. Jesus Christ, Son of God, Saviour. To Pastor, a good and innocent son, who lived 4 years, 5 months and 26 days. Vitalis and Marcellina, his parents.

3. In eternal sleep (*somno aeternali*). Aurelius Gemellus, who lived . . . years and 8 months and 18 days. His mother made this for her

scriptions before Constantine, and mostly confined to members of the family. The Autun inscription (probably from the fourth century) ends with the petition of Pectorius to his departed parents, to think of him as often as they look upon Christ. See Marriott, p. 185.

[1] Dr. McCaul, of Toronto (as quoted in Smith and Cheetham, I. 856) says: "I recollect but two examples in Christian epitaphs of the first six centuries of the address to the reader for his prayers, so common in mediæval times."

[2] Luke 23: 43; Phil. 1: 23; 2 Cor. 5: 8.

[3] *Prima, vivis in gloria Dei et in pace Domini nostri.*" Scratched in the mortar round a grave in the cemetery of Thraso, in Rome, quoted by Northcote, p. 89. He also quotes Paulinus of Nola, who represents a whole host of saints going forth from heaven to receive the soul of St. Felix as soon as it had left the body, and conducting it in triumph before the throne of God. A distinction, however, was made by Tertullian and other fathers between Paradise or Abraham's bosom, whither the pious go, and heaven proper. Comp. Roller's discussion of the idea of *refrigerium* which often meets us in the epitaphs, *Les Catacombes*, I. 225 sqq.

dearest well-deserving son. In peace. I commend [to thee], Bassilla, the innocence of Gemellus.

4. Lady Bassilla [= Saint Bassilla], we, Crescentius and Micina, commend to thee our daughter Crescen [tina], who lived 10 months and . . . days.

5. Matronata Matrona, who lived a year and 52 days. Pray for thy parents.

6. Anatolius made this for his well-deserving son, who lived 7 years, 7 months and 20 days. May thy spirit rest well in God. Pray for thy sister.

7. Regina, mayest thou live in the Lord Jesus (*vivas in Domino Jesu*).

8. To my good and sweetest husband Castorinus, who lived 61 years, 5 months and 10 days; well-deserving. His wife made this. Live in God!

9. Amerimnus to his dearest, well-deserving wife, Rufina. May God refresh thy spirit.

10. Sweet Faustina, mayest thou live in God.

11. Refresh, O God, the soul of . . . .

12. Bolosa, may God refresh thee, who lived 31 years; died on the 19th of September. In Christ.

13. Peace to thy soul, Oxycholis.

14. Agape, thou shalt live forever.

15. In Christ. To Paulinus, a neophyte. In peace. Who lived 8 years.

16. Thy spirit in peace, Filmena.

17. In Christ. Æstonia, a virgin; a foreigner, who lived 41 years and 8 days. She departed from the body on the 26th of February.

18. Victorina in peace and in Christ.

19. Dafnen, a widow, who whilst she lived burdened the church in nothing.

20. To Leopardus, a neophyte, who lived 3 years, 11 months. Buried on the 24th of March. In peace.

21. To Felix, their well-deserving son, who lived 23 years and 10 days; who went out of the world a virgin and a neophyte. In peace. His parents made this. Buried on the 2^d of August.

22. Lucilianus to Bacius Valerius, who lived 9 years, 8 [months], 22 days. A catechumen.

23. Septimius Prætextatus Cæcilianus, servant of God, who has led a worthy life. If I have served Thee [O Lord], I have not repented, and I will give thanks to Thy name. He gave up his soul to God (at the age of) thirty-three years and six months. [In the crypt of St.

Cecilia in St. Callisto. Probably a member of some noble family, the third name is mutilated. De Rossi assigns this epitaph to the beginning of the third century.]

24. Cornelius. Martyr. Ep. [iscopus].

II. THE AUTUN INSCRIPTION.

This Greek inscription was discovered A. D. 1839 in the cemetery Saint Pierre l'Estrier near Autun (Augustodunum, the ancient capital of Gallia Æduensis), first made known by Cardinal Pitra, and thoroughly discussed by learned archæologists of different countries. See the *Spicilegium Solesmense* (ed. by Pitra), vols. I.–III., Raf. Garrucci, *Monuments d' epigraphie ancienne*, Paris 1856, 1857; F. Lenormant, *Mémoire sur l' inscription d' Autun*, Paris 1855; H. B. Marriott, *The Testimony of the Catacombs*, Lond. 1870, pp. 113–188. The Jesuit fathers Secchi and Garrucci find in it conclusive evidence of transubstantiation and purgatory, but Marriott takes pains to refute them. Comp. also Schultze, *Katak.* p. 118. The Ichthys-symbol figures prominently in the inscription, and betrays an early origin, but archæologists differ: Pitra, Garrucci and others assign it to A. D. 160–202; Kirchhoff, Marriott, and Schultze, with greater probability, to the end of the fourth or the beginning of the fifth century, Lenormant and Le Blant to the fifth or sixth. De Rossi observes that the characters are not so old as the ideas which they express. The inscription has some gaps which must be filled out by conjecture. It is a memorial of Pectorius to his parents and friends, in two parts; the first six lines are an acrostic, (*Ichthys*), and contain words of the dead (probably the mother); in the second part the son speaks. The first seems to be older. Schultze conjectures that it is an old Christian hymn. The inscription begins with 'Ιχθύος ο [ὑρανίου ἄγ] ιον [or perhaps θεῖον] γένος, and concludes with μνήσεο Πεκτορίου, who prepared the monument for his parents. The following is the translation (partly conjectural) of Marriott (*l. c.* 118):

'Offspring of the heavenly ICHTHYS, see that a heart of holy reverence be thine, now that from Divine waters thou hast received, while yet among mortals, a fount of life that is to immortality. Quicken thy soul, beloved one, with ever-flowing waters of wealth-giving wisdom, and receive the honey-sweet food of the Saviour of the saints. Eat with a longing hunger, holding Ichthys in thine hands.'

'To Ichthys . . . . Come nigh unto me, my Lord [and] Saviour [be thou my Guide] I entreat Thee, Thou Light of them for whom the hour of death is past.'

'Aschandius, my Father, dear unto mine heart, and thou [sweet Mother, and all] that are mine . . . . remember Pectorius.'

§ 87. *Lessons of the Catacombs.*

The catacombs represent the subterranean Christianity of the ante-Nicene age. They reveal the Christian life in the face of death and eternity. Their vast extent, their solemn darkness, their labyrinthine mystery, their rude epitaphs, pictures, and sculptures, their relics of handicraft, worship, and martyrdom give us a lively and impressive idea of the social and domestic condition, the poverty and humility, the devotional spirit, the trials and sufferings, the faith and hope of the Christians from the death of the apostles to the conversion of Constantine. A modern visitor descending alive into this region of the dead, receives the same impression as St. Jerome more than fifteen centuries ago: he is overcome by the solemn darkness, the terrible silence, and the sacred associations; only the darkness is deeper, and the tombs are emptied of their treasures. "He who is thoroughly steeped in the imagery of the catacombs," says Dean Stanley, not without rhetorical exaggeration, "will be nearer to the thoughts of the early church than he who has learned by heart the most elaborate treatise even of Tertullian or of Origen."[1]

The discovery of this subterranean necropolis has been made unduly subservient to polemical and apologetic purposes both by Roman Catholic and Protestant writers. The former seek and find in it monumental arguments for the worship of saints, images, and relics, for the cultus of the Virgin Mary, the primacy of Peter, the seven sacraments, the real presence, even for transubstantiation, and purgatory; while the latter see there the evidence of apostolic simplicity of life and worship, and an illustration of Paul's saying that God chose the foolish, the weak, and the despised things of the world to put to shame them that are wise and strong and mighty.[1]

---

[1] *Study of Ecclesiastical History*, prefixed to his *Lectures on the History of the Eastern Church*, p. 59.

[1] The apologetic interest for Romanism is represented by Marchi, De Rossi, Garrucci, Le Blant, D. de Richemond, Armellini, Bartoli. Maurus. Wolter (*Die röm. Katakomben und die Sakramente der kath. Kirche*, 1866), Martigny

A full solution of the controversial questions would depend upon the chronology of the monuments and inscriptions, but this is exceedingly uncertain. The most eminent archæologists hold widely differing opinions. John Baptist de Rossi, of Rome, the greatest authority on the Roman Catholic side, traces some paintings and epitaphs in the crypts of St. Lucina and St. Domitilla back even to the close of the first century or the beginning of the second. On the other hand, J. H. Parker, of Oxford, an equally eminent archæologist, maintains that "fully three-fourths of the fresco-paintings belong to the latest restorations of the eighth and ninth centuries," and that "of the remaining fourth a considerable number are of the sixth century." He also asserts that in the catacomb pictures "there are no religious subjects before the time of Constantine," that "during the fourth and fifth centuries they are entirely confined to Scriptural subjects," and that there is "not a figure of a saint or martyr before the sixth century, and very few before the eighth, when they became abundant." [1] Renan assigns the earliest pictures of the catacombs to the fourth century, very few (in Domitilla) to the third. [2] Theodore Mommsen deems De Rossi's argument for the early date of the *Cœmeterium Domitillæ* before A. D. 95 inconclusive, and traces it rather to the times of Hadrian and Pius than to those of the Flavian emperors. [3]

(*Dictionaire*, etc., 1877), A. Kuhn (1877), Northcote and Brownlow (1879), F. X. Kraus (*Real=Encykl. der christl. Alterthümer*, 1880 sqq.), Diepolder (1882), and among periodicals, by De Rossi's *Bulletino*, the *Civiltà Cattolica*, the *Revue de l'art chrétien*, and the *Revue archéologique*. Among the Protestant writers on the catacombs are Piper, Parker, Maitland, Lundy, Withrow, Becker, Stanley, Schultze, Heinrici, and Roller. See among others: Heinrici, *Zur Deutung der Bildwerke altchristlicher Grabstätten*, in the "Studien und Kritiken" for 1882, p. 720–743, and especially Piper, *Monumentale Theologie*.

[1] *Catacombs*, Pref. p. xi. The writer of the article *Catacombs* in the "Encycl. Brit." v. 214 (ninth ed.), is of the same opinion: "It is tolerably certain that the existing frescos are restorations of the eighth, or even a later century, from which the character of the earlier work can only very imperfectly be discovered." He then refers to Parker's invaluable photographs taken in the catacombs by magnesian light, and condemns, with Milman, the finished drawings in Perret's costly work as worthless to the historian, who wants truth and fidelity.

[2] *Marc-Aurèle*, p. 543.   [3] "Contemp. Rev." for May, 1871, p. 170.

But in any case it is unreasonable to seek in the catacombs for a complete creed any more than in a modern grave-yard. All we can expect there is the popular elements of eschatology, or the sentiments concerning death and eternity, with incidental traces of the private and social life of those times. Heathen, Jewish, Mohammedan, and Christian cemeteries have their characteristic peculiarities, yet all have many things in common which are inseparable from human nature. Roman Catholic cemeteries are easily recognized by crosses, crucifixes, and reference to purgatory and prayers for the dead; Protestant cemeteries by the frequency of Scripture passages in the epitaphs, and the expressions of hope and joy in prospect of the immediate transition of the pious dead to the presence of Christ. The catacombs have a character of their own, which distinguishes them from Roman Catholic as well as Protestant cemeteries.

Their most characteristic symbols and pictures are the Good Shepherd, the Fish, and the Vine. These symbols almost wholly disappeared after the fourth century, but to the mind of the early Christians they vividly expressed, in childlike simplicity, what is essential to Christians of all creeds, the idea of Christ and his salvation, as the only comfort in life and in death. The Shepherd, whether from the Sabine or the Galilean hills, suggested the recovery of the lost sheep, the tender care and protection, the green pasture and fresh fountain, the sacrifice of life: in a word, the whole picture of a Saviour.[1] The popu-

---

[1] Stanley, l. c., p. 283: "What was the popular Religion of the first Christians? It was, in one word, the Religion of the Good Shepherd. The kindness, the courage, the grace, the love, the beauty of the Good Shepherd was to them, if we may so say, Prayer Book and Articles, Creeds and Canons, all in one. They looked on that figure, and it conveyed to them all that they wanted. As ages passed on, the Good Shepherd faded away from the mind of the Christian world, and other emblems of the Christian faith have taken his place. Instead of the gracious and gentle Pastor, there came the Omnipotent Judge or the Crucified Sufferer, or the Infant in His Mother's arms, or the Master in His Parting Supper, or the figures of innumerable saints and angels, or the elaborate expositions of the various forms of theological controversy."

larity of this picture enables us to understand the immense popularity of the Pastor of Hermas, a religious allegory which was written in Rome about the middle of the second century, and read in many churches till the fourth as a part of the New Testament (as in the Sinaitic Codex). The Fish expressed the same idea of salvation, under a different form, but only to those who were familiar with the Greek (the anagrammatic meaning of *Ichthys*) and associated the fish with daily food and the baptismal water of regeneration. The Vine again sets forth the vital union of the believer with Christ and the vital communion of all believers among themselves.

Another prominent feature of the catacombs is their hopeful and joyful eschatology. They proclaim in symbols and words a certain conviction of the immortality of the soul and the resurrection of the body, rooted and grounded in a living union with Christ in this world.[1] These glorious hopes comforted and strengthened the early Christians in a time of poverty, trial, and persecution. This character stands in striking contrast with the preceding and contemporary gloom of paganism, for which the future world was a blank, and with the succeeding gloom of the mediæval eschatology which presented the future world to the most serious Christians as a continuation of penal sufferings. This is the chief, we may say, the only *doctrinal*, lesson of the catacombs.

On some other points they incidentally shed new light, especially on the spread of Christianity and the origin of Christian art. Their immense extent implies that Christianity was

---

[1] See the concluding chapter in the work of Roller, II. 347 sqq. Raoul-Rochette characterizes the art of the Catacombs as "*un système d'illusions consolantes.*" Schultze sees in the sepulchral symbols chiefly *Auferstehungsgedanken* and *Auferstehungshoffnungen*. Heinrici dissents from him by extending the symbolism to the present life as a life of hope in Christ. "*Nicht der Gedanke an die Auferstehung des Fleisches für sich, sondern die christliche Hoffnung überhaupt, wie sie aus der sicheren Lebensgemeinschaft mit Christus erblüht und Leben wie Sterben des Gläubigen beherrscht, bedingt die Wahl der religiös bedeutsamen Bilder. Sie sind nicht Symbole der einstigen Auferstehung, sondern des unverlierbaren Heilsbesitzes in Christus.*" ("Studien und Krit." 1842, p. 729).

numerically much stronger in heathen Rome than was generally supposed.[1] Their numerous decorations prove conclusively, either that the primitive Christian aversion to pictures and sculptures, inherited from the Jews, was not so general nor so long continued as might be inferred from some passages of ante-Nicene writers, or, what is more likely, that the popular love for art inherited from the Greeks and Romans was little affected by the theologians, and ultimately prevailed over the scruples of theorizers.

The first discovery of the catacombs was a surprise to the Christian world, and gave birth to wild fancies about the incalculable number of martyrs, the terrors of persecution, the subterranean assemblies of the early Christians, as if they lived and died, by necessity or preference, in darkness beneath the earth. A closer investigation has dispelled the romance, and deepened the reality.

There is no contradiction between the religion of the ante-Nicene monuments and the religion of the ante-Nicene literature. They supplement and illustrate each other. Both exhibit to us neither the mediæval Catholic nor the modern Protestant, but the post-apostolic Christianity of confessors and martyrs,— simple, humble, unpretending, unlearned, unworldly, strong in death and in the hope of a blissful resurrection; free from the distinctive dogmas and usages of later times; yet with that strong love for symbolism, mysticism, asceticism, and popular superstitions which we find in the writings of Justin Martyr, Tertullian, Clement of Alexandria, and Origen.

[1] Theodore Mommsen (in "The Contemp. Rev." for May, 1871, p. 167): "The enormous space occupied by the burial vaults of Christian Rome, in their extent not surpassed even by the system of cloacæ or sewers of Republican Rome, is certainly the work of that community which St. Paul addressed in his Epistle to the Romans—a living witness of its immense development, corresponding to the importance of the capital."

CHAPTER VIII.

CHRISTIAN LIFE IN CONTRAST WITH PAGAN CORRUPTION.

§ 88. *Literature.*

I. SOURCES: The works of the APOSTOLIC FATHERS. The Apologies of JUSTIN. The practical treatises of TERTULLIAN. The Epistles of CYPRIAN. The Canons of Councils. The APOSTOLICAL CONSTITUTIONS and CANONS. The Acts of Martyrs.—On the condition of the Roman Empire: the Histories of TACITUS, SUETONIUS, and DION CASSIUS, the writings of SENECA, HORACE, JUVENAL, PERSIUS, MARTIAL.

II. LITERATURE: W. CAVE: *Primitive Christianity, or the Religion of the Ancient Christians in the first ages of the Gospel.* London, fifth ed. 1689.

G. ARNOLD: *Erste Liebe, d. i. Wahre Abbildung der ersten Christen nach ihrem lebendigen Glauben und heil. Leben.* Frankf. 1696, and often since.

NEANDER: *Denkwürdigkeiten aus der Geschichte des christlichen Lebens* (first 1823), vol. i. third ed. Hamb. 1845. The same in English by Ryland: *Neander's Memorials of Christian Life,* in Bohn's Library, 1853.

L. COLEMAN: *Ancient Christianity exemplified in the private, domestic, social, and civil Life of the Primitive Christians,* etc. Phil. 1853.

C. SCHMIDT: *Essai historique sur la société dans le monde Romain, et sur la transformation par le Christianisme.* Par. 1853. The same transl. into German by A. V. Richard. Leipz. 1857.

E. L. CHASTEL: *Études historiques sur l'influence de la charité durant les premiers siècles chrét.* Par. 1853. Crowned by the French Académie. The same transl. into English (*The Charity of the Primitive Churches*), by G. A. Matile. Phila. 1857.

A. Fr. VILLEMAIN: *Nouveaux essais sur l'infl. du Christianisme dans le monde Grec et Latin.* Par. 1853.

BENJ. CONSTANT MARTHA (Member of the *Académie des sciences morales et politiques,* elected in 1872): *Les Moralistes sous l'Empire romain.* Paris 1854, second ed. 1866 (Crowned by the French Academy).

FR. J. M. TH. CHAMPAGNY: *Les premiers siècles de la charité.* Paris, 1854. Also his work *Les Antonins.* Paris, 1863, third ed. 1874, 3 vols.

311

J. Denis: *Histoire des theories et des idées morales dans l'antiquité.* Paris, 1856, 2 tom.

P. Janet: *Histoire de la philosophie morale et politique.* Paris, 1858, 2 tom.

G. Ratzinger: *Gesch. der kirchlichen Armenpflege.* Freib. 1859.

W. E. H. Lecky: *History of European Morals from Augustus to Charlemagne.* Lond. and N. Y. 1869, 2 vols., 5th ed. Lond. 1882. German transl. by *Dr. H. Jalowicz.*

Marie-Louis-Gaston Boissier: *La Religion romaine d'Auguste aux Antonins.* Paris, 1874, 2 vols.

Bestmann: *Geschichte der christlichen Sitte.* Nördl. Bd. I. 1880.

W. Gass: *Geschichte der christlichen Ethik.* Berlin, 1881{vol. I. 49–107).

G. Uhlhorn: *Die christliche Liebesthätigkeit in der alten Kirche.* Stuttg. 1881. English translation (*Christian Charity in the Ancient Church*). Edinb. and N. York, 1883 (424 pages).

Charles L. Brace: *Gesta Christi: or a History of humane Progress under Christianity.* N. York, 1883 (500 pages).

§ 89. *Moral Corruption of the Roman Empire.*

Besides the Lit. quoted in § 88, comp. the historical works on the Roman Empire by Gibbon, Merivale, and Ranke; also J. J. A. Ampère's *Histoire Romaine à Rome* (1856–64, 4 vols.).

Friedlaender's *Sittengeschichte Roms* (from Augustus to the Antonines. Leipzig, 3 vols., 5th ed. 1881); and Marquardt and Mommsen's *Handbuch der römischen Alterthümer* (Leipz. 1871, second ed. 1876, 7 vols., divided into *Staatsrecht, Staatsverwaltung, Privatleben*).

Christianity is not only the revelation of truth, but also the fountain of holiness under the unceasing inspiration of the spotless example of its Founder, which is more powerful than all the systems of moral philosophy. It attests its divine origin as much by its moral workings as by its pure doctrines. By its own inherent energy, without noise and commotion, without the favor of circumstances, nay, in spite of all possible obstacles, it has gradually wrought the greatest moral reformation, we should rather say, regeneration of society which history has ever seen; while its purifying, ennobling, and cheering effects upon the private life of countless individuals are beyond the reach of the historian, though recorded in God's book of life to be opened on the day of judgment.

To appreciate this work, we must first review the moral condition of heathenism in its mightiest embodiment in history.

When Christianity took firm foothold on earth, the pagan civilization and the Roman empire had reached their zenith. The reign of Augustus was the golden age of Roman literature; his successors added Britain and Dacia to the conquests of the Republic; internal organization was perfected by Trajan and the Antonines. The fairest countries of Europe, and a considerable part of Asia and Africa stood under one imperial government with republican forms, and enjoyed a well-ordered jurisdiction. Piracy on the seas was abolished; life and property were secure. Military roads, canals, and the Mediterranean Sea facilitated commerce and travel; agriculture was improved, and all branches of industry flourished. Temples, theatres, aqueducts, public baths, and magnificent buildings of every kind adorned the great cities; institutions of learning disseminated culture; two languages with a classic literature were current in the empire, the Greek in the East, the Latin in the West; the book trade, with the manufacture of paper, was a craft of no small importance, and a library belonged to every respectable house. The book stores and public libraries were in the most lively streets of Rome, and resorted to by literary people. Hundreds of slaves were employed as scribes, who wrote simultaneously at the dictation of one author or reader, and multiplied copies almost as fast as the modern printing press.[1] The excavations of Pompeii and Herculaneum reveal a high degree of convenience and taste in domestic life even in provincial towns;

---

[1] Friedlaender, III. 369 sqq. (5th ed.), gives much interesting information about the book trade in Rome, which was far more extensive than is generally supposed, and was facilitated by slave-labor. Books were cheap. The first book of Martial (over 700 verses in 118 poems) cost in the best outfit only 5 denarii (80 cts.) Julius Cæsar conceived the plan of founding public libraries, but was prevented from carrying it into effect. In the fourth century there were no less than twenty-eight public libraries in Rome. The ease and enjoyment of reading, however, were considerably diminished by the many errors, the absence of division and punctuation. Asinius Pollio introduced the custom of public readings of new works before invited circles.

and no one can look without amazement at the sublime and eloquent ruins of Rome, the palaces of the Cæsars, the Mausoleum of Hadrian, the Baths of Caracalla, the Aqueducts, the triumphal arches and columns, above all the Colosseum, built by Vespasian, to a height of one hundred and fifty feet, and for more than eighty thousand spectators. The period of eighty-four years from the accession of Nerva to the death of Marcus Aurelius has been pronounced by high authority " the most happy and prosperous period in the history of the world." [1]

But this is only a surface view. The inside did not correspond to the outside. Even under the Antonines the majority of men groaned under the yoke of slavery or poverty; gladiatorial shows brutalized the people; fierce wars were raging on the borders of the empire; and the most virtuous and peaceful of subjects—the Christians—had no rights, and were liable at any moment to be thrown before wild beasts, for no other reason than the profession of their religion. The age of the full bloom of the Græco-Roman power was also the beginning of its decline. This imposing show concealed incurable moral putridity and indescribable wretchedness. The colossal piles of architecture owed their erection to the bloody sweat of innumerable slaves, who were treated no better than so many beasts of burden; on the Flavian amphitheatre alone toiled twelve thousand Jewish prisoners of war; and it was built to gratify the cruel taste of the people for the slaughter of wild animals and human beings made in the image of God. The influx of wealth from conquered nations diffused the most extravagant luxury, which collected for a single meal peacocks from Samos, pike from Pessinus, oysters from Tarentum, dates from Egypt, nuts from Spain, in short the rarest dishes from all parts of the world, and resorted to emetics to stimulate appetite and to lighten the stomach. " They eat," says Seneca, " and then they vomit; they vomit, and then they eat." Apicius, who lived under Tiberius, dissolved pearls in the wine he drank,

---

[1] Gibbon, *Decline and Fall,* ch. III.   Renan expresses the same view.

squandered an enormous fortune on the pleasures of the table, and then committed suicide.[1] He found imperial imitators in Vitellius and Heliogabalus (or Elagabal). A special class of servants, the cosmetes, had charge of the dress, the smoothing of the wrinkles, the setting of the false teeth, the painting of the eye-brows, of wealthy patricians. Hand in hand with this luxury came the vices of natural and even unnatural sensuality, which decency forbids to name. Hopeless poverty stood in crying contrast with immense wealth; exhausted provinces, with revelling cities. Enormous taxes burdened the people, and misery was terribly increased by war, pestilence, and famine. The higher or ruling families were enervated, and were not strengthened or replenished by the lower. The free citizens lost physical and moral vigor, and sank to an inert mass. The third class was the huge body of slaves, who performed all kinds of mechanical labor, even the tilling of the soil, and in times of danger were ready to join the enemies of the empire. A proper middle class of industrious citizens, the only firm basis of a healthy community, cannot coëxist with slavery, which degrades free labor. The army, composed

[1] Either from disgust of life, or because he thought he could not live of the remaining ten million of sesterces, after he had wasted sixty or a hundred million. Seneca, *Ad Helv.* x. 9. Heliogabalus chose Apicius as his model. These, however, are exceptional cases, and became proverbial. See on this whole subject of Roman luxury the third volume of Friedlaender's *Sittengeschichte*, pp. 1–152. He rather modifies the usual view, and thinks that Apicius had more imitators among French epicures under Louis XIV., XV., and XVI. than among the Roman nobles, and that some petty German princes of the eighteenth century, like King August of Saxony (who wasted eighty thousand thalers on a single opera), and Duke Karl of Württemberg, almost equalled the heathen emperors in extravagance and riotous living, at the expense of their poor subjects. The wealth of the old Romans was much surpassed by that of some modern Russian and English noblemen, French bankers, and American merchant princes, but had a much greater purchasing value. The richest Romans were Ca. Lentulus, and Narcissus (a freedman of Nero), and their fortune amounted to four hundred million sesterces (from sixty-five to seventy million marks); while Mazarin left two hundred million francs, Baron James Rothschild (d. 1868) two thousand million francs (*l. c.* p. 13 sqq.). The architecture of the imperial age surpassed all modern palaces in extravagance and splendor, but in parks and gardens the modern English far surpass the ancient Romans (p. 78 sqq.).

largely of the rudest citizens and of barbarians, was the strength
of the nation, and gradually stamped the government with the
character of military despotism. The virtues of patriotism,
and of good faith in public intercourse, were extinct. The
basest avarice, suspicion and envy, usuriousness and bribery,
insolence and servility, everywhere prevailed.

The work of demoralizing the people was systematically
organized and sanctioned from the highest places downwards.
There were, it is true, some worthy emperors of old Roman
energy and justice, among whom Trajan, Antoninus Pius, and
Marcus Aurelius stand foremost; all honor to their memory.
But the best they could do was to check the process of internal
putrefaction, and to conceal the sores for a little while; they
could not heal them. Most of the emperors were coarse military despots, and some of them monsters of wickedness. There
is scarcely an age in the history of the world, in which so many
and so hideous vices disgraced the throne, as in the period
from Tiberius to Domitian, and from Commodus to Galerius.
"The annals of the emperors," says Gibbon, "exhibit a strong
aud various picture of human nature, which we should vainly
seek among the mixed and doubtful characters of modern history. In the conduct of those monarchs we may trace the
utmost lines of vice and virtue; the most exalted perfection
and the meanest degeneracy of our own species." [1] "Never,
probably," says Canon Farrar, "was there any age or any place
where the worst forms of wickedness were practised with a
more unblushing effrontery than in the city of Rome under the
government of the Cæsars." [2] We may not even except the
infamous period of the papal pornocracy, and the reign of
Alexander Borgia, which were of short duration, and excited
disgust and indignation throughout the church.

The Pagan historians of Rome have branded and immortal-
ized the vices and crimes of the Cæsars: the misanthropy,
cruelty, and voluptuousness of Tiberius; the ferocious madness

[1] *Decline and Fall*, ch. III.   [2] *Seekers after God*, p. 37.

of Caius Caligula, who had men tortured, beheaded, or sawed
in pieces for his amusement, who seriously meditated the butch-
ery of the whole senate, raised his horse to the dignity of consul
and priest, and crawled under the bed in a storm; the bottom-
less vileness of Nero, "the inventor of crime," who poisoned
or murdered his preceptors Burrhus and Seneca, his half-brother
and brother-in-law Britannicus, his mother Agrippina, his wife
Octavia, his mistress Poppæa, who in sheer wantonness set fire
to Rome, and then burnt innocent Christians for it as torches in
his gardens, figuring himself as charioteer in the infernal spectacle; the swinish gluttony of Vitellius, who consumed millions of money in mere eating; the refined wickedness of
Domitian, who, more a cat than a tiger, amused himself most
with the torments of the dying and with catching flies; the
shameless revelry of Commodus with his hundreds of concubines, and ferocious passion for butchering men and beasts on the
arena; the mad villainy of Heliogabalus, who raised the lowest
men to the highest dignities, dressed himself in women's clothes,
married a dissolute boy like himself, in short, inverted all the
laws of nature and of decency, until at last he was butchered
with his mother by the soldiers, and thrown into the muddy
Tiber. And to fill the measure of impiety and wickedness,
such imperial monsters were received, after their death, by a
formal decree of the Senate, into the number of divinities, and
their abandoned memory was celebrated by festivals, temples,
and colleges of priests! The emperor, in the language of
Gibbon, was at once "a priest, an atheist, and a god." Some
added to it the dignity of amateur actor and gladiator on the
stage. Domitian, even in his lifetime, caused himself to be
called "*Dominus et Deus noster,*" and whole herds of animals
to be sacrificed to his gold and silver statues. It is impossible
to imagine a greater public and official mockery of all religion.

The wives and mistresses of the emperors were not much
better. They revelled in luxury and vice, swept through the
streets in chariots drawn by silver-shod mules, wasted fortunes
on a single dress, delighted in wicked intrigues, aided their

husbands in dark crimes, and shared at last in their tragic fate. Messalina, the wife of Claudius, was murdered by the order of her husband in the midst of her nuptial orgies with one of her favorites; and the younger Agrippina, the mother of Nero, after poisoning her husband, was murdered by her own son, who was equally cruel to his wives, kicking one of them to death when she was in a state of pregnancy. These female monsters were likewise deified, and elevated to the rank of Juno or Venus.

From the higher regions the corruption descended into the masses of the people, who by this time had no sense for anything but *"Panem et Circenses,"* and, in the enjoyment of these, looked with morbid curiosity and interest upon the most flagrant vices of their masters.

No wonder that Tacitus, who with terse eloquence and old Roman severity exposes the monstrous characters of Nero and other emperors to eternal infamy, could nowhere, save perhaps among the barbarian Germans, discover a star of hope, and foreboded the fearful vengeance of the gods, and even the speedy destruction of the empire. And certainly nothing could save it from final doom, whose approach was announced with ever-growing distinctness by wars, insurrections, inundations, earthquakes, pestilence, famine, irruption of barbarians, and prophetic calamities of every kind. Ancient Rome, in the slow but certain process of dissolution and decay, teaches the

> ". . sad moral of all human tales;
> 'Tis but the same rehearsal of the past;
> First freedom, and then glory—when that fails,
> Wealth, vice, corruption, barbarism at last."

§ 90. *Stoic Morality.*

ED. ZELLER: *The Stoics, Epicureans, and Sceptics. Translated from the German by O. J. Reichel.* London (Longman, Green & Co.), 1870. Chs. x–xii treat of the Stoic Ethics and Religion.

F. W. FARRAR (Canon of Westminster): *Seekers after God.* London (Macmillan & Co.), first ed. n. d. (1869), new ed. 1877 (Seneca, Epictetus, and Marcus Aurelius, 336 pages).

Comp. also the essays on *Seneca and Paul* by FLEURY, AUBERTIN, BAUR, LIGHTFOOT, and REUSS (quoted in vol. I. 283).

Let us now turn to the bright side of heathen morals, as exhibited in the teaching and example of Epictetus, Marcus Aurelius, and Plutarch—three pure and noble characters—one a slave, the second an emperor, the third a man of letters, two of them Stoics, one a Platonist. It is refreshing to look upon a few green spots in the moral desert of heathen Rome. We may trace their virtue to the guidance of conscience (the good demon of Socrates), or to the independent working of the Spirit of God, or to the indirect influence of Christianity, which already began to pervade the moral atmosphere beyond the limits of the visible church, and to infuse into legislation a spirit of humanity and justice unknown before, or to all these causes combined. It is certain that there was in the second century a moral current of unconscious Christianity, which met the stronger religious current of the church and facilitated her ultimate victory.

It is a remarkable fact that two men who represent the extremes of society, the lowest and the highest, were the last and greatest teachers of natural virtue in ancient Rome. They shine like lone stars in the midnight darkness of prevailing corruption. Epictetus the slave, and Marcus Aurelius, the crowned ruler of an empire, are the purest among the heathen moralists, and furnish the strongest " testimonies of the naturally Christian soul."

Both belonged to the school of Zeno.

The Stoic philosophy was born in Greece, but grew into manhood in Rome. It was predestinated for that stern, grave, practical, haughty, self-governing and heroic character which from the banks of the Tiber ruled over the civilized world.[1]

---

[1] Zeller, *l. c.* p. 37 : " Nearly all the most important Stoics before the Christian era belong by birth to Asia Minor, to Syria, and to the islands of the Eastern Archipelago. Then follow a line of Roman Stoics, among whom the Phrygian Epictetus occupies a prominent place ; but Greece proper is exclusively represented by men of third or fourth-rate capacity."

In the Republican period Cato of Utica lived and died by his own hand a genuine Stoic in practice, without being one in theory. Seneca, the contemporary of St. Paul, was a Stoic in theory, but belied his almost Christian wisdom in practice, by his insatiable avarice, anticipating Francis Bacon as " the wisest, brightest, meanest of mankind." [1] Half of his ethics is mere rhetoric. In Epictetus and Marcus Aurelius the Stoic theory and practice met in beautiful harmony, and freed from its most objectionable features.   They were the last and the best of that school which taught men to live and to die, and offered an asylum for individual virtue and freedom when the Roman world at large was rotten to the core.

Stoicism is of all ancient systems of philosophy both nearest to, and furthest from, Christianity : nearest in the purity and sublimity of its maxims and the virtues of simplicity, equanimity, self-control, and resignation to an all-wise Providence ; furthest in the spirit of pride, self-reliance, haughty contempt,

---

[1] Niebuhr says of Seneca : " He acted on the principle that he could dispense with the laws of morality which he laid down for others." Macaulay : "The business of the philosopher was to declaim in praise of poverty, with two millions sterling at usury ; to meditate epigrammatic conceits about the evils of luxury in gardens which moved the envy of sovereigns ; to rant about liberty while fawning on the insolent and pampered freedman of a tyrant ; to celebrate the divine beauty of virtue with the same pen which had just before written a defense of the murder of a mother by a son." Farrar (*l. c.* p. 161) : " In Seneca's life, we see as clearly as in those of many professed Christians that it is impossible to be at once worldly and righteous. His utter failure was due to the vain attempt to combine in his own person two opposite characters—that of a Stoic and that of a courtier . . . . In him we see some of the most glowing pictures of the nobility of poverty combined with the most questionable avidity in the pursuit of wealth." For a convenient collection of Seneca's resemblances to Scripture, see Farrar, ch. XV., 174–185. The most striking passages are : " A sacred spirit dwells within us, the observer and guardian of all our evil and our good . . . there is no good man without God." *Ep. ad Lucil.* 41. Comp. 1 Cor. 3 : 16. " Not one of us is without fault . . . no man is found who can acquit himself." *De Ira* I. 14 ; II. 27. Comp. 1 John 1 : 8. " Riches . . . . the greatest source of human trouble." *De Tranqu. An.* 8. Comp. 1 Tim. 6 : 10. " You must live for another, if you wish to live for yourself." *Ep.* 48. Comp. Rom. 12 : 10. " Let him who hath conferred a favor hold his tongue." *De Benef.* II. 11. Comp. Matt. 6 : 3.

and cold indifference. Pride is the basis of Stoic virtue, while humility is the basis of Christian holiness; the former is inspired by egotism, the latter by love to God and man; the Stoic feels no need of a Saviour, and calmly resorts to suicide when the house smokes; while the Christian life begins with a sense of sin, and ends with triumph over death; the resignation of the Stoic is heartless apathy and a surrender to the iron necessity of fate; the resignation of the Christian, is cheerful submission to the will of an all-wise and all-merciful Father in heaven; the Stoic sage resembles a cold, immovable statue, the Christian saint a living body, beating in hearty sympathy with every joy and grief of his fellow-men. At best, Stoicism is only a philosophy for the few, while Christianity is a religion for all.

§ 91. *Epictetus.*

EPICTETI. *Dissertationum ab Arriano digestarum Libri IV. Euiusdem Enchiridion et ex deperditis Sermonibus Fragmenta ... recensuit ..* JOH. SCHWEIGHÄUSER. Lips. 1799, 1800. 5 vols. The Greek text with a Latin version and notes.

The Works of EPICTETUS. *Consisting of his Discourses, in four books, the Enchiridion, and Fragments. A translation from the Greek, based on that of Mrs. Elizabeth Carter, by* THOMAS WENTWORTH HIGGINSON. Boston (Little, Brown & Co.), 1865. A fourth ed. of Mrs. Carter's translation was published in 1807, with introduction and notes.

The Discourses of EPICTETUS, *with the Enchiridion and Fragments. Translated, with Notes, etc., by* GEORGE LONG. London (George Bell & Sons), 1877.

There are also other English, as well as German and French, versions.

Epictetus was born before the middle of the first century, at Hierapolis, a city in Phrygia, a few miles from Colossæ and Laodicea, well known to us from apostolic history. He was a compatriot and contemporary of Epaphras, a pupil of Paul, and founder of Christian churches in that province.[1] There is

---

[1] Col. 1: 7; 4: 12, 13.

a bare possibility that he had a passing acquaintance with him, if not with Paul himself. He came as a slave to Rome with his master, Epaphroditus, a profligate freedman and favorite of Nero (whom he aided in committing suicide), and was afterwards set at liberty. He rose above his condition. " Freedom and slavery," he says in one of his Fragments, " are but names of virtue and of vice, and both depend upon the will. No one is a slave whose will is free." He was lame in one foot and in feeble health. The lameness, if we are to credit the report of Origen, was the result of ill treatment, which he bore heroically. When his master put his leg in the torture, he quietly said : " You will break my leg ; " and when the leg was broken, he added : " Did I not tell you so ? " This reminds one of Socrates who is reported to have borne a scolding and subsequent shower from Xantippe with the cool remark : After the thunder comes the rain. Epictetus heard the lectures of Musonius Rufus, a distinguished teacher of the Stoic philosophy under Nero and Vespasian, and began himself to teach. He was banished from Rome by Domitian, with all other philosophers, before A. D. 90. He settled for the rest of his life in Nicopolis, in Southern Epirus, not far from the scene of the battle of Actium. There he gathered around him a large body of pupils, old and young, rich and poor, and instructed them, as a second Socrates, by precept and example, in halls and public places. The emperor Hadrian is reported to have invited him back to Rome (117), but in vain. The date of his death is unknown.

Epictetus led from principle and necessity a life of poverty and extreme simplicity, after the model of Diogenes, the arch-Cynic. His only companions were an adopted child with a nurse. His furniture consisted of a bed, a cooking vessel and earthen lamp. Lucian ridicules one of his admirers, who bought the lamp for three thousand drachmas, in the hope of becoming a philosopher by using it. Epictetus discouraged marriage and the procreation of children. Marriage might do well in a " community of wise men," but " in the present state of things," which he compared to " an army in battle array," it is likely to withdraw the philosopher from the service of God.[1] This view, as well as the reason assigned, resembles the advice of St. Paul, with the great difference, that the apostle had the highest conception of the institution of marriage as reflecting the mystery of Christ's union with the church. " Look at me," says Epictetus, "who am without a city, without a house, without possessions, without a slave; I sleep on the ground; I have no wife, no children, no prætorium, but only the earth and the heavens, and one poor cloak. And what do I want? Am I not without sorrow? Am I not without fear? Am I not free? . . . Did I ever blame God or man? . . . Who, when he sees me, does not think that he sees his king and master?" His epitaph fitly describes his character: "I was Epictetus, a slave, and maimed in body, and a beggar for poverty, and dear to the immortals."

Epictetus, like Socrates, his great exemplar, wrote nothing himself, but he found a Xenophon. His pupil and friend, Flavius Arrianus, of Nicomedia, in Bithynia, the distinguished historian of Alexander the Great, and a soldier and statesman under Hadrian, handed to posterity a report of the oral instructions and familiar conversations ($\delta\iota\alpha\tau\rho\iota\beta\alpha\iota$) of his teacher. Only four of the original eight books remain. He also collected his chief maxims in a manual (Enchiridion). His biography of that remarkable man is lost.

Epictetus starts, like Zeno and Cleanthes, with a thoroughly practical view of philosophy, as the art and exercise of virtue, in accordance with reason and the laws of nature. He bases virtue on faith in God, as the supreme power of the universe, who directs all events for benevolent purposes. The philosopher is a teacher of righteousness, a physician and surgeon of the sick who feel their weakness, and are anxious to be cured. He

---

[1] *Disc.* III. 22. Comp. 1 Cor. 7: 35; but also Eph. 5: 28–33. Farrar, *l. c.*, p. 213, thinks that the philosopher and the apostle agree in recommending celibacy as "a counsel of perfection." But this is the Roman Catholic, not the Scripture view.

is a priest and messenger of the gods to erring men, that they might learn to be happy even in utter want of earthly possessions. If we wish to be good, we must first believe that we are bad. Mere knowledge without application to life is worthless. Every man has a guardian spirit, a god within him who never sleeps, who always keeps him company, even in solitude; this is the Socratic *daimonion*, the personified conscience. We must listen to its divine voice. "Think of God more often than you breathe. Let discourse of God be renewed daily, more surely than your food." The sum of wisdom is to desire nothing but freedom and contentment, and to bear and forbear. All unavoidable evil in the world is only apparent and external, and does not touch our being. Our happiness depends upon our own will, which even Zeus cannot break. The wise man joyously acquiesces in what he cannot control, knowing that an all-wise Father rules the whole. "We ought to have these two rules always in readiness: that there is nothing good or evil except in the will; and that we ought not to lead events, but to follow them."[1] If a brother wrongs me, that is his fault; my business is to conduct myself rightly towards him. The wise man is not disturbed by injury and injustice, and loves even his enemies. All men are brethren and children of God. They own the whole world; and hence even banishment is no evil. The soul longs to be freed from the prison house of the body and to return to God.

Yet Epictetus does not clearly teach the immortality of the soul. He speaks of death as a return to the elements in successive conflagrations. Seneca approaches much more nearly the Platonic and Socratic, we may say Christian, view of immortality. The prevailing theory of the Stoics was, that at the end of the world all individual souls will be resolved into the primary substance of the Divine Being.[2]

---

[1] *Discourses*, III. 10. Here E. discusses the manner in which we ought to bear sickness.

[2] The only point about which the Stoics were undecided was, whether all souls would last until that time as separate souls, or whether, as Chrysippus held, only the souls of the wise would survive." Zeller, *l. c.*, p. 205.

Epictetus nowhere alludes directly to Christianity, but he speaks once of "Galileans," who by enthusiasm or madness were free from all fear.[1] He often recurs to his predecessors, Socrates, Diogenes, Zeno, Musonius Rufus. His ethical ideal is a Cynic philosopher, naked, penniless, wifeless, childless, without want or desire, without passion or temper, kindly, independent, contented, imperturbable, looking serenely or indifferently at life and death. It differs as widely from the true ideal as Diogenes who lived in a tub, and sought with a lantern in day-light for "a man," differs from Christ who, indeed, had not where to lay his head, but went about doing good to the bodies and souls of men.

Owing to the purity of its morals, the *Enchiridion* of Epictetus was a favorite book. Simplicius, a Neo-Platonist, wrote an elaborate commentary on it; and monks in the middle ages reproduced and Christianized it. Origen thought Epictetus had done more good than Plato. Niebuhr says: "His greatness cannot be questioned, and it is impossible for any person of sound mind not to be charmed by his works." Higginson says: "I am acquainted with no book more replete with high conceptions of the deity and noble aims of man." This is, of course, a great exaggeration, unless the writer means to confine his comparison to heathen works.

§ 92. *Marcus Aurelius.*

Μάρκου ᾿Αντωνίνου τοῦ αὐτοκράτορος τῶν εἰς ἑαυτὸν βιβλία ιβ´ (*De Rebus suis libri* xii). Ed. by THOMAS GATAKER, with a Latin Version and Notes (including those of Casaubon). Trajecti ad Rhenum, 1697, 2 vols. fol. The second vol. contains critical dissertations. (The

---

[1] *Disc.* IV. 7: "Through madness (ὑπὸ μανίας) it is possible for a man to be so disposed towards these things and through habit (ὑπὸ ἔθους), as the Galileans." By Galileans he no doubt means Christians, and the allusion is rather contemptuous, like the allusion of Marcus Aurelius to the martyrs, with this difference that the emperor attributes to obstinacy what Epictetus attributes to "habit." But Schweighäuser (II. 913 sq.) suspects that the reading ὑπὸ ἔθους is false, and that Arrian wrote ὑπὸ ἀπονοίας, ὡς οἱ Γαλ., so that Epictetus ascribed to the Christians fury and desperation or *dementia*. To the Greeks the gospel is foolishness, 1 Cor. 1 : 22.

first ed. appeared at Cambridge, 1652, in 1 vol.) English translation
by GEORGE LONG, revised ed. London, 1880.

See the liter. quoted in § 20, p. 52 sq. (especially Renan's *Marc-
Aurèle*, 1882).

Marcus Aurelius, the last and best representative of Stoicism,
ruled the Roman Empire for twenty years (A. D. 161–180) at
the height of its power and prosperity. He was born April 26,
121, in Rome, and carefully educated and disciplined in Stoic
wisdom. Hadrian admired him for his good nature, docility,
and veracity, and Antoninus Pius adopted him as his son and
successor. He learned early to despise the vanities of the
world, maintained the simplicity of a philosopher in the
splendor of the court, and found time for retirement and
meditation amid the cares of government and border wars, in
which he was constantly engaged. Epictetus was his favorite
author. He left us his best thoughts, a sort of spiritual auto-
biography, in the shape of a diary which he wrote, not without
some self-complacency, for his own improvement and enjoyment during the last years of his life (172–175) in the military
camp among the barbarians. He died in Panonia of the pestilence which raged in the army (March 17, 180).[1] His last
words were: "Weep not for me, weep over the pestilence and
the general misery,[2] and save the army. Farewell!" He
dismissed his servants and friends, even his son, after a last
interview, and died alone.

The philosophic emperor was a sincere believer in the gods,
their revelations and all-ruling providence. His morality and
religion were blended. But he had no clear views of the
divinity. He alternately uses the language of the polytheist,
the deist, and the pantheist. He worshipped the deity of the
universe and in his own breast. He thanks the gods for his
good parents and teachers, for his pious mother, for a wife,

[1] According to less probable accounts he died of suicide, or of poison administered to him by order of his son, Commodus. See Renan, p. 485.

[2] "*Quid me fletis, et non magis de pestilentia et communi morte cogitatis?*"
Capitolinus, *M. Aurelius*.

whom he blindly praises as "amiable, affectionate, and pure,"
and for all the goods of life. His motto was "never to wrong
any man in deed or word."[1] He claimed no perfection, yet
was conscious of his superiority, and thankful to the gods that
he was better than other men. He traced the sins of men merely
to ignorance and error. He was mild, amiable, and gentle; in
these respects the very reverse of a hard and severe Stoic, and
nearly approaching a disciple of Jesus. We must admire his
purity, truthfulness, philanthropy, conscientious devotion to
duty, his serenity of mind in the midst of the temptations of
power and severe domestic trials, and his resignation to the will
of providence. He was fully appreciated in his time, and universally beloved by his subjects. We may well call him among
the heathen the greatest and best man of his age.[2] "It seems"
(says an able French writer, Martha), "that in him the philosophy of heathenism grows less proud, draws nearer and nearer
to a Christianity which it ignored or which it despised, and is
ready to fling itself into the arms of the 'Unknown God.' In
the sad *Meditations* of Aurelius we find a pure serenity, sweetness, and docility to the commands of God, which before him
were unknown, and which Christian grace has alone surpassed.
If he has not yet attained to charity in all that fullness of
meaning which Christianity has given to the world, he has

---

[1] *Medit.* v. 31.

[2] So Renan, *Marc-Aurèle*, p. 488, without qualification: "*Avec lui, la philosophie a régné. Un moment, grâce à lui, le monde a été gouverné par l'homme le meilleur et le plus grand de son siècle.*" But elsewhere he puts Antoninus Pius above Aurelius. "Of the two," he says (*Conférences d'Angleterre*, translated by Clara Erskine Clement, p. 140 sq.): "I consider Antonine the greatest. His goodness did not lead him into faults: he was not tormented with that internal trouble which disturbed, without ceasing, the heart of his adopted son. This strange malady, this restless study of himself, this demon of scrupulousness, this fever of perfection, are signs of a less strong and distinguished nature. As the finest thoughts are those which are not written, Antonine had in this respect also a superiority over Marcus Aurelius. But let us add, that we should be ignorant of Antonine, if Marcus Aurelius had not transmitted to us that exquisite portrait of his adopted father, in which he seems to have applied himself through humility, to painting the picture of a better man than himself."

already gained its unction, and one cannot read his book, unique in the history of Pagan philosophy, without thinking of the sadness of Pascal and the gentleness of Fénélon."

The Meditations of Marcus Aurelius are full of beautiful moral maxims, strung together without system. They bear a striking resemblance to Christian ethics. They rise to a certain universalism and humanitarianism which is foreign to the heathen spirit, and a prophecy of a new age, but could only be realized on a Christian basis. Let us listen to some of his most characteristic sentiments:

" It is sufficient to attend to the demon [the good genius] within, and to reverence it sincerely. And reverence for the demon consists in keeping it pure from passion and thoughtlessness and dissatisfaction with what comes from God and men." [1] " Do not act as if thou wert going to live ten thousand years. Death hangs over thee. While thou livest, while it is in thy power, be good." [2] " Do not disturb thyself. Make thyself all simplicity. Does any one do wrong? It is to himself that he does the wrong. Has anything happened to thee? Well; out of the universe from the beginning everything which happens has been apportioned and spun out to thee. In a word, thy life is short. Thou must turn to profit the present by the aid of reason and justice. Be sober in thy relaxation. Either it is a well-arranged universe or a chaos huddled together, but still a universe." [3] " A man must stand erect, and not be kept erect by others." [4] " Have I done something for the general interest? Well, then, I have had my reward. Let this always be present to my mind, and never stop [doing good]." [5] " What is thy art? to be good." [6] " It is a man's duty to comfort himself, and to wait for the natural dissolution, and not to be vexed at the delay." [7] " O Nature: from thee are all things, in thee are all things, to thee all things return." [8] " Willingly give thyself up to Clotho" [one of the fates], " allowing her to spin thy thread into whatever things she pleases. Every thing is only

[1] *Medit.* II. 13.   [2] IV. 17.   [3] IV. 26, 27.   [4] III. 5.
[5] IX. 4.   [6] IX. 5.   [7] V. 10.   [8] IV. 23.

for a day, both that which remembers and that which is remembered."[1] " Consider that before long thou wilt be nobody and nowhere, nor will any of the things exist which thou now seest, nor any of those who are now living. For all things are formed by nature to change and be turned, and to perish, in order that other things in continuous succession may exist."[2] "It is best to leave this world as early as possible, and to bid it friendly farewell."[3]

These reflections are pervaded by a tone of sadness; they excite emotion, but no enthusiasm; they have no power to console, but leave an aching void, without hope of an immortality, except a return to the bosom of mother nature. They are the rays of a setting, not of a rising, sun; they are the swansong of dying Stoicism. The end of that noble old Roman was virtually the end of the antique world.[4]

The cosmopolitan philosophy of Marcus Aurelius had no sympathy with Christianity, and excluded from its embrace the most innocent and most peaceful of his subjects. He makes but one allusion to the Christians, and unjustly traces their readiness for martyrdom to "sheer obstinacy" and a desire for "theatrical display."[5] He may have had in view some fanatical enthusiasts who rushed into the fire, like Indian gymnosophists, but possibly such venerable martyrs as Polycarp and those of Southern Gaul in his own reign. Hence the strange phenomenon that the wisest and best of Roman emperors permitted (we cannot say, instigated, or even authorized) some of the most cruel persecutions of Christians, especially in Lugdunum and

---

[1] IV. 34, 35.   [2] XII. 21.   [3] IX. 2, 3; XI. 3.

[4] The significant title of Renan's book is *Marc-Aurèle et la fin du monde antique*.

[5] XI. 3: "What a soul that is which is ready, if at any moment it must be separated from the body, and ready either to be extinguished or dispersed, or continue to exist; but so that this readiness comes from a man's own judgment, not *from mere obstinacy, as with the Christians*, but considerately and with dignity, and in a way to persuade another without scenic show (ἀτραγῴδως)." I have availed myself in these extracts of Long's excellent translation, but compared them with the Greek original in Gataker's edition.

Vienne. We readily excuse him on the ground of ignorance. He probably never saw the Sermon on the Mount, nor read any of the numerous Apologies addressed to him. But persecution is not the only blot on his reputation. He wasted his affections upon a vicious and worthless son, whom he raised in his fourteenth year to full participation of the imperial power, regardless of the happiness of millions, and upon a beautiful but faithless and wicked wife, whom he hastened after her death to cover with divine honors. His conduct towards Faustina was either hypocritical or unprincipled.[1] After her death he preferred a concubine to a second wife and stepmother of his children.

His son and successor left the Christians in peace, but was one of the worst emperors that disgraced the throne, and undid all the good which his father had done.[2]

Aristotle was the teacher of Alexander; Seneca, the teacher of Nero; Marcus Aurelius, the father of Commodus.

§ 93. *Plutarch.*

Πλουτάρχου τοῦ Χαιρωνέως τὰ Ἠθικά. Ed. Tauchnitz Lips. The same with a Latin version and notes in

---

[1] At his earnest request the obsequious Senate declared Faustina a goddess; she was represented in her temples with the attributes of Juno, Venus, and Ceres; and it was decreed that on the day of their nuptials the youth of both sexes should pay their vows before the altar of this adulterous woman. See Gibbon, ch. IV. A bas-relief in the museum of the Capitol at Rome represents Faustina borne to heaven by a messenger of the gods, and her husband looking at her with admiration and love. Renan apologizes for his favorite hero on the ground of the marvellous beauty of Faustina, and excuses her, because she naturally grew tired of the dull company of an ascetic philosopher!

[2] Renan thus describes the sudden relapse (p. 490): "*Horrible déception pour les gens de bien! Tant de vertu, tant d'amour n'aboutissant qu'à mettre le monde entre les mains d'un équarrisseur de bêtes, d'un gladiateur! Après cette belle apparition d'un monde élyséen sur la terre, retomber dans l'enfer des Césars, qu'on croyait fermé pour toujours! La foi dans le bien fut alors perdue. Après Caligula, après Néron, après Domitien, on avait pu espérer encore. Les expériences n'avaient pas été décisives. Maintenant, c'est après le plus grand effort de rationalisme gouvernemental, après quatre-ving quatre ans d'un régime excellent, après Nerva, Trajan, Adrien, Antonin, Marc-Aurèle, que le règne du mal recommence, pire que jamais. Adieu, vertu; adieu, raison. Puisque Marc-Aurèle n'a pas pu sauver le monde, qui le sauvera?*"

PLUTARCHI *Chœronensis Moralia, id est, Opera, exceptis vitis, reliqua.*
Ed. by DANIEL WYTTENBACH. Oxon. 1795–1800, 8 vols. (including 2 Index vols.). French ed. by Dübner, in the Didot collection.

PLUTARCH'S *Morals. Translated from the Greek by several Hands.*
London, 1684–'94, 5th ed. 1718. The same as *corrected and revised by* WILLIAM W. GOODWIN (Harvard University). *With an introduction by Ralph Waldo Emerson.* Boston, 1870, 5 vols.

OCTAVE GREARD: *De la moralité de Plutarque.* Paris, 1866.

RICHARD CHENEVIX TRENCH (Archbishop of Dublin): *Plutarch, his Life, his Parallel Lives, and his Morals.* London (Macmillan & Co.), 2nd ed. 1874.

W. MÖLLER: *Ueber die Religion des Plutarch.* Kiel, 1881.

JULIA WEDGWOOD: *Plutarch and the unconscious Christianity of the first two centuries.* In the "Contemporary Review" for 1881, pp. 44–60.

Equally remarkable, as a representative of "unconscious Christianity" and "seeker after the unknown God," though from a different philosophical standpoint, is the greatest biographer and moralist of classical antiquity.

It is strange that Plutarch's contemporaries are silent about him. His name is not even mentioned by any Roman writer. What we know of him is gathered from his own works. He lived between A. D. 50 and 125, mostly in his native town of Chæroneia, in Bœotia, as a magistrate and priest of Apollos. He was happily married, and had four sons and a daughter, who died young. His *Conjugal Precepts* are full of good advice to husbands and wives. The letter of consolation he addressed to his wife on the death of a little daughter, Timoxena, while she was absent from home, gives us a favorable impression of his family life, and expresses his hope of immortality. "The souls of infants," he says at the close of this letter, "pass immediately into a better and more divine state." He spent some time in Rome (at least twice, probably under Vespasian and Domitian), lectured on moral philosophy to select audiences, and collected material for his Parallel Lives of Greeks and Romans. He was evidently well-bred, in good circumstances, familiar with books, different countries, and human nature and society in all its phases. In his philosophy he stands midway between Platonism and Neo-Platonism. He was "a Platonist with an Oriental tinge." [1] He was equally opposed to Stoic pantheism and Epicurean naturalism, and adopted the Platonic dualism of God and matter. He recognized a supreme God, and also the subordinate divinities of the Hellenic religion. The gods are good, the demons are divided between good and bad, the human soul combines both qualities. He paid little attention to metaphysics, and dwelt more on the practical questions of philosophy, dividing his labors between historical and moral topics. He was an utter stranger to Christianity, and therefore neither friendly nor hostile. There is in all his numerous writings not a single allusion to it, although at his time there must have been churches in every considerable city of the empire. He often speaks of Judaism, but very superficially, and may have regarded Christianity as a Jewish sect. But his moral philosophy makes a very near approach to Christian ethics.

His aim, as a writer, was to show the greatness in the acts and in the thoughts of the ancients, the former in his " Parallel Lives," the latter in his " Morals," and by both to inspire his contemporaries to imitation. They constitute together an encyclopædia of well-digested Greek and Roman learning. He was not a man of creative genius, but of great talent, extensive information, amiable spirit, and universal sympathy. Emerson calls him " the chief example of the illumination of the intellect by the force of morals." [1]

Plutarch endeavored to build up morality on the basis of religion. He is the very opposite of Lucian, who as an architect of ruin, ridiculed and undermined the popular religion. He was a strong believer in God, and his argument against atheism is well worth quoting. " There has never been," he says, "a state of atheists. You may travel over the world, and you may find cities without walls, without king, without

---

[1] So Trench calls him, *l. c.* p. 112. The best account of his philosophy is given by Zeller in his *Philosophie der Griechen,* Part III., 141–182; and more briefly by Ueberweg, *Hist. of Phil.* (Eng. Ver.) I. 234–236.

[1] Introduction to Goodwin's ed. p. xi.

mint, without theatre or gymnasium; but you will never find a
city without God, without prayer, without oracle, without sacrifice. Sooner may a city stand without foundations, than a state
without belief in the gods. This is the bond of all society and
the pillar of all legislation."[1]

In his treatise on *The Wrong Fear of the Gods*, he contrasts
superstition with atheism as the two extremes which often meet,
and commends piety or the right reverence of the gods as the
golden mean. Of the two extremes he deems superstition the
worse, because it makes the gods capricious, cruel, and revenge-
ful, while they are friends of men, saviours ($\sigma\omega\tau\tilde{\eta}\rho\varepsilon\varsigma$), and not
destroyers. (Nevertheless superstitious people can more easily
be converted to true faith than atheists who have destroyed all
religious instincts.)

His remarkable treatise on *The Delays of Divine Justice in
punishing the wicked*,[2] would do credit to any Christian theologian. It is his solution of the problem of evil, or his
theodicy. He discusses the subject with several of his relatives
(as Job did with his friends), and illustrates it by examples.
He answers the various objections which arise from the delay of
justice, and vindicates Providence in his dealings with the
sinner. He enjoins first modesty and caution in view of our
imperfect knowledge. God only knows best *when* and *how* and
how much to punish. He offers the following considerations:
1) God teaches us to moderate our anger, and never to punish
in a passion, but to imitate his gentleness and forbearance.
2) He gives the wicked an opportunity to repent and reform.
3) He permits them to live and prosper that he may use them
as executioners of his justice on others. He often punishes the
sinner by the sinner. 4) The wicked are sometimes spared that
they may bless the world by a noble posterity. 5) Punishment
is often deferred that the hand of Providence may be more
conspicuous in its infliction. Sooner or later sin will be
punished, if not in this world, at least in the future world, to

[1] *Adv. Colotem* (an Epicurean), c. 31 (*Moralia*, ed. Tauchnitz, VI. 265).
[2] *De Sera Numinis Vindicta.* In Goodwin's ed. vol. IV. 140–188.

which Plutarch points as the final solution of the mysteries of Providence. He looked upon death as a good thing for the good soul, which shall then live indeed; while the present life " resembles rather the vain illusions of some dream."

The crown of Plutarch's character is his humility, which was so very rare among ancient philosophers, especially the Stoics, and which comes from true self-knowledge. He was aware of the native depravity of the soul, which he calls " a storehouse and treasure of many evils and maladies." [1] Had he known the true and radical remedy for sin, he would no doubt have accepted it with gratitude.

We do not know how far the influence of these saints of ancient paganism, as we may call Epictetus, Marcus Aurelius, and Plutarch, extended over the heathens of their age, but we do know that their writings had and still have an elevating and ennobling effect upon Christian readers, and hence we may infer that their teaching and example were among the moral forces that aided rather than hindered the progress and final triumph of Christianity. But this religion alone could bring about such a general and lasting moral reform as they themselves desired.

§ 94. *Christian Morality.*

The ancient world of classic heathenism, having arrived at the height of its glory, and at the threshold of its decay, had exhausted all the resources of human nature left to itself, and possessed no recuperative force, no regenerative principle. A regeneration of society could only proceed from religion. But the heathen religion had no restraint for vice, no comfort for the poor and oppressed; it was itself the muddy fountain of immorality. God, therefore, who in his infinite mercy desired not the destruction but the salvation of the race, opened in the midst of this hopeless decay of a false religion a pure fountain

---

[1] Ποικίλον τι καὶ πολυπαθὲς κακῶν ταμεῖον καὶ θησαύρισμα, ὡς φησι Δημόκριτος. *Animi ne an corporis affectiones sint pejores,* c. 2 (in Wyttenbach's ed. Tom. III. p. 17).

of holiness, love, and peace, in the only true and universal religion of his Son Jesus Christ.

In the cheerless waste of pagan corruption the small and despised band of Christians was an oasis fresh with life and hope. It was the salt of the earth, and the light of the world. Poor in this world's goods, it bore the imperishable treasures of the kingdom of heaven. Meek and lowly in heart, it was destined, according to the promise of the Lord, without a stroke of the sword, to inherit the earth. In submission it conquered; by suffering and death it won the crown of life.

The superiority of the principles of Christian ethics over the heathen standards of morality even under its most favorable forms is universally admitted. The superiority of the example of Christ over all the heathen sages is likewise admitted. The power of that peerless example was and is now as great as the power of his teaching. It is reflected in every age and every type of purity and goodness. But every period, while it shares in the common virtues and graces, has its peculiar moral physiognomy. The ante-Nicene age excelled in unworldliness, in the heroic endurance of suffering and persecution, in the contempt of death, and the hope of resurrection, in the strong sense of community, and in active benevolence.

Christianity, indeed, does not come " with observation." Its deepest workings are silent and inward. The operations of divine grace commonly shun the notice of the historian, and await their revelation on the great day of account, when all that is secret shall be made known. Who can measure the depth and breadth of all those blessed experiences of forgiveness, peace, gratitude, trust in God, love for God and love for man, humility and meekness, patience and resignation, which have bloomed as vernal flowers on the soil of the renewed heart since the first Christian Pentecost? Who can tell the number and the fervor of Christian prayers and intercessions which have gone up from lonely chambers, caves, deserts, and martyrs' graves, in the silent night and the open day, for friends and foes, for all classes of mankind, even for cruel persecutors, to

the throne of the exalted Saviour?   But where this Christian
life has taken root in the depths of the soul it must show itself
in the outward conduct, and exert an elevating influence on
every calling and sphere of action.   The Christian morality
surpassed all that the noblest philosophers of heathendom had
ever taught or labored for as the highest aim of man.   The
masterly picture of it in the anonymous Epistle to Diognetus
is no mere fancy sketch, but a faithful copy from real life.[1]

When the apologists indignantly repel the heathen calumnies,
and confidently point to the unfeigned piety, the brotherly love,
the love for enemies, the purity and chastity, the faithfulness
and integrity, the patience and gentleness, of the confessors of
the name of Jesus, they speak from daily experience and personal observation.   " We, who once served lust," could Justin
Martyr say without exaggeration, " now find our delight only
in pure morals; we, who once followed sorcery, have now consecrated ourselves to the eternal good God; we, who once loved
gain above all, now give up what we have for the common use,
and share with every needy one; we, who once hated and killed
each other; we, who would have no common hearth with
foreigners for difference of customs, now, since the appearance
of Christ, live with them, pray for our enemies, seek to convince those who hate us without cause, that they may regulate
their life according to the glorious teaching of Christ, and
receive from the all-ruling God the same blessings with ourselves."   Tertullian could boast that he knew no Christians
who suffered by the hand of the executioner, except for their
religion.   Minutius Felix tells the heathens[2]: " You prohibit
adultery by law, and practise it in secret; you punish wickedness only in the overt act; we look upon it as criminal even in
thought.   You dread the inspection of others; we stand in
awe of nothing but our own consciences as becomes Christians.
And finally your prisons are overflowing with criminals; but
they are all heathens, not a Christian is there, unless he be an

[1] See § 2, p. 9. sq.   [2] *Octavius*, cap. 35.

apostate." Even Pliny informed Trajan, that the Christians, whom he questioned on the rack respecting the character of their religion, had bound themselves by an oath never to commit theft, robbery, nor adultery, nor to break their word—and this, too, at a time when the sins of fraud, uncleanness, and lasciviousness of every form abounded all around. Another heathen, Lucian, bears testimony to their benevolence and charity for their brethren in distress, while he attempts to ridicule this virtue as foolish weakness in an age of unbounded selfishness.

The humble and painful condition of the church under civil oppression made hypocrisy more rare than in times of peace, and favored the development of the heroic virtues. The Christians delighted to regard themselves as soldiers of Christ, enlisted under the victorious standard of the cross against sin, the world, and the devil. The baptismal vow was their oath of perpetual allegiance;[1] the Apostles' creed their parole;[2] the sign of the cross upon the forehead, their mark of service;[3] temperance, courage, and faithfulness unto death, their cardinal virtues; the blessedness of heaven, their promised reward. "No soldier," exclaims Tertullian to the Confessors,. "goes with his sports or from his bed-chamber to the battle; but from the camp, where he hardens and accustoms himself to every inconvenience. Even in peace warriors learn to bear labor and fatigue, going through all military exercises, that neither soul nor body may flag. . . . . Ye wage a good warfare, in which the living God is the judge of the combat, the Holy Spirit the leader, eternal glory the prize." To this may be added the eloquent passage of Minutius Felix[4]: "How fair a spectacle in the sight of God is a Christian entering the lists with affliction, and with noble firmness combating menaces and tortures, or with a disdainful smile marching to death through the clamors of the people, and the insults of the executioners; when he bravely maintains his liberty against kings and princes, and

---

[1] *Sacramentum militiæ Christianæ.*
[2] *Symbolum*, or, *tessera militaris.*
[3] *Character militaris, stigma militare.*
[4] *Octavius*, cap. 37

submits to God, whose servant he is; when, like a conqueror, he triumphs over the judge that condemns him. For he certainly is victorious who obtains what he fights for. He fights under the eye of God, and is crowned with length of days. You have exalted some of your stoical sufferers to the skies; such as Scævola who, having missed his aim in an attempt to kill the king, voluntarily burned the mistaking hand. Yet how many among us have suffered not only the hand, but the whole body to be consumed without a complaint, when their deliverance was in their own power! But why should I compare our elders with your Mutius, or Aquilius, or Regulus, when our very children, our sons and daughters, inspired with patience, despise your racks and wild beasts, and all other instruments of cruelty? Surely nothing but the strongest reasons could persuade people to suffer at this rate; and nothing else but Almighty power could support them under their sufferings."

Yet, on the other hand, the Christian life of the period before Constantine has been often unwarrantably idealized. In a human nature essentially the same, we could but expect the same faults which we found even in the apostolic churches. The Epistles of Cyprian afford incontestable evidence, that, especially in the intervals of repose, an abatement of zeal soon showed itself, and, on the reopening of persecution, the Christian name was dishonored by hosts of apostates. And not seldom did the most prominent virtues, courage in death, and strictness of morals, degenerate into morbid fanaticism and unnatural rigor.

§ 95. *The Church and Public Amusements.*

TERTULLIAN: *De Spectaculis.* On the Roman Spectacles see the abundant references in FRIEDLAENDER, II. 255–580 (5th ed.)

Christianity is anything but sanctimonious gloominess and misanthropic austerity. It is the fountain of true joy, and of that peace which "passeth all understanding." But this joy wells up from the consciousness of pardon and of fellowship

with God, is inseparable from holy earnestness, and has no concord with worldly frivolity and sensual amusement, which carry
the sting of a bad conscience, and beget only disgust and bitter
remorse. "What is more blessed," asks Tertullian, "than
reconciliation with God our Father and Lord; than the revelation of the truth, the knowledge of error; than the forgiveness
of so great past misdeeds? Is there a greater joy than the disgust with earthly pleasure, than contempt for the whole world,
than true freedom, than an unstained conscience, than contentment in life and fearlessness in death?"

Contrast with this the popular amusements of the heathen:
the theatre, the circus, and the arena. They were originally
connected with the festivals of the gods, but had long lost their
religious character and degenerated into nurseries of vice. The
theatre, once a school of public morals in the best days of
Greece, when Aeschylos and Sophocles furnished the plays, had
since the time of Augustus room only for low comedies and
unnatural tragedies, with splendid pageantry, frivolous music,
and licentious dances.[1] Tertullian represents it as the temple
of Venus and Bacchus, who are close allies as patrons of lust
and drunkenness.[2] The circus was devoted to horse and chariot
races, hunts of wild beasts, military displays and athletic games,
and attracted immense multitudes. "The impatient crowd,"
says the historian of declining Rome,[3] "rushed at the dawn of
day to secure their places, and there were many who passed a
sleepless and anxious night in the adjacent porticos. From the
morning to the evening, careless of the sun or of the rain, the
spectators, who sometimes amounted to the number of four
hundred thousand, remained in eager attention; their eyes fixed
on the horses and charioteers, their minds agitated with hope

[1] Friedlaender, II. 391: "*Neben den gewaltigen Aufregungen, die Circus und
Arena boten, konnte die Bühne ihre Anziehungskraft für die Massen nur durch
unedle Mittel behaupten. durch rohe Belustigung und raffinirten Sinnenkitzel: und
so hat sie, statt dem verderblichen Einfluss jener anderen Schauspiele die Wage zu
halten, zur Corruption und Verwilderung Roms nicht am wenigsten beigetragen.*"
[2] De Spectac. c. 10. Comp.Minut. Felix, Octav. c. 37.
[3] Gibbon, ch. XXXI. (vol. III. 384, ed. Smith).

and fear for the success of the colors which they espoused; and the happiness of Rome appeared to hang on the event of a race. The same immoderate ardor inspired their clamors and their applause as often as they were entertained with the hunting of wild beasts and the various modes of theatrical representation."

The most popular, and at the same time the most inhuman and brutalizing of these public spectacles were the gladiatorial fights in the arena. There murder was practised as an art, from sunrise to sunset, and myriads of men and beasts were sacrificed to satisfy a savage curiosity and thirst for blood. At the inauguration of the Flavian amphitheatre from five to nine thousand wild beasts (according to different accounts) were slain in one day. No less than ten thousand gladiators fought in the feasts which Trajan gave to the Romans after the conquest of Dacia, and which lasted four months (A. D. 107). Under Probus (A. D. 281) as many as a hundred lions, a hundred lionesses, two hundred leopards, three hundred bears, and a thousand wild boars were massacred in a single day.[1] The spectacles of the worthless Carinus (284) who selected his favorites and even his ministers from the dregs of the populace, are said to have surpassed those of all his predecessors. The gladiators were condemned criminals, captives of war, slaves, and professional fighters; in times of persecution innocent Christians were not spared, but thrown before lions and tigers. Painted savages from Britain, blonde Germans from the Rhine and Danube, negroes from Africa, and wild beasts, then much more numerous than now, from all parts of the world, were brought to the arena. Domitian arranged fights of dwarfs and women.

The emperors patronized these various spectacles as the surest means of securing the favor of the people, which clamored for "*Panem et Circenses.*" Enormous sums were wasted on them from the public treasury and private purses. Augustus set the example. Nero was so extravagantly liberal in this direction

---

[1] Gibbon, ch. XII. (I. 646).

that the populace forgave his horrible vices, and even wished his return from death. The parsimonious Vespasian built the most costly and colossal amphitheatre the world has ever seen, incrusted with marble, decorated with statues, and furnished with gold, silver, and amber. Titus presented thousands of Jewish captives after the capture of Jerusalem to the provinces of the East for slaughter in the arena. Even Trajan and Marcus Aurelius made bountiful provision for spectacles, and the latter, Stoic as he was, charged the richest senators to gratify the public taste during his absence from Rome. Some emperors, as Nero, Commodus, and Caracalla, were so lost to all sense of dignity and decency that they delighted and gloried in histrionic and gladiatorial performances. Nero died by his own hand, with the explanation: " What an artist perishes in me." Commodus appeared no less than seven hundred and thirty-five times on the stage in the character of Hercules, with club and lion's skin, and from a secure position killed countless beasts and men.

The theatrical passion was not confined to Rome, it spread throughout the provinces. Every considerable city had an amphitheatre, and that was the most imposing building, as may be seen to this day in the ruins at Pompeii, Capua, Puteoli, Verona, Nismes, Autun (Augustodunum), and other places.[1]

Public opinion favored these demoralizing amusements almost without a dissenting voice.[2] Even such a noble heathen as Cicero commended them as excellent schools of courage and contempt of death. Epictetus alludes to them with indifference. Seneca is the only Roman author who, in one of his latest writings, condemned the bloody spectacles from the standpoint of humanity, but without effect. Paganism had no proper conception of the sanctity of human life; and even the Stoic

---

[1] See the long list of amphitheatres in Friedlaender, II. 502-566.

[2] Friedlaender, II. 370: " *In der ganzen römischen Literatur begegnen wir kaum einer Aeusserung des Abscheus, den die heutige Welt gegen diese unmenschlichen Lustbarkeiten empfindet. In der Regel werden die Fechterspiele mit der grössten Gleichgiltigkeit erwähnt. Die Kinder spielen Gladiatoren wie jetzt in Andalusien Stier und Matador.*"

philosophy, while it might disapprove of bloody games as brutal and inhuman, did not condemn them as the sin of murder.

To this gigantic evil the Christian church opposed an inexorable Puritanic rigor in the interest of virtue and humanity. No compromise was possible with such shocking public immorality. Nothing would do but to flee from it and to warn against it. The theatrical spectacles were included in " the pomp of the devil," which Christians renounced at their baptism. They were forbidden, on pain of excommunication, to attend them. It sometimes happened that converts, who were overpowered by their old habits and visited the theatre, either relapsed into heathenism, or fell for a long time into a state of deep dejection. Tatianus calls the spectacles terrible feasts, in which the soul feeds on human flesh and blood. Tertullian attacked them without mercy, even before he joined the rigorous Montanists. He reminds the catechumens, who were about to consecrate themselves to the service of God, that " the condition of faith and the laws of Christian discipline forbid, among other sins of the world, the pleasures of the public shows." They excite, he says, all sorts of wild and impure passions, anger, fury, and lust; while the spirit of Christianity is a spirit of meekness, peace, and purity. " What a man should not say he should not hear. All licentious speech, nay, every idle word is condemned by God. The things which defile a man in going out of his mouth, defile him also when they go in at his eyes and ears. The true wrestlings of the Christian are to overcome unchastity by chastity, perfidy by faithfulness, cruelty by compassion and charity." Tertullian refutes the arguments with which loose Christians would plead for those fascinating amusements; their appeals to the silence of the Scriptures, or even to the dancing of David before the ark, and to Paul's comparison of the Christian life with the Grecian games. He winds up with a picture of the fast approaching day of judgment, to which we should look forward. He inclined strongly to the extreme view, that all art is a species of fiction and falsehood, and inconsistent with

Christian truthfulness. In two other treatises[1] he warned the Christian women against all display of dress, in which the heathen women shone in temples, theatres, and public places. Visit not such places, says he to them, and appear in public only for earnest reasons. The handmaids of God must distinguish themselves even outwardly from the handmaids of Satan, and set the latter a good example of simplicity, decorum, and chastity.

The opposition of the Church had, of course, at first only a moral effect, but in the fourth century it began to affect legislation, and succeeded at last in banishing at least the bloody gladiatorial games from the civilized world (with the single exception of Spain and the South American countries, which still disgrace themselves by bull-fights). Constantine, even as late as 313, committed a great multitude of defeated barbarians to the wild beasts for the amusement of the people, and was highly applauded for this generous act by a heathen orator; but after the Council of Nicæa, in 325, he issued the first prohibition of those bloody spectacles in times of peace, and kept them out of Constantinople.[2] "There is scarcely," says a liberal historian of moral progress, "any other single reform so important in the moral history of mankind as the suppression of the gladiatorial shows, and this feat must be almost exclusively ascribed to the Christian church. When we remember how extremely few of the best and greatest men of the Roman world had absolutely condemned the games of the amphitheatre, it is impossible to regard, without the deepest admiration, the unwavering and uncompromising consistency of the patristic denunciations."[3]

§ 96. *Secular Callings and Civil Duties.*

As to the various callings of life, Christianity gives the instruction: "Let each man abide in that calling wherein he was

---

[1] *De Habitu Muliebri*, and *De Cultu Feminarum*.
[2] On the action of his successors, see vol. III. 122 sq.
[3] Lecky, *Hist. of Europ. Morals*, II. 36 sq.

called." [1] It forbids no respectable pursuit, and only requires that it be followed in a new spirit to the glory of God and the benefit of men. This is one proof of its universal application —its power to enter into all the relations of human life and into all branches of society, under all forms of government. This is beautifully presented by the unknown author of the Epistle to Diognetus. Tertullian protests to the heathens: [2] "We are no Brahmins nor Indian gymnosophists, no hermits, no exiles from life.[3] We are mindful of the thanks we owe to God, our Lord and Creator; we despise not the enjoyment of his works; we only temper it, that we may avoid excess and abuse. We dwell, therefore, with you in this world, not without markets and fairs, not without baths, inns, shops, and every kind of intercourse. We carry on commerce and war,[4] agriculture and trade with you. We take part in your pursuits, and give our labor for your use."

But there were at that time some callings which either ministered solely to sinful gratification, like that of the stage-player, or were intimately connected with the prevailing idolatry, like the manufacture, decoration, and sale of mytho-logical images and symbols, the divination of astrologers, and all species of magic. These callings were strictly forbidden in the church, and must be renounced by the candidate for baptism. Other occupations, which were necessary indeed, but commonly perverted by the heathens to fraudulent purposes— inn-keeping, for example—were elevated by the Christian spirit. Theodotus at Ancyra made his house a refuge for the Christians and a place of prayer in the Diocletian persecution, in which he himself suffered martyrdom.

In regard to military and civil offices under the heathen government, opinion was divided. Some, on the authority of such passages as Matt. 5: 39 and 26: 52, condemned all war as unchristian and immoral; anticipating the views of the Mennonites and Friends. Others appealed to the good

---

[1] 1 Cor. 7: 20.   [2] *Apol.* c. 42.   [3] *Exules vitæ.*
[4] "*Militamus,*" which proves that many Christians served in the army.

centurion of Capernaum and Cornelius of Cæsarea, and held the military life consistent with a Christian profession. The tradition of the *legio fulminatrix* indicates that there were Christian soldiers in the Roman armies under Marcus Aurelius, and at the time of Diocletian the number of Christians at the court and in civil office was very considerable.

But in general the Christians of those days, with their lively sense of foreignness to this world, and their longing for the heavenly home, or the millennial reign of Christ, were averse to high office in a heathen state. Tertullian expressly says, that nothing was more alien to them than politics.[1] Their conscience required them to abstain scrupulously from all idolatrous usages, sacrifices, libations, and flatteries connected with public offices; and this requisition must have come into frequent collision with their duties to the state, so long as the state remained heathen. They honored the emperor as appointed to earthly government by God, and as standing nearest of all men to him in power; and they paid their taxes, as Justin Martyr expressly states, with exemplary faithfulness. But their obedience ceased whenever the emperor, as he frequently did, demanded of them idolatrous acts. Tertullian thought that the empire would last till the end of the world, then supposed to be near at hand, and would be irreconcilable with the Christian profession. Against the idolatrous worship of the emperor he protests with Christian boldness: "Augustus, the founder of the empire, would never be called Lord; for this is a surname of God. Yet I will freely call the emperor so, only not in the place of God. Otherwise I am free from him; for I have only one Lord, the almighty and eternal God, who also is the emperor's Lord. . . . . Far be it from me to call the emperor God, which is not only the most shameful, but the most pernicious flattery."

The comparative indifference and partial aversion of the Christians to the affairs of the state, to civil legislation and

---

[1] *Apol.* c. 38: " *Nec ulla res aliena magis quam publica.*"

administration exposed them to the frequent reproach and contempt of the heathens. Their want of patriotism was partly the result of their superior devotion to the church as their country, partly of their situation in a hostile world. It must not be attributed to an "indolent or criminal disregard for the public welfare" (as Gibbon intimates), but chiefly to their just abhorrence of the innumerable idolatrous rites connected with the public and private life of the heathens. While they refused to incur the guilt of idolatry, they fervently and regularly prayed for the emperor and the state, their enemies and persecutors.[1] They were the most peaceful subjects, and during this long period of almost constant provocation, abuse, and persecutions, they never took part in those frequent insurrections and rebellions which weakened and undermined the empire. They renovated society from within, by revealing in their lives as well as in their doctrine a higher order of private and public virtue, and thus proved themselves patriots in the best sense of the word.

The patriotism of ancient Greece and republican Rome, while it commands our admiration by the heroic devotion and sacrifice to the country, was after all an extended selfishness, and based upon the absolutism of the State and the disregard of the rights of the individual citizen and the foreigner. It was undermined by causes independent of Christianity. The amalgamation of different nationalities in the empire extinguished sectionalism and exclusivism, and opened the wide view of a universal humanity. Stoicism gave this cosmopolitan sentiment a philosophical and ethical expression in the writings of Seneca, Epictetus, and Marcus Aurelius. Terence embodied it in his famous line: "*Homo sum: humani nihil a me alienum puto.*" But Christianity first taught the fatherhood of God, the redemption by Christ, the common brotherhood of believers, the duty of charity for all men made in the image of God. It is true that monasticism, which began to develop itself already in

---

[1] See the prayer for rulers in the newly discovered portions of the Epistle of Clement of Rome, quoted in § 66, p. 228.

the third century, nursed indifference to the state and even to the family, and substituted the total abandonment of the world for its reformation and transformation. It withdrew a vast amount of moral energy and enthusiasm from the city to the desert, and left Roman society to starvation and consumption. But it preserved and nursed in solitude the heroism of self-denial and consecration, which, in the collapse of the Roman empire, became a converting power of the barbarian conquerors, and laid the foundation for a new and better civilization. The decline and fall of the Roman empire was inevitable; Christianity prolonged its life in the East, and diminished the catastrophe of its collapse in the West, by converting and humanizing the barbarian conquerors.[1] St. Augustin pointed to the remarkable fact that amid the horrors of the sack of Rome by the Goths, "the churches of the apostles and the crypts of the martyrs were sanctuaries for all who fled to them, whether Christian or pagan," and "saved the lives of multitudes who impute to Christ the ills that have befallen their city."[2]

§ 97. *The Church and Slavery.*

See Lit. vol. I. § 48, p. 444, especially WALLON'S *Histoire de l'esclavage* (Paris, new ed. 1879, 3 vols). Comp. also V. LECHLER: *Sklaverei und Christenthum.* Leipzig, 1877, 1878; THEOD. ZAHN: *Sklaverei und Christenthum in der alten Welt.* Heidelberg, 1879. OVERBECK: *Verh. d. alten Kirche zur Sclaverei im röm. Reiche.* 1875.

[1] Gibbon, ch. 36, admits this in part. "If the decline of the Roman empire was hastened by the conversion of Constantine, the victorious religion broke the violence of the fall, and mollified the ferocious temper of the conquerors." Milman says of the Church: "If treacherous (?) to the interests of the Roman empire, it was true to those of mankind" (III. 48). Lecky (II. 153) says: "It is impossible to deny that the Christian priesthood contributed materially both by their charity and by their arbitration, to mitigate the calamities that accompanied the dissolution of the empire; and it is equally impossible to doubt that their political attitude greatly increased their power for good. Standing between the conflicting forces, almost indifferent to the issue, and notoriously exempt from the passions of the combat, they obtained with the conqueror, and used for the benefit of the conquered, a degree of influence they would never have possessed had they been regarded as Roman patriots."

[2] *De Civ. Dei,* I. c. 1.

Heathenism had no conception of the general and natural rights of men. The ancient republics consisted in the exclusive dominion of a minority over an oppressed majority. The Greeks and Romans regarded only the free, *i. e.* the free-born rich and independent citizens as men in the full sense of the term, and denied this privilege to the foreigners, the laborers, the poor, and the slaves. They claimed the natural right to make war upon all foreign nations, without distinction of race, in order to subject them to their iron rule. Even with Cicero the foreigner and the enemy are synonymous terms. The barbarians were taken in thousands by the chance of war (above 100,000 in the Jewish war alone) and sold as cheap as horses. Besides, an active slave-trade was carried on in the Euxine, the eastern provinces, the coast of Africa, and Britain. The greater part of mankind in the old Roman empire was reduced to a hopeless state of slavery, and to a half brutish level. And this evil of slavery was so thoroughly interwoven with the entire domestic and public life of the heathen world, and so deliberately regarded, even by the greatest philosophers, Aristotle for instance, as natural and indispensable, that the abolition of it, even if desirable, seemed to belong among the impossible things.

Yet from the outset Christianity has labored for this end; not by impairing the right of property, not by outward violence, nor sudden revolution; this, under the circumstances, would only have made the evil worse; but by its moral power, by preaching the divine descent and original unity of all men, their common redemption through Christ, the duty of brotherly love, and the true freedom of the spirit. It placed slaves and masters on the same footing of dependence on God and of freedom in God, the Father, Redeemer, and Judge of both. It conferred inward freedom even under outward bondage, and taught obedience to God and for the sake of God, even in the enjoyment of outward freedom. This moral and religious freedom must lead at last to the personal and civil liberty of the individual. Christianity redeems not only the soul but the body also, and the process of regeneration will end in the resurrection and glorification of the entire natural world.

In the period before us, however, the abolition of slavery, save in isolated cases of manumission, was utterly out of question, considering only the enormous number of the slaves. The world was far from ripe for such a step. The church, in her persecuted condition, had as yet no influence at all over the machinery of the state and the civil legislation. And she was at that time so absorbed in the transcendent importance of the higher world and in her longing for the speedy return of the Lord, that she cared little for earthly freedom or temporal happiness. Hence Ignatius, in his epistle to Polycarp, counsels servants to serve only the more zealously to the glory of the Lord, that they may receive from God the higher freedom; and not to attempt to be redeemed at the expense of their Christian brethren, lest they be found slaves to their own caprice. From this we see that slaves, in whom faith awoke the sense of manly dignity and the desire of freedom, were accustomed to demand their redemption at the expense of the church, as a right, and were thus liable to value the earthly freedom more than the spiritual. Tertullian declares the outward freedom worthless without the ransom of the soul from the bondage of sin. "How can the world," says he, "make a servant free? All is mere show in the world, nothing truth. For the slave is already free, as a purchase of Christ; and the freedman is a servant of Christ. If thou takest the freedom which the world can give for true, thou hast thereby become again the servant of man, and hast lost the freedom of Christ, in that thou thinkest it bondage." Chrysostom, in the fourth century, was the first of the fathers to discuss the question of slavery at large in the spirit of the apostle Paul, and to recommend, though cautiously, a gradual emancipation.

But the church before Constantine labored with great success to elevate the intellectual and moral condition of the slaves, to adjust inwardly the inequality between slaves and masters, as the first and efficient step towards the final outward abolition of the evil, and to influence the public opinion even of the heathens.   Here the church was aided by a concurrent movement in philosophy and legislation.   The cruel views of Cato, who advised to work the slaves, like beasts of burden, to death rather than allow them to become old and unprofitable, gave way to the milder and humane views of Seneca, Pliny, and Plutarch, who very nearly approach the apostolic teaching.   To the influence of the later Stoic philosophy must be attributed many improvements in the slave-code of imperial Rome.   But the most important improvements were made from the triumph of Constantine to the reign of Justinian, under directly Christian influences.   Constantine issued a law in 315, forbidding the branding of slaves on the face to prevent the disfiguration of the figure of celestial beauty (*i. e.* the image of God).[1]   He also facilitated emancipation, in an edict of 316, by requiring only a written document, signed by the master, instead of the previous ceremony in the presence of the prefect and his lictor.

It is here to be considered, first of all, that Christianity spread freely among the slaves, except where they were so rude and degraded as to be insensible to all higher impressions.   They were not rarely (as Origen observes) the instruments of the conversion of their masters, especially of the women, and children, whose training was frequently intrusted to them.   Not a few slaves died martyrs, and were enrolled among the saints; as Onesimus, Eutyches, Victorinus, Maro, Nereus, Achilleus, Blandina, Potamiæna, Felicitas.   Tradition makes Onesimus, the slave of Philemon, a bishop.   The church of St. Vital at Ravenna—the first and noblest specimen of Byzantine architecture in Italy—was dedicated by Justinian to the memory of a martyred slave.   But the most remarkable instance is that of Callistus, who was originally a slave, and rose to the chair of St. Peter in Rome (218–223).   Hippolytus, who acquaints us with his history, attacks his doctrinal and disciplinarian

---

[1] "*Facies, quæ ad similitudinem pulchritudinis est coelestis figurata.*"   *Cod. Just.* IX 17, 17.

views, but does not reproach him for his former condition. Callistus sanctioned the marriages between free Christian women and Christian slaves. Celsus cast it up as a reproach to Christianity, that it let itself down so readily to slaves, fools, women, and children. But Origen justly saw an excellence of the new religion in this very fact, that it could raise this despised and, in the prevailing view, irreclaimable class of men to the level of moral purity and worth. If, then, converted slaves, with the full sense of their intellectual and religious superiority, still remained obedient to their heathen masters, and even served them more faithfully than before, resisting decidedly only their immoral demands (like Potamiæna, and other chaste women and virgins in the service of voluptuous masters)—they showed, in this very self-control, the best proof of their ripeness for civil freedom, and at the same time furnished the fairest memorial of that Christian faith, which raised the soul, in the enjoyment of sonship with God and in the hope of the blessedness of heaven, above the sufferings of earth. Euelpistes, a slave of the imperial household, who was carried with Justin Martyr to the tribunal of Rusticus, on being questioned concerning his condition, replied: "I am a slave of the emperor, but I am also a Christian, and have received liberty from Jesus Christ; by his grace I have the same hope as my brethren." Where the owners of the slaves themselves became Christians, the old relation virtually ceased; both came together to the table of the Lord, and felt themselves brethren of one family, in striking contrast with the condition of things among their heathen neighbors as expressed in the current proverb: "As many enemies as slaves." [1] Clement of Alexandria frequently urges that "slaves are men like ourselves," though he nowhere condemns the institution itself. That there actually were such

---

[1] "*Totidem esse hostes, quot servos.*" Seneca, *Ep.* 47. From the time of the Servile Wars the Romans lived in constant fear of slave conspiracies and insurrections. The slaves formed nearly one half of the population, and in some agricultural districts, as in Sicily and Calabria, they were largely in the majority.

cases of fraternal fellowship, like that which St. Paul recommended to Philemon, we have the testimony of Lactantius, at the end of our period, who writes, in his *Institutes*, no doubt from life: "Should any say: Are there not also among you poor and rich, servants and masters, distinctions among individuals? No; we call ourselves brethren for no other reason than that we hold ourselves all equal. For since we measure everything human not by its outward appearance, but by its intrinsic value, we have, notwithstanding the difference of outward relations, no slaves, but we call them and consider them brethren in the Spirit and fellow-servants in religion."[1] The same writer says: "God would have all men equal. . . . With him there is neither servant nor master. If he is the same Father to all, we are all with the same right free. So no one is poor before God, but he who is destitute of righteousness; no one rich, but he who is full of virtues."[2]

The testimony of the catacombs, as contrasted with pagan epitaphs, shows that Christianity almost obliterated the distinction between the two classes of society. Slaves are rarely mentioned. "While it is impossible," says De Rossi, "to examine the pagan sepulchral inscriptions of the same period without finding mention of a slave or a freedman, I have not met with one well-ascertained instance among the inscriptions of the Christian tombs."[3]

The principles of Christianity naturally prompt Christian slave-holders to actual manumission. The number of slave-holders before Constantine was very limited among Christians, who were mostly poor. Yet we read in the Acts of the mar-

---

[1] Lib. v. c. 15 (ed. Fritzsche. Lips. 1842, p. 257).

[2] *Inst.* v. 14 (p. 257): "*Deus enim, qui homines generat et inspirat, omnes aequos, id est pares esse voluit; eandem conditionem vivendi omnibus posuit; omnes ad sapientiam genuit; omnibus immortalitatem spopondit, nemo a beneficiis coelestibus segregatur. . . . . Nemo apud eum servus est, nemo dominus; si enim cunctis idem Pater est, aequo jure omnes liberi sumus.*"

[3] "*Bulletino* for 1866, p. 24. V. Schultze (*Die Katakomben*, p. 258) infers from the monuments that in the early Christian congregations slavery was reduced to a minimum.

tyrdom of the Roman bishop Alexander, that a Roman prefect, Hermas, converted by that bishop, in the reign of Trajan, received baptism at an Easter festival with his wife and children and twelve hundred and fifty slaves, and on this occasion gave all his slaves their freedom and munificent gifts besides.[1] So in the martyrology of St. Sebastian, it is related that a wealthy Roman prefect, Chromatius, under Diocletian, on embracing Christianity, emancipated fourteen hundred slaves, after having them baptized with himself, because their sonship with God put an end to their servitude to man.[2] Several epitaphs in the catacombs mention the fact of manumission. In the beginning of the fourth century St. Cantius, Cantianus, and Cantianilla, of an old Roman family, set all their slaves, seventy-three in number, at liberty, after they had received baptism.[3] St. Melania emancipated eight thousand slaves; St. Ovidius, five thousand; Hermes, a prefect in the reign of Trajan, twelve hundred and fifty.[4]

These legendary traditions may indeed be doubted as to the exact facts in the case, and probably are greatly exaggerated; but they are nevertheless conclusive as the exponents of the spirit which animated the church at that time concerning the duty of Christian masters. It was felt that in a thoroughly Christianized society there can be no room for despotism on the one hand and slavery on the other.

After the third century the manumission became a solemn act, which took place in the presence of the clergy and the congregation. It was celebrated on church festivals, especially on Easter. The master led the slave to the altar; there the document of emancipation was read, the minister pronounced the blessing, and the congregation received him as a free brother with equal rights and privileges. Constantine found this custom already established, and African councils of the fourth

---

[1] *Acta Sanct. Boll.* Maj. tom. i. p. 371.

[2] *Acta Sanct.* Ian. tom. iii. 275.

[3] *Acta Sanct.* Maj. tom. vi. 777.

[4] Champagny, *Charité chrét.* p. 210 (as quoted by Lecky, II. 74).

century requested the emperor to give it general force.   He placed it under the superintendence of the clergy.

NOTES.

H. WALLON, in his learned and able *Histoire de l'esclavage dans l'antiquité* (second ed. Paris, 1879, 3 vols.), shows that the gospel in such passages as Matt. 23: 8; Gal. 3: 28; Col. 3: 11; 1 Cor. 12: 13 sounded the death knell of slavery, though it was very long in dying, and thus sums up the teaching of the ante-Nicene church (III. 237): "*Minutius Félix, Tertullien et tous ceux qui ont écrit dans cette période où l'Église a surtout souffert, invoquent de même cette communauté de nature, cette communauté de patrie dans la république du monde, en un language familier à la philosophie, mais qui trouvait parmi les chrétiens avec une sanction plus haute et un sens plus complet, une application plus sérieuse. Devant ce droit commun des hommes, fondé sur le droit divin, le prétendu droit des gens n'était plus qu' une monstrueuse injustice.*" For the views of the later fathers and the influence of the church on the imperial legislation, see ch. VIII. to X. in his third volume.

LECKY discusses the relation of Christianity to slavery in the second vol. of his *History of European Morals*, pp. 66–90, and justly remarks: "The services of Christianity in this sphere were of three kinds. It supplied a new order of relations, in which the distinction of classes was unknown. It imparted a moral dignity to the servile classes, and it gave an unexampled impetus to the movement of enfranchisement."

§ 98. The Heathen Family.

In ancient Greece and Rome the state was the highest object of life, and the only virtues properly recognized—wisdom, courage, moderation, and justice—were political virtues.   Aristotle makes the state, that is the organized body of free citizens [1] (foreigners and slaves are excluded), precede the family and the individual, and calls man essentially a " political animal."   In Plato's ideal commonwealth the state is everything and owns everything, even the children.

This political absolutism destroys the proper dignity and rights of the individual and the family, and materially hinders the development of the domestic and private virtues.   Marriage was allowed no moral character, but merely a political import for the preservation of the state, and could not be legally contracted except by free citizens.   Socrates, in instructing his son

<hr>

[1] Κοινωνία τῶν ἐλευθέρων.

concerning this institution, tells him, according to Xenophon, that we select only such wives as we hope will yield beautiful children. Plato recommends even community of women to the class of warriors in his ideal republic, as the best way to secure vigorous citizens. Lycurgus, for similar reasons, encouraged adultery under certain circumstances, requiring old men to lend their young and handsome wives to young and strong men.

Woman was placed almost on the same level with the slave. She differs, indeed, from the slave, according to Aristotle, but has, after all, really no will of her own, and is hardly capable of a higher virtue than the slave. Shut up in a retired apartment of the house, she spent her life with the slaves. As human nature is essentially the same in all ages, and as it is never entirely forsaken by the guidance of a kind Providence, we must certainly suppose that female virtue was always more or less maintained and appreciated even among the heathen. Such characters as Penelope, Nausicaa, Andromache, Antigone, Iphigenia, and Diotima, of the Greek poetry and history, bear witness of this. Plutarch's advice to married people, and his letter of consolation to his wife after the death of their daughter, breathe a beautiful spirit of purity and affection. But the general position assigned to woman by the poets, philosophers, and legislators of antiquity, was one of social oppression and degradation. In Athens she was treated as a minor during lifetime, and could not inherit except in the absence of male heirs. To the question of Socrates: "Is there any one with whom you converse less than with the wife?" his pupil, Aristobulus, replies: "No one, or at least very few." If she excelled occasionally, in Greece, by wit and culture, and, like Aspasia, Phryne, Laïs, Theodota, attracted the admiration and courtship even of earnest philosophers like Socrates, and statesmen like Pericles, she generally belonged to the disreputable class of the *hetœrœ* or *amicœ*. In Corinth they were attached to the temple of Aphrodite, and enjoyed the sanction of religion for the practice of vice.[1] These dissolute women were esteemed above house-

---

[1] Their name ἑταῖραι was an Attic euphonism for πόρναι. In the temple of

wives, and became the proper and only representatives of some sort of female culture and social elegance. To live with them openly was no disgrace even for married men.[1] How could there be any proper conception and abhorrence of the sin of licentiousness and adultery, if the very gods, a Jupiter, a Mars, and a Venus, were believed to be guilty of those sins! The worst vices of earth were transferred to Olympus.

Modesty forbids the mention of a still more odious vice, which even depraved nature abhors, which yet was freely discussed and praised by ancient poets and philosophers, practised with neither punishment nor dishonor, and likewise divinely sanctioned by the example of Apollo and Hercules, and by the lewdness of Jupiter with Ganymede. [2]

Aphrodite at Corinth more than a thousand *hetæræ* were employed as *hierodulæ*. and were the ruin of foreigners (Strabo, VIII. 6, 20). Κορινϑία κόρη was a synonym for *hetæra*, and expressive of the acme of voluptuousness. A full account of these *hetæræ* and of the whole domestic life of the ancient Greeks may be found in Becker's *Charicles*, transla'ed by Metcalf, third ed. London, 1866. Becker says (p. 242), that in the period of the greatest refinement of classical Greece, "sensuality, if not the mother, was at all events the nurse of the Greek perception of the beautiful." Plato himself, even in his ideal state, despaired of restricting his citizens to the lawful intercourse of marriage.

[1] Aspasia bewitched Pericles by her beauty and genius; and Socrates acknowledged his deep obligation to the instructions of a courtesan named Diotima.

[2] Lecky (II. 311) derives this unnatural vice of Greece from the influence of the public games, which accustomed men to the contemplation of absolute nudity, and awoke unnatural passions. See the thirteenth book of Athenæus, Grote on the *Symposium* of Plato, and the full account in Döllinger's *Heidenthum und Judenthum*, 1857, p. 684 sqq. He says: "*Bei den Griechen tritt das Laster der Pœderastie mit allen Symptomen einer grossen nationalen Krankheit, gleichsam eines ethischen Miasma auf ; es zeigt sich als ein Gefühl, das stärker and heftiger wirkte, als die Weiberliebe bei andern Völkern, massloser, leidenschaftlicher in seinen Ausbrüchen war. . . . . In der ganzen Literatur der vorchristlichen Periode ist kaum ein Schriftsteller zu finden, der sich entschieden dagegen erklärt hätte. Vielmehr war die ganze Gesellschaft davon angesteckt, und man athmete das Miasma, so zu sagen, mit der Luft ein.*" Even Socrates and Plato gave this morbid vice the sanction of their great authority, if not in practice, at least in theory. Comp. Xenophon's *Mem.* VIII. 2, Plato's *Charmides*, and his descriptions of Eros, and Döllinger, *l. c.* p. 686 sq. Zeno, the founder of the austere sect of Stoics, was praised for the moderation with which he practiced this vice.

The Romans were originally more virtuous, domestic, and chaste, as they were more honest and conscientious, than the Greeks. With them the wife was honored by the title *domina*, *matrona*, *materfamilias*. At the head of their sacerdotal system stood the flamens of Jupiter, who represented marriage in its purity, and the vestal virgins, who represented virginity. The Sabine women interceding between their parents and their husbands, saved the republic; the mother and the wife of Coriolanus by her prayers averted his wrath, and raised the siege of the Volscian army; Lucretia who voluntarily sacrificed her life to escape the outrage to her honor offered by king Tarquin, and Virginia who was killed by her father to save her from slavery and dishonor, shine in the legendary history of Rome as bright examples of unstained purity. But even in the best days of the republic the legal status of woman was very low. The Romans likewise made marriage altogether subservient to the interest of the state, and allowed it in its legal form to free citizens alone. The proud maxims of the republic prohibited even the legitimate nuptials of a Roman with a foreign queen; and Cleopatra and Berenice were, as strangers, degraded to the position of concubines of Mark Antony and Titus. According to ancient custom the husband bought his bride from her parents, and she fulfilled the *coëmption* by purchasing, with three pieces of copper, a just introduction to his house and household deities. But this was for her simply an exchange of one servitude for another. She became the living property of a husband who could lend her out, as Cato lent his wife to his friend Hortensius, and as Augustus took Livia from Tiberius Nero. "Her husband or master," says Gibbon,[1] "was invested with the plenitude of paternal power. By his judgment or caprice her behavior was approved or censured, or chastised; he exercised the jurisdiction of life and death; and it was allowed, that in cases of adultery or drunkenness, the sentence might be properly inflicted. She acquired and inherited for the sole profit of her lord; and so

[1] Chapter XLIV., where he discusses at length the Roman code of laws.

clearly was woman defined, not as a *person*, but as a *thing*, that, if the original title were deficient, she might be claimed like other movables, by the use and possession of an entire year."

Monogamy was the rule both in Greece and in Rome, but did not exclude illegitimate connexions. Concubinage, in its proper legal sense, was a sort of secondary marriage with a woman of servile or plebeian extraction, standing below the dignity of a matron and above the infamy of a prostitute. It was sanctioned and regulated by law; it prevailed both in the East and the West from the age of Augustus to the tenth century, and was preferred to regular marriage by Vespasian, and the two Antonines, the best Roman emperors. Adultery was severely punished, at times even with sudden destruction of the offender; but simply as an interference with the rights and property of a free *man*. The wife had no legal or social protection against the infidelity of her husband. The Romans worshipped a peculiar goddess of domestic life; but her name *Viriplaca*, the appeaser of husbands, indicates her partiality. The intercourse of a husband with the slaves of his household and with public prostitutes was excluded from the odium and punishment of adultery. We say nothing of that unnatural abomination alluded to in Rom. 1 : 26, 27, which seems to have passed from the Etruscans and Greeks to the Romans, and prevailed among the highest as well as the lowest classes. The women, however, were almost as corrupt as their husbands, at least in the imperial age. Juvenal calls a chaste wife a *" rara avis in terris."* Under Augustus free-born daughters could no longer be found for the service of Vesta, and even the severest laws of Domitian could not prevent the six priestesses of the pure goddess from breaking their vow. The pantomimes and the games of Flora, with their audacious indecencies, were favorite amusements. " The unblushing, undisguised obscenity of the Epigrams of Martial, of the Romances of Apuleius and Petronius, and of some of the Dialogues of Lucian, reflected but too faithfully the spirit of their times." [1]

[1] Lecky, II. 321.

Divorce is said to have been almost unknown in the ancient days of the Roman republic, and the marriage tie was regarded as indissoluble. A senator was censured for kissing his wife in the presence of their daughter. But the merit of this virtue is greatly diminished if we remember that the husband always had an easy outlet for his sensual passions in the intercourse with slaves and concubines. Nor did it outlast the republic. After the Punic war the increase of wealth and luxury, and the influx of Greek and Oriental licentiousness swept away the stern old Roman virtues. The customary civil and religious rites of marriage were gradually disused; the open community of life between persons of similar rahk was taken as sufficient evidence of their nuptials; and marriage, after Augustus, fell to the level of any partnership, which might be dissolved by the abdication of one of the associates. "Passion, interest, or caprice," says Gibbon on the imperial age, "suggested daily motives for the dissolution of marriage; a word, a sign, a message, a letter, the mandate of a freedman, declared the separation; the most tender of human connections was degraded to a transient society of profit or pleasure." [1]

---

[1] Gibbon (ch. XLIV.) confirms the statement by several examples, to which more might be added. Mæcenas, "*qui uxores millies duxit*" (Seneca, *Ep.* 114) was as notorious for his levity in forming and dissolving the nuptial tie, as famous for his patronage of literature and art. Martial (*Epigr.* VI. 7), though in evident poetical exaggeration, speaks of ten husbands in one month. Juvenal (*Satir.* VI. 229) exposes a matron, who in five years submitted to the embraces of eight husbands. Jerome (*Ad Gerontiam*) "saw at Rome a triumphant husband bury his twenty-first wife, who had interred twenty-two of his less sturdy predecessors." These are extreme cases, and hardly furnish a sufficient basis for a general judgment of the state of society in Rome, much less in the provinces. We should not forget the noble and faithful Roman women even in the days of imperial corruption, as Mallonia, who preferred suicide to the embraces of Tiberius; Helvia, the mother of Seneca, and Paulina his wife, who opened her veins to accompany him to the grave; the elder Arria who, when her husband Pætus was condemned to death under Claudius (42), and hesitated to commit suicide, plunged the dagger in her breast, and, drawing it out, said to him with her dying breath: "My Pætus, it does not pain" (*Pœte, non dolet*); and her worthy daughter, Cæcinia Arria, the wife of Thrasea, who was condemned to death (66), and her granddaughter Fannia, who accompanied her husband Helvidius Priscus twice into

Various remedies were tardily adopted as the evil spread, but they proved inefficient, until the spirit of Christianity gained the control of public opinion and improved the Roman legislation, which, however, continued for a long time to fluctuate between the custom of heathenism and the wishes of the church.

Another radical evil of heathen family life, which the church had to encounter throughout the whole extent of the Roman Empire, was the absolute tyrannical authority of the parent over the children, extending even to the power of life and death, and placing the adult son of a Roman citizen on a level with the movable things and slaves, " whom the capricious master might alienate or destroy, without being responsible to any earthly tribunal."

With this was connected the unnatural and monstrous custom of exposing poor, sickly, and deformed children to a cruel death, or in many cases to a life of slavery and infamy—a custom expressly approved, for the public interest, even by a Plato, an Aristotle, and a Seneca! " Monstrous offspring," says the great Stoic philosopher, " we destroy ; children too, if born feeble and ill-formed, we drown. It is not wrath, but reason, thus to separate the useless from the healthy." " The exposition of children "—to quote once more from Gibbon—" was the prevailing and stubborn vice of antiquity: it was sometimes prescribed,

banishment, and suffered a third for his sake after his execution (93). See Pliny, *Epist.* III. 16; Tacitus, *Ann.* XVI. 30–34; Friedlaender, I. 459 sqq. Nor should we overlook the monumental evidences of conjugal devotion and happiness in numerous Roman epitaphs. See Friedlaender, I. 463. Yet sexual immorality reached perhaps its lowest depths in imperial Rome, far lower than in the worst periods of the dark ages, or in England under Charles II., or in France under Louis XIV. and XV. And it is also certain, as Lecky says (II. 326), " that frightful excesses of unnatural passion, of which the most corrupt of modern courts present no parallel, were perpetrated with but little concealment on the Palatine." Prenuptial unchastity of men was all but universal among the Romans, according to Cicero's testimony. Even Epictetus, the severest among the Stoic moralists, enjoins only moderation, not entire abstinence, from this form of vice. Lampridius relates of Alexander Severus, who otherwise legislated against vice, that he provided his unmarried provincial governors with a concubine as a part of their outfit, because " they could not exist without one " (*quod sine concubinis esse non possent*)."

often permitted, almost always practised with impunity by the nations who never entertained the Roman ideas of paternal power; and the dramatic poets, who appeal to the human heart, represent with indifference a popular custom which was palliated by the motives of economy and compassion. . . . The Roman Empire was stained with the blood of infants, till such murders were included, by Valentinian and his colleagues, in the letter and spirit of the Cornelian law. The lessons of jurisprudence and Christianity had been insufficient to eradicate this inhuman practice, till their gentle influence was fortified by the terrors of capital punishment."[1]

§ 99. *The Christian Family.*

Such was the condition of the domestic life of the ancient world, when Christianity, with its doctrine of the sanctity of marriage, with its injunction of chastity, and with its elevation of woman from her half-slavish condition to moral dignity and equality with man, began the work of a silent transformation, which secured incalculable blessings to generations yet unborn. It laid the foundation for a well-ordered family life. It turned the eye from the outward world to the inward sphere of affection, from the all-absorbing business of politics and state-life into the sanctuary of home; and encouraged the nurture of those virtues of private life, without which no true public virtue can exist. But, as the evil here to be abated, particularly the degradation of the female sex and the want of chastity, was so deeply rooted and thoroughly interwoven in the whole life of the old world, this ennobling of the family, like the abolition of slavery, was necessarily a very slow process. We cannot wonder, therefore, at the high estimate of celibacy, which in the eyes of many seemed to be the only radical escape from the impurity and misery of married life as it generally stood among the heathen. But, although the fathers are much more frequent and enthusiastic in the praise of virginity than in that of marriage,

[1] Ch. XLIV. See a good chapter on the exposure of children in Brace, *Gesta Christi*, p. 72–83.

yet their views on this subject show an immense advance upon the moral standard of the greatest sages and legislators of Greece and Rome.

CHASTITY before marriage, in wedlock, and in celibacy, in man as well as in woman, so rare in paganism, was raised to the dignity of a cardinal virtue and made the corner-stone of the family. Many a female martyr preferred cruel torture and death to the loss of honor. When St. Perpetua fell half dead from the horns of a wild bull in the arena, she instinctively drew together her dress, which had been torn in the assault. The acts of martyrs and saints tell marvellous stories, exaggerated no doubt, yet expressive of the ruling Christian sentiment, about heroic resistance to carnal temptation, the sudden punishment of unjust charges of impurity by demoniacal possession or instant death, the rescue of courtesans from a life of shame and their radical conversion and elevation even to canonical sanctity.[1] The ancient councils deal much with carnal sins so fearfully prevalent, and unanimously condemn them in every shape and form. It is true, chastity in the early church and by the unanimous consent of the fathers was almost identified with celibacy, as we shall see hereafter; but this excess should not blind us to the immense advance of patristic over heathen morals.

WOMAN was emancipated, in the best sense of the term, from the bondage of social oppression, and made the life and light of a Christian home. Such pure and heroic virgins as the martyred Blandina, and Perpetua, and such devoted mothers as Nonna, Anthusa, and Monica, we seek in vain among the ancient Greek and Roman maidens and matrons, and we need not wonder that the heathen Libanius, judging from such examples as

---

[1] Among the converted courtesans of the ancient church in the Roman calendar are St. Mary Magdalene, St. Mary of Egypt, St. Afra, St. Pelagia, St. Thais, and St. Theodota. See Charles de Bussy, *Les Courtisanes saintes.* St. Vitalius, it is said, visited dens of vice every night, gave money to the inmates to keep them from sin, and offered up prayers for their conversion. A curious story is told of St. Serapion, who went to such a place by appointment, and prayed and prayed and prayed till the unfortunate courtesan was converted and fell half dead at his feet. See Lecky, II. 338.

the mother of his pupil Chrysostom, reluctantly exclaimed: "What women have these Christians!" The schoolmen of the middle ages derived from the formation of woman an ingenious argument for her proper position: Eve was not taken from the feet of Adam to be his slave, nor from his head to be his ruler, but from his side to be his beloved partner.[1]

At the same time here also we must admit that the ancient church was yet far behind the ideal set up in the New Testament, and counterbalanced the elevation of woman by an extravagant over-estimate of celibacy. It was the virgin far more than the faithful wife and mother of children that was praised and glorified by the fathers; and among the canonized saints of the Catholic calendar there is little or no room for husbands and wives, although the patriarchs, Moses, and some of the greatest prophets (Isaiah, Ezekiel), and apostles (Peter taking the lead) lived in honorable wedlock.

MARRIAGE was regarded in the church from the beginning as a sacred union of body and soul for the propagation of civil society, and the kingdom of God, for the exercise of virtue and the promotion of happiness. It was clothed with a sacramental or semi-sacramental character on the basis of Paul's comparison of the marriage union with the relation of Christ to his church.[2]

---

[1] This beautiful idea (often attributed to Matthew Henry, the commentator) was first suggested by Augustin. *De Genesi ad Literam*, l. IX. c. 13 (in Migne's ed. of *Opera*, III. col. 402), and fully stated by Peter the Lombard, *Sentent.* l. II. Dist. XVIII. (*de formatione mulieris*): "*Mulier de viro, non de qualibet parte corporis viri, sed de latere eius formata est, ut ostenderetur quia in consortium creabatur dilectionis, ne forte si fuisset de capite facta, viro ad dominationem videretur preferenda; aut si de pedibus, ad servitutem subjicienda. Quia igitur viro nec domina, nec ancilla parabatur, sed socia, nec capite, nec de pedibus, sed de latere fuerat producenda, ut juxta se ponendam cognosceret quam de suo latere sumptam didicisset.*" And again by Thomas Aquinas, *Summa Theol.* Pars. 1. Quaest. XCII. Art. III. (in Migne's ed. I. col. 1231).

[2] Eph. 5: 28–32. The Vulgate translates τὸ μυστήριον in ver. 32 by *sacramentum*, and thus furnished a quasi-exegetical foundation to the Catholic doctrine of the sacrament of marriage. The passage is so used by the Council of Trent and in the Roman Catechism. Ellicott (*in loc.*) judges that "the words cannot possibly be urged in favor of the *sacramental* nature of marriage, but that the very fact of the comparison does place marriage on a far holier and higher basis than modern theories are disposed to admit." Bengel refers "the

It was in its nature indissoluble except in case of adultery, and this crime was charged not only to the woman, but to the man as even the more guilty party, and to every extra-connubial carnal connection. Thus the wife was equally protected against the wrongs of the husband, and chastity was made the general law of the family life.

We have a few descriptions of Christian homes from the ante-Nicene age, one from an eminent Greek father, another from a married presbyter of the Latin church.

Clement of Alexandria enjoins upon Christian married persons united prayer and reading of the Scriptures,[1] as a daily morning exercise, and very beautifully says: "The mother is the glory of her children, the wife is the glory of her husband, both are the glory of the wife, God is the glory of all together."[2]

Tertullian, at the close of the book which he wrote to his wife, draws the following graphic picture, which, though somewhat idealized, could be produced only from the moral spirit of the gospel and actual experience:[3] "How can I paint the happiness of a marriage which the church ratifies, the oblation (the celebration of the communion) confirms, the benediction seals, angels announce, the Father declares valid. Even upon earth, indeed, sons do not legitimately marry without the consent of their fathers. What a union of two believers—one hope, one vow, one discipline, and one worship! They are brother and sister, two fellow-servants, one spirit and one flesh. Where there is one flesh, there is also one spirit. They pray together, fast together, instruct, exhort, and support each other. They go together to the church of God, and to the table of the Lord. They share each other's tribulation, persecution, and revival. Neither conceals anything from the other; neither avoids, neither annoys the other. They delight to visit the sick, supply

---

mystery" not to marriage, but to the union of Christ with the church ("*non matrimonium humanum sed ipsa conjunctio Christi et ecclesiæ*"). Meyer refers it to the preceding quotation from Genesis; Estius and Ellicott to the intimate conjugal relationship.

[1] Εὐχὴ καὶ ἀνάγνωσις.   [2] *Pædag.* III. 250.   [3] *Ad Uxorem*, l. II. c. 8.

the needy, give alms without constraint, and in daily zeal lay their offerings before the altar without scruple or hindrance. They do not need to keep the sign of the cross hidden, nor to express slyly their Christian joy, nor to suppress the blessing. Psalms and hymns they sing together, and they vie with each other in singing to God. Christ rejoices when he sees and hears this. He gives them his peace. Where two are together in his name, there is he; and where he is, there the evil one cannot come."

A large sarcophagus represents a scene of family worship: on the right, four men, with rolls in their hands, reading or singing; on the left, three women and a girl playing a lyre.

For the conclusion of a marriage, Ignatius[1] required "the consent of the bishop, that it might be a marriage for God, and not for pleasure. All should be done to the glory of God." In Tertullian's time,[2] as may be inferred from the passage just quoted, the solemnization of marriage was already at least a religious act, though not a proper sacrament, and was sealed by the celebration of the holy communion in presence of the congregation. The Montanists were disposed even to make this benediction of the church necessary to the validity of marriage among Christians. All noisy and wanton Jewish and heathen nuptial ceremonies, and at first also the crowning of the bride, were discarded; but the nuptial ring, as a symbol of union, was retained.

In the catacombs the marriage ceremony is frequently represented by the man and the woman standing side by side and joining hands in token of close union, as also on heathen documents. On a gilded glass of the fourth century, the couple join hands over a small nuptial altar, and around the figures are inscribed the words (of the priest): "May ye live in God."[3]

---

[1] *Ad Polyc.* c. 5. In the Syr. version, c. 2.

[2] Tert. *Ad Uxor.* II. 8; comp. *De Monog.* c. 11; *De Pudic.* c. 4.

[3] *Vivatis in Deo.* See the picture in Northcote and Brownlow, II. 303. In other and later pictures the ceremony is presided over by Christ, who either crowns the married couple, or is represented by his monogram. *Ibid.* p. 302.

MIXED MARRIAGES with heathens, and also with heretics, were unanimously condemned by the voice of the church in agreement with the Mosaic legislation, unless formed before conversion, in which case they were considered valid.[1] Tertullian even classes such marriages with adultery. What heathen, asks he, will let his wife attend the nightly meetings of the church, and the slandered supper of the Lord, take care of the sick even in the poorest hovels, kiss the chains of the martyrs in prison, rise in the night for prayer, and show hospitality to strange brethren? Cyprian calls marriage with an unbeliever a prostitution of the members of Christ. The Council of Elvira in Spain (306) forbade such mixed marriages on pain of excommunication, but did not dissolve those already existing. We shall understand this strictness, if, to say nothing of the heathen marriage rites, and the wretchedly loose notions on chastity and conjugal fidelity, we consider the condition of those times, and the offences and temptations which met the Christian in the constant sight of images of the household gods, mythological pictures on the walls, the floor, and the furniture; in the libations at table; in short, at every step and turn in a pagan house.

SECOND MARRIAGE.—From the high view of marriage, and also from an ascetic over-estimate of celibacy, arose a very prevalent aversion to re-marriage, particularly of widows. The Shepherd of Hermas allows this reunion indeed, but with the reservation, that continuance in single life earns great honor with the Lord. Athenagoras goes so far as to call the second marriage a "decent adultery."[2]

The Montanists and Novatians condemned re-marriage, and made it a subject of discipline.

---

[1] According to 1 Cor. 7 : 12, 16.

[2] *Legat.* 33 : Ὁ δεύτερος γάμος εὐπρεπής ἐστι μοιχεία. According to Origen, digamists may be saved, but will not be crowned by Christ (*Hom.* XVII. *in Luc.*). Theophilus, *Ad Autol.* III. 15, says that with the Christians ἐγκράτεια ἀσκεῖται, μονογαμία τηρεῖται. Perhaps even Irenæus held a similar view, to judge from the manner in which he speaks of the woman of Samaria (John 4 : 7), "*quæ in uno viro non mansit, sed fornicata est in multis nuptiis.*" *Adv. Haer.* III. 17, § 2.

Tertullian came forward with the greatest decision, as advocate of monogamy against both successive and simultaneous polygamy.[1] He thought thus to occupy the true middle ground between the ascetic Gnostics, who rejected marriage altogether, and the Catholics, who allowed more than one.[2] In the earlier period of his life, when he drew the above picture of Christian marriage, before his adoption of Montanism, he already placed a high estimate on celibacy as a superior grade of Christian holiness, appealing to 1 Cor. 7: 9, and advised at least his wife, in case of his death, not to marry again, especially with a heathen; but in his Montanistic writings, " De Exhortatione Castitatis " and " De Monogamia," he repudiates second marriage from principle, and with fanatical zeal contends against it as unchristian, as an act of polygamy, nay of " stuprum" and " adulterium." He opposes it with all sorts of acute argument; now, on the ground of an ideal conception of marriage as a spiritual union of two souls for time and eternity; now, from an opposite sensuous view; and again, on principles equally good against all marriage and in favor of celibacy. Thus, on the one hand, he argues, that the second marriage impairs the spiritual fellowship with the former partner, which should continue beyond the grave, which should show itself in daily intercessions and in yearly celebration of the day of death, and which hopes even for outward re-union after the resurrection.[3] On the other hand, however, he places the essence of marriage in the communion of flesh,[4] and regards it as a mere concession, which God makes to

[1] Comp. Hauber: *Tertullian's Kampf gegen die zweite Ehe*, in the "Studien und Kritiken" for 1845, p. 607 sqq.

[2] De Monog. 1: " *Hæretici nuptias auferunt, psychici ingerunt; illi nec semel, isti non semel nubunt.*"

[3] De Exhort. Cast. c. 11: " *Duplex rubor est, quia in secundo matrimonio duæ uxores eundem circumstant maritum, una spiritu, alia in carne. Neque enim pristinam poteris odisse, cui etiam religiosiorem reservas affectionem ut jam receptæ apud Dominum, pro cujus spiritu postulas, pro qua oblationes annuas reddis. Stabis ergo ad Dominum cum tot uxoribus quot in oratione commemoras, et offeres pro duabus,*" etc.

[4] De Exhort. Cast. c. 9: " *Leges videntur matrimonii et stupri differentiam facere, per diversitatem illiciti, non per conditionem rei ipsius . . . . Nuptiæ ipsæ ex eo constant quod est stuprum.*"

our sensuality, and which man therefore should not abuse by repetition. The ideal of the Christian life, with him, not only for the clergy, but the laity also, is celibacy. He lacks clear perception of the harmony of the moral and physical elements which constitutes the essence of marriage; and strongly as he elsewhere combats the Gnostic dualism, he here falls in with it in his depreciation of matter and corporeity, as necessarily incompatible with spirit. His treatment of the exegetical arguments of the defenders of second marriage is remarkable. The levirate law, he says, is peculiar to the Old Testament economy. To Rom. 7: 2 he replies, that Paul speaks here from the position of the Mosaic law, which, according to the same passage, is no longer binding on Christians. In 1 Cor. ch. 7, the apostle allows second marriage only in his subjective, human judgment, and from regard to our sensuous infirmity; but in the same chapter (ver. 40) he recommends celibacy to all, and that on the authority of the Lord, adding here, that he also has the Holy Spirit, *i. e.* the principle, which is active in the new prophets of Montanism. The appeal to 1 Tim. 3: 2; Tit. 1: 6, from which the right of laymen to second marriage was inferred, as the prohibition of it there related only to the clergy, he met with the doctrine of the universal priesthood of believers, which admitted them all both to the privileges and to the obligations of priests. But his reasoning always amounts in the end to this : that the state of original virgin purity, which has nothing at all to do with the sensual, is the best. The true chastity consists, therefore, not in the chaste spirit of married partners, but in the entire continence of *"virgines"* and *"spadones."* The desire of posterity, he, contrary to the Old Testament, considers unworthy of a Christian, who, in fact, ought to break away entirely from the world, and renounce all inheritance in it. Such a morality, forbidding the same that it allows, and rigorously setting as an ideal what it must in reality abate at least for the mass of mankind, may be very far above the heathen level, but is still plainly foreign to the deeper substance and the world-sanctifying principle of Christianity.

The Catholic church, indeed, kept aloof from this Montanistic extravagance, and forbade second marriage only to the clergy (which the Greek church does to this day); yet she rather advised against it, and leaned very decidedly towards a preference for celibacy, as a higher grade of Christian morality.[1]

As to the relation of PARENTS and CHILDREN, Christianity exerted from the beginning a most salutary influence. It restrained the tyrannical power of the father. It taught the eternal value of children as heirs of the kingdom of heaven, and commenced the great work of education on a religious and moral basis. It resisted with all energy the exposition of children, who were then generally devoured by dogs and wild beasts, or, if found, trained up for slavery or doomed to a life of infamy. Several apologists, the author to the Epistle of Diognetus, Justin Martyr,[2] Minutius Felix, Tertullian, and Arnobius speak with just indignation against this unnatural custom. Athenagoras declares abortion and exposure to be equal to murder.[3] No heathen philosopher had advanced so far. Lactantius also puts exposure on a par with murder even of the worst kind, and admits no excuse on the ground of pity or poverty, since God provides for all his creatures.[4] The Christian spirit of

---

[1] "*Non prohibemus secundas nuptias*," says Ambrose, "*sed non suademus*." None of the fathers recommends re-marriage or even approves of it. Jerome represented the prevailing view of the Nicene age. He took the lowest view of marriage as a mere safeguard against fornication and adultery, and could conceive of no other motive for second or third marriage but animal passion. "The first Adam," he says, "had one wife; the second Adam had no wife. Those who approve of digamy hold forth a third Adam, who was twice married, whom they follow" (*Contra Jovin.* 1). Gregory of Nazianzum infers from the analogy of marriage to the union of Christ with his church that second marriage is to be reproved, as there is but one Christ and one church (*Orat.* XXXI).

[2] *Apol.* I. 27 and 29.   [3] *Apol.* c. 35.

[4] *Inst. Div.* vi. 20 (p. 48 ed. Lips.): "Let no one imagine that even this is allowed, to strangle newly-born children, which is the greatest impiety; for God breathes into their souls for life, and not for death. But men (that there may be no crime with which they may not pollute their hands) deprive souls as yet innocent and simple of the light which they themselves have not given. Can they be considered innocent who expose their own offspring as a prey to dogs, and as far as it depends upon themselves, kill them in a more cruel

humanity gradually so penetrated the spirit of the age that the better emperors, from the time of Trajan, began to direct their attention to the diminution of these crying evils ; but the best legal enactments would never have been able to eradicate them without the spiritual influence of the church. The institutions and donations of Trajan, Antonius Pius, Septimius Severus, and private persons, for the education of poor children, boys and girls, were approaches of the nobler heathen towards the genius of Christianity. Constantine proclaimed a law in 315 throughout Italy "to turn parents from using a parricidal hand on their new-born children, and to dispose their hearts to the best sentiments." The Christian fathers, councils, emperors, and lawgivers united their efforts to uproot this monstrous evil and to banish it from the civilized world.[1]

§ 100. *Brotherly Love, and Love for Enemies.*

SCHAUBACH : *Das Verhältniss der Moral des classischen Alterthums zur christlichen, beleuchtet durch vergleichende Erörterung der Lehre von der Feindesliebe*, in the "Studien und Kritiken" for 1851, p. 59–121. Also the works of SCHMIDT, CHASTEL, UHLHORN, etc., quoted at § 88.

IT is generally admitted, that selfishness was the soul of heathen morality. The great men of antiquity rose above its sordid forms, love of gain and love of pleasure, but were the more

---

manner than if they had strangled them ? Who can doubt that he is impious who gives occasion for the pity of others ? For, although that which he has wished should befall the child—namely, that it should be brought up—he has certainly consigned his own offspring either to servitude or to the brothel ? But who does not understand, who is ignorant what things may happen, or are accustomed to happen, in the case of each sex, even through error ? For this is shown by the example of Œdipus alone, confused with twofold guilt. It is therefore as wicked to expose as it is to kill. But truly parricides complain of the scantiness of their means, and allege that they have not enough for bringing up more children ; as though, in truth, their means were in the power of those who possess them, or God did not daily make the rich poor, and the poor rich. Wherefore, if any one on account of poverty shall be unable to bring up children, it is better to abstain from marriage than with wicked hands to mar the work of God."

[1] For further details see Brace, *l. c.* 79 sqq., and Terme et Monfalcon, *Hist. des enfants trouvés.* Paris, 1840.

under the power of ambition and love of fame. It was for fame that Miltiades and Themistocles fought against the Persians; that Alexander set out on his tour of conquest; that Herodotus wrote his history, that Pindar sang his odes, that Sophocles composed his tragedies, that Demosthenes delivered his orations, that Phidias sculptured his Zeus. Fame was set forth in the Olympian games as the highest object of life; fame was held up by Æschylus as the last comfort of the suffering; fame was declared by Cicero, before a large assembly, the ruling passion of the very best of men.[1] Even the much-lauded patriotism of the heroes of ancient Greece and Rome was only an enlarged egotism. In the catalogue of classical virtues we look in vain for the two fundamental and cardinal virtues, love and humility. The very word which corresponds in Greek to humility[2] signifies generally, in classical usage, a mean, abject mind. The noblest and purest form of love known to the heathen moralist is friendship, which Cicero praises as the highest good next to wisdom. But friendship itself rested, as was freely admitted, on a utilitarian, that is, on an egotistic basis, and was only possible among persons of equal or similar rank in society. For the stranger, the barbarian, and the enemy, the Greek and Roman knew no love, but only contempt and hatred. The *jus talionis*, the return of evil for evil, was universally acknowledged throughout the heathen world as a just principle and maxim, in direct opposition to the plainest injunctions of the New Testament.[3] We must offend those who offend us, says Æschylus.[4] Not to take revenge was regarded as a sign of weakness and cowardice. To return evil for good is devilish; to return good for good is human and common to all religions; to return good

<hr>

[1] *Pro Archia poeta*, c. 11: " *Trahimur omnes laudis studio, et optimus quisque maxime gloria ducitur.*"

[2] Ταπεινός, ταπεινόφρων, ταπεινότης, ταπεινοφροσύνη.

[3] Matt. 5: 23, 24, 44; 6: 12; 18: 21. Rom. 12: 17, 19, 20. 1 Cor. 13: 7. 1 Thess. 5: 15. 1 Pet. 3: 9.

[4] *Prom. Vinct.* v. 1005, comp. 1040. Many passages of similar import from Homer, Hesiod, Sophocles, Euripides, etc., see quoted on p. 81 sqq. of the article of Schaubach referred to above.

for evil is Christlike and divine, and only possible in the Christian religion.

On the other hand, however, we should suppose that every Christian virtue must find some basis in the noblest moral instincts and aspirations of nature; since Christianity is not against nature, but simply above it and intended for it. Thus we may regard the liberality, benevolence, humanity and magnanimity which we meet with in heathen antiquity, as an approximation to, and preparation for, the Christian virtue of charity. The better schools of moralists rose more or less above the popular approval of hatred of the enemy, wrath and revenge. Aristotle and the Peripatetics, without condemning this passion as wrong in itself, enjoined at least moderation in its exercise. The Stoics went further, and required complete apathy or suppression of all strong and passionate affections. Cicero even declares placability and clemency one of the noblest traits in the character of a great man,[1] and praises Cæsar for forgetting nothing except injuries. Seneca, Epictetus, Plutarch, and Marcus Aurelius, who were already indirectly and unconsciously under the influence of the atmosphere of Christian morality, decidedly condemn anger and vindictiveness, and recommend kindness to slaves, and a generous treatment even of enemies.

But this sort of love for an enemy, it should be remembered, in the first place, does not flow naturally from the spirit of heathenism, but is, as it were, an accident and exception; secondly, it is not enjoined as a general duty, but expected only from the great and the wise; thirdly, it does not rise above the conception of magnanimity, which, more closely considered, is itself connected with a refined form of egotism, and with a noble pride that regards it below the dignity of a gentleman to notice the malice of inferior men;[2] fourthly, it is commended only in its

---

[1] De Offic. I. 25: "Nihil enim laudabilius, nihil magno et præclaro viro dignius placabilitate et clementia."

[2] Comp. Seneca, De ira II. 32: "Magni animi est injurias despicere. Ille magnus et nobilis est, qui more magnæ feræ latratus minutorum canum securus exaudit."

negative aspect as refraining from the right of retaliation, not as active benevolence and charity to the enemy, which returns good for evil; and finally, it is nowhere derived from a religious principle, the love of God to man, and therefore has no proper root, and lacks the animating soul.

No wonder, then, that in spite of the finest maxims of a few philosophers, the imperial age was controlled by the coldest selfishness, so that, according to the testimony of Plutarch, friendship had died out even in families, and the love of brothers and sisters was supposed to be possible only in a heroic age long passed by. The old Roman world was a world without charity. Julian the Apostate, who was educated a Christian, tried to engraft charity upon heathenism, but in vain. The idea of the infinite value of each human soul, even the poorest and humblest, was wanting, and with it the basis for true charity.

It was in such an age of universal egotism that Christianity first revealed the true spirit of love to man as flowing from the love of God, and exhibited it in actual life. This cardinal virtue we meet first within the Church itself, as the bond of union among believers, and the sure mark of the genuine disciple of Jesus. "That especially," says Tertullian to the heathen, in a celebrated passage of his *Apologeticus*, "which love works among us, exposes us to many a suspicion. 'Behold,' they say, 'how they love one another!' Yea, verily this must strike them; for *they* hate each other. 'And how ready they are to die for one another!' Yea, truly; for *they* are rather ready to kill one another. And even that we call each other 'brethren,' seems to them suspicious for no other reason, than that, among them, all expressions of kindred are only feigned. We are even *your* brethren, in virtue of the common nature, which is the mother of us all; though ye, as evil brethren, deny your human nature. But how much more justly are those called and considered brethren, who acknowledge the one God as their Father; who have received the one Spirit of holiness; who have awaked from the same darkness of uncertainty to the light of the same truth? ... And we, who are united in spirit and in soul, do not hesitate to have also all things common, except wives. For we break fellowship just where other men practice it."

This brotherly love flowed from community of life in Christ. Hence Ignatius calls believers "Christ-bearers" and "God-bearers."[1] The article of the Apostles' Creed : "I believe in the communion of saints;" the current appellation of "brother" and "sister;" and the fraternal kiss usual on admission into the church, and at the Lord's Supper, were not empty forms, nor even a sickly sentimentalism, but the expression of true feeling and experience, only strengthened by the common danger and persecution. A travelling Christian, of whatever language or country, with a letter of recommendation from his bishop,[2] was everywhere hospitably received as a long known friend. It was a current phrase : In thy brother thou hast seen the Lord himself. The force of love reached beyond the grave. Families were accustomed to celebrate at appointed times the memory of their departed members; and this was one of the grounds on which Tertullian opposed second marriage.

The brotherly love expressed itself, above all, in the most self-sacrificing beneficence to the poor and sick, to widows and orphans, to strangers and prisoners, particularly to confessors in bonds. It magnifies this virtue in our view, to reflect, that the Christians at that time belonged mostly to the lower classes, and in times of persecution often lost all their possessions. Every congregation was a charitable society, and in its public worship took regular collections for its needy members. The offerings at the communion and love-feasts, first held on the evening, afterwards on the morning of the Lord's Day, were considered a part of worship.[3] To these were added numberless private charities, given in secret, which eternity alone will reveal. The church at Rome had under its care a great multitude of widows, orphans,

---

[1] Χριστοφόροι, θεοφόροι.

[2] Γράμματα τετυπωμένα or κοινωνικά; epistolæ or literæ formatæ ; so called, because composed after a certain τύπος or forma, to guard against frequent forgeries.

[3] Comp. James 1: 27; Hebr. 13: 1–3, 16.

blind, lame, and sick,[1] whom the deacon Laurentius, in the Decian persecution, showed to the heathen prefect, as the most precious treasures of the church. It belonged to the idea of a Christian housewife, and was particularly the duty of the deaconesses, to visit the Lord, to clothe him, and give him meat and drink, in the persons of his needy disciples. Even such opponents of Christianity as Lucian testify to this zeal of the Christians in labors of love, though they see in it nothing but an innocent fanaticism. "It is incredible," says Lucian, "to see the ardor with which the people of that religion help each other in their wants. They spare nothing. Their first legislator has put into their heads that they are all brethren."[2]

This beneficence reached beyond the immediate neighborhood. Charity begins at home, but does not stay at home. In cases of general distress the bishops appointed special collections, and also fasts, by which food might be saved for suffering brethren. The Roman church sent its charities great distances abroad.[3] Cyprian of Carthage, who, after his conversion, sold his own estates for the benefit of the poor, collected a hundred thousand sestertia, or more than three thousand dollars, to redeem Christians of Numidia, who had been taken captive by neighboring barbarians; and he considered it a high privilege "to be able to ransom for a small sum of money him, who has redeemed us from the dominion of Satan with his own blood." A father, who refused to give alms on account of his children, Cyprian charged with the additional sin of binding his children to an earthly inheritance, instead of pointing them to the richest and most loving Father in heaven.

Finally, this brotherly love expanded to love even for enemies, which returned the heathens good for evil, and not rarely, in persecutions and public misfortunes, heaped coals of fire on their heads. During the persecution under Gallus (252), when the pestilence raged in Carthage, and the heathens threw out their dead and sick upon the streets, ran away from them for

[1] Cornelius, in Euseb. *H. E.* VI. 43.   [2] *De Morte Peregr.* c. 13.
[3] Dionysius of Corinth, in Eus. IV. 23.

fear of the contagion, and cursed the Christians as the supposed
authors of the plague, Cyprian assembled his congregation, and
exhorted them to love their enemies; whereupon all went to
work; the rich with their money, the poor with their hands,
and rested not, till the dead were buried, the sick cared for, and
the city saved from desolation. The same self-denial appeared
in the Christians of Alexandria during a ravaging plague under
the reign of Gallienus. These are only a few prominent mani-
festations of a spirit which may be traced through the whole
history of martyrdom and the daily prayers of the Christians for
their enemies and persecutors. For while the love of friends,
says Tertullian, is common to all men, the love of enemies is a
virtue peculiar to Christians.[1] "You forget," he says to the
heathens in his Apology, "that, notwithstanding your persecutions, far from conspiring against you, as our numbers would
perhaps furnish us with the means of doing, we pray for you
and do good to you; that, if we give nothing for your gods, we
do give for your poor, and that our charity spreads more alms
in your streets than the offerings presented by your religion in
your temples."

The organized congregational charity of the ante-Nicene age
provided for all the immediate wants. When the state professed
Christianity, there sprang up permanent charitable institutions
for the poor, the sick, for strangers, widows, orphans, and helpless old men.[2] The first clear proof of such institutions we find
in the age of Julian the Apostate, who tried to check the progress of Christianity and to revive paganism by directing the
high priest of Galatia, Arsacius, to establish in every town a
Xenodochium to be supported by the state and also by private
contributions; for, he said, it was a shame that the heathen

---

[1] *Ad Scapulam*, c. 1 : " *Ita enim disciplina jubemur diligere inimicos quoque et
orare pro iis qui nos persequuntur, ut haec sit perfecta et propria bonitas nostra,
non communis. Amicos enim diligere omnium est, inimicos autem solorum Christianorum.*"

[2] Nosocomia, Ptochotrophia, Xenodochia, Cherotrophia, Orphanotrophia,
Brephotrophia, Gerontocomia (for old men).

should be left without support from their own, while "among the Jews no beggar can be found, and the godless Galilæans" (*i. e.* the Christians) "nourish not only their own, but even our own poor." A few years afterwards (370) we hear of a celebrated hospital at Cæsarea, founded by St. Basilius, and called after him "Basilias," and similar institutions all over the province of Cappadocia. We find one at Antioch at the time of Chrysostom, who took a practical interest in it. At Constantinople there were as many as thirty-five hospitals. In the West such institutions spread rapidly in Rome, Sicily, Sardinia, and Gaul.[1]

§ 101. *Prayer and Fasting.*

In regard to the importance and the necessity of prayer, as the pulse and thermometer of spiritual life, the ancient church had but one voice. Here the plainest and the most enlightened Christians met; the apostolic fathers, the steadfast apologists, the realistic Africans, and the idealistic Alexandrians. Tertullian sees in prayer the daily sacrifice of the Christian, the bulwark of faith, the weapon against all the enemies of the soul. The believer should not go to his bath nor take his food without prayer; for the nourishing and refreshing of the spirit must precede that of the body, and the heavenly must go before the earthly. "Prayer," says he, "blots out sins, repels temptations, quenches persecutions, comforts the desponding, blesses the highminded, guides the wanderers, calms the billows, feeds the poor, directs the rich, raises the fallen, holds up the falling, preserves them that stand." Cyprian requires prayer by day and by night; pointing to heaven, where we shall never cease to pray and give thanks. The same father, however, falls already into that false, unevangelical view, which represents prayer as a meritorious work and a satisfaction to be rendered to God.[2] Clement of

---

[1] See Uhlhorn, Book III. ch. 4 (p. 319 sqq.).

[2] *De Orat. Domin.* 33: "*Cito orationes ad Deum adscendunt, quas ad Deum merita operis nostri imponunt.*" *De Lapsis* 17: "*Dominus orandus est, Dominus nostra satisfactione placandus est.*" *Epist.* xl. 2: "*Preces et orationes, quibus Dominus longa et continua satisfactione placandus est.*"

Alexandria conceives the life of a genuine Christian as an unbroken prayer. "In every place he will pray, though not
openly, in the sight of the multitude. Even on his walks, in
his intercourse with others, in silence, in reading, and in labor,
he prays in every way. And though he commune with God
only in the chamber of his soul, and call upon the Father only
with a quiet sigh, the Father is near him." The same idea we
find in Origen, who discourses in enthusiastic terms of the
mighty inward and outward effects of prayer, and with all his
enormous learning, regards prayer as the sole key to the spiritual
meaning of the Scriptures.

The order of human life, however, demands special times for
this consecration of the every-day business of men. The Christians generally followed the Jewish usage, observed as times of
prayer the hours of nine, twelve, and three, corresponding also
to the crucifixion of Christ, his death, and his descent from the
cross; the cock-crowing likewise, and the still hour of midnight
they regarded as calls to prayer.

With prayer for their own welfare, they united intercessions
for the whole church, for all classes of men, especially for the
sick and the needy, and even for the unbelieving. Polycarp
enjoins on the church of Philippi to pray for all the saints, for
kings and rulers, for haters and persecutors, and for the enemies
of the cross. "We pray," says Tertullian, "even for the emperors and their ministers, for the holders of power on earth, for
the repose of all classes, and for the delay of the end of the
world."

With the free outpourings of the heart, without which living
piety cannot exist, we must suppose, that, after the example of
the Jewish church, standing forms of prayer were also used,
especially such as were easily impressed on the memory and
could thus be freely delivered. The familiar " ex pectore " and
" sine monitore " of Tertullian prove nothing against this; for a
prayer committed to memory may and should be at the same
time a prayer of the heart, as a familiar psalm or hymn may be
read or sung with ever new devotion. The general use of the

Lord's Prayer in the ancient church in household and public worship is beyond all doubt. The *Didache* (ch. 8) enjoins it three times a day. Tertullian, Cyprian, Origen, wrote special treatises upon it. They considered it the model prayer, prescribed by the Lord for the whole church. Tertullian calls it the "regular and usual prayer, a brief summary of the whole gospel, and foundation of all the other prayers of the Christians." The use of it, however, was restricted to communicants; because the address presupposes the worshipper's full sonship with God, and because the fourth petition was taken in a mystical sense, as referring to the holy Supper, and was therefore thought not proper for catechumens.

As to posture in prayer; kneeling or standing, the raising or closing of the eyes, the extension or elevation of the hands, were considered the most suitable expressions of a bowing spirit and a soul directed towards God. On Sunday the standing posture was adopted, in token of festive joy over the resurrection from sin and death. But there was no uniform law in regard to these forms. Origen lays chief stress on the lifting of the soul to God and the bowing of the heart before him; and says that, where circumstances require, one can worthily pray sitting, or lying, or engaged in business.

After the Jewish custom, FASTING was frequently joined with prayer, that the mind, unencumbered by earthly matter, might devote itself with less distraction to the contemplation of divine things. The apostles themselves sometimes employed this wholesome discipline,[1] though without infringing the gospel freedom by legal prescriptions. As the Pharisees were accustomed to fast twice in the week, on Monday and Thursday, the Christians appointed Wednesday and especially Friday, as days of half-fasting or abstinence from flesh,[2] in commemoration of the passion and crucifixion of Jesus. They did this with reference to the Lord's words: "When the bridegroom shall be taken away from them, then will they fast."[3]

[1] Comp. Acts 13: 2; 14: 23; 2 Cor. 6: 5.
[2] *Semijejunium, abstinentia.*
[3] Matt. 9: 15.

In the second century arose also the custom of Quadragesimal fasts before Easter, which, however, differed in length in different countries; being sometimes reduced to forty hours, sometimes extended to forty days, or at least to several weeks. Perhaps equally ancient are the nocturnal fasts or vigils before the high festivals, suggested by the example of the Lord and the apostles.[1] But the Quatemporal fasts[2] are of later origin, though founded likewise on a custom of the Jews after the exile. On special occasions the bishops appointed extraordinary fasts, and applied the money saved to charitable purposes; a usage which became often a blessing to the poor. Yet hierarchical arrogance and Judaistic legalism early intruded here, even to the entire destruction of the liberty of a Christian man.[3]

This rigidity appeared most in the Montanists. Besides the usual fasts, they observed special *Xerophagiæ*,[4] as they were called; seasons of two weeks for eating only dry, or properly uncooked food, bread, salt, and water. The Catholic church, with true feeling, refused to sanction these excesses as a general rule, but allowed ascetics to carry fasting even to extremes. A confessor in Lyons, for example, lived on bread and water alone, but forsook that austerity when reminded that he gave offence to other Christians by so despising the gifts of God.

Against the frequent over-valuation of fasting, Clement of Alexandria quotes the word of Paul: The kingdom of God is not meat and drink, therefore neither abstinence from wine and flesh, but righteousness and peace and joy in the Holy Spirit.

§ 102. *Treatment of the Dead.*

Comp. Chapter VII. on the Catacombs.

The pious care of the living for the beloved dead is rooted in the noblest instincts of human nature, and is found among all nations, ancient and modern, even among barbarians. Hence

---

[1] Luke 6: 12. Acts 16: 25. [2] From *quatuor tempora.*
[3] Comp. Matt. 9: 15; Gal. 4: 9; 5: 1.
[4] Ξηροφαγίαι, *aridus victus.* See Tertullian, *De Jejuu,* 15; Hippolytus, *Philos.* VIII. 19.

the general custom of surrounding the funeral with solemn rites and prayers, and giving the tomb a sacred and inviolable character. The profane violation of the dead and robbery of graves were held in desecration, and punished by law.[1] No traditions and laws were more sacred among the Egyptians, Greeks, and Romans than those that guarded and protected the shades of the departed who can do no harm to any of the living. "It is the popular belief," says Tertullian, "that the dead cannot enter Hades before they are buried." Patroclus appears after his death to his friend Achilles in a dream, and thus exhorts him to provide for his speedy burial:

> "Achilles, sleepest thou, forgetting me?
> Never of me unmindful in my life,
> Thou dost neglect me dead. O, bury me
> Quickly, and give me entrance through the gates
> Of Hades; for the souls, the forms of those
> Who live no more, repulse me, suffering not
> That I should join their company beyond
> The river, and I now must wander round
> The spacious portals of the House of Death."[2]

Christianity intensified this regard for the departed, and gave it a solid foundation by the doctrine of the immortality of the soul and the resurrection of the body. Julian the Apostate traced the rapid spread and power of that religion to three causes: benevolence, care of the dead, and honesty.[3] After the persecution under Marcus Aurelius, the Christians in Southern Gaul were much distressed because the enraged heathens would not deliver them the corpses of their brethren for burial.[4] Sometimes the vessels of the church were sold for the purpose. During the ravages of war, famine, and pestilence, they considered it their duty to bury the heathen as well as their fellow-

[1] And it occurs occasionally even among Christian nations. The corpse of the richest merchant prince of New York, Alexander T. Stewart (d. 1876), was stolen from St. Mark's grave-yard, and his splendid mausoleum in Garden City on Long Island is empty.

[2] *Iliad* XXIII. 81–88, in Bryant's translation (II. 284).

[3] *Epist.* XLIX. ad Arsacium, the pagan high-priest in Galatia.

[4] Eus. IX. 8.

Christians. When a pestilence depopulated the cities in the
reign of the tyrannical persecutor Maximinus, "the Christians
were the only ones in the midst of such distressing circumstances
that exhibited sympathy and humanity in their conduct. They
continued the whole day, some in the care and burial of the
dead, for numberless were they for whom there was none to
care; others collected the multitude of those wasting by the
famine throughout the city, and distributed bread among all.
So that the fact was cried abroad, and men glorified the God of
the Christians, constrained, as they were by the facts, to acknowledge that these were the only really pious and the only real
worshippers of God."[1] Lactantius says: "The last and greatest
office of piety is the burying of strangers and the poor; which
subject these teachers of virtue and justice have not touched
upon at all, as they measure all their duties by utility. We will
not suffer the image and workmanship of God to lie exposed as
a prey to beasts and birds; but we will restore it to the earth,
from which it had its origin; and although it be in the case of
an unknown man, we will fulfil the office of relatives, into
whose place, since they are wanting, let kindness succeed; and
wherever there shall be need of man, there we will think that
our duty is required."[2]

The early church differed from the pagan and even from the
Jewish notions by a cheerful and hopeful view of death, and
by discarding lamentations, rending of clothes, and all signs of
extravagant grief. The terrors of the grave were dispelled by the
light of the resurrection, and the idea of death was transformed
into the idea of a peaceful slumber. No one, says Cyprian,
should be made sad by death, since in living is labor and peril,
in dying peace and the certainty of resurrection; and he quotes
the examples of Enoch who was translated, of Simeon who
wished to depart in peace, several passages from Paul, and the
assurance of the Lord that he went to the Father to prepare
heavenly mansions for us.[3] The day of a believer's death, espe-

---

[1] Eusebius, *H. E.* V. 1.   [2] *Instit. Div.* VI. c. 12   [3] *Testim. l.* III. c. 58

cially if he were a martyr, was called the day of his heavenly birth. His grave was surrounded with symbols of hope and of victory; anchors, harps, palms, crowns. The primitive Christians always showed a tender care for the dead; under a vivid impression of the unbroken communion of saints and the future resurrection of the body in glory. For Christianity redeems the body as well as the soul, and consecrates it a temple of the Holy Spirit. Hence the Greek and Roman custom of burning the corpse (*crematio*) was repugnant to Christian feeling and the sacredness of the body.[1] Tertullian even declared it a symbol of the fire of hell, and Cyprian regarded it as equivalent to apostasy. In its stead, the church adopted the primitive Jewish usage of burial (*inhumatio*),[2] practiced also by the Egyptians and Babylonians. The bodies of the dead were washed,[3] wrapped in linen cloths,[4] sometimes embalmed,[5] and then, in the presence of ministers, relatives, and friends, with prayer and singing of psalms, committed as seeds of immortality to the bosom of the earth. Funeral discourses were very common as early as the Nicene period.[6] But in the times of persecution the interment was often necessarily performed as hastily and secretly as possible. The death-days of martyrs the church celebrated annually at their graves with oblations, love feasts, and the Lord's Supper. Families likewise commemorated their departed members in the domestic circle. The current prayers for the dead were originally only thanksgivings for the grace of God

[1] Comp. 1 Cor. 3: 16; 6: 19; 2 Cor. 6: 16. Burial was the prevailing Oriental and even the earlier Roman custom before the empire, and was afterwards restored, no doubt under the influence of Christianity. Minucius Felix says (*Octav.* c. 34): " *Vetcrem et meliorem consuetudinem humandi frequentamus.*" Comp. Cicero, *De Leg.* II. 22; Pliny, *Hist. Nat.* VII. 54; Augustin, *De Civ. Dei* I. 12, 13. Sometimes dead Christians were burned during the persecution by the heathen to ridicule their hope of a resurrection.

[2] Comp. Gen. 23: 19; Matt. 27: 60; John 11: 17; Acts 5 6; 8: 2.

[3] Acts 9: 37.

[4] Matt. 27: 59; Luke 23: 53; John 11: 44.

[5] John 19: 39 sq.; 12: 7.

[6] We have the funeral orations of Eusebius at the death of Constantine, of Gregory of Nazianzum on his father, brother, and sister, of Ambrose on Theodosius.

manifested to them. But they afterwards passed into intercessions, without any warrant in the teaching of the apostles, and
in connection with questionable views in regard to the intermediate state. Tertullian, for instance, in his argument against
second marriage, says of the Christian widow, she prays for the
soul of her departed husband,[1] and brings her annual offering
on the day of his departure.

The same feeling of the inseparable communion of saints gave
rise to the usage, unknown to the heathens, of consecrated places
of common burial.[2] For these cemeteries, the Christians, in the
times of persecution, when they were mostly poor and enjoyed
no corporate rights, selected remote, secret spots, and especially
subterranean vaults, called at first *crypts*, but after the sixth
century commonly termed *catacombs*, or resting-places, which
have been discussed in a previous chapter.

We close with a few stanzas of the Spanish poet Prudentius
(d. 405), in which he gives forcible expression to the views and
feelings of the ancient church before the open grave :[3]

> "No more, ah, no more sad complaining;
>   Resign these fond pledges to earth:
> Stay, mothers, the thick-falling tear-drops;
>   This death is a heavenly birth.

> Take, Earth, to thy bosom so tender,—
>   Take, nourish this body. How fair,
> How noble in death! We surrender
>   These relics of man to thy care.

> This, this was the home of the spirit,
>   Once built by the breath of our God;
> And here, in the light of his wisdom,
>   Christ, Head of the risen, abode.

---

[1] "*Pro anima ejus orat.*" Compare, however, the prevailing cheerful tone
of the epigraphs in the catacombs, p. 301–303.

[2] Κοιμητήρια, *cimeteria, dormitoria, areæ.*

[3] From his *Iam mœsta quiesce querela,* the concluding part of his tenth
Cathemerinon, Opera, ed. Obbarius (1845), p. 41; Schaff, *Christ in Song,* p. 506
(London ed.). Another version by E. Caswall: "Cease, ye tearful mourners,
Thus your hearts to rend: Death is life's beginning Rather than its end."

Guard well the dear treasure we lend thee
The Maker, the Saviour of men:
Shall never forget His beloved,
But claim His own likeness again."

§ 103. *Summary of Moral Reforms.*

Christianity represents the thoughts and purposes of God in history. They shine as so many stars in the darkness of sin and error. They are unceasingly opposed, but make steady progress and are sure of final victory. Heathen ideas and practices with their degrading influences controlled the ethics, politics, literature, and the house and home of emperor and peasant, when the little band of despised and persecuted followers of Jesus of Nazareth began the unequal struggle against overwhelming odds and stubborn habits. It was a struggle of faith against superstition, of love against selfishness, of purity against corruption, of spiritual forces against political and social power.

Under the inspiring influence of the spotless purity of Christ's teaching and example, and aided here and there by the nobler instincts and tendencies of philosophy, the Christian church from the beginning asserted the individual rights of man, recognized the divine image in every rational being, taught the common creation and common redemption, the destination of all for immortality and glory, raised the humble and the lowly, comforted the prisoner and captive, the stranger and the exile, proclaimed chastity as a fundamental virtue, elevated woman to dignity and equality with man, upheld the sanctity and inviolability of the marriage tie, laid the foundation of a Christian family and happy home, moderated the evils and undermined the foundations of slavery, opposed polygamy and concubinage, emancipated the children from the tyrannical control of parents, denounced the exposure of children as murder, made relentless war upon the bloody games of the arena and the circus, and the shocking indecencies of the theatre, upon cruelty and oppression and every vice, infused into a heartless and loveless world the spirit of love and brotherhood, transformed sinners into saints, frail women into heroines, and lit up the darkness of the tomb by the bright ray of unending bliss in heaven.

Christianity reformed society from the bottom, and built upwards until it reached the middle and higher classes, and at last the emperor himself. Then soon after the conversion of Constantine it began to influence legislation, abolished cruel institutions, and enacted laws which breathe the spirit of justice and humanity. We may deplore the evils which followed in the train of the union of church and state, but we must not overlook its many wholesome effects upon the Justinian code which gave Christian ideas an institutional form and educational power for whole generations to this day. From that time on also began the series of charitable institutions for widows and orphans, for the poor and the sick, the blind and the deaf, the intemperate and criminal, and for the care of all unfortunate,—institutions which we seek in vain in any other but Christian countries.

Nor should the excesses of asceticism blind us against the moral heroism of renouncing rights and enjoyments innocent in themselves, but so generally abused and poisoned, that total abstinence seemed to most of the early fathers the only radical and effective cure. So in our days some of the best of men regard total abstinence rather than temperance, the remedy of the fearful evils of intemperance.

Christianity could not prevent the irruption of the Northern barbarians and the collapse of the Roman empire. The process of internal dissolution had gone too far; nations as well as individuals may physically and morally sink so low that they are beyond the possibility of recovery. Tacitus, the heathen Stoic in the second century, and Salvianus, the Christian presbyter in the fifth, each a Jeremiah of his age, predicted the approaching doom and destruction of Roman society, looked towards the savage races of the North for fresh blood and new vigor. But the Keltic and Germanic conquerors would have turned Southern Europe into a vast solitude (as the Turks have laid waste the fairest portions of Asia), if they had not embraced the principles, laws, and institutions of the Christian church.

CHAPTER IX.

ASCETIC TENDENCIES.

§ 104. Ascetic Virtue and Piety.

AD. MÖHLER (R. C.): *Geschichte des Mönchthums in der Zeit seiner ersten Entstehung u. ersten Ausbildung*, 1836 ("Vermischte Schriften," ed. Döllinger. Regensb. 1839, II. p. 165 sqq.).

Is. TAYLOR (Independent): *Ancient Christianity*, 4th ed. London, 1844, I. 133-299 (anti-Puseyite and anti Catholic).

H. RUFFNER (Presbyt.): *The Fathers of the Desert; or an Account of the Origin and Practice of Monkery among heathen nations; its passage into the church; and some wonderful Stories of the Fathers concerning the primitive Monks and Hermits.* N. York, 1850. 2 vols.

OTTO ZÖCKLER (Lutheran): *Kritische Geschichte der Askese.* Frkf. and Erlangen, 1863 (434 pages).

P. E. LUCIUS: *Die Therapeuten und ihre Stellung in der Geschichte der Askese.* Strasburg, 1879.

H. WEINGARTEN: *Ueber den Ursprung des Mönchthums im nach-Konstantinischen Zeitalter.* Gotha, 1877. And his article in Herzog's "Encykl." new ed. vol. X. (1882) p. 758 sqq. (abridged in Schaff's Herzog, vol. II. 1551 sqq. N. Y. 1883).

AD. HARNACK: *Das Mönchthum, seine Ideale und seine Geschichte.* Giessen, 1882.

The general literature on Monasticism is immense, but belongs to the next period. See vol. III. 147 sq., and the list of books in Zöckler, *l. c.* p. 10-16.

HERE we enter a field where the early church appears most remote from the free spirit of evangelical Protestantism and modern ethics, and stands nearest the legalistic and monastic ethics of Greek and Roman Catholicism. Christian life was viewed as consisting mainly in certain outward exercises, rather than an inward disposition, in a multiplicity of acts rather than a life of faith. The great ideal of virtue was, according to the prevailing notion of the fathers and councils, not so much to transform the world and sanctify the natural things and relations created by God, as to flee from the world into monastic seclusion, and voluntarily renounce property and marriage. The Pauline doctrine of faith and of justification by grace alone steadily retreated, or rather, it was never yet rightly enthroned in the general thought and life of the church. The qualitative view of morality yielded more and more to quantitative calculation by the number of outward meritorious and even supererogatory works, prayer, fasting, alms-giving, voluntary poverty, and celibacy. This necessarily brought with it a Judaizing self-righteousness and over-estimate of the ascetic life, which developed, by an irresistible impulse, into the hermit-life and monasticism of the Nicene age. All the germs of this asceticism appear in the second half of the third century, and even earlier.

Asceticism in general is a rigid outward self-discipline, by which the spirit strives after full dominion over the flesh, and a superior grade of virtue.[1] It includes not only that true moderation or restraint of the animal appetites, which is a universal Christian duty, but total abstinence from enjoyments in themselves lawful, from wine, animal food, property, and marriage, together with all kinds of penances and mortifications of the body. In the union of the abstractive and penitential elements, or of self-denial and self-punishment, the catholic asceticism stands forth complete in light and shade; exhibiting, on the one hand, wonderful examples of heroic renunciation

---

[1] Ἄσκησις, from ἀσκέω, to exercise, to strengthen; primarily applied to athletic and gymnastic exercises, but used also, even by the heathens and by Philo, of moral self-discipline. Clement of Alex. represents the whole Christian life as an ἄσκησις (Strom. IV. 22) and calls the patriarch Jacob an ἀσκητής (Pædag. I. 7). But at the same time the term ἀσκηταί was applied from the middle of the second century by Athenagoras, Tertullian, Origen, Eusebius, Athanasius, Epiphanius, Jerome, etc., to a special class of self-denying Christians. Clement of Alex. styles them ἐκλεκτῶν ἐκλεκτότεροι (Quis Dives salv. 36; Strom. VIII. 15). Thus "ascetics" assumed the same meaning as "religious" in the middle ages. Zöckler takes a comprehensive view of asceticism, and divides it into eight branches, 1) the asceticism of penal discipline and self-castigation; 2) of domestic life; 3) of diet (fasting, abstinence); 4) of sexual life (celibacy); 5) of devotion; 6) of contemplation; 7) of practical life; 8) of social life (solitude, poverty, obedience).

of self and the world, but very often, on the other, a total misapprehension and perversion of Christian morality; the renunciation involving more or less a Gnostic contempt of the gifts
and ordinances of the God of nature, and the penance or self-
punishment running into practical denial of the all-sufficient
merits of Christ. The ascetic and monastic tendency rests
primarily upon a lively, though morbid sense of the sinfulness
of the flesh and the corruption of the world; then upon the
desire for solitude and exclusive occupation with divine things;
and finally, upon the ambition to attain extraordinary holiness
and merit. It would anticipate upon earth the life of angels in
heaven.[1] It substitutes an abnormal, self-appointed virtue and
piety for the normal forms prescribed by the Creator; and not
rarely looks down upon the divinely-ordained standard with
spiritual pride. It is a mark at once of moral strength and
moral weakness. It presumes a certain degree of culture, in
which man has emancipated himself from the powers of nature
and risen to the consciousness of his moral calling; but thinks
to secure itself against temptation only by entire separation
from the world, instead of standing in the world to overcome it
and transform it into the kingdom of God.

Asceticism is by no means limited to the Christian church,
but it there developed its highest and noblest form. We observe
kindred phenomena long before Christ; among the Jews, in the
Nazarites, the Essenes, and the cognate Therapeutæ,[2] and still
more among the heathens, in the old Persian and Indian religions, especially among the Buddhists, who have even a fully
developed system of monastic life, which struck some Roman

---

[1] Matt. 22: 30. Hence the frequent designation of monastic life as a *vita
angelica.*

[2] As described by Philo in his tract *De vita contemplativa* (περὶ βίου
θεωρητικοῦ). Eusebius (II. 17) mistook the Therapeutæ for Christian ascetics,
and later historians for Christian monks. It was supposed that Philo was
converted by the Apostle Peter. This error was not dispelled till after the
Reformation. Lucius, in his recent monograph, sees in that tract an apology
of Christian asceticism written at the close of the third century under the
name of Philo. But Weingarten (in Herzog X. 761 sqq.) again argues for
the Jewish, though post-Philonic origin of that book.

missionaries as the devil's caricature of the Catholic system. In Egypt the priests of Serapis led a monastic life.[1] There is something in the very climate of the land of the Pharaohs, in its striking contrast between the solitude of the desert and the fertility of the banks of the Nile, so closely bordering on each other, and in the sepulchral sadness of the people, which induces men to withdraw from the busy turmoil and the active duties of life. It is certain that the first Christian hermits and monks were Egyptians. Even the Grecian philosophy was conceived by the Pythagoreans, the Platonists, and the Stoics, not as theoretical knowledge merely, but also as practical wisdom, and frequently joined itself to the most rigid abstemiousness, so that "philosopher" and "ascetic" were interchangeable terms. Several apologists of the second century had by this practical philosophy, particularly the Platonic, been led to Christianity; and they on this account retained their simple dress and mode of life. Tertullian congratulates the philosopher's cloak on having now become the garb of a better philosophy. In the show of self-denial the Cynics, the followers of Diogenes, went to the extreme; but these, at least in their later degenerate days, concealed under the guise of bodily squalor, untrimmed nails, and uncombed hair, a vulgar cynical spirit, and a bitter hatred of Christianity.

In the ancient church there was a special class of Christians of both sexes who, under the name of "ascetics" or "abstinents,"[2] though still living in the midst of the community, retired from society, voluntarily renounced marriage and property, devoted themselves wholly to fasting, prayer, and religious contemplation, and strove thereby to attain Christian perfection. Sometimes they formed a society of their own,[3] for mutual im-

---

[1] The Serapis monks have been made known by the researches of Letronne, Boissier, and especially Brunet de Presle (*Mémoire sur le Sérapeum de Memphis*, 1852 and 1865). Weingarten derives Christian monasticism from this source, and traces the resemblance of the two. Pachomius was himself a monk of Serapis before his conversion. See Revillout, *Le reclus du Serapeum* (Paris 1880, quoted by Weingarten in Herzog X. 784).

[2] Ἀσκηταί, *continentes;* also παρθένοι, *virgines.*   [3] Ἀσκητήριον.

provement, an *ecclesiola in ecclesia*, in which even children could be received and trained to abstinence. They shared with the confessors the greatest regard from their fellow-Christians, had a separate seat in the public worship, and were considered the fairest ornaments of the church. In times of persecution they sought with enthusiasm a martyr's death as the crown of perfection.

While as yet each congregation was a lonely oasis in the desert of the world's corruption, and stood in downright opposition to the surrounding heathen world, these ascetics had no reason for separating from it and flying into the desert. It was under and after Constantine, and partly as the result of the union of church and state, the consequent transfer of the world into the church, and the cessation of martyrdom, that asceticism developed itself to anchoretism and monkery, and endeavored thus to save the virgin purity of the church by carrying it into the wilderness. The first Christian hermit, Paul of Thebes, is traced back to the middle of the third century, but is lost in the mist of fable; St. Anthony, the real father of monks, belongs to the age of Constantine.[1] At the time of Cyprian[2] there was as yet no absolutely binding vow. The early origin and wide spread of this ascetic life are due to the deep moral earnestness of Christianity, and the prevalence of sin in all the social relations of the then still thoroughly pagan world. It was the

---

[1] Paul of Thebes withdrew in his sixteenth year, under the Decian persecution (250), to a cavern in the lower Thebais, and lived there for one hundred and thirteen years, fed by a raven, and known only to God until St. Anthony, about 350, revealed his existence to the world. But his biography is a pious romance of Jerome, the most zealous promoter of asceticism and monasticism in the West. "The Life of St. Anthony" (d. about 356) is usually ascribed to St. Athanasius, and has undoubtedly a strong historic foundation. Eusebius never mentions him, for the two passages in the *Chronicon* (ed. Schöne II. 192, 195) belong to the continuation of Jerome. But soon after the middle of the fourth century Anthony was regarded as the patriarch of monasticism, and his biography exerted great influence upon Gregory of Nazianzum, Jerome, and Augustin. See vol. III. 179 sqq. Weingarten denies the Athanasian authorship of the biography, but not the historic existence of Anthony (in Herzog, revised ed. vol. X. 774).

[2] Epist. LXII.

excessive development of the negative, world-rejecting element in Christianity, which preceded its positive effort to transform and sanctify the world.

The ascetic principle, however, was not confined, in its influence, to the proper ascetics and monks. It ruled more or less the entire morality and piety of the ancient and mediæval church; though, on the other hand, there were never wanting in her bosom protests of the free evangelical spirit against moral narrowness and excessive regard to the outward works of the law. The ascetics were but the most consistent representatives of the old catholic piety, and were commended as such by the apologists to the heathens. They formed the spiritual nobility, the flower of the church, and served especially as examples to the clergy.

§ 105. *Heretical and Catholic Asceticism.*

But we must now distinguish two different kinds of asceticism in Christian antiquity: a heretical and an orthodox or catholic. The former rests on heathen philosophy, the latter is a development of Christian ideas.

The heretical asceticism, the beginnings of which are resisted in the New Testament itself,[1] meets us in the Gnostic and Manichæan sects. It is descended from Oriental and Platonic ideas, and is based on a dualistic view of the world, a confusion of sin with matter, and a perverted idea of God and the creation. It places God and the world at irreconcilable enmity, derives the creation from an inferior being, considers the human body substantially evil, a product of the devil or the demiurge, and makes it the great moral business of man to rid himself of the same, or gradually to annihilate it, whether by excessive abstinence or by unbridled indulgence. Many of the Gnostics placed the fall itself in the first gratification of the sexual desire, which subjected man to the dominion of the Hyle.

---

[1] 1 Tim. 4: 3; Col. 2: 16 sqq. Comp. Rom. 14.

The orthodox or catholic asceticism starts from a literal and overstrained construction of certain passages of Scripture. It admits that all nature is the work of God and the object of his love, and asserts the divine origin and destiny of the human body, without which there could, in fact, be no resurrection, and hence no admittance to eternal glory.[1] It therefore aims not to mortify the body, but perfectly to control and sanctify it. For the metaphysical dualism between spirit and matter, it substitutes the ethical conflict between the spirit and the flesh. But in practice it exceeds the simple and sound limits of the Bible, falsely substitutes the bodily appetites and affections, or sensuous nature, as such, for the flesh, or the principle of selfishness, which resides in the soul as well as the body; and thus, with all its horror of heresy, really joins in the Gnostic and Manichæan hatred of the body as the prison of the spirit. This comes out especially in the depreciation of marriage and the family life, that divinely appointed nursery of church and state, and in excessive self-inflictions, to which the apostolic piety affords not the remotest parallel. The heathen Gnostic principle of separation from the world and from the body,[2] as a means of self-redemption, after being theoretically exterminated, stole into the church by a back door of practice, directly in face of the Christian doctrine of the high destiny of the body and perfect redemption through Christ.

The Alexandrian fathers furnished a theoretical basis for this asceticism in the distinction of a lower and higher morality, which corresponds to the Platonic or Pythagorean distinction between the life according to nature and the life above nature, or the practical and contemplative life. It was previously suggested by Hermas about the middle of the second century.[3] Ter-

---

[1] The 51st Apostolic Canon, while favoring asceticism as a useful discipline, condemns those who "abhor" things in themselves innocent, as marriage, or flesh, or wine, and "blasphemously slander God's work, forgetting that all things are very good, and that God made man, male and female." The Canon implies that there were such heretical ascetics in the church, and they are threatened with excommunication.

[2] *Entweltlichung* and *Entleiblichung*.

[3] *Pastor Hermæ. Simil.* V. 3. "If you do any good beyond or outside of

tullian made a corresponding opposite distinction of mortal and venial sins.[1] Here was a source of serious practical errors, and an encouragement both to moral laxity and ascetic extravagance The ascetics, and afterwards the monks, formed or claimed to be a moral nobility, a spiritual aristocracy, above the common Christian people; as the clergy stood in a separate caste of inviolable dignity above the laity, who were content with a lower grade of virtue. Clement of Alexandria, otherwise remarkable for his elevated ethical views, requires of the sage or gnostic, that he excel the plain Christian not only by higher knowledge, but also by higher, emotionless virtue, and stoical superiority to all bodily conditions; and he inclines to regard the body, with Plato, as the grave and fetter[2] of the soul. How little he understood the Pauline doctrine of justification by faith, may be inferred from a passage in the *Stromata*, where he explains the word of Christ: "Thy faith hath saved thee," as referring, not to faith simply, but to the Jews only, who lived according to the law; as if faith was something to be added to the good works, instead of being the source and principle of the holy life.[3] Origen goes still further, and propounds quite distinctly the catholic doctrine of two kinds of morality and piety, a lower for all Christians, and a higher for saints or the select few.[4] He

what is commanded by God (ἐκτὸς τῆς ἐντολῆς τοῦ θεοῦ), you will gain for yourself more abundant glory (δόξαν περισσοτέραν), and will be more honored by God than you would otherwise be."

[1] *Peccata irremissibilia* and *remissibilia*, or *mortalia* and *venialia*.

[2] Τάφος, δεσμός.

[3] *Strom.* VI. 14: "When we hear, 'Thy faith hath saved thee' (Mark 5: 34), we do not understand him to say absolutely that those who have believed in any way whatever shall be saved, unless also works follow. But it was to the Jews alone that he spoke this utterance, who kept the law and lived blamelessly, who wanted only faith in the Lord."

[4] *In Ep. ad Rom.* c. iii. ed. de la Rue iv. p. 507: "*Donec quis hoc tantum facit, quod debet*, i. e. *quæ præcepta sunt, inutilis servus. Si autem addas aliquid ad præceptum, tunc non jam inutilis servus eris, sed dicetur ad te: Euge serve bone et fidelis. Quid autem sit quod addatur præceptis et supra debitum fiat Paulus ap. dixit: De virginibus autem præceptum Domini non habeo, consilium autem do, tamquam misericordiam assecutus a Domino* (1 Cor. 7: 25). *Hoc opus super præceptum est. Et iterum præceptum est, ut hi qui evangelium nunciant, de evangelio vivant. Paulus autem dicit, quia nullo horum usus sum: et ideo non inutilis erit servus, sed fidelis et prudens.*"

includes in the higher morality works of supererogation,[1] *i. e.* works not enjoined indeed in the gospel, yet recommended as counsels of perfection,[2] which were supposed to establish a peculiar merit and secure a higher degree of blessedness.   He who does only what is required of all is an unprofitable servant;[3] but he who does more, who performs, for example, what Paul, in 1 Cor. 7: 25, merely recommends, concerning the single state, or like him, resigns his just claim to temporal remuneration for spiritual service, is called a good and faithful servant.[4]

Among these works were reckoned martyrdom, voluntary poverty, and voluntary celibacy.   All three, or at least the last two of these acts, in connection with the positive Christian virtues, belong to the idea of the higher perfection, as distinguished from the fulfilment of regular duties, or ordinary morality.   To poverty and celibacy was afterwards added absolute obedience; and these three things were the main subjects of the *consilia evangelica* and the monastic vow.

The ground on which these particular virtues were so strongly urged is easily understood.   Property, which is so closely allied to the selfishness of man and binds him to the earth, and sexual intercourse, which brings out sensual passion in its greatest strength, and which nature herself covers with the veil of modesty;—these present themselves as the firmest obstacles to that perfection, in which God alone is our possession, and Christ alone our love and delight.

In these things the ancient heretics went to the extreme. The Ebionites made poverty the condition of salvation.   The Gnostics were divided between the two excesses of absolute self-denial and unbridled self-indulgence.   The Marcionites, Carpocratians, Prodicians, false Basilidians, and Manichæans objected to individual property, from hatred to the material world; and

---

[1] *Opera supererogatoria.*

[2] Matt. 19: 21; Luke 14: 26; 1 Cor. 7; 8 sq. 25.   Hence *consilia evangelica*, in distinction from *præcepta.*

[3] Luke 17: 10.   [4] Matt. 25: 21.

Epiphanes, in a book "on Justice" about 125, defined virtue as a community with equality, and advocated the community of goods and women.   The more earnest of these heretics entirely prohibited marriage and procreation as a diabolical work, as in the case of Saturninus, Marcion, and the Encratites; while other Gnostic sects substituted for it the most shameless promiscuous intercourse, as in Carpocrates, Epiphanes, and the Nicolaitans.

The ancient church, on the contrary, held to the divine institution of property and marriage, and was content to recommend the voluntary renunciation of these intrinsically lawful pleasures to the few elect, as means of attaining Christian perfection.   She declared marriage holy, virginity more holy.   But unquestionably even the church fathers so exalted the higher holiness of virginity, as practically to neutralize, or at least seriously to weaken, their assertion of the holiness of marriage.   The Roman church, in spite of the many Bible examples of married men of God from Abraham to Peter, can conceive no real holiness without celibacy, and therefore requires celibacy of its clergy without exception.

§ 106. *Voluntary Poverty.*

The recommendation of voluntary poverty was based on a literal interpretation of the Lord's advice to the rich young ruler, who had kept all the commandments from his youth up: "If thou wouldest be perfect, go, sell that thou hast, and give to the poor, and thou shalt have treasure in heaven: and come, follow me."[1]   To this were added the actual examples of the poverty of Christ and his apostles, and the community of goods in the first Christian church at Jerusalem.   Many Christians, not of the ascetics only, but also of the clergy, like Cyprian, accordingly gave up all their property at their conversion, for the benefit of the poor.   The later monastic societies sought to represent in their community of goods the original equality and the perfect brotherhood of men.

Yet on the other hand, we meet with more moderate views.

[1] Matt. 19 : 21.

Clement of Alexandria, for example, in a special treatise on the right use of wealth,[1] observes, that the Saviour forbade not so much the possession of earthly property, as the love of it and desire for it; and that it is possible to retain the latter, even though the possession itself be renounced. The earthly, says he, is a material and a means for doing good, and the unequal distribution of property is a divine provision for the exercise of Christian love and beneficence. The true riches are the virtue, which can and should maintain itself under all outward conditions; the false are the mere outward possession, which comes and goes.

§ 107. *Voluntary Celibacy.*

The old catholic exaggeration of celibacy attached itself to four passages of Scripture, viz. Matt. 19: 12; 22: 30; 1 Cor. 7: 7 sqq.; and Rev. 14: 4; but it went far beyond them, and unconsciously admitted influences from foreign modes of thought. The words of the Lord in Matt. 22: 30 (Luke 20: 35 sq.) were most frequently cited; but they expressly limit unmarried life to the angels, without setting it up as the model for men. Rev. 14: 4 was taken by some of the fathers more correctly in the symbolical sense of freedom from the pollution of idolatry. The example of Christ, though often urged, cannot here furnish a rule; for the Son of God and Saviour of the world was too far above all the daughters of Eve to find an equal companion among them, and in any case cannot be conceived as holding such relations. The whole church of the redeemed is his pure bride. Of the apostles some at least were married, and among them Peter, the oldest and most prominent of all. The advice of Paul in 1 Cor. ch. 7 is so cautiously given, that even here the view of the fathers found but partial support; especially if balanced with the Pastoral Epistles, where marriage is presented as the proper condition for the clergy. Nevertheless he was frequently made the apologist of celibacy by orthodox and

---

[1] Τίς ὁ σωζόμενος πλούσιος.

heretical writers.[1] Judaism—with the exception of the paganizing Essenes, who abstained from marriage—highly honors the
family life; it allows marriage even to the priests and the high-
priests, who had in fact to maintain their order by physical
reproduction; it considers unfruitfulness a disgrace or a curse.

Heathenism, on the contrary, just because of its own degradation of woman, and its low, sensual conception of marriage, frequently includes celibacy in its ideal of morality, and associates it
with worship. The noblest form of heathen virginity appears
in the six Vestal virgins of Rome, who, while girls of from six
to ten years, were selected for the service of the pure goddess,
and set to keep the holy fire burning on its altar; but, after
serving thirty years, were allowed to return to secular life and
marry. The penalty for breaking their vow of chastity was to
be buried alive in the campus sceleratus.

The ascetic depreciation of marriage is thus due, at least in
part, to the influence of heathenism. But with this was associated the Christian enthusiasm for angelic purity in opposition
to the horrible licentiousness of the Græco-Roman world. It
was long before Christianity raised woman and the family life
to the purity and dignity which became them in the kingdom of
God. In this view, we may the more easily account for many
expressions of the church fathers respecting the female sex, and
warnings against intercourse with women, which to us, in the
present state of European and American civilization, sound perfectly coarse and unchristian. John of Damascus has collected
in his Parallels such patristic expressions as these: "A woman
is an evil." "A rich woman is a double evil." "A beautiful
woman is a whited sepulchre." "Better is a man's wickedness
than a woman's goodness." The men who could write so, must

---

[1] Thus, for example, in the rather worthless apocryphal *Acta Pauli et Theclæ*,
which are first mentioned by Tertullian (*De Baptismo*, c. 17, as the production
of a certain Asiatic presbyter), and must therefore have existed in the second
century. There Paul is made to say : Μακάριοι οἱ ἐγκρατεῖς, ὅτι αὐτοῖς λαλήσει
ὁ θεός . . μακάριοι οἱ ἔχοντες γυναῖκας ὡς μὴ ἔχοντες, ὅτι αὐτοί κληρονομήσουσι τὸν
θεόν . . . μακάρια τὰ σώματα τῶν παρθένων, ὅτι αὐτὰ εὐαρεστήσουσιν τῷ Θεῷ καὶ οὐκ
ἀπολέσουσιν τὸν μισθὸν τῆς ἁγνείας αὐτῶν. See Tischendorf: *Acta Apostolorum
Apocrypha*. Lips. 1851, p. 42 sq.

have forgotten the beautiful passages to the contrary in the proverbs of Solomon; yea, they must have forgotten their own mothers.

On the other hand, it may be said, that the preference given to virginity had a tendency to elevate woman in the social sphere and to emancipate her from that slavish condition under heathenism, where she could be disposed of as an article of merchandise by parents or guardians, even in infancy or childhood. It should not be forgotten that many virgins of the early church devoted their whole energies as deaconesses to the care of the sick and the poor, or exhibited as martyrs a degree of passive virtue and moral heroism altogether unknown before. Such virgins Cyprian, in his rhetorical language, calls "the flowers of the church, the masterpieces of grace, the ornament of nature, the image of God reflecting the holiness of our Saviour, the most illustrious of the flock of Jesus Christ, who commenced on earth that life which we shall lead once in heaven."

The excessive regard for celibacy and the accompanying depreciation of marriage date from about the middle of the second century, and reach their height in the Nicene age.

Ignatius, in his epistle to Polycarp, expresses himself as yet very moderately: "If any one can remain in chastity of the flesh to the glory of the Lord of the flesh" [or, according to another reading, "of the flesh of the Lord], let him remain thus without boasting;[1] if he boast, he is lost, and if it be made known, beyond the bishop,[2] he is ruined." What a stride from this to the obligatory celibacy of the clergy! Yet the admonition leads us to suppose, that celibacy was thus early, in the beginning of the second century, in many cases, boasted of as meritorious, and allowed to nourish spiritual pride. Ignatius is

---

[1] Ἐν ἀκαυχησίᾳ μενέτω.

[2] Ἐὰν γνωσθῇ πλὴν τοῦ ἐπισκόπου, according to the larger Greek recension, c. 5, with which the Syriac (c. 2) and Armenian versions agree. But the shorter Greek recension reads πλέον for πλήν, which would give the sense: "If he think himself (on that account) above the (married) bishop; si majorem se episcopo censeat."

the first to call voluntary virgins brides of Christ and jewels of Christ.

Justin Martyr goes further. He points to many Christians of both sexes who lived to a great age unpolluted; and he desires celibacy to prevail to the greatest possible extent. He refers to the example of Christ, and expresses the singular opinion, that the Lord was born of a virgin only to put a limit to sensual desire, and to show that God could produce without the sexual agency of man. His disciple Tatian ran even to the Gnostic extreme upon this point, and, in a lost work on Christian perfection, condemned conjugal cohabitation as a fellowship of corruption destructive of prayer. At the same period Athenagoras wrote, in his Apology: "Many may be found among us, of both sexes, who grow old unmarried, full of hope that they are in this way more closely united to God."

Clement of Alexandria is the most reasonable of all the fathers in his views on this point. He considers eunuchism a special gift of divine grace, but without yielding it on this account preference above the married state. On the contrary, he vindicates with great decision the moral dignity and sanctity of marriage against the heretical extravagances of his time, and lays down the general principle, that Christianity stands not in outward observances, enjoyments, and privations, but in righteousness and peace of heart. Of the Gnostics he says, that, under the fair name of abstinence, they act impiously towards the creation and the holy Creator, and repudiate marriage and procreation on the ground that a man should not introduce others into the world to their misery, and provide new nourishment for death. He justly charges them with inconsistency in despising the ordinances of God and yet enjoying the nourishment created by the same hand, breathing his air, and abiding in his world. He rejects the appeal to the example of Christ, because Christ needed no help, and because the church is his bride. The apostles also he cites against the impugners of marriage. Peter and Philip begot children; Philip gave his daughters in marriage; and even Paul hesitated not to speak of a female companion (rather only of his right to lead about such an one, as well as Peter). We seem translated into an entirely different, Protestant atmosphere, when in this genial writer we read : The perfect Christian, who has the apostles for his patterns, proves himself truly a man in this, that he chooses not a solitary life, but marries, begets children, cares for the household, yet under all the temptations which his care for wife and children, domestics and property, presents, swerves not from his love to God, and as a Christian householder exhibits a miniature of the all-ruling Providence.

But how little such views agreed with the spirit of that age, we see in Clement's own stoical and Platonizing conception of the sensual appetites, and still more in his great disciple Origen, who voluntarily disabled himself in his youth, and could not think of the act of generation as anything but polluting. Hieracas, or Hierax, of Leontopolis in Egypt, who lived during the Diocletian persecution, and probably also belonged to the Alexandrian school, is said to have carried his asceticism to a heretical extreme, and to have declared virginity a condition of salvation under the gospel dispensation. Epiphanius describes him as a man of extraordinary biblical and medical learning, who knew the Bible by heart, wrote commentaries in the Greek and Egyptian languages, but denied the resurrection of the material body and the salvation of children, because there can be no reward without conflict, and no conflict without knowledge (1 Tim. 2 : 11). He abstained from wine and animal food, and gathered around him a society of ascetics, who were called Hieracitæ.[1] Methodius was an opponent of the spiritualistic, but not of the ascetic Origen, and wrote an enthusiastic plea for virginity, founded on the idea of the church as the pure, unspotted,

---

[1] Epiphan. *Hær.* 67 ; August. *Hær.* 47. Comp. Neander, Walch, and the articles of Harnack in Herzog (VI. 100), and Salmon in Smith & Wace (III. 24). Epiphanius, the heresy hunter, probably exaggerated the doctrines of Hieracas, although he treats his asceticism with respect. It is hardly credible that he should have excluded married Christians and all children from heaven unless he understood by it only the highest degree of blessedness, as Neander suggests.

ever young, and ever beautiful bride of God.   Yet, quite remarkably, in his " Feast of the Ten Virgins," the virgins express themselves respecting the sexual relations with a minuteness which, to our modern taste, is extremely indelicate and
offensive.

As to the Latin fathers: The views of Tertullian for and
against marriage, particularly against second marriage, we have
already noticed.[1]   His disciple Cyprian differs from him in his
ascetic principles only by greater moderation in expression, and,
in his treatise *De Habitu Virginum*, commends the unmarried
life on the ground of Matt. 19: 12; 1 Cor. 7, and Rev. 14: 4.

Celibacy was most common with pious virgins, who married
themselves only to God or to Christ,[2] and in the spiritual delights of this heavenly union found abundant compensation for
the pleasures of earthly matrimony.   But cases were not rare
where sensuality, thus violently suppressed, asserted itself under
other forms; as, for example, in indolence and ease at the expense of the church, which Tertullian finds it necessary to censure; or in the vanity and love of dress, which Cyprian rebukes;
and, worst of all, in a desperate venture of asceticism, which
probably often enough resulted in failure, or at least filled the
imagination with impure thoughts.   Many of these heavenly
brides[3] lived with male ascetics, and especially with unmarried
clergymen, under pretext of a purely spiritual fellowship, in so
intimate intercourse as to put their continence to the most peril-
ous test, and wantonly challenge temptation, from which we
should rather pray to be kept.   This unnatural and shameless
practice was probably introduced by the Gnostics; Irenæus at
least charges it upon them.   The first trace of it in the church
appears early enough, though under a rather innocent allegorical
form, in the *Pastor Hermœ*, which originated in the Roman
church.[4]   It is next mentioned in the Pseudo-Clementine Epis-

---

[1] See § 99. p. 367.   [2] *Nuptæ Deo, Christo.*

[3] Ἀδελφαί, *sorores* (1 Cor. 9: 5); afterwards cleverly called γιναίκες συνείσακτοι,
mulieres subintroductae, extraneae.

[4] *Simil.* IX. c. 11 (ed. Gebhardt & Harnack, p. 218).   The *Virgines,*

tles *Ad Virgines*. In the third century it prevailed widely in the East and West. The worldly-minded bishop Paulus of Antioch favored it by his own example. Cyprian of Carthage came out earnestly,[1] and with all reason, against the vicious practice, in spite of the solemn protestation of innocence by these " sisters," and their appeal to investigations through midwives. Several councils, at Elvira, Ancyra, Nicæa, &c., felt called upon to forbid this pseudo-ascetic scandal. Yet the intercourse of clergy with "*mulieres subintroductæ*" rather increased than diminished with the increasing stringency of the celibate laws, and has at all times more or less disgraced the Roman priesthood.

§ 108. *Celibacy of the Clergy.*

G. Calixtus (Luth.): *De conjug. clericorum.* Helmst. 1631; ed. emend. *H. Ph. Kr. Henke*, 1784, 2 Parts.

Lud. Thomassin (Rom. Cath., d. 1696): *Vetus et Nova Ecclesiæ Disciplina.* Lucae, 1728, 3 vols. fol.; Mayence, 1787, also in French. P. I. L. II. c. 60–67.

Fr. Zaccaria (R. C.): *Storia polemica del celibato sacro.* Rom. 1774; and *Nuova giustificazione del celibato sacro.* Fuligno, 1785.

F. W. Carové (Prot.): *Vollständige Sammlung der Cölibatsgesetze.* Francf. 1823.

J. Ant. & Aug. Theiner (R. C.): *Die Einführung der erzwungenen Ehelosigkeit bei den Geistlichen u. ihre Folgen.* Altenb. 1828; 2 vols.; second ed. Augsburg, 1845. In favor of the abolition of enforced celibacy.

who doubtless symbolically represent the Christian graces (*fides, abstinentia, potestas, patientia, simplicitas, innocentia, castitas, hilaritas, veritas, intelligentia, concordia,* and *caritas,* comp. c. 15), there say to Hermas, when he proposes an evening walk: Οὐ δύνασαι ἀφ' ἡμῶν ἀναχωρῆσαι . . . . Μεθ' ἡμῶν κοιμηθήσῃ ὡς ἀδελφός, καὶ οὐχ' ὡς ἀνήρ· ἡμέτερος γὰρ ἀδελφὸς εἶ· Καὶ τοῦ λοιποῦ μέλλομεν μετὰ σοῦ κατοικεῖν, λίαν γὰρ σε ἀγαπῶμεν. Then the first of these virgins. *fides,* comes to the blushing Hermas, and begins to kiss him. The others do the same; they lead him to the tower (symbol of the church), and sport with him. When night comes on, they retire together to rest, with singing and prayer; καὶ ἔμεινα, he continues, μετ' αὐτῶν τὴν νύκτα καὶ ἐκοιμήθην παρὰ τὸν πύργον. Ἐστρωσαν δὲ αἱ παρθένοι τοὺς λινοὺς χιτῶνας ἑαυτῶν χαμαί, καὶ ἐμὲ ἀνέκλιναν εἰς τὸ μέσον αὐτῶν, καὶ οὐδὲν ὅλως ἐποίουν εἰ μὴ προσηύχοντο· κἀγὼ μετ' αὐτῶν ἀδιαλείπτως προσηυχόμην. It cannot be conceived that the apostolic Hermas wrote such silly stuff. It sounds much more like a later Hermas towards the middle of the second century.

[1] *Ep.* LXII., also V. and VI.

TH. FR. KLITSCHE (R. C.): *Geschichte des Cölibats* (from the time of the Apostles to Gregory VII.) Augsb. 1830.

A. MÖHLER: *Beleuchtung der (badischen) Denkschrift zur Aufhebung des Cölibats.* In his 'Gesammelte Schriften." Regensb. 1839, vol. I. 177 sqq.

C. J. HEFELE (R. C.): *Beiträge zur Kirchengesch.* Vol. I. 122–139.

A. DE ROSKOVANY (R. C.): *Cœlibatus et Breviarium . . . . a monumentis omnium sæculorum demonstrata.* Pest, 1861. 4 vols. A collection of material and official decisions. Schulte calls it "*ein gänzlich unkritischer Abdruck von Quellen.*"

HENRY C. LEA (Prot.): *An Historical Sketch of Sacerdotal Celibacy in the Christian Church.* Philadelphia, 1867 ; 2d ed. enlarged, Boston, 1884 (682 pp.) ; the only impartial and complete history down to 1880.

PROBST (R. C.): *Kirchliche Disciplin,* 1870.

J. FRIED. VON. SCHULTE (Prof. of jurisprudence in Bonn, and one of the leaders among the Old Catholics): *Der Cölibatszwang und dessen Aufhebung.* Bonn 1876 (96 pages). Against celibacy.

All the above works, except that of Lea, are more or less controversial. Comp. also, on the Roman Cath. side, art. *Celibacy,* MARTIGNY, and in KRAUS, "Real-Encykl. der christl. Alterthümer" (1881) I. 304–307 by FUNK, and in the new ed. of WETZER & WELTE'S "Kirchenlexicon ; " on the Prot. side, BINGHAM, Book IV. ch. V. ; HERZOG², III. 299–303 ; and SMITH & CHEETHAM, I. 323–327.

As the clergy were supposed to embody the moral ideal of Christianity, and to be in the full sense of the term the heritage of God, they were required to practise especially rigid sexual temperance after receiving their ordination. The virginity of the church of Christ, who was himself born of a virgin, seemed, in the ascetic spirit of the age, to recommend a virgin priesthood as coming nearest his example, and best calculated to promote the spiritual interests of the church.

There were antecedents in heathenism to sacerdotal celibacy. Buddhism rigorously enjoined it under a penalty of expulsion. The Egyptian priests were allowed one, but forbidden a second marriage, while the people practiced unrestrained polygamy. The priestesses of the Delphic Apollo, the Achaian Juno, the Scythian Diana, and the Roman Vesta were virgins.

In the ante-Nicene period sacerdotal celibacy did not as yet become a matter of law, but was left optional, like the vow of chastity among the laity. In the Pastoral Epistles of Paul marriage, if not expressly enjoined, is at least allowed to all ministers of the gospel (bishops and deacons), and is presumed to exist as the rule.[1] It is an undoubted fact that Peter and several apostles, as well as the Lord's brothers, were married,[2] and that Philip the deacon and evangelist had four daughters.[3] It is also self-evident that, if marriage did not detract from the authority and dignity of an apostle, it cannot be inconsistent with the dignity and purity of any minister of Christ. The marriage relation implies duties and privileges, and it is a strange perversion of truth if some writers under the influence of dogmatic prejudice have turned the apostolic marriages, and that between Joseph and Mary into empty forms. Paul would have expressed himself very differently if he had meant to deny to the clergy the conjugal intercourse after ordination, as

[1] The passages 1 Tim. 3: 2, 12; Tit. 1: 5, where St. Paul directs that presbyter-bishops and deacons must be husbands of "one wife" (μιᾶς γυναικὸς ἀνδρις), are differently interpreted. The Greek church takes the words both as commanding (δεῖ) one marriage of the clergy (to the exclusion, however, of bishops who must be unmarried), and as prohibiting a second marriage. The Roman church understands Paul as conceding one marriage to the weakness of the flesh, but as intimating the better way of total abstinence (Comp. 1 Cor. 7: 7, 32, 33). Protestant commentators are likewise divided; some refer the two passages to simultaneous, others to successive polygamy. The former view was held even by some Greek fathers, Theodore of Mopsueste and Theodoret; but the parallel expression ἑνὸς ἀνδρὸς γυνή, 1 Tim. 5: 9, seems to favor the latter view, since it is very unlikely that polyandry existed in apostolic churches. And yet Paul expressly allows without a censure second marriage after the death of the former husband or wife, Rom. 7: 2, 3; 1 Cor. 7: 39; 1 Tim. 5: 14. For this reason some commentators (Matthies, Hofmann, Huther in Meyer's Com.) understand the apostle as prohibiting concubinage or all illegitimate connubial intercourse.

[2] 1 Cor. 9: 5: "Have we no right (ἐξουσίαν) to lead about a wife that is a believer (ἀδελφὴν γυναῖκα), even as the rest of the apostles (οἱ λοιποὶ ἀπ.) and the brothers of the Lord (οἱ ἀδελφοὶ τ. Κυρίου), and Cephas?" The definite article seems to indicate that the majority, if not all, the apostles and brothers of the Lord were married. The only certain exception is John, and probably also Paul, though he may have been a widower. Tertullian in his blind zeal argued that γυναῖκα is to be rendered mulierem, not uxorem (De Monog. c. 8), but his contemporary, Clement of Alex., does not question the true interpretation, speaks of Peter, Paul, and Philip, as married, and of Philip as giving his daughters in marriage. Tradition ascribes to Peter a daughter, St. Petronilla.

[3] Acts 21: 8, 9.

was done by the fathers and councils in the fourth century. He expressly classes the prohibition of marriage (including its consequences) among the doctrines of demons or evil spirits that control the heathen religions, and among the signs of the apostacy of the latter days.[1] The Bible represents marriage as the first institution of God dating from the state of man's innocency, and puts the highest dignity upon it in the Old and New Covenants. Any reflection on the honor and purity of the married state and the marriage bed reflects on the patriarchs, Moses, the prophets, and the apostles, yea, on the wisdom and goodness of the Creator.[2]

There was an early departure from these Scripture views in the church under the irresistible influence of the ascetic enthusiasm for virgin purity. The undue elevation of virginity necessarily implied a corresponding depreciation of marriage.

The scanty documents of the post-apostolic age give us only incidental glimpses into clerical households, yet sufficient to prove the unbroken continuance of clerical marriages, especially in the Eastern churches, and at the same time the superior estimate put upon an unmarried clergy, which gradually limited or lowered the former.

Polycarp expresses his grief for Valens, a presbyter in Philippi, "and his wife," on account of his covetousness.[3] Irenæus mentions a married deacon in Asia Minor who was ill-rewarded for his hospitality to a Gnostic heretic, who seduced his wife.[4] Rather unfortunate examples. Clement of Alexandria, one of the most enlightened among the ante-Nicene fathers, describes the true ideal of a Christian Gnostic as one who marries and has children, and so attains to a higher excellence, because he con-

---

[1] 1 Tim. 4: 1–3.

[2] Comp. Heb. 13: 4: "*Let* marriage *be* had in honor among all, and *let* the bed *be* undefiled" (τίμιος ὁ γάμος ἐν πᾶσι, καὶ ἡ κοίτη ἀμίαντος).

[3] *Ep. ad Phil.* c. 11. Some think that *incontinence* or *adultery* is referred to; but the proper reading is φιλαργυρία, *avaritia*, not πλεονεξία.

[4] *Adv. Hær.* 1. 13, 5 (ed. Stieren I. 155).

quers more temptations than that of the single state.[1] Tertullian, though preferring celibacy, was a married priest, and exhorted his wife to refrain after his death from a second marriage in order to attain to that ascetic purity which was impossible during their married life.[2] He also draws a beautiful picture of the holy beauty of a Christian family. An African priest, Novatus —another unfortunate example—was arraigned for murdering his unborn child.[3] There are also examples of married bishops. Socrates reports that not even bishops were bound in his age by any law of celibacy, and that many bishops during their episcopate begat children.[4] Athanasius says:[5] "Many bishops have not contracted matrimony; while, on the other hand, monks have become fathers. Again, we see bishops who have children, and monks who take no thought of having posterity." The father of Gregory of Nazianzum (d. 390) was a married bishop, and his mother, Nonna, a woman of exemplary piety, prayed earnestly for male issue, saw her future son in a prophetic vision, and dedicated him, before his birth, to the service of God, and he became the leading theologian of his age. Gregory of Nyssa (d. about 394) was likewise a married bishop, though he gave the preference to celibacy. Synesius, the philosophic disciple of Hypatia of Alexandria, when pressed to accept the bishopric of Ptolemais (A. D. 410), declined at first, because he was unwilling to separate from his wife, and desired numerous offspring : but

---

[1] *Strom.* VII. 12, p. 741.

[2] *Ad Uxor.* I. 7 : " *Ut quod in matrimonio non valuimus, in viduitate sectemur.* This clearly implies the continuance of sexual intercourse. Tertullian lays down the principle : " *Defuncto viro matrimonium defungitur.*"

[3] Cyprian, *Epist.* 52, cap. 2, Oxf. ed. and ed. Hartel (*al.* 48). He paints his schismatical opponent in the darkest colors, and charges him with kicking his wife in a state of pregnancy, and thus producing a miscarriage, but he does not censure him for his marriage.

[4] *Hist. Eccl.* V. 22 : "In the East all clergymen, and even the bishops themselves abstain from their wives: but this they do of their own accord, there being no law in force to make it necessary ; for there have been among them many bishops who have had children by their lawful wives during their episcopate."

[5] In a letter to the Egyptian monk Dracontius, who had scruples about accepting a call to the episcopate.

he finally accepted the office without a separation. This proves that his case was already exceptional. The sixth of the Apostolical Canons directs: " Let not a bishop, a priest, or a deacon cast off his own wife under pretence of piety; but if he does cast her off, let him be suspended. If he go on in it, let him be deprived." The Apostolical Constitutions nowhere prescribe clerical celibacy, but assume the single marriage of bishop, priest, and deacon as perfectly legitimate.[1]

The inscriptions on the catacombs bear likewise testimony to clerical marriages down to the fifth century.[2]

[1] This is substantially also the position of Eusebius, Epiphanius, and Chrysostom, as far as we may.infer from allusions, and their expositions of 1 Tim. 3 : 2, although all preferred celibacy as a higher state. See Funk, *l. c.* p. 305. The Synod of Gangra, after the middle of the fourth century, anathematized (*Can.* 4) those who maintained that it was wrong to attend the eucharistic services of priests living in marriage. See Hefele I. 782, who remarks against Baronius, that the canon means such priests as not only had wives, but lived with them in conjugal intercourse (*mit denselben ehelich leben*). The *Codex Ecclesiae Rom.* ed. by Quesnel omits this canon.

[2] Lundy (*Monumental Christianity*, N. Y. 1876, p. 343 sqq.) quotes the following inscriptions of this kind from Gruter, Bosio, Arringhi, Burgon, and other sources:

"The place of the Presbyter Basil and his Felicitas.
      They made it for themselves."

"Susanna, once the happy daughter of the Presbyter Gabinus,
Here lies in peace joined with her father."

"Gaudentius, the Presbyter, for himself and his wife Severa, a virtuous woman, who lived 42 years, 3 months, 10 days. Buried on the 4th after the nones of April, Timasius and Promus being consuls."

"Petronia, the wife of a Levite, type of modesty. In this place I lay my bones; spare your tears, dear husband and daughters, and believe that it is forbidden to weep for one who lives in God. Buried in peace, on the third before the nones of October."

The names of three children appear on the same tablet, and are no doubt those referred to by Petronia as hers, with the consular dates of their burial. Her own interment was A.D. 472.

Gruter and Le Blant both publish a very long and elaborate inscription at Narbonne, A. D. 427, to the effect that Rusticus the Bishop, son of Bonosius, a Bishop, nephew of Aratoris, another Bishop, etc., in connection with the presbyter Ursus and the deacon Hermetus, began to build the church; and that Montanus the sub-deacon finished the apse, etc.

At the same time the tendency towards clerical celibacy set in very early, and made steady and irresistible progress, especially in the West. This is manifest in the qualifications of the facts and directions just mentioned. For they leave the impression that there were not many *happy* clerical marriages and model pastors' wives in the early centuries; nor could there be so long as the public opinion of the church, contrary to the Bible, elevated virginity above marriage.

1. The first step in the direction of clerical celibacy was the prohibition of *second* marriage to the clergy, on the ground that Paul's direction concerning "the husband of *one* wife" is a restriction rather than a command. In the Western church, in the early part of the third century, there were many clergymen who had been married a second or even a third time, and this practice was defended on the ground that Paul allowed re-marriage, after the death of one party, as lawful without any restriction or censure. This fact appears from the protest of the Montanistic Tertullian, who makes it a serious objection to the Catholics, that they allow digamists to preside, to baptize, and to celebrate the communion.[1] Hippolytus, who had equally rigoristic views on discipline, reproaches about the same time the Roman bishop Callistus with admitting to sacerdotal and episcopal office those who were married a second and even a third time, and permitting the clergy to marry after having been ordained.[2] But the rigorous practice prevailed, and was legalized in the Eastern church. The Apostolical Constitutions expressly forbid bishops, priests, and deacons to marry a second time. They also forbid clergymen to marry a concubine, or a slave, or a widow, or a divorced woman, and extend the prohibition of second marriage even to cantors, readers, and porters. As to the deaconess, she must be "a pure virgin, or a widow who has been but once married, faithful and well esteemed."[3]

---

[1] He asks the Catholics with indignation: "*Quot enim et digami præsident apud vos, insultantes utique apostolo, certe non erubescentes, cum hæc sub illis leguntur? . . . . Digamus tinguis? digamus offers?*" De Monog. c. 12.

[2] *Philosoph.* IX. 12.

[3] *Const. Ap.* VI. 17.

The Apostolical Canons give similar regulations, and declare
that the husband of a second wife, of a widow, a courtezan, an
actress, or a slave was ineligible to the priesthood.[1]

2. The second step was the prohibition of marriage and conjugal intercourse *after* ordination.   This implies the incompati-
bility of the priesthood with the duties and privileges of marriage.   Before the Council of Elvira in Spain (306) no distinction
was made in the Latin church between marriages before and
after ordination.[2]   But that rigoristic council forbade nuptial
intercourse to priests of all ranks upon pain of excommunication.[3]
The Council of Arles (314) passed a similar canon.[4]   And so
did the Council of Ancyra (314), which, however, allows deacons
to marry as deacons, in case they stipulated for it before taking
orders.[5]   This exception was subsequently removed by the 27th

---

[1] *Can.* 17, 18, 19, 27.   The Jewish high-priests were likewise required to
marry a virgin of their own people.   Lev. 21 : 16.

[2] Admitted by Prof. Funk (R. Cath.), who quotes Innocent, *Ep. ad Episc.
Maced.* c. 2; Leo I. *Ep.* XII. c. 5.   He also admits that Paul's direction excludes such a distinction.   See Kraus, *Real-Enc.* I. 304 sq.

[3] *Can.* 33 : " *Placuit in totum prohibere episcopis, presbyteris, et diaconibus, vel
omnibus clericis positis in ministerio, abstinere se a conjugibus suis, et non generare
filios; quicunque vero fecerit, ab honore clericatus exterminetur.*"   Hefele says
(I. 168): "This celebrated canon contains the first law of celibacy."   It is
strange that the canon in its awkward latinity seems to *prohibit* the clergy *to
abstain* from their wives, when in fact it means to prohibit the *intercourse.*   On
account of the words *positis in ministerio*, some would see here only a prohibition of sexual commerce at the time of the performance of clerical functions,
as in the Jewish law; but this was self-understood, and would not come up to
the disciplinary standard of that age.   How little, however, even in Spain,
that first law on celibacy was obeyed, may be inferred from the letter of Pope
Siricius to Bishop Himerius of Tarragona, that there were, at the close of the
fourth century, *plurimi sacerdotes Christi et levitæ* living in wedlock.

[4] *Can.* 6 (29, see Hefele I. 217): " *Præterea, quod dignum, pudicum et honestum
est, suademus fratribus, ut sacerdotes et levitæ cum uxoribus suis non coëant, quia
ministerio quotidiano occupantur.   Quicunque contra hanc constitutionem fecerit, a
cleritatus honore deponatur.*"

[5] *Can.* 10 (Hefele, *Conciliengesch.* I. p. 230, 2te Aufl).   The canon is adopted
in the *Corpus juris can.* c. 8. Dist. 28.   The Synod of Neo-Cæsarea, between
314-325, can. 1, forbids the priests to marry on pain of deposition.   This does
not conflict with the other canon, and likewise passed into the Canon Law, c.
9, Dist. 28.   See Hefele, I. 244.

Apostolic Canon, which allows only the lectors and cantors (belonging to the minor orders) to contract marriage.[1]

At the Œcumenical Council of Nicæa (325) an attempt was made, probably under the lead of Hosius, bishop of Cordova—the connecting link between Elvira and Nicæa—to elevate the Spanish rule to the dignity and authority of an œcumenical ordinance, that is, to make the prohibition of marriage after ordination and the strict abstinence of married priests from conjugal intercourse, the universal law of the Church; but the attempt was frustrated by the loud protest of Paphnutius, a venerable bishop and confessor of a city in the Upper Thebaid of Egypt, who had lost one eye in the Diocletian persecution, and who had himself never touched a woman. He warned the fathers of the council not to impose too heavy a burden on the clergy, and to remember that marriage and conjugal intercourse were venerable and pure. He feared more harm than good from excessive rigor. It was sufficient, if unmarried clergymen remain single according to the ancient tradition of the church; but it was wrong to separate the married priest from his legitimate wife, whom he married while yet a layman. This remonstrance of a strict ascetic induced the council to table the subject and to leave the continuance or discontinuance of the married relation to the free choice of every clergyman. It was a prophetic voice of warning.[2]

The Council of Nicæa passed no law in favor of celibacy; but it strictly prohibited in its third canon the dangerous and scandalous practice of unmarried clergymen to live with an unmar-

---

[1] "Of those who come into the clergy unmarried, we permit only the readers and singers, if they are so minded, to marry afterward."

[2] This important incident of Paphnutius rests on the unanimous testimony of the well informed historians Socrates (*Hist. Eccl.* I. 11), Sozomen (*H. E.* I. 23), and Gelasius Cyzic. (*Hist. Conc. Nic.* II. 32); see Mansi, Harduin, and Hefele (I. 431–435). It agrees moreover with the directions of the Apost. Const. and Canons, and with the present practice of the Eastern churches on this subject. The objections of Baronius, Bellarmine, Valesius, and other Romanists are unfounded and refuted by Natalis Alexander, and Hefele (*l. c.*). Funk (R. C.) says: "*Die Einwendungen, die gegen den Bericht vorgebracht wurden, sind völlig nichtig*" (utterly futile).

ried woman,[1] unless she be "a mother or sister or aunt or a person above suspicion."[2] This prohibition must not be confounded with prohibition of nuptial intercourse any more than those spiritual concubines are to be identified with regular wives. It proves, however, that nominal clerical celibacy must have extensively prevailed at the time.

The Greek Church substantially retained the position of the fourth century, and gradually adopted the principle and practice of limiting the law of celibacy to bishops (who are usually taken from monasteries), and making a single marriage the rule for the lower clergy; the marriage to take place *before* ordination, and not to be repeated. Justinian excluded married men from the episcopate, and the Trullan Synod (A. D. 692) legalized the existing practice. In Russia (probably since 1274), the single marriage of the lower clergy was made obligatory. This is an error in the opposite direction. Marriage, as well as celibacy, should be left free to each man's conscience.

3. The Latin Church took the third and last step, the *absolute prohibition* of clerical marriage, including even the lower orders. This belongs to the next period; but we will here briefly anticipate the result. Sacerdotal marriage was first prohibited by Pope Siricius (A. D. 385), then by Innocent I. (402), Leo I. (440), Gregory I. (590), and by provincial Synods of Carthage (390 and 401), Toledo (400), Orleans (538), Orange (441), Arles (443 or 452), Agde (506), Gerunda (517). The great teachers of the Nicene and post-Nicene age, Jerome, Augustin, and Chrysostom, by their extravagant laudations of the superior sanctity of virginity, gave this legislation the weight of their authority. St. Jerome, the author of the Latin standard

---

[1] Euphoniously called συνείσακτος, *subintroducta* (introduced as a companion), ἀγαπητή, *soror*. See Hefele, I. 380. Comp. on this canon W. Bright, *Notes on the Canons of the First Four General Councils.* Oxford, 1882, pp. 8, 9. A Council of Antioch had deposed Paul of Samosata, bishop of Antioch, for this nasty practice, and for heresy. Euseb. *H. E.* VII. 30.

[2] Notwithstanding this canonical prohibition the disreputable practice continued. Chrysostom wrote a discourse "against persons ἔχοντας παρθένους συνεισάκτους," and another urging the dedicated virgins not to live with them. Jerome complains of the "*pestis agapetarum*" (*Ep.* XXII. 14).

version of the Bible, took the lead in this ascetic crusade against marriage, and held up to the clergy as the ideal aim of the saint, to "cut down the wood of marriage by the axe of virginity." He was willing to praise marriage, but only as the nursery of virgins.[1]

Thus celibacy was gradually enforced in the West under the combined influence of the sacerdotal and hierarchical interests to the advantage of the hierarchy, but to the injury of morality.[2]

For while voluntary abstinence, or such as springs from a special gift of grace, is honorable and may be a great blessing to the church, the forced celibacy of the clergy, or celibacy as a universal condition of entering the priesthood, does violence to nature and Scripture, and, all sacramental ideas of marriage to the contrary notwithstanding, degrades this divine ordinance, which descends from the primeval state of innocence, and symbolizes the holiest of all relations, the union of Christ with his church. But what is in conflict with nature and nature's God is also in conflict with the highest interests of morality. Much, therefore, as Catholicism has done to raise woman and the family life from heathen degradation, we still find, in general, that in

---

[1] *Ep.* XXII. "*Laudo nuptias, laudo conjugium, sed quia mihi virgines generant.*" Comp. *Ep.* CXXIII.

[2] And the Roman church seems to care more for the power, than for the purity of the clergy. Gregory VII., who used all his unflinching energy to enforce celibacy, said openly: "*Non liberari potest ecclesia a servitude laicorum, nisi liberentur clerici ab uxoribus.*" As clerical celibacy is a matter of discipline, not of doctrine, the Pope might at any time abolish it, and Aeneas Sylvius, before he ascended the chair of Peter as Pius II. (1458 to 1464), remarked that marriage had been denied to priests for good and sufficient reasons, but that still stronger ones now required its restoration. The United Greeks and Maronites are allowed to retain their wives. Joseph II. proposed to extend the permission. During the French Revolution, and before the conclusion of the Concordat (1801), many priests and nuns were married. But the hierarchical interest always defeated in the end such movements, and preferred to keep the clergy aloof from the laity in order to exercise a greater power over it. "The Latin church," says Lea in his *History of Celibacy*, "is the most wonderful structure in history, and ere its leaders can consent to such a reform they must confess that its career, so full of proud recollections, has been an error."

Evangelical Protestant countries, woman occupies a far higher grade of intellectual and moral culture than in exclusively Roman Catholic countries. Clerical marriages are probably the most happy as a rule, and have given birth to a larger number of useful and distinguished men and women than those of any other class of society.[1]

[1] Comp. this History, Vol. VI., § 79, p. 473 sqq.

CHAPTER X.

MONTANISM.

§ 109. *Literature.*

SOURCES:

The prophetic utterances of MONTANUS, PRISCA (or PRISCILLA) and MAXIMILLA, scattered through Tertullian and other writers, collected by F. MÜNTER (*Effata et Oracula Montanistarum*, Hafniæ, 1829), and by BONWETSCH, in his *Gesch. des Mont.* p. 197–200. TERTULLIAN'S writings after A. D. 201, are the chief source, especially *De Corona Militis; De Fuga in Persec.; De Cult. Feminarum; De Virg. Velandis; De Exhort. Castitatis; De Monogamia; De Paradiso; De Jejuniis; De Pudicitia; De Spectaculis; De Spe Fidelium.* His seven books *On Ecstasy*, mentioned by Jerome, are lost. In his later anti-heretical writings (*Adv. Marcionem; Adv. Valentin.; Adv. Praxean; De Anima; De Resurr. Carnis*), Tertullian occasionally refers to the new dispensation of the Spirit. On the chronology of his writings see Uhlhorn: *Fundamenta chronologiæ Tertullianeæ* (Gött. 1852), Bonwetsch: *Die Schriften Tertullians nach der Zeit ihrer Abfassung* (Bonn, 1878), and Harnack, in Brieger's "Zeitschrift für K. gesch." No. II.

IRENÆUS: *Adv. Hær.* III. 11, 9; IV. 33, 6 and 7. (The references to Montanism are somewhat doubtful). EUSEBIUS: *H. E.* V. 3. EPIPHAN.: *Hær.* 48 and 49.

The anti-Montanist writings of Apolinarius (Apollinaris) of Hierapolis, Melito of Sardes, Miltiades (περὶ τοῦ μὴ δεῖν προφήτην ἐν ἐκστάσει λαλεῖν), Apollonius, Serapion, Gaius, and an anonymous author quoted by Eusebius are lost. Comp. on the sources Soyres, *l. c.* p. 3–24, and Bonwetsch, *l. c.* p. 16–55.

WORKS:

THEOPH. WERNSDORF: *Commentatio de Montanistis Sœculi II. vulgo creditis hœreticis.* Dantzig, 1781. A vindication of Montanism as being essentially agreed with the doctrines of the primitive church and unjustly condemned. Mosheim differs, but speaks favorably of it. So also Soyres. Arnold had espoused the cause of M. before, in his *Kirchen–und Ketzerhistorie.*

415

MOSHEIM: *De Rebus Christ. ante Const. M.* p. 410–425 (Murdock's transl. I. 501–512).

WALCH: *Ketzerhistorie*, I. 611–666.

KIRCHNER: *De Montanistis.* Jenæ, 1832.

NEANDER: *Antignosticus oder Geist aus Tertullian's Schriften.* Berlin, 1825 (2d ed. 1847), and the second ed. of his *Kirchengesch.* 1843, Bd. II. 877–908 (Torrey's transl. Boston ed. vol. I. 506–526). Neander was the first to give a calm and impartial philosophical view of Montanism as the realistic antipode of idealistic Gnosticism.

A. SCHWEGLER: *Der Montanismus und die christl. Kirche des 2ten Jahrh.* Tüb. 1841. Comp. his *Nach-apost. Zeitalter* (Tüb. 1846). A very ingenious philosophical *a-priori* construction of history in the spirit of the Tübingen School. Schwegler denies the historical existence of Montanus, wrongly derives the system from Ebionism, and puts its essence in the doctrine of the Paraclete and the new supernatural epoch of revelation introduced by him. Against him wrote GEORGII in the "Deutsche Jahrbücher für Wissenschaft und Kunst," 1842.

HILGENFELD: *Die Glossolalie in der alten Kirche.* Leipz. 1850.

BAUR: *Das Wesen des Montanismus nach den neusten Forschungen*, in the "Theol. Jahrbücher." Tüb. 1851, p. 538 sqq.; and his *Gesch. der Christl. Kirche*, I. 235–245, 288–295 (3d ed. of 1863). Baur, like Schwegler, lays the chief stress on the doctrinal element, but refutes his view on the Ebionitic origin of Mont., and reviews it in its conflict with Gnosticism and episcopacy.

NIEDNER: *K. Gesch.* 253 sqq., 259 sqq.

ALBRECHT RITSCHL: *Entstehung der altkathol. Kirche*, second ed. 1857, p. 402–550. R. justly emphasizes the practical and ethical features of the sect.

P. GOTTWALD: *De Montanismo Tertulliani.* Vratisl. 1862.

A. REVILLE: *Tertullien et le Montanisme*, in the "Revue des deux mondes," Nov. 1864. Also his essay in the "Nouvelle Revue de Theologie" for 1858.

R. A. LIPSIUS: *Zur Quellenkritik des Epiphanios.* Wien, 1865; and *Die Quellen der ältesten Ketzergeschichte.* Leipz. 1875.

EMILE STRÖHLIN: *Essai sur le Montanisme.* Strasbourg, 1870.

JOHN DE SOYRES: *Montanism and the Primitive Church* (Hulsean prize essay). Cambridge, 1878 (163 pages). With a useful chronological table.

G. NATHANAEL BONWETSCH (of Dorpat): *Die Geschichte des Montanismus.* Erlangen, 1881 (201 pages). The best book on the subject.

RENAN: *Marc-Aurèle* (1882), ch. XIII. p. 207–225. Also his essay *Le Montanisme*, in the "Revue des deux mondes," Feb. 1881.

W. BELCK: *Geschichte des Montanismus.* Leipzig, 1883.

HILGENFELD: *D. Ketzergesch. des Urchristenthums.* Leipzig, 1884. (pp. 560–600.)

The subject is well treated by Dr. MÖLLER in Herzog (revis. ed.

Bd. X. 255–262); Bp. HEFELE in Wetzer & Welter, Bd. VII. 252–268, and in his *Conciliengesch.* revised ed. Bd. I. 83 sqq.; and by Dr. SALMOND in Smith & Wace, III. 935–945.
Comp. also the Lit. on Tertullian, § 196 (p. 818).

§ 110. *External History of Montanism.*

All the ascetic, rigoristic, and chiliastic elements of the ancient church combined in Montanism. They there asserted a claim to universal validity, which the catholic church was compelled, for her own interest, to reject; since she left the effort after extraordinary holiness to the comparatively small circle of ascetics and priests, and sought rather to lighten Christianity than add to its weight, for the great mass of its professors. Here is the place, therefore, to speak of this remarkable phenomenon, and not under the head of doctrine, or heresy, where it is commonly placed. For Montanism was not, originally, a departure from the faith, but a morbid overstraining of the practical morality and discipline of the early church. It was an excessive supernaturalism and puritanism against Gnostic rationalism and catholic laxity. It is the first example of an earnest and well-meaning, but gloomy and fanatical hyper-Christianity, which, like all hyper-spiritualism, is apt to end in the flesh.

Montanism originated in Asia Minor, the theatre of many movements of the church in this period; yet not in Ephesus or any large city, but in some insignificant villages of the province of Phrygia, once the home of a sensuously mystic and dreamy nature-religion, where Paul and his pupils had planted congregations at Colossæ, Laodicea, and Hierapolis.[1] The movement

---

[1] Neander first pointed to the close connection of Montanism with the Phrygian nationality, and it is true as far as it goes, but does not explain the spread of the system in North Africa. Schwegler and Baur protested against Neander's view, but Renan justly reasserts it: " *La Phrygie était un des pays de l'antiquité les plus portés aux rêveries religieuses. Les Phrygiens passaient, en général pour niais et simples. Le christianisme eut chez eux, dès l'origine, un charactère essentiellement mystique et ascétique. Déjà, dans l'épître aux Colossiens, Paul combat des erreurs où les signes précurseurs du gnosticisme et les excès d'un ascétisme mal entendu semblent se mêler. Presque partout ailleurs, le christianisme fut une religion de grandes villes; ici, comme dans la Syrie au delà du Jourdain, ce fut une religion de bourgades et de campagnards.*"

was started about the middle of the second century during the reign of Antoninus Pius or Marcus Aurelius, by a certain Montanus.[1] He was, according to hostile accounts, before his conversion, a mutilated priest of Cybele, with no special talents nor culture, but burning with fanatical zeal. He fell into somnambulistic ecstasies, and considered himself the inspired organ of the promised Paraclete or Advocate, the Helper and Comforter in these last times of distress. His adversaries wrongly inferred from the use of the first person for the Holy Spirit in his oracles, that he made himself directly the Paraclete, or, according to Epiphanius, even God the Father. Connected with him were two prophetesses, Priscilla and Maximilla, who left their husbands. During the bloody persecutions under the Antonines, which raged in Asia Minor, and caused the death of Polycarp (155), all three went forth as prophets and reformers of the Christian life, and proclaimed the near approach of the age of the Holy Spirit and of the millennial reign in Pepuza, a small village of Phrygia, upon which the new Jerusalem was to come down. Scenes took place similar to those under the preaching of the first Quakers, and the glossolalia and prophesying in the Irvingite congregations. The frantic movement soon far exceeded the intention of its authors, spread to Rome and North Africa, and threw the whole church into commotion. It gave rise to the first Synods which are mentioned after the apostolic age.

The followers of Montanus were called Montanists, also Phrygians, Cataphrygians (from the province of their origin), Pepu-

---

[1] The chronology is uncertain, and varies between 126–180. See the note of Renan in *Marc-Aur.* p. 209, Hefele (I. 85), Soyres (p. 25–29 and 157), and Bonwetsch (140–145). Eusebius assigns the rise of Montanism to the year 172, which is certainly too late; Epiphanius is confused, but leans to 157. Soyres dates it back as far as 130, Hefele to 140, Neander, Bonwetsch, and Möller (in Herzog, new ed. X. 255) to 156, Renan to 167. The recent change of the date of Polycarp's martyrdom from 167 to 155, establishes the fact of persecutions in Asia Minor under Antoninus Pius. Hefele thinks that the Pastor Hermæ, which was written before 151 under Pius I., already combats Montanist opinions. Bonwetsch puts the death of Montanus and Maximilla between 180 and 200. The name Montanus occurs on Phrygian inscriptions.

ziani, Priscillianists (from Priscilla, not to be confounded with the Priscillianists of the fourth century). They called themselves *spiritual* Christians ($\pi\nu\epsilon\nu\mu\alpha\tau\iota\varkappa\sigma\iota'$), in distinction from the psychic or carnal Christians ($\psi\nu\chi\iota\varkappa\sigma\iota'$).

The bishops and synods of Asia Minor, though not with one voice, declared the new prophecy the work of demons, applied exorcism, and cut off the Montanists from the fellowship of the church. All agreed that it was supernatural (a natural interpretation of such psychological phenomena being then unknown), and the only alternative was to ascribe it either to God or to his great Adversary. Prejudice and malice invented against Montanus and the two female prophets slanderous charges of immorality, madness and suicide, which were readily believed. Epiphanius and John of Damascus tell the absurd story, that the sacrifice of an infant was a part of the mystic worship of the Montanists, and that they made bread with the blood of murdered infants.[1]

Among their literary opponents in the East are mentioned Claudius Apolinarius of Hierapolis, Miltiades, Appollonius, Serapion of Antioch, and Clement of Alexandria.

The Roman church, during the episcopate of Eleutherus (177–190), or of Victor (190–202), after some vacillation, set itself likewise against the new prophets at the instigation of the presbyter Caius and the confessor Praxeas from Asia, who, as Tertullian sarcastically says, did a two-fold service to the devil at Rome by driving away prophecy and bringing in heresy (patripassianism), or by putting to flight the Holy Spirit and crucifying God the Father. Yet the opposition of Hippolytus to Zephyrinus and Callistus, as well as the later Novatian schism, show that the disciplinary rigorism of Montanism found energetic advocates in Rome till after the middle of the third century.

The Gallic Christians, then severely tried by persecution,

---

[1] Renan says of these slanders (p. 214): "*Ce sont là les calomnies ordinaires, qui ne manquent jamais sous la plume des écrivains orthodoxes, quand il s'agit de noircir les dissidents.*"

took a conciliatory posture, and sympathized at least with the moral earnestness, the enthusiasm for martyrdom, and the chiliastic hopes of the Montanists. They sent their presbyter (afterwards bishop) Irenæus to Eleutherus in Rome to intercede in their behalf. This mission seems to have induced him or his successor to issue letters of peace, but they were soon afterwards recalled. This sealed the fate of the party.[1]

In North Africa the Montanists met with extensive sympathy, as the Punic national character leaned naturally towards gloomy and rigorous acerbity.[2] Two of the most distinguished female martyrs, Perpetua and Felicitas, were addicted to them, and died a heroic death at Carthage in the persecution of Septimius Severus (203).

Their greatest conquest was the gifted and fiery, but eccentric and rigoristic Tertullian. He became in the year 201 or 202, from ascetic sympathies, a most energetic and influential advocate of Montanism, and helped its dark feeling towards a twilight of philosophy, without, however, formally seceding from the Catholic Church, whose doctrines he continued to defend against the heretics. At all events, he was not excommunicated, and his orthodox writings were always highly esteemed. He is the only theologian of this schismatic movement, which started in purely practical questions, and we derive the best of our knowledge of it from his works. Through him, too, its principles reacted in many respects on the Catholic Church; and that not only in North Africa, but also in Spain, as we may see from the harsh decrees of the Council of Elvira in 306. It is singular that Cyprian, who, with all his high-church tendencies and abhorrence of schism, was a daily reader of Tertullian,

---

[1] Tertullian, who mentions these "*litteras pacis jam emissas*" in favor of the Montanists in Asia (*Adv. Prax.* 1). leaves us in the dark as to the name of the "episcopus Romanus" from whom they proceeded and of the other by whom they were recalled, and as to the cause of this temporary favor. Victor condemned the Quartodecimanians with whom the Montanists were affiliated. Irenæus protested against it. See Bonwetsch, p. 173 sq.

[2] This disposition, an ἦθος πικρόν, σκυθρωπόν, and σκληρόν, even Plutarch notices in the Carthaginians (in his Πολιτικὰ παραγγέλματα, c. 3), and contrasts with the excitable and cheerful character of the Athenians.

makes no allusion to Montanism. Augustin relates that Tertullian left the Montanists, and founded a new sect, which was
called after him, but was, through his (Augustin's) agency,
reconciled to the Catholic congregation of Carthage.[1]

As a separate sect, the Montanists or Tertullianists, as they
were also called in Africa, run down into the sixth century.
At the time of Epiphanius the sect had many adherents in
Phrygia, Galatia, Cappadocia, Cilicia, and in Constantinople.
The successors of Constantine, down to Justinian (530), repeatedly enacted laws against them. Synodical legislation about
the validity of Montanist baptism is inconsistent.[2]

§ 111. *Character and Tenets of Montanism.*

I. In doctrine, Montanism agreed in all essential points
with the Catholic Church, and held very firmly to the traditional rule of faith.[3] Tertullian was thoroughly orthodox according to the standard of his age. He opposed infant baptism
on the assumption that mortal sins could not be forgiven after
baptism; but infant baptism was not yet a catholic dogma, and
was left to the discretion of parents. He contributed to the development of the orthodox doctrine of the Trinity, by asserting
against Patripassianism a personal distinction in God, and the
import of the Holy Spirit. Montanism was rooted neither, like
Ebionism, in Judaism, nor, like Gnosticism, in heathenism, but
in Christianity; and its errors consist in a morbid exaggeration
of Christian ideas and demands. Tertullian says, that the administration of the Paraclete consists only in the reform of discipline, in deeper understanding of the Scriptures, and in effort
after higher perfection; that it has the same faith, the same

---

[1] *De Hæresibus,* § 6.

[2] See Hefele, *Conciliengesch.,* I. 754. He explains the inconsistency by the
fact that the Montanists were regarded by some orthodox, by others heretical,
in the doctrine of the Trinity.

[3] This was acknowledged by its opponents. Epiphanius, *Hær.* XLVIII. 1,
says, the Cataphrygians receive the entire Scripture of the Old and New Testament, and agree with the Catholic church in their views on the Father, the
Son, and the Holy Spirit.

God, the same Christ, and the same sacraments with the Catholics. The sect combated the Gnostic heresy with all decision, and forms the exact counterpart of that system, placing Christianity chiefly in practical life instead of theoretical speculation, and looking for the consummation of the kingdom of God on this earth, though not till the millennium, instead of transferring it into an abstract ideal world. Yet between these two systems, as always between opposite extremes, there were also points of contact; a common antagonism, for example, to the present order of the world, and the distinction of a pneumatic and a psychical church.

Tertullian conceived religion as a process of development, which he illustrates by the analogy of organic growth in nature. He distinguishes in this process four stages :—(1.) Natural religion, or the innate idea of God; (2.) The legal religion of the Old Testament; (3.) The gospel during the earthly life of Christ; and (4.) the revelation of the Paraclete; that is, the spiritual religion of the Montanists, who accordingly called themselves the *pneumatics*, or the *spiritual* church, in distinction from the *psychical* (or *carnal*) Catholic church. This is the first instance of a theory of development which assumes an advance beyond the New Testament and the Christianity of the apostles; misapplying the parables of the mustard seed and the leaven, and Paul's doctrine of the growth of the church *in* Christ (but not *beyond* Christ). Tertullian, however, was by no means rationalistic in his view. On the contrary, he demanded for all new revelations the closest agreement with the traditional faith of the church, the *regula fidei*, which, in a genuine Montanistic work, he terms "*immobilis et irreformabilis.*" Nevertheless he gave the revelations of the Phrygian prophets on matters of practice an importance which interfered with the sufficiency of the Scriptures.

II. In the field of PRACTICAL LIFE and DISCIPLINE, the Montanistic movement and its expectation of the near approach of the end of the world came into conflict with the reigning Catholicism; and this conflict, consistently carried out, must of

course show itself to some extent in the province of doctrine.
Every schismatic tendency is apt to become in its progress more
or less heretical.

1. Montanism, in the first place, sought a forced continuance
of the MIRACULOUS GIFTS of the apostolic church, which gradually disappeared as Christianity became settled in humanity,
and its supernatural principle was naturalized on earth.[1] It asserted, above all, the continuance of *prophecy*, and hence it went
generally under the name of the *nova prophetia*. It appealed
to Scriptural examples, John, Agabus, Judas, and Silas, and for
their female prophets, to Miriam and Deborah, and especially
to the four daughters of Philip, who were buried in Hierapolis,
the capital of Phrygia. Ecstatic oracular utterances were mistaken for divine inspirations. Tertullian calls the mental status
of those prophets an "*amentia*," an "*excidere sensu*," and describes it in a way which irresistibly reminds one of the phenomena of magnetic clairvoyance. Montanus compares a man
in the ecstasy with a musical instrument, on which the Holy
Spirit plays his melodies. "Behold," says he in one of his oracles, in the name of the Paraclete, "the man is as a lyre, and I
sweep over him as a plectrum. The man sleeps; I wake.
Behold, it is the Lord who puts the hearts of men out of themselves, and who gives hearts to men."[2] As to its matter, the
Montanistic prophecy related to the approaching heavy judgments of God, the persecutions, the millennium, fasting, and
other ascetic exercises, which were to be enforced as laws of the
church.

The Catholic church did not deny, in theory, the continuance
of prophecy and the other miraculous gifts, but was disposed

---

[1] In this point, as in others, Montanism bears a striking affinity to Irvingism,
but differs from it by its democratic, anti-hierarchical constitution. Irvingism
asserts not only the continuance of the apostolic gifts, but also of all the apostolic offices, especially the twelvefold apostolate, and is highly ritualistic.

[2] Epiph. *Hær.* xlviii. 4: ἰδού, ὁ ἄνθρωπος ὡσεὶ λύρα, κἀγὼ ἐφίπταμαι ὡσεὶ
πλῆκτρον. ὁ ἄνθρωπος κοιμᾶται, κἀγὼ γρηγορῶ, ἰδού, κύριος ἐστιν ὁ ἐξιστάνων καρδίας
ἀνθρώπων καὶ διδοὺς καρδίαν ἀνθρώποις.

to derive the Montanistic revelations from satanic inspirations,[1] and mistrusted them all the more for their proceeding not from the regular clergy, but in great part from unauthorized laymen and fanatical women.

2. This brings us to another feature of the Montanistic movement, the assertion of the UNIVERSAL PRIESTHOOD of Christians, even of females, against the special priesthood in the Catholic church. Under this view it may be called a democratic reaction against the clerical aristocracy, which from the time of Ignatius had more and more monopolized all ministerial privileges and functions. The Montanists found the true qualification and appointment for the office of teacher in direct endowment by the Spirit of God, in distinction from outward ordination and episcopal succession. They everywhere proposed the supernatural element and the free motion of the Spirit against the mechanism of a fixed ecclesiastical order.

Here was the point where they necessarily assumed a schismatic character, and arrayed against themselves the episcopal hierarchy. But they only brought another kind of aristocracy into the place of the condemned distinction of clergy and laity. They claimed for their prophets what they denied to the Catholic bishops. They put a great gulf between the true spiritual Christians and the merely psychical ; and this induced spiritual pride and false pietism. Their affinity with the Protestant idea of the universal priesthood is more apparent than real ; they go on altogether different principles.

3. Another of the essential and prominent traits of Montanism was a visionary MILLENNARIANISM, founded indeed on the Apocalypse and on the apostolic expectation of the speedy return of Christ, but giving it extravagant weight and a materialistic coloring. The Montanists were the warmest millennarians in the ancient church, and held fast to the speedy return of Christ in glory, all the more as this hope began to give

[1] Tert. *De Jejun.* 11 : "*Spiritus diaboli est, dicis, o psychice.*" Tertullian himself, however, always occupied an honorable rank among the church writers, though not numbered among the church *fathers* in the technical sense.

way to the feeling of a long settlement of the church on earth, and to a corresponding zeal for a compact, solid episcopal organization. In praying, "Thy kingdom come," they prayed for the end of the world. They lived under a vivid impression of the great final catastrophe, and looked therefore with contempt upon the present order of things, and directed all their desires to the second advent of Christ. Maximilla says: "After me there is no more prophecy, but only the end of the world." [1]

The failure of these predictions weakened, of course, all the other pretensions of the system. But, on the other hand, the abatement of faith in the near approach of the Lord was certainly accompanied with an increase of worldliness in the Catholic church. The millennarianism of the Montanists has reappeared again and again in widely differing forms.

4. Finally, the Montanistic sect was characterized by fanatical severity in ASCETICISM and CHURCH DISCIPLINE. It raised a zealous protest against the growing looseness of the Catholic penitential discipline, which in Rome particularly, under Zephyrinus and Callistus, to the great grief of earnest minds, established a scheme of indulgence for the grossest sins, and began, long before Constantine, to obscure the line between the church and the world. Tertullian makes the restoration of a rigorous discipline the chief office of the new prophecy.[2]

But Montanism certainly went to the opposite extreme, and fell from evangelical freedom into Jewish legalism; while the Catholic church in rejecting the new laws and burdens defended the cause of freedom. Montanism turned with horror from all

---

[1] Bonwetsch, p. 149: "*Das Wesen des Montanismus ist eine Reaktion angesichts der nahen Parusie gegen Verweltlichung der Kirche.*" Baur, too, emphasizes this point and puts the chief difference between Montanism and Gnosticism in this, that the latter looked at the beginning, the former at the end of all things. "*Wie die Gnosis den Anfangspunkt ins Auge fasst, von welchem alles ausgeht, die absoluten Principien, durch welche der Selbstoffenbarungsprocess Gottes und der Gang der Weltentwicklung bedingt ist, so ist im Montanismus der Hauptpunkt um welchen sich alles bewegt, das Ende der Dinge, die Katastrophe, welcher der Weltverlauf entgegengeht.*" (*K. Gesch.* I. 235).

[2] *De Monog.* c. 2, he calls the Paraclete "*novae disciplinæ institutor,*" but in c. 4 he says, correcting himself: "*Paracletus restitutor potius, quam institutor disciplinæ.*"

the enjoyments of life, and held even art to be incompatible with Christian soberness and humility. It forbade women all ornamental clothing, and required virgins to be veiled. It courted the blood-baptism of martyrdom, and condemned concealment or flight in persecution as a denial of Christ. It multiplied fasts and other ascetic exercises, and carried them to extreme severity, as the best preparation for the millennium. It prohibited second marriage as adultery, for laity as well as clergy, and inclined even to regard a single marriage as a mere concession on the part of God to the sensuous infirmity of man. It taught the impossibility of a second repentance, and refused to restore the lapsed to the fellowship of the church. Tertullian held all mortal sins (of which he numbers seven), committed after baptism, to be unpardonable,[1] at least in this world, and a church, which showed such lenity towards gross offenders, as the Roman church at that time did, according to the corroborating testimony of Hippolytus, he called worse than a "den of thieves," even a "*spelunca mœchorum et fornicatorum.*"[2]

The Catholic church, indeed, as we have already seen, opened the door likewise to excessive ascetic rigor, but only as an exception to her rule; while the Montanists pressed their rigoristic demands as binding upon all. Such universal asceticism was simply impracticable in a world like the present, and the sect itself necessarily dwindled away. But the religious earnestness which animated it, its prophecies and visions, its millennarianism, and the fanatical extremes into which it ran, have since reappeared, under various names and forms, and in new combinations, in Novatianism, Donatism, the spiritualism of the Fran-

---

[1] Comp. *De Pud.* c. 2 and 19.

[2] *De Pudic.* c. 1: "*Audio etiam edictum esse propositum, et quidem peremptorium. Pontifex scilicet maximus, quod est episcopus episcoporum* (so he calls, ironically, the Roman bishop; in all probability he refers to Zephyrinus or Callistus), *edicit: Ego et moechiœ et fornicationis delicta pœnitentia functis dimitto. . . . . Absit, absit a sponsa Christi tale praeconium! Illa, quœ vera est, quœ pudica, quœ sancta, carebit etiam aurium macula. Non habet quibus hoc repromittit, et si habuerit, non repromittat, quoniam et terrenum Dei templum citius spelunca latronum* (Matt. 21: 13) *appellari potuit a Domino quam moechorum et fornicatorum.*"

ciscans, Anabaptism, the Camisard enthusiasm, Puritanism, Quakerism, Quietism, Pietism, Second Adventism, Irvingism, and so on, by way of protest and wholesome reaction against various evils in the church.[1]

[1] Comp. on these analogous phenomena Soyres, p. 118 sqq. and 142 sqq. He also mentions Mormonism as an analogous movement, and so does Renan (*Marc-Aurèle*, p. 209), but this is unjust to Montanism, which in its severe ascetic morality differs widely from the polygamous pseudo-theocracy in Utah. Montanism much more nearly resembles Irvingism, whose leaders are eminently pure and devout men (as Irving, Thiersch, W. W. Andrews).

CHAPTER XI.

§ 112. *Judaism and Heathenism within the Church.*

HAVING described in previous chapters the moral and intellectual victory of the church over avowed and consistent Judaism and heathenism, we must now look at her deep and mighty struggle with those enemies in a hidden and more dangerous form: with Judaism and heathenism concealed in the garb of Christianity and threatening to Judaize and paganize the church. The patristic theology and literature can never be thoroughly understood without a knowledge of the heresies of the patristic age, which play as important a part in the theological movements of the ancient Greek and Latin churches as Rationalism with its various types in the modern theology of the Protestant churches of Europe and America.

Judaism, with its religion and its sacred writings, and Græco-Roman heathenism, with its secular culture, its science, and its art, were designed to pass into Christianity to be transformed and sanctified. But even in the apostolic age many Jews and Gentiles were baptized only with water, not with the Holy Spirit and fire of the gospel, and smuggled their old religious notions and practices into the church. Hence the heretical tendencies, which are combated in the New Testament, especially in the Pauline and Catholic Epistles.[1]

The same heresies meet us at the beginning of the second century, and thenceforth in more mature form and in greater extent in almost all parts of Christendom. They evince, on the one hand, the universal import of the Christian religion in his-

---

[1] Comp. vol. I. 564 sqq., and my *History of the Apost. Church.* ? 165–169.

tory, and its irresistible power over all the more profound and earnest minds of the age. Christianity threw all their religious ideas into confusion and agitation. They were so struck with the truth, beauty, and vigor of the new religion, that they could no longer rest either in Judaism or in heathenism; and yet many were unable or unwilling to forsake inwardly their old religion and philosophy. Hence strange medleys of Christian and unchristian elements in chaotic ferment. The old religions did not die without a last desperate effort to save themselves by appropriating Christian ideas. And this, on the other hand, exposed the specific truth of Christianity to the greatest danger, and obliged the church to defend herself against misrepresentation, and to secure herself against relapse to the Jewish or the heathen level.

As Christianity was met at its entrance into the world by two other religions, the one relatively true, and the other essentially false, heresy appeared likewise in the two leading forms of EBIONISM and GNOSTICISM, the germs of which, as already observed, attracted the notice of the apostles. The remark of Hegesippus, that the church preserved a virginal purity of doctrine to the time of Hadrian, must be understood as made only in view of the open advance of Gnosticism in the second century, and therefore as only relatively true. The very same writer expressly observes, that heresy had been already secretly working from the days of Simon Magus. Ebionism is a Judaizing, pseudo-Petrine Christianity, or, as it may equally well be called, a Christianizing Judaism; Gnosticism is a paganizing or pseudo-Pauline Christianity, or a pseudo-Christian heathenism.

These two great types of heresy are properly opposite poles. Ebionism is a particularistic contraction of the Christian religion; Gnosticism, a vague expansion of it. The one is a gross realism and literalism; the other, a fantastic idealism and spiritualism. In the former the spirit is bound in outward forms; in the latter it revels in licentious freedom. Ebionism makes salvation depend on observance of the law; Gnosticism, on speculative knowledge. Under the influence of Judaistic legalism, Christianity must stiffen and petrify; under the influence of Gnostic speculation, it must dissolve into empty notions and fancies. Ebionism denies the divinity of Christ, and sees in the gospel only a new law; Gnosticism denies the true humanity of the Redeemer, and makes his person and his work a mere phantom, a docetistic illusion.

The two extremes, however, meet; both tendencies from opposite directions reach the same result—the denial of the incarnation, of the true and abiding union of the divine and the human in Christ and his kingdom; and thus they fall together under St. John's criterion of the antichristian spirit of error. In both Christ ceases to be mediator and reconciler, and his religion makes no specific advance upon the Jewish and the heathen, which place God and man in abstract dualism, or allow them none but a transient and illusory union.

Hence, there were also some forms of error, in which Ebionistic and Gnostic elements were combined. We have a Gnostic or theosophic Ebionism (the pseudo-Clementine), and a Judaizing Gnosticism (in Cerinthus and others). These mixed forms also we find combated in the apostolic age. Indeed, similar forms of religious syncretism we meet with even before the time and beyond the field of Christianity, in the Essenes, the Therapeutæ, and the Platonizing Jewish philosopher, Philo.

§ 113. *Nazarenes and Ebionites (Elkesaites, Mandœans).*

I. IRENÆUS: *Adv. Hœr.* I. 26. HIPPOLYTUS: *Refut. omnium Hœr.*, or *Philosophumena*, l. IX. 13–17. EPIPHANIUS: *Hœr.* 29, 30, 53. Scattered notices in JUSTIN M., TERTULLIAN, ORIGEN, HEGESIPPUS, EUSEBIUS, and JEROME. Several of the Apocryphal Gospels, especially that of the Hebrews. The sources are obscure and conflicting. Comp. the collection of fragments from Elxai, the Gospel of the Hebrews, etc. in Hilgenfeld's *Novum Test. extra Canonem receptum.* Lips. 1866.

II. GIESELER: *Nazaräer u. Ebioniten* (in the fourth vol. of Stäudlin's and Tzschirner's "Archiv." Leipz. 1820).

CREDNER: *Ueber Essœer und Ebioniten und einen theilweisen Zusammenhang derselben* (in Winer's "Zeitschrift für wissensch. Theol." Sulzbach, 1829).

BAUR: *De Ebionitarum Origine et Doctrina ab Essæis repetenda.* Tüb. 1831.

SCHLIEMANN: *Die Clementinen u. der Ebionitismus.* Hamb. 1844, p. 362-552.

RITSCHL: *Ueber die Secte der Elkesaiten* (in Niedner's "Zeitschr. für hist. Theol." 1853, No. 4).

D. CHWOLSOHN: *Die Ssabier und der Ssabismus.* St. Petersburg, 1856, 2 vols.

UHLHORN: *Ebioniten* and *Elkesaiten,* in Herzog, new ed., vol. IV. (1879), 13 sqq. and 184 sqq.

G. SALMON: *Elkesai, Elkesaites,* in Smith & Wace, vol. II. (1880) p. 95-98.

M. N. SIOUFFI: *Études sur la religion des Soubbas ou Sabéens, leurs dogmes, leurs moeurs.* Paris, 1880.

K. KESSLER: *Mandæer,* in Herzog, revised ed., IX. (1881), p. 205-222.

AD. HILGENFELD: *Ketzergesch. des Urchristenthums,* Leip., 1884 (421 sqq.).

The Jewish Christianity, represented in the apostolic church by Peter and James, combined with the Gentile Christianity of Paul, to form a Christian church, in which "neither circumcision availeth anything, nor uncircumcision, but a new creature in Christ."

I. A portion of the Jewish Christians, however, adhered even after the destruction of Jerusalem, to the national customs of their fathers, and propagated themselves in some churches of Syria down to the end of the fourth century, under the name of NAZARENES; a name perhaps originally given in contempt by the Jews to all Christians as followers of Jesus of Nazareth.[1] They united the observance of the Mosaic ritual law with their belief in the Messiahship and divinity of Jesus, used the Gospel of Matthew in Hebrew, deeply mourned the unbelief of their brethren, and hoped for their future conversion in a body, and for a millennial reign of Christ on the earth. But they indulged no antipathy to the apostle Paul, and never denounced the Gentile Christians as heretics for not observing the law. They were, therefore, not heretics, but stunted separatist Christians; they stopped at the obsolete position of a narrow and anxious

---

[1] The heathen enemies of Christianity, as Julian the Apostate, called them sometimes "Galileans." So also Epictetus in the only passage, in which he alludes to the Christians.

Jewish Christianity, and shrank to an insignificant sect. Jerome says of them, that, wishing to be Jews and Christians alike, they were neither one nor the other.

II. From these Nazarenes we must carefully distinguish the *heretical* Jewish Christians, or the EBIONITES, who were more numerous. Their name comes not, as Tertullian first intimated,[1] from a supposed founder of the sect, Ebion, of whom we know nothing, but from the Hebrew word, אֶבְיוֹן, *poor*. It may have been originally, like "Nazarene" and "Galilean," a contemptuous designation of all Christians, the majority of whom lived in needy circumstances;[2] but it was afterwards confined to this sect; whether in reproach, to denote the poverty of their doctrine of Christ and of the law, as Origen more ingeniously than correctly explains it; or, more probably, in honor, since the Ebionites regarded themselves as the genuine followers of the poor Christ and his poor disciples, and applied to themselves alone the benediction on the poor in spirit. According to Epiphanius, Ebion spread his error first in the company of Christians which fled to Pella after the destruction of Jerusalem; according to Hegesippus in Eusebius, one Thebutis, after the death of the bishop Symeon of Jerusalem, about 107, made schism among the Jewish Christians, and led many of them to apostatize, because he himself was not elected to the bishopric.

We find the sect of the Ebionites in Palestine and the surrounding regions, on the island of Cyprus, in Asia Minor, and even in Rome. Though it consisted mostly of Jews, Gentile Christians also sometimes attached themselves to it. It continued into the fourth century, but at the time of Theodoret was entirely extinct. It used a Hebrew Gospel, now lost, which was probably a corruption of the Gospel of Matthew.

The characteristic marks of Ebionism in all its forms are: degradation of Christianity to the level of Judaism; the princi

---

[1] *Præscr. Hæret.* c. 13.

[2] Minut. Felix, *Octav.* 36: " *Ceterum quod plerique* PAUPERES *dicimur non est infamia nostra, sed gloria; animus enim ut luxu solvitur, ita frugalitate firmatur.*"

ple of the universal and perpetual validity of the Mosaic law;
and enmity to the apostle Paul. But, as there were different
sects in Judaism itself, we have also to distinguish at least two
branches of Ebionism, related to each other as Pharisaism and
Essenism, or, to use a modern illustration, as the older deistic
and the speculative pantheistic rationalism in Germany, or the
practical and the speculative schools in Unitarianism.

1. The common EBIONITES, who were by far the more numerous, embodied the Pharisaic legalism, and were the proper successors of the Judaizers opposed in the Epistle to the Galatians.
Their doctrine may be reduced to the following propositions:

(*a*) Jesus is, indeed, the promised Messiah, the son of David,
and the supreme lawgiver, yet a mere man, like Moses and
David, sprung by natural generation from Joseph and Mary.
The sense of his Messianic calling first arose in him at his baptism by John, when a higher spirit joined itself to him. Hence,
Origen compared this sect to the blind man in the Gospel, who
called to the Lord, without seeing him: "Thou son of David,
have mercy on me."

(*b*) Circumcision and the observance of the whole ritual law
of Moses are necessary to salvation for all men.

(*c*) Paul is an apostate and heretic, and all his epistles are to
be discarded. The sect considered him a native heathen, who
came over to Judaism in later life from impure motives.

(*d*) Christ is soon to come again, to introduce the glorious
millennial reign of the Messiah, with the earthly Jerusalem for
its seat.

2. The second class of Ebionites, starting with Essenic notions, gave their Judaism a speculative or theosophic stamp, like
the errorists of the Epistle to the Colossians. They form the
stepping-stone to Gnosticism. Among these belong the ELKE-
SAITES.[1] They arose, according to Epiphanius, in the reign of
Trajan, in the regions around the Dead Sea, where the Essenes
lived. Their name is derived from their supposed founder,

---

[1] Ἐλκεσσαῖοι (Epiphanius); Ἠλχασσαί (Hippolytus); Ἐλκεσαιταί (Origen).
Also Σαμψαῖοι, from שֶׁמֶשׁ, sun.

Elxai or Elkasai, and is interpreted : "hidden power," which (according to Gieseler's suggestion) signifies the Holy Spirit.[1] This seems to have been originally the title of a book, which pretended, like the book of Mormon, to be revealed by an angel, and was held in the highest esteem by the sect. This secret writing, according to the fragments in Origen, and in the "*Philosophumena*" of Hippolytus, contains the groundwork of the remarkable pseudo-Clementine system.[2] (See next section.) It is evidently of Jewish origin, represents Jerusalem as the centre of the religious world, Christ as a creature and the Lord of angels and all other creatures, the Holy Spirit as a female, enjoins circumcision as well as baptism, rejects St. Paul, and justifies the denial of faith in time of persecution. It claims to date from the third year of Trajan (101). This and the requirement of circumcision would make it considerably older than the Clementine *Homilies*. A copy of that book was brought to Rome from Syria by a certain Alcibiades about A. D. 222, and excited attention by announcing a new method of forgiveness of sins.

3. A similar sect are the MANDÆANS, from *Manda, knowledge* (γνῶσις), also SABIANS, *i. e. Baptists* (from *sâbi*, to baptize, to wash), and MUGHTASILAH, which has the same meaning. On account of their great reverence for John the Baptist, they were called "Christians of John."[3] Their origin is uncertain. A remnant of them still exists in Persia on the eastern banks of the Tigris. Their sacred language is an Aramaic dialect of some importance for comparative philology.[4] At present they speak Arabic and Persian. Their system is very complicated with the prevalence of the heathen element, and comes nearest to Manichæism.[5]

---

[1] Δύναμις κεκαλυμμένη, חֵיל כְּסִי. Comp. the δύναμις ἄσαρκος in the Clem. *Homilies*, XVII. 16. Other derivations: from Elkesi, a village in Galilee (Delitzsch); from אֵל שַׁדַּי ; from אֶלְכָחֲשִׁים = *apostatæ*.

[2] See the fragments collected in Hilgenfeld's *Nov. Test. extra Canonem receptum*, III. 153–167.

[3] *Johanneschristen, Chrétiens de Saint Jean.*

[4] *Mandäische Grammatik*, by Th. Nöldeke. Halle, 1875.

[5] For further particulars see the article of Kessler in Herzog, above quoted.

§ 114. *The Pseudo-Clementine Ebionism.*

I. SOURCES:

1. Τὰ Κλημέντια, or more accurately, Κλήμεντος τῶν Πέτρου ἐπιδημιῶν κηρυγμάτων ἐπιτομή, first published (without the twentieth and part of the nineteenth homily) by *Cotelier* in "Patres Apost." Par. 1672; *Clericus* in his editions of Cotelier, 1698, 1700, and 1724; again by *Schwegler*, Stuttg. 1847 (the text of Clericus); then first entire, with the missing portion, from a new codex in the Ottobonian Library in the Vatican, by *Alb. R. M. Dressel* (with the Latin trans. of Cotelier and notes), under the title: *Clementis Romani quae feruntur Homiliae Viginti nunc primum integræ.* Gott. 1853; and by *Paul de Lagarde : Clementina Græce.* Leipz. 1865.

2. CLEMENTIS ROM. RECOGNITIONES ('Αναγνωρισμοί or 'Αναγνώσεις), in ten books, extant only in the Latin translation of Rufinus (d. 410); first published in Basel, 1526; then better by *Cotelier, Gallandi,* and by *Gersdorf* in his "Bibl. Patr. Lat." Lips. 1838. Vol. I. In Syriac, ed. by P. DE LAGARDE (*Clementis Romani Recognitiones Syriace*). Lips. 1861. An English translation of the Recognitions of Clement by Dr. *Thomas Smith,* in the "Ante-Nicene Christian Library," Edinburgh, vol. III. (1868), pp. 137–471. The work in the MSS. bears different titles, the most common is *Itinerarium St. Clementis.*

3. CLEMENTIS EPITOME DE GESTIS PETRI (Κλήμ. ἐπισκ. Ῥώμης περὶ τῶν πράξεων ἐπιδημιῶν τε καὶ κηρυγμάτων Πέτρου ἐπιτομή), first at Paris, 1555; then critically edited by *Cotelier, l. c. ;* and more completely with a second epitome by *A. R. M. Dressel : Clementinorum Epitomæ duæ,* with valuable critical annotations by *Fr. Wieseler.* Lips. 1859. The two *Epitomes* are only a summary of the *Homilies.*

II. WORKS.

NEANDER and BAUR, in their works on *Gnosticism* (vid. the following section), and in their Church Histories.

SCHLIEMANN: *Die Clementinen nebst den verwandten Schriften, u. der Ebionitismus.* Hamb. 1844.

AD. HILGENFELD: *Die Clementinischen Recognitionem n. Homilien nach ihrem Ursprung n. Inhalt.* Jena, 1848. Art. by the same in the "Theol. Jahrbücher" for 1854 (483 sqq.), and 1868 (357 sqq.); and *Die Apost. Väter.* Halle 1853, p. 287–302.

G. UHLHORN: *Die Homilien n. Recognitionen des Clemens Romanus.* Gött. 1854. Comp. the same author's article "Clementinen," in *Herzog,* second ed., vol. III. (1878), p. 277–286.

RITSCHL: *Die Entstehung der altkath. Kirche* 1857 (second ed. p. 206–270).

J. LEHMANN: *Die Clementinischen Schriften mit besonderer Rücksicht auf ihr liter. Verhältniss.* Gotha 1869. He mediates between Hilgenfeld and Uhlhorn. (See a review by Lipsius in the "Protest.

Kirchenztg," 1869, 477–482, and by Lagarde in his " *Symmicta*," I. 1877, pp. 2–4 and 108–112, where Lehmann is charged with plagiarism).

R. A. LIPSIUS: *Die Quellen der römischen Petrus-Sage kritish untersucht.* Kiel 1872. Lipsius finds the basis of the whole Clementine literature in the strongly anti-Pauline *Acta Petri.*

A. B. LUTTERBECK: *Die Clementinen und ihr Verh. z. Unfehlbarkeitsdogma.* Giessen, 1872.

The system of the pseudo-Clementine *Homilies* exhibits Ebionism at once in its theosophic perfection, and in its internal dissolution. It represents rather an individual opinion, than a sect, but holds probably some connection, not definitely ascertained, with the Elkesaites, who, as appears from the " *Philosophumena*," branched out even to Rome. It is genuinely Ebionitic or Judaistic in its monotheistic basis, its concealed antagonism to Paul, and its assertion of the essential identity of Christianity and Judaism, while it expressly rejects the Gnostic fundamental doctrine of the demiurge. It cannot, therefore, properly be classed, as it is by Baur, among the Gnostic schools.

The twenty Clementine *Homilies* bear the celebrated name of the Roman bishop Clement, mentioned in Phil. 4: 3, as a helper of Paul, but evidently confounded in the pseudo-Clementine literature with Flavius Clement, kinsman of the Emperor Domitian. They really come from an unknown, philosophically educated author, probably a Jewish Christian, of the second half of the second century. They are a philosophico-religious romance, based on some historical traditions, which it is now impossible to separate from apocryphal accretions. The conception of Simon as a magician was furnished by the account in the eighth chapter of Acts, and his labors in Rome were mentioned by Justin Martyr. The book is prefaced by a letter of Peter to James, bishop of Jerusalem, in which he sends him his sermons, and begs him to keep them strictly secret; and by a letter of the pseudo-Clement to the same James, in which he relates how Peter, shortly before his death, appointed him (Clement) his successor in Rome, and enjoined upon him to send to James a work composed at the instance of Peter, entitled " *Clementis*

Epitome prædicationum Petri in peregrinationibus.[1]   By these epistles it was evidently designed to impart to the pretended extract from the itinerant sermons and disputations of Peter, the highest apostolical authority, and at the same time to explain the long concealment of them.[2]

The substance of the *Homilies* themselves is briefly this: Clement, an educated Roman, of the imperial family, not satisfied with heathenism, and thirsting for truth, goes to Judæa, having heard, under the reign of Tiberius, that Jesus had appeared there.   In Cæsarea he meets the apostle Peter, and being instructed and converted by him, accompanies him on his missionary journeys in Palestine, to Tyre, Tripolis, Laodicea, and Antioch.   He attends upon the sermons of Peter and his long, repeated disputations with Simon Magus, and, at the request of the apostle, commits the substance of them to writing.   Simon Peter is thus the proper hero of the romance, and appears throughout as the representative of pure, primitive Christianity, in opposition to Simon Magus, who is portrayed as a " man full of enmity," and a "deceiver," the author of all anti-Jewish heresies, especially of the Marcionite Gnosticism.   The author was acquainted with the four canonical Gospels, and used them, Matthew most, John least; and with them another work of the same sort, probably of the Ebionitic stamp, but now unknown.[3]

It has been ingeniously conjectured by Baur (first in 1831),

---

[1] Κλήμεντος τῶν Πέτρου ἐπιδημιῶν κηρυγμάτων ἐπιτομή.

[2] The Tübingen School, under the lead of Dr. Baur, has greatly exaggerated the importance of these heretical fictions which the unknown author never intended to present as solid facts.   Thus Hilgenfeld says (*l. c.* p. 1) : " There is scarcely a single writing which is of so great importance for the history of Christianity in its first age, and which has already given such brilliant disclosures [?] at the hands of the most renowned critics in regard to the earliest history of the Christian Church, as the writings ascribed to the Roman Clement, the *Recognitions* and *Homilies*."   Their importance is confined to the history of heresy, which with the Tübingen school is the most interesting portion of ancient church history.

[3] The Tübingen school first denied the use of the fourth Gospel, but the discovery of the missing portion by Dressel in 1853 has settled this point, for it contains (*Hom.* XIX. 22) a clear quotation from John 9: 1-3.

and adopted by his pupils, that the pseudo-Clementine Peter combats, under the mask of the Magician, the apostle Paul (nowhere named in the Homilies), as the first and chief corrupter of Christianity.[1] This conjecture, which falls in easily with Baur's view of the wide-spread and irreconcilable antagonism of Petrinism and Paulinism in the primitive church, derives some support from several malicious allusions to Paul, especially the collision in Antioch. Simon Magus is charged with claiming that Christ appeared to him in a vision, and called him to be an apostle, and yet teaching a doctrine contrary to Christ, hating his apostles, and denouncing Peter, the firm rock and foundation of the church, as "self-condemned"[2] But this allusion is probably only an incidental sneer at Paul. The whole design of the *Homilies*, and the account given of the origin, history and doctrine of Simon, are inconsistent with such an identification of the heathen magician with the Christian apostle. Simon Magus is described in the *Homilies*[3] as a Samaritan, who studied Greek in Alexandria, and denied the supremacy of God and the resurrection of the dead, substituted Mount Gerizim for Jerusalem, and declared himself the true Christ. He carried with him a companion or mistress, Helena, who descended from the highest heavens, and was the primitive essence and wisdom. If Paul had been intended, the writer would have effectually concealed and defeated his design by such and other traits, which find not the remotest parallel in the history and doctrine of Paul, but are directly opposed to the statements in his Epistles and in the Acts of the Apostles.

In the *Recognitions* the anti-Pauline tendency is moderated, yet Paul's labors are ignored, and Peter is made the apostle of the Gentiles.

The doctrine which pseudo-Clement puts into the mouth of

---

[1] The hypothesis has been most fully carried out by Lipsius in his article on Simon Magus in Schenkel's "Bibellexicon," vol. V. 301–321.

[2] Comp. *Hom.* XVII. 19 (p. 351 sq. ed. Dressel) with Gal. 2: 11, where Paul uses the same word κατεγνωμένος of Peter.

[3] *Hom.* II. 22 sqq. (p. 57 sqq.).

Peter, and very skilfully interweaves with his narrative, is a confused mixture of Ebionitic and Gnostic, ethical and metaphysical ideas and fancies. He sees in Christianity only the restoration of the pure primordial religion,[1] which God revealed in the creation, but which, on account of the obscuring power of sin and the seductive influence of demons, must be from time to time renewed. The representatives of this religion are the pillars of the world: Adam, Enoch, Noah, Abraham, Isaac, Jacob, Moses, and Christ. These are in reality only seven different incarnations of the same Adam or primal man, the true prophet of God, who was omniscient and infallible. What is recorded unfavorable to these holy men, the drunkenness of Noah, the polygamy of the patriarchs, the homicide of Moses, and especially the blasphemous history of the fall of Adam, as well as all unworthy anthropopathical passages concerning God, were foisted into the Old Testament by the devil and his demons. Thus, where Philo and Origen resorted to allegorical interpretation, to remove what seems offensive in Scripture, pseudo-Clement adopts the still more arbitrary hypothesis of diabolical interpolations. Among the true prophets of God, again, he gives Adam, Moses, and Christ peculiar eminence, and places Christ above all, though without raising him essentially above a prophet and lawgiver. The history of religion, therefore, is not one of progress, but only of return to the primitive revelation. Christianity and Mosaism are identical, and both coincide with the religion of Adam. Whether a man believe in Moses or in Christ, it is all the same, provided he blaspheme neither. But to know both, and find in both the same doctrine, is to be rich in God, to recognize the new as old, and the old as become new. Christianity is an advance only in its extension of the gospel to the Gentiles, and its consequent universal character.

As the fundamental principle of this pure religion, our author lays down the doctrine of one God, the creator of the world. This is thoroughly Ebionitic, and directly opposed to the dual-

---

[1] The πρώτη τῇ ἀνθρωπότητι παραδοθεῖσα σωτήριος θρησκεία.

ism of the demiurgic doctrine of the Gnostics. But then he makes the whole stream of created life flow forth from God in a long succession of sexual and ethical antitheses and syzygies, and return into him as its absolute rest; here plainly touching the pantheistic emanation-theory of Gnosticism. God himself one from the beginning, has divided everything into counterparts, into right and left, heaven and earth, day and night, light and darkness, life and death. The monad thus becomes the dyad. The better came first, the worse followed; but from man onward the order was reversed. Adam, created in the image of God, is the true prophet; his wife, Eve, represents false prophecy. They were followed, first, by wicked Cain, and then by righteous Abel. So Peter appeared after Simon Magus, as light after darkness, health after sickness. So, at the last, will antichrist precede the advent of Christ. And finally, the whole present order of things loses itself in the future; the pious pass into eternal life; the ungodly, since the soul becomes mortal by the corruption of the divine image, are annihilated after suffering a punishment, which is described as a purifying fire.[1] When the author speaks of *eternal* punishment, he merely accommodates himself to the popular notion. The fulfilling of the law, in the Ebionitic sense, and knowledge, on a half-Gnostic principle, are the two parts of the way of salvation. The former includes frequent fasts, ablutions, abstinence from animal food, and voluntary poverty; while early marriage is enjoined, to prevent licentiousness. In declaring baptism to be absolutely necessary to the forgiveness of sin, the author approaches the catholic system. He likewise adopts the catholic principle involved, that salvation is to be found only in the external church.

As regards ecclesiastical organization, he fully embraces the monarchical episcopal view. The bishop holds the place of Christ in the congregation, and has power to bind and loose. Under him stand the presbyters and deacons. But singularly, and again in true Ebionitic style, James, the brother of the

---

[1] Πῦρ καθάρσιον, *ignis purgatorius*.

Lord, bishop of Jerusalem, which is the centre of Christendom, is made the general vicar of Christ, the visible head of the whole church, the bishop of bishops.   Hence even Peter must give him an account of his labors; and hence, too, according to the introductory epistles, the sermons of Peter and Clement's abstract of them were sent to James for safe-keeping, with the statement, that Clement had been named by Peter as his successor at Rome.

It is easy to see that this appeal to a pseudo-Petrine primitive Christianity was made by the author of the Homilies with a view to reconcile all the existing differences and divisions in Christendom.   In this effort he, of course, did not succeed, but rather made way for the dissolution of the Ebionitic element still existing in the orthodox catholic church.

Besides these *Homilies*, of which the *Epitome* is only a poor abridgement, there are several other works, some printed, some still unpublished, which are likewise forged upon Clement of Rome, and based upon the same historical material, with unimportant deviations, but are in great measure free, as to doctrine, from Judaistic and Gnostic ingredients, and come considerably nearer the line of orthodoxy.

The most important of these are the *Recognitions* of Clement, in ten books, mentioned by Origen, but now extant only in a Latin translation by Rufinus.   They take their name from the narrative, in the last books, of the reunion of the scattered members of the Clementine family, who all at last find themselves together in Christianity, and are baptized by Peter.

On the question of priority between these two works, critics are divided, some making the *Recognitions* an orthodox, or at least more nearly orthodox, version of the *Homilies;*[1] others regarding the *Homilies* as a heretical corruption of the *Recognitions.*[2] But in all probability both works are based upon older

---

[1] Clericus, Möhler, Schliemann, Uhlhorn, Schwegler, partly also Lehmann. Uhlhorn has since modified his view (1876).

[2] Particularly Hilgenfeld and Ritschl, and among older writers, Cave and Whiston. Salmon also assigns the priority of composition to the *Recognitions.*

and simpler Jewish-Christian documents, under the assumed names of Peter and Clement.[1]

As to their birth-place, the *Homilies* probably originated in East Syria, the *Recognitions* in Rome. They are assigned to the second half of the second century.

In a literary point of view, these productions are remarkable, as the first specimens of Christian romance, next to the "*Pastor Hermæ.*" They far surpass, in matter, and especially in moral earnestness and tender feeling, the heathen romances of a Chariton and an Achilles Tatios, of the fourth or fifth centuries. The style, though somewhat tedious, is fascinating in its way, and betrays a real artist in its combination of the didactic and historical, the philosophic and the poetic elements.

NOTES.

Lagarde (in the Preface to his edition of the *Clementina*, p. 22) and G. E. Steitz (in a lengthy review of Lagarde in the "Studien und Kritiken" for 1867, No. III. p. 556 sqq.) draw a parallel between the pseudo-Clementine fiction of Simon and the German story of Faust, the magician, and derive the latter from the former through the medium of the *Recognitions*, which were better known in the church than the *Homilies*. George Sabellicus, about A. D. 1507, called himself *Faustus junior, magus secundus*. Clement's father is called Faustus, and his two brothers, Faustinus and Faustinianus (in the *Recognitions* Faustus and Faustinus), were brought up with Simon the magician, and at first associated with him. The characters of Helena and Homunculus appear in both stories, though very differently. I doubt whether these resemblances are sufficient to establish a connection between the two otherwise widely divergent popular fictions.

§ 115. *Gnosticism. The Literature.*

SOURCES:

I. Gnostic (of the Valentinian school in the wider sense): PISTIS SOPHIA; *Opus gnosticum e codice Coptico descriptum lat. vertit M. G. Schwartze, ed. J. H. Petermann.* Berl. 1851. Of the middle of the

---

[1] The Περίοδοι Πέτρου διὰ Κλήμεντος, and the still older Κηρύγματα Πέτρου (about A. D. 140–145), the contents of which are mentioned in *Recogn.* III. 75, and the oldest *Acta Petri*, parts of which are preserved in the apocryphal *Acta Petri et Pauli.* See Lipsius, *Quellen der röm. Petrus-Sage*, 1872, pp. 14 sqq. Uhlhorn assents in his last art. in the new ed. of Herzog, III. 285. Dr. Salmon (in Smith and Wace, I. 571) likewise assumes that both are drawn from a common original, but that the author of *Homilies* borrowed the biographical portions from *Recognitions*.

third century. An account of the fall and repentance of Sophia and the mystery of redemption. Comp. the article of *Köstlin* in the "Tüb. Theol. Jahrbücher," 1854.—The Apocryphal Gospels, Acts, and Apocalypses are to a large extent of Gnostic origin, *e. g.* the Acts of St. Thomas (a favorite apostle of the Gnostics), John, Peter, Paul, Philip, Matthew, Andrew, Paul and Thecla. Some of them have been worked over by Catholic authors, and furnished much material to the legendary lore of the church. They and the stories of monks were the religious novels of the early church. See the collections of the apocryphal literature of the N. T. by Fabricius, Thilo, Tischendorf, Max Bonnet, D. William Wright, G. Phillips, S. C. Malan, Zahn, and especially Lipsius: *Die Apokryphen Apostelgeschichten und Apostellegenden* (Braunschweig, 1883, 2 vols.) Comp. the Lit. quoted in vol. I. 90 sq.; 188 sq., and in Lipsius, I. 34 sqq.

II. Patristic (with many extracts from lost Gnostic writings): IRENÆUS: *Adv. Hœreses.* The principal source, especially for the Valentinian Gnosticism. HYPPOLYTUS: *Refutat. omnium Hœresium (Philosophumena),* ed. Duncker and Schneidewin. Gott. 1859. Based partly on Irenæus, partly on independent reading of Gnostic works. TERTULLIAN: *De Prœscriptionibus Hœreticorum; Adv. Valentin; Scorpiace; Adv. Marcionem.* The last is the chief authority for Marcionism. CLEMENS ALEX.: *Stromata.* Scattered notices of great value. ORIGENES: *Com. in Evang. Joh.* Furnishes much important information and extracts from Heracleon. EPIPHANIUS: Πανάριον. Full of information, but uncritical and fanatically orthodox. EUSEBIUS: *Hist Eccl.* THEODORET: *Fabulœ Hœr.*

See FR. OEHLER'S *Corpus Haereseologicum* (a collection of the ancient anti-heretical works of Epiphanius, Philastrus, Augustin, etc.). Berol. 1856–1861, 5 vols.

III. Neo-Platonist: PLOTINUS: Πρὸς τοὺς γνωστικούς (or *Ennead.* II. 9).

IV. Critical: R. A. LIPSIUS: *Zur Quellen-Kritik des Epiphanios.* Wien 1865. *Die Quellen der ältesten Ketzergeschichte.* Leipz. 1875 (258 pp.)

AD. HARNACK: *Zur Quellen-Kritik der Geschichte des Gnosticismus.* Leipz. 1873. Comp. his article in Brieger's "Zeitschrift für K. Gesch." for 1876, I. Also HILGENFELD: *Ketzergesch.* p. 1–83.

WORKS:

MASSUET (R. C.): *Dissert. de Gnosticorum rebus,* prefixed to his edition of Irenæus; also in Stieren's edition of Iren. vol. II. pp. 54–180.

MOSHEIM: *Comment. de rebus ante Const. M.* pp. 333 sqq.

NEANDER: *Genet. Entwicklung der gnost. Systeme.* Berl. 1818. Comp. the more mature exposition in his *Ch. Hist.* He first opened a calm philosophical treatment of Gnosticism.

JAQUES MATTER: *Histoire critique du Gnosticisme et de son influence*

sur les sectes religieuses et philosophiques des six premiers siècles
Par. 1828 ; second ed. much enlarged. Strasb. and Par. 1844, in 1
vols.

BURTON : *Bampton Lectures on the Heresies of the Apost. Age.* Oxf. 1830.
MÖHLER (R. C.) : *Der Ursprung des Gnosticismus.* Tüb. 1831 (in his
"Vermischte Schriften," I. pp. 403 sqq.)

BAUR : *Die christliche Gnosis in ihrer geschichtl. Entwicklung.* Tüb.
1835. A masterly philosophical analysis, which includes also the
systems of Jacob Böhme, Schelling, Schleiermacher, and Hegel.
Comp. his *Kirchengesch.* vol. I. 175–234.

NORTON : *History of the Gnostics.* Boston, 1845.

H. ROSSEL : *Gesch. der Untersuch. über den Gnostic.;* in his "Theol.
Nachlass," published by Neander. Berl. 1847, vol. 2ⁿᵈ, p. 179 sqq.

THIERSCH : *Kritik der N. Tlichen Schriften.* Erl. 1845 (chap. 5, pp. 231
sqq. and 268 sqq.)

R. A. LIPSIUS : *Der Gnosticismus, sein Wesen, Ursprung und Entwick-
lungsgang.* Leipz. 1860 (from Ersch and Gruber's "Allgem. Encycl."
1. Sect. vol. 71). Comp. his critical work on the sources of Gn.
quoted above.

E. WILH. MÖLLER : *Geschichte der Kosmologie in der griechischen Kirche
bis auf Origenes. Mit Specialuntersuchungen über die gnostischen
Systeme.* Halle, 1860 (pp. 189–473).
In Ersch und Gruber's Encykl. 1860.

C. W. KING : *The Gnostics and their Remains* (with illustrations of
Gnostic symbols and works of art). Lond., 1864.

HENRY L. MANSEL (Dean of St. Paul's, d. 1871) : *The Gnostic Heresies,*
ed. by J. B. Lightfoot. London, 1875.

J. B. LIGHTFOOT : *The Colossian Heresy,* Excursus in his *Com. on Colossians and Philemon.* London, 1875, pp. 73–113. This is the best
account of Gnosticism, written by an Englishman, but confined to
the apostolic age.

RENAN : *L' église chrétienne* (Paris, 1879), Chap. IX. and X. p. 140–185,
and XVIII. p. 350–363.

J. L. JACOBI : *Gnosis,* in the new ed. of Herzog, vol. V. (1879), 204–247,
condensed in Schaff's "Rel. Encycl.," 1882, vol. I. 877 sqq.

G. SALMON, in SMITH and WACE, II. 678–687.

G. KOFFMANE : *Die Gnosis nach ihrer Tendenz und Organisation.* Breslau, 1881. (Theses, 33 pages).

AD. HILGENFELD : *Die Ketzergeschichte des Urchristenthums.* Leipzig, 1884
(p. 162 sqq.).

A number of monographs on individual Gnostics, see below.

§ 116. *Meaning, Origin and Character of Gnosticism.*

The Judaistic form of heresy was substantially conquered in
the apostolic age. More important and more widely spread in

the second period was the paganizing heresy, known by the name of GNOSTICISM. It was the Rationalism of the ancient church; it pervaded the intellectual atmosphere, and stimulated the development of catholic theology by opposition.

The Greek word *gnosis* may denote all schools of philosophical or religious knowledge, in distinction from superficial opinion or blind belief. The New Testament makes a plain distinction between true and false gnosis. The true consists in a deep insight into the essence and structure of the Christian truth, springs from faith, is accompanied by the cardinal virtues of love and humility, serves to edify the church, and belongs among the gifts of grace wrought by the Holy Spirit.[1] In this sense, Clement of Alexandria and Origen aimed at gnosis, and all speculative theologians who endeavor to reconcile reason and revelation, may be called Christian Gnostics. The false gnosis,[2] on the contrary, against which Paul warns Timothy, and which he censures in the Corinthians and Colossians, is a morbid pride of wisdom, an arrogant, self-conceited, ambitious knowledge, which puffs up, instead of edifying,[3] runs into idle subtleties and disputes, and verifies in its course the apostle's word: "Professing themselves to be wise, they became fools."[4]

In this bad sense, the word applies to the error of which we now speak, and which began to show itself at least as early as the days of Paul and John. It is a one-sided intellectualism on a dualistic heathen basis. It rests on an over-valuation of knowledge or gnosis, and a depreciation of faith or pistis. The Gnostics contrasted themselves by this name with the Pistics, or the mass of believing Christians. They regarded Christianity as consisting essentially in a higher knowledge; fancied themselves the sole possessors of an esoteric, philosophical religion, which made them genuine, spiritual men, and looked down with contempt upon the mere men of the soul and of the body. They constituted the intellectual aristocracy, a higher caste in

---

[1] Λόγος γνώσεως, λόγος σοφίας, 1 Cor. 12: 8; comp. 13: 2, 12; Jno. 17: 3.
[2] Ψευδώνυμος γνῶσις, 1 Tim. 6: 20.
[3] 1 Cor. 8: 1.   [4] Rom. 1: 22.

the church. They, moreover, adulterated Christianity with sundry elements entirely foreign, and thus quite obscured the true essence of the gospel.[1]

We may parallelize the true and false, the believing and unbelieving forms of Gnosticism with the two forms of modern Rationalism and modern Agnosticism. There is a Christian Rationalism which represents the doctrines of revelation as being in harmony with reason, though transcending reason in its present capacity; and there is an anti-Christian Rationalism which makes natural reason (*ratio*) the judge of revelation, rejects the specific doctrines of Christianity, and denies the supernatural and miraculous. And there is an Agnosticism which springs from the sense of the limitations of thought, and recognizes faith as the necessary organ of the supernatural and absolute;[2] while the unbelieving Agnosticism declares the infinite and absolute to be unknown and unknowable, and tends to indifferentism and atheism.[3]

We now proceed to trace the origin of Gnosticism.

As to its substance, Gnosticism is chiefly of heathen descent. It is a peculiar translation or transfusion of heathen philosophy and religion into Christianity. This was perceived by the church-fathers in their day. Hippolytus particularly, in his "*Philosophumena*," endeavors to trace the Gnostic heresies to the various systems of Greek philosophy, making Simon Magus, for example, dependent on Heraclitus, Valentine on Pythagoras and Plato, Basilides on Aristotle, Marcion on Empedocles; and hence he first exhibits the doctrines of the Greek philosophy from Thales down. Of all these systems Platonism had the greatest influence, especially on the Alexandrian Gnostics; though not so much in its original Hellenic form, as in its later

[1] Baur takes too comprehensive a view of Gnosticism, and includes in it all systems of Christian philosophy of religion down to Schelling and Hegel.

[2] Sir William Hamilton and Dean Mansel.

[3] Hume, Spencer, Comte. As to Kant, he started from Hume, but checked the scepticism of the theoretical reason by the categorical imperative of the practical reason. See Calderwood's article "Agnosticism" in Schaff's "Rel. Encycl." vol. I.

orientalized eclectic and mystic cast, of which Neo-Platonism was another fruit. The Platonic speculation yielded the germs of the Gnostic doctrine of æons, the conceptions of matter, of the antithesis of an ideal and a real world, of an ante-mundane fall of souls from the ideal world, of the origin of sin from matter, and of the needed redemption of the soul from the fetters of the body. We find also in the Gnostics traces of the Pythagorean symbolical use of numbers, the Stoic physics and ethics, and some Aristotelian elements.

But this reference to Hellenic philosophy, with which Massuet was content, is not enough. Since Beausobre and Mosheim the East has been rightly joined with Greece, as the native home of this heresy. This may be inferred from the mystic, fantastic, enigmatic form of the Gnostic speculation, and from the fact, that most of its representatives sprang from Egypt and Syria. The conquests of Alexander, the spread of the Greek language and literature, and the truths of Christianity, produced a mighty agitation in the eastern mind, which reacted on the West. Gnosticism has accordingly been regarded as more or less parallel with the heretical forms of Judaism, with Essenism, Therapeutism, Philo's philosophico-religious system, and with the Cabbala, the origin of which probably dates as far back as the first century. The affinity of Gnosticism also with the Zoroastrian dualism of a kingdom of light and a kingdom of darkness is unmistakable, especially in the Syrian Gnostics. Its alliance with the pantheistic, docetic, and ascetic elements of Buddhism, which had advanced at the time of Christ to western Asia, is equally plain. Parsic and Indian influence is most evident in Manichæism, while the Hellenic element there amounts to very little.

Gnosticism, with its syncretistic tendency, is no isolated fact. It struck its roots deep in the mighty revolution of ideas induced by the fall of the old religions and the triumph of the new. Philo, of Alexandria, who was a contemporary of Christ, but wholly ignorant of him, endeavored to combine the Jewish religion, by allegorical exposition, or rather imposition, with

Platonic philosophy ; and this system, according as it might be prosecuted under the Christian or the heathen influence, would prepare the way either for the speculative theology of the Alexandrian church fathers, or for the heretical Gnosis. Still more nearly akin to Gnosticism is Neo-Platonism, which arose a little later than Philo's system, but ignored Judaism, and derived its ideas exclusively from eastern and western heathenism. The Gnostic syncretism, however, differs materially from both the Philonic and the Neo-Platonic by taking up Christianity, which the Neo-Platonists directly or indirectly opposed. This the Gnostics regarded as the highest stage of the development of religion, though they so corrupted it by the admixture of foreign matter, as to destroy its identity.

Gnosticism is, therefore, the grandest and most comprehensive form of speculative religious syncretism known to history. It consists of Oriental mysticism, Greek philosophy, Alexandrian, Philonic, and Cabbalistic Judaism, and Christian ideas of salvation, not merely mechanically compiled, but, as it were, chemically combined. At least, in its fairly developed form in the Valentinian system, it is, in its way, a wonderful structure of speculative or rather imaginative thought, and at the same time an artistic work of the creative fancy, a Christian mythological epic. The old world here rallied all its energies, to make out of its diverse elements some new thing, and to oppose to the real, substantial universalism of the catholic church an ideal, shadowy universalism of speculation. But this fusion of all systems served in the end only to hasten the dissolution of eastern and western heathenism, while the Christian element came forth purified and strengthened from the crucible.

The Gnostic speculation, like most speculative religions, failed to establish a safe basis for practical morals. On the one side, a spiritual pride obscured the sense of sin, and engendered a frivolous antinomianism, which often ended in sensuality and debaucheries. On the other side, an over-strained sense of sin often led the Gnostics, in glaring contrast with the pagan deification of nature, to ascribe nature to the devil, to abhor the body as the seat of evil, and to practice extreme austerities upon themselves.

This ascetic feature is made prominent by Möhler, the Roman Catholic divine. But he goes quite too far, when he derives the whole phenomenon of Gnosticism (which he wrongly views as a forerunner of Protestantism) directly and immediately from Christianity. He represents it as a hyper-Christianity, an exaggerated contempt for the world,[1] which, when seeking for itself a speculative basis, gathered from older philosophemes, theosophies, and mythologies, all that it could use for its purpose.

The number of the Gnostics it is impossible to ascertain. We find them in almost all portions of the ancient church; chiefly where Christianity came into close contact with Judaism and heathenism, as in Egypt, Syria, and Asia Minor; then in Rome, the rendezvous of all forms of truth and falsehood; in Gaul, where they were opposed by Irenæus; and in Africa, where they were attacked by Tertullian, and afterwards by Augustin, who was himself a Manichæan for several years. They found most favor with the educated, and threatened to lead astray the teachers of the church. But they could gain no foothold among the people; indeed, as esoterics, they stood aloof from the masses; and their philosophical societies were, no doubt, rarely as large as the catholic congregations.

The flourishing period of the Gnostic schools was the second century. In the sixth century, only faint traces of them remained; yet some Gnostic and especially Manichæan ideas continue to appear in several heretical sects of the middle ages, such as the Priscillianists, the Paulicians, the Bogomiles, and the Catharists; and even the history of modern theological and philosophical speculation shows kindred tendencies.

§ 117. *The System of Gnosticism. Its Theology.*

Gnosticism is a heretical philosophy of religion, or, more exactly, a mythological theosophy, which reflects intellectually the peculiar, fermenting state of that remarkable age of transition

---

[1] He calls Gnosticism a " *Verteufelung der Natur.*"

from the heathen to the Christian order of things. If it were merely an unintelligible congeries of puerile absurdities and impious blasphemies, as it is grotesquely portrayed by older historians,[1] it would not have fascinated so many vigorous intellects and produced such a long-continued agitation in the ancient church. It is an attempt to solve some of the deepest metaphysical and theological problems. It deals with the great antitheses of God and world, spirit and matter, idea and phenomenon; and endeavors to unlock the mystery of the creation; the question of the rise, development, and end of the world; and of the origin of evil.[2] It endeavors to harmonize the creation of the material world and the existence of evil with the idea of an absolute God, who is immaterial and perfectly good. This problem can only be solved by the Christian doctrine of redemption; but Gnosticism started from a false basis of dualism, which prevents a solution.

In form and method it is, as already observed, more Oriental than Grecian. The Gnostics, in their daring attempt to unfold the mysteries of an upper world, disdained the trammels of reason, and resorted to direct spiritual intuition. Hence they speculate not so much in logical and dialectic mode, as in an imaginative, semi-poetic way, and they clothe their ideas not in the simple, clear, and sober language of reflection, but in the many-colored, fantastic, mythological dress of type, symbol, and allegory. Thus monstrous nonsense and the most absurd conceits are chaotically mingled up with profound thoughts and poetic intuitions.

This spurious supernaturalism which substitutes the irrational for the supernatural, and the prodigy for the miracle, pervades

---

[1] Even some of the more recent writers, as Bishop Kaye (*Eccl. History of the Second and Third Centuries*), and the translators of Irenæus in the "Ante-Nicene Christian Library" (Edinb. 1868, vol. 1st, Introductory Notice) have the same idea of the Gnostic systems as an impenetrable wilderness of absurdities. But Mansel, Lightfoot, and Salmon show a clear knowledge of the subject, and agree substantially with Neander's account.

[2] Πόθεν τὸ κακόν. or ἡ κακία; *unde malum?* See Tertullian, *De Præscript.* 7; *Adv. Marc.* I. 2; Euseb. *H. E.* V. 27; Baur, *Gnosis*, p. 19.

the pseudo-historical romances of the Gnostic Gospels and Acts. These surpass the Catholic traditions in luxuriant fancy and incredible marvels. "Demoniacal possessions," says one who has mastered this literature,[1] "and resurrections from the dead, miracles of healing and punishment are accumulated without end; the constant repetition of similar events gives the long stories a certain monotony, which is occasionally interrupted by colloquies, hymns and prayers of genuine poetic value. A rich apparatus of visions, angelic appearances, heavenly voices, speaking animals, defeated and humbled demons is unfolded, a superterrestrial splendor of light gleams up, mysterious signs from heaven, earthquakes, thunder and lightning frighten the impious; fire, earth, wind and water obey the pious; serpents, lions, leopards, tigers, and bears are tamed by a word of the apostles and turn upon their persecutors; the dying martyrs are surrounded by coronets, roses, lilies, incense, while the abyss opens to swallow up their enemies."

The highest source of knowledge, with these heretics, was a secret tradition, in contrast with the open, popular tradition of the Catholic church. In this respect, they differ from Protestant sects, which generally discard tradition altogether and appeal to the Bible only, as understood by themselves. They appealed also to apocryphal documents, which arose in the second century in great numbers, under eminent names of apostolic or pre-Christian times. Epiphanius, in his 26th Heresy, counts the apocrypha of the Gnostics by thousands, and Irenæus found among the Valentinians alone a countless multitude of such writings.[2] And finally, when it suited their purpose, the Gnostics employed single portions of the Bible, without being able to agree either as to the extent or the interpretation of the same. The Old Testament they generally rejected, either entirely, as

---

[1] Dr. Lipsius, *Die Apokryphen Apostelgeschichten und Apostellegenden* (1883), vol. I. p. 7.

[2] *Adv. Haer.* I. c. 20. § 1: Ἀμίθητον πλῆθος ἀποκρύφων καὶ νόθων γραφῶν, ἃς αὐτοὶ ἔπλασαν, παρεισφέρουσιν εἰς κατάπληξιν τῶν ἀνοήτων καὶ τὰ τῆς ἀληθείας μὴ ἐπισταμένων γράμματα.

in the case of the Marcionites and the Manichæans, or at least in great part; and in the New Testament they preferred certain books or portions, such as the Gospel of John, with its profound spiritual intuitions, and either rejected the other books, or wrested them to suit their ideas. Marcion, for example, thus mutilated the Gospel of Luke, and received in addition to it only ten of Paul's Epistles, thus substituting an arbitrary canon of eleven books for the catholic Testament of twenty-seven. In interpretation they adopted, even with far less moderation than Philo, the most arbitrary and extravagant allegorical principles; despising the letter as sensuous, and the laws of language and exegesis as fetters of the mind. The number 30 in the New Testament, for instance, particularly in the life of Jesus, is made to denote the number of the Valentinian æons; and the lost sheep in the parable is Achamoth. Even to heathen authors, to the poems of Homer, Aratus, Anacreon, they applied this method, and discovered in these works the deepest Gnostic mysteries.[1] They gathered from the whole field of ancient mythology, astronomy, physics, and magic, everything which could serve in any way to support their fancies.

The common characteristics of nearly all the Gnostic systems are (1) Dualism; the assumption of an eternal antagonism between God and matter. (2) The demiurgic notion; the separation of the creator of the world or the demiurgos from the proper God. (3) Docetism; the resolution of the human element in the person of the Redeemer into mere deceptive appearance.[2]

We will endeavor now to present a clear and connected view of the theoretical and practical system of Gnosticism in general, as it comes before us in its more fully developed forms, especially the Valentinian school.

1. THE GNOSTIC THEOLOGY. The system starts from absolute primal being. God is the unfathomable abyss,[3] locked up within himself, without beginning, unnamable, and incomprehensible; on the one hand, infinitely exalted above every exist-

---

[1] Hippol. *Philos.* IV. 46, V. 8, 13, 20.

[2] Δόκητις, φάντασμα.   [3] Βυθός.

ence; yet, on the other hand, the original æon, the sum of all ideas and spiritual powers. Basilides would not ascribe even existence to him, and thus, like Hegel, starts from absolute nonentity, which, however, is identical with absolute being.[1] He began where modern Agnosticism ends.

2. KOSMOLOGY. The abyss opens; God enters upon a process of development, and sends forth from his bosom the several æons; that is, the attributes and unfolded powers of his nature, the ideas of the eternal spirit-world, such as mind, reason, wisdom, power, truth, life.[2] These emanate from the absolute in a certain order, according to Valentine in pairs with sexual polarity. The further they go from the great source, the poorer and weaker they become. Besides the notion of emanation,[3] the Gnostics employed also, to illustrate the self-revelation of the absolute, the figure of the evolution of numbers from an original unit, or of utterance in tones gradually diminishing to the faint echo.[4] The cause of the procession of the æons is, with some, as with Valentine, the self-limiting love of God; with others, metaphysical necessity. The whole body of æons forms the ideal world, or light-world, or spiritual fulness, the *Pleroma*, as opposed to the *Kenoma*, or the material world of emptiness. The one is the totality of the divine powers and attributes, the other the region of shadow and darkness. Christ belongs to the Pleroma, as the chief of the æons; the Demiurge or Creator belongs to the Kenoma. In opposition to the incipient form of this heresy, St. Paul taught that *Jesus Christ* is the whole pleroma

---

[1] So in the old Hindu philosophy, absolute Being is regarded as the ground of all existence. It is itself devoid of qualities, incapable of definition, inconceivable, neither one thing nor another thing, yet containing in itself the possibilities of all things: and out from its dark depths the universe was evolved through some mysterious impulse. The Vedas describe it thus: "It is neither Brahma, nor Vishnoo, nor Sivan, but something back of these, without passion, neither great nor small, neither male nor female, but something far beyond."

[2] Νοῦς, λόγος, σοφία, δύναμις, ἀλήθεια, ζωή, etc.

[3] Ἱροβολή (from προβάλλω), a putting forward, a projection.

[4] Basilides and Saturninus use the former illustration; Marcos uses the latter.

of the Godhead (Col. 1: 19; 2: 9), and the church the reflected pleroma of Christ (Eph. 1: 22).

The material visible world is the abode of the principle of evil. This cannot proceed from God; else he were himself the author of evil. It must come from an opposite principle. This is *Matter* (ὕλη), which stands in eternal opposition to God and the ideal world. The Syrian Gnostics, and still more the Manichæans, agreed with Parsism in conceiving Matter as an intrinsically evil substance, the raging kingdom of Satan, at irreconcilable warfare with the kingdom of light. The Alexandrian Gnostics followed more the Platonic idea of the ὕλη, and conceived this as κένωμα, emptiness, in contrast with πλήρωμα, the divine, vital fulness, or as the μὴ ὄν, related to the divine being as shadow to light, and forming the dark limit beyond which the mind cannot pass. This Matter is in itself dead, but becomes animated by a union with the Pleroma, which again is variously described. In the Manichæan system there are powers of darkness, which seize by force some parts of the kingdom of light. But usually the union is made to proceed from above. The last link in the chain of divine æons, either too weak to keep its hold on the ideal world, or seized with a sinful passion for the embrace of the infinite abyss, falls as a spark of light into the dark chaos of matter, and imparts to it a germ of divine life, but in this bondage feels a painful longing after redemption, with which the whole world of æons sympathizes. This weakest æon is called by Valentine the lower Wisdom, or Achamoth[1], and marks the extreme point, where spirit must surrender itself to matter, where the infinite must enter into the finite, and thus form a basis for the real world. The myth of Achamoth is grounded in the thought, that the finite is incompatible with the absolute, yet in some sense demands it to account for itself.

Here now comes in the third principle of the Gnostic specula-

---

[1] Ἡ κάτω σοφία, Ἀχαμώθ (Iren. I. 4; in Stieren, I. 44), הַחָכְמוֹת, or אַכִּימוּת, the Chaldaic form of the Hebrew חָכְמָה.

tion, namely, the world-maker, commonly called the *Demiurge*,[1] termed by Basilides "Archon" or world-ruler, by the Ophites, "Jaldabaoth," or son of chaos. He is a creature of the fallen æon, formed of physical material, and thus standing between God and Matter. He makes out of Matter the visible sensible world, and rules over it. He has his throne in the planetary heavens, and presides over time and over the sidereal spirits. Astrological influences were generally ascribed to him. He is the God of Judaism, the Jehovah, who imagines himself to be the supreme and only God. But in the further development of this idea the systems differ; the anti-Jewish Gnostics, Marcion and the Ophites, represent the Demiurge as an insolent being, resisting the purposes of God; while the Judaizing Gnostics, Basilides and Valentine, make him a restricted, unconscious instrument of God to prepare the way for redemption.

3. CHRISTOLOGY and SOTERIOLOGY. Redemption itself is the liberation of the light-spirit from the chains of dark Matter, and is effected by *Christ*, the most perfect æon, who is the mediator of return from the sensible phenomenal world to the supersensuous ideal world, just as the Demiurge is the mediator of apostacy from the Pleroma to the Kenoma. This redeeming æon, called by Valentine σωτήρ or Ἰησοῦς, descends through the sphere of heaven, and assumes the ethereal appearance of a body; according to another view, unites himself with the man Jesus, or with the Jewish Messiah, at the baptism, and forsakes him again at the passion. At all events, the redeemer, however conceived in other respects, is allowed no actual contact with sinful matter. His human birth, his sufferings and death, are explained by Gnosticism after the manner of the Indian mythology, as a deceptive appearance, a transient vision, a spectral form, which he assumed only to reveal himself to the sensuous nature of man. Reduced to a clear philosophical definition, the Gnostic Christ is really nothing more than the ideal spirit of man himself, as in the mythical gospel-theory of Strauss. The

---

[1] Δημιουργός, a term used by Plato in a similar sense.

Holy Ghost is commonly conceived as a subordinate æon. The central fact in the work of Christ is the communication of the Gnosis to a small circle of the initiated, prompting and enabling them to strive with clear consciousness after the ideal world and the original unity. According to Valentine, the heavenly Soter brings Achamoth after innumerable sufferings into the Pleroma, and unites himself with her—the most glorious æon with the lowest—in an eternal spirit-marriage. With this, all disturbance in the heaven of æons is allayed, and a blessed harmony and inexpressible delight are restored, in which all spiritual (pneumatic) men, or genuine Gnostics, share. Matter is at last entirely consumed by a fire breaking out from its dark bosom.

4. The ANTHROPOLOGY of the Gnostics corresponds with their theology. Man is a microcosm, consisting of spirit, body, and soul, reflecting the three principles, God, Matter, and Demiurge, though in very different degrees. There are three classes of men: the *spiritual*,[1] in whom the divine element, a spark of light from the ideal world, predominates; the *material*,[2] bodily, carnal, physical, in whom matter, the gross sensuous principle, rules; and the *psychical*,[3] in whom the demiurgic, quasi-divine principle, the mean between the two preceding, prevails.

These three classes are frequently identified with the adherents of the three religions respectively; the spiritual with the Christians, the carnal with the heathens, the psychical with the Jews. But they also made the same distinction among the professors of any one religion, particularly among the Christians; and they regarded themselves as the genuine spiritual men in the full sense of the word; while they looked upon the great mass of Christians[4] as only psychical, not able to rise from blind faith to true knowledge, too weak for the good, and too tender for the evil, longing for the divine, yet unable to attain it, and thus hovering between the Pleroma of the ideal world and the Kenoma of the sensual.

Ingenious as this thought is, it is just the basis of that un-

---

[1] Πνευματικοί.   [2] Σωματικοί, φυσικοί, σαρκικοί, ὑλικοί.   [3] Ψυχικοί.   [4] Οἱ πολλοί.

christian distinction of esoteric and exoteric religion, and that pride of knowledge, in which Gnosticism runs directly counter to the Christian virtues of humility and love.

§ 118. *Ethics of Gnosticism.*

All the Gnostic heretics agree in disparaging the divinely created body, and over-rating the intellect. Beyond this, we perceive among them two opposite tendencies: a gloomy asceticism, and a frivolous antinomianism; both grounded in the dualistic principle, which falsely ascribes evil to matter, and traces nature to the devil. The two extremes frequently met, and the Nicolaitan maxim in regard to the abuse of the flesh[1] was made to serve asceticism first, and then libertinism.

The ascetic Gnostics, like Marcion, Saturninus, Tatian, and the Manichæans, were pessimists. They felt uncomfortable in the sensuous and perishing world, ruled by the Demiurge, and by Satan; they abhorred the body as formed from Matter, and forbade the use of certain kinds of food and all nuptial intercourse, as an adulteration of themselves with sinful Matter; like the Essenes and the errorists noticed by Paul in the Colossians and Pastoral Epistles. They thus confounded sin with matter, and vainly imagined that, matter being dropped, sin, its accident, would fall with it. Instead of hating sin only, which God has not made, they hated the world, which he has made.

The licentious Gnostics, as the Nicolaitans, the Ophites, the Carpocratians, and the Antitactes, in a proud conceit of the exaltation of the spirit above matter, or even on the diabolical principle, that sensuality must be overcome by indulging it, bade defiance to all moral laws, and gave themselves up to the most shameless licentiousness. It is no great thing, said they, according to Clement of Alexandria, to restrain lust; but it is surely a great thing not to be conquered by lust, when one indulges in it. According to Epiphanius there were Gnostic sects in Egypt, which, starting from a filthy, materialistic pantheism

---

[1] Δεῖ καταχρῆσθαι τῇ σαρκί, the flesh must be abused to be conquered.

and identifying Christ with the generative powers of nature, practised debauchery as a mode of worship, and after having, as they thought, offered and collected all their strength, blasphemously exclaimed: " I am Christ." From these pools of sensuality and Satanic pride arose the malaria of a vast literature, of which, however, fortunately, nothing more than a few names has come down to us.

§ 119. *Cultus and Organization.*

In cultus, the Gnostic docetism and hyper-spiritualism led consistently to naked intellectual simplicity; sometimes to the rejection of all sacraments and outward means of grace; if not even, as in the Prodicians, to blasphemous self-exaltation above all that is called God and worshiped.[1]

But with this came also the opposite extreme of a symbolic and mystic pomp, especially in the sect of the Marcosians. These Marcosians held to a two-fold baptism, that applied to the human Jesus, the Messiah of the psychical, and that administered to the heavenly Christ, the Messiah of the spiritual; they decorated the baptistery like a banquet-hall; and they first introduced extreme unction. As early as the second century the Basilideans celebrated the feast of Epiphany. The Simonians and Carpocratians used images of Christ and of their religious heroes in their worship. The Valentinians and Ophites sang in hymns the deep longing of Achamoth for redemption from the bonds of Matter. Bardesanes is known as the first Syrian hymn-writer. Many Gnostics, following their patriarch, Simon, gave themselves to magic, and introduced their arts into their worship; as the Marcosians did in the celebration of the Lord's Supper.

Of the outward organization of the Gnostics (with the exception of the Manichæans, who will be treated separately), we can say little. Their aim was to resolve Christianity into a magnificent speculation; the practical business of organization

[1] Comp. 2 Thess. 2: 4.

was foreign to their exclusively intellectual bent. Tertullian charges them with an entire want of order and discipline.[1] They formed, not so much a sect or party, as a multitude of philosophical schools, like the modern Rationalists. Many were unwilling to separate at all from the Catholic church, but assumed in it, as theosophists, the highest spiritual rank. Some were even clothed with ecclesiastical office, as we must no doubt infer from the Apostolic Canons (51 or 50), where it is said, with evident reference to the gloomy, perverse asceticism of the Gnostics : " If a bishop, a priest, or a deacon, or any ecclesiastic abstain from marriage, from flesh, or from wine, not for practice in self-denial, but from disgust,[2] forgetting that God made everything very good, that he made also the male and the female, in fact, even blaspheming the creation ; [3] he shall either retract his error, or be deposed and cast out of the church. A layman also shall be treated in like manner." Here we perceive the polemical attitude which the Catholic church was compelled to assume even towards the better Gnostics.

§ 120. *Schools of Gnosticism.*

The arbitrary and unbalanced subjectivity of the Gnostic speculation naturally produced a multitude of schools. These Gnostic schools have been variously classified.

Geographically they may be reduced to two great families, the Egyptian or Alexandrian, and the Syrian, which are also intrinsically different. In the former (Basilides, Valentine, the Ophites), Platonism and the emanation theory prevail, in the latter (Saturninus, Bardesanes, Tatian), Parsism and dualism. Then, distinct in many respects from both these is the more practical school of Marcion, who sprang neither from Egypt nor from Syria, but from Asia Minor, where St. Paul had left the strong imprint of his free gospel in opposition to Jewish legalism and bondage.

Examined further, with reference to its doctrinal character,

---

[1] *De Præscr. Hæret.*, c. 41.   [2] βδελυρία.   [3] βλασφημῶν διαβάλλει τὴν δημιουργίαν.

Gnosticism appears in three forms, distinguished by the preponderance of the heathen, the Jewish, and the Christian elements respectively in its syncretism. The Simonians, Nicolaitans, Ophites, Carpocratians, Prodicians, Antitactes, and Manichæans belong to a paganizing class; Cerinthus, Basilides, Valentine, and Justin (as also the Pseudo-Clementine Homilies, though these are more properly Ebionitic), to a Judaizing; Saturninus, Marcion, Tatian, and the Encratites, to a Christianizing division. But it must be remembered here, that this distinction is only relative; all the Gnostic systems being, in fact, predominantly heathen in their character, and essentially opposed alike to the pure Judaism of the Old Testament and to the Christianity of the New. The Judaism of the so-called Judaizing Gnostics is only of an apocryphal sort, whether of the Alexandrian or the Cabalistic tinge.[1]

The ethical point of view, from which the division might as well be made, would give likewise three main branches: the speculative or theosophic Gnostics (Basilides, Valentine), the practical and ascetic (Marcion, Saturninus, Tatian), and the antinomian and libertine (Simonians, Nicolaitans, Ophites, Carpocratians, Antitactes).

Having thus presented the general character of Gnosticism, and pointed out its main branches, we shall follow chiefly the chronological order in describing the several schools, beginning with those which date from the age of the apostles.

---

[1] Gibbon, who devotes four pages (Ch. XV.) to the Gnostics, dwells exclusively on the anti-Jewish feature, and makes them express his own aversion to the Old Testament. He calls them (from very superficial knowledge, but with his masterly skill of insinuation) "the most polite. the most learned, and the most wealthy of the Christian name," and says that, being mostly averse to the pleasures of sense, "they morosely arraigned the polygamy of the patriarchs, the gallantries of David, and the seraglio of Solomon," and were at a loss to reconcile "the conquest of Canaan, and the extirpation of the unsuspecting natives with the common notions of humanity and justice."

§ 121. Simon Magus and the Simonians.

I. Commentaries on Acts 8: 9–24. JUSTIN MARTYR: Apol. I. 26 and 56. The pseudo-Clementine *Homilies* and *Recognitions*. IRENÆUS, I. 23. HIPPOLYTUS, VI. 2–15, etc.

II. SIMSON: *Leben und Lehre Simon des Magiers*, in the "Zeitschrift für hist. Theologie" for 1841.

HILGENFELD: *Der Magier Simon*, in the "Zeischrift für wissenschaftl. Theologie" for 1868.

LIPSIUS: *Simon d. Mag.* in Schenkel's "Bibel-Lexikon," vol. V. (1875), p. 301–321. Comp. the literature quoted there, p. 320.

Simon Magus is a historical character known to us from the eighth chapter of the Acts of the Apostles.[1] He was probably a native of Gitthon, in Samaria, as Justin Martyr, himself a Samaritan, reports;[2] but he may nevertheless be identical with the contemporaneous Jewish magician of the same name, whom Josephus mentions as a native of Cyprus and as a friend of Procurator Felix, who employed him to alienate Drusilla, the beautiful wife of king Azizus of Emesa, in Syria, from her husband, that he might marry her.[3]

[1] The Tübingen school, which denies the historical character of the Acts, resolves also the story of Simon into a Jewish Christian fiction, aimed at the apostle Paul as the real heretic and magician. So Baur, Zeller, and Volkmar. Lipsius ingeniously carries out this Simon-Paul hypothesis, and declares (*l. c.* p. 303): "*Der Kern der Sage ist nichts als ein vollständig ausgeführtes Zerrbild des Heidenapostels, dessen Züge bis in's einzelne hinein die Person, die Lehre, und die Lebenschicksale des Paulus persifliren sollen.*" But the book of Acts gives the earliest record of Simon and is the production, if not of Luke, as we believe with the unanimous testimony of antiquity, at all events of a writer friendly to Paul, and therefore utterly unlikely to insert an anti-Pauline fiction which would stultify the greater part of his own book. Comp. the remarks above, § 114, p. 438.

[2] *Apol.* I. 26 (Σίμωνα μέν τινα Σαμαρέα, τὸν ἀπὸ κώμης λεγομένης Γιττῶν); comp. *Clem. Hom.* I. 15; II. 22 (ἀπὸ Γιτθῶν); Hippol. *Philos.* VI. 7 (ὁ Γιττηνός). There was such a place as Γίτται, not far from Flavia Neapolis (Nablus), Justin's birth-place. It is now called Kuryet Jît (Dschit). See Robinson's *Pal.* II. 308, and Otto's note on the passage in Justin (*Opera* I. 78).

[3] According to Josephus, *Ant.* XX. 7, 2. The identity is assumed by Neander, De Wette, Hilgenfeld. There was on the island of Cyprus a city named Κίτιον (Thucyd. I. 112, 1), which Justin M. may possibly have confounded with Gitthon, in Samaria, as he confounded *Simo* and *Semo* on the statue in Rome. But it is much more likely that Josephus was mistaken on a question of Samaria than Justin, a native of Flavia Neapolis (the ancient Shechem).

Simon represented himself as a sort of emanation of the deity
("the Great Power of God"),[1] made a great noise among the
half-pagan, half-Jewish Samaritans by his sorceries, was baptized by Philip about the year 40, but terribly rebuked by Peter
for hypocrisy and abuse of holy things to sordid ends.[2] He
thus affords the first instance in church history of a confused
syncretism in union with magical arts; and so far as this goes,
the church fathers are right in styling him the patriarch, or, in
the words of Irenæus, the "magister" and "progenitor" of all
heretics, and of the Gnostics in particular. Besides him, two
other contemporaneous Samaritans, Dositheus and Menander,
bore the reputation of heresiarchs. Samaria was a fertile soil
of religious syncretism even before Christ, and the natural
birth-place of that syncretistic heresy which goes by the name
of Gnosticism.

The wandering life and teaching of Simon were fabulously
garnished in the second and third centuries by Catholics and
heretics, but especially by the latter in the interest of Ebionism
and with bitter hostility to Paul. In the pseudo-Clementine
romances he represents all anti-Jewish heresies. Simon the
Magician is contrasted, as the apostle of falsehood, with Simon
Peter, the apostle of truth; he follows him, as darkness follows
the light, from city to city, in company with Helena (who had
previously been a prostitute at Tyre, but was now elevated to
the dignity of divine intelligence); he is refuted by Peter in
public disputations at Cæsarea, Antioch, and Rome; at last he
is ignominiously defeated by him after a mock-resurrection and
mock-ascension before the Emperor Nero; he ends with suicide,
while Peter gains the crown of martyrdom.[3] There is a bare

[1] ἡ Δίναμις τοῦ θεοῦ ἡ Μεγάλη, Acts 8: 10. According to the Clementine
Homilies (II. 22) and *Recognitions* (II. 7), Simon called himself "the Supreme
Power of God" (ἀνωτάτη δίναμις, *Virtus Suprema*).

[2] The memory of this incident is perpetuated in the name of *simony* for profane traffic in ecclesiastical offices.

[3] The legendary accounts, both catholic and heretical, vary considerably.
Justin M. reports Simon's visit to Rome, but assigns it to the reign of Claudius
(41–54), and says nothing of an encounter with Peter. Other reports put the

possibility that, like other heretics and founders of sects, he may have repaired to Rome (before Peter); but Justin Martyr's account of the statue of Simon is certainly a mistake.[1]

The Gnosticism which Irenæus, Hippolytus, and other fathers ascribe to this Simon and his followers is crude, and belongs to the earlier phase of this heresy. It was embodied in a work entitled "The Great Announcement" or "Proclamation,"[2] of which Hippolytus gives an analysis.[3] The chief ideas are "the great power," "the great idea," the male and female principle. He declared himself an incarnation of the creative world-spirit, and his female companion, Helena, the incarnation of the receptive world-soul. Here we have the Gnostic conception of the syzygy.

The sect of the Simonians, which continued into the third century, took its name, if not its rise, from Simon Magus, worshipped him as a redeeming genius, chose, like the Cainites, the most infamous characters of the Old Testament for its heroes, and was immoral in its principles and practices. The name, however, is used in a very indefinite sense, for various sorts of Gnostics.

journey in the reign of Nero (54–68). According to Hippolytus, Simon was buried alive at his own request, being confident of rising again on the third day, as a pseudo-Christ. According to the Apostolical Constitutions, he attempted to fly, but fell and broke his thigh and ankle-bone in answer to the prayers of Peter, and died in consequence of this injury. According to Arnobius, he attempted to ascend in a fiery chariot, like Elijah, but broke his leg, and in the confusion of shame committed suicide by throwing himself from a high mountain. See Lipsius, *l. c.* p. 310.

[1] He reports (*Apol.* I. 26 and 56) that Simon Magus made such an impression by his magical arts upon the Roman Senate and people that they paid him divine homage, and erected a statue to him on the island of the Tiber. But he mistook *Semo Sancus* or *Sangus*, a Sabine-Roman divinity unknown to him, for *Simo Sanctus*. For in 1574 a statue was found in the place described, with the inscription: *Semoni Sanco Deo Fidio sacrum*, etc. The mistake is repeated by Irenæus *Adv. Hær.* I. 23, 1, Tertullian *Apol.* 13, and Eusebius, but Hippolytus who resided at Rome does not mention it. See Otto's note on Just. I. 26, *Opera* I. 79 sq. (ed. III).

[2] Ἀπόφασις μεγάλη.   [3] *Philos.* VI. 6 sqq.

§ 122. The Nicolaitans.

IRENÆUS: *Adv. Hær.* I. 26, 3; CLEMENT OF ALEX.: *Strom.* III. 4 (and in Euseb. *H. E.* III. 29); HIPPOLYTUS: *Philos.* VII. 24; EPIPHANIUS: *Hær.* I. 2, 25.

The Nicolaitans are mentioned as a licentious sect in the Apocalypse (2: 6, 15). They claimed as their founder Nicolas, a proselyte of Antioch and one of the seven deacons of the congregation of Jerusalem (Acts 6: 5). He is supposed to have apostatized from the true faith, and taught the dangerous principle that the flesh must be abused,[1] that is, at least as understood by his disciples, one must make the whole round of sensuality, to become its perfect master.

But the views of the fathers are conflicting. Irenæus (who is followed substantially by Hippolytus) gives a very unfavorable account.

"The Nicolaitanes," he says, "are the followers of that Nicolas who was one of the seven first ordained to the diaconate by the apostles. They lead lives of unrestrained indulgence. The character of these men is very plainly pointed out in the Apocalypse of John, where they are represented as teaching that it is a matter of indifference to practice adultery, and to eat things sacrificed to idols. Wherefore the Word has also spoken of them thus: ' But this thou hast, that thou hatest the deeds of the Nicolaitanes, which I also hate.' "

Clement of Alexandria says that Nicolas was a faithful husband, and brought up his children in purity, but that his disciples misunderstood his saying (which he attributes also to the Apostle Matthias), "that we must fight against the flesh and abuse it."[2]

---

[1] Δεῖ καταχρῆσθαι τῇ σαρκί.

[2] He adds the curious statement (*Strom.* III. c. 4) that on a certain occasion Nicolas was sharply reproved by the Apostles as a jealous husband, and repelled the charge by offering to allow his beautiful wife to become the wife of any other person. Extremely improbable.

§ 123. *Cerinthus.*

IREN. I. (25) 26, § 1; III. 3, § 4; III. 11, § 1; HIPPOL. VII. 21; EUSEB. III. 28; IV. 14. Comp. DORNER: *Lehre v. der Person Christi*, I. 314 sq. Art. Cerinth in "Smith and Wace," I. 447.

Cerinthus[1] appeared towards the close of the first century in Asia Minor, and came in conflict with the aged Apostle John, who is supposed by Irenæus to have opposed his Gnostic ideas in the Gospel and Epistles. The story that John left a public bath when he saw Cerinthus, the enemy of the truth, fearing that the bath might fall in, and the similar story of Polycarp meeting Marcion and calling him "the first born of Satan," reveal the intense abhorrence with which the orthodox church-men of those days looked upon heresy.[2]

Cerinthus was (according to the uncertain traditions collected by Epiphanius) an Egyptian and a Jew either by birth or con-version, studied in the school of Philo in Alexandria, was one of the false apostles who opposed Paul and demanded circum-cision (Gal. 2: 4; 2 Cor. 11: 13), claimed to have received an-gelic revelations, travelled through Palestine and Galatia, and once came to Ephesus. The time of his death is unknown.

His views, as far as they can be ascertained from confused accounts, assign him a position between Judaism and Gnosticism proper. He rejected all the Gospels except a mutilated Mat-thew, taught the validity of the Mosaic law and the millennial kingdom. He was so far strongly Judaistic, and may be counted among the Ebionites; but in true Gnostic style he dis-tinguished the world-maker from God, and represented the for-mer as a subordinate power, as an intermediate, though not exactly hostile, being. In his Christology he separates the earthly man Jesus, who was a son of Joseph and Mary, from the heavenly Christ,[3] who descended upon the man Jesus in the

---

[1] Κήρινθος.

[2] Both recorded by Irenæus III. c. 3, § 4, as illustrating Tit. 3: 10. But the same story of John in the bath is also told of Ebion, whose very existence is doubtful.

[3] ὁ ἄνω Χριστός. He also calls the Holy Spirit ἡ ἄνω δύναμις, the power from on high which came down upon Jesus. Valentine called the Jewish

form of a dove at the baptism in the Jordan, imparted to him the genuine knowledge of God and the power of miracles, but forsook him in the passion, to rejoin him only at the coming of the Messianic kingdom of glory. The school of Valentine made more clearly the same distinction between the Jesus of the Jews and the divine Saviour, or the lower and the higher Christ —a crude anticipation of the modern distinction (of Strauss) between the Christ of history and the Christ of faith. The millennium has its centre in Jerusalem, and will be followed by the restoration of all things.[1]

The Alogi, an obscure anti-trinitarian and anti-chiliastic sect of the second century, regarded Cerinthus as the author of the Apocalypse of John on account of the chiliasm taught in it. They ascribed to him also the fourth Gospel, although it is the best possible refutation of all false Gnosticism from the highest experimental Gnosis of faith.

Simon Magus, the Nicolaitans, and Cerinthus belong to the second half of the first century. We now proceed to the more developed systems of Gnosticism, which belong to the first half of the second century, and continued to flourish till the middle of the third.

The most important and influential of these systems bear the names of Basilides, Valentinus, and Marcion. They deserve, therefore, a fuller consideration. They were nearly contemporaneous, and matured during the reigns of Hadrian and Antoninus Pius. Basilides flourished in Alexandria A.D. 125; Valentine came to Rome in 140; Marcion taught in Rome between 140 and 150.

§ 124. *Basilides.*

Besides the sources in Irenæus, Hippolytus (L. VII. 20–27), Clemens Alex. (Strom. VII.), Eusebius (IV. 7), and Epiphanius, comp. the following monographs:

Messiah ὁ κάτω Χριστός. The best account of Cerinth's Christology is given by Dorner.

[1] The chiliastic eschatology of Cerinthus is omitted by Irenæus, who was himself a chiliast, though of a higher spiritual order, but it is described by Caius, Dionysius (in Eusebius), Theodoret, and Augustin.

JACOBI: *Basilidis philosophi Gnostici Sentent. ex Hippolyti lib. nuper reperto illustr.* Berlin, 1852. Comp. his article *Gnosis* in Herzog, vol. V. 219–223, and in Brieger's " Zeitschrift für Kirchengesch." for 1876–77 (I. 481–544).

UHLHORN: *Das Basilidianische System.* Göttingen, 1855. The best analysis.

BAUR in the Tübinger "Theol. Jahrbücher" for 1856, pp. 121–162.

HOFSTEDE DE GROOT: *Basilides as witness for the Gospel of John*, in Dutch, and in an enlarged form in German. Leipz. 1868. Apologetic for the genuineness of the fourth Gospel.

Dr. HORT in Smith and Wace, "Dictionary of Christian Biography" (Lond. 1877). I. 268–281 (comp. " Abrasax," p. 9–10). Very able.

HILGENFELD, in his "Zeitschrift für wissensch. Theol." 1878, XXI. 228–250, and the lit. there given.

Basilides (*Βασιλείδης*) produced the first well-developed system of Gnosis; but it was too metaphysical and intricate to be popular. He claimed to be a disciple of the apostle Matthias and of an interpreter (ἑρμηνεύς) of St. Peter, named Glaucias. He taught in Alexandria during the reign of Hadrian (A.D. 117–138). His early youth fell in the second generation of Christians, and this gives his quotations from the writings of the New Testament considerable apologetic value. He wrote (according to his opponent, Agrippa Castor) "twenty-four books (βιβλία) on the Gospel." This work was probably a commentary on the canonical Gospels, for Clement of Alexandria quotes from "the thirty-third book" of a work of Basilides which he calls " *Exegetica.*" [1]

His doctrine is very peculiar, especially according to the extended and original exhibition of it in the " *Philosophumena.*" Hippolytus deviates in many respects from the statements of Irenæus and Epiphanius, but derived his information probably from the works of Basilides himself, and he therefore must be

---

[1] Comp. Euseb. *Hist. Eccl.* IV. 7 and Clem. Alex. *Strom.* IV. 12. p. 599 sq. Origen (*Hom. in Luc.* I : 1) says that Basilides "had the audacity (ἐτόλμησεν) to write a Gospel according to Basilides;" but he probably mistook the commentary for an apocryphal Gospel. Hippolytus expressly asserts that Basilides, in his account of all things concerning the Saviour after "the birth of Jesus" agreed with "the Gospels."

chiefly followed.[1] The system is based on the Egyptian astronomy and the Pythagorean numerical symbolism. It betrays also the influence of Aristotle; but Platonism, the emanation-theory, and dualism do not appear.

Basilides is monotheistic rather than dualistic in his primary idea, and so far differs from the other Gnostics, though later accounts make him a dualist. He starts from the most abstract notion of the absolute, to which he denies even existence, thinking of it as infinitely above all that can be imagined and conceived.[2] This ineffable and unnamable God,[3] not only super-existent, but non-existent,[4] first forms by his creative word (not by emanation) the world-seed or world-embryo,[5] that is, chaos, from which the world develops itself according to arithmetical relations, in an unbroken order, like the branches and leaves of the tree from the mustard seed, or like the many-colored peacock from the egg. Everything created tends upwards towards God, who, himself unmoved, moves all,[6] and by the charm of surpassing beauty attracts all to himself.

In the world-seed Basilides distinguishes three kinds of sonship,[7] of the same essence with the non-existent God, but growing weaker in the more remote gradations; or three races of

---

[1] The prevailing opinion is that Hippolytus gives the system of Basilides himself, Irenæus that of his school. So Jacobi, Uhlhorn, Baur, Schaff (first ed.), Möller, Mansel, Hort. The opposite view is defended by Hilgenfeld, Lipsius, Volkmar and Scholten. The reasoning of Hort in favor of the former view, *l. c.* p. 269 sq., is based on the extracts of Clement of Alex. from the ἐξηγητικά of Basilides. He assumes the priority of the Valentinian system, from which Basilides proceeded to construct his own by contrast. But history puts Valentinus about a decade later.

[2] Herein, as already remarked, he resembles Hegel, who likewise begins with the idea of absolute non-entity, and reconstructs the universe *ex nihilo*. In both systems "nothing" must be understood in a non-natural sense, as opposed to all definite, concrete being or form of existence. It is in fact identical with the most abstract conception of pure being. *Nichts ist Sein*, and *Sein ist Nichts*, but, set in motion by a dialectic process, they produce the *Werden*, and the *Werden* results in *Dasein*. And here again the latest German philosophy meets with the oldest Hindu mythology. See the note on p. 453.

[3] ἄρρητος, ἀκατονόμαστος.   [4] ὁ οὐκ ὢν θεός.

[5] πανσπερμία—a Stoic idea.   [6] ἀκίνητος κινητής.   [7] υἱότης τριμερής.

children of God, a pneumatic, a psychic, and a hylic. The first sonship liberates itself immediately from the world-seed, rises with the lightning-speed of thought to God, and remains there as the blessed spirit-world, the Pleroma. It embraces the seven highest genii,[1] which, in union with the great Father, form the first ogdoad, the type of all the lower circles of creation. The second sonship, with the help of the Holy Spirit, whom it produces, and who bears it up, as the wing bears the bird, strives to follow the first,[2] but can only attain the impenetrable firmament,[3] that is the limit of the Pleroma, and could endure the higher region no more than the fish the mountain air. The third sonship, finally, remains fixed in the world-seed, and in need of purification and redemption.

Next Basilides makes two archons or world-rulers (demiurges) issue from the world-seed. The first or great archon, whose greatness and beauty and power cannot be uttered, creates the ethereal world or the upper heaven, the ogdoad, as it is called; the second is the maker and ruler of the lower planetary heaven below the moon, the hebdomad. Basilides supposed in all three hundred and sixty-five heavens or circles of creation,[4] corresponding to the days of the year, and designated them by the mystic name *Abrasax*, or *Abraxas*,[5] which, according to the numerical value of the Greek letters, is equal to 365.[6] This

---

[1] νοῦς, λόγος, φρόνησις, σοφία, δίναμις, δικαιοσύνη, and εἰρήνη.

[2] Hence it is called μιμητική. [3] στερέωμα. [4] κτίσεις, ἀρχαί, δυνάμεις, ἐξουσίαι.

[5] Ἀβρασάξ, or Ἀβραξάς. Abraxas is a euphonic inversion, which seems to date from the Latin translator of Irenæus.

[6] Thrice α=3; β=2; ρ=100; σ=200; ξ=60. Epiphanius mentions that the Basilidians referred the word to the 365 parts (μέλη) of the human body as well as to the days of the year. But modern writers are inclined to think that the engravers of the Abrasax gems and the Basilidians received the mystic name from an older common source. Dr. Hort suggests the derivation from *Ab-razach, Ab-zarach, i. e.* "the father of effulgence," a name appropriate to a solar deity. According to Movers, *Serach* was a Phœnician name for Adonis, whose worship was connected with the seasons of the year. Comp. Bellermann, *Ueber die Gemmen der Alten mit dem Abraxasbilde* (Berlin, 1817, '19); King, *The Gnostics and their Remains* (London, 1864), Hort, *l. c.*, Matter, "Abraxas," etc. in Herzog, I. 103–107, and Kraus, in his "Real-Encykl. der christl. Alterthümer," I. 6–10 (with illustrations).

name also denotes the great archon or ruler of the 365 heavens. It afterwards came to be used as a magical formula, with all sorts of strange figures, the "Abraxas gems," of which many are still extant.

Each of the two archons, however, according to a higher ordinance, begets a son, who towers far above his father, communicates to him the knowledge received from the Holy Spirit, concerning the upper spirit-world and the plan of redemption, and leads him to repentance. With this begins the process of the redemption or return of the sighing children of God, that is, the pneumatics, to the supra-mundane God. This is effected by Christianity, and ends with the consummation, or apokatastasis of all things. Like Valentine, Basilides also properly held a threefold Christ—the son of the first archon, the son of the second archon, and the son of Mary. But all these are at bottom the same principle, which reclaims the spiritual natures from the world-seed to the original unity. The passion of Christ was necessary to remove the corporeal and psychical elements, which he brought with him from the primitive medley and confusion (σύγχυσις ἀρχική). His body returned, after death, into shapelessness (ἀμορφία); his soul rose from the grave, and stopped in the hebdomad, or planetary heaven, where it belongs; but his spirit soared, perfectly purified, above all the spheres of creation, to the blessed first sonship (υἱότης) and the fellowship of the non-existent or hyper-existent God.

In the same way with Jesus, the first-fruits, all other pneumatic persons must rise purified to the place where they by nature belong, and abide there. For all that continues in its place is imperishable; but all that transgresses its natural limits is perishable. Basilides quotes the passage of Paul concerning the groaning and travailing of the creation expecting the revelation of the sons of God (Rom. 8 : 19). In the process of redemption he conceded to faith (pistis) more importance than most of the Gnostics, and his definition of faith was vaguely derived from Hebrews 11 : 1.

In his moral teaching Basilides inculcated a moderate asceticism, from which, however, his school soon departed. He used some of Paul's Epistles and the canonical Gospels; quoting, for example, John 1: 9 ("The true light, which enlightens every man, was coming into the world"), to identify his idea of the world seed with John's doctrine of the Logos as the light of the world.[1] The fourth Gospel was much used and commented upon also by the Ophites, Perates, and Valentinians before the middle of the second century. The Gnostics were alternately attracted by the mystic Gnosis of that Gospel (especially the Prologue), and repelled by its historic realism, and tried to make the best use of it. They acknowledged it, because they could not help it. The other authorities of Basilides were chiefly the secret tradition of the apostle Matthias, and of a pretended interpreter of Peter, by the name of Glaucias.

His son ISIDORE was the chief, we may say the only important one, of his disciples. He composed a system of ethics and other books, from which Clement of Alexandria has preserved a few extracts. The Basilidians, especially in the West, seem to have been dualistic and docetic in theory, and loose, even dissolute in practice. They corrupted and vulgarized the high-pitched and artificial system of the founder. The whole life of Christ was to them a mere sham. It was Simon of Cyrene who was crucified; Jesus exchanged forms with him on the way, and, standing unseen opposite in Simon's form, mocked those who crucified him, and then ascended to heaven. They held it prudent to repudiate Christianity in times of persecution, regarding the noble confession of martyrs as casting pearls before swine,

---

[1] *Philosoph.*, VII. 22. He also quoted John 2: 4, "My hour is not yet come," and Luke 1: 35, "A Holy Spirit shall come upon thee, and a power of the Most High shall overshadow thee." It is true that Hippolytus sometimes mixes up the opinions of the master with those of his followers. But there is no ambiguity here where Basilides is introduced with φησί, "he says," while when quoting from the school he uses the formula "according to them" (κατ' αὐτούς). The joint testimony of those early heretics (to whom we must add the pseudo-Clementine Homilies and the heathen Celsus) is overwhelming against the Tübingen hypothesis of the late origin of the fourth Gospel. See vol. I. p. 707, and Abbott, *Authorship of the Fourth Gospel*. p. 85 sqq.

and practiced various sorts of magic, in which the Abraxas gems did them service. The spurious Basilidian sect maintained itself in Egypt till the end of the fourth century, but does not seem to have spread beyond, except that Marcus, a native of Memphis, is reported by Sulpicius Severus to have brought some of its doctrines to Spain.

§ 125. *Valentinus.*

I. The sources are: 1) Fragments of VALENTINUS; PTOLOMEY'S *Epistola ad Floram ;* and exegetical fragments of HERACLEON. 2) The patristic accounts and refutations of IRENÆUS (I. 1–21 and throughout his whole work); HIPPOLYTUS (VI. 29–37); TERTULLIAN (*Adv. Valentinianos*); EPIPHANIUS, (*Hær.* XXXI; in Oehler's ed. I. 305–386). The last two depend chiefly upon Irenæus. See on the sources Lipsius and Heinrici (p. 5–148).

II. REN. MASSUET: *Dissert. de Hæreticis*, Art. I. *De Valentino*, in his ed. of Irenæus, and in Stieren's ed. Tom. II. p. 54–134. Very learned and thorough.

GEORGE HEINRICI: *Die. Valentinianische Gnosis und die heilige Schrift.* Berlin, 1871 (192 pages).

Comp. NEANDER (whose account is very good, but lacks the additional information furnished by Hippolytus); ROSSEL, *Theol. Schriften* (Berlin, (1847), p. 280 sqq.; BAUR, *K. Gesch.* I. 195–204; and JACOBI, in Herzog,[2] vol. V. 225–229.

Valentinus or Valentine[1] is the author of the most profound and luxuriant, as well as the most influential and best known of the Gnostic systems. Irenæus directed his work chiefly against it, and we have made it the basis of our general description of Gnosticism.[2] He founded a large school, and spread his doctrines in the West. He claimed to have derived them from Theodas or Theudas, a pupil of St. Paul.[3] He also pretended to have received revelations from the Logos in a vision. Hippolytus calls him a Platonist and Pythagorean rather than a

---

[1] Οὐαλεντῖνος or Βαλεντῖνος.

[2] "No other system, says Baur (I. 203), "affords us such a clear insight into the peculiar character of the Gnosis, the inner connection of its view of the world, and the deeper intellectual character of the whole."

[3] Clemens Alex. *Strom.* l. VII. p. 898 (ed. Potter). Nothing certain is known of Theudas.

Christian. He was probably of Egyptian Jewish descent and Alexandrian education.[1] Tertullian reports, perhaps from his own conjecture, that he broke with the orthodox church from disappointed ambition, not being made a bishop.[2] Valentine came to Rome as a public teacher during the pontificate of Hyginus (137–142), and remained there till the pontificate of Anicetus (154).[3] He was then already celebrated; for Justin Martyr, in his lost "Syntagma against all Heresies," which he mentions in his "First Apology" (140), combated the Valentinians among other heretics before A. D. 140. At that time Rome had become the centre of the church and the gathering place of all sects. Every teacher who wished to exercise a general influence on Christendom naturally looked to the metropolis. Valentine was one of the first Gnostics who taught in Rome, about the same time with Cerdo and Marcion; but though he made a considerable impression by his genius and eloquence, the orthodoxy of the church and the episcopal authority were too firmly settled to allow of any great success for his vagaries. He was excommunicated, and went to Cyprus, where he died about A. D. 160.

His system is an ingenious theogonic and cosmogonic epos. It describes in three acts the creation, the fall, and the redemption; first in heaven, then on earth. Great events repeat themselves in different stages of being. He derived his material from his own fertile imagination, from Oriental and Greek speculations, and from Christian ideas. He made much use of the Prologue of John's Gospel and the Epistles to the Colossians and Ephesians; but by a wild exegesis he put his own pantheistic and mythological fancies into the apostolic words, such as Logos, Only Begotten, Truth, Life, Pleroma, Ecclesia.

---

[1] Epiph. *Hær.* XXXI. 2. The Jewish extraction may be inferred from some of his terms, as "Achamoth."

[2] *De Præsc. Hær.* c. 30, and *Adv. Valent.* c. 4. Tertullian and the orthodox polemics generally are apt to trace all heresies to impure personal motives.

[3] Iren. III. 4, 3. Comp. Euseb. *H. E.* IV. 10, 11 (quoting from Irenæus). All authorities agree that he taught at Rome before the middle of the second century.

Valentine starts from the eternal primal Being, which he significantly calls Bythos or Abyss.[1] It is the fathomless depth in which the thinking mind is lost, the ultimate boundary beyond which it cannot pass. The Bythos is unbegotten, infinite, invisible, incomprehensible, nameless, the absolute agnoston ; yet capable of evolution and development, the universal Father of all beings. He continues for immeasurable ages in silent contemplation of his own boundless grandeur, glory, and beauty. This "Silence" or "Solitude" ($\dot{\eta}$ $\sigma\iota\gamma\dot{\eta}$) is his Spouse or $\sigma\dot{v}\zeta\nu\gamma\upsilon\varsigma$. It is the silent self-contemplation, the slumbering consciousness of the Infinite. He also calls it "Thought" ($\dot{\epsilon}\nu\nu\omicron\iota\alpha$), and "Grace" ($\chi\acute{\alpha}\rho\iota\varsigma$).[2] The pre-mundane Bythos includes, therefore, at least according to some members of the school, the female as well as the male principle; for from the male principle alone nothing could spring. According to Hippolytus, Valentine derived this sexual duality from the essential nature of love, and said : "God is all love; but love is not love except there is some object of affection."[3] He grappled here with a pre-mundane mystery, which the orthodox theology endeavors to solve by the doctrine of the immanent eternal trinity in the divine essence : God is love, therefore God is triune : a loving subject, a beloved object, and a union of the two. "*Ubi amor, ibi trinitas.*"

After this eternal silence, God enters upon a process of evolution or emanation, *i. e.* a succession of generations of antithetic and yet supplementary ideas or principles. From the Abyss emanate thirty æons in fifteen pairs,[4] according to the law of sexual polarity, in three generations, the first called the ogdoad, the second the decad, the third the dodecad. The Æons are the unfolded powers and attributes of the divinity. They corre-

---

[1] $\beta\upsilon\vartheta\acute{o}\varsigma$, also $\pi\rho\omicron\pi\acute{\alpha}\tau\omega\rho$, $\pi\rho\omicron\alpha\rho\chi\dot{\eta}$, $\alpha\dot{\upsilon}\tau\omicron\pi\acute{\alpha}\tau\omega\rho$.

[2] Iren. I. 1, ₰ 1 ; Tert. *Adv. Val.* c. 7.

[3] *Philos.* VI. 24. There seems, however, to have been a difference of opinion among the Valentinians on the companionship of the Bythos, for in ch. 25 we read : "The Father alone, without copulation, has produced an offspring . . . . he alone possesses the power of self-generation."

[4] $\sigma\dot{\upsilon}\zeta\upsilon\gamma\omicron\iota$. The same number of æons as in Hesiod's theogony.

spond to the dynameis in the system of Basilides. God begets first the masculine, productive Mind or Reason (ὁ νοῦς),[1] with the feminine, receptive Truth (ἡ ἀλήθεια); these two produce the Word (ὁ λόγος) and the Life (ἡ ζωή), and these again the (ideal) Man (ὁ ἄνθρωπος) and the (ideal) Church (ἡ ἐκκλησία). The influence of the fourth Gospel is unmistakable here, though of course the terminology of John is used in a sense different from that of its author. The first two syzygies constitute the sacred *Tetraktys*, the root of all things.[2] The Nous and the Aletheia produce ten æons (five pairs); the Logos and the Zoë, twelve æons (six pairs). At last the Nous or Monogenes and the Aletheia bring forth the heavenly Christ (ὁ ἄνω Χριστός) and the (female) Holy Spirit (τὸ πνεῦμα ἅγιον), and therewith complete the number thirty. These æons constitute together the *Pleroma*, the plenitude of divine powers, an expression which St. Paul applied to the historical Christ (Col. 2: 9). They all partake in substance of the life of the Abyss; but their form is conditioned by the Horos (ὅρος), the limiting power of God. This genius of limitation stands between the Pleroma and the Hysterema outside, and is the organizing power of the universe, and secures harmony.[3] If any being dares to transcend its fixed boundaries and to penetrate beyond revelation into the hidden being of God, it is in danger of sinking into nothing. Two actions are ascribed to the Horos, a negative by which he limits every being and sunders from it foreign elements, and the positive by which he forms and establishes it.[4] The former action is emphatically called Horos, the latter is called Stauros (cross, post), because he stands firm and immovable, the guardian of

[1] Also called ὁ πατήρ (as immediately proceeding from the προπάτωρ), the Father, also ὁ μονογενής, the Only Begotten (comp. John 1: 18), and the ἀρχή as the Beginning of all things (comp. ἐν ἀρχῇ, John 1: 1).

[2] The ἱερὰ τετρακτύς of the Pythagoreans. Tert. (c. 7): "*prima quadriga Valentinianæ factionis, matrix et origo cunctorum.*"

[3] "*Es ist eine tiefe Idee des Valentinianischen Systems,*" says Neander (II. 722), "*dass, wie alles Dasein in der Selbstbeschränkung des Bythos seinen Grund hat, so das Dasein aller geschaffenen Wesen auf Beschränkung beruht.*"

[4] The ἐνεργεία μεριστικὴ καὶ διοριστική, and the ἐνεργεία ἑδραστικὴ καὶ στηριστική.

the Æons, so that nothing can come from the Hysterema into the neighborhood of the æons in the Pleroma.

The process of the fall and redemption takes place first in the ideal world of the Pleroma, and is then repeated in the lower world. In this process the lower Wisdom or *Sophia*, also called *Achamoth* or *Chakmuth* plays an important part.[1] She is the mundane soul, a female æon, the weakest and most remote member of the series of æons (in number the twenty-eighth), and forms, so to speak, the bridge which spans the abyss between God and the real world. Feeling her loneliness and estrangement from the great Father, she wishes to unite herself immediately, without regard to the intervening links, with him who is the originating principle of the universe, and alone has the power of self-generation. She jumps, as it were by a single bound, into the depth of the eternal Father, and brings forth of herself alone an abortion ($\xi \kappa \tau \rho \omega \mu a$), a formless and inchoate substance,[2] of which Moses speaks when he says: "The earth was without form and void." By this sinful passion she introduces confusion and disturbance into the Pleroma.[3] She wanders about outside of it, and suffers with fear, anxiety, and despair on account of her abortion. This is the fall; an act both free and necessary.

But Sophia yearns after redemption; the æons sympathize with her sufferings and aspirations; the eternal Father himself commands the projection of the last pair of æons, Christ and the Holy Spirit, "for the restoration of Form, the destruction of the abortion, and for the consolation and cessation of the groans of Sophia." They comfort and cheer the Sophia, and separate

---

[1] Usually identified with *Chocmah*, but by Lipsius and Jacobi with *Chakmuth*, the world-mother, which has a place in the system of Bardesanes. The idea of Sophia as the mediatrix of creation is no doubt borrowed from the Proverbs and the Wisdom of Solomon.

[2] οὐσία ἄμορφος καὶ ἀκατασκεύαστος. *Philos.* VI. 28 (30 ed. Duncker and Schneidewin, I. 274). The Thohuvabohu of Genesis.

[3] "Ignorance having arisen within the Pleroma in consequence of Sophia, and shapelessness (ἀμορφία) in consequence of the offspring of Sophia, confusion arose in the pleroma (θόρυβος ἐγένετο ἐν πληρώματι)." *Philos.* VI. 26 (31 in Duncker and Schneidewin).

the abortion from the Pleroma. At last, the thirty æons together project in honor of the Father the æon Soter or Jesus, "the great High Priest," "the Joint Fruit of the Pleroma," and "send him forth beyond the Pleroma as a Spouse for Sophia, who was outside, and as a rectifier of those sufferings which she underwent in searching after Christ." After many sufferings, Sophia is purged of all passions and brought back as the bride of Jesus, together with all pneumatic natures, into the ideal world. The demiurge, the fiery and jealous God of the Jews, as "the friend of the bridegroom,"[1] with the psychical Christians on the border of the Pleroma, remotely shares the joy of the festival, while matter sinks back into nothing.

In Valentine's Christology, we must distinguish properly three redeeming beings: (1) The ἄνω Χριστός or heavenly Christ, who, after the fall of Sophia, emanates from the æon μονογενής, and stands in conjunction with the female principle, the πνεῦμα ἅγιον. He makes the first announcement to the æons of the plan of redemption, whereupon they strike up anthems of praise and thanksgiving in responsive choirs. (2) The σωτήρ or Ἰησοῦς, produced by all the æons together, the star of the Pleroma. He forms with the redeemed Sophia the last and highest syzygy. (3) The κάτω Χριστός, the psychical or Jewish Messiah, who is sent by the Demiurge, passes through the body of Mary as water through a pipe, and is at last crucified by the Jews, but, as he has merely an apparent body, does not really suffer. With him Soter, the proper redeemer, united himself in the baptism in the Jordan, to announce his divine gnosis on earth for a year, and lead the pneumatic persons to perfection.

NOTES.

Dr. Baur, the great critical historian of ancient Gnosticism and the master spirit of modern Gnosticism, ingeniously reproduces the Valentinian system in Hegelian terminology. I quote the chief part, as a fair specimen of his historic treatment, from his *Kirchengeschichte*, vol. I. 201 sqq. (comp. his *Gnosis*, p. 124 sqq.):

---

[1] ὁ φίλος τοῦ νυμφίου, John 3: 29.

" *Der Geist, oder Gott als der Geist an sich, geht aus sich heraus, in dieser Sebstoffenbarung Gottes entsteht die Welt, die in ihrem Unterschied von Gott auch wieder an sich mit Gott eins ist. Wie man aber auch dieses immanente Verhältniss von Gott und Welt betrachten mag, als Selbstoffenbarung Gottes oder als Weltentwicklung, es ist an sich ein rein geistiger, im Wesen des Geistes begründeter Process. Der Geist stellt in den Aeonen, die er aus sich hervorgehen lässt, sein eigenes Wesen aus sich heraus und sich gegenüber; da aber das Wesen des Geistes an sich das Denken und Wissen ist, so kann der Process seiner Selbstoffenbarung nur darin bestehen, dass er sich dessen bewusst ist, was er an sich ist. Die Aeonen des Pleroma sind die höchsten Begriffe des geistigen Seins und Lebens, die allgemeinen Denkformen, in welchen der Geist das, was er an sich ist, in bestimmter concreter Weise für das Bewusstsein ist. Mit dem Wissen des Geistes von sich, dem Selbstbewusstsein des sich von sich unterscheidenden Geistes, ist aber auch schon nicht blos ein Princip der Differenzirung, sondern, da Gott und Welt an sich Eins sind, auch ein Princip der Materialisirung des Geistes gesetzt. Je grösser der Abstand der das Bewusstsein des Geistes vermittelnden Begriffe von dem absoluten Princip ist, um so mehr verdunkelt sich das geistige Bewusstsein, der Geist entäussert sich seiner selbst, er ist sich selbst nicht mehr klar und durchsichtig, das Pneumatische sinkt zum Psychischen herab, das Psychische verdichtet sich zum Materiellen, und mit dem Materiellen verbindet sich in seinem Extrem auch der Begriff des Dämonischen und Diabolischen. Da aber auch das Psychische an sich pneumatischer Natur ist, und Keime des geistigen Lebens überall zurückgeblieben sind, so muss das Pneumatische die materielle Verdunklung des geistigen Bewusstseins auf der Stufe des psychischen Lebens wieder durchbrechen und die Decke abwerfen, die in der Welt des Demiurg auf dem Bewusstsein des Geistes liegt. Die ganze Weltentwicklung ist die Continuität desselben geistigen Processes, es muss daher auch einen Wendepunkt geben, in welchem der Geist aus seiner Selbstentäuserung zu sich selbst zurückkehrt und wieder zum klaren Bewusstsein dessen, was er an sich ist, kommt. Diess ist der gnostische Begriff der christlichen Offenbarung. Die Wissenden im Sinne der Gnostiker, die Pneumatischen, die als solche auch das wahrhaft christliche Bewusstsein in sich haben, sind ein neues Moment des allgemeinen geistigen Lebens, die höchste Stufe der Selbstoffenbarung Gottes und der Weltentwicklung. Diese Periode des Weltverlaufs beginnt mit der Erscheinung Christi und endet zuletzt damit, dass durch Christus und die Sophia alles Geistige in das Pleroma wieder aufgenommen wird. Da Christus, wie auf jeder Stufe der Weltentwicklung, so auch schon in den höchsten Regionen der Aeonenwelt, in welcher alles seinen Ausgangspunkt hat, und von Anfang an auf dieses Resultat des Ganzen angelegt ist, als das wiederherstellende, in der Einheit mit dem Absoluten erhaltende Princip thätig ist, so hat er in der Weltanschauung der Gnostiker durchaus die Bedeutung eines absoluten Weltprincips.*"

§ 126. *The School of Valentinus. Heracleon, Ptolemy, Marcos,*
Bardesanes, Harmonius.

Of all the forms of Gnosticism, that of Valentinus was the
most popular and influential, more particularly in Rome. He
had a large number of followers, who variously modified his
system. Tertullian says, his heresy "fashioned itself into as
many shapes as a courtesan who usually changes and adjusts her
dress every day."

The school of Valentinus divided chiefly into two branches,
an Oriental,[1] and an Italian. The first, in which Hippolytus
reckons one AXIONICOS, not otherwise known, and ARDESIANES
(᾽Αρδησιάνης, probably the same with Bardesanes), held the
body of Jesus to be pneumatic and heavenly, because the Holy
Spirit, *i. e.* Sophia and the demiurgic power of the Highest,
came upon Mary. The Italian school—embracing HERACLEON
and PTOLEMY—taught that the body of Jesus was psychical,
and that for this reason the Spirit descended upon him in the
baptism. Some Valentinians came nearer the orthodox view,
than their master.

HERACLEON was personally instructed by Valentine, and
probably flourished between 170 and 180 somewhere in Italy.
He has a special interest as the earliest known commentator of
the Gospel of John. Origen, in commenting on the same book,
has preserved us about fifty fragments, usually contradicting
them. They are chiefly taken from the first two, the fourth,
and the eighth chapters.[2] Heracleon fully acknowledges the
canonical authority of the fourth Gospel, but reads his own system into it. He used the same allegorical method, as Origen,
who even charges him with adhering too much to the letter,
and not going deep enough into the spiritual sense. He finds
in John the favorite Valentinian ideas of logos, life, light, love,
conflict with darkness, and mysteries in all the numbers, but

---

[1] Διδασκαλία ἀνατολική. Hippol. VI. 35 (p. 286).
[2] They are collected by Grabe, *Spicil.* II. 83–117, and by Stieren, in his ed.
of Iren. Tom. I. 938–971 Clement of Alexandria (*Strom.* IV. 9) quotes also
from a Commentary of Heracleon on Luke 12: 8.

deprives the facts of historical realness. The woman of Samaria, in the fourth chapter, represents the redemption of the Sophia; the water of Jacob's well is Judaism; her husband is her spiritual bridegroom from the Pleroma; her former husbands are the Hyle or kingdom of the devil. The nobleman in Capernaum (4: 47) is the Demiurge, who is not hostile, but short-sighted and ignorant, yet ready to implore the Saviour's help for his subjects; the nobleman's son represents the psychics, who will be healed and redeemed when their ignorance is removed. The fact that John's Gospel was held in equal reverence by the Valentinians and the orthodox, strongly favors its early existence before their separation, and its apostolic origin.[1]

PTOLEMY is the author of the Epistle to Flora, a wealthy Christian lady, whom he tried to convert to the Valentinian system.[2] He deals chiefly with the objection that the creation of the world and the Old Testament could not proceed from the highest God. He appeals to an apostolic tradition and to the words of Christ, who alone knows the Father of all and first revealed him (John 1: 18). God is the only good (Matt. 19: 17), and hence he cannot be the author of a world in which there is so much evil. Irenæus derived much of his information from the contemporary followers of Ptolemy.

Another disciple of Valentine, MARCOS, who taught likewise in the second half of the second century, probably in Asia Minor, perhaps also in Gaul, blended a Pythagorean and Cabbalistic numerical symbolism with the ideas of his master, introduced a ritual abounding in ceremonies, and sought to attract beautiful and wealthy women by magical arts. His followers were called MARCOSIANS.[3]

---

[1] Baur (I. 203) significantly ignores Heracleon's Commentary, which is fatal to his hypothesis of the late origin of the fourth Gospel.

[2] The *Epistola ad Floram* is preserved by Epiphanius (*Hær.* XXIII. § 3). Stieren, in a Latin inaugural address (1843), denied its genuineness, but Rossel in an Appendix to Neander's *Church History* (Germ. ed. II. 1249–1254, in Torrey's translation I. 725–728), and Heinrici (*l. c.* p. 75 sqq.) defend it.

[3] Marcos and the Marcosians are known to us from Clement of Alex. and

The name of COLARBASUS, which is often connected with Marcos, must be stricken from the list of the Gnostics; for it originated in confounding the Hebrew *Kol-Arba*, "the Voice of Four," *i. e.* the divine Tetrad at the head of the Pleroma, with a person.[1]

Finally, in the Valentinian school is counted also BARDE-SANES or BARDAISAN (son of Daisan, $Bαρδησάνης$).[2] He was a distinguished Syrian scholar and poet, and lived at the court of the prince of Edessa at the close of the second and in the early part of the third century.[3] But he can scarcely be numbered among the Gnostics, except in a very wide sense. He was at first orthodox, according to Epiphanius, but became corrupted by contact with Valentinians. Eusebius, on the contrary, makes him begin a heretic and end in orthodoxy. He also reports, that Bardesanes wrote against the heresy of Marcion in the Syriac language. Probably he accepted the common Christian faith with some modifications, and exercised freedom on speculative doctrines, which were not yet clearly developed in the Syrian church of that period.[4] His numerous works are

Iren. (I. 13–21). Hippolytus (VI. 39 sqq., p. 296 sqq.) and Epiphanius depend here almost entirely on Irenæus, who speak of Marcos as still living.

[1] It is to be derived from קוֹל, *voice* (not from כֹּל, *all*), and אַרְבַּע, *four*. The confusion was first discovered by Heumann (1743), and more fully explained by Volkmar, *Die Colarbasus-Gnosis*, in Niedner's "*Zeitschrift für hist. Theol.*" 1855, p. 603–616. Comp. Baur, I. 204, note, and Hort in Smith and Wace, I. 594 sq.

[2] Comp. AUG. HAHN: *Bardesanes, Gnosticus Syrorum primus hymnologus.* Lips. 1819. A. MERX: *Bardes. v. Edessa.* Halle, 1863. LIPSIUS: In the "*Zeitschrift für wissenschaftl. Theol.*" 1863, p. 435 sqq. A. HILGENFELD: *Bardesanes, der letzte Gnostiker.* Leipz. 1864. K. MACKE: *Syrische Lieder gnostischen Ursprungs*, in the "*Tüb. Theol. Quartalschrift*" for 1874. Dr. HORT: *Bardaisan*, in Smith and Wace, I. 256–260 (very thorough).

[3] Eusebius (IV. 30) and Jerome (*De Vir. illustr.* 33), misled by the common confusion of the earlier and later Antonines, assign him to the reign of Marcus Aurelius (161–180), but according to the Chronicle of Edessa (Assemani, *Bibl. Or.* I. 389) he was born July 11, 155, and according to Barhebræus (*Chron. Eccl.* ed. Abbeloos and Lamy, 1872, p. 79) he died in 223, aged 68 years. Hilgenfeld, Jacobi and Hort adopt the later date.

[4] Dr. Hort (p. 252) thinks that "there is no reason to suppose that Bardaisan rejected the ordinary faith of Christians, as founded on the Gospels and the

lost, with the exception of a "Dialogue on Fate," which has recently been published in full.[1] It is, however, of uncertain date, and shows no trace of the Gnostic mythology and dualism, ascribed to him. He or his son Harmonius (the accounts vary) is the father of Syrian hymnology, and composed a book of one hundred and fifty hymns (after the Psalter), which were used on festivals, till they were superseded by the orthodox hymns of St. Ephræm the Syrian, who retained the same metres and tunes.[2] He enjoyed great reputation, and his sect is said to have spread to the Southern Euphrates, and even to China.

His son HARMONIUS, of Edessa, followed in his steps. He is said to have studied philosophy at Athens. He shares with Bardesanes (as already remarked) the honor of being the father of Syrian hymnology.

§ 127. *Marcion and his School.*

I. JUSTIN M.: *Apol.* I. c. 26 and 58. He wrote also a special work against Marcion, which is lost. IRENÆUS: I. 28. IV. 33 sqq. and several other passages. He likewise contemplated a special treatise against Marcion (III. 12). TERTULLIAN: *Adv. Marcionem Libri* V.

writings of the Apostles, except on isolated points." The varying modern constructions of his system on a Gnostic basis are all arbitrary.

[1] Περὶ εἱμαρμένης. It was formerly known only from a Greek extract in Eusebius's *Præparatio Evang.* (VI. 9, 10). The Syriac original was discovered among the Nitrian MSS. of the British Museum, and published by Cureton, in *Spicilegium Syriacum*, London 1855, with an English translation and notes. Merx gives a German translation with notes (p. 25-55). The treatise is either identical with the *Book of the Laws of Countries*, or an extract from it. Dr. Hort doubts its genuineness.

[2] Ephræm the Syrian speaks of a book of 150 hymns, by which Bardesanes had beguiled the people, and makes no mention of Harmonius; but Sozomen and Theodoret report that Harmonius was the first to adapt the Syrian language to metrical forms and music, and that his hymns and tunes were used till the time of Ephræm. Dr. Hort explains this contradiction, which has not received sufficient attention, by supposing that the book of hymns was really written by Harmonius, perhaps in his father's lifetime, and at his suggestion. But it is equally possible that Bardesanes was the author and Harmonius the editor, or that both were hymnists. The testimony of Ephræm cannot easily be set aside as a pure error. Fragments of hymns of Bardesanes have been traced in the *Acta Thomæ* by K. Macke in the article quoted above. The Syriac hymns of Ephræm are translated into German by Zingerle (1838), and into English by H. Burgess (1853).

HIPPOL.: *Philos.* VII. 29 (ed. Duncker and Schneidewin, pp. 382–394). EPIPHANIUS: *Hær.* XLII. PHILASTER: *Hær.* XLV. The Armenian account of ESNIG in his "Destruction of Heretics" (5th century), translated by Neumann, in the "Zeitschrift für histor. Theologie," Leipzig, vol. IV. 1834. Esnig gives Marcionism more of a mystic and speculative character than the earlier fathers, but presents nothing which may not be harmonized with them.

II. NEANDER (whose account is too charitable), BAUR (I. 213–217), MÖLLER (*Gesch. der Kosmologie,* 374–407), FESSLER (in Wetzer and Welte, VI. 816–821), JACOBI (in Herzog, V. 231–236), SALMON (in Smith and Wace, III. 816–824). AD. HILGENFELD: *Cerdon und Marcion,* in his "Zeitschrift für wissenschaftl. Theol." Leipz. 1881, pp. 1–37.

III. On the critical question of Marcion's canon and the relation of his mutilated Gospel of Luke to the genuine Gospel of Luke, see the works on the Canon, the critical Introductions, and especially VOLKMAR: *Das Evangelium Marcions, Text und Kritik* (Leipz. 1852), and SANDAY: *The Gospels in the Second Century* (London, 1876). The last two have conclusively proved (against the earlier view of Baur, Ritschl, and the author of "Supernat. Rel.") the priority of the canonical Luke. Comp. vol. I. 668.

MARCION was the most earnest, the most practical, and the most dangerous among the Gnostics, full of energy and zeal for reforming, but restless, rough and eccentric. He has a remote connection with modern questions of biblical criticism and the canon. He anticipated the rationalistic opposition to the Old Testament and to the Pastoral Epistles, but in a very arbitrary and unscrupulous way. He could see only superficial differences in the Bible, not the deeper harmony. He rejected the heathen mythology of the other Gnostics, and adhered to Christianity as the only true religion; he was less speculative, and gave a higher place to faith. But he was utterly destitute of historical sense, and put Christianity into a radical conflict with all previous revelations of God; as if God had neglected the world for thousands of years until he suddenly appeared in Christ. He represents an extreme anti-Jewish and pseudo-Pauline tendency, and a magical supranaturalism, which, in fanatical zeal for a pure primitive Christianity, nullifies all history, and turns the gospel into an abrupt, unnatural, phantom-like appearance.

Marcion was the son of a bishop of Sinope in Pontus, and gave in his first fervor his property to the church, but was excommunicated by his own father, probably on account of his heretical opinions and contempt of authority.[1] He betook himself, about the middle of the second century, to Rome (140–155), which originated none of the Gnostic systems, but attracted them all. There he joined the Syrian Gnostic, CERDO, who gave him some speculative foundation for his practical dualism. He disseminated his doctrine by travels, and made many disciples from different nations. He is said to have intended to apply at last for restoration to the communion of the Catholic Church, when his death intervened.[2] The time and place of his death are unknown. He wrote a recension of the Gospel of Luke and the Pauline Epistles, and a work on the contradictions between the Old and New Testaments. Justin Martyr regarded him as the most formidable heretic of his day. The abhorrence of the Catholics for him is expressed in the report of Irenæus, that Polycarp of Smyrna, meeting with Marcion in Rome, and being asked by him : " Dost thou know me?" answered : " I know the first-born of Satan."[3]

Marcion supposed two or three primal forces (ἀρχαί): the good or gracious God (ϑεὸς ἀγαϑός), whom Christ first made known ; the evil matter (ὕλη), ruled by the devil, to which heathenism belongs ; and the righteous world-maker (δημιουργὸς δίκαιος), who is the finite, imperfect, angry Jehovah of the Jews. Some writers reduce his principles to two ; but he did not identify the demiurge with the hyle. He did not go into any further speculative analysis of these principles ; he rejected the pagan emanation theory, the secret tradition, and the allegorical interpretation of the Gnostics ; in his system he has no Pleroma,

---

[1] Epiphanius and others mention, as a reason, his seduction of a consecrated virgin ; but this does not agree well with his asceticism, and Irenæus and Tertullian bring no charge of youthful incontinence against him.

[2] So Tertullian ; but Irenæus tells a similar story of Cerdo. Tertullian also reports that Marcion was repeatedly (*semel et iterum*) excommunicated.

[3] *Adv. Hær.* iii. c. 3, § 4 : Ἐπιγινώσκω τὸν πρωτότοκον τοῦ Σατανᾶ.

no Æons, no Dynameis, no Syzygies, no suffering Sophia; he excludes gradual development and growth; everything is unprepared, sudden and abrupt.

His system was more critical and rationalistic than mystic and philosophical.[1] He was chiefly zealous for the consistent practical enforcement of the irreconcilable dualism which he established between the gospel and the law, Christianity and Judaism, goodness and righteousness.[2] He drew out this contrast at large in a special work, entitled "*Antitheses.*" The God of the Old Testament is harsh, severe and unmerciful as his law; he commands, "Love thy neighbor, but hate thine enemy," and returns "an eye for an eye, and a tooth for a tooth;" but the God of the New Testament commands, "Love thine enemy." The one is only just, the other is good. Marcion rejected all the books of the Old Testament, and wrested Christ's word in Matt. 5: 17 into the very opposite declaration: "I am come not to fulfil the law and the prophets, but to destroy them." In his view, Christianity has no connection whatever with the past, whether of the Jewish or the heathen world, but has fallen abruptly and magically, as it were, from heaven.[3] Christ, too, was not born at all, but suddenly descended into the city of Capernaum in the fifteenth year of the reign of Tiberius, and appeared as the revealer of the good God, who sent him.

---

[1] The Armenian bishop, Esnig, however, brings it nearer to the other forms of Gnosticism. According to him Marcion assumed three heavens; in the highest dwelt the good God, far away from the world, in the second the God of the Law, in the lowest his angels; beneath, on the earth, lay Hyle, or Matter, which he calls also the power ($\delta\acute{v}v\alpha\mu\iota\varsigma$) or essence ($o\acute{v}\sigma\acute{\iota}a$) of the earth. The Hyle is a female principle, and by her aid, as his spouse, the Jewish God of the Law made this world, after which he retired to his heaven, and each ruled in his own domain, he with his angels in heaven, and Hyle with her sons on earth. Möller (p. 378) is disposed to accept this account as trustworthy. Salmon thinks it such a system as Marcion may have learned from Cerdo, but he must have made little account of the mystic element, else it would be mentioned by the earlier writers.

[2] "*Separatio legis et evangelii proprium et principale opus est Marcionis.*" Tertullian, *Adv. Marc.* I. 19.

[3] "*Subito Christus, subito Joannes. Sic sunt omnia apud Marcionem, q͞ e suum et plenum habent ordinem apud creatorem.*" Tert. IV. 11.

He has no connection with the Messiah, announced by the Demiurge in the Old Testament; though he called himself the Messiah by way of accommodation. His body was a mere appearance, and his death an illusion, though they had a real meaning.[1] He cast the Demiurge into Hades, secured the redemption of the soul (not of the body), and called the apostle Paul to preach it. The other apostles are Judaizing corrupters of pure Christianity, and their writings are to be rejected, together with the catholic tradition. In over-straining the difference between Paul and the other apostles, he was a crude forerunner of the Tübingen school of critics.

Marcion formed a canon of his own, which consisted of only eleven books, an abridged and mutilated Gospel of Luke, and ten of Paul's epistles. He put Galatians first in order, and called Ephesians the Epistle to the Laodicæans. He rejected the pastoral epistles, in which the forerunners of Gnosticism are condemned, the Epistle to the Hebrews, Matthew, Mark, John, the Acts, the Catholic Epistles, and the Apocalypse.

Notwithstanding his violent antinomianism, Marcion taught and practiced the strictest ascetic self-discipline, which revolted not only from all pagan festivities, but even from marriage, flesh, and wine. (He allowed fish). He could find the true God in nature no more than in history. He admitted married persons to baptism only on a vow of abstinence from all sexual intercourse.[2] He had a very gloomy, pessimistic view of the world and the church, and addressed a disciple as " his partner in tribulation, and fellow-sufferer from hatred."

In worship he excluded wine from the eucharist, but retained the sacramental bread, water-baptism, anointing with oil, and the mixture of milk and honey given to the newly baptized.[3]

---

[1] Renan (L'église chrét., p. 358) says of the shadowy narrative of Christ's life which Marcion elaborated on the basis of his mutilated Luke: " Si Jesus ne nous avait été connu que par des textes de ce genre, on aurait pu douter s'il avait vraiment existé, ou s'il n' était pas une fiction A PRIORI, dégagée de tout lien avec la réalité. Dans un pareil système, le Christ ne naissait pas (la naissance, pour Marcion, était une souillure), ne souffrait pas, ne mourait pas."

[2] Tertullian, I. 29; IV. 10.   [3] Tert. I. 14.

Epiphanius reports that he permitted females to baptize. The Marcionites practiced sometimes vicarious baptism for the dead.[1] Their baptism was not recognized by the church.

The Marcionite sect spread in Italy, Egypt, North Africa, Cyprus, and Syria; but it split into many branches. Its wide diffusion is proved by the number of antagonists in the different countries.

The most noteworthy Marcionites are PREPO, LUCANUS (an Assyrian), and APELLES. They supplied the defects of the master's system by other Gnostic speculations, and in some instances softened down its antipathy to heathenism and Judaism. Apelles acknowledged only one first principle. Ambrosius, a friend of Origen, was a Marcionite before his conversion. These heretics were dangerous to the church because of their severe morality and the number of their martyrs. They abstained from marriage, flesh, and wine, and did not escape from persecution, like some other Gnostics.

Constantine forbade the Marcionites freedom of worship public and private, and ordered their meeting-houses to be handed over to the Catholic Church.[2] The Theodosian code mentions them only once. But they existed in the fifth century when Theodoret boasted to have converted more than a thousand of these heretics, and the Trullan Council of 692 thought it worth while to make provision for the reconciliation of Marcionites. Remains of them are found as late as the tenth century.[3] Some of their principles revived among the Paulicians, who took refuge in Bulgaria, and the Cathari in the West.

§ 128. *The Ophites. The Sethites. The Peratæ. The Cainites.*

I. HIPPOLYTUS: *Philosoph.* Bk. V. 1–23. He begins his account of the Heresies with the Naasseni, or Ophites, and Peratæ (the first four books being devoted to the systems of heathen philosophy).

---

[1] So they understood, 1 Cor. 15: 29.   [2] Euseb. *Vit. Const.* III. 64.

[3] Flügel's *Mani,* p. 160, 167 (quoted by Salmon). Prof. Jacobi (in Herzog, V. 236) quotes a letter of Hasenkamp to Lavater of the year 1774, and later authorities, to prove the lingering existence of similar opinions in Bosnia and Herzegowina.

IRENÆUS: *Adv. Hær.* I. 30 (ed. Stieren, I. 266 sqq.). EPIPHAN.
Hær. 37 (in Oehler's ed. I. 495 sqq.).

II. MOSHEIM: *Geschichte der Schlangenbrüder.* Helmstädt, 1746, '48.

E. W. MÖLLER: *Geschichte der Kosmologie.* Halle, 1860. *Die
ophitische Gnosis*, p. 190 sqq.

BAXMANN: *Die Philosophumena und die Peraten*, in Niedner's "Zeitschrift für die hist. Theol." for 1860.

LIPSIUS: *Ueber das ophitische System.* In "Zeitschrift für wissenschaftl.
Theologie" for 1863 and '64.

JACOBI in Herzog, new ed., vol. V. 240 sq.

GEORGE SALMON: "Cainites," in Smith and Wace, vol. I. 380–82.
Articles "Ophites and "Peratæ" will probably appear in vol. IV.,
not yet published.

The origin of the OPHITES,[1] or, in Hebrew, NAASENES,[2] *i. e.*
Serpent-Brethren, or Serpent-Worshippers, is unknown, and is
placed by Mosheim and others before the time of Christ. In
any case, their system is of purely heathen stamp. Lipsius has
shown their connection with the Syro-Chaldaic mythology.
The sect still existed as late as the sixth century; for in 530
Justinian passed laws against it.

The accounts of their worship of the serpent rest, indeed, on
uncertain data; but their name itself comes from their ascribing
special import to the serpent as the type of gnosis, with reference to the history of the fall (Gen. 3: 1), the magic rod of Moses (Ex. 4: 2, 3), and the healing power of the brazen serpent
in the wilderness (Num. 21: 9; comp. John 3: 14). They made
use of the serpent on amulets.

That mysterious, awe-inspiring reptile, which looks like the
embodiment of a thunderbolt, or like a fallen angel tortuously
creeping in the dust, represents in the Bible the evil spirit, and
its motto, *Eritis sicut Deus*, is the first lie of the father of lies,
which caused the ruin of man; but in the false religions it is
the symbol of divine wisdom and an object of adoration; and
the *Eritis sicus dii* appears as a great truth, which opened the
path of progress. The serpent, far from being the seducer of
the race, was its first schoolmaster and civilizer by teaching it

---

[1] 'Οφιανοί, from ὄφις, serpent, Serpentini.   [2] From נָחָשׁ.

the difference between good and evil. So the Ophites regarded the fall of Adam as the transition from the state of unconscious bondage to the state of conscious judgment and freedom; therefore the necessary entrance to the good, and a noble advance of the human spirit. They identified the serpent with the Logos, or the mediator between the Father and the Matter, bringing down the powers of the upper world to the lower world, and leading the return from the lower to the higher. The serpent represents the whole winding process of development and salvation.[1] The Manichæans also regarded the serpent as the direct image of Christ.[2]

With this view is connected their violent opposition to the Old Testament. Jaldabaoth,[3] as they termed the God of the Jews and the Creator of the world, they represented as a malicious, misanthropic being. In other respects, their doctrine strongly resembles the Valentinian system, except that it is much more pantheistic, unchristian, and immoral, and far less developed.

The Ophites again branch out in several sects, especially three.

The SETHITES considered the third son of Adam the first pneumatic man and the forerunner of Christ. They maintained three principles, darkness below, light above, and spirit between.

The PERATÆ or PERATICS[4] (Transcendentalists) are described by Hippolytus as allegorizing astrologers and as mystic tritheists, who taught three Gods, three Logoi, three Minds, three Men. Christ had a three-fold nature, a three-fold body, and

---

[1] As Baur (*K. Gesch.* I. 195) expresses it: " *Die Schlange ist mit Einem Wort der durch die Gegensätze dialectisch sich hindurchwindende Weltentwicklungsprocess relbst.*"

[2] Augustin, *De Hær.* c. 17 and 46.

[3] יַלְדָּא בָהוּת, product of chaos.

[4] From περάω, to pass across, to go beyond (the boundary of the material world). We know their system from the confused account of Hippolytus, *Philos.* l. v. 7 sqq. He says, that their blasphemy against Christ has for many years escaped notice. Irenæus, Tertullian, and Epiphanius are silent about the Peratæ. Clement of Alex. mentions them.

a three-fold power. He descended from above, that all things triply divided might be saved.[1]

The CAINITES boasted of the descent from Cain the fratricide, and made him their leader[2]. They regarded the God of the Jews and Creator of the world as a positively evil being, whom to resist is virtue. Hence they turned the history of salvation upside down, and honored all the infamous characters of the Old and New Testaments from Cain to Judas as spiritual men and martyrs to truth. Judas Iscariot alone among the apostles had the secret of true knowledge, and betrayed the psychic Messiah with good intent to destroy the empire of the evil God of the Jews. Origen speaks of a branch of the Ophites, who were as great enemies of Jesus as the heathen Celsus, and who admitted none into their society who had not first cursed his name. But the majority seem to have acknowledged the goodness of Jesus and the benefit of his crucifixion brought about by the far-sighted wisdom of Judas. A book entitled "the Gospel of Judas" was circulated among them.

No wonder that such blasphemous travesty of the Bible history, and such predilection for the serpent and his seed was connected with the most unbridled antinomianism, which changed

---

[1] The following specimen of Peratic transcendental nonsense is reported by Hippolytus (v. 12): "According to them, the universe is the Father, Son, [and] Matter; [but] each of these three has endless capacities in itself. Intermediate, then, between the Matter and the Father sits the Son, the Word, the Serpent, always being in motion towards the unmoved Father, and [towards] matter itself in motion. And at one time he is turned towards the Father, and receives the powers into his own person; but at another time takes up these powers, and is turned towards Matter. And Matter, [though] devoid of attribute, and being unfashioned, moulds [into itself] forms from the Son which the Son moulded from the Father. But the Son derives shape from the Father after a mode ineffable, and unspeakable, and unchangeable. . . . No one can be saved or return [into heaven] without the Son, and the Son is the Serpent. For as he brought down from above the paternal marks, so again he carries up from thence those marks, roused from a dormant condition, and rendered paternal characteristics, substantial ones from the unsubstantial Being, transferring them hither from thence."

[2] Καϊνοι (Hippol. VIII. 20), Καϊανισταί (Clem. Alex. Strom. VII. 17), Καϊανοί (Epiph. Hær. 38), Caiani, Cainæi.

vice into virtue. They thought it a necessary part of "perfect knowledge" to have a complete experience of all sins, including even unnamable vices.

Some have identified the Ophites with the false teachers denounced in the Epistle of Jude as filthy dreamers, who "defile the flesh, and set at naught dominion, and rail at dignities," who "went in the way of Cain, and ran riotously in the error of Balaam for hire, and perished in the gainsaying of Korah," as "wandering stars, for whom the blackness of darkness has been reserved forever." The resemblance is certainly very striking, and those heretics may have been the forerunners of the Ophites of the second century.

§ 129. *Saturninus* (*Satornilos*).

Iren. I. 24, § 1, 2; ch. 28. Hippol. VII. 3, 28 (depending on Iren.). Tert. *Præsc. Hær.* 46. Hegesippus in *Euseb.* IV. 22, 29. Epiph. *Hær.* XXIII. Theod. *Fab. Hær.* I. 3. Comp. Möller, *l. c.*, p. 367–373.

Contemporary with Basilides under Hadrian, was Saturninus or Satornilos,[1] in Antioch. He was, like him, a pupil of Menander. His system is distinguished for its bold dualism between God and Satan, the two antipodes of the universe, and for its ascetic severity.[2] God is the unfathomable abyss, absolutely unknown ($\vartheta\varepsilon\grave{o}\varsigma$ $\check{a}\gamma\nu\omega\sigma\tau o\varsigma$). From him emanates by degrees the spirit-world of light, with angels, archangels, powers, and dominions. On the lowest degree are the seven planetary spirits ($\check{a}\gamma\gamma\varepsilon\lambda o\iota$ $\varkappa o\sigma\mu o\varkappa\rho\acute{a}\tau o\rho\varepsilon\varsigma$) with the Demiurge or God of the Jews at the head. Satan, as the ruler of the hyle, is eternally opposed to the realm of light. The seven planetary spirits invade the realm of Satan, and form out of a part of the hyle the material world with man, who is filled by the highest

---

[1] This second form, says Renan (*L'égl. chrét*, p. 177), is common in inscriptions.

[2] So Mosheim, Neander, Baur, Gieseler, Renan. But Möller (p. 371) disputes the dualism of Saturninus, and maintains that Satan and the God of the Jews are alike subordinate, though antagonistic beings. But so is Ahriman in the Parsee dualism, and the Demiurge in all the Gnostic systems.

God with a spark of light (σπινϑήρ). Satan creates in opposition a hylic race of men, and incessantly pursues the spiritual race with his demons and false prophets. The Jewish God, with his prophets, is unable to overcome him. Finally the good God sends the æon *Nous* in an unreal body, as *Soter* on earth, who teaches the spiritual men by gnosis and strict abstinence from marriage and carnal food to emancipate themselves from the vexations of Satan, and also from the dominion of the Jewish God and his star-spirits, and to rise to the realm of light.

<h2 style="text-align:center">§ 130. Carpocrates.</h2>

Iren. I. 25 (24). Hippol. VII. 32 (D. & Schn. p. 398 sqq.). Clem. Alex. *Strom.* III. 511. Epiphanius, *Hær.* XXV.

Carpocrates also lived under Hadrian, probably at Alexandria, and founded a Gnostic sect, called by his own name, which put Christ on a level with heathen philosophers, prided itself on its elevation above all the popular religions, and sank into unbridled immorality. The world is created by angels greatly inferior to the unbegotten Father. Jesus was the son of Joseph, and just like other men, except that his soul was steadfast and pure, and that he perfectly remembered those things which he had witnessed within the sphere of the unbegotten God. For this reason a power descended upon him from the Father, that by means of it he might escape from the creators of the world. After passing through them all, and remaining in all points free, he ascended again to the Father. We may rise to an equality with Jesus by despising in like manner the creators of the world.

The Carpocratians, say Irenæus and Hippolytus, practiced also magical arts, incantations, and love-potions, and had recourse to familiar spirits, dream-sending demons, and other abominations, declaring that they possess power to rule over the princes and framers of this world. But they led a licentious life, and abused the name of Christ as a means of hiding their wickedness. They were the first known sect that used pictures of Christ, and they derived them from a pretended original of Pontius Pilate.[1]

EPIPHANES, a son of Carpocrates, who died at the age of seventeen, was the founder of "monadic" Gnosticism, which in opposition to dualism seems to have denied the independent existence of evil, and resolved it into a fiction of human laws. He wrote a book on "Justice," and defined it to be equality. He taught that God gave his benefits to all men alike and in common, and thence derived the community of goods, and even of women. He was worshipped by his adherents after his death as a god, at Same in Cephalonia, by sacrifices, libations, banquets, and singing of hymns. Here we have the worship of genius in league with the emancipation of the flesh, which has been revived in modern times. But it is not impossible that Clement of Alexandria, who relates this fact, may have made a similar mistake as Justin Martyr in the case of Simon Magus, and confounded a local heathen festival of the moon known as τὰ Ἐπιφάνεια or ὁ Ἐπιφανής with a festival in honor of Epiphanes.[2]

§ 131. *Tatian and the Encratites.*

I. TATIAN: Λόγος πρὸς Ἕλληνας (*Oratio adversus Græcos*), ed. S. Worth, Oxon. 1700 (an excellent ed.); in Otto's *Corpus Apol.*, vol. VI., Jenæ 1851; and in Migne's *Patrologia Græca*, Tom. VI. fol. 803–888. Eng. transl. by Pratten & Dods in the "Ante-Nicene Library," vol. III. (Edinb. 1867). A Commentary of St. Ephræm on Tatian's *Diatessaron* (Τὸ διὰ τεσσάρων), was found in an Armenian translation in the Armenian Convent at Venice, translated into Latin in 1841 by Aucher, and edited by *Mösinger* (Prof. of Biblical Learning in Salzburg) under the title "*Evangelii Concordantis Expositio facta a Sancto Ephræmo Doctore Syro.*" Venet. 1876. The *Diatessaron* itself was found in an Arabic translation in 1886, and published by P. AUG. CIASCA: *Tatiani Evangeliorum Harmoniæ Arabice*, Rom. 1888. A new and more critical edition of the *Oratio ad Gr.*, by ED. SCHWARTZ, Lips., 1888 (105 pp).

[1] Hippol. *Philos.* VII. 32: εἰκόνας κατασκευάζουσι τοῦ Χριστοῦ λέγοντες ὑπὸ Πιλάτου τῷ καιρῷ ἐκείνῳ γενέσθαι.

[2] This was the conjecture of Mosheim, which has been worked out and modified by Volkmar in a monthly periodical of the *Wissenschaftl. Verein* at Zürich, 1856. He maintains that the deity worshipped at Same was the new appearing moon, ὁ Ἐπιφανής.

ORTHODOX Notices of Tatian: IREN. I. 28, 1; III. 23, 8 sqq. (in Stieren, I. 259, 551 sq.). HIPPOL.: VIII. 16 (very brief). CLEM. ALEX.: *Strom.* l. III. EUSEB.: *H.E.* IV. 16, 28, 29; VI. 13. EPIPHANIUS, *Hær.* 46 (Tatian) and 47 (Encratites). The recently discovered work of MACARIUS MAGNES (Paris 1876), written about 400, contains some information about the Encratites which agrees with Epiphanius.

II. H. A. DANIEL: *Tatian der Apologet.* Halle 1837.

JAMES DONALDSON: *A Critical History of Christian Liter.*, etc. Lond. vol. IIIrd. (1866), which is devoted to Tatian, etc., p. 3–62.

THEOD. ZAHN: *Tatian's Diatessaron.* Erlangen, 1881. (The first part of *Forschungen zur Gesch. des neutestamentl. Kanons*).

AD. HARNACK: *Tatian's Diatessaron*, in Brieger's "Zeitschrift für Kirchengesch." 1881, p. 471–505; *Die Oratio des Tatian nebst einer Ein. tung über die Zeit dieses Apologeten, in " Texte und Untersuch-ungen zur Gesch. der altchristl. Literatur,"* vol. I. No. 2, p. 196–231. Leipz., 1883, and his art., "Tatian," in "Encycl. Brit." xxiii. (1888).

FR. XAV. FUNK (R. C.): *Zur Chronologie Tatian's*, in the Tübing. "Theol. Quartalschrift," 1883, p. 219–234.

TATIAN, a rhetorician of Syria, was converted to Catholic Christianity by Justin Martyr in Rome, but afterwards strayed into Gnosticism, and died A. D. 172.[1] He resembles Marcion in his anti-Jewish turn and dismal austerity. Falsely interpreting 1 Cor. 7 : 5, he declared marriage to be a kind of licentiousness and a service of the devil. Irenæus says, that Tatian, after the martyrdom of Justin, apostatised from the church, and elated with the conceit of a teacher, and vainly puffed up as if he surpassed all others, invented certain invisible æons similar to those of Valentine, and asserted with Marcion and Saturninos that marriage was only corruption and fornication. But his extant apologetic treatise against the Gentiles, and his Gospel-Harmony (recently recovered), which were written between 153 and 170, show no clear traces of Gnosticism, unless it be the omission of the genealogies of Jesus in the " Diatessaron." He was not so much anti-catholic as hyper-catholic, and hyper-ascetic. We shall return to him again in the last chapter.

---

[1] The chronology is not certain. Zahn and Harnack put his birth at A. D. 110, his conversion at 150, his death at 172. Funk puts the birth and conversion about 10 years later.

His followers, who kept the system alive till the fifth century, were called, from their ascetic life, ENCRATITES, or ABSTAINERS, and from their use of water for wine in the Lord's Supper, HYDROPARASTATÆ or AQUARIANS.[1] They abstained from flesh, wine, and marriage, not temporarily (as the ancient catholic ascetics) for purposes of devotion, nor (as many modern total abstainers from intoxicating drink) for the sake of expediency or setting a good example, but permanently and from principle on account of the supposed intrinsic impurity of the things renounced. The title "Encratites," however, was applied indiscriminately to all ascetic sects of the Gnostics, especially the followers of Saturninus, Marcion, and Severus (Severians, of uncertain origin). The Manichæans also sheltered themselves under this name. Clement of Alexandria refers to the Indian ascetics as the forerunners of the Encratites.

The practice of using mere water for wine in the eucharist was condemned by Clement of Alexandria, Cyprian, and Chrysostom, and forbidden by Theodosius in an edict of 382. A certain class of modern abstinence men in America, in their abhorrence of all intoxicating drinks, have resorted to the same heretical practice, and substituted water or milk for the express ordinance of our Lord.

§ 132. *Justin the Gnostic.*

HIPPOLYTUS: *Philos.* V. 23–27 (p. 214–233), and X. 15 (p. 516–519).

Hippolytus makes us acquainted with a Gnostic by the name of JUSTIN, of uncertain date and origin.[2] He propagated his doctrine secretly, and bound his disciples to silence by solemn oaths. He wrote a number of books, one called *Baruch*, from which Hippolytus gives an abstract. His gnosis is mostly based upon a mystical interpretation of Genesis, and has a somewhat

---

[1] 'Εγκρατῖται, also 'Εγκρατεῖς, 'Εγκρατηταί, *Continentes*, the abstemious; or, 'Υδροπαραστάται, *Aquarii*.

[2] Lipsius regards him as one of the earliest, Salmon (in "Smith & Wace," III. 587), with greater probability, as one of the latest Gnostics. The silence of Irenæus favors the later date.

Judaizing cast. Hippolytus, indeed, classes him with the Naassenes, but Justin took an opposite view of the serpent as the cause of all *evil* in history. He made use also of the Greek mythology, especially the tradition of the twelve labors of Hercules. He assumes three original principles, two male and one female. The first is the Good Being; the second Elohim, the Father of the creation; the third is called Eden and Israel, and has a double form, a woman above the middle and a snake below. Elohim falls in love with Eden, and from their intercourse springs the spirit-world of twenty angels, ten paternal and ten maternal, and these people the world. The chief of the two series of angels are Baruch, who is the author of all good, and is represented by the tree of life in Paradise, and Naas, the serpent, who is the author of all evil, and is represented by the tree of knowledge. The four rivers are symbols of the four divisions of angels. The Naas committed adultery with Eve, and a worse crime with Adam; he adulterated the laws of Moses and the oracles of the prophets; he nailed Jesus to the cross. But by this crucifixion Jesus was emancipated from his material body, rose to the good God to whom he committed his spirit in death, and thus he came to be the deliverer.

§ 133. *Hermogenes.*

TERTULLIAN: *Adv. Hermogenem.* Written about A. D. 206. One of his two tracts against H. is lost. HIPPOLYTUS: *Philos.* VIII. 17 (p. 432). Comp. NEANDER: *Antignosticus*, p. 448; KAYE: *Tertullian*, p. 532; HAUCK: *Tertullian*, p. 240; SALMOND: in "Smith & Wace," III. 1-3.

HERMOGENES was a painter in Carthage at the end of the second and beginning of the third century. Tertullian describes him as a turbulent, loquacious, and impudent man, who "married more women than he painted."[1] He is but remotely connected with Gnosticism by his Platonic dualism and denial of the creation out of nothing. He derived the world, including the soul of man, from the formless, eternal matter,[2] and

---

[1] This was enough to condemn him in the eyes of a Montanist.

[2] Hippol. *l. c.* : ἔφη τὸν θεὸν ἐξ ὕλης συγχρόνου καὶ ἀγεννήτου πάντα πεποιηκέναι.

explained the ugly in the natural world, as well as the evil in the spiritual, by the resistance of matter to the formative influence of God. In this way only he thought he could account for the origin of evil. For if God had made the world out of nothing, it must be all good. He taught that Christ on his ascension left his body in the sun, and then ascended to the Father.[1] But otherwise he was orthodox and did not wish to separate from the church.

§ 134. *Other Gnostic Sects.*

The ancient fathers, especially Hippolytus and Epiphanius, mention several other Gnostic sects under various designations.

1. The DOCETÆ or DOCETISTS taught that the body of Christ was not real flesh and blood, but merely a deceptive, transient phantom, and consequently that he did not really suffer and die and rise again. Hippolytus gives an account of the system of this sect. But the name applied as well to most Gnostics, especially to Basilides, Saturninus, Valentinus, Marcion, and the Manichæans. Docetism was a characteristic feature of the first antichristian errorists whom St. John had in view (1 John 4: 2; 2 John 7).[2]

2. The name ANTITACTÆ or ANTITACTES, denotes the licentious antinomian Gnostics, rather than the followers of any single master, to whom the term can be traced.[3]

3. The PRODICIANS, so named from their supposed founder, PRODICUS, considered themselves the royal family,[4] and, in crazy self-conceit, thought themselves above the law, the sabbath, and every form of worship, even above prayer itself, which was becoming only to the ignorant mass. They resembled the Nicolaitans and Antitactæ, and were also called Adamites,

---

[1] This foolish notion he proved from Ps. 19: " He hath placed his tabernacle in the sun."

[2] For a fuller account see two good articles of Dr. Salmon on *Docetæ* and *Docetism,* in "Smith & Wace," I. 865–870.

[3] See Clement of Alex., *Strom.* III. 526. From ἀντιτάσσεσθαι, to defy, rebel against, the law.

[4] Εὐγενεῖς.

Barbelitæ, Borboriani, Coddiani, Phibionitæ, and by other unintelligible names.[1]

Almost every form of immorality and lawlessness seems to have been practiced under the sanction of religion by the baser schools of Gnosticism, and the worst errors and organized vices of modern times were anticipated by them. Hence we need not be surprised at the uncompromising opposition of the ancient fathers to this radical corruption and perversion of Christianity.

§ 135. *Mani and the Manichæans.*

SOURCES.

I. Oriental Sources : The most important, though of comparatively late date. (a) Mohammedan (Arabic): *Kitâb al Fihrist.* A history of Arabic literature to 987, by an Arab of Bagdad, usually called IBN ABI JAKUB AN-NADÎM; brought to light by Flügel, and published after his death by Rödiger and Müller, in 2 vols. Leipz. 1871–'72. Book IX. section first, treats of Manichæism. Flügel's transl. see below. Kessler calls Fihrist a *"Fundstätte allerersten Ranges."* Next to it comes the relation of the Mohamedan philosopher AL-SHAHRASTANÎ (d. 1153), in his *History of Religious Parties and Philosophical Sects,* ed. Cureton, Lond. 1842, 2 vols. (I. 188–192); German translation by Haarbrücker. Halle, 1851. On other Mohammedan sources see Kessler in Herzog[2], IX. 225 sq. (b) Persian sources, relating to the life of Mani; the *Shâhnâmeh* (the Kings' Book) of FIRDAUSÎ, ed. by Jul. Mohl. Paris, 1866 (V. 472–475). See Kessler, *ibid.* 225. (c) Christian Sources: In Arabic, the Alexandrian Patriarch EUTYCHIUS (d. 916), *Annales,* ed. Pococke. Oxon. 1628; BARHEBRÆUS (d. 1286), in his *Historia Dynastiarum,* ed. Pococke. In Syriac: EPHRÆM SYRUS (d. 393), in various writings. ESNIG or ESNIK, an Armenian bishop of the 5th century, who wrote against Marcion and Mani (German translation from the Armenian by C. Fr. Neumann in Illgen's "Zeitschrift für die hist. Theol." 1834, p. 77–78).

II. Greek Sources: EUSEBIUS (*H. E.* VII. 31, a brief account). EPIPHANIUS (*Hær.* 66). CYRIL OF JERUSAL. (*Catech.* VI. 20 sqq.). TITUS OF BOSTRA (πρὸς Μανιχαίους, ed. P. de Lagarde, 1859). PHOTIUS: *Adv. Manichæos* (Cod. 179 *Biblioth.*). JOHN OF DAMASCUS: *De Hæres.* and *Dial.*

---

[1] See Clem. Alex., *Strom.* I. f. 304; III. f. 438; VII. f. 722; and Epiphan., *Hær.* 26 (Oehler's ed. I. 169 sqq.).

III. Latin Sources: ARCHELAUS (Bishop of Cascar in Mesopotamia, d. about 278): *Acta Disputationis cum Manete hæresiarcha;* first written in Syriac, and so far belonging to the Oriental Christian sources (comp. Jerome, *De vir. ill.* 72), but extant only in a Latin translation, which seems to have been made from the Greek, edited by Zacagni (Rom. 1698) and Routh (in *Reliquiæ Sacræ,* vol. V. 3–206), Engl. transl. in Clark's "Ante-Nicene Library" (vol. XX. 272–419).

These Acts purport to contain the report of a disputation between Archelaus and Mani before a large assembly, which was in full sympathy with the orthodox bishop, but (as Beausobre first proved) they are in form a fiction from the first quarter of the fourth century (about 320) by a Syrian ecclesiastic (probably of Edessa), yet based upon Manichæan documents, and containing much information about Manichæan doctrines. They consist of various pieces, and were the chief source of information to the West. Mani is represented (ch. 12) as appearing in a many-colored cloak and trousers, with a sturdy staff of ebony, a Babylonian book under his left arm, and with a mien of an old Persian master. In his defense he quotes freely from the N. T. At the end he makes his escape to Persia (ch. 55). Comp. H. v. ZITTWITZ: *Die Acta Archelai et Manetis untersucht,* in Kahnis' "Zeitschrift für hist. Theol." 1873, No. IV. OBLASINSKI: *Acta Disput. Arch.,* etc. Lips. 1874 (inaugural dissert.). AD. HARNACK: *Die Acta Archelai und das Diatessaron Tatians,* in "Texte und Untersuch. zur Gesch. der altchristl. Lit." vol. I. Heft. 3 (1883), p. 137–153. Harnack tries to prove that the Gospel quotations of Archelaus are taken from Tatian's Diatessaron. Comp. also his *Dogmengeschichte,* I. (1886), 681–694.

ST. AUGUSTIN (d. 430, the chief Latin authority next to the translation of Archelaus): *Contra Epistolam Manichœi; Contra Faustum Manich.,* and other anti-Manichæan writings, in the 8th vol. of the Benedictine edition of his *Opera.* English translation in Schaff's "Nicene and Post-Nicene Library," Vol. IV., N. York, 1887.

Comp. also the Acts of Councils against the Manich. from the fourth century onward, in Mansi and Hefele.

MODERN WORKS:

*ISAAC DE BEAUSOBRE (b. 1659 in France, pastor of the French church in Berlin, d. 1738): *Histoire crit. de Manichée et du Manichéisme.* Amst. 1734 and '39. 2 vols. 4°. Part of the first vol. is historical, the second doctrinal. Very full and scholarly. He intended to write a third volume on the later Manichæans.

*F. CHR. BAUR: *Das Manichäische Religionssystem nach den Quellen neu untersucht und entwickelt.* Tüb. 1831 (500 pages). A comprehensive philosophical and critical view. He calls the Manich. system a "*glühend prächtiges Natur-und Weltgedicht.*"

TRECHSEL: *Ueber Kanon, Kritik, und Exegese der Manichäer.* **Bern,** 1832.

D. CHWOLSON: *Die Ssabier und der Ssabismus.* Petersb. 1856, 2 vols.

*GUST. FLÜGEL (d. 1870): *Mani, seine Lehre und seine Schriften. Aus dem Fihrist des Abi Jakub an-Nadim* (987). Leipz. 1862. Text, translation, and Commentary, 440 pages.

FR. SPIEGEL: *Eranische Alterthumskunde,* vol. II. 1873, p. 185–232.

ALEX. GEYLER: *Das System des Manichäisimus und sein Verh. zum Buddhismus.* Jena, 1875.

*K. KESSLER: *Untersuchungen zur Genesis des manich. Rel. systems.* Leipz. 1876. By the same: *Mâni oder Beiträge zur Kenntniss der Religionsmischung im Semitismus.* Leipz. 1882. See also his thorough art. *Mâni und die Manichäer,* in "Herzog," new ed., vol. IX. 223–259 (abridged in Schaff's "Encycl." II. 1396–1398).

G. T. STOKES: *Manes,* and *Manichœans* in "Smith and Wace," III. 792–801.

AD. HARNACK: *Manichœism,* in the 9th ed. of the "Encycl. Britannica," vol. XV. (1883), 481–487.

The accounts of Mosheim, Lardner, Schröckh, Walch, Neander, Gieseler.

We come now to the latest, the best organized, the most consistent, tenacious and dangerous form of Gnosticism, with which Christianity had to wage a long conflict. Manichæism was not only a school, like the older forms of Gnosticism, but a rival religion and a rival church. In this respect it resembled Islam which at a later period became a still more formidable rival of Christianity; both claimed to be divine revelations, both engrafted pseudo-Christian elements on a heathen stock, but the starting point was radically different: Manichæism being anti-Jewish and dualistic, Mohammedanism, pseudo-Jewish and severely and fanatically monotheistic.

First the external history.

The origin of Manichæism is matter of obscure and confused tradition. It is traced to MANI (MANES, MANICHÆUS),[1] a

---

[1] Μάνης, Μάνητος, Μάνεντος, Μανιχαῖος, *Manes* (gen. *Manetis*), *Manichœans* (the last form always used by St. Augustin). The name is either of Persian or Semitic origin, but has not yet been satisfactorily explained. Kessler identifies it with *Mânâ, Manda, i. e.* knowledge, γνῶσις, of the Mandæans. According to the *Acta Archelai* he was originally called *Cubricus,* which Kessler regards as a corruption of the Arabic *Shuraik.*

Persian philosopher, astronomer, and painter,[1] of the third century (215–277), who came over to Christianity, or rather
introduced some Christian elements into the Zoroastrian religion,
and thus stirred up an intellectual and moral revolution among
his countrymen. According to Arabic Mohammedan sources,
he was the son of Fatak (Πάτεκιος), a high-born Persian of
Hamadan (Ecbatana), who emigrated to Ctesiphon in Babylonia.
Here he received a careful education. He belonged originally
to the Judaizing Gnostic sect of the Mandæans or Elkesaites
(the Mogtasilah, *i. e.* Baptists); but in his nineteenth and again
in his twenty-fourth year (238) a new religion was divinely
revealed to him. In his thirtieth year he began to preach his
syncretistic creed, undertook long journeys and sent out disciples.
He proclaimed himself to be the last and highest prophet of God
and the Paraclete promised by Christ (as Mohammed did six
hundred years later). He began his "*Epistola Fundamenti,*" in
which he propounded his leading doctrines, with the words:
"Mani, the apostle of Jesus Christ, by the providence of God
the Father. These are the words of salvation from the eternal
and living source." He composed many books in the Persian
and Syriac languages and in an alphabet of his own invention,
but they are all lost.[2]

At first Mani found favor at the court of the Persian king
Shapur I. (Sapor), but stirred up the hatred of the priestly cast
of the Magians. He fled to East India and China and became
acquainted with Buddhism. Indeed, the name of Buddha is
interwoven with the legendary history of the Manichæan system.
His disputations with Archelaus in Mesopotamia are a fiction,
like the pseudo-Clementine disputations of Simon Magus with

---

[1] At least, according to Persian accounts; but the Arabs, who hate painting,
and the church fathers are silent about his skill as a painter.

[2] Among these are mentioned the *Book of Mysteries*, the *Book of Giants*, the
Book of Precepts for Hearers (*Capitula* or *Epistola Fundamenti*, from which
Augustin gives large extracts), *Shâhpûrakân* (*i. e.* belonging to King
Shâhpûr), the *Book of Life*, the *Gospel* or the *Living Gospel*. See Kessler, *l. c.*
p. 249 sqq.

Peter, but on a better historic foundation and with an orthodox aim of the writer. [1]

In the year 270 Mani returned to Persia, and won many followers by his symbolic (pictorial) illustrations of the doctrines, which he pretended had been revealed to him by God. But in a disputation with the Magians, he was convicted of corrupting the old religion, and thereupon was crucified, or flayed alive by order of king Behram I. (Veranes) about 277 ; his skin was stuffed and hung up for a terror at the gate of the city Djondishapur (or Gundeshapur), since called "the gate of Mani." [2] His followers were cruelly persecuted by the king.

Soon after Mani's horrible death his sect spread in Turkistan, Mesopotamia, North Africa, Sicily, Italy and Spain. As it moved westward it assumed a more Christian character, especially in North Africa. It was everywhere persecuted in the Roman empire, first by Diocletian (A. D. 287), and afterwards by the Christian emperors. Nevertheless it flourished till the sixth century and even later. Persecution of heresy always helps heresy unless the heretics are exterminated.

The mysteriousness of its doctrine, its compact organization, the apparent solution of the terrible problem of evil, and the show of ascetic holiness sometimes were the chief points of attraction. Even such a profound and noble spirit as St. Augustin was nine years an auditor of the sect before he was converted to the Catholic church. He sought there a deeper

---

[1] Beausobre (vol. I. Pref. p. viii) : " Les Actes de cette Dispute sont évidemment une fiction pareille à celle de cet imposteur, qui a pris le nom de Clément Romain, et qui a introduit S. Pierre disputant contre Simon le Magicien."

[2] The cruel death of Mani and the maltreatment of his corpse are well attested, but his being skinned alive is perhaps a later Christian tradition. The Disput. Archelai (c. 55) towards the close gives this account : " He was apprehended and brought before the king, who, being inflamed with the strongest indignation against him, and fired with the desire of avenging two deaths upon him—namely, the death of his own son, and the death of the keeper of the prison—gave orders that he should be flayed alive and hung before the gate of the city, and that his skin should be dipped in certain medicaments and inflated : his flesh, too, he commanded to be given as a prey to the birds." See the different accouuts in Beausobre, I. 205 sq.

philosophy of religion and became acquainted with the gifted and eloquent Faustus of Numidia, but was disappointed and found him a superficial charlatan. Another Manichæan, by the name of Felix, he succeeded in converting to the Catholic faith in a public disputation of two days at Hippo. His connection with Manichæism enabled him in his polemic writings to refute it and to develop the doctrines of the relation of knowledge and faith, of reason and revelation, the freedom of will, the origin of evil and its relation to the divine government. Thus here, too, error was overruled for the promotion of truth.

Pope Leo I. searched for these heretics in Rome, and with the aid of the magistrate brought many to punishment. Valentinian III. punished them by banishment, Justinian by death. The violent and persistent persecutions at last destroyed their organization. But their system extended its influence throughout the middle ages down to the thirteenth century, re-appearing, under different modifications, with a larger infusion of Christian elements, in the Priscillianists, Paulicians, Bogomiles, Albigenses, Catharists and other sects, which were therefore called "New Manichæans." Indeed some of the leading features of Manichæism—the dualistic separation of soul and body, the ascription of nature to the devil, the pantheistic confusion of the moral and physical, the hypocritical symbolism, concealing heathen views under Christian phrases, the haughty air of mystery, and the aristocratic distinction of esoteric and exoteric—still live in various forms even in modern systems of philosophy and sects of religion.[1]

§ 136. *The Manichœan System.*

Manichæism is a compound of dualistic, pantheistic, Gnostic, and ascetic elements, combined with a fantastic philosophy of nature, which gives the whole system a materialistic character, notwithstanding its ascetic abhorrence of matter. The me-

---

[1] The Mormons or Latter-Day Saints of Utah present an interesting parallel, especially in their hierarchical organization; while in their polygamy they as strongly contrast with the ascetic Manichæans, and resemble the Mohammedans.

taphysical foundation is a radical dualism between good and evil, light and darkness, derived from the Persian Zoroastrism (as restored by the school of the Magasæans under the reign of the second Sassanides towards the middle of the second century). The prominent ethical feature is a rigid asceticism which strongly resembles Buddhism.[1] The Christian element is only a superficial varnish (as in Mohammedanism). The Jewish religion is excluded altogether (while in Mohammedanism it forms a very important feature), and the Old Testament is rejected, as inspired by the devil and his false prophets. The chief authorities were apocryphal Gospels and the writings of Mani.

1. The Manichæan THEOLOGY begins with an irreconcilable antagonism between the kingdom of light and the kingdom of darkness. And this is identified with the ethical dualism between good and bad. These two kingdoms stood opposed to each other from eternity, remaining unmingled. Then Satan who with his demons was born from darkness, began to rage and made an assault upon the kingdom of light. From this incursion resulted the present world, which exhibits a mixture of the two elements, detached portions of light imprisoned in darkness. Adam was created in the image of Satan, but with a strong spark of light, and was provided by Satan with Eve as his companion, who represents seductive sensuousness, but also with a spark of light, though smaller than that in Adam. Cain and Abel are sons of Satan and Eve, but Seth is the offspring of Adam by Eve, and full of light. Thus mankind came into existence with different shares of light, the men with more, the women with less. Every individual man is at once a son of light and of darkness, has a good soul, and a body substantially evil, with an evil soul corresponding to it. The redemption of the light from the bonds of the darkness is effected by Christ, who

---

[1] Kessler (followed by Harnack) derives Manichæism exclusively from Chaldæan sources, but must admit the strong affinity with Zoroastric and Buddhist ideas and customs. The Fihrist says that Mani derived his doctrine from Parsism and Christianity. On the Buddhistic element, see Baur, p. 433–445.

is identical with the sun spirit, and by the Holy Ghost, who has his seat in the ether. These two beings attract the light-forces out of the material world, while the prince of darkness, and the spirits imprisoned in the stars, seek to keep them back. The sun and moon are the two shining ships (*lucidæ naves*) for conducting the imprisoned light into the eternal kingdom of light. The full moon represents the ship laden with light; the new moon, the vessel emptied of its cargo; and the twelve signs of the zodiac also serve as buckets in this pumping operation.

The Manichæan christology, like the Gnostic, is entirely docetic, and, by its perverted view of body and matter, wholly excludes the idea of an incarnation of God. The teachings of Christ were compiled and falsified by the apostles in the spirit of Judaism. Mani, the promised Paraclete, has restored them. The goal of history is an entire separation of the light from the darkness; a tremendous conflagration consumes the world, and the kingdom of darkness sinks into impotence.

Thus Christianity is here resolved into a fantastic dualistic, and yet pantheistic philosophy of nature; moral regeneration is identified with a process of physical refinement; and the whole mystery of redemption is found in light, which was always worshipped in the East as the symbol of deity. Unquestionably there pervades the Manichæan system a kind of groaning of the creature for redemption, and a deep sympathy with nature, that hieroglyphic of spirit; but all is distorted and confused. The suffering Jesus on the cross (*Jesus patibilis*) is here a mere illusion, a symbol of the world-soul still enchained in matter, and is seen in every plant which works upwards from the dark bosom of the earth towards the light, towards bloom and fruit, yearning after freedom. Hence the class of the "perfect" would not kill nor wound a beast, pluck a flower, nor break a blade of grass. The system, instead of being, as it pretends, a liberation of light from darkness, is really a turning of light into darkness.

2. The MORALITY of the Manichæans was severely ascetic, based on the fundamental error of the intrinsic evil of matter and

the body; the extreme opposite of the Pelagian view of the essential moral purity of human nature.[1] The great moral aim is, to become entirely unworldly in the Buddhistic sense; to renounce and destroy corporeity; to set the good soul free from the fetters of matter. This is accomplished by the most rigid and gloomy abstinence from all those elements which have their source in the sphere of darkness. It was, however, only required of the elect, not of catechumens. A distinction was made between a higher and lower morality similar to that in the catholic church. The perfection of the elect consisted in a threefold seal or preservative (*signaculum*).[2]

(a) The *signaculum oris*, that is, purity in words and in diet, abstinence from all animal food and strong drink, even in the holy supper, and restriction to vegetable diet, which was furnished to the perfect by the "hearers," particularly olives, as their oil is the food of light.

(b) The *signaculum manuum:* renunciation of earthly property, and of material and industrial pursuits, even agriculture; with a sacred reverence for the divine light-life diffused through all nature.

(c) The *signaculum sinus*, or celibacy, and abstinence from any gratification of sensual desire. Marriage, or rather procreation, is a contamination with corporeity, which is essentially evil.

This unnatural holiness of the elect at the same time atoned for the unavoidable daily sins of the catechumens who paid them the greatest reverence. It was accompanied, however, as in the Gnostics, with an excessive pride of knowledge, and if we are to believe the catholic opponents, its fair show not rarely concealed refined forms of vice.

[1] Schleiermacher correctly represents Manichæism and Pelagianism as the two fundamental heresies in anthropology and soteriology · the one makes man *essentially evil* (in body), and thus denies the *possibility* of redemption; the other makes man *essentially good*, and thus denies the *necessity* of redemption.

[2] The meaning of *signaculum* is not *criterion* (as Baur explains, *l. c.* p. 248), but *seal* (as is clear from the corresponding Arabic *hatâm* in the Fihrist). See Kessler.

3. ORGANIZATION. Manichæism differed from all the Gnostic schools in having a fixed, and that a strictly hierarchical, organization. This accounts in large measure for its tenacity and endurance. At the head of the sect stood twelve apostles, or magistri, among whom Mani and his successors, like Peter and the pope, held the chief place. Under them were seventy-two bishops, answering to the seventy-two (strictly seventy) disciples of Jesus; and under these came presbyters, deacons and itinerant evangelists.[1] In the congregation there were two distinct classes, designed to correspond to the catechumens and the faithful in the catholic church: the " hearers;"[2] and the " perfect," the esoteric, the priestly caste,[3] which represents the last stage in the process of liberation of the spirit and its separation from the world, the transition from the kingdom of matter into the kingdom of light, or in Buddhistic terms, from the world of Sansara into Nirwana.

4. The WORSHIP of the Manichæans was, on the whole, very simple. They had no sacrifices, but four daily prayers, preceded by ablutions, and accompanied by prostrations, the worshipper turned towards the sun or moon as the seat of light. They observed Sunday, in honor of the sun, which was with them the same with the redeemer; but, contrary to the custom of the catholic Christians, they made it a day of fasting. They had weekly, monthly, and yearly fasts. They rejected the church festivals, but instead celebrated in March with great pomp the day of the martyrdom of their divinely appointed teacher, Mani.[4] The sacraments were mysteries of the elect, of which even Augustin could learn very little. Hence it has been disputed whether they used baptism or not, and whether

---

[1] The organization of the Mormons is similar.

[2] *Auditores, catechumeni*, in Arabic *sammaûn*.

[3] *Electi, perfecti, catharistæ*, ἐκλεκτοί, τέλειοι, in the Fihrist *siddikûn*. Faustus terms them the *sacerdotale genus*.

[4] The feast of "the chair," βῆμα, *cathedra*. The Mormons likewise celebrate the martyrdom of their founder, Joseph Smith; who was killed by the mob at Carthage, Illinois (June 27, 1844).

SECOND PERIOD. A. D. 100–311.

they baptized by water, or by oil. Probably they practised water
baptism and anointing, and regarded the latter as a higher
spiritual baptism, or distinguished both as baptism and confirmation in the catholic church.[1] They also celebrated a kind of
holy supper, sometimes even under disguise in catholic churches,
but without wine (because Christ had no blood), and regarding
it perhaps, according to their pantheistic symbolism, as the
commemoration of the light-soul crucified in all nature. Their
sign of recognition was the extension of the right hand as a
symbol of the common deliverance from the kingdom of darkness by the redeeming hand of the spirit of the sun.

[1] Gieseler and Neander are disposed to deny the use of water-baptism by the
Manichæans, Beausobre, Thilo, Baur, and Kessler assert it. The passages in
Augustin are obscure and conflicting. See Baur, *l. c.* p. 273–281. The older
Gnostic sects (the Marcionites and Valentinians), and the New Manichæans
practised a baptismal rite by water. Some new light is thrown on this disputed question by the complete Greek text of the Gnostic Acts of Thomas,
recently published by Max Bonnet of Montpellier (*Acta Thomæ*, Lips. 1883).
Here both baptism and anointing are repeatedly mentioned, p. 19 (in a thanksgiving to Christ: καθαρίσας αὐτοὺς τᾷ σῷ λουτρῷ καὶ ἀλείψας αὐτοὺς τῷ σῷ ἐλείῳ
ἀπὸ τῆς περιεχούσης αὐτοὺς πλάνης), 20, 35, 68 (where, however, the pouring of
oil is mentioned *before* water-baptism), 73, 32 (ἀλείψας . . . καὶ ἐβάπτισεν αὐτοὺς
. . . ἀνελθόντων δὲ αὐτῶν ἐκ τῶν ὑδάτων λαβὼν ἄρτον καὶ ποτήριον εὐλόγησεν εἰπών
. . .). Comp. the discussion of Lipsius in *Die Apokryphen Apostelgeschichten
und Apostellegenden* (Braunschweig, 1883), p. 331, where he asserts: "*Die Was-
sertaufe stand bei den Manichæern ebenso wie bei den meisten älteren gnostichen
Secten in Uebung.*"

CHAPTER XII.

THE DEVELOPMENT OF CATHOLIC THEOLOGY IN CONFLICT WITH HERESY.

§ 137. *Catholic Orthodoxy.*

I. Sources: The doctrinal and polemical writings of the ante-Nicene fathers, especially JUSTIN MARTYR, IRENÆUS, HIPPOLYTUS, TERTULLIAN, CYPRIAN, CLEMENT OF ALEX., and ORIGEN.

II. Literature: The relevant sections in the works on Doctrine History by PETAVIUS, MÜNSCHER, NEANDER, GIESELER, BAUR, HAGENBACH, SHEDD, NITZSCH, HARNACK (first vol. 1886 ; 2d ed. 1888).

JOS. SCHWANE (R. C.): *Dogmengeschichte der vornicänischen Zeit.* Münster, 1862.

EDM. DE PRESSENSÉ: *Heresy and Christian Doctrine,* transl. by Annie Harwood. Lond. 1873.

The special literature see below. Comp. also the Lit. in Ch. XIII.

BY the wide-spread errors described in the preceding chapter, the church was challenged to a mighty intellectual combat, from which she came forth victorious, according to the promise of her Lord, that the Holy Spirit should guide her into the whole truth. To the subjective, baseless, and ever-changing speculations, dreams, and fictions of the heretics, she opposed the substantial, solid realities of the divine revelation. Christian theology grew, indeed, as by inward necessity, from the demand of faith for knowledge. But heresy, Gnosticism in particular, gave it a powerful impulse from without, and came as a fertilizing thunder-storm upon the field. The church possessed the truth from the beginning, in the experience of faith, and in the holy scriptures, which she handed down with scrupulous fidelity from generation to generation. But now came the task of developing the substance of the Christian truth in theoretical form,[1] fortifying it on all sides, and presenting it in clear light

---

[1] λογικώτερον, as Eusebius has it.

before the understanding. Thus the Christian polemic and dogmatic theology, or the church's logical apprehension of the doctrines of salvation, unfolded itself in this conflict with heresy; as the apologetic literature and martyrdom had arisen through Jewish and heathen persecution.

From this time forth the distinction between catholic and heretical, orthodoxy and heterodoxy, the faith of the church and dissenting private opinion, became steadily more prominent. Every doctrine which agreed with the holy scriptures and the faith of the church, was received as catholic; that is, universal, and exclusive.[1] Whatever deviated materially from this standard, every arbitrary notion, framed by this or that individual, every distortion or corruption of the revealed doctrines of Christianity, every departure from the public sentiment of the church, was considered heresy.[2]

Almost all the church fathers came out against the contemporary heresies, with arguments from scripture, with the tradition of the church, and with rational demonstration, proving them inwardly inconsistent and absurd.

But in doing this, while they are one in spirit and purpose, they pursue two very different courses, determined by the differences between the Greek and Roman nationality, and by peculiarities of mental organization and the appointment of Providence. The Greek theology, above all the Alexandrian, represented by Clement and Origen, is predominantly idealistic and speculative, dealing with the objective doctrines of God, the incarnation, the trinity, and christology; endeavoring to supplant the false gnosis by a true knowledge, an orthodox philosophy, resting on the Christian pistis. It was strongly influenced by Platonic speculation in the Logos doctrine. The Latin theology, particularly the North African, whose most distinguished rep-

---

[1] The term *catholic* is first used in its ecclesiastical sense by Ignatius, the zealous advocate of episcopacy. *Ad Smyrn.* c. 8: ὅπου ἂν ᾖ Χριστὸς Ἰησοῦς, ἐκεῖ ἡ καθολικὴ ἐκκλησία, *ubi est Christus Jesus, illic Catholica Ecclesia.* So also in the Letter of the Church of Smyrna on the martyrdom of Polycarp (155), in Eusebius, *H. E.* IV. 15.

[2] From αἵρεσις. See notes below.

resentatives are Tertullian and Cyprian, is more realistic and practical, concerned with the doctrines of human nature and of salvation, and more directly hostile to Gnosticism and philosophy. With this is connected the fact, that the Greek fathers were first philosophers; the Latin were mostly lawyers and statesmen; the former reached the Christian faith in the way of speculation, the latter in the spirit of practical morality. Characteristically, too, the Greek church built mainly upon the apostle John, pre-eminently the contemplative "divine;" the Latin upon Peter, the practical leader of the church. While Clement of Alexandria and Origen often wander away into cloudy, almost Gnostic speculation, and threaten to resolve the real substance of the Christian ideas into thin spiritualism, Tertullian sets himself implacably against Gnosticism and the heathen philosophy upon which it rests. "What fellowship," he asks, "is there between Athens and Jerusalem, the academy and the church, heretics and Christians?" But this difference was only relative. With all their spiritualism, the Alexandrians still committed themselves to a striking literalism; while, in spite of his aversion to philosophy, Tertullian labored with profound speculative ideas which came to their full birth in Augustin.

Irenæus, who sprang from the Eastern church, and used the Greek language, but labored in the West, holds a kind of mediating position between the two branches of the church, and may be taken as, on the whole, the most moderate and sound representative of ecclesiastical orthodoxy in the ante-Nicene period. He is as decided against Gnosticism as Tertullian, without overlooking the speculative want betrayed in that system. His refutation of the Gnosis,[1] written between 177 and 192, is the leading polemic work of the second century. In the first book of this work Irenæus gives a full account of the Valentinian system of Gnosis; in the second book he begins his refutation in philosophical and logical style; in the third,

[1] Ἔλεγχος καὶ ἀνατροπὴ τῆς ψευδωνύμου γνώσεως.

he brings against the system the catholic tradition and the holy scriptures, and vindicates the orthodox doctrine of the unity of God, the creation of the world, the incarnation of the Logos, against the docetic denial of the true humanity of Christ and the Ebionitic denial of his true divinity; in the fourth book he further fortifies the same doctrines, and, against the antinomianism of the school of Marcion, demonstrates the unity of the Old and New Testaments; in the fifth and last book he presents his views on eschatology, particularly on the resurrection of the body—so offensive to the Gnostic spiritualism—and at the close treats of Antichrist, the end of the world, the intermediate state, and the millennium.

His disciple Hippolytus gives us, in the " *Philosophumena,*" a still fuller account, in many respects, of the early heresies, and traces them up to their sources in the heathen systems of philosophy, but does not go so deep into the exposition of the catholic doctrines of the church.

The leading effort in this polemic literature was, of course, to develop and establish positively the Christian truth; which is, at the same time, to refute most effectually the opposite error. The object was, particularly, to settle the doctrines of the rule of faith, the incarnation of God, and the true divinity and true humanity of Christ. In this effort the mind of the church, under the constant guidance of the divine word and the apostolic tradition, steered with unerring instinct between the threatening cliffs. Yet no little indefiniteness and obscurity still prevailed in the scientific apprehension and statement of these points. In this stormy time, too, there were as yet no general councils to settle doctrinal controversy by the voice of the whole church. The dogmas of the trinity and the person of Christ, did not reach maturity and final symbolical definition until the following period, or the Nicene age.

NOTES ON HERESY.

The term *heresy* is derived from αἱρεσις, which means originally either *capture* (from αἱρέω), or *election, choice* (from αἱρέομαι), and assumed the additional idea of arbitrary opposition to public opinion and authority. In the N. Test. it designates a chosen way of life, a school or sect or party, not necessarily in a bad sense, and is applied to the Pharisees, the Sadducees, and even the Christians as a Jewish sect (Acts 5: 17; 15: 5; 24: 5, 14; 26: 5; 28: 22); then it signifies discord, arising from difference of opinion (Gal. 5: 20; 1 Cor. 11: 19); and lastly error (2 Pet. 2: 1, αἱρέσεις ἀπωλείας, destructive heresies, or sects of perdition). This passage comes nearest to the ecclesiastical definition. The term *heretic* (αἱρετικὸς ἄνθρωπος) occurs only once, Tit 3: 10, and means a factious man, a sectary, a partisan, rather than an errorist.

Constantine the Great still speaks of the Christian church as a sect, ἡ αἵρεσις ἡ καθολική, ἡ ἁγιωτάτη αἵρεσις (in a letter to Chrestus, bishop of Syracuse, in Euseb, *H. E.* X. c. 5, § 21 and 22, in Heinichen's ed. I, 491). But after him church and sect became opposites, the former term being confined to the one ruling body, the latter to dissenting minorities.

The fathers commonly use *heresy* of false teaching, in opposition to Catholic doctrine, and *schism* of a breach of discipline, in opposition to Catholic government. The ancient heresiologists—mostly uncritical, credulous, and bigoted, though honest and pious, zealots for a narrow orthodoxy—unreasonably multiplied the heresies by extending them beyond the limits of Christianity, and counting all modifications and variations separately. Philastrius or Philastrus, bishop. of Brescia or Brixia (d. 387), in his *Liber de Hœresibus*, numbered 28 Jewish and 128 Christian heresies; Epiphanius of Cyprus (d. 403), in his Πανάριον. 80 heresies in all, 20 before and 60 after Christ; Augustin (d. 430), 88 Christian heresies, including Pelagianism; Prœdestinatus, 90, including Pelagianism and Nestorianism. (Pope Pius IX. condemned 80 modern heresies, in his Syllabus of Errors, 1864.) Augustin says that it is "altogether impossible, or at any rate most difficult" to define heresy, and wisely adds that the *spirit* in which error is held, rather than error itself, constitutes heresy. There are innocent as well as guilty errors. Moreover, a great many people are better than their creed or no-creed, and a great many are worse than their creed, however orthodox it may be. The severest words of our Lord were directed against the hypocritical orthodoxy of the Pharisees. In the course of time heresy was defined to be a religious error held in wilful and persistent opposition to the truth after it has been defined and declared by the church in an authoritative manner, or *"pertinax defensio dogmatis ecclesiæ universalis judicio condemnati."* Speculations on open questions of theology are no heresies. Origen was no heretic in his age, but was condemned long after his death.

In the present divided state of Christendom there are different kinds of orthodoxy and heresy. Orthodoxy is conformity to a recognized creed or standard of public doctrine; heresy is a wilful departure from it. The Greek church rejects the Roman dogmas of the papacy, of the double procession of the Holy Ghost, the immaculate conception of the

Virgin Mary, and the infallibility of the Pope, as heretical, because con‐ trary to the teaching of the first seven œcumenical councils. The Ro‐ man church anathematized, in the Council of Trent, all the distinctive doctrines of the Protestant Reformation. Evangelical Protestants on the other hand regard the unscriptural traditions of the Greek and Roman churches as heretical. Among Protestant churches again there are minor doctrinal differences, which are held with various degrees of exclusiveness or liberality according to the degree of departure from the Roman Catholic church. Luther, for instance, would not tolerate Zwingli's view on the Lord's Supper, while Zwingli was willing to fraternize with him notwithstanding this difference. The Lutheran Formula of Concord, and the Calvinistic Synod of Dort rejected and condemned doctrines which are now held with impunity in orthodox evangelical churches. The danger of orthodoxy lies in the direction of exclusive and uncharitable bigotry, which contracts the truth; the danger of liberalism lies in the direction of laxity and indifferentism, which obliterates the eternal distinction between truth and error.

The apostles, guided by more than human wisdom, and endowed with more than ecclesiastical authority, judged severely of every essential de‐ parture from the revealed truth of salvation. Paul pronounced the anathema on the Judaizing teachers, who made circumcision a term of true church membership (Gal. 1: 8), and calls them sarcastically "dogs" of the "concision" (Phil. 3: 2, βλέπετε τοὺς κύνας .... τῆς κατατομῆς). He warned the elders of Ephesus against "grievous wolves" (λύκοι βαρεῖς) who would after his departure enter among them (Acts 20: 29); and he characterizes the speculations of the rising gnosis falsely so called (ψευδώνυμος γνῶσις) as "doctrines of demons" (διδασκαλίαι δαιμονίων, 1 Tim. 4: 1; comp. 6: 3-20; 2 Tim. 3: 1 sqq.; 4: 3 sqq.). John warns with equal earnestness and severity against all false teachers who deny the fact of the incarnation, and calls them antichrists (1 John 4: 3; 2 John 7); and the second Epistle of Peter and the Epistle of Jude de‐ scribe the heretics in the darkest colors.

We need not wonder, then, that the ante-Nicene fathers held the gnostic heretics of their days in the greatest abhorrence, and called them servants of Satan, beasts in human shape, dealers in deadly poison, rob‐ bers, and pirates. Polycarp (Ad Phil. c. 7), Ignatius (Ad Smyrn. c. 4), Justin M. (Apol. I. c. 26), Irenæus (Adv. Hær. III. 3, 4), Hippolytus, Tertullian, even Clement of Alexandria, and Origen occupy essentially the same position of uncompromising hostility towards heresy as the fathers of the Nicene and post-Nicene ages. They regard it as the tares sown by the devil in the Lord's field (Matt. 13: 3–6 sqq). Hence Tertullian infers, "That which was first delivered is of the Lord and is true; whilst that is strange and false which was afterwards introduced" (Praescr. c. 31: "Ex ipso ordine manifestatur, id esse dominicum et verum quod sit prius traditum, id autem extraneum et falsum quod sit posterius inmissum"). There is indeed a necessity for heresies and sects (1 Cor. 11: 19), but "woe to that man through whom the offence cometh" (Matt. 18: 7). "It was necessary," says Tertullian (*ib.* 30), "that the Lord should be betrayed; but woe to the traitor."

Another characteristic feature of patristic polemics is to trace heresy to mean motives, such as pride, disappointed ambition, sensual lust, and avarice. No allowance is made for different mental constitutions, educational influences, and other causes. There are, however, a few noble exceptions. Origen and Augustin admit the honesty and earnestness at least of some teachers of error.

We must notice two important points of difference between the ante-Nicene and later heresies, and the mode of punishing heresy.

1. The chief ante-Nicene heresies were undoubtedly radical perversions of Christian truth and admitted of no kind of compromise. Ebionism, Gnosticism, and Manichæism were essentially anti-Christian. The church could not tolerate that medley of pagan sense and nonsense without endangering its very existence. But Montanists, Novatians, Donatists, Quartodecimanians, and other sects who differed on minor points of doctrine or discipline, were judged more mildly, and their baptism was acknowledged.

2. The punishment of heresy in the ante-Nicene church was purely ecclesiastical, and consisted in reproof, deposition, and excommunication. It had no effect on the civil status.

But as soon as church and state began to be united, temporal punishments, such as confiscation of property, exile, and death, were added by the civil magistrate with the approval of the church, in imitation of the Mosaic code, but in violation of the spirit and example of Christ and the apostles. Constantine opened the way in some edicts against the Donatists, A. D. 316. Valentinian I. forbade the public worship of Manichæans (371). After the defeat of the Arians by the second Œcumenical Council, Theodosius the Great enforced uniformity of belief by legal penalties in fifteen edicts between 381 and 394. Honorius (408), Arcadius, the younger Theodosius, and Justinian (529) followed in the same path. By these imperial enactments heretics, *i. e.* open dissenters from the imperial state-religion, were deprived of all public offices, of the right of public worship, of receiving or bequeathing property, of making binding contracts; they were subjected to fines, banishment, corporeal punishment, and even death. See the Theos. Code, Book XVI. tit. V. *De Hæreticis.* The first sentence of death by the sword for heresy was executed on Priscillian and six of his followers who held Manichæan opinions (385). The better feeling of Ambrose of Milan and Martin of Tours protested against this act, but in vain. Even the great and good St. Augustin, although he had himself been a heretic for nine years, defended the *principle* of religious persecution, on a false exegesis of *Cogite eos intrare,* Luke 14: 23 (*Ep.* 93 *ad Vinc.; Ep.* 185 *ad Bonif. , Retract.* II. 5.). Had he foreseen the crusade against the Albigenses and the horrors of the Spanish Inquisition, he would have retracted his dangerous opinion.   A theocratic or Erastian state-church theory—whether Greek Catholic or Roman Catholic or Protestant—makes all offences against the church offences against the state, and requires their punishment with more or less severity according to the prevailing degree of zeal for orthodoxy and hatred of heresy.   But in the overruling Providence of God which brings good out of every evil, the bloody persecution of heretics—one of the darkest chapters in church history—has produced the sweet fruit of religious liberty.   See vol. III. 138–146.

§ 138. *The Holy Scriptures and the Canon.*

The works on the Canon by REUSS, WESTCOTT, (6th ed., 1889), ZAHN, (1888).   HOLTZMANN: *Kanon u. Tradition*, 1859.   SCHAFF: *Companion to the Greek Testament and the English Version.*   N. York and London, 1883; third ed. 1888.   GREGORY: *Prolegomena* to Tischendorf's 8th ed. of the Greek Test.   Lips., 1884.   A. HARNACK: *Das N. Test. um das jahr* 200.   Leipz., 1889.

The question of the source and rule of Christian knowledge lies at the foundation of all theology.   We therefore notice it here before passing to the several doctrines of faith.

1. This source and this rule of knowledge are the holy scriptures of the Old and New Covenants.[1]   Here at once arises the inquiry as to the number and arrangement of the sacred writings, or the canon, in distinction both from the productions of enlightened but not inspired church teachers, and from the very numerous and in some cases still extant apocryphal works (Gospels, Acts, Epistles, and Apocalypses), which were composed in the first four centuries, in the interest of heresies or for the satisfaction of idle curiosity, and sent forth under the name of an apostle or other eminent person.   These apocrypha, however, did not all originate with Ebionites and Gnostics ; some were merely designed either to fill chasms in the history of Jesus and the apostles by fictitious stories, or to glorify Christianity by *vaticinia post eventum*, in the way of pious fraud at that time freely allowed.

The canon of the Old Testament descended to the church from the Jews, with the sanction of Christ and the apostles. The Jewish Apocrypha were included in the Septuagint and passed from it into Christian versions.   The New Testament

---

[1] Called simply ἡ γραφή, αἱ γραφαί, *scriptura, scripturæ.*

canon was gradually formed, on the model of the Old, in the course of the first four centuries, under the guidance of the same Spirit, through whose suggestion the several apostolic books had been prepared. The first trace of it appears in the second Epistle of Peter (3 : 15), where a collection of Paul's epistles[1] is presumed to exist, and is placed by the side of "the other scriptures."[2] The apostolic fathers and the earlier apologists commonly appeal, indeed, for the divinity of Christianity to the Old Testament, to the oral preaching of the apostles, to the living faith of the Christian churches, the triumphant death of the martyrs, and the continued miracles. Yet their works contain quotations, generally without the name of the author, from the most important writings of the apostles, or at least allusions to those writings, enough to place their high antiquity and ecclesiastical authority beyond all reasonable doubt.[3] The heretical canon of the Gnostic Marcion, of the middle of the second century, consisting of a mutilated Gospel of Luke and ten of Paul's epistles, certainly implies the existence of an orthodox canon at that time, as heresy always presupposes truth, of which it is a caricature.

The principal books of the New Testament, the four Gospels, the Acts, the thirteen Epistles of Paul, the first Epistle of Peter, and the first of John, which are designated by Eusebius as "Homologumena," were in general use in the church after the middle of the second century, and acknowledged to be apostolic, inspired by the Spirit of Christ, and therefore authoritative and canonical. This is established by the testimonies

---

[1] ἐν πάσαις ταῖς ἐπιστολαῖς.   [2] τὰς λοιπὰς (not τὰς ἄλλας) γραφάς.

[3] Comp. Clement of Rome, Ad Cor. c. 47; Polycarp, Ad Phil. 3; Ignatius, Ad Eph. 12; Ad Philad. 5; Barnabas, Ep. c. 1; Papias, testimonies on Matthew and Mark, preserved in Euseb. III. 39; Justin Martyr, Apol. I. 61; Dial. c. Tryph. 63, 81, 103, 106, and his frequent quotations from the so called "Memoirs by the Apostles;" Tatian, Diatessaron, etc. To these must be added the testimonies of the early heretics, as Basilides (125), Valentine (140), Heracleon, etc. See on this subject the works on the Canon, and the critical Introductions to the N. T. The Didache quotes often from Matthew, and shows acquaintance with other books ; Chs. 1, 3, 7, 8, 9, 10, 11, 13, 14, 16. See Schaff, Did., p. 81 sqq.

of Justin Martyr, Tatian, Theophilus of Antioch, Irenæus, Tertullian, Clement of Alexandria, and Origen, of the Syriac Peshito (which omits only Jude, 2 Peter, 2 and 3 John, and the Revelation), the old Latin Versions (which include all books but 2 Peter, Hebrews, and perhaps James and the Fragment of Muratori;[1] also by the heretics, and the heathen opponent Celsus—persons and documents which represent in this matter the churches in Asia Minor, Italy, Gaul, North Africa, Egypt, Palestine, and Syria. We may therefore call these books the original canon.

Concerning the other seven books, the "Antilegomena" of Eusebius, viz. the Epistle to the Hebrews,[2] the Apocalypse,[3] the second Epistle of Peter, the second and third Epistles of John, the Epistle of James, and the Epistle of Jude,—the tradition of the church in the time of Eusebius, the beginning of the fourth century, still wavered between acceptance and rejection. But of the two oldest manuscripts of the Greek Testament which date from the age of Eusebius and Constantine, one—the Sinaitic— contains all the twenty-seven books, and the other—the Vatican—was probably likewise complete, although the last chapters of Hebrews (from 11 : 14), the Pastoral Epistles, Philemon, and Revelation are lost. There was a second class of Antilegomena, called by Eusebius "spurious" (νόθα), consisting of several post-apostolic writings, viz. the catholic Epistle of Barnabas, the first Epistle of Clement of Rome to the Corinthians, the Epistle

---

[1] The Muratorian Canon (so called from its discoverer and first publisher, Muratori, 1740) is a fragment of Roman origin, though translated from the Greek, between A. D. 170 and 180, begins with Mark, passes to Luke as the *third* Gospel, then to John, Acts, *thirteen* Epistles of Paul, mentions *two* Epp. of John, one of Jude, and the *Apocalypses* of John and Peter; thus omitting James, Hebrews, third John, first and second Peter, and mentioning instead an apocryphal Apocalypse of Peter, but adding that "some of our body will not have it read in the church." The interesting fragment has been much discussed by Credner, Kirchhofer, Reuss, Tregelles, Hilgenfeld, Westcott, Hesse, Harnack, Overbeck, Salmon, and Zahn.

[2] Which was regarded as canonical indeed, but not as genuine or Pauline in the West.

[3] Which has the strongest external testimony, that of Justin, Irenæus, etc., in its favor, and came into question only in the third century turough some anti-chiliasts on dogmatical grounds.

of Polycarp to the Philippians, the Shepherd of Hermas, the lost Apocalypse of Peter, and the Gospel of the Hebrews ; which were read at least in some churches, but were afterwards generally separated from the canon. Some of them are even incorporated in the oldest manuscripts of the Bible, as the Epistle of Barnabas and a part of the Shepherd of Hermas (both in the original Greek) in the Codex Sinaiticus, and the first Epistle of Clement of Rome in the Codex Alexandrinus.

The first express definition of the New Testament canon, in the form in which it has since been universally retained, comes from two African synods, held in 393 at Hippo, and 397 at Carthage, in the presence of Augustin, who exerted a commanding influence on all the theological questions of his age. By that time, at least, the whole church must have already become nearly unanimous as to the number of the canonical books; so that there seemed to be no need even of the sanction of a general council. The Eastern church, at all events, was entirely independent of the North African in the matter. The Council of Laodicea (363) gives a list of the books of our New Testament with the exception of the Apocalypse. The last canon which contains this list, is probably a later addition, yet the long-established ecclesiastical use of all the books, with some doubts as to the Apocalypse, is confirmed by the scattered testimonies of all the great Nicene and post Nicene fathers, as Athanasius (d. 373), Cyril of Jerusalem (d. 386), Gregory of Nazianzum (d. 389), Epiphanius of Salamis (d. 403), Chrysostom (d. 407), etc.[1] The name *Novum Testamentum*,[2] also *Novum Instrumentum* (a juridical term conveying the idea of legal validity), occurs first in Tertullian, and came into general use instead of the more correct term *New Covenant*. The books were currently divided into two parts, " the Gospel[3] " and " the

---

[1] See lists of patristic canons in Charteris, *Canonicity*. p. 12 sqq.

[2] διαθήκη, covenant, comp. Matt. 26: 28, where the Vulgate translates, " *testamentum*," instead of *fœdus*.

[3] τὰ εὐαγγελικὰ καὶ τὰ ἀποστολικά, or τὸ εὐαγγέλιον καὶ ὁ ἀπόστολος ; *instrumentum wangelicum, apostolicum,* or *evangelium, apostolus.* Hence the Scripture lessons in the liturgical churches are divided into "Gospels" and " Epistles."

Apostle,"[3] and the Epistles, in the second part, into Catholic or General, and Pauline. The Catholic canon thus settled remained untouched till the time of the Reformation when the question of the Apocrypha and of the Antilegomena was reopened and the science of biblical criticism was born. But the most thorough investigations of modern times have not been able to unsettle the faith of the church in the New Testament, nor ever will.

2. As to the origin and character of the apostolic writings, the church fathers adopted for the New Testament the somewhat mechanical and magical theory of inspiration applied by the Jews to the Old; regarding the several books as composed with such extraordinary aid from the Holy Spirit as secured their freedom from errors (according to Origen, even from faults of memory). Yet this was not regarded as excluding the writer's own activity and individuality. Irenæus, for example, sees in Paul a peculiar style, which he attributes to the mighty flow of thought in his ardent mind. The Alexandrians, however, enlarged the idea of inspiration to a doubtful breadth. Clement of Alexandria calls the works of Plato inspired, because they contain truth; and he considers all that is beautiful and good in history, a breath of the infinite, a tone, which the divine Logos draws forth from the lyre of the human soul.

As a production of the inspired organs, of divine revelation, the sacred scriptures, without critical distinction between the Old and New Covenants, were acknowledged and employed against heretics as an infallible source of knowledge and an unerring rule of Christian faith and practice. Irenæus calls the Gospel a pillar and ground of the truth. Tertullian demands scripture proof for every doctrine, and declares, that heretics cannot stand on pure scriptural ground. In Origen's view nothing deserves credit which cannot be confirmed by the testimony of scripture.

3. The exposition of the Bible was at first purely practical, and designed for direct edification. The controversy with the Gnostics called for a more scientific method. Both the orthodox and

heretics, after the fashion of the rabbinical and Alexandrian Judaism, made large use of allegorical and mystical interpretation, and not rarely lost themselves amid the merest fancies and wildest vagaries. The fathers generally, with a few exceptions, (Chrysostom and Jerome) had scarcely an idea of grammatical and historical exegesis.

Origen was the first to lay down, in connection with the allegorical method of the Jewish Platonist, Philo, a formal theory of interpretation, which he carried out in a long series of exegetical works remarkable for industry and ingenuity, but meagre in solid results. He considered the Bible a living organism, consisting of three elements which answer to the body, soul, and spirit of man, after the Platonic psychology. Accordingly, he attributed to the scriptures a threefold sense; (1) a somatic, literal, or historical sense, furnished immediately by the meaning of the words, but only serving as a veil for a higher idea; (2) a psychic or moral sense, animating the first, and serving for general edification; (3) a pneumatic or mystic and ideal sense, for those who stand on the high ground of philosophical knowledge. In the application of this theory he shows the same tendency as Philo, to spiritualize away the letter of scripture, especially where the plain historical sense seems unworthy, as in the history of David's crimes; and instead of simply bringing out the sense of the Bible, he puts into it all sorts of foreign ideas and irrelevant fancies. But this allegorizing suited the taste of the age, and, with his fertile mind and imposing learning, Origen was the exegetical oracle of the early church, till his orthodoxy fell into disrepute. He is the pioneer, also, in the criticism of the sacred text, and his " Hexapla " was the first attempt at a Polyglot Bible.

In spite of the numberless exegetical vagaries and differences in detail, which confute the Tridentine fiction of a " *unanimis consensus patrum*," there is still a certain unanimity among the fathers in their way of drawing the most important articles of faith from the Scriptures. In their expositions they all follow one dogmatical principle, a kind of *analogia fidei.* This brings us to tradition.

NOTES ON THE CANON.

I. THE STATEMENTS OF EUSEBIUS.

The accounts of Eusebius (d. 340) on the apostolic writings in several passages of his Church History (especially III. 25 ; comp. II. 22, 23 ; III. 3, 24 ; V. 8 ; VI. 14, 25) are somewhat vague and inconsistent, yet upon the whole they give us the best idea of the state of the canon in the first quarter of the fourth century just before the Council of Nicæa (325).

He distinguishes four classes of sacred books of the Christians (*H. E.* III. 25, in Heinichen's ed. vol. I. 130 sqq. ; comp. his note in vol. III. 87 sqq.).

1. HOMOLOGUMENA, *i. e.* such as were *universally acknowledged* (ὁμολογούμενα) : 22 Books of the 27 of the N. T., viz. : 4 Gospels, Acts, 14 Pauline Epistles (including Hebrews), 1 Peter, 1 John, Revelation. He says : "Having arrived at this point, it is proper that we should give a summary catalogue of the afore-mentioned (III. 24) writings of the N. T. (ἀνακεφαλαιώσασθαι τὰς δηλωθείσας τῆς καινῆς διαθήκης γραφάς). First, then, we must place the sacred quaternion (or quartette, τετρακτύν) of the Gospels, which are followed by the book of the Acts of the Apostles (ἡ τῶν πράξεων τῶν ἀποστόλων γραφή). After this we must reckon the Epistles of Paul, and next to them we must maintain as genuine (κυρωτέον, the verb. adj. from κυρόω, *to ratify*), the Epistle circulated as the former of John (τὴν φερομένην Ἰωάννου προτέραν), and in like manner that of Peter (καὶ ὁμοίως τὴν Πέτρου ἐπιστολήν). In addition to these books, if it seem proper (εἴγε φανείη), we must place the Revelation of John (τὴν ἀποκάλυψιν Ἰωάννου), concerning which we shall set forth the different opinions in due course. And these are reckoned among those which are *generally received* (ἐν ὁμολογουμένοις)."

In Bk. III. ch. 3, Eusebius speaks of "fourteen Epp." of Paul (τοῦ δὲ Παύλου πρόδηλοι καὶ σαφεῖς αἱ δεκατέσσαρες), as commonly received, but adds that "some have rejected the Ep. to the *Hebrews*, saying that it was disputed as not being one of Paul's epistles."

On the Apocalypse, Eusebius vacillates according as he gives the public belief of the church or his private opinion. He first counts it among the Homologumena, and then, in the same passage (III. 25), among the spurious books, but in each case with a qualifying statement (εἰ φανείη), leaving the matter to the judgment of the reader. He rarely quotes the book, and usually as the "Apocalypse of John," but in one place (III. 39) he intimates that it was probably written by "the second John," which must mean the "Presbyter John," so called, as distinct from the Apostle—an opinion which has found much favor in the Schleiermacher school of critics. Owing to its mysterious character, the Apocalypse is, even to this day, the most popular book of the N. T. with a few, and the most unpopular with the many. It is as well attested as any other book, and the most radical modern critics (Baur, Renan) admit its apostolic authorship and composition before the destruction of Jerusalem.

2. ANTILEGOMENA, or *controverted* books, yet "familiar to most people of the church" (ἀντιλεγόμενα, γνώριμα δ' ὅμως τοῖς πολλοῖς, III. 25). These are five (or seven), viz., one Epistle of James, one of Jude, 2 Peter, 2 and 3 John ("whether they really belong to the Evangelist or to another John").

To these we may add (although Eusebius does not do it expressly) the Hebrews and the Apocalypse, the former as not being generally acknowledged as Pauline, the latter on account of its supposed chiliasm, which was offensive to Eusebius and the Alexandrian school.

3. SPURIOUS Books (νόθα), such as the Acts of Paul, the Revelation of Peter, the Shepherd (Hermas), the Ep. of Barnabas, the so-called "Doctrines of the Apostles," and the Gospel according to the Hebrews, "in which those Hebrews who have accepted Christ take special delight."

To these he adds inconsistently, as already remarked, the Apocalypse of John, "which some, as I said, reject (ἥν τινες ἀθετοῦσιν), while others reckon it among the books generally received (τοῖς ὁμολογουμένοις)." He ought to have numbered it with the Antilegomena.

These νόθα, we may say, correspond to the Apocrypha of the O. T., pious and useful, but not canonical.

4. HERETICAL Books. These, Eusebius says, are worse than spurious books, and must be "set aside as altogether worthless and impious." Among these he mentions the Gospels of Peter, and Thomas, and Matthias, the Acts of Andrew, and John, and of the other Apostles.

II. ECCLESIASTICAL DEFINITIONS OF THE CANON.

Soon after the middle of the fourth century, when the church became firmly settled in the Empire, all doubts as to the Apocrypha of the Old Testament and the Antilegomena of the New ceased, and the acceptance of the Canon in its Catholic shape, which includes both, became an article of faith. The first Œcumenical Council of Nicæa did not settle the canon, as one might expect, but the scriptures were regarded without controversy as the sure and immovable foundation of the orthodox faith. In the last (20th or 21st) Canon of the Synod of Gangra, in Asia Minor (about the middle of the fourth century), it is said: "To speak briefly, we desire that what has been handed down to us by the divine scriptures and the Apostolic traditions should be observed in the church." Comp. Hefele, *Conciliengesch.* I. 789.

The first Council which expressly legislated on the number of canonical books is that of LAODICEA in Phrygia, in Asia Minor (held between A. D. 343 and 381, probably about 363). In its last canon (60 or 59), it enumerates the canonical books of the Old Testament, and then all of the New, *with the exception of the Apocalypse*, in the following order:

"And these are the Books of the New Testament: Four Gospels, according to Matthew, according to Mark, according to Luke, according to John; Acts of the Apostles; Seven Catholic Epistles, One of James, Two of Peter, Three of John, One of Jude; Fourteen Epistles of Paul, One to the Romans, Two to the Corinthians, One to the Galatians, One to the Ephesians, One to the Philippians, One to the Colossians, Two to the Thessalonians, One to the Hebrews, Two to Timothy, One to Titus, and One to Philemon."

This catalogue is omitted in several manuscripts and versions, and probably is a later insertion from the writings of Cyril of Jerusalem. Spittler, Herbst, and Westcott deny, Schröckh and Hefele defend, the Laodicean origin of this catalogue. It resembles that of the 85th of the Apostolical Canons which likewise omits the Apocalypse, but inserts two Epistles of Clement and the pseudo-Apostolical Constitutions.

On the Laodicean Council and its uncertain date, see Hefele, *Conciliengeschichte*, revised ed. vol. I. p. 746 sqq., and Westcott, on the *Canon of the N. T.*, second ed., p. 382 sqq.

In the Western church, the third provincial Council of CARTHAGE (held A. D. 397) gave a full list of the canonical books of both Testaments, which should be read as divine Scriptures to the exclusion of all others in the churches. The N. T. books are enumerated in the following order: "Four Books of the Gospels, One Book of the Acts of the Apostles, Thirteen Epp. of the Apostle Paul, One Ep. of the same [Apostle] to the Hebrews, Two Epistles of the Apostle Peter, Three of John, One of James, One of Jude, One Book of the Apocalypse of John." This canon had been previously adopted by the African Synod of Hippo regius, A. D. 393, at which Augustin, then presbyter, delivered his discourse *De Fide et Symbolo*. The acts of that Council are lost, but they were readopted by the third council of Carthage, which consisted only of forty-three African bishops, and can claim no general authority. (See Westcott, p. 391, Charteris, p. 20, and Hefele, II. 53 and 68, revised ed.)

Augustin, (who was present at both Councils), and Jerome (who translated the Latin Bible at the request of Pope Damasus of Rome) exerted a decisive influence in settling the Canon for the Latin church.

The Council of Trent (1546) confirmed the traditional view with an anathema on those who dissent. "This fatal decree," says Dr. Westcott (p. 426 sq.), "was ratified by fifty-three prelates, among whom was not one German, not one scholar distinguished for historical learning, not one who was fitted by special study for the examination of a subject in which the truth could only be determined by the voice of antiquity."

For the Greek and Roman churches the question of the Canon is closed, although no *strictly* œcumenical council representing the entire church has pronounced on it. But Protestantism claims the liberty of the ante-Nicene age and the right of renewed investigation into the origin and history of every book of the Bible. Without this liberty there can be no real progress in exegetical theology.

§ 139. *Catholic Tradition.*

IRENÆUS: *Adv. Hær.* Lib. I. c. 9, ¾ 5; I. 10, 1; III. 3, 1, 2; III. 4, 2;
IV. 33, 7. TERTULL.: *De Præscriptionibus Hæreticorum ;* especially
c. 13, 14, 17–19, 21, 35, 36, 40, 41; *De Virgin. veland.* c. 1; *Adv.
Prax.* c. 2; on the other hand, *Adv. Hermog.* c. 22; *De Carne
Christi,* c. 7; *De Resurr. Carnis,* c. 3. NOVATIAN: *De Trinitate* 3;
De Regula Fidei. CYPRIAN: *De Unitate Eccl.;* and on the other
hand, *Epist.* 74. ORIGEN: *De Princip.* lib. I. Præf. ¾ 4–6. CYRIL
of Jerus.: Κατηχήσεις (written 348).
J. A. DANIEL: *Theol. Controversen* (the doctrine of the Scriptures as
the source of knowledge). Halle, 1843.
J. J. JACOBI: *Die kirchl. Lehre von d. Tradition u. heil. Schrift in ihrer
Entwickelung dargestellt.* Berl. I. 1847.
PH. SCHAFF: *Creeds of Christendom,* vol. I. p. 12 sqq.; II. 11–44.
Comp. Lit. in the next section.

Besides appealing to the Scriptures, the fathers, particularly
Irenæus and Tertullian, refer with equal confidence to the "rule
of faith;"[1] that is, the common faith of the church, as orally
handed down in the unbroken succession of bishops from Christ
and his apostles to their day, and above all as still living in the
original apostolic churches, like those of Jerusalem, Antioch,
Ephesus, and Rome. Tradition is thus intimately connected
with the primitive episcopate. The latter was the vehicle of
the former, and both were looked upon as bulwarks against
heresy.

Irenæus confronts the secret tradition of the Gnostics with the
open and unadulterated tradition of the catholic church, and
points to all churches, but particularly to Rome, as the visible
centre of the unity of doctrine. All who would know the truth,
says he, can see in the whole church the tradition of the apostles;
and we can count the bishops ordained by the apostles, and
their successors down to our time, who neither taught nor knew
any such heresies. Then, by way of example, he cites the first

[1] κανὼν τῆς πίστεως, or τῆς ἀληθείας, παράδοσις τῶν ἀποστόλων, or παρ.
ἀποστολική, κανὼν ἐκκλησιαστικός, τὸ ἀρχαῖον τῆς ἐκκλησίας, σύστημα, regula fidei,
regula veritatis, traditio apostolica, lex fidei, fides catholica. Sometimes these
terms are used in a wider sense, and embrace the whole course of catechetical
instruction.

twelve bishops of the Roman church from Linus to Eleutherus, as witnesses of the pure apostolic doctrine. He might conceive of a Christianity without scripture, but he could not imagine a Christianity without living tradition; and for this opinion he refers to barbarian tribes, who have the gospel, "*sine charta et atramento,*" written in their hearts.

Tertullian finds a universal antidote for all heresy in his celebrated prescription argument, which cuts off heretics, at the outset, from every right of appeal to the holy scriptures, on the ground, that the holy scriptures arose in the church of Christ, were given to her, and only in her and by her can be rightly understood. He calls attention also here to the tangible succession, which distinguishes the catholic church from the arbitrary and ever-changing sects of heretics, and which in all the principal congregations, especially in the original sees of the apostles, reaches back without a break from bishop to bishop, to the apostles themselves, from the apostles to Christ, and from Christ to God. "Come, now," says he, in his tract on Prescription, "if you would practise inquiry to more advantage in the matter of your salvation, go through the apostolic churches, in which the very chairs of the apostles still preside, in which their own authentic letters are publicly read, uttering the voice and representing the face of every one. If Achaia is nearest, you have Corinth. If you are not far from Macedonia, you have Philippi, you have Thessalonica. If you can go to Asia, you have Ephesus. But if you live near Italy, you have Rome, whence also we [of the African church] derive our origin. How happy is the church, to which the apostles poured out their whole doctrine with their blood," etc.

To estimate the weight of this argument, we must remember that these fathers still stood comparatively very near the apostolic age, and that the succession of bishops in the oldest churches could be demonstrated by the living memory of two or three generations. Irenæus, in fact, had been acquainted in his youth with Polycarp, a disciple of St. John. But for this very reason we must guard against overrating this testimony, and employing it in behalf of traditions of later origin, not grounded in the scriptures.

Nor can we suppose that those fathers ever thought of a blind and slavish subjection of private judgment to ecclesiastical authority, and to the decision of the bishops of the apostolic mother churches. The same Irenæus frankly opposed the Roman bishop Victor. Tertullian, though he continued essentially orthodox, contested various points with the catholic church from his later Montanistic position, and laid down, though at first only in respect to a conventional custom—the veiling of virgins—the genuine Protestant principle, that the thing to be regarded, especially in matters of religion, is not custom but truth.[1] His pupil, Cyprian, with whom biblical and catholic were almost interchangeable terms, protested earnestly against the Roman theory of the validity of heretical baptism, and in this controversy declared, in exact accordance with Tertullian, that custom without truth was only time-honored error.[2] The Alexandrians freely fostered all sorts of peculiar views, which were afterwards rejected as heretical; and though the παράδοσις ἀποστολική plays a prominent part with them, yet this and similar expressions have in their language a different sense, sometimes meaning simply the holy scriptures. So, for example, in the well-known passage of Clement: "As if one should be changed from a man to a beast after the manner of one charmed by Circe; so a man ceases to be God's and to continue faithful to the Lord, when he sets himself up against the church tradition, and flies off to positions of human caprice."

In the substance of its doctrine this apostolic tradition agrees with the holy scriptures, and though derived, as to its form, from the oral preaching of the apostles, is really, as to its con-

---

[1] "Christus veritatem se, non consuetudinem cognominavit. . . . . Hacreses non tam novitas quam veritas revincit. Quodcunque adversus veritatem sapit hoc erit hæresis, etiam vetus consuetudo." De Virg. vel. c. 1.

[2] "Consuetudo sine veritate vetustas erroris est." Ep. 74 (contra Stephanum), c. 9.

tents, one and the same with those apostolic writings. In this view the apparent contradictions of the earlier fathers, in ascribing the highest authority to both scripture and tradition in matters of faith, resolve themselves. It is one and the same gospel which the apostles preached with their lips, and then laid down in their writings, and which the church faithfully hands down by word and writing from one generation to another.[1]

§ 140. *The Rule of Faith and the Apostles' Creed.*

RUFINUS (d. 410): *Expos. in Symbolum Apostolorum.* In the Append. to Fell's ed. of Cyprian, 1682; and in *Rufini Opera*, Migne's "Patrologia," Tom. XXI. fol. 335–386.

JAMES USSHER (Prot. archbishop of Armagh, d. 1655): *De Romanæ Ecclesiæ Symbolo Apostolico vetere, aliisque fidei formulis.* London, 1647. In his *Works*, Dublin 1847, vol. VII. p. 297 sqq. Ussher broke the path for a critical history of the creed on the basis of the oldest MSS. which he discovered.

JOHN PEARSON (Bp. of Chester, d. 1686): *Exposition of the Creed*, 1659, in many editions (revised ed. by Dr. E. Burton, Oxf. 1847; New York 1851). A standard work of Anglican theology.

PETER KING (Lord Chancellor of England, d. 1733): *History of the Apostles' Creed.* Lond. 1702.

HERM. WITSIUS (Calvinist, d. at Leyden, 1708): *Exercitationes sacrae in Symbolum quod Apostolorum dicitur.* Amstel. 1700. Basil. 1739. 4°. English translation by *Fraser*. Edinb. 1823, in 2 vols.

ED. KÖLLNER (Luth.): *Symbolik aller christl. Confessionen.* Part I. Hamb. 1837, p. 6–28.

*AUG. HAHN: *Bibliothek der Symbole und Glaubensregeln der apostolisch-katholischen* [in the new ed. *der alten*] *Kirche.* Breslau, 1842 (pp. 222). Second ed. revised and enlarged by his son, G. LUDWIG HAHN. Breslau, 1877 (pp. 300).

J. W. NEVIN: *The Apostles' Creed*, in the "Mercersburg Review," 1849. Purely doctrinal.

---

[1] So Paul uses the word παράδοσις, 2 Thess. 2: 15: "hold the traditions which ye were taught, whether by *word* (διὰ λόγου), or by *epistle* of ours (δι' ἐπιστολῆς ἡμῶν); comp. 3: 6 (κατὰ τὴν παράδοσιν ἥν παρελάβετε παρ' ἡμῶν); 1 Cor. 11: 2. In all other passages, however, where the word παράδοσις, *traditio*, occurs, it is used in an unfavorable sense of extra-scriptural teaching, especially that of the Pharisees. Comp. Matt. 15: 2, 6; Mark 7: 3, 5, 9, 13; Gal. 1: 14; Col. 2: 8. The Reformers attached the same censure to the mediæval traditions of the Roman church, which obscured and virtually set aside the written word of God.

PET. MEYERS (R. C.): *De Symboli Apostolici Titulo, Origine et antiquissimis ecclesiae temporibus Auctoritate.* Treviris, 1849 (pp. 210). A learned defense of the Apostolic origin of the Creed.

W. W. HARVEY: *The History and Theology of the three Creeds (the Apostles', the Nicene, and the Athanasian).* Lond. 1854. 2 vols.

*CHARLES A. HEURTLEY: *Harmonia Symbolica.* Oxford, 1858.

MICHEL NICOLAS: *Le Symbole des apôtres. Essai historic.* Paris, 1867. (Sceptical).

*J. RAWSON LUMBY: *The History of the Creeds (ante-Nicene, Nicene and Athanasian).* London, 1873, 2d ed. 1880.

*C. A. SWAINSON: *The Nicene and the Apostles' Creed.* London, 1875.

*C. P. CASPARI (Prof. in Christiania): *Quellen zur Gesch. des Tauf. symbols und der Glaubensregel.* Christiania, 1866–1879. 4 vols. Contains new researches and discoveries of MSS.

*F. J. A. HORT: *Two Dissertations on* μονογενὴς θεός, *and on the "Constantinopolitan Creed and other Eastern Creeds of the Fourth Century.* Cambr. and Lond. 1876. Of great critical value.

F. B. WESTCOTT: *The Historic Faith.* London, 1883.

PH. SCHAFF: *Creeds of Christendom,* vol. I. 3–42, and II. 10–73. (4th ed. 1884.

In the narrower sense, by apostolic tradition or the rule of faith (κανὼν τῆς πίστεως, *regula fidei*) was understood a doctrinal summary of Christianity, or a compend of the faith of the church. Such a summary grew out of the necessity of catechetical instruction and a public confession of candidates for baptism. It became equivalent to a *symbolum,* that is, a sign of recognition among catholic Christians in distinction from unbelievers and heretics. The confession of Peter (Matt. 16 : 16) gave the key-note, and the baptismal formula (Matt. 28 : 19) furnished the trinitarian frame-work of the earliest creeds or baptismal confessions of Christendom.

There was at first no prescribed formula of faith binding upon all believers. Each of the leading churches framed its creed (in a sort of independent congregational way), according to its wants, though on the same basis of the baptismal formula, and possibly after the model of a brief archetype which may have come down from apostolic days. Hence we have a variety of such rules of faith, or rather fragmentary accounts of them, longer or shorter, declarative or interrogative, in the ante-Nicene writers, as Irenæus of Lyons (180), Tertullian of Carthage

(200), Cyprian of Carthage (250), Novatian of Rome (250), Origen of Alexandria (250), Gregory Thaumaturgus (270), Lucian of Antioch (300), Eusebius of Cæsarea (325), Marcellus of Ancyra (340), Cyril of Jerusalem (350), Epiphanius of Cyprus (374), Rufinus of Aquileja (390), and in the Apostolic Constitutions).[1] Yet with all the differences in form and extent there is a substantial agreement, so that Tertullian could say that the *regula fidei* was "*una omnino, sola immobilis et irreformabilis.*" They are variations of the same theme. We may refer for illustration of the variety and unity to the numerous orthodox and congregational creeds of the Puritan churches in New England, which are based upon the Westminster standards.

The Oriental forms are generally longer, more variable and metaphysical, than the Western, and include a number of dogmatic terms against heretical doctrines which abounded in the East. They were all replaced at last by the Nicene Creed (325, 381, and 451), which was clothed with the authority of œcumenical councils and remains to this day the fundamental Creed of the Greek Church. Strictly speaking it is the only œcumenical Creed of Christendom, having been adopted also in the West, though with a clause (*Filioque*) which has become a wall of division. We shall return to it in the next volume.

The Western forms—North African, Gallican, Italian—are shorter and simpler, have less variety, and show a more uniform type. They were all merged into the Roman Symbol, which became and remains to this day the fundamental creed of the Latin Church and her daughters.

This Roman symbol is known more particularly under the honored name of the *Apostles' Creed*. For a long time it was believed (and is still believed by many in the Roman church) to be the product of the Apostles who prepared it as a summary of their teaching before parting from Jerusalem (each contributing one of the twelve articles by higher inspiration).[2] This tradition

---

[1] See a collection of these ante-Nicene rules of faith in Hahn, Denzinger, Heurtley, Caspari, and Schaff (II. 11–41).

[2] This obsolete opinion, first mentioned by Ambrose and Rufinus is still de-

which took its rise in the fourth century,[1] is set aside by the variations of the ante-Nicene creeds and of the Apostles' Creed itself. Had the Apostles composed such a document, it would have been scrupulously handed down without alteration. The creed which bears this name is undoubtedly a gradual growth. We have it in two forms.

The earlier form as found in old manuscripts,[2] is much shorter and may possibly go back to the third or even the second century. It was probably imported from the East, or grew in Rome, and is substantially identical with the Greek creed of Marcellus of Ancyra (about 340), inserted in his letter to Pope Julius I. to prove his orthodoxy,[3] and with that con-

---

fended by Pet. Meyers, *l. c.* and by Abbé Martigny in his French *Dictionary of Christ. Antiquities* (sub *Symbole des apôtres*). Longfellow, in his *Divine Tragedy* (1871) makes poetic use of it, and arranges the Creed in twelve articles, with the names of the supposed apostolic authors. The apostolic origin was first called in question by Laurentius Valla, Erasmus, and Calvin. See particulars in Schaff's *Creeds*, I. 22–23.

[1] Rufinus speaks of it as an ancestral tradition (*tradunt majores nostri*) and supports it by a false explanation of *symbolum*, as "*collatio, hoc est quod plures in unum conferunt.*" See Migne, XXI. fol. 337.

[2] In the Græco-Latin Codex Laudianus (Cod. E of the Acts) in the Bodleian Library at Oxford, from the sixth century, and known to the Venerable Bede (731). The Creed is attached at the end, is written in uncial letters, and was first made known by Archbishop Ussher. Heurtley (p. 61 sq.) gives a facsimile. It is reprinted in Caspari, Hahn (second ed. p. 16), and Schaff (II. 47). Another copy is found in a MS. of the eighth century in the British Museum, published by Swainson, *The Nic. and Ap. Creeds*, p. 161, and by Hahn in a *Nachtrag* to the Preface, p. xvi. This document, however, inserts *catholicam* after *ecclesiam*. Comp. also the form in the *Explanatio Symboli ad initiandos*, by Ambrose in Caspari, II. 48 and 128, and Schaff, II. 50. The Creed of Aquileja, as given by Rufinus, has a few additions, but marks them as such so that we can infer from it the words of the Roman Creed. With these Latin documents agree the Greek in the Psalterium of King Aethelstan, and of Marcellus (see next note).

[3] In Epiphanius, *Hær.* LXXII. It is assigned to A. D. 341, by others to 337. It is printed in Schaff (II. 47), Hahn, and in the first table below. It contains, according to Caspari, the original form of the Roman creed as current at the time in the Greek portion of the Roman congregation. It differs from the oldest Latin form only by the omission of πατέρα, and the addition of ζωὴν αἰώνιον.

tained in the Psalter of King Aethelstan.[1] Greek was the ruling language of the Roman Church and literature down to the third century.[2]

The longer form of the Roman symbol, or the present received text, does not appear before the sixth or seventh century. It has several important clauses which were wanting in the former, as "he descended into hades,"[3] the predicate "catholic" after ecclesiam,[4] "the communion of saints,"[5] and "the life ever-

---

[1] The *Psalterium Aethelstani*, in the Cotton Library of the British Museum, written in Anglo-Saxon letters, first published by Ussher, then by Heurtley, Caspari, and Hahn (p. 15). It differs from the text of Marcellus by the insertion of πατέρα and the omission of ζωὴν αἰώνιον, in both points agreeing with the Latin text.

[2] On the Greek original of the Roman symbol Caspari's researches (III. 267–466) are conclusive. Harnack (in Herzog [2], vol. I. 567) agrees: " *Der griechische Text ist als das Original zu betrachten; griechisch wurde das Symbol zu Rom eine lange Zeit hindurch ausschliesslich tradirt. Dann trat der lateinisch übersetzte Text als Parallelform hinzu.*" Both are disposed to trace the symbol to Johannean circles in Asia Minor on account of the term "only begotten" (μονογενής), which is used of Christ only by John.

[3] *Descendit ad inferna*, first found in Arian Creeds (εἰς ᾅδου or εἰς τὸν ᾅδην) about A. D. 360; then in the Creed of Aquileja, about A. D. 390; then in the Creed of Venantius Fortunatus, 590, in the Sacramentarium Gallicanum, 650, and in the ultimate text of the Apostles' Creed in Pirminius, 750. See the table in Schaff's *Creeds*, II. 54, and critical note on p. 46. Rufinus says expressly that this clause was not contained in the Roman creed, and explains it wrongly as being identical with "buried." *Com.* c. 18 (in Migne, f. 356): "*Sciendum sane est, quod in Ecclesiæ Romanæ Symbolo non habetur additum, 'descendit ad inferna:' sed neque in Orientis Ecclesiis habetur hic sermo: via tamen verbi eadem videtur esse in eo, quod 'sepultus' dicitur.*" The article of the descent is based upon Peter's teaching, Acts 2: 31 ("he was not *left* in Hades," εἰς ᾅδου, consequently he *was* there); 1 Pet. 3: 19; 4: 6; and the promise of Christ to the dying robber, Luke 23: 43 ("to day thou shalt be with Me in paradise," ἐν τᾷ παραδείσῳ), and undoubtedly means a self exhibition of Christ to the spirits of the departed. The translation "descended into *hell*" is unfortunate and misleading. We do not know whether Christ was in hell; but we do know from his own lips that he was in paradise between his death and resurrection. The term Hades is much more comprehensive than Hell (Gehenna), which is confined to the state and place of the lost.

[4] It is found first in the Sacramentarium Gallicanum, 650. The older creeds of Cyprian, Rufinus, Augustin, read simply *sanctam ecclesiam*, Marcellus ἁγίαν ἐκκλησίαν.

[5] *Sanctorum communionem.* After 650.

lasting."[1] These additions were gathered from the provincial versions (Gallican and North African) and incorporated into the older form.

The Apostles' Creed then, in its present shape, is post-apostolic; but, in its contents and spirit, truly apostolic. It embodies the faith of the ante-Nicene church, and is the product of a secondary inspiration, like the *Gloria in Excelsis* and the *Te-deum*, which embody the devotions of the same age, and which likewise cannot be traced to an individual author or authors. It follows the historical order of revelation of the triune God, Father, Son, and Holy Spirit, beginning with the creation and ending with the resurrection and life eternal. It clusters around Christ as the central article of our faith. It sets forth living facts, not abstract dogmas, and speaks in the language of the people, not of the theological school. It confines itself to the fundamental truths, is simple, brief, and yet comprehensive, and admirably adapted for catechetical and liturgical use. It still forms a living bond of union between the different ages and branches of orthodox Christendom, however widely they differ from each other, and can never be superseded by longer and fuller creeds, however necessary these are in their place. It has the authority of antiquity and the dew of perennial youth, beyond any other document of post-apostolic times. It is the only strictly œcumenical Creed of the West, as the Nicene Creed is the only œcumenical Creed of the East.[2] It is the Creed of creeds, as the Lord's Prayer is the Prayer of prayers.

NOTE.

The legendary formulas of the Apostles' Creed which appear after the sixth century, distribute the articles to the several apostles arbitrarily

[1] Contained in Marcellus and Augustin, but wanting in Rufinus and in the Psalter of Aethelstan. See on all these additions and their probable date the tables in my *Creeds of Christendom*, II. 54 and 55.

[2] We usually speak of *three* œcumenical creeds; but the Greek church has never adopted the Apostles' Creed and the Athanasian Creed, although she holds the doctrines therein contained. The Nicene Creed was adopted in the West, and so far is universal, but the insertion of the formula *Filioque* created and perpetuates the split between the Greek and Latin churches.

and with some variations. The following is from one of the pseudo-Augustinian sermons (see Hahn, p.47 sq.):

" Decimo die post ascensionem discipulis prae timore Judaeorum congregatis Dominus promissum Paracletum misit: quo veniente ut candens ferrum inflammati omniumque linguarum peritia repleti Symbolum composuerunt.

PETRUS dixit: *Credo in Deum Patrem omnipotentem—creatorem cœli et terræ.*

ANDREAS dixit: *Et in Jesum Christum, Filium ejus—unicum Dominum nostrum.*

JACOBUS dixit: *Qui conceptus est de Spiritu Sancto—natus ex Maria Virgine.*

JOANNES dixit: *Passus sub Pontio Pilato—crucifixus, mortuus et sepultus.*

THOMAS dixit: *Descendit ad inferna—tertia die resurrexit a mortuis.*

JACOBUS dixit: *Adscendit ad cœlos—sedet ad dexteram Dei Patris omnipotentis.*

PHILIPPUS dixit: *Inde venturus est judicare vivos et mortuos.*

BARTHOLOMÆUS dixit: *Credo in Spiritum Sanctum.*

MATTHÆUS dixit: *Sanctam Ecclesiam catholicam— Sanctorum communionem.*

SIMON dixit: *Remissionem peccatorum.*

THADDEUS dixit: *Carnis resurrectionem.*

MATTHIAS dixit: *Vitam aeternam.*"

§ 141. *Variations of the Apostles' Creed.*

We present two tables which show the gradual growth of the Apostles' Creed, and its relation to the Ante-Nicene rules of faith and the Nicene Creed in its final form.[1]

---

[1] The second table is transferred from the author's *Creeds of Christendom*, vol. II. 40 and 41 (by permission of the publishers, Messrs. Harpers). In the same work will be found other comparative illustrative and chronological tables of the oldest symbols. See vol. I. 21 and 28 sq.; and vol. II. 54, 55.

II. COMPARATIVE TABLE OF THE APOSTLES' CREED,

SHOWING THE DIFFERENT STAGES OF ITS GROWTH TO ITS PRESENT FORM. THE ADDITIONS ARE ENCLOSED IN BRACKETS.

FORMULA MARCELLI ANCYRANI. About A.D. 340.	FORMULA ROMANA. From the 3d or 4th Century.	FORMULA AQUILEIENSIS. From Rufinus (400).	FORMULA RECEPTA. Since the 6th or 7th Century. (Later additions in brackets).	THE RECEIVED TEXT.
Πιστεύω εἰς Θεὸν παντοκράτορα.	Credo in DEUM PATREM omnipotentem.	Credo in DEO PATRE omnipotente, [invisibili et impassibili].	Credo in DEUM PATREM omnipotentem, [Creatorem coeli et terræ].	I believe in GOD THE FATHER Almighty, [Maker of heaven and earth]
Καὶ εἰς Χριστὸν Ἰησοῦν, τὸν υἱὸν αὐτοῦ τὸν μονογενῆ, τὸν κύριον ἡμῶν,	Et in CHRISTUM JESUM, Filium ejus unicum, Dominum nostrum;	Et in CHRISTO JESU, unico filio ejus, Domino nostro;	Et in JESUM CHRISTUM, Filium ejus unicum, Dominum nostrum;	And in JESUS CHRIST, his only begotten Son, our Lord;
τὸν γεννηθέντα ἐκ Πνεύματος ἁγίου καὶ Μαρίας τῆς παρθένου,	qui natus est de Spiritu Sancto et Maria Virgine;	qui natus est de Spiritu Sancto ex Maria Virgine;	qui [conceptus] est de Spiritu Sancto, natus ex Maria Virgine;	who was [conceived] by the Holy Ghost, born of the Virgin Mary;
τὸν ἐπὶ Ποντίου Πιλάτου σταυρωθέντα καὶ ταφέντα,	crucifixus est sub Pontio Pilato, et sepultus;	crucifixus sub Pontio Pilato, et sepultus;	[passus] sub Pontio Pilato, crucifixus, [mortuus], et sepultus;	[suffered] under Pontius Pilate, was crucified, [dead], and buried.
		[descendit ad inferna] ;	[descendit ad inferna] ;	[He descended into Hades] ;
καὶ τῇ τρίτῃ ἡμέρᾳ ἀναστάντα ἐκ τῶν νεκρῶν,	tertia die resurrexit a mortuis;	tertia die resurrexit a mortuis;	tertia die resurrexit a rrortuis;	the third day He rose from the dead;
ἀναβάντα εἰς τοὺς οὐρανοὺς,	ascendit in coelos;	ascendit in coelos ;	ascendit ad coelos ·	He ascended into heaven;
καὶ καθήμενον ἐν δεξιᾷ τοῦ πατρός,	sedet ad dexteram Patris;	sedet ad dexteram Patris;	sedet ad dexteram Dei Patris [omnipotentis] ;	and sitteth on the right hand of God the Father [Almighty];
ὅθεν ἔρχεται κρίνειν ζῶντας καὶ νεκρούς.	inde venturus judicare vivos et mortuos.	inde venturus est judicare vivos et mortuos.	inde venturus judicare vivos et mortuos.	from thence He shall come to judge the quick and the dead.
Καὶ εἰς τὸ Ἅγιον Πνεῦμα,	Et in SPIRITUM SANCTUM;	Et in SPIRITU SANCTO.	[Credo] in SPIRITUM SANCTUM;	[I believe] in the HOLY GHOST;
ἁγίαν ἐκκλησίαν,	Sanctam Ecclesiam;	Sanctam Ecclesiam ;	Sanctam Ecclesiam [catholicam], [sanctorum communionem] ;	the holy [catholic] church, [the communion of saints] ;
ἄφεσιν ἁμαρτιῶν, σαρκὸς ἀνάστασιν,	remissionem peccatorum; carnis resurrectionem.	remissionem peccatorum; [hujus] carnis resurrectionem.	remissionem peccatorum; carnis resurrectionem;	the forgiveness of sins; the resurrection of the body;
[ζωὴν αἰώνιον].			[vitam æternam. Amen].	[and the life everlasting. Amen].

COMPARATIVE TABLE OF THE ANTE-NICENE RULES OF FAITH,

AS RELATED TO THE APOSTLES' CREED AND THE NICENE CREED.

THE APOSTLES' CREED. (Rome.) About A.D. 340. Later additions are in italics.	IRENÆUS. (Gaul.) A.D. 170.	TERTULLIAN. (North Africa.) A.D. 200.	CYPRIAN. (Carthage.) A.D. 250.	NOVATIAN. (Rome.) A.D. 250.	ORIGEN. (Alexandria.) A.D. 230.
I believe 1. in GOD THE FATHER Almighty, *Maker of heaven and earth;*	We believe 1. . . . in ONE GOD THE FATHER Almighty, who made heaven and earth, and the sea, and all that in them is:	We believe 1. . . . in ONE GOD, the Creator of the world, who produced all out of nothing . . .	I believe 1. in GOD THE FATHER;	We believe 1. in GOD THE FATHER and Almighty Lord;	[We believe in] 1. ONE GOD, who created and framed every thing . . . Who in the last days sent
2. And in JESUS CHRIST, His only Son, our Lord;	2. And in one CHRIST JESUS, the Son of God [our Lord];	2. And in the Word, his Son, JESUS CHRIST;	2. in his SON CHRIST;	2. in the Son of God, CHRIST JESUS, our Lord God;	2. Our Lord JESUS CHRIST . . . born of the Father before all creation . . .
3. who was *conceived* by the Holy Ghost, born of the Virgin Mary;	3. Who became flesh [of the Virgin] for our salvation;	3. Who through the Spirit and power of God the Father descended into the Virgin Mary, was made flesh in her womb, and born of her;			3. born of the Virgin and the Holy Ghost, made incarnate while remaining God . . .
4. *suffered* under Pontius Pilate, was crucified, *dead,* and buried;	4. and his suffering [under Pontius Pilate];	4. Was fixed on the cross [under Pontius Pilate], was dead and buried;			4. suffered in truth, died;
5. *He descended into Hades;* the third day he rose from the dead;	5. and his rising from the dead;	5. rose again the third day;			5. rose from the dead;
6. He ascended into heaven, and sitteth on the right hand of *God* the Father *Almighty;*	6. and his bodily assumption into heaven;	6. was taken up into heaven and sitteth at the right hand of God the Father;			6. was taken up . . .
7. from thence he shall come to judge the quick and the dead.	7. and his coming from heaven in the glory of the Father to comprehend all things under one head, . . . and to execute righteous judgment over all.	7. He will come to judge the quick and the dead.			
8. And *I believe* in THE HOLY GHOST;	8. And in THE HOLY GHOST . . .	8. And in THE HOLY GHOST, the Paraclete, the Sanctifier, sent by Christ from the Father.	8. in THE HOLY GHOST;	8. in THE HOLY GHOST (promised of old to the Church, and granted in the appointed and fitting time).	8. THE HOLY GHOST, united in honor and dignity with the Father and the Son.
9. the holy *Catholic* Church; *the communion of saints;*					
10. the forgiveness of sins;			10. { I believe the forgiveness of sins,		
11. the resurrection of the body;	11. And that Christ shall come from heaven to raise up all flesh, . . . and to adjudge the impious and unjust . . . to eternal fire,	11. And that Christ will, after the restoration of the flesh, receive his saints			
12. *and the life everlasting.*[1]	12. and to give . . . to the just and holy immortality and eternal glory.	12. into the enjoyment of eternal life and the promises of heaven, and judge the wicked with eternal fire.	12. and eternal life through the holy Church.		

[1] The Roman Creed according to Rufinus (390) ends with *carnis resurrectionem*; but the Greek version of the Roman Creed by Marcellus (341) with ζωὴν αἰώνιον.

THE APOSTLES' CREED.	GREGORY. (Neo-Cæsarea.) A.D. 270.	LUCIAN. (Antioch.) A.D. 300.	EUSEBIUS. (Cæsarea, Pal.) A.D. 325.	CYRIL. (Jerusalem.) A.D. 350.	NICÆNO-CONSTANTINOPOLITAN CREED. A.D. 325 and 381.
			We believe	We believe	We [I] believe
1. I believe in GOD THE FATHER Almighty, *Maker of heaven and earth;*	1. [We believe in] ONE GOD THE FATHER.	1. [We believe in] ONE GOD THE FATHER Almighty, Maker and Provider of all things;	1. in ONE GOD THE FATHER Almighty, Maker of all things visible and invisible;	1. in ONE GOD THE FATHER Almighty, Maker of heaven and earth, and of all things visible and invisible;	1. in ONE GOD THE FATHER Almighty, Maker of heaven and earth, *and of all things visible and invisible;*
2. And in JESUS CHRIST, His only Son, our Lord;	2. one LORD, ... God of God, the image and likeness of the Godhead, ... the Wisdom and Power which produces all creation, the true Son of the true Father ...	2. And in one Lord JESUS CHRIST his Son, begotten of the Father before all ages, God of God, Wisdom, Life, Light ...	2. And in one LORD JESUS CHRIST, the Word of God, God of God, Light of Light, Life of Life, the only-begotten Son, the first-born of every creature, begotten of God the Father before all ages; by whom all things were made;	2. And in one LORD JESUS CHRIST, the only-begotten Son of God, begotten of the Father before all ages, very God, by whom all things were made;	2. And in one Lord JESUS CHRIST, the only-begotten Son of God, begotten of the Father *before all worlds;* [God of God], Light of Light, very God of very God, begotten, not made, being of one substance with the Father (ὁμοούσιον τῷ Πατρί); by whom all things were made;
3. who was *conceived* by the Holy Ghost, born of the Virgin Mary,		3. who was born of a Virgin, according to the Scriptures, and became man ...	3. who for our salvation was made flesh and lived among men;	3. who was made flesh, and became man;	3. who, for us men, and for our salvation, came down *from heaven,* and was incarnate *by the Holy Ghost and [of, or] the Virgin Mary,* and was made man;
4. *suffered* under Pontius Pilate, was crucified, *dead,* and buried; *He descended into Hades;*		4. who suffered for us;	4. and suffered;	4. was crucified, and was buried;	4. *He was crucified for us under Pontius Pilate,* and suffered, *and was buried;*
5. the third day he rose from the dead;		5. and rose for us on the third day;	5. and rose on the third day;	5. rose on the third day;	5. and the third day he rose again, *according to the Scriptures;*
6. He ascended into heaven, and sitteth on the right hand of *God the* Father *Almighty;*		6. and ascended into heaven, and sitteth on the right hand of God the Father;	6. and ascended to the Father;	6. and ascended into heaven, and sitteth on the right hand of the Father;	6. and ascended into heaven, *and sitteth on the right hand of the Father;*
7. from thence he shall come to judge the quick and the dead.		7. and again is coming with glory and power, to judge the quick and the dead;	7. and will come again with glory, to judge the quick and the dead.	7. and will come again in glory, to judge the quick and the dead; whose kingdom shall have no end;	7. and he shall come again, *with glory,* to judge the quick and the dead; *whose kingdom shall have no end;*
8. And *I believe* in THE HOLY GHOST;	8. one HOLY GHOST, ... the minister of sanctification, in whom is revealed God the Father, who is over all things and through all things, and God the Son, who is through all things,— a-perfect Trinity, not divided nor differing in glory, eternity, and sovereignty. ...	8. And in THE HOLY GHOST, given for consolation and sanctification and perfection to those who believe ...	8. We believe also in THE HOLY GHOST.	8. And in one HOLY GHOST, the Advocate, who spake in the Prophets.	8. And [I believe] in THE HOLY GHOST, *the Lord, and Giver of life, Who proceedeth from the Father* [and the Son, *Filioque*], *who with the Father and the Son together is worshiped and glorified, who spake by the Prophets.*
9. the holy *Catholic* Church; *the communion of saints;*				9. And in one baptism of repentance for the remission of sins;	9. *And* [I believe] *in one holy Catholic and Apostolic Church;*
10. the forgiveness of sins;				10. and in one holy Catholic Church;	10. we [I] acknowledge one baptism *for the remission of sins;*
11. the resurrection of the body;				11. and in the resurrection of the flesh;	11. *and we* [I] *look for the resurrection of the dead;*
12. *and the life everlasting.*				12. and in life everlasting (ζωὴν αἰώνιον).	12. *and the life of the world to come* (ζωὴν τοῦ μέλλοντος αἰῶνος).

The words in *italics* in the last column are additions of the second œcumenical Council (381); the words in brackets are Western changes.

§ 142. *God and the Creation.*

E. Wilh. Möller: *Geschichte der Kosmologie in der griechischen Kirche bis auf Origenes.* Halle, 1860. P. 112–188; 474–560. The greater part of this learned work is devoted to the cosmological theories of the Gnostics.

In exhibiting the several doctrines of the church, we must ever bear in mind that Christianity entered the world, not as a logical system but as a divine-human fact; and that the New Testament is not only a theological text-book for scholars but first and last a book of life for all believers. The doctrines of salvation, of course, lie in these facts of salvation, but in a concrete, living, ever fresh, and popular form. The logical, scientific development of those doctrines from the word of God and Christian experience is left to the theologians. Hence we must not be surprised to find in the period before us, even in the most eminent teachers, a very indefinite and defective knowledge, as yet, of important articles of faith, whose practical force those teachers felt in their own hearts and impressed on others, as earnestly as their most orthodox successors. The centre of Christianity is the divine-human person and the divine-human work of Christ. From that centre a change passed through the whole circle of existing religious ideas, in its first principles and its last results, confirming what was true in the earlier religion, and rejecting the false.

Almost all the creeds of the first centuries, especially the Apostles' and the Nicene, begin with confession of faith in God, the Father Almighty, Maker of heaven and earth, of the visible and the invisible. With the defence of this fundamental doctrine laid down in the very first chapter of the Bible, Irenæus opens his refutation of the Gnostic heresies. He would not have believed the Lord himself, if he had announced any other God than the Creator. He repudiates everything like an *a priori* construction of the idea of God, and bases his knowledge wholly on revelation and Christian experience.

We begin with the general idea of God, which lies at the

bottom of all religion. This is refined, spiritualized, and invigorated by the manifestation in Christ. We perceive the advance particularly in Tertullian's view of the irresistible leaning of the human soul towards God, and towards the only true God. "God will never be hidden," says he, "God will never fail mankind; he will always be recognized, always perceived, and seen, when man wishes. God has made all that we are, and all in which we are, a witness of himself. Thus he proves himself God, and the one God, by his being known to all; since another must first be proved. The sense of God is the original dowry of the soul; the same, and no other, in Egypt, in Syria, and in Pontus; for the God of the Jews all souls call their God." But nature also testifies of God. It is the work of his hand, and in itself good; not as the Gnostics taught, a product of matter, or of the devil, and intrinsically bad. Except as he reveals himself, God is, according to Irenæus, absolutely hidden and incomprehensible. But in creation and redemption he has communicated himself, and can, therefore, not remain entirely concealed from any man.

Of the various arguments for the existence of God, we find in this period the beginnings of the cosmological and physico-theological methods. In the mode of conceiving the divine nature we observe this difference; while the Alexandrians try to avoid all anthropomorphic and anthropopathic notions, and insist on the immateriality and spirituality of God almost to abstraction, Tertullian ascribes to him even corporeality; though probably, as he considers the non-existent alone absolutely incorporeal, he intends by corporeality only to denote the substantiality and concrete personality of the Supreme Being.[1]

The doctrine of the unity of God, as the eternal, almighty, omnipresent, just, and holy creator and upholder of all things, the Christian church inherited from Judaism, and vindicated

---

[1] "*Omne quod est corpus est sui generis. Nihil est incorporale, nisi quod non est. Habente igitur anima invisible corpus,*" etc. (*De Carne Christi*, c. 11). "*Quis enim negabit, Deum corpus esse, etsi Deus spiritus est? Spiritus enim corpus sui generis in sua effigie.*" (*Adv. Prax.* c. 7).

against the absurd polytheism of the pagans, and particularly against the dualism of the Gnostics, which supposed matter co-eternal with God, and attributed the creation of the world to the intermediate Demiurge.   This dualism was only another form of polytheism, which excludes absoluteness, and with it all proper idea of God.

As to creation : Irenæus and Tertullian most firmly rejected the hylozoic and demiurgic views of paganism and Gnosticism, and taught, according to the book of Genesis, that God made the world, including matter, not, of course, out of any material, but out of nothing, or, to express it positively, out of his free, almighty will, by his word.[1]   This free will of God, a will of *love*, is the supreme, absolutely unconditioned, and all-conditioning cause and final reason of all existence, precluding every idea of physical force or of emanation.   Every creature, since it proceeds from the good and holy God, is in itself, as to its essence, good.[2]   Evil, therefore, is not an original and substantial entity, but a corruption of nature, and hence can be destroyed by the power of redemption.   Without a correct doctrine of creation there can be no true doctrine of redemption, as all the Gnostic systems show.

Origen's view of an eternal creation is peculiar.   His thought is not so much that of an endless succession of new worlds, as that of ever new metamorphoses of the original world, revealing from the beginning the almighty power, wisdom and goodness of God.   With this is connected his Platonic view of the pre-existence of the soul.   He starts from the idea of an intimate relationship between God and the world, and represents the latter as a necessary revelation of the former.   It would be impious and absurd to maintain that there was a time when God did not show forth his essential attributes which make up his very being.   He was never idle or quiescent.   God's being is identical with his goodness and love, and his will is identical with his nature.

---

[1] Comp. Gen. c. 1 and 2; Psalm 33: 9; 148: 5; John 1: 3; Col. 1: 15; Heb. 1: 2; 11: 3; Rev. 4: 11.

[2] Gen. 1: 31; comp. Ps. 104: 24; 1 Tim. 4: 4.

He *must* create according to his nature, and he *will* create. Hence what is a necessity is at the same time a free act. Each world has a beginning and an end which are comprehended in the divine Providence. But what was before the first world? Origen connects the idea of time with that of the world, but cannot get beyond the idea of an endless succession of time. God's eternity is above time, and yet fills all time. Origen mediates the transition from God to the world by the eternal generation of the Logos who is the express image of the Father and through whom God creates first the spiritual and then the material world. And this generation is itself a continued process; God always (άεί) begets his Son, and never was without his Son as little as the Son is without the Father.[1]

§ 143. *Man and the Fall.*

It was the universal faith of the church that man was made in the image of God, pure and holy, and fell by his own guilt and the temptation of Satan who himself fell from his original state. But the extent of sin and the consequences of the fall were not fully discussed before the Pelagian controversy in the fifth century. The same is true of the metaphysical problem concerning the origin of the human soul. Yet three theories appear already in germ.

Tertullian is the author of *traducianism*,[2] which derives soul and body from the parents through the process of generation.[3]

[1] For a full exposition of Origen's cosmology see Möller, *l. c.* p. 536–560. He justly calls it a "*kirchlich-wissenschaftliches Gegenbild der gnostischen Weltanschauung.*" Comp. also Huetius (*Origeniana*), Neander, Dorner, Redepenning.

[2] From *tradux*, a branch for propagation, frequently used by Tertullian, *Adv. Val. nt.* c. 25, etc.

[3] Tertullian, *De Anima*, c. 27: "*Ex uno homine tota hæc animarum redundantia.*" Cap. 36: "*Anima in utero seminata pariter cum carne pariter cum ipsa sortitur et sexum,*" *i. e.* "the soul, being sown in the womb at the same time with the body, receives likewise along with it its sex;" and this takes place so simultaneously "that neither of the two substances can be alone regarded as the cause of the sex (*ita pariter, ut in causa sexus neutra substantia teneatur*)." In Tertullian this theory was connected with a somewhat materialistic or strongly realistic tendency of thought.

It assumes that God's creation *de nihilo* was finished on the sixth day, and that Adam's soul was endowed with the power of reproducing itself in individual souls, just as the first created seed in the vegetable world has the power of reproduction in its own kind. Most Western divines followed Tertullian in this theory because it most easily explains the propagation of original sin by generation,[1] but it materializes sin which originates in the mind. Adam had fallen inwardly by doubt and disobedience before he ate of the forbidden fruit.

The Aristotelian theory of *creationism* traces the origin of each individual soul to a direct agency of God and assumes a subsequent corruption of the soul by its contact with the body, but destroys the organic unity of soul and body, and derives sin from the material part. It was advocated by Eastern divines, and by Jerome in the West. Augustin wavered between the two theories, and the church has never decided the question.

The third theory, that of *pre-existence*, was taught by Origen, as before by Plato and Philo. It assumes the pre-historic existence and fall of every human being, and thus accounts for original sin and individual guilt; but as it has no support in scripture or human consciousness—except in an *ideal* sense—it was condemned under Justinian, as one of the Origenistic heresies. Nevertheless it has been revived from time to time as an isolated speculative opinion.[2]

The cause of the Christian faith demanded the assertion both of

---

[1] "*Tradux animœ tradux peccati.*"

[2] Notably in our century by one of the profoundest and soundest evangelical divines, Dr. Julius Müller, in his masterly work on *The Christian Doctrine of Sin*. (Urwick's translation, Edinb. 1868, vol. II. pp. 357 sqq., comp. pp. 73, 147, 397). He assumes that man in a transcendental, pre-temporal or extra-temporal existence, by an act of free self-decision, fixed his moral character and fate for his present life. This conclusion, he thinks, reconciles the fact of the universalness of sin with that of individual guilt, and accords with the unfathomable depth of our consciousness of guilt and the mystery of that inextinguishable melancholy and sadness which is most profound in the noblest natures. But Müller found no response, and was opposed by Rothe, Dorner, and others. In America, the theory of pre-existence was independently advocated by Dr. Edward Beecher in his book: *The Conflict of Ages*. Boston, 1853.

man's need of redemption, against Epicurean levity and Stoical self-sufficiency, and man's capacity for redemption, against the Gnostic and Manichæan idea of the intrinsic evil of nature, and against every form of fatalism.

The Greek fathers, especially the Alexandrian, are very strenuous for the freedom of the will, as the ground of the accountability and the whole moral nature of man, and as indispensable to the distinction of virtue and vice. It was impaired and weakened by the fall, but not destroyed. In the case of Origen freedom of choice is the main pillar of his theological system. Irenæus and Hippolytus cannot conceive of man without the two inseparable predicates of intelligence and ·freedom. And Tertullian asserts expressly, against Marcion and Hermogenes, free will as one of the innate properties of the soul,[1] like its derivation from God, immortality, instinct of dominion, and power of divination.[2] On the other side, however, Irenæus, by his Pauline doctrine of the casual connection of the original sin of Adam with the sinfulness of the whole race, and especially Tertullian, by his view of hereditary sin and its propagation by generation, looked towards the Augustinian system which the greatest of the Latin fathers developed in his controversy with the Pelagian heresy, and which exerted such a powerful influence upon the Reformers, but had no effect whatever on the Oriental church and was practically disowned in part by the church of Rome.[3]

---

[1] " *Inesse nobis* τὸ αὐτεξούσιον *naturaliter, jam et Marcioni ostendimus et Hermogeni.*" *De Anima,* c. 21. Comp. *Adv. Marc.* II. 5 sqq.

[2] " *Definimus animam Dei flatu natam, immortalem, corporalem, effigiatam, substantia simplicem, de suo sapientem, varie procedentem, liberam arbitrii, accidentiis obnoxiam, per ingenia mutabilem, rationalem, dominatricem, divinatricem, ex una redundantem.*" *De Anima,* c. 22.

[3] See vol. III. p. 783 sqq.

§ 144. Christ and the Incarnation.

Literature.

*DIONYS. PETAVIUS (or Denis Petau, Prof. of Theol. in Paris, d. 1652): *Opus de theologicis dogmatibus*, etc. Par. 1644–50, in 5 vols. fol. Later ed. of Antw. 1700; by Fr. Ant. Zacharia, Venice, 1757 (in 7 vols. fol); with additions by C. Passaglia, and C. Schrader, Rome, 1857 (incomplete); and a still later one by J. B. Thomas, Bar le Duc, 1834, in 8 vols. Petau was a thoroughly learned Jesuit and the father of Doctrine History (*Dogmengeschichte*). In the section *De Trinitate* (vol. II.), he has collected most of the passages of the ante-Nicene and Nicene fathers, and admits a progressive development of the doctrine of the divinity of Christ, and of the trinity, for which the Anglican, G. Bull, severely censures him.

*GEORGE BULL (Bishop of St. David's, d. 1710): *Defensio Fidei Nicænae de æterna Divinitate Filii Dei, ex scriptis catholic. doctorum qui intra tria ecclesiæ Christianæ secula floruerunt.* Oxf. 1685. (Loud. 1703; again 1721; also in Bp. Bull's complete *Works*, ed. by Edw. Burton, Oxf. 1827, and again in 1846 (vol. V., Part I. and II.); English translation in the "Library of Anglo-Catholic Theology," (Oxford 1851, 2 vols.). Bishop Bull is still one of the most learned and valuable writers on the early doctrine of the Trinity, but he reads the ante-Nicene fathers too much through the glass of the Nicene Creed, and has to explain and to defend the language of more than one half of his long list of witnesses.

MARTINI: *Gesch. des Dogmas von der Gottheit Christi in den ersten vier Jahrh.* Rost. 1809 (rationalistic).

AD. MÖHLER (R. C.): *Athanasius der Gr.* Mainz. 1827, second ed. 1844 (Bk 1. *Der Glaube der Kirche der drei ersten Jahrh. in Betreff der Trinität*, etc., p. 1–116).

EDW. BURTON: *Testimonies of the ante-Nicene Fathers to the Divinity of Christ.* Second ed. Oxf. 1829.

*F. C. BAUR (d. 1860): *Die christl. Lehre von der Dreieinigkeit u. Menschwerdung Gottes in ihrer geschichtlichen Entwicklung.* Tüb. 1841–43. 3 vols. (I. p. 129–341). Thoroughly independent, learned, critical, and philosophical.

G. A. MEIER: *Die Lehre von der Trinität in ihrer hist. Entwicklung.* Hamb. 1844. 2 vols. (I. p. 45–134).

*ISAAC A. DORNER: *Entwicklungsgeschichte der Lehre von der Person Christi* (1839), 2d ed. Stuttg. u. Berl. 1845–56. 2 vols. (I. pp. 122–747). A masterpiece of exhaustive and conscientious learning, and penetrating and fair criticism. Engl. translation by W. I. Alexander and D. W. Simon. Edinb. 1864, 5 vols.

Robt. Is. Wilberforce (first Anglican, then, since 1854, R. C.): *The Doctrine of the Incarnation of our Lord Jesus Christ, in its relation to Mankind and to the Church* (more doctrinal than historical). 4th ed. Lond. 1852. (Ch. V. pp. 93–147.) Republ. from an earlier ed., Philad. 1849.

Ph. Schaff: *The Conflict of Trinitarianism and Unitarianism in the ante-Nicene age*, in the "Bibl. Sacra." Andover, 1858, Oct.

M. F. Sadler: *Emmanuel, or, The Incarnation of the Son of God the Foundation of immutable Truth.* London 1867 (Doctrinal).

Henry Parry Liddon (Anglican, Canon of St. Paul's Cathedral): *The Divinity of our Lord and Saviour Jesus Christ.* (The Bampton Lectures for 1866). London 1867, 9th ed. 1882. Devout, able, and eloquent.

Ph. Schaff: *Christ and Christianity.* N. Y. 1885, p. 45–123. A sketch of the history of Christology to the present time.

Comp. the relevant sections in the doctrine—histories of Hagenbach, Thomasius, Harnack, etc.

The Messiahship and Divine Sonship of Jesus of Nazareth, first confessed by Peter in the name of all the apostles and the eye-witnesses of the divine glory of his person and his work, as the most sacred and precious fact of their experience, and after the resurrection adoringly acknowledged by the sceptical Thomas in that exclamation, "My Lord and my God!"—is the foundation stone of the Christian church;[1] and the denial of the mystery of the incarnation is the mark of antichristian heresy.[2]

The whole theological energy of the ante-Nicene period concentrated itself, therefore, upon the doctrine of Christ as the God-man and Redeemer of the world. This doctrine was the kernel of all the baptismal creeds, and was stamped upon the entire life, constitution and worship of the early church. It was not only expressly asserted by the fathers against heretics, but also professed in the daily and weekly worship, in the celebration of baptism, the eucharist and the annual festivals, especially Easter. It was embodied in prayers, doxologies and hymns of praise. From the earliest record Christ was the object not of admiration which is given to finite persons and things, and presupposes equality, but of prayer, praise and adoration which is due only to an infinite, uncreated, divine being. This is evident

---

[1] Matt. 16: 16–19 sqq.   [2] 1 John 4: 1–3.

from several passages of the New Testament,[1] from the favorite symbol of the early Christians, the *Ichthys*,[2] from the *Tersanctus*, the *Gloria in Excelsis*, the hymn of Clement of Alexandria in praise of the Logos,[3] from the testimony of Origen, who says : "We sing hymns to the Most High alone, and His Only Begotten, who is the Word and God ; and we praise God and His Only Begotten;"[4] and from the heathen testimony of the younger Pliny who reports to the Emperor Trajan that the Christians in Asia were in the habit of singing "hymns to Christ as their God."[5] Eusebius, quoting from an earlier writer (probably Hippolytus) against the heresy of Artemon, refers to the testimonies of Justin, Miltiades, Tatian, Clement, and "many others" for the divinity of Christ, and asks : "Who knows not the works of Irenæus and Melito, and the rest, in which Christ is announced as God and man ? Whatever psalms and hymns of the brethren were written by the faithful from the beginning, celebrate Christ as the Word of God, by asserting his divinity."[6] The same faith was sealed by the sufferings and death of "the noble army" of confessors and martyrs, who confessed Christ to be God, and died for Christ as God.[7]

---

[1] Comp. Matt. 2: 11; 9: 18; 17: 14, 15; 28: 9, 17; Luke 17: 15, 16; 23: 42; John 20: 28; Acts 7: 59, 60; 9: 14, 21; 1 Cor. 1: 2; Phil. 2: 10; Hebr. 1: 6; 1 John 5: 13–15; Rev. 5: 6–13, etc.

[2] See p. 279.   [3] See p. 230.   [4] *Contra Cels.* l. VIII. c. 67.

[5] "*Carnem Christo quasi Deo dicere,*" *Epp.* X. 97. A heathen mock-crucifix which was discovered in 1857 in Rome, represents a Christian as worshipping a crucified ass as "his God." See above, p. 272.

[6] τὸν λόγον τοῦ θεοῦ τὸν Χριστὸν ὑμνοῦσι θεολογοῦντες. *Hist. Eccl.* V. 28.

[7] Comp. Ruinart, *Acta Mart.;* Prudentius, *Peristeph.*, Liddon, *l. c.*, pp. 400 sqq. "If there be one doctrine of our faith" (says Canon Liddon, p. 406) "which the martyrs especially confessed at death, it is the doctrine of our Lord's Divinity..... The learned and the illiterate, the young and the old, the noble and the lowly, the slave and his master united in this confession. Sometimes it is wrung from the martyr reluctantly by cross-examination, sometimes it is proclaimed as a truth with which the Christian heart is full to bursting, and which, out of the heart's abundance, the Christian mouth cannot but speak. Sometimes Christ's Divinity is professed as belonging to the great Christian contradiction of the polytheism of the heathen world around. Sometimes it is explained as involving Christ's unity with the Father, against the pagan imputation of ditheism; sometimes it is proclaimed as justifying the

Life and worship anticipated theology, and Christian experience contained more than divines could in clear words express. So a child may worship the Saviour and pray to Him long before he can give a rational account of his faith. The instinct of the Christian people was always in the right direction, and it is unfair to make them responsible for the speculative crudities, the experimental and tentative statements of some of the ante-Nicene teachers. The divinity of Christ then, and with this the divinity of the Holy Spirit, were from the first immovably fixed in the mind and heart of the Christian Church as a central article of faith.

But the logical definition of this divinity, and of its relation to the Old Testament fundamental doctrine of the unity of the divine essence—in a word, the church dogma of the trinity—was the work of three centuries, and was fairly accomplished only in the Nicene age. In the first efforts of reason to grapple with these unfathomable mysteries, we must expect mistakes, crudities, and inaccuracies of every kind.

In the Apostolic Fathers we find for the most part only the simple biblical statements of the deity and humanity of Christ, in the practical form needed for general edification. Of those fathers Ignatius is most deeply imbued with the conviction, that the crucified Jesus is God incarnate, and indeed frequently calls him, without qualification, God.[1]

worship which, as the heathens knew, Christians paid to Christ." Many illustrations are given.

[1] *Ad. Eph.* c. 18: ὁ γὰρ Θεὸς ἡμῶν Ιησοῦς ὁ Χριστὸς ἐκνοφορήθη ὑπὸ Μαρίας (*Deus noster Jesus Christus conceptus est ex Maria*); c. 7 : ἐν σαρκὶ γενόμενος Θεός. Ignatius calls the blood of Jesus the "blood of God" (ἐν αἵματι θεοῦ), *Ad Eph.* 1. He desires to imitate the sufferings of "his God," μιμητὴς εἶναι τοῦ πάθους τοῦ Θεοῦ μου, *Ad Rom.* 6. Polycarp calls Christ the eternal Son of God, to whom all things in heaven and earth are subject (*Ad Phil.* c. 2, 8, and his last prayer in *Martyr. Polyc.* c. 14). The anonymous author of the Epistle to Diognetus (c. 7, 8) teaches that the Father sent to men, not one of his servants, whether man or angel, but the very architect and author of all things, by whom all has been ordered, and on whom all depends; he sent him as God, and because he is God, his advent is a revelation of God. On the Christology of the Apost. Fathers comp., besides Dorner, Schwane's *Ante-Nicene Doctrine History*, pp. 60 ff., and Liddon's *Lectures on the Divinity of Christ*, pp. 379 and 411 sqq.

The scientific development of Christology begins with Justin and culminates in Origen. From Origen then proceed two opposite modes of conception, the Athanasian and the Arian; the former at last triumphs in the council of Nicæa A. D. 325, and confirms its victory in the council of Constantinople, 381. In the Arian controversy the ante-Nicene conflicts on this vital doctrine came to a head and final settlement.

The doctrine of the Incarnation involves three elements: the divine nature of Christ; his human nature; and the relation of the two to his undivided personality.

§ 145. *The Divinity of Christ.*

The dogma of the DIVINITY of Christ is the centre of interest. It comes into the foreground, not only against rationalistic Monarchianism and Ebionism, which degrade Christ to a second Moses, but also against Gnosticism, which, though it holds him to be superhuman, still puts him on a level with other æons of the ideal world, and thus, by endlessly multiplying sons of God, after the manner of the heathen mythology, pantheistically dilutes and destroys all idea of a specific sonship. The development of this dogma started from the Old Testament idea of the word and the wisdom of God; from the Jewish Platonism of Alexandria; above all, from the Christology of Paul, and from the Logos-doctrine of John. This view of John gave a mighty impulse to Christian speculation, and furnished it ever fresh material. It was the form under which all the Greek fathers conceived the divine nature and divine dignity of Christ before his incarnation. The term Logos was peculiarly serviceable here, from its well-known double meaning of "reason" and "word," *ratio* and *oratio;* though in John it is evidently used in the latter sense alone.[1]

[1] On the Logos doctrine of Philo, which probably was known to John much has been written by Gfrörer (1831), Dähne (1834), Grossmann (1829 and 1841), Dorner (1845), Langen, (1867), Heinze (1872), Schürer (1874), Siegfried (1875), Soulier, Pahud, Klasen, and others.

JUSTIN MARTYR developed the first Christology, though not as a novelty, but in the consciousness of its being generally held by Christians.[1] Following the suggestion of the double meaning of Logos and the precedent of a similar distinction by Philo, he distinguishes in the Logos, that is, the divine being of Christ, two elements: the immanent, or that which determines the revelation of God to himself within himself;[2] and the transitive, in virtue of which God reveals himself outwardly.[3] The act of the procession of the Logos from God[4] he illustrates by the figure of generation,[5] without division or diminution of the divine substance; and in this view the Logos is the only and absolute Son of God, the only-begotten. The generation, however, is not with him an eternal act, grounded in metaphysical necessity, as with Athanasius in the later church doctrine. It took place before the creation of the world, and proceeded from the free will of God.[6] This begotten, ante-mundane (though it would seem not strictly eternal) Logos he conceives as a hypostatical being, a person numerically distinct from the Father; and to the agency of this person before his incarnation[7] Justin attributes the creation and support of the universe, all the theophanies (Christophanies) of the Old Testament, and all that is true and rational in the world. Christ is the Reason of reasons, the incarnation of the absolute and eternal reason. He is a true object of worship. In his efforts to reconcile this view with monotheism, he at one time asserts the moral unity of the two divine persons, and at another decidedly subordinates the Son to the

---

[1] For thorough discussions of Justin's Logos doctrine see Semisch, *Justin der Märtyrer*, II. 289 sqq.; Dorner, *Entwicklungsgesch.* etc. I. 415–435; Weizsäcker. *Die Theologie des Märt. Justinus*, in Dorner's "Jahrbücher für deutsche Theol." Bd XII. 1867, p. 60 sqq.; and M. von Engelhardt, *Das Christenthum Justins des Märt.* (1878), p. 107–120, and his art. in the revised ed. of Herzog, vol. VII. (1880), p. 326.

[2] Λόγος ἐνδιάθετος. [3] Λόγος προφορικός. [4] προέρχεσθαι. [5] γεννᾶν, γεννᾶσθαι.

[6] He calls Christ "the first begotten of God," πρωτότοκος τοῦ θεοῦ and the πρῶτον γέννημα (but not κτίσμα or ποίημα τοῦ θεοῦ. See *Apol.* I. 21, 23, 33, 46, 63; and Engelhardt, *l. c.* p. 116–120: "*Der Logos ist vorweltlich, aber nicht ewig.*" [7] Λόγος ἄσαρκος.

Father. Justin thus combines hypostasianism, or the theory of
the independent, personal (hypostatical) divinity of Christ, with
subordinationism; he is, therefore, neither Arian nor Athanasian;
but his whole theological tendency, in opposition to the heresies,
was evidently towards the orthodox system, and had he lived
later, he would have subscribed the Nicene creed.[1] The same
may be said of Tertullian and of Origen.

In this connection we must also mention Justin's remarkable
doctrine of the " Logos spermatikos," or the Divine Word disseminated among men. He recognized in every rational soul
something Christian, a germ (σπέρμα) of the Logos, or a spark
of the absolute Reason. He therefore traced all the elements of
truth and beauty which are scattered like seeds not only among
the Jews but also among the heathen to the influence of Christ
before his incarnation. He regarded the heathen sages, Socrates,
(whom he compares to Abraham), Plato, the Stoics, and some of
the poets and historians as unconscious disciples of the Logos, as
Christians before Christ.[2]

Justin derived this idea no doubt from the Gospel of John
(1: 4, 5, 9, 10), though he only quotes one passage from it
(3: 3–5). His pupil Tatian used it in his Diatessaron.[3]

---

[1] See the proof in the monograph of Semisch.

[2] Comp. *Apol.* II. 8, 10, 13. He says that the moral teaching of the Stoics
and some of the Greek poets was admirable on account of the seed of the
Logos implanted in every race of men (διὰ τὸ ἔμφυτον παντὶ γένει ἀνθρώπων
σπέρμα τοῦ λόγου), and mentions as examples Heraclitus, Musonius, and others,
who for this reason were hated and put to death.

[3] On the relation of Justin to John's Gospel, see especially the very careful
examination of Ezra Abbot, *The Authorship of the Fourth Gospel* (Boston, 1880),
pp. 29–56. He says (p. 41): "While Justin's conceptions in regard to the
Logos were undoubtedly greatly affected by Philo and the Alexandrian philosophy, the doctrine of the *incarnation* of the Logos was utterly foreign to that
philosophy, and could only have been derived, it would seem, from the Gospel
of John. He accordingly speaks very often in language similar to that of
John (1: 14) of the Logos as 'made flesh,' or as 'having become man.' That
in the last phrase he should prefer the term 'man' to the Hebraistic 'flesh'
can excite no surprise. With reference to the deity of the Logos and his
instrumental agency in creation, compare also especially *Apol.* II. 6, 'through
him God created all things' (δι' αὐτοῦ πάντα ἔκτισε) *Dial.* c. 56, and *Apol.*

The further development of the doctrine of the Logos we find in the other apologists, in Tatian, Athenagoras, Theophilus of Antioch, and especially in the Alexandrian school.

CLEMENT of Alexandria speaks in the very highest terms of the Logos, but leaves his independent personality obscure. He makes the Logos the ultimate principle of all existence, without beginning, and timeless; the revealer of the Father, the sum of all intelligence and wisdom, the personal truth, the speaking as well as the spoken word of creative power, the proper author of the world, the source of light and life, the great educator of the human race, at last becoming man, to draw us into fellowship with him and make us partakers of his divine nature.

ORIGEN felt the whole weight of the Christological and trinitarian problem and manfully grappled with it, but obscured it by foreign speculations. He wavered between the *homo-ousian*, or orthodox, and the *homoi-ousian* or subordinatian theories, which afterwards came into sharp conflict with each other in the Arian controversy.[1] On the one hand he brings the Son as near as possible to the essence of the Father; not only making him the

---

I. 63, with John 1: 1-3 Since the Fathers who immediately followed Justin, as Theophilus, Irenæus, Clement, Tertullian, unquestionably founded their doctrine of the incarnation of the Logos on the Gospel of John, the presumption is that Justin did the same. He professes to hold his view, in which he owns that some Christians do not agree with him 'because we have been commanded by Christ himself not to follow the doctrines of men, but those which were proclaimed by the blessed prophets and *taught* by HIM.' (*Dial.* c. 48). Now, as Canon Westcott observes, 'the Synoptists do not anywhere declare Christ's pre-existence.' And where could Justin suppose himself to have found this doctrine taught by Christ except in the Fourth Gospel? Compare *Apol.* I. 46: 'That Christ is the first-born of God, being the Logos [the divine Reason] of which every race of men have been partakers [comp. John 1: 4, 5, 9], we *have been taught* and have declared before. And those who have lived according to Reason are Christians, even though they were deemed atheists; as for example, Socrates and Heraclitus and those like them among the Greeks.'"

[1] Comp. here Neander, Baur, Dorner (I. 635-695), the monographs on Origen by Redepenning (II. 295-307), and Thomasius, H. Schultz, *Die Christologie des Origenes*, in the "Jahrb. f. Protest. Theol." 1875, No. II. and III., and the art. of Möller in Herzog² XI. 105 sqq.

absolute personal wisdom, truth, righteousness, reason,[1] but also expressly predicating eternity of him, and propounding the church dogma of the *eternal* generation of the Son. This generation he usually represents as proceeding from the will of the Father; but he also conceives it as proceeding from his essence; and hence, at least in one passage, he already applies the term *homo-ousios* to the Son, thus declaring him coëqual in essence or nature with the Father.[2] This idea of eternal generation, however, has a peculiar form with him, from its close connection with his doctrine of an eternal creation. He can no more think of the Father without the Son, than of an almighty God without creation, or of light without radiance.[3] Hence he describes this generation not as a single, instantaneous act, but, like creation, ever going on.[4] But on the other hand he distinguishes the essence of the Son from that of the Father; speaks of a difference of substance;[5] and makes the Son decidedly inferior to the Father, calling him, with reference to John i. 1, merely ϑεός without the article, that is, God in a relative or secondary sense (*Deus de Deo*), also δεύτερος ϑεός, but the Father God in the absolute sense, ὁ ϑεός (*Deus per se*), or αὐτόϑεος, also the fountain and root of the divinity.[6] Hence, he also taught, that the Son should not be directly addressed in prayer, but the Father through the Son in the Holy Spirit.[7] This must be limited, no doubt, to *absolute* worship, for he elsewhere recognizes prayer

---

[1] αὐτοσοφία, αὐτοαλήθεια, αὐτοδικαιοσύνη, αὐτοδύναμις, αὐτόλογος, etc. *Contra Cels.* III. 41; V. 39. Origen repeatedly uses the term "God Jesus," ϑεὸς Ἰησοῦς, without the article, *ibid.* V. 51; VI. 66.

[2] In a fragment on the Ep. to the Hebrews (IV. 697, de la Rue): ἀπόρροια ὁμοούσιος.

[3] *De Princip.* IV. 28: "*Sicut lux numquam sine splendore esse potuit, ita nec Filius quidem sine Patre intelligi potest*"

[4] *De Princ.* I. 2, 4: "*Est æterna et sempiterna generatio, sicut splendor generatur a luce.*" *Hom. in Jerem.* IX. 4: ἀεὶ γεννᾶ ὁ Πατὴρ τὸν Υἱόν.

[5] ἐτιρότης τῆς οὐσίας or τοῦ ὑποκειμένου, which the advocates of his orthodoxy, probably without reason, take as merely opposing the Patripassian conception of the ὁμοουσία. Redepenning, II. 300–306, gives the principal passages for the homo-ousia and the hetero-ousia.

[6] πηγή, ῥίζα τῆς θεότητος.   [7] *De Orat.* c. 15.

to the Son and to the Holy Spirit.[1] Yet this subordination of the Son formed a stepping-stone to Arianism, and some disciples of Origen, particularly Dionysius of Alexandria, decidedly approached that heresy. Against this, however, the deeper Christian sentiment, even before the Arian controversy, put forth firm protest, especially in the person of the Roman Dionysius, to whom his Alexandrian namesake and colleague magnanimously yielded.

In a simpler way the western fathers, including here Irenæus and Hippolytus, who labored in the West, though they were of Greek training, reached the position, that Christ must be one with the Father, yet personally distinct from him. It is commonly supposed that they came nearer the *homo-ousion* than the Greeks. This can be said of Irenæus, but not of Tertullian. And as to Cyprian, whose sphere was exclusively that of church government and discipline, he had nothing peculiar in his speculative doctrines.

IRENÆUS, after Polycarp, the most faithful representative of the Johannean school, keeps more within the limits of the simple biblical statements, and ventures no such bold speculations as the Alexandrians, but is more sound and much nearer the Nicene standard. He likewise uses the terms "Logos" and "Son of God" interchangeably, and concedes the distinction, made also by the Valentinians, between the inward and the uttered word,[2] in reference to man, but contests the application of it to God, who is above all antitheses, absolutely simple and unchangeable, and in whom before and after, thinking and speaking, coincide. He repudiates also every speculative or *a priori* attempt to explain the derivation of the Son from the Father; this he holds to be an incomprehensible mystery.[3] He is content to

---

[1] For example, *Ad Rom.* I. p. 472: "*Adorare alium quempiam praeter Patrem et Filium et Spiritum sanctum, impietatis est crimen.*" *Contra Cels.* VIII. 67. He closes his Homilies with a doxology to Christ.

[2] The λόγος ἐνδιάθετος and λόγος προφορικός.

[3] *Adv. Hær.* II. 28, 6: "*Si quis nobis dixerit: quomodo ergo Filius prolatus a Patre est? dicimus ei—nemo novit nisi solus, qui generavit Pater et qui natus est Filius.*"

define the actual distinction between Father and Son, by saying
that the former is God revealing himself, the latter, God revealed;
the one is the ground of revelation, the other is the actual,
appearing revelation itself. Hence he calls the Father the
invisible of the Son, and the Son the visible of the Father.
He discriminates most rigidly the conceptions of generation and
of creation. The Son, though begotten of the Father, is still
like him, distinguished from the created world, as increate,
without beginning, and eternal. All this plainly shows that
Irenæus is much nearer the Nicene dogma of the substantial
identity of the Son with the Father, than Justin and the Alexandrians. If, as he does in several passages, he still subordinates
the Son to the Father, he is certainly inconsistent; and that for
want of an accurate distinction between the eternal Logos and
the actual Christ.[1] Expressions like, " My Father is greater
than I," which apply only to the Christ of history, he refers
also, like Justin and Origen, to the eternal Word. On the
other hand, he has been charged with leaning in the opposite
direction towards the Sabellian and Patripassian views, but
unjustly.[2] Apart from his frequent want of precision in expression, he steers in general, with sure biblical and churchly
tact, equally clear of both extremes, and asserts alike the essential unity and the eternal personal distinction of the Father and
the Son.

The incarnation of the Logos Irenæus represents both as a
restoration and redemption from sin and death, and as the completion of the revelation of God and of the creation of man.
In the latter view, as finisher, Christ is the perfect Son of Man,
in whom the likeness of man to God, the *similitudo Dei*, regarded
as moral duty, in distinction from the *imago Dei*, as an essential
property, becomes for the first time fully real. According to
this the incarnation would be grounded in the original plan of

---

[1] The λόγος ἄσαρκος and the λόγος ἔνσαρκος.

[2] As Duncker in his monograph: *Die Christologie des heil. Irenæus*, p. 50
sqq., has unanswerably shown.

God for the education of mankind, and independent of the fall; it would have taken place even without the fall, though in some other form. Yet Irenæus does not expressly say this; speculation on abstract possibilities was foreign to his realistic cast of mind.

TERTULLIAN cannot escape the charge of subordinationism. He bluntly calls the Father the whole divine substance, and the Son a part of it;[1] illustrating their relation by the figures of the fountain and the stream, the sun and the beam. He would not have two suns, he says, but he might call Christ God, as Paul does in Rom 9 : 5. The sunbeam, too, in itself considered, may be called sun, but not the sun a beam. Sun and beam are two distinct things (*species*) in one essence (*substantia*), as God and the Word, as the Father and the Son. But we should not take figurative language too strictly, and must remember that Tertullian was specially interested to distinguish the Son from the Father in opposition to the Patripassian Praxeas. In other respects he did the church Christology material service. He propounds a threefold hypostatical existence of the Son (*filiatio*): (1) The pre-existent, eternal immanence of the Son in the Father; they being as inseparable as reason and word in man, who was created in the image of God, and hence in a measure reflects his being;[2] (2) the coming forth of the Son with the Father for the purpose of the creation; (3) the manifestation of the Son in the world by the incarnation.[3]

With equal energy HIPPOLYTUS combated Patripassianism, and insisted on the recognition of different hypostases with equal claim to divine worship. Yet he, too, is somewhat trammelled with the subordination view.[4]

---

[1] *Adv. Prax.* c. 9 : "*Pater tota substantia est, Filius vero derivatio totius et portio, sicut ipse profitetur : Quia Pater major Me est*" (John 14 : 28).

[2] Hence he says (*Adv. Prax.* c. 5), by way of illustration : "*Quodcunque cogitaveris, sermo est; quodcunque senseris ratio est. Loquoris illud in animo necesse est, et dum loqueris, conlocutorem pateris sermonem, in quo inest haec ipsa ratio qua cum eo cogitans loquaris, per quem loquens cogitas.*"

[3] In German terminology this progress in the filiation (*Hypostasirung*) may be expressed : *die werdende Persönlichkeit, die gewordene Persönlichkeit, die erscheinende Persönlichkeit.* [4] See the exposition of Döllinger, *Hippol.* p. 195 sqq.

On the other hand, according to his representation in the *Philosophumena*, the Roman bishops Zephyrinus and especially Callistus favored Patripassianism. The later popes, however, were firm defenders of hypostasianism. One of them, Dionysius, A. D. 262, as we shall see more fully when speaking of the trinity, maintained at once the *homo-ousion* and eternal generation against Dionysius of Alexandria, and the hypostatical distinction against Sabellianism, and sketched in bold and clear outlines the Nicene standard view.

§ 146. *The Humanity of Christ.*

Passing now to the doctrine of the Saviour's HUMANITY, we find this asserted by IGNATIUS as clearly and forcibly as his divinity. Of the Gnostic Docetists of his day, who made Christ a spectre, he says, they are bodiless spectres themselves, whom we should fear as wild beasts in human shape, because they tear away the foundation of our hope.[1] He attaches great importance to the flesh, that is, the full reality of the human nature of Christ, his true birth from the virgin, and his crucifixion under Pontius Pilate ; he calls him God incarnate ;[2] therefore is his death the fountain of life.

IRENÆUS refutes Docetism at length. Christ, he contends against the Gnostics, must be a man, like us, if he would redeem us from corruption and make us perfect. As sin and death came into the world by a man, so they could be blotted out legitimately and to our advantage only by a man ; though of course not by one who should be a mere descendant of Adam, and thus himself in need of redemption, but by a second Adam, supernaturally begotten, a new progenitor of our race, as divine as he is human. A new birth unto life must take the place of the old birth unto death. As the completer, also, Christ must enter into fellowship with us, to be our teacher and pattern. He made himself equal

---

[1] *Ep. ad Smyrn.* c. 2–5.

[2] ἐν σαρκὶ γενόμενος θεός (*ad Ephes.* c. 7) ; also ἕνωσις σαρκὸς καὶ πνεύματος. Comp. Rom. 1: 3, 4 ; 9: 5 ; 1 John 4: 1–3.

with man, that man, by his likeness to the Son, might become precious in the Father's sight. Irenæus conceived the humanity of Christ not as a mere corporeality, though he often contends for this alone against the Gnostics, but as true humanity, embracing body, soul, and spirit. He places Christ in the same relation to the regenerate race, which Adam bears to the natural, and regards him as the absolute, universal man, the prototype and summing up [1] of the whole race. Connected with this is his beautiful thought, found also in Hippolytus in the tenth book of the Philosophumena, that Christ made the circuit of all the stages of human life, to redeem and sanctify all. To apply this to advanced age, he singularly extended the life of Jesus to fifty years, and endeavored to prove this view from the Gospels, against the Valentinians. [2] The full communion of Christ with men involved his participation in all their evils and sufferings, his death, and his descent into the abode of the dead.

TERTULLIAN advocates the entire yet sinless humanity of Christ against both the Docetistic Gnostics [3] and the Patripassians. [4] He accuses the former of making Christ who is all truth, a half lie, and by the denial of his flesh resolving all his work in the flesh, his sufferings and his death, into an empty show, and subverting the whole scheme of redemption. Against the Patripassians he argues, that God the Father is incapable of suffering, and is beyond the sphere of finiteness and change. In the humanity, he expressly includes the soul; and this, in his view, comprises the reason also; for he adopts not the trichotomic, but the dychotomic division. The body of Christ, before the exaltation, he conceived to have been even homely, on a misapprehension of Isa. 53: 2, where the suffering Messiah is

---

[1] ἀνακεφαλαίωσις, recapitulatio, a term frequently used by Irenæus. Comp. Rom. 13: 9; Eph. 1: 10.

[2] Adv. Hær. II. 22, § 4–6. He appeals to tradition and to the loose conjecture of the Jews that Christ was near fifty years, John 8: 57. The Valentinian Gnostics allowed only thirty years to Christ, corresponding to the number of their æons.

[3] Adv. Marcionem, and De Carne Christi.   [4] Adv. Praxean.

figuratively said to have "no form nor comeliness." This unnatural view agreed with his aversion to art and earthly splendor, but was not commonly held by the Christian people if we are to judge from the oldest representations of Christ under the figure of a beautiful Shepherd carrying the lamb in his arms or on his shoulders.

CLEMENT of Alexandria likewise adopted the notion of the uncomely personal appearance of Jesus, but compensated it with the thought of the moral beauty of his soul. In his effort, however, to idealize the body of the Lord, and raise it above all sensual desires and wants, he almost reaches Gnostic Docetism.

The Christology of ORIGEN is more fully developed in this part, as well as in the article of the divine nature, and peculiarly modified by his Platonizing view of the pre-existence and pre-Adamic fall of souls and their confinement in the prison of corporeity; but he is likewise too idealistic, and inclined to substitute the superhuman for the purely human. He conceives the incarnation as a gradual process, and distinguishes two stages in it—the assumption of the soul, and the assumption of the body. The Logos, before the creation of the world, nay, from the beginning, took to himself a human soul, which had no part in the ante-mundane apostasy, but clave to the Logos in perfect love, and was warmed through by him, as iron by fire. Then this fair soul, married to the Logos, took from the Virgin Mary a true body, yet without sin; not by way of punishment, like the fallen souls, but from love to men, to effect their redemption. Again, Origen distinguishes various forms of the manifestation of this human nature, in which the Lord became all things to all men, to gain all. To the great mass he appeared in the form of a servant; to his confidential disciples and persons of culture, in a radiance of the highest beauty and glory, such as, even before the resurrection, broke forth from his miracles and in the transfiguration on the Mount. In connection with this comes Origen's view of a gradual spiritualization and deification of the body of Christ, even to the ubiquity which he ascribes to it in its exalted state.[1]

On this insufficient ground his opponents charged him with teaching a double Christ (answering to the lower Jesus and the higher Soter of the Gnostics), and a merely temporary validity in the corporeity of the Redeemer.

Origen is the first to apply to Christ the term God-man,[2] which leads to the true view of the relation of the two natures.

§ 147. *The Relation of the Divine and the Human in Christ.*

The doctrine of the MUTUAL RELATION of the divine and the human in Christ did not come into special discussion nor reach a definite settlement until the Christological (Nestorian and Eutychian) controversies of the fifth century.

Yet IRENÆUS, in several passages, throws out important hints. He teaches unequivocally a true and indissoluble union of divinity and humanity in Christ, and repels the Gnostic idea of a mere external and transient connection of the divine Soter with the human Jesus. The foundation for that union he perceives in the creation of the world by the Logos, and in man's original likeness to God and destination for permanent fellowship with Him. In the act of union, that is, in the supernatural generation and birth, the divine is the active principle, and the seat of personality; the human, the passive or receptive; as, in general, man is absolutely dependent on God, and is the vessel to receive the revelations of his wisdom and love. The medium and bond of the union is the Holy Spirit, who took the place of the masculine agent in the generation, and overshadowed the virgin womb of Mary with the power of the Highest. In this connection he calls Mary the counterpart of Eve the "mother of all living" in a higher sense; who, by her

---

[1] The view of the ubiquity of Christ's body was adopted by Gregory of Nyssa, revived by Scotus Erigena, but in a pantheistic sense, and by Luther, who made it a support to his doctrine of the Lord's Supper. See *Creeds of Christendom*, vol. I. p. 286 sqq.   [2] Θεάνθρωπος.

believing obedience, became the cause of salvation both to herself
and the whole human race,[1] as Eve by her disobedience induced
the apostasy and death of mankind;—a fruitful but questionable
parallel, suggested but not warranted by Paul's parallel between
Adam and Christ, afterwards frequently pushed too far, and
turned, no doubt, contrary to its original sense, to favor the
idolatrous worship of the blessed Virgin. Irenæus seems[2] to
conceive the incarnation as progressive, the two factors reaching
absolute communion (but neither absorbing the other) in the ascension; though before this, at every stage of life, Christ was a
perfect man, presenting the model of every age.

ORIGEN, the author of the term "God-man," was also the first
to employ the figure, since become so classical, of an iron warmed
through by fire, to illustrate the pervasion of the human nature
(primarily the soul) by the divine in the presence of Christ.

§ 148. *The Holy Spirit.*

ED. BURTON: *Testimonies of the Ante-Nicene Fathers to the Divinity of
the Holy Ghost.* Oxf. 1831 (*Works,* vol. II).

K. F. A. KAHNIS: *Die Lehre vom heil. Geiste.* Halle, 1847. (Pt. I. p.
149–356. Incomplete).

NEANDER: *Dogmengeschichte,* ed. by Jacobi, I. 181–186.

The doctrine of Justin Mart. is treated with exhaustive thoroughness by
SEMISCH, in his monograph (Breslau, 1840), II. 305–332. Comp.
also M. v. ENGELHARDT: *Das Christenthum Justins* (Erlangen,
1878), p. 143–147.

The doctrine of the Holy Spirit was far less developed, and
until the middle of the fourth century was never a subject of
special controversy. So in the Apostles' Creed, only one article[3] is
devoted to the third person of the holy Trinity, while the confession of the Son of God, in six or seven articles, forms the body of
the symbol. Even the original Nicene Creed breaks off abruptly
with the words: "And in the Holy Spirit;" the other clauses
being later additions. Logical knowledge appears to be here

---

[1] "*Et sibi et universo generi humano causa facta est salutis.*" *Adv. Hær.* III.
22, § 4.

[2] At least according to Dorner, I. 495.   [3] *Credo in Spiritum Sanctum.*

still further removed than in Christology from the living substance of faith. This period was still in immediate contact with the fresh spiritual life of the apostolic, still witnessed the lingering operations of the extraordinary gifts, and experienced in full measure the regenerating, sanctifying, and comforting influences of the divine Spirit in life, suffering, and death ; but, as to the theological definition of the nature and work of the Spirit, it remained in many respects confused and wavering down to the Nicene age.

Yet rationalistic historians go quite too far when, among other accusations, they charge the early church with making the Holy Spirit identical with the Logos. To confound the functions, as in attributing the inspiration of the prophets, for example, now to the Holy Spirit, now to the Logos, is by no means to confound the persons. On the contrary, the thorough investigations of recent times show plainly that the ante-Nicene fathers, with the exception of the Monarchians and perhaps Lactantius, agreed in the two fundamental points, that the Holy Spirit, the sole agent in the application of redemption, is a supernatural divine being, and that he is an independent person ; thus closely allied to the Father and the Son, yet hypostatically different from them both. This was the practical conception, as demanded even by the formula of baptism. But instead of making the Holy Spirit strictly coördinate with the other divine persons, as the Nicene doctrine does, it commonly left him subordinate to the Father and the Son.

So in JUSTIN, the pioneer of scientific discovery in Pneumatology as well as in Christology. He refutes the heathen charge of atheism with the explanation, that the Christians worship the Creator of the universe, in the second place the Son,[1] in the third rank[2] the prophetic Spirit; placing the three divine hypostases in a descending gradation as objects of worship. In another passage, quite similar, he interposes the host of good angels between the Son and the Spirit, and thus favors the inference

---

[1] ἐν δευτέρᾳ χώρᾳ.   [2] ἐν τρίτῃ τάξει, Apol. I. 13.

that he regarded the Holy Ghost himself as akin to the angels
and therefore a created being.[1] But aside from the obscurity
and ambiguity of the words relating to the angelic host, the co-
ordination of the Holy Ghost with the angels is utterly precluded
by many other expressions of Justin, in which he exalts the
Spirit far above the sphere of all created being, and challenges
for the members of the divine trinity a worship forbidden to
angels. The leading function of the Holy Spirit, with him, as
with other apologists, is the inspiration of the Old Testament
prophets.[2] In general the Spirit conducted the Jewish theocracy,
and qualified the theocratic officers. All his gifts concentrated
themselves finally in Christ; and thence they pass to the faithful
in the church. It is a striking fact, however, that Justin in only
two passages refers the new moral life of the Christian to the
Spirit; he commonly represents the Logos as its fountain. He
lacks all insight into the distinction of the Old Testament Spirit
and the New, and urges their identity in opposition to the Gnostics.

[1] *Apol.* I. 6: Ἐκεῖνόν τε (*i. e.* Θεὸν), καὶ τὸν παρ' αὐτοῦ Υἱὸν ἐλθόντα καὶ
διδάξαντα ἡμᾶς ταῦτα καὶ τὸν τῶν ἄλλων ἐπομένων καὶ ἐξομοιουμένων ἀγαθῶν
ἀγγέλων στρατὸν, Πνεῦμά τε τὸ προφητικὸν σεβόμεθα καὶ προσκυνοῦμεν. This passage has been variously explained. The questions arise, whether ἄγγελος here
is not to be taken in the wider sense, in which Justin often uses it, and even
applies it to Christ; whether στρατόν depends on σεβόμεθα, and not rather on
διδάξαντα, so as to be co-ordinate with ἡμᾶς, or with ταῦτα, and not with Υἱόν
and Πνεῦμα. Still others suspect that στρατόν is a false reading for στρατηγόν,
which would characterize Christ as the leader of the angelic host. It is impossible to co-ordinate the host of angels with the Father, Son, and Spirit, as
objects of worship, without involving Justin in gross self-contradiction (*Apol.*
I. 17: Θεὸν μόνον προσκυνοῦμεν, etc.). We must either join στρατόν with ἡμᾶς,
in the sense that Christ is the teacher, not of men only, but also of the host of
angels; or with ταῦτα in the sense that the Son of God taught us (διδάξαντα
ἡμᾶς) about these things (ταῦτα, *i. e.* evil spirits, compare the preceding chapter
I. 5), but also concerning the good angels—τὸν ἀγγέλων στρατόν being in this
case elliptically put for τὰ περὶ τοῦ ... ἀγγέλων στρατοῦ. The former is more
natural, although a more careful writer than Justin would in this case have
said ταῦτα ἡμᾶς instead of ἡμᾶς ταῦτα. For a summary of the different interpretations see Otto's notes in the third ed. of Justin's *Opera*, I. 20–23.

[2] Hence the frequent designation, τὸ Πνεῦμα προφητικόν, together with the
other, Πνεῦμα ἅγιον; and hence also even in the Symb. Nic. Constantin. the
definition: Πνεῦμα ... τὸ λαλῆσαν διὰ τῶν προφητῶν, "who spoke through the
prophets."

In CLEMENT of Alexandria we find very little progress beyond this point. Yet he calls the Holy Spirit the third member of the sacred triad, and requires thanksgiving to be addressed to him as to the Son and the Father.[1]

ORIGEN vacillates in his Pneumatology still more than in his Christology between orthodox and heterodox views. He ascribes to the Holy Spirit eternal existence, exalts him, as he does the Son, far above all creatures, and considers him the source of all charisms,[2] especially as the principle of all the illumination and holiness of believers under the Old Covenant and the New. But he places the Spirit in essence, dignity, and efficiency below the Son, as far as he places the Son below the Father; and though he grants in one passage[3] that the Bible nowhere calls the Holy Spirit a creature, yet, according to another somewhat obscure sentence, he himself inclines towards the view, which, however, he does not avow, that the Holy Spirit had a beginning (though, according 'to his system, not in time but from eternity), and is the first and most excellent of all the beings produced by the Logos.[4] In the same connection he adduces three opinions concerning the Holy Spirit; one regarding him as not having an origin; another, ascribing to him no separate personality; and a third, making him a being originated by the Logos. The first of these opinions he rejects because the Father alone is without origin (ἀγέννητος); the second he rejects because in Matt. 12 : 32 the Spirit is plainly distinguished from the Father and the Son; the third he takes for the true and scriptural view, because everything was made

---

[1] Paed. III. p. 311 : Εὐχαριστοῦντας αἰνεῖν τῷ μόνῳ Πατρὶ καὶ Υἱῷ—σὺν καὶ τῷ ἁγίῳ Πνεύματι.

[2] Not as ὕλη τῶν χαρισμάτων, as Neander and others represent it, but as τὴν ὕλην τῶν χαρισμ. παρέχον, as offering the substance and fulness of the spiritual gifts; therefore as the ἀρχή and πηγή of them. In Joh. II. § 6.

[3] De Princip. I. 3, 3.

[4] In Joh. tom. II. § 6 : τιμιώτερον—this comparative, by the way, should be noticed as possibly saying more than the superlative, and perhaps designed to distinguish the Spirit from all creatures—πάντων τῶν ὑπὸ τοῦ Πατρὸς διὰ Χριστοῦ γεγεννημένων.

by the Logos.[1]   Indeed, according to Matt. 12 : 32, the Holy
Spirit would seem to stand above the Son ; but the sin against
the Holy Ghost is more heinous than that against the Son of
Man, only because he who has received the Holy Spirit stands
higher than he who has merely the reason from the Logos.

Here again IRENÆUS comes nearer than the Alexandrians to
the dogma of the perfect substantial identity of the Spirit with
the Father and the Son ; though his repeated figurative (but for
this reason not so definite) designation of the Son and Spirit as
the "hands" of the Father, by which he made all things, implies
a certain subordination.   He differs from most of the Fathers in
referring the Wisdom of the book of Proverbs not to the Logos
but to the Spirit; and hence must regard him as eternal.   Yet he
was far from conceiving the Spirit a mere power or attribute;
he considered him an independent personality, like the Logos.
"With God," says he,[2] "are ever the Word and the Wisdom, the
Son and the Spirit, through whom and in whom he freely made
all things, to whom he said, ' Let us make man in our image,
after our likeness.' "   But he speaks more of the operations than
of the nature of the Holy Ghost.   The Spirit predicted in the
prophets the coming of Christ; has been near to man in all
divine ordinances; communicates the knowledge of the Father
and the Son; gives believers the consciousness of sonship; is
fellowship with Christ, the pledge of imperishable life, and the
ladder on which we ascend to God.

In the Montanistic system the Paraclete occupies a peculiarly
important place.   He appears there as the principle of the
highest stage of revelation, or of the church of the consummation.   TERTULLIAN made the Holy Spirit the proper essence of
the church, but subordinated him to the Son, as he did the Son
to the Father, though elsewhere he asserts the "unitas substantiæ."   In his view the Spirit proceeds "a Patre per Filium,"
as the fruit from the root through the stem.   The view of the
Trinity presented by Sabellius contributed to the suppression of
these subordinatian ideas.

[1] According to John 1: 3.   [2] Adv. Hær. IV. 20, § 1.

§ 149. *The Holy Trinity.*

Comp. the works quoted in § 144, especially PETAVIUS, BULL, BAUR, and DORNER.

Here now we have the elements of the dogma of the Trinity, that is, the doctrine of the living, only true God, Father, Son, and Spirit, of whom, through whom, and to whom are all things. This dogma has a peculiar, comprehensive, and definitive import in the Christian system, as a brief summary of all the truths and blessings of revealed religion. Hence the baptismal formula (Matt. 28 : 19), which forms the basis of all the ancient creeds, is trinitarian; as is the apostolic benediction also (2 Cor. 13 : 14). This doctrine meets us in the Scriptures, however, not so much in direct statements and single expressions, of which the two just mentioned are the clearest, as in great living facts; in the history of a threefold revelation of the living God in the creation and government, the reconciliation and redemption, and the sanctification and consummation of the world—a history continued in the experience of Christendom. In the article of the Trinity the Christian conception of God completely defines itself, in distinction alike from the abstract monotheism of the Jewish religion, and from the polytheism and dualism of the heathen. It has accordingly been looked upon in all ages as the sacred symbol and the fundamental doctrine of the Christian church, with the denial of which the divinity of Christ and the Holy Spirit, and the divine character of the work of redemption and sanctification, fall to the ground.

On this scriptural basis and the Christian consciousness of a threefold relation we sustain to God as our Maker, Redeemer, and Sanctifier, the church dogma of the Trinity arose; and it directly or indirectly ruled even the ante-Nicene theology, though it did not attain its fixed definition till in the Nicene age. It is primarily of a practical religious nature, and speculative only in a secondary sense. It arose not from the field of metaphysics, but from that of experience and worship; and not as an abstract, isolated dogma, but in inseparable connection with the study of Christ and of the Holy Spirit; especially in connection with Christology, since all theology proceeds from "God in Christ reconciling the world unto himself." Under the condition of monotheism, this doctrine followed of necessity from the doctrine of the divinity of Christ and of the Holy Spirit. The unity of God was already immovably fixed by the Old Testament as a fundamental article of revealed religion in opposition to all forms of idolatry. But the New Testament and the Christian consciousness as firmly demanded faith in the divinity of the Son, who effected redemption, and of the Holy Spirit, who founded the church and dwells in believers; and these apparently contradictory interests could be reconciled only in the form of the Trinity;[1] that is, by distinguishing in the one and indivisible essence of God[2] three hypostases or persons;[3] at the same time allowing for the insufficiency of all human conceptions and words to describe such an unfathomable mystery.

The Socinian and rationalistic opinion, that the church doctrine of the Trinity sprang from Platonism[4] and Neo-Platonism[5] is therefore radically false. The Indian Trimurti, altogether pantheistic in spirit, is still further from the Christian Trinity. Only thus much is true, that the Hellenic philosophy operated from without, as a stimulating force, upon the form of the whole patristic theology, the doctrines of the Logos and the Trinity among the rest; and that the deeper minds of heathen

---

[1] τριάς, first in Theophilus; trinitas, first in Tertullian; from the fourth century more distinctly μονοτριάς, μονὰς ἐν τριάδι, triunitas.

[2] οὐσία, φύσις, substantia; sometimes also, inaccurately, ὑπόστασις.

[3] τρεῖς ὑποστάσεις, τρία πρόσωπα, personæ.

[4] Comp. Plato, Ep. 2 and 6, which, however, are spurious or doubtful. Legg. IV. p. 185: Ὁ θεὸς ἀρχήν τε καὶ τελευτὴν καὶ μεσὰ τῶν ὄντων ἁπάντων ἔχων.

[5] Plotinus (in Enn. V. 1) and Porphyry (in Cyril. Alex. c. Jul.) who, however, were already unconsciously affected by Christian ideas, speak of τρεῖς ὑποστάσεις but in a sense altogether different from that of the church.

antiquity showed a presentiment of a threefold distinction in the divine essence; but only a remote and vague presentiment which, like all the deeper instincts of the heathen mind, serves to strengthen the Christian truth. Far clearer and more fruitful suggestions presented themselves in the Old Testament, particularly in the doctrines of the Messiah, of the Spirit, of the Word, and of the Wisdom of God, and even in the system of symbolical numbers, which rests on the sacredness of the numbers three (God), four (the world), seven and twelve (the union of God and the world, hence the covenant numbers. But the mystery of the Trinity could be fully revealed only in the New Testament after the completion of the work of redemption and the outpouring of the Holy Spirit. The historical manifestation of the Trinity is the condition of the knowledge of the Trinity.

Again, it was primarily the œconomic or transitive trinity, which the church had in mind; that is, the trinity of the revelation of God in the threefold work of creation, redemption, and sanctification; the trinity presented in the apostolic writings as a living fact. But from this, in agreement with both reason and Scripture, the immanent or ontologic trinity was inferred; that is, an eternal distinction in the essence of God itself, which reflects itself in his revelation, and can be understood only so far as it manifests itself in his works and words. The divine nature thus came to be conceived, not as an abstract, blank unity, but as an infinite fulness of life; and the Christian idea of God (as John of Damascus has remarked) in this respect combined Jewish monotheism with the truth which lay at the bottom of even the heathen polytheism, though distorted and defaced there beyond recognition.

Then for the more definite illustration of this trinity of essence, speculative church teachers of subsequent times appealed to all sorts of analogies in nature, particularly in the sphere of the finite mind, which was made after the image of the divine, and thus to a certain extent authorizes such a parallel. They found a sort of triad in the universal law of thesis, antithesis, and synthesis; in the elements of the syllogism; in the three persons of grammar; in the combination of body, soul, and spirit in man; in the three leading faculties of the soul; in the nature of intelligence and knowledge as involving a union of the thinking subject and the thought object; and in the nature of love, as likewise a union between the loving and the loved.[1] These speculations began with Origen and Tertullian; they were pursued by Athanasius and Augustin; by the scholastics and mystics of the Middle Ages; by Melanchthon, and the speculative Protestant divines down to Schleiermacher, Rothe and Dorner, as well as by philosophers from Böhme to Hegel; and they are not yet exhausted, nor will be till we reach the beatific vision. For the holy Trinity, though the most evident, is yet the deepest of mysteries, and can be adequately explained by no analogies from finite and earthly things.

As the doctrines of the divinity of Christ and of the Holy Spirit were but imperfectly developed in logical precision in the ante-Nicene period, the doctrine of the Trinity, founded on them, cannot be expected to be more clear. We find it first in the most simple biblical and practical shape in all the creeds of the first three centuries: which, like the Apostles' and the Nicene, are based on the baptismal formula, and hence arranged in trinitarian order. Then it appears in the trinitarian doxologies used in the church from the first; such as occur even in the epistle of the church at Smyrna on the martyrdom of Polycarp.[2] Clement of Rome calls "God, the Lord Jesus Christ, and the Holy Spirit" the object of "the faith and hope of the elect."[3]

[1] "Ubi amor, ibi trinitas," says St. Augustin.

[2] C. 14, where Polycarp concludes his prayer at the stake with the words, δι᾽ οὗ (i. e. Christ) σοί (i. e. the Father) σὺν αὐτῷ (Christ) καὶ Πνεύματι ἁγίῳ δόξα καὶ νῦν καὶ εἰς τοὺς μέλλοντας αἰῶνας. Comp. at the end of c. 22: ὁ κύριος ᾽Ιησ. Χριστός . . . ᾧ ἡ δόξα, σὺν Πατρὶ καὶ ἁγίῳ Πνεύματι, εἰς τοὺς αἰῶνας τῶν αἰώνων. "Dominus Jesus Christus, cui sit gloria cum Patre et Spiritu Sancto in sæcula sæculorum. Amen." I quote the text from Funk, Patr. Apost. I. 298 and 308.

[3] In the Const. MS. Ad Cor. 58: ζῇ ὁ θεὸς καὶ ζῇ ὁ κύριος ᾽Ιησοῦς Χριστὸς καὶ τὸ πνεῦμα ἅγιον, ἥ τε πίστις καὶ ἡ ἐλπὶς τῶν ἐκλεκτῶν. "As surely as God liveth . . . so surely," etc.

The sentiment, that we rise through the Holy Spirit to the Son, through the Son to the Father, belongs likewise to the age of the immediate disciples of the apostles.[1]

JUSTIN MARTYR repeatedly places Father, Son, and Spirit together as objects of divine worship among the Christians (though not as being altogether equal in dignity), and imputes to Plato a presentiment of the doctrine of the Trinity. Athenagoras confesses his faith in Father, Son, and Spirit, who are one as to power (κατὰ δύναμιν), but whom he distinguishes as to order or dignity (τάξις), in subordinatian style. Theophilus of Antioch (180) is the first to denote the relation of the three divine persons[2] by the term Triad.

ORIGEN conceives the Trinity as three concentric circles, of which each succeeding one circumscribes a smaller area. God the Father acts upon all created being; the Logos only upon the rational creation; the Holy Ghost only upon the saints in the church. But the sanctifying work of the Spirit leads back to the Son, and the Son to the Father, who is consequently the ground and end of all being, and stands highest in dignity as the compass of his operation is the largest.

IRENÆUS goes no further than the baptismal formula and the trinity of revelation; proceeding on the hypothesis of three successive stages in the development of the kingdom of God on earth, and of a progressive communication of God to the world. He also represents the relation of the persons according to Eph. 4 : 6; the Father as above all, and the head of Christ; the Son as through all, and the head of the church; the Spirit as in all, and the fountain of the water of life.[3] Of a supramundane trinity of essence he betrays but faint indications.

TERTULLIAN advances a step. He supposes a distinction in God himself; and on the principle that the created image affords a key to the uncreated original, he illustrates the distinction in the divine nature by the analogy of human thought; the neces-

---

[1] In Irenæus: *Adv. Hær.* V. 36, 2.
[2] Θεός, Λόγος, and Σοφία. By Σοφία, like Irenæus, he means the Holy Spirit.
[3] *Adv. Hær.* V. 18, 2.

sity of a self-projection, or of making one's self objective in word, for which he borrows from the Valentinians the term προβολή, or *prolatio rei alterius ex altera*,[1] but without connecting with it the sensuous emanation theory of the Gnostics. Otherwise he stands, as already observed, on subordinatian ground, if his comparisons of the trinitarian relation to that of root, stem, and fruit; or fountain, flow, and brook; or sun, ray, and raypoint, be dogmatically pressed.[2] Yet he directly asserts also the essential unity of the three persons.[3]

Tertullian was followed by the schismatic but orthodox NOVATIAN, the author of a special treatise *De Trinitate*, drawn from the Creed, and fortified with Scripture proofs against the two classes of Monarchians.

The Roman bishop DIONYSIUS (A. D. 262), a Greek by birth,[4] stood nearest the Nicene doctrine. He maintained distinctly, in the controversy with Dionysius of Alexandria, at once the unity of essence and the real personal distinction of the three members of the divine triad, and avoided tritheism, Sabellianism, and subordinatianism with the instinct of orthodoxy, and also with the art of anathematizing already familiar to the popes. His view has come down to us in a fragment in Athanasius, where it is said: "Then I must declare against those who annihilate the most sacred doctrine of the church by

---

[1] *Adv. Praxean*, c. 8.

[2] "*Tertius*"—says he, *Adv. Prax.* c. 8—"*est Spiritus a Deo et Filio, sicut tertius a radice fructus ex frutice, et tertius a fonte rivus ex flumine, et tertius a sole apex ex radio. Nihil tamen a matrice alienatur, a qua proprietates suas ducit. Ita trinitas* [here this word appears for the first time, comp. c. 2: οἰκονομία *quae unitatem in trinitatem disponit*] *per consertos* [al. *consortes*] *et connexos gradus a Patre decurrens et monarchiæ nihil obstrepit et οἰκονομίας statum protegit.*"

[3] C. 2: "*Tres autem non statu, sed gradu, nec substantia, sed forma, nec potestate, sed specie, unius autem substantiæ, et unius status, et unius potestatis, quia unus Deus, ex quo et gradus isti et formæ et species, in nomine Patris et Filii et Spiritus Sancti deputantur.*"

[4] Nothing is known of him except his effective effort against the Sabellian heresy. He was consecrated after the death of Xystus, July 22. 259, during the persecution of Valerian. He acted with Dionysius of Alexandria in condemning and degrading Paul of Samosata, in 264. He died Dec. 26, 269.

dividing and dissolving the unity of God into three powers, separate hypostases, and three deities. This notion [some tritheistic view, not further known to us] is just the opposite of the opinion of Sabellius. For while the latter would introduce the impious doctrine, that the Son is the same as the Father, and the converse, the former teach in some sense three Gods, by dividing the sacred unity into three fully separate hypostases. But the divine Logos must be inseparably united with the God of all, and in God also the Holy Ghost must dwell so that the divine triad must be comprehended in one, viz. the all-ruling God, as in a head."[1] Then Dionysius condemns the doctrine, that the Son is a creature, as "the height of blasphemy," and concludes: "The divine adorable unity must not be thus cut up into three deities; no more may the transcendant dignity and greatness of the Lord be lowered by saying, the Son is created; but we must believe in God the almighty Father, and in Jesus Christ his Son, and in the Holy Ghost, and must consider the Logos inseparably united with the God of all; for he says, 'I and my Father are one'; and 'I am in the Father and the Father in me.' In this way are both the divine triad and the sacred doctrine of the unity of the Godhead preserved inviolate."

§ 150. *Antitrinitarians. First Class: The Alogi, Theodotus, Artemon, Paul of Samosata.*

The works cited at § 144, p. 543.

SCHLEIERMACHER: *Ueber den Gegensatz der sabellianischen u. athanasianischen Vorstellung von der Trinität* (*Werke zur Theol.* Vol. II.). A rare specimen of constructive criticism (in the interest of Sabellianism).

LOBEG. LANGE: *Geschichte u. Lehrbegriff der Unitarier vor der nicänischen Synode.* Leipz. 1831.

JOS. SCHWANE (R. C.): *Dogmengesch. der vornicän. Zeit* (Münster, 1862), pp. 142–156; 199–203. Comp. his art. *Antitrinitarier* in "Wetzer und Welte," new ed. I. 971–976.

[1] Τὴν θείαν τριάδα εἰς ἕνα ὥσπερ εἰς κορυφήν τινα (τὸν θεὸν τῶν ὅλων, τὸν παντοκράτορα λέγω) συνκεφαλαιοῦσθαί τε καὶ συνάγεσθαι πᾶσα ἀνάγκη. Athanasius, *De Sent. Dionysii*, c. 4 sqq. (*Opera*, I. 252); *De Decr. Syn. Nic.* 26 (Routh, *Reliqu. Sacræ*, iii. p. 384, ed. alt.).

FRIEDR. NITZSCH: *Dogmengeschichte*, Part I. (Berlin, 1870), 194-210.
AD. HARNACK: *Monarchianismus.* In Herzog[2], vol. X. (1882), 178-213.
    A very elaborate article. Abridged in Schaff's Herzog, II. 1548 sqq.
AD. HILGENFELD : *Ketzergeschichte des Urchristenthums* (1884) p. 608-628.

That this goal was at last happily reached, was in great part
due again to those controversies with the opponents of the
church doctrine of the Trinity, which filled the whole third
century. These Antitrinitarians are commonly called *Monarchians* from (μοναρχία)[1] or *Unitarians*, on account of the stress
they laid upon the numerical, personal unity of the Godhead.

But we must carefully distinguish among them two opposite
classes : the rationalistic or dynamic Monarchians, who denied
the divinity of Christ, or explained it as a mere "power"
(δύναμις); and the patripassian or modalistic Monarchians, who
identified the Son with the Father, and admitted at most only
a modal trinity, that is a threefold mode of revelation, but not a
tripersonality.

The first form of this heresy, involved in the abstract Jewish
monotheism, deistically sundered the divine and the human, and
rose little above Ebionism. After being defeated in the church
this heresy arose outside of it on a grander scale, as a pretended
revelation, and with marvellous success, in Mohammedanism
which may be called the pseudo-Jewish and pseudo-Christian
Unitarianism of the East.

The second form proceeded from the highest conception of
the deity of Christ, but in part also from pantheistic notions
which approached the ground of Gnostic docetism.

The one prejudiced the dignity of the Son, the other the

---

[1] The designation *Monarchiani* as a sectarian name is first used by Tertullian,
Adv. Prax. c. 10 (*"vanissimi isti Monarchiani"*) ; but the Monarchians themselves used μοναρχία in the good sense (*Adv. Prax.* 3. "*Monarchiam, inquiunt,
tenemus*"), in which it was employed by the orthodox fathers in opposition to
dualism and polytheism. Irenæus wrote (according to Jerome) a book "*De
Monarchia, sive quod Deus non sit auctor malorum.*" In a somewhat different
sense, the Greek fathers in opposition to the Latin *Filioque* insist on the
μοναρχία of the Father, *i. e.* the sovereign dignity of the first Person of the
Trinity, as the root and fountain of the Deity.

dignity of the Father; yet the latter was by far the more profound and Christian, and accordingly met with the greater acceptance.

The Monarchians of the first class saw in Christ a mere man, filled with divine power; but conceived this divine power as operative in him, not from the baptism only, according to the Ebionite view, but from the beginning; and admitted his supernatural generation by the Holy Spirit. To this class belong:

1. The ALOGIANS or ALOGI,[1] a heretical sect in Asia Minor about A. D. 170, of which very little is known. Epiphanius gave them this name because they rejected the Logos doctrine and the Logos Gospel, together with the Apocalypse. " What good," they said, " is the Apocalypse to me, with its seven angels and seven seals? What have I to do with the four angels at Euphrates, whom another angel must loose, and the host of horsemen with breastplates of fire and brimstone?" They seem to have been jejune rationalists opposed to chiliasm and all mysterious doctrines. They absurdly attributed the writings of John to the Gnostic, Cerinthus, whom the aged apostle opposed.[2] This is the first specimen of negative biblical criticism, next to Marcion's mutilation of the canon.[3]

---

[1] From ἀ privative and λόγος, which may mean both irrational, and opponents of the Logos doctrine. The designation occurs first in Epiphanius, who invented the term (Hær. 51, c. 3) to characterize sarcastically their unreasonable rejection of the Divine Reason preached by John.

[2] Hence Epiphanius asks (Hær. 51, 3): πῶς ἔσται Κηρίνθου τὰ κατὰ Κηρίνθου λέγοντα?

[3] Comp. on the Alogi, Iren. Adv. Hær. III. 11. 9 (alii . . . simul evangelium [Joannis] et propheticum repellunt spiritum;" but the application of this passage is doubtful); Epiphanius, Hær. 51 and 54. M. Merkel, Historisch-kritische Aufklärung der Streitigkeiten der Aloger über die Apokalypsis, Frankf. and Leipz. 1782; by the same: Umständlicher Beweis dass die Apok. ein untergeschobenes Buch sei, Leipz. 1785; F. A. Heinichen, De Alogis, Theodotianis atque Artemonites, Leipzig, 1829; Neander, Kirchengesch.I. II. 906, 1003; Dorner, l. c. Bd. II. 500–503; Schaff, Alogians in "Smith and Wace," I. 87; Lipsius, Quellen der ältesten Ketzergeschichte, 93 and 214; Schwane, l. c. 145–148; Döllinger, Hippolytus and Callistus. 273–288 (in Plummer's transl.); Zahn, in the "Zeitschrift für hist. Theol." 1875, p. 72 sq.; Harnack, in Herzog², 183–186. Harnack infers from Irenæus that the Alogi were churchly or catholic opponents

2. The THEODOTIANS; so called from their founder, the tanner THEODOTUS. He sprang from Byzantium; denied Christ in a persecution, with the apology that he denied only a man; but still held him to be the supernaturally begotten Messiah. He gained followers in Rome, but was excommunicated by the bishop Victor (192–202). After his death his sect chose the confessor Natalis bishop, who is said to have afterwards penitently returned into the bosom of the Catholic church. A younger Theodotus, the "money-changer," put Melchizedek as mediator between God and the angels, above Christ, the mediator between God and men; and his followers were called Melchizedekians.[1]

3. The ARTEMONITES, or adherents of ARTEMON or AR-TEMOS, who came out somewhat later at Rome with a similar opinion, declared the doctrine of the divinity of Christ an innovation and a relapse to heathen polytheism; and was excommunicated by Zephyrinus (202–217) or afterwards. The Artemonites were charged with placing Euclid and Aristotle above Christ, and esteeming mathematics and dialectics higher than the gospel. This indicates a critical intellectual turn, averse to mystery, and shows that Aristotle was employed by some against the divinity of Christ,·as Plato was engaged for it.

Their assertion, that the true doctrine was obscured in the Roman church only from the time of Zephyrinus,[2] is explained

of the Montanistic prophecy as well as the millennarian Gnosticism of Cerinth at a time before the canon was fixed; but it is doubtful whether Irenæus refers to them at all, and in the year 170 the fourth Gospel was undoubtedly recognized throughout the Catholic church.

[1] On the older Theodotus see Hippol. *Philos.*, VII. 35; X. 23 (in D. and Schn. p. 406 and 526); Epiph., *Hær.* 54; Philastr., *Hær.* 50; Pseudo Tert., *Hær.* 28; Euseb., *H. E.* V. 28. On the younger Theodotus, see Hippol., VII. 36; Euseb., V. 28; Pseudo-Tert., 29; Epiph., *Hær.* 55 (*Contra Melchisedecianos*).

[2] Euseb. V. 28. Eusebius derived his information from an anonymous book which Nicephorus (IV. 21) calls μικρὸν λαβύρινθον, "the little labyrinth," and which Photius (*Bibl.* c. 48) ascribes to Caius, but which was probably written by Hippolytus of Rome. See the note of Heinichen in Tom. III. 243 sq., and Döllinger, *Hippolytus*, p. 3 (Engl. transl.).

by the fact brought to light recently through the *Philoso-phumena* of Hippolytus, that Zephyrinus (and perhaps his predecessor Victor), against the vehement opposition of a portion of the Roman church, favored Patripassianism, and probably in behalf of this doctrine condemned the Artemonites.[1]

4. PAUL OF SAMOSATA, from 260 bishop of Antioch, and at the same time a high civil officer,[2] is the most famous of these rationalistic Unitarians, and contaminated one of the first apostolic churches with his heresy. He denied the personality of the Logos and of the Holy Spirit, and considered them merely powers of God, like reason and mind in man ; but granted that the Logos dwelt in Christ in larger measure than in any former messenger of God, and taught, like the Socinians in later times, a gradual elevation of Christ, determined by his own moral development, to divine dignity.[3] He admitted that Christ remained free from sin, conquered the sin of our forefathers, and then became the Saviour of the race. To introduce his Christology into the mind of the people, he undertook to alter the church hymns, but was shrewd enough to accommodate himself to the orthodox formulas, calling Christ, for example, "God from the Virgin,"[4] and ascribing to him even *homo-ousia* with the Father, but of course in his own sense.[5]

---

[1] The sources of our fragmentary information about Artemon are Epiphanius, *Hær.* 65, c. 1–4; Euseb., *H. E.* V. 28; VII. 30; Theodoret, *Hær. Fab.* II. 8. Comp. Kapp, *Historia Artemonis*, 1737, Schleiermacher, Dorner, and Harnack.

[2] "Ducenarius procurator." He was viceroy of the queen of Palmyra, to which Antioch belonged at that time.

[3] A θεοποίησις ἐκ προκοπῆς, or α γεγονέναι θεὸν ἐξ ἀνθρώπου. He anticipated the doctrine of the Socinians who were at first frequently called *Samosatenians* (*e. g.* in the Second Helvetic Confession). They teach that Christ began as a man and ended as a God, being elevated after the resurrection to a quasi-divinity, so as to become an object of adoration and worship. But the logical tendency of Socinianism is towards mere humanitarianism. The idea of divinity necessarily includes aseity and eternity. A divinity communicated in time is only a finite being.

[4] Θεὸς ἐκ τῆς παρθένου.

[5] Probably he meant the impersonal, pre-existent Logos. But the Synod of Antioch declined the term ὁμοούσιος in this impersonal (Sabellian) sense.

The bishops under him in Syria accused him not only of heresy but also of extreme vanity, arrogance, pompousness, avarice, and undue concern with secular business; and at a third synod held in Antioch A. D. 269 or 268, they pronounced his deposition. The number of bishops present is variously reported (70, 80, 180). Domnus was appointed successor. The result was communicated to the bishops of Rome, Alexandria, and to all the churches. But as Paul was favored by the queen Zenobia of Palmyra, the deposition could not be executed till after her subjection by the emperor Aurelian in 272, and after consultation with the Italian bishops.[1]

His overthrow decided the fall of the Monarchians; though they still appear at the end of the fourth century as condemned heretics, under the name of Samosatians, Paulianists, and Sabellians.

§ 151. *Second Class of Antitrinitarians: Praxeas, Noëtus, Callistus, Beryllus.*

The second class of Monarchians, called by Tertullian " Patripassians" (as afterwards a branch of the Monophysites was called " Theopaschites "),[2] together with their unitarian zeal felt the deeper Christian impulse to hold fast the divinity of Christ; but they sacrificed to it his independent personality, which they merged in the essence of the Father. They taught that the one supreme God by his own free will, and by an act of self-limitation became man, so that the Son is the Father veiled in the flesh. They knew no other God but the one manifested in Christ, and charged their opponents with ditheism.

---

[1] Sources: The fragmentary acts of the Synod of Antioch in Eusebius, VII. 27–30; Jerome, *De Viris ill.* 71; Epiphanius, *Hær.* 65 (or 45 κατὰ τοῦ Παύλου τοῦ Σαμοσατέως, in Oehler's ed. II. 2, p. 380–397); five fragments of sermons of Paul of doubtful genuineness, in Ang. Mai's *Vet. Script. Nova Coll.* VII. 68 sq.; scattered notices in Athanasius, Hilary, and other Nicene fathers; Theodoret *Fab. Hær.* II. 8. Comp. Dorner and Harnack.

[2] The Orientals usually call them "Sabellians" from their most prominent representative.

They were more dangerous than the rationalistic Unitarians, and for a number of years had even the sympathy and support of the papal chair. They had a succession of teachers in Rome, and were numerous there even at the time of Epiphanius towards the close of the fourth century.

1. The first prominent advocate of the Patripassian heresy was PRAXEAS of Asia Minor. He came to Rome under Marcus Aurelius with the renown of a confessor; procured there the condemnation of Montanism; and propounded his Patripassianism, to which he gained even the bishop Victor.[1] But Tertullian met him in vindication at once of Montanism and of hypostasianism with crushing logic, and sarcastically charged him with having executed at Rome two commissions of the devil: having driven away the Holy Ghost, and having crucified the Father. Praxeas, constantly appealing to Is. 45: 5; Jno. 10: 30 ("I and my Father are one"), and 14: 9 ("He that hath seen me hath seen the Father"), as if the whole Bible consisted of these three passages, taught that the Father himself became man, hungered, thirsted, suffered, and died in Christ. True, he would not be understood as speaking directly of a suffering (*pati*) of the Father, but only of a sympathy (*copati*) of the Father with the Son; but in any case he lost the independent personality of the Son. He conceived the relation of the Father to the Son as like that of the spirit to the flesh. The same subject, as spirit, is the Father; as flesh, the Son. He thought the Catholic doctrine tritheistic.[2]

---

[1] Pseudo-Tert.: "*Praxeas hæresim introduxit quam Victorinus* [probably= *Victor*] *corroborare curavit.*" It is certain from Hippolytus, that Victor's successors, Zephyrinus and Callistus sympathized with Patripassianism.

[2] The chief source: Tertullian, *Adv. Praxean* (39 chs., written about 210). Comp. Pseudo-Tertull. 20. Hippolytus strangely never mentions Praxeas. Hence some have conjectured that he was identical with Noëtus, who came likewise from Asia Minor; others identify him with Epigonus, or with Callistus, and regard Praxeas as a nickname. The proper view is that Praxeas appeared in Rome before Epigonus, probably under Eleutherus, and remained but a short time. On the other hand Tertullian nowhere mentions the names of Noëtus, Epigonus, Cleomenes, and Callistus.

2. NOËTUS of Smyrna published the same view about A. D. 200, appealing also to Rom. 9 : 5, where Christ is called "the one God over all." When censured by a council he argued in vindication of himself, that his doctrine enhanced the glory of Christ.[1] The author of the *Philosophumena* places him in connection with the pantheistic philosophy of Heraclitus, who, as we here for the first time learn, viewed nature as the harmony of all antitheses, and called the universe at once dissoluble and indissoluble, originated and unoriginated, mortal and immortal; and thus Noëtus supposed that the same divine subject must be able to combine opposite attributes in itself.[2]

Two of his disciples, Epigonus and Cleomenes,[3] propagated this doctrine in Rome under favor of Pope Zephyrinus.

3. CALLISTUS (pope Calixtus I.) adopted and advocated the doctrine of Noëtus. He declared the Son merely the manifestation of the Father in human form; the Father animating the Son, as the spirit animates the body,[4] and suffering with him on the cross. "The Father," said he, "who was in the Son, took flesh and made it God, uniting it with himself and made it one. Father and Son were therefore the name of the one God, and this one person[5] cannot be two; thus the Father suffered with the Son." He considered his opponents "ditheists,"[6] and they in return called his followers "Callistians."

These and other disclosures respecting the church at Rome during the first quarter of the third century, we owe, as already observed, to the ninth book of the *Philosophumena* of Hip-

---

[1] τί οὖν κακὸν ποιῶ, he asked, δοξάζων τὸν Χριστόν.

[2] On Noëtus see *Hippol.*, *Philos.* IX. 7–9 (p. 440–442), and his tract against Noëtus ('Ομιλία εἰς τὴν αἵρεσιν Νοήτου τινός, perhaps the last chapter of his lost work against the 32 heresies). Epiphanius, *Hær.* 57, used both these books, but falsely put Noëtus back from the close of the second century to about 130.

[3] Not his teachers, as was supposed by former historians, including Neander. See Hippolytus, IX. 7.

[4] John 14: 11.

[5] πρόσωπον. Callistus, however, rectified this statement, which seems to be merely an inference of Hippolytus.   [6] δίθεοι.

polytus, who was, however, it must be remembered, the leading opponent and rival of Callistus, and in his own doctrine of the Trinity inclined to the opposite subordinatian extreme. He calls Callistus, evidently with passion, an "unreasonable and treacherous man, who brought together blasphemies from above and below, only to speak against the truth, and was not ashamed to fall now into the error of Sabellius, now into that of Theodotus" (of which latter, however, he shows no trace, but the very opposite).[1] Callistus differed from the ditheistic separation of the Logos from God, but also from the Sabellian confusion of the Father and the Son, and insisted on the mutual indwelling (περιχώρησις) of the divine Persons; in other words, he sought the way from modalistic unitarianism to the Nicene trinitarianism; but he was not explicit and consistent in his statements. He excommunicated both Sabellius and Hippolytus; the Roman church sided with him, and made his name one of the most prominent among the ancient popes.[2]

After the death of Callistus, who occupied the papal chair between 218 and 223 or 224, Patripassianism disappeared from the Roman church.

4. BERYLLUS of Bostra (now Bosra and Bosseret), in Arabia

---

[1] Döllinger here dissents from, Harnack agrees with, the charge of Hippolytus.

[2] On Callistus see Hippol. IX. 11, 12 (p. 450–462) and c. 27 (p. 528–530). Comp. Döllinger, *Hippol. und Callistus*, ch. IV. (Engl. transl. p. 183 sqq., especially p. 215), and other works on Hippolytus; also Langen, *Gesch. der röm. Kirche*, p. 192–216. Döllinger charges Hippolytus with misrepresenting the views of Callistus; while Bishop Wordsworth (*St. Hippolytus and the Church of Rome*, ch. XIV. p. 214 sqq.), charges Callistus with the Sabellian heresy, and defends the orthodoxy of Hippolytus by such easy reasoning as this (p. 254): "Callistus is asserted by Hippolytus to have been a heretic. No church historian affirms Callistus to have been orthodox. All church history that has spoken of Hippolytus,—and his name is one of the most celebrated in its annals,—has concurred in bearing witness to the soundness of his faith." Harnack (in Herzog X. 202) considers the formula of Callistus as the bridge from the original monarchianism of the Roman church to the hypostasis-christology ("*die Brücke, auf welcher die ursprünglich monarchianisch gesinnten römischen Christen, dem Zuge der Zeit und der kirchlichen Wissenschaft folgend, zur Anerkennung der Hypostasen-Christologie übergegangen sind*").

Petræa. From him we have only a somewhat obscure and very variously interpreted passage preserved in Eusebius.[1] He denied the personal pre-existence[2] and in general the independent divinity[3] of Christ, but at the same time asserted the indwelling of the divinity of the Father[4] in him during his earthly life. He forms, in some sense, the stepping-stone from simple Patripassianism to Sabellian modalism. At an Arabian synod in 244, where the presbyter Origen, then himself accused of heresy, was called into consultation, Beryllus was convinced of his error by that great teacher, and was persuaded particularly of the existence of a human soul in Christ, in place of which he had probably put his πατρικὴ θεότης, as Apollinaris in a later period put the λόγος. He is said to have thanked Origen afterwards for his instruction. Here we have one of the very few theological disputations which have resulted in unity instead of greater division.[5]

§ 152. *Sabellianism.*

SOURCES: HIPPOLYTUS: *Philos.* IX. 11 (D. and Schn. p. 450, 456, 458). Rather meagre, but important. EPIPHAN.: *Hœr.* 62. The fragments of letters of DIONYSIUS OF ALEX. in Athanasius, *De Sentent. Dion.*, and later writers, collected in Routh, *Reliqu. sacr.* NOVATIAN: *De Trinit.* EUSEB.: *Contra Marcellum.* The references in the writings of ATHANASIUS (*De Syn.* ; *De Decr. Nic. Syn.* ; *Contra Arian.*). BASIL M.: *Ep.* 207, 210, 214, 235. GREGORY NAZ.: λόγος κατὰ 'Αρείου κ. Σαβελλίου.

Comp. SCHLEIERMACHER, NEANDER, BAUR, DORNER, HARNACK, *l. c.*, and ZAHN, *Marcellus von Ancyra* (Gotha, 1867); NITZSCH, *Dogmengesch.* I. 206-209, 223-225.

[1] *H. E.* VI. 33.
[2] ἰδία οὐσίας περιγραφή, *i. e.* a circumscribed, limited, separate existence.
[3] ἰδία θεότης.   [4] ἡ πατρικὴ θεότης.
[5] The Acts of the Synod of Bostra, known to Eusebius and Jerome, are lost. Our scanty information on Beryllus is derived from Eusebius, already quoted, from Jerome, *De Vir. ill.* c. 60, and from a fragment of Origen in the Apology of Pamphilus, Orig. *Opera*, IV. 22 (ed. Bened.) Comp. Ullmann, *De Beryllo Bostr.*, Hamb. 1835. Fock, *Dissert. de Christologia Berylli*, 1843; Kober, *Beryll v. B.* in the Tüb. "Theol. Quartalschrift," for 1848. Also Baur, Dorner (1. 545 sqq.), Harnack, and Hefele (*Conc. Gesch.* I. 109).

5. SABELLIUS is by far the most original, profound, and ingenious of the ante-Nicene Unitarians, and his system the most plausible rival of orthodox trinitarianism. It revives from time to time in various modifications.[1] We know very little of his life. He was probably a Lybian from the Pentapolis. He spent some time in Rome in the beginning of the third century, and was first gained by Callistus to Patripassianism, but when the latter became bishop he was excommunicated.[2] The former fact is doubtful. His doctrine spread in Rome, and especially also in the Pentapolis in Egypt. Dionysius, bishop of Alexandria, excommunicated him in 260 or 261[3] at a council in that city, and, in vehement opposition to him, declared in almost Arian terms for the hypostatical independence and subordination of the Son in relation to the Father. This led the Sabellians to complain of that bishop to Dionysius of Rome, who held a council in 262, and in a special treatise controverted Sabellianism, as well as subordinatianism and tritheism, with nice orthodox tact.[4] The bishop of Alexandria very cheerfully yielded, and retracted his assertion of the creaturely inferiority of the Son in favor of the orthodox *homo-ousios.* Thus the strife was for a while allayed, to be renewed with still greater violence by Arius half a century later.

The system of Sabellius is known to us only from a few fragments, and some of these not altogether consistent, in Athanasius and other fathers.

While the other Monarchians confine their inquiry to the relation of Father and Son, Sabellius embraces the Holy Spirit

[1] We will only mention Marcellus of Ancyra, Schleiermacher, and Bushnell. Schleiermacher's doctrine of the trinity is a very ingenious improvement of Sabellianism.

[2] This we learn from Hippolytus, who introduces him rather incidentally (in his account of Callistus) as a man well known at his time in the Roman church.

[3] Sabellius must have been an old man at that time.

[4] Comp. the close of § 149, p. 570.

in his speculation, and reaches a trinity, not a simultaneous trinity of essence, however, but only a successive trinity of revelation. He starts from a distinction of the monad and the triad in the divine nature. His fundamental thought is, that the unity of God, without distinction in itself, unfolds or extends itself[1] in the course of the world's development in three different forms and periods of revelation,[2] and, after the completion of redemption, returns into unity. The Father reveals himself in the giving of the law or the Old Testament economy (not in the creation also, which in his view precedes the trinitarian revelation); the Son, in the incarnation; the Holy Ghost, in inspiration. The revelation of the Son ends with the ascension; the revelation of the Spirit goes on in regeneration and sanctification. He illustrates the trinitarian relation by comparing the Father to the disc of the sun, the Son to its enlightening power, the Spirit to its warming influence. He is said also to have likened the Father to the body, the Son to the soul, the Holy Ghost to the spirit of man; but this is unworthy of his evident speculative discrimination. His view of the Logos,[3] too, is peculiar. The Logos is not identical with the Son, but is the monad itself in its transition to triad; that is, God conceived as vital motion and creating principle, the speaking God,[4] in distinction from the silent God.[5] Each πρόσωπον is another διαλέγεσθαι, and the three πρόσωπα together are only successive evolutions of the Logos or the worldward aspect of the divine nature. As the Logos proceeded from God, so he returns at last into him, and the process of trinitarian development[6] closes.

Athanasius traced the doctrine of Sabellius to the Stoic philosophy. The common element is the pantheistic leading

---

[1] ἡ μονὰς πλατυνθεῖσα γέγονε τριάς.

[2] ὀνόματα, πρόσωπα,—not in the orthodox sense of hypostasis, however, but in the primary sense of mask, or part (in a play)—, also μορφαί, σχήματα.

[3] Which was for the first time duly brought out by Dr. Baur.

[4] Θεὸς λαλῶν.   [5] Θεὸς σιωπῶν.

[6] διάλεξις.

view of an expansion and contraction[1] of the divine nature immanent in the world. In the Pythagorean system also, in the Gospel of the Egyptians, and in the pseudo-Clementine Homilies, there are kindred ideas. But the originality of Sabellius cannot be brought into question by these. His theory broke the way for the Nicene church doctrine, by its full co-ordination of the three persons. He differs from the orthodox standard mainly in denying the trinity of essence and the permanence of the trinity of manifestation; making Father, Son, and Holy Ghost only temporary phenomena, which fulfil their mission and return into the abstract monad.

§ 153. Redemption.

COTTA: *Histor. doctrinœ de redemptione sanguine J. Chr. facta*, in Ger hard: *Loci theol.*, vol. IV. p. 105–134.

ZIEGLER: *Hist. dogmatis de redemptione.* Gott. 1791. Rationalistic.

K. BAEHR: *Die Lehre der Kirche vom Tode Jesu in den drei ersten Jahrh.*, Sulzb. 1832. Against the orthodox doctrine of the *satisfactio vicaria*.

F. C. BAUR: *Die christl. Lehre von der Versöhnung in ihrer geschichtl. Entw. von der ältesten Zeit bis auf die neueste.* Tüb. 1838. 764 pages, (See pp. 23–67). Very learned, critical, and philosophical, but resulting in Hegelian pantheism.

L. DUNCKER: *Des heil. Irenæus Christologie.* Gött. 1843 (p. 217 sqq.; purely objective).

BAUMGARTEN CRUSIUS: *Compendium der christl. Dogmengeschichte.* Leipz. 2d Part 1846, § 95 sqq. (p. 257 sqq.)

ALBRECHT RITSCHL (Prof. in Göttingen): *Die christl. Lehre von der Rechtfertigung und Versöhnung*, Bonn, 1870, second revised ed. 1882, sqq., 3 vols. The first vol. (pages 656) contains the *history of* the doctrine, but devotes only a few introductory pages to our period (p. 4), being occupied chiefly with the Anselmic, the orthodox Lutheran and Calvinistic, and the modern German theories of redemption. Ritschl belonged originally to the Tübingen school, but pursues now an independent path, and lays greater stress on the ethical forces in history.

The work of the triune God, in his self-revelation, is the salvation, or redemption and reconciliation of the world: nega-

---

[1] ἔκτασις, or πλατυτμός, and συστολή.

tively, the emancipation of humanity from the guilt and power of sin and death; positively, the communication of the right-eousness and life of fellowship with God. First, the discord between the Creator and the creature must be adjusted; and then man can be carried onward to his destined perfection. Reconciliation with God is the ultimate aim of every religion. In heathenism it was only darkly guessed and felt after, or anticipated in perverted, fleshly forms. In Judaism it was divinely promised, typically foreshadowed, and historically pre-pared. In Christianity it is revealed in objective reality, according to the eternal counsel of the love and wisdom of God, through the life, death, and resurrection of Christ, and is being continually applied subjectively to individuals in the church by the Holy Spirit, through the means of grace, on condition of repentance and faith. Christ is, exclusively and absolutely, the Saviour of the world, and the Mediator between God and man.

The apostolic scriptures, in the fulness of their inspiration, everywhere bear witness of this salvation wrought through Christ, as a living fact of experience. But it required time for the profound ideas of a Paul and a John to come up clearly to the view of the church; indeed, to this day they remain un-fathomed. Here again experience anticipated theology. The church lived from the first on the atoning sacrifice of Christ. The cross ruled all Christian thought and conduct, and fed the spirit of martyrdom. But the primitive church teachers lived more in the thankful enjoyment of redemption than in logical reflection upon it. We perceive in their exhibitions of this blessed mystery the language rather of enthusiastic feeling than of careful definition and acute analysis. Moreover, this doc-trine was never, like Christology and the doctrine of the Trinity, a subject of special controversy within the ancient church. The œcumenical symbols touch it only in general terms. The Apostles' Creed presents it in the article on the forgiveness of sins on the ground of the divine-human life, death, and resurrection of Christ. The Nicene Creed says, a little more definitely, that Christ became man for our salvation,[1] and died for us, and rose again.

Nevertheless, all the essential elements of the later church doctrine of redemption may be found, either expressed or implied, before the close of the second century. The negative part of the doctrine, the subjection of the devil, the prince of the kingdom of sin and death, was naturally most dwelt on in the patristic period, on account of the existing conflict of Christianity with heathenism, which was regarded as wholly ru'ed by Satan and demons. Even in the New Testament, particularly in Col. 2: 15, Heb. 2: 14, and 1 John 3: 8, the victory over the devil is made an integral part of the work of Christ. But this view was carried out in the early church in a very peculiar and, to some extent, mythical way; and in this form continued current, until the satisfaction theory of Anselm gave a new turn to the development of the dogma. Satan is supposed to have acquired, by the disobedience of our first parents, a legal claim (whether just or unjust) upon mankind, and held them bound in the chains of sin and death (comp. Hebr. 2: 14, 15). Christ came to our release. The victory over Satan was conceived now as a legal ransom by the payment of a stipulated price, to wit, the death of Christ; now as a cheat upon him,[2] either intentional and deserved, or due to his own infatuation.[3]

The theological development of the doctrine of the work of Christ began with the struggle against Jewish and heathen influences, and at the same time with the development of the doctrine of the person of Christ, which is inseparable from that of his work, and indeed fundamental to it. Ebionism, with its deistic and legal spirit, could not raise its view above the prophetic office of Christ to the priestly and the kingly, but saw in him only a new teacher and legislator. Gnosticism, from

---

[1] διὰ τὴν ἡμετέραν σωτηρίαν.   [2] 1 Cor. 2: 8, misapprehended.

[3] This strange theory is variously held by Irenæus, Origen, Gregory of Nyssa, Gregory Nazianzen, Ambrose, Augustin, Leo the Great and Gregory the Great. See Baur, ch. I. and II. p. 30–118.

the naturalistic and pantheistic position of heathendom, looked upon redemption as a physical and intellectual process, liberating the spirit from the bonds of matter, the supposed principle of evil; reduced the human life and passion of Christ to a vain show; and could ascribe at best only a symbolical virtue to his death. For this reason even Ignatius, Irenæus, and Tertullian, in their opposition to docetism, insist most earnestly on the reality of the humanity and death of Jesus, as the source of our reconciliation with God.[1]

In JUSTIN MARTYR appear traces of the doctrine of satisfaction, though in very indefinite terms. He often refers to the Messianic fifty-third chapter of Isaiah.[2]

The anonymous author of the Epistle to an unknown heathen, Diognetus, which has sometimes been ascribed to Justin, but is probably of much earlier date, has a beautiful and forcible passage on the mystery of redemption, which shows that the root of the matter was apprehended by faith long before a logical analysis was attempted. "When our wickedness," he says,[3] "had reached its height, and it had been clearly shown that its reward—punishment and death—was impending over us . . . . God himself took on Him the burden of our iniquities. He gave His own Son as a ransom for us, the holy One for transgressors, the blameless One for the wicked, the righteous One for the unrighteous, the incorruptible One for the corruptible, the immortal One for them that are mortal. For what other thing was capable of covering our sins than His righteousness? By what other one was it possible that we, the wicked and ungodly, could be justified, than by the only Son of God? O sweet exchange! O unsearchable operation! O benefits surpassing all expectation! that the wickedness of many should be hid in a single righteous One, and that the righteousness of One should justify many transgressors!"

---

[1] Comp. § 146.

[2] *Apol.* I. 50, etc. See von Engelhardt, p. 182.

[3] *Ep. ad Diognetum*, c. 9.

IRENÆUS is the first of all the church teachers to give a careful analysis of the work of redemption, and his view is by far the deepest and soundest we find in the first three centuries. Christ, he teaches, as the second Adam, repeated in himself the entire life of man, from childhood to manhood, from birth to death and hades, and as it were summed up that life and brought it under one head,[1] with the double purpose of restoring humanity from its fall and carrying it to perfection. Redemption comprises the taking away of sin by the perfect obedience of Christ; the destruction of death by victory over the devil; and the communication of a new divine life to man. To accomplish this work, the Redeemer must unite in himself the divine and human natures; for only as God could he do what man could not, and only as man could he do in a legitimate way, what man should. By the voluntary disobedience of Adam the devil gained a power over man, but in an unfair way, by fraud.[2] By the voluntary obedience of Christ that power was wrested from him by lawful means.[3] This took place first in the temptation, in which Christ renewed or recapitulated the struggle of Adam with Satan, but defeated the seducer, and thereby liberated man from his thraldom. But then the whole life of Christ was a continuous victorious conflict with Satan, and a constant obedience to God. This obedience completed itself in the suffering and death on the tree of the cross, and thus blotted out the disobedience which the first Adam had committed on the tree of knowledge. This, however, is only the negative side. To this is added, as already remarked, the communication of a new divine principle of life, and the perfecting of the idea of humanity first effected by Christ.

ORIGEN differs from Irenæus in considering man, in consequence of sin, the lawful property of Satan, and in representing

---

[1] This, as already intimated in a former connection, is the sense of his frequent expression: ἀνακεφαλαιοῦν, ἀνακεφαλαίωσις, recapitulare, recapitulatio.

[2] *Dissuasio.*

[3] By *suadela,* persuasion, announcement of truth, not overreaching or deception.

the victory over Satan as an outwitting of the enemy, who had no claim to the sinless soul of Jesus, and therefore could not keep it in death. The ransom was paid, not to God, but to Satan, who thereby lost his right to man. Here Origen touches on mythical Gnosticism. He contemplates the death of Christ, however, from other points of view also, as an atoning sacrifice of love offered to God for the sins of the world; as the highest proof of perfect obedience to God; and as an example of patience. He singularly extends the virtue of this redemption to the whole spirit world, to fallen angels as well as men, in connection with his hypothesis of a final restoration. The only one of the fathers who accompanies him in this is Gregory of Nyssa.

Athanasius, in his early youth, at the beginning of the next period, wrote the first systematic treatise on redemption and answer to the question " *Cur Deus homo ?* " [1] But it was left for the Latin church, after the epoch-making treatise of Anselm, to develop this important doctrine in its various aspects.

§ 154. *Other Doctrines.*

The doctrine of the *subjective* appropriation of salvation, including faith, justification, and sanctification, was as yet far less perfectly formed than the objective dogmas; and in the nature of the case, must follow the latter. If any one expects to find in this period, or in any of the church fathers, Augustin himself not excepted, the Protestant doctrine of justification by faith *alone*, as the "*articulus stantis aut cadentis ecclesiæ*," he will be greatly disappointed. The incarnation of the Logos, his true divinity and true humanity, stand almost unmistakably in the foreground, as the fundamental truths. Paul's doctrine

---

[1] λόγος περὶ τῆς ἐνανθρωπήσεως τοῦ λόγου. It was written before the outbreak of the Arian controversy. The Athanasian authorship has been contested without good reason; but another work with the similar title: Περὶ τῆς σαρκώσεως τοῦ θεοῦ λόιου, is pseudo-Athanasian, and belongs to the younger Apollinaris of Laodicea. See Ritschl, I. 8 sq.

of justification, except perhaps in Clement of Rome, who joins it with the doctrine of James, is left very much out of view, and awaits the age of the Reformation to be more thoroughly established and understood. The fathers lay chief stress on sanctification and good works, and show the already existing germs of the Roman Catholic doctrine of the meritoriousness and even the supererogatory meritoriousness of Christian virtue. It was left to modern evangelical theology to develop more fully the doctrines of soteriology and subjective Christianity.

The doctrine of the *church*, as the communion of grace, we have already considered in the chapter on the constitution of the church,[1] and the doctrine of the sacraments, as the objective means of appropriating grace, in the chapter on worship.[2]

§ 155. *Eschatology. Immortality and Resurrection.*

I. GENERAL Eschatology:

CHR. W. FLÜGGE: *Geschichte des Glaubens an Unsterblichkeit, Auferstehung, Gericht und Vergeltung.* 3 Theile, Leipz. 1794–1800. Part III. in 2 vols. gives a history of the Christian doctrine. Not completed.

WILLIAM ROUNSEVILLE ALGER (Unitarian): *A Critical History of the Doctrine of a Future Life. With a Complete Literature on the Subject.* Philad. 1864, tenth ed. with six new chs. Boston, 1878. He treats of the patristic doctrine in Part Fourth, ch. I. p. 394–407. The Bibliographical Index by Prof. EZRA ABBOT, of Cambridge, contains a classified list of over 5000 books on the subject, and is unequalled in bibliographical literature for completeness and accuracy.

EDM. SPIESS: *Entwicklungsgeschichte der Vorstellungen vom Zustand nach dem Tode.* Jena, 1877. This book of 616 pages omits the Christian eschatology.

II. GREEK and ROMAN Eschatology:

C. FR. NÄGELSBACH: *Die homerische Theologie in ihrem Zusammenhang dargestellt.* Nürnberg, 1840.

The same: *Die nachhomerische Theologie des griechischen Volksglaubens bis auf Alexander.* Nürnberg, 1857.

AUG. ARNDT: *Die Ansichten der Alten über Leben, Tod und Unsterblichkeit.* Frankfurt a. M. 1874.

LEHRS: *Vorstellungen der Griechen über das Fortleben nach dem Tode.* Second ed. 1875.

---

[1] See especially § 53, p. 168 sqq.   [2] See §§ 66 to 74, p. 235 sqq.

LUDWIG FRIEDLAENDER: *Sittengeschichte Roms,* fifth ed. Leipz. 1881, vol. III. p. 681–717 (*Der Unsterblichkeitsglaube*).

III. JEWISH Eschatology:

A. KAHLE: *Biblische Eschatologie des Alten Testaments.* Gotha, 1870.

A. WAHL: *Unsterblichkeits-und Vergeltungslehre des alttestamentlichen Hebraismus.* Jena, 1871.

Dr. FERDINAND WEBER (d. 1879): *System der Altsynagogalen Palästinischen Theologie aus Targum, Midrasch und Talmud.* Ed. by Franz Delitzsch and Georg Schnedermann. Leipzig, 1880. See chs. XXI. 322–332; XXIV. 371–386.

AUG. WÜNSCHE: *Die Vorstellungen vom Zustande nach dem Tode nach Apokryphen, Talmud, und Kirchenvätern.* In the "Jahrbücher für Protest. Thecl." Leipz. 1880.

BISSELL: *The Eschatology of the Apocrypha.* In the "Bibliotheca Sacra," 1879.

IV. CHRISTIAN Eschatology:

See the relevant chapters in FLÜGGE, and ALGER, as above.

Dr. EDWARD BEECHER: *History of Opinions on the Scriptural Doctrine of Retribution.* New York, 1878 (334 pages).

The relevant sections in the Doctrine Histories of MÜNSCHER, NEANDER, GIESELER, BAUR, HAGENBACH (H. B. Smith's ed. vol. I. 213 sqq. and 368 sqq.), SHEDD, FRIEDRICH NITZSCH (I. 397 sqq.)

A large number of monographs on Death, Hades, Purgatory, Resurrection, Future Punishment. See the next sections.

Christianity—and human life itself, with its countless problems and mysteries—has no meaning without the certainty of a future world of rewards and punishments, for which the present life serves as a preparatory school. Christ represents himself as "the Resurrection and the Life," and promises "eternal life" to all who believe in Him. On his resurrection the church is built, and without it the church could never have come into existence. The resurrection of the body and the life everlasting are among the fundamental articles of the early baptismal creeds. The doctrine of the future life, though last in the logical order of systematic theology, was among the first in the consciousness of the Christians, and an unfailing source of comfort and strength in times of trial and persecution. It stood in close connection with the expectation of the Lord's glorious reappearance. It is the subject of Paul's first Epistles, those to the Thessalonians, and is prominently discussed in the fifteenth chapter of First

Corinthians. He declares the Christians "the most pitiable," because the most deluded and uselessly self-sacrificing, "of all men," if their hope in Christ were confined to this life.

The ante-Nicene church was a stranger in the midst of a hostile world, and longed for the unfading crown which awaited the faithful confessor and martyr beyond the grave. Such a mighty revolution as the conversion of the heathen emperor was not dreamed of even as a remote possibility, except perhaps by the far-sighted Origen. Among the five causes to which Gibbon traces the rapid progress of the Christian religion, he assigns the second place to the doctrine of the immortality of the soul. We know nothing whatever of a future world which lies beyond the boundaries of our observation and experience, except what God has chosen to reveal to us. Left to the instincts and aspirations of nature, which strongly crave after immortality and glory, we can reach at best only probabilities; while the gospel gives us absolute certainty, sealed by the resurrection of Christ.

1. The HEATHEN notions of the future life were vague and confused. The Hindoos, Babylonians, and Egyptians had a lively sense of immortality, but mixed with the idea of endless migrations and transformations. The Buddhists, starting from the idea that existence is want, and want is suffering, make it the chief end of man to escape such migrations, and by various mortifications to prepare for final absorption in Nirwana. The popular belief among the ancient Greeks and Romans was that man passes after death into the Underworld, the Greek *Hades*, the Roman *Orcus*. According to Homer, Hades is a dark abode in the interior of the earth, with an entrance at the Western extremity of the Ocean, where the rays of the sun do not penetrate. Charon carries the dead over the stream Acheron, and the three-headed dog Cerberus watches the entrance and allows none to pass out. There the spirits exist in a disembodied state and lead a shadowy dream-life. A vague distinction was made between two regions in Hades, an

Elysium (also "the Islands of the Blessed") for the good, and
Tartarus for the bad.   "Poets and painters," says Gibbon,
"peopled the infernal regions with so many phantoms and
monsters, who dispensed their rewards and punishments with so
little equity, that a solemn truth, the most congenial to the
human heart, was oppressed and disgraced by the absurd mixture of the wildest fictions.   The eleventh book of the Odyssey
gives a very dreary and incoherent account of the infernal
shades.   Pindar and Virgil have embellished the picture; but
even those poets, though more correct than their great model,
are guilty of very strange inconsistencies." [1]

Socrates, Plato, Cicero, Seneca, and Plutarch rose highest
among the ancient philosophers in their views of the future
life, but they reached only to belief in its probability—not in
its certainty.   Socrates, after he was condemned to death, said to
his judges : " Death is either an eternal sleep, or the transition
to a new life ; but in neither case is it an evil ; " [2] and he drank
with playful irony the fatal hemlock.   Plato, viewing the
human soul as a portion of the eternal, infinite, all-pervading
deity, believed in its pre-existence *before* this present life, and
thus had a strong ground of hope for its continuance after
death.   All the souls (according to his *Phædon* and *Gorgias*)
pass into the spirit-world, the righteous into the abodes of bliss,
where they live forever in a disembodied state, the wicked into
Tartarus for punishment and purification (which notion prepared the way for purgatory).   Plutarch, the purest and noblest
among the Platonists, thought that immortality was inseparably
connected with belief in an all-ruling Providence, and looked
with Plato to the life beyond as promising a higher knowledge
of, and closer conformity to God, but only for those few who
are here purified by virtue and piety.   In such rare cases,
departure might be called an ascent to the stars, to heaven,
to the gods, rather than a descent to Hades.   He also, at the
death of his daughter, expresses his faith in the blissful state of

---

[1] *Decline and Fall of the R. Emp.* ch. **XV**   [2] Plato, *Apol.* 40.

infants who die in infancy. Cicero, in his *Tusculan Questions* and treatise *De Senectute*, reflects in classical language "the ignorance, the errors, and the uncertainty of the ancient philosophers with regard to the immortality of the soul." Though strongly leaning to a positive view, he yet found it no superfluous task to quiet the fear of death in case the soul should perish with the body. The Stoics believed only in a limited immortality, or denied it altogether, and justified suicide when life became unendurable. The great men of Greece and Rome were not influenced by the idea of a future world as a motive of action. During the debate on the punishment of Catiline and his fellow-conspirators, Julius Cæsar openly declared in the Roman Senate that death dissolves all the ills of mortality, and is the boundary of existence beyond which there is no more care nor joy, no more punishment for sin, nor any reward for virtue. The younger Cato, the model Stoic, agreed with Cæsar; yet before he made an end to his life at Utica, he read Plato's *Phædon*. Seneca once dreamed of immortality, and almost approached the Christian hope of the birth-day of eternity, if we are to trust his rhetoric, but afterwards he awoke from the beautiful dream and committed suicide. The elder Pliny, who found a tragic death under the lava of Vesuvius, speaks of the future life as an invention of man's vanity and selfishness, and thinks that body and soul have no more sensation after death than before birth; death becomes doubly painful if it is only the beginning of another indefinite existence. Tacitus speaks but once of immortality, and then conditionally; and he believed only in the immortality of fame. Marcus Aurelius, in sad resignation, bids nature, "Give what thou wilt, and take back again what and when thou wilt."

These were noble and earnest Romans. What can be expected from the crowd of frivolous men of the world who moved within the limits of matter and sense, and made present pleasure and enjoyment the chief end of life? The surviving wife of an Epicurean philosopher erected a monument to him, with the inscription, " to the eternal sleep."[1] Not a few heathen epitaphs openly profess the doctrine that death ends all; while, in striking contrast with them, the humble Christian inscriptions in the catacombs express the confident hope of future bliss and glory in the uninterrupted communion of the believer with Christ and God.

Yet the scepticism of the educated and half-educated could not extinguish the popular belief in the imperial age. The number of cheerless and hopeless materialistic epitaphs is, after all, very small as compared with the many thousands which reveal no such doubt, or express a belief in some kind of existence beyond the grave.[2]

Of a resurrection of the body the Greeks and Romans had no conception, except in the form of shades and spectral outlines, which were supposed to surround the disembodied spirits, and to make them to some degree recognizable. Heathen philosophers, like Celsus, ridiculed the resurrection of the body as useless, absurd, and impossible.

2. The JEWISH doctrine is far in advance of heathen notions and conjectures, but presents different phases of development.

(a) The Mosaic writings are remarkably silent about the future life, and emphasize the present rather than future consequences of the observance or non-observance of the law (because it had a civil or political as well as spiritual import); and hence the Sadducees accepted them, although they denied the resurrection (perhaps also the immortality of the soul). The Pentateuch contains, however, some remote and significant hints of immortality, as in the tree of life with its symbolic import;[3] in the mysterious translation of Enoch as a reward for his piety;[4] in the prohibition of necromancy;[5] in the

---

[1] See Friedlaender, l. c. 682 sq.

[2] See Friedlaender, p. 685. So in our age, too, the number of sceptics, materialists, and atheists, though by no means inconsiderable, is a very small minority compared with the mass of believers in a future life.

[3] Gen. 2: 9; 3: 22, 24.   [4] Gen. 5: 24.

[5] Deut. 18: 11; comp. 1 Sam. 28: 7.

patriarchal phrase for dying: "to be gathered to his fathers," or "to his people;"[1] and last, though not least, in the self-designation of Jehovah as "the God of Abraham, Isaac, and Jacob," which implies their immortality, since "God is not the God of the dead, but of the living."[2] What has an eternal meaning for God must itself be eternal.

(b) In the later writings of the Old Testament, especially during and after the exile, the doctrine of immortality and resurrection comes out plainly.[3] Daniel's vision reaches out even to the final resurrection of "many of them that sleep in the dust of the earth to everlasting life," and of "some to shame and everlasting contempt," and prophesies that "they that are wise shall shine as the brightness of the firmament, and they that turn many to righteousness as the stars forever and ever."[4]

But before Christ, who first revealed true life, the Hebrew Sheol, the general receptacle of departing souls, remained, like the Greek Hades, a dark and dreary abode, and is so described in the Old Testament.[5] Cases like Enoch's translation and Elijah's ascent are altogether unique and exceptional, and imply the meaning that death is contrary to man's original destination, and may be overcome by the power of holiness.

(c) The Jewish Apocrypha (the Book of Wisdom, and the Second Book of Maccabees), and later Jewish writings (the Book of Enoch, the Apocalypse of Ezra) show some progress:

---

[1] Gen. 25: 8; 35: 29: 49: 29, 33.   [2] Ex. 3: 6, 16; comp. Matt. 22: 32.

[3] Comp. the famous Goël-passage, Job 19: 25-27, which strongly teaches the immortality of the soul and the future rectification of the wrongs of this life; Eccles. 12: 7 ("the spirit shall return to God who gave it"), and ver. 14 ("God shall bring every work into judgment, with every secret thing, whether it be good or whether it be evil").

[4] Dan. 12: 2, 3; comp. Isa. 65: 17; 66: 22-24.

[5] See the passages sub *Sheol* in the Hebrew Concordance. The very name *Sheol* (שְׁאוֹל) expresses either the inexorable demand and insatiability of death (if derived from שָׁאַל, to ask pressingly, to urge), or the subterranean character of the region, an abyss (if derived from שָׁעַל, to be hollow, comp. *hell, hollow, Höhle*), and is essentially the same as the Greek *Hades* and the

they distinguish between two regions in Sheol—Paradise or Abraham's Bosom for the righteous, and Gehinnom or Gehenna for the wicked; they emphasize the resurrection of the body, and the future rewards and punishments.

(d) The Talmud adds various fanciful embellishments. It puts Paradise and Gehenna in close proximity, measures their extent, and distinguishes different departments in both corresponding to the degrees of merit and guilt. Paradise is sixty times as large as the world, and Hell sixty times as large as Paradise, for the bad preponderate here and hereafter. According to other rabbinical testimonies, both are well nigh boundless. The Talmudic descriptions of Paradise (as those of the Koran) mix sensual and spiritual delights. The righteous enjoy the vision of the Shechina and feast with the patriarchs, and with Moses and David of the flesh of leviathan, and drink wine from the cup of salvation. Each inhabitant has a house according to his merit. Among the punishments of hell the chief place is assigned to fire, which is renewed every week after the Sabbath. The wicked are boiled like the flesh in the pot, but the bad Israelites are not touched by fire, and are otherwise tormented. The severest punishment is reserved for idolaters, hypocrites, traitors, and apostates. As to the duration of future punishment the school of Shammai held that it was everlasting; while the school of Hillel inclined to the milder view of a possible redemption after repentance and purification.

Roman *Orcus*. The distinction of two regions in the spirit-world (Abraham's Bosom or Paradise, and Gehenna, comp. Luke 16: 22, 23) does not appear clearly in the canonical books, and is of later origin. Oehler (*Theol. des A. Test.*, I. 264) says: "*Von einem Unterschied des Looses der im Todtenreich Befindlichen ist im Alten Test. nirgends deutlich geredet. Wie vielmehr dort Alles gleich werde, schildert Hiob. 3: 17–19. Nur in Jes. 14: 15; Ez. 32: 23, wo den gestürzten Eroberern die äusserste Tiefe (יַרְכְּתֵי־בוֹר) angewiesen wird, kann man die Andeutung verschiedener Abstufungen des Todtenreichs finden, etwa in dem Sinn, wie Josephus (Bell. Jud. III. 8, 5) den Selbstmördern einen, ᾅδης σκοτιώτερος in Aussicht stellt. Sonst ist nur von einer Sonderung nach Völkern und Geschlechtern die Rede, nicht von einer Sonderung der Gerechten und Ungerechten*"

Some Rabbis taught that hell will cease, and that the sun will burn up and annihilate the wicked.[1]

3. The CHRISTIAN doctrine of the future life differs from the heathen, and to a less extent also from the Jewish, in the following important points:

(*a*) It gives to the belief in a future state the absolute certainty of divine revelation, sealed by the fact of Christ's resurrection, and thereby imparts to the present life an immeasurable importance, involving endless issues.

(*b*) It connects the resurrection of the body with the immortality of the soul, and thus gives concrete completion to the latter, and saves the whole individuality of man from destruction.

(*c*) It views death as the punishment of sin, and therefore as something terrible, from which nature shrinks. But its terror has been broken, and its sting extracted by Christ.

(*d*) It qualifies the idea of a future state by the doctrine of sin and redemption, and thus makes it to the believer a state of absolute holiness and happiness, to the impenitent sinner a state of absolute misery. Death and immortality are a blessing to the one, but a terror to the other; the former can hail them with joy; the latter has reason to tremble.

(*e*) It gives great prominence to the general judgment, after the resurrection, which determines the ultimate fate of all men according to their works done in this earthly life.

But we must distinguish, in this mysterious article, what is of faith, and what is private opinion and speculation.

The return of Christ to judgment with its eternal rewards and punishment is the centre of the eschatological faith of the church. The judgment is preceded by the general resurrection, and followed by life everlasting.

---

[1] See these and other curious particulars with references in Wünsche, *l. c.* p. 361 sqq., and 494 sqq. He confesses, however, that it is exceedingly difficult to present a coherent system from the various sayings of the Rabbis. The views of the Essenes differed from the common Jewish notions; they believed only in the immortality of the soul, and greeted death as a deliverance from the prison of the body.

This faith is expressed in the œcumenical creeds.

The Apostles' Creed :

"He shall come to judge the quick and the dead," and "I believe in the resurrection of the body and life everlasting."

The Nicene Creed :

"He shall come again, with glory, to judge the quick and the dead; whose kingdom shall have no end." "And we look for the resurrection of the dead, and the life of the world to come."

The Athanasian Creed, so called, adds to these simple statements a damnatory clause at the beginning, middle, and end, and makes salvation depend on belief in the orthodox catholic doctrine of the Trinity and the Incarnation, as therein stated. But that document is of much later origin, and cannot be traced beyond the sixth century.

The liturgies which claim apostolic or post-apostolic origin, give devotional expression to the same essential points in the eucharistic sacrifice.

The Clementine liturgy :

"Being mindful, therefore, of His passion and death, and resurrection from the dead, and return into the heavens, and His future second appearing, wherein He is to come with glory and power to judge the quick and the dead, and to recompense to every one according to his works."

The liturgy of James :

"His second glorious and awful appearing, when He shall come with glory to judge the quick and the dead, and render to every one according to his works."

The liturgy of Mark :

"His second terrible and dreadful coming, in which He will come to judge righteously the quick and the dead, and to render to each man according to his works."

All that is beyond these revealed and generally received articles must be left free. The time of the Second Advent, the preceding revelation of Antichrist, the millennium before or after the general judgment, the nature of the disembodied state between death and resurrection, the mode and degree of future punishment, the proportion of the saved and lost, the fate of the heathen and all who die ignorant of Christianity, the locality of heaven and hell, are open questions in eschatology about which wise and good men in the church have always differed, and will differ to the end. The Bible speaks indeed of *ascending* to heaven and *descending* to hell, but this is simply the unavoidable popular language, as when it speaks of the rising and setting sun. We do the same, although we know that in the universe of God there is neither above nor below, and that the sun does not move around the earth. The supernatural world may be very far from us, beyond the stars and beyond the boundaries of the visible created world (if it has any boundaries), or very near and round about us. At all events there is an abundance of room for all God's children. "In my Father's house are many mansions. I go to prepare a place for you" (John 14: 2). This suffices for faith.

§ 156. *Between Death and Resurrection.*

DAV. BLONDEL: *Traité de la créance des Pères touchant l'état des ames après cette vie.* Charenton, 1651.

J. A. BAUMGARTEN: *Historia doctrinæ de Statu Animarum separatarum.* Hal. 1754.

HÖPFNER: *De Origine dogm. de Purgatorio.* Hal. 1792.

J. A. ERNESTI: *De veterum Patrum opinione de Statu Animarum a corpore sejunctar.* Lips. 1794.

HERBERT MORTIMER LUCKOCK (Canon of Ely, high-Anglican): *After Death. An Examination of the Testimony of Primitive Times respecting the State of the Faithful Dead, and their Relationship to the Living.* London, third ed. 1881. Defends prayers for the dead.

Among the darkest points in eschatology is the middle state, or the condition of the soul between death and resurrection. It is difficult to conceive of a disembodied state of happiness or woe without physical organs for enjoyment and suffering. Justin Martyr held that the souls retain their sensibility after death, otherwise the bad would have the advantage over the good. Origen seems to have assumed some refined, spiritual corporeity which accompanies the soul on its lonely journey, and is the germ of the resurrection body ; but the speculative opinions of that profound thinker were looked upon with suspicion, and some of them were ultimately condemned. The idea of the sleep of the soul (psychopannychia) had some advocates, but was expressly rejected by Tertullian.[1] Others held that the soul died with the body, and was created anew at the resurrection.[2] The prevailing view was that the soul continued in a conscious, though disembodied state, by virtue either of inherent or of communicated immortality. The nature of that state depends upon the moral character formed in this life either for weal or woe, without the possibility of a change except in the same direction.

The catholic doctrine of the *status intermedius* was chiefly derived from the Jewish tradition of the Sheol, from the parable of Dives and Lazarus (Luke 16 : 19 sqq.), and from the passages of Christ's descent into Hades.[3] The utterances of the ante-Nicene fathers are somewhat vague and confused, but receive light from the more mature statements of the Nicene and post-Nicene fathers, and may be reduced to the following points :[4]

1. The pious who died before Christ from Abel or Adam down to John the Baptist (with rare exceptions, as Enoch, Moses, and Elijah) were detained in a part of Sheol,[5] waiting

---

[1] *De Anima*, c. 58. The doctrine of the psychopannychia was renewed by the Anabaptists, and refuted by Calvin in one of his earliest books. (Paris, 1534.)

[2] Eusebius, VI. 37, mentions this view as held by some in Arabia.

[3] Luke 23 : 43 ; Acts 2 : 31 ; 1 Pet. 3 : 19 ; 4 : 6.

[4] Comp. among other passages, Justin M., *Dial.* c. 5, 72, 80, 99, 105 (Engelhardt, *l. c.* p 308) ; Irenæus, IV. 27, 2 ; V. 31 ; Tertullian, *De Anima*, c. 7, 31, 50, 55, 58 ; *Adv. Marc.* IV. 34 ; Cyprian, *Ep.* 52 ; Clemens Alex., *Strom.* VI. 762 sq. ; Origen, *Contra Cels.* V. 15 ; *Hom. in Luc.* XIV. (Tom. III. 948) ; *Hom. in Ez* I. (III. 360) ; Ambrose, *De Bono Mortis*, and *Ep.* 20.

[5] The mediæval scholastics called that part of Sheol the *Limbus Patrum*, and assumed that it was emptied by Christ at his descent, and replaced by *Purgatory*, which in turn will be emptied at the second Advent, so that after the judgment there will be only heaven and hell. The evangelical confessions

for the first Advent, and were released by Christ after the crucifixion and transferred to Paradise. This was the chief aim and result of the *descensus ad inferos*, as understood in the church long before it became an article of the Apostles' Creed, first in Aquileja (where, however, Rufinus explained it wrongly, as being equivalent to burial), and then in Rome. Hermas of Rome and Clement of Alexandria supposed that the patriarchs and Old Testament saints, before their translation, were baptized by Christ and the apostles. Irenæus repeatedly refers to the descent of Christ to the spirit-world as the only means by which the benefits of the redemption could be made known and applied to the pious dead of former ages.[1]

2. Christian martyrs and confessors, to whom were afterwards added other eminent saints, pass immediately after death into heaven to the blessed vision of God.[2]

3. The majority of Christian believers, being imperfect, enter for an indefinite period into a preparatory state of rest and happiness, usually called Paradise (comp. Luke 23 : 41) or Abraham's Bosom (Luke 16 : 23). There they are gradually purged of remaining infirmities until they are ripe for heaven, into which nothing is admitted but absolute purity. Origen assumed a constant progression to higher and higher regions of knowledge and bliss. (After the fifth or sixth century, certainly since Pope Gregory I., Purgatory was substituted for Paradise).

4. The locality of Paradise is uncertain : some imagined it agree with the Roman Catholic in the twofold state after the judgment, but deny the preceding state of purgatory between heaven and hell. They allow, however, different degrees of holiness and happiness as well as guilt and punishment before and after the judgment.

[1] *Adv. Hær.* IV. 27,§ 2 : "It was for this reason that the Lord descended into the regions beneath the earth, preaching His advent to them also, and [declaring] the remission of sins to those who believe in Him. Now all those believed in Him who had hope towards him, that is, those who proclaimed His advent, and submitted to His dispensations, the righteous men, the prophets, and the patriarchs, to whom He remitted sins in the same way, as He did to us, which sins we should not lay to their charge, if we would not despise the grace of God." This passage exists only in the Latin version.

[2] The Gnostics taught that all souls return immediately to God, but this was rejected as heretical. Justin, *Dial.* 80.

to be a higher region of Hades beneath the earth, yet "afar off" from Gehenna, and separated from it by "a great gulf" (comp. Luke 16 : 23, 26) ;[1] others transferred it to the lower regions of heaven above the earth, yet clearly distinct from the final home of the blessed.[2]

5. Impenitent Christians and unbelievers go down to the lower regions of Hades (Gehenna, Tartarus, Hell) into a preparatory state of misery and dreadful expectation of the final judgment. From the fourth century Hades came to be identified with Hell, and this confusion passed into many versions of the Bible, including that of King James.

6. The future fate of the heathen and of unbaptized children was left in hopeless darkness, except by Justin and the Alexandrian fathers, who extended the operations of divine grace beyond the limits of the visible church. Justin Martyr must have believed, from his premises, in the salvation of all those heathen who had in this life followed the light of the Divine Logos and died in a state of unconscious Christianity, or preparedness for Christianity. For, he says, "those who lived with the Logos were Christians, although they were esteemed atheists, as Socrates and Heraclitus,[2] and others like them."[3]

---

[1] So apparently Tertullian, who calls Gehenna " a reservoir of secret fire under the earth," and Paradise "the place of divine bliss appointed to receive the spirits of the saints, separated from the knowledge of this world by that fiery zone [i. e. the river Pyriphlegeton as by a sort of enclosure."] *Apol.* c. 47.

[2] So Irenæus, *Adv. Hær.* V. 5, § 1 : " Wherefore also the elders who were disciples of the apostles tell us that those who were translated were transferred to that place (for paradise has been prepared for righteous men, such as have the Spirit; in which place also Paul the apostle, when he was caught up, heard words which are unspeakable as regards us in our present condition), and that there shall they who have been translated remain until the consummation [of all things], as a prelude to immortality."

[3] *Apol.* I. 46 : οἱ μετὰ Λόγου βιώσαντες Χριστιανοί εἰσι, κἂν ἄθεοι ἐνομίσθησαν, οἷον ἐν Ἕλλησι Σωκράτης καὶ Ἡράκλειτος καὶ οἱ ὅμοιοι αὐτοῖς. Comp. *Apol.* I. 20, 44; *Apol.* II. 8, 13. He does not say anywhere expressly that the nobler heathen are saved ; but it follows from his view of the Logos spermaticos (see p. 550). It was renewed in the sixteenth century by Zwingli, and may be consistently held by all who make salvation depend on eternal election rather than on water-baptism. God is not bound by his own ordinances, and may save whom and when and how he pleases.

7. There are, in the other world, different degrees of happiness and misery according to the degrees of merit and guilt. This is reasonable in itself, and supported by scripture.

8. With the idea of the imperfection of the middle state and the possibility of progressive amelioration, is connected the commemoration of the departed, and prayer in their behalf. No trace of the custom is found in the New Testament nor in the canonical books of the Old, but an isolated example, which seems to imply habit, occurs in the age of the Maccabees, when Judas Maccabæus and his company offered prayer and sacrifice for those slain in battle, "that they might be delivered from sin."[1] In old Jewish service-books there are prayers for the blessedness of the dead.[2] The strong sense of the communion of saints unbroken by death easily accounts for the rise of a similar custom among the early Christians. Tertullian bears clear testimony to its existence at his time. "We offer," he says, "oblations for the dead on the anniversary of their birth," i. e. their celestial birth-day.[3] He gives it as a mark of a Christian widow, that she prays for the soul of her husband, and requests for him refreshment and fellowship in the first resurrection; and that she offers sacrifice on the anniversaries of his falling asleep.[4] Eusebius narrates that at the tomb of Constantine a vast crowd of people, in company with the priests of God, with tears and great lamentation offered their prayers to God for the emperor's soul.[5] Augustin calls prayer for the pious dead in the eucharistic sacrifice an observance of the uni-

---

[1] 2 Macc. 12: 39 sqq. Roman Catholic divines use this passage (besides Matt. 5: 26; 12: 32 and 1 Cor. 3: 13-15) as an argument for the doctrine of purgatory. But it would prove too much for them; for the sin here spoken of was not venial, but the deadly sin of idolatry, which is excluded from purgatory and from the reach of efficacious intercession.

[2] See specimens in Luckock, l. c. p. 58 sqq.

[3] De Cor. Mil. c. 3: "Oblationes pro defunctis, pro natalitiis annua die facimus." Comp. the notes in Oehler's ed. Tom. I. 422.

[4] De Monog. c. 10: "Pro anima ejus orat et refrigerium interim adpostulat ei et in prima resurrectione consortium."

[5] Vita Const. IV. 71: σὺν κλαυθμῷ πλείονι τὰς εὐχὰς ὑπὲρ τῆς βασιλέως ψυχῆς ἀπεδίδοσαν τῷ θεῷ.

versal church, handed down from the fathers.[1] He himself remembered in prayer his godly mother at her dying request.

This is confirmed by the ancient liturgies, which express in substance the devotions of the ante-Nicene age, although they were not committed to writing before the fourth century. The commemoration of the pious dead is an important part in the eucharistic prayers. Take the following from the Liturgy of St. James: "Remember, O Lord God, the spirits of whom we have made mention, and of whom we have not made mention, who are of the true faith,[2] from righteous Abel unto this day; do Thou Thyself give them rest there in the land of the living, in Thy kingdom, in the delight of Paradise,[3] in the Bosom of Abraham and of Isaac and of Jacob, our holy fathers; whence pain ·and grief and lamentation have fled away: there the light of Thy countenance looks upon them, and gives them light for evermore." The Clementine Liturgy in the eighth book of the "Apostolical Constitutions" has likewise a prayer "for those who rest in faith," in these words: "We make an offering to Thee for all Thy saints who have pleased Thee from the beginning of the world, patriarchs, prophets, just men, apostles, martyrs, confessors, bishops, elders, deacons, sub-deacons, singers, virgins, widows, laymen, and all whose names Thou Thyself knowest."

9. These views of the middle state in connection with prayers for the dead show a strong tendency to the Roman Catholic doctrine of Purgatory, which afterwards came to prevail in the

---

[1] *Sermo* 172. He also inferred from the passage on the unpardonable sin (Matt. 12: 32) that other sins may be forgiven in the future world. *De Civit. Dei.* XXI. 24. In the Council of Chalcedon (452), Dioscurus was charged with a breach of trust for not having executed the will of a saintly woman who had left large sums of money to monasteries, hospitals, and alms-houses, in the hope of being benefited by the prayers of the faithful recipients.

[2] τῶν πνευμάτων . . . . ὀρθοδόξων. The Greek church lays great stress on orthodoxy; but it has here evidently a very wide meaning, as it includes the faith of Abel and all Old Testament saints.

[3] Not Purgatory. This shows the difference between the ante-Nicene and post-Nicene faith. See below.

West through the great weight of St. Augustin and Pope Gregory I. But there is, after all, a considerable difference. The ante-Nicene idea of the middle state of the pious excludes, or at all events ignores, the idea of penal suffering, which is an essential part of the Catholic conception of purgatory. It represents the condition of the pious as one of comparative happiness, inferior only to the perfect happiness after the resurrection. Whatever and wherever Paradise may be, it belongs to the heavenly world; while purgatory is supposed to be a middle region between heaven and hell, and to border rather on the latter. The sepulchral inscriptions in the catacombs have a prevailingly cheerful tone, and represent the departed souls as being "in peace" and "living in Christ," or "in God."[1] The same view is substantially preserved in the Oriental church, which holds that the souls of the departed believers may be aided by the prayers of the living, but are nevertheless "in light and rest, with a foretaste of eternal happiness.[2]

Yet alongside with this prevailing belief, there are traces of the purgatorial idea of suffering the temporal consequences of sin, and a painful struggle after holiness. Origen, following in the path of Plato, used the term "purgatorial fire,"[3] by which the remaining stains of the soul shall be burned away; but he understood it figuratively, and connected it with the consuming fire at the final judgment, while Augustin and Gregory I. transferred it to the middle state. The common people and most of the fathers understood it of a material fire; but this is not a matter of faith, and there are Roman divines[4] who confine

---

[1] Sometimes, however, this is expressed in the form of a wish or prayer: "Mayest thou live in God" (*Vivas in Deo*, or *in Christo*); "May God refresh thy spirit" (*Deus refrigeret spiritum tuum*); "Mayest thou have eternal light in Christ," etc. Comp. § 86, p. 301–303.

[2] Longer Russian Catechism, in Schaff's *Creeds*, vol. II. p. 503.

[3] πῦρ καθάρσιον. It is mentioned also before Origen in the Clementine *Homilies*, IX. 13. The Scripture passage on which the term *ignis purgatorius* was based, is 1 Cor. 3: 13, 15, "the *fire* shall prove each man's work .... he himself shall be saved; yet so as through *fire* (ὡς διὰ πυρός).

[4] As Möhler, Klee, and others.

the purgatorial sufferings to the mind and the conscience. A material fire would be very harmless without a material body. A still nearer approach to the Roman purgatory was made by Tertullian and Cyprian, who taught that a special satisfaction and penance was required for sins committed after baptism, and that the last farthing must be paid (Matt. 5 : 20) before the soul can be released from prison and enter into heaven.

§ 157. *After Judgment. Future Punishment.*

The doctrine of the Fathers on future punishment is discussed by Dr. EDWARD BEECHER, *l. c.*, and in the controversial works called forth by Canon FARRAR's *Eternal Hope* (Five Sermons preached in Westminster Abbey, Nov. 1877. Lond., 1879.) See especially

Dr. PUSEY: " *What is of Faith as to Everlasting Punishment ?* " *A Reply to Dr. Farrar's Challenge.* Oxf. and Lond., second ed. 1880 (284 pages).

Canon F. W. FARRAR: *Mercy and Judgment : A few last words on Christian Eschatology with reference to Dr. Pusey's " What is of Faith ?* " London and N. York, 1881 (485 pages). See chs. II., III., IX.–XII. Farrar opposes with much fervor "the current opinions about Hell," and reduces it to the smallest possible dimensions of time and space, but expressly rejects Universalism. He accepts with Pusey the Romanizing view of "future purification" (instead of "probation"), and thus increases the number of the saved by withdrawing vast multitudes of imperfect Christians from the awful doom.

After the general judgment we have nothing revealed but the boundless prospect of æonian life and æonian death. This is the ultimate boundary of our knowledge.

There never was in the Christian church any difference of opinion concerning the righteous, who shall inherit eternal life and enjoy the blessed communion of God forever and ever. But the final fate of the impenitent who reject the offer of salvation admits of three answers to the reasoning mind : everlasting punishment, annihilation, restoration (after remedial punishment and repentance).

1. EVERLASTING PUNISHMENT of the wicked always was, and always will be the orthodox theory. It was held by the Jews at the time of Christ, with the exception of the Sadducees,

who denied the resurrection.[1] It is endorsed by the highest
authority of the most merciful Being, who sacrificed his own
life for the salvation of sinners.[2]

[1] The point is disputed, but the 4th Maccabees, the 4th Esdras, the Book of
Enoch, the Apocalypse of Baruch, and the Psalms of Solomon, contain very
strong passages, which Dr. Pusey has collected, *l, c.* 48–100, and are not in-
validated by the reply of Farrar, ch. VIII. 180–221. Josephus (whose testimony Farrar arbitrarily sets aside as worthless) attests the belief of the Pharisees and Essenes in eternal punishment, *Ant.* XVIII. 1, 3; *Bell. Jud.* II. 8,
11. Rabbi Akiba (about 120) limited the punishment of Gehenna to twelve
months; but only for the Jews. The Talmud assigns certain classes to everlasting punishment, especially apostates and those who despise the wisdom of
the Rabbis. The chief passage is *Rosh Hoshanah,* f. 16 and 17: "There will
be three divisions on the day of judgment, the perfectly righteous, the perfectly
wicked, and the intermediate class. The first will be at once inscribed and
sealed to life eternal; the second at once to Gehenna (Dan. 12: 2); the third
will descend into Gehenna and keep rising and sinking" (Zech. 12: 10). This
opinion was endorsed by the two great schools of Shammai and Hillel, but
Hillel inclined to a liberal and charitable construction (see p. 596). Farrar
maintains that Gehenna does not necessarily and usually mean hell in our
sense, but 1) for Jews, or the majority of Jews, a short punishment, followed
by forgiveness and escape; 2) for worse offenders a long but still terminable
punishment; 3) for the worst offenders, especially Gentiles—punishment followed by *annihilation.* He quotes several modern Jewish authorities of the
rationalistic type, *e. g.* Dr. Deutsch, who says: "There is not a word in the
Talmud that lends any support to the damnable dogma of endless torment."
But Dr. Ferd. Weber who is as good authority, says, that some passages in the
Talmud teach total annihilation of the wicked, others teach everlasting punishment, *e. g. Pesachim* 54ª: "The fire of Gehenna is never extinguished." *Syst.
der altsynag. Paläst. Theologie,* p. 375. The Mohammedans share the Jewish
belief, but change the inhabitants: the Koran assigns Paradise to the orthodox
Moslems, and Hell to all unbelievers (Jews, Gentiles, and Christians), and to
apostates from Islam.

[2] Matt. 12: 32 (the unpardonable sin); 26: 24 (Judas had better never been
born); 25: 46 ("eternal punishment" contrasted with "eternal life"); Mark
9: 48 ("Gehenna, where their worm dieth not, and the fire is not quenched").
In the light of these solemn declarations we must interpret the passages of
Paul (Rom. 5: 12 sqq.; 14: 9; 1 Cor. 15: 22, 28), which look towards universal restoration. The exegetical discussion lies outside of our scope, but as
the meaning of αἰώνιος has been drawn into the patristic discussion, it is necessary to remark that the argumentative force lies not in the etymological and
independent meaning of the word, which is limited to an æon, but in its connection with future punishment as contrasted with future reward, which no
man doubts to be everlasting (Matt. 25: 46). On the exegetical question see
M. Stuart, *l. c.,* and especially the excursus of Taylor Lewis on *Olamic* and
Æonian words in Scripture, in Lange's Com. on *Ecclesiastes* (Am. ed. p. 44–51).

Consequently the majority of the fathers who speak plainly on this terrible subject, favor this view.

Ignatius speaks of "the unquenchable fire;"[1] Hermas, of some "who will not be saved," but "shall utterly perish," because they will not repent.[2]

Justin Martyr teaches that the wicked or hopelessly impenitent will be raised at the judgment to receive eternal punishment. He speaks of it in twelve passages. "Briefly," he says, "what we look for, and have learned from Christ, and what we teach, is as follows. Plato said to the same effect, that Rhadamanthus and Minos would punish the wicked when they came to them ; we say that the same thing will take place ; but that the judge will be Christ, and that their souls will be united to the same bodies, and will undergo an *eternal* punishment (αἰωνίαν κόλασιν); *and not*, as Plato said, a period of only a thousand years (χιλιονταετῇ περίοδον)."[3] In another place: "We believe that all who live wickedly and do not repent, will be punished in eternal fire" (ἐν αἰωνίῳ πυρί).[4] Such language is inconsistent with the annihilation theory for which Justin M. has been claimed.[5] He does, indeed, reject with several other ante-Nicene writers, the Platonic idea that the soul is in itself and independently immortal,[6] and hints at the *possibility* of the final destruction of the wicked,[7] but he puts that possi-

---

[1] *Ep. ad Eph.* c. 16 : ὁ τοιοῦτος, ῥυπαρὸς γενόμενος, εἰς τὸ πῦρ τὸ ἄσβεστον χωρήσει.

[2] *Vis.* III. 2, 7 ; *Simil.* VIII. 9 (ed. Funk, I. p. 256, 488 sq.). Dr. Pusey claims also Polycarp (?), Barnabas, and the spurious second Ep. of Clement, and many martyrs (from their Acts) on his side, p. 151-166.

[3] *Apol.* I. 8. (Comp. Plato, *Phædr.* p. 249 A ; *De Republ.* p. 615 A.)

[4] *Apol.* I. 21: comp. c. 28, 45, 52; II. 2, 7, 8, 9; *Dial.* 45, 130. Also v. Engelhardt, p. 206, and Donaldson, II. 321.

[5] By Petavius, Beecher (p. 206), Farrar (p. 236), and others.

[6] *Dial. c. Tr.* 4. 5 ; comp. Apol. I. 21. Tatian, his disciple, says against the Platonists (*Adv. Græc.* c. 13) : "The soul is not immortal in itself, O Greeks, but mortal (οὐκ ἔστιν ἀθάνατος ἡ ψυχὴ καθ᾽ ἑαυτήν, θνητὴ δέ). Yet it is possible for it not to die." Irenæus, Theophilus of Antioch, Arnobius, and Lactantius held the same view. See Nitzsch, I. 351-353.

[7] In *Dial.* c. 5, he puts into the mouth of the aged man by whom he was converted, the sentence: "Such as are worthy to see God die no more, but

bility countless ages beyond the final judgment, certainly beyond the Platonic millennium of punishment, so that it loses all practical significance and ceases to give relief.

Irenæus has been represented as holding inconsistently all three theories, or at least as hesitating between the orthodox view and the annihilation scheme. He denies, like Justin Martyr, the necessary and intrinsic immortality of the soul, and makes it dependent on God for the continuance in life as well as for life itself.[1] But in paraphrasing the apostolic rule of faith he mentions eternal punishment, and in another place he accepts as certain truth that "eternal fire is prepared for sinners," because "the Lord openly affirms, and the other

others shall undergo punishment *as long as it shall please Him that they shall exist and be punished.*" But just before he had said: "I do not say that all souls die: for that would be a godsend to the wicked. What then? the souls of the pious remain in a better place, while those of the unjust and wicked are in a worse, waiting for the time of judgment." Comp. the note of Otto on the passage, *Op.* II. 26.

[1] *Adv. Hær.* II. 34, § 3: "*omnia quæ facta sunt . . . perseverant quoadusque ea Deus et esse et perseverare voluerit.*" Irenæus reasons that whatever is created had a beginning, and therefore *may* have an end. Whether it will continue or not, depends upon man's gratitude or ingratitude. He who preserves the gift of life and is grateful to the Giver, shall receive length of days forever and ever (*accipiet et in sæculum sæculi longitudinem dierum*); but he who casts it away and becomes ungrateful to his Maker, "*deprives himself of perseverance forever*" (*ipse se privat in sæculum sæculi perseverantia*). From this passage, which exists only in the imperfect Latin version, Dodwell, Beecher (p. 260), and Farrar (241) infer that Irenæus taught annihilation, and interpret *perseverantia* to mean continued existence; while Massuet (see his note in Stieren I. 415), and Pusey (p. 183) explain *perseverantia* of continuance in *real* life in God, or eternal *happiness*. The passage, it must be admitted, is not clear, for *longitudo dierum* and *perseverantia* are not identical, nor is *perseverantia* equivalent to *existentia* or *vita*. In Bk. IV. 20, 7, Irenæus says that Christ "became the dispenser of the paternal grace for the benefit of man . . . lest man, falling away from God altogether, should *cease to exist*" (*cessaret esse*); but he adds, "the life of man consists in beholding God" (*vita autem hominis visio Dei*). In the fourth Pfaffian Fragment ascribed to him (Stieren I. 889), he says that Christ "will come at the end of time to destroy all evil (εἰς τὸ καταργῆσαι πᾶν τὸ κακὸν) and to reconcile all things (εἰς τὸ ἀποκαταλλάξαι τὰ πάντα, from Col. 1: 20) that there may be an end of all impurity." This passage, like 1 Cor. 15: 28 and Col. 1: 20, looks towards universal restoration rather than annihilation, but admits, like the Pauline passages, of an interpretation consistent with eternal punishment. See the long note in Stieren.

Scriptures prove" it.[1]   Hippolytus approves the eschatology of the Pharisees as regards the resurrection, the immortality of the soul, the judgment and conflagration, everlasting life and "everlasting punishment;" and in another place he speaks of "the rayless scenery of gloomy Tartarus, where never shines a beam from the radiating voice of the Word."[2] According to Tertullian the future punishment "will continue, not for a long time, but forever."[3]   It does credit to his feelings when he says that no innocent man can rejoice in the punishment of the guilty, however just, but will grieve rather.   Cyprian thinks that the fear of hell is the only ground of the fear of death to any one, and that we should have before our eyes the fear of God and eternal punishment much more than the fear of men and brief suffering.[4]

The generality of this belief among Christians is testified by Celsus, who tells them that the heathen priests threaten the same "eternal punishment" as they, and that the only question was which was right, since both claimed the truth with equal confidence.[5]

II. The final ANNIHILATION of the wicked removes all discord from the universe of God at the expense of the natural immortality of the soul, and on the ground that sin will ultimately destroy the sinner, and thus destroy itself.

This theory is attributed to Justin Martyr, Irenæus, and others, who believed only in a conditional immortality which may be forfeited; but, as we have just seen, their utterances in favor of eternal punishment are too clear and strong to justify the inference which they might have drawn from their psychology.

---

[1] *Adv. Hær.* III. 4, 1; II. 28, 7. See Pusey, p. 177–181. Ziegler (*Irenäus,* p. 312) says that Irenæus teaches the eternity of punishment in several passages, or presupposes it, and quotes III. 23, 3; IV. 27, 4; 28, 1; IV. 33, 11; 39, 4; 40, 1 and 2.   [2] *Philos.* IX. 23, 30.

[3] *Apol.* c. 45. Comp. *De Test. An.* 4; *De Spect.* 19, 30. Pusey, 184 sq.

[4] *De Mortal.* 10; *Ep.* VIII. 2. Pusey, 190. He quotes also the Recognitions of Clement, and the Clementine Homilies (XI. 11) on this side.

[5] Orig. *C. Cels.* VIII. 48. Origen in his answer does not deny the fact, but aims to prove that the truth is with the Christians.

Arnobius, however, seems to have believed in actual annihilation; for he speaks of certain souls that "are engulfed and burned up," or "hurled down and having been reduced to nothing, vanish in the frustration of a perpetual destruction."[1]

III. The APOKATASTASIS or final restoration of all rational beings to holiness and happiness. This seems to be the most satisfactory speculative solution of the problem of sin, and secures perfect harmony in the creation, but does violence to freedom with its power to perpetuate resistance, and ignores the hardening nature of sin and the ever increasing difficulty of repentance. If conversion and salvation are an ultimate necessity, they lose their moral character, and moral aim.

Origen was the first Christian Universalist. He taught a final restoration, but with modesty as a speculation rather than a dogma, in his youthful work *De Principiis* (written before 231), which was made known in the West by the loose version of Rufinus (398).[2] In his later writings there are only faint traces of it; he seems at least to have modified it, and exempted Satan from final repentance and salvation, but this defeats the end of the theory.[3] He also obscured it by his other theory of the necessary mutability of free will, and the constant succession of fall and redemption.[4]

Universal salvation (including Satan) was clearly taught by Gregory of Nyssa, a profound thinker of the school of

[1] *Adv. Gent.* II. 14. The theory of conditional immortality and the annihilation of the wicked has been recently renewed by a devout English author, Rev. Edward White, *Life in Christ.* Dr. R. Rothe also advocates annihilation, but not till after the conversion of the wicked has become a moral impossibility. See his posthumous *Dogmatik,* ed. by Schenkel, II. 335.

[2] *De Princ.* I. 6, 3. Comp. *In Jer. Hom.* 19; *C. Cels.* VI. 26.

[3] It is usually asserted from Augustin down to Nitzsch (I. 402), that Origen included Satan in the ἀποκατάστασις τῶν πάντων, but *In Ep. ad Rom.* l. VIII. 9 (*Opera* IV. 634) he says that Satan will not be converted, not even at the end of the world, and in a letter *Ad quosdam amicos Alex.* (*Opera* I. 5, quoted by Pusey, p. 125): "Although they say that the father of malice and of the perdition of those who shall be cast out of the kingdom of God, can be saved; which no one can say, even if bereft of reason."

[4] After the apokatastasis has been completed in certain æons, he speaks of πάλιν ἄλλη ἀρχή. See the judicious remarks of Neander, I. 656 (Am. ed.)

Origen (d. 395), and, from an exegetical standpoint, by the eminent Antiochian divines Diodorus of Tarsus (d. 394) and Theodore of Mopsuestia (d. 429), and many Nestorian bishops.[1] In the West also at the time of Augustin (d. 430) there were, as he says, " multitudes who did not believe in eternal punishment." But the view of Origen was rejected by Epiphanius, Jerome, and Augustin, and at last condemned as one of the Origenistic errors under the Emperor Justinian (543).[2]

Since that time universalism was regarded as a heresy, but is tolerated in Protestant churches as a private speculative opinion or charitable hope.[3]

[1] Nitzsch (I. 403 sq.) includes also Gregory Nazianzen, and possibly Chrysostom among universalists. So does Farrar more confidently (249 sqq., 271 sqq.). But the passages on the other side are stronger, see Pusey, 209 sqq., 244 sqq., and cannot be explained from mere "accommodation to the popular view." It is true, however, that Chrysostom honored the memory of Origen, and eulogized his teacher Diodorus, of Tarsus, and his comments on 1 Cor. 15 : 28 look towards an apokatastasis. Pusey speaks too disparagingly of Diodor and Theodore of Mopsuestia, as the fathers of Nestorianism, and unjustly asserts that they denied the incarnation (223-226). They and Chrysostom were the fathers of a sound grammatical exegesis against the allegorizing extravagances of the Origenistic school.

[2] Pusey contends (125-137), that Origen was condemned by the fifth Œcumenical Council, 553, but Hefele conclusively proves that the fifteen anathematisms against Origen were passed by a local Synod of Constantinople in 543 under Mennas. See his *Conciliengesch.*, second ed., II. 859 sqq. The same view was before advocated by Dupin, Walch, and Döllinger.

[3] At least in the Lutheran church of Germany and in the church of England. Bengel very cautiously intimates the apokatastasis, and the Pietists in Würtemberg generally hold it. Among recent divines Schleiermacher, the Origen of Germany, is the most distinguished Universalist. He started not, like Origen, from freedom, but from the opposite Calvinistic theory of a particular election of individuals and nations, which necessarily involves a particular reprobation or prætermission rather, but only for a time, until the election shall reach at last the fulness of the Gentiles and the whole of Israel. Satan was no obstacle with him, as he denied his personal existence. A denomination of recent American origin, the Universalists, have a creed of three articles called the Winchester Confession (1803), and one article teaches the ultimate restoration of " the whole family of mankind to holiness and happiness."

§ 158. *Chiliasm.*

CORRODI: *Kritische Geschichte des Chiliasmus.* 1781. Second ed. Zürich, 1794. 4 vols. Very unsatisfactory.

MÜNSCHER: *Lehre vom tausendjährigen Reich in den 3 ersten Jahrh.* (in Henke's "Magazin," VI. 2, p. 233 sqq.)

D. T. TAYLOR: *The Voice of the Church on the Coming and Kingdom of the Redeemer; a History of the Doctrine of the Reign of Christ on Earth.* Revised by Hastings. Second ed. Peace Dale, R. I. 1855. Pre-millennial.

W. VOLCK: *Der Chiliasmus. Eine historisch-exeget. Studie.* Dorpat, 1869 Millennarian.

A. KOCH: *Das tausendjährige Reich.* Basel, 1872. Millennarian against Hengstenberg.

C. A. BRIGGS: *Origin and History of Premillennarianism.* In the "Lutheran Quarterly Review," Gettysburg, Pa., for April, 1879. 38 pages. Anti-millennial, occasioned by the "Prophetic Conference" of Pre-millennarians, held in New York, Nov. 1878. Discusses the ante-Nicene doctrine.

GEO. N. H. PETERS: *The Theocratic Kingdom of our Lord Jesus, the Christ.* N. York, announced for publ. in 3 vols. 1884. Pre-millennarian.

A complete critical history is wanting, but the *controversial* and *devotional* literature on the subject is very large, especially in the English language. We mention –1) on the millennial side (embracing widely different shades of opinion). (*a*) English and American divines: Jos. Mede (1627), Twisse, Abbadie, Beverly T. Burnet, Bishop Newton, Edward Irving, Birks, Bickersteth, Horatio and Andrew Bonar (two brothers), E. B. Elliott (*Horæ Apoc.*), John Cumming, Dean Alford, Nathan Lord, John Lillie, James H. Brooks, E. R. Craven, Nath. West, J. A. Seiss, S. H. Kellogg, Peters, and the writings of the Second Adventists, the Irvingites, and the Plymouth Brethren. (*b*) German divines: Spener (*Hoffnung besserer Zeiten*), Peterson, Bengel (*Erklärte Offenbarung Johannis,* 1740), Oetinger, Stilling, Lavater, Auberlen (on *Dan. and Revel.*), Martensen, Rothe, von Hofmann, Löhe, Delitzsch, Volck, Luthardt. 2) On the anti-millennial side—(*a*) English and American: Bishop Hall, R. Baxter, David Brown (*Christ's Second Advent*), Fairbairn, Urwick, G. Bush, Mos. Stuart (on *Revel.*), Cowles (on *Dan.* and *Revel.*), Briggs, etc. (*b*) German: Gerhard, Maresius, Hengstenberg, Keil, Kliefoth, Philippi, and many others. See the articles "Millennarianism" by Semisch, and "Pre-Millennarianism" by Kellog, in Schaff-Herzog, vols. II. and III., and the literature there given.

The most striking point in the eschatology of the ante-Nicene age is the prominent chiliasm, or millennarianism, that is the belief of a visible reign of Christ in glory on earth with the risen saints for a thousand years, before the general resurrection and judgment.[1] It was indeed not the doctrine of the church embodied in any creed or form of devotion, but a widely current opinion of distinguished teachers, such as Barnabas, Papias, Justin Martyr, Irenæus, Tertullian, Methodius, and Lactantius; while Caius, Origen, Dionysius the Great, Eusebius (as afterwards Jerome and Augustin) opposed it.

The Jewish chiliasm rested on a carnal misapprehension of the Messianic kingdom, a literal interpretation of prophetic figures, and an overestimate of the importance of the Jewish people and the holy city as the centre of that kingdom. It was developed shortly before and after Christ in the apocalyptic literature, as the Book of Enoch, the Apocalypse of Baruch, 4th Esdras, the Testaments of the Twelve Patriarchs, and the Sibylline Books. It was adopted by the heretical sect of the Ebionites, and the Gnostic Cerinthus.[2]

The Christian chiliasm is the Jewish chiliasm spiritualized and fixed upon the second, instead of the first, coming of Christ. It distinguishes, moreover, two resurrections, one before and another after the millennium, and makes the millennial reign of Christ only a prelude to his eternal reign in heaven, from which it is separated by a short interregnum of Satan. The millennium is expected to come not as the legitimate result of a historical process but as a sudden supernatural revelation.

The advocates of this theory appeal to the certain promises

---

[1] *Chiliasm* (from χίλια ἔτη, a thousand years, Rev. 20: 2, 3) is the Greek, *millennarianism* or *millennialism* (from *mille anni*), the Latin term for the same theory. The adherents are called *Chiliasts*, or *Millennarians*, also *Pre-millennarians*, or *Pre-millennialists* (to indicate the belief that Christ will appear again *before* the millennium), but among them many are counted who simply believe in a golden age of Christianity which is yet to come. *Post-millennarians* or *Anti-millennarians* are those who put the Second Advent after the millennium.

[2] See Euseb. *H. E.* III. 27 and 28.

of the Lord,[1] but particularly to the hieroglyphic passage of the Apocalypse, which teaches a millennial reign of Christ upon this earth after the first resurrection and before the creation of the new heavens and the new earth.[2]

In connection with this the general expectation prevailed that the return of the Lord was near, though uncertain and unascertainable as to its day and hour, so that believers may be always ready for it.[3] This hope, through the whole age of persecution, was a copious fountain of encouragement and comfort under the pains of that martyrdom which sowed in blood the seed of a bountiful harvest for the church.

Among the Apostolic Fathers BARNABAS is the first and the only one who expressly teaches a pre-millennial reign of Christ on earth. He considers the Mosaic history of the creation a type of six ages of labor for the world, each lasting a thousand years, and of a millennium of rest; since with God "one day is as a thousand years." The millennial sabbath on earth will be followed by an eighth and eternal day in a new world, of which the Lord's Day (called by Barnabas "the eighth day") is the type.[4]

PAPIAS of Hierapolis, a pious but credulous cotemporary of Polycarp, entertained quaint and extravagant notions of the

[1] Matt. 5: 4; 19: 28; Luke 14: 12 sqq.

[2] Rev. 20: 1–6. This is the only strictly millennarian passage in the whole Bible. Commentators are still divided as to the literal or symbolical meaning of the millennium, and as to its beginning in the past or in the future. But a number of other passages are drawn into the service of the millennarian theory, as affording indirect support, especially Isa. 11: 4–9; Acts 3: 21; Rom. 11: 15. Modern Pre-millennarians also appeal to what they call the unfulfilled prophecies of the Old Testament regarding the restoration of the Jews in the holy land. But the ancient Chiliasts applied those prophecies to the Christian church as the true Israel.

[3] Comp. Matt. 24: 33, 36; Mark 13: 32; Acts 1: 7; 1 Thess. 5: 1, 2; 2 Pet. 3: 10; Rev. 1: 3; 3: 3.

[4] Barn. *Epist.* ch. 15. He seems to have drawn his views from Ps. 90: 4, 2 Pet. 3: 8, but chiefly from Jewish tradition. He does not quote the Apocalypse. See Otto in Hilgenfeld's "Zeitschrift für wissenschaftliche Theologie," 1877, p. 525–529, and Funk's note in *Patr. Apost.* I. 46.

happiness of the millennial reign, for which he appealed to apostolic tradition. He put into the mouth of Christ himself a highly figurative description of the more than tropical fertility of that period, which is preserved and approved by Irenæus, but sounds very apocryphal.[1]

JUSTIN MARTYR represents the transition from the Jewish Christian to the Gentile Christian chiliasm. He speaks repeatedly of the second parousia of Christ in the clouds of heaven, surrounded by the holy angels. It will be preceded by the near manifestation of the man of sin ($\check{\alpha}\nu\vartheta\rho\omega\pi\sigma\varsigma$ $\tau\tilde{\eta}\varsigma$ $\dot{\alpha}\nu\sigma\mu\dot{\iota}\alpha\varsigma$) who speaks blasphemies against the most high God, and will rule three and a half years. He is preceded by heresies and false prophets.[2] Christ will then raise the patriarchs, prophets,

---

[1] *Adv. Hær.* V. 33, § 3 (ed. Stieren I. 809), quoted from the fourth book of "*The Oracles of the Lord:*" "The days will come when vines shall grow, each having ten thousand branches, and in each branch ten thousand twigs, and in each true twig ten thousand shoots, and in every one of the shoots ten thousand clusters, and on every one of the clusters ten thousand grapes, and every grape when pressed will give five-and-twenty measures of wine. And when any one of the saints shall lay hold of a cluster, another shall cry out, 'I am a better cluster, take me; bless the Lord through me.' In like manner [He said], 'that a grain of wheat shall produce ten thousand ears, and that every ear shall have ten thousand grains, and every grain shall yield ten pounds of pure, fine flour; and that apples, and seeds, and grass shall produce in similar proportions; and that all animals, feeding on the productions of the earth, shall then live in peace and harmony, and be in perfect subjection to man.'" These words were communicated to Papias by "the presbyters, who saw John the disciple of the Lord," and who remembered having heard them from John as coming from the Lord. There is a similar description of the Messianic times in the twenty-ninth chapter of the Apocalypse of Baruch, from the close of the first or beginning of the second century, as follows: "The earth shall yield its fruits, one producing ten thousand, and in one vine shall be a thousand bunches, and one bunch shall produce one thousand grapes, and one grape shall produce one thousand berries, and one berry shall yield a measure of wine. And those who have been hungry shall rejoice, and they shall again see prodigies every day. For spirits shall go forth from my sight to bring every morning the fragrance of spices, and at the end of the day clouds dropping the dew of health. And it shall come to pass, at that time, that the treasure of manna shall again descend from above, and they shall eat of it in these years." See the Latin in Fritzsche's ed. of the *Libri Apoc. V. T.*, p. 666.

[2] *Dial. c. Tryph.* c. 32, 51, 110. Comp. Dan. 7: 25 and 2 Thess. 2: 8.

and pious Jews, establish the millennium, restore Jerusalem, and reign there in the midst of his saints; after which the second and general resurrection and judgment of the world will take place. He regarded this expectation of the earthly perfection of Christ's kingdom as the key-stone of pure doctrine, but adds that many pure and devout Christians of his day did not share this opinion.[1] After the millennium the world will be annihilated, or transformed.[2] In his two *Apologies*, Justin teaches the usual view of the general resurrection and judgment, and makes no mention of the millennium, but does not exclude it.[3] The other Greek Apologists are silent on the subject, and cannot be quoted either for or against chiliasm.

IRENÆUS, on the strength of tradition from St. John and his disciples, taught that after the destruction of the Roman empire, and the brief raging of antichrist (lasting three and a half years or 1260 days), Christ will visibly appear, will bind Satan, will reign at the rebuilt city of Jerusalem with the little band of faithful confessors and the host of risen martyrs over the nations of the earth, and will celebrate the millennial sabbath of preparation for the eternal glory of

[1] *Dial.* c. 80 and 81. He appeals to the prophecies of Isaiah (65: 17 sqq.), Ezekiel, Ps. 90: 4, and the Apocalypse of "a man named John, one of the apostles of Christ." In another passage, *Dial.* c. 113, Justin says that as Joshua led Israel into the holy land and distributed it among the tribes, so Christ will convert the diaspora and distribute the goodly land, yet not as an earthly possession, but give us (($\dot{\eta}\mu\tilde{\iota}\nu$)) an eternal inheritance. He will shine in Jerusalem as the eternal light, for he is the King of Salem after the order of Melchisedek, and the eternal priest of the Most High. But he makes no mention of the loosing of Satan after the millennium. Comp. the discussion of Justin's eschatology by M. von Engelhardt, *Das Christenthum Justins des Märt.* (1878), p. 302–307, and by Donaldson, *Crit. Hist. of Christ. Lit.* II. 316–322.

[2] This point is disputed. Semisch contends for annihilation, Weizsäcker for transformation, von Engelhardt (p. 309) leaves the matter undecided. In the *Dial.* c. 113 Justin says that God through Christ will renew ($\kappa\alpha\iota\nu\upsilon\rho\gamma\epsilon\tilde{\iota}\nu$) the heaven and the earth; in the *Apologies*, that the world will be burnt up.

[3] *Apol.* I. 50, 51, 52. For this reason Donaldson (II. 263), and Dr. Briggs (*l. c.* p. 21) suspect that the chiliastic passages in the *Dialogue* (at least ch. 81) are an interpolation, or corrupted, but without any warrant. The omission of Justin in Jerome's lists of Chiliasts can prove nothing against the testimony of all the manuscripts.

heaven; then, after a temporary liberation of Satan, follows the final victory, the *general* resurrection, the judgment of the world, and the consummation in the new heavens and the new earth.[1]

TERTULLIAN was an enthusiastic Chiliast, and pointed not only to the Apocalypse, but also to the predictions of the Montanist prophets.[2] But the Montanists substituted Pepuza in Phrygia for Jerusalem, as the centre of Christ's reign, and ran into fanatical excesses, which brought chiliasm into discredit, and resulted in its condemnation by several synods in Asia Minor.[3]

After Tertullian, and independently of Montanism, chiliasm was taught by COMMODIAN towards the close of the third century,[4] LACTANTIUS,[5] and VICTORINUS of Petau,[6] at the beginning of the fourth. Its last distinguished advocates in the East were METHODIUS (d., a martyr, 311), the opponent of Origen,[7] and APOLLINARIS of Laodicea in Syria.

We now turn to the anti-Chiliasts. The opposition began during the Montanist movement in Asia Minor. Caius of Rome attacked both Chiliasm and Montanism, and traced the former to the hated heretic Cerinthus.[8] The Roman church seems never to have sympathized with either, and prepared itself for a comfortable settlement and normal development in this world. In Alexandria, Origen opposed chiliasm as a

---

[1] *Adv. Hær.* V. 23–36. On the eschatology of Irenæus see Ziegler, *Iren. der B. v. Lyon* (Berl. 1871), 298–320; and Kirchner, *Die Eschatol. d. Iren.* in the "Studien und Kritiken" for 1863, p. 315–358.

[2] *De Res. Carn.* 25; *Adv. Marc.* III. 24; IV. 29, etc. He discussed the subject in a special work, *De Spe Fidelium*, which is lost.

[3] See § 111, p. 424 sq.

[4] *Instruct. adv. Gentium Deos*, 43, 44, with the Jewish notion of fruitful millennial marriages.

[5] *Instit.* VII. 24; *Epit.* 71, 72. He quotes from the Sibylline books, and expects the speedy end of the world, but not while the city of Rome remains.

[6] In his Commentary on Revelation, and the fragment *De Fabrica Mundi* (part of a Com. on Genesis). Jerome classes him among the Chiliasts.

[7] In his *Banquet of the Ten Virgins*, IX. 5, and *Discourse on Resurrection*.

[8] Euseb. *H. E.* II. 25 (against the Montanist Proclus), and III. 28 (against chiliasm).

Jewish dream, and spiritualized the symbolical language of the prophets.[1] His distinguished pupil, Dionysius the Great (d. about 264), checked the chiliastic movement when it was revived by Nepos in Egypt, and wrote an elaborate work against it, which is lost. He denied the Apocalypse to the apostle John, and ascribed it to a presbyter of that name.[2] Eusebius inclined to the same view.

But the crushing blow came from the great change in the social condition and prospects of the church in the Nicene age. After Christianity, contrary to all expectation, triumphed in the Roman empire, and was embraced by the Cæsars themselves, the millennial reign, instead of being anxiously waited and prayed for, began to be dated either from the first appearance of Christ, or from the conversion of Constantine and the downfall of paganism, and to be regarded as realized in the glory of the dominant imperial state-church. Augustin, who himself had formerly entertained chiliastic hopes, framed the new theory which reflected the social change, and was generally accepted. The apocalyptic millennium he understood to be the present reign of Christ in the Catholic church, and the first resurrection, the translation of the martyrs and saints to heaven, where they participate in Christ's reign.[3] It was consistent with this theory that towards the close of the first millennium of the Christian era there was a wide-spread expectation in Western Europe that the final judgment was at hand.

From the time of Constantine and Augustin chiliasm took its place among the heresies, and was rejected subsequently even by the Protestant reformers as a Jewish dream.[4] But it was re-

---

[1] *De Princ.* II. 11. He had, however, in view a very sensuous idea of the millennium with marriages and luxuriant feasts.

[2] Euseb. VII. 24, 25.   [3] *De Civit. Dei*, XX. 6–10.

[4] The Augsburg Confession, Art. XVII., condemns the Anabaptists and others "who now scatter Jewish opinions that, before the resurrection of the dead, the godly shall occupy the kingdom of the world, the wicked being everywhere suppressed." The 41st of the Anglican Articles, drawn up by Cranmer (1553), but omitted afterwards in the revision under Elizabeth (1563), describes the millennium as "a fable of Jewish dotage."

vived from time to time as an article of faith and hope by pious
individuals and whole sects, often in connection with historic
pessimism, with distrust in mission work, as carried on by
human agencies, with literal interpretations of prophecy, and
with peculiar notions about Antichrist, the conversion and
restoration of the Jews, their return to the Holy Land, and also
with abortive attempts to calculate "the times and seasons" of
the Second Advent, which "the Father hath put in his own
power" (Acts 1: 7), and did not choose to reveal to his own
Son in the days of his flesh.   In a free spiritual sense, however,
millennarianism will always survive as the hope of a golden
age of the church on earth, and of a great sabbath of history
after its many centuries of labor and strife.   The church militant ever longs after the church triumphant, and looks "for
new heavens and a new earth, wherein dwelleth righteousness"
(2 Pet. 3: 13).   "There remaineth a sabbath rest for the people
of God."   (Heb. 4: 9).

CHAPTER XIII.

ECCLESIASTICAL LITERATURE OF THE ANTE-NICENE AGE, AND
BIOGRAPHICAL SKETCHES OF THE CHURCH-FATHERS.

§ 159. *Literature.*

I. *General Patristic Collections.*

The *Benedictine* editions, repeatedly published in Paris, Venice, etc., are
the best as far as they go, but do not satisfy the present state of
criticism. Jesuits (Petavius, Sirmond, Harduin), and Dominicans
(Combefis, Le Quien) have also published several fathers. These
and more recent editions are mentioned in the respective sections.
Of patristic collections the principal ones are :

MAXIMA BIBLIOTHECA *veterum Patrum*, etc. Lugd. 1677, 27 tom. fol.
Contains the less voluminous writers, and only in the Latin translation.

A. GALLANDI (Andreas Gallandius, Oratorian, d. 1779): *Bibliotheca
Græco-Latina veterum Patrum*, etc. Ven. 1765–88, 14 tom. fol.
Contains in all 380 ecclesiastical writers (180 more than the *Bibl
Max.*) in Greek and Latin, with valuable dissertations and notes.

ABBÉ MIGNE (Jacques Paul, b. 1800, founder of the Ultramontane
L'Univers religeux and the Cath. printing establishment at Montrouge, consumed by fire 1868): *Patrologiae cursus completus sive
Bibliotheca universalis, integra, uniformis, commoda, oeconomica,
omnium SS. Patrum, Doctorum, Scriptorumque ecclesiasticorum.*
Petit Montrouge (near Paris), 1844–1866 (Garnier Frères). The
cheapest and most complete patristic library, but carelessly
edited, and often inaccurate, reaching down to the thirteenth
century, the Latin in 222, the Greek in 167 vols., reprinted from the
Bened. and other good editions, with Prologomena, Vitae, Dissertations, Supplements, etc. Some of the plates were consumed by fire
in 1868, but have been replaced. To be used with great caution.

Abbé HOROY : *Bibliotheca Patristica ab anno MCCXVI. usque ad Con-
cilii Tridentini Tempora.* Paris, 1879 sqq. A continuation of Migne.
Belongs to mediaeval history.

A new and critical edition of the Latin Fathers has been under-
taken by the Imperial Academy of Vienna in 1866, under the title :
Corpus scriptorum ecclesiasticorum Latinorum. The first volume
contains the works of Sulpicius Severus, ed. by C. HALM, 1866 ; the
second Minucius Felix and Jul. Firmicus Maternus, by the same,

621

1867 ; Cyprian by HARTEL, 1876 ; Arnobius by REIFFERSCHEID ; Commodianus by DOMBART ; Salvianus by PAULY ; Cassianus by PETSCHENIG ; Priscillian by SCHEPSS, etc. So far 18 vols. from 1866 to 1889.

A new and critical edition of the Greek fathers is still more needed.

Handy editions of the older fathers by OBERTHÜR, RICHTER, GERSDORF, etc.

Special collections of patristic fragments by GRABE (*Spicilegium Patrum*), ROUTH (*Reliquiae Sacrae*), ANGELO MAI (*Scriptorum vet. nova Collectio*, Rom. 1825–'38, 10 t.; *Spicilegium roman.* 1839–'44, 10 t.; *Nova Patrum Bibliotheca*, 1852 sqq. 7 t.) ; Card. PITRA (*Spicilegium Solesmense*, 1852 sqq. 5 t.), LIVERANI (*Spicileg. Liberianum*, 1865), and others.

II. *Separate Collections of the ante-Nicene Fathers.*

PATRES APOSTOLICI, best critical editions, one Protestant by OSCAR VON GEBHARDT, HARNACK, and ZAHN (ed. II. Lips. 1876–'78, in 3 parts) ; another by HILGENFELD (ed. II. Lips. 1876 sqq. in several parts) ; one by Bp. LIGHTFOOT (Lond. 1869 sqq.) ; and one, R. Catholic, by Bp. HEFELE, fifth ed. by Prof. FUNK, Tübingen (1878 and '81, 2 vols.). See § 161.

CORPUS APOLOGETARUM CHRISTIANORUM SECULI II., ED. OTTO. Jenae, 1847–'50 ; Ed. III. 1876 sqq. A new critical ed. by O. V. GEBHARDT and E. SCHWARTZ. Lips. 1888 sqq.

ROBERTS and DONALDSON : *Ante-Nicene Christian Library.* Edinburgh 1857–1872. 24 vols. Authorized reprint, N. York, 1885–'86, 8 vols.

III. *Biographical, critical, doctrinal. Patristics and Patrology.*

ST. JEROME (d. 419) : *De Viris illustribus.* Comprises, in 135 numbers, brief notices of the biblical and ecclesiastical authors, down to A. D. 393. Continuations by GENNADIUS (490), ISIDOR (636), ILDEFONS (667), and others.

PHOTIUS (d. 890) : Μυριοβίβλιον, ἡ βιβλιοϑήκη, ed. *J. Becker*, Berol. 1824, 2 t. fol., and in Migne, *Phot. Opera*, t. III. and IV. Extracts of 280 Greek authors, heathen and Christian, whose works are partly lost. See a full account in Hergenröther's *Photius*, III. 13–31.

BELLARMIN (R. C.) : *Liber de scriptoribus ecclesiasticis* (from the O. T. to A. D. 1500). Rom. 1613 and often.

TILLEMONT (R. C.) : *Memoirs pour servir à l'histoire ecclés.* Par. 1693 sqq. 16 vols. The first six centuries.

L. E. DUPIN (R. C. d. 1719) : *Nouvelle Bibliothèque des auteurs ecclesiastiques, contenant l'histoire de leur vie,* etc. Par. 1688–1715, 47 vols. 8°, with continuations by Coujet, Petit-Didier to the 18th century, and Critiques of R. Simon, 61 vols., 9th ed. Par. 1698 sqq.; another edition, but incomplete, Amstel. 1690–1713, 20 vols. 4°.

REMI CEILLIER (R. C. d. 1761): *Histoire générale des auteurs sacrés et ecclesiastiques.* Par. 1729–'63, 23 vols. 4°; new ed. with additions, Par. 1858–1865 in 14 vols. More complete and exact, but less liberal than Dupin; extends to the middle of the thirteenth century.

WILL. CAVE (Anglican, d. 1713): *Scriptorum ecclesiasticorum Historia literaria, a Christo nato usque ad saecul. XIV.* Lond. 1688–98, 2 vols.; Geneva, 1720; Colon. 1722; best edition superintended by WATERLAND, Oxf. 1740–43, reprinted at Basle 1741–'45. This work is arranged in the centurial style (saeculum Apostolicum, s. Gnosticum, s. Novatianum, s. Arianum, s. Nestorianum, s. Eutychianum, s. Monotheleticum, etc.) W. CAVE: *Lives of the most eminent fathers of the church that flourished in the first four centuries.* Best ed. revised by HENRY CARY. Oxf. 1840, 3 vols.

CHAS. OUDIN (first a monk, then a Protestant, librarian to the University at Leyden, died 1717) : *Commentarius de scriptoribus ecclesiae antiquis illorumque scriptis, a Bellarmino, Possevino, Caveo, Dupin et aliis omissis, ad ann.* 1460. Lips. 1722. 3 vols. fol.

JOHN ALB. FABRICIUS ("the most learned, the most voluminous and the most useful of bibliographers," born at Leipsic 1668, Prof. of Eloquence at Hamburg, died 1736): *Bibliotheca Graeca, sive notitia scriptorum veterum Graecorum;* ed. III. Hamb. 1718–'28, 14 vols.; ed. IV. by G. CHR. HARLESS, with additions. Hamb. 1790–'1811, in 12 vols. (incomplete). This great work of forty years' labor embraces all the Greek writers to the beginning of the eighteenth century, but is inconveniently arranged. (A valuable supplement to it is S. F. G. HOFFMANN : *Bibliographisches Lexicon der gesammten Literatur der Griechen.* Leipz. 3 vols.), 2nd ed. 1844–'45. J. A. FABRICIUS published also a *Bibliotheca Latina mediae et infimae aetatis,* Hamb. 1734–'46, in 6 vols. (enlarged by *Mansi,* Padua, 1754, 3 tom.), and a *Bibliotheca ecclesiastica,* Hamb. 1718, in 1 vol. fol., which contains the catalogues of ecclesiastical authors by Jerome, Gennadius, Isidore, Ildefondus, Trithemius (d. 1515) and others.

C. T. G. SCHÖNEMANN : *Bibliotheca historico-literaria patrum Latinorum a Tertulliano usque ad Gregorium M. et Isidorum Hispalensem.* Lips. 1792, 2 vols. A continuation of Fabricius' *Biblioth. Lat.*

G. LUMPER (R. C.): *Historia theologico-critica de vita, scriptis et doctrina SS. Patrum trium primorum saeculorum.* Aug. Vind. 1783–'99, 13 t. 8°.

A. MÖHLER (R. C. d. 1838): *Patrologie, oder christliche Literärgeschichte.* Edited by REITHMAYER. Regensb. 1840, vol. I. Covers only the first three centuries.

J. FESSLER (R. C.): *Institutiones patrologicae.* Oenip. 1850—'52, 2 vols.

J. C. F. BÄHR : *Geschichte der römischen Literatur.* Karlsruhe, 1836, 4th ed. 1868.

Fr. Böhringer (d. 1879): *Die Kirche Christi u. ihre Zeugen, oder die K. G. in Biographien.* Zür. 1842 (2d ed. 1861 sqq. and 1873 sqq.), 2 vols. in 7 parts (to the sixteenth century).

Joh. Alzog (R. C., Prof. in Freiburg, d. 1878): *Grundriss der Patrologie oder der älteren christl. Literärgeschichte.* Frieburg, 1866; second ed. 1869; third ed. 1876; fourth ed. 1888.

James Donaldson: *A Critical History of Christian Literature and Doctrine from the death of the Apostles to the Nicene Council.* London, 1864–'66. 3 vols. Very valuable, but unfinished.

Jos. Schwane (R. C.): *Dogmengeschichte der patristischen Zeit.* Münster, 1866.

Adolf Ebert: *Geschichte der christlich-lateinischen Literatur von ihren Anfängen bis zum Zeitalter Karls des Grossen.* Leipzig, 1872 (624 pages). The first vol. of a larger work on the general history of mediæval literature. The second vol. (1880) contains the literature from Charlemagne to Charles the Bald.

Jos. Nirschl (R. C.): *Lehrbuch der Patrologie und Patristik.* Mainz. Vol. I. 1881 (VI. and 384).

George A. Jackson: *Early Christian Literature Primers.* N. York, 1879–1883, in 4 little vols., containing extracts from the fathers.

Fr. W. Farrar: *Lives of the Fathers. Sketches of Church History in Biographies.* Lond. and N. York, 1889, 2 vols.

IV. *On the Authority and Use of the Fathers.*

Dallaeus (Daillé, Calvinist): *De usu Patrum in decidendis controversiis.* Genev. 1656 (and often). Against the superstitious and slavish R. Catholic overvaluation of the fathers.

J. W. Eberl (R. C.): *Leitfaden zum Studium der Patrologie.* Augsb. 1854.

J. J. Blunt (Anglican): *The Right Use of the Early Fathers.* Lond. 1857, 3rd ed. 1859. Confined to the first three centuries, and largely polemical against the depreciation of the fathers, by Daillé, Barbeyrat, and Gibbon.

V. *On the Philosophy of the Fathers.*

H. Ritter: *Geschichte der christl. Philosophie.* Hamb. 1841 sqq. 2 vols.

Joh. Huber (d. 1879 as an Old Catholic): *Die Philosophie der Kirchenväter.* München, 1859.

A. Stöckl (R. C.): *Geschichte der Philosophie der patristischen Zeit.* Würzb. 1858, 2 vols.; and *Geschichte der Philosophie des Mittelalters.* Mainz, 1864–1866. 3 vols.

Friedr. Ueberweg: *History of Philosophy* (Engl. transl. by Morris & Porter). N. Y. 1876 (first vol.).

VI. *Patristic Dictionaries.*

J. C. SUICER (d. in Zurich, 1660): *Thesaurus ecclesiasticus e Patribus Graecis.* Amstel., 1682, second ed., much improved, 1728. 2 vols. fol. (with a new title page. Utr. 1746).

DU CANGE (Car. Dufresne a Benedictine, d. 1688): *Glossarium ad scriptores mediae et infimae Graecitatis.* Lugd. 1688. 2 vols. By the same: *Glossarium ad scriptores mediae et infimae Latinitatis.* Par. 1681, again 1733, 6 vols. fol., re-edited by *Carpenter* 1766, 4 vols., and by *Henschel*, Par. 1840–'50, 7 vols. A revised English edition of Du Cange by E. A. Dayman was announced for publication by John Murray (London), but has not yet appeared, in 1889.

E. A. SOPHOCLES: *A glossary of Latin and Byzantine Greek.* Boston, 1860, enlarged ed. 1870. A new ed. by Jos. H. Thayer, 1888.

G. KOFFMANE : *Geschichte des Kirchenlateins.* Breslau, 1879 sqq.

WM. SMITH and HENRY WACE (Anglicans): *A Dictionary of Christian Biography, Literature, Sects and Doctrines.* London, vol. I. 1877–1887, 4 vols. By far the best patristic biographical Dictionary in the English or any other language. A noble monument of the learning of the Church of England.

E. C. RICHARDSON (Hartford, Conn.): *Bibliographical Synopsis of the Ante-Nicene Fathers.* An appendix to the Am Ed. of the Ante-Nicene Fathers, N. York, 1887. Very complete.

§ 160. *A General Estimate of the Fathers.*

As Christianity is primarily a religion of divine facts, and a new moral creation, the literary and scientific element in its history held, at first, a secondary and subordinate place. Of the apostles, Paul alone received a learned education, and even he made his rabbinical culture and great natural talents subservient to the higher spiritual knowledge imparted to him by revelation. But for the very reason that it is a new life, Christianity must produce also a new science and literature; partly from the inherent impulse of faith towards deeper and clearer knowledge of its object for its own satisfaction; partly from the demands of self-preservation against assaults from without; partly from the practical want of instruction and direction for the people. The church also gradually appropriated the classical culture, and made it tributary to her theology. Throughout the middle ages she was almost the sole vehicle and guardian of literature and art, and she is the mother of the best elements of the

modern European and American civilization. We have already
treated of the mighty intellectual labor of our period on the
field of apologetic, polemic, and dogmatic theology. In this
section we have to do with patrology, or the biographical and
bibliographical matter of the ancient theology and literature.

The ecclesiastical learning of the first six centuries was cast
almost entirely in the mould of the Graeco-Roman culture.
The earliest church fathers, even Clement of Rome, Hermas,
and Hippolytus, who lived and labored in and about Rome,
used the Greek language, after the example of the apostles,
with such modifications as the Christian ideas required. Not
till the end of the second century, and then not in Italy, but in
North Africa, did the Latin language also become, through
Tertullian, a medium of Christian science and literature. The
Latin church, however, continued for a long time dependent on
the learning of the Greek. The Greek church was more excitable, speculative, and dialectic; the Latin more steady, practical, and devoted to outward organization; though we have
on both sides striking exceptions to this rule, in the Greek
Chrysostom, who was the greatest pulpit orator, and the Latin
Augustin, who was the profoundest speculative theologian among
the fathers.

The patristic literature in general falls considerably below the
classical in elegance of form, but far surpasses it in the sterling
quality of its matter. It wears the servant form of its master,
during the days of his flesh, not the splendid, princely garb of
this world. Confidence in the power of the Christian truth
made men less careful of the form in which they presented it.
Besides, many of the oldest Christian writers lacked early education, and had a certain aversion to art, from its manifold
perversion in those days to the service of idolatry and immorality. But some of them, even in the second and third centuries, particularly Clement and Origen, stood at the head of their
age in learning and philosophical culture; and in the fourth
and fifth centuries, the literary productions of an Athanasius, a

Gregory, a Chrysostom, an Augustin, and a Jerome, excelled the contemporaneous heathen literature in every respect. Many fathers, like the two Clements, Justin Martyr, Athenagoras, Theophilus, Tertullian, Cyprian, and among the later ones, even Jerome and Augustin, embraced Christianity after attaining adult years; and it is interesting to notice with what enthusiasm, energy, and thankfulness they laid hold upon it.

The term "church-father" originated in the primitive custom of transferring the idea of father to spiritual relationships, especially to those of teacher, priest, and bishop. In the case before us the idea necessarily includes that of antiquity, involving a certain degree of general authority for all subsequent periods and single branches of the church. Hence this title of honor is justly limited to the more distinguished teachers of the first five or six centuries, excepting, of course, the apostles, who stand far above them all as the inspired organs of Christ. It applies, therefore, to the period of the œcumenical formation of doctrines, before the separation of Eastern and Western Christendom. The line of the Latin fathers is generally closed with Pope Gregory I. (d. 604), the line of the Greek with John of Damascus (d. about 754).

Besides antiquity, or direct connection with the formative age of the whole church, learning, holiness, orthodoxy, and the approbation of the church, or general recognition, are the qualifications for a church father. These qualifications, however, are only relative. At least we cannot apply the scale of fully developed orthodoxy, whether Greek, Roman, or Evangelical, to the ante-Nicene fathers. Their dogmatic conceptions were often very indefinite and uncertain. In fact the Roman church excludes a Tertullian for his Montanism, an Origen for his Platonic and idealistic views, an Eusebius for his semi-Arianism, also Clement of Alexandria, Lactantius, Theodoret, and other distinguished divines, from the list of "fathers" (*Patres*), and designates them merely "ecclesiastical writers" (*Scriptores Ecclesiastici*).

In strictness, not a single one of the ante-Nicene fathers fairly agrees with the Roman standard of doctrine in all points. Even Irenæus and Cyprian differed from the Roman bishop, the former in reference to Chiliasm and Montanism, the latter on the validity of heretical baptism. Jerome is a strong witness against the canonical value of the Apocrypha. Augustin, the greatest authority of Catholic theology among the fathers, is yet decidedly evangelical in his views on sin and grace, which were enthusiastically revived by Luther and Calvin, and virtually condemned by the Council of Trent. Pope Gregory the Great repudiated the title "ecumenical bishop" as an antichristian assumption, and yet it is comparatively harmless as compared with the official titles of his successors, who claim to be the Vicars of Christ, the vicegerents of God Almighty on earth, and the infallible organs of the Holy Ghost in all matters of faith and discipline. None of the ancient fathers and doctors knew anything of the modern Roman dogmas of the immaculate conception (1854) and papal infallibility (1870). The "unanimous consent of the fathers" is a mere illusion, except on the most fundamental articles of general Christianity. We must resort here to a liberal conception of orthodoxy, and duly consider the necessary stages of progress in the development of Christian doctrine in the church.

On the other hand the theology of the fathers still less accords with the Protestant standard of orthodoxy. We seek in vain among them for the evangelical doctrines of the exclusive authority of the Scriptures, justification by faith alone, the universal priesthood of the laity; and we find instead as early as the second century a high estimate of ecclesiastical traditions, meritorious and even overmeritorious works, and strong sacerdotal, sacramentarian, ritualistic, and ascetic tendencies, which gradually matured in the Greek and Roman types of catholicity. The Church of England always had more sympathy with the fathers than the Lutheran and Calvinistic Churches, and professes to be in full harmony with the creed, the episcopal polity, and liturgical worship of antiquity before the separation of the east and the west; but the difference is only one of degree; the Thirty-Nine Articles are as thoroughly evangelical as the Augsburg Confession or the Westminster standards; and even the modern Anglo-Catholic school, the most churchly and churchy of all, ignores many tenets and usages which were considered of vital importance in the first centuries, and holds others which were unknown before the sixteenth century. The reformers were as great and good men as the fathers, but both must bow before the apostles. There is a steady progress of Christianity, an ever-deepening understanding and an ever-widening application of its principles and powers, and there are yet many hidden treasures in the Bible which will be brought to light in future ages.

In general the excellences of the church fathers are very various. Polycarp is distinguished, not for genius or learning, but for patriarchal simplicity and dignity; Clement of Rome, for the gift of administration; Ignatius, for impetuous devotion to episcopacy, church unity, and Christian martyrdom; Justin, for apologetic zeal and extensive reading; Irenæus, for sound doctrine and moderation; Clement of Alexandria, for stimulating fertility of thought; Origen, for brilliant learning and bold speculation; Tertullian, for freshness and vigor of intellect, and sturdiness of character; Cyprian, for energetic churchliness; Eusebius, for literary industry in compilation; Lactantius, for elegance of style. Each had also his weakness. Not one compares for a moment in depth and spiritual fulness with a St. Paul or St. John; and the whole patristic literature, with all its incalculable value, must ever remain very far below the New Testament. The single epistle to the Romans or the Gospel of John is worth more than all commentaries, doctrinal, polemic, and ascetic treatises of the Greek and Latin fathers, schoolmen, and reformers.

The ante-Nicene fathers may be divided into five or six classes :

(1.) The apostolic fathers, or personal disciples of the apostles. Of these, Polycarp, Clement, and Ignatius are the most eminent.

(2.) The apologists for Christianity against Judaism and heathenism: Justin Martyr and his successors to the end of the second century.

(3.) The controversialists against heresies within the church: Irenæus, and Hippolytus, at the close of the second century and beginning of the third.

(4). The Alexandrian school of philosophical theology: Clement and Origen, in the first half of the third century.

(5.) The contemporary but more practical North African school of Tertullian and Cyprian.

(6). Then there were also the germs of the Antiochian school, and some less prominent writers, who can be assigned to no particular class.

Together with the genuine writings of the church fathers there appeared in the first centuries, in behalf both of heresy and of orthodoxy, a multitude of apocryphal Gospels, Acts, and Apocalypses, under the names of apostles and of later celebrities; also Jewish and heathen prophecies of Christianity, such as the Testaments of the Twelve Patriarchs, the Books of Hydaspes, of Hermas Trismegistos, and of the Sibyls. The frequent use made of such fabrications of an idle imagination even by eminent church teachers, particularly by the apologists, evinces not only great credulity and total want of literary criticism, but also a very imperfect development of the sense of truth, which had not yet learned utterly to discard the *pia fraus* as immoral falsehood.

NOTES.

The Roman church extends the line of the *Patres*, among whom she further distinguishes a small number of *Doctores ecclesiae*, emphatically so-called, down late into the middle ages, and reckons in it Anselm, Bernard of Clairvaux, Thomas Aquinas, Bonaventura, and the divines of the Council of Trent, resting on her claim to exclusive catholicity, which is recognized neither by the Greek nor the Evangelical church. The marks of a *Doctor Ecclesiæ* are:

1) *eminens eruditio;* 2) *doctrina orthodoxa;* 3) *sanctitas vitae;* 4) *expressa ecclesiae declaratio.* The Roman Church recognizes as *Doctores Ecclesiae* the following Greek fathers : Athanasius, Basil the Great, Gregory of Nazianzen, Chrysostom, Cyril of Alexandria, and John of Damascus, and the following Latin fathers : Ambrose, Jerome, Augustin, Hilarius of Poitiers, Leo I. and Gregory I., together with the mediæval divines Anselm, Thomas Aquinas, Bonaventura and Bernard of Clairvaux. The distinction between *doctores ecclesiae* and *patres ecclesiae* was formally recognized by Pope Boniface VIII. in a decree of 1298, in which Ambrose, Augustin, Jerome,, and Gregory the Great are designated as *magni doctores ecclesiae,* who deserve a higher degree of veneration. Thomas Aquinas, Bonaventura, and St. Bernard were added to the list by papal decree in 1830, Hilary in 1852, Alfonso Maria da Liguori in 1871. Anselm of Canterbury and a few others are called *doctores* in the liturgical service, without special decree. The long line of popes has only furnished two fathers, Leo I. and Gregory I. The Council of Trent first speaks of the "*unanimis consensus patrum,*" which is used in the same sense as "*doctrina ecclesiæ.*"

§ 161. *The Apostolic Fathers.*

Sources :

PATRUM APOSTOLICORUM OPERA. Best editions by O. VON GEBHARDT, A. HARNACK, TH. ZAHN, Lips. 1876–'8, 3 vols. (being the third ed. of Dressel much improved) ; by FR. XAV. FUNK (R. C.), Tüb. 1878 and 1881, 2 vols. (being the 5th and enlarged edition of Hefele) ; by A. HILGENFELD (Tübingen school) : *Novum Testamentum extra canonem receptum,* Lips. 1866, superseded by the revised ed. appearing in parts (Clemens R., 1876 ; Barnabas, 1877 ; Hermas, 1881) ; and by Bishop LIGHTFOOT, Lond. and Cambr. 1869, 1877, and 1885 (including Clement of Rome, Ignatius and Polycarp, with a full critical apparatus, English translations and valuable notes ; upon the whole the best edition as far as it goes.)

Older editions by B. COTELERIUS (COTELIER, R. C.), Par. 1672, 2 vols. fol., including the spurious works ; republ. and ed. by J. CLERICUS (LE CLERC), Antw. 1698, 2nd ed. Amst. 1724, 2 vols. ; TH. ITTIG, 1699 ; FREY, Basel, 1742 ; R. RUSSEL, Lond. 1746, 2 vols. (the genuine works) ; HORNEMANN, Havniæ, 1828 ; GUIL. JACOBSON, Oxon. 1838, ed. IV. 1866, 2 vols. (very elegant and accurate, with valuable notes, but containing only Clemens, Ignatius, Polycarp, and the *Martyria* of Ign. and Polyc.) ; C. J. HEFELE (R. C.), Tüb. 1839, ed. IV. 1855, 1 vol. (very handy, with learned and judicious prolegomena and notes) ; A. R. M. DRESSEL. Lips. 1857, second ed. 1863 (more complete, and based on new MSS. Hefele's and Dressel's edd. are superseded by the first two above mentioned.

English translations of the Apost. Fathers by Archbishop W. WAKE
(d. 1737), Lond. 1693, 4th ed. 1737, and often republished (in admirable style, though with many inaccuracies) ; by ALEX. ROBERTS
and JAMES DONALDSON, in the first vol. of Clark's "Ante-Nicene
Christian Library," Edinb. 1867 (superior to Wake in accuracy,
but inferior in old English flavor) ; by CHS. H. HOOLE, Lond. 1870
and 1872; best by Lightfoot (Clement R. in Appendix, 1877). An
excellent German translation by H. SCHOLZ, Gütersloh, 1865 (in
the style of Luther's Bible version).

WORKS:

The *Prolegomena* to the editions just named, particularly those of the
first four.

A. SCHWEGLER: *Das nachapostolische Zeitalter.* Tüb. 1846. 2 vols.
A very able but hypercritical reconstruction from the Tübingen
school, full of untenable hypotheses, assigning the Gospels, Acts,
the Catholic and later Pauline Epistles to the post-apostolic age,
and measuring every writer by his supposed Petrine or Pauline
tendency, and his relation to Ebionism and Gnosticism.

A. HILGENFELD : *Die apostolischen Väter.* Halle, 1853.

J. H. B. LÜBKERT : *Die Theologie der apostolischen Väter,* in the " Zeitschrift für hist. Theol." Leipz. 1854.

Abbé FREPPEL (Prof. at the Sorbonne) : *Les Pères Apostoliques et leur
époque,* second ed. Paris, 1859. Strongly Roman Catholic.

LECHLER : *Das. apost. u. nachapost. Zeitalter.* Stuttgart, 1857, p. 476–
495 ; 3d ed., thoroughly revised (Leipz., 1885), p. 526–608.

JAMES DONALDSON (LL. D.) : *A Critical History of Christian Literature,*
etc. Vol. I. The Apost. Fathers. Edinburgh, 1864. The same,
separately publ. under the title: *The Apostolic Fathers : A critical
account of their genuine writings and of their doctrines.* London,
1874 (412 pages). Ignatius is omitted. A work of honest and sober
Protestant learning.

GEORGE A. JACKSON: *The Apostolic Fathers and the Apologists of the
Second Century.* New York 1879. Popular, with extracts (pages
203).

J. M. COTTERILL : *Peregrinus Proteus.* Edinburgh, 1879. A curious
book, by a Scotch Episcopalian, who tries to prove that the two
Epistles of Clement, the Epistle to Diognetus, and other ancient
writings, were literary frauds perpetrated by Henry Stephens and
others in the time of the revival of letters in the sixteenth century.

JOSEF SPRINZL (R. C.) : *Die Theologie der apost. Väter.* Wien, 1880.
Tries to prove the entire agreement of the Ap. Fathers with the
modern Vatican theology.

The "apostolic," or rather post-apostolic "fathers"[1] were the first church teachers after the apostles, who had enjoyed in part personal intercourse with them, and thus form the connecting link between them and the apologists of the second century. This class consists of Barnabas, Clement of Rome, Ignatius, Polycarp, and, in a broader sense, Hermas, Papias, and the unknown authors of the Epistle to Diognetus, and of the *Didache*.

Of the outward life of these men, their extraction, education, and occupation before conversion, hardly anything is known. The distressed condition of that age was very unfavorable to authorship; and more than this, the spirit of the primitive church regarded the new life in Christ as the only true life, the only one worthy of being recorded. Even of the lives of the apostles themselves before their call we have only a few hints. But the pious story of the martyrdom of several of these fathers, as their entrance into perfect life, has been copiously written. They were good men rather than great men, and excelled more in zeal and devotion to Christ than in literary attainments. They were faithful practical workers, and hence of more use to the church in those days than profound thinkers or great scholars could have been. "While the works of Tacitus, Sueton, Juvenal, Martial, and other contemporary heathen authors are filled with the sickening details of human folly, vice, and crime, these humble Christian pastors are ever burning with the love of God and men, exhort to a life of purity and holiness in imitation of the example of Christ, and find abundant strength and comfort amid trial and persecution in their faith, and the hope of a glorious immortality in heaven."[2]

---

[1] The usual name is probably derived from Tertullian, who calls the followers of the apostles, *Apostolici*, (*De Carne*, 2; *Præscr. Hær.* 30). Westcott calls them *sub-apostolic*, Donaldson, *ep-apostolic*.

[2] "The most striking feature of these writings," says Donaldson (p. 105)," is the deep living piety which pervades them. It consists in the warmest love to God, the deepest interest in man, and it exhibits itself in a healthy, vigorous, manly morality."

The extant works of the apostolic fathers are of small compass, a handful of letters on holy living and dying, making in
all a volume of about twice the size of the New Testament.
Half of these (several Epistles of Ignatius, the Epistle of Barnabas, and the Pastor of Hermas) are of doubtful genuineness;
but they belong at all events to that. obscure and mysterious
transition period between the end of the first century and the
middle of the second. They all originated, not in scientific
study, but in practical religious feeling, and contain not analyses
of doctrine so much as simple direct assertions of faith and
exhortations to holy life; all, excepting **Hermas** and the
Didache, in the form of epistles after the model of Paul's.[1]
Yet they show the germs of the apologetic, polemic, dogmatic,
and ethic theology, as well as the outlines of the organization
and the cultus of the ancient Catholic church. Critical research
has to assign to them their due place in the external and internal development of the church; in doing this it needs very
great caution to avoid arbitrary construction.

If we compare these documents with the canonical Scriptures
of the New Testament, it is evident at once that they fall far
below in original force, depth, and fulness of spirit, and afford

---

[1] Like the N. T. Epistles, the writings of the Apostolic fathers generally
open with an inscription and Christian salutation, and conclude with a benediction and doxology. The Ep. of Clement to the Corinthians beginning thus
(ch. I.) : "The church of God, which sojournes in Rome to the church of God
which sojournes in Corinth, to them that are called and sanctified by the
will of God, through our Lord Jesus Christ: Grace and peace from Almighty
God, through Jesus Christ, be multiplied unto you." (comp. 1 Cor. 1 : 2, 3;
2 Pet. 1 : 2.) It concludes (ch. 65, formerly ch. 59): "The grace of our
Lord Jesus Christ be with you, and with all men everywhere who are called
of God through Him, through whom be glory, honor, power, majesty, and eternal dominion unto Him from the ages past to the ages of ages. Amen."—The
Ep. of Polycarp begins: "Polycarp, and the presbyters that are with him, to
the church of God sojourning in Philippi: Mercy unto you and peace from
God Almighty and from the Lord Jesus Christ our Saviour, be multiplied;"
and it concludes: "Grace be with you all. Amen." The Ep. of Barnabas
opens and closes in a very general way, omitting the names of the writer and
readers. The inscriptions and salutations of the Ignatian Epistles are longer
and overloaded, even in the Syriac recension.

in this a strong indirect proof of the inspiration of the apostles. Yet they still shine with the evening red of the apostolic day, and breathe an enthusiasm of simple faith and fervent love and fidelity to the Lord, which proved its power in suffering and martyrdom. They move in the element of living tradition, and make reference oftener to the oral preaching of the apostles than to their writings; for these were not yet so generally circulated; but they bear a testimony none the less valuable to the genuineness of the apostolic writings, by occasional citations or allusions, and by the coincidence of their reminiscences with the facts of the gospel history and the fundamental doctrines of the New Testament. The epistles of Barnabas, Clement, and Polycarp, and the Shepherd of Hermas, were in many churches read in public worship.[1] Some were even incorporated in important manuscripts of the Bible.[2] This shows that the sense of the church, as to the extent of the canon, had not yet become everywhere clear. Their authority, however, was always but sectional and subordinate to that of the Gospels and the apostolic Epistles. It was a sound instinct of the church, that the writings of the disciples of the apostles, excepting those of Mark and Luke, who were peculiarly associated with Peter and Paul, were kept out of the canon of the New Testament. For by the wise ordering of the Ruler of history, there is an impassable gulf between the inspiration of the apostles and the illumination of the succeeding age, between the standard authority of holy Scripture and the derived validity of the teaching of the church. "The Bible"—to adopt an illustration of a

[1] Comp. Euseb. *H. E.* III. 16; IV. 23, as regards the epistle of Clement, which continued to be read in the church of Corinth down to the time of Dionysius, A. D. 160, and even to the time of Eusebius and Jerome, in the fourth century. The *Pastor Hermæ* is quoted by Irenæus IV. 3, as "*scriptura*," and is treated by Clement of Alex. and Origen (*Ad Rom. Comment.* X. c. 31) as "*scriptura valde utilis et divinitus inspirata.*"

[2] The Codex Alexandrinus (A) of the fifth century contains, after the Apocalypse, the Epistle of Clemens Romanus to the Corinthians, with a fragment of a homily; and the Codex Sinaiticus of the fourth century gives, at the close, the Epistle of Barnabas complete in Greek, and also a part of the Greek *Pastor Hermæ.*

distinguished writer [1]—"is not like a city of modern Europe, which subsides through suburban gardens and groves and mansions into the open country around, but like an Eastern city in the desert, from which the traveler passes by a single step into a barren waste." The very poverty of these post-apostolic writings renders homage to the inexhaustible richness of the apostolic books which, like the person of Christ, are *divine* as well as human in their origin, character, and effect. [2]

§ 162. *Clement of Rome.*

(I.) *The Epistle of* CLEMENS ROM. *to the Corinthians.* Only the first is genuine, the second so-called Ep. of Cl. is a homily of later date. Best editions by PHILOTHEOS BRYENNIOS (Τοῦ ἐν ἁγίοις πατρὸς ἡμῶν Κλήμεντος ἐπισκόπου 'Ρώμης αἱ δύο πρὸς Καρινθίους ἐπιστολαί, etc. 'Εν Κωνσταντινοπόλει, 1875. With prolegomena, commentary and fac-similes at the end, 188 pp. text, and ρξθ' or 169 prolegomena); HILGENFELD (second ed. Leipz. 1876, with prolegomena, textual notes and conjectures); VON GEBHARDT & HARNACK (sec. ed. 1876, with proleg., notes, and Latin version); FUNK (1878, with Latin version and notes); and LIGHTFOOT (with notes, Lond. 1869, and Appendix containing the newly-discovered portions, and an English Version, 1877).

All the older editions from the Alexandrian MS. first published by Junius, 1633, are partly superseded by the discovery of the new and complete MS. in Constantinople, which marks an epoch in this chapter of church history.

(II.) R. A. LIPSIUS: *De Clementis Rom. Epistola ad Corinth. priore dis-quisitio.* Lips. 1856 (188 pages). Comp. his review of recent editions in the "Jenaer Literaturzeitung," Jan. 13, 1877.

B. H. COWPER: *What the First Bishop of Rome taught. The Ep. of Clement of R. to the Cor., with an Introduction and Notes.* London, 1867.

JOS. MULLOOLY: *St. Clement Pope and Martyr, and his Basilica in Rome.* Rome, second ed. 1873. The same in Italian. Discusses the supposed house and basilica of Clement, but not his works.

---

[1] Ascribed to Archbishop Whately.

[2] Baur, Schwegler, and the other Tübingen critics show great want of spiritual discernment in assigning so many N. T. writings, even the Gospel of John to the borrowed moonlight of the post-apostolic age. They form the opposite extreme to the Roman overestimate of patristic teaching as being of equal authority with the Bible.

JACOBI: *Die beiden Briefe des Clemens v. Rom.*, in the "Studien und Kritiken" for 1876, p. 707 sqq.

FUNK: *Ein theologischer Fund*, in the Tüb. "Theol. Quartalschrift," 1876, p. 286 sqq.

DONALDSON: *The New MS. of Clement of Rome.* In the "Theolog. Review," 1877, p. 35 sqq.

WIESELER: *Der Brief des röm. Clemens an die Kor.*, in the "Jahrbücher für deutsche Theol." 1877. No. III.

RENAN: *Les évangiles.* Paris 1877. Ch. XV. 311–338.

C. J. H. ROPES: *The New MS. of Clement of Rome*, in the "Presb. Quarterly and Princeton Review," N. York 1877, p. 325–343. Contains a scholarly examination of the new readings, and a comparison of the concluding prayer with the ancient liturgies.

The relevant sections in HILGENFELD (*Apost. Väter*, 85–92), DONALDSON (*Ap. Fath.*, 113–190), SPRINZL (*Theol. d. apost. Väter*, 21 sqq., 57 sqq.), SALMON in Smith and Wace, I. 554 sqq., and UHLHORN in Herzog[2], sub *Clemens Rom.* III. 248–257.

Comp. full lists of editions, translations, and discussions on Clement, before and after 1875, in the Prolegomena of von Gebhardt & Harnack, XVIII.–XXIV.; Funk, XXXII.–XXXVI.; Lightfoot, p. 28 sqq., 223 sqq., and 393 sqq., and Richardson, *Synopsis*, 1 sqq.

The first rank among the works of the post-Apostolic age belongs to the " Teaching of the Apostles," discovered in 1883.[1] Next follow the letters of Clement, Ignatius, and Polycarp.

I. CLEMENT, a name of great celebrity in antiquity, was a disciple of Paul and Peter, to whom he refers as the chief examples for imitation. He may have been the same person who is mentioned by Paul as one of his faithful fellow-workers in Philippi (Phil. 4 : 3); or probably a Roman who was in some way connected with the distinguished Flavian family, and through it with the imperial household, where Christianity found an early lodgment.[2] His Epistle betrays a man of classical culture, exe-

---

[1] See above p. 184 sq., and my monograph, third revised edition, 1889.

[2] There are six different conjectures. 1) Clement was the Philippian Clement mentioned by Paul. So Origen, Eusebius, Jerome. He may have been a Greek or a Roman laboring for a time in Philippi and afterwards in Rome. 2) A distant relative of the emperor Tiberius. So the pseudo-Clementine romances which are historically confused and worthless. 3) The Consul Flavius Clemens, Domitian's cousin, who was put to death by him for "atheism," *i. e.* the Christian faith, A. D. 95, while his wife Domitilla (who founded the oldest Christian cemetery in Rome) was banished to an island.

cutive wisdom, and thorough familiarity with the Septuagint
Bible. The last seems to indicate that he was of Jewish parentage.[1]
What we know with certainty is only this, that he stood at the
head of the Roman congregation at the close of the first century.
Yet tradition is divided against itself as to the time of his
administration; now making him the first successor of Peter,
now, with more probability, the third. According to Eusebius
he was bishop from the twelfth year of Domitian to the third
of Trajan (A. D. 92 to 101). Considering that the official distinction between bishops and presbyters was not yet clearly
defined in his time, he may have been co-presbyter with Linus
and Anacletus, who are represented by some as his predecessors,
by others as his successors.[2]

Later legends have decked out his life in romance, both in
the interest of the Catholic church and in that of heresy. They
picture him as a noble and highly educated Roman who, dis-
satisfied with the wisdom and art of heathenism, journeyed to
Palestine, became acquainted there with the apostle Peter, and
was converted by him; accompanied him on his missionary
tours; composed many books in his name; was appointed by

So Hilgenfeld, and, less confidently, Harnack. But our Clement died a natural
death, and if he had been so closely related to the emperor. the fact would
have been widely spread in the church. 4) A nephew of Flavius Clemens.
So the martyr acts of Nereus and Achilles, and Cav. de Rossi. 5) A son of
Flavius Clemens. So Ewald. But the sons of the Consul, whom Domitian
appointed his successors on the throne, were mere boys when Clement was
bishop of Rome. 6) A Jewish freedman or son of a freedman belonging to
the household of Flavius Clemens. Plausibly advocated by Lightfoot (p. 265).
The imperial household seems to have been the centre of the Roman church
from the time of Paul's imprisonment (Phil. 4: 22). Slaves and freedmen
were often very intelligent and cultivated. Hermas (*Vis.* I. 1) and Pope
Callistus (*Philos.* IX. 12) were formerly slaves. Funk concludes: *res non
liquet.* So also Uhlhorn in Herzog.

[1] Renan (p. 313) thinks that he was a Roman Jew. So also Lightfoot. But
Justin Martyr had the same familiarity with the Old Testament, though he
was a Gentile by birth and education.

[2] See § 52, p. 166. Bryennios discusses this question at length in his
Prolegomena, and comes to the conclusion that Clement was the third bishop
of Rome, and the author of both Epistles to the Corinthians. He identifies
him with the Clement in Phil. 4: 3.

him his successor as bishop of Rome, with a sort of supervision over the whole church; and at last, being banished under Trajan to the Taurian Chersonesus, died the glorious death of a martyr in the waves of the sea. But the oldest witnesses, down to Eusebius and Jerome, know nothing of his martyrdom. The *Acta Martyrii Clementis* (by Simon Metaphrastes) make their appearance first in the ninth century. They are purely fictitious, and ascribe incredible miracles to their hero.

It is very remarkable that a person of such vast influence in truth and fiction, whose words were law, who preached the duty of obedience and submission to an independent and distracted church, whose vision reached even to unknown lands beyond the Western sea, should inaugurate, at the threshold of the second century, that long line of pontiffs who have outlasted every dynasty in Europe, and now claim an infallible authority over the consciences of two hundred millions of Christians.[1]

II. From this Clement we have a Greek epistle to the Corinthians. It is often cited by the church fathers, then disappeared, but was found again, together with the fragments of the second epistle, in the Alexandrian codex of the Bible (now in the British Museum), and published by Patricius Junius (Patrick Young) at Oxford in 1633.[2] A second, less ancient, but more perfect manuscript from the eleventh century,

---

[1] "*Clément Romain,*" says the sceptical Renan, once a student of Roman Catholic theology in St. Sulpice, "*ne fut pas seulement un personnage réel, ce fut un personnage de premier ordre, un vrai chef d'Église, un évêque, avant que l'épiscopat fût nettement constitué, j' oserais presque dire un pape, si ce mot ne faisait ici un trop fort anachronisme. Son autorité passa pour la plus grande de toutes en Italie, en Grèce, en Macédonie, durant les dix dernières années du Ier siècle. À la limite de l' âge apostolique, il fut comme un apôtre, un épigone de la grande génération des disciples de Jésus, une des colonnes de cette Eglise de Rome, qui, depuis la destruction de Jérusalem, devenait de plus en plus le centre du christianisme.*"

[2] The Alexandrian Bible codex dates from the fifth century, and was presented by Cyril Lucar, of Constantinople, to King Charles I. in 1628. Since 1633 the Ep. of Cl. has been edited about thirty times from this single MS. It lacks the concluding chapters (57–66) in whole or in part, and is greatly blurred and defaced. It was carefully re-examined and best edited by Tischendorf (1867 and 1873), Lightfoot (1869 and 1877), Laurent (1870), and Gebhardt (in his first ed. 1875). Their conjectures have been sustained in great

containing the missing chapters of the first (with the oldest
written prayer) and the whole of the second Epistle (together
with other valuable documents), was discovered by Philotheos
Bryennios,[1] in the convent library of the patriarch of Jerusalem
in Constantinople, and published in 1875.[2] Soon afterwards a
complete Syriac translation was found in the library of Jules
Mohl, of Paris (d. 1876).[3] We have thus three independent

part by the discovery of the Constantinopolitan MS.   See the critical *Addenda*
in the Append. of Lightfoot, p. 396 sqq.

[1] At that time metropolitan of Serræ (*μετροπολιτης Σερρῶν*)—an ancient see
(Heraclea), in Macedonia—afterwards of Nicomedia. This Eastern prelate was
most cordially welcomed by the scholars of the West, Catholic and Protestant,
to an honored place in the republic of Christian learning.   His discovery
is of inestimable value.   In his prolegomena and notes—all in Greek—he
shows considerable knowledge of the previous editions of Clement (except that
of Lightfoot, 1869) and of modern German literature.   It is amusing to find
familiar names turned into Greek, as Neander (*ὁ Νέανδρος*), Gieseler (*ὁ
Ρισελέριος*), Hefele (*ὁ Ἔφελος*), Dressel (*ὁ Δρεσσέλιος*), Hilgenfeld (*ὁ Ἱλγεμφέλδος*),
Jacobson (*ὁ Ἰακωβσόνιος*), Tischendorf (*Κωνσταντῖνος ὁ Τισενδόρφιος*), Thiersch
(*ὁ Θείρσιος*), Schroeckh (*ὁ Σροίκχιος*), Schwegler (*ὁ Σουέγλερος*), Schliemann
(*ὁ Σλιμάννος*), Reithmayr (*ὁ Ρεϊθμάϋρος*), Uhlhorn (*ὁ Οὐλχόρνιος ἐν τῇ Real
Encykl. von Herzog ἐν λέξ.   Clemens von Rom τομ. β'. σελ* 721 ; p. *ξζ'*), etc. He
complains, however, of " the higher" or " lofty criticism" (*ὑψηλὴ κριτική*) and
the " episcophobia" (*ἐπισκοφοβία*) of certain Germans, and his own criticism is
checked by his reverence for tradition, which leads him to accept the Second
Epistle of Clement as genuine, contrary to the judgment of the best scholars.

[2] The Constantinopolitan codex belongs to the library of the Convent of
the Holy Sepulchre (*τοῦ Παναγίου Τάφου*) in the Fanar or Phanar, the Greek
district of Constantinople, whose inhabitants, the Fanariotes, were originally
employed as secretaries and transcribers of documents.   It is a small 8vo
parchment of 120 leaves, dates from A. D. 1056, is clearly and carefully written
in cursive characters, with accents, spiritus, punctuation (but without jota sub-
scriptum), and contains in addition the second Epistle of Clement in full, the
Greek Ep. of Barnabas, the larger Greek recension of the 12 Ignatian Epistles,
the " Teaching of the Twelve Apostles" (*διδαχὴ τῶν δώδεκα ἀποστόλων*), and a
work of Chrysostom (a Synopsis of the Old and New Testaments).   The value
of this text consists chiefly in the new matter of the first Ep. (about one-
tenth of the whole, from the close of ch. 57 to the end), and the remainder of
the second.   It presents nearly four hundred variations.   The Constantinopolitan codex is preferred by Hilgenfeld, the Alexandrian by Lightfoot, Gebhardt and Harnack.   The *Didache* is far more important, but was not published
till 1883.

[3] This MS., which escaped the attention of French scholars, is now in Cambridge.   It was written in the year 1170, in the convent of Mar Saliba, at

texts (A, C, S), derived, it would seem, from a common parent of the second century. The newly discovered portions shed new light on the history of papal authority and liturgical worship, as we have pointed out in previous chapters.[1]

This first (and in fact the only) Epistle to the Corinthians was sent by the Church of God in Rome, at its own impulse, and unasked, to the Church of God in Corinth, through three aged and faithful Christians : Claudius Ephebus, Valerius Biton, and Fortunatus.[2] It does not bear the name of Clement, and is written in the name of the Roman congregation, but was universally regarded as his production.[3] It stood in the highest esteem in ancient times, and continued in public use in the Corinthian church and in several other churches down to the beginning of the fourth century.[4] This accounts for its incor-

Edessa. It contains, with the exception of the Apocalypse, the entire New Testament in the Harclean recension (616) of the Philoxenian version (508), and the two Epistles of Clement between the Catholic and Pauline Epistles (instead of at the close, as in the Alexandrian Cod.), as if they were equal in authority to the canonical books. Bishop Lightfoot (Appendix to *S. Clement*, p. 238) says, that this Syriac version is conscientious and faithful, but with a tendency to run into paraphrase, and that it follows the Alex. rather than the Constantinopolitan text, but presents also some independent readings.

[1] See § 50, p. 157, and § 66, p. 226, 228.

[2] Mentioned at the close in ch. 65 (which in the Alex. text is ch. 59). Claudius and Valerius may have been connected with the imperial household as freedmen (comp. Phil. 4 : 22). Fortunatus has been identified by some with the one mentioned 1 Cor. 16 : 17, as a younger member of the household of Stephanas in Corinth.

[3] By the author of the Catalogue of contents prefixed to the Alexandrian codex, generally called Cod. A ; by Dionysius of Corinth, in his letter to Soter of Rome (Euseb. IV. 23) ; Irenæus (*Adv. Hær*. III. 3, § 3) ; Clement of Alexandria, who often quotes from it ; Origen (*Comm. in Joan.* VI. § 36 and other places) ; Eusebius (*H. E.* III. 16 ; IV. 23 ; V. 6) ; Jerome (*De Viris illustr.* c. 15). Polycarp already used it, as appears from the similarity of several passages. All modern critics (with the exception of Baur, Schwegler, Volkmar, and Cotterill) admit the Clementine origin, which is supported by the internal evidence of style and doctrine. Cotterill's *Peregrinus Proteus* (1879), which puts the Clementine Epistles in their present shape among the Stephanic fabrications, is an ingenious literary curiosity, but no serious argument. Renan says (p. 319) : "*Peu d' écrits sont aussi authentiques.*"

[4] Dionysius of Corinth (A. D. 170) first mentions the liturgical use of the Epistle in his church. Eusebius (III. 16) testifies from his own knowledge

poration in the Alexandrian Bible Codex, but it is properly put after the Apocalypse and separated from the apostolic epistles.

And this indicates its value. It is not apostolical, not inspired—far from it—but the oldest and best among the subapostolic writings both in form and contents. It was occasioned by party differences and quarrels in the church of Corinth, where the sectarian spirit, so earnestly rebuked by Paul in his first Epistle, had broken out afresh and succeeded in deposing the regular officers (the presbyter-bishops). The writer exhorts the readers to harmony and love, humility, and holiness, after the pattern of Christ and his apostles, especially Peter and Paul, who had but recently sealed their testimony with their blood. He speaks in the highest terms of Paul who, " after instructing the whole [Roman] world in righteousness, and after having reached the end of the West, and borne witness before the rulers, departed into the holy place, leaving the greatest example of patient endurance." [1] He evinces the calm dignity and executive wisdom of the Roman church in her original simplicity, without hierarchical arrogance; and it is remarkable how soon that church recovered after the terrible ordeal of the Neronian persecution, which must have been almost an annihilation. He appeals to the word of God as the final authority, but quotes as freely from the Apocrypha as from the canonical Scriptures (the Septuagint). He abounds in free reminiscences of the teaching of Christ and the Apostles.[2] He refers to Paul's (First) Epistle

that it was read in very many churches ($\dot{\epsilon}\nu$ $\pi\lambda\epsilon\dot{\iota}\sigma\tau\alpha\iota\varsigma$ $\dot{\epsilon}\kappa\kappa\lambda\eta\sigma\dot{\iota}\alpha\iota\varsigma$) both in former times and in his own day. Comp. Jerome, *De Vir. ill.* c. 15.

[1] Ch. 5. The $\tau\dot{\epsilon}\rho\mu\alpha$ $\tau\tilde{\eta}\varsigma$ $\delta\dot{\upsilon}\sigma\epsilon\omega\varsigma$ must be Spain, whither Paul intended to go, Rom. 15 : 24, 28. To a Roman writing in Rome, Spain or Britain was the Western terminus of the earth. Comp. Strabo II. c. 1, 4; III. 2. The $\dot{\eta}\gamma o\dot{\upsilon}\mu\epsilon\nu o\iota$ are the Roman magistrates; others refer the word specifically to Tigellinus and Nymphidius, the prefects of the prætorium in 67, or to Helius and Polycletus, who ruled in Rome during the absence of Nero in Greece in 67.

[2] Funk gives a list of quotations and parallel passages, *Patr. Apost.* I. 566–570. From this it appears that 157 are from the O. T., including the Apocrypha and (apparently) the Assumption of Moses, 158 from the N. T., but only three of the latter are strict quotations (ch. 46 from Matt. 26 : 24, and Luke 17 : 2; ch. 2 and 61 from Tit. 3 : 1). Clement mentions by name only

to the Corinthians, and shows great familiarity with his letters, with James, First Peter, and especially the Epistle to the Hebrews, from which he borrows several expressions. Hence he is mentioned—with Paul, Barnabas, and Luke—as one of the supposed authors of that anonymous epistle. Origen conjectured that Clement or Luke composed the Hebrews under the inspiration or dictation of Paul.

Clement bears clear testimony to the doctrines of the Trinity ("God, the Lord Jesus Christ, and the Holy Spirit, who are the faith and the hope of the elect"), of the Divine dignity and glory of Christ, salvation only by his blood, the necessity of repentance and living faith, justification by grace, sanctification by the Holy Spirit, the unity of the church, and the Christian graces of humility, charity, forbearance, patience, and perseverance. In striking contrast with the bloody cruelties practiced by Domitian, he exhorts to prayer for the civil rulers, that God "may give them health, peace, concord, and stability for the administration of the government he has given them."[1] We have here the echo of Paul's exhortation to the Romans (ch. 13) under the tyrant Nero. Altogether the Epistle of Clement is worthy of a disciple of the apostles, although falling far short of their writings in original simplicity, terseness, and force.

III. In regard to its theology, this epistle belongs plainly to the school of Paul, and strongly resembles the Epistle to the Hebrews, while at the same time it betrays the influence of Peter also; both these apostles having, in fact, personally

---

one book of the N. T., the ἐπιστολὴ τοῦ μακαρίου Παύλου, with evident reference to 1 Cor. 1; 10 sqq. Comp. also the lists of Scripture quotations in the ed. of Bryennios (p. 159–165), and G. and H. p. 144–155.

[1] "When we remember," says Lightfoot, p. 268 sq., "that this prayer issued from the fiery furnace of persecution after experience of a cruel and capricious tyrant like Domitian, it will appear truly sublime—sublime in its utterances, and still more sublime in its silence. Who would have grudged the Church of Rome her primacy, if she had always spoken thus?" Ropes (*l. c.* p. 343): "The sublimity of this prayer gains a peculiar significance when we remember that it was Domitian in whose behalf it was offered."

labored in the church of Rome, in whose name the letter is written, and having left the stamp of their mind upon it. There is no trace in it of an antagonism between Paulinism and Petrinism.[1] Clement is the only one of the apostolic fathers, except perhaps Polycarp, who shows some conception of the Pauline doctrine of justification by faith. "All (the saints of the Old Testament)," says he,[2] "became great and glorious, not through themselves, nor by their works, nor by their righteousness, but by the will of God. Thus we also, who are called by the will of God in Christ Jesus, are righteous not of ourselves, neither through our wisdom, nor through our understanding, nor through our piety, nor through our works, which we have wrought in purity of heart, but by faith, by which the almighty God justified all these from the beginning ; to whom be glory to all eternity." And then Clement, precisely like Paul in the sixth chapter of Romans, derives sanctification from justification, and continues : "What, then, should we do, beloved brethren ? Should we be slothful in good works and neglect love ? By no means ! But with zeal and courage we will hasten to fulfil every good work. For the Creator and Lord of all things himself rejoices in his works." Among the good works he especially extols love, and describes it in a strain which reminds one of Paul's 13th chapter of 1 Corinthians : "He who has love in Christ obeys the commands of Christ. Who can declare the bond of the love of God, and tell the greatness of its beauty ? The height to which it leads is unspeakable. Love unites us with God ; covers a multitude of sins ; beareth all things, endureth all things. There is

---

[1] Renan (p. 314) calls his epistle "*un beau morceau neutre, dont les disciples de Pierre et ceux de Paul durent se contenter également. Il est probale qu 'il fut un des agents les plus énergetiques de la grande œuvre qué etait en train de s' accomplir, je veux dire, de la réconciliation posthume de Pierre et de Paul de la fusior des deux partis, sans l'union desquels l'œuvre du Christ ne pouvait que périr.*"

[2] Ch. 32. An echo of Paul's teaching is found in Polycarp, *Ad Phil.* c. 1, where he refers to "the firm root of their faith, preached to them from olden times, which remains to this day, and bears fruit in our Lord Jesus Christ."

nothing mean in love, nothing haughty. It knows no division; it is not refractory; it does everything in harmony. In love have all the elect of God become perfect. Without love nothing is pleasing to God. In love has the Lord received us; for the love which he cherished towards us, Jesus Christ our Lord gave his blood for us according to the will of God, and his flesh for our flesh, and his soul for our soul."[1] Hence all his zeal for the unity of the church. "Wherefore are dispute, anger, discord, division, and war among you? Or have we not one God and one Christ and one Spirit, who is poured out upon us, and one calling in Christ? Wherefore do we tear and sunder the members of Christ, and bring the body into tumult against itself, and go so far in delusion, that we forget that we are members one of another?"[2]

Very beautifully also he draws from the harmony of the universe an incitement to concord, and incidentally expresses here the remarkable sentiment, perhaps suggested by the old legends of the Atlantis, the *orbis alter*, the *ultima Thule*, etc., that there are other worlds beyond the impenetrable ocean, which are ruled by the same laws of the Lord.[3]

But notwithstanding its prevailing Pauline character, this epistle lowers somewhat the free evangelical tone of the Gentile apostle's theology, softens its anti-Judaistic sternness, and blends it with the Jewish-Christian counterpart of St. James, showing that the conflict between the Pauline and Petrine views was

---

[1] Ch. 49.   [2] Ch. 46. Comp. Eph. 4: 3 sqq.

[3] Ch. 20: Ὠκέανος ἀνθρώποις ἀπέραντος καὶ οἱ μετ᾽ αὐτὸν κόσμοι ταῖς αὐταῖς ταγαῖς τοῦ δεσπότου διευθύνονται. Lightfoot (p. 84) remarks on this passage: "Clement may possibly be referring to some known, but hardly accessible land, lying without the pillars of Hercules. But more probably he contemplated some unknown land in the far west beyond the ocean, like the fabled Atlantis of Plato, or the real America of modern discovery." Lightfoot goes on to say that this passage was thus understood by Irenæus (II. 28, 2), Clement of Alexandria (*Strom.* V. 12), and Origen (*De Princ.* II. 6; *In Ezech.* VIII. 3), but that, at a later date, this opinion was condemned by Tertullian (*De Pall.* 2 *Hermog.* 25), Lactantius (*Inst.* II. 24), and Augustin (*De Civit. Dei* XVI. 9). For centuries the idea of Cosmas Indicopleustes that the earth was a plain surface and a parallelogram, prevailed in Christian literature.

substantially settled at the end of the first century in the Roman church, and also in that of Corinth.

Clement knows nothing of an episcopate above the presbyterate; and his epistle itself is written, not in his own name, but in that of the church at Rome. But he represents the Levitical priesthood as a type of the Christian teaching office, and insists with the greatest decision on outward unity, fixed order, and obedience to church rulers. He speaks in a tone of authority to a sister church of apostolic foundation, and thus reveals the easy and as yet innocent beginning of the papacy.[1] A hundred years after his death his successors ventured, in their own name, not only to exhort, but to excommunicate whole churches for trifling differences.

The interval between Clement and Paul, and the transition from the apostolic to the apocryphal, from faith to superstition, appears in the indiscriminate use of the Jewish Apocrypha, and in the difference between Paul's treatment of scepticism in regard to the resurrection, and his disciple's treatment of the same subject.[2] Clement points not only to the types in nature, the changes of the seasons and of day and night, but also in full earnest to the heathen myth of the miraculous bird, the phœnix in Arabia, which regenerates itself every five hundred years. When the phœnix—so runs the fable—approaches death, it makes itself a nest of frankincense, myrrh, and other spices; from its decaying flesh a winged worm arises, which, when it becomes strong, carries the reproductive nest from Arabia to Heliopolis in Egypt, and there flying down by day, in the sight of all, it lays it, with the bones of its predecessors, upon the altar of the sun. And this takes place, according to the reckoning of the priests, every five hundred years. After Clement other fathers also used the phœnix as a symbol of the resurrection.[3]

[1] See especially chs. 56, 58, 59, 63, of the Constantinopolitan and Syrian text.

[2] Clement, *Ad Cor.* c. 25.   Contrast with this account the fifteenth chapter of Paul's first epistle to the Corinthians.

[3] Tertullian (*De Resurrect.* 13), Origen (*C. Cels.* IV. 72), Ambrose (*Hexaëm.* V. 23, 79), Epiphanius, Rufinus, and other patristic writers. The Phœnix was

IV. As to the *time* of its composition, this epistle falls certainly after the death of Peter and Paul, for it celebrates their martyrdom; and probably after the death of John (about 98); for one would suppose, that if he had been living, Clement would have alluded to him, in deference to superior authority, and that the Corinthian Christians would have applied to an apostle for counsel, rather than to a disciple of the apostles in distant Rome. The persecution alluded to in the beginning of the epistle refers to the Domitian as well as the Neronian; for he speaks of "sudden and *repeated* calamities and reverses which have befallen us." [1] He prudently abstains from naming the imperial persecutors, and intercedes at the close for the civil rulers. Moreover, he calls the church at Corinth at that time "firmly established and ancient." [2] With this date the report

a favorite symbol of renovation and resurrection, and even of Christ himself, among the early Christians, and appears frequently on coins, medals, rings, cups, and tombstones. But in this point they were no more superstitious than the most intelligent heathen contemporaries. Herodotus heard the marvelous story of the burial of the parent bird by the offspring from Egyptian priests, II. 73. Ovid and other Latin poets refer to it, and Claudian devotes a poem to it. Tacitus (*Ann.* VI. 28), Pliny (*H. Nat.* X. 2), and Dion Cassius LVIII. 27) record that the Phœnix actually reappeared in Egypt, A. D. 34, after an interval of 250 years. According to Pliny the bird was also brought to Rome by a decree of Claudius, and exhibited in the comitium, in the year of the city 800 (A. D. 47). This, of course, was a fraud, but many, and among them probably Clement, who may have seen the wonderful bird from Egypt at the time, took it for genuine. But an inspired writer like Paul would never have made use of such a heathen fable as an argument for a Christian truth. "It is now known," says Lightfoot, "that the story owes its origin to the symbolic and pictorial representations of astronomy. The appearance of the phœnix is the recurrence of a period marked by the heliacal rising of some prominent star or constellation." See on the whole subject Henrichsen, *De Phœnicis Fabula* (Havn. 1825), Cowper, Gebhardt and Harnack, Funk, and Lightfoot on ch. 25 of the Clementine Ep., Piper, *Mythologie und Symbolik der christl. Kunst* (1847) I. 446 sqq., and Lepsius, *Chronologie der Aegypter* (1849) 180 sq.

[1] Ch. 1. The usual reading is: γενομένας, which refers to past calamities. So Cod. C. The Alex. MS. is here defective, probably [γενομ] ένας. Lightfoot reads with the Syrian version γινομένας, "which are befalling us" (267 and 399), and refers the passage to the *continued* perils of the church under *Domitian*.

[2] βεβαιοτάτην καὶ ἀρχαίαν, c. 47.

of Eusebius agrees, that Clement did not take the bishop's chair in Rome till 92 or 93.[1]

§ 163. *The Pseudo-Clementine Works.*

The most complete collection of the genuine and spurious works of Clement in Migne's *Patrol. Græca,* Tom. I. and II.

The name of Clement has been forged upon several later writings, both orthodox and heretical, to give them the more currency by the weight of his name and position. These pseudo-Clementine works supplanted in the church of Rome the one genuine work of Clement, which passed into oblivion with the knowledge of the Greek language. They are as follows:

1. A SECOND EPISTLE TO THE CORINTHIANS, falsely so called, formerly known only in part (12 chapters), since 1875 in full (20 chapters).[2] It is greatly inferior to the First Epistle

---

[1] The later date (93–97) is assigned to the Epistle by Cotelier, Tillemont, Lardner, Möhler, Schliemann, Bunsen, Ritschl, Lipsius, Hilgenfeld, Donaldson, Bryennios, Harnack, Uhlhorn, Lightfoot (who puts the letter soon after the martyrdom of Flavius Clement, A. D. 95), Funk (who puts it after the death of Domitian, 96). But other writers, including Hugo Grotius, Grabe, Hefele, Wieseler, B. H. Cowper, assign the Epistle to an earlier date, and infer from ch. 41 that it must have been written before 70, when the temple service in Jerusalem was still celebrated. "Not everywhere, brethren," says Clement, "are the daily sacrifices offered (προσφέρονται θυσίαι), or the vows, or the sin-offerings, or the trespass-offerings, but *in Jerusalem only;* and even there they are not offered (προσφέρεται) in every place, but only at the altar before the sanctuary, after the victim to be offered has been examined by the high-priest and the ministers already mentioned." This argument is very plausible, but not conclusive, since Josephus wrote A. D. 93 in a similar way of the sacrifices of the temple, using the *præsens historicum,* as if it still existed, *Ant.* III. 10. In ch. 6 Clement seems to refer to the destruction of Jerusalem when he says that "jealousy and strife have overthrown great cities and uprooted great nations." Cowper (*l. c.* p. 16) mentions the absence of any allusion to the Gospel of John as another argument. But the Synoptic Gospels are not named either, although the influence of all the Gospels and nearly all the Epistles can be clearly traced in Clement.

[2] Ed. in full by Bryennios, Const. 1875, p. 113–142 with Greek notes; by Funk, with a Latin version (I. 144–171), and by Lightfoot with an English version (380–390).

in contents and style, and of a later date, between 120 and 140, probably written in Corinth; hence its connection with it in MSS.[1] It is no epistle at all, but a homily addressed to "brothers and sisters." It is the oldest known specimen of a post-apostolic sermon, and herein alone lies its importance and value.[2] It is an earnest, though somewhat feeble exhortation to active Christianity and to fidelity in persecution, meantime contending with the Gnostic denial of the resurrection. It is orthodox in sentiment, calls Christ "God and the Judge of the living and the dead," and speaks of the great moral revolution wrought by him in these words (ch. 1): "We were deficient in understanding, worshipping stocks and stones, gold and silver and brass, the works of men; and our whole life was nothing else but death. . . . Through Jesus Christ we have received sight, putting off by his will the cloud wherein we were wrapped. He mercifully saved us. . . . He called us when we were not, and willed that out of nothing we should attain a real existence."

2. Two Encyclical Letters on Virginity. They were first discovered by J. J. Wetstein in the library of the Remonstrants at Amsterdam, in a Syriac Version written A. D. 1470, and published as an appendix to his famous Greek Testament,

---

[1] It is first mentioned by Eusebius, but with the remark that it was not used by ancient writers (*H. E.* III. 38). Irenæus, Clement of Alex., and Origen know only one Ep. of Clement. Dionysius of Corinth, in a letter to Bishop Soter of Rome, calls it, indeed, "the former" (προτέρα), but with reference to a later epistle of Soter to the Corinthians (Euseb. *H. E.* IV. 23). Bryennios, the discoverer of the complete copy, still vindicates the Clementine authorship of the homily, and so does Sprinzl (p. 28), but all other modern scholars give it up. Wocher (1830) assigned it to Dionysius of Corinth, Hilgenfeld first to Soter of Rome, afterwards (*Clem. Ep.* ed. II. 1876, p. xlix) to Clement of Alex. in his youth during his sojourn in Corinth, Harnack (1877) to a third Clement who lived in Rome between the Roman and the Alexandrian Clement, Lightfoot (*App.* p. 307) and Funk (*Prol.* xxxix) to an unknown Corinthian before A. D. 140, on account of the allusion to the Isthmian games (c. 7) and the connection with the Ep. of Clement. Comp. above p. 225.

[2] Lightfoot (p. 317) calls it a testimony "of the lofty moral earnestness and triumphant faith which subdued a reluctant world, and laid it prostrate at the feet of the cross," but "almost worthless as a literary work."

1752.[1] They commend the unmarried life, and contain exhortations and rules to ascetics of both sexes. They show the early development of an asceticism which is foreign to the apostolic teaching and practice. While some Roman Catholic divines still defend the Clementine origin,[2] others with stronger arguments assign it to the middle or close of the second century.[3]

3. The APOSTOLICAL CONSTITUTIONS and CANONS.[4] The so-called LITURGIA S. CLEMENTIS is a part of the eighth book of the Constitutions.

4. The PSEUDO-CLEMENTINA, or twenty Ebionitic homilies and their Catholic reproduction, the RECOGNITIONS.[5]

5. FIVE DECRETAL LETTERS, which pseudo-Isidore has placed at the head of his collection. Two of them are addressed to James, the Lord's Brother, are older than the pseudo-Isidore, and date from the second or third century; the three others were fabricated by him. They form the basis for the most gigantic and audacious literary forgery of the middle ages—the Isidorian Decretals—which subserved the purposes of the papal hierarchy.[6] The first Epistle to James gives an account of the appointment of Clement by Peter as his successor in the see of Rome, with directions concerning the functions of the church-officers and the general administration of the church. The second Epistle to James refers to the administration of the eucharist, church furniture, and other ritualistic matters. They are attached to the pseudo-Clementine Homilies and Recognitions. But it is remarkable that in the

---

[1] Best edition with Latin version by Beelen: *S. Clementis R. Epistolæ binæ de Virginitate.* Louvain, 1856. German translation by Zingerle (1827), French by Villecourt (1853), English in the "Ante-Nicene Library."

[2] Villecourt, Beelen, Möhler, Champagny, Brück.

[3] Mansi, Hefele, Alzog, Funk (*Prol.* XLII. sq.). Also all the Protestant critics except Wetstein, the discoverer. Lightfoot (*l. c.* p. 15 sq.) assigns the document to the beginning of the third century. Eusebius nowhere mentions it.

[4] See § 56, p. 183 sqq.   [5] See § 114, p. 435 sqq.

[6] They originated in the east of France between A. D. 829 and 847.

Homilies James of Jerusalem appears as the superior of Peter of Rome, who must give an account of his doings, and entrust to him his sermons for safe keeping.

§ 164. *Ignatius of Antioch.*

Comp. §§ 17 and 45 (p. 47 sqq. and 149 sqq.).

SOURCES:

I. The Epistles.

W. CURETON: *The Ancient Syriac Version of the Epistles of S. Ignatius to S. Polycarp, the Ephesians, and the Romans.* With transl. and notes. Lond. and Berl., 1845. Also in LIGHTFOOT II. 659–676.

C. C. J. BUNSEN: *Die 3 ächten u. die 4 unächten Briefe des Ignatius von Ant. Hergestellter u. vergleichender Text mit Anmerkk.* Hamb., 1847.

W. CURETON: *Corpus Ignatianum: a complete collection of the Ignatian Epistles, genuine, interpolated, and spurious; together with numerous extracts from them as quoted by eccles. writers down to the tenth century; in Syriac, Greek, and Latin, an Engl. transl. of the Syriac text, copious notes, and introd.* Lond. and Berl., 1849.

J. H. PETERMANN: *S. Ignatii quæ feruntur Epistolæ, una cum ejusdem martyrio, collatis edd. Græcis, versionibusque Syriaca, Armeniaca, Latinis.* Lips., 1849.

THEOD. ZAHN: *Ignatii et Polycarpi Epistulæ, Martyria, Fragmenta.* Lips. 1876 (the second part of *Patrum Apostolorum Opera*, ed. Gebhardt, Harnack and Zahn). This is the best critical ed. of the shorter Greek text. Funk admits its superiority (*"non hesitans dico, textum quem exhibuit Zahn, prioribus longe præstare,"* Prol., p. lxxv.).

FR. XAV. FUNK: *Opera Patrum Apost.*, vol. I. Tub., 1878.

J. B. LIGHTFOOT: *The Apost. Fathers.* P. II. vol. I. and II. Lond. 1885.

English translations of all the Epistles of Ignatius (Syriac, and Greek in both recensions) by ROBERTS, DONALDSON, and CROMBIE, in Clark's "Ante-Nicene Library, (1867), and by LIGHTFOOT (1885).

Earlier Engl. translations by WHISTON (1711) and CLEMENTSON (1827). German translations by M. I. WOCHER (1829) and JOS. NIRSCHL (*Die Briefe des heil. Ign. und sein Martyrium,* 1870).

II. The Martyria.

ACTA MARTYRII S. IGNATII (Μαρτύρριον τοῦ ἁγίου ἱερομάρτυρος Ἰγνατίου τοῦ Θεοφόρου), ed. by Ussher (from two Latin copies, 1647), Cotelier (Greek, 1672), Ruinart (1689), Grabe, Ittig, Smith, Gallandi, Jacobson, Hefele, Dressel, Cureton, Mösinger, Petermann, Zahn (pp. 301 sqq.), (Funk (I. 254-265; II. 218-275), and Lightfoot (II. 473-536). A Syriac version was edited by Cureton (*Corpus Ignat.* 222-225, 252-255), and more fully by Mösinger (*Supplementum Corporis Ignat.,* 1872). An Armenian Martyr. was edited by Petermann, 1849. The Martyrium Colbertinum (from the codex Colbertinus in Paris) has seven chapters. There are several later and discordant recensions, with many interpolations. The Acts of Ignatius profess to be written by two of his deacons and travelling companions; but they were unknown to Eusebius, they contradict the Epistles, they abound in unhistorical statements, and the various versions conflict with each other. Hence recent Protestant critics reject them; and even the latest Roman Catholic editor admits that they must have been written *after* the second century. Probably not before the fifth. Comp. the investigation of Zahn, *Ign.* v. *Ant.*, p. 1–74; Funk, *Proleg.* p. lxxix. sqq., and Lightfoot, II. 363–536.

The patristic statements concerning Ignatius are collected by Cureton, Bunsen, Petermann, Zahn, p. 326–381, and Lightfoot, I. 127–221.

CRITICAL DISCUSSIONS.

Joh. Dallæus (Daillé): *De scriptis quæ sub Dionysii Areopagitæ et Ignatii nominibus circumferuntur, libri duo.* Genev., 1666. Against the genuineness.

*J. Pearson: *Vindiciæ Ignatianæ.* Cambr., 1672. Also in Cleric. ed. of the *Patres Apost.* II. 250–440, and in Migne's *Patrol. Gr.*, Tom. V. Republished with annotations by *E. Churton*, in the Anglo-Cath. Library, Oxf., 1852, 2 vols.

* R. Rothe: *Anfänge der christl. Kirche.* Wittenb., 1837. I., p. 715 sqq. For the shorter Greek recension.

Baron von Bunsen (at that time Prussian ambassador in England): *Ignatius von Ant. u. seine Zeit. 7 Sendschreiben an Dr. Neander.* Hamb., 1847. For the Syriac version.

Baur: *Die Ignatianischen Briefe u. ihr neuster Kritiker.* Tüb., 1848. Against Bunsen and against the genuineness of all recensions.

Denzinger (R. C.): *Ueber die Æchtheit des bisherigen Textes der Ignatian. Briefe.* Würzb., 1849.

*G. Uhlhorn: *Das Verhältniss der syrischen Recension der Ignatian. Br. zu der kürzeren griechischen.* Leipz., 1851 (in the "Zeitschr. für hist. Theol."); and his article "Ignatius" in Herzog's Theol. Encykl., vol. vi. (1856), p. 623 sqq., and in the second ed., vol. vi. 688–694. For the shorter Greek recension.

Thiersch: *Kirche im apost. Zeitalter.* Frankf. u. Erl., 1852, p. 320 sqq.

Lipsius: *Ueber die Æchtheit der syr. Recens. der Ignat. Br.* Leipz., 1856 (in Niedner's "Zeitschr. für hist. Theol."). For the Syriac version. But he afterwards changed his view in Hilgenfeld's "Zeitschrift f. wiss. Theol." 1874, p. 211.

Vaucher: *Recherches critiques sur les lettres d'Ignace d'Antioche.* Genève, 1856.

Merx: *Meletemata Ignatiana.* Hal. 1861.

*Theod. Zahn: *Ignatius von Antiochien.* Gotha, 1873. (631 pages.) For the short Greek recension. The best vindication. Comp. the Proleg. to his ed., 1876.

RENAN: *Les Évangiles* (1877), ch. XXII. 485–498, and the introduction, p. x sqq. Comp. also his notice of Zahn in the "Journal des Savants" for 1874. Against the genuineness of all Ep. except Romans. See in reply Zahn, Proleg. p. x.

F. X. FUNK: *Die Echtheit der Ignatianischen Briefe.* Tübingen 1883.

LIGHTFOOT: *St. Paul's Ep. to the Philippians* (Lond. 1873), Excurs. on the Chr. Ministry, p. 208–211, and 232–236. "The short Greek of the Ignatian letters is probably corrupt or spurious: but from internal evidence this recension can hardly have been made later than the middle of the second century" (p. 210). On p. 232, note, he expressed his preference with Lipsius for the short Syriac text. But since then he has changed his mind in favor of the short Greek recension. See his *S. Ignatius* and *S. Polycarp*, London, 1885, Vol. I., 315–414. He repeats and reinforces Zahn's arguments.

CANON R. TRAVERS SMITH: *St. Ignatius* in Smith and Wace III. (1882), 209–223. For the short Greek recension.

On the chronology:

JOS. NIRSCHL: *Das Todesjahr des Ignatius v. A. und die drei oriental. Feldzüge des Kaisers Trajan* (1869); ADOLF HARNACK: *Die Zeit des Ignatius und die Chronologie der Antiochenischen Bischöfe bis Tyrannus* (Leipzig, 1878); and WIESELER: *Die Christenverfolgungen der Cæsaren* (Gütersloh, 1878), p. 125 sqq.

On the theology of Ignatius, comp. the relevant sections in MÖHLER, HILGENFELD, ZAHN (422–494), NIRSCHL, and SPRINZL.

I. Life of Ignatius.

IGNATIUS, surnamed Theophŏrus,[1] stood at the head of the Church of Antioch at the close of the first century and the beginning of the second, and was thus contemporaneous with Clement of Rome and Simeon of Jerusalem. The church of Antioch was the mother-church of Gentile Christianity; and the city was the second city of the Roman empire. Great numbers of Chris-

---

[1] Θεοφόρος, "bearer of God." The titles of the Epistles call him Ἰγνάτιος ὁ καὶ Θεοφόρος, adding simply the Greek to the Latin name. The *Martyrium Ignatii*, c. 2, makes him explain the term, in answer to a question of Trajan, as meaning "one who has Christ in his breast." The still later legend (in Symeon Metaphrastes and the *Menæa Græca*), by changing the accent (Θεόφορος, Theophŏrus), gives the name the passive meaning, "one carried by God," because Ignatius was the child whom Christ took up in his arms and set before his disciples as a pattern of humility (Matt. 18: 2). So the *Acta Sanctorum*, 1 Febr. I. 28. The Syrians called him *Nurono*, the Fiery, in allusion to his Latin name from *ignis*.

tians and a host of heretical tendencies were collected there, and pushed the development of doctrine and organization with great rapidity.

As in the case of Rome, tradition differs concerning the first episcopal succession of Antioch, making Ignatius either the second or the first bishop of this church after Peter, and calling him now a disciple of Peter, now of Paul, now of John. The Apostolic Constitutions intimate that Evodius and Ignatius presided contemporaneously over that church, the first being ordained by Peter, the second by Paul.[1] Baronius and others suppose the one to have been the bishop of the Jewish, the other of the Gentile converts. Thiersch endeavors to reconcile the conflicting statements by the hypothesis, that Peter appointed Evodius presbyter, Paul Ignatius, and John subsequently ordained Ignatius bishop. But Ignatius himself and Eusebius say nothing of his apostolic discipleship ; while the testimony of Jerome and the Martyrium Colbertinum that he *and Polycarp* were fellow-disciples of St. John, is contradicted by the Epistle of Ignatius to Polycarp, according to which he did not know Polycarp till he came to Smyrna on his way to Rome.[2] According to later story, Ignatius was the first patron of sacred music, and introduced the antiphony in Antioch.

But his peculiar glory, in the eyes of the ancient church, was his martyrdom. The minute account of it, in the various versions of the *Martyrium S. Ignatii*, contains many embellishments of pious fraud and fancy; but the fact itself is confirmed by general tradition. Ignatius himself says, in his Epistle to the

---

[1] *Ap. Const.* VII. 46: 'Αντιοχείας Εὐόδιος μὲν ὑπ' ἐμοῦ Πέτρου, 'Ιγνάτιος δὲ ὑπὸ Παύλου κεχειροτόνηται. According to Eusebius (*Chron.*, ed. Schœne II., p. 158) and Jerome, Ignatius was "*Antiochiæ secundus episcopus.*" Comp. Zahn, *Ign. v. A.*, p. 56 sqq., and Harnack, *Die Zeit des Ign.*, p. 11 sq.

[2] Comp. Zahn, p. 402, who rejects this tradition as altogether groundless: "*Es fehlt bei Ignatius auch jede leiseste Spur davon, dass er noch aus apostolischem Mund die Predigt gehört habe.*" He calls himself five times the least among the Antiochian Christians, and not worthy to be one of their number. From this, Zahn infers that he was converted late in life from determined hostility to enthusiastic devotion, like Paul (comp. 1 Cor. 15: 8–10).

Romans, according to the Syriac version: "From Syria to Rome I fight with wild beasts, on water and on land, by day and by night, chained to ten leopards [soldiers],[1] made worse by signs of kindness. Yet their wickednesses do me good as a disciple; but not on this account am I justified. Would that I might be glad of the beasts made ready for me. And I pray that they may be found ready for me. Nay, I will fawn upon them, that they may devour me quickly, and not, as they have done with some, refuse to touch me from fear. Yea, and if they will not voluntarily do it, I will bring them to it by force."

The Acts of his martyrdom relate more minutely, that Ignatius was brought before the Emperor Trajan at Antioch in the ninth year of his reign (107–108), was condemned to death as a Christian, was transported in chains to Rome, was there thrown to lions in the Coliseum for the amusement of the people, and that his remains were carried back to Antioch as an invaluable treasure.[2] The transportation may be accounted for as designed to cool the zeal of the bishop, to terrify other Christians on the way, and to prevent an outbreak of fanaticism in the church of Antioch.[3] But the chronological part of the statement makes difficulty. So far as we know, from coins and other ancient documents, Trajan did not come to Antioch on his Parthian expedition till the year 114 or 115. We must therefore either place the martyrdom later,[4] or suppose, what is much more pro-

---

[1] Ὅ ἐστι στρατιωτῶν τάγμα is added here for explanation by the two Greek versions, and by Eusebius also, *H. E.* III. 36.

[2] ϑησαυρὸς ἄτιμος, *Mart.* c. 6.

[3] Lucian, in his satire *on the Death of Peregrinus*, represents this Cynic philosopher as a hypocritical bishop and confessor, who while in prison received and sent messages, and was the centre of attention and correspondence among the credulous and good-natured Christians in Syria and Asia Minor. The coincidence is so striking that Zahn and Renan agree in the inference that Lucian knew the story of Ignatius, and intended to mimic him in the person of Peregrinus Proteus, as he mimicked the martyrdom of Polycarp. See Renan, *Les évangiles*, p. 430 sq.

[4] Grabe proposes to read, in the *Martyr.* c. 2, δεκάτῳ ἐννάτῳ ἔτει, for ἐννάτῳ, which would give the year 116. Tillemont and others escape the difficulty by supposing, without good reason, a double Parthian expedition of Trajan, one

bable, that Ignatius did not appear before the emperor himself
at all, but before his governor.[1] Eusebius, Chrysostom, and
other ancient witnesses say nothing of an imperial judgment,
and the Epistle to the Romans rather implies that Ignatius was
not condemned by the emperor at all; for otherwise it would
have been useless for him to forbid them to intercede in his behalf. An appeal was possible from a lower tribunal, but not
from the emperor's.

II. His Letters.

On his journey to Rome, Bishop Ignatius, as a prisoner of
Jesus Christ, wrote seven epistles to various churches, mostly in
Asia Minor. Eusebius and Jerome put them in the following
order: (1) To the Ephesians; (2) to the Magnesians; (3) to the
Trallians; (4) to the Romans; (5) to the Philadelphians; (6) to
the Smyrneans; (7) to Polycarp, bishop of Smyrna. The first
four were composed in Smyrna; the other three later in Troas.
These seven epistles, in connection with a number of other decidedly spurious epistles of Ignatius, have come down to us in
two Greek versions, a longer and a shorter. The shorter is
unquestionably to be preferred to the longer, which abounds
with later interpolations. Besides these, to increase the confusion of controversy, a Syriac translation has been made known
in 1845, which contains only three of the former epistles—those
to Polycarp, to the Ephesians, and to the Romans—and these
in a much shorter form. This version is regarded by some as
an exact transfer of the original; by others, with greater probability, as a mere extract from it for practical and ascetic purposes.

---

in 107 and another in 115 or 116. Comp. Francke: *Zur Geschichte Trajan's*,
1837, p. 253 sqq., and Büdinger, *Untersuchungen zur röm. Kaisergesch.* I. 153
sqq. Nirschl assumes even three oriental expeditions of Trajan. Wieseler
and Frank defend the traditional date (107); Harnack puts the martyrdom
down to the reign of Hadrian or Antoninus Pius, but without solid reasons
Zahn (p. 58) leaves it indefinite between 107 and 116, Lightf. between 110 and 118.

[1] So Uhlhorn, Zahn (248 sq.), Funk (XLVII.). Comp. Lightfoot (II. 390).

The question therefore lies between the shorter Greek copy
and the Syriac version. The preponderance of testimony is for
the former, in which the letters are no loose patch-work, but
were produced each under its own impulse, were known to
Eusebius (probably even to Polycarp),[1] and agree also with the
Armenian version of the fifth century, as compared by Petermann. The three Syriac epistles, however, though they lack
some of the strongest passages on episcopacy and on the divinity
of Christ, contain the outlines of the same life-picture, and especially the same fervid enthusiasm for martyrdom, as the seven
Greek epistles.

III. His Character and Position in history.

Ignatius stands out in history as the ideal of a catholic martyr, and as the earliest advocate of the hierarchical principle in
both its good and its evil points. As a writer, he is remarkable
for originality, freshness and force of ideas, and for terse, spark-
ling and sententious style; but in apostolic simplicity and soundness, he is inferior to Clement and Polycarp, and presents a
stronger contrast to the epistles of the New Testament. Clement
shows the calmness, dignity and governmental wisdom of the
Roman character. Ignatius glows with the fire and impetuosity
of the Greek and Syrian temper which carries him beyond the
bounds of sobriety. He was a very uncommon man, and made
a powerful impression upon his age. He is the incarnation, as it
were, of the three closely connected ideas: the glory of martyrdom, the omnipotence of episcopacy, and the hatred of heresy
and schism. Hierarchical pride and humility, Christian charity
and churchly exclusiveness are typically represented in Ignatius.

[1] Polycarp writes to the Philippians (ch. 13), that he had sent them the
Epistles of Ignatius (τὰς ἐπιστολὰς Ἰγνατίου, τὰς πεμφθείσας ἡμῖν ὑπ' αὐτοῦ καὶ
ἄλλας . . ἐπέμψαμεν ὑμῖν). Zahn and Funk maintain that this *sylloge Polycarp-
iana* consisted of six epistles, and excluded that to the Romans. (Ussher excluded the Ep. to Polycarp). Irenæus quotes a passage from the Epistle to the
Romans, *Adv. Hær.* V. 28, § 4. Origen speaks of several letters of Ignatius,
and quotes a passage from Romans and another from Ephesians, *Prol. in Cant.
Cantic.* and *Hom. VI. in Luc.* (III. 30 and 938, Delarue). Zahn (p. 513) finds
also traces of Ignatius in Clement of Alexandria and Lucian's book *De Morte
Peregrini*, which was written soon after the martyrdom of Polycarp.

As he appears personally in his epistles, his most beautiful and venerable trait is his glowing love for Christ as God incarnate, and his enthusiasm for martyrdom. If great patriots thought it sweet to die for their country, he thought it sweeter and more honorable to die for Christ, and by his blood to fertilize the soil for the growth of His Church. "I would rather die for Christ," says he, "than rule the whole earth." "It is glorious to go down in the world, in order to go up into God." He beseeches the Romans: "Leave me to the beasts, that I may by them be made partaker of God. I am a grain of the wheat of God, and I would be ground by the teeth of wild beasts, that I may be found pure bread of God. Rather fawn upon the beasts, that they may be to me a grave, and leave nothing of my body, that, when I sleep, I may not be burdensome to any one. Then will I truly be a disciple of Christ, when the world can no longer even see my body. Pray the Lord for me, that through these instruments I may be found a sacrifice to God."[1] And further on: "Fire, and cross, and exposure to beasts, scattering of the bones, hewing of the limbs, crushing of the whole body, wicked torments of the devil, may come upon me, if they only make me partaker of Jesus Christ. . . . My love is crucified, and there is no fire in me, which loves earthly stuff. . . . I rejoice not in the food of perishableness, nor in the pleasures of this life. The bread of God would I have, which is the flesh of Christ; and for drink I wish his blood, which is imperishable love."[2]

From these and similar passages, however, we perceive also that his martyr-spirit exceeds the limits of the genuine apostolic soberness and resignation, which is equally willing to depart or to remain according to the Lord's good pleasure.[3] It degenerates into boisterous impatience and morbid fanaticism. It resembles the lurid torch rather than the clear calm light. There mingles also in all his extravagant professions of humility and

---

[1] *Ad Rom.* c. 2, according to the Syriac text; c. 4, in the Greek.
[2] Ch. 4 (Syr.), or 5-7 (Gr.).
[3] Comp. Phil. 1: 23, 24, and Matt. 26: 39.

entire unworthiness a refined spiritual pride and self-commend-
ation. And, finally, there is something offensive in the tone of
his epistle to Polycarp, in which he addresses that venerable
bishop and apostolic disciple, who at that time must have
already entered upon the years of ripe manhood, not as a colleague
and brother, but rather as a pupil, with exhortations and warnings, such as: " Strive after more knowledge than thou hast."
" Be wise as the serpents." " Be more zealous than thou art."
" Flee the arts of the devil."[1] This last injunction goes even
beyond that of Paul to Timothy: " Flee youthful lusts,"[2] and
can hardly be justified by it. Thus, not only in force and depth
of teaching, but also in life and suffering, there is a significant
difference between an apostolic and a post-apostolic martyr.

The doctrinal and churchly views of the Ignatian epistles are
framed on a peculiar combination and somewhat materialistic
apprehension of John's doctrine of the incarnation, and Paul's
idea of the church as the body of Jesus Christ. In the "catholic
church"—an expression introduced by him—that is, the episcopal orthodox organization of his day, the author sees, as it were,
the continuation of the mystery of the incarnation, on the reality
of which he laid great emphasis against the Docetists; and in
every bishop, a visible representative of Christ, and a personal
centre of ecclesiastical unity, which he presses home upon his
readers with the greatest solicitude and almost passionate
zeal. He thus applies those ideas of the apostles directly to the
outward organization, and makes them subservient to the principle and institution of the growing hierarchy. Here lies the
chief importance of these epistles; and the cause of their high
repute with catholics and prelatists,[3] and their unpopularity with

---

[1] Τὰς κακοτεχνίας φεῦγε, according to all the MSS., even the Syriac. Bunsen
proposes to read κακοτέχνους, in the sense of seductive women, coquettes, instead
of κακοτεχνίας. But this, besides being a mere conjecture, would not materially
soften the warning.

[2] 2 Tim. ii. 22.

[3] Such Roman Catholic writers as Nirschl and Sprinzl find the whole theology and church polity of Rome in Ignatius. Episcopalians admire him for
his advocacy of episcopacy; but he proves too little and too much for them;

anti-episcopalians, and modern critics of the more radical school.[1]

It is remarkable that the idea of the episcopal hierarchy which we have developed in another chapter, should be first clearly and boldly brought out, not by the contemporary Roman bishop Clement,[2] but by a bishop of the Eastern church; though it was transplanted by him to the soil of Rome, and there sealed with his martyr blood. Equally noticeable is the circumstance, that these oldest documents of the hierarchy soon became so interpolated, curtailed, and mutilated by pious fraud, that it is to-day almost impossible to discover with certainty the genuine Ignatius of history under the hyper- and pseudo-Ignatius of tradition.

§ 165. *The Ignatian Controversy.*

Of all the writings of the apostolic fathers none have been so much discussed, especially in modern times, as the Ignatian Epistles. This arises partly from the importance of their contents to the episcopal question, partly from the existence of so many different versions. The latter fact seems to argue as strongly *for* the hypothesis of a genuine *basis* for all, as *against* the supposition of the *full* integrity of any one of the

too little because Ignatius knows nothing of a diocesan, but only of a congregational episcopacy; too much because he requires absolute obedience to the bishop as the representative of Christ himself, while the Presbyters represent the apostles. Moreover the Ignatian episcopacy is free from the sacerdotal idea which came in later with Cyprian, but is intimated in Clement of Rome.

[1] Calvin, who, however, knew only the spurious and worthless longer recension, calls the Ignatian Epistles abominable trash (*Inst.* l. 1, c. 13, § 29); Dr. W. D. Killen, who ought to know better, from strong anti-prelatic feeling, speaks of Ignatius, even according to the shorter Syriac recension, as an " anti-evangelical formalist, a puerile boaster, a mystic dreamer and crazy fanatic." (*Ancient Church*, 1859, p. 414). Neander is far more moderate, yet cannot conceive that a martyr so near the apostolic age should have nothing more important to say than " such things about obedience to the bishops " (*Ch. H.* I. 192, note, Bost. ed.). Baur and the Tübingen critics reject the entire Ignatian literature as a forgery. Rothe on the other hand is favorably impressed with the martyr-enthusiasm of the Epistles, and Zahn (an orthodox Lutheran) thinks the Ignatian epistles in the shorter Greek recension worthy of a comparison with the epistles of St. Paul (p. 400).

[2] Still less by the apostle Peter, the alleged first Pope of Rome; on the contrary, he enters a solemn protest against hierarchical tendencies for all time to come, 1 Pet. 5: 1–4.

extant texts. Renan describes the Ignatian problem as the most difficult in early Christian literature, next to that of the Gospel of John (*Les Évang.* p. x).

The Ignatian controversy has passed through three periods, the first from the publication of the spurious Ignatius to the publication of the shorter Greek recension (A. D. 1495 to 1644); the second from the discovery and publication of the shorter Greek recension to the discovery and publication of the Syrian version (A. D. 1644 to 1845), which resulted in the rejection of the larger Greek recension; the third from the discovery of the Syrian extract to the present time (1845–1883), which is favorable to the shorter Greek recension.

1. The LARGER GREEK RECENSION OF SEVEN EPISTLES with eight additional ones. Four of them were published in Latin at Paris, 1495, as an appendix to another book; eleven more by Faber Stapulensis, also in Latin, at Paris, 1498; then all fifteen in Greek by Valentine Hartung (called Paceus or Irenæus) at Dillingen, 1557; and twelve by Andreas Gesner at Zurich, 1560. The Catholics at first accepted them all as genuine works of Ignatius; and Hartung, Baronius, Bellarmin defended at least twelve; but Calvin and the Magdeburg Centuriators rejected them all, and later Catholics surrendered at least eight as utterly untenable. These are two Latin letters of Ignatius to St. John and one to the Virgin Mary with an answer of the Virgin; and five Greek letters of Ignatius to Maria Castabolita, with an answer, to the Tarsenses, to the Antiochians, to Hero, a deacon of Antioch, and to the Philippians. These letters swarm with offences against history and chronology. They were entirely unknown to Eusebius and Jerome. They are worthless forgeries, clothed with the name and authority of Ignatius. It is a humiliating fact that the spurious Ignatius and his letters to St. John and the Virgin Mary should in a wretched Latin version have so long transplanted and obscured the historical Ignatius down to the sixteenth century. No wonder that Calvin spoke of this fabrication with such contempt. But in like manner the Mary of history gave way to a Mary of fiction, the real Peter to a pseudo-Peter, and the real Clement to a pseudo-Clement. Here, if anywhere, we see the necessity and use of historical criticism for the defense of truth and honesty.

2. The SHORTER GREEK RECENSION of the seven Epistles known to Eusebius was discovered in a Latin version and edited by Archbishop Ussher at Oxford, 1644 (*Polycarpi et Ignatii Epistolæ*), and in Greek by Isaac Vossius, from a Medicean Codex in 1646, again by Th. Ruinart from the Codex Colbertinus (together with the *Martyrium*) in 1689. We have also fragments of a Syrian version (in Cureton), and of an Armenian version apparently from the Syrian (printed in Constantinople in 1783, and compared by Petermann). Henceforth the longer Greek recension found very few defenders (the eccentric Whiston, 1711, and more recently Fr. C. Meier, 1836), and their arguments were conclusively refuted by R. Rothe in his *Anfänge*, 1837, and by K. Fr. L. Arndt in the "Stu-

dien und Kritiken," 1839). It is generally given up even by Roman Catholic scholars (as Petavius, Cotelier, Dupin, Hefele, Funk). But as regards the genuineness of the shorter Greek text there are three views among which scholars are divided.

(a) Its genuineness and integrity are advocated by Pearson (*Vindiciæ Ignatianæ*, 1672, against the doubts of the acute Dallæus), latterly by Gieseler, Möhler (R. C.), Rothe (1837), Huther (1841), Düsterdieck (1843), Dorner (1845), and (since the publication of the shorter Syriac version) by Jacobson, Hefele (R. C., 1847 and 1855), Denzinger (R. C., 1849), Petermann (1849), Wordsworth, Churton (1852), and most thoroughly by Ulhhorn, (1851 and '56), and Zahn (1873, *Ign. v. Ant.* 495–541). The same view is adopted by Wieseler (1878), Funk (in *Patr. Apost.* 1878, Prol LX. sqq., and his monograph, 1883), Canon Travers Smith, (in Smith and Wace, 1882), and Lightfoot (1885).

(b) The friends of the three Syriac epistles (see below under No. 3) let only so many of the seven epistles stand as agree with those. Also Lardner (1743), Mosheim (1755), Neander (1826), Thiersch (1852), Lechler (1857), Robertson and Donaldson (1867), are inclined to suppose at least interpolation.

(c) The shorter recension, though older than the longer, is likewise spurious. The letters were forged in the later half of the second century for the purpose of promoting episcopacy and the worship of martyrs. This view is ably advocated by two very different classes of divines: first by Calvinists in the interest of Presbyterianism or anti-prelacy, Claudius Salmasius (1645), David Blondel (1646), Dallæus (1666), Samuel Bassnage, and by Dr. Killen of Belfast (1859 and 1883) ; next by the Tübingen school of critics in a purely historical interest, Dr. Baur (1835, then against Rothe, 1838, and against Bunsen, 1848 and 1853), Schwegler (1846), and more thoroughly by Hilgenfeld (1853). The Tübingen critics reject the whole Ignatian literature as unhistorical tendency writings, partly because the entire historical situation implied in it and the circuitous journey to Rome are in themselves improbable, partly because it advocates a form of church government and combats Gnostic heresies, which could not have existed in the age of Ignatius. This extreme scepticism is closely connected with the whole view of the Tübingen school in regard to the history of primitive Christianity, and offers no explanation of the stubborn fact that Ignatius was a historical character of a strongly marked individuality and wrote a number of letters widely known and appreciated in the early church. Renan admits the genuineness of the Ep. to the Romans, but rejects the six others as fabrications of a zealous partizan of orthodoxy and episcopacy about A. D. 170. He misses in them *le génie, le caractère individuel*, but speaks highly of the Ep. to the Romans, in which the enthusiasm of the martyr has found "*son expression la plus exaltée*" (p. 489).

(d) We grant that the integrity of these epistles, even in the shorter copy, is not beyond all reasonable doubt. As the manuscripts of them con tain, at the same time, decidedly spurious epistles (even the Armenian translation has thirteen epistles), the suspicion arises, that the seven genuine also have not wholly escaped the hand of the forger. Yet there are, in any case, very strong arguments for their genuineness and substantial integrity; viz. (1) The testimony of the fathers, especially of Eusebius. Even Polycarp alludes to epistles of Ignatius. (2) The raciness and freshness of their contents, which a forger could not well imitate. (3) The small number of citations from the New Testament, indicating the period of the immediate disciples of the apostles. (4) Their way of combating the Judaists and Docetists (probably Judaizing Gnostics of the school of Cerinthus), showing us Gnosticism as yet in the first stage of its development. (5) Their dogmatical indefiniteness, particularly in regard to the Trinity and Christology, notwithstanding very strong expressions in favor of the divinity of Christ. (6) Their urgent recommendation of episcopacy as an institution still new and fresh, and as a centre of *congregational* unity in distinction from the *diocesan* episcopacy of Irenæus and Tertullian. (7) Their entire silence respecting a Roman primacy, even in the epistle to the Romans, where we should most expect it. The Roman *church* is highly recommended indeed, but the Roman *bishop* is not even mentioned. In any case these epistles must have been written before the middle of the second century, and reflect the spirit of their age in its strong current towards a hierarchical organization and churchly orthodoxy on the basis of the glory of martyrdom.

3. The SYRIAC VERSION contains only three epistles (to Polycarp, to the Ephesians, and to the Romans), and even these in a much reduced form, less than half of the corresponding Greek Epistles. It has the subscription : "Here end *the three epistles* of the bishop and martyr Ignatius," on which, however, Bunsen lays too great stress ; for, even if it comes from the translator himself, and not from a mere transcriber, it does not necessarily exclude the existence of other epistles (comp. Petermann, *l. c. p.* xxi.). It was discovered in 1839 and '43 by the Rev. Henry Tattam in a monastery of the Libyan desert, together with 365 other Syriac manuscripts, now in the British Museum ; published first by Cureton in 1845, and again in 1849, with the help of a third MS. discovered in 1847 ; and advocated as genuine by him, as also by Lee (1846), Bunsen (1847), Ritschl (1851 and 1857), Weiss (1852), and most fully by Lipsius (1856), also by E. de Pressensé (1862), Böhringer (1873), and at first by Lightfoot.

Now, it is true, that all the considerations we have adduced in favor of the shorter Greek text, except the first, are equally good, and some of them even better, for the genuineness of the Syrian Ignatius, which has the additional advantage of lacking many of the most offensive passages (though not in the epistle to Polycarp).

But against the Syriac text is, in the first place, the external testimony of antiquity, especially that of Eusebius, who confessedly knew of and used seven epistles, whereas the oldest of the three manuscripts of this version, according to Cureton, belongs at the earliest to the sixth century, a period, when the longer copy also had become circulated through all the East, and that too in a Syriac translation, as the fragments given by Cureton show. Secondly, the internal testimony of the fact, that the Syriac text, on close examination, by the want of a proper sequence of thoughts and sentences betrays the character of a fragmentary *extract* from the Greek ; as Baur (1848), Hilgenfeld (1853), and especially Uhlhorn (1851), and Zahn (1873, p. 167–241), by an accurate comparison of the two, have proved in a manner hitherto unrefuted and irrefutable. The short Syriac Ignatius has vanished like a dream. Even Lipsius and Lightfoot have given up or modified their former view. The great work of Lightfoot on Ignatius and Polycarp (1885) which goes into all the details and gives all the documents, may be regarded as a full and final settlement of the Ignatian problem in favor of the shorter Greek recension.

The only genuine Ignatius, as the question now stands, is the Ignatius of the shorter seven Greek epistles.

§ 166. *Polycarp of Smyrna.*

Comp. ¿ 19 and the lit. there quoted.

S. POLYCARPI, *Smyrnæorum episcopi et hieromartyris, ad Philippenses Epistola,* first published in Latin by *Faber Stapulensis* (Paris 1498), then with the Greek original by *Petrus Halloisius* (Halloix), Duæi, 1633 ; and *Jac. Usserius* (Ussher), Lond. 1647 : also in all the editions of the Apost. Fath., especially those of *Jacobson* (who compared several manuscripts), *Zahn* (1876), *Funk* (1878), and *Lightfoot* (1885).

MARTYRIUM S. POLYCARPI (*Epistola circularis ecclesiæ Smyrnensis*), first completed ed. in Gr. & Lat. by Archbp. *Ussher,* Lond. 1647, then in all the ed. of the *Patr. Apost.,* especially that of *Jacobson* (who here also made use of three new codices), of *Zahn,* and *Funk.*

L. DUCHESNE: *Vita Sancti Polycarpi Smyrnæorum episcopi auctore Pionio Primum græce edita.* Paris 1881. The same also in the second vol. of Funk's *Patr. Apost.* (1881) pp. LIV.–LVIII. 315–347. It is, according to Funk, from the fourth or fifth century, and shows not what Polycarp really was, but how he appeared to the Christians of a later age.

ZAHN: *Ign. v. Ant.* p. 495–511 ; and Proleg. to his ed. of Ign. and Pol. (1876), p. XLII–LV.

DONALDSON: *Ap. Fath.* 191–247.

RENAN *L'église chrétienne* (1879), ch. IX. and X. p. 437–466.

LIGHTFOOT : *S. Ign. and S. Polycarp,* (1885), vol. I. 417–704.

POLYCARP, born about A. D. 69 or earlier, a disciple of the apostle John, a younger friend of Ignatius, and the teacher of

Irenæus (between 130 and 140), presided as presbyter-bishop over the church of Smyrna in Asia Minor in the first half of the second century; made a journey to Rome about the year 154, to adjust the Easter dispute; and died at the stake in the persecution under Antoninus Pius A. D. 155, at a great age, having served the Lord six and eighty years.[1] He was not so original and intellectually active as Clement or Ignatius, but a man of truly venerable character, and simple, patriarchal piety. His disciple Irenæus of Lyons (who wrote under Eleutherus, 177–190), in a letter to his fellow-pupil Florinus, who had fallen into the error of Gnosticism, has given us most valuable reminiscences of this "blessed and apostolic presbyter," which show how faithfully he held fast the apostolic tradition, and how he deprecated all departure from it. He remembered vividly his mode of life and personal appearance, his discourses to the people, and his communications respecting the teaching and miracles of the Lord, as he had received them from the mouth of John and other eye-witnesses, in agreement with the Holy Scriptures.[2] In another place, Irenæus says of Polycarp, that he had all the time taught what he had learned from the apostles, and what the church handed down; and relates, that he once called the Gnostic Marcion in Rome, "the first-born of Satan."[3] This is by no means incredible in a disciple of John, who, with all his mildness, forbids his people to salute the deniers of the true divinity and humanity of the Lord;[4] and it is confirmed by a passage in the epistle of Polycarp to the Philippians,[5] where he says: "Whoever doth not confess, that Jesus Christ is come in the flesh, is antichrist,[6] and whoever doth not confess the mystery of the cross, is of the devil; and he, who wrests the words of the Lord according to his own pleasure, and saith, there is no resurrection and judgment, is the first-born of Satan. Therefore would we forsake the empty babbling of this crowd

---

[1] On the change of date from 166 or 167 to 155 or 156, in consequence of Waddington's researches, see p. 50.

[2] Eusebius, *H. E.* V. 20. [3] *Adv. Hær.* iii. 3, § 4. [4] 2 John 10.

[5] Ch. 7. [6] Comp. 1 John 4: 3.

and their false teachings, and turn to the word which hath been given us from the beginning, watching in prayer,[1] continuing in fasting, and most humbly praying God, that he lead us not into temptation,[2] as the Lord hath said : ' The spirit is willing, but the flesh is weak.' " [3]

This epistle to the Philippians consists of fourteen short chapters, and has been published in full since 1633.   It is the only document that remains to us from this last witness of the Johannean age, who wrote several letters to neighboring congregations.   It is mentioned first by his pupil Irenæus ;[4] it was still in public use in the churches of Asia Minor in the time of Jerome as he reports ; and its contents corrrespond with the known life and character of Polycarp ; its genuineness there is no just reason to doubt.[5]   It has little merit as a literary production, but is simple and earnest, and breathes a noble Christian spirit. It was written after the death of Ignatius (whose epistles are mentioned, c. 13) in the name of Polycarp and his presbyters ; commends the Philippians for the love they showed Ignatius in bonds and his companions, and for their adherence to the ancient faith ; and proceeds with simple, earnest exhortation to love, harmony, contentment, patience, and perseverance, to prayer even for enemies and persecutors ; also giving special directions for deacons, presbyters, youths, wives, widows, and virgins ; with strokes against Gnostic Docetic errors.   Of Christ it speaks in high terms, as the Lord, who sits at the right hand of God to whom everything in heaven and earth is subject ; whom

---

[1] Comp. 1 Pet. 4 : 17.   [2] Matt. 6 : 13.   [3] Matt. 26 : 41.

[4] *Adv. Hær.* III. 3, § 4.   Comp. Euseb. *H. E.* III. 36, and Jerome *De Vir. ill.* c. 17.

[5] Nor has its integrity been called in question with sufficient reason by Dallæus, and more recently by Bunsen, Ritschl (in the second ed of his *Entstehung der altkath. Kirche,* p. 584–600), Renan (*Journal des savants,* 1874, and less confidently in *L'église chret.,* 1879, p. 442 sqq.), and the author of *Supernatural Religion* (I. 274–278).   But the genuineness and integrity of the Ep. are ably vindicated by Zahn (1873) and by Lightfoot ("Contemp. Rev.," Feb. 1875, p. 838–852).   The testimony of Irenæus, who knew it (*Adv. Hær.* III. 3, § 4), is conclusive.   Renan urges chiefly the want of originality and force against it.

every living being serves; who is coming to judge the quick and
the dead; whose blood God will require of all, who believe not
on him.[1] Polycarp guards with sound feeling against being considered equal with the apostles: " I write these things, brethren,
not in arrogance, but because ye have requested me. For
neither I, nor any other like me, can attain the wisdom of the
blessed and glorious Paul, who was among you, and in the
presence of the then living accurately and firmly taught the
word of truth, who also in his absence wrote you an epistle,[2]
from which ye may edify yourselves in the faith given to you,
which is the mother of us all,[3] hope following after, and love to
God and to Christ, and to neighbors leading further.[4] For
when any one is full of these virtues, he fulfills the command of
righteousness ; for he, who has love, is far from all sin." [5] This
does not agree altogether with the system of St. Paul. But it
should be remembered that Polycarp, in the very first chapter,
represents faith and the whole salvation as the gift of free grace.[6]

The epistle is interwoven with many reminiscences of the
Synoptical Gospels and the epistles of Paul, John and First
Peter, which give to it considerable importance in the history
of the canon.[7]

The *Martyrium S. Polycarpi* (22 chs.), in the form of a circu-
lar letter of the church of Smyrna to the church of Philomelium
in Phrygia, and all "parishes of the Catholic church," appears,
from ch. 18, to have been composed before the first annual celebration of his martyrdom. Eusebius has incorporated in his church
history the greater part of this beautiful memorial, and Ussher
first published it complete in the Greek original, 1647. It
contains an edifying description of the trial and martyrdom of

---

[1] Ch. 2. [2] Ἐπιστολάς must here probably be understood, like the Latin
literae, of one epistle. [3] Gal. 4 : 26. [4] προαγούσης. [5] Ch. 3.

[6] Χάριτί ἐστε σεσωσμένοι οὐκ ἐξ ἔργων, ἀλλά θελήματι θεοῦ, διὰ Ἰησοῦ Χριστοῦ,
comp. Eph. 2: 8, 9.

[7] Funk (I. 573 sq.), counts only 6 quotations from the O. T., but 68 remi-
niscences of passages in Matthew (8), Mark (1), Luke (1), Acts (4), Romans,
Cor., Gal., Eph., Phil., Col., Thess., 1 and 2 Tim., James (1), 1 Pet. (10), 2
Pet. (1?) 1 and 2 John. Comp. the works on the canon of the N. T.

Polycarp, though embellished with some marvellous additions of legendary poesy. When, for example, the pile was kindled, the flames surrounded the body of Polycarp, like the full sail of a ship, without touching it; on the contrary it shone, unhurt, with a gorgeous color, like white baken bread, or like gold and silver in a crucible, and gave forth a lovely fragrance as of precious spices. Then one of the executioners pierced the body of the saint with a spear, and forthwith there flowed such a stream of blood that the fire was extinguished by it. The narrative mentions also a dove which flew up from the burning pile; but the reading is corrupt, and Eusebius, Rufinus, and Nicephorus make no reference to it.[1] The sign of a dove (which is frequently found on ancient monuments) was probably first marked on the margin, as a symbol of the pure soul of the martyr, or of the power of the Holy Spirit which pervaded him; but the insertion of the word dove in the text suggests an intended contrast to the eagle, which flew up from the ashes of the Roman emperors, and proclaimed their apotheosis, and may thus be connected with the rising worship of martyrs and saints.

Throughout its later chapters this narrative considerably exceeds the sober limits of the Acts of the Apostles in the description of the martyrdom of Stephen and the elder James, and serves to illustrate, in this respect also, the undeniable difference, notwithstanding all the affinity, between the apostolic and the old catholic literature.[2]

---

[1] All sorts of corrections, accordingly, have been proposed for περιστερά in ch. 16; e. g. ἐπ' ἀριστερᾷ, a sinistra, or περὶ στέρνα, or περίπτερα αἵματος (scintillarum instar sanguinis), or περὶ στύρακα, (circa hastile, around the spike). Comp. Hefele: Patr. Ap. p. 288 (4th ed.) note 4; and Funk (5th ed.) 299. Funk reads περὶ στύρακα, which gives good sense. So also the ed. of Gebh. and Harn.

[2] Keim (1873), and Lipsius (1876) reject the whole Martyrium. Steitz (1861), Zahn (1876), and Funk (Prol. XCVII.) the last two chapters as later additions. Donaldson (p. 198 sqq.) assumes several interpolations, which make it unreliable as a historical document, but admits that it is superior to the later martyria by its greater simplicity and the probability of the most part of the narrative, especially the circumstances of the flight and capture of Polycarp.

NOTES.

I. Of all the writings of the Apostolic Fathers the Epistle of Polycarp is the least original, but nearest in tone to the Pastoral Epistles of Paul, and fullest of reminiscences from the New Testament. We give the first four chapters as specimens.

I. " POLYCARP AND THE PRESBYTERS WITH HIM TO THE CONGREGATION OF GOD WHICH SOJOURNS AT PHILIPPI. MERCY AND PEACE BE MULTIPLIED UPON YOU, FROM GOD ALMIGHTY, AND FROM JESUS CHRIST OUR SAVIOUR.

1. " I have greatly rejoiced with you in the joy you have had in our Lord Jesus Christ, in receiving those examples of true charity, and having accompanied, as it well became you, those who were bound with holy chains [Ignatius and his fellow-prisoners, Zosimus and Rufus; comp. ch. 9]; who are the diadems of the truly elect of God and our Lord; and that the strong root of your faith, spoken of in the earliest times, endureth until now, and bringeth forth fruit unto our *Lord Jesus Christ,* who suffered for our sins, but *whom God raised from the dead, having loosed the pains of Hades* [Acts 2: 24]; *in whom though ye see Him not, ye believe, and believing rejoice with joy unspeakable and full of glory* [1 Pet. 1: 8]; into which joy many desire to enter; knowing that *by grace ye are saved,* not *by works* [Eph. 2: 8, 9], but by the will of God through Jesus Christ.

2. " *Wherefore, girding up your loins, serve the Lord in fear* [1 Pet. 1: 13] and truth, as those who have forsaken the vain, empty talk and error of the multitude, and *believed in Him who raised up our Lord Jesus Christ from the dead, and gave him glory* [1 Pet. 1: 21], and a throne at His right hand [comp. Heb. 1: 3; 8: 1; 12: 2]; to whom all things in heaven and on earth are subject. Him every spirit serves. His blood will God require of those who do not believe in Him. But He who raised Him up from the dead will raise up us also, if we do His will, and walk in His commandments, and love what He loved, keeping ourselves from all unrighteousness, covetousness, love of money, evil-speaking, false-witness; *not rendering evil for evil, or reviling for reviling* [1 Pet. 3: 9]; or blow for blow, or cursing for cursing, *remembering the words of the Lord Jesus* [comp. Acts 20: 35] in His teaching: *Judge not, that ye be not judged; forgive, and it shall be forgiven unto you; be merciful, that ye may obtain mercy; with what measure ye mete, it shall be measured to you again* [Matt. 7: 1, 2; Luke 6: 36-38], and once more, *Blessed are the poor, and those that are persecuted for righteosness' sake, for theirs is the kingdom of God* [Luke 6: 20; Matt. 5: 3, 10].

3. " These things, brethren, I write to you concerning righteousness, not because I take anything on myself, but because ye have invited me thereto. For neither I, nor any such as I, can come up to the wisdom of the blessed and glorified Paul. He, when among you, accurately and steadfastly taught the word of truth in the presence of those who were then alive; and when absent from you, he wrote you a letter, which, if you

carefully study, you will find to be the means of building you up in that faith which has been given you, and which, being followed by hope and preceded by love towards God, and Christ, and our neighbor, is *the mother of us all* [Gal. 4: 26]. For if any one be inwardly possessed of these graces, he has fulfilled the command of righteousness, since he that has love is far from all sin.

4. "But *the love of money is a beginning* [ἀρχή, *instead of root, ῥίζη*] *of all kinds of evil*, [1 Tim. 6: 10]. Knowing, therefore, that *as we brought nothing into the world, so we can carry nothing out*, [1 Tim. 6: 7], let us arm ourselves with the armor of righteousness; and let us teach, first of all, ourselves to walk in the commandments of the Lord. Next teach your wives to walk in the faith given to them, and in love and purity tenderly loving their own husbands in all truth, and loving all equally in all chastity; and to train up their children in the knowledge and fear of God [comp. Eph. 6: 11, 13, 14]. Let us teach the widows to be discreet as respects the faith of the Lord, praying continually for all, being far from all slandering, evil-speaking, false-witnessing, love of money, and every kind of evil; knowing that they are the altar of God, that He clearly perceives all things, and that nothing is hid from Him, neither reasonings, nor reflections, nor any one of the secret things of the heart."

II. From the *Martyrium Polycarpi.* When the Proconsul demanded that Polycarp should swear by the genius of Cæsar and renounce Christ, he gave the memorable answer:

"Eighty and six years have I served Christ, nor has He ever done me any harm. How, then, could I blaspheme my King who saved me" (τὸν βασιλέα μου τὸν σώσαντά με)? Ch. 9.

Standing at the stake with his hands tied to the back, as the fagots were kindled, Polycarp lifted up his voice and uttered this sublime prayer as reported by disciples who heard it (ch. 14):

"Lord God Almighty, Father of Thy beloved and blessed Son, Jesus Christ, through whom we have received the grace of knowing Thee; God of angels and powers, and the whole creation, and of the whole race of the righteous who live in Thy presence; I bless Thee for deigning me worthy of this day and this hour that I may be among Thy martyrs and drink of the cup of my Lord Jesus Christ, unto the resurrection of eternal life of soul and body in the incorruption of the Holy Spirit. Receive me this day into Thy presence together with them, as a fair and acceptable sacrifice prepared for Thyself in fulfillment of Thy promise, O true and faithful God. Wherefore I praise Thee for all Thy mercies; I bless Thee, I glorify Thee, through the eternal High-Priest, Jesus Christ, Thy beloved Son, with whom to Thyself and the Holy Spirit, be glory both now and forever. Amen."

For a good popular description of Polycarp, including his letter and martyrdom, see *The Pupils of St. John the Divine, by the Author of the Heir of Redcliffe*, in Macmillan's "Sunday Library," London 1863.

§ 167. *Barnabas.*

EDITIONS.

First editions in Greek and Latin, except the first four chapters and part of the fifth, which were known only in the Latin version, by Archbishop USSHER (Oxf. 1643, destroyed by fire 1644), LUC. D'ACHERY (Par. 1645), and ISAAC VOSS (Amstel. 1646).

First complete edition of the Greek original from the *Codex Sinaiticus,* to which it is appended, by TISCHENDORF in the facsimile ed. of that Codex, Petropoli, 1862, Tom. IV. 135–141, and in the *Novum Testam. Sinait.* 1863. The text dates from the fourth century. It was discovered by Tischendorf in the Convent of St. Catharine at Mt. Sinai, 1859, and is now in the library of St. Petersburg.

A new MS. of the Greek B. from the eleventh century (1056) was discovered in Constantinople by BRYENNIOS, 1875, together with the Ep. of Clement, and has been utilized by the latest editors, especially by Hilgenfeld.

O. V. GEBHARDT, HARNACK, and ZAHN: *Patr. Ap.* 1876. Gebhardt ed. the text from Cod. Sin. Harnack prepared the critical commentary. In the small ed. of 1877 the Const. Cod. is also compared.

HEFELE—FUNK: *Patr. Ap.* 1878, p. 2–59.

AD. HILGENFELD: *Barnabæ Epistula. Integram Grœce iterum edidit, veterem interpretationem Latinam, commentarium criticum et adnotationes addidit A. H. Ed. altera et valde aucta.* Lips. 1877. Dedicated to Bryennios, " *Orientalis Ecclesiæ splendido lumini,*" who being prevented by the Oriental troubles from editing the new MS., sent a collation to H. in Oct. 1876 (*Prol.* p. XIII). The best critical edition. Comp. Harnack's review in Schürer's "Theol. Lit. Ztg." 1877, f. 473–'77.

J. G. MÜLLER (of Basle): *Erklärung des Barnabasbriefes.* Leipz. 1869. An Appendix to De Wette's Com. on the N. T.

English translations by WAKE (1693), ROBERTS and DONALDSON (in Ante-Nic. Lib. 1867), HOOLE (1872), RENDALL (1877), SHARPE (1880, from the Sinait. MS). German translations by HEFELE (1840), SCHOLZ (1865), MAYER (1869), RIGGENBACH (1873).

CRITICAL DISCUSSIONS.

C. JOS. HEFELE (R. C.): *Das Sendschreiben des Apostels Barnabas, auf's Neue untersucht und erklärt.* Tüb. 1840.

JOH. KAYSER: *Ueber den sogen. Barnabasbrief.* Paderborn, 1866.

DONALDSON: *Ap. Fathers* (1874), p. 248–317.

K. WIESELER: *On the Origin and Authorship of the Ep. of B.,* in the "Jahrbücher für Deutsche Theol.," 1870, p. 603 sqq.

O. BRAUNSBERGER (R. C.): *Der Apostel Barnabas. Sein Leben und der ihm beigelegte Brief wissenschaftlich gewürdigt.* Mainz, 1876.

W. CUNNINGHAM : *The Ep. of St. Barnabas.* London, 1876.
SAMUEL SHARPE : *The Ep. of B. from the Sinaitic MS.* London, 1880.
J. WEISS : *Der Barnabasbrief kritisch untersucht.* Berlin, 1888.
MILLIGAN in Smith and Wace, I. 260–265; Harnack in Herzog² II.
101–105.

Other essays by HENKE (1827), RÖRDAM (1828), ULLMANN
(1828), SCHENKEL (1837), FRANKE (1840), WEIZSÄCKER (1864),
HEYDECKE (1874). On the relation of Barnabas to Justin Martyr
see M. von Engelhardt : *Das Christenthum Justins d. M.* (1878), p.
375–394.

The doctrines of B. are fully treated by HEFELE, KAYSER,
DONALDSON, HILGENFELD, BRAUNSBERGER, and SPRINZL.

Comp. the list of books from 1822–1875 in HARNACK'S *Prol.* to the
Leipz. ed. of *Barn. Ep.* p. xx sqq.; and in RICHARDSON, *Synopsis*,
16–19 (down to 1887).

The CATHOLIC EPISTLE OF BARNABAS, so called, is anonymous, and omits all allusion to the name or residence of the
readers. He addresses them not as their teacher, but as one
among them.[1] He commences in a very general way : " All
hail, ye sons and daughters, in the name of our Lord Jesus
Christ, who loved us, in peace ; " and concludes : " Farewell, ye
children of love and peace, The Lord of glory and all grace be
with your spirit. Amen."[2] For this reason, probably, Origen
called it a " Catholic " Epistle, which must be understood,
however, with limitation. Though not addressed to any particular congregation, it is intended for a particular class of
Christians who were in danger of relapsing into Judaizing
errors.

1. CONTENTS. The epistle is chiefly doctrinal (ch. 1–17),
and winds up with some practical exhortations to walk " in the
way of light," and to avoid "the way of darkness" (ch. 18–21).[3]

---

[1] οὐχ ὡς διδάσκαλος, ἀλλ᾽ ὡς εἷς ἐξ ὑμῶν, ch. 1 ; comp. 4 : πολλὰ θέλων γράφειν,
οὐχ ὡς διδάσκαλος.

[2] The Cod. Sinaiticus omits "Amen," and adds at the close : Ἐπιστολὴ
Βαρνάβα.

[3] The last chapters are derived either from the *Didache*, or from a still older
work, *Duæ Viæ vel Judicium Petri*, which may have been the common source
of both. See my work on the *Didache*, p. 227 sqq., 305, 309, 312 sq., 317.

It has essentially the same object as the Epistle to the Hebrews, though far below it in depth, originality and unction. It shows that Christianity is the all-sufficient, divine institution for salvation, and an abrogation of Judaism, with all its laws and ceremonies. Old things have passed away; all things are made new. Christ has indeed given us a law; but it is a *new* law, without the yoke of constraint.[1] The tables of Moses are broken that the love of Christ may be sealed in our hearts.[2] It is therefore sin and folly to assert that the old covenant is still binding. Christians should strive after higher knowledge and understand the difference.

By Judaism, however, the author understands not the Mosaic and prophetic writings in their true spiritual sense, but the carnal misapprehension of them. The Old Testament is, with him, rather a veiled Christianity, which he puts into it by a mystical allegorical interpretation, as Philo, by the same method, smuggled into it the Platonic philosophy. In this allegorical conception he goes so far, that he actually seems to deny the literal historical sense. He asserts, for example, that God never willed the sacrifice and fasting, the Sabbath observance and temple-worship of the Jews, but a purely spiritual worship; and that the laws of food did not relate at all to the eating of clean and unclean animals, but only to intercourse with different classes of men, and to certain virtues and vices. His chiliasm likewise rests on an allegorical exegesis, and is no proof of a Judaizing tendency any more than in Justin, Irenæus, and Tertullian. He sees in the six days of creation a type of six historical millennia of work to be followed first by the seventh millennium of rest, and then by the eighth millennium of eternity, the latter being foreshadowed by the weekly Lord's Day. The carnal Jewish interpretation of the Old Testament is a diabolical perversion. The Christians, and not the Jews, are the true Israel of God and the righteous owners of the Old Testament Scriptures.

[1] Ch. 2: ὁ καινὸς νόμος τοῦ Κυρίου ἡμῶν ᾽Ι. Χ., ἄνευ (ἄτερ) ζυγοῦ ἀνάγκης ὤν.

[2] Ch. 4: συνετρίβη αὐτῶν ἡ διαθήκη, ἵνα ἡ τοῦ ἠγαπημένου ᾽Ιησοῦ ἐγκατασφραγισθῇ εἰς τὴν καρδίαν ἡμῶν ἐν ἐλπίδι τῆς πίστεως αὐτοῦ.

Barnabas proclaims thus an absolute separation of Christianity from Judaism. In this respect he goes further than any post-apostolic writer. He has been on that ground charged with unsound ultra-Paulinism bordering on antinomianism and heretical Gnosticism. But this is unjust. He breathes the spirit of Paul, and only lacks his depth, wisdom, and discrimination. Paul, in Galatians and Colossians, likewise takes an uncompromising attitude against Jewish circumcision, sabbatarianism, and ceremonialism, if made a ground of justification and a binding yoke of conscience; but nevertheless he vindicated the Mosaic law as a preparatory school for Christianity. Barnabas ignores this, and looks only at the negative side. Yet he, too, acknowledges the new *law* of Christ. He has some profound glances and inklings of a Christian philosophy. He may be called an orthodox Gnostic. He stands midway between St. Paul and Justin Martyr, as Justin Martyr stands between Barnabas and the Alexandrian school. Clement and Origen, while averse to his chiliasm, liked his zeal for higher Christian knowledge and his allegorizing exegesis which obscures every proper historical understanding of the Old Testament.

The Epistle of Barnabas has considerable historical, doctrinal, and apologetic value. He confirms the principal facts and doctrines of the gospel. He testifies to the general observance of Sunday on "the eighth day," as the joyful commemoration of Christ's resurrection, in strict distinction from the Jewish Sabbath on the seventh. He furnishes the first clear argument for the canonical authority of the Gospel of Matthew (without naming it) by quoting the passage: "Many are called, but few are chosen," with the solemn formula of Scripture quotation: "as it is written."[1] He introduces also (ch. 5) the words of

---

[1] Cap. 4 at the close: προσέχωμεν μήποτε, ὡς γέγραπται, πολλοὶ κλητοὶ, ὀλίγοι δὲ ἐκλεκτοὶ εὑρεθῶμεν. From Matt. 22: 14. As long as the fourth chapter of this epistle existed only in Latin, the words: "*sicut scriptum est*" were suspected by Dr. Credner and other critics as an interpolation. Hilgenfeld (1853) suggested that the original had simply καθὼς φησιν, and Dressel, in his first edition of the *Apostolic Fathers* (1857), remarked *in loc:* "*Voces ' sicut scriptum est' glos-*

Christ, that he did not come "to call just men, but sinners," which are recorded by Matthew (9: 13). He furnishes parallels to a number of passages in the Gospels, Pauline Epistles, First Peter, and the Apocalypse. His direct quotations from the Old Testament, especially the Pentateuch, the Psalms, and Isaiah, are numerous; but he quotes also IV. Esdras and the Book of Enoch.[1]

2. AUTHORSHIP. The Epistle was first cited by Clement of Alexandria, and Origen, as a work of the apostolic Barnabas, who plays so prominent a part in the early history of the church.[2] Origen seems to rank it almost with the inspired Scriptures. In the Sinaitic Bible, of the fourth century, it follows as the "Epistle of Barnabas," immediately after the Apocalypse (even on the same page 135, second column), as if it were a regular part of the New Testament. From this we may infer that it was read in some churches as a secondary ecclesiastical book, like the Epistle of Clement, the Epistle of Polycarp, and the Pastor of Hermas. Eusebius and Jerome likewise ascribe it to Barnabas, but number it among the "spurious," or

sam olent." But the discovery of the Greek original in the Sinaitic MS. of the Bible has settled this point, and the Constantinopolitan MS. confirms it. The attempt of Strauss and other sceptics to refer the quotation to the apocryphal fourth Book of Esdras, which was probably written by a Jewish Christian after the destruction of Jerusalem, and contains the passage: 'Many are *born*, but few will be *saved*," is only worth mentioning as an instance of the stubbornness of preconceived prejudice.

[1] Funk (I. 364–366) gives nine quotations from Genesis, thirteen from Exodus, six from Deuteronomy, fourteen from the Psalms, twenty-six from Isaiah, etc., also one from IV. Esdras, four from Enoch. Comp. the list in Anger's *Synopsis Evang.* (1852), Gebh. and Harn., 217–230.

[2] See Acts 1: 23; 4: 37; 9: 26 sq.; 11: 22, 30; 14: 4, 14; 15: 2, etc. Clement of Alex. quotes the Epistle seven times (four times under the name of Barnabas), in his *Stromata*, Origen, his pupil, three or four times (*Contra Cels.* I. 63; *De Princ.* III. 2; *Ad Rom.* I. 24). Tertullian does not mention the epistle, but seems to have known it (comp. *Adv. Marc.* III. 7; *Adv. Jud.* 14); he, however, ascribes the Ep. to the Hebrews to Barnabas (*De Pudic.* c. 20). Hefele and Funk find probable allusions to it in Irenæus, Justin Martyr, Ignatius, and Hermas; but these are uncertain. On the life and labors of Barnabas see especially Hefele and Braunsberger (p. 1–135).

"apocryphal" writings.[1] They seem to have doubted the authority, but not the authenticity of the epistle. The historical testimony therefore is strong and unanimous in favor of Barnabas, and is accepted by all the older editors and several of the later critics.[2]

But the internal evidence points with greater force to a post-apostolic writer.[3] The Epistle does not come up to the position and reputation of Barnabas, the senior companion of Paul, unless we assume that he was a man of inferior ability and gradually vanished before the rising star of his friend from Tarsus. It takes extreme ground against the Mosaic law, such as we can hardly expect from one who stood as a mediator between the Apostle of the Gentiles and the Jewish Apostles, and who in the collision at Antioch sided with Peter and Mark against the bold champion of freedom; yet we should remember that this was only a temporary inconsistency, and that no doubt a reaction afterwards took place in his mind. The author in order to glorify the grace of the Saviour, speaks of the apostles of Christ before their conversion as over-sinful,[4] and

---

[1] In *H. E.* III. 25, Eusebius counts it among the "spurious" books (ἐν τοῖς νόθοις . . . ἡ φερομένη Βαρνάβα ἐπιστολή), but immediately afterwards and in VI. 14, among the "doubtful" (ἀντιλεγόμενα), and Jerome (*De Vir. ill.* c. 6), "*inter apocryphas scripturas.*"

[2] Voss, Dupin, Gallandi, Cave, Pearson, Lardner, Henke, Rördam, Schneckenburger, Franke, Gieseler, Credner, Bleek (formerly), De Wette, Möhler, Alzog, Sprinzl ("genuine, but not inspired"), Sharpe. The interpolation hypothesis of Schenkel (1837) and Heydeke (1874) is untenable; the book must stand or fall as a whole.

[3] So Ussher, Daillé, Cotelier, Tillemont, Mosheim, Neander, Ullmann, Baur, Hilgenfeld, Hefele, Döllinger, Kayser, Donaldson, Westcott, Müller, Wieseler, Weizsäcker, Braunsberger, Harnack, Funk. Hefele urges eight arguments against the genuineness; but five of them are entirely inconclusive. See Milligan, *l. c.*, who examines them carefully and concludes that the authenticity of the Epistle is more probable than is now commonly supposed.

[4] Or "sinners above all sin," ὑπὲρ πᾶσαν ἁμαρτίαν ἀνομωτέρους, *homines omni peccato iniquiores*, c. 5. Paul might call himself in genuine humility "the chief of sinners" (1 Tim. 1: 15), with reference to his former conduct as a persecutor; but he certainly would not have used such a term of all the apostles, nor would it be true of any of them but Judas.

indulges in artificial and absurd allegorical fancies.[1] He also wrote after the destruction of Jerusalem when Barnabas in all probability was no more among the living, though the date of his death is unknown, and the inference from Col. 4: 10 and 1 Pet. 5: 13 is uncertain.

These arguments are not conclusive, it is true, but it is quite certain that if Barnabas wrote this epistle, he cannot be the author of the Epistle to the Hebrews, and *vice versa*. The difference between the two is too great for the unity of the authorship. The ancient church showed sound tact in excluding that book from the canon; while a genuine product of the apostolic Barnabas[2] had a claim to be admitted into it as well as the anonymous Epistle to the Hebrews or the writings of Mark and Luke.

The author was probably a converted Jew from Alexandria (perhaps by the name Barnabas, which would easily explain the confusion), to judge from his familiarity with Jewish literature, and, apparently, with Philo and his allegorical method in handling the Old Testament. In Egypt his Epistle was first known and most esteemed; and the Sinaitic Bible which contains it was probably written in Alexandria or Cæsarea in Palestine. The readers were chiefly Jewish Christians in Egypt and the East, who overestimated the Mosaic traditions and ceremonies.[3]

[1] He is also charged with several blunders concerning Jewish history and worship which can hardly be expected from Barnabas the Levite. Comp. chs. 7, 8, 9, 10, 15. But this is disproved by Braunsberger (p. 253 sqq.), who shows that the epistle gives us interesting archæological information in those chapters, although he denies the genuineness.

[2] He is twice called an apostle, Acts 14: 4, 14, being included with Paul in ἀπόστολοι.

[3] So Neander, Möhler, Hefele (1840), Funk, Güdemann. On the other hand, Lardner, Donaldson, Hilgenfeld, Kayser, Riggenbach, Hefele (1868), Braunsberger, Harnack contend that Barnabas and his readers were *Gentile* Christians, because he distinguishes himself and his readers (ἡμεῖς) from the Jews chs. 2, 3, 4, 8, 10, 14, 16. But the same distinction is uniformly made by John in the Gospel, and was quite natural after the final separation between the church and the synagogue. The mistakes in Jewish history are doubtful and less numerous than the proofs of the writer's familiarity with it. The strongest passage is ch. 16: "Before we became believers in God, the house of our heart

3. TIME of composition. The work was written after the destruction of Jerusalem and the temple, which is alluded to as an accomplished fact;[1] yet probably before the close of the first century, certainly before the reconstruction of Jerusalem under Hadrian (120).[2]

§ 168. *Hermas.*

EDITIONS.

The older editions give only the imperfect Latin Version, first published by FABER STAPULENSIS (Par. 1513). Other Latin MSS. were discovered since. The Greek text (brought from Mt. Athos by Constantine Simonides, and called *Cod. Lipsiensis*) was first published by R. ANGER, with a preface by G. DINDORF (Lips. 1856); then by TISCHENDORF, in Dressel's *Patres Apost.*, Lips 1857 (p. 572–637); again in the second ed. 1863, where Tischendorf, in consequence of the intervening discovery of the Cod. Sinaiticus retracted his former objections to the originality of the Greek Hermas from

was . . . full of *idolatry* and the house of *demons,* because we did what was contrary to God's will." But even this, though more applicable to heathen, is not inapplicable to Jews; nor need we suppose that there were *no* Gentiles among the readers. Towards the close of the second century there were probably very few unmixed congregations. Lipsius and Volkmar seek the readers in Rome, Müller in Asia Minor, Schenkel, Hilgenfeld, Harnack, and Funk in Alexandria or Egypt. There is a similar difference of opinion concerning the readers of the Epistle to the Hebrews.

[1] Ch. 16 compared with the explanation of Daniel's prophecy of the little horn in ch. 4.

[2] Hefele, Kayser, Baur, Müller, Lipsius, put the composition between 107 and 120 (before the building of Ælia Capitolina under Hadrian), and Braunsberger between 110 and 137; but Hilgenfeld, Reuss (*Gesch. d. N. T.*, 4th ed., 1864, p. 233), Ewald (*Gesch. d. Volkes Israel*, VII. 136), Weizsäcker ("in Jahrb. für Deutsch. Theol.," 1865, p. 391, and 1871, p. 569), Wieseler (*Ibid.* 1870, p. 603-614), and Funk (*Prol.* p. VI.), at the close of the first century, or even before 79. Wieseler argues from the author's interpretation of Daniel's prophecy concerning the ten kingdoms and the little horn (ch. 4 and 16), that the Ep. was written under Domitian, the eleventh Rom. emperor, and "the little horn" of Daniel. Weiszäcker and Cunningham refer the little horn to Vespasian (79–79), Hilgenfeld to Nerva; but even in the last case the Ep. would have been written before A. D. 98, when Nerva died. Milligan concludes that it was written very soon after the destruction of Jerusalem. But in fresh view of that terrible judgment, we can scarcely account for the danger of apostasy to Judaism. The author's aim seems to pre-suppose a revival of Judaism and of Jewish tendencies within the Christian Church.

Mt. Athos, which he had pronounced a mediæval retranslation from the Latin (see the *Proleg.*, *Appendix and Preface* to the second ed.). The Ποιμὴν ὅρασις is also printed in the fourth vol. of the large edition of the Codex Sinaiticus, at the close (pp. 142–148), Petersb. 1862. The texts from Mt. Athos and Mt. Sinai substantially agree. An Ethiopic translation appeared in Leipz. 1860, ed. with a Latin version by ANT. D' ABBADIE. Comp. DILLMANN in the "Zeitschrift d. D. Morgenländ. Gesellschaft" for 1861; SCHODDE: *Hêrmâ Nabî, the Ethiop. V. of P. H. examined.* Leipz. 1876 (criticised by Harnack in the "Theol. Lit. Ztg.," 1877, fol. 58), and G. and H's *Proleg.* XXXIV. sqq.

O. v. GEBHARDT, and HARNACK : *Patrum Apost. Opera,* Fascic. III. Lips. 1877. Greek and Latin. A very careful recension of the text (from the Sinaitic MS.) by v. Gebhardt, with ample Prolegomena (84 pages), and a critical and historical commentary by Harnack.

FUNK's fifth ed. of Hefele's *Patres Apost.* I. 334–563. Gr. and Lat. Follows mostly the text of Von Gebhardt.

AD. HILGENFELD : *Hermæ Pastor. Græce e codicibus Sinaitico et Lipsiensi . . . restituit,* etc. *Ed. altera emendata et valde aucta.* Lips. 1881. With Prolegomena and critical annotations (257 pp.). By the same : *Hermæ Pastor Græce integrum ambitu.* Lips., 1887 (pp. 130). From the Athos and Sinaitic MSS.

S. P. LAMBROS (Prof. in Athens): *A Collation of the Athos Codex of the Shepherd of Hermas, together with an Introduction.* Translated and edited by J. A. ROBINSON, Cambridge, 1888.

English translations by WAKE (1693, from the Latin version) ; F. CROMBIE (vol. I. of the "Ante-Nicene Christian Library," 1867, from the Greek of the Sinait. MS.), by CHARLES H. HOLE (1870, from Hilgenfeld's first ed. of 1866,) and by ROBINSON (1888).

ESSAYS.

C. REINH. JACHMANN : *Der Hirte des Hermas.* Königsberg, 1835.

ERNST GAÂB : *Der Hirte des Hermas.* Basel, 1866 (pp. 203).

THEOD. ZAHN : *Der Hirt des Hermas.* Gotha 1868. (Comp. also his review of Gaâb in the *Studien und Kritiken* for 1868, pp. 319–349).

CHARLES H. HOOLE (of Christ Church, Oxf.) : *The Shepherd of Hermas translated into English, with an Introduction and Notes.* Lond., Oxf. and Cambr. 1870 (184 pages).

GUST. HEYNE : *Quo tempore Hermæ Pastor scriptus sit.* Regimonti, 1872.

J. DONALDSON : *The Apostolical Fathers* (1874) p. 318–392.

H. M. BEHM : *Der Verfasser der Schrift., welche d. Titel "Hirt" führt.* Rostock, 1876 (71 pp.).

BRÜLL : *Der Hirt des Hermas. Nach Ursprung und Inhalt untersucht.* Freiburg i. B. 1882. The same : *Ueber den Ursprung des ersten Clemensbriefs und des Hirten des Hermas.* 1882.

Ad. Link : *Christi Person und Werk im Hirten des Hermas.* Marburg, 1886. *Die Einheit des Pastor Hermæ.* Marb. 1888. Defends the unity of Hermas against Hilgenfeld.

P. Baumgärtner : *Die Einheit des Hermas-Buches.* Freiburg, 1889. He mediates between Hilgenfeld and Link, and holds that the book was written by one author, but at different times.

I. The Shepherd of Hermas[1] has its title from the circumstance that the author calls himself Hermas and is instructed by the angel of repentance in the costume of a shepherd. It is distinguished from all the productions of the apostolic fathers by its literary form. It is the oldest Christian allegory, an apocalyptic book, a sort of didactic religious romance. This accounts in part for its great popularity in the ancient church. It has often been compared with Bunyan's Pilgrim's Progress and Dante's Divina Commedia, though far inferior in literary merit and widely different in theology from either. For a long time it was only known in an old, inaccurate Latin translation, which was first published by Faber Stapulensis in 1513; but since 1856 and 1862, we have it also in the original Greek, in two texts, one hailing from Mount Athos, re-discovered and compared by Lambros, and another (incomplete) from Mount Sinai.

II. Character and Contents. The Pastor Hermæ is a sort of system of Christian morality in an allegorical dress, and a call to repentance and to renovation of the already somewhat slumbering and secularized church in view of the speedily approaching day of judgment. It falls into three books:[2]

(1) *Visions;* four visions and revelations, which were given to the author, and in which the church appears to him first in the form of a venerable matron in shining garments with a book, then as a tower, and lastly as a virgin. All the visions have for their object to call Hermas and through him the church to repentance, which is now possible, but will close when the church tower is completed.

It is difficult to decide whether the writer actually had or imagined himself to have had those visions, or invented them as

---

[1] *Pastor Hermæ,* 'Ο Ποιμήν. Comp. *Vis.* I. 1, 2, 4; II. 2.

[2] This division, however, is made by later editors.

a pleasing and effective mode of instruction, like Dante's vision and Bunyan's dream.

(2) *Mandats*, or twelve commandments, prescribed by a guardian angel in the garb of a shepherd.

(3) *Similitudes*, or ten parables, in which the church again appears, but now in the form of a building, and the different virtues are represented under the figures of stones and trees. The similitudes were no doubt suggested by the parables of the gospel, but bear no comparison with them for beauty and significance.

The scene is laid in Rome and the neighborhood. The Tiber is named, but no allusion is made to the palaces, the court, the people and society of Rome, or to any classical work. An old lady, virgins, and angels appear, but the only persons mentioned by name are Hermas, Maximus, Clement and Grapte.

The literary merit of the Shepherd is insignificant. It differs widely from apostolic simplicity and has now only an antiquarian interest, like the pictures and sculptures of the catacombs. It is prosy, frigid, monotonous, repetitious, overloaded with uninteresting details, but animated by a pure love of nature and an ardent zeal for doing good. The author was a self-made man of the people, ignorant of the classics and ignored by them, but endowed with the imaginative faculty and a talent for popular religious instruction. He derives lessons of wisdom and piety from shepherd and sheep, vineyards and pastures, towers and villas, and the language and events of every-day life.

The first Vision is a fair specimen of the book, which opens like a love story, but soon takes a serious turn. The following is a faithful translation:

1. " He who had brought me up, sold me to a certain Rhoda at Rome.[1] Many years after, I met her again and began to love her as a sister. Some time after this, I saw her bathing in the river Tiber, and

[1] So v. Gebh. and Hilgenf. ed. II., with Cod. Sin. But the MSS. vary considerably. The Vatican MS. reads: *vendidit quandam puellam Romæ*. The words εἰς 'Ρώμην would indicate that the writer was not from Rome; but he often confounds εἰς and ἐν.

I gave her my hand and led her out of the river. And when I beheld her beauty, I thought in my heart, saying: 'Happy should I be, if I had a wife of such beauty and goodness.' This was my only thought, and nothing more.

"After some time, as I went into the villages and glorified the creatures of God, for their greatness, and beauty, and power, I fell asleep while walking. And the Spirit seized me and carried me through a certain wilderness through which no man could travel, for the ground was rocky and impassable, on account of the water.

"And when I had crossed the river, I came to a plain; and falling upon my knees, I began to pray unto the Lord and to confess my sins. And while I was praying, the heaven opened, and I beheld the woman that I loved saluting me from heaven, and saying: 'Hail, Hermas!' And when I beheld her, I said unto her: 'Lady, what doest thou here?' But she answered and said: 'I was taken up, in order that I might bring to light thy sins before the Lord.' And I said unto her: 'Hast thou become my accuser?' 'No,' said she; 'but hear the words that I shall say unto thee. God who dwells in heaven, and who made the things that are out of that which is not, and multiplied and increased them on account of his holy church, is angry with thee because thou hast sinned against me.' I answered and said unto her: 'Have I sinned against thee? In what way? Did I ever say unto thee an unseemly word? Did I not always consider thee as a lady? Did I not always respect thee as a sister? Why doest thou utter against me, O Lady, these wicked and foul lies?' But she smiled and said unto me: 'The desire of wickedness has entered into thy heart. Does it not seem to thee an evil thing for a just man, if an evil desire enters into his heart? Yea, it is a sin, and a great one (said she). For the just man devises just things, and by devising just things is his glory established in the heavens, and he finds the Lord merciful unto him in all his ways; but those who desire evil things in their hearts, bring upon themselves death and captivity, especially they who set their affection upon this world, and who glory in their wealth, and lay not hold of the good things to come. The souls of those that have no hope, but have cast themselves and their lives away, shall greatly regret it. But do thou pray unto God, and thy sins shall be healed, and those of thy whole house and of all the saints.'

2. "After she had spoken these words, the heavens were closed, and I remained trembling all over and was sorely troubled. And I said within myself: 'If this sin be set down against me, how can I be saved? or how can I propitiate God for the multitude of my sins? or with what words shall I ask the Lord to have mercy upon me?'

"While I was meditating on these things, and was musing on them in my heart, I beheld in front of me a great white chair made out of fleeces of wool; and there came an aged woman, clad in very shining raiment, and having a book in her hand, and she sat down by herself on the chair and saluted me, saying: 'Hail, Hermas!" And I, sorrowing and weeping, said unto her: 'Hail, Lady!' And she said unto me: 'Why art thou sorrowful, O Hermas, for thou wert wont to be patient, and good-tempered, and always smiling? Why is thy countenance cast down? and why art thou not cheerful?' And I said unto her: 'O Lady, I have been reproached by a most excellent woman, who said unto me that I sinned against her.' And she said unto me: 'Far be it from the servant of God to do this thing. But of a surety a desire after her must have come into thy heart. Such an intent as this brings a charge of sin against the servant of God; for it is an evil and horrible intent that a devout and tried spirit should lust after an evil deed; and especially that the chaste Hermas should do so—he who abstained from every evil desire, and was full of all simplicity, and of great innocence!'

3. "'But [she continued] God is not angry with thee on account of this, but in order that thou mayest convert thy house, which has done iniquity against the Lord, and against you who art their parent. But thou, in thy love for your children (φιλότεκνος ὤν) didst not rebuke thy house, but didst allow it to become dreadfully wicked. On this account is the Lord angry with thee; but He will heal all the evils that happened aforetime in thy house; for through the sins and iniquities of thy household thou hast been corrupted by the affairs of this life. But the mercy of the Lord had compassion upon thee, and upon thy house, and will make thee strong and establish thee in His glory. Only be not slothful, but be of good courage and strengthen thy house. For even as the smith, by smiting his work with the hammer, accomplishes the thing that he wishes, so shall the daily word of righteousness overcome all iniquity. Fail not, therefore, to rebuke thy children, for I know that if they will repent with all their heart, they will be written in the book of life, together with the saints.'

"After these words of hers were ended, she said unto me: 'Dost thou wish to hear me read?' I said unto her: 'Yea, Lady, I do wish it.' She said unto me: 'Be thou a hearer, and listen to the glories of God.' Then I heard, after a great and wonderful fashion, that which my memory was unable to retain; for all the words were terrible, and beyond man's power to bear. The last words, however, I remembered; for they were profitable for us, and gentle: 'Behold the God of power, who by his invisible strength, and His great wisdom, has created the world, and by His magnificent counsel hath crowned His creation with glory, and by His mighty word has fixed the heaven, and founded the earth upon the waters, and by His own wisdom and foresight has formed His holy church, which He has also blessed! Behold, He removes the heavens from their places, and the mountains, and the hills, and the stars, and everything becomes smooth before His elect, that He may give unto them the blessing which He promised them with great glory and joy, if only they shall keep with firm faith the laws of God which they have received.'

4. "When, therefore, she had ended her reading, and had risen up

from the chair, there came four young men, and took up the chair, and departed towards the east.   Then she called me, and touched my breast, and said unto me: 'Hast thou been pleased with my reading?'   And I said unto her: 'Lady, these last things pleased me; but the former were hard and harsh.'   But she spake unto me, saying: 'These last are for the righteous; but the former are for the heathen and the apostates." While she was yet speaking with me, there appeared two men, and they took her up in their arms and departed unto the east, whither also the chair had gone.   And she departed joyfully; and as she departed, she said: 'Be of good courage, O Hermas!'

III. The THEOLOGY of Hermas is ethical and practical.   He is free from speculative opinions and ignorant of theological technicalities.   He views Christianity as a new *law* and lays chief stress on practice.   Herein he resembles James, but he ignores the "liberty" by which James distinguishes the "perfect" Christian law from the imperfect old law of bondage.   He teaches not only the merit, but the supererogatory merit of good works and the sin-atoning virtue of martyrdom.   He knows little or nothing of the gospel, never mentions the word, and has no idea of justifying faith, although he makes faith the chief virtue and the mother of virtues.   He dwells on man's duty and performance more than on God's gracious promises and saving deeds.   In a word, his Christianity is thoroughly legalistic and ascetic, and further off from the evangelical spirit than any other book of the apostolic fathers.   Christ is nowhere named, nor his example held up for imitation (which is the true conception of Christian life); yet he appears as "the Son of God," and is represented as pre-existent and strictly divine.[1] The word Christian never occurs.

But this meagre view of Christianity, far from being heretical or schismatic, is closely connected with catholic orthodoxy as

---

[1] In the *Visions* and *Mandates* the person of the Redeemer is mentioned only three times; in the *Similitudes* Hermas speaks repeatedly of the "Son of God," and seems to identify his pre-existent divine nature with the Holy Spirit. *Sim.* IX. 1 τὸ πνεῦμα τό ἅγιον . . . ὁ θεὸς τοῦ θεοῦ ἐστίν. But a passage in a parable must not be pressed and it is differently explained. Comp. Hilgenfeld, *Ap. Väter*, 166 sq., Harnack's notes on *Sim.* V. 5 and IX. 1 ; the different view of Zahn, 139 sqq. and 245 sqq., and especially Link's monograph quoted above (p. 680).

far as we can judge from hints and figures. Hermas stood in close normal relation to the Roman congregation (either under Clement or Pius), and has an exalted view of the "holy church," as he calls the church universal. He represents her as the first creature of God for which the world was made, as old and ever growing younger; yet he distinguishes this ideal church from the real and represents the latter as corrupt. He may have inferred this conception in part from the Epistle to the Ephesians, the only one of Paul's writings with which he shows himself familiar. He requires water-baptism as indispensable to salvation, even for the pious Jews of the old dispensation, who received it from the apostles in Hades.[1] He does not mention the eucharist, but this is merely accidental. The whole book rests on the idea of an exclusive church out of which there is no salvation. It closes with the characteristic exhortation of the angel : "Do good works, ye who have received earthly blessings from the Lord, that the building of the tower (the church) may not be finished while ye loiter ; for the labor of the building has been interrupted for your sakes. Unless, therefore, ye hasten to do right, the tower will be finished, and ye will be shut out."

Much of the theology of Hermas is drawn from the Jewish apocalyptic writings of pseudo-Enoch, pseudo-Esdras, and the lost Book of Eldad and Medad.[2] So his doctrine of angels. He teaches that six angels were first created and directed the

---

[1] This is the natural interpretation of the curious passage *Simil.* IX. 16: "These apostles and teachers who preached the name of the Son of God, after having fallen asleep in the power and faith of the Son of God, preached to those also who were asleep and gave to them the seal of preaching. They descended therefore into the water with them and again ascended (κατέβησαν οὖν μετ' αὐτῶν εἰς τὸ ὕδωρ καὶ πάλιν ἀνέβησαν). But these descended alive and again ascended alive; but those who had fallen asleep before descended dead (νεκροί) and ascended alive (ξῶντες)." This imaginary *post-mortem* baptism is derived from the preaching of Christ in Hades, 1 Pet. 3: 19; 4: 6. Clement of Alex. quotes this passage with approbation, but supposed that Christ as well as the apostles baptized in Hades. *Strom.* II. 9. 44; VI. 6, 45, 46. Cotelier and Donaldson (p. 380) are wrong in interpreting Hermas as meaning merely a metaphorical and mystical baptism, or the divine blessings symbolized by it.

[2] The last is expressly quoted in the Second Vision.

building of the church. Michael, their chief, writes the law in the hearts of the faithful; the angel of repentance guards the penitent against relapse and seeks to bring back the fallen. Twelve good spirits which bear the names of Christian virtues, and are seen by Hermas in the form of Virgins, conduct the believer into the kingdom of heaven; twelve unclean spirits named from the same number of sins, hinder him. Every man has a good and an evil genius. Even reptiles and other animals have a presiding angel. The last idea Jerome justly condemns as foolish.

It is confusing and misleading to judge Hermas from the apostolic conflict between Jewish and Gentile Christianity.[1] That conflict was over. John shows no traces of it in his Gospel and Epistles. Clement of Rome mentions Peter and Paul as inseparable. The two types had melted into the one Catholic family, and continued there as co-operative elements in the same organization, but were as yet very imperfectly understood, especially the free Gospel of Paul. Jewish and pagan features reappeared, or rather they never disappeared, and exerted their influence for good and evil. Hence there runs through the whole history of Catholicism a legalistic or Judaizing, and an evangelical or Pauline tendency; the latter prevailed in the Reformation and produced Protestant Christianity. Hermas stood nearest to James and furthest from Paul; his friend Clement of Rome stood nearer to Paul and further off from James: but neither one nor the other had any idea of a hostile conflict between the apostles.

IV. Relation to the Scriptures. Hermas is the only one

---

[1] As is done by the Tübingen School, but without unanimity. Schwegler, and, with qualifications, Hilgenfeld and Lipsius represent Hermas as an Ebionite, while Ritschl on the contrary assigns him to the school of Paul. There is no trace whatever in Hermas of the essential features of Ebionism— circumcision, the sabbath, the antipathy to Paul;—nor on the other hand of an understanding of the specific doctrines of Paul. Uhlhorn hits the point (*l. c.* p. 13): "*Hermas ist ein Glied der damaligen orthodoxen Kirche, und seine Auffassung der christlichen Lehre die eines einfachen Gemeindegliedes ohne bestimmte Ausprägung irgend eines Parteicharakters.*"

of the apostolic fathers who abstains from quoting the Old Testament Scriptures and the words of our Lord. This absence is due in part to the prophetic character of the Shepherd, for prophecy is its own warrant, and speaks with divine authority. There are, however, indications that he knew several books of the New Testament, especially the Gospel of Mark, the Epistle of James, and the Epistle to the Ephesians. The name of Paul is nowhere mentioned, but neither are the other apostles. It is wrong, therefore, to infer from this silence an anti-Pauline tendency. Justin Martyr likewise omits the name, but shows acquaintance with the writings of Paul.[1]

V. RELATION TO MONTANISM. The assertion of the prophetic gift and the disciplinarian rigorism Hermas shares with the Montanists; but they arose half a century later, and there is no historic connection. Moreover his zeal for discipline does not run into schismatic excess. He makes remission and absolution after baptism difficult, but not impossible; he ascribes extra merit to celibacy and seems to have regretted his own unhappy marriage, but he allows second marriage as well as second repentance, at least till the return of the Lord which, with Barnabas, he supposes to be near at hand. Hence Tertullian as a Montanist denounced Hermas.

VI. AUTHORSHIP AND TIME OF COMPOSITION. Five opinions are possible. (a) The author was the friend of Paul to whom he sends greetings in Rom. 16 : 14, in the year 58. This is the oldest opinion and accounts best for its high authority.[2] (b) A contemporary of Clement, presbyter-bishop of Rome, A. D. 92–

---

[1] See the list of Scripture allusions of Hermas in Gebhardt's ed. p. 272–274; in Funk's ed. I. 575–578; Hilgenfeld, *Die Ap. Väter*, 182–184; Zahn, *Hermæ Pastore N. T. illustratus*, Gött. 1867; and *D. Hirt d. H.* 391–482. Zahn discovers considerable familiarity of H. with the N. T. writings. On the relation of Hermas to John see Holtzmann, in Hilgenfeld's "Zeitschrift für wissensch. Theol.," 1875, p. 40 sqq.

[2] So Origen (his opinion, *puto enim*, etc.), Eusebius, Jerome, probably also Irenæus and Clement of Alexandria; among recent writers Cotelier, Cave, Lardner, Gallandi, Lumper, Lachmann, Sprinzl.

101. Based upon the testimony of the book itself.[1] (c) A brother of Bishop Pius of Rome (140). So asserts an unknown author of 170 in the Muratorian fragment of the canon.[2] But he may have confounded the older and younger Hermas with the Latin translator.   (d) The book is the work of two or three authors, was begun under Trajan before 112 and completed by the brother of Pius in 140.[3]   (e) Hermas is a fictitious name to lend apostolic authority to the Shepherd. (f) Barely worth mentioning is the isolated assertion of the Ethiopian version that the apostle Paul wrote the Shepherd under the name of Hermas which was given to him by the inhabitants of Lystra.

We adopt the second view, which may be combined with the first. The author calls himself Hermas and professes to be a contemporary of the Roman Clement, who was to send his book to foreign churches.[4] This testimony is clear and must outweigh

---

[1] Gaâb, Zahn, Caspari, Alzog, Salmon (in "Dict. of Chr. Biog." II. 912 sqq.).

[2] "*Pastorem vero nuperrime temporibus nostris in urbe Roma Herma* (*Hermas*) *conscripsit, sedente* [*in*] *cathedra urbis Romae ecclesiae Pio episcopo, fratre ejus. Et ideo legi eum quidem opportet, se*[*d*] *publicare vero in ecclesia populo neque inter prophetas completum* [read: *completos*] *numero, neque inter apostolos, in finem temporum potest.*" The same view is set forth in a poem of pseudo-Tertullian against Marcion :

"*Post hunc* [*Hyginus*] *deinde Pius, Hermas, cui germine frater,*
Angelicus Pastor, qui tradita verba locutus."

It is also contained in the Liberian Catalogue of Roman bishops (A. D. 354), and advocated by Mosheim, Schröckh, Credner, Hefele, Lipsius, Ritschl, Heyne, v. Gebhardt, Harnack, Brüll, Funk, Uhlhorn, Baumgärtner. Others assume that the brother of Pius was the author, but simulated an elder Hermas.

[3] Hilgenfeld designates these authors H. a= Hermas apocalypticus ; H. p. = Hermas pastoralis ; H. s.= Hermas secundarius. See *Prol.* p. XXI. sq. Thiersch, Count de Champagny (*Les Antonins*, ed. III. 1875, T. I, p. 144) and Guéranger likewise assumed more than one author. But the book is a unit. Comp. Harnack versus Hilgenfeld in the "Theol. Literatur-Zeitung" for 1882, f. 249 sqq., Link, Baumgärtner, Lambros, quoted above.

[4] In *Vis.* II. 4 Hermas receives the command to write "two books and to send one to Clement and one to Grapte ; " and Clement was to send the books to foreign cities (εἰς τὰς ἔξω πόλεις). This seems to imply that he was the well known bishop of Rome. Grapte was a deaconess, having charge of

every other. If the Hermas mentioned by Paul was a young disciple in 58, he may well have lived to the age of Trajan, and he expressly represents himself as an aged man at the time when he wrote.

We further learn from the author that he was a rather unfortunate husband and the father of bad children, who had lost his wealth in trade through his own sins and those of his neglected sons, but who awoke to repentance and now came forward himself as a plain preacher of righteousness, though without any official position, and apparently a mere layman.[1] He had been formerly a slave and sold by his master to a certain Christian lady in Rome by the name of Rhoda. It has been inferred from his Greek style that he was born in Egypt and brought up in a Jewish family.[2] But the fact that he first mistook the aged woman who represents the church, for the heathen Sibyl, rather suggests that he was of Gentile origin. We may infer the same from his complete silence about the prophetic Scriptures of the Old Testament. He says nothing of his conversion.

widows and orphans. The opinion of Origen that Clement and Grapte represent the spiritual and literal methods of interpretation is merely an allegorical fancy. Donaldson and Harnack assume that Clement is an unknown person, but this is inconsistent with the assumed authority of that person.

[1] He is told in the Second *Vision*, ch. 2: "Your seed, O Hermas, has sinned against God, and they have blasphemed against the Lord, and in their great wickedness they have betrayed their parents . . . and their iniquities have been filled up. But make known these words to all your children, and to your wife who is to be your sister. For she does not restrain her tongue, with which she commits iniquity; but on hearing these words she will control herself, and will obtain mercy." The words "who is to be your sister" probably refer to future continence or separation. Tillemont and Hefele regard Hermas as a presbyter, but Fleury, Hilgenfeld, Thiersch, Zahn, Uhlhorn and Salmon as a layman. He always speaks of presbyters as if he were not one of them, and severely censures the Roman clergy. Justin Martyr was also a lay-preacher, but with more culture.

[2] Zahn infers from the Jewish Greek idiom of Hermas that he grew up in Jewish circles, and was perhaps acquainted with the Hebrew language. On the other hand Harnack supposes (Notes on *Vis.* I. 1) that Hermas was descended from Christian parents, else he would not have omitted to inform us of his conversion in the house of Rhoda. Hilgenfeld (p. 138) makes Hermas a Jew, but his master, who sold him, a Gentile. Robinson conjectures that he was a Greek slave (*Sim.* IX.) and wrote reminiscences of his youth.

The book was probably written at the close of the first or early in the second century. It shows no trace of a hierarchical organization, and assumes the identity of presbyters and bishops; even Clement of Rome is not called a bishop.[1] The state of the church is indeed described as corrupt, but corruption began already in the apostolic age, as we see from the Epistles and the Apocalypse. At the time of Irenæus the book was held in the highest esteem, which implies its early origin.

VII. AUTHORITY and VALUE. No product of post-apostolic literature has undergone a greater change in public esteem. The Shepherd was a book for the times, but not for all times. To the Christians of the second and third century it had all the charm of a novel from the spirit-world, or as Bunyan's Pilgrims' Progress has at the present day. It was even read in public worship down to the time of Eusebius and Jerome, and added to copies of the Holy Scriptures (as the Codex Sinaiticus, where it follows after the Ep. of Barnabas). Irenæus quotes it as " divine Scripture."[2] The Alexandrian fathers, who with all

---

[1] The church officers appear as a plurality of πρεσβύτεροι, or *seniores*, or *præsides*, of equal rank, but Clement of Rome is supposed to have a certain supervision in relation to foreign churches. *Vis.* II., 2, 4 ; III., 9 ; *Simil.* IX., 31. In one passage (*Vis.* III., 5) Hermas mentions four officers, " apostles, bishops, teachers, and deacons." The " bishops" here include presbyters, and the " teachers" are either all preachers of the gospel or the presbyter-bishops in their teaching (as distinct from their ruling) capacity and function. In other passages he names only the ἀπόστολοι and διδάσκαλοι, *Sim.* IX., 15, 16, 25 ; comp. Paul's ποιμένες καὶ διδάσκαλοι, Eph. 4: 11. The statements of Hermas on church organization are rather loose and indefinite. They have been discussed by Hilgenfeld and Harnack in favor of presbyterianism, by Hefele and Rothe in favor of episcopacy. Lightfoot, who identifies Hermas with the brother of bishop Pius (140), says: " Were it not known that the writer's own brother was bishop of Rome (?), we should be at a loss what to say about the constitution of the Roman church in his day." (*Com. on Philipp.*, p. 218.)

[2] *Adv. Hær.* IV. 20, ₰ 2 : εἶπεν ἡ γραφὴ ἡ λέγουσα. Then follows a quotation from *Mand.* I. 1 : "First of all believe that there is one God who created and prepared and made all things out of nothing." Possibly the wrong reference was a slip of memory in view of familiar passages, 2 Macc. 7 : 28 (πάντα . . ἐξ οὐκ ὄντων ἐποίησεν) ; Heb. 11 : 3 ; Mark 12: 29 (ὁ θεὸς εἰς ἐστί) ; James 2 : 18 Hilgenfeld thinks that the Hermas was known also to the author of the κήρυγμα Πέτρου and pseudo-Clement.

their learning were wanting in sound critical discrimination, regarded it as "divinely inspired," though Origen intimates that others judged less favorably.[1] Eusebius classes it with the "spurious," though orthodox books, like the Epistle of Barnabas, the Acts of Paul, etc.; and Athanasius puts it on a par with the Apocrypha of the Old Testament, which are useful for catechetical instruction.

In the Latin church where it originated, it never rose to such high authority. The Muratorian canon regards it as apocryphal, and remarks that " it should be read,[2] but not publicly used in the church or numbered among the prophets or the apostles." Tertullian, who took offence at its doctrine of the possibility of a second repentance, and the lawfulness of second marriage, speaks even contemptuously of it.[3] So does Jerome in one passage, though he speaks respectfully of it in another.[4] Ambrose and Augustin ignore it. The decree of Pope Gelasius I. (about 500) condemns the book as apocryphal. Since that time it shared the fate of all Apocrypha, and fell into entire neglect. The Greek original even disappeared for centuries, until it turned up unexpectedly in the middle of the nineteenth century to awaken a new interest, and to try the ingenuity of scholars as one of the links in the development of catholic Christianity.

NOTE.

The Pastor Hermæ has long ceased to be read for devotion or entertainment. We add some modern opinions. Mosheim (who must have

[1] See the quotations from Clement of Alex. and Origen in G. and H. *Prol.*, p. LIII.–LVI. Zahn says that "the history of the ecclesiastical authority of Hermas in the East begins with an unbounded recognition of the same as a book resting on divine revelation."

[2] In private only, or in the church? The passage is obscure and disputed.

[3] On account of this comparative mildness (*Mand.* IV., 1), Tertullian calls Hermas sarcastically "*ille apocryphus Pastor mœchorum.*" *De Pud.* c. 20; comp. c. 10.

[4] Jerome calls the Shepherd "*revera utilis liber,*" which was publicly read in certain churches of Greece, and quoted by many ancient writers as an authority, but "almost unknown among the Latins" (*apud Latinos' pœne ignotus*). *Op.* II. 846. In another passage, *Op.* VI. 604, he condemns the view of the angelic supervision of animals (*Vis.* IV. 2).

read it very superficially) pronounced the talk of the heavenly spirits in Hermas to be more stupid and insipid than that of the barbers of his day, and concluded that he was either a fool or an impostor. The great historian Niebuhr, as reported by Bunsen, used to say that he pitied the Athenian [why not the Roman?] Christians who were obliged to listen to the reader of such a book in the church. Bunsen himself pronounces it " a well-meant but silly romance."

On the other hand, some Irvingite scholars, Dr. Thiersch and Mr. Gaâb, have revived the old belief in a supernatural foundation for the visions, as having been really seen and recorded in the church of Rome during the apostolic age, but afterwards modified and mingled with errors by the compiler under Pius. Gaâb thinks that Hermas was gifted with the power of vision, and inspired in the same sense as Swedenborg.

Westcott ascribes " the highest value" to the Shepherd, " as showing in what way Christianity was endangered by the influence of Jewish principles as distinguished from Jewish forms." *Hist. of the Canon of the N. T.* p. 173 (second ed.)

Donaldson (a liberal Scotch Presbyterian) thinks that the Shepherd "ought to derive a peculiar interest from its being the first work extant, the main effort of which is to direct the soul to God. The other religious books relate to internal workings in the church—this alone specially deals with the great change requisite to living to God. . . . Its creed is a very short and simple one. Its great object is to exhibit the morality implied in conversion, ... and it is well calculated to awaken a true sense of the spiritual foes that are ever ready to assail him." (*Ap. Fath.*, p. 339). But he also remarks (p. 336) that "nothing would more completely show the immense difference between ancient Christian feeling and modern, than the respect in which ancient, and a large number of modern Christians hold this work."

George A. Jackson (an American Congregationalist) judges even more favorably (*Ap. Fath.*, 1879, p. 15): " Reading the ' Shepherd,' and remembering that it appeared in the midst of a society differing little from that satirized by Juvenal, we no longer wonder at the esteem in which it was held by the early Christians, but we almost join with them in calling it an inspired book."

Mr. Hoole, of Oxford, agrees with the judgment of Athanasius, and puts its literary character on the same footing as the pious but rude art of the Roman catacombs.

Dr. Salmon, of Dublin, compares Hermas with Savonarola, who sincerely believed: (*a*) that the church of his time was corrupt and worldly; (*b*) that a time of great tribulation was at hand, in which the dross should be purged away; (*c*) that there was still an intervening time for repentance; (*d*) that he himself was divinely commissioned to be a preacher of that repentance.

§ 169. *Papias.*

(I.) The fragments of PAPIAS collected in ROUTH: *Reliquiae Sacrae*, ed. II., Oxf., 1846, vol. I., 3–16. VON GEBHARDT and HARNACK: *Patres Apost.*, Appendix: *Papiæ Fragmenta*, I., 180–196. English translation in *Roberts* and *Donaldson*, "Ante-Nicene Library," I., 441–448.

Passages on Papias in IRENÆUS: *Adv. Hær.*, v. 33, ⸹ 3, 4. EUSEB. *H. E.* III. 36, 39; *Chron.* ad Olymp. 220, ed. Schöne II. 162. Also a few later notices; see Routh and the Leipz. ed. of *P. A.* The *Vita S. Papiæ*, by the Jesuit Halloix, Duæi, 1633, is filled with a fanciful account of the birth, education, ordination, episcopal and literary labors of the saint, of whom very little is really known.

(II.) Separate articles on Papias, mostly connected with the Gospel question, by SCHLEIERMACHER (on his testimonies concerning Matthew and Mark in the "Studien und Kritiken" for 1832, p. 735); TH. ZAHN (*ibid.* 1866, No. IV. p. 649 sqq.); G. E. STEITZ (in the "Studien und Kritiken" for 1868, No. I. 63–95, and art. Papias in Herzog's "Encyc." ed. I. vol. XI., 78–86; revised by LEIMBACH in ed. II. vol. XI. 194–206); JAMES DONALDSON (*The Apost. Fathers* 1874, p. 393–402); Bishop LIGHTFOOT (in the "Contemporary Review" for Aug., 1875, pp. 377–403; a careful examination of the testimonies of Papias concerning the Gospels of Mark and Matthew against the misstatements in "Supernatural Religion"); LEIMBACH (*Das Papiasfragment*, 1875); WEIFFENBACH (*Das Papiasfragment*, 1874 and 1878); HILGENFELD ("Zeitschrift für wissensch. Theol.," 1875, 239 sqq.); LÜDEMANN (*Zur Erklärung des Papiasfragments*, in the "Jahrbücher für protest. Theol.," 1879, p. 365 sqq.); H. HOLTZMANN (*Papias und Johannes*, in Hilgenfeld's "Zeitschrift für wissensch. Theologie," 1880, pp. 64–77). Comp. also WESTCOTT on the *Canon of the N. T.*, p. 59–68.

PAPIAS, a disciple of John[1] and friend of Polycarp, was bishop of Hierapolis, in Phrygia, till towards the middle of the second century. According to a later tradition in the "Paschal Chronicle," he suffered martyrdom at Pergamon about the same time with Polycarp at Smyrna. As the death of the latter has recently been put back from 166 to 155, the date of Papias must undergo a similar change; and as his contemporary friend was at least 86 years old, Papias was probably born about A. D. 70, so that he may have known St. John, St. Philip the Evan-

---

[1] See note at the end of the section.

gelist, and other primitive disciples who survived the destruction of Jerusalem.

Papias was a pious, devout and learned student of the Scriptures, and a faithful traditionist, though somewhat credulous
and of limited comprehension.[1] He carried the heavenly treasure in an earthen vessel. His associations give him considerable
weight. He went to the primitive sources of the Christian
faith. "I shall not regret," he says, "to subjoin to my interpretations [of the Lord's Oracles], whatsoever I have at any
time accurately ascertained and treasured up in my memory, as
I have received it from the elders ($\pi a \rho \grave{a}\ \tau \tilde{\omega} \nu\ \pi \rho \varepsilon \sigma \beta \upsilon \tau \acute{\varepsilon} \rho \omega \nu$) and
have recorded it to give additional confirmation to the truth, by
my testimony. For I did not, like most men, delight in those
who speak much, but in those who teach the truth; nor in those
who record the commands of others [or new and strange com-
mands], but in those who record the commands given by the
Lord to our faith, and proceeding from truth itself. If then
any one who had attended on the elders came, I made it a point
to inquire what were the words of the elders; what Andrew, or
what Peter said, or Philip, or Thomas, or James, or John, or
Matthew, or any other of the disciples of our Lord; and what
things Aristion and the elder John, the disciples of the Lord,
say. For I was of opinion that I could not derive so much
benefit from books as from the living and abiding voice."[2] He
collected with great zeal the oral traditions of the apostles and
their disciples respecting the discourses and works of Jesus, and

---

[1] Eusebius, *H. E.* III. 39, says that he was $\sigma \phi \acute{o} \delta \rho a\ \sigma \mu \iota \kappa \rho \grave{o} \varsigma\ \tau \grave{o} \nu\ \nu o \tilde{\upsilon} \nu$, "very
small-minded," and that this appears from his writings; but he was no doubt
unfavorably influenced in his judgment by the strong millennarianism of
Papias, which he mentions just before; and even if well founded, it would not
invalidate his testimony as to mere facts. In another place (III. 36), Eusebius
calls him a man of comprehensive learning and knowledge of the Scriptures
($\grave{a} \nu \grave{\eta} \rho\ \tau \grave{a}\ \pi \acute{a} \nu \tau a\ \acute{o} \tau \iota\ \mu \acute{a} \lambda \iota \sigma \tau a\ \lambda o \gamma \iota \acute{\omega} \tau a \tau o \varsigma\ \kappa a \grave{\iota}\ \tau \tilde{\eta} \varsigma\ \gamma \rho a \phi \tilde{\eta} \varsigma\ \varepsilon \mathring{\upsilon} \delta \acute{\eta} \mu \omega \nu$, *omni doctrinæ
genere instructissimus et in scriptura sacra versatus*). Learning, piety, and good
sense are not always combined. The passage, however, is wanting in some
MSS. of Eusebius. See the note of Heinichen, vol. I. 141 sqq.

[2] $\pi a \rho \grave{a}\ \zeta \acute{\omega} \sigma \eta \varsigma\ \phi \omega \nu \tilde{\eta} \varsigma\ \kappa a \grave{\iota}\ \mu \varepsilon \nu o \acute{\upsilon} \sigma \eta \varsigma$. Eus. III. 39 (Heinichen, I. 148).

published them in five books under the title: "*Explanation of the Lord's Discourses.*"[1]

Unfortunately this book, which still existed in the thirteenth century, is lost with the exception of valuable and interesting fragments preserved chiefly by Irenæus and Eusebius. Among these are his testimonies concerning the Hebrew Gospel of Matthew and the Petrine Gospel of Mark, which figure so prominently in all the critical discussions on the origin of the Gospels.[2] The episode on the woman taken in adultery which is found in some MSS. of John 7: 53–8: 11, or after Luke 21: 38, has been traced to the same source and was perhaps to illustrate the word of Christ, John 8: 15 ("I judge no man"); for Eusebius reports that Papias "set forth another narrative concerning a woman who was maliciously accused before the Lord of many sins, which is contained in the Gospel according to the Hebrews."[3] If so, we are indebted to him for the preservation of a precious fact which at once illustrates in a most striking manner our Saviour's absolute purity in dealing with sin, and his tender compassion toward the sinner. Papias was an enthusiastic chiliast, and the famous parable of the fertility of the millennium which he puts in the Lord's mouth and which Irenæus accepted in good faith, may have been intended as an explanation of the Lord's word concerning the fruit of the

---

[1] Λογίων κυριακῶν ἐξήγησις, *Explanatio sermonum Domini.* The word ἐξήγησις here no doubt means interpretation of some already existing gospel record, since Anastasius of Sinai (d. 599) classes Papias among Biblical exegetes or interpreters. He probably took as his text the canonical Gospels, and gave his own comments on the Lord's Discourses therein contained, together with additional sayings which he had derived, directly or indirectly, from personal disciples of Christ. Although this work has disappeared for several centuries, it may possibly yet be recovered either in the original, or in a Syriac or Armenian version. The work was still extant in 1218 in the MSS. collection of the church at Nismes, according to Gallandi and Pitra. It is also mentioned thrice in the Catalogue of the Library of the Benedictine Monastery of Christ Church, Canterbury, contained in the Cottonian MS. of the thirteenth or fourteenth century. Donaldson, p. 402. On the meaning of λόγια see Vol. I. 622 sq.

[2] See vol. I. p. 622, 633 sq.

[3] The plural (ἐπὶ πολλαῖς ἁμαρτίαις, *H. E.* III. 39) is no argument against the conjecture. Cod. D reads ἁμαρτίᾳ instead of μοιχείᾳ in John 8: 3.

vine which he shall drink new in his Father's kingdom, Matt.
26: 29.[1] His chiliasm is no proof of a Judaizing tendency, for
it was the prevailing view in the second century. He also
related two miracles, the resurrection of a dead man which took
place at the time of Philip (the Evangelist), as he learned from
his daughters, and the drinking of poison without harm by
Justus Barsabas.

Papias proves the great value which was attached to the oral
traditions of the apostles and their disciples in the second century. He stood on the threshold of a new period when the last
witnesses of the apostolic age were fast disappearing, and when
it seemed to be of the utmost importance to gather the remaining fragments of inspired wisdom which might throw light on
the Lord's teaching, and guard the church against error.

But he is also an important witness to the state of the canon
before the middle of the second century. He knew the first two
Gospels, and in all probability also the Gospel of John, for he
quoted, as Eusebius expressly says, from the first Epistle of
John, which is so much like the fourth Gospel in thought and
style that they stand or fall as the works of one and the same
author.[2] He is one of the oldest witnesses to the inspiration and

---

[1] See above, § 158, p. 616. Card. Pitra, in the first vol. of his *Spicileg. Solesm.*,
communicates a similar fragment, but this is, as the title and opening words
intimate, a translation of Irenæus, not of Papias. The authoress of " *The
Pupils of St. John*," p. 203, remarks on that description of Papias : " Understood literally, this is of course utterly unlike anything we know of our blessed
Lord's unearthly teaching; yet it does sound like what a literal and narrow
mind, listening to mere word-of mouth narrative, might make of the parable
of the Vine, and of the Sower, or of the Grain of Mustard-seed; and we also
see how providential and how merciful it was that the real words of our Lord
were so early recorded by two eye-witnesses, and by two scholarly men, under
the guidance of the Holy Spirit, instead of being left to the versions that good
but dull-minded believers might make of them."

[2] A mediæval tradition assigns to Papias an account of the origin, and even
a part in the composition, of the Gospel of John as his amanuensis. So a note
prefixed to John's Gospel in a MS. of the ninth century, rediscovered by Pitra
and Tischendorf in 1866 in the Vatican library. The note is, in Tischendorf's
opinion, older than Jerome, and is as follows : "*Evangelium johannis manifesta-
tum et datum est ecclesiis ab johanne adhuc in corpore constituto, sicut papios nomine
hierapolitanus discipulus johannis carus in exotericis [exegeticis], id est in extremis,*

credibility of the Apocalypse of John, and commented on a part of it.[1] He made use of the first Epistle of Peter, but is silent as far as we know concerning Paul and Luke. This has been variously explained from accident or ignorance or dislike, but best from the nature of his design to collect only words of the Lord. Hermas and Justin Martyr likewise ignore Paul, and yet knew his writings. That Papias was not hostile to the great apostle may be inferred from his intimacy with Polycarp, who lauds Paul in his Epistle.

NOTES.

The relation of Papias to the Apostle John is still a disputed point. Irenæus, the oldest witness and himself a pupil of Polycarp, calls Papias Ἰωάννου μὲν ἀκουστὴς, Πολυκάρπου δὲ ἑταῖρος (*Adv. Hær.* V. 33, 4). He must evidently mean here the Apostle John. Following him, Jerome and later writers (Maximus Confessor, Andrew of Crete and Anastasius Sinaita) call him a disciple of the Apostle John, and this view has been defended with much learning and acumen by Dr. Zahn (1866), and, independently of him, by Dr. Milligan (on *John the Presbyter*, in Cowper's "Journal of Sacred Literature" for Oct., 1867, p. 106 sqq.), on the assumption of the identity of the Apostle John with "Presbyter John;" comp. 2 and 3 John, where the writer calls himself ὁ πρεσβύτερος. Riggenbach (on John the Ap. and John the Presbyter, in the "Jahrbücher für Deutsche Theologie," 1868, pp. 319–334), Hengstenberg, Leimbach, take the same view (also Schaff in *History of the Apost. Ch.*, 1853, p. 421).

On the other hand, Eusebius (*H. E.* III. 39) infers that Papias distinguishes between John the Apostle and "the Presbyter John" (ὁ πρεσβύτερος Ἰωάννης) so called, and that he was a pupil of the Presbyter only. He bases the distinction on a fragment he quotes from the introduction to the "*Explanation of the Lord's Discourses*," where Papias says that he ascertained the primitive traditions: τί Ἀνδρέας ἢ τί Πέτρος εἶπεν [in the past tense], ἢ τί Φίλιππος ἢ τί Θωμᾶς ἢ Ἰάκωβος ἢ τί Ἰωάννης [the Apostle] ἢ Ματθαῖος, ἢ τις ἕτερος τῶν τοῦ κυρίου μαθητῶν, ἅ τε Ἀριστίων καὶ ὁ

quinque libris retulit. Discripsit vero evangelium dictante johanne recte," etc. The last sentence is probably a mistaken translation of the Greek. See Lightfoot in the "Contemp. Rev.," Oct. 1875, p. 854; Charteris, *Canonicity*, p. 168. Another testimony is found in a fragment of a Greek commentator in the Proœmium of the *Catena Patrum Græcorum in S. Johannem*, ed. by Corderius. Antwerp, 1630, according to which John dictated his Gospel to Papias of Hierapolis. See Papiæ Frag. in Gebh. and Harn.'s ed. p. 194. This tradition is discredited by the silence of Eusebius, but it shows that in the opinion of the mediæval church Papias was closely connected with the Gospel of John.

[1] Andreas of Cæsarea, *In Apoc.* c. 34, Serm. 12. See v. G. and H. p. 189.

πρεσβύτερος 'Ιωάννης, οἱ τοῦ κυρίου [not τῶν ἀποστόλων] μαθηταί, λέγουσιν [present tense]. Here two Johns seem to be clearly distinguished; but the Presbyter John, together with an unknown Aristion, is likewise called a disciple of the Lord (not of the Apostles). The distinction is maintained by Steitz, Tischendorf, Keim, Weiffenbach, Lüdemann, Donaldson, Westcott, and Lightfoot. In confirmation of this view, Eusebius states that two graves were shown at Ephesus bearing the name of John (III. 39: δύο ἐν 'Εφέσῳ γενέσθαι μνήματα, καὶ ἑκάτερον 'Ιωάννου ἔτι νῦν λέγεσθαι). But Jerome, De Vir. ill. c. 9, suggests, that both graves were only memories of the Apostle. Beyond this, nothing whatever is known of this mysterious Presbyter John, and it was a purely critical conjecture of the anti-millennarian Dionysius of Alexandria that he was the author of the Apocalypse (Euseb. VII. 25). The substance of the mediæval legend of " Prester John" was undoubtedly derived from another source.

In any case, it is certainly possible that Papias, like his friend Polycarp, may have seen and heard the aged apostle who lived to the close of the first or the beginning of the second century. It is therefore unnecessary to charge Irenæus with an error either of name or memory. It is more likely that Eusebius misunderstood Papias, and is responsible for a fictitious John, who has introduced so much confusion into the question of the authorship of the Johannean Apocalypse.

§ 170. *The Epistle to Diognetus.*

Editions.

EPISTOLA AD DIOGNETUM, ed. *Otto* (with Lat. transl., introduction and critical notes), ed. II. Lips. 1852.

In the Leipz. edition of the Apost. Fathers, by *O. v. Gebhardt* and *Ad Harnack*, I. 216–226; in the Tübingen ed. of *Hefele-Funk*, I. pp 310–333.

W. A. HOLLENBERG: *Der Brief an Diognet.* Berl. 1853.

E. M. KRENKEL: *Epistola ad Diogn.* Lips. 1860.

English translation: in Kitto's " Journal of S. Lit." 1852, and in vol. I of the "Ante-Nicene Library." Edinb. 1867.

French versions by *P. le Gras*, Paris 1725; *M. de Genoude*, 1838; *A Kayser*, 1856.

Discussions.

OTTO: *De Ep. ad Diognetum.* 1852.

A. KAYSER: *La Lettre à Diognète.* 1856 (in " Révue de Théologie ").

G. J. SNOECK: *Specimen theologicum exhibens introductionem in Epistolan ad Diogn.* Lugd. Bat. 1861.

DONALDSON: *A Critical Hist. of Christian Liter.*, etc. Lond., 1866, II. 126 sqq. He was inclined to assume that Henry Stephens, the first editor, manufactured the Ep., but gave up the strange hypothesis, which was afterwards reasserted by COTTERILL in his *Peregrinus Proteus*, 1879.

FRANZ OVERBECK : *Ueber den pseudo-justinischen Brief an Diognet.* Basel 1872. And again with additions in his *Studien zur Geschichte der alten Kirche* (Schloss-Chemnitz, 1875), p. 1–92. He represents the Ep. (like Donaldson) as a post-Constantinian fiction, but has been refuted by Hilgenfeld, Keim, Lipsius, and Dräseke.

JOH. DRÄSEKE : *Der Brief an Diognetos.* Leipz. 1881 (207 pp.). Against Overbeck and Donaldson. The Ep. was known and used by Tertullian, and probably composed in Rome by a Christian Gnostic (perhaps Appelles). Unlikely.

HEINR. KIHN (R. C.) : *Der Ursprung des Briefes an Diognet.* Freiburg i. B. 1882 (XV. and 168 pages).

SEMISCH : art. *Diognet.* in Herzog[2] III. 611–615 (and in his *Justin der Märt.*, 1840, vol. I. 172 sqq.) ; SCHAFF, in McClintock and Strong, III. 807 sq., and BIRKS, in Smith and Wace, II. 162–167.

The Ep. to D. has also been discussed by Neander, Hefele, Credner, Möhler, Bunsen, Ewald, Dorner, Hilgenfeld, Lechler, Baur, Harnack, Zahn, Funk, Lipsius, Keim (especially in *Rom nnd das Christhum*, 460–468).

1. The short but precious document called the EPISTLE TO DIOGNETUS was unknown in Christian literature[1] until Henry Stephens, the learned publisher of Paris, issued it in Greek and Latin in 1592, under the name of Justin Martyr.[2] He gives no account of his sources. The only Codex definitely known is the Strassburg Codex of the thirteenth century, and even this (after having been thoroughly compared by Professor Cunitz for Otto's edition), was destroyed in the accidental

---

[1] Not even Eusebius or Jerome or Photius make any mention of it. Möhler (*Patrol.* p. 170) refers to Photius, but Photius speaks of Justin Martyr, with whose writings he was well acquainted. See Hergenröther, *Photius*, III. 19 sq.

[2] ΙΟΥΣΤΙΝΟΥ ΤΟΥ φιλοσόφου καὶ μάρτυρος 'Επιστολὴ πρὸς Διόγνητον, καὶ Λόγος πρὸς 'Έλληνας. *Iustini Philosophi et Martyris Ep. ad Diognetum, et Oratio ad Græcos, nunc primum luce et latinitate donatæ ab Henrico Stephano. Eiusdem Henr. Stephani annotationibus additum est Io. Iacobi Beureri de quorundam locorum partim interpretatione partim emendatione iudicium. Tatiani, discipuli Iustini, quædam. Excudebat Henricus Stephanus. Anno MDXCII.* The copy of Stephens is still preserved in the University library at Leiden. The copy of Beurer is lost, but was probably made from the Strassburg Codex, with which it agrees in the readings published by Stephens in his appendix, and by Sylburg in his notes.

fire at Strassburg during the siege of 1870.[1] So great is the mystery hanging over the origin of this document, that some modern scholars have soberly turned it into a post-Constantinian fiction in imitation of early Christianity, but without being able to agree upon an author, or his age, or his nationality.

Yet this most obscure writer of the second century is at the same time the most brilliant; and while his name remains unknown to this day, he shed lustre on the Christian name in times when it was assailed and blasphemed from Jew and Gentile, and could only be professed at the risk of life. He must be ranked with the "great unknown" authors of Job and the Epistle to the Hebrews, who are known only to God.

2. DIOGNETUS was an inquiring heathen of high social position and culture, who desired information concerning the origin and nature of the religion of the Christians, and the secret of their contempt of the world, their courage in death, their brotherly love, and the reason of the late origin of this new fashion, so different from the gods of the Greeks and the superstition of the Jews. A Stoic philosopher of this name instructed Marcus Aurelius in his youth (about 133) in painting and composition, and trained him in Attic simplicity of life, and " whatever else of the kind belongs to Grecian discipline." Perhaps he taught him also to despise the Christian martyrs, and to trace their heroic courage to sheer obstinacy. It is quite probable that our Diognetus was identical with the imperial tutor ; for he wished especially to know what enabled these Christians "to despise the world and to make light of death."[2]

---

[1] " *Epistulæ ad Diognetum unum tantummodo exemplar antiquius ad nostram usque pervenit memoriam: codicem dico Ioannis Reuchlini quondam, postea Argentoratensem, qui misero illo incendio die nono ante Calendas Septembres anni MDCCCLXX cum tot aliis libris pretiosis in cineres dilapsus est.*" Von Gebhardt and Harnack, p. 205. They assert, p. 208, that the copies of Stephens and Beurer were taken from the Cod. of Strassburg. Otto (*Prol.* p. 3) speaks of " *tres codices, Argentoratensis, apographon Stephani, apographon Beureri.*"

[2] Comp. *Ep. ad Diog.,* c. 1, with Marcus Aur. *Medit.,* IX. 3 (his only allusion to Christianity, quoted p. 329). Marcus Aurelius gratefully remembers his teacher Diognetus, *Medit.,* I. 6. Diognetus was not a rare name; but the one of our Epistle was a person of social prominence, as the term κράτιστος,

3. The EPISTLE before us is an answer to the questions of this noble heathen. It is a brief but masterly vindication of Christian life and doctrine from actual experience. It is evidently the product of a man of genius, fine taste and classical culture. It excels in fresh enthusiasm of faith, richness of thought, and elegance of style, and is altogether one of the most beautiful memorials of Christian antiquity, unsurpassed and hardly equalled by any genuine work of the Apostolic Fathers.[1]

4. CONTENTS. The document consists of twelve chapters. It opens with an address to Diognetus who is described as exceedingly desirous to learn the Christian doctrine and mode of worship in distinction from that of the Greeks and the Jews. The writer, rejoicing in this opportunity to lead a Gentile friend to the path of truth, exposes first the vanity of idols (ch. 2), then the superstitions of the Jews (ch. 3, 4); after this he gives by contrasts a striking and truthful picture of Christian life which moves in this world like the invisible, immortal soul in the visible, perishing body (ch. 5 and 6),[2] and sets forth the benefits of Christ's coming (ch. 7). He next describes the miserable condition of the world before Christ (ch. 8), and answers the question why He appeared so late (ch. 9). In this connec-

---

honorable, implies. Otto and Ewald identify the two. Keim and Dräseke (p. 141) admit that our Diognetus belonged to the imperial court, but put him later.

[1] Ewald (*Geschichte des Volkes Israel*, Bd. VII. p. 150) places it first among all the early Christian epistles which were not received into the N. T., and says that it combines perfectly "the fulness and art of Greek eloquence with the purest love of truth, and the ease and grace of words with the elevating seriousness of the Christian." Bunsen: "Indisputably, after Scripture, the finest monument of sound Christian feeling, noble courage, and manly eloquence." Semisch (in Herzog) calls it "*ein Kleinod des christl. Alterthums, welchem in Geist und Fassung kaum ein zweites Schriftwerk der nachapostolischen Zeit gleichsteht.*" Keim (*Rom und das Christenthum*, p. 463 sq.) calls it "*das lieblichste, ja ein fast zauberhaftes Wort des zweiten Jahrhunderts*," and eloquently praises "*die reine, klassische Sprache, den schönen, korrekten Satzbau, die rhetorische Frische, die schlagenden Antithesen, den geistreichen Ausdruck, die logische Abrundung ... die unmittelbare, liebeswarme, begeisterte, wenn schon mit Bildung durchsättigte Frömmigkeit.*"

[2] Quoted above, § 2, p. 9.

tion occurs a beautiful passage on redemption, fuller and clearer than any that can be found before Irenæus.[1] He concludes with an account of the blessings and moral effects which flow from the Christian faith (ch. 10). The last two chapters which were probably added by a younger contemporary, and marked as such in the MS., treat of knowledge, faith and spiritual life with reference to the tree of knowledge and the tree of life in paradise. Faith opens the paradise of a higher knowledge of the mysteries of the supernatural world.

The Epistle to Diognetus forms the transition from the purely practical literature of the Apostolic Fathers to the reflective theology of the Apologists. It still glows with the ardor of the first love. It is strongly Pauline.[2] It breathes the spirit of freedom and higher knowledge grounded in faith. The Old Testament is ignored, but without any sign of Gnostic contempt.

5. AUTHORSHIP and TIME of composition. The author calls himself "a disciple of the Apostles,"[3] but this term occurs in the appendix, and may be taken in a wider sense. In the MS. the letter is ascribed to Justin Martyr, but its style is more elegant, vigorous and terse than that of Justin, and the thoughts are more original and vigorous.[4] It belongs, however, in all probability, to the same age, that is, to the middle of the second century, rather earlier than later. Christianity appears in it as something still new and unknown to the aristocratic society, as a stranger in the world, everywhere exposed to calumny and persecution of Jews and Gentiles. All this suits the reign of Antoninus Pius and of Marcus Aurelius. If Diognetus was the teacher of the latter as already suggested, we would have an indication of Rome, as the probable place of composition.

Some assign the Epistle to an earlier date under Trajan or

---

[1] See above, § 153, p. 587.

[2] "As if no less a person than Paul himself had returned to life for that age." Ewald, VII. 149.

[3] Ἀποστόλων γενόμενος μαθητής, ch. 11.

[4] The Justinian authorship is defended by Cave, Fabricius, and Otto, but refuted by Semisch, Hefele, Keim, and others.

Hadrian,[1] others to the reign of Marcus Aurelius,[2] others to the close of the second century or still later.[3] The speculations about the author begin with Apollos in the first, and end with Stephens in the sixteenth, century. He will probably remain unknown.[4]

§ 171. *Sixtus of Rome.*

Enchiridion SIXTI *philosophi Pythagorici*, first ed. by Symphor. Champerius, Lugd. 1507 (under the title: *Sixtii Xysti Anulus*); again at Wittenberg with the *Carmina aurea* of Pythagoras, 1514; by Beatus Rhenanus, Bas. 1516; in the "Maxima Bibliotheca Vet. Patrum," Lugd. 1677, Tom. III. 335–339 (under the title *Xysti vel Sexti Pythagorici philosophi ethnici Sententiæ, interprete Rufino Presbytero Aquilejensi*); by U. G. Siber, Lips. 1725 (under the name of Sixtus II. instead of Sixtus I.); and by GILDEMEISTER (Gr., Lat. and Syr.), Bonn 1873.

A Syriac Version in P. LAGARDII *Analecta Syriaca*, Lips. and Lond. 1858 (p. 1–31, only the Syriac text, derived from seven MSS. of the Brit. Museum, the oldest before A. D. 553, but mutilated).

The book is discussed in the "Max. Bibl." *l. c.*; by FONTANINUS: *Historia liter. Aquilejensis* (Rom. 1742); by FABRICIUS, in the *Bibliotheca Græca*, Tom. I. 870 sqq. (ed. Harles, 1790); by EWALD: *Geschichte des Volkes Israel*, vol. VII. (Göttingen, 1859), p. 321–326; and by TOBLER in *Annulus Rufini, Sent. Sext.* (Tübingen 1878).

XYSTUS, or as the Romans spelled the name, SEXTUS or SIXTUS I., was the sixth bishop of Rome, and occupied this position about ten years under the reign of Hadrian (119–128).[5]

---

[1] Tillemont and Möhler to the first century, Hefele and Ewald to the reign of Hadrian (120–130). Westcott (*Can. N. T.* p. 76): Not before Trajan, and not much later; everything betokens an early age.

[2] So Keim, who suggests the bloody year 177.

[3] So Hilgenfeld, Lipsius, Gass, Zahn, Dräseke (under Septimus Severus, between 193—211). Overbeck's hypothesis of a post-Constantinian date is exploded.

[4] Justin M. (the MS. tradition); Marcion before his secession from the church (Bunsen); Quadratus (Dorner); Apelles, the Gnostic in his old age (Dräseke, p. 141). The writer of the art. in Smith and Wace, II. 162, identifies the author with one Ambrosius, "a chief man of Greece who became a Christian, and all his fellow councillors raised a clamor against him," and refers to Cureton's *Spicil. Syriacum*, p. 61–69. The Stephanic hypothesis of and Cotterill is a literary and moral impossibility.

[5] Irenæus (*Adv. Hær.* l. III. c. 3, § 3) mentions him as the Roman bishop after Clement, Evaristus, and Alexander. Eusebius (*H. E.* IV. 5) relates that

Little or nothing is known about him except that he was supposed to be the author of a remarkable collection of moral and
religious maxims, written in Greek, translated into Latin by
Rufinus and extensively read in the ancient church. The sentences are brief and weighty after the manner of the Hebrew
Proverbs and the Sermon on the Mount. They do not mention
the prophets or apostles, or even the name of Christ, but are full
of God and sublime moral sentiments, only bordering somewhat
on pantheism.[1] If it is the production of a heathen philosopher,
he came nearer the genius of Christian ethics than even Seneca,
or Epictetus, or Plutarch, or Marcus Aurelius; but the product
has no doubt undergone a transformation in Christian hands,
and this accounts for its ancient popularity, and entitles it to a
place in the history of ecclesiastical literature. Rufinus took
great liberties as translator; besides, the MSS. vary very much.

Origen first cites in two places the *Gnomœ* or *Sententiœ* of
SEXTUS (γνῶμαι Σέξτου), as a work well known and widely
read among the Christians of his times, *i. e.*, in the first half of
the second century, but he does not mention that the writer was
a bishop, or even a Christian. Rufinus translated them with
additions, and ascribes them to Sixtus, bishop of Rome and
martyr. But Jerome, who was well versed in classical literature,
charges him with prefixing the name of a Christian bishop to
the product of a christless and most heathenish Pythagorean
philosopher, Xystus, who is admired most by those who teach
Stoic apathy and Pelagian sinlessness. Augustin first regarded
the author as one of the two Roman bishops Sixti, but afterwards retracted his opinion, probably in consequence of Jerome's
statement. Maximus the Confessor and John of Damascus ascribe
it to Xystus of Rome. Gennadius merely calls the work *Xysti
Sententiœ*. Pope Gelasius declares it spurious and written by

he ruled the Roman church for ten years. Jaffé (*Regesta Pontificum Rom.*
p. 3) puts his pontificate between 119 and 128. The second Pope of that name
died a martyr A. D. 257 or 258. The two have been sometimes confounded as
authors of the *Enchiridion.* Siber published it under the name of Sixtus II.

[1] See specimens in the Notes.

heretics.[1] More recent writers (as Fontanini, Brucker, Fabricius, Mosheim) agree in assigning it to the elder QUINTUS SEXTUS or SEXTIUS (Q. S. PATER), a Stoic philosopher who declined the dignity of Roman Senator offered to him by Julius Cæsar and who is highly lauded by Seneca. He abstained from animal food, and subjected himself to a scrupulous self-examination at the close of every day. Hence this book was entirely ignored by modern church historians.[2] But Paul de Lagarde, who published a Syriac Version, and Ewald have again directed attention to it and treat it as a genuine work of the first Pope Xystus. Ewald puts the highest estimate on it. "The Christian conscience," he says, "appears here for the first time before all the world to teach all the world its duty, and to embody the Christian wisdom of life in brief pointed sentences."[3] But it seems impossible that a Christian sage and bishop should write a system of Christian Ethics or a collection of Christian proverbs without even mentioning the name of Christ.

NOTES.

The following is a selection of the most important of the 430 Sentences of Xystus from the *Bibliotheca Maxima Veterum Patrum*, Tom. III. 335–339. We add some Scripture parallels:

"1. *Fidelis homo, electus homo est.* 2. *Electus homo, homo Dei est.* 3. *Homo Dei est, qui Deo dignus est.* 4. *Deo dignus est, qui nihil indigne agit.* 5. *Dubius in fide, infidelis est.* 6. *Infidelis homo, mortuus est corpore vivente.* 7. *Vere fidelis est, qui non peccat, atque etiam, in minimis caute agit.* 8. *Non est minimum in humana vita, negligere minima.* 9. *Omne peccatum impietatem puta. Non enim manus, vel oculus peccat, vel aliquod huiusmodi membrum, sed male uti manu vel oculo, peccatum est.* 10. *Omne membrum corporis, quod invitat te contra pudicitiam agere, abjiciendum est.*

[1] See the references in the *Biblioth. Max.* III. 525; and in Fontanini and Fabricius, *l. c.*

[2] Neander, Gieseler, Baur, Donaldson, and others do not even mention the book.

[3] *Geschichte Israels*, vol. VII. p. 322. Compare his review of Lagardii *Analecta Syriaca* in the "Göttingen Gel. Anzeigen," 1859, p. 261–269. Both Ewald and P. de Lagarde, his successor, characteristically ignore all previous editions and discussions.

Melius est uno membro vivere, quam cum duobus puniri [Comp. Matt. 5:
29]. . . .

"15. *Sapiens vir, et pecuniæ contemptor, similis est Deo.*   16. *Rebus
mundanis in causis tantum necessariis utere.*   17. *Quæ mundi sunt, mundo :
et quæ Dei sunt, reddantur Deo* [Comp. Matt. 22: 21].   18. *Certus esto,
quod animam tuam fidele depositum acceperis à Deo.*   19. *Cum loqueris Deo,
scito quod judiceris à Deo.*   20. *Optimam purificationem putato, nocere
nemini.*   21. *Anima purificatur Dei verbo per sapientiam.* . . .

"28. *Quæcumque fecit Deus, pro hominibus ea fecit.*   29. *Angelus minister
est Dei ad hominem.*   30. *Tam pretiosus est homo apud Deum, quam angelus.*   31. *Primus beneficus est Deus : secundus est is, qui beneficii eius fit
particeps homo.   Vive igitur ita, tanquam qui sis secundus post Deum, et
electus ab eo.*   32. *Habes, inquam, in te aliquid simile Dei, et ideo utere
teipso velut templo Dei, propter illud quod in te simile est Dei* [1 Cor. 3 :
16, 17]. . . .

"40. *Templum sanctum est Deo mens pii, et altare est optimum ei cor mundum et sine peccato.*   41. *Hostia soli Deo acceptabilis, benefacere hominibus
pro Deo.*   42. *Deo gratiam præstat homo, qui quantum possibile est vivit
secundum Deum.* . . .

"47. *Omne tempus, quo Deo non cogitas, hoc puta te perdidisse.*   48. *Corpus
quidem tuum incedat in terra, anima autem semper sit apud Deum.*   49. *In-
tellige quæ sint bona, ut bene agas.*   50. *Bona cogitatio hominis Deum non
latet et ideo cogitatio tua pura sit ab omni malo.*   51. *Dignus esto eo, qui te
dignatus est filium dicere, et age omnia ut filius Dei.*   52. *Quod Deum patrem
vocas, huius in actionibus tuis memor esto.*   53. *Vir castus et sine peccato,
potestatem accepit a Deo esse filius Dei* [Comp. John 1: 13].   54. *Bona
mens chorus est Dei.*   55. *Mala mens chorus est dæmonum malorum.* . . .

78. *Fundamentum pietatis est continentia : culmen autem pietatis amor
Dei.*   79. *Pium hominem habeto tanquam teipsum.*   80. *Opta tibi evenire
non quod vis, sed quod expedit.*   81. *Qualem vis esse proximum tuum tibi,
talis esto et tu tuis proximis* [Luke 6 : 31]. . . .

"86. *Si quid non vis scire Deum, istud nec agas, nec cogites,*   87. *Prius-
quam agas quodcunque agis, cogita Deum, ut lux eius pæcedat actus tuos.* . . .

"96. *Deus in bonis actibus hominibus dux est.*   97. *Neminem inimicum
deputes.*   98. *Dilige omne quod eiusdem tecum naturæ est, Deum vero plus
quam animam dilige.*   99. *Pessimum est peccatoribus, in unum convenire
cum peccant.*   100. *Multi cibi impediunt castitatem, et incontinentia ciborum
immundum facit hominem.*   101. *Animantium omnium usus quidem in
cibis indifferens, abstinere vero rationabilius est.*   102. *Non cibi per os in-
feruntur polluunt hominem, sed ea quæ ex malis actibus proferuntur* [Mark
7: 18–21]. . . .

"106. *Mali nullius autor est Deus.*   107. *Non amplius possideas quam usus
corporis poscit.* . . .

"115. *Ratio quæ in te est, vitæ tuæ lux est* [Matt. 6 : 22].   116. *Ea pete
a Deo, quæ accipere ab homine non potes.* . . .

"122. *Nil pretiosum ducas, quod auferre a te possit homo malus.* 123. *Hoc solum bonum putato, quod Deo dignum est.* 124. *Quod Deo dignum est, hoc et viro bono.* 125. *Quicquid non convenit ad beatudinem Dei, non conveniat nomini Dei.* 126. *Ea debes velle, quæ et Deus vult.* 127. *Filius Dei est, qui haec sola pretiosa ducit quæ et Deus.* 139. *Semper apud Deum mens est sapientis.* 137. *Sapientis mentem Deus inhabitat.* . . .

"181. *Sapiens vir etiamsi nudus sit, sapiens apud te habeatur.* 182. *Neminem propterea magni œstimes, quod pecunia divitiisque abundet.* 183. *Difficile est divitem salvari* [Matt. 19 : 23]. . . .

"187. *Age magna, non magna pollicens.* 188. *Non eris sapiens, si te reputaveris sapientem.* 189. *Non potest bene vivere qui non integre credit.* 190. *In tribulationibus quis sit fidelis, agnoscitur.* 191. *Finem vitae existima vivere secundum Deum.* 192. *Nihil putes malum, quod non sit turpe.* . . .

"198. *Malitia est œgritudo animæ.* 199. *Animæ autem mors iniustitia et impietas.* 200. *Tunc te putato fidelem, cum passionibus animæ carueris.* 201. *Omnibus hominibus ita utere, quasi communis omnium post Deum curator.* 202. *Qui hominibus male utitur, seipso male utitur.* 203. *Qui nihil mali vult, fidelis est.* . . .

"214. *Verba tua pietate semper plena sint.* 215. *In actibus tuis ante oculos pone Deum.* 216. *Nefas est Deum patrem invocare, et aliquid inhonestum agere.* . . .

"261. *Ebrietatem quasi insaniam fuge.* 262. *Homo qui a ventre vincitur, belluæ similis est.* 263. *Ex carne nihil oritur bonum.* . . .

"302. *Omne quod malum est, Deo inimicum est.* 303. *Qui sapit in te, hunc dicito esse hominem.* 304. *Particeps Dei est vir sapiens.* 305. *Ubi est quod sapit in te, ibi est et bonum tuum.* 306. *Bonum in carne non quæras.* 307. *Quod animæ non nocet, nec homini.* 308. *Sapientem hominem tanquam Dei ministrum honora post Deum.* . . .

"390. *Quæcunque dat mundus, nemo firmiter tenet.* 391. *Quæcumque dat Deus nemo auferre potest.* 392. *Divina sapientia vera est scientia.* . . .

"403. *Animae ascensus ad Deum per Dei verbum est.* 404. *Sapiens sequitur Deum, et Deus animam sapientis.* 405. *Gaudet rex super his quos regit, gaudet ergo Deus super sapiente. Inseparabilis est et ab his quos regit ille, qui regit, ita ergo et Deus ab anima sapientis quam tuetur et regit.* 406. *Regitur a Deo vir sapiens, et idcirco beatus est.* . . .

"424. *Si non diligis Deum, non ibis ad Deum.* 425. *Consuesce teipsum semper respicere ad Deum.* 426. *Intuendo Deum videbis Deum.* 427. *Videns Deum facies mentem tuam qualis est Deus.* 428. *Excole quod intra te est, nec ei ex libidine corporis contumeliam facias.* 429. *Incontaminatum custodi corpus tuum, tanquam si indumentum acceperis à Deo, et sicut vestimentum corporis immaculatum servare stude.* 430. *Sapiens mens speculum est Dei.*"

§ 172. *The Apologists. Quadratus and Aristides.*

On the Apologetic Lit. in general, see § 28, p. 85 sq., and § 37, p. 104.

We now proceed to that series of ecclesiastical authors who, from the character and name of their chief writings are called APOLOGISTS. They flourished during the reigns of Hadrian, Antoninus, and Marcus Aurelius, when Christianity was exposed to the literary as well as bloody persecution of the heathen world. They refuted the charges and slanders of Jews and Gentiles, vindicated the truths of the Gospel, and attacked the errors and vices of idolatry. They were men of more learning and culture than the Apostolic Fathers. They were mostly philosophers and rhetoricians, who embraced Christianity in mature age after earnest investigation, and found peace in it for mind and heart. Their writings breathe the same heroism, the same enthusiasm for the faith, which animated the martyrs in their sufferings and death.

The earliest of these Apologists are QUADRATUS and ARISTIDES, who wrote against the heathen, and ARISTO of Pella, who wrote against the Jews, all in the reign of Hadrian (117–137).

QUADRATUS (Κοδράτης) was a disciple of the apostles, and bishop (presbyter) of Athens. His *Apology* is lost. All we know of him is a quotation from Eusebius who says: "QUADRATUS addressed a discourse to Ælius Hadrian, as an apology for the religion that we profess; because certain malicious persons attempted to harass our brethren. The work is still in the hands of some of the brethren, as also in our own; from which any one may see evident proof, both of the understanding of the man, and of his apostolic faith. This writer shows the antiquity of the age in which he lived, in these passages: 'The deeds of our Saviour,' says he, 'were always before you, for they were true miracles; those that were healed, those that were raised from the dead, who were seen, not only when healed and when raised, but were always present. They remained living a long time, not only whilst our Lord was on earth, but likewise when he left the earth. So that some of them have also lived to our own times.' Such was Quadratus."

ARISTIDES (Ἀριστείδης) was an eloquent philosopher at Athens who is mentioned by Eusebius as a contemporary of Quadratus.[1] His *Apology* likewise disappeared long ago, but a fragment of it was recently recovered in an Armenian translation and published by the Mechitarists in 1878[2]. It was addressed to Hadrian, and shows that the preaching of Paul in Athens had taken root. It sets forth the Christian idea of God as an infinite and indescribable Being who made all things and cares for all things, whom we should serve and glorify as the only God; and the idea of Christ, who is described as "the Son of the most high God, revealed by the Holy Spirit, descended from heaven, born of a Hebrew Virgin. His flesh he received from the Virgin, and he revealed himself in the human nature as the Son of God. In his goodness which brought the glad tidings, he has won the whole world by his life-giving preaching. [It was he who according to the flesh was born from the race of the Hebrews, of the mother of God, the Virgin Mariam.][3] He selected twelve apostles and taught the whole world by his mediatorial, light-giving truth. And he was cru-

---

[1] *Hist. Eccl.* IV. 3.

[2] The discovery has called forth a considerable literature which is mentioned by Harnack, *Texte und Untersuchungen*, etc., I., p. 110, note 23. The first part is the most important. See a French translation by Gautier, in the "Revue de théol. et de philos.," 1879, p. 78–82; a German translation by Himpel in the "Tübing. Theol. Quartalschrift," 1880, reprinted by Harnack, pp. 111 and 112. The art. Aristides in the first vol. of Smith and Wace (p. 160) is behind the times. Bücheler and Renan doubt the genuineness of the document; Gautier, Baunard, Himpel, Harnack defend it; but Harnack assumes some interpolation, as the term *theotokos*, of the Virgin Mary. The Armenian MS. is dated 981, and the translation seems to have been made from the Greek in the fifth century. At the time of Eusebius the work was still well known in the church. But the second piece, which the Mechitarists also ascribe to Aristides, is a homily of later date, apparently directed against Nestorianism.

[3] The bracketed sentence sounds repetitious and like a post-Nicene interpolation.

cified, being pierced with nails by the Jews; and he rose from the dead and ascended to heaven. He sent the apostles into all the world and instructed all by divine miracles full of wisdom. Their preaching bears blossoms and fruits to this day, and calls the whole world to illumination."

A curious feature in this document is the division of mankind into four parts, Barbarians, Greeks, Jews, and Christians.

ARISTO OF PELLA, a Jewish Christian of the first half of the second century, was the author of a lost apology of Christianity against Judaism.[1]

§ 173. Justin the Philosopher and Martyr.

Editions of Justin Martyr.

* JUSTINI *Philosophi et Martyris Opera omnia*, in the CORPUS APOLOGE-TARUM *Christianorum sæculi secundi*, ed. *Jo. Car. Th. de Otto*, Jen. 1847, 3d ed. 1876–'81. 5 vols. 8vo. Contains the genuine, the doubtful, and the spurious works of Justin Martyr with commentary, and Maran's Latin Version.

Older ed. (mostly incomplete) by *Robt. Stephanus*, Par., 1551; *Sylburg*, Heidelb., 1593; *Grabe*, Oxon., 1700 (only the *Apol. I.*); *Prudent. Maranus*, Par., 1742 (the Bened. ed.), republ. at Venice, 1747, and in Migne's *Patrol. Gr.* Tom. VI. (Paris, 1857), c. 10–800 and 1102–1680, with additions from Otto. The *Apologies* were also often published separately, *e. g.* by Prof. *B. L. Gildersleeve*, N. Y. 1877, with introduction and notes.

On the MSS. of Justin see Otto's *Proleg.*, p. xx. sqq., and Harnack, *Texte.* Of the genuine works we have only two, and they are corrupt, one in Paris, the other in Cheltenham, in possession of Rev. F. A. Fenwick (see Otto, p. xxiv.).

English translation in the Oxford "Library of the Fathers," Lond., 1861, and another by G. J. Davie in the "Ante-Nicene Library," Edinb. Vol. II., 1867 (465 pages), containing the *Apologies*, the *Address to the Greeks*, the *Exhortation*, and the *Martyrium*, translated by M. Dods; the *Dialogue with Trypho*, and *On the Sole Government of God*, trsl. by G. Reith; and also the writings of Athenagoras, trsl. by B. P. Pratten. Older translations by Wm. Reeves, 1709, Henry Brown, 1755, and J. Chevallier, 1833 (ed. II., 1851). On German and other versions see Otto, *Prol.* LX. sqq.

Works on Justin Martyr.

Bp. KAYE: *Some Account of the Writings and Opinions of Justin Martyr.* Cambr., 1829, 3d ed., 1853.

---

[1] See above, § 38, p. 107, and Harnack. *l. c.* I. 115–130.

C. A. CREDNER: *Beiträge zur Einleitung in die bibl. Schriften.* Halle, vol. I., 1832 (92–267); also in vol. II., 1838 (on the quotations from the O. T., p. 17–98; 104–133; 157–311). Credner discusses with exhaustive learning Justin's relation to the Gospels and the Canon of the N. T., and his quotations from the Septuagint. Comp. also his *Geschichte des N. T. Canon*, ed. by Volkmar, 1860.

*C. SEMISCH: *Justin der Märtyrer.* Breslau, 1840 and 1842, 2 vols. Very thorough and complete up to date of publication. English translation by *Ryland*, Edinb., 1844, 2 vols. Comp. SEMISCH: *Die apostol. Denkwürdigkeiten des Just. M.* (Hamb. and Gotha, 1848), and his article *Justin* in the first ed. of Herzog, VII. (1857), 179–186.

FR. BÖHRINGER: *Die Kirchengesch. in Biographien.* Vol. I. Zürich, 1842, ed. II., 1861, p. 97–270.

AD. HILGENFELD: *Krit. Untersuchungen über die Evangelien Justin's.* Halle, 1850. Also: *Die Ap. Gesch. u. der M. Just.* in his "Zeitschr. f. wiss. Theol.," 1872, p. 495–509, and *Ketzergesch.*, 1884, pp. 21 sqq.

*J. C. TH. OTTO: *Zur Characteristik des heil. Justinus.* Wien, 1852. His art. *Justinus der Apologete*, in "Ersch and Gruber's Encyklop." Second Section, 30th part (1853), pp. 39–76. Comp. also his Prolegomena in the third ed. of Justin's works. He agrees with Semisch in his general estimate of Justin.

C. G. SEIBERT: *Justinus, der Vertheidiger des Christenthums vor dem Thron der Cæsaren.* Elberf., 1859.

CH. E. FREPPEL (R. C. Bp.): *Les Apologistes Chrétiens du II.ᵉ siècle.* Par., 1860.

L. SCHALLER: *Les deux Apologies de Justin M. au point de vie dogmatique.* Strasb., 1861.

B. AUBÉ: *De l' apologetique Chrétienne au II.ᵉ siècle.* Par., 1861; and *S. Justin philosophe et martyr*, 1875.

E. DE PRESSENSÉ, in the third vol. of his *Histoire des trois premiers siècles*, or second vol. of the English version (1870), which treats of Martyrs and Apologists, and his art. in Lichtenberger VII. (1880) 576–583.

EM. RUGGIERI: *Vita e dottrina di S. Giustino.* Rom., 1862.

*J. DONALDSON: *Hist. of Ante-Nicene Christian Literature.* Lond., vol. II. (1866), which treats of Justin M., pp. 62–344.

*C. WEIZSÄCKER: *Die Theologie des Märtyrers Justinus* in the "Jahrbücher fur Deutsche Theologie. Gotha, 1867 (vol. XII., I. pp. 60–120).

RENAN: *L'église chrétienne* (Par., 1879), ch. XIX., pp. 364–389, and ch. XXV. 480 sqq.

*MORITZ VON ENGELHARDT (d. 1881): *Das Christenthum Justins des Märtyrers.* Erlangen, 1878. (490 pages, no index.) With an instructive critical review of the various treatments of Irenæus and his place in history (p. 1–70). See also his art. *Justin* in Herzog², VII.

G. F. PURVES: *The Testimony of Justin M. to Early Christianity.* New York. 1888.

ADOLF STÄHELIN : *Justin der Märtyrer und sein neuster Beurtheiler.* Leip-
    zig, 1880 (67 pages).   A careful review of Engelhardt's monograph.
HENRY SCOTT HOLLAND: Art. *Justinus Martyr,* in Smith and Wace III.
    (1880), 560–587.
AD. HARNACK : *Die Werke des Justin,* in "Texte und Untersuchungen,"
    etc.   Leipz., 1882.   I. 130–195.
The relation of Justin to the Gospels is discussed by Credner, Semisch,
    Hilgenfeld, Norton, Sanday, Westcott, Abbot; his relation to the
    Acts by Overbeck (1872) and Hilgenfeld; his relation to the
    Pauline Epistles by H. D. Tjeenk Willink (1868), Alb. Thoma
    (1875), and v. Engelhardt (1878).

The most eminent among the Greek Apologists of the second
century is FLAVIUS JUSTINUS, surnamed "Philosopher and
Martyr."[1] He is the typical apologist, who devoted his whole
life to the defense of Christianity at a time when it was most
assailed, and he sealed his testimony with his blood.   He is also
the first Christian philosopher or the first philosophic theologian.
His writings were well known to Irenæus, Hippolytus, Eusebius, Epiphanius, Jerome, and Photius, and the most important
of them have been preserved to this day.

I. His LIFE.   Justin was born towards the close of the first
century, or in the beginning of the second, in the Græco-Roman
colony of Flavia Neapolis, so called after the emperor Flavius
Vespasian, and built near the ruins of Sychem in Samaria (now
Nablous).   He calls himself a Samaritan, but was of heathen
descent, uncircumcised, and ignorant of Moses and the prophets
before his conversion.   Perhaps he belonged to the Roman
colony which Vespasian planted in Samaria after the destruction of Jerusalem.   His grandfather's name was Greek (Bac-
chius), his father's (Priscus) and his own, Latin.   His education
was Hellenic.   To judge from his employment of several
teachers and his many journeys, he must have had some means,
though he no doubt lived in great simplicity and may have
been aided by his brethren.

---

[1] Tertullian (*Adv. Valent.* 5) first calls him *philosophus et martyr,* Hippolytus
(*Philos.* VIII. 16), "Just. Martyr;" Eusebius (*H. E.* IV. 12), "a genuine lover
of the true philosophy," who "in the garb of a philosopher proclaimed the
divine word and defended the faith by writings" (IV. 17).

His conversion occurred in his early manhood. He himself tells us the interesting story.[1] Thirsting for truth as the greatest possession, he made the round of the systems of philosophy and knocked at every gate of ancient wisdom, except the Epicurean which he despised. He first went to a Stoic, but found him a sort of agnostic who considered the knowledge of God impossible or unnecessary; then to a Peripatetic, but he was more anxious for a good fee than for imparting instruction; next to a celebrated Pythagorean, who seemed to know something, but demanded too much preliminary knowledge of music, astronomy and geometry before giving him an insight into the highest truths. At last he threw himself with great zeal into the arms of Platonism under the guidance of a distinguished teacher who had recently come to his city.[2] He was overpowered by the perception of immaterial things and the contemplation of eternal ideas of truth, beauty, and goodness. He thought that he was already near the promised goal of this philosophy—the vision of God—when, in a solitary walk not far from the sea-shore, a venerable old Christian of pleasant countenance and gentle dignity, entered into a conversation with him, which changed the course of his life. The unknown friend shook his confidence in all human wisdom, and pointed him to the writings of the Hebrew prophets who were older than the philosophers and had seen and spoken the truth, not as reasoners, but as witnesses. More than this: they had foretold the coming of Christ, and their prophecies were fulfilled in his life and work. The old man departed, and Justin saw him no more, but he took his advice and soon found in the prophets of the Old Testament as illuminated and confirmed by the Gospels, the true and infallible philosophy which rests upon the firm ground of

[1] *Dial. c. Tryph. Jud.* c. 2–8. The conversion occurred before the Bar-Cochba war, from which Tryphon was flying when Justin met him. Archbishop Trench has reproduced the story in thoughtful poetry (*Poems*, Lond. 1865, p. 1–10).

[2] This city may be Flavia Neapolis, or more probably Ephesus, where the conversation with Trypho took place, according to Eusebius (IV. 18). Some have located the scene at Corinth, others at Alexandria. Mere conjectures.

revelation. Thus the enthusiastic Platonist became a believing Christian.

To Tatian also, and Theophilus at Antioch, and Hilary, the Jewish prophets were in like manner the bridge to the Christian faith. We must not suppose, however, that the Old Testament alone effected his conversion; for in the Second *Apology*, Justin distinctly mentions as a means the practical working of Christianity. While he was yet a Platonist, and listened to the calumnies against the Christians, he was struck with admiration for their fearless courage and steadfastness in the face of death.[1]

After his conversion Justin sought the society of Christians, and received from them instruction in the history and doctrine of the gospel. He now devoted himself wholly to the spread and vindication of the Christian religion. He was an itinerant evangelist or teaching missionary, with no fixed abode and no regular office in the church.[2] There is no trace of his ordination; he was as far as we know a lay-preacher, with a commission from the Holy Spirit; yet he accomplished far more for the good of the church than any known bishop or presbyter of his day. "Every one," says he, "who can preach the truth and does not preach it, incurs the judgment of God." Like Paul, he felt himself a debtor to all men, Jew and Gentile, that he might show them the way of salvation. And, like Aristides, Athenagoras, Tertullian, Heraclas, Gregory Thaumaturgus, he retained his philosopher's cloak,[3] that he might the more readily

---

[1] *Apol.* II. 12, 13.

[2] Tillemont and Maran (in Migne's ed. col. 114) infer from his mode of describing baptism (*Apol.* I. 65) that he baptized himself, and consequently was a priest. But Justin speaks in the name of the Christians in that passage (" *We* after we have thus washed him," etc.) and throughout the *Apology;* besides baptism was no exclusively clerical act, and could be performed by laymen. Equally inconclusive is the inference of Maran from the question of the prefect to the associates of Justin (in the Acts of his martyrdom): " *Christianos vos ferit Justinus?* "

[3] τρίβων, τριβώνιον, *pallium*, a threadbare cloak, adopted by philosophers and afterwards by monks (the cowl) as an emblem of severe study or austere life, or both.

discourse on the highest themes of thought; and when he appeared in early morning (as he himself tells us), upon a public walk, many came to him with a "Welcome, philosopher!"[1] He spent some time in Rome where he met and combated Marcion. In Ephesus he made an effort to gain the Jew Trypho and his friends to the Christian faith.

He labored last, for the second time, in Rome. Here, at the instigation of a Cynic philosopher, Crescens, whom he had convicted of ignorance about Christianity, Justin, with six other Christians, about the year 166, was scourged and beheaded. Fearlessly and joyfully, as in life, so also in the face of death, he bore witness to the truth before the tribunal of Rusticus, the prefect of the city, refused to sacrifice, and proved by his own example the steadfastness of which he had so often boasted as a characteristic trait of his believing brethren. When asked to explain the mystery of Christ, he replied: "I am too little to say something great of him." His last words were: "We desire nothing more than to suffer for our Lord Jesus Christ; for this gives us salvation and joyfulness before his dreadful judgment seat, at which all the world must appear."

Justin is the first among the fathers who may be called a learned theologian and Christian thinker. He had acquired considerable classical and philosophical culture before his conversion, and then made it subservient to the defense of faith. He was not a man of genius and accurate scholarship, but of respectable talent, extensive reading, and enormous memory. He had some original and profound ideas, as that of the spermatic Logos, and was remarkably liberal in his judgment of the noble heathen and the milder section of the Jewish Christians. He lived in times when the profession of Christ was a crime under the Roman law against secret societies and prohibited religions. He had the courage of a confessor in life and of a martyr in death. It is impossible not to admire his fearless devotion to the cause of truth and the defense of his persecuted brethren.

[1] Φιλόσοφε, χαῖρε!

If not a great man, he was (what is better) an eminently good and useful man, and worthy of an honored place in "the noble army of martyrs."[1]

II. WRITINGS. To his oral testimony Justin added extensive literary labors in the field of apologetics and polemics. His pen was incessantly active against all the enemies of Christian truth, Jews, Gentiles, and heretics.

(1) His chief works are apologetic, and still remain, namely, his two *Apologies* against the heathen, and his *Dialogue with the Jew Trypho*. The *First* or larger *Apology* (68 chapters) is addressed to the Emperor Antoninus Pius (137–161) and his adopted sons, and was probably written about A. D. 147, if not earlier; the *Second* or smaller *Apology* (25 chapters) is a supplement to the former, perhaps its conclusion, and belongs to the same reign (not to that of Marcus Aurelius).[2] Both are a de-

---

[1] I add the estimate of Pressensé (*Martyrs and Apologists*, p. 251): "The truth never had a witness more disinterested, more courageous, more worthy of the hatred of a godless age and of the approval of Heaven. The largeness of his heart and mind equalled the fervor of his zeal, and both were based on his Christian charity. Justin derived all his eloquence from his heart; his natural genius was not of rare order, but the experiences of his early life, illumined by revelation, became the source of much fruitful suggestion for himself, and gave to the Church a heritage of thought which, ripened and developed at Alexandria, was to become the basis of the great apology of Christianity. If we except the beautiful doctrine of the Word *germinally present in every man*, there was little originality in Justin's theological ideas. In exegesis he is subtle, and sometimes puerile; in argument he flags, but where his heart speaks, he stands forth in all his moral greatness, and his earnest, generous words are ever quick and telling. Had he remained a pagan he would have lived unnoted in erudite mediocrity. Christianity fired and fertilized his genius, and it is the glowing soul which we chiefly love to trace in all his writings."

[2] The year of composition cannot be fixed with absolute certainty. The *First Apology* is addressed "To the Emperor (αὐτοκράτορι) Titus Aelius Adrianus Antoninus, Pius, Augustus Cæsar; and to Verissimus, his son, philosopher [*i. e.* Marcus Aurelius]; and to Lucius, the philosopher [?]—son by nature of a Cæsar [*i. e.* Cæsar Aelius Verus] and of Pius by adoption; and to the sacred Senate;—and to the whole Roman people," etc. The address violates the curial style, and is perhaps (as Mommsen and Volkmar suspect) a later addition, but no one doubts its general correctness. From the title "Verissimus," which Marcus Aurelius ceased to bear after his adoption by

fense of the Christians and their religion against heathen calumnies and persecutions. He demands nothing but justice for his brethren, who were condemned without trial, simply as Christians and suspected criminals. He appeals from the lower courts and the violence of the mob to the highest tribunal of law, and feels confident that such wise and philosophic rulers as he addresses would acquit them after a fair hearing. He ascribes the persecutions to the instigation of the demons who tremble for their power and will soon be dethroned.

The *Dialogue* (142 chapters) is more than twice as large as the two *Apologies*, and is a vindication of Christianity from Moses and the prophets against the objections of the Jews. It was written after the former (which are referred to in ch. 120), but also in the reign of Antoninus Pius, *i. e.*, before A. D. 161, pro-

Antonine in 138, and from the absence of the title "Cæsar," which he received in 139, the older critics have inferred that it must have been written shortly after the death of Hadrian (137), and Eusebius, in the *Chronicon*, assigns it to 141. The early date is strengthened by the fact that in the *Dialogue*, which was written *after* the *Apologies*, the Bar-Cochba war (132–135) is represented as still going on, or at all events as recent (φυγὼν τὸν νῦν γενόμενον πόλεμον, *ex bello nostra œtate profugus*, ch. I; comp. ch. 9). But, on the other hand, Marcus Aurelius was not really associated as co-regent with Antonine till 147, and in the book itself Justin seems to imply two regents. Lucius Verus, moreover, was born 130, and could not well be addressed in his eighth year as "philosopher;" Eusebius, however, reads "Son of the philosopher Cæsar;" and the term φιλόσοφος was used in a very wide sense. Of more weight is the fact that the first *Apology* was written *after* the *Syntagma* against Marcion, who flourished in Rome between 139–145, though this chronology, too, is not quite certain. Justin says that he was writing 150 years after the birth of the Saviour; if this is not simply a round number, it helps to fix the date. For these reasons modern critics decide for 147–150 (Volkmar, Baur, Von Engelhardt, Hort, Donaldson, Holland), or 150 (Lipsius and Renan), or 160 (Keim and Aubé). The smaller *Apology* was written likewise under Antoninus Pius (so Neander, Otto, Volkmar, Hort, contrary to Eusebius, IV. 15, 18, and the older view, which puts it in the reign of Marcus Aurelius); for it presupposes two rulers, but only one autocrat, while after his death there were two "Augusti" or autocrats. See on the chronology Volkmar, *Die Zeit Just. des M.*, in the "Theol. Jahrb." of Tübingen, 1855 (Nos. 2 and 4); Hort *On the Date of Justin M.*, in the "Journal of Classic and Sacred Philology," June 1856; Donaldson, II. 73 sqq.; Engelhardt, *l. c.* 71–80; Keim, *Rom. u. d. Christenth.*, p. 425; Renan, *l. c.* p. 367, note, and Harnack, *Texte und Unters.*, etc. I. 172 sq.

bably about A. D. 148.[1] In the *Apologies* he speaks like a philosopher to philosophers; in the *Dialogue* as a believer in the Old Testament with a son of Abraham. The disputation lasted two days, in the gymnasium just before a voyage of Justin, and turned chiefly on two questions, how the Christians could profess to serve God, and yet break his law, and how they could believe in a human Saviour who suffered and died. Trypho, whom Eusebius calls "the most distinguished among the Hebrews of his day," was not a fanatical Pharisee, but a tolerant and courteous Jew, who evasively confessed at last to have been much instructed, and asked Justin to come again, and to remember him as a friend. The book is a storehouse of early interpretation of the prophetic Scriptures.

The polemic works, *Against all Heresies*, and *Against Marcion*, are lost. The first is mentioned in the *First Apology;* of the second, Irenæus has preserved some fragments; perhaps it was only a part of the former.[2] Eusebius mentions also a *Psalter* of Justin, and a book *On the Soul*, which have wholly disappeared.

(2) Doubtful works which bear Justin's name, and may have been written by him: An address *To the Greeks;*[3] a treatise *On the Unity of God;* another *On the Resurrection*.

(3) Spurious works attributed to him: The *Epistle to Diognetus*, probably of the same date, but by a superior writer,[4] the *Exhortation to the Greeks*,[5] the *Deposition of the True Faith*, the epistle *To Zenas and Serenus*, the *Refutation of some Theses of Aristotle*, the *Questions to the Orthodox*, the *Questions of the Christians to the Heathens*, and the *Questions of the Heathens*

---

[1] Hort puts the *Dial.* between 142 and 148; Volkmar in 155; Keim between 160–164; Englehardt in 148 or after.

[2] On these anti-heretical works see Harnack, *Zur Quellenkritik des Gnosticismus* (1873), Lipsius, *Die Quellen der ältesten Ketzergeschichte* (1875), and Hilgenfeld, *D. Ketzergesch. des Urchristenthums* (1884, p. 21 sqq.).

[3] *Oratio ad Graecos*, λόγος πρὸς Ἕλληνας.   [4] See above, § 170, p. 702.

[5] *Cohortatio ad Græcos*, λόγος παραινετικὸς πρὸς Ἕλληνας. Based on Julius Africanus, as proved by Donaldson, and independently by Schürer in the "Zeitschrift für Kirchengesch." Bd. II. p. 319.

to the Christians. Some of these belong to the third or later centuries.[1]

The genuine works of Justin are of unusual importance and interest. They bring vividly before us the time when the church was still a small sect, despised and persecuted, but bold in faith and joyful in death. They everywhere attest his honesty and earnestness, his enthusiastic love for Christianity, and his fearlessness in its defense against all assaults from without and perversions from within. He gives us the first reliable account of the public worship and the celebration of the sacraments. His reasoning is often ingenious and convincing, but sometimes rambling and fanciful, though not more so than that of other writers of those times. His style is fluent and lively, but diffuse and careless. He writes under a strong impulse of duty and fresh impression without strict method or aim at rhetorical finish and artistic effect. He thinks pen in hand, without looking backward or forward, and uses his memory more than books. Only occasionally, as in the opening of the *Dialogue,* there is a touch of the literary art of Plato, his old master.[1] But the lack of careful elaboration is made up by freshness and truthfulness. If the emperors of Rome had read the books addressed to them they must have been strongly impressed, at least with the honesty of the writer and the innocence of the Christians.[2]

III. THEOLOGY. As to the sources of his religious knowledge,

---

[1] On these doubtful and spurious writings see Maranus, Otto, Semisch, Donaldson, and Harnack (*l. c.* 190–193).

[2] Comp. Otto *De Justiniana dictione,* in the *Proleg.* LXIII–LXXVI. Renan's judgment is interesting, but hardly just. He says (p. 365): " *Justin n'était un grand esprit; il manquait à la fois de philosophie et de critique; son exégèse surtout passerait aujour d' hui pour très défectueuse; mais il fait preuve d'un sens général assez droit; il avait cette espèce de crédulité médiocre qui permet de raissonner sensément sur des prémisses puériles et de s'arrêter à temps de façon à n'être qu'à moitié absurde.*" On the next page he says: " *Justin était un esprit faible; mais c'était un noble et bon cœur.*" Donaldson justly remarks (II. 15 sq.) that the faults of style and reasoning attributed to Justin and other Apologists may be paralleled in Plutarch and all other contemporaries, and that more learned and able writers could not have done better than present the same arguments in a more elaborate and polished form.

Justin derived it partly from the Holy Scriptures, partly from the living church tradition. He cites, most frequently, and generally from memory, hence often inaccurately, the Old Testament prophets (in the Septuagint), and the "Memoirs" of Christ, or "Memoirs by the Apostles," as he calls the canonical Gospels, without naming the authors.[1] He says that they were publicly read in the churches with the prophets of the Old Testament. He only quotes the words and acts of the Lord. He makes most use of Matthew and Luke, but very freely, and from John's Prologue (with the aid of Philo whom he never names) he derived the inspiration of the Logos-doctrine, which is the heart of his theology.[2] He expressly mentions the Revelation of John. He knew no fixed canon of the New Testament, and, like Hermas and Papias, he nowhere notices Paul; but several allusions to passages of his Epistles (Romans, First Corinthians, Ephesians, Colossians, etc.), can hardly be mistaken, and his controversy with Marcion must have implied a full knowledge of the ten Epistles which that heretic included in his canon. Any dogmatical inference from this silence is the less admissible, since, in the genuine writings of Justin, not one of the apostles or evangelists is expressly named except John once, and Simon Peter twice, and "the sons of Zebedee whom Christ called Boanerges," but reference is always made directly to Christ and to the prophets and apostles in general.[3] The last

---

[1] ἀπομνημονεύματα τῶν ἀποστόλων, a designation peculiar to Justin, and occurring in the *Apologies* and the *Dialogue*, but nowhere else, borrowed, no doubt, from Xenophon's *Memorabilia* of Socrates. Four times he calls them simply "Memoirs," four times "Memoirs of (or by) the Apostles;" once "Memoirs made by the Apostles," which constitute the one *Gospel* (τὸ εὐαγγέλιον, *Dial.* c. 10), and which "are called Gospels" (ἃ καλεῖται εὐαγγέλια, *Apol.* I. 66, a decisive passage), once, quoting from Mark, "Peter's Memoirs." After long and thorough discussion the identity of these Memoirs with our canonical Gospels is settled notwithstanding the doubts of the author of *Supernatural Religion*. It is possible, however, that Justin may have used also some kind of gospel harmony such as his pupil Tatian actually prepared.

[2] One unquestionable quotation from John (3: 3–5) is discussed in vol. I. 703 sq. If he did not cite the words of John, he evidently moved in his thoughts.

[3] See the list of Justin's Scripture quotations or allusions in Otto's edition.

are to him typified in the twelve bells on the border of the high priest's garment which sound through the whole world. But this no more excludes Paul from apostolic dignity than the names of the twelve apostles on the foundation stones of the new Jerusalem (Rev. 21: 14). They represent the twelve tribes of Israel, Paul the independent apostolate of the Gentiles.

Justin's exegesis of the Old Testament is apologetic, typological and allegorical throughout. He finds everywhere references to Christ, and turned it into a text book of Christian theology. He carried the whole New Testament into the Old without discrimination, and thus obliterated the difference. He had no knowledge of Hebrew,[1] and freely copied the blunders and interpolations of the Septuagint. He had no idea of grammatical or historical interpretation. He used also two or three times the Sibylline Oracles and Hystaspes for genuine prophecies, and appeals to the Apocryphal Acts of Pilate as an authority. We should remember, however, that he is no more credulous, inaccurate and uncritical than his contemporaries and the majority of the fathers.

Justin forms the transition from the apostolic fathers to the church fathers properly so called. He must not be judged by the standard of a later orthodoxy, whether Greek, Roman, or Evangelical, nor by the apostolic conflict between Jewish and Gentile Christianity, or Ebionism and Gnosticism, which at that time had already separated from the current of Catholic Christianity. It was a great mistake to charge him with Ebionism. He was a converted Gentile, and makes a sharp distinction between the church and the synagogue as two antagonistic organizations. He belongs to orthodox Catholicism as modified

---

579–592. The most numerous are from the Pentateuch, Isaiah, Matthew, and Luke. Of profane authors he quotes Plato, Homer, Euripides, Xenophon, and Menander.

[1] Donaldson (II. 148) infers from his Samaritan origin, and his attempts in one or two cases to give the etymology of Hebrew words (*Apol.* I. 33), that he must have known a little Hebrew, but it must have been a very little indeed: at all events he never appeals to the Hebrew text.

by Greek philosophy. The Christians to him are the true
people of God and heirs of all the promises. He distinguishes
between Jewish Christians who would impose the yoke of the
Mosaic law (the Ebionites), and those who only observe it
themselves, allowing freedom to the Gentiles (the Nazarenes);
the former he does not acknowledge as Christians, the latter he
treats charitably, like Paul in Romans ch. 14 and 15. The
only difference among orthodox Christians which he mentions is
the belief in the millennium which he held, like Barnabas,
Irenæus and Tertullian, but which many rejected. But, like all
the ante-Nicene writers, he had no clear insight into the distinction between the Old Testament and the New, between the law
and the gospel, nor any proper conception of the depth of sin
and redeeming grace, and the justifying power of faith. His
theology is legalistic and ascetic rather than evangelical and
free. He retained some heathen notions from his former studies,
though he honestly believed them to be in full harmony with
revelation.

Christianity was to Justin, theoretically, the *true philosophy*,[1]
and, practically, a *new law* of holy living and dying.[2] The
former is chiefly the position of the *Apologies*, the latter that of
the *Dialogue*.

He was not an original philosopher, but a philosophizing
eclectic, with a prevailing love for Plato, whom he quotes more
frequently than any other classical author. He may be called,
in a loose sense, a Christian Platonist. He was also influenced
by Stoicism. He thought that the philosophers of Greece had
borrowed their light from Moses and the prophets. But his
relation to Plato after all is merely external, and based upon
fancied resemblances. He illuminated and transformed his
Platonic reminiscences by the prophetic Scriptures, and especially by the Johannean doctrine of the Logos and the incar-

[1] He calls the Christian religion (*Dial.* c. 8) μόνη φιλοσοφία ἀσφαλής τε καὶ
σύμφορος, *sola philosophia tuta atque utilis*.

[2] τελευταῖος νόμος καὶ διαθήκη κυριωτάτη πασῶν, *novissima lex et fœdus omnium
firmissimum*. *Dial.* c. 11.

nation. This is the central idea of his philosophical theology. Christianity is the highest reason. The Logos is the pre-existent, absolute, personal Reason, and Christ is the embodiment of it, the Logos incarnate. Whatever is rational is Christian, and whatever is Christian is rational.[1] The Logos endowed all men with reason and freedom, which are not lost by the fall. He scattered seeds (σπέρματα) of truth before his incarnation, not only among the Jews, but also among the Greeks and barbarians, especially among philosophers and poets, who are the prophets of the heathen. Those who lived reasonably (οἱ μετὰ λόγου βιώσαντες) and virtuously in obedience to this preparatory light were Christians in fact, though not in name; while those who lived unreasonably (οἱ ἄνευ λόγου βιώσαντες) were Christless and enemies of Christ.[2] Socrates was a Christian as well as Abraham, though he did not know it. None of the fathers or schoolmen has so widely thrown open the gates of salvation. He was the broadest of broad churchmen.

This extremely liberal view of heathenism, however, did not blind him to the prevailing corruption. The mass of the Gentiles are idolaters, and idolatry is under the control of the devil and the demons. The Jews are even worse than the heathen, because they sin against better knowledge. And worst of all are the heretics, because they corrupt the Christian truths. Nor did he overlook the difference between Socrates and Christ, and between the best of heathen and the humblest Christian. "No one trusted Socrates," he says, "so as to die for his doctrine; but Christ, who was partially known by Socrates, was trusted not only by philosophers and scholars, but also by artizans and people altogether unlearned."

The Christian faith of Justin is faith in God the Creator, and

---

[1] Very different from the principle of Hegel: All that is rational is real, and all that is real is rational.

[2] He calls them ἄχρηστοι (useless), Apol. I. 46; with reference to the frequent confusion of Χριστός with χρηστός, good. Comp. Apol. I. 4: Χριστιανοὶ εἶναι κατηγορούμεθα· τὸ δὲ χρηστὸν μισεῖσθαι οὐ δίκαιον. Justin knew, however, the true derivation of Χριστός, see Apol. II. 6.

in his Son Jesus Christ the Redeemer, and in the prophetic Spirit.   All other doctrines which are revealed through the prophets and apostles, follow as a matter of course.   Below the deity are good and bad angels; the former are messengers of God, the latter servants of Satan, who caricature Bible doctrines in heathen mythology, invent slanders, and stir up persecutions against Christians, but will be utterly overthrown at the second coming of Christ.   The human soul is a creature, and hence perishable, but receives immortality from God, eternal happiness as a reward of piety, eternal fire as a punishment of wickedness.   Man has reason and free will, and is hence responsible for all his actions; he sins by his own act, and hence deserves punishment.   Christ came to break the power of sin, to secure forgiveness and regeneration to a new and holy life.

Here comes in the practical or ethical side of this Christian philosophy.   It is wisdom which emanates from God and leads to God.   It is a new law and a new covenant, promised by Isaiah and Jeremiah, and introduced by Christ.   The old law was only for the Jews, the new is for the whole world; the old was temporary and is abolished, the new is eternal; the old commands circumcision of the flesh, the new, circumcision of the heart; the old enjoins the observance of one day, the new sanctifies all days; the old refers to outward performances, the new to spiritual repentance and faith, and demands entire consecration to God.

IV. From the time of Justin Martyr, the PLATONIC PHILOSOPHY continued to exercise a direct and indirect influence upon Christian theology, though not so unrestrainedly and naïvely as in his case.[1]   We can trace it especially in Clement of Alex-

---

[1] On the general subject of the relation of Platonism to Christianity, see Ackermann, *Das Christliche im Plato* (1835, Engl. transl. by Asbury, with preface by Shedd, 1861); Baur, *Socrates und Christus* (1837, and again ed. by Zeller, 1876); Tayler Lewis, *Plato against the Atheists* (1845); Hampden, *The Fathers of the Greek Philosophy* (1862); Cocker, *Christianity and Greek Philosophy* (1870), Ueberweg's *History of Philosophy* (Engl. transl. 1872), and an excellent art. of Prof. W. S. Tyler, of Amherst College, in the third vol. of Schaff-Herzog's *Rel. Encycl.* (1883, p. 1850–'53).   On the relation of Justin to Platonism and heathenism, see von Engelhardt, *l. c.* 447–484.

andria and Origen, and even in St. Augustin, who confessed that it kindled in him an incredible fire. In the scholastic period it gave way to the Aristotelian philosophy, which was better adapted to clear, logical statements. But Platonism maintained its influence over Maximus, John of Damascus, Thomas Aquinas, and other schoolmen, through the pseudo-Dionysian writings which first appear at Constantinople in 532, and were composed probably in the fifth century. They represent a whole system of the universe under the aspect of a double hierarchy, a heavenly and an earthly, each consisting of three triads.

The Platonic philosophy offered many points of resemblance to Christianity. It is spiritual and idealistic, maintaining the supremacy of the spirit over matter, of eternal ideas over all temporary phenomena, and the pre-existence and immortality of the soul ; it is theistic, making the supreme God above all the secondary deities, the beginning, middle, and end of all things; it is ethical, looking towards present and future rewards and punishments ; it is religious, basing ethics, politics, and physics upon the authority of the Lawgiver and Ruler of the universe; it leads thus to the very threshold of the revelation of God in Christ, though it knows not this blessed name nor his saving grace, and obscures its glimpses of truth by serious errors. Upon the whole the influence of Platonism, especially as represented in the moral essays of Plutarch, has been and is to this day elevating, stimulating, and healthy, calling the mind away from the vanities of earth to the contemplation of eternal truth, beauty, and goodness. To not a few of the noblest teachers of the church, from Justin the philosopher to Neander the historian, Plato has been a schoolmaster who led them to Christ.

NOTES.

The theology and philosophy of Justin are learnedly discussed by Maran, and recently by Möhler and Freppel in the Roman Catholic interest, and in favor of his full orthodoxy. Among Protestants his orthodoxy was first doubted by the authors of the "Magdeburg Centuries," who judged him from the Lutheran standpoint.

Modern Protestant historians viewed him chiefly with reference to the conflict between Jewish and Gentile Christianity. Credner first endeavored to prove, by an exhaustive investigation (1832), that Justin was a Jewish Christian of the Ebionitic type, with the Platonic Logos-doctrine attached to his low creed as an appendix. He was followed by the Tübingen critics, Schwegler (1846), Zeller, Hilgenfeld, and Baur himself (1853). Baur, however, moderated Credner's view, and put Justin rather *between* Jewish and Gentile Christianity, calling him a Pauline in fact, but not in name (*" er ist der Sache nach Pauliner, aber dem Namen nach will er es nicht sein"*). This shaky judgment shows the unsatisfactory character of the Tübingen construction of Catholic Christianity as the result of a conflux and compromise between Ebionism and Paulinism.

Ritschl (in the second ed. of his *Entstehung der altkatholischen Kirche,* 1857) broke loose from this scheme and represented ancient Catholicism as a development of *Gentile* Christianity, and Justin as the type of the *"katholisch werdende Heidenchristenthum,"* who was influenced by Pauline ideas, but unable to comprehend them in their depth and fulness, and thus degraded the standpoint of freedom to a new form of legalism. This he calls a *"herabgekommener* or *abgeschwächter Paulinismus."* Engelhardt goes a step further, and explains this degradation of Paulinism from the influences of Hellenic heathenism and the Platonic and Stoic modes of thought. He says (p. 485) : " Justin was at once a Christian and a heathen. We must acknowledge his Christianity and his heathenism in order to understand him." Harnack (in a review of E., 1878) agrees with him, and lays even greater stress on the heathen element. Against this Stähelin (1880) justly protests, and vindicates his truly Christian character.

Among recent French writers, Aubé represents Justin's theology superficially as nothing more than popularized heathen philosophy. Renan (p. 389) calls his philosophy *" une sorte d'eclectisme fondé sur un rationalisme mystic."* Freppel returns to Maran's treatment, and tries to make the philosopher and martyr of the second century even a Vatican Romanist of the nineteenth.

For the best estimates of his character and merits see Neander, Semisch, Otto, von Engelhardt, Stähelin, Donaldson (II. 147 sqq.), and Holland (in Smith and Wace).

§ 174. *The Other Greek Apologists. Tatian.*

Lit. on the later Greek Apologists:

Otto: *Corpus Apologetarum Christ.* Vol. VI. (1861): Tatiani Assyrii *Opera*; vol. VII.: Athenagoras; vol. VIII. : Theophilus; vol. IX. : Hermias, Quadratus, Aristides, Aristo, Miltiades, Melito, Apollinaris (*Reliquiæ*). Older ed. by Maranus, 1742, reissued by Migne, 1857, in Tom. VI. of his " Patrol. Gr." A new ed. by O. v. Gebhardt and E. Schwartz, begun Leipz. 1888.

The third vol. of DONALDSON'S *Critical History of Christ. Lit. and Doctr.*, etc. (Lond. 1866) is devoted to the same Apologists. Comp. also KEIM'S *Rom und das Christenthum* (1881), p. 439–495; and on the MSS. and early traditions HARNACK'S *Texte*, etc. Band I. Heft. 1 and 2 (1882), and SCHWARTZ in his ed. (1888).

On TATIAN see § 131, p. 493–496.

TATIAN of Assyria (110–172) was a pupil of Justin Martyr whom he calls a most admirable man ($\vartheta\alpha\upsilon\mu\alpha\sigma\iota\dot{\omega}\tau\alpha\tau\circ\varsigma$), and like him an itinerant Christian philosopher; but unlike him he seems to have afterwards wandered to the borders of heretical Gnosticism, or at least to an extreme type of asceticism. He is charged with having condemned marriage as a corruption and denied that Adam was saved, because Paul says: "We all die in Adam." He was an independent, vigorous and earnest man, but restless, austere, and sarcastic.[1] In both respects he somewhat resembles Tertullian. Before his conversion he had studied mythology, history, poetry, and chronology, attended the theatre and athletic games, became disgusted with the world, and was led by the Hebrew Scriptures to the Christian faith.[2]

We have from him an apologetic work addressed *To the Greeks*.[3] It was written in the reign of Marcus Aurelius, pro-

[1] Comp. Donaldson, III. 27 sqq.

[2] He tells his conversion himself, *Ad Gr.* c. 29 and 30. The following passage (29) is striking: "While I was giving my most earnest attention to the matter [the discovery of the truth], I happened to meet with certain barbaric writings, too old to be compared with the opinions of the Greeks, and too divine to be compared with their errors; and I was led to put faith in these by the unpretending cast of the language, the inartificial character of the writers, the foreknowledge displayed of future events, the excellent quality of the precepts, and the declaration of the government of the universe as centred in one Being. And, my soul being taught of God, I discerned that the former class of writings lead to condemnation, but that these put an end to the slavery that is in the world, and rescue us from a multiplicity of rulers and ten thousand tyrants, while they give us, not indeed what we had not before received, but what we had received, but were prevented by error from retaining."

[3] Πρὸς Ἕλληνας, *Oratio ad Græcos*. The best critical edition by Ed. Schwartz, Leipsig, 1888. On the MSS. see also Otto's *Proleg.*, and Harnack's *Texte*, etc. Bd. I. Heft. I. p. 1–97. English translation by B. P. Pratten, in the "Ante-Nicene Library," III. 1–48; Am. ed. II., 59 sqq. The specimens below are from this version, compared with the Greek.

bably in Rome, and shows no traces of heresy. He vindicates
Christianity as the " philosophy of the barbarians," and exposes
the contradictions, absurdities, and immoralities of the Greek mythology from actual knowledge and with much spirit and acute-
ness, but with vehement contempt and bitterness. He proves
that Moses and the prophets were older and wiser than the
Greek philosophers, and gives much information on the antiquity of the Jews. Eusebius calls this " the best and most useful of his writings," and gives many extracts in his *Præparatio
Evangelica*.

The following specimens show his power of ridicule and
his radical antagonism to Greek mythology and philosophy :

Ch. 21.—*Doctrines of the Christians and Greeks respecting God compared.*

" We do not act as fools, O Greeks, nor utter idle tales, when we announce that God was born in the form of a man. (ἐν ἀνθρώπου μορφῇ
γεγονέναι). I call on you who reproach us to compare your mythical accounts with our narrations. Athene, as they say, took the form of Dei-
phobus for the sake of Hector, and the unshorn Phœbus for the sake of
Admetus fed the trailing-footed oxen, and the spouse of Zeus came as an
old woman to Semelé. But, while you treat seriously such things, how
can you deride us? Your Asclepios died, and he who ravished fifty virgins in one night at Thespiæ, lost his life by delivering himself to the de-
vouring flame. Prometheus, fastened to Caucasus, suffered punishment
for his good deeds to men. According to you, Zeus is envious, and hides
the dream from men, wishing their destruction. Wherefore, looking at
your own memorials, vouchsafe us your approval, though it were only as
dealing in legends similar to your own. We, however, do not deal in
folly, but your legends are only idle tales. If you speak of the origin
of the gods, you also declare them to be mortal. For what reason is
Hera now never pregnant? Has she grown old? or is there no one to
give you information? Believe me now, O Greeks, and do not resolve
your myths and gods into allegory. If you attempt to do this, the divine
nature as held by you is overthrown by your own selves; for, if the
demons with you are such as they are said to be, they are worthless as to
character; or, if regarded as symbols of the powers of nature, they are
not what they are called. But I cannot be persuaded to pay religious
homage to the natural elements, nor can I undertake to persuade my
neighbor. And Metrodorus of Lampsacus, in his treatise concerning
Homer, has argued very foolishly, turning everything into allegory. For
he says that neither Hera, nor Athene, nor Zeus are what those persons
suppose who consecrate to them sacred enclosures and groves, but parts

of nature and certain arrangements of the elements. Hector also, and Achilles, and Agamemnon, and all the Greeks in general, and the Barbarians with Helen and Paris, being of the same nature, you will of course say are introduced merely for the sake of the machinery of the poem, not one of these personages having really existed.

But these things we have put forth only for argument's sake; for it is not allowable even to compare our notions of God with those who are wallowing in matter and mud."

Ch. 25. *Boastings and quarrels of the philosophers.*

"What great and wonderful things have your philosophers effected? They leave uncovered one of their shoulders; they let their hair grow long; they cultivate their beards; their nails are like the claws of wild beasts. Though they say that they want nothing, yet, like Proteus [the Cynic, Proteus Peregrinus known to us from Lucian], they need a currier for their wallet, and a weaver for their mantle, and a woodcutter for their staff, and they need the rich [to invite them to banquets], and a cook also for their gluttony. O man competing with the dog [cynic philosopher], you know not God, and so have turned to the imitation of an irrational animal. You cry out in public with an assumption of authority, and take upon you to avenge your own self; and if you receive nothing, you indulge in abuse, for philosophy is with you the art of getting money. You follow the doctrines of Plato, and a disciple of Epicurus lifts up his voice to oppose you. Again, you wish to be a disciple of Aristotle, and a follower of Democritus rails at you. Pythagoras says that he was Euphorbus, and he is the heir of the doctrine of Pherecydes, but Aristotle impugns the immortality of the soul. You who receive from your predecessors doctrines which clash with one another, you the inharmonious, are fighting against the harmonious. One of you asserts "that God is body," but I assert that He is without body; "that the world is indestructible," but I assert that it is to be destroyed; "that a conflagration will take place at various times," but I say that it will come to pass once for all; "that Minos and Rhadamanthus are judges," but I say that God Himself is Judge; "that the soul alone is endowed with immortality," but I say that the flesh also is endowed with it. What injury do we inflict upon you, O Greeks? Why do you hate those who follow the word of God, as if they were the vilest of mankind? It is not we who eat human flesh—they among you who assert such a thing have been suborned as false witnesses; it is among you that Pelops is made a supper for the gods, although beloved by Poseidon ; and Kronos devours his children, and Zeus swallows Metis."

Of great importance for the history of the canon and of exegesis is Tatian's *Diatessaron* or Harmony of the Four Gospels, once widely circulated, then lost, but now measurably recovered.[1] Theodoret found more than two hundred copies of it in his diocese.   Ephræm the Syrian wrote a commentary on it which was preserved in an Armenian translation by the Mechitarists at Venice, translated into Latin by Aucher (1841), and published with a learned introduction by Mösinger (1876).   From this commentary Zahn has restored the text (1881).   Since then an Arabic translation of the *Diatessaron* itself has been discovered and published by Ciasca (1888).   The *Diatessaron* begins with the Prologue of John (*In principio erat Verbum,* etc.), follows his order of the festivals, assuming a two years' ministry, and makes a connected account of the life of Christ from the four Evangelists.   There is no heretical tendency, except perhaps in the omission of Christ's human genealogies in Matthew and Luke, which may have been due to the influence of a docetic spirit. This *Diatessaron* conclusively proves the existence and ecclesiastical use of the four Gospels, no more and no less, in the middle of the second century.

§ 175. *Athenagoras.*

OTTO, vol. VII.; MIGNE, VI. 890–1023.   Am. ed. by W. B. OWEN, N. Y., 1875.

CLARISSE: *De Athenagoræ vita, scriptis, doctrina* (Lugd. Bat. 1819); DONALDSON, III. 107–178; HARNACK, *Texte,* I. 176 sqq., and his art. "Athen." in Herzog,[2] I. 748–750; SPENCER MANSEL in Smith andᵢWace, I. 204–207; RENAN, *Marc-Aurèle,* 382–386.

ATHENAGORAS was " a Christian philosopher of Athens," during the reign of Marcus Aurelius (A. D., 161–180), but is otherwise entirely unknown and not even mentioned by Eusebius, Jerome, and Photius.[2]   His philosophy was Platonic, but

---

[1] Τὸ διὰ τεσσάρων.   Eusebius, *H. E.* IV. 29, and Theodoret, *Fab. Hær.* I. 20, notice the Diatessaron.   Comp. Mösinger's introduction to his ed. of *Ephræm's Com.* (Venet. 1876), Zahn's *Tatian's Diatessaron* (1881), and Ciasca's edition of the Arabic version (1888) noticed p. 493.

[2] The account of Philippus Sidetes, deacon of Chrysostom, as preserved by Nicephorus Callistus, is entirely unreliable.   It makes Athenagoras the first head of the school of Alexandria under Hadrian, and the teacher of Clement of Alex.—a palpable chronological blunder—and states that he addressed his

modified by the prevailing eclecticism of his age. He is less original as an apologist than Justin and Tatian, but more elegant and classical in style.

He addressed an *Apology* or *Intercession in behalf of the Christians* to the Emperors Marcus Aurelius and Commodus.[1] He reminds the rulers that all their subjects are allowed to follow their customs without hindrance except the Christians who are vexed, plundered and killed on no other pretence than that they bear the name of their Lord and Master. We do not object to punishment if we are found guilty, but we demand a fair trial. A name is neither good nor bad in itself, but becomes good or bad according to the character and deeds under it. We are accused of three crimes, atheism, Thyestean banquets (cannibalism), Oedipodean connections (incest). Then he goes on to refute these charges, especially that of atheism and incest. He does it calmly, clearly, eloquently, and conclusively. By a divine law, he says, wickedness is ever fighting against virtue. Thus Socrates was condemned to death, and thus are stories invented against us. We are so far from committing the excesses of which we are accused, that we are not permitted to lust after a woman in thought. We are so particular on this point that we either do not marry at all, or we marry for the sake of children, and only once in the course of our life. Here comes out his ascetic tendency which he shares with his age. He even condemns second marriage as " decent adultery." The Christians are more humane than the heathen, and condemn, as murder, the practices of abortion, infanticide, and gladiatorial shows.

Apology to Hadrian and Antoninus, which is contradicted by the inscription. But in a fragment of Methodius, *De Resurrectione*, there is a quotation from the *Apology* of Athenagoras (c. 24) with his name attached.

[1] Πρεσβεία (embassy) περὶ Χριστιανῶν, *Legatio* (also *Supplicatio, Intercessio*) *pro Christianis*. Some take the title in its usual sense, and assume that Athenagoras really went as a deputation to the emperor. The book was often copied in the fifteenth century, and there are seventeen MSS. extant; the three best contain also the treatise on the Resurrection. Both were edited by Henry Stephens, 1557, and often since. The objections against the genuineness are weak and have been refuted.

Another treatise under his name, " *On the Resurrection of the Dead*," is a masterly argument drawn from the wisdom, power, and justice of God, as well as from the destiny of man, for this doctrine which was especially offensive to the Greek mind. It was a discourse actually delivered before a philosophical audience. For this reason perhaps he does not appeal to the Scriptures.

All historians put a high estimate on Athenagoras. " He writes," says Donaldson, " as a man who is determined that the real state of the case should be exactly known. He introduces similes, he occasionally has an antithesis, he quotes poetry, but always he has his main object distinctly before his mind, and he neither makes a useless exhibition of his own powers, nor distracts the reader by digressions. His *Apology* is the best defence of the Christians produced in that age." Spencer Mansel declares him " decidedly superior to most of the Apologists, elegant, free from superfluity of language, forcible in style, and rising occasionally into great powers of description, and in his reasoning remarkable for clearness and cogency."

Tillemont found traces of Montanism in the condemnation of second marriage and the view of prophetic inspiration, but the former was common among the Greeks, and the latter was also held by Justin M. and others. Athenagoras says of the prophets that they were in an ecstatic condition of mind and that the Spirit of God " used them as if a flute-player were breathing into his flute." Montanus used the comparison of the plectrum and the lyre.

§ 176. *Theophilus of Antioch.*

OTTO, vol. VIII. MIGNE, VI. col. 1023–1168.

DONALDSON, *Critical History*, III. 63–106.   RENAN, *Marc-Aur.* 386 sqq.

THEOD. ZAHN : *Der Evangelien-commentar des Theophilus von Antiochien.* Erlangen 1883 (302 pages). The second part of his *Forschungen zur Gesch. des neutestam. Kanons und der altkirchlichen Lit.* Also his *Supplementum Clementinum*, 1884, p. 198–276 (in self-defense against Harnack).

HARNACK, *Texte*, etc. Bd. I., Heft II., 282–298., and Heft. IV. (1883), p. 97–175 (on the Gospel Commentary of Theoph.. against Zahn).

A. HAUCK : *Zur Theophilusfrage*, Leipz. 1844, and in Herzog,[2] xv. 544.

W. BORNEMANN : *Zur Theophilusfrage;* In ''Brieger's Zeitschrift f. Kirchen-Geschichte*,*'' 1888, p. 169–283.

THEOPHILUS was converted from heathenism by the study of the Scriptures, and occupied the episcopal see at Antioch, the sixth from the Apostles, during the later part of the reign of Marcus Aurelius. He died about A. D. 181.[1]

His principal work, and the only one which has come down to us, is his three books to Autolycus, an educated heathen friend.[2] His main object is to convince him of the falsehood of idolatry, and of the truth of Christianity. He evinces extensive knowledge of Grecian literature, considerable philosophical talent, and a power of graphic and elegant composition. His treatment of the philosophers and poets is very severe and contrasts unfavorably with the liberality of Justin Martyr. He admits elements of truth in Socrates and Plato, but charges them with having stolen the same from the prophets. He thinks that the Old Testament already contained all the truths which man requires to know. He was the first to use the term "triad" for the holy Trinity, and found this mystery already in the words: " Let us make man " (Gen. 1: 26); for, says he, " God spoke to no other but to his own Reason and his own Wisdom," that is, to the Logos and the Holy Spirit hypostatized.[3] He also first

---

[1] Eusebius *H. E.* IV. 20, and in his *Chron.* ad ann. IX. M. Aurelii. His supposed predecessors were Peter, Evodius, Ignatius, Heron, Cornelius, and Eros. Comp. Harnack, *Die Zeit des Ignat. und die Chronologie der Antiochen. Bischöfe bis Tyrannus* (Leipz. 1878 p. 56). Jerome (*De Vir. ill.* 25; *Ep. ad Algas.*, and *Praef. in Com. Matth.*), Lactantius (*Inst. div.* I. 23), and Gennadius of Massila (*De Vir. ill.* 34) likewise mention Theophilus and his writings, but the later Greeks, even Photius, seem to have forgotten him. See Harnack, *Texte*, I. 282 sqq. Renan calls him *"un docteur très fécond, un catechiste doné d'un grand talent d'exposition, un polémiste habile selon les idées du temps."*

[2] Θεοφίλου πρὸς Αὐτόλυκον, *Theophili ad Autolycum.* We have three MSS. of his books *Ad Autolycum*, the best from the eleventh century, preserved in Venice. See Otto, and Donaldson, p. 105. The first printed edition appeared at Zürich, 1546. Three English translations, by J. Betty, Oxf. 1722, by W. B Flower, Lond. 1860, and Marcus Dods, Edinb. 1867 (in the "Ante-Nicene Libr." III. 49–133).

[3] *Ad Autol.* II. 15 (in Migne VI. 1077), where the first three days of creation are called τύποι τῆς τριάδος, τοῦ θεοῦ, καὶ τοῦ λόγου αὐτοῦ, καὶ τῆς σοφίας αὐτοῦ. Comp. c. 18 (col. 1081), where the trinity is found in Gen. 1: 26. In the Gospel Com. of Th. the word *trinitas* occurs five times (see Zahn, *l. c.* 143). Among Latin writers, Tertullian is the first who uses the term *trinitas* (*Adv Prax.* 4; *De Pud.* 21).

quoted the Gospel of John by *name*,[1] but it was undoubtedly known and used before by Tatian, Athenagoras, Justin, and by the Gnostics, and can be traced as far back as 125 within the lifetime of many personal disciples of the Apostle.   Theophilus describes the Christians as having a sound mind, practising self-restraint, preserving marriage with one, keeping chastity, expelling injustice, rooting out sin, carrying out righteousness as a habit, regulating their conduct by law, being ruled by truth, preserving grace and peace, and obeying God as king. They are forbidden to visit gladiatorial shows and other public amusements, that their eyes and ears may not be defiled.   They are commanded to obey authorities and to pray for them, but not to worship them.

The other works of Theophilus, polemical and exegetical, are lost.   Eusebius mentions a book against Hermogenes, in which he used proofs from the Apocalypse of John, another against Marcion and "certain catechetical books" (κατηχητικὰ βιβλία).   Jerome mentions in addition commentaries on the Proverbs, and on the Gospel, but doubts their genuineness. There exists under his name, though only in Latin, a sort of exegetical Gospel Harmony, which is a later compilation of uncertain date and authorship.

NOTES.

Jerome is the only ancient writer who mentions a Commentary or Commentaries of Theophilus on the Gospel, but adds that they are inferior to his other books in elegance and style; thereby indicating a doubt as to their genuineness. *De Vir ill.* 25: "*Legi sub nomine eius* [*Theophili*] IN EVANGELIUM *et in Proverbia Salomonis* COMMENTARIOS, *qui mihi cum superiorum voluminum* [the works *Contra Marcionem, Ad Autolycum*, and *Contra Hermogenem*] *elegantia et phrasi non videntur congruere.*" He alludes to the Gospel Commentary in two other passages (in the Pref. to his *Com. on Matthew*, and *Ep.* 121 (*ad Algasiam*), and quotes from it the exposition of the parable of the unjust steward (Luke 16: 1 sqq.). Eusebius may possibly have included the book in the κατηχητικά βιβλία which he ascribes to Theophilus.

[1] *Ad Autol.* II. 22: "The Holy Scriptures teach us, and all who were moved by the Spirit, among whom John says: 'In the beginning was the Word (Logos), and the Word was with God.'" He then quotes John 1: 3.

A Latin Version of this Commentary was first published (from MSS. not indicated and since lost) by Marg. de la Bigne in *Sacræ Bibliothecæ Patrum*, Paris 1576, Tom. V. col. 169–196; also by Otto in the *Corp. Apol.* VIII. 278–324, and with learned notes by Zahn in the second vol. of his *Forschungen zur Gesch. des neutest. Kanons* (1883), p. 31–85. The Commentary begins with an explanation of the symbolical import of the four Gospels as follows : " *Quatuor evangelia quatuor animalibus figurata Jesum Christum demonstrant. Matthæus enim salvatorem nostrum natum passumque homini comparavit. Marcus leonis gerens figuram a solitudine incipit dicens : ' Vox clamantis in deserto : parate viam Domini,' sane qui regnat invictus. Joannes habet similitudinem aquilæ, quod ab imis alta petiverit ; ait enim : ' In principio erat Verbum, et verbum erat apud Deum, et Deus erat Verbum ; hoc erat in principio apud Deum ;' vel quia Christus resurgens volavit ad cœlos. Lucas vituli speciem gestat, ad cuius instar salvator noster est immolatus, vel quod sacerdotii figurat officium.*" The position of Luke as the fourth is very peculiar and speaks for great antiquity. Then follows a brief exposition of the genealogy of Christ by Matthew with the remark that Matthew traces the origin " *per reges,*" Luke " *per sacerdotes.*" The first book of the Commentary is chiefly devoted to Matthew, the second and third to Luke, the fourth to John. It concludes with an ingenious allegory representing Christ as a gardener (who appeared to Mary Magdalene, John 20 : 15), and the church as his garden full of rich flowers) as follows (see Zahn, p. 85) : " *Hortus Domini est ecclesia catholica, in qua sunt rosae martyrum, lilia virginum, violae viduarum, hedera coniugum ; nam illa, quæ æstimabat eum hortulanum esse significabat scilicet eum plantantem diversis virtutibus credentium vitam. Amen.*"

Dr. Zahn, in his recent monograph (1883), which abounds in rare patristic learning, vindicates this Commentary to Theophilus of Antioch and dates the translation from the third century. If so, we would have here a work of great apologetic as well as exegetical importance, especially for the history of the canon and the text; for Theophilus stood midway between Justin Martyr and Irenæus and would be the oldest Christian exegete. But a Nicene or post-Nicene development of theology and church organization is clearly indicated by the familiar use of such terms as *regnum Christi catholicum, catholica doctrina, catholicum dogma, sacerdos, peccatum originale, monachi, sœculares, pagani.* The suspicion of a later date is confirmed by the discovery of a MS. of this commentary in Brussels, with an anonymous preface which declares it to be a compilation. Harnack, who made this discovery, ably refutes the conclusions of Zahn, and tries to prove that the commentary ascribed to Theophilus is a Latin work by an anonymous author of the fifth or sixth century (470–520). Zahn (1884) defends in part his former position against Harnack, but admits the weight of the argument furnished by the Brussels MS. Hauck holds that the commentary was written after A. D. 200, but was used by Jerome. Bornemann successfully defends Harnack's view against Zahn and Hauck, and puts the work between 450 and 700.

§ 177. *Melito of Sardis.*

(I.) Euseb. *H. E.* IV. 13, 26; V. 25. Hieron.: *De Vir. ill.* 24. The remains of Melito in Routh, *Reliq. Sacr.* I. 113–153; more fully in Otto, *Corp. Ap.* IX. (1872), 375–478. His second Apology, of doubtful genuineness, in Cureton, *Spicilegium Syriacum*, Lond. 1855 (Syriac, with an English translation), and in Pitra, *Spicil. Solesm.* II. (with a Latin translation by Renan, which was revised by Otto, *Corp. Ap.* vol. IX.); German transl. by Welte in the Tüb. "Theol. Quartalschrift" for 1862.

(II.) Piper in the *Studien und Kritiken* for 1838, p. 54–154. Uhlhorn in "Zeitschrift für hist. Theol." 1866. Donaldson, III. 221–239 Steitz in Herzog² IX. 537–539. Lightfoot in "Contemp. Review," Febr. 1876. Harnack, *Texte*, etc., I. 240–278. Salmon in Smith and Wace III. 894–900. Renan, *Marc-Aurèle*, 172 sqq. (Comp. also the short notice in *L'église chrét.*, p. 436).

Melito, bishop of Sardis,[1] the capital of Lydia, was a shining light among the churches of Asia Minor in the third quarter of the second century. Polycrates of Ephesus, in his epistle to bishop Victor of Rome (d. 195), calls him a "eunuch who, in his whole conduct, was full of the Holy Ghost, and sleeps in Sardis awaiting the episcopate from heaven (or visitation, τὴν ἀπὸ τῶν οὐρανῶν ἐπισκοπήν) on the day of the resurrection." The term "eunuch" no doubt refers to voluntary celibacy for the kingdom of God (Matt. 19: 12).[2] He was also esteemed as a prophet. He wrote a book on prophecy, probably against the pseudo-prophecy of the Montanists; but his relation to Montanism is not clear. He took an active part in the paschal and other controversies which agitated the churches of Asia Minor. He was among the chief supporters of the Quartadeciman practice which was afterwards condemned as schismatic

---

[1] This is the English spelling. The Germans and French spell *Sardes* (*Gr. αἱ Σάρδεις*, but also Σάρδις in Herodotus).

[2] Renan thinks of an act of self-mutilation (in *L'église chrét.* 436): "*Comme plus tard Origène, il voulut que sa chasteté fût en quelque sorte matériellement constatée.*" But St. John, too, is called *spado* by Tertullian (*De Monog.* 17) and *eunuchus* by Jerome (*In Es.* c. 56). Athenagoras uses εὐνουχία for male continence, *Leg.* c. 33: τὸ ἐν παρθενείᾳ καὶ ἐν εὐνουχίᾳ μεῖναι, *in virginitate et eunuchi statu manere.*

and heretical. This may be a reason why his writings fell into oblivion. Otherwise he was quite orthodox according to the standard of his age, and a strong believer in the divinity of Christ, as is evident from one of the Syrian fragments (see below).

Melito was a man of brilliant mind and a most prolific author. Tertullian speaks of his elegant and eloquent genius.[1] Eusebius enumerates no less than eighteen or twenty works from his pen, covering a great variety of topics, but known to us now only by name.[2] He gives three valuable extracts. There must have been an uncommon literary fertility in Asia Minor after the middle of the second century.[3]

[1] "*Elegans et declamatorium ingenium*," in his lost book on *Ecstasis*, quoted by Jerome, *De Vir. ill.* 24. Harnack draws a comparison between Melito and Tertullian; they resembled each other in the variety of topics on which they wrote, and in eloquence, but not in elegance of style.

[2] Eusebius (IV. 26) mentions first his *Apology* for the faith addressed to the emperor of the Romans, and then the following: "Two works *On the Passover*, and those *On the Conduct of Life and the Prophets* (τὸ περὶ πολιτείας καὶ προφητῶν, perhaps two separate books, perhaps καί for τῶν), one *On the Church*, and another discourse *On the Lord's Day* (περὶ κυριακῆς), one also *On the Nature* (περὶ φύσεως, *al.* Faith, πίστεως) *of Man*, and another *On his Formation* (περὶ πλάσεως), a work *On the Subjection of the Senses to Faith* [ὁ περὶ ὑπακοῆς πίστεως αἰσθητηρίων, which Rufinus changes into two books ' *de obedientia fidei; de sensibus,*' so also Nicephorus]. Besides these, a treatise *On the Soul, the Body, and the Mind.* A dissertation also, *On Baptism;* one also *On Truth and Faith, and* [probably another on] *the Generation of Christ.* His discourse *On Prophecy,* and that *On Hospitality.* A treatise called *The Key* (ἡ κλείς), his works *On the Devil,* and *The Revelation of John.* The treatise *On God Incarnate* (περὶ ἐνσωμάτου θεοῦ, comp. ἐνσωμάτωσις = incarnation), and last of all, the discourse (βιβλίδιον) addressed to Antonine." He then adds still another book called Ἐκλογαί, and containing extracts from the Old Testament. Some of these titles may indicate two distinct books, as τὰ περὶ τοῦ διαβόλου, καὶ τῆς ἀποκαλύψεως Ἰωάννου. So Rufinus and Jerome understood this title. See Heinichen's notes. Other works were ascribed to him by later writers, as *On the Incarnation of Christ* (περὶ σαρκώσεως Χριστοῦ), *On the Cross, On Faith,* and two decidedly spurious works, *De Passione S. Joannis,* and *De Transitu b. Mariæ.*

[3] Comp. Euseb. IV. 21, 25. Renan says (p. 192): "*Jamais peut-être le christianisme n'a plus écrit que durant le IIe siècle en Asie. La culture littéraire était extrêmement répandue dans cette province; l'art d'écrire y était fort commun, et le christianisme en profitait. La littérature des Pères d l'Église commençait. Les siècles suivants ne dépassèrent pas ces premiers essais de l'éloquence chrétienne; mais, au point de vue de l'orthodoxie, les livres de ces Pères du IIe siècle offraient*

The *Apology* of Melito was addressed to Marcus Aurelius, and written probably at the outbreak of the violent persecutions in 177, which, however, were of a local or provincial character, and not sanctioned by the general government. He remarks that Nero and Domitian were the only imperial persecutors, and expresses the hope that, Aurelius, if properly informed, would interfere in behalf of the innocent Christians. In a passage preserved in the " Paschal Chronicle " he says: " We are not worshipers of senseless stones, but adore one only God, who is before all and over all, and His Christ truly God the Word before all ages."

A Syriac Apology bearing his name[1] was discovered by Tattam, with other Syrian MSS. in the convents of the Nitrian desert (1843), and published by Cureton and Pitra (1855). But it contains none of the passages quoted by Eusebius, and is more an attack upon idolatry than a defense of Christianity, but may nevertheless be a work of Melito under an erroneous title.

To Melito we owe the first Christian list of the Hebrew Scriptures. It agrees with the Jewish and the Protestant canon, and omits the Apocrypha. The books of Esther and Nehemiah are also omitted, but may be included in Esdras. The expressions " the Old Books," " the Books of the Old Covenant," imply that the church at that time had a canon of the New Covenant. Melito made a visit to Palestine to seek information on the Jewish canon.

---

plus d'une pierre el'achoppement. La lecture en devint suspecte; on les copia de moins en moins, et ainsi presque tons ces beaux écrits disparurent, pour faire place aux écrivains classiques, postérieurs au concile de Nicée, écrivains plus corrects comme doctrine, mais, en général, bien moins originaux que ceux du IIe siècle.

[1] Under the heading, "The oration of Melito the Philosopher, held before Antoninus Cæsar, and he spoke [?] to Cæsar that he might know God, and he showed him the way of truth, and began to speak as follows." Ewald (in the "Gött. Gel. Anz." 1856, p. 655 sqq.) and Renan (*M. Aur.* 184, note) suggest that it is no apology, but Melito's tract $\pi\epsilon\rho\grave{\iota}\ \grave{\alpha}\lambda\eta\vartheta\epsilon\acute{\iota}\alpha\varsigma$, as this word very often occurs. Jacobi, Otto, and Harnack ascribe it to a different author, probably from Syria.

He wrote a commentary on the Apocalypse, and a "Key" (ἡ κλείς), probably to the Scriptures.[1]

The loss of this and of his books "on the Church" and "on the Lord's Day" are perhaps to be regretted most.

Among the Syriac fragments of Melito published by Cureton is one from a work "On Faith," which contains a remarkable christological creed, an eloquent expansion of the *Regula Fidei*.[2] The Lord Jesus Christ is acknowledged as the perfect Reason, the Word of God; who was begotten before the light; who was Creator with the Father; who was the Fashioner of man; who was all things in all; Patriarch among the patriarchs, Law in the law, Chief Priest among the priests, King among the kings, Prophet among the prophets, Archangel among the angels; He piloted Noah, conducted Abraham, was bound with Isaac, exiled with Jacob, was Captain with Moses; He foretold his own sufferings in David and the prophets; He was incarnate in the Virgin; worshipped by the Magi; He healed the lame, gave sight to the blind, was rejected by the people, condemned by Pilate, hanged upon the tree, buried in the earth, rose from the dead and appeared to the apostles, ascended to heaven; He is the Rest of the departed, the Recoverer of the lost, the Light of the blind, the Refuge of the afflicted, the Bridegroom of the Church, the Charioteer of the cherubim, the Captain of angels; God who is of God, the Son of the Father, the King for ever and ever.

[1] A Latin work under the title *Melitonis Clavis Sanctæ Scripturæ* was mentioned by Labbé in 1653 as preserved in the library of Clermont College, and was at last, after much trouble, recovered in Strassburg and elsewhere, and published by Cardinal Pitra in the *Spicilegium Solesm.* 1855 (Tom. II. and III.). But, unfortunately, it turned out to be no translation of Melito's κλείς at all, but a mediæval glossary of mystic interpretation of the Scriptures compiled from Gregory I. and other Latin fathers. This was conclusively proven by Steitz in the "Studien und Kritiken" for 1857, p. 584–596. Renan assents (p. 181, note): "*L'ouvrage latin que dom Pitra a publié comme étant la Clef de Meliton, est une compilation de passages des Pères latins pouvant servir à l'explication allégorique des écritures qui figure pour la première fois dans la Bible de Théodulphe.*"

[2] *Spicileg. Solesm.* T. II. p. LIX.

§ 178. *Apolinarius of Hierapolis. Miltiades.*

CLAUDIUS APOLINARIUS,[1] bishop of Hierapolis in Phrygia, a successor of Papias, was a very active apologetic and polemic writer about A. D. 160–180. He took a leading part in the Montanist and Paschal controversies. Eusebius puts him with Melito of Sardis among the orthodox writers of the second century, and mentions four of his "many works" as known to him, but since lost, namely an "*Apology*" addressed to Marcus Aurelius (before 174), "*Five books against the Greeks*," "*Two books on Truth*," "*Two books against the Jews*." He also notices his later books "*Against the heresy of the Phrygians*" (the Montanists), about 172.[2]

Apolinarius opposed the Quartodeciman observance of Easter, which Melito defended.[3] Jerome mentions his familiarity with heathen literature, but numbers him among the Chiliasts.[4] The

---

[1] This is the spelling of the ancient Greek authors who refer to him. Latin writers usually spell his name *Apollinaris* or *Apollinarius.* There are several noted persons of this name: 1) the legendary ST. APOLLINARIS, bishop of Ravenna (50–78?), who followed St. Peter from Antioch to Rome, was sent by him to Ravenna, performed miracles, died a martyr, and gave name to a magnificent basilica built in the sixth century. See *Acta Sanct.* Jul. V. 344. 2) APOLLINARIS THE ELDER, presbyter at Laodicea in Syria (not in Phrygia), an able classical scholar and poet, about the middle of the fourth century. 3) APOLLINARIS THE YOUNGER, son of the former, and bishop of Laodicea between 362 and 380, who with his father composed Christian classics to replace the heathen classics under the reign of Julian, and afterwards originated the christological heresy which is named after him. See my article in Smith and Wace I. 134 sq.

[2] *H. E.* IV. 27; repeated by Jerome, *De Viris ill.* 26. Two extracts of a work not mentioned by Eusebius are preserved in the *Chron. Pasch.* Copies of three of his apologetic books, πρὸς Ἕλληνας, περὶ εὐσεβείας, περὶ ἀληθείας, are mentioned by Photius. The last two are probably identical, as they are connected by καί. See the fragments in Routh, I. 159–174. Comp. Donaldson III. 243; Harnack, *Texte*, I. 232–239, and Smith and Wace I. 132.

[3] See above, p. 214 sq., and *Chron. Pasch.* I. 13.

[4] *De Vir. ill.* 18; *Com. in Ezech.* c. 36. In the latter place Jerome mentions Irenæus as the first, and Apollinaris as the last, of the Greek Chiliasts ("*ut Græcos nominem, et primum extremumque conjugam, Iren. et Ap.*"); but this is a palpable error, for Barnabas and Papias were Chiliasts before Irenæus; Methodius and Nepos long after Apolinarius. Perhaps he meant Apollinaris of Laodicea, in Syria.

latter is doubtful on account of his opposition to Montanism. Photius praises his style. He is enrolled among the saints.[1]

MILTIADES was another Christian Apologist of the later half of the second century whose writings are entirely lost. Eusebius mentions among them an " Apology" addressed to the rulers of the world, a treatise " against the Greeks," and another " against the Jews ;" but he gives no extracts.[2] Tertullian places him between Justin Martyr and Irenæus.[3]

§ 179. *Hermias.*

Ερμείου φιλοσόφου Διασυρμὸς τῶν ἔξω φιλοσόφων, HERMIÆ PHILOSOPHI *Gentilium Philosophorum Irrisio,* ten chapters. Ed. princeps with Lat. vers. Basel, 1553, Zurich, 1560. Worth added it to his Tatian, Oxf. 1700. In Otto and Maranus (Migne, VI. col. 1167–1180). DONALDSON, III. 179–181.

Under the name of the " philosopher" HERMIAS ('Ερμείας or 'Ερμίας), otherwise entirely unknown to us, we have a " *Mockery of Heathen Philosophers,*" which, with the light arms of wit and sarcasm, endeavors to prove from the history of philosophy, by exposing the contradictions of the various systems, the truth of Paul's declaration, that the wisdom of this world is foolishness with God. He derives the false philosophy from the demons. He first takes up the conflicting heathen notions about the soul, and then about the origin of the world, and ridicules them. The following is a specimen from the discussion of the first topic :

" I confess I am vexed by the reflux of things. For now I am immortal, and I rejoice; but now again I become mortal, and I weep; but straightway I am dissolved into atoms. I become water, and I become air: I become fire: then after a little I am neither air nor fire: one

---

[1] *Acta Sanct.* Febr. II. 4. See Wetzer and Welte[2] I. 1086.

[2] *H. E.* V. 17. Jerome, *De Vir. ill.* 39. Comp. Harnack, *Texte,* I. 278–282, and Salmon, in Smith and Wace III. 916.

[3] *Adv. Valent.* 5. Miltiades is here called " *ecclesiarum sophista,*" either honorably=*rhetor* or *philosophus* (See Otto and Salmon), or with an implied censure (" *mit einem üblen Nebengeschmack,*" as Harnack thinks). The relation of Miltiades to Montanism is quite obscure, but probably he was an opponent.

makes me a wild beast, one makes me a fish. Again, then, I have dolphins for my brothers. But when I see myself, I fear my body, and I no longer know how to call it, whether man, or dog, or wolf, or bull, or bird, or serpent, or dragon, or chimæra. I am changed by the philosophers into all the wild beasts, into those that live on land and on water, into those that are winged, many-shaped, wild, tame, speechless, and gifted with speech, rational and irrational. I swim, fly, creep, run, sit; and there is Empedocles too, who makes me a bush."

The work is small and unimportant.[1] Some put it down to the third or fourth century; but the writer calls himself a "philosopher" (though he misrepresents his profession), has in view a situation of the church like that under Marcus Aurelius, and presents many points of resemblance with the older Apologists and with Lucian who likewise ridiculed the philosophers with keen wit, but from the infidel heathen standpoint. Hence we may well assign him to the later part of the second century.

§ 180. *Hegesippus*.

(I.) EUSEB. *H. E.* II. 23; III. 11, 16, 19, 20, 32; IV. 8, 22. Collection of fragments in GRABE, *Spicil.* II. 203–214; ROUTH, *Reliq. S.* I. 205–219; HILGENFELD, in his "Zeitschrift für wissenschaftliche Theol." 1876 and 1878.

(II.) The *Annotationes in Heges. Fragm.* by ROUTH, I. 220–292 (very valuable). DONALDSON: *L. c.* III. 182–213. NÖSGEN: *Der kirchl. Standpunkt des Heg.* in Brieger's "Zeitschrift für Kirchengesch." 1877 (p. 193–233). Against Hilgenfeld. ZAHN: *Der griech. Irenæus und der ganze Hegesippus im* 16*ten Jahr., ibid.* p. 288–291. H. DANNREUTHER: *Du Témoignage d' Hégésippe sur l'église chrétienne au deux premiers siècles.* Nancy 1878. See also his art. in Lichtenberger's "Encycl." VI. 126–129. FRIEDR. VOGEL: *De Hegesippo, qui dicitur, Josephi interprete.* Erlangen 1881. W. MILLIGAN: *Hegesippus,* in Smith and Wace II. (1880) 875–878. C. WEIZSÄCKER: *Hegesippus,* in Herzog[2] V. 695–700. CASPARI: *Quellen,* etc., III. 345–348. The orthodoxy of Hegesippus has been denied by the Tübingen critics, Baur, Schwegler, and, more moderately by Hilgenfeld, but defended by Dorner, Donaldson, Nösgen, Weizsäcker, Caspari and Milligan.

Contemporary with the Apologists, though not of their class, were Hegesippus (d. about 180), and Dionysius of Corinth (about 170).

---

[1] Hase aptly calls it "*eine oberflächlich witzige Belustigung über paradoxe Philosopheme.*"

HEGESIPPUS was an orthodox Jewish Christian[1] and lived during the reigns of Hadrian, Antoninus, and Marcus Aurelius. He travelled extensively through Syria, Greece, and Italy, and was in Rome during the episcopate of Anicetus. He collected " Memorials "[2] of the apostolic and post-apostolic churches. He used written sources and oral traditions. Unfortunately this work which still existed in the sixteenth century,[3] is lost, but may yet be recovered. It is usually regarded as a sort of church history, the first written after the Acts of St. Luke. This would make Hegesippus rather than Eusebius " the father of church history." But it seems to have been only a collection of reminiscences of travel without regard to chronological order (else the account of the martyrdom of James would have been put in the first instead of the fifth book.) He was an antiquarian rather than a historian. His chief object was to prove the purity and catholicity of the church against the Gnostic heretics and sects.

Eusebius has preserved his reports on the martyrdom of St. James the Just, Simeon of Jerusalem, Domitian's inquiry for the descendants of David and the relatives of Jesus, the rise of heresies, the episcopal succession, and the preservation of the orthodox doctrine in Corinth and Rome. These scraps of history command attention for their antiquity ; but they must be received with critical caution. They reveal a strongly Jewish type of piety, like that of James, but by no means Judaizing heresy. He was not an Ebionite, nor even a Nazarene, but decidedly catholic. There is no trace of his insisting on circumcision or the observance of the law as necessary to salvation. His use of " the Gospel according to the Hebrews" implies no heretical bias. He derived all the heresies and schisms from Judaism. He laid great stress on the regular apostolic succession of bishops. In every city he set himself to inquire for two things : purity of

---

[1] Eusebius (IV. 22) expressly calls him "a convert from the Hebrews," and this is confirmed by the strongly Jewish coloring of his account of James, quoted in full, vol. I. 276 sq. He was probably from Palestine.

[2] Ὑπομνήματα, or Συγγάμματα, in five books.

[3] In the library of the convent of St. John at Patmos. See Zahn, l. c.

doctrine and the unbroken succession of teachers from the times of the apostles. The former depended in his view on the latter. The result of his investigation was satisfactory in both respects. He found in every apostolic church the faith maintained. " The church of Corinth," he says, " continued in the true faith, until Primus was bishop there [the predecessor of Dionysius], with whom I had familiar intercourse, as I passed many days at Corinth, when I was about sailing to Rome, during which time we were mutually refreshed in the true doctrine. After coming to Rome, I stayed with Anicetus, whose deacon was Eleutherus. After Anicetus, Soter succeeded, and after him Eleutherus. In every succession, however, and in every city, the doctrine prevails according to what is announced by the law and the prophets and the Lord."[1] He gives an account of the heretical corruption which proceeded from the unbelieving Jews, from Thebuthis and Simon Magus and Cleobius and Dositheus, and other unknown or forgotten names, but " while the sacred choir of the apostles still lived, the church was undefiled and pure, like a virgin, until the age of Trajan, when those impious errors which had so long crept in darkness ventured forth without shame into open daylight."[2] He felt perfectly at home in the Catholic church of his day which had descended from, or rather never yet ascended the lofty mountain-height of apostolic knowledge and freedom. And as Hegesippus was satisfied with the orthodoxy of the Western churches, so Eusebius was satisfied with the orthodoxy of Hegesippus, and nowhere intimates a doubt.

[1] Euseb. IV. 22.

[2] *Ibid.* III. 32. This passage has been used by Baur and his school as an argument against the Pastoral and other apostolic epistles which warn against the Gnostic heresy, but it clearly teaches that its open manifestation under Trajan was preceded by its secret working as far back as Simon Magus. Hegesippus, therefore, only confirms the N. T. allusions, which likewise imply a distinction between present beginnings and future developments of error.

§ 181. *Dionysius of Corinth.*

EUSEB.: *H. E.* II. 25; III. 4; IV. 21, 23. HIERON.: *De Vir. ill.* 27. ROUTH: *Rel. S.* I. 177–184 (the fragments), and 185–201 (the annotations). Includes Pinytus Cretensis and his *Ep. ad Dion.* (*Eus.* IV. 23). DONALDSON III. 214–220. SALMON in Smith and Wace II. 848 sq.

DIONYSIUS was bishop of Corinth (probably the successor of Primus) in the third quarter of the second century, till about A. D. 170. He was a famous person in his day, distinguished for zeal, moderation, and a catholic and peaceful spirit. He wrote a number of pastoral letters to the congregations of Lacedæmon, Athens, Nicomedia, Rome, Gortyna in Crete, and other cities. One is addressed to Chrysophora, "a most faithful sister." They are all lost, with the exception of a summary of their contents given by Eusebius, and four fragments of the letter to Soter and the Roman church. They would no doubt shed much light on the spiritual life of the church. Eusebius says of him that he "imparted freely not only to his own people, but to others abroad also, the blessings of his divine (or inspired) industry."[1] His letters were read in the churches.

Such active correspondence promoted catholic unity and gave strength and comfort in persecution from without and heretical corruption within. The bishop is usually mentioned with honor, but the letters are addressed to the church; and even the Roman bishop Soter, like his predecessor Clement, addressed his own letter in the name of the Roman church to the church of Corinth. Dionysius writes to the Roman Christians: "To-day we have passed the Lord's holy day, in which we have read your epistle.[2] In reading it we shall always have our minds stored with admonition, as we shall also from that written to us before by Clement." He speaks very highly of the liberality of the church of Rome in aiding foreign brethren condemned to the mines, and sending contributions to every city.

Dionysius is honored as a martyr in the Greek, as a confessor in the Latin church.

[1] ἐνθέου φιλοπονίας, Euseb. IV. 23. [2] ὑμῶν τὴν ἐπιστολήν. Euseb. II. 23.

§ 182. *Irenæus.*

Editions of his Works.

S. Irenæi *Episcopi Lugdun. Opera quae supersunt omnia,* ed. A. Stieren. Lips. 1853, 2 vols. The second volume contains the Prolegomena of older editors, and the disputations of Maffei and Pfaff on the Fragments of Irenæus. It really supersedes all older ed., but not the later one of Harvey.

S. Irenæi *libros quinque adversus Hæreses edidit* W. Wigan Harvey. Cambr. 1857, in 2 vols. Based upon a new and careful collation of the Cod. Claromontanus and Arundel, and embodying the original Greek portions preserved in the *Philosoph.* of Hippolytus, the newly discovered Syriac and Armenian fragments, and learned Prolegomena.

Older editions by *Erasmus,* Basel 1526 (from three Latin MSS. since lost, repeated 1528, 1534); *Gallasius,* Gen. 1570 (with the use of the Gr. text in Epiphan.); *Grynæus,* Bas. 1571 (worthless); *Fevardentius (Feuardent),* Paris 1575, improved ed. Col. 1596, and often; *Grabe,* Oxf. 1702; and above all *Massuet,* Par. 1710, Ven. 1734, 2 vois. fol., and again in Migne's "Patrol. Græco-Lat." Tom. VII. Par. 1857 (the Bened. ed., the best of the older, based on three MSS., with ample Proleg. and 3 Dissertations).

English translation by A. Roberts and W. H. Rambaut, 2 vols., in the "Ante-Nicene Library," Edinb. 1868. Another by John Keble, ed. by Dr. Pusey, for the Oxford "Library of the Fathers," 1872.

Biographical and Critical.

Ren. Massuet (R. C.): *Dissertationes in Irenaei libros (de hereticis, de Irenaei vita, gestis et scriptis, de Ir. doctrina)* prefixed to his edition of the *Opera,* and reprinted in Stieren and Migne. Also the Proleg. of Harvey, on Gnosticism, and the Life and Writings of Iren.

H. Dodwell: *Dissert. in Iren.* Oxon. 1689.

Tillemont: *Mémoirs,* etc. III. 77–99.

Deyling: *Irenæus, evangelicæ veritatis confessor ac testis.* Lips. 1721. (Against Massuet.)

Stieren: Art. *Irenæus* in "Ersch and Gruber's Encykl." IInd sect. Vol. XXIII. 357–386.

J. Beaven: *Life and Writings of Irenæus.* Lond. 1841.

J. M. Prat (R. C.): *Histoire de St. Irenée.* Lyon and Paris 1843.

L. Duncker: *Des heil. Irenaeus Christologie.* Gött. 1843. Very valuable.

K. Graul: *Die Christliche Kirche an der Schwelle des Irenæischen Zeitalters.* Leipz. 1860. (168 pages.) Introduction to a biography which never appeared.

Ch. E. Freppel (bishop of Angers, since 1869): *Saint Irénée et l'élo-quence chrétienne dans la Gaule aux deux premiers siècles.* Par. 1861.

G. Schneemann: *Sancti Irenœi de ecclesiœ Romanœ principatu testimo-nium.* Freib. i. Br. 1870.

Böhringer: *Die Kirche Christi und ihre Zeugen,* vol. II. new ed. 1873.

Heinrich Ziegler: *Irenœus der Bischof von Lyon.* Berlin 1871. (320 p.)

R. A. Lipsius: *Die Zeit des Irenœus von Lyon und die Entstehung der altkatholischen Kirche,* in Sybel's "Histor. Zeitschrift." München 1872, p. 241 sqq. See his later art. below.

A. Guilloud: *St. Irenée et son temps.* Lyon 1876.

Bp. Lightfoot: *The Churches of Gaul,* in the "Contemporary Review" for Aug. 1876.

C. J. H. Ropes: *Irenœus of Lyons,* in the Andover "Bibliotheca Sacra" for April 1877, p. 284–334. A learned discussion of the nation·ality of Irenæus (against Harvey).

J. Quarry: *Irenœus; his testimony to early Conceptions of Christianity.* In the "British Quarterly Review" for 1879, July and Oct.

Renan: *Marc Aurèle.* Paris 1882, p. 336–344.

Th. Zahn: art. *Iren.* in Herzog [2], VII. 129–140 (abridged in Schaff-Her-zog), chiefly chronological; and R. A. Lipsius in Smith and Wace, III. 253–279. Both these articles are very important; that of Lip-sius is fuller.

Comp. also the *Ch. Hist.* of Neander, and Baur, and the *Patrol.* of Möhler, and Alzog.

Special doctrines and relations of Irenæus have been discussed by Baur, Dorner, Thiersch, Höfling, Hopfenmiller, Körber, Ritschl, Kirchner, Zahn, Harnack, Leimbach, Reville, Hackenschmidt. See the lit. in Zahn's art. in Herzog [2].

A full and satisfactory monograph of Irenæus and his age is still a desideratum.

Almost simultaneously with the apology against false religions without arose the polemic literature against the heresies, or various forms of pseudo-Christianity, especially the Gnostic; and upon this was formed the dogmatic theology of the church. At the head of the old catholic controversialists stand Irenæus and his disciple Hippolytus, both of Greek education, but both be-longing, in their ecclesiastical relations and labors, to the West.

Asia Minor, the scene of the last labors of St. John, produced a luminous succession of divines and confessors who in the first three quarters of the second century reflected the light of the setting sun of the apostolic age, and may be called the pupils of St. John. Among them were Polycarp of Smyrna, Papias of

Hierapolis, Apolinarius of Hierapolis, Melito of Sardis, and others less known but honorably mentioned in the letter of Polycrates of Ephesus to bishop Victor of Rome (A. D. 190).

The last and greatest representative of this school is IRENÆUS, the first among the fathers properly so called, and one of the chief architects of the Catholic system of doctrine.

I. LIFE AND CHARACTER. Little is known of Irenæus except what we may infer from his writings. He sprang from Asia Minor, probably from Smyrna, where he spent his youth.[1] He was born between A. D. 115 and 125.[2] He enjoyed the in-

---

[1] Harvey derives from the alleged familiarity of Irenæus with Hebrew and the Syriac Peshito the conclusion that he was a Syrian, but Ropes denies the premise and defends the usual view of his Greek nationality. See also Caspari, *Quellen zur Gesch. des Taufsymb.* III. 343 sq.

[2] The change of Polycarp's martyrdom from 166 to 155 necessitates a corresponding change in the chronology of Irenæus, his pupil, who moreover says that the Apocalypse of John was written at the end of Domitian's reign (d. 96), "almost within our age" (σχεδὸν ἐπὶ τῆς ἡμετέρας γενεᾶς, *Adv. Hær.* v. 30, 3). Zahn (in Herzog) decides for 115, Lipsius (in Smith and Wace) for 130 or 125, as the date of his birth. Dodwell favored the year 97 or 98; Grabe 108, Tillemont and Lightfoot 120, Leimbach, Hilgenfeld, and Ropes 126, Oscar von Gebhardt 126-130, Harvey 130, Massuet, Dupin, Böhringer, Kling 140 (quite too late), Ziegler 142-147 (impossible). The late date is derived from a mistaken understanding of the reference to the old age of Polycarp (πάνυ γηραλέος, but this, as Zahn and Lightfoot remark, refers to the time of his martyrdom, not the time of his acquaintance with Irenæus), and from the assumption of the wrong date of his martyrdom (166 instead of 155 or 156). The term πρώτη ἡλικία, "first age," which Irenæus uses of the time of his acquaintance with Polycarp (III. 3, § 4; comp. Euseb. *H. E.* IV. 14), admits of an extension from boyhood to youth and early manhood; for Irenæus counts five ages of a man's life (*Adv. Hær.* II. 22, § 4; 24, § 4—*infans, parvulus, puer, juvenis, senior*), and includes the thirtieth year in the youth, by calling Christ a *juvenis* at the time of his baptism. Hence Zahn and Lipsius conclude that the πρώτη ἡλικία of Irenæus's connection with Polycarp is not the age of childhood, but of early young-manhood. "*Als junger Mann*," says Zahn, "*etwa zwischen dem* 18. *und* 35. *Lebensjahre, will Ir. sich des Umgangs mit Pol erfreut haben.*" Another hint is given in the letter of Iren. to Florinus, in which he reminds him of their mutual acquaintance with Polycarp in lower Asia in their youth when Florinus was at "the royal court" (αὐλὴ βασιλική). Lightfoot conjectures that this means by anticipation the court of Antoninus Pius, when he was proconsul of Asia Minor, A. D. 136, two years before he ascended the imperial throne (Waddington, *Fastes des provinces Asiatiques,* p. 714). But Zahn reasserts

struction of the venerable Polycarp of Smyrna, the pupil of John, and of other "Elders," who were mediate or immediate disciples of the apostles. The spirit of his preceptor passed over to him. "What I heard from him," says he, "that wrote I not on paper, but in my heart, and by the grace of God I constantly bring it afresh to mind." Perhaps he also accompanied Polycarp on his journey to Rome in connexion with the Easter controversy (154). He went as a missionary to Southern Gaul which seems to have derived her Christianity from Asia Minor. During the persecution in Lugdunum and Vienne under Marcus Aurelius (177), he was a presbyter there and witnessed the horrible cruelties which the infuriated heathen populace practiced upon his brethren.[1] The aged and venerable bishop, Pothinus, fell a victim, and the presbyter took the post of danger, but was spared for important work.

He was sent by the Gallican confessors to the Roman bishop Eleutherus (who ruled A. D. 177–190), as a mediator in the Montanistic disputes.[2]

After the martyrdom of Pothinus he was elected bishop of Lyons (178), and labored there with zeal and success, by tongue and pen, for the restoration of the heavily visited church, for the spread of Christianity in Gaul, and for the defence and development of its doctrines. He thus combined a vast missionary and literary activity. If we are to trust the account of Gregory of Tours, he converted almost the whole population of Lyons and sent notable missionaries to other parts of pagan France.

After the year 190 we lose sight of Irenæus. Jerome speaks of him as having flourished in the reign of Commodus, i. e., between 180 and 192. He is reported by later tradition (since the fourth or fifth century) to have died a martyr in the persecution under Septimus Severus, A. D. 202, but the silence of Tertullian,

the more natural explanation of Dodwell, that the court of Emperor Hadrian is meant, who twice visited Asia Minor as emperor between the years 122 and 130.

[1] See above, § 20, p. 55 sq.

[2] Either during, or after the persecution. Euseb. V. S.; Jerome, De Vir. ill. c. 35.

Hippolytus, Eusebius, and Epiphanius makes this point extremely doubtful. He was buried under the altar of the church of St. John in Lyons.[1] This city became again famous in church history in the twelfth century as the birthplace of the Waldensian martyr church, the *Pauperes de Lugduno*.

II. His character and position. Irenæus is the leading representative of catholic Christianity in the last quarter of the second century, the champion of orthodoxy against Gnostic heresy, and the mediator between the Eastern and Western churches. He united a learned Greek education and philosophical penetration with practical wisdom and moderation. He is neither very original nor brilliant, but eminently sound and judicious. His individuality is not strongly marked, but almost lost in his catholicity. He modestly disclaims elegance and eloquence, and says that he had to struggle in his daily administrations with the barbarous Celtic dialect of Southern Gaul; but he nevertheless handles the Greek with great skill on the most abstruse subjects.[2] He is familiar with Greek poets (Homer, Hesiod, Pindar, Sophocles) and philosophers (Thales, Pythagoras, Plato), whom he occasionally cites. He is perfectly at home in the Greek Bible and in the early Christian writers, as Clement of Rome, Polycarp, Papias, Ignatius, Hermas, Justin M., and

---

[1] "The story that his bones were dug up and thrown into the street by the Calvinists in 1562 has been abundantly refuted." *Encycl. Brit.*, ninth ed XIII. 273.

[2] This is evident from the very passage in which he makes that apology to his friend (*Adv. Hær.*, Pref. § 3): "Thou wilt not require from me, who dwell among the Celts (ἐν Κελτοῖς), and am accustomed for the most part to use a barbarous dialect (βάρβαρον διάλεκτον) any skill in discourse which I have not learned, nor any power of composition which I have not practised, nor any beauty of style nor persuasiveness of which I know nothing. But thou wilt accept lovingly what I write lovingly to thee in simplicity, truthfully, and in my own way (ἁπλῶς καὶ ἀληθῶς καὶ ἰδιωτικῶς); whilst thou thyself (as being more competent than I am) wilt expand those ideas of which I send thee, as it were, only the seeds and principles (σπέρματα καὶ ἀρχάς); and in the comprehensiveness of thine understanding, wilt develop to their full extent the points on which I briefly touch, so as to set with power before thy companions those things which I have uttered in weakness." Jerome praises the style of Irenæus as "*doctissimus et eloquentissimus*," and Massuet (*Diss.* II. § 51) adds that his "Greek text as far as preserved, is elegant, polished, and grave."

Tatian.[1] His position gives him additional weight, for he is linked by two long lives, that of his teacher and grand-teacher, to the fountain head of Christianity. We plainly trace in him the influence of the spirit of Polycarp and John. "The true way to God," says he, in opposition to the false Gnosis, "is love. It is better to be willing to know nothing but Jesus Christ the crucified, than to fall into ungodliness through over-curious questions and paltry subtleties." We may trace in him also the strong influence of the anthropology and soteriology of Paul. But he makes more account than either John or Paul of the outward visible church, the episcopal succession, and the sacraments; and his whole conception of Christianity is predominantly legalistic. Herein we see the catholic churchliness which so strongly set in during the second century.

Irenæus is an enemy of all error and schism, and, on the whole, the most orthodox of the ante-Nicene fathers.[2] We must, however, except his eschatology. Here, with Papias and most of his contemporaries, he maintains the pre-millennarian views which were subsequently abandoned as Jewish dreams by the catholic church. While laboring hard for the spread and defense of the church on earth, he is still "gazing up into heaven," like the men of Galilee, anxiously waiting for the return of the Lord and the establishment of his kingdom. He is also strangely mistaken about the age of Jesus from a false inference of the question of the Jews, John 8: 57.

Irenæus is the first among patristic writers who makes full use of the New Testament. The Apostolic Fathers reëcho the oral traditions; the Apologists are content with quoting the Old Testament prophets and the Lord's own words in the Gospels as proof of divine revelation; but Irenæus showed the

---

[1] Harvey claims for him also Hebrew and Syriac scholarship; but this is disputed.

[2] Bishop Lightfoot ("Contemp. Rev." May, 1875, p. 827) says that Irenæus "on all the most important points conforms to the standard which has satisfied the Christian church ever since." Renan (p. 341) calls him "le modèle de l'homme ecclésiastique accompli."

unity of the Old and New Testaments in opposition to the Gnostic separation, and made use of the four Gospels and nearly all Epistles in opposition to the mutilated canon of Marcion.[1]

With all his zeal for pure and sound doctrine, Irenæus was liberal towards subordinate differences, and remonstrated with the bishop of Rome for his unapostolic efforts to force an outward uniformity in respect to the time and manner of celebrating Easter.[2] We may almost call him a forerunner of Gallicanism in its protest against ultramontane despotism. " The apostles have ordained," says he in the third fragment, which appears to refer to that controversy, " that we make conscience with no one of food and drink, or of particular feasts, new moons, and sabbaths. Whence, then, controversies; whence schisms? We keep feasts but with the leaven of wickedness and deceit, rending asunder the church of God, and we observe the outward, to the neglect of the higher, faith and love." He showed the same moderation in the Montanistic troubles. He was true to his name *Peaceful* (Εἰρηναῖος) and to his spiritual ancestry.

III. HIS WRITINGS.   (1.) The most important work of Irenæus is his Refutation of Gnosticism, in five books.[3] It was

---

[1] See the long list of his Scripture quotations in Stieren, I. 996–1005, and the works on the Canon of the N. T.

[2] Comp. § 62, p. 217 sq.

[3] Ἔλεγχος καὶ ἀνατροπὴ τῆς ψευδωνύμου γνώσεως (1 Tim. 6 : 20), *i. e. A Refutation and Subversion of Knowledge falsely so called;* cited, since Jerome, under the simpler title: *Adversus Hœreses* (πρὸς αἱρέσεις). The Greek original of the work, together with the five books of Hegesippus, was still in existence in the sixteenth century, and may yet be recovered. See Zahn in Brieger's " Zeitschrift für K. Gesch." 1877, p. 288–291. But so far we only have fragments of it preserved in Hippolytus (*Philosophumena*), Eusebius, Theodoret, and especially in Epiphanius (*Hœr.* XXXI. c. 9–33). We have, however, the entire work in a slavishly literal translation into barbarous Latin, crowded with Grecisms, but for this very reason very valuable. Three MSS. of the Latin version survive, the oldest is the Codex Claromontanus of the tenth or eleventh century. This and the Arundel MS. are now in England (see a description in Harvey's Preface, I. VIII. sqq. with fac-similes). Besides, we have now fragments of a Syrian version, derived from the Nitrian MSS. of the British Museum, and fragments of an Armenian translation, published by Pitra in his *Spicilegium Solesmense,* vol. I. (1852), both incorporated in Harvey's edition,

composed during the pontificate of Eleutherus, that is between the years 177 and 190.[1] It is at once the polemic theological master-piece of the ante-Nicene age, and the richest mine of informa-tion respecting Gnosticism and the church doctrine of that age. It contains a complete system of Christian divinity, but en-veloped in polemical smoke, which makes it very difficult and tedious reading. The work was written at the request of a friend who wished to be informed of the Valentinian heresy and to be furnished with arguments against it. Valentinus and Marcion had taught in Rome about A. D. 140, and their doctrines had spread to the south of France. The first book contains a minute exposition of the gorgeous speculations of Valentinus and a general view of the other Gnostic sects; the second an exposure of the unreasonableness and contradictions of these heresies; especially the notions of the Demiurge as distinct from the Creator, of the Aeons, the Pleroma and Kenoma, the emanations, the fall of Achamoth, the formation of the lower world of mat-ter, the sufferings of the Sophia, the difference between the three classes of men, the Somatici, Psychici, and Pneumatici. The last three books refute Gnosticism from the Holy Scripture and Christian tradition which teach the same thing; for the same gospel which was first orally preached and transmitted was sub-sequently committed to writing and faithfully preserved in all the apostolic churches through the regular succession of the bishops and elders; and this apostolic tradition insures at the same time the correct interpretation of Scripture against heretical perversion. To the ever-shifting and contradictory opinions of the heretics Irenæus opposes the unchanging faith of the catholic

vol. II. 431–469. They agree closely with the Latin Version. An attempt to restore the Greek text from the Latin, for the better understanding of it, has been made on the first four chapters of the third book by H. W. J. Thiersch ("Stud. u. Kritiken," 1842). Semler's objections to the genuineness have been so thoroughly refuted by Chr. G. F. Walch (*De authentia librorum Irenæi*, 1774), that Möhler and Stieren might have spared themselves the trouble.

[1] Eleutherus is mentioned, III. 3, 3, as then occupying the see of Rome. Lipsius fixes the composition between A. D. 180 and 185, Harvey between 182 and 188 (I. CLVIII).

church which is based on the Scriptures and tradition, and compacted together by the episcopal organization. It is the same argument which Bellarmin, Bossuet, and Möhler use against divided and distracted Protestantism, but Protestantism differs as much from old Gnosticism as the New Testament from the apocryphal Gospels, and as sound, sober, practical sense differs from mystical and transcendental nonsense. The fifth book dwells on the resurrection of the body and the millennial kingdom. Irenæus derived his information from the writings of Valentinus and Marcion and their disciples, and from Justin Martyr's *Syntagma*.[1]

The interpretation of Scripture is generally sound and sober, and contrasts favorably with the fantastic distortions of the Gnostics. He had a glimpse of a theory of inspiration which does justice to the human factor. He attributes the irregularities of Paul's style to his rapidity of discourse and the impetus of the Spirit which is in him.[2]

(2.) The Epistle to Florinus, of which Eusebius has preserved an interesting and important fragment, treated *On the Unity of God, and the Origin of Evil*.[3] It was written probably after the work against heresies, and as late as 190.[4] Florinus was an older friend and fellow-student of Irenæus, and for some time presbyter in the church of Rome, but was deposed on account of his apostasy to the Gnostic heresy. Irenæus reminded him very

---

[1] On the sources of the history of heresies see especially the works of Lipsius, and Harnack, quoted on p. 443, and Harvey's Preliminary Observations in vol. I.

[2] *Adv. Hær.* III. 7, § 2.

[3] Περὶ μοναρχίας ἢ περὶ τοῦ μὴ εἶναι τὸν Θεὸν ποιητὴν κακῶν. Euseb. *H. E.* V. 20, comp. ch. 15.

[4] Leimbach and Lightfoot regard the letter as one of the earliest writings of Irenæus, but Lipsius (p. 263) puts it down to about A. D. 190 or after, on the ground of the Syriac fragment from a letter of Irenæus to Victor of Rome (190–202) concerning "Florinus, a presbyter and partisan of the error of Valentinus, who published an abominable book." See the fragment in Harvey, II. 457. Eusebius makes no mention of such a letter, but there is no good reason to doubt its genuineness.

touchingly of their common studies at the feet of the patriarchal Poiycarp, when he held some position at the royal court (probably during Hadrian's sojourn at Smyrna), and tried to bring him back to the faith of his youth, but we do not know with what effect.

(3.) *On the Ogdoad*[1] against the Valentinian system of Aeons, in which the number eight figures prominently with a mystic meaning. Eusebius says that it was written on account of Florinus, and that he found in it " a most delightful remark," as follows : " I adjure thee, whoever thou art, that transcribest this book, by our Lord Jesus Christ and by his gracious appearance, when he shall come to judge the quick and the dead, to compare what thou hast copied, and to correct it by this original manuscript, from which thou hast carefully transcribed. And that thou also copy this adjuration, and insert it in the copy." The carelessness of transcribers in those days is the chief cause of the variations in the text of the Greek Testament which abounded already in the second century. Irenæus himself mentions a remarkable difference of reading in the mystic number of Antichrist (666 and 616), on which the historic interpretation of the book depends (Rev. 13 : 18).

(4.) A book *On Schism,* addressed to Blastus who was the head of the Roman Montanists and also a Quartodeciman.[2] It referred probably to the Montanist troubles in a conciliatory spirit.

(5.) Eusebius mentions[3] several other treatises which are entirely lost, as *Against the Greeks* (or *On Knowledge*), *On Apostolic Preaching,* a *Book on Various Disputes,*[4] and on the *Wis-*

---

[1] Περὶ ὀγδοάδος. Euseb. V. 20.

[2] Περὶ σχίσματος. Also mentioned by Euseb. *l. c.* Comp. V. 14; Pseudo-Tertullian *Adv. Hær.* 22; and the Syriac fragment in Harvey II. 456; also the critical discussion of the subject and date by Lipsius, 264 sq.

[3] *H. E.* V. 26.

[4] βιβλίον διαλέξεων διαφόρων. Harvey and Lipsius make this out to have been a collection of homilies on various texts of scripture.

dom of Solomon. In the Syriac fragments some other lost works
are mentioned.

(6.) Irenæus is probably the author of that touching account
of the persecution of 177, which the churches of Lyons and
Vienne sent to the churches in Asia Minor and Phrygia, and
which Eusebius has in great part preserved. He was an eye-
witness of the cruel scene, yet his name is not mentioned, which
would well agree with his modesty; the document breathes his
mild Christian spirit, reveals his aversion to Gnosticism, his indulgence for Montanism, his expectation of the near approach of
Antichrist. It is certainly one of the purest and most precious
remains of ante-Nicene literature and fully equal, yea superior
to the " Martyrdom of Polycarp," because free from superstitious
relic-worship.[1]

(7.) Finally, we must mention four more Greek fragments of
Irenæus, which Pfaff discovered at Turin in 1715, and first published. Their genuineness has been called in question by some
Roman divines, chiefly for doctrinal reasons.[2] The first treats
of the true knowledge,[3] which consists not in the solution of
subtle questions, but in divine wisdom and the imitation of
Christ; the second is on the eucharist;[4] the third, on the duty
of toleration in subordinate points of difference, with reference
to the Paschal controversies;[5] the fourth, on the object of the

---

[1] Eusebius, *H. E.* V. 1 and 2; also in Routh's *Reliquiæ S.* I. 295 sqq., with
notes. It has often been translated. Comp. on this document the full discussion of Donaldson, III. 250–286, and the striking judgment of Renan (*l. c.* p.
340), who calls it " *un des morceaux les plus extraordinaires que possède aucune
litterature,*" and " *la perle de la litterature chrétienne au IIe siecle.*" He attributes
it to Irenæus; Harvey denies it to him; Donaldson leaves the authorship in
doubt.

[2] Harvey (I. CLXXII) accepts them all as "possessing good external authority, and far more convincing internal proof of genuineness, than can
always be expected in such brief extracts."

[3] γνῶσις ἀληθινή, perhaps the same treatise as the one mentioned by
Eusebius under the title περὶ τῆς ἐπιστήμης.

[4] Discussed in §69, p. 242.

[5] This Lipsius (p. 266) considers to be the only one of the four fragments
which is undoubtedly genuine.

incarnation, which is stated to be the purging away of sin and the annihilation of all evil.[1]

§ 183. *Hippolytus.*

(I.) S. HIPPOLYTI *episcopi et martyris Opera, Grœce et Lat.* ed. J. A-FABRICIUS, Hamb. 1716–18, 2 vols. fol.; ed. GALLANDI in "Biblioth. Patrum," Ven. 1760, Vol. II.; MIGNE: *Patr. Gr.*, vol. x. col. 583–982. P. ANT. DE LAGARDE: HIPPOLYTI *Romani quœ feruntur omnia Grœce*, Lips. et Lond. 1858 (216 pages). Lagarde has also published some Syriac and Arabic fragments, of Hippol., in his *Analecta Syriaca* (p. 79–91) and Appendix, Leipz. and Lond. 1858. Patristic notices of Hippolytus. EUSEB.: *H. E.* VI. 20, 22; PRUDENTIUS in the 11th of his *Martyr Hymns* (περὶ στεφάνων); HIERON.: *De Vir. ill.* c. 61; PHOTIUS, Cod. 48 and 121. EPIPHANIUS barely mentions Hippol. (*Hœr.* 31). THEODORET quotes several passages and calls him "holy Hippol. bishop and martyr" (*Hœr. Fab.* III. 1 and *Dial.* I., II. and III.). See Fabricius, *Hippol.* I. VIII.–XX.

S. HIPPOLYTI Epis. et Mart. *Refutationis omnium haeresium librorum decem quœ supersunt*, ed. DUNCKER et SCHNEIDEWIN. Gött. 1859. The first ed. appeared under the name of Origen: Ὠριγένους Φιλοσοφύμενα, ἢ κατὰ πασῶν αἱρέεων ἔλεγχος. ORIGENIS *Philosophumena, sive omnium hæresium refutatio. E codice Parisino nunc primum* ed. EMMANUEL MILLER. Oxon. (Clarendon Press), 1851. Another ed. by Abbe CRUICE, Par. 1860. An English translation by J. H. MACMAHON, in the "Ante-Nicene Christian Library," Edinb. 1868.

A MS. of this important work from the 14th century was discovered at Mt. Athos in Greece in 1842, by a learned Greek, Minoïdes Mynas (who had been sent by M. Villemain, minister of public instruction under Louis Philippe, to Greece in search of MSS.), and deposited in the national library at Paris. The first book had been long known among the works of Origen, but had justly been already denied to him by Huet and De la Rue; the second and third, and beginning of the fourth, are still wanting; the tenth lacks the conclusion. This work is now universally ascribed to Hippolytus.

Canones S. HIPPOLYTI *Arabice e codicibus Romanis cum versione Latina*, ed. D. B. DE HANEBERG. Monach. 1870. The canons are very rigoristic, but "certain evidence as to their authorship is wanting."

O. BARDENHEWER: *Des heil. Hippolyt von Rom. Commentar zum B. Daniel.* Freib. i. B. 1877.

(II.) E. F. KIMMEL: *De Hippolyti vita et scriptis.* Jen. 1839. MÖHLER: *Patrol.* p. 584 sqq. Both are confined to the older confused sources of information.

---

[1] See § 157, p. 609, and Stieren's ed. I. 889.

Since the discovery of the *Philosophumena* the following books and tracts
on Hippolytus have appeared, which present him under a new light:

BUNSEN : *Hippolytus and his Age.* Lond. 1852. 4 vols. (German in 2
vols. Leipz. 1855); 2d ed. with much irrelevant and heterogeneous
matter (under the title: *Christianity and Mankind*). Lond. 1854.
7 vols.

JACOBI in the "Deutsche Zeitschrift," Berl. 1851 and '53; and Art.
"Hippolytus" in Herzog's Encykl. VI. 131 sqq. (1856), and in Herzog [2] VI. 139–149.

BAUR, in the "Theol. Jahrb." Tüb. 1853. VOLKMAR and RITSCHL,
ibid. 1854.

GIESELER, in the "Stud. u. Krit." for 1853.

DÖLLINGER (R. Cath., but since 1870 an Old Cath.): *Hippolytus und
Callistus, oder die röm. Kirche in der ersten Hälfte des dritten Jahrh.*
Regensburg 1853. English translation by ALFRED PLUMMER, Edinb.
1876 (360 pages). The most learned book on the subject. An apology for Callistus and the Roman see, against Hippolytus the supposed first anti-Pope.

CHR. WORDSWORTH (Anglican): *St. Hippolytus and the Church of Rome
in the earlier part of the third century.* London 1853. Second and
greatly enlarged edition, 1880. With the Greek text and an English
version of the 9th and 10th books. The counter-part of Döllinger.
An apology for Hippolytus against Callistus and the papacy.

L'ABBÉ CRUICE (chanoine hon. de Paris): *Etudes sur de nouv. doc. hist.
des Philosophumena.* Paris 1853 (380 p.)

W. ELFE TAYLER : *Hippol. and the Christ. Ch. of the third century.*
Lond. 1853. (245 p.)

LE NORMANT: *Controverse sur les Philos. d'Orig.* Paris 1853. In "Le
Correspondant," Tom. 31 p. 509–550. For Origen as author.

G. VOLKMAR : *Hippolytus und die röm. Zeitgenossen.* Zürich 1855.
(174 pages.)

CASPARI : *Quellen zur Gesch. des Taufsymbols und der Glaubensregel.*
Christiania, vol. III. 349 sqq. and 374–409. On the writings of H.

LIPSIUS: *Quellen der ältesten Ketzergesch.* Leipzig 1875.

DE SMEDT (R. C.): *De Auctore Philosophumenon.* In "Dissertationes
Selectæ." Ghent, 1876.

G. SALMON: *Hipp. Romanus* in Smith and Wace III. 85–105 (very good.)

I. LIFE OF HIPPOLYTUS. This famous person has lived
three lives, a real one in the third century as an opponent of the
popes of his day, a fictitious one in the middle ages as a canonized saint, and a literary one in the nineteenth century after the
discovery of his long lost work against heresies. He was undoubtedly one of the most learned and eminent scholars and

theologians of his time. The Roman church placed him in the number of her saints and martyrs, little suspecting that he would come forward in the nineteenth century as an accuser against her. But the statements of the ancients respecting him are very obscure and confused. Certain it is, that he received a thorough Grecian education, and, as he himself says, in a fragment preserved by Photius, heard the discourses of Irenæus (in Lyons or in Rome). His public life falls in the end of the second century and the first three decennaries of the third (about 198 to 236), and he belongs to the western church, though he may have been, like Irenæus, of Oriental extraction. At all events he wrote all his books in Greek.[1]

Eusebius is the first who mentions him, and he calls him indefinitely, bishop, and a contemporary of Origen and Beryl of Bostra; he evidently did not know where he was bishop, but he gives a list of his works which he saw (probably in the library of Cæsarea). Jerome gives a more complete list of his writings, but no more definite information as to his see, although he was well acquainted with Rome and Pope Damasus. He calls him martyr, and couples him with the Roman senator Apollonius. An old catalogue of the popes, the Catalogus Liberianus (about A. D. 354), states that a "presbyter" Hippolytus was banished, together with the Roman bishop Pontianus, about 235, to the unhealthy island of Sardinia, and that the bodies of both were deposited on the same day (Aug. 13), Pontianus in the cemetery of Callistus, Hippolytus on the Via Tiburtina (where his statue was discovered in 1551). The translation of Pontianus was effected by Pope Fabianus about 236 or 237. From this statement we would infer that Hippolytus died in the mines of Sardinia and was thus counted a martyr, like all those confessors who died in prison. He may, however, have returned and suf-

---

[1] Dr. Caspari (III. 351 note 153) thinks it probable that Hippolytus came from the East to Rome in very early youth, and grew up there as a member, and afterwards officer of the Greek part of the Roman congregation. Lipsius (p. 40 sqq.) supposes that Hippolytus was a native of Asia Minor, and a pupil there of Irenæus in 170. But this is refuted by Harnack and Caspari (p. 409)

fered martyrdom elsewhere. The next account we have is from the Spanish poet Prudentius who wrote in the beginning of the fifth century. He represents Hippolytus in poetic description as a Roman presbyter (therein agreeing with the Liberian Catalogue) who belonged to the Novatian party[1] (which, however, arose several years after the death of Hippolytus), but in the prospect of death regretted the schism exhorted his numerous followers to return into the bosom of the catholic church, and then, in bitter allusion to his name and to the mythical Hippolytus, the son of Theseus, was bound by the feet to a team of wild horses and dragged to death over stock and stone. He puts into his mouth as his last words: "These steeds drag my limbs after them; drag Thou, O Christ, my soul to Thyself."[2] He places the scene of his martyrdom at Ostia or Portus where the Prefect of Rome happened to be at that time who condemned him for his Christian profession. Prudentius also saw the subterranean grave-chapel in Rome and a picture which represented his martyrdom (perhaps intended originally for the mythological Hippolytus).[3] But as no such church is found in the early lists of Roman churches, it may have been the church of St. Lawrence, the famous gridiron-martyr, which adjoined the tomb of Hippolytus. Notwithstanding the chronological error about the Novatian schism and the extreme improbability of such a horrible death under Roman laws and customs, there is an important element of truth in this legend, namely the schismatic position

---

[1] He calls it *schisma Novati*, instead of *Novatiani*. The two names are often confounded, especially by Greek writers, including Eusebius.

[2] *Ultima vox audita senis venerabilis hæc est :*
"*Hi rapiant artus, tu rape, Christe, animam.*"

[3] No. XI. of the *Peristephanon Liber*. Plummer, in Append. C. to Döllinger, p. 345–351, gives the poem in full (246 lines) from Dressel's text (1860). Baronius charged Prudentius with confounding three different Hippolytis and transferring the martyrdom of Hippolytus, the Roman officer, guard, and disciple of St. Lawrence, upon the bishop of that name. Döllinger severely analyses the legend of Prudentius, and derives it from a picture of a martyr torn to pieces by horses, which may have existed near the church of the martyr St. Lawrence (p. 58).

of Hippolytus which suits the *Philosophumena*, perhaps also his connection with Portus. The later tradition of the catholic church (from the middle of the seventh century) makes him bishop of Portus Romanus (now Porto) which lies at the Northern mouth of the Tiber, opposite Ostia, about fifteen miles from Rome.[1] The Greek writers, not strictly distinguishing the city from the surrounding country, call him usually bishop of Rome.[2]

These are the vague and conflicting traditions, amounting to this that Hippolytus was an eminent presbyter or bishop in Rome or the vicinity, in the early part of the third century, that he wrote many learned works and died a martyr in Sardinia or Ostia. So the matter stood when a discovery in the sixteenth century shed new light on this mysterious person.

In the year 1551, a much mutilated marble statue, now in the Lateran Museum, was exhumed at Rome near the basilica of St. Lawrence on the Via Tiburtina (the road to Tivoli). This statue is not mentioned indeed by Prudentius, and was perhaps originally designed for an entirely different purpose, possibly for a Roman senator; but it is at all events very ancient, probably from the middle of the third century.[3] It represents a venerable

---

[1] So first the *Paschal Chronicle*, and Anastasius.

[2] Salmon says: "Of the fragments collected in De Lagarde's edition the majority are entitled merely of 'Hippolytus,' or 'of Hippolytus, bishop and martyr,' but about twenty describe him as 'bishop of Rome,' and only three place him elsewhere. The earliest author who can be named as so describing him is Apollinaris in the fourth century. . . . Hippol. likewise appears as pope and bishop of Rome in the Greek menologies, and is also honored with the same title by the Syrian, Coptic, and Abyssinian churches." See the authorities in Döllinger.

[3] The reasons for this early age are: (1) The artistic character of the statue, which ante-dates the decline of art, which began with Constantine. (2) The paschal cycle, which gives the list of the paschal full moons accurately for the years 217–223, but for the next eight years wrongly, so that the table after that date became useless, and hence must have been written soon after 222. (3) The Greek language of the inscription, which nearly died out in Rome in the fourth century, and gave way to the Latin as the language of the Roman church. Dr. Salmon fixes the date of the erection of the statue at 235, very

man clothed with the Greek pallium and Roman toga, seated in a bishop's chair. On the back of the cathedra are engraved in uncial letters the paschal cycle, or easter-table of Hippolytus for seven series of sixteen years, beginning with the first year of Alexander Severus (222), and a list of writings, presumably written by the person whom the statue represents. Among these writings is named a work *On the All,* which is mentioned in the tenth book of the *Philosophumena* as a product of the writer.[1] This furnishes the key to the authorship of that important work.

Much more important is the recent discovery and publication (in 1851) of one of his works themselves, and that no doubt the most valuable of them all, viz. the *Philosophumena,* or *Refutation of all Heresies.*   It is now almost universally acknowledged that this work comes not from Origen, who never was a bishop, nor from the antimontanistic and antichiliastic presbyter Caius, but from Hippolytus ; because, among other reasons, the author, in accordance with the Hippolytus-statue, himself refers to a work *On the All,* as his own, and because Hippolytus is declared by the fathers to have written a work *Adversus omnes Hæreses.*[2]   The entire matter of the work, too, agrees with the scattered statements of antiquity respecting his ecclesiastical position ; and at the same time places that position in a much clearer light, and gives us a better understanding of those statements.[3]

shortly after the banishment of Hippolytus. A cast of the Hippolytus-statue is in the library of the Union Theol. Seminary in New York, procured from Berlin through Professor Piper.

[1] Περὶ τοῦ παντός. See the list of books in the notes.

[2] On the chair of the statue, it is true, the *Philosophumena* is not mentioned, and cannot be concealed under the title Πρὸς Ἕλληνας, which is connected by καί with the work against Plato. But this silence is easily accounted for, partly from the greater rarity of the book, partly from its offensive opposition to two Roman popes.

[3] The authorship of Hippolytus is proved or conceded by Bunsen, Gieseler, Jacobi, Döllinger, Duncker, Schneidewin, Caspari, Milman, Robertson, Wordsworth, Plummer, Salmon. Cardinal Newman denies it on doctrinal grounds, but offers no solution. The only rival claimants are Origen (so the first editor, Miller, and Le Normant), and Cajus (so Baur and Cruice, the latter hesitating

The author of the *Philosophumena* appears as one of the most prominent of the clergy in or near Rome in the beginning of the third century; probably a bishop, since he reckons himself among the successors of the apostles and the guardians of the doctrine of the church. He took an active part in all the doctrinal and ritual controversies of his time, but severely opposed the Roman bishops Zephyrinus (202–218) and Callistus (218–223), on account of their Patripassian leanings, and their loose penitential discipline. The latter especially, who had given public offence by his former mode of life, he attacked without mercy and not without passion. He was, therefore, if not exactly a schismatical counter-pope (as Döllinger supposes), yet the head of a disaffected and schismatic party, orthodox in doctrine, rigoristic in discipline, and thus very nearly allied to the Montanists before him, and to the later schism of Novatian. It is for this reason the more remarkable, that we have no account respecting the subsequent course of this movement, except the later unreliable tradition, that Hippolytus finally returned into the bosom of the catholic church, and expiated his schism by martyrdom, either in the mines of Sardinia or near Rome (A. D. 235, or rather 236, under the persecuting emperor Maximinus the Thracian).

II. His Writings. Hippolytus was the most learned divine

between Caius and Tertullian). Origen is out of the question, because of the difference of style and theology, and because he was no bishop and no resident at Rome, but only a transient visitor (under Zephyrinus, about 211). The only claim of Caius is the remark of Photius, based on a marginal note in his MS., but doubted by himself, that Caius wrote a work περὶ τοῦ παντός and an anti-heretical work called " The Labyrinth," and that he was " a presbyter of Rome," and also declared by some " a bishop of the heathen." But Caius was an anti-Chiliast, and an opponent of Montanism; while Hippolytus was probably a Chiliast, like Irenæus, and accepted the Apocalypse as Johannean, and sympathized with the disciplinary rigorism of the Montanists, although he mildly opposed them. See Döllinger, *l. c.* p. 250 sqq. (Engl. translation), Volkmar, *l. c.* p. 60–71 ; and Wordsworth, *l. c.* p. 16–28. Two other writers have been proposed as authors of the *Philosophumena*, but without a shadow of possibility, namely Tertullian by the Abbé Cruice, and the schismatic Novatian by the Jesuit Torquati Armellini, in a dissertation *De prisca refutatione haereseon Origenis nomine ac philosophumenon tituto recens vulgata*, Rom., 1862 (quoted by Plummer, p. 354).

and the most voluminous writer of the Roman church in the third century; in fact the first great scholar of that church, though like his teacher, Irenæus, he used the Greek language exclusively. This fact, together with his polemic attitude to the Roman bishops of his day, accounts for the early disappearance of his works from the remembrance of that church. He is not so much an original, productive author, as a learned and skilful compiler. In the philosophical parts of his *Philosophumena* he borrows largely from Sextus Empiricus, word for word, without acknowledgment; and in the theological part from Irenæus. In doctrine he agrees, for the most part, with Irenæus, even to his chiliasm, but is not his equal in discernment, depth, and moderation. He repudiates philosophy, almost with Tertullian's vehemence, as the source of all heresies; yet he employs it to establish his own views. On the subject of the trinity he assails Monarchianism, and advocates the hypostasian theory with a zeal which brought down upon him the charge of ditheism. His disciplinary principles are rigoristic and ascetic. In this respect also he is akin to Tertullian, though he places the Montanists, like the Quartodecimanians, but with only a brief notice, among the heretics. His style is vigorous, but careless and turgid. Caspari calls Hippolytus "the Roman Origen." This is true as regards learning and independence, but Origen had more genius and moderation.

The principal work of Hippolytus is the *Philosophumena* or *Refutation of all Heresies*. It is, next to the treatise of Irenæus, the most instructive and important polemical production of the ante-Nicene church, and sheds much new light, not only upon the ancient heresies, and the development of the church doctrine, but also upon the history of philosophy and the condition of the Roman church in the beginning of the third century. It furthermore affords valuable testimony to the genuineness of the Gospel of John, both from the mouth of the author himself, and through his quotations from the much earlier Gnostic Basilides, who was a later contemporary of John (about A. D. 125). The composition falls some years after the death of Callistus, between the years 223 and 235. The first of the ten books gives an outline of the heathen philosophies which he regards as the sources of all heresies; hence the title *Philosophumena* which answers the first four books, but not the last six. It is not in the Athos-MS., but was formerly known and incorporated in the works of Origen. The second and third books, which are wanting, treated probably of the heathen mysteries, and mathematical and astrological theories. The fourth is occupied likewise with the heathen astrology and magic, which must have exercised great influence, particularly in Rome. In the fifth book the author comes to his proper theme, the refutation of all the heresies from the times of the apostles to his own. He takes up thirty-two in all, most of which, however, are merely different branches of Gnosticism and Ebionism. He simply states the heretical opinions from lost writings, without introducing his own reflection, and refers them to the Greek philosophy, mysticism, and magic, thinking them sufficiently refuted by being traced to those heathen sources. The ninth book, in refuting the doctrine of the Noëtians and Callistians, makes remarkable disclosures of events in the Roman church. He represents Pope Zephyrinus as a weak and ignorant man who gave aid and comfort to the Patripassian heresy, and his successor Callistus, as a shrewd and cunning manager who was once a slave, then a dishonest banker, and became a bankrupt and convict, but worked himself into the good graces of Zephyrinus and after his death obtained the object of his ambition, the papal chair, taught heresy and ruined the discipline by extreme leniency to offenders. Here the author shows himself a violent partizan, and must be used with caution.

The tenth book, made use of by Theodoret, contains a brief recapitulation and the author's own confession of faith, as a positive refutation of the heresies. The following is the most important part relating to Christ:

"This Word (Logos) the Father sent forth in these last days no longer to speak by a prophet, nor willing that He should be only guessed at from obscure preaching, but bidding Him be manifested face to face, in order that the world should reverence Him when it beheld Him, not giving His commands in the person of a prophet, nor alarming the soul by an angel, but Himself present who had spoken.

"Him we know to have received a body from the Virgin and to have refashioned the old man by a new creation, and to have passed in His life through every age, in order that He might be a law to every age, and by His presence exhibit His own humanity as a pattern to all men,[1] and thus convince man that God made nothing evil, and that man possesses free will, having in himself the power of volition or non-volition, and being able to do both. Him we know to have been a man of the same nature with ourselves.

"For, if He were not of the same nature, He would in vain exhort us to imitate our Master. For if that man was of another nature, why does He enjoin the same duties on me who am weak? And how can He be good and just? But that He might be shown to be the same as we, He underwent toil and consented to suffer hunger and thirst, and rested in sleep, and did not refuse His passion, and became obedient unto death, and manifested His resurrection, having consecrated in all these things His own humanity, as first fruits, in order that thou when suffering mayest not despair, acknowledging thyself a man of like nature and waiting for the appearance of what thou gavest to Him.[2]

"Such is the true doctrine concerning the Deity, O ye Greeks and Barbarians, Chaldæans and Assyrians, Egyptians and Africans, Indians and Ethiopians, Celts, and ye warlike Latins, and all ye inhabitants of Europe, Asia, and Africa, whom I exhort, being a disciple of the man-loving Word and myself a lover of men ($\lambda\acute{o}\gamma ov$ $\acute{v}\pi\acute{a}\rho\chi\omega v$ $\mu\alpha\vartheta\eta\tau\grave{\eta}\varsigma$ $\kappa\alpha\grave{\iota}$ $\varphi\iota\lambda\acute{a}\nu\vartheta\rho\omega\pi o\varsigma$). Come ye and learn from us, who is the true God, and what is His well-ordered workmanship, not heeding the sophistry of artificial speeches, nor the vain professions of plagiarist heretics, but the grave simplicity of unadorned truth. By this knowledge ye will escape the coming curse of the judgment of fire, and the dark rayless aspect of Tartarus, never illuminated by the voice of the Word. . . .

"Therefore, O men, persist not in your enmity, nor hesitate to retrace your steps. For Christ is the God who is over all ($\acute{o}$ $\kappa\alpha\tau\grave{a}$ $\pi\acute{a}\nu\tau\omega v$ $\vartheta\epsilon\acute{o}\varsigma$, comp. Rom. 9: 5), who commanded men to wash away sin [in baptism],[3] regenerating the old man, having called him His image from the beginning, showing by a figure His love to thee. If thou obeyest His holy commandment and becomest an imitator in goodness of Him who is

---

[1] This idea is borrowed from Irenæus.

[2] The reading here is disputed.

[3] The passage is obscure: $\acute{o}\varsigma$ $\tau\grave{\eta}v$ $\acute{a}\mu\alpha\rho\tau\acute{\iota}\alpha v$ $\acute{\epsilon}\xi$ $\acute{a}\nu\vartheta\rho\acute{\omega}\pi\omega v$ $\acute{a}\pi o\pi\lambda\acute{\upsilon}\nu\epsilon\iota v$ $\pi\rho o\sigma\acute{\epsilon}\tau\alpha\xi\epsilon$. Wordsworth translates: "who commanded us to wash away sin from man;" Macmahon: "He has arranged to wash away sin from human beings." Bunsen changes the reading thus: "For Christ is He whom the God of all has ordered to wash away the sins of mankind." Hippolytus probably refers to the command to repent and be baptized for the forgiveness of sin.

good, thou wilt become like Him, being honored by Him. For God has a need and craving for thee, having made thee divine for His glory."

Hippolytus wrote a large number of other works, exegetical, chronological, polemical, and homiletical, all in Greek, which are mostly lost, although considerable fragments remain. He prepared the first continuous and detailed commentaries on several books of the Scriptures, as the Hexaëmeron (used by Ambrose), on Exodus, Psalms, Proverbs, Ecclesiastes, the larger prophets (especially Daniel), Zechariah, also on Matthew, Luke, and the Apocalypse. He pursued in exegesis the allegorical method, like Origen, which suited the taste of his age.

Among his polemical works was one *Against Thirty-two Heresies*, different from the *Philosophumena*, and described by Photius as a "little book," [1] and as a synopsis of lectures which Hippolytus heard from Irenæus. It must have been written in his early youth. It began with the heresy of Dositheus and ended with that of Noëtus.[2] His treatise *Against Noëtus* which is still preserved, presupposes previous sections, and formed probably the concluding part of that synopsis.[3] If not, it must

---

[1] βιβλιδάριον. The more usual diminutive of βιβλίς or βίβλος is βιβλίδιον.

[2] Lipsius, in his *Quellenkritik des Epiphanios*, has made the extraordinary achievement of a partial reconstruction of this work from unacknowledged extracts in the anti-heretical writings of Epiphanius, Philaster, and Pseudo-Tertullian.

[3] As suggested by Fabricius (I., 235), Neander (I. 682, Engl. ed.), and Lipsius. It bears in the MS. the title "Homily of Hippolytus against the Heresy of one Noëtus" ὁμιλία Ἱππολ. εἰς τὴν αἵρεσιν Νοήτου τινός, and was first printed by Vossius in Latin, and then by Fabricius in Greek from a Vatican MS. (vol. II. 5–20, in Latin, vol. I. 235–244), and by P. de Lagarde in Greek (*Hippol. Opera Gr.* p. 43–57). Epiphanius made a mechanical use of it. It presupposes preceding sections by beginning: "Certain *others* are privily introducing *another* doctrine, having become disciples of one Noëtus." The only objection to the identification is that Photius describes the entire work against thirty-two Heresies as a *little* book (βιβλιδάριον). Hence Lipsius suggests that this was not the σύνταγμα itself, but only a summary of its contents, such as was frequently attached to anti-heretical works. Döllinger (p. 191 sqq.) shows the doctrinal agreement of the treatise against Noëtus with the corresponding section of the *Philosophumena*, and finds both heretical on the subject of the Trinity and the development of the Logos as a subordinate Divine personality called into existence before the world by an act of the

have been the conclusion of a special work against the **Mon-**
archian heretics,[1] but no such work is mentioned.

The book *On the Universe*[2] was directed against Platonism.
It made all things consist of the four elements, earth, air, fire,
and water. Man is formed of all four elements, his soul, of air.
But the most important part of this book is a description of
Hades, as an abode under ground where the souls of the departed are detained until the day of judgment: the righteous in
a place of light and happiness called Abraham's Bosom; the
wicked in a place of darkness and misery; the two regions
being separated by a great gulf. The entrance is guarded by an
archangel. On the judgment day the bodies of the righteous
will rise renewed and glorified, the bodies of the wicked with
all the diseases of their earthly life for everlasting punishment.
This description agrees substantially with the eschatology of
Justin Martyr, Irenæus, and Tertullian.[3]

The anonymous work called *The Little Labyrinth,*[4] mentioned

Father's will, which doctrine afterwards became a main prop of Arianism.
Döllinger finds here the reason for the charge of partial Valentinianism raised
against Hippolytus, as his doctrine of the origination of the Logos was confounded with the Gnostic emanation theory.

[1] So Volkmar (*l. c.* p. 165 : " *Der Cod. Vatic.* ' *Contra Noëtum*' ist der Schluss
nicht jener kürzeren Häreseologie, sondern einer andern, von Epiphanius noch
vorgefundenen Schrift desselben Hippolyt, wie es scheint, gegen alle Monarchianer.''
Caspari (III. 400 sq.) decides for the same view.

[2] Περὶ τῆς τοῦ παντὸς αἰτίας (or οὐσίας, as Hippol. himself gives the title,
Philos. X. 32 ed. D. and Schn.), or Περὶ τοῦ παντός (on the Hippolytus-statue).
Greek and Latin in Fabricius I. 220–222. Greek in P. de Lagarde, p. 68–73.
The book was a sort of Christian cosmogony and offset to Plato's *Timæus.*

[3] Comp. Döllinger, p. 330 sqq. He connects the view of Hippolytus on the
intermediate state with his chiliasm, which does not admit that the souls of
the righteous ever can attain to the kingdom of heaven and the beatific vision
before the resurrection. Wordsworth on the other hand denies that Hippol.
believed in a millennium and "the Romish doctrine of Purgatory," and accepts his view of Hades as agreeing with the Burial Office of the Church of
England, and the sermons of Bishop Bull on the state of departed souls.
Hippol. p. 210–216. He also gives, in Appendix A, p. 306–308, an addition
to the fragment of the book *On the Universe*, from a MS. in the Bodleian
library.

[4] Σμικρὸς Λαβύρινθος (Theodoret, *Hær. Fab.* II. 5) or σπούδασμα κατὰ τῆς
'Αρτέμωνος αἱρέσεως (Euseb. *H. E.* V. 28).

by Eusebius and Theodoret as directed against the rationalistic heresy of Artemon, is ascribed by some to Hippolytus, by others to Caius. But *The Labyrinth* mentioned by Photius as a work of Caius is different and identical with the tenth book of the *Philosophumena*, which begins with the words, "The labyrinth of heresies." [1]

The lost tract on the *Charismata* [2] dealt probably with the Montanistic claims to continued prophecy. Others make it a collection of apostolical canons.

The book on *Antichrist* [3] which has been almost entirely recovered by Gudius, represents Antichrist as the complete counterfeit of Christ, explains Daniel's four kingdoms as the Babylonian, Median, Grecian, and Roman, and the apocalyptic number of the beast as meaning Λατεῖνος, *i. e.*, heathen Rome. This is one of the three interpretations given by Irenæus who, however, preferred *Teitan*.

In a commentary on the *Apocalypse* [4] he gives another interpretation of the number, namely *Dantialos* (probably because Antichrist was to descend from the tribe of Dan). The woman in the twelfth chapter is the church; the sun with which she is clothed, is our Lord; the moon, John the Baptist; the twelve stars, the twelve apostles; the two wings on which she was to fly, hope and love. Armageddon is the valley of Jehoshaphat. The five kings (17 : 13) are Nebuchadnezzar, Cyrus, Darius, Alexander, and his four successors; the sixth is the Roman empire, the seventh will be Antichrist. In his commentary on *Daniel* he fixes the consummation at A. D. 500, or A. M. 6000, on the assumption that Christ appeared in the year of the world 5500, and that a sixth millennium must yet be completed before

---

[1] Caspari, III. 404 sq., identifies the two books.

[2] Περὶ χαρισμάτων ἀποστολικὴ παράδοσις. On the Hippolytus-statue.

[3] Περὶ τοῦ σωτῆρος ἡμῶν Ἰησοῦ Χριστοῦ καὶ περὶ ἀντιχρίστου, in Fabricius I. 4–36 (Gr. and Lat.), and in P. de Lagarde, 1–36 (Greek only).

[4] Included in Jerome's list, and mentioned by Jacob of Edessa and by Syncellus. Fragments from an Arabic *Catena* on the Apocalypse in Lagarde's *Anal. Syr.*, Append. p. 24–27. See Salmon in Smith and Wace, III. 105.

the beginning of the millennial sabbath, which is prefigured by the divine rest after creation. This view, in connection with his relation to Irenæus, and the omission of chiliasm from his list of heresies, makes it tolerably certain that he was himself a chiliast, although he put off the millennium to the sixth century after Christ.[1]

We conclude this section with an account of a visit of Pope Alexander III. to the shrine of St. Hippolytus in the church of St. Denis in 1159, to which his bones were transferred from Rome under Charlemagne.[2] "On the threshold of one of the chapels the Pope paused to ask, whose relics it contained. 'Those of St. Hippolytus,' was the answer. ' Non credo, non credo,' replied the infallible authority, ' the bones of St. Hippolytus were never removed from the holy city.' But St. Hippolytus, whose dry bones apparently had as little reverence for the spiritual progeny of Zephyrinus and Callistus as the ancient bishop's tongue and pen had manifested towards these saints themselves, was so very angry that he rumbled his bones inside the reliquary with a noise like thunder. To what lengths he might have gone if rattling had not sufficed we dare not conjecture. But the Pope, falling on his knees, exclaimed in terror, ' I believe, O my Lord Hippolytus, I believe, pray be quiet.' And he built an altar of marble there to appease the disquieted saint."

NOTES.

The questions concerning the literary works of Hippolytus, and especially his ecclesiastical status are not yet sufficiently solved. We add a few additional observations.

I. THE LIST OF BOOKS on the back of the Hippolytus-statue has been discussed by Fabricius, Cave, Döllinger, Wordsworth, and Volkmar. See the three pictures of the statue with the inscriptions on both sides in Fabricius, I. 36–38, and a fac-simile of the book titles in the frontispiece of Wordsworth's work. It is mutilated and reads—with the conjectural supplements in brackets and a translation—as follows :

[1] See Döllinger, p. 330 sqq. (Engl. ed.)

[2] We are indebted for this curious piece of information to Dr. Salmon, who refers to Benson, in the "Journal of Classical and Sacred Philology," I. 190.

[πρὸς τοὺς Ἰουδα] ίους.	Against the Jews.
[περὶ παρϑε] νίας.	On Virginity.
[Or, perhaps, εἰς παροιμίας.]	[Or, On the Proverbs.]
[εἰς τοὺς ψ]αλμούς.	On the Psalms.
[εἰς τὴν ἐ]γγαστρίμυϑον.	On the Ventriloquist [the witch at Endor?]
[ἀπολογία] ὑπὲρ τοῦ κατὰ Ἰωάννην	Apology of the Gospel according to John,
εὐαγγελίου καὶ ἀποκαλύψεως.	and the Apocalypse.
περὶ χαρισμάτων.	On Spiritual Gifts.
ἀποστολικὴ παράδοσις.	Apostolic Tradition.
χρονικῶν [sc. βίβλος].	Chronicles [Book of].
πρὸς Ἕλληνας,	Against the Greeks,
καὶ πρὸς Πλάτωνα,	and against Plato,
ἢ καὶ περὶ τοῦ παντός.	or also On the All.
προτρεπτικὸς πρὸς σεβήρειναν.	A hortatory address to Severina. [Perhaps the Empress Severa, second wife of Elogabalus].
ἀπόδε[ι]ξις χρόνων τοῦ πάσχα.	Demonstration of the time of the Pascha according to the order in the table.
κατὰ [τὰ] ἐν τῷ πίνακι.	
ᾠδαί [ε]ἰς πάσας τὰς γραφάς.	Hymns on all the Scriptures.
περὶ ϑ[εο]ῦ, καὶ σαρκὸς ἀναστάσεως.	Concerning God, and the resurrection of the flesh.
περὶ τοῦ ἀγαθοῦ, καὶ πόϑεν τὸ κακόν.	Concerning the good, and the origin of evil.

Comp. on this list Fabricius I. 79–89; Wordsworth p. 233–240; Volkmar, p. 2 sqq.

Eusebius and Jerome give also lists of the works of Hippolytus, some being the same, some different, and among the latter both mention one *Against Heresies*, which is probably identical with the *Philosophumena*. On the *Canon Pasch.* of Hippol. see the tables in Fabricius, I. 137–140.

II. Was Hippolytus a *bishop*, and *where?*

Hippolytus does not call himself a bishop, nor a "bishop of Rome," but assumes episcopal authority, and describes himself in the preface to the first book as "a successor of the Apostles, a partaker with them in the same grace and principal sacerdocy (ἀρχιεράτεια), and doctorship, and as numbered among the guardians of the church." Such language is scarcely applicable to a mere presbyter. He also exercised the power of excommunication on certain followers of the Pope Callistus. But where was his bishopric? This is to this day a point in dispute.

(1.) He was bishop of Portus, the seaport of Rome. This is the traditional opinion in the Roman church since the seventh century, and is advocated by Ruggieri (*De Portuensi S. Hippolyti, episcopi et martyris, Sede*, Rom. 1771), Simon de Magistris (*Acta Martyrum ad Ostia Tiberina*, etc. Rom. 1795), Baron Bunsen, Dean Milman, and especially by Bishop

Wordsworth. In the oldest accounts, however, he is represented as a Roman "presbyter." Bunsen combined the two views on the unproved assumption that already at that early period the Roman suburban bishops, called *cardinales episcopi*, were at the same time members of the Roman presbytery. In opposition to this Dr. Döllinger maintains that there was no bishop in Portus before the year 313 or 314; that Hippolytus considered himself the rightful bishop of Rome, and that he could not be simultaneously a member of the Roman presbytery and bishop of Portus. But his chief argument is that from silence which bears with equal force against his own theory. It is true that the first bishop of Portus on record appears at the Synod of Arles, 314, where he signed himself *Gregorius episcopus de loco qui est in Portu Romano*. The episcopal see of Ostia was older, and its occupant had (according to St. Augustin) always the privilege of consecrating the bishop of Rome. But it is quite possible that Ostia and Portus which were only divided by an island at the mouth of the Tiber formed at first one diocese. Prudentius locates the martyrdom of Hippolytus at Ostia or Portus (both are mentioned in his poem). Moreover Portus was a more important place than Döllinger will admit. The harbor whence the city derived its name *Portus* (also *Portus Ostiensis*, *Portus Urbis*, *Portus Romœ*) was constructed by the Emperor Claudius (perhaps Augustus, hence *Portus Augusti*), enlarged by Nero and improved by Trajan (hence *Portus Trajani*), and was the landing place of Ignatius on his voyage to Rome (*Martyr. Ign.* c. 6 : τοῦ καλουμένου Πόρτου) where he met Christian brethren. Constantine surrounded it with strong walls and towers. Ostia may have been much more important as a commercial emporium and naval station (see Smith's *Dict. of Gr. and Rom. Geogr.* vol. II. 501–504) ; but Cavalier de Rossi, in the *Bulletino di Archeol.*, 1866, p. 37 (as quoted by Wordsworth, p. 264, sec[d] ed.), proves from 13 inscriptions that " the site and name of Portus are celebrated in the records of the primitive [?] church," and that "the name is more frequently commemorated than that of Ostia." The close connection of Portus with Rome would easily account for the residence of Hippolytus at Rome and for his designation as Roman bishop. In later times the seven suburban bishops of the vicinity of Rome were the suffragans of the Pope and consecrated him. Finally, as the harbor of a large metropolis attracts strangers from every nation and tongue, Hippolytus might with propriety be called " bishop of the nations" (ἐπίσκοπος ἐθνῶν). We conclude then that the Portus-hypothesis is not impossible, though it cannot be proven.

(2.) He was bishop of the Arabian Portus Romanus, now Aden on the Red Sea. This was the opinion of Stephen Le Moyne (1685), adopted by Cave, Tillemont, and Basnage, but now universally given up as a baseless conjecture, which rests on a misapprehension of Euseb. VI. 20, where Hippolytus is accidentally collocated with Beryllus, bishop of Bostra in Arabia. Adan is nowhere mentioned as an episcopal see, and our Hippolytus belonged to the West, although he may have been of eastern origin, like Irenæus.

(3.) Rome. Hippolytus was no less than the first Anti-Pope and claimed to be the legitimate bishop of Rome. This is the theory of Döllinger, derived from the *Philosophumena* and defended with much learning and acumen. The author of the *Philosophumena* was undoubtedly a resident of Rome, claims episcopal dignity, never recognized Callistus as bishop, but treated him merely as the head of a heretical school (διδασκαλεῖον) or sect, calls his adherents " Callistians," some of whom he had excommunicated, but admits that Callistus had aspired to the episcopal throne and " imagined himself to have obtained" the object of his ambition after the death of Zephyrinus, and that his school formed the majority and claimed to be the catholic church. Callistus on his part charged Hippolytus, on account of his view of the independent personality of the Logos, with the heresy of ditheism (a charge which stung him to the quick), and probably proceeded to excommunication. All this looks towards an open schism. This would explain the fact that Hippolytus was acknowledged in Rome only as a presbyter, while in the East he was widely known as bishop, and even as bishop of Rome. Dr. Döllinger assumes that the schism continued to the pontificate of Pontianus, the successor of Callistus, was the cause of the banishment of the two rival bishops to the pestilential island of Sardinia (in 235), and brought to a close by their resignation and reconciliation; hence their bones were brought back to Rome and solemnly deposited on the same day. Their death in exile was counted equivalent to martyrdom. Dr. Caspari of Christiania who has shed much light on the writings of Hippolytus, likewise believes that the difficulty between Hippolytus and Callistus resulted in an open schism and mutual excommunication (*l. c.* III. 330). Langen (*Gesch. der röm. Kirche*, Bonn. 1881, p. 229) is inclined to accept Döllinger's conclusion as at least probable.

This theory is plausible and almost forced upon us by the *Philosophumena*, but without any solid support outside of that polemical work. History is absolutely silent about an Anti-Pope before Novatianus, who appeared fifteen years after the death of Hippolytus and shook the whole church by his schism (251), although he was far less conspicuous as a scholar and writer. A schism extending through three pontificates (for Hippolytus opposed Zephyrinus as well as Callistus) could not be hidden and so soon be forgotten, especially by Rome which has a long memory of injuries done to the chair of St. Peter and looks upon rebellion against authority as the greatest sin. The name of Hippolytus is not found in any list of Popes and Anti-Popes, Greek or Roman, while that of Callistus occurs in all. Even Jerome who spent over twenty years from about 350 to 372, and afterwards four more years in Rome and was intimate with Pope Damasus, knew nothing of the see of Hippolytus, although he knew some of his writings. It seems incredible that an Anti-Pope should ever have been canonized by Rome as a saint and martyr. It is much easier to conceive that the divines of the distant East were mistaken. The oldest authority which Döllinger adduces for the designation

"bishop of Rome," that of Presbyter Eustratius of Constantinople about
A. D. 582 (see p. 84), is not much older than the designation of Hippolytus as bishop of Portus, and of no more critical value.

(4.) Dr. Salmon offers a modification of the Döllinger-hypothesis by
assuming that Hippolytus was a sort of independent bishop of a
Greek-speaking congregation in Rome. He thus explains the enigmati-
cal expression ἐθνῶν ἐπίσκοπος, which Photius applies to Caius, but which
probably belongs to Hippolytus. But history knows nothing of two independent and legitimate bishops in the city of Rome. Moreover there
still remains the difficulty that Hippolytus notwithstanding his open
resistance rose afterwards to such high honors in the papal church. We
can only offer the following considerations as a partial solution : first,
that he wrote in Greek which died out in Rome, so that his books became unknown; secondly, that aside from those attacks he did, like the
schismatic Tertullian, eminent service to the church by his learning and
championship of orthodoxy and churchly piety; and lastly, that he was
believed (as we learn from Prudentius) to have repented of his schism
and, like Cyprian, wiped out his sin by his martyrdom.

III. But no matter whether Hippolytus was bishop or presbyter in
Rome or Portus, he stands out an irrefutable witness against the claims
of an *infallible papacy* which was entirely unknown in the third century.
No wonder that Roman divines of the nineteenth century (with the exception of Döllinger who seventeen years after he wrote his book on
Hippolytus seceded from Rome in consequence of the Vatican decree of
infallibility) deny his authorship of this to them most obnoxious book.
The Abbé Cruice ascribes it to Caius or Tertullian, the Jesuit Armellini
to Novatian, and de Rossi (1866) hesitatingly to Tertullian, who, however,
was no resident of Rome, but of Carthage. Cardinal Newman declares it
"simply incredible" that a man so singularly honored as St. Hippolytus
should be the author of " that malignant libel on his contemporary popes,"
who did not scruple " in set words to call Pope Zephyrinus a weak and
venal dunce, and Pope Callistus a sacrilegious swindler, an infamous convict, and an heresiarch *ex cathedra*." (*Tracts, Theological and Ecclesiastical*,
1874, p. 222, quoted by Plummer, p. XIV. and 340.) But he offers no
solution, nor can he. Dogma *versus* history is as unavailing as the
pope's bull against the comet. Nor is Hippolytus, or whoever wrote that
"malignant libel" alone in his position. The most eminent ante-Nicene
fathers, and the very ones who laid the foundations of the catholic system, Irenæus, Tertullian, and Cyprian (not to speak of Origen, and of
Novatian, the Anti-Pope), protested on various grounds against Rome.
And it is a remarkable fact that the learned Dr. Döllinger who, in 1853,
so ably defended the Roman see against the charges of Hippolytus
should, in 1870, have assumed a position not unlike that of Hippolytus, against the error of papal infallibility.

§ 184. *Caius of Rome.*

EUSEB.: *H. E.* II. 25; III. 28, 31; VI. 20.   HIERON.: *De Vir. ill.* 59.
THEODOR.: *Fab. Hær.* II. 3; III. 2.   PHOTIUS: *Biblioth. Cod.* 48.
Perhaps also *Martyr. Polyc.*, c. 22, where a Caius is mentioned as a
pupil or friend of Irenæus.
ROUTH: *Rel. S.* II. 125–158 (comp. also I. 397–403).   BUNSEN: *Analecta
Ante-Nicæna* I. 409 sq.   CASPARI: *Quellen*, etc., III. 330, 349, 374
sqq.   HARNACK in Herzog², III. 63 sq.   SALMON in Smith and
Wace I. 384–386.   Comp. also HEINICHEN'S notes on Euseb. II. 25
(in *Comment.* III. 63–67), and the Hippolytus liter., § 183, especially
DÖLLINGER (250 sq.) and VOLKMAR (60–71).

Among the Western divines who, like Irenæus and Hippolytus, wrote exclusively in Greek, must be mentioned CAIUS
who flourished during the episcopate of Zephyrinus in the first
quarter of the third century.   He is known to us only from a
few Greek fragments as an opponent of Montanism and Chiliasm.   He was probably a Roman presbyter.   From his name,[1]
and from the fact that he did not number Hebrews among
the Pauline Epistles, we may infer that he was a native of Rome
or at least of the West.   Eusebius calls him a very learned
churchman or ecclesiastic author at Rome,[2] and quotes four times
his disputation with Proclus (διάλογος πρὸς Πρόκλον), the leader
of one party of the Montanists.[3]   He preserves from it the notice
that Philip and his four prophetic daughters are buried at Hierapolis in Phrygia, and an important testimony concerning the monuments or trophies (τρόπαια) of Peter and Paul, the founders of
the Roman church, on the Vatican hill and the Ostian road.
This is nearly all that is certain and interesting about

---

[1] The name, however, was common, and the New Testament mentions four
Caii (Acts 19: 29; 20: 4; Rom. 16: 24; 1 Cor. 1: 14; 3 John 1), Eusebius
five.

[2] ἀνὴρ ἐκκλησιαστικός and λογιώτατος (II. 25 and VI. 20).   The former term
does not necessarily imply an office, but is rendered by Valesius *vir catholicus*,
by Heinichen (Euseb. *Com.* III. 64) *ein rechtgläubiger Schriftsteller*.

[3] No doubt the same with the "*Proculus noster*" commended by Tertullian,
Adv. Val. 5.   Comp. Jerome (c. 59): "*Proculum Montani sectatorem*."   His
followers were Trinitarians; another party of the Montanists were Monarchians.

Caius. Jerome, as usual in his catalogue of illustrious men,
merely repeats the. statements of Eusebius, although from his
knowledge of Rome we might expect some additional information. Photius, on the strength of a marginal note in the MS. of
a supposed work of Caius *On the Universe*, says that he was a
"presbyter of the Roman church during the episcopate of Victor
and Zephyrinus, and that he was elected bishop of the Gentiles
(ἐθνῶν ἐπίσκοπος)." He ascribes to him that work and also
The Labyrinth, but hesitatingly. His testimony is too late to be
of any value, and rests on a misunderstanding of Eusebius and
a confusion of Caius with Hippolytus, an error repeated by
modern critics.[1] Both persons have so much in common—age,
residence, title—that they have been identified (Caius being supposed to be simply the prænomen of Hippolytus).[2] But this
cannot be proven ; Eusebius clearly distinguishes them, and
Hippolytus was no opponent of Chiliasm, and only a moderate
opponent of Montanism ; while Caius wrote against the Chiliastic dreams of Cerinthus ; but he did not deny, as has been
wrongly inferred from Eusebius, the Johannean authorship of
the Apocalypse ; he probably meant pretended revelations
(ἀποκαλύψεις) of that heretic. He and Hippolytus no doubt
agreed with the canon of the Roman church, which recognized
thirteen epistles of Paul (excluding Hebrews) and the Apocalypse of John.

Caius has been surrounded since Photius with a mythical halo
of authorship, and falsely credited with several works of Hippolytus, including the recently discovered *Philosophumena*.
The Muratorian fragment on the canon of the New Testament
was also ascribed to him by the discoverer (Muratori, 1740) and
recent writers. But this fragment is of earlier date (A. D. 170),
and written in Latin, though perhaps originally in Greek. It
is as far as we know the oldest Latin church document of Rome,
and of very great importance for the history of the canon.[3]

[1] See above § 183, p. 762 sq.

[2] So Lightfoot in the "Journal of Philology," I. 98. and Salmon. *l. c.*, p. 386.

[3] See the document and the discussion about the authorship in Routh, I. 393

§ 185. *The Alexandrian School of Theology.*

J. G. MICHAELIS : *De Scholæ Alexandrinæ prima origine, progressu, ac præcipuis doctoribus.* Hal. 1739.

H. E. FR. GUERIKE: *De Schola quæ Alexandriæ floruit catechetica commentatio historica et theologica.* Hal. 1824 and '25. 2 Parts (pp. 119 and 456). The second Part is chiefly devoted to Clement and Origen.

C. F. W. HASSELBACH : *De Schola, quæ Alex. floruit, catech.* Stettin 1826. P. 1. (against Guerike), and *De discipulorum . . . s. De Catechumenorum ordinibus,* Ibid. 1839.

J. MATTER : *L'Histoire de l'École d'Alexandrie,* second ed. Par. 1840. 3 vols.

J. SIMON : *Histoire de l'École d'Alexandrie.* Par. 1845.

E. VACHEROT : *Histoire critique de l'École d'Alexandrie.* Par. 1851. 3 vols.

NEANDER : I. 527–557 (Am. ed.) ; GIESELER I. 208–210 (Am. ed.)

RITTER : *Gesch. der christl. Philos.* I. 421 sqq.

UEBERWEG: *History of Philosophy,* vol. I. p. 311–319 (Engl. transl. 1875).

REDEPENNING in his *Origenes* I. 57–83, and art. in Herzog [2] I. 290–292. Comp. also two arts. on the Jewish, and the New-Platonic schools of Alexandria, by M. NICOLAS in Lichtenberger's " Encyclopédie " I. 159–170.

CH. BIGG : *The Christian Platonists of Alexandria.* Lond. 1886.

Alexandria, founded by Alexander the Great three hundred and twenty-two years before Christ, on the mouth of the Nile, within a few hours' sail from Asia and Europe, was the metropolis of Egypt, the flourishing seat of commerce, of Grecian and Jewish learning, and of the greatest library of the ancient world, and was destined to become one of the great centres of Christianity,

---

sqq., the article of Salmon in Smith and Wace III. 1000 sqq., and the different works on the Canon. Most of the writers on the subject, including Salmon, regard the fragment as a translation from a Greek original, since all other documents of the Roman Church down to Zephyrinus and Hippolytus are in Greek. Hilgenfeld and P. de Lagarde have attempted a re-translation. But Hesse (*Das Murator. Fragment,* Giessen, 1873, p. 25–39), and Caspari (*Quellen,* III. 410 sq.) confidently assert the originality of the Latin for the reason that the re-translation into the Greek does not clear up the obscurities. The Latin barbarisms occur also in other Roman writers. Caspari, however, thinks that it was composed by an African residing in Rome, on the basis of an older Greek document of the Roman church. He regards it as the oldest ecclesiastical document in the Latin language ("*das älteste in lateinischer Sprache geschriebene originale kirchliche Schriftstück*").

the rival of Antioch and Rome. There the religious life of Palestine and the intellectual culture of Greece commingled and prepared the way for the first school of theology which aimed at a philosophic comprehension and vindication of the truths of revelation. Soon after the founding of the church which tradition traces to St. Mark, the Evangelist, there arose a " Catechetical school" under the supervision of the bishop.[1] It was originally designed only for the practical purpose of preparing willing heathens and Jews of all classes for baptism. But in that home of the Philonic theology, of Gnostic heresy, and of Neo-Platonic philosophy, it soon very naturally assumed a learned character, and became, at the same time, a sort of theological seminary, which exercised a powerful influence on the education of many bishops and church teachers, and on the development of Christian science. It had at first but a single teacher, afterwards two or more, but without fixed salary, or special buildings. The more wealthy pupils paid for tuition, but the offer was often declined. The teachers gave their instructions in their dwellings, generally after the style of the ancient philosophers.

The first superintendent of this school known to us was PANTÆNUS, a converted Stoic philosopher, about A. D. 180. He afterwards labored as a missionary in India, and left several commentaries, of which, however, nothing remains but some scanty fragments.[2] He was followed by CLEMENT, to A. D. 202; and Clement, by ORIGEN, to 232, who raised the school to the summit of its prosperity, and founded a similar one at Cæsarea

---

[1] Eusebius (V. 10; VI. 3, 6) calls it τὸ τῆς κατηχήσεως διδασκαλεῖον, and διδασκαλεῖον τῶν ἱερῶν λόγων. Sozomen (III. 15), τὸ ἱερὸν διδασκαλεῖον τῶν ἱερῶν μαθημάτων; Jerome (Catal. 38), and Rufinus (H. E. II. 7), ecclesiastica schola.

[2] Clemens calls him "the Sicilian bee" (σικελικὴ μέλιττα, perhaps with reference to his descent from Sicily). Jerome (Catal. 36) says of him: "Hujus multi quidem in S. Scripturam exstant commentarii, sed magis viva voce ecclesiis profuit." Comp. on him Redepenning; Origenes I. 63 sqq., and Möller in Herzog[2] XI. 182. The two brief relics of Pantænus are collected and accompanied with learned notes by Routh, Rel. S. I. 375–383.

in Palestine. The institution was afterwards conducted by Origen's pupils, HERACLAS (d. 248), and DIONYSIUS (d. 265), and last by the blind but learned DIDYMUS (d. 395), until, at the end of the fourth century, it sank for ever amidst the commotions and dissensions of the Alexandrian church, which at last prepared the way for the destructive conquest of the Arabs (640). The city itself gradually sank to a mere village, and Cairo took its place (since 969). In the present century it is fast rising again, under European auspices, to great commercial importance.

From this catechetical school proceeded a peculiar theology, the most learned and genial representatives of which were Clement and Origen. This theology is, on the one hand, a regenerated Christian form of the Alexandrian Jewish religious philosophy of Philo; on the other, a catholic counterpart, and a positive refutation of the heretical Gnosis, which reached its height also in Alexandria, but half a century earlier. The Alexandrian theology aims at a reconciliation of Christianity with philosophy, or, subjectively speaking, of *pistis* with *gnosis;* but it seeks this union upon the basis of the Bible, and the doctrine of the church. Its centre, therefore, is the Divine Logos, viewed as the sum of all reason and all truth, before and after the incarnation. Clement came from the Hellenic philosophy to the Christian faith; Origen, conversely, was led by faith to speculation. The former was an aphoristic thinker, the latter a systematic. The one borrowed ideas from various systems; the other followed more the track of Platonism. But both were Christian philosophers and churchly gnostics. As Philo, long before them, in the same city, had combined Judaism with Grecian culture, so now they carried the Grecian culture into Christianity. This, indeed, the apologists and controversialists of the second century had already done, as far back as Justin the "philosopher." But the Alexandrians were more learned, and made much freer use of the Greek philosophy. They saw in it not sheer error, but in one view a gift of God, and an intellectual schoolmaster for Christ, like the law in the moral and religious sphere. Clement compares it to a wild olive tree, which can be ennobled by faith; Origen (in the fragment of an epistle to Gregory Thaumaturgus), to the jewels, which the Israelites took with them out of Egypt, and turned into ornaments for their sanctuary, though they also wrought them into the golden calf. Philosophy is not necessarily an enemy to the truth, but may, and should be its handmaid, and neutralize the attacks against it. The elements of truth in the heathen philosophy they attributed partly to the secret operation of the Logos in the world of reason, partly to acquaintance with the writings of Moses and the prophets.

So with the Gnostic heresy. The Alexandrians did not sweepingly condemn it, but recognized the desire for deeper religious knowledge, which lay at its root, and sought to meet this desire with a wholesome supply from the Bible itself. To the γνῶσις ψευδώνυμος they opposed a γνῶσις ἀληθινή. Their maxim was, in the words of Clement: "No faith without knowledge, no knowledge without faith;" or: "Unless you believe, you will not understand."[1] Faith and knowledge have the same substance, the saving truth of God, revealed in the Holy Scriptures, and faithfully handed down by the church; they differ only in form. Knowledge is our consciousness of the deeper ground and consistency of faith. The Christian knowledge, however, is also a gift of grace, and has its condition in a holy life. The ideal of a Christian gnostic includes perfect love as well as perfect knowledge, of God. Clement describes him as one "who, growing grey in the study of the Scriptures, and preserving the orthodoxy of the apostles and the church, lives strictly according to the gospel."

The Alexandrian theology is intellectual, profound, stirring, and full of fruitful germs of thought, but rather unduly idealistic and spiritualistic, and, in exegesis, loses itself in arbitrary allegorical fancies. In its efforts to reconcile revelation and philosophy it took up, like Philo, many foreign elements, especially of the Platonic stamp, and wandered into speculative views

---

[1] Is. 7: 9 according to the LXX: ἐὰν μὴ πιστεύσητε, οὐδὲ μὴ συνῆτε.

which a later and more orthodox, but more narrow-minded and less productive age condemned as heresies, not appreciating the immortal service of this school to its own and after times.

§ 186. *Clement of Alexandria.*

(I.) CLEMENTIS ALEX. *Opera omnia Gr. et Lat.* ed. POTTER (bishop of Oxford). Oxon. 1715. 2 vols. Reprinted Venet. 1757. 2 vols. fol., and in MIGNE'S "*Patr. Gr.*" vols. VIII. and IX., with various additions and the comments of Nic. LE Nourry. For an account of the MSS. and editions of Clement see FABRICIUS; *Biblioth. Græca,* ed. Harles, vol. VII. 109 sqq.

Other edd. by VICTORINUS (Florence, 1550); SYLBURG (Heidelb. 1592); HEINSIUS (Græco-Latin., Leyden, 1616); KLOTZ (Leipz. 1831–34, 4 vols., only in Greek, and very incorrect); W. DINDORF (Oxf. 1868–69, 4 vols.).

English translation by WM. WILSON in Clark's "Ante-Nicene Library," vols. IV. and V. Edinb. 1867.

(II.) EUSEBIUS: *Hist. Eccl.* V. 11; VI. 6, 11, 13. HIERONYMUS: *De Vir. ill.* 38; PHOTIUS: *Biblioth.* 109–111. See the *Testimonia Veterum de Cl.* collected in Potter's ed. at the beginning of vol. I. and in Migne's ed. VIII. 35–50.

(III.) HOFSTEDE DE GROOT: *Dissert. de Clem. Alex.* Groning. 1826. A. F. DAEHNE: DE γνώσει CLEM AL. Hal. 1831.

F. R. EYLERT: *Clem. v. Alex. als Philosoph und Dichter.* Leipz. 1832.

Bishop KAYE: *Some Account of the Writings and Opinions of Clement of Alex.* Lond. 1835.

KLING: *Die Bedeutung des Clem. Alex. für die Entstehung der Theol.* ("Stud. u. Krit." for 1841, No. 4).

H. J. REINKENS: *De Clem. Alex. homine, scriptore, philosopho, theologo.* Wratisl. (Breslau) 1851.

H. REUTER: *Clementis Alex. Theol. moralis.* Berl. 1853.

LÆMMER: *Clem. Al. de Logo doctrina.* Lips. 1855.

Abbé COGNAT: *Clement d'Alexandrie.* Paris 1859.

J. H. MÜLLER: *Idées dogm. de Clement d'Alex.* Strasb. 1861.

CH. E. FREPPEL (R. C.): *Clément d'Alexandrie.* Paris, 1866, second ed. 1873.

C. MERK: *Clemens v. Alex. in s. Abhängigkeit von der griech. Philosophie.* Leipz. 1879.

FR. JUL. WINTER: *Die Ethik des Clemens v. Alex.* Leipz. 1882 (first part of *Studien zur Gesch. der christl. Ethik*).

JACOBI in Herzog[2] III. 269–277, and WESTCOTT in Smith and Wace I. 559–567.

THEOD. ZAHN: *Supplementum Clementinum.* Third Part of his *Forschungen zur Gesch. des N. T. lichen Kanons.* Erlangen 1884.

I. Titus Flavius Clemens[1] sprang from Greece, probably from Athens. He was born about 150, and brought up in heathenism. He was versed in all branches of Hellenic literature and in all the existing systems of philosophy ; but in these he found nothing to satisfy his thirst for truth. In his adult years, therefore, he embraced the Christian religion, and by long journeys East and West he sought the most distinguished teachers, " who preserved the tradition of pure saving doctrine, and implanted that genuine apostolic seed in the hearts of their pupils." He was captivated by Pantænus in Egypt, who, says he, " like the Sicilian bee, plucked flowers from the apostolic and prophetic meadow, and filled the souls of his disciples with genuine, pure knowledge." He became presbyter in the church of Alexandria, and about A. D. 189 succeeded Pantænus as president of the catechetical school of that city. Here he labored benignly some twelve years for the conversion of heathens and the education of the Christians, until, as it appears, the persecution under Septimius Severus in 202 compelled him to flee. After this we find him in Antioch, and last (211) with his former pupil, the bishop Alexander, in Jerusalem. Whether he returned thence to Alexandria is unknown. He died before the year 220, about the same time with Tertullian. He has no place, any more than Origen, among the saints of the Roman church, though he frequently bore this title of honor in ancient times. His name is found in early Western martyrologies, but was omitted in the martyrology issued by Clement VIII. at the suggestion of Baronius. Benedict XIV. elaborately defended the omission (1748), on the ground of unsoundness in doctrine.

II. Clement was the father of the Alexandrian Christian philosophy. He united thorough biblical and Hellenic learning with genius and speculative thought. He rose, in many points,

---

[1] Κλήμης. It is strange that he, and not his distinguished Roman name-sake, should be called *Flavius*. Perhaps he was descended from a freedman of Titus Flavius Clemens, the nephew of the Emperor Vespasian and Consul in 95, who with his wife Domitilla was suddenly arrested and condemned on the charge of "atheism," *i. e.* Christianity, by his cousin, the emperor Domitian.

far above the prejudices of his age, to more free and spiritual views. His theology, however, is not a unit, but a confused eclectic mixture of true Christian elements with many Stoic, Platonic, and Philonic ingredients. His writings are full of repetition, and quite lacking in clear, fixed method. He throws out his suggestive and often profound thoughts in fragments, or purposely veils them, especially in the *Stromata*, in a mysterious darkness, to conceal them from the exoteric multitude, and to stimulate the study of the initiated or philosophical Christians. He shows here an affinity with the heathen mystery cultus, and the Gnostic arcana. His extended knowledge of Grecian literature and rich quotations from the lost works of poets, philosophers, and historians give him importance also in investigations regarding classical antiquity. He lived in an age of transition when Christian thought was beginning to master and to assimilate the whole domain of human knowledge. " And when it is frankly admitted " (says Dr. Westcott) " that his style is generally deficient in terseness and elegance; that his method is desultory; that his learning is undigested : we can still thankfully admire his richness of information, his breadth of reading, his largeness of sympathy, his lofty aspirations, his noble conception of the office and capacities of the Faith."

III. The three leading works which he composed during his residence as teacher in Alexandria, between the years 190 and 195, represent the three stages in the discipline of the human race by the divine Logos, corresponding to the three degrees of knowledge required by the ancient mystagogues,[1] and are related to one another very much as apologetics, ethics, and dogmatics, or as faith, love, and mystic vision, or as the stages of the Christian cultus up to the celebration of the sacramental mysteries. The " Exhortation to the Greeks," [2] in three books, with almost a waste of learning, points out the unreasonableness and immo-

---

[1] The ἀποκάθαρσις, and the μύησις, and the ἐπότεία, *i. e.* purification, initiation, vision.

[2] Λόγος προτρεπτικός πρὸς ῾Ελληνας, *Cohortatio ad Grœcos*, or *ad Gentes*.

rality, but also the nobler prophetic element, of heathenism, and seeks to lead the sinner to repentance and faith.   The " Tutor" or " Educator" [1] unfolds the Christian morality with constant reference to heathen practices, and exhorts to a holy walk, the end of which is likeness to God.   The Educator is Christ, and the children whom he trains, are simple, sincere believers.   The " Stromata " or " Miscellanies," [2] in seven books (the eighth, containing an imperfect treatise on logic, is spurious), furnishes a guide to the deeper knowledge of Christianity, but is without any methodical arrangement, a heterogeneous mixture of curiosities of history, beauties of poetry, reveries of philosophy, Christian truths and heretical errors (hence the name).   He compares it to a thick-grown, shady mountain or garden, where fruitful and barren trees of all kinds, the cypress, the laurel, the ivy, the apple, the olive, the fig, stand confusedly grouped together, that many may remain hidden from the eye of the plunderer without escaping the notice of the laborer, who might transplant and arrange them in pleasing order.   It was, probably, only a prelude to a more comprehensive theology.   At the close the author portrays the ideal of the true gnostic, that is, the perfect Christian, assigning to him, among other traits, a stoical elevation above all sensuous affections.   The inspiring thought of Clement is that Christianity satisfies all the intellectual and moral aspirations and wants of man.

Besides these principal works we have, from Clement also, an able and moderately ascetic treatise, on the right use of wealth.[3]   His ethical principles are those of the Hellenic

[1] Παιδαγωγός.   This part contains the hymn to Christ at the close.

[2] Στρωματεῖς, Stromata, or pieces of tapestry, which, when curiously woven, and in divers colors, present an apt picture of such miscellaneous composition.

[3] Τίς ὁ σωζόμενος πλούσιος, Quis dives salvus, or salvetur ? an excellent commentary on the words of the Lord in Mark 10 : 17 sqq.   A most practical topic for a rich city like Alexandria, or any other city and age, especially our own, which calls for the largest exercise of liberality for literary and benevolent objects.   See the tract in Potter's ed. II. 935–961 (with a Latin version).   It ends with the beautiful story of St. John and the young robber, which Eusebius has inserted in his Church History (III. 23).

philosophy, inspired by the genius of Christianity. He does not run into the excesses of asceticism, though evidently under its influence. His exegetical works,[1] as well as a controversial treatise on prophecy against the Montanists, and another on the passover, against the Judaizing practice in Asia Minor, are all lost, except some inconsiderable fragments.

To Clement we owe also the oldest Christian hymn that has come down to us; an elevated but somewhat turgid song of praise to the Logos, as the divine educator and leader of the human race.[2]

§ 187. *Origen.*

(I.) ORIGENIS *Opera omnia Græce et Lat.* *Ed.* CAROL. ET VINC. DE LA RUE. Par. 1733–'59, 4 vols. fol. The only complete ed., begun by the Benedictine Charles D. L. R., and after his death completed by his nephew Vincent. Republ. in Migne's *Patrol. Gr.* 1857, 8 vols., with additions from Galland (1781), Cramer (1840–44), and Mai (1854).

Other editions by J. MERLINUS (ed. princeps, Par. 1512–'19, 2 vols. fol., again in Venice 1516, and in Paris 1522; 1530, only the Lat. text) ; by ERASMUS and BEATUS RHENANUS (Bas. 1536, 2 vols. fol. ; 1545; 1551; 1557; 1571); by the Benedictine G. GENEBRARD (Par. 1574; 1604; 1619 in 2 vols. fol,. all in Lat.); by CORDERIUS (Antw. 1648, partly in Greek); by P. D. HUETIUS, or HUET, afterwards Bp. of Avranges (Rouen, 1668, 2 vols. fol., the Greek writings, with very learned dissertations, *Origeniana ;* again Paris 1679; Cologne 1685); by MONTFAUCON (only the *Hexapla,* Par. 1713, '14, 2 vols. fol., revised and improved ed. by FIELD, Oxf. 1875); by LOMMATSCH (Berol. 1837–48, 25 vols. oct.).

English translation of select works of Origen by F. CROMBIE in Clark's "Ante-Nicene Library," Edinb. 1868, and N. York 1885.

(II.) EUSEBIUS: *Hist. Eccles.* VI. 1–6 and passim. HIERONYMUS: *De Vir. ill.* 54 ; *Ep.* 29, 41, and often. GREGORIUS THAUMAT.: *Oratio panegyrica in Origenem.* PAMPHILUS: *Apologia Orig.* RUFINUS: *De Adulteratione librorum Origenis.* All in the last vol. of Delarue's ed.

---

[1] Ὑποτυπώσεις, *Adumbrationes, Outlines,* or a condensed survey of the contents of the Old and New Testament Scriptures. See the analysis of the fragments by Westcott, in Smith and Wace, III. 563 sq., and Zahn, *l. c.* 64–103.

[2] ὑμνος τοῦ σωτῆρος Χριστοῦ, written in an anapæstic measure. See § 66, p. 230. The other hymn added to the "Tutor'" written in trimeter iambics, and addressed to the παιδαγωγός, is of later date.

(III.) P. D. HUETIUS: *Origeniana*. Par. 1679, 2 vols. (and in Delarue's
ed. vol. 4th). Very learned, and apologetic for Origen.

G. THOMASIUS: *Origenes. Ein Beitrag zur Dogmengesch.* Nürnb. 1837.

E. RUD. REDEPENNING: *Origenes. Eine Darstellung seines Lebens und
seiner Lehre.* Bonn 1841 and '46, in 2 vols. (pp. 461 and 491).

BÖHRINGER: *Origenes und sein Lehrer Klemens, oder die Alexandrinische
innerkirchliche Gnosis des Christenthums.* Bd. V. of *Kirchengesch.*
in *Biographieen.* Second ed. Leipz. 1873.

CH. E. FREPPEL (R. C.): *Origène.* Paris 1868, second ed. 1875.

Comp. the articles of SCHMITZ in Smith's "Dict. of Gr. and Rom. Biogr."
III. 46–55 ; MÖLLER in Herzog[2] vol. XI. 92–109 ; WESTCOTT in
"Dict. of Chr. Biogr," IV. 96–142 ; FARRAR, in "Lives of the
Fathers," I. 291–330.

Also the respective sections in BULL (*Defens. Fid. Nic.* ch. IX. in
Delarue, IV. 339–357), NEANDER, BAUR, and DORNER (especially
on Origen's doctrine of the Trinity and Incarnation); and on his
philosophy, RITTER, HUBER, UEBERWEG.

I. LIFE AND CHARACTER. ORIGENES,[1] surnamed "Adamantius" on account of his industry and purity of character,[2] is
one of the most remarkable men in history for genius and learning, for the influence he exerted on his age, and for the controversies and discussions to which his opinions gave rise. He was
born of Christian parents at Alexandria, in the year 185, and
probably baptized in childhood, according to Egyptian custom
which he traced to apostolic origin.[3] Under the direction of his
father, Leonides,[4] who was probably a rhetorician, and of the
celebrated Clement at the catechetical school, he received a pious
and learned education. While yet a boy, he knew whole sections
of the Bible by memory, and not rarely perplexed his father
with questions on the deeper sense of Scripture. The father
reproved his curiosity, but thanked God for such a son, and

---

[1] Ὠριγένης, *Origenes,* probably derived from the name of the Egyptian divinity Or or Horus (as Phœbigena from Phœbus, Diogenes from Zeus). See
Huetius I. 1, 2 ; Redepenning. I. 421 sq.

[2] Ἀδαμάντιος (also Χαλκέντερος). Jerome understood the epithet to indicate
his unwearied industry, Photius the irrefragable strength of his arguments.
See Redepenning, I. 430.

[3] So Möller (*l. c.* 92) and others. But it is only an inference from Origen's
view. There is no record as far as I know of his baptism.

[4] Λεωνίδης, Eus. VI. 1. So Neander and Gieseler. Others spell the name
Leonidas (Redepenning and Möller).

often, as he slept, reverentially kissed his breast as a temple of the Holy Spirit. Under the persecution of Septimius Severus in 202, he wrote to his father in prison, beseeching him not to deny Christ for the sake of his family, and strongly desired to give himself up to the heathen authorities, but was prevented by his mother, who hid his clothes. Leonides died a martyr, and, as his property was confiscated, he left a helpless widow with seven children. Origen was for a time assisted by a wealthy matron, and then supported himself by giving instruction in the Greek language and literature, and by copying manuscripts.

In the year 203, though then only eighteen years of age, he was nominated by the bishop Demetrius, afterwards his opponent, president of the catechetical school of Alexandria, left vacant by the flight of Clement. To fill this important office, he made himself acquainted with the various heresies, especially the Gnostic, and with the Grecian philosophy; he was not even ashamed to study under the heathen Ammonius Saccas, the celebrated founder of Neo-Platonism. He learned also the Hebrew language, and made journeys to Rome (211), Arabia, Palestine (215), and Greece. In Rome he became slightly acquainted with Hippolytus, the author of the *Philosophumena*, who was next to himself the most learned man of his age. Döllinger thinks it all but certain that he sided with Hippolytus in his controversy with Zephyrinus and Callistus, for he shared (at least in his earlier period) his rigoristic principles of discipline, had a dislike for the proud and overbearing bishops in large cities, and held a subordinatian view of the Trinity, but he was far superior to his older contemporary in genius, depth, and penetrating insight.[1]

When his labors and the number of his pupils increased he gave the lower classes of the catechetical school into the charge of his pupil Heraclas, and devoted himself wholly to the more advanced students. He was successful in bringing many emi-

---

[1] See Döllinger, *Hippolytus and Callistus*, p. 236 sqq. (Plummer's translation).

nent heathens and heretics to the Catholic church ; among them a wealthy Gnostic, Ambrosius, who became his most liberal patron, furnishing him a costly library for his biblical studies, seven stenographers, and a number of copyists (some of whom were young Christian women), the former to note down his dictations, the latter to engross them. His fame spread far and wide over Egypt. Julia Mammæa, mother of the Emperor Alexander Severus, brought him to Antioch in 218, to learn from him the doctrines of Christianity. An Arabian prince honored him with a visit for the same purpose.

His mode of life during the whole period was strictly ascetic. He made it a matter of principle to renounce every earthly thing not indispensably necessary. He refused the gifts of his pupils, and in literal obedience to the Saviour's injunction he had but one coat, no shoes, and took no thought of the morrow. He rarely ate flesh, never drank wine ; devoted the greater part of the night to prayer and study, and slept on the bare floor. Nay, in his youthful zeal for ascetic holiness, he even committed the act of self-emasculation, partly to fulfil literally the mysterious words of Christ, in Matt. 19 : 12, for the sake of the kingdom of God, partly to secure himself against all temptation and calumny which might arise from his intercourse with many female catechumens.[1] By this inconsiderate and misdirected heroism, which he himself repented in his riper years, he incapacitated himself, according to the canons of the church, for the clerical office. Nevertheless, a long time afterwards, in 228, he was ordained presbyter by two friendly bishops, Alexander of Jerusalem, and Theoctistus of Cæsarea in Palestine, who had, even before this, on a former visit of his, invited him while a layman, to teach publicly in their churches, and to expound the Scriptures to their people.

[1] This fact rests on the testimony of Eusebius (vi. 8), who was very well informed respecting Origen ; and it has been defended by Engelhardt, Redepenning, and Neander, against the unfounded doubts of Baur and Schnitzer. The comments of Origen on the passage in Matthew speak for rather than against the fact. See also Möller (p. 93).

But this foreign ordination itself, and the growing reputation of Origen among heathens and Christians, stirred the jealousy of the bishop Demetrius of Alexandria, who charged him besides, and that not wholly without foundation, with corrupting Christianity by foreign speculations. This bishop held two councils, A. D. 231 and 232, against the great theologian, and enacted, that he, for his false doctrine, his self-mutilation, and his violation of the church laws, be deposed from his offices of presbyter and catechist, and excommunicated. This unrighteous sentence, in which envy, hierarchical arrogance, and zeal for orthodoxy joined, was communicated, as the custom was, to other churches. The Roman church, always ready to anathematize, concurred without further investigation; while the churches of Palestine, Arabia, Phœnicia, and Achaia, which were better informed, decidedly disapproved it.

In this controversy Origen showed a genuine Christian meekness. "We must pity them," said he of his enemies, "rather than hate them; pray for them, rather than curse them; for we are made for blessing, and not for cursing." He betook himself to his friend, the bishop of Cæsarea in Palestine, prosecuted his studies there, opened a new philosophical and theological school, which soon outshone that of Alexandria, and labored for the spread of the kingdom of God. The persecution under Maximinus Thrax (235) drove him for a time to Cappadocia. Thence he went to Greece, and then back to Palestine. He was called into consultation in various ecclesiastical disputes, and had an extensive correspondence, in which were included even the emperor Philip the Arabian, and his wife. Though thrust out as a heretic from his home, he reclaimed the erring in foreign lands to the faith of the church. At an Arabian council, for example, he convinced the bishop Beryllus of his christological error, and persuaded him to retract (A. D. 244).

At last he received an honorable invitation to return to Alexandria, where, meantime, his pupil Dionysius had become bishop. But in the Decian persecution he was cast into prison, cruelly tortured, and condemned to the stake; and though he regained his liberty by the death of the emperor, yet he died some time after, at the age of sixty-nine, in the year 253 or 254, at Tyre, probably in consequence of that violence. He belongs, therefore, at least among the confessors, if not among the martyrs. He was buried at Tyre.

It is impossible to deny a respectful sympathy, veneration and gratitude to this extraordinary man, who, with all his brilliant talents and a host of enthusiastic friends and admirers, was driven from his country, stripped of his sacred office, excommunicated from a part of the church, then thrown into a dungeon, loaded with chains, racked by torture, doomed to drag his aged frame and dislocated limbs in pain and poverty, and long after his death to have his memory branded, his name anathematized, and his salvation denied;[1] but who nevertheless did more than all his enemies combined to advance the cause of sacred learning, to refute and convert heathens and heretics, and to make the church respected in the eyes of the world.

II. His Theology. Origen was the greatest scholar of his age, and the most gifted, most industrious, and most cultivated of all the ante-Nicene fathers. Even heathens and heretics admired or feared his brilliant talent and vast learning. His knowledge embraced all departments of the philology, philosophy, and theology of his day. With this he united profound and fertile thought, keen penetration, and glowing imagination. As a true divine, he consecrated all his studies by prayer, and turned them, according to his best convictions, to the service of truth and piety.

He may be called in many respects the Schleiermacher of the Greek church. He was a guide from the heathen philosophy and the heretical Gnosis to the Christian faith. He exerted an

---

[1] Stephen Binet, a Jesuit, wrote a little book, *De salute Origenis*, Par. 1629, in which the leading writers on the subject debate the question of the salvation of Origen, and Baronius proposes a descent to the infernal regions to ascertain the truth; at last the final revision of the heresy-trial is wisely left with the secret counsel of God. See an account of this book by Bayle, *Diction. sub* "Origene," Tom. III. 541, note D. Origen's "gravest errors," says Westcott (*l. c.* iv. 139), "are attempts to solve that which is insoluble."

immeasurable influence in stimulating the development of the catholic theology and forming the great Nicene fathers, Athanasius, Basil, the two Gregories, Hilary, and Ambrose, who consequently, in spite of all his deviations, set great value on his services. But his best disciples proved unfaithful to many of his most peculiar views, and adhered far more to the reigning faith of the church. For—and in this too he is like Schleiermacher—he can by no means be called orthodox, either in the Catholic or in the Protestant sense. His leaning to idealism, his predilection for Plato, and his noble effort to reconcile Christianity with reason, and to commend it even to educated heathens and Gnostics, led him into many grand and fascinating errors. Among these are his extremely ascetic and almost docetistic conception of corporeity, his denial of a material resurrection, his doctrine of the pre-existence and the pre-temporal fall of souls (including the pre-existence of the *human* soul of Christ), of eternal creation, of the extension of the work of redemption to the inhabitants of the stars and to all rational creatures, and of the final restoration of all men and fallen angels. Also in regard to the dogma of the divinity of Christ, though he powerfully supported it, and was the first to teach expressly the eternal generation of the Son, yet he may be almost as justly considered a forerunner of the Arian *heteroousion*, or at least of the semi-Arian *homoiousion*, as of the Athanasian *homoousion*.

These and similar views provoked more or less contradiction during his lifetime, and were afterwards, at a local council in Constantinople in 543, even solemnly condemned as heretical.[1] But such a man might in such an age hold erroneous opinions without being a heretic. For Origen propounded his views always with modesty and from sincere conviction of their agreement with Scripture, and that in a time when the church doctrine was as yet very indefinite in many points. For this reason

---

[1] Not at the fifth ecumenical council of 553, as has been often, through confusion, asserted. See Hefele, *Conciliengesch.* vol. II. 790 sqq. and 859 sqq. Möller, however, in Herzog² xi. 113, again defends the other view of Noris and Ballerini. See the 15 anathematisms in Mansi, *Conc.* ix. 534.

even learned Roman divines, such as Tillemont and Möhler, have shown Origen the greatest respect and leniency; a fact
the more to be commended, since the Roman church has refused
him, as well as Clement of Alexandria and Tertullian, a place
among the saints and the fathers in the stricter sense.

Origen's greatest service was in exegesis. He is father of the
critical investigation of Scripture, and his commentaries are still
useful to scholars for their suggestiveness. Gregory Thaumaturgus says, he had "received from God the greatest gift, to
be an interpreter of the word of God to men." For that age
this judgment is perfectly just. Origen remained the exegetical
oracle until Chrysostom far surpassed him, not indeed in originality and vigor of mind and extent of learning, but in sound,
sober tact, in simple, natural analysis, and in practical application of the text. His great defect is the neglect of the grammatical and historical sense and his constant desire to find a hidden
mystic meaning. He even goes further in this direction than
the Gnostics, who everywhere saw transcendental, unfathomable
mysteries. His hermeneutical principle assumes a threefold
sense—somatic, psychic, and pneumatic; or literal, moral, and
spiritual. His allegorical interpretation is ingenious, but often
runs far away from the text and degenerates into the merest
caprice; while at times it gives way to the opposite extreme of a
carnal literalism, by which he justifies his ascetic extravagance.[1]

Origen is one of the most important witnesses of the ante-
Nicene text of the Greek Testament, which is older than
the received text. He compared different MSS. and noted
textual variations, but did not attempt a recension or lay down
any principles of textual criticism. The value of his testimony
is due to his rare opportunities and life-long study of the Bible
before the time when the traditional Syrian and Byzantine text
was formed.

---

[1] His exegetical method and merits are fully discussed by Huetius, and by
Redepenning (I. 296–324), also by Diestel, *Gesch. des A. T. in der christl.
Kirche*, 1869, p. 36 sq. and 53 sq.

§ 188. *The Works of Origen.*

Origen was an uncommonly prolific author, but by no means an idle bookmaker. Jerome says, he wrote more than other men can read. Epiphanius, an opponent, states the number of his works as six thousand, which is perhaps not much beyond the mark, if we include all his short tracts, homilies, and letters, and count them as separate volumes. Many of them arose without his coöperation, and sometimes against his will, from the writing down of his oral lectures by others. Of his books which remain, some have come down to us only in Latin translations, and with many alterations in favor of the later orthodoxy. They extend to all branches of the theology of that day.

1. His biblical works were the most numerous, and may be divided into critical, exegetical, and hortatory.

Among the critical were the *Hexapla*[1] (the *Sixfold* Bible) and the shorter *Tetrapla* (the *Fourfold*), on which he spent eight-and-twenty years of the most unwearied labor. The Hexapla was the first polyglott Bible, but covered only the Old Testament, and was designed not for the critical restoration of the original text, but merely for the improvement of the received Septuagint, and the defense of it against the charge of inaccuracy. It contained, in six columns, the original text in two forms, in Hebrew and in Greek characters, and the four Greek versions of the Septuagint, of Aquila, of Symmachus, and of Theodotion. To these he added, in several books, two or three other anonymous Greek versions.[2] The order was determined

---

[1] Τὰ ἑξαπλᾶ, also in the singular form τὸ ἑξαπλοῦν, *Hexaplum* (in later writers). Comp. Fritzsche in Herzog[2] I. 285.

[2] Called *Quinta* (ε΄), *Sexta* (ϛ΄), and *Septima* (ζ΄). This would make nine columns in all, but the name *Enneapla* never occurs. *Octapla* and *Heptapla* are used occasionally, but very seldom. The following passage from Habakkuk 2: 4 (quoted Rom. 1: 17) is found complete in all the columns:

Τὸ Ἑβραικόν.	Τὸ Ἑβραικὸν Ἑλληνικοῖς γράμμασιν.	Ἀκύλας.	Σύμμαχος.	Οἱ Ο΄. (LXX.)	Θεοδοτίων.	Ε΄.	Σ΄.	Ζ΄.
וצדיק באמונתו יחיה	ουσαδικ βημουναθω ιειε.	καὶ δίκαιος ἐν πιστει αὐτοῦ ζήσεται.	ὁ δὲ δίκαιος τῇ εαυτοῦ πίστει ζήσει.	ὁ δὲ δίκαιος ἐκ πίστεως μοῦ ζήσεται.	ὁ δὲ δίκαιος τῇ εαυτοῦ πίστει ζήσει.	ὁ δὲ δίκαιος τῇ εαυτοῦ πίστει ζήσει.	ὁ δὲ δίκαιος τῇ εαυτοῦ πίστει ζήσει.	ὁ δὲ δίδαιος τῇ εαυτοῦ πίστει ζήσει.

by the degree of literalness. The Tetrapla[1] contained only the four versions of Aquila, Symmachus, the Septuagint, and Theodotion. The departures from the standard he marked with the critical signs *asterisk* (*) for alterations and additions, and *obelos* (ഗ) for proposed omissions. He also added marginal notes, *e. g.*, explanations of Hebrew names. The voluminous work was placed in the library at Cæsarea, was still much used in the time of Jerome (who saw it there), but doubtless never transcribed, except in certain portions, most frequently the Septuagint columns (which were copied, for instance, by Pamphilus and Eusebius, and regarded as the standard text), and was probably destroyed by the Saracens in 653. We possess, therefore, only some fragments of it, which were collected and edited by the learned Benedictine Montfaucon (1714), and more recently by an equally learned Anglican scholar, Dr. Field (1875).[2]

His *commentaries* covered almost all the books of the Old and New Testaments, and contained a vast wealth of original and profound suggestions, with the most arbitrary allegorical and mystical fancies. They were of three kinds: (*a*) Short notes on single difficult passages for beginners;[3] all these are lost, except what has been gathered from the citations of the fathers (by Delarue under the title Ἐκλογαί, *Selecta*). (*b*) Extended expositions of whole books, for higher scientific study;[4] of, these we have a number of important fragments in the original, and in the translation of Rufinus. In the Commentary on

---

[1] τὰ τετραπλᾶ, or τετραπλοῦν, or τὸ τετρασέλιδον, Tetrapla, Tetraplum.

[2] BERNARDUS DE MONTFAUCON: *Hexaplorum Origenis quæ supersunt.* Paris 1713 and 1714, 2 vols. fol. He added a Latin version to the Hebrew and Greek texts. C. F. BAHRDT issued an abridged edition, Leipz. 1769 and '70, in 2 vols. FRIDERICUS FIELD: *Origenis Hexaplorum quæ supersunt.* Oxon. 1875. This is a thorough revision of Montfaucon's edition with valuable additions, including the *Syro-Hexapla*, or Syriac translation of the Hexaplar recension of the Septuagint made in 617. See a good article on the Hexapla by Dr. Charles Taylor in Smith and Wace III. 14–23, and especially the Prolegomena of Field. See also Fritzsche in Herzog[2] I. 285–298.

[3] Σημειώσεις, σχόλια, scholia.

[4] Τόμοι, volumina, also commentarii.

John the Gnostic exegeses of Heracleon is much used. (c) Hortatory or practical applications of Scripture for the congregation or Homilies.[1] They were delivered extemporaneously, mostly in Cæsarea and in the latter part of his life, and taken down by stenographers. They are important also to the history of pulpit oratory. But we have them only in part, as translated by Jerome and Rufinus, with many unscrupulous retrenchments and additions, which perplex and are apt to mislead investigators.

2. Apologetic and polemic works. The refutation of Celsus's attack upon Christianity, in eight books, written in the last years of his life, about 248, is preserved complete in the original, and is one of the ripest and most valuable productions of Origen, and of the whole ancient apologetic literature.[2] And yet he did not know who this Celsus was, whether he lived in the reign of Nero or that of Hadrian, while modern scholars assign him to the period A. D. 150 to 178. His numerous polemic writings against heretics are all gone.

3. Of his dogmatic writings we have, though only in the inaccurate Latin translation of Rufinus, his juvenile production, De Principiis, i. e. on the fundamental doctrines of the Christian faith, in four books.[3] It was written in Alexandria, and became the chief source of objections to his theology. It was the first attempt at a complete system of dogmatics, but full of his peculiar Platonizing and Gnosticizing errors, some of

---

[1] Ὁμιλίαι.

[2] Comp. § 32, p. 89 sqq. A special ed. by W. Selwyn: Origenis Contra Celsum libri I–IV. Lond. 1877. English version by Crombie, 1868. The work of Celsus restored from Origen by Keim, Celsus' Wahres Wort, Zürich 1873.

[3] Περὶ ἀρχῶν. The version of Rufinus with some fragments of a more exact rival version in Delarue I. 42–195. A special ed. by Redepenning, Origenes de Princip., Lips. 1836. Comp. also K. F. Schnitzer, Orig. über die Grundlehren des Christenthums, ein Wiederherstellungsversuch, Stuttgart 1836. Rufinus himself confesses that he altered or omitted several pages, pretending that it had been more corrupted by heretics than any other work of Origen. Tillemont well remarks that Rufinus might have spared himself the trouble of alteration, as we care much less about his views than those of the original.

which he retracted in his riper years. In this work Origen treats in four books, first, of God, of Christ, and of the Holy Spirit; in the second book, of creation and the incarnation, the resurrection and the judgment; in the third, of freedom, which he very strongly sets forth and defends against the Gnostics; in the fourth, of the Holy Scriptures, their inspiration and authority, and the interpretation of them; concluding with a recapitulation of the doctrine of the trinity. His *Stromata*, in imitation of the work of the same name by Clemens Alex., seeems to have been doctrinal and exegetical, and is lost with the exception of two or three fragments quoted in Latin by Jerome. His work on the *Resurrection* is likewise lost.

4. Among his practical works may be mentioned a treatise on prayer, with an exposition of the Lord's Prayer,[1] and an exhortation to martyrdom,[2] written during the persecution of Maximin (235-238), and addressed to his friend and patron Ambrosius.

5. Of his letters, of which Eusebius collected over eight hundred, we have, besides a few fragments, only an answer to Julius Africanus on the authenticity of the history of Susanna.

Among the works of Origen is also usually inserted the *Philocalia*, or a collection, in twenty-seven chapters, of extracts from his writings on various exegetical questions, made by Gregory Nazianzen and Basil the Great.[3]

§ 189. *Gregory Thaumaturgus.*

I. S. GREGORII *episcopi Neocœsariensis Opera omnia*, ed. G. VOSSIUS, Mag. 1604; better ed. by FRONTO DUCÆUS, Par. 1622, fol.; in

---

[1] Περὶ εὐχῆς, *De Oratione.* Delarue, I. 195-272. Separate ed. Oxf. 1635, with a Latin version. Origen omits (as do Tertullian and Cyprian) the doxology of the Lord's Prayer, not finding it in his MSS. This is one of the strongest negative proofs of its being a later interpolation from liturgical usage.

[2] Εἰς μαρτύριον προτρεπτικὸς λόγος, or Περὶ μαρτυρίου, *De Martyrio.* First published by Wetstein, Basel, 1574; in Delarue, I. 273-310, with Latin version and notes.

[3] First published in Latin by Genebrardus, Paris 1574, and in Greek and Latin by Delarue, who, however, omits those extracts, which are elsewhere given in their appropriate places.

GALLANDI, "Bibl. Vet. Patrum" (1766–77), Tom. III., p. 385–470; and in *Migne*, "Patrol. Gr." Tom. X. (1857), 983-1343. Comp. also a Syriac version of Gregory's κατὰ μέρος πίστις in R. DE LAGARDE'S *Analecta Syriaca*, Leipz. 1858, pp. 31–67.

II. GREGORY OF NYSSA: Βίος καὶ ἐγκώμιον ῥηθὲν εἰς τὸν ἅγιον Γρηγόριον τὸν Θαυματουργόν. In the works of Gregory of Nyssa, (Migne, vol. 46). A eulogy full of incredible miracles, which the author heard from his grandmother.

English translation by S. D. F. SALMOND, in Clark's "Ante-Nicene Library," vol. xx. (1871), p. 1-156.

C. P. CASPARI: *Alte und neue Quellen zur Gesch. des Taufsymbols und der Glaubensregel.* Christiania, 1879, p. 1–160.

VICTOR RYSSEL: *Gregorius Thaumaturgus. Sein Leben und seine Schriften.* Leipzig, 1880 (160 pp.). On other biographical essays of G., see Ryssel, pp. 59 sqq. Contains a translation of two hitherto unknown Syriac writings of Gregory.

W. MÖLLER in Herzog[2], **V.** 404 sq. H. R. REYNOLDS in Smith & Wace, II. 730–737.

Most of the Greek fathers of the third and fourth centuries stood more or less under the influence of the spirit and the works of Origen, without adopting all his peculiar speculative views. The most distinguished among his disciples are Gregory Thaumaturgus, Dionysius of Alexandria, surnamed the Great, Heraclas, Hieracas, Pamphilus; in a wider sense also Eusebius, Gregory of Nyssa and other eminent divines of the Nicene age.

GREGORY, surnamed THAUMATURGUS, "the wonder-worker," was converted from heathenism in his youth by Origen at Cæsarea, in Palestine, spent eight years in his society, and then, after a season of contemplative retreat, labored as bishop of Neo-Cæsarea in Pontus from 244 to 270 with extraordinary success. He could thank God on his death-bed, that he had left to his successor no more unbelievers in his diocese than he had found Christians in it at his accession; and those were only seventeen. He must have had great missionary zeal and executive ability. He attended the Synod of Antioch in 265, which condemned Paul of Samosata.

Later story represents him as a "second Moses," and attributed extraordinary miracles to him. But these are not mentioned till a century after his time, by Gregory of Nyssa and Basil, who made him also a champion of the Nicene orthodoxy before the Council of Nicæa. Eusebius knows nothing of them, nor of his trinitarian creed, which is said to have been communicated to him by a special revelation in a vision.[1] This creed is almost too orthodox for an admiring pupil of Origen, and seems to presuppose the Arian controversy (especially the conclusion). It has probably been enlarged. Another and fuller creed ascribed to him, is the work of the younger Apollinaris at the end of the fourth century.[2]

Among his genuine writings is a glowing eulogy on his beloved teacher Origen, which ranks as a masterpiece of later Grecian eloquence.[3] Also a simple paraphrase of the book of Ecclesiastes.[4] To these must be added two books recently published in a Syriac translation, one on the co-equality of the Father, Son, and Holy Spirit, and the other on the impassibility and the passibility of God.

NOTES.

I. The DECLARATION OF FAITH (ἐκθεσις πίστεως κατὰ ἀποκάλυψιν) is said to have been revealed to Gregory in a night vision by St. John, at the request of the Virgin Mary, and the autograph of it was, at the time of Gregory of Nyssa (as he says), in possession of the church of Neocæsarea. It is certainly a very remarkable document and the most explicit statement of the doctrine of the Trinity from the ante-Nicene age. Caspari (in his *Alte und neue Quellen*, etc., 1879, pp. 25–64), after an elaborate discussion, comes to the conclusion that the creed contains nothing inconsistent with a pupil of Origen, and that it was written by Gregory in opposition to Sabellianism and Paul of Samosata, and with reference to

---

[1] The ᾽Εκθεσις τῆς πίστεως κατὰ ἀποκάλυψιν is rejected as spurious by Gieseler and Baur, defended by Hahn, Caspari, and Ryssel. It is given in Mansi, *Conc.* I., 1030, in Hahn, *Bibl. der Symbole der alten Kirche*, second ed. p. 183, and by Caspari, p. 10–17, in Greek and in two Latin versions with notes.

[2] The κατὰ μέρος πίστις (*i. e.* the faith set forth piece for piece, or in detail, not in part only) was first published in the Greek original by Angelo Mai, *Scriptorum Vet. Nova Collectio*, VII. 170–176. A Syriac translation in the *Analecta Syriaca*, ed. by P. de Lagarde, pp. 31–42. See Caspari, *l. c.* pp. 65–116, who conclusively proves the Apollinarian origin of the document. A third trinitarian confession from Gregory διάλεξις πρὸς Αἰλιανόν, is lost.

[3] Best separate edition by Bengel, Stuttgart, 1722. It is also published in the 4th vol. of Delarue's ed. of Origen, and in Migne, *Patr. Gr.* X. col. 1049–1104. English version in Ante-Nic. Lib., XX., 36–80.

[4] In Migne, Tom. X. col. 987–1018.

the controversy between Dionysius of Alexandria and Dionysius of Rome on the Trinity, between A. D. 260 and 270. But I think it more probable that it has undergone some enlargement at the close by a later hand. This is substantially also the view of Neander, and of Dorner (*Entwicklungsgesch. der L. v. d. Pers. Christi*, I. 735–737). The creed is at all events a very remarkable production and a Greek anticipation of the Latin *Quicunque* which falsely goes under the name of the " Athanasian Creed." We give the Greek with a translation. See Mansi, *Conc.* I. 1030; Migne, *Patr. Gr.* X. col. 983; Caspari, *l. c.;* comp. the comparative tables in Schaff's *Creeds of Christendom*, II. 40 and 41.

GREGORY THAUMAT. DECLARATION OF FAITH.

Εἷς Θεός, Πατὴρ λόγου ζῶντος, σοφίας ὑφεστώσης καὶ δυνάμεως καὶ χαρακτῆρος ἀϊδίου, τέλειος τελείου γεννήτωρ, Πατὴρ Υἱοῦ μονογενοῦς.

There is one God, the Father of the living Word, (who is his) subsisting Wisdom and Power and eternal Impress (Image) : perfect Begetter of the Perfect [Begotten], Father of the only begotten Son.

Εἷς Κύριος, μόνος ἐκ μονου, Θεὸς ἐκ Θεοῦ, χαρακτὴρ καὶ εἰκὼν τῆς θεότητος, λόγος ἐνεργός, σοφία τῆς τῶν ὅλων συστάσεως περιεκτικὴ καὶ δύναμις τῆς ὅλης κτίσεως ποιητική, Υἱὸς ἀληθινὸς ἀληθινοῦ Πατρός, ἀόρατος ἀοράτου καὶ ἄφθαρτος ἀφθάρτου καὶ ἀθάνατος ἀθανάτου καὶ ἀίδιος ἀϊδίου.

There is one Lord, Only of Only, God of God, the Image and Likeness of the Godhead, the efficient Word, Wisdom comprehensive of the system of all things, and Power productive of the whole creation ; true Son of the true Father, Invisible of Invisible, and Incorruptible of Incorruptible, and Immortal of Immortal, and Eternal of Eternal.

Καὶ ἓν Πνεῦμα Ἅγιον, ἐκ Θεοῦ τὴν ὕπαρξιν ἔχον, καὶ δι' Υἱοῦ πεφηνὸς (δηλαδὴ τοῖς ἀνθρώποις), εἰκὼν τοῦ Υἱοῦ τελείου τελεία, ζωή, ζώντων αἰτία, πηγὴ ἁγία, ἁγιότης, ἁγιασμοῦ χορηγός· ἐν ᾧ φανεροῦται Θεὸς ὁ Πατὴρ ὁ ἐπὶ πάντων καὶ ἐν πᾶσι, καὶ Θεὸς ὁ Υἱὸς ὁ διὰ πάντων· τριὰς τελεία, δόξῃ καὶ ἀϊδιότητι καὶ βασιλείᾳ μὴ μεριζομένη μηδὲ ἀπαλλοτριουμένη.

And there is one Holy Ghost, having his existence from God, and being manifested (namely, to mankind) by the Son ; the perfect Likeness of the perfect Son : Life, the Cause of the living ; sacred Fount ; Holiness, the Bestower of sanctification ; in whom is revealed God the Father, who is over all things and in all things, and God the Son, who is through all things : a perfect Trinity, in glory and eternity and dominion, neither divided nor alien.

Οὔτε οὖν κτιστόν τι ἢ δοῦλον ἐν τῇ τριάδι, οὔτε ἐπείσακτον, ὡς πρότερον μὲν οὐχ ὑπάρχον, ὕστερον δὲ ἐπεισελθόν· οὔτε οὖν ἐνέλιπέ ποτε Υἱὸς Πατρί, οὔτε Υἱῷ Πνεῦμα, ἀλλὰ ἄτρεπτος καὶ ἀναλλοίωτος ἡ αὐτὴ τριὰς ἀεί.

There is therefore nothing created or subservient in the Trinity, nor superinduced, as though not before existing, but introduced afterward. Nor has the Son ever been wanting to the Father, nor the Spirit to the Son, but there is unvarying and unchangeable the same Trinity forever.

II. The MIRACLES ascribed to Gregory Thaumaturgus in the fourth century, one hundred years after his death, by the enlightened and philosophic Gregory of Nyssa, and defended in the nineteenth century by Cardinal Newman of England as credible (*Two Essays on Bibl. and Eccles. Miracles.* Lond. 3d ed., 1873, p. 261-270), are stupendous and surpass all that are recorded of the Apostles in the New Testament.

Gregory not only expelled demons, healed the sick, banished idols from a heathen temple, but he moved large stones by a mere word, altered the course of the Armenian river Lycus, and, like Moses of old, even dried up a lake. The last performance is thus related by St. Gregory of Nyssa: Two young brothers claimed as their patrimony the possession of a lake. (The name and location are not given.) Instead of dividing it between them, they referred the dispute to the Wonderworker, who exhorted them to be reconciled to one another. The young men however, became exasperated, and resolved upon a murderous duel, when the man of God, remaining on the banks of the lake, by the power of prayer, transformed the whole lake into dry land, and thus settled the conflict.

Deducting all these marvellous features, which the magnifying distance of one century after the death of the saint created, there remains the commanding figure of a great and good man who made a most powerful impression upon his and the subsequent generations.

§ 190. *Dionysius the Great.*

(I.) S. DIONYSII *Episcopi Alexandrini quæ supersunt Operum et Episto larum fragmenta,* in MIGNE's "Patrol. Gr." Tom. X. col. 1237-1344 and Addenda, col. 1575-1602. Older collections of the fragments by SIMON DE MAGISTRIS, Rom. 1796, and ROUTH, *Rel. Sacr.*, vol. IV. 393-454. Add PITRA, *Spicil. Solesm.* I. 15 sqq.—English translation by SALMOND in Clark's "Ante-Nicene Library," vol. xx. (1871), p. 161-266.

(II.) EUSEBIUS: *H. E.* III. 28; VI. 41, 45, 46; VII. 2, 4, 7, 9, 11, 22, 24, 26, 27, 28. ATHANASIUS: *De Sent. Dionys.* HIERONYM.: *De Vir. ill.* 69.

(III.) TH. FÖRSTER: *De Doctrina et Sententiis Dionysii Magni Episcopi Alex.* Berl. 1865. And in the "Zeitschrift für hist. Theol." 1871. DR. DITTRICH (R. C.): *Dionysius der Grosse von Alexandrien.* Freib. i. Breisg. 1867 (130 pages). WEIZSÄCKER in Herzog[2] III. 615 sq. WESTCOTT in Smith and Wace I. 850 sqq.

DIONYSIUS OF ALEXANDRIA—so distinguished from the contemporary Dionysius of Rome—surnamed "the Great,"[1]

---

[1] First by Eusebius in the Prœem. to Bk. VII: ὁ μέγας ᾿Αλεξανδρέων ἐπίσκοπος Διονύσιος. Athanasius (*De Seut. Dion.* 6) calls him "teacher of the Catholic church" (τῆς καθολ. ἐκκλησίας διδάσκαλος).

was born about A. D. 190,[1] of Gentile parents, and brought up to a secular profession with bright prospects of wealth and renown, but he examined the claims of Christianity and was won to the faith by Origen, to whom he ever remained faithful. He disputes with Gregory Thaumaturgus the honor of being the chief disciple of that great teacher; but while Gregory was supposed to have anticipated the Nicene dogma of the trinity, the orthodoxy of Dionysius was disputed. He became Origen's assistant in the Catechetical School (233), and after the death of Heraclas bishop of Alexandria (248). During the violent persecution under Decius (249–251) he fled, and thus exposed himself, like Cyprian, to the suspicion of cowardice. In the persecution under Valerian (247), he was brought before the præfect and banished, but he continued to direct his church from exile. On the accession of Gallienus he was allowed to return (260). He died in the year 265.

His last years were disturbed by war, famine and pestilence, of which he gives a lively account in the Easter encyclical of the year 263.[2] "The present time," he writes, "does not appear a fit season for a festival ... All things are filled with tears, all are mourning, and on account of the multitudes already dead and still dying, groans are daily heard throughout the city ... There is not a house in which there is not one dead ... After this, war and famine succeeded which we endured with the heathen, but we bore alone those miseries with which they afflicted us ... But we rejoiced in the peace of Christ which he gave to us alone ... Most of our brethren by their exceeding great love and affection not sparing themselves and adhering to one another, were constantly superintending the sick, ministering to their wants without fear and cessation, and healing them in Christ." The heathen, on the contrary, repelled the sick or cast them half-dead into the street. The same self-denying charity in contrast with heathen selfishness mani-

---

[1] When invited in 265 to attend the Synod of Antioch, he declined on account of the infirmities of old age. Eus. VII. 27.

[2] Preserved by Eusebius VII. 22.

fested itself at Carthage during the raging of a pestilence, under the persecuting reign of Gallus (252), as we learn from Cyprian.

Dionysius took an active part in the christological, chiliastic, and disciplinary controversies of his time, and showed in them moderation, an amiable spirit of concession, and practical churchly tact, but also a want of independence and consistency. He opposed Sabellianism, and ran to the brink of tritheism, but in his correspondence with the more firm and orthodox Dionysius of Rome he modified his view, and Athanasius vindicated his orthodoxy against the charge of having sowed the seeds of Arianism. He wished to adhere to Origen's christology, but the church pressed towards the Nicene formula. There is nothing, however, in the narrative of Athanasius which implies a recognition of Roman supremacy. His last christological utterance was a letter concerning the heresy of Paul of Samosata; he was prevented from attending the Synod of Antioch in 264, which condemned and deposed Paul. He rejected, with Origen, the chiliastic notions, and induced Nepos and his adherents to abandon them, but he denied the apostolic origin of the Apocalypse and ascribed it to the " Presbyter John," of doubtful existence. He held mild views on discipline and urged the Novatians to deal gently with the lapsed and to preserve the peace of the church. He also counselled moderation in the controversy between Stephen and Cyprian on the validity of heretical baptism, though he sided with the more liberal Roman theory.

Dionysius wrote many letters and treatises on exegetic, polemic, and ascetic topics, but only short fragments remain, mostly in Eusebius. The chief books were *Commentaries on Ecclesiastes*, and *Luke; Against Sabellius* (christological); *On Nature* (philosophical) ; *On the Promises* (against Chiliasm); *On Martyrdom*. He compared the style of the fourth Gospel and of the Apocalypse to deny the identity of authorship, but he saw only the difference and not the underlying unity.[1] " All the

[1] In Euseb. VII. 25. Dionysius concludes the comparison with praising

fragments of Dionysius," says Westcott, " repay careful perusal.
They are uniformly inspired by the sympathy and large-heart-
edness which he showed in practice."

Dionysius is commemorated in the Greek church on October
3, in the Roman on November 17.

§ 191. *Julius Africanus.*

(I.) The fragments in ROUTH: *Rel. Sacr.* II. 221–509. Also in GAL-
LANDI, Tom. II., and MIGNE, "Patr. Gr.," Tom. X. col. 35–108.

(II.) EUSEBIUS: *H. E.* VI. 31. JEROME: *De Vir. ill.* 63. SOCRATES:
H. E. II. 35. PHOTIUS: *Bibl.* 34.

(III.) FABRICIUS: "Bibl. Gr." IV. 240 (ed. Harles). G. SALMON in
Smith and Wace I. 53–57. AD. HARNACK in Herzog[2] VII. 296–
298. Also PAULY'S "Real-Encykl." IV. 501 sq.; NICOLAI'S " Griech.
Lit. Gesch." II. 584; and Smith's "Dict. of Gr. and Rom. Biogr."
I. 56 sq.

JULIUS AFRICANUS,[1] the first Christian chronographer and
universal historian, an older friend of Origen, lived in the first
half of the second century at Emmaus (Nicopolis), in Palestine,[2]
made journeys to Alexandria, where he heard the lectures of
Heraclas, to Edessa, Armenia and Phrygia, and was sent on an
embassy to Rome in behalf of the rebuilding of Emmaus which
had been ruined (221). He died about A. D. 240 in old age.
He was not an ecclesiastic, as far as we know, but a philosopher
who pursued his favorite studies after his conversion and made

the pure Greek of the Gospel and contrasting with it "the barbarous idioms
and solecisms" of the Apocalypse; yet the style of the Gospel is thoroughly
Hebrew in the inspiring soul and mode of construction. He admits, however,
that the author of the Apocalypse "saw a revelation and received knowledge
and prophecy," and disclaims the intention of depreciating the book; only he
cannot conceive that it is the product of the same pen as the fourth Gospel.
He anticipated the theory of the Schleiermacher school of critics who defend
the Johannean origin of the Gospel and surrender the Apocalypse; while the
Tübingen critics and Renan reverse the case. See on this subject vol. I.
716 sq.

[1] Suidas calls him *Sextus Africanus.* Eusebius calls him simply Ἀφρικανός.

[2] Not the Emmaus known from Luke 24 : 16, which was only sixty stadia
from Jerusalem, but another Emmaus, 176 stadia (22 Roman miles) from
Jerusalem.

them useful to the church. He may have been a presbyter, but certainly not a bishop.[1] He was the forerunner of Eusebius, who in his *Chronicle* has made copious use of his learned labor and hardly gives him sufficient credit, although he calls his chronography "a most accurate and labored performance." He was acquainted with Hebrew. Socrates classes him for learning with Clement of Alexandria and Origen.

His chief work is his chronography, in five books. It commenced with the creation (B. C. 5499) and came down to the year 221, the fourth year of Elagabalus. It is the foundation of the mediæval historiography of the world and the church. We have considerable fragments of it and can restore it in part from the *Chronicle* of Eusebius. A satisfactory estimate of its merits requires a fuller examination of the Byzantine and oriental chronography of the church than has hitherto been made. Earlier writers were concerned to prove the antiquity of the Christian religion against the heathen charge of novelty by tracing it back to Moses and the prophets who were older than the Greek philosophers and poets. But Africanus made the first attempt at a systematic chronicle of sacred and profane history. He used as a fixed point the accession of Cyrus, which he placed Olymp. 55, 1, and then counting backwards in sacred history, he computed 1237 years between the exodus and the end of the seventy years' captivity or the first year of Cyrus. He followed the Septuagint chronology, placed the exodus A. M. 3707, and counted 740 years between the exodus and Solomon. He fixed the Lord's birth in A. M. 5500, and 10 years before our Dionysian era, but he allows only one year's public ministry and thus puts the crucifixion A. M. 5531. He makes the 31 years of the Saviour's life the complement of the 969 years of Methuselah. He understood the 70 weeks of Daniel to be 490 lunar years, which are equivalent to 475 Julian years. He treats the dark-

---

[1] Two Syrian writers, Barsalibi and Ebedjesu, from the end of the twelfth century, call him bishop of Edessa; but earlier writers know nothing of this title, and Origen addresses him as "brother."

ness at the crucifixion as miraculous, since an eclipse of the sun
could not have taken place at the full moon.

Another work of Africanus, called *Cesti* (Κεστοί) or Varie-
gated Girdles, was a sort of universal scrap-book or miscellaneous
collection of information on geography, natural history, medicine, agriculture, war, and other subjects of a secular character.
Only fragments remain. Some have unnecessarily denied his
authorship on account of the secular contents of the book, which
was dedicated to the Emperor Alexander Severus.

Eusebius mentions two smaller treatises of Africanus, a letter
to Origen, "in which he intimates his doubts on the history of
Susanna, in Daniel, as if it were a spurious and fictitious composition," and "a letter to Aristides on the supposed discrepancy
between the genealogies of Christ in Matthew and Luke, in
which he most clearly establishes the consistency of the two
evangelists, from an account which had been handed down from
his ancestors."

The letter to Origen is still extant and takes a prominent
rank among the few specimens of higher criticism in the literature of the ancient church. He urges the internal improba-
bilities of the story of Susanna, its omission from the Hebrew
canon, the difference of style as compared with the canonical
Daniel, and a play on Greek words which shows that it was
originally written in Greek, not in Hebrew. Origen tried at
great length to refute these objections, and one of his arguments
is that it would be degrading to Christians to go begging to the
Jews for the unadulterated Scriptures.

The letter to Aristides on the genealogies solves the difficulty
by assuming that Matthew gives the natural, Luke the legal,
descent of our Lord. It exists in fragments, from which F.
Spitta has recently reconstructed it.[1]

---

[1] *Der Brief des Jul. Africanus an Aristides kritisch untersucht und hergestellt.*
Halle 1877.

§ 192. *Minor Divines of the Greek Church.*

A number of divines of the third century, of great reputation in their day, mostly of Egypt and of the school of Origen, deserve a brief mention, although only few fragments of their works have survived the ravages of time.

I. HERACLAS and his brother Plutarch (who afterwards died a martyr) were the oldest distinguished converts and pupils of Origen, and older than their teacher. Heraclas had even before him studied the New-Platonic philosophy under Ammonius Saccas. He was appointed assistant of Origen, and afterwards his successor in the Catechetical School. After the death of Demetrius, the jealous enemy of Origen, Heraclas was elected bishop of Alexandria and continued in that high office sixteen years (A. D. 233–248). We know nothing of his administration, nor of his writings. He either did not adopt the speculative opinions of Origen, or prudently concealed them, at least he did nothing to recall his teacher from exile. He was succeeded by Dionysius the Great. Eusebius says that he was "devoted to the study of the Scriptures and a most learned man, not unacquainted with philosophy," but is silent about his conduct to Origen during and after his trial for heresy.[1]

II. Among the successors of Heraclas and Dionysius in the Catechetical School was THEOGNOSTUS, not mentioned by Eusebius, but by Athanasius and Photius. We have from him a brief fragment on the blasphemy against the Holy Ghost, and a few extracts from his *Hypotyposeis* (Adumbrations).[2]

III. PIERIUS probably succeeded Theognostus, while Theonas was bishop of Alexandria (d. 300), and seems to have outlived the Diocletian persecution. He was the teacher of Pamphilus, and called "the younger Origen."[3]

---

[1] *Hist. Eccl.* VI. 15, 26, 35; *Chron.* ad ann. Abr. 2250, 2265.

[2] In Routh, *Reliquiæ Sacræ* III. 407–422. Cave puts Theognostus *after* Pierius, about A. D. 268, but Routh corrects him (p. 408).

[3] Euseb. VII. 32 towards the close; Hieron. *De Vir. ill.* 76; *Præf. in Hos.;*

IV. PAMPHILUS, a great admirer of Origen, a presbyter and theological teacher at Cæsarea in Palestine, and a martyr of the persecution of Maximinus (309), was not an author himself, but one of the most liberal and efficient promoters of Christian learning. He did invaluable service to future generations by founding a theological school and collecting a large library, from which his pupil and friend Eusebius (hence called "Eusebius *Pampili*"), Jerome, and many others, drew or increased their useful information. Without that library the church history of Eusebius would be far less instructive than it is now. Pamphilus transcribed with his own hand useful books, among others the Septuagint from the Hexapla of Origen.[1] He aided poor students, and distributed the Scriptures. While in prison, he wrote a defense of Origen, which was completed by Eusebius in six books, but only the first remains in the Latin version of Rufinus, whom Jerome charges with wilful alterations. It is addressed to the confessors who were condemned to the mines of Palestine, to assure them of the orthodoxy of Origen from his own writings, especially on the trinity and the person of Christ.[2]

V. PETER, pupil and successor of Theonas, was bishop of

Photius, *Cod.* 118, 119. Eusebius knew Pierius personally, and says that he was greatly celebrated for his voluntary poverty, his philosophical knowledge, and his skill in expounding the Scriptures in public assemblies. Jerome calls him "*Origenes junior.*" He mentions a long treatise of his on the prophecies of Hosea. Photius calls him Παμφίλου τοῦ μάρτυρος ὑφηγητής. See Routh, *Rel. S.* III. 425–431.

[1] "Jerome says (*De Vir. ill.* 75): *Pamphilus . . . tanto bibliothecæ divinæ amore flagravit, ut maximam partem Origenis voluminum sua manu descripserit, quæ usque hodie in Cæsariensi bibliotheca habentur. Sed et in duodecim prophetas viginti quinque ἐξηγήσεων Origenis volumina manu ejus exarata reperi, quæ tanto amplector et servo gaudio, ut Crœsi opes habere me credam. Si enim lœtitia est, unam epistolam habere martyris, quanto magis tot millia versuum quæ mihi videtur sui sanguinis signasse vestigiis.*"

[2] See Routh's *Rel. S.* vol. III. 491–512, and vol. IV. 339–392; also in Delarue's *Opera Orig.* vol. IV., and in the editions of Lommatsch and Migne. Eusebius wrote a separate work on the life and martyrdom of his friend and the school which he founded, but it is lost. See *H. E.* VII. 32; comp. VI. 32; VIII. 13, and especially *De Mart. Pal.* c. 11, where he gives an account of his martyrdom and the twelve who suffered with him. The *Acta Passionis S. Pamph.* in the *Act SS.* Bolland. Junii I. 64.

Alexandria since A. D. 300, lived during the terrible times of the Diocletian persecution, and was beheaded by order of Maximinus in 311. He held moderate views on the restoration of the lapsed, and got involved in the Meletian schism which engaged much of the attention of the Council of Nicæa. Meletius, bishop of Lycopolis, taking advantage of Peter's flight from persecution, introduced himself into his diocese, and assumed the character of primate of Egypt, but was deposed by Peter in 306 for insubordination. We have from Peter fifteen canons on discipline, and a few homiletical fragments in which he rejects Origen's views of the pre-existence and ante-mundane fall of the soul as heathenish, and contrary to the Scripture account of creation. This dissent would place him among the enemies of Origen, but Eusebius makes no allusion to it, and praises him for piety, knowledge of the Scriptures, and wise administration.[1]

VI. HIERACAS (Hierax), from Leontopolis in Egypt, towards the end of the third century, belongs only in a wider sense to the Alexandrian school, and perhaps had no connexion with it at all. Epiphanius reckons him among the Manichæan heretics. He was, at all events, a perfectly original phenomenon, distinguished for his varied learning, allegorical exegesis, poetical talent, and still more for his eccentric asceticism. Nothing is left of the works which he wrote in the Greek and Egyptian languages. He is said to have denied the historical reality of the fall and the resurrection of the body, and to have declared celibacy the only sure way to salvation, or at least to the highest degree of blessedness. His followers were called *Hieracitæ*.[2]

---

[1] *H. E.* VIII. 13; IX. 6. The fragments in Routh, IV. 23–82. Peter taught in a sermon on the soul, that soul and body were created together on the same day, and that the theory of pre-existence is derived from "the Hellenic philosophy, and is foreign to those who would lead a godly life in Christ" (Routh, p. 49 sq.).

[2] Our information about Hierax is almost wholly derived from Epiphanius, *Hær.* 67, who says that he lived during the Diocletian persecution. Eusebius knows nothing about him; for the Egyptian bishop Hierax whom he mentions in two places (VII. 21 and 30), was a contemporary of Dionysius of Alexandria, to whom he wrote a paschal letter about 262.

§ 193. Opponents of Origen. Methodius.

(I.) Μεθοδίου ἐπισκόπου καὶ μάρτυρος τὰ εὑρισκόμενα πάντα. In *Gallandi's*
"Vet. Patr. Biblioth." Tom. III.; in *Migne's* "Patrol. Gr." Tom.
XVIII. col. 9–408; and by *A. Jahn* (*S. Methodii Opera, et S. Metho-*
dius Platonizans, Hal. 1865, 2 pts.). The first ed. was publ. by *Com-*
befis, 1644, and more completely in 1672. English translation in
Clark's "Ante-Nicene Libr.," vol. XIV. (Edinb. 1869.)

(II.) HIERONYMUS: *De Viris ill.* 83, and in several of his Epp. and Comment. EPIPHANIUS: *Hær.* 64. SOCRATES: *H. E.* VI. 31. PHO-
TIUS: *Bibl.* 234–237.

Eusebius is silent about Method., perhaps because of his opposition to
Origen; while Photius, perhaps for the same reason, pays more attention to him than to Origen, whose *De Principiis* he pronounces blasphemous, *Bibl.* 8. Gregory of Nyssa, Arethas, Leontius Byzantius,
Maximus, the *Martyrologium Romanum* (XIV. Kal. Oct.) and the
Menologium Græcum (ad diem 20 Junii), make honorable mention
of him.

(III.) LEO ALLATIUS: *Diatribe de Methodiorum Scriptis,* in his ed. of the
Convivium in 1656. FABRIC. "Bibl. Gr.," ed. Harles, VII. 260 sqq.
W. MÖLLER in Herzog², IX. 724–726. (He discusses especially the
relation of Methodius to Origen.) G. SALMON in Smith and Wace,
III. 909–911.

The opposition of Demetrius to Origen proceeded chiefly from
personal feeling, and had no theological significance. Yet it
made a pretext at least of zeal for orthodoxy, and in subsequent
opponents this motive took the principal place. This was the
case, so early as the third century, with Methodius, who may
be called a forerunner of Epiphanius in his orthodox war against
Origen, but with this difference that he was much more
moderate, and that in other respects he seems to have been an
admirer of Plato whom he imitated in the dramatic dress of
composition, and of Origen whom he followed in his allegorical
method of interpretation. He occupied the position of Christian realism against the speculative idealism of the Alexandrian
teacher.

METHODIUS (also called Eubulius) was bishop first of Olympus and then of Patara (both in the province of Lycia, Asia

Minor, on the southern coast), and died a martyr in 311 or earlier, in the Diocletian persecution.[1]

His principal work is his *Symposium* or *Banquet of Ten Virgins*.[2] It is an eloquent but verbose and extravagant eulogy on the advantages and blessings of voluntary virginity, which he describes as "something supernaturally great, wonderful, and glorious," and as "the best and noblest manner of life." It was unknown before Christ (the ἀρχιπάρθενος). At first men were allowed to marry sisters, then came polygamy, the next progress was monogamy, with continence, but the perfect state is celibacy for the kingdom of Christ, according to his mysterious hint in Matt. 19 : 12, the recommendation of Paul, 1 Cor. 7 : 1, 7, 34, 40, and the passage in Revelation 14 : 1–4, where "a hundred and forty-four thousand virgins" are distinguished from the innumerable multitude of other saints (7 : 9).

The literary form is interesting. The Ten Virgins are, of course, suggested by the parable in the gospel. The conception of the Symposium and the dialogue are borrowed from Plato, who celebrated the praises of Eros, as Methodius the praises of virginity. Methodius begins with a brief dialogue between Eubulios or Eubulion (*i. e.* himself) and the virgin Gregorion who was present at a banquet of the ten virgins in the gardens of Arete (*i. e.* personified virtue) and reports to him ten discourses which these virgins successively delivered in praise of

[1] Jerome makes him bishop of Tyre ("*Meth. Olympi Lyciæ et postea Tyri episcopus*"); but as all other authorities mention Patara as his second diocese, "Tyre" is probably the error of a transcriber for "Patara," or for "Myra," which lies nearly midway between Olympus and Patara, and probably belonged to the one or the other diocese before it became an independent see. It is not likely that Tyre in Phœnicia should have called a bishop from so great a distance. Jerome locates the martyrdom of Methodius at "Chalcis in Greece" (in Eubœa). But Sophronius, the Greek translator, substitutes "in the East" for "in Greece." Perhaps (as Salmon suggests, p. 909) Jerome confounded Methodius of Patara with a Methodius whose name tradition has preserved as a martyr at Chalcis in the Decian persecution. This confusion is all the more probable as he did not know the time of the martyrdom, and says that some assign it to the Diocletian persecution ("*ad extremum novissimæ persecutionis*"), others to the persecution "*sub Decio et Valeriano.*"

[2] Συμπόσιον τῶν δέκα παρθένων, *Symposium*, or *Convivium Decem Virginum*.

chastity. At the end of the banquet the victorious Thecla, chief of the virgins (St. Paul's apocryphal companion), standing on the right hand of Arete, begins to sing a hymn of chastity to which the virgins respond with the oft-repeated refrain,

> "I keep myself pure for Thee, O Bridegroom,
> And holding a lighted torch, I go to meet Thee."[1]

Then follows a concluding dialogue between Eubulios and Gregorion on the question, whether chastity ignorant of lust is preferable to chastity which feels the power of passion and overcomes it, in other words, whether a wrestler who has no opponents is better than a wrestler who has many and strong antagonists and continually contends against them without being worsted. Both agree in giving the palm to the latter, and then they betake themselves to "the care of the outward man," expecting to resume the delicate discussion on the next day.

The taste and morality of virgins discussing at great length the merits of sexual purity are very questionable, at least from the standpoint of modern civilization, but the enthusiastic praise of chastity to the extent of total abstinence was in full accord with the prevailing asceticism of the fathers, including Origen, who freed himself from carnal temptation by an act of violence against nature.

The work *On the Resurrection*, likewise in the form of a dialogue, and preserved in large extracts by Epiphanius and Photius, was directed against Origen and his views on creation, pre-existence, and the immateriality of the resurrection body. The orthodox speakers (Eubulios and Auxentios) maintain that the soul cannot sin without the body, that the body is not a fetter of the soul, but its inseparable companion and an instrument for good as well as evil, and that the earth will not be destroyed, but purified and transformed into a blessed abode for the risen saints. In a book *On Things Created*[2] he refutes

---

[1] ἁγνεύω σοι, καὶ λαμπάδας φαεσφόρους κρατοῦσα, Νυμφίε, ὑπαντάσω σοι.

[2] Περὶ τῶν γενητῶν, known to us only from extracts in Photius, *Cod.* 235. Salmon identifies this book with the *Xeno* mentioned by Socrates, *H. E.* VI. 13, as an attack upon Origen.

Origen's view of the eternity of the world, who thought it necessary to the conception of God as an Almighty Creator and Ruler,
and as the unchangeable Being.

The *Dialogue On Free Will*[1] treats of the origin of matter,
and strongly resembles a work on that subject ($\pi\epsilon\rho\grave{\iota}\ \tau\tilde{\eta}\varsigma\ \ddot{\upsilon}\lambda\eta\varsigma$)
of which Eusebius gives an extract and which he ascribes to
Maximus, a writer from the close of the second century.[2]

Other works of Methodius, mentioned by Jerome, are:
Against Porphyry (10,000 lines); *Commentaries* on *Genesis* and
Canticles; De Pythonissa (on the witch of Endor, against
Origen's view that Samuel was laid under the power of Satan
when he evoked her by magical art). A Homily for Palm
Sunday, and a Homily on the Cross are also assigned to him.
But there were several Methodii among the patristic writers.

§ 194. *Lucian of Antioch.*

(I.) LUCIANI *Fragmenta* in Routh, *Rel. s.* IV. 3–17.

(II.) EUSEB. *H. E.* VIII. 13; IX. 6 (and Rufinus's Eus. IX. 6). HIER.
De Vir. ill. 77, and in other works. SOCRAT.: *H. E.* II. 10. So-
ZOM.: *H. E.* III. 5. EPIPHAN.: *Ancoratus*, c. 33. THEODOR.: *H. E.*
I. 3. PHILOSTORGIUS: *H. E.*, II. 14, 15. CHRYSOSTOM'S *Hom. in
Lucian*, (in *Opera ed. Montfaucon*, T. II. 524 sq; Migne, "Patr. Gr."
I. 520 sqq.) RUINART: *Acta Mart.*, p. 503 sq.

(III.) *Acta Sanct.* Jan. VII. 357 sq. BARON. *Ann.* ad ann. 311. Brief
notices in TILLEMONT, CAVE, FABRICIUS, NEANDER, GIESELER,
HEFELE (*Conciliengesch.* vol. I). HARNACK: *Luc. der Märt.* in
Herzog[2] VIII. (1881), pp. 767–772. J. T. STOKES, in *Smith & Wace*,
III., 748 and 749.

On his textual labors see the critical Introductions to the Bible.

I. LUCIAN was an eminent presbyter of Antioch and martyr
of the Diocletian persecution, renewed by Maximin. Very
little is known of him. He was transported from Antioch to
Nicomedia, where the emperor then resided, made a noble con-

---

[1] Περὶ αὐτεξουσίου, *De libero arbitrio.* Freedom of the will is strongly em-
phasized by Justin Martyr, Origen, and all the Greek fathers.

[2] *Prœp. Evang.* VII. 22; comp. *H. E.* V. 27; and Routh, *Rel. S.* II. 87.
Möller and Salmon suppose that Methodius borrowed from Maximus, and
merely furnished the rhetorical introduction.

fession of his faith before the judge and died under the tortures in prison (311). His memory was celebrated in Antioch on the 7th of January. His piety was of the severely ascetic type.

His memory was obscured by the suspicion of unsoundness in the faith. Eusebius twice mentions him and his glorious martyrdom, but is silent about his theological opinions. Alexander of Alexandria, in an encyclical of 321, associates him with Paul of Samosata and makes him responsible for the Arian heresy ; he also says that he was excommunicated or kept aloof from the church (ἀποσυνάγωγος ἔμεινε) during the episcopate of Domnus, Timæus, and Cyrillus ; intimating that his schismatic condition ceased before his death. The charge brought against him and his followers is that he denied the *eternity* of the Logos, and the human *soul* of Christ (the Logos taking the place of the rational soul). Arius and the Arians speak of him as their teacher. On the other hand Pseudo-Athanasius calls him a great and holy martyr, and Chrysostom preached a eulogy on him Jan. 1, 387. Baronius defends his orthodoxy, other Catholics deny it.[1] Some distinguished two Lucians, one orthodox, and one heretical ; but this is a groundless hypothesis.

The contradictory reports are easily reconciled by the assumption that Lucian was a critical scholar with some peculiar views on the Trinity and Christology which were not in harmony with the later Nicene orthodoxy, but that he wiped out all stains by his heroic confession and martyrdom.[2]

II. The creed which goes by his name and was found after his death, is quite orthodox as far as it goes, and was laid with three similar creeds before the Synod of Antioch held A. D. 341, with the intention of being substituted for the Creed of Nicæa.[3]

---

[1] See Baron. *Annal.* ad ann. 311; De Broglie, *L'église et l'empire*, I. 375; Newman, *Arians of the Fourth Century*, 414.

[2] Hefele, *Conciliengesch.*, vol. I., p. 258 sq. (2nd ed.), assumes to the same effect that Lucian first sympathized with his countryman, Paul of Samosata, in his humanitarian Christology, and hence was excommunicated for a while, but afterwards renounced this heresy, was restored, and acquired great fame by his improvement of the text of the Septuagint and by his martyrdom.

[3] This Synod is recognized as legitimate and orthodox, and its twenty-five

It resembles the creed of Gregorius Thaumaturgus, is strictly trinitarian and acknowledges Jesus Christ " as the Son of God, the only begotten God,[1] through whom all things were made, who was begotten of the Father before all ages, God of God, Whole of Whole, One of One, Perfect of Perfect, King of Kings, Lord of Lords, the living Word, Wisdom, Life, True Light, Way, Truth, Resurrection, Shepherd, Door, unchangeable and unalterable, the immutable Likeness of the Godhead, both of the substance and will and power and glory of the Father, the first-born of all creation,[2] who was in the beginning with God, the Divine Logos, according to what is said in the Gospel : ' And the Word was God (John 1 : 1), through whom all things were made ' (ver. 3), and in whom ' all things consist ' (Col. 1 ; 17) : who in the last days came down from above, and was born of a Virgin, according to the Scriptures, and became man, the Mediator between God and man," etc.[3]

III. Lucianus is known also by his critical revision of the text of the Septuagint and the Greek Testament. Jerome

canons are accepted, although it confirmed the previous deposition of Athanasius for violating a canon. See a full acccount in Hefele, *l. c.* I. 502–530.

[1] τὸν μονογενῆ θεόν. Comp. the Vatican and Sinaitic reading of John 1: 18, μονογενὴς θεός (without the article), instead of ὁ μονογενὴς υἱός. The phrase μονογενὴς θεός was widely used in the Nicene age, not only by the orthodox, but also by Arian writers in the sense of one who is both θεός (divine) and μονογενής. See Hort's *Two Dissertations* on this subject, Cambr., 1876. In the usual punctuation of Lucian's creed, τὸν μονογενῆ is connected with the preceding τὸν υἱὸν αὐτοῦ, and separated from θεόν, so as to read " his Son the only begotten, God," etc.

[2] πρωτότοκον (not πρωτόκτιστον, first-created) πάσης κτίσεως, from Col. 1 : 17.

[3] See the creed in full in Athanasius, *Ep. de Synodis Arimini et Seleucidæ celebratis*, ? 23 (*Opera* ed. Montf. I. ii. 735); Mansi, *Conc.* II. 1339–'42; Schaff, *Creeds of Christendom*, II. 25–28; and Hahn, *Bibl. der Symb.*, ed. II., p. 184–'87. Hefele, *l. c.*, gives a German version. It is not given as a creed of Lucian by Athanasius or Socrates (*H. E.* II. 10), or Hilarius (in his Latin version, *De Syn. sive de Fide Orient.*, ? 29); but Sozomenus reports (*H. E.* III. 5) that the bishops of the Synod of Antioch ascribed it to him, and also that a Semi-Arian synod in Caria, 367, adopted it under his name (VI. 12). It is regarded as genuine by Cave, Basnage, Bull, Hahn, Dorner, but questioned either in whole or in part by Routh (I. 16), Hefele, Keim, Harnack, and Caspari ; but the last two acknowledge an authentic basis of Lucian which was enlarged by the Antiochian synod. The concluding anathema is no doubt a later addition.

mentions that copies were known in his day as "*exemplaria Lucianea*," but in other places he speaks rather disparagingly of the texts of Lucian, and of Hesychius, a bishop of Egypt (who distinguished himself in the same field). In the absence of definite information it is impossible to decide the merits of his critical labors. His Hebrew scholarship is uncertain, and hence we do not know whether his revision of the Septuagint was made from the original.[1]

As to the New Testament, it is likely that he contributed much towards the Syrian recension (if we may so call it), which was used by Chrysostom and the later Greek fathers, and which lies at the basis of the *textus receptus*.[2]

§ 195. *The Antiochian School.*

KIHN (R. C.): *Die Bedeutung der antioch. Schule.* Weissenburg, 1856.

C. HORNUNG: *Schola Antioch.* Neostad. ad S. 1864.

JOS. HERGENRÖTHER (Cardinal): *Die Antioch. Schule.* Würzb. 1866.

DIESTEL: *Gesch. des A. Test. in der christl. Kirche.* Jena, 1869 (pp. 126–141).

W. MÖLLER in Herzog[2], I. 454–457.

Lucian is the reputed founder of the ANTIOCHIAN SCHOOL of theology, which was more fully developed in the fourth century. He shares this honor with his friend Dorotheus, likewise a presbyter of Antioch, who is highly spoken of by Eusebius as a biblical scholar acquainted with Hebrew.[3] But the real founders

---

[1] On his labors in regard to the Sept., see Simeon Metaphrastes and Suidas, quoted in Routh IV. 3 sq.; Field's ed. of the *Hexapla* of Origen; Nestle in the "Zeitschr. d. D. Morgenl. Gesellsch.," 1878, 465–508; and the prospectus to the proposed ed. of the Sept. by P. de Lagarde.

[2] Dr. Hort, *Introd. and Append.* to Westcott and Hort's *Greek Test.* (Lond. and N. York, 1881), p. 138, says of Lucian: "Of known names his has a better claim than any other to be associated with the early Syrian revision; and the conjecture derives some little support from a passage of Jerome . . . *Praetermitto eos codices quos a Luciano et Hesychio nuncupatos adscrit perversa contentio,*" etc. Dr. Scrivener, who denies such a Syrian recension as an *ignis fatuus*, barely alludes to Lucian in his *Introduction to the Criticism of the N. Test.*, 3rd ed., Cambr., 1883, pp. 515, 517.

[3] Euseb. *H. E.* VII. 32 (in the beginning) speaks of Δωρόθεος as having known him personally. He calls him "a learned man (λόγιον ἄνδρα) who was honored

of that school are Diodorus, bishop of Tarsus (c. A. D. 379–394), and Theodorus, bishop of Mopsuestia (393–428), both formerly presbyters of Antioch.

The Antiochian School was not a regular institution with a continuous succession of teachers, like the Catechetical School of Alexandria, but a theological tendency, more particularly a peculiar type of hermeneutics and exegesis which had its centre in Antioch. The characteristic features are, attention to the revision of the text, a close adherence to the plain, natural meaning according to the use of language and the condition of the writer, and justice to the human factor. In other words, its exegesis is grammatical and historical, in distinction from the allegorical method of the Alexandrian School. Yet, as regards textual criticism, Lucian followed in the steps of Origen. Nor did the Antiochians disregard the spiritual sense, and the divine element in the Scriptures. The grammatico-historical exegesis is undoubtedly the only safe and sound basis for the understanding of the Scriptures as of any other book; and it is a wholesome check upon the wild licentiousness of the allegorizing method which often substitutes imposition for exposition. But it may lead to different results in different hands, according to the spirit of the interpreter. The Arians and Nestorians claimed descent from, or affinity with, Lucian and his school; but from the same school proceeded also the prince of commentators among the fathers, John Chrysostom, the eulogist of Lucian and Diodorus, and the friend and fellow student of Theodore of Mopsuestia. Theodoret followed in the same line.

After the condemnation of Nestorius, the Antiochian theology continued to be cultivated at Nisibis and Edessa among the Nestorians.

with the rank of presbyter of Antioch" at the time of bishop Cyrillus, and "a man of fine taste in sacred literature, much devoted to the study of the Hebrew language, so that he read the Hebrew Scriptures with great facility." He adds that he "was of a very liberal mind and not unacquainted with the preparatory studies pursued among the Greeks, but in other respects a eunuch by nature, having been such from his birth."

NOTES.

Cardinal Newman, when still an Anglican (in his book on *Arians of the Fourth Century*, p. 414) made the Syrian School of biblical criticism responsible for the Arian heresy, and broadly maintained that the "mystical interpretation and orthodoxy will stand or fall together." But Cardinal Hergenröther, who is as good a Catholic and a better scholar, makes a proper distinction between use and abuse, and gives the following fair and discriminating statement of the relation between the Antiochian and Alexandrian schools, and the critical and mystical method of interpretation to which a Protestant historian can fully assent. (*Handbuch der allgem. Kirchengeschichte*. Freiburg i. B. 2nd ed. 1879, vol. I. p. 281.)

"*Die Schule von Antiochien hatte bald den Glanz der Alexandrinischen erreicht, ja sogar überstrahlt. Beide konnten sich vielfach ergänzen, da jede ihre eigenthümliche Entwicklung, Haltung und Methode hatte, konnten aber auch eben wegen iherer Verschiedenheit leicht unter sich in Kampf und auf Abwege von der Kirchenlehre gerathen. Während bei den Alexandrinern eine speculativ-intuitive, zum Mystischen sich hinneigende Richtung hervortrat, war bei den Antiochenern eine logisch-reflectirende, durchaus nüchterne Verstandesrichtung vorherrschend. Während jene enge an die platonische Philosophie sich anschlossen und zwar vorherrschend in der Gestalt, die sie unter dem hellenistischen Juden Philo gewonnen hatte, waren die Antiochener einem zum Stoicismus hinneigenden Eklekticismus, dann der Aristotelischen Schule ergeben, deren scharfe Dialektik ganz ihrem Geiste zusagte. Demgemäss wurde in der alexandrinischen Schule vorzugsweise die allegorisch-mystische Erklärung der heiligen Schrift gepflegt, in der Antiochenischen dagegen die buchstäbliche, grammatisch-logische und historische Interpretation, ohne dass desshalb der mystische Sinn und insbesondere die Typen des Alten Bundes gänzlich in Abrede gestellt worden wären. Die Origenisten suchen die Unzulänglichkeit des blossen buchstäblichen Sinnes und die Nothwendigkeit der allegorischen Auslegung nachzuweisen, da der Wortlaut vieler biblischen Stellen Falsches, Widersprechendes, Gottes Unwürdiges ergebe; sie fehlten hier durch das Uebermass des Allegorisirens und durch Verwechslung der figürlichen Redeweisen, die dem Literalsinne angehören, mit der mystischen Deutung; sie verflüchtigten oft den historischen Gehalt der biblischen Erzählung, hinter deren äusserer Schale sie einen verborgenen Kern suchen zu müssen glaubten. Damit stand ferner in Verbindung, dass in der alexandrinischen Schule das Moment des Uebervernünftigen, Unaussprechlichen, Geheimnissvollen in den göttlichen Dingen stark betont wurde, während die Antiochener vor Allem das Vernunftgemässe, dem menschlichen Geiste Entsprechende in den Dogmen hervorhoben, das Christenthum als eine das menschliche Denken befriedigende Wahrheit nachzuweisen suchten. Indem sie aber dieses Streben verfolgten, wollten die hervorragenden Lehrer der antiochenischen Schule keineswegs den übernatürlichen Char-*

akter und die Mysterien der Kirchenlehre bestreiten, sie erkannten diese in der Mehrzahl an, wie Chrysotomus und Theodoret ; aber einzelne Gelehrte konnten über dem Bemühen, die Glaubenslehren leicht verständlich und begreiflich zu machen, ihren Inhalt verunstalten und zerstören."

§ 196. Tertullian and the African School.

Comp. the liter. on Montanism, § 109, p. 415.

(I.) TERTULLIANI *quœ supersunt omnia.* Ed. FRANC. OEHLER. Lips. 1853, 3 vols. The third vol. contains dissertations *De Vita et Scriptis Tert.* by NIC. Le Nourry, Mosheim, Noesselt, Semler, Kaye. Earlier editions by *Beatus Rhenanus,* Bas. 1521 ; *Pamelius,* Antwerp, 1579 ; *Rigaltius* (Rigault), Par. 1634 and Venet. 1744 ; *Semler,* Halle, 1770–3. 6 vols. ; *Oberthür,* 1780 ; *Leopold,* in Gersdorf's "Biblioth. patrum eccles. Latinorum selecta" (IV–VII.), Lips. 1839–41 ; and *Migne,* Par. 1884. A new ed. by REIFFERSCHEID will appear in the Vienna "Corpus Scriptorum eccles. Lat."

English transl. by P. HOLMES and others in the "Ante-Nicene Christian Library," Edinb. 1868 sqq. 4 vols. German translation by K. A. H. KELLNER. Köln, 1882, 2 vols.

(II.) EUSEB. H. G. II. 2, 25 ; III. 20 ; V. 5. JEROME : DE VIRIS ILL. c. 53.

(III.) NEANDER : *Antignosticus, Geist des Tertullianus u. Einleitung in dessen Schriften.* Berl. 1825, 2d ed. 1849.

J. KAYE : *Eccles. Hist. of the second and third Centuries, illustrated from the Writings of Tertullian.* 3d ed. Lond. 1845.

CARL HESSELBERG : *Tertullian's Lehre aus seinen Schriften entwickelt.* 1. *Th. Leben und Schriften.* Dorpat 1848 (136 pages).

P. GOTTWALD : *De Montanismo Tertulliani.* Breslau, 1863.

HERMANN RÖNSCH : *Das Neue Testament Tertullian's.* Leipz. 1871 (731 pages.) A reconstruction of the text of the old Latin version of the N. T. from the writings of Tertullian.

AD. EBERT : *Gesch. der Christl. lat. Lit.* Leipz. 1874, sqq. I. 24–31.

A. HAUCK : *Tertullian's Leben und Schriften, Erlangen,* 1877 (410 pages.) With judicious extracts from all his writings.

(IV.) On the chronology of Tertullian's works see NÖSSELT : *De vera œtate et doctrina Scriptorum Tertull.* (in Oehler's ed. III. 340–619) ; UHLHORN : *Fundamenta Chronologiœ Tertullianeœ* (Göttingen 1852) ; BONWETSCH : *Die Schriften Tertullians nach der Zeit ihrer Abfassung* (Bonn 1879, 89 pages) ; HARNACK : *Zur Chronologie der Schriften Tertullians* (Leipz. 1878) ; NOELDECHEN : *Abfassungszeit der Schriften Tertullians* (Leipz. 1888).

(V.) On special points: OEHNINGER : *Tertullian und seine Auferstehungslehre* (Augsb. 1878, 34 pp). F. J. SCHMIDT : *De Latinitate Tertulliani* (Erlang. 1877). M. KLUSSMANN : *Curarum Tertullianearum, part. I. et II.* (Halle 1881). G. R. HAUSCHILD : *Tertullian's Psychologie* (Frankf. a. M. 1880, 78 pp.). By the same : *Die Grund-*

sätze u. Mittel der Wortbildung bei Tertullian (Leipz. 1881, 56 pp); LUDWIG : *Tert's Ethik.* (Leipz. 1885). Special treatises on Tertullian, by Hefele, Engelhardt, Leopold, Schaff (in Herzog), Ebert, Kolberg.

The Western church in this period exhibits no such scientific productiveness as the Eastern. The apostolic church was predominantly Jewish, the ante-Nicene church, Greek, the post-Nicene, Roman. The Roman church itself was first predominantly Greek, and her earliest writers—Clement, Hermas, Irenæus, Hippolytus—wrote exclusively in Greek. Latin Christianity begins to appear in literature at the end of the second century, and then not in Italy, but in North Africa, not in Rome, but in Carthage, and very characteristically, not with converted speculative philosophers, but with practical lawyers and rhetoricians. This literature does not gradually unfold itself, but appears at once under a fixed, clear stamp, with a strong realistic tendency. North Africa also gave to the Western church the fundamental book—the Bible in its first Latin Version, the so-called *Itala*, and this was the basis of Jerome's *Vulgata* which to this day is the recognized standard Bible of Rome. There were, however, probably several Latin versions of portions of the Bible current in the West before Jerome.

I. Life of Tertullian.

QUINTUS SEPTIMIUS FLORENS TERTULLIANUS is the father of the Latin theology and church language, and one of the greatest men of Christian antiquity. We know little of his life but what is derived from his book and from the brief notice of Jerome in his catalogue of illustrious men. But few writers have impressed their individuality so strongly in their books as this African father. In this respect, as well as in others, he resembles St. Paul, and Martin Luther. He was born about the year 150, at Carthage, the ancient rival of Rome, where his father was serving as captain of a Roman legion under the proconsul of Africa. He received a liberal Græco-Roman education; his writings manifest an extensive acquaintance with historical, philosophical, poetic, and antiquarian literature, and with juridical terminology and all the arts of an advocate. He seems to have devoted himself to politics and forensic eloquence, either in Carthage or in Rome. Eusebius calls him "a man accurately acquainted with the Roman laws,"[1] and many regard him as identical with the Tertyllus, or Tertullianus, who is the author of several fragments in the Pandects.

To his thirtieth or fortieth year he lived in heathen blindness and licentiousness.[2] Towards the end of the second century he embraced Christianity, we know not exactly on what occasion, but evidently from deepest conviction, and with all the fiery energy of his soul; defended it henceforth with fearless decision against heathens, Jews, and heretics; and studied the strictest morality of life. His own words may be applied to himself: "*Fiunt, non nascuntur Christiani.*" He was married, and gives us a glowing picture of Christian family life, to which we have before referred; but in his zeal for every form of self-denial, he set celibacy still higher, and advised his wife, in case he should die before her, to remain a widow, or, at least never to marry an unbelieving husband; and he afterwards put second marriage even on a level with adultery. He entered the ministry of the Catholic church,[3] first probably in Carthage, perhaps in Rome, where at all events he spent some time;[4] but, like Clement of Alexandria and Origen, he never rose above the rank of presbyter.

Some years after, between 199 and 203, he joined the puritanic, though orthodox, sect of the Montanists. Jerome attri-

---

[1] *H. E.* II. 2. He adds that Tertullian was "particularly distinguished among the eminent men of Rome," and quotes a passage from his *Apology,* "which is also translated into the Greek."

[2] *De Resurr. Carn.* c. 59, he confesses: "*Ego me scio neque alia carne adulteria commisisse, neque nunc alia carne ad continentiam eniti.*" Comp. also *Apolog.,* c. 18 and 25; *De Anima,* c. 2; *De Pœnit.,* c. 4 and 12; *Ad Scapul.,* c. 5.

[3] This fact, however, rests only on the authority of Jerome, and does not appear from Tertullian's own writings. Roman Catholic historians, with their dislike to married priests, have made him a layman on the insufficient ground of the passage: "*Nonne et Laici sacerdotes sumus?*" *De Exhort. Cast.,* c. 7.

[4] *De Cultu Femin.,* c. 7. Comp. Euseb. II. 2.

butes this change to personal motives, charging it to the envy
and insults of the Roman clergy, from whom he himself experienced many an indignity.[1] But Tertullian was inclined to
extremes from the first, especially to moral austerity. He was
no doubt attracted by the radical contempt for the world, the
strict asceticism, the severe discipline, the martyr enthusiasm,
and the chiliasm of the Montanists, and was repelled by the
growing conformity to the world in the Roman church, which
just at that period, under Zephyrinus and Callistus, openly took
under its protection a very lax penitential discipline, and at the
same time, though only temporarily, favored the Patripassian
error of Praxeas, an opponent of the Montanists. Of this man
Tertullian therefore says, in his sarcastic way: He has executed in Rome two works of the devil; has driven out prophecy
(the Montanistic) and brought in heresy (the Patripassian); has
turned off the Holy Ghost and crucified the Father.[2] Tertullian now fought the catholics, or the psychicals, as he frequently
calls them, with the same inexorable sternness with which he
had combated the heretics. The departures of the Montanists,
however, related more to points of morality and discipline than
of doctrine; and with all his hostility to Rome, Tertullian
remained a zealous advocate of the catholic faith, and wrote,
even from his schismatic position, several of his most effective
works against the heretics, especially the Gnostics. Indeed, as
a divine, he stood far above this fanatical sect, and gave it by
his writings an importance and an influence in the church itself
which it certainly would never otherwise have attained.

He labored in Carthage as a Montanist presbyter and an
author, and died, as Jerome says, in decrepit old age, according
to some about the year 220, according to others not till 240; for
the exact time, as well as the manner of his death, are unknown.
His followers in Africa propagated themselves, under the name

---

[1] *De Vir. illustr.*, c. 53: "*Hic* [*Tert.*] *cum usque ad mediam ætatem presbyter ecclesiæ permansisset, invidia et contumeliis clericorum Romanæ ecclesiæ ad Montani dogma delapsus in multis libris novæ propheticæ meminit.*"

[2] *Adv. Prax.* c. 1.

of "Tertullianists," down to the time of Augustin in the fifth century, and took perhaps a middle place between the proper Montanists and the catholic church. That he ever returned into the bosom of Catholicism is an entirely groundless opinion.

Strange that this most powerful defender of old catholic orthodoxy and the teacher of the high-churchly Cyprian, should have been a schismatic and an antagonist of Rome. But he had in his constitution the tropical fervor and acerbity of the Punic character, and that bold spirit of independence in which his native city of Carthage once resisted, through more than a hundred years' war,[1] the rising power of the seven-hilled city on the Tiber. He truly represents the African church, in which a similar antagonism continued to reveal itself, not only among the Donatists, but even among the leading advocates of Catholicism. Cyprian died at variance with Rome on the question of heretical baptism; and Augustin, with all his great services to the catholic system of faith, became at the same time, through his anti-Pelagian doctrines of sin and grace, the father of evangelical Protestantism and of semi-Protestant Jansenism.

Hippolytus presents several interesting points of contact. He was a younger contemporary of Tertullian, though they never met as far as we know. Both were champions of catholic orthodoxy against heresy, and yet both opposed to Rome. Hippolytus charged two popes with heresy as well as laxity of discipline; and yet in view of his supposed repentance and martyrdom (as reported by Prudentius nearly two hundred years afterwards), he was canonized in the Roman church; while such honor was never conferred upon the African, though he was a greater and more useful man.

II. Character. Tertullian was a rare genius, perfectly original and fresh, but angular, boisterous and eccentric; full of glowing fantasy, pointed wit, keen discernment, polemic dexterity, and moral earnestness, but wanting in clearness, moderation, and symmetrical development. He resembled a foaming

---

[1] B. C. 264–146.

mountain torrent rather than a calm, transparent river in the valley. His vehement temper was never fully subdued, although he struggled sincerely against it.[1] He was a man of strong convictions, and never hesitated to express them without fear or favor.

Like almost all great men, he combined strange contrarieties of character. Here we are again reminded of Luther ; though the reformer had nothing of the ascetic gloom and rigor of the African father, and exhibits instead with all his gigantic energy, a kindly serenity and childlike simplicity altogether foreign to the latter. Tertullian dwells enthusiastically on the divine foolishness of the gospel, and has a sublime contempt for the world, for its science and its art; and yet his writings are a mine of antiquarian knowledge, and novel, striking, and fruitful ideas. He calls the Grecian philosophers the patriarchs of all heresies, and scornfully asks : " What has the academy to do with the church ? what has Christ to do with Plato—Jerusalem with Athens ?" He did not shrink from insulting the greatest natural gift of God to man by his "*Credo quia absurdum est.*" And yet reason does him invaluable service against his antagonists.[2] He vindicates the principle of church authority and tradition with great force and ingenuity against all heresy ; yet, when a Montanist, he claims for himself with equal energy the right of private judgment and of individual protest.[3] He has a vivid sense of the corruption of human nature and the absolute need of moral regeneration ; yet he declares the soul to be born Christian, and unable to find rest except in Christ. " The testi-

[1] Comp. his own painful confession in *De Patient.* c. 1 : "*Miserrimus ego semper æger caloribus impatientiæ.*"

[2] In a similar manner Luther, though himself one of the most original and fruitful thinkers, sometimes unreasonably abuses reason as the devil's mistress.

[3] In this apparent contradiction Luther resembles Tertullian : he fought Romanism with private judgment, and Zwinglians, Anabaptists, and all sectarians ("*Schwarm—und Rottengeister,*" as he called them) with catholic authority ; he denounced "the damned heathen Aristotle," as the father of Popish scholasticism, and used scholastic distinctions in support of the ubiquity of Christ's body against Zwingli.

monies of the soul," says he, "are as true as they are simple; as simple as they are popular; as popular as they are natural; as natural as they are divine." He is just the opposite of the genial, less vigorous, but more learned and comprehensive Origen. He adopts the strictest supranatural principles; and yet he is a most decided realist, and attributes body, that is, as it were, a corporeal, tangible substantiality, even to God and to the soul; while the idealistic Alexandrian cannot speak spiritually enough of God, and can conceive the human soul without and before the existence of the body. Tertullian's theology revolves about the great Pauline antithesis of sin and grace, and breaks the road to the Latin anthropology and soteriology afterwards developed by his like-minded, but clearer, calmer, and more considerate countryman, Augustin. For his opponents, be they heathens, Jews, heretics, or catholics, he has as little indulgence and regard as Luther. With the adroitness of a special pleader he entangles them in self-contradictions, pursues them into every nook and corner, overwhelms them with arguments, sophisms, apophthegms, and sarcasms, drives them before him with unmerciful lashings, and almost always makes them ridiculous and contemptible. His polemics everywhere leave marks of blood. It is a wonder that he was not killed by the heathens, or excommunicated by the Catholics.

His style is exceedingly characteristic, and corresponds with his thought. It is terse, abrupt, laconic, sententious, nervous, figurative, full of hyperbole, sudden turns, legal technicalities, African provincialisms, or rather antiquated or vulgar latinisms.[1] It abounds in latinized Greek words, and new expres-

---

[1] According to Niebuhr, a most competent judge of Latin antiquities. Provinces and colonies often retain terms and phrases after they die out in the capital and in the mother country. Renan says with reference to Tertullian (*Marc-Aurèle*, p. 456): "*La 'lingua volgata' d'Afrique contribua ainsi dans une large part à la formation de la langue ecclésiastique de l' Occident, et ainsi elle exerça une influence décisive sur nos langues modernes. Mais il résulta de là une autre conséquence; cest que les textes fondamentaux de la littérature latine chrétienne furent écrits dans une langue que lettrés d'Italie trouvèrent barbare et corrompue, ce qui plus tard donna occasion de la part des rhéteurs à des objections et à des épigrammes*

sions, in roughnesses, angles, and obscurities; sometimes, like a grand volcanic eruption, belching precious stones and dross in strange confusion; or like the foaming torrent tumbling over the precipice of rocks and sweeping all before it. His mighty spirit wrestles with the form, and breaks its way through the primeval forest of nature's thinking. He had to create the church language of the Latin tongue.[1]

In short, we see in this remarkable man, both intellectually and morally, the fermenting of a new creation, but not yet quite set free from the bonds of chaotic darkness and brought into clear and beautiful order.

NOTES.

I. Gems from Tertullian's writings.

The philosophy of persecution:

"SEMEN EST SANGUIS CHRISTIANORUM." (*Apol.* c. 50.)

The human soul and Christianity (made for Christ, yet requiring a new birth):

"TESTIMONIUM ANIMÆ NATURALITER CHRISTIANÆ." (*De Test. Anim.* c. 2; see the passages quoted § 40, p. 120.)

"FIUNT, NON NASCUNTUR CHRISTIANI." (*Apol.* 18. *De Test. Anim.* 1.)

Christ the Truth, not Habit (*versus* traditionalism):

"CHRISTUS VERITAS EST, NON CONSUETUDO." (*De Virg. vel.* 1.)

General priesthood of the laity (*versus* an exclusive hierarchy):

"NONNE ET LAICI SACERDOTES SUMUS?" (*De Exhort. Cast.* 7.)

Religious Liberty, an inalienable right of man (*versus* compulsion and persecution):

"HUMANI JURIS ET NATURALIS POTESTATIS EST UNICUIQUE QUOD PUTAVERIT COLERE." (*Ad Scap.* 2; comp. *Apol.* 14 and the passages quoted § 13, p. 35.)

---

sans fin." Comp. the works of Rönsch, Vercellone, Kaulen, Ranke, and Ziegler on the Itala and Vulgata.

[1] Ruhnken calls Tertullian " *Latinitatis pessimum auctorem* " and Bishop Kaye "the harshest and most obscure of writers," but Niebuhr, (*Lectures on Ancient History*, vol. II. p. 54), Oehler (*Op.* III. 720), and Holmes (the translator of Tert. against Marcion, p. ix.) judge more favorably of his style, which is mostly " the terse and vigorous expression of terse and vigorous thought." Renan (*Marc Aurèle*, p. 456) calls Tertullian the strangest literary phenomenon : " *un mélange inouï de talent, de fausseté d'esprit, d'éloquence et de mauvais goût ; grand écrivain, si l'on admet que sacrifier toute grammaire et toute correction à l' effet sois bien écrire.*" Cardinal Newman calls him " the most powerful writer of the early centuries " (*Tracts, Theol. and Eccles.*, p. 219).

Dr. Baur (*Kirchengesch.* I. 428) says: "It is remarkable how already the oldest Christian Apologists, in vindicating the Christian faith, were led to assert the Protestant principle of freedom of faith and conscience" [and we must add, of public worship], "as an inherent attribute of the conception of religion against their heathen opponents." Then he quotes Tertullian, as the first who gave clear expression to this principle.

II. Estimates of Tertullian as a man and an author.

NEANDER (*Ch. Hist.* I. 683 sq., Torrey's translation): "Tertullian presents special claims to attention, both as the first representative of the theological tendency in the North-African church, and as a representative of the Montanistic mode of thinking. He was a man of an ardent and profound spirit, of warm and deep feelings; inclined to give himself up, with his whole soul and strength, to the object of his love, and sternly to repel everything that was foreign from this. He possessed rich and various stores of knowledge; which had been accumulated, however, at random, and without scientific arrangement. His profoundness of thought was not united with logical clearness and sobriety: an ardent, unbridled imagination, moving in a world of sensuous images, governed him. His fiery and passionate disposition, and his previous training as an advocate and rhetorician, easily impelled him, especially in controversy, to rhetorical exaggerations. When he defends a cause, of whose truth he was convinced, we often see in him the advocate, whose sole anxiety is to collect together all the arguments which can help his case, it matters not whether they are true arguments or only plausible sophisms; and in such cases the very exuberance of his wit sometimes leads him astray from the simple feeling of truth. What must render this man a phenomenon presenting special claims to the attention of the Christian historian is the fact, that Christianity is the inspiring soul of his life and thoughts; that out of Christianity an entirely new and rich inner world developed itself to his mind: but the leaven of Christianity had first to penetrate through and completely refine that fiery, bold and withal rugged nature. We find the new wine in an old bottle; and the tang which it has contracted there, may easily embarrass the inexperienced judge. Tertullian often had more within him than he was able to express: the overflowing mind was at a loss for suitable forms of phraseology. He had to *create* a language for the new spiritual matter,—and that out of the rude Punic Latin,—without the aid of a logical and grammatical education, and as he was hurried along in the current of thoughts and feelings by his ardent nature. Hence the often difficult and obscure phraseology; but hence, too, the original and striking turns in his mode of representation. And hence this great church-teacher, who unites great gifts with great failings, has been so often misconceived by those who could form no friendship with the spirit which dwelt in so ungainly a form."

HASE (*Kirchengesch.* p. 91, tenth ed.) : "*Die lateinische Kirche hatte fast nur Übersetzungen, bis Tertullianus, als Heide Rhetor und Sachwalter zu Rom, mit reicher griechischer Gelehrsamkeit, die auch der Kirchenvater gern sehen liess, Presbyter in seiner Vaterstadt Karthago, ein strenger, düsterer, feuriger Character, dem Christenthum aus punischem Latein eine Literatur errang, in welcher geistreiche Rhetorik, genialer so wie gesuchter Witz, derb sinnliches Anfassen des Idealen, tiefes Gefühl und juridische Verstandesansicht mit einander ringen. Er hat der afrikanischen Kirche die Losung angegeben: Christus sprach: Ich bin die Wahrheit, nicht, das Herkommen. Er hat das Gottesbewusstsein in den Tiefen der Seele hochgehalten, aber ein Mann der Auctorität hat er die Thorheit des Evangeliums der Weltweisheit seiner Zeitgenossen, das Unglaubliche der Wunder Gottes dem gemeinen Weltverstande mit stolzer Ironie entgegengehalten. Seine Schriften, denen er unbedenklich Fremdes angeeignet und mit dem Gepräge seines Genius versehen hat, sind theils polemisch mit dem höchsten Selbstvertraun der katholischen Gesinnung gegen Heiden, Juden und Häretiker, theils erbaulich; so jedoch, dass auch in jenen das Erbauliche, in diesen das Polemische für strenge Sitte und Zucht vorhanden ist.*"

HAUCK (*Tertullian's Leben und Schriften*, p. 1) : "*Unter den Schriftstellern der lateinischen Christenheit ist Tertullian einer der bedeutendsten und intressantesten. Er ist der Anfänger der lateinischen Theologie, der nicht nur ihrer Sprache seinen Stempel aufgeprägt hat, sondern sie auch auf die Bahn hinwies, welche sie lange einhielt. Seine Persönlichkeit hat ebensoviel Anziehendes als Abstossendes ; denn wer könnte den Ernst seines sittlichen Strebens, den Reichthum und die Lebhaftigkeit seines Geistes, die Festigkeit seiner Ueberzeugung und die stürmische Kraft seiner Beredtsamkeit verkennen? Allein ebensowenig lässt sich übersehen, dass ihm in allen Dingen das Mass fehlte. Seine Erscheinung hat nichts Edles ; er war nicht frei von Bizzarem, ja Gemeinem. So zeigen ihn seine Schriften, die Denkmäler seines Lebens Er war ein Mann, der sich in unaufhörlichem Streite bewegte : sein ganzes Wesen trägt die Spuren hievon.*"

Cardinal HERGENRÖTHER, the first Roman Catholic church historian now living (for Döllinger was excommunicated in 1870), says of Tertullian (in his *Kirchengesch.* I. 168, second ed., 1879): "*Strenge und ernst, oft beissend sarkastisch, in der Sprache gedrängt und dunkel, der heidnischen Philosophie durchaus abgeneigt, mit dem römischen Rechte sehr vertraut, hat er in seinen zahlreichen Schriften Bedeutendes für die Darstellung der kirchlichen Lehre geleistet, und ungeachtet seines Uebertritts zu den Montanisten betrachteten ihn die späteren african-ischen Schriftsteller, auch Cyprian, als Muster und Lehrer.*"

PRESSENSÉ (*Martyrs and Apologists*, p. 375): "The African nationality gave to Christianity its most eloquent defender, in whom the intense vehemence, the untempered ardor of the race, appear purified indeed, but not subdued. No influence in the early ages could equal that of Tertullian; and his writings breathe a spirit of such undying power that they can never grow old, and even now render living, controversies which have been silent for fifteen centuries. We must seek the man in his own pages, still aglow with his enthusiasm and quivering with his passion, for the details of his personal history are very few. The man is, as it were, absorbed in the writer, and we can well understand it, for his writings embody his whole soul. Never did a man more fully infuse his entire moral life into his books, and act through his words."

§ 197. *The Writings of Tertullian.*

Tertullian developed an extraordinary literary activity in two languages between about 190 and 220. His earlier books in the Greek language, and some in the Latin, are lost. Those which remain are mostly short; but they are numerous, and touch nearly all departments of religious life. They present a graphic picture of the church of his day. Most of his works, according to internal evidence, fall in the first quarter of the third century, in the Montanistic period of his life, and among these many of his ablest writings against the heretics; while, on the other hand, the gloomy moral austerity, which predisposed him to Montanism, comes out quite strongly even in his earliest productions.[1]

His works may be grouped in three classes : apologetic; polemic or anti-heretical ; and ethic or practical ; to which may be added as a fourth class the expressly Montanistic tracts against the Catholics. We can here only mention the most important :

1. In the APOLOGETIC works against heathens and Jews, he pleads the cause of all Christendom, and deserves the thanks of all Christendom. Preëminent among them is the *Apologeticus* (or *Apologeticum*).[2] It was composed in the reign of Septimius Severus, between 197 and 200. It is unquestionably one of the most beautiful monuments of the heroic age of the church. In

---

[1] On the chronological order see Notes.

[2] Comp. H. A. Woodham: *Tert. Liber Apologeticus with English Notes and an Introduction to the Study of Patristical and Ecclesiastical Latinity*, Cambridge, 1850. Am. ed. of *Select Works of Tert.*, by F. A. March, New York, 1876. p. 26–46.

this work, Tertullian enthusiastically and triumphantly repels the attacks of the heathens upon the new religion, and demands for it legal toleration and equal rights with the other sects of the Roman empire.   It is the first plea for religious liberty, as an *inalienable right* which God has given to every man, and which the civil government in its own interest should not only tolerate but respect and protect.   He claims no support, no favor, but simply justice.   The church was in the first three centuries a self-supporting and self-governing society (as it ought always to be), and no burden, but a blessing to the state, and furnished to it the most peaceful and useful citizens.   The cause of truth and justice never found a more eloquent and fearless defender in the very face of despotic power, and the blazing fires of persecution, than the author of this book.   It breathes from first to last the assurance of victory in apparent defeat.

"We conquer," are his concluding words to the prefects and judges of the Roman empire, " We conquer in dying; we go forth victorious at the very time we are subdued. . . . Many of your writers exhort to the courageous bearing of pain and death, as Cicero in the *Tusculans*, as Seneca in his *Chances*, as Diogenes, Pyrrhus, Callinicus. And yet their words do not find so many disciples as Christians do, teachers not by words, but by their deeds.   That very obstinacy you rail against is the preceptress. For who that contemplates it is not excited to inquire what is at the bottom of it?   Who, after inquiry, does not embrace our doctrines?   And, when he has embraced them, desires not to suffer that he may become partaker of the fulness of God's grace, that he may obtain from God complete forgiveness, by giving in exchange his blood?   For that secures the remission of all offences.   On this account it is that we return thanks on the very spot for your sentences.   As the divine and human are ever opposed to each other, when we are condemned by you, we are acquitted by the Highest."

The relation of the *Apologeticus* to the *Octavius* of Minucius Felix will be discussed in the next section.   But even if Tertullian should have borrowed from that author (as he undoubtedly borrowed, without acknowledgment, much matter from Irenæus, in his book against the Valentinians), he remains one of the most original and vigorous writers.[1]   Moreover the plan is different ;

[1] Ebert, who was the first to assert the priority of *Octavius*, nevertheless ad-

Minucius Felix pleads for Christianity as a philosopher before
philosophers, to convince the intellect ; Tertullian as a lawyer
and advocate before judges, to induce them to give fair play to
the Christians, who were refused even a hearing in the courts.

The beautiful little tract " *On the Testimony of the Soul*," (6
chapters) is a supplement to the *Apologeticus,* and furnishes one
of the strongest positive arguments for Christianity.   Here the
human soul is called to bear witness to the one true God : it
springs from God, it longs for God ; its purer and nobler instincts and aspirations, if not diverted and perverted by selfish
and sinful passions, tend upwards and heavenwards, and find rest
and peace only in God.   There is, we may say, a pre-established
harmony between the soul and the christian religion ; they are
made for each other ; the human soul is constitutionally
Christian.   And this testimony is universal, for as God is everywhere, so the human soul is everywhere.   But its testimony
turns against itself if not heeded.

" Every soul," he concludes, " is a culprit as well as a witness: in the
measure that it testifies for truth, the guilt of error lies on it; and on the
day of judgment it will stand before the court of God, without a word
to say.   Thou proclaimedst God, O soul, but thou didst not seek to know
Him ; evil spirits were detested by thee, and yet they were the objects of
thy adoration ; the punishments of hell were foreseen by thee, but no
care was taken to avoid them ; thou hadst a savor of Christianity, and
withal wert the persecutor of Christians."

2. His POLEMIC works are occupied chiefly with the refutation
of the Gnostics.   Here belongs first of all his thoroughly
catholic tract, " *On the Prescription of Heretics.*" [1]   It is of a
general character and lays down the fundamental principle of
the church in dealing with heresy.   Tertullian cuts off all errors
and neologies at the outset from the right of legal contest and

mits (*Gesch. der christl. lat. Lit.* I. 32) : " *Tertullian ist einer der genialsten,
originellsten und fruchtbarsten unter den christlich-lateinischen Autoren.*"

[1] *Præscriptio*, in legal terminology, means an exception made before the
merits of a case are discussed, showing *in limine* that the plaintiff ought not to
be heard.   This book has been most admired by R. Catholics as a masterly
vindication of the catholic rule of faith against heretical assailants; but its
force is weakened by Tertullian's Montanism.

appeal to the holy Scriptures, because these belong only to the catholic church as the legitimate heir and guardian of Christianity. Irenæus had used the same argument, but Tertullian gave it a legal or forensic form. The same argument, however, turns also against his own secession; for the difference between heretics and schismatics is really only relative, at least in Cyprian's view. Tertullian afterwards asserted, in contradiction with this book, that in religious matters not custom nor long possession, but truth alone, was to be consulted.

Among the heretics, he attacked chiefly the Valentinian Gnostics, and Marcion. The work against Marcion (A. D. 208) is his largest, and the only one in which he indicates the date of composition, namely the 15th year of the reign of Septimius Severus (A. D. 208).[1] He wrote three works against this famous heretic; the first he set aside as imperfect, the second was stolen from him and published with many blunders before it was finished. In the new work (in five books), he elaborately defends the unity of God, the Creator of all, the integrity of the Scriptures, and the harmony of the Old and New Testaments. He displays all his power of solid argument, subtle sophistry, ridicule and sarcasm, and exhausts his vocabulary of vituperation. He is more severe upon heretics than Jews or Gentiles. He begins with a graphic description of all the physical abnormities of Pontus, the native province of Marcion, and the gloomy temper, wild passions, and ferocious habits of its people, and then goes on to say:

"Nothing in Pontus is so barbarous and sad as the fact that Marcion was born there, fouler than any Scythian, more roving than the Sarmatian, more inhuman than the Massagete, more audacious than an Amazon, darker than the cloud of the Euxine, colder than its winter, more brittle than its ice, more deceitful than the Ister, more craggy than Caucasus. Nay, more, the true Prometheus, Almighty God, is mangled by Marcion's blasphemies. Marcion is more savage than even the beasts of that barbarous region. For what beaver was ever a greater emasculator than he who has abolished the nuptial bond? What Pontic mouse ever

[1] English translation by Peter Holmes, in the "Ante-Nicene Libr.," vol. VII., 1868 (478 pages).

had such gnawing powers as he who has gnawed the Gospel to pieces? Verily, O Euxine, thou hast produced a monster more credible to philosophers than to Christians. For the cynic Diogenes used to go about, lantern in hand, at mid-day, to find a man; whereas Marcion has quenched the light of his faith, and so lost the God whom he had found."

The tracts " On Baptism," " On the Soul," " On the Flesh of Christ," " On the Resurrection of the Flesh," " Against Hermogenes," " Against Praxeas," are concerned with particular errors, and are important to the doctrine of baptism, to Christian psychology, to eschatology, and christology.

3. His numerous PRACTICAL or ASCETIC treatises throw much light on the moral life of the early church, as contrasted with the immorality of the heathen world. Among these belong the books " On Prayer," " On Penance," " On Patience,"—a virtue, which he extols with honest confession of his own natural impatience and passionate temper, and which he urges upon himself as well as others,—the consolation of the confessors in prison (Ad Martyres), and the admonition against visiting theatres (De Spectaculis), which he classes with the pomp of the devil, and against all share, direct or indirect, in the worship of idols (De Idololatria).

4. His strictly MONTANISTIC or anti-catholic writings, in which the peculiarities of this sect are not only incidentally touched, as in many of the works named above, but vindicated expressly and at large, are likewise of a practical nature, and contend, in fanatical rigor, against the restoration of the lapsed (De Pudicitia), flight in persecutions, second marriage (De Monogamia, and De Exhortatione Castitatis), display of dress in females (De Cultu Feminarum), and other customs of the " Psychicals," as he commonly calls the Catholics in distinction from the sectarian Pneumatics. His plea, also, for excessive fasting (De Jejuniis), and his justification of a Christian soldier, who was discharged for refusing to crown his head (De Corona Militis), belong here Tertullian considers it unbecoming the followers of Christ, who, when on earth, wore a crown of thorns for us, to adorn their

heads with laurel, myrtle, olive, or with flowers or gems. We may imagine what he would have said to the tiara of the pope in his mediæval splendor.

NOTES.

The chronological order of Tertullian's work can be approximately determined by the frequent allusions to the contemporaneous history of the Roman empire, and by their relation to Montanism. See especially Uhlhorn, Hauck, Bonwetsch, and also Bp. Kaye (in Oehler's ed. of the *Opera* III. 709-718.) We divide the works into three classes, according to their relation to Montanism.

(1) Those books which belong to the author's catholic period before A. D. 200; viz.: *Apologeticus* or *Apologeticum* (in the autumn of 197, according to Bonwetsch; 198, Ebert; 199, Hesselberg; 200, Uhlhorn); *Ad Martyres* (197); *Ad Nationes* (probably soon after *Apol.*); *De Testimonio Animæ; De Pœnitentia; De Oratione; De Baptismo* (which according to cap. 15, was preceded by a Greek work against the validity of *Heretical Baptism*); *Ad Uxorem; De Patientia; Adv. Judæos; De Praescriptione Hæreticorum; De Spectaculis* (and a lost work on the same subject in the Greek language).

Kaye puts *De Spectaculis* in the Montanistic period. *De Praescriptione* is also placed by some in the Montanistic period before or after *Adv. Marcionem*. But Bonwetsch (p. 46) puts it between 199 and 206, probably in 199. Hauck makes it almost simultaneous with *De Baptismo*. He also places *De Idololatria* in this period.

(2) Those which were certainly not composed till after his transition to Montanism, between A. D. 200 and 220; viz.: *Adv. Marcionem* (5 books, composed in part at least in the 15th year of the Emperor Septimius Severus, *i. e.* A. D. 207 or 208; comp. I. 15); *De Anima; De Carne Christi; De Resurrectione Carnis; Adv. Praxean; Scorpiace* (*i. e.* antidote against the poison of the Gnostic heresy); *De Corona Militis; De Virginibus velandis; De Exhortatione Castitatis; De Pallio* (208 or 209); *De Fuga in persecutione; De Monogamia; De Jejuniis; De Pudicitia; Ad Scapulam* (212); *De Ecstasi* (lost); *De Spe Fidelium* (likewise lost).

Kellner (1870) assigns *De Pudicitia, De Monogamia, De Jejunio,* and *Adv. Praxean* to the period between 218 and 222.

(3) Those which probably belong to the Montanistic period; viz.: *Adv. Valentinianos; De cultu Feminarum* (2 libri); *Adv. Hermogenem.*

§ 198: *Minucius Felix.*

(I.) M. MINUCII FELICIS *Octavius,* best ed. by CAR. HALM, Vienna 1867 (in vol. II. of the "Corpus Scriptorum eccles. Latin."), and BERNH. DOMBART, with German translation and critical notes, 2d ed. Erlangen 1881. Halm has compared the only MS. of this book, formerly in the Vatican library now in Paris, very carefully ("*tanta diligentia ut de nullo jam loco dubitari possit quid in codice uno scriptum inveniatur*").

Ed. princeps by *Faustus Sabäus* (Rom. 1543, as the eighth book of Arnobius *Adv. Gent*); then by *Francis Balduin* (Heidelb. 1560, as an independent work). Many edd. since, by *Ursinus* (1583), *Meursius* (1598), *Wowerus* (1603), *Rigaltius* (1643), *Gronovius* (1709, 1743), *Davis* (1712), *Lindner* (1760, 1773), *Russwurm* (1824), *Lübkert* (1836), *Muralt* (1836), *Migne* (1844, in "Patrol." III. col. 193 sqq.), *Fr. Oehler* (1847, in Gersdorf's "Biblioth. Patr. ecclesiast. selecta," vol. XIII). *Kayser* (1863), *Cornelissen* (Lugd. Bat. 1882), etc.

English translations by H. A. HOLDEN (Cambridge 1853), and R. E. WALLIS in Clark's "Ante-Nic. Libr." vol. XIII. p. 451–517.

(II.) JEROME: *De vir. ill.* c. 58, and *Ep.* 48 *ad Pammach.*, and *Ep.* 70 *ad Magn.* LACTANT.: *Inst. Div.* V. 1, 22.

(III.) Monographs, dissertations and prolegomena to the different editions of M. Fel., by *van Hoven* (1766, also in Lindner's ed. II. 1773); MEIER (Turin, 1824,) NIC. LE NOURRY, and LUMPER (in Migne, "Patr. Lat." III. 194–231; 371–652); RÖREN (*Minuciania*,) Bedburg, 1859); BEHR (on the relation of M. F. to Cicero, Gera 1870); RÖNSCH (*in Das N. T.* Tertull.'s, 1871, p. 25 sqq.); PAUL P. DE FÊLICE (*Études sur l'Octavius*, Blois, 1880); KEIM (in his *Celsus*, 1873, 151–168, and in *Rom. und das Christenthum*, 1881, 383 sq., and 468–486); AD. EBERT (1874, in *Gesch. der christlich-latein. Lit.* I. 24–31); G. LŒSCHE (on the relation of M. F. to Athenagoras, in the "Jahrb. für Prot. Theol." 1882, p. 168–178); RENAN (*Marc-Aurèle*, 1882, p. 389–404); RICHARD KÜHN: *Der Octavius des Minucius Felix. Eine heidnisch philosophische Auffassung vom Christenthum.* Leipz. 1882 (71 pages). See also the art. of MANGOLD in Herzog[2] X. 12–17 (abridged in Schaff-Herzog); G. SALMON in Smith and Wace III. 920–924.

(IV.) On the relation of Minuc. Fel. to Tertullian: Ad. EBERT: *Tertullian's Verhältniss zu Minucius Felix, nebst einem Anhang über Commodian's Carmen apologeticum* (1868, in the 5th vol. of the "Abhandlungen der philol. histor. Classe der K. sächs. Ges. der Wissenschaften"); W. HARTEL (in Zeitschrift für d. öester. Gymnas. 1869, p. 348–368, against Ebert); E. KLUSSMANN ("Jenaer Lit. Zeitg," 1878); BONWETSCH (in *Die Schriften Tert.*, 1878, p. 21;) V. SCHULTZE (in "Jahrb. für Prot. Theol." 1881, p. 485–506; P. SCHWENKE (*Ueber die Zeit des Min. Fel.* in "Jahrb. für Prot. Theol.'" 1883, p. 263–294).

In close connection with Tertullian, either shortly before, or shortly after him, stands the Latin Apologist Minucius Felix.[1]

---

[1] Jerome puts him after Tertullian (and Cyprian), Lactantius before Tertullian.

Converts are always the most zealous, and often the most effective promoters of the system or sect which they have deliberately chosen from honest and earnest conviction. The Christian Apologists of the second century were educated heathen philosophers or rhetoricians before their conversion, and used their secular learning and culture for the refutation of idolatry and the vindication of the truths of revelation. In like manner the Apostles were Jews by birth and training, and made their knowledge of the Old Testament Scriptures subservient to the gospel. The Reformers of the sixteenth century came out of the bosom of mediæval Catholicism, and were thus best qualified to oppose its corruptions and to emancipate the church from the bondage of the papacy.[1]

I. MARCUS MINUCIUS FELIX belongs to that class of converts, who brought the rich stores of classical culture to the service of Christianity. He worthily opens the series of Latin writers of the Roman church which had before spoken to the world only in the Greek tongue. He shares with Lactantius the honor of being the Christian Cicero.[2] He did not become a clergyman, but apparently continued in his legal profession. We know nothing of his life except that he was an advocate in Rome, but probably of North African descent.[3]

II. We have from him an apology of Christianity in the form of a dialogue under the title *Octavius*.[4] The author makes

---

[1] We may also refer to more recent analogies: the ablest champions of Romanism—as Hurter, Newman, Manning, Brownson—owe their intellectual and moral equipment to Protestantism ; while the Old Catholic leaders of the opposition to Vatican Romanism—as Döllinger, Friedrich, Reinkens, Reusch, Langen, von Schulte—were formerly eminent teachers in the Roman church.

[2] Jerome describes him as "*insignis causidicus Romani fori*," but he depended on Lactantius, who may have derived this simply from the introduction to the book, where the author speaks of taking advantage of the court holidays for an excursion to Ostia. The *gens Minucia* was famous in Rome, and an inscription (Gruter, p. 918) mentions one with the cognomen *Felix.*

[3] From Cirta (now Constantine). This we must infer from the fact that he calls Corn. Fronto "*Cirtensis noster,*" *Octav.* c. 9; comp. c. 31, "*tuus Fronto.*"

[4] In 40 (*al.* 41) short chapters which, in Halm's edition, cover 54 pages, oct. The book was written several years after the Dialogue and after the death of

with his friend Octavius Januarius, who had, like himself, been converted from heathen error to the Christian truth, an excursion from Rome to the sea-bath at Ostia. There they meet on a promenade along the beach with Cæcilius Natalis, another friend of Minucius, but still a heathen, and, as appears from his reasoning, a philosopher of the sceptical school of the New Academy. Sitting down on the large stones which were placed there for the protection of the baths, the two friends in full view of the ocean and inhaling the gentle sea breeze, begin, at the suggestion of Cæcilius, to discuss the religious question of the day. Minucius sitting between them is to act as umpire (chaps. 1–4).

Cæcilius speaks first (chs. 5–15), in defence of the heathen, and in opposition to the Christian, religion. He begins like a sceptic or agnostic concerning the existence of a God as being doubtful, but he soon shifts his ground, and on the principle of expediency and utility he urges the duty of worshipping the ancestral gods. It is best to adhere to what the experience of all nations has found to be salutary. Every nation has its peculiar god or gods; the Roman nation, the most religious of all, allows the worship of all gods, and thus attained to the highest power and prosperity. He charges the Christians with presumption for claiming a certain knowledge of the highest problems which lie beyond human ken; with want of patriotism for forsaking the ancestral traditions; with low breeding (as Celsus did). He ridicules their worship of a crucified malefactor and the instrument of his crucifixion, and even an ass's head. He repeats the lies of secret crimes, as promiscuous incest, and the murder of innocent children, and quotes for these slanders the authority of the celebrated orator Fronto. He objects to their religion that it has no temples, nor altars, nor images. He attacks their doctrines of one God, of the destruction of the present world, the resurrection and judgment,

Octavius (c. 1: "*discedens* or *decedens vir eximius et sanctus immensum sui deside rium nobis reliquit,*" etc.).

as irrational and absurd. He pities them for their austere habits and their aversion to the theatre, banquets, and other innocent enjoyments. He concludes with the re-assertion of human ignorance of things which are above us, and an exhortation to leave those uncertain things alone, and to adhere to the religion of their fathers, " lest either a childish superstition should be introduced, or all religion should be overthrown."

In the second part (ch. 16–38), Octavius refutes these charges, and attacks idolatry ; meeting each point in proper order. He vindicates the existence and unity of the Godhead, the doctrine of creation and providence, as truly rational, and quotes in confirmation the opinions of various philosophers (from Cicero). He exposes the absurdity of the heathen mythology, the worship of idols made of wood and stone, the immoralities of the gods, and the cruelties and obscene rites connected with their worship. The Romans have not acquired their power by their religion, but by rapacity and acts of violence. The charge of worshipping a criminal and his cross, rests on the ignorance of his innocence and divine character. The Christians have no temples, because they will not limit the infinite God, and no images, because man is God's image, and a holy life the best sacrifice. The slanderous charges of immorality are traced to the demons who invented and spread them among the people, who inspire oracles, work false miracles and try in every way to draw men into their ruin. It is the heathen who practice such infamies, who cruelly expose their new-born children or kill them by abortion. The Christians avoid and abhor the immoral amusements of the theatre and circus where madness, adultery, and murder are exhibited and practiced, even in the name of the gods. They find their true pleasure and happiness in God, his knowledge and worship.

At the close of the dialogue (chs. 39–40), Cæcilius confesses himself convinced of his error, and resolves to embrace Christianity, and desires further instruction on the next day. Minucius expresses his satisfaction at this result, which made a decision on his part unnecessary. Joyful and thankful for the joint

victory over error, the friends return from the sea-shore to
Ostia.[1]

III. The apologetic value of this work is considerable, but
its doctrinal value is very insignificant. It gives us a lively
idea of the great controversy between the old and the new
religion among the higher and cultivated classes of Roman
society, and allows fair play and full force to the arguments on
both sides. It is an able and eloquent defense of monotheism
against polytheism, and of Christian morality against heathen
immorality. But this is about all. The exposition of the
truths of Christianity is meagre, superficial, and defective. The
unity of the Godhead, his all-ruling providence, the resurrection
of the body, and future retribution make up the whole creed of
Octavius. The Scriptures, the prophets and apostles are ignored,[2] the doctrines of sin and grace, Christ and redemption,
the Holy Spirit and his operations are left out of sight, and the
name of Christ is not even mentioned; though we may reasonably infer from the manner in which the author repels the
charge of worshipping "a crucified malefactor," that he regarded Christ as more than a mere man (ch. 29). He leads
only to the outer court of the temple. His object was purely
apologetic, and he gained his point.[3] Further instruction is not
excluded, but is solicited by the converted Cæcilius at the
close, "as being necessary to a perfect training."[4] We have
therefore no right to infer from this silence that the author was
ignorant of the deeper mysteries of faith.[5]

[1] "*Post hæc læti hilaresque discessimus, Cæcilius quod crediderit, Octavius gau-
dere [ad gaudendum] quod vicerit, ego [Minuc. Fel.] et quod hic crediderit et hic
vicerit.*"

[2] The only traces are in chs. 29 and 34, which perhaps allude to Jer. 17: 5
and 1 Cor. 15: 36, 42.

[3] Keim supposes that he intended to refute Celsus (but he is nowhere mentioned); De Félice, that he aimed at Fronto (who is twice mentioned); Kühn
better: public opinion, the ignorant prejudice of the higher classes against
Christianity.

[4] C. 40: "*Etiam nunc tamen aliqua consubsidunt non obstrepentia veritati, sed
perfectæ institutioni necessaria, de quibus crastino, quod iam sol occasui declivis est,
ut de toto (or et die toto) congruentius, promptius requiremus.*"

[5] Renan (p. 402) takes a different view, namely that Minucius was a liberal

His philosophic stand-point is eclectic with a preference for Cicero, Seneca, and Plato. Christianity is to him both theoretically and practically the true philosophy which teaches the only true God, and leads to true virtue and piety. In this respect he resembles Justin Martyr.[1]

IV. The literary form of *Octavius* is very pleasing and elegant. The diction is more classical than that of any contemporary Latin writer heathen or Christian. The book bears a strong resemblance to Cicero's *De Natura Deorum*, in many ideas, in style, and the urbanity, or gentlemanly tone. Dean Milman says that it "reminds us of the golden days of Latin prose." Renan calls it "the pearl of the apologetic literature of the last years of Marcus Aurelius." But the date is under dispute, and depends in part on its relation to Tertullian.

V. Time of composition. *Octavius* closely resembles Tertullian's *Apologeticus*, both in argument and language, so that one book presupposes the other; although the aim is different, the former being the plea of a philosopher and refined gentleman, the other the plea of a lawyer and ardent Christian. The older opinion (with some exceptions[2]) maintained the priority of *Apologeticus*, and consequently put *Octavius* after A. D. 197 or 200 when the former was written. Ebert reversed the order and tried to prove, by a careful critical comparison, the originality

---

Christian of the Deistic stamp, a man of the world "*qui n'empêche ni la gaieté, ni le talent, ni le goût aimable de la vie, ni la recherche de l'élégance du style. Que nous sommes loin de l'ébionite ou même du juif de Galilée! Octavius, c'est Cicéron, ou mieux Fronton, devenu chrétien. En réalité, c'est par la culture intellectuelle qu'il arrive au déisme. Il aime la nature, il se plaît a la conversation des gens biens élevés. Des hommes faits sur ce modèle n'auraient créé ni l'Évangile ni l'Apocalypse; mais, réciproquement, sans de tels adhérents, l'Évangile, l'Apocalypse, les épîtres de Paul fussent restés les éscrits secrets d'une secte fermée, qui, comme les esséniens ou les thérapeutes, eut finalement disparu.*" Kühn, also, represents Minucius as a philosopher rather than a Christian, and seems to explain his silence on the specific doctrines of Christianity from ignorance. But no educated Christian could be ignorant of Christ and His work, nor of the prophets and apostles who were regularly read in public worship.

[1] On the philosophy of Minucius, see the analysis of Kühn, p. 21 sqq.; 58 sqq.
[2] Blondel (1641), Daillé (1660), Rösler (1777), Russwurm (1824), doubted the priority of Tertullian. See Kühn, *l. c.*, p. v.

of *Octavius.*[1] His conclusion is adopted by the majority of recent German writers,[2] but has also met with opposition.[3] If Tertullian used Minucius, he expanded his suggestions ; if Minucius used Tertullian, he did it by way of abridgement.

It is certain that Minucius borrowed from Cicero (also from Seneca, and, perhaps, from Athenagoras),[4] and Tertullian (in his *Adv. Valent.*) from Irenæus ; though both make excellent use of their material, reproducing rather than copying it ; but Tertullian is beyond question a far more original, vigorous, and important writer. Moreover the Roman divines used the Greek language from Clement down to Hippolytus towards the middle of the third century, with the only exception, perhaps, of Victor (190–202). So far the probability is for the later age of Minucius.

But a close comparison of the parallel passages seems to favor his priority ; yet the argument is not conclusive.[5] The priority of Minucius has been inferred also from the fact that he twice

[1] In his essay on the subject (1866), Ebert put *Octavius* between 160 and the close of the second century; in his more recent work on the *History of Christ. Lat. Lit.* (1874), vol. I., p. 25, he assigns it more definitely to between 179 and 185 ("*Anfang oder Mitte der achtziger Jahre des 2. Jahrh.*"). He assumes that Minucius used Athenagoras who wrote 177.

[2] Ueberweg (1866), Rönsch (*Das n. T. Tertull.* 1871), Keim (1873), Caspari (1875, III. 411), Herzog (1876), Hauck (1877), Bonwetsch (1878), Mangold (in Herzog[2] 1882), Kühn (1882), Renan (1882), Schwenke (1883). The last (pp. 292 and 294) puts the oral dialogue even so far back as Hadrian (before 137), and the composition before the death of Antoninus Pius (160).

[3] Hartel (1869), Jeep (1869), Klussmann (1878), Schultze (1881), and Salmon (1883). Hartel, while denying that Tertullian borrowed from Minucius, leaves the way open for an independent use of an older book by both. Schultze puts Minucius down to the reign of Domitian (300–303), which is much too late.

[4] Renan (p. 390) calls Minucius (although he puts him before Tertullian) a habitual plagiarist who often copies from Cicero without acknowledgment. Dombart (p. 135 sqq.), and Schwenke (p. 273 sqq.) prove his dependence on Seneca.

[5] The crucial test of relative priority applied by Ebert is the relation of the two books to Cicero. Minucius wrote with Cicero open before him ; Tertullian shows no fresh reading of Cicero ; consequently if the parallel passages contain traces of Cicero, Tertullian must have borrowed them from Minucius. But these traces in Tertullian are very few, and the inference is disputable. The application of this test has led Hartel and Salmon (in Smith and Wace, III. 922) to the opposite conclusion. And Schultze proves 1) that Minucius used other works of Tertullian besides the *Apologeticus*, and 2) that Minucius.

mentions Fronto (the teacher and friend of Marcus Aurelius), apparently as a *recent* celebrity, and Fronto died about 168. Keim and Renan find allusions to the persecutions under Marcus Aurelius (177), and to the attack of Celsus (178), and hence put *Octavius* between 178 and 180.[1] But these assumptions are unfounded, and they would lead rather to the conclusion that the book was not written before 200; for about twenty years elapsed (as Keim himself supposes) before the Dialogue actually was recorded on paper.

An unexpected argument for the later age of Minucius is furnished by the recent French discovery of the name of *Marcus Cæcilius Quinti F. Natalis*, as the chief magistrate of Cirta (Constantine) in Algeria, in several inscriptions from the years 210 to 217.[2] The heathen speaker Cæcilius Natalis of our Dialogue hailed from that very city (chs. 9 and 31). The identity of the two persons can indeed not be proven, but is at least very probable.

Considering these conflicting possibilities and probabilities, we conclude that *Octavius* was written in the first quarter of the third century, probably during the peaceful reign of Alexander Severus (A. D. 222–235). The last possible date is the year 250, because Cyprian's book *De Idolorum Vanitate*, written about that time, is largely based upon it.[3]

in copying from Cicero, makes the same kind of verbal changes in copying from Tertullian.

[1] Chs. 29, 33, 37. I can find in these passages no proof of any *particular* violent persecution. Tortures are spoken of in ch. 37, but to these the Christians were always exposed. Upon the whole the situation of the church appears in the introductory chapters, and throughout the Dialogue, as a comparatively quiet one, such as we know it to have been at intervals between the imperial persecutions. This is also the impression of Schultze and Schwenke. Minucius is silent about the argument so current under Marcus Aurelius, that the Christians are responsible for all the public calamities.

[2] Mommsen, *Corp. Lat. Inscript.* VIII. 6996 and 7094–7098; *Recueil* de Constantine, 1869, p. 695. See an article by Dessau in "Hermes," 1880, t. xv., p. 471–74; Salmon, *l. c.*, p. 924; and Renan, *l. c.*, p. 390 sq. Renan admits the possible identity of this Cæcilius with the friend of Minucius, but suggests in the interest of his hypothesis that he was the son.

[3] V. Schultze denies Cyprian's authorship; but the book is attested by Jerome and Augustin.

§ 199. *Cyprian.*

Comp. §§ 22, 47 and 53.

(I.) S. CYPRIANI *Opera omnia.* Best critical ed. by W. HARTEL, Vin·
dob. 1868–'71, 3 vols. oct. (in the Vienna " Corpus Scriptorum eccle·
siast. Latinorum "); based upon the examination of 40 MSS.

Other edd. by *Sweynheym* and *Pannartz,* Rom. 1471 (ed.
princeps),
again Venice 1477; by *Erasmus,* Bas. 1520 (first critical ed., often reprinted); by *Paul Manutius,* Rom. 1563; by *Morell,* Par. 1564; by
Rigault (Rigaltius), Par. 1648; *John Fell,* Bp. of Oxford, Oxon. 1682
(very good, with Bishop Pearson's *Annales Cyprianici*), again
Amst. 1700 and since; the Benedictine ed. begun by *Baluzius*
and completed by *Prud. Maranus,* Par. 1726, 1 vol. fol. (a magnificent ed., with textual emendations to satisfy the Roman curia), reprinted in Venice, 1758, and in *Migne's* "Patrol. Lat." (vol. IV.
Par. 1844, and part of vol. V. 9–80, with sundry additions); a convenient manual ed. by *Gersdorf,* Lips. 1838 sq. (in *Gersdorf's* "Biblioth. Patrum Lat." Pars II. and III.)

English translations by N. MARSHALL, Lond., 1717; in the Oxf. "Library of the Fathers," Oxf. 1840; and by R. G. WALLIS in "Ante-
Nicene Lib." Edinb. 1868, 2 vols.; N. York ed. vol. V. (1885).

(II.) *Vita Cypriani* by PONTIUS, and the *Acta Proconsularia Martyrii
Cypr.,* both in Ruinart's *Acta Mart.* II., and the former in most ed.
of his works.

(III.) J. PEARSON: *Annales Cyprianici.* Oxon. 1682, in the ed. of Fell.
A work of great learning and acumen, determining the chronological order of many Epp. and correcting innumerable mistakes.

H. DODWELL: *Dissertationes Cyprianicæ tres.* Oxon. 1684; Amst. 1700;
also in Tom. V of Migne's "Patr. Lat." col. 9–80.

A. F. GERVAISE: *Vie de St. Cyprien.* Par. 1717.

F. W. RETTBERG: *Cyprianus nach seinem Leben u. Wirken.* Gött. 1831.

G. A. POOLE: *Life and Times of Cyprian.* Oxf. 1840 (419 pages). High-
church Episcop. and anti-papal.

AEM. BLAMPIGNON: *Vie de Cyprien.* Par. 1861.

CH. E. FREPPEL (Ultramontane): *Saint Cyprien et l' église d' Afrique
au troisième siècle.* Paris, 1865, 2d ed. 1873.

AD. EBERT: *Geschichte der christl. latein. Literatur.* Leipz. 1874, vol. I.
54–61.

J. PETERS (R. C.): *Der heil. Cyprian. Leben u. Wirken.* Regensb. 1877.

B. FECHTRUP: *Der h. Cyprian, Leben u. Lehre,* vol. I. Münster, 1878.

OTTO RITSCHL: *Cyprian von Karthago und die Verfassung der Kirche.*
Göttingen 1885.

Articles on special topics connected with Cyprian by J. W. NEVIN
and VARIEN (both in " Mercersburg Review " for 1852 and '53);
PETERS (Ultramontane: *Cyprian's doctrine on the Unity of the*

Church in opposition to the schisms of Carthage and Rome, Luxemb 1870); Jos. Hub. Reinkens (Old Cath. Bp.: *Cypr's. Doctr. on the Unity of the Church.* Würzburg, 1873).

I. Life of Cyprian.

Thascius Cæcilius Cyprianus, bishop and martyr, and the impersonation of the catholic church of the middle of the third century, sprang from a noble and wealthy heathen family of Carthage, where he was born about the year 200, or earlier. His deacon and biographer, Pontius, considers his earlier life not worthy of notice in comparison with his subsequent greatness in the church. Jerome tells us, that he stood in high repute as a teacher of rhetoric.[1] He was, at all events, a man of commanding literary, rhetorical, and legal culture, and of eminent administrative ability, which afterwards proved of great service to him in the episcopal office. He lived in worldly splendor to mature age, nor was he free from the common vices of heathenism, as we must infer from his own confessions. But the story, that he practised arts of magic arises perhaps from some confusion, and is at any rate unattested. Yet, after he became a Christian, he believed, like Tertullian and others, in visions and dreams, and had some only a short time before his martyrdom.

A worthy presbyter, Cæcilius, who lived in Cyprian's house, and afterwards at his death committed his wife and children to him, first made him acquainted with the doctrines of the Christian religion, and moved him to read the Bible. After long resistance Cyprian forsook the world, entered the class of catechumens, sold his estates for the benefit of the poor,[2] took a vow of chastity, and in 245 or 246 received baptism, adopting, out of gratitude to his spiritual father, the name of Cæcilius.

He himself, in a tract soon afterwards written to a friend,[3]

---

[1] *Catal.* c. 67 : " *Cyprianus Afer primum gloriose rhetoricam docuit.*"

[2] Pontius, in his *Vita*, a very unsatisfactory sketch, prefixed to the editions of the works of Cyprian, places this act of renunciation (Matt. 19 : 21) before his baptism, " *inter fidei prima rudimenta.*" Cyprian's gardens, however, together with a villa, were afterwards restored to him, " *Dei indulgentia.*" that is, very probably, through the liberality of his Christian friends.

[3] *De Gratia Dei, ad Donatum,* c. 3, 4.

gives us the following oratorical description of his conversion :
" While I languished in darkness and deep night, tossing upon
the sea of a troubled world, ignorant of my destination, and far
from truth and light, I thought it, according to my then habits,
altogether a difficult and hard thing that a man could be born
anew, and that, being quickened to new life by the bath of saving water, he might put off the past, and, while preserving the
identity of the body, might transform the man in mind and
heart. How, said I, is such a change possible ? How can one
at once divest himself of all that was either innate or acquired
and grown upon him ? . . . Whence does he learn frugality, who
was accustomed to sumptuous feasts ? And how shall he who
shone in costly apparel, in gold and purple, come down to common and simple dress ? He who has lived in honor and station,
cannot bear to be private and obscure. . . . But when, by the aid
of the regenerating water,[1] the stain of my former life was
washed away, a serene and pure light poured from above into my
purified breast. So soon as I drank the spirit from above
and was transformed by a second birth into a new man, then the
wavering mind became wonderfully firm ; what had been closed
opened ; the dark became light ; strength came for that which
had seemed difficult ; what I had thought impossible became
practicable."

Cyprian now devoted himself zealously, in ascetic retirement,
to the study of the Scriptures and the church teachers, especially
Tertullian, whom he called for daily with the words : " Hand me
the master ! "[2] The influence of Tertullian on his theological
formation is unmistakable, and appears at once, for example, on
comparing the tracts of the two on prayer and on patience, or
the work of the one on the vanity of idols with the apology of
the other. It is therefore rather strange that in his own writings

---

[1] " *Undæ genitalis auxilio*," which refers of course to baptism.

[2] " *Da magistrum !*" So Jerome relates in his notice on Tertullian, *Cat.* c.
53, on the testimony of an old man, who had heard it in his youth from the
" *notarius beati Cypriani.*" As to the time, Cyprian might have personally
known Tertullian, who lived at least till the year 220 or 230.

we find no acknowledgment of his indebtedness, and, as far as I recollect, no express allusion whatever to Tertullian and the Montanists. But he could derive no aid and comfort from him in his conflict with schism.

Such a man could not long remain concealed. Only two years after his baptism, in spite of his earnest remonstrance, Cyprian was raised to the bishopric of Carthage by the acclamations of the people, and was thus at the same time placed at the head of the whole North African clergy. This election of a neophyte was contrary to the letter of the ecclesiastical laws (comp. 1 Tim. 3 : 6), and led afterwards to the schism of the party of Novatus. But the result proved, that here, as in the similar elevation of Ambrose, Augustin, and other eminent bishops of the ancient church, the voice of the people was the voice of God.

For the space of ten years, ending with his triumphant martyrdom, Cyprian administered the episcopal office in Carthage with exemplary energy, wisdom, and fidelity, and that in a most stormy time, amidst persecutions from without and schismatic agitations within. The persecution under Valerian brought his active labors to a close. He was sent into exile for eleven months, then tried before the Proconsul, and condemned to be beheaded. When the sentence was pronounced, he said: "Thanks be to God," knelt in prayer, tied the bandage over his eyes with his own hand, gave to the executioner a gold piece, and died with the dignity and composure of a hero. His friends removed and buried his body by night. Two chapels were erected on the spots of his death and burial. The anniversary of his death was long observed; and five sermons of Augustin still remain in memory of Cyprian's martyrdom, Sept. 14, 258.

II. Character and Position.

As Origen was the ablest scholar, and Tertullian the strongest writer, so Cyprian was the greatest bishop, of the third century. He was born to be a prince in the church. In executive talent, he even surpassed all the Roman bishops of his time; and he bore himself towards them, also, as "frater" and "collega," in the spirit of full equality. Augustin calls him by eminence, "the catholic bishop and catholic martyr;" and Vincentius of Lirinum, "the light of all saints, all martyrs, and all bishops." His stamp of character was more that of Peter than either of Paul or John.

His peculiar importance falls not so much in the field of theology, where he lacks originality and depth, as in church organization and discipline. While Tertullian dealt mainly with heretics, Cyprian directed his polemics against schismatics, among whom he had to condemn, though he never does in fact, his venerated teacher, who died a Montanist. Yet his own conduct was not perfectly consistent with his position; for in the controversy on heretical baptism he himself exhibited his master's spirit of opposition to Rome. He set a limit to his own exclusive catholic principle of tradition by the truly Protestant maxims : "*Consuetudo sine veritate vetustas erroris est*, and, *Non est de consuetudine præscribendum, sed ratione vincendum.*" In him the idea of the old catholic hierarchy and episcopal autocracy, both in its affinity and in its conflict with the idea of the papacy, was personally embodied, so to speak, and became flesh and blood. The unity of the church, as the vehicle and medium of all salvation, was the thought of his life and the passion of his heart. But he contended with the same zeal for an independent episcopate as for a Roman primacy; and the authority of his name has been therefore as often employed against the papacy as in its favor. On both sides he was the faithful organ of the churchly spirit of the age.

It were great injustice to attribute his high churchly principles to pride and ambition, though temptations to this spirit unquestionably beset a prominent position like his. Such principles are entirely compatible with sincere personal humility before God. It was the deep conviction of the divine authority, and the heavy responsibility of the episcopate, which lay at the bottom both of his first "*nolo episcopari*," and of his subsequent hierarchical feeling. He was as conscientious in discharging the duties, as he was jealous in maintaining the rights, of his office. Notwithstanding his high conception of the dignity of a bishop, he took counsel of his presbyters in everything, and respected the rights of his people. He knew how to combine strictness and moderation, dignity and gentleness, and to inspire love and confidence as well as esteem and veneration. He took upon himself, like a father, the care of the widows and orphans, the poor and sick. During the great pestilence of 252 he showed the most self-sacrificing fidelity to his flock, and love for his enemies. He forsook his congregation, indeed, in the Decian persecution, but only, as he expressly assured them, in pursuance of a divine admonition, and in order to direct them during his fourteen months of exile by pastoral epistles. His conduct exposed him to the charge of cowardice. In the Valerian persecution he completely washed away the stain of that flight with the blood of his calm and cheerful martyrdom.

He exercised first rigid discipline, but at a later period—not in perfect consistency—he moderated his disciplinary principles in prudent accommodation to the exigencies of the times. With Tertullian he prohibited all display of female dress, which only deformed the work of the Creator ; and he warmly opposed all participation in heathen amusements,—even refusing a converted play-actor permission to give instruction in declamation and pantomime. He lived in a simple, ascetic way, under a sense of the perishableness of all earthly things, and in view of the solemn eternity, in which alone also the questions and strifes of the church militant would be perfectly settled. " Only above," says he in his tract *De Mortalitate*, which he composed during the pestilence, " only above are true peace, sure repose, constant, firm, and eternal security ; there is our dwelling, there our home. Who would not fain hasten to reach it ? There a great multitude of beloved awaits us ; the numerous host of fathers, brethren, and children. There is a glorious choir of apostles ; there the number of exulting prophets ; there the countless multitude of martyrs, crowned with victory after warfare and

suffering; there triumphing virgins; there the merciful enjoying their reward. Thither let us hasten with longing desire;
let us wish to be soon with them, soon with Christ. After the
earthly comes the heavenly; after the small follows the great;
after perishableness, eternity."

III. His writings.

As an author, Cyprian is far less original, fertile and vigorous
than Tertullian, but is clearer, more moderate, and more elegant
and rhetorical in his style. He wrote independently only on the
doctrines of the church, the priesthood, and sacrifice.

(1.) His most important works relate to practical questions on
church government and discipline. Among these is his tract on
the *Unity of the Church* (A.D. 251), that "magna charta" of the
old catholic high-church spirit, the commanding importance of
which we have already considered. Then eighty-one *Epistles*,[1]
some very long, to various bishops, to the clergy and the
churches of Africa and of Rome, to the confessors, to the lapsed,
&c.; comprising also some letters from others in reply, as from
Cornelius of Rome and Firmilian of Cæsarea. They give us a
very graphic picture of his pastoral labors, and of the whole
church life of that day. To the same class belongs also his treatise: *De Lapsis* (A.D. 250) against loose penitential discipline.

(2.) Besides these he wrote a series of moral works, *On the
Grace of God* (246); *On the Lord's Prayer* (252); *On Mortality* (252); against worldly-mindedness and pride of dress in
consecrated virgins (*De Habitu Virginum*); a glowing call to
Martyrdom; an exhortation to liberality (*De Opere et Eleemosynis*, between 254 and 256), with a touch of the "opus operatum"
doctrine; and two beautiful tracts written during his controversy
with pope Stephanus: *De Bono Patientiæ*, and *De Zelo et
Livore* (about 256), in which he exhorts the excited minds to
patience and moderation.

(3.) Least important are his two apologetic works, the product

[1] The order of them varies in different editions, occasioning frequent confusion in citation.

of his Christian pupilage. One is directed against heathenism
(*de Idolorum Vanitate*), and is borrowed in great part, often ver-
bally, from Tertullian and Minucius Felix. The other, against
Judaism (*Testimonia adversus Judæos*), also contains no new
thoughts, but furnishes a careful collection of Scriptural proofs
of the Messiahship and divinity of Jesus.

NOTE.—Among the pseudo-Cyprianic writings is a homily against dice-play-
ing and all games of chance (*Adversus Aleatores*, in Hartel's ed. III. 92–103),
which has been recently vindicated for Bishop Victor of Rome (190–202), an
African by birth and an exclusive high churchman. It is written in the tone
of a papal encyclical and in rustic Latin. See HARNACK : *Der pseudo-cyprian.
Tractat De Aleatoribus*, Leipzig 1888. PH. SCHAFF: *The Oldest Papal Encyclical*,
in *The Independent*, N. York, Feb. 28, 1889.

§ 200. *Novatian.*

Comp. § 58, p. 196 sq. and § 183, p. 773.

(I.) NOVATIANI, *Presbyteri Romani, Opera quae exstant omnia.* Ed. by
Gagnæus (Par. 1545, in the works of Tertullian) ; *Gelenius* (Bas.
1550 and 1562) ; *Pamelius* (Par. 1598); *Gallandi* (Tom III.) ; *Edw.
Welchman* (Oxf. 1724); *J. Jackson* (Lond. 1728, the best ed.); *Migne*
(in "Patrol. Lat." Tom. III. col. 861–970). Migne's ed. includes
the dissertation of *Lumper* and the Commentary of *Gallandi.*
English translation by R. E. WALLIS in Clark's "Ante-Nicene
Library," vol. II. (1869), p. 297–395; comp. vol. I. 85 sqq.

(II.) EUSEB.: *H. E.* VI. 43, 44, 45. HIERON.: *De Vir. ill.* 66 and 70 ; *Ep.*
36 *ad Damas. ; Apol. adv. Ruf.* II. 19. SOCRATES: *H. E.* IV. 28.
The *Epistles* of CYPRIAN and CORNELIUS referring to the schism of
Novatian (Cypr. *Ep.* 44, 45, 49, 52, 55, 59, 60, 68, 69, 73). EPIPHA-
NIUS: *Haer.* 59 ; SOCRATES: *H. E.* IV. 28. THEODOR.: *Hær. Fab.*
III. 5. PHOTIUS: *Biblioth.* 182, 208, 280.

(III.) WALCH : *Ketzerhistorie* II. 185–288. SCHŒNEMANN : *Biblioth.
Hist. lit. Patr. Latinorum*, I. 135–142. LUMPER : *Dissert. de Vita,
Scriptis, et Doctrina Nov.*, in Migne's ed. III. 861–884. NEANDER,
I. 237–248, and 687 (Am ed.). CASPARI: *Quellen zur Gesch. des
Taufsymbols*, III. 428–430, 437–439. JOS. LANGEN (Old Cath.):
Gesch. der röm. Kirche (Bonn 1881), p. 289–314. HARNACK ; *Nova-
tian* in Herzog² X. (1882), p. 652–670. Also the works on Cyprian,
especially FECHTRUP. See lit. § 199. On Novatian's doctrine of the
trinity and the person of Christ see DORNER'S *Entwicklungsgesch. der
L. v. d. Pers. Christi* (1851), I. 601–604. (" *Dem Tertullian nahe
stehend, von ihm abhängig, aber auch ihn verflachend ist Novatian.*")

NOVATIAN, the second Roman anti-Pope (Hippolytus being

probably the first), orthodox in doctrine, but schismatic in discipline, and in both respects closely resembling Hippolytus and Tertullian, flourished in the middle of the third century and became the founder of a sect called after his name.[1] He was a man of unblemished, though austere character, considerable biblical and philosophical learning, speculative talent, and eloquence.[2] He is moreover, next to Victor and Minucius Felix, the first Roman divine who used the Latin Language, and used it with skill. We may infer that at his time the Latin had become or was fast becoming the ruling language of the Roman church, especially in correspondence with North Africa and the West; yet both Novatian and his rival Cornelius addressed the Eastern bishops in Greek. The epitaphs of five Roman bishops of the third century, Urbanus, Anteros, Fabianus, Lucius, and Eutychianus (between 223 and 283), in the cemetery of Callistus are Greek, but the epitaph of Cornelius (251–253) who probably belonged to the noble Roman family of that name, is Latin ("Cornelius Martyr E. R. X.")[3]

At that time the Roman congregation numbered forty presbyters, seven deacons, seven sub-deacons, forty-two acolytes, besides exorcists, readers and janitors, and an "innumerable multitude of the people," which may have amounted perhaps to about 50,000 members.[4]

We know nothing of the time and place of the birth and death of Novatian. He was probably an Italian. The later account of his Phrygian origin deserves no credit, and may have arisen from the fact that he had many followers in Phrygia, where they united with the Montanists. He was converted in

---

[1] *Novatiani*, in the East also Καθαροί, which is equivalent to *Puritans*.

[2] Jerome calls him and Tertullian *eloquentissimi viri* (*Ad Dam. Ep.* 36). Eusebius speaks unfavorably of him on account of his severe discipline, which seemed to deny mercy to poor sinners.

[3] On the subject of the official language of the Roman Church. see especially the learned and conclusive investigations of Caspari, *l. c.* III. 430 sqq., and the inscriptions in De Rossi, *Rom. sotter.* I. 277 sqq., 293, and II. 76 sqq. Also Harnack : *D. Pseudo-Cyprian. Tractat De Aleatoribus*, 1888. Cornelius was not buried officially by the Roman Church, but by private members of the same.

[4] See the letter of Cornelius to Fabius, preserved by Euseb. VI. 33.

adult age, and received only clinical baptism by sprinkling on the sick bed without subsequent episcopal confirmation, but was nevertheless ordained to the priesthood and rose to the highest rank in the Roman clergy. He conducted the official correspondence of the Roman see during the vacancy from the martyrdom of Fabian, January 21, 250, till the election of Cornelius, March, 251. In his letter to Cyprian, written in the name of "the presbyters and deacons abiding at Rome,"[1] he refers the question of the restoration of the lapsed to a future council, but shows his own preference for a strict discipline, as most necessary in peace and in persecution, and as "the rudder of safety in the tempest."[2]

He may have aspired to the papal chair to which he seemed to have the best claim. But after the Decian persecution had

---

[1] *Ep.* XXX. of Cyprian (Oxf. and Hartel's edd.). English version in "Ante-Nic. Libr.," Cyprian's works, I. 85–92. That this letter was written by Novatian, appears from Cyprian's *Ep.* LV. (*ad Antonianum*) cap. 4, where Cyprian quotes a passage from the same, and then adds: "*Additum est etiam Novatiano tunc scribente,*" etc.

[2] Ch. 2. Comp. also ch. 3, where he says: "Far be it from the Roman Church to slacken her vigor with so profane a facility, and to loosen the nerves of her severity by overthrowing the majesty of faith; so that when the wrecks of your ruined brethren are not only lying, but are falling around, remedies of a too hasty kind, and certainly not likely to avail, should be afforded for communion; and by a false mercy, new wounds should be impressed on the old wounds of their transgression; so that even repentance should be snatched from these wretched beings, to their greater overthrow." And in ch. 7: "Whosoever shall deny me before men, him will I also deny before my Father and before his angels. For God, as He is merciful, so He exacts obedience to his precepts, and indeed carefully exacts it; and as he invites to the banquet, so the man that hath not a wedding garment he binds hands and feet, and casts him out beyond the assembly of the saints. He has prepared heaven but he has also prepared hell. He has prepared places of refreshment, but he has also prepared eternal punishment. He has prepared the light that none can approach unto, but he has also prepared the vast and eternal gloom of perpetual night." At the close he favors an exception in case of impending death of the penitent lapsed, to whom cautious help should be administered, "that neither ungodly men should praise our smooth facility, nor truly penitent men accuse our severity as cruel." This letter relieves Novatian of the reproach of being chiefly influenced in his schism by personal motives, as Pope Cornelius (Euseb. VI. 43), and Roman historians maintain (also Harnack, in Herzog[2] X. 661).

ceased his rival Cornelius, unknown before, was elected by a majority of the clergy and favored the lenient discipline towards the Fallen which his predecessors Callistus and Zephyrinus had exercised, and against which Hippolytus had so strongly protested twenty or thirty years before. Novatian was elected anti-Pope by a minority and consecrated by three Italian bishops.[1] He was excommunicated by a Roman council, and Cornelius denounced him in official letters as "a deceitful, cunning and savage beast." Both parties appealed to foreign churches. Fabian of Antioch sympathized with Novatian, but Dionysius of Alexandria, and especially Cyprian who in the mean time had relaxed his former rigor and who hated schism like the very pest, supported Cornelius, and the lax and more charitable system of discipline, together with worldly conformity triumphed in the Catholic church. Nevertheless the Novatian schism spread East and West and maintained its severe discipline and orthodox creed in spite of imperial persecution down to the sixth century. Novatian died a martyr according to the tradition of his followers. The controversy turned on the extent of the power of the Keys and the claims of justice to the purity of the church and of mercy towards the fallen. The charitable view prevailed by the aid of the principle that out of the church there is no salvation.

Novatian was a fruitful author. Jerome ascribes to him works *On the Passover; On the Sabbath; On Circumcision; On the Priest (De Sacerdote); On Prayer; On the Jewish Meats; On Perseverance;*[2] *On Attilus* (a martyr of Pergamus); and *" On the Trinity."*

Two of these books are preserved. The most important is

---

[1] " *Ex exigna et vilissima Italiæ parte.*" See Jaffé *Regesta Pontif. Rom.* p. 7. Cornelius, in his letter to Fabian (Euseb. VI. 43), describes these three bishops as contemptible ignoramuses, who were intoxicated when they ordained Novatian "by a shadowy and empty imposition of hands."

[2] *De Instantia*, probably in persecution, not in prayer. See Caspari, p. 428, note 284 *versus* Lardner and Lumper, who explain it of Perseverance in *prayer*: but this was no doubt treated in *De Oratione*, for which, however, the Vatican Cod. reads *De Ordinatione*.

his *Liber de Trinitate* (31 chs.), composed A. D. 256. It has sometimes been ascribed to Tertullian or Cyprian. Jerome calls it a "great work," and an extract from an unknown work of Tertullian on the same subject. Novatian agrees essentially with Tertullian's subordinatian trinitarianism. He ably vindicates the divinity of Christ and of the Holy Spirit, strives to reconcile the divine threeness with unity, and refutes the Monarchians, especially the Sabellians by biblical and philosophical arguments.

In his *Epistola de Cibus Judaicis* (7 chapters) written to his flock from a place of retirement during persecution, he tries to prove by allegorical interpretation, that the Mosaic laws on food are no longer binding upon Christians, and that Christ has substituted temperance and abstinence for the prohibition of unclean animals, with the exception of meat offered to idols, which is forbidden by the Apostolic council (Acts 15).

§ 201. *Commodian.*

I.) COMMODIANUS : *Instructiones adversus Gentium Deos pro Christiana Disciplina*, and *Carmen Apologeticum adversus Judæos et Gentes.* The *Instructiones* were discovered by Sirmond, and first edited by *Rigault* at Toul, 1650; more recently by *Fr. Oehler* in Gersdorf's " Biblioth. P. Lat.," vol. XVIII., Lips. 1847 (p. 133–194,) and by *Migne*, "Patrol." vol. V. col. 201–262.

The second work was discovered and published by Card. *Pitra* in the "Spicilegium Solesmense," Tom. I. Par. 1852, p. 21–49 and Excurs. 537–543, and with new emendations of the corrupt text in Tom. IV. (1858), p. 222–224 ; and better by *Rönsch* in the "Zeitschrift für hist. Theol." for 1872.

Both poems were edited together by E. LUDWIG : *Commodiani Carmina*, Lips. 1877 and 1878 ; and by B. DOMBART, Vienna.

English translation of the first poem (but in prose) by R. E. WALLIS in Clark's " Ante-Nicene Library," vol. III. (1870 , pp. 434–474.

(II.) DODWELL : *Dissert. de ætate Commod.* Prolegg. in *Migne*, V. 189–200. ALZOG : *Patrol.* 340–342. J. L. JACOBI in Schneider's "Zeitschrift für christl. Wissenschaft und christl. Leben " for 1853, pp. 203–209. AD. EBERT, in an appendix to his essay on Tertullian's relation to Minucius Felix, Leipz. 1868, pp. 69–102; in his *Gesch. der christl. lat. Lit.*, I. 86–93 ; also his art. in Herzog [2] III. 325 sq. LEIMBACH, in an Easter Programme on Commodian's *Carmen apol.*

adv. Gentes et Judæos, Schmalkalden, 1871 (he clears up many points). HERMANN RÖNSCH, in the "Zeitschrift für historische Theologie " for 1872, No. 2. pp. 163–302 (he presents a revised Latin text with philological explanations). YOUNG in Smith and Wace, I. 610–611.

COMMODIAN was probably a clergyman in North Africa.[1] He was converted from heathenism by the study of the Scriptures, especially of the Old Testament.[2] He wrote about the middle of the third century two works in the style of vulgar African latinity, in uncouth versification and barbarian hexameter, without regard to quantity and hiatus. They are poetically and theologically worthless, but not unimportant for the history of practical Christianity, and reveal under a rude dress with many superstitious notions, an humble and fervent Christian heart. Commodian was a Patripassian in christology and a Chiliast in eschatology. Hence he is assigned by Pope Gelasius to the apocryphal writers. His vulgar African latinity is a landmark in the history of the Latin language and poetry in the transition to the Romance literature of the middle ages.

The first poem is entitled "Instructions for the Christian Life," written about A. D. 240 or earlier.[3] It is intended to convert heathens and Jews, and gives also exhortations to catechumens, believers, and penitents. The poem has over twelve hundred verses and is divided into eighty strophes, each of which is an acrostic, the initial letters of the lines composing the title or

---

[1] In the MSS. of the second poem he is called a bishop. Commodian gives no indication of his clerical status, but it may be fairly inferred from his learning. In the last section of his second poem he calls himself *Gazæus*. Ebert understands this geographically, from the city of Gaza in Syria. But in this case he would have written in Greek or in Syriac. The older interpretation is preferable, from Gaza (γάζα), *treasure*, or *gazophylacium* (γαζοφυλάκιον) *treasury*, which indicates either his possession of the treasure of saving truth or his dependence for support on the treasury of the church.

[2] Ebert suggests that he was a Jewish proselyte; but in the introduction to the first poem he says that he formerly worshipped the *gods* (*deos vanos*), which he believed to be demons, like most of the patristic writers.

[3] The author upbraids the Gentiles for persevering in unbelief after Christianity had existed for 200 years (VI. 2). Ebert dates the *Instructions* back as far as 239. Alzog puts it down much later.

subject of the section. The first 45 strophes are apologetic, and aimed at the heathen, the remaining 35 are parenetic and addressed to Christians. The first part exhorts unbelievers to repent in view of the impending end of the world, and gives prominence to chiliastic ideas about Antichrist, the return of the Twelve Tribes, the first resurrection, the millennium, and the last judgment. The second part exhorts catechumens and various classes of Christians. The last acrostic which again reminds the reader of the end of the world, is entitled " *Nomen Gazœi*,"[1] and, if read backwards, gives the name of the author : *Commodianus mendicus Christi.*[2]

2. The second work which was only brought to light in 1852, is an "Apologetic Poem against Jews and Gentiles," and was written about 249. It exhorts them (like the first part of the "Instructions" to repent without delay in view of the approaching end of the world. It is likewise written in uncouth hexameters, and discusses in 47 sections the doctrine of God, of man, and of the Redeemer (vers. 89–275) ; the meaning of the names of Son and Father in the economy of salvation (276–573) ; the obstacles to the progress of Christianity(574–611) ; it warns Jews and Gentiles to forsake their religion(612–783), and gives a description of the last things (784–1053).

The most interesting part of this second poem is the conclusion. It contains a fuller description of Antichrist than the first poem. The author expects that the end of the world will soon come with the seventh persecution ; the Goths will conquer Rome and redeem the Christians ; but then Nero will appear as the heathen Antichrist, reconquer Rome, and rage against the Christians three years and a-half ; he will be conquered in turn by the Jewish and real Antichrist from the east, who after the

---

[1] See above p. 854. Note 1.
[2] The last five lines are (see Migne V. col. 261, 262) :
" *ostenduntur illis, et legunt gesta de cœlo*
Memoria *prisca debito et merita digno.*
Merces *in perpetuo secundum facta tyranno.*
omnia *non possum comprehendere parvo libello.*
curiositas *docti inveniet nomen in isto.*"

defeat of Nero and the burning of Rome will return to Judæa, perform false miracles, and be worshipped by the Jews. At last Christ appears, that is God himself (from the Monarchian standpoint of the author), with the lost Twelve Tribes as his army, which had lived beyond Persia in happy simplicity and virtue; under astounding phenomena of nature he will conquer Antichrist and his host, convert all nations and take possession of the holy city of Jerusalem. The concluding description of the judgment is preserved only in broken fragments. The idea of a double Antichrist is derived from the two beasts of the Apocalypse, and combines the Jewish conception of the Antimessiah, and the heathen Nero-legend. But the remarkable feature is that the second Antichrist is represented as a Jew and as defeating the heathen Nero, as he will be defeated by Christ. The same idea of a double antichrist appears in Lactantius.[1]

§ 202. *Arnobius.*

(I.) ARNOBII (*oratoris*) *adversus Nationes* (*or Gentes*) *libri septem. Best ed.* by REIFFERSCHEID, Vindob. 1875. (vol. IV. of the "Corpus Scriptorum Ecclesiasticorum Latinorum," issued by the Academy of Vienna.)

Other editions: by *Faustus Sabœus,* Florence 1543 (ed. princeps); Bas. (Frobenius) 1546; Paris 1580, 1666, 1715; Antw. 1582; Rom. 1583; Genev. 1597; Lugd. Bat. 1598, 1651; by *Orelli,* Lips. 1816; *Hildebrand,* Halle, 1844; *Migne,* "Patrol. Lat." v. 1844, col. 350 sqq. *Fr. Oehler* (in Gersdorf's "Bibl. Patr. Lat."), Lips. 1846. On the text see the Prolegg of Oehler and Reifferscheid.

English Version by A. HAMILTON BRYCE and HUGH CAMPBELL, in Clark's "Ante-Nic. Libr." vol. XIX. (Edinb. 1871). German transl. by BENARD (1842), and ALLEKER (1858).

(II.) HIERONYMUS: *De Vir. ill.* 79; *Chron.* ad ann. 325 (xx. Constantini); *Ep.* 46, and 58, ad Paulinum.

(III.) The learned *Dissertatio prævia* of the Benedictine LE NOURRY in Migne's ed. v. 365–714. NEANDER: I. 687–689. MÖHLER (R. C.): *Patrol.* I. 906–916. ALZOG (R. C.): *Patrologie* (3d ed.), p. 205–210. *Zink: Zur Kritik und Erklärung des Arnob.,* Bamb. 1873. EBERT, *Gesch. der christl. lat. Lit. I.* 61–70. HERZOG in Herzog[2] I. 692 sq. MOULE in Smith and Wace I. 167–169.

---

[1] *Inst. Div.* VII. 16 sqq.

ARNOBIUS, a successful teacher of rhetoric with many pupils (Lactantius being one of them), was first an enemy, then an advocate of Christianity. He lived in Sicca, an important city on the Numidian border to the Southwest of Carthage, in the latter part of the third and the beginning of the fourth century. He was converted to Christ in adult age, like his more distinguished fellow-Africans, Tertullian and Cyprian. " O blindness," he says, in describing the great change, " only a short time ago I was worshipping images just taken from the forge, gods shaped upon the anvil and by the hammer. . . . When I saw a stone made smooth and smeared with oil, I prayed to it and addressed it as if a living power dwelt in it, and implored blessings from the senseless stock. And I offered grievious insult even to the gods, whom I took to be such, in that I considered them wood, stone, and bone, or fancied that they dwelt in the stuff of such things. Now that I have been led by so great a teacher into the way of truth, I know what all that is, I think worthily of the Worthy, offer no insult to the Godhead, and give every one his due. . . . Is Christ, then, not to be regarded as God ? And is He who in other respects may be deemed the very greatest, not to be honored with divine worship, from whom we have received while alive so great gifts, and from whom, when the day comes, we expect greater gifts ? " [1]

The contrast was very startling indeed, if we remember that Sicca bore the epithet "Veneria," as the seat of the vile worship of the goddess of lust in whose temple the maidens sacrificed their chastity, like the Corinthian priestesses of Aphrodite. He is therefore especially severe in his exposure of the sexual immoralities of the heathen gods, among whom Jupiter himself takes the lead in all forms of vice.[2]

[1] *Adv. Nat.* 1, 39, ed. Reifferscheid, p. 26.
[2] In book V. 22 he details the crimes of Jupiter who robbed Ceres, Leda, Danae, Europa, Alcmena, Electra, Latona, Laodamia, and "a thousand other virgins and a thousand matrons, and with them the boy Catamitus, of their honor and chastity," and who was made a collection of "all impurities of the stage."

We know nothing of his subsequent life and death. Jerome, the only ancient writer who mentions him, adds some doubtful particulars, namely that he was converted by visions or dreams, that he was first refused admission to the Church by the bishop of Sicca, and hastily wrote his apology in proof of his sincerity. But this book, though written soon after his conversion, is rather the result of an inward impulse and strong conviction than outward occasion.

We have from him an Apology of Christianity in seven books of unequal length, addressed to the Gentiles. It was written A. D. 303 [1], at the outbreak of the Diocletian persecution; for he alludes to the tortures, the burning of the sacred Scriptures and the destruction of the meeting houses, which were the prominent features of that persecution.[2] It is preserved in only one manuscript (of the ninth or tenth century), which contains also the "Octavius" of Minucius Felix.[3] The first two books are apologetic, the other five chiefly polemic. Arnobius shows great familiarity with Greek and Roman mythology and literature, and quotes freely from Homer, Plato, Cicero, and Varro. He ably refutes the objections to Christianity, beginning with the popular charge that it brought the wrath of the gods and the many public calamities upon the Roman empire. He exposes at length the absurdities and immoralities of the heathen mythology. He regards the gods as real, but evil beings.

The positive part is meagre and unsatisfactory. Arnobius seems as ignorant about the Bible as Minucius Felix. He never quotes the Old Testament, and the New Testament only once.[4]

---

[1] He says that Christianity had then existed three hundred years (I. 13), and that the city of Rome was one thousand and fifty years old (II. 71). The last date leaves a choice between A. D. 296 or 303, according as we reckon by the Varronian or the Fabian era.

[2] IV. 36; comp. I. 26; II. 77; III. 36, etc.   Comp. Euseb. *H. E.* VIII. 2.

[3] In the Nation. Libr. of Paris, No. 1661. The copy in Brussels is merely a transcript. The MS., though well written, is very corrupt, and leaves room for many conjectures. Reifferscheid has carefully compared it at Paris in 1867.

[4] "Has that well-known word (*illud vulgatum*) never struck your ears, that the wisdom of man is foolishness with God?'" II. 6; comp. 1 Cor. 3: 19.

He knows nothing of the history of the Jews, and the Mosaic worship, and confounds the Pharisees and Sadducees. Yet he is tolerably familiar, whether from the Gospels or from tradition, with the history of Christ. He often refers in glowing language to his incarnation, crucifixion, and exaltation. He represents him as the supreme teacher who revealed God to man, the giver of eternal life, yea, as God, though born a man, as God on high, God in his inmost nature, as the Saviour God, and the object of worship.[1] Only his followers can be saved, but he offers salvation even to his enemies. His divine mission is proved by his miracles, and these are attested by their unique character, their simplicity, publicity and beneficence. He healed at once a hundred or more afflicted with various diseases, he stilled the raging tempest, he walked over the sea with unwet foot, he astonished the very waves, he fed five thousand with five loaves, and filled twelve baskets with the fragments that remained, he called the dead from the tomb. He revealed himself after the resurrection "in open day to countless numbers of men;" "he appears even now to righteous men of unpolluted mind who love him, not in any dreams, but in a form of pure simplicity."[2]

His doctrine of God is Scriptural, and strikingly contrasts with the absurd mythology. God is the author and ruler of all things, unborn, infinite, spiritual, omnipresent, without passion, dwelling in light, the giver of all good, the sender of the Saviour.

As to man, Arnobius asserts his free will, but also his ignorance and sin, and denies his immortality. The soul outlives the body, but depends solely on God for the gift of eternal duration. The wicked go to the fire of Gehenna, and will ultimately be

---

[1] The strongest passages for the divinity of Christ are I. 37, 39, 42 and 53. In the last passage he says (Reifferscheid, p. 36): "*Deus ille sublimis fuit* [*Christus*], *deus radice ab intima, deus ab incognitis regnis et ab omnium principe deo sospitator est missus.*"

[2] "*per puræ speciem simplicitatis,*" I. 46. This passage speaks against the story, that Arnobius was converted by a dream.

consumed or annihilated.   He teaches the resurrection of the
flesh, but in obscure terms.

Arnobius does not come up to the standard of Catholic orthodoxy, even of the ante-Nicene age.   Considering his apparent
ignorance of the Bible, and his late conversion, we need not be
surprised at this.   Jerome now praises, now censures him, as
unequal, prolix, and confused in style, method, and doctrine.
Pope Gelasius in the fifth century banished his book to the
apocryphal index, and since that time it was almost forgotten,
till it was brought to light again in the sixteenth century.
Modern critics agree in the verdict that he is more successful in
the refutation of error than in the defense of truth.

But the honesty, courage, and enthusiasm of the convert for
his new faith are as obvious as the defects of his theology. If he
did not know or clearly understand the doctrines of the Bible,
he seized its moral tone.[1]   " We have learned," he says, " from
Christ's teaching and his laws, that evil ought not to be re-
quited with evil (comp. Matt. 5 : 39), that it is better to suffer
wrong than to inflict it, that we should rather shed our own
blood than stain our hands and our conscience with that of
another. An ungrateful world is now for a long period enjoying
the benefit of Christ ; for by his influence the rage of savage
ferocity has been softened, and restrained from the blood of a
fellow-creature.   If all would lend an ear to his salutary and
peaceful laws, the world would turn the use of steel to occupations of peace, and live in blessed harmony, maintaining inviolate the sanctity of treaties."[2] He indignantly asks the heathen,
" Why have our writings deserved to be given to the flames, and
our meetings to be cruelly broken up? In them prayer is offered
to the supreme God, peace and pardon are invoked upon all in

---

[1] I must differ from Ebert (p. 69), who says that Christianity produced no
moral change in his heart. "*In seinem Stil ist Arnobius durchaus Heide, und
auch dies ist ein Zeugniss für die Art seines Christenthums, das eben eine innere
Umwandlung nicht bewirkt hatte. Das Gemüth hat an seinem Ausdruck nirgends
einen Antheil.*"

[2] I. 9.

authority, upon soldiers, kings, friends, enemies, upon those still in life, and those released from the bondage of the flesh. In them all that is said tends to make men humane, gentle, modest, virtuous, chaste, generous in dealing with their substance, and inseparably united to all that are embraced in our brotherhood."[1] He uttered his testimony boldly in the face of the last and most cruel persecution, and it is not unlikely that he himself was one of its victims.

The work of Arnobius is a rich store of antiquarian and mythological knowledge, and of African latinity.

§ 203. *Victorinus of Petau.*

(I.) *Opera* in the "Max. Biblioth. vet. Patrum." Lugd. Tom. III., in *Gallandi's* "Bibl. PP.," Tom. IV.; and in *Migne's* "Patrol. Lat.," V. 281–344 (*De Fabrica Mundi*, and *Scholia in Apoc. Joannis*).

English translation by R. E. WALLIS, in Clark's "Ante-Nicene Library," Vol. III., 388–433; N. York ed. VII. (1886).

(II.) JEROME: *De. Vir. ill.*, 74. CASSIODOR.: *Justit. Div. Lit.*, c. 9. CAVE: *Hist. Lit.*, I., 147 sq. LUMPER'S *Proleg.*, in Migne's ed., V. 281–302. ROUTH: *Reliq.*, S. I., 65; III., 455–481.

VICTORINUS, probably of Greek extraction, was first a rhetorician by profession, and became bishop of Petavium, or Petabio,[2] in ancient Panonia (Petau, in the present Austrian Styria). He died a martyr in the Diocletian persecution (303). We have only fragments of his writings, and they are not of much importance, except for the age to which they belong. Jerome says that he understood Greek better than Latin, and that his works are excellent for the sense, but mean as to the style. He counts him among the Chiliasts, and ascribes to him commentaries on Genesis, Exodus, Leviticus, Isaiah, Ezekiel, Habakkuk, Canticles, the Apocalypse, a book Against all Heresies, "*et multa alia.*" Several poems are also credited to him, but without good reason.[3]

---

[1] IV. 36.

[2] *Vict. Petavionensis* or *Petabionensis;* not *Pictaviensis* (from Poictiers), as in the Rom. Martyrologium and Baronius. John Launoy (d. 1678) is said to have first corrected this error.

[3] *Carmina de Jesu Christo Deo et homine; Lignum Vitœ;* also the hymns *De*

1. The fragment on the *Creation of the World* is a series of notes on the account of creation, probably a part of the commentary on Genesis mentioned by Jerome. The days are taken literally. The creation of angels and archangels preceded the creation of man, as light was made before the sky and the earth. The seven days typify seven millennia; the seventh is the millennial sabbath, when Christ will reign on earth with his elect. It is the same chiliastic notion which we found in the Epistle of Barnabas, with the same opposition to Jewish sabbatarianism. Victorinus compares the seven days with the seven eyes of the Lord (Zech. 4: 10), the seven heavens (comp. Ps. 33: 6), the seven spirits that dwelt in Christ (Isa. 11 : 2, 3), and the seven stages of his humanity : his nativity, infancy, boyhood, youth, young-manhood, mature age, death. This is a fair specimen of these allegorical plays of a pious imagination.

2. The scholia on the *Apocalypse of John* are not without interest for the history of the interpretation of this mysterious book.[1] But they are not free from later interpolations of the fifth or sixth century. The author assigns the Apocalypse to the reign of Domitian (herein agreeing with Irenæus), and combines the historical and allegorical methods of interpretation. He also regards the visions in part as synchronous rather than successive. He comments only on the more difficult passages.[2] We select the most striking points.

The woman in ch. 12 is the ancient church of the prophets and apostles; the dragon is the devil. The woman sitting on the seven hills (in ch. 17), is the city of Rome. The beast from the abyss is the Roman empire; Domitian is counted as the sixth, Nerva as the seventh, and Nero revived as the eighth Roman

---

Cruce or *De Paschate*, in Tertullian's and Cyprian's works. Routh, III. 483, denies the genuineness; so also Lumper in Migne V. 294.

[1] Comp. Lücke, *Einleitung in die Offenb. Joh.*, pp. 972-982 (2nd ed.); and Bleek, *Vorlesungen über die Apok.*, p. 34 sq. Lücke and Bleek agree in regarding this commentary as a work of Victorinus, but with later interpolations. Bleek assumes that it was originally more pronounced in its chiliasm.

[2] As Cassiodorus remarks: "*Difficillima quædam loca breviter tractavit.*"

King.[1] The number 666 (13 : 18) means in Greek *Teitan*[2] (this is the explanation preferred by Irenæus), in Latin *Diclux*. Both names signify Antichrist, according to the numerical value of the Greek and Roman letters. But Diclux has this meaning by contrast, for Antichrist, " although he is cut off from the supernal light, yet transforms himself into an angel of light, daring to call himself light."[3] To this curious explanation is added, evidently by a much later hand, an application of the mystic number to the Vandal king Genseric (γενσήρικος), who in the fifth century laid waste the Catholic church of North Africa and sacked the city of Rome.

The exposition of ch. 20 : 1–6 is not so strongly chiliastic, as the corresponding passage in the Commentary on Genesis, and hence some have denied the identity of authorship. The first resurrection is explained spiritually with reference to Col. 3 : 1, and the author leaves it optional to understand the thousand years as endless or as limited. Then he goes on to allegorize about the numbers : ten signifies the decalogue, and hundred the crown of virginity ; for he who keeps the vow of virginity completely, and fulfils the precepts of the decalogue, and destroys the impure thoughts within the retirement of his own

---

[1] This explanation of 17 : 10, 11 rests on the expectation of the return of Nero as Antichrist, and was afterwards justly abandoned by Andreas and Arethas, but has been revived again, though with a different counting of the emperors, by the modern champions of the Nero-hypothesis. See the discussion in vol. I, 864 sqq.

[2] T=300 ; E=5 ; I=10 ; T=300: A=1 ; N=50 ; in all 666. Dropping the final n, we get Teita=616, which was the other reading in 13: 18, mentioned by Irenæus. Titus was the destroyer of Jerusalem, but in unconscious fulfilment of Christ's prophecy ; he was no persecutor of the church, and was one of the best among the Roman emperors.

[3] D=500 ; I=1 ; C=100 ; L=50 ; V=5 ; X=10 ; in all=666. "*Id est quod Græce sonat* τειτάν, *nempe id quod Latine dicitur* DICLUX, *quo nomine per antiphrasin expresso intelligimus antichristum, qui cum a luce superna abscissus sit et ea privatus, transfigurat tamen se in angelum lucis, audens sese dicere lucem. Item invenimus in quodam codice Græco* άντεμος." The last name is perhaps a corruption for 'Αντειμος, which occurs on coins of Mœsia for a ruling dynasty, or may be meant for a designation of character: *honori contrarius*. See Migne, V. 339, and Lücke, p. 978.

heart, is the true priest of Christ, and reigns with him; and "truly in his case the devil is bound." At the close of the notes on ch. 22, the author rejects the crude and sensual chiliasm of the heretic Cerinthus. " For the kingdom of Christ," he says, " is now eternal in the saints, although the glory of the saints shall be manifested after the resurrection."[1] This looks like a later addition, and intimates the change which Constantine's reign produced in the mind of the church as regards the millennium. Henceforth it was dated from the incarnation of Christ.[2]

§ 204. Eusebius, Lactantius, Hosius.

On EUSEBIUS see vol. III. 871–879.—Add to Lit. the exhaustive article of Bp. LIGHTFOOT in Smith and Wace, II. (1880), p. 308–348; Dr. SALMON, on the Chron. of Eus. ibid. 354–355; and SEMISCH in Herzog[2] IV. 390–398.

On LACTANTIUS see vol. III. 955–959.—Add to Lit. EBERT: Gesch. der christl. lat. Lit. I. (1874), p. 70–86; and his art. in Herzog[2] VIII. 364–366; and E. S. FFOULKES in Smith and Wace III. 613–617.

On HOSIUS, see § 55 p. 179 sqq.; and vol. III. 627, 635, 636.—Add to Lit. P. BONIF. GAMS (R. C.): Kirchengesch. v. Spanien, Regensb. 1862 sqq., Bd II. 137–309 (the greater part of the second vol. is given to Hosius); W. MÖLLER in Herzog[2] VI. 326–328; and T. D. C. MORSE in Smith and Wace III. 162–174.

At the close of our period we meet with three representative divines, in close connection with the first Christian emperor who effected the politico-ecclesiastical revolution known as the union of church and state. Their public life and labors belong to the next period, but must at least be briefly foreshadowed here.

EUSEBIUS, the historian, LACTANTIUS, the rhetorician, and HOSIUS, the statesman, form the connecting links between the ante-Nicene and Nicene ages; their long lives—two died octogenarians, Hosius a centenarian—are almost equally divided between the two; and they reflect the lights and shades of both.[3]

---

[1] " Nam regnum Christi nunc est sempiternum in sanctis, cum fuerit gloria post resurrectionem manifestata sanctorum." (Migne V. 344.)

[2] Comp. § 188, p. 612 sqq.

[3] Eusebius died A. D. 340; Lactantius between 320 and 330; Hosius between 357 and 360.

Eusebius was bishop of Cæsarea and a man of extensive and useful learning, and a liberal theologian; Lactantius, a professor of eloquence in Nicomedia, and a man of elegant culture; Hosius, bishop of Cordova and a man of counsel and action.[1] They thus respectively represented the Holy Land, Asia Minor, and Spain; we may add Italy and North Africa, for Lactantius was probably a native Italian and a pupil of Arnobius of Sicca, and Hosius acted to some extent for the whole western church in Eastern Councils. With him Spain first emerges from the twilight of legend to the daylight of church history; it was the border land of the west which Paul perhaps had visited, which had given the philosopher Seneca and the emperor Trajan to heathen Rome, and was to furnish in Theodosius the Great the strong defender of the Nicene faith.

Eusebius, Lactantius, and Hosius were witnesses of the cruelties of the Diocletian persecution, and hailed the reign of imperial patronage. They carried the moral forces of the age of martyrdom into the age of victory. Eusebius with his literary industry saved for us the invaluable monuments of the first three centuries down to the Nicene Council; Lactantius bequeathed to posterity, in Ciceronian Latin, an exposition and vindication of the Christian religion against the waning idolatry of Greece and Rome, and the tragic memories of the imperial persecutors; Hosius was the presiding genius of the synods of

---

[1] Hosius left no literary work. The only document we have from his pen is his letter to the Arian Emperor Constantius, preserved by Athanasius (*Hist. Arian.* 44). See Gams, *l. c.* II. 215 sqq. It begins with this noble sentence: "I was a confessor of the faith long before your grandfather Maximian persecuted the church. If you persecute me, I am ready to suffer all rather than to shed innocent blood and to betray the truth." Unfortunately, in his extreme old age he yielded under the infliction of physical violence, and subscribed an Arian creed, but bitterly repented before his death. Athanasius expressly says (*l. c.* 45), that "at the approach of death, as it were by his last testament, he abjured the Arian heresy, and gave strict charge that no one should receive it." It is a disputed point whether he died at Sirmium in 357, or was permitted to return to Spain, and died there about 359 or 360. We are only informed that he was over a hundred years old, and over sixty years a bishop. Athan. *l. c.; Sulpicius Severus, Hist.* II. 55.

Elvira (306), Nicæa (325), and Sardica (347), the friend of Athanasius in the defense of orthodoxy and in exile.

All three were intimately associated with Constantine the Great, Eusebius as his friend and eulogist, Lactantius as the tutor of his eldest son, Hosius as his trusted counsellor who probably suggested to him the idea of convening the first œcumenical synod; he was we may say for a few years his ecclesiastical prime minister. They were, each in his way, the emperor's chief advisers and helpers in that great change which gave to the religion of the cross the moral control over the vast empire of Rome. The victory was well deserved by three hundred years of unjust persecution and heroic endurance, but it was fraught with trials and temptations no less dangerous to the purity and peace of the church than fire and sword.

ILLUSTRATIONS FROM THE CATACOMBS.

ALLEGORICAL REPRESENTATION OF CHRIST AS THE GOOD SHEPHERD.

(See p. 276.)

THE GOOD SHEPHERD. (FRESCO CEILING, FROM BOSIO.)

In the centre, "The Good Shepherd." The subjects, beginning at the top and going to the right, are: (1.) The Paralytic carrying his Bed; (2.) Five Baskets full of Fragments; (3.) Raising of Lazarus; (4.) Daniel in the Lion's Den; (5.) Jonah swallowed by the Fish; (6.) Jonah vomited Forth; (7.) Moses striking the Rock; (8.) Noah and the Dove.

ALLEGORICAL REPRESENTATION OF CHRIST UNDER THE TYPE OF ORPHEUS.

(See p. 276.)

ORPHEUS. (Fresco Ceiling in the Crypt of St. Domitilla.)

Orpheus in the centre, playing the Lyre to the enchanted Animals, surrounded by landscapes and Scripture Scenes, viz., beginning at the right: (1.) The Raising of the mummy-like Corpse of Lazarus; (2.) Daniel in the Lion's Den; (3.) Moses smiting the Rock; (4.) David with the Sling.

ALPHABETICAL INDEX

Christ, 555; against Noëtus and Callistus, 578; on future punishment, 609; on Hades, 768; his life and writings, 757 sqq
Holy Scriptures and the canon, 516 sqq
Holy Spirit, doctrine of the, 560 sqq
Homologumena, 522
Hort, 529, 815
Hosius, 181, 864 sqq
Humanity of Christ, 555 sqq
Hydroparastatæ, 495
Hymns, 226 sqq

ICHTHYS, 279
Ignatius of Antioch, his life and martyrdom, 47 sqq.; on the episcopate, 145, 158 sq.; on celibacy, 399; on the divinity of Christ, 547; on the humanity of Christ, 556 sq.; his epistles, 651 sqq
Ignatian controversy, 660 sqq
Immersion, see Baptism
Immortality of the soul, 590 sqq
Incarnation, doctrine of the, 545
Infant baptism, see Baptism
Irenæus, on the number of martyrs, 79; on episcopacy, 149; on primacy, 159 sq., 171; on the paschal controversy, 213, 217 sq.; on the eucharist, 242; on infant baptism, 259; on Gnosticism, 443; on tradition, 525; on God and creation, 538, 540; his christology, 553, 556, 559 sq.; on the Holy Spirit, 563; on the Trinity, 569; on redemption, 587; on future punishment, 609; on chiliasm, 617; his life and writings, 746 sqq
Irvingism compared with Montanism, 427
Isidore, 471
Italy, Christianity in, 29

JACHMANN, 679
Jackson, George A., 632, 692
Jacobi, 758, 781, and passim
Jaldabaoth. See Gnosticism.
Jamblichus, 98
Janitors, 132
Jason and Papiscus, 88, 107
Jerome, passim, especially in Ch. XIII

Jerusalem, again destroyed, 37 sq
Jewish (literary) opposition, 87 sq
Jewish persecution, 36 sqq
John and the Easter controversy, 219 sq
Josephus, 87 sq, and passim
Judaism and heathenism within the Church, 428
Judaism, argument against, 107
Julia Mammæa, 59
Julius Africanus, 803 sqq
Justin Martyr, on the spread of Christianity, 22; apologetics against the heathen, 107, 114, 119; on Sunday observance, 203; on public worship, 223; on the eucharist, 235, 242; on baptism, 247 sq.; on celibacy, 400; on the Logos and the divinity of Christ, 548 sqq.; on the Holy Spirit, 561; on the Trinity, 569; on redemption, 586; on future punishment, 608; on chiliasm, 616; his life and writings, 710 sqq
Justin the Gnostic, 495 sq

KAYE, 781, 818, 833
Keim, 51, 64, 85, 93, 701, 841, and passim
Kneelers, 189
Kosmology, 453 sqq
Kühn, 834, 839

LACTANTIUS, 66, 105, 864 sqq
Lagarde, Paul de, 184, 442, 703, 705, 757, 761, 797
Lapsi, 60, 76, 189 sqq
Laurentius, 63
Lecky, on the spread of Christianity, 18 sq.; on persecution, 81 on the decline of the Roman Empire, 347; on Greek vice, 356
Legio fulminatrix, 56
Leonides, 57, 786
Libellatici, 60, 76
Lightfoot, Bp., 121, 126, 133, 135, 136, 225, 636, 643, 653, 690, 747, 748
Lipsius, 163, 164, 443, 444, 461, 636, 747
Literary opposition to Christianity, 86 sq.; Jewish opposition, 87 sq.; Josephus and the Talmud, 87 sq.; Pagan opposition, 88 sq
Liturgy of Clement, 226
Logos, doctrine of the, 548 sqq